Cecil Bell

THE MOTORIST'S ROAD ATLAS OF GREAT BRITAIN

THE MOTORIST'S ROAD ATLAS OF GREAT BRITAIN

CHANCELLOR
PRESS

The representation in this atlas of a road or track is not evidence of the existence of a right of way. Based upon the Ordnance Survey maps with the sanction of the Controller of Her Majesty's Stationery Office, © Crown Copyright.

Previously published by George Philip Ltd

This 1992 edition published by
Chancellor Press
Michelin House
81 Fulham Road
London SW3 6RB

Cartography by George Philip Ltd

Printed in Hong Kong

MORECAMBE
HEYSHAM
LANCASTER
Heysham Lake
Shoulder of Lune
Cockerham Sands
FLEETWOOD
Cleveleys
Thornton
BISPHAM
BLACKPOOL
NORTH SHORE
SOUTH SHORE
St. Anne's
Lytham St. Anne's
Kirkham
FYLDE
M55
Higher Penwortham
Hesketh Bank
SOUTHPORT
Birkdale Sands
Formby Hills
Formby
Ormskirk
Skelmersdale
Maghull
M58
Crosby
Litherland
Kirkby
BOOTLE
ST. HELENS
MERSEYSIDE
WALLASEY
LIVERPOOL
M57
Prescot
Huyton
BIRKENHEAD

Contents

Journey Planning

Motorways	II
Motorway service areas	III
M25 London orbital motorway	IV-V
Distance table	VI-VII
Local radio stations	VIII
Key map and map symbols	1

Road Maps

England, Wales and Scotland	2-64

London Maps

London approaches – North	65-68
London approaches – South	69-72
Central London streets	73-80

Town and City Plans 81-112

Aberdeen, Bath 81, Birmingham 82-84, Blackpool, Bolton 85, Bournemouth 86, Bradford 86-7, Brighton 87, Bristol 88, Cambridge, Canterbury 89, Cardiff 90, Cheltenham, Chester 89, Coventry, Croydon 91, Derby, Dundee, Durham 92, Edinburgh 93, Exeter 92, Glasgow 94, Gloucester, Kingston upon Hull 95 , Leeds 96, Leicester, Lincoln 97, Liverpool 98, Manchester 99-100, Middlesbrough, Milton Keynes 101, Newcastle 102-103, Newport (Gwent), Northampton, Norwich 103, Nottingham 104, Oxford, Peterborough, Plymouth 105, Portsmouth, Reading 106, Rochester and the Medway towns, Salisbury 107, Scarborough, Sheffield 108, Shrewsbury, Southampton 109, Southend 110, Stoke-on-Trent 111, Stratford-upon-Avon 110, Swansea 112, Torquay 111, Windsor, York 112

Indexes

Index to road maps	1-48
Index to London maps	49-61

II MOTORWAYS

MAP SYMBOLS
Motorways
Main Primary Routes
Scale 1: 4 350 000
20 0 20 40 Miles
20 0 20 40 60 Kms
Orkney Islands
Scrabster
Wick
Isle of Lewis
A9
Ullapool
A835
North Uist
Inverness
A96
South Uist
Isle of Skye
A82
Aberdeen
Barra
Mallaig
A87
A9
A94
Eigg
Fort William
Coll
Tiree
A828
Dundee
Mull
Oban
Perth
A816
A83
M90
M9
Colonsay
M80
M8
Edinburgh
Glasgow
Berwick
Islay
Ardrossan
M74
A1
A7
Arran
Ayr
A83
A74
A77
Londonderry
A2
A26
Newcastle
Cairnryan
A75
A6
Larne
A69
M2
Carlisle
A1(M)
Stranraer
A5
A29
M6
Dungannon
Belfast
A66
Darlington
M1
Sligo
A1
A2
Isle of Man
A595
Douglas
A1
Scarborough
Ripon
Heysham
A65
York
Fleetwood
M55
Bradford
Leeds
M62
Hull
Blackpool
M61
M65
M18
M66
M62
A1 (M)
M180
Manchester
Doncaster
M58
M1
M57
M62
A628
M18
A46
Anglesey
Liverpool
M56
Sheffield
Galway
Dublin
M53
Lincoln
Dun Laoghaire
Holyhead
A55
M6
A1
A16
M1
A6
A17
Stoke
A5
A49
Derby
Nottingham
A50
Norwich
Limerick
M69
Leicester
A43
A47
Shrewsbury
Peterborough
M54
A10
Wolverhampton
M6
A1
Birmingham
Coventry
A11
Aberystwyth
A487
A46
Northampton
Cambridge
Rosslare
M40
M45
A12
Warwick
A6
Ipswich
Killarney
A49
M1
M5
A439
A1 (M)
Felixstowe
Banbury
Harwich
Cork
M50
M11
Fishguard
A40
Gloucester
Oxford
M25
A40
M40
LONDON
Swindon
M4
Pembroke
M4
Swansea
Reading
Sheerness
Ramsgate
M32
Canterbury
Cardiff
Bristol
M4
M2
Dover
M20
Maidstone
A36
A34
M25
Ashford
M5
Crawley
M23
Folkestone
M3
Winchester
A3
A23
Taunton
A303
A33
A259
Southampton
M27
Brighton
A39
A31
Newhaven
Lymington
Portsmouth
M5
A30
A35
Exeter
Poole
Weymouth
Isle of Wight
Torquay
Plymouth
A38
Penzance
Isles of Scilly

All motorway service areas are listed below, together with symbols indicating special facilities.

- *Overnight accommodation available*
- *Hot meals or snacks available at night*
- *Repair facilities*
- C *Facilities for young children*
- *Picnic area*
- *Tourist Information Centre*

M1

	Between Access Numbers	Overnight accommodation	Hot meals at night	Repair	C Young children	Picnic area	Tourist Information
Scratchwood	2 – 4	✓	✓	✓	✓		
Toddington	11 – 12	✓	✓	✓	✓	✓	
Newport Pagnall	14 – 15	✓	✓	✓	✓		
Rothersthorpe	Turn off at exit 15A		✓	✓	✓		
Watford Gap	16 – 17		✓	✓	✓		
Leicester Forest East	21 – 22		✓	✓	✓		
Leicester Markfield	Turn off at exit 22	✓	✓		✓	✓	
Trowell	25 – 26		✓	✓	✓	✓	✓
Woodall	30 – 31		✓	✓	✓		✓
Woolley Edge	38 – 39	✓	✓	✓	✓	✓	

M2

	Between Access Numbers	Overnight accommodation	Hot meals at night	Repair	C Young children	Picnic area	Tourist Information
Farthing Corner	4 – 5	✓	✓	✓	✓	✓	✓

M3

	Between Access Numbers	Overnight accommodation	Hot meals at night	Repair	C Young children	Picnic area	Tourist Information
Fleet	4 – 5		✓	✓	✓	✓	

M4

	Between Access Numbers	Overnight accommodation	Hot meals at night	Repair	C Young children	Picnic area	Tourist Information
Heston	2 – 3	✓	✓	✓	✓	✓	
Chieveley	Turn off at exit 13		✓	✓	✓	✓	
Membury	14 – 15		✓	✓	✓	✓	
Leigh Delamere	17 – 18	✓	✓	✓	✓	✓	
Aust	Turn off at exit 21	✓	✓	✓	✓	✓	
Cardiff West	Turn off at exit 33	✓	✓	✓	✓	✓	✓ (*Summer only*)
Sarn Park	Turn off at exit 36	✓	✓		✓		✓
Swansea	Turn off at exit 47	✓	✓	✓	✓	✓	
Pont Abraham	49		✓		✓	✓	✓

M5

	Between Access Numbers	Overnight accommodation	Hot meals at night	Repair	C Young children	Picnic area	Tourist Information
Frankley	3 – 4	✓	✓	✓	✓	✓	
Strensham	7 – 8		✓	✓	✓	✓	
Michaelwood	13 – 14		✓		✓	✓	
Gordano	Turn off at exit 19	✓	✓	✓	✓	✓	✓
Sedgemoor	21 – 22	✓	✓		✓	✓	✓ (*Summer only*)
Taunton Deane	25 – 26	✓	✓	✓	✓	✓	
Exeter	Turn off at exit 30	✓	✓	✓	✓	✓	✓

M6

	Between Access Numbers	Overnight accommodation	Hot meals at night	Repair	C Young children	Picnic area	Tourist Information
Corley	3 – 4		✓	✓	✓		
Hilton Park	10A – 11	✓	✓	✓	✓	✓	✓
Keele	15 – 16		✓	✓	✓		✓
Sandbach	16 – 17		✓	✓	✓		✓
Knutsford	18 – 19		✓	✓	✓	✓	
Charnock Richard	27 – 28	✓	✓	✓	✓		✓
Forton	32 – 33	✓	✓	✓	✓	✓	✓
Burton *(Northbound only)*	35 - 36		✓	✓	✓	✓	
Killington *(Southbound only)*	36-37		✓	✓	✓	✓	✓
Tebay West *(Northbound only)*	38 – 39	✓ (*Caravan site*)	✓	✓	✓	✓	
Southwaite	41 – 42	✓	✓	✓	✓	✓	✓

M8

	Between Access Numbers	Overnight accommodation	Hot meals at night	Repair	C Young children	Picnic area	Tourist Information
Harthill	4 – 5		✓		✓		

M9

	Between Access Numbers	Overnight accommodation	Hot meals at night	Repair	C Young children	Picnic area	Tourist Information
Stirling	Turn off at exit 9	✓	✓	✓	✓	✓	✓

M23

	Between Access Numbers	Overnight accommodation	Hot meals at night	Repair	C Young children	Picnic area	Tourist Information
Pease Pottage	11		✓		✓		

M25

	Between Access Numbers	Overnight accommodation	Hot meals at night	Repair	C Young children	Picnic area	Tourist Information
South Mimms	Turn off at exit 23		✓		✓		✓
Thurrock	30 – 31		✓		✓		

M27

	Between Access Numbers	Overnight accommodation	Hot meals at night	Repair	C Young children	Picnic area	Tourist Information
Rownhams	3 – 4	✓	✓	✓	✓	✓	✓

M42

	Between Access Numbers	Overnight accommodation	Hot meals at night	Repair	C Young children	Picnic area	Tourist Information
Tamworth	Turn off at exit 10	✓	✓		✓	✓	

M61

	Between Access Numbers	Overnight accommodation	Hot meals at night	Repair	C Young children	Picnic area	Tourist Information
Anderton	6 – 8		✓	✓	✓	✓	

M62

	Between Access Numbers	Overnight accommodation	Hot meals at night	Repair	C Young children	Picnic area	Tourist Information
Burtonwood	7 – 9		✓	✓	✓		
Birch	18 – 19	✓	✓	✓	✓	✓	
Hartshead Moor	25 – 26		✓	✓	✓		✓
Ferrybridge	Turn off at exit 33	✓	✓	✓	✓		

M74

	Between Access Numbers	Overnight accommodation	Hot meals at night	Repair	C Young children	Picnic area	Tourist Information
Bothwell *(Southbound only)*	4 – 5		✓		✓	✓	
Hamilton *(Northbound only)*	5 – 6	✓	✓		✓	✓	✓

M90

	Between Access Numbers	Overnight accommodation	Hot meals at night	Repair	C Young children	Picnic area	Tourist Information
Kinross	6	✓	✓		✓	✓	✓ (*Summer only*)

		Overnight accommodation	Hot meals at night	Repair	C Young children	Picnic area	Tourist Information
Washington	Tyne & Wear	✓	✓	✓	✓		

Parking, toilets and fuel are available at all times, and although all have hot meals available during the day some have only vending machine facilities at night.

IV M25 - LONDON ORBITAL MOTORWAY

Chesham
Amersham
Beaconsfield
Chorleywood
RICKMANSWORTH
WATFORD
Bushey
BARNET
Potters Bar
FINCHLEY
HENDON
HARROW
WEMBLEY
Hampstead
WILLESDEN
Ruislip
UXBRIDGE
SLOUGH
WINDSOR
Hayes
Southall
Ealing
Acton
Hammersmith
Fulham
Chelsea
Kensington
WESTMINSTER
HOUNSLOW
Brentford
Heathrow Airport
Richmond
Twickenham
Wimbledon
KINGSTON
Feltham
Staines
Egham
Sunbury
CHERTSEY
Weybridge
Walton-on-Thames
Esher
Surbiton
New Malden
Sutton
Epsom
Cobham
WOKING
Leatherhead
Banstead
Chobham
Ashtead
Wandsworth
Stanmore
Edgware
Northwood
Radlett
Borehamwood
Elstree
Gerrards Cross
Datchet
Ashford
Shepperton
Byfleet
Oxshott

CHESHUNT
Epping
ENFIELD
Loughton
Chigwell
Chingford
Edmonton
TOTTENHAM
Walthamstow
Woodford
Leyton
Hackney
ISLINGTON
ILFORD
Barking
ROMFORD
Hornchurch
DAGENHAM
BRENTWOOD
Billericay
Laindon
Upminster
Rainham
Purfleet
Grays
Tilbury
Northfleet
GRAVESEND
DARTFORD
Erith
Bexley
Sidcup
WOOLWICH
Greenwich
Lewisham
Catford
Bromley
Beckenham
CROYDON
ORPINGTON
Swanley
West Kingsdown
Kemsing
Otford
SEVENOAKS
Westerham
Caterham
Coulsdon
Whyteleafe
Biggin Hill
Dartford Tunnel
Woolwich Ferry
CITY OF LONDON
Thames
Miles
Kilometres

Distances in these tables are based on Primary Routes as far as possible and are not necessarily the shortest distances between any two towns.

DISTANCES

DISTANCES IN MILES

	LONDON	Aberdeen	Aberystwyth	Birmingham	Bournemouth	Brighton	Bristol	Cambridge	Cardiff	Carlisle	Chester	Derby	Dover	Edinburgh	Exeter	Fishguard	Fort William	Glasgow	Harwich	Holyhead
LONDON		806	341	179	169	89	183	84	249	484	298	198	117	608	275	422	818	634	114	420
Aberdeen	501		724	658	903	895	789	742	792	349	571	634	924	198	911	795	254	241	848	692
Aberystwyth	212	450		193	328	425	206	354	177	375	153	222	459	526	325	90	708	525	460	182
Birmingham	111	409	120		237	267	132	161	163	309	117	63	296	460	259	283	642	459	267	246
Bournemouth	105	561	204	147		148	124	251	195	554	351	306	278	705	132	375	887	703	283	463
Brighton	55	556	264	166	92		217	180	288	573	386	286	130	697	275	468	906	723	203	509
Bristol	114	490	128	82	77	135		233	71	439	237	195	314	591	121	251	722	589	314	340
Cambridge	52	461	220	100	156	112	145		290	417	269	155	204	544	351	436	750	566	106	391
Cardiff	155	492	110	101	121	179	44	180		443	237	225	385	587	192	180	776	608	359	341
Carlisle	301	217	233	192	344	356	273	259	275		222	304	602	151	571	444	333	150	523	341
Chester	185	355	95	73	218	240	147	167	147	138		114	415	373	357	243	555	372	375	137
Derby	123	394	138	39	190	178	121	96	140	189	71		315	436	315	312	637	454	261	251
Dover	73	574	285	184	173	81	195	127	239	374	258	196		726	391	539	935	752	203	538
Edinburgh	378	123	327	286	438	433	367	338	365	94	232	271	451		723	616	233	72	650	489
Exeter	171	566	202	161	82	171	75	218	119	355	222	196	243	449		372	904	721	389	460
Fishguard	262	494	56	176	233	291	156	271	112	276	151	194	335	383	231		777	594	533	272
Fort William	508	158	440	399	551	563	480	466	482	207	345	396	581	145	562	483		183	856	671
Glasgow	394	150	326	285	437	449	366	352	378	93	231	282	467	45	448	369	114		673	488
Harwich	71	527	286	166	176	126	195	66	223	325	233	162	126	404	242	331	532	418		497
Holyhead	261	430	113	153	288	316	211	243	212	212	85	156	334	304	286	169	417	303	309	
Hull	168	348	229	143	255	223	226	124	244	155	132	98	251	225	301	285	362	250	181	217
Inverness	537	105	482	445	594	590	528	497	524	253	387	430	601	159	603	529	66	176	563	463
Leeds	190	322	173	111	261	251	206	148	212	115	78	74	269	199	268	229	322	210	214	163
Leicester	98	417	151	39	166	153	112	68	139	208	94	28	171	294	187	207	415	301	134	183
Lincoln	136	382	189	85	217	191	163	86	190	180	123	51	213	259	238	245	387	273	152	208
Liverpool	205	334	104	94	235	260	164	184	164	116	17	88	278	210	239	160	323	211	250	94
Manchester	192	332	133	81	228	247	167	154	172	115	38	58	265	209	242	189	322	210	220	123
Newcastle	271	230	270	209	348	326	295	231	310	58	175	164	344	107	370	326	257	143	297	260
Norwich	107	487	267	155	212	162	221	60	237	287	210	139	169	364	277	331	494	380	63	299
Nottingham	123	388	154	50	189	178	132	84	152	185	87	16	196	265	207	210	392	278	150	172
Oxford	56	464	157	62	92	99	66	79	107	256	128	98	129	341	139	207	461	340	134	202
Penzance	282	683	313	268	193	269	186	329	230	466	333	307	354	560	111	342	673	559	353	397
Plymouth	213	614	244	199	124	213	117	260	161	397	264	238	285	491	42	273	604	490	284	328
Preston	216	302	144	105	256	271	185	198	190	85	49	100	289	179	266	200	292	180	264	125
Sheffield	162	358	158	75	227	217	163	124	176	145	78	36	235	235	248	214	352	240	190	163
Southampton	79	530	202	128	32	60	75	136	119	322	194	164	149	416	111	231	520	415	150	283
Stranraer	410	235	342	301	453	465	382	368	384	109	247	298	483	133	464	385	199	85	434	321
Swansea	196	506	76	126	162	220	85	216	41	289	151	165	280	383	160	71	496	382	264	189
Worcester	114	428	98	26	131	168	60	116	75	211	88	65	187	305	135	155	418	304	182	152
York	196	309	197	134	273	251	215	157	242	116	102	89	269	186	290	253	323	211	223	187

IN KILOMETRES

Hull	Inverness	Leeds	Leicester	Lincoln	Liverpool	Manchester	Newcastle	Norwich	Nottingham	Oxford	Penzance	Plymouth	Preston	Sheffield	Southampton	Stranraer	Swansea	Worcester	York	
270	864	306	158	219	330	309	436	172	198	90	454	343	348	261	127	660	315	183	315	**LONDON**
560	169	518	671	615	538	534	370	784	624	747	1099	988	486	576	853	378	814	689	497	**Aberdeen**
369	776	278	243	304	167	214	435	430	248	253	504	393	232	254	325	550	122	158	317	**Aberystwyth**
230	716	179	63	137	151	130	336	249	80	100	431	320	169	121	206	484	203	42	216	**Birmingham**
410	956	420	267	349	378	367	560	341	304	148	311	200	412	365	51	729	261	211	439	**Bournemouth**
359	950	404	246	307	418	398	525	261	286	159	433	343	436	349	97	748	354	270	404	**Brighton**
364	850	332	180	262	264	269	475	356	212	106	299	188	298	262	121	615	137	97	346	**Bristol**
200	800	238	109	138	296	248	372	97	135	127	529	418	319	200	219	592	348	187	253	**Cambridge**
393	843	341	224	306	264	277	499	381	245	172	370	259	306	283	192	618	66	121	389	**Cardiff**
249	407	185	335	290	187	185	93	462	298	412	750	639	137	233	518	175	465	340	187	**Carlisle**
212	623	126	151	198	27	61	282	338	140	206	536	425	79	126	312	398	243	142	164	**Chester**
158	692	119	45	82	142	93	264	224	26	158	494	383	161	58	264	480	266	105	143	**Derby**
404	967	433	275	343	447	426	554	272	315	208	570	459	465	378	240	777	451	301	433	**Dover**
362	256	320	473	417	338	336	172	586	426	549	901	790	288	378	669	214	616	491	299	**Edinburgh**
484	970	431	301	383	385	389	595	446	333	224	179	68	428	399	179	747	257	217	467	**Exeter**
459	851	369	333	394	257	304	525	533	338	333	550	439	322	344	372	620	114	249	407	**Fishguard**
583	106	518	668	623	520	518	414	795	631	742	1083	972	470	566	837	320	798	673	520	**Fort William**
402	283	338	484	439	340	338	230	612	447	547	900	789	290	386	668	137	615	489	340	**Glasgow**
291	906	344	216	245	402	354	478	101	241	216	568	457	425	306	241	698	429	293	359	**Harwich**
349	745	262	295	335	151	198	418	481	277	325	639	528	201	262	455	517	304	245	301	**Holyhead**
	615	90	145	61	196	151	190	240	148	262	663	552	180	103	412	425	433	272	63	**Hull**
382		579	729	673	605	604	428	842	682	816	1159	1049	555	634	925	417	872	747	552	**Inverness**
56	358		158	108	119	64	148	277	116	272	613	502	90	58	378	360	369	220	39	**Leeds**
90	453	98		82	187	138	301	187	42	119	480	369	206	105	225	510	282	109	174	**Leicester**
38	418	67	51		192	137	245	169	56	201	562	451	185	72	307	465	340	192	124	**Lincoln**
122	376	74	116	119		55	253	360	167	251	563	452	50	119	357	362	270	169	158	**Liverpool**
94	375	40	86	85	34		212	306	119	230	568	457	48	64	325	360	295	164	103	**Manchester**
118	266	92	187	152	157	132		414	254	412	774	663	203	206	518	262	517	378	127	**Newcastle**
149	523	174	116	105	224	190	257		198	224	626	515	354	241	299	637	439	283	293	**Norwich**
92	424	72	26	35	104	74	158	123		156	512	401	167	64	262	473	283	122	134	**Nottingham**
163	507	169	74	125	156	143	256	139	97		402	291	272	217	106	587	230	95	291	**Oxford**
412	720	381	298	349	350	353	481	389	318	250		126	597	560	357	925	436	396	645	**Penzance**
343	652	312	229	280	281	284	412	320	249	181	78		486	447	246	814	325	285	534	**Plymouth**
112	345	56	128	115	31	30	126	220	104	169	371	302		113	375	312	322	203	126	**Preston**
64	394	36	65	45	74	40	128	150	40	135	348	278	70		323	490	336	163	90	**Sheffield**
256	575	235	140	191	222	202	322	186	163	66	222	153	233	201		679	257	193	398	**Southampton**
264	259	224	317	289	225	224	163	396	294	365	575	506	194	254	422		641	515	362	**Stranraer**
269	542	229	175	211	168	183	321	273	176	143	271	202	200	209	160	398		161	418	**Swansea**
169	464	137	68	119	105	102	235	176	76	59	246	177	126	101	120	320	100		257	**Worcester**
39	343	24	108	77	98	64	79	182	83	181	401	332	78	56	247	225	260	160		**York**

Aberdeen
BBC Radio Aberdeen FM 93.1, 93.8 & 94.5 MHz
North Sound FM 96.9 MHz. MV 1035 kHz

Ayr
West Sound FM 96.7 & 97.5 MHz. MV 1035 kHz

Barnsley
Radio Hallam FM 102.9 MHz
Classic Gold MW 1305 kHz

Basingstoke & Andover
Radio 210 FM 102.9 MHz

Bath
GWR FM 103.0 MHz

Bedford
BBC Radio Bedfordshire FM 95.5, 103.8 & 104.5MHz
MW 630 & 1161 kHz
Chiltern Radio FM 96.9 & 97.6 MHz

Belfast
Downtown Radio FM 97.4, 96.6, 96.4 & 102.4 MHz
MW 1026 kHz

Birmingham
BBC Radio WM (West Midlands) FM 95.6 MHz. MW 828 & 1458 kHz
BRMB Radio FM 96.4 MHz. MW 1152 kHz
Buzz FM FM 102.4 MHz

Borders/Peebles
Radio Borders FM 103.1, 97.5, 96.8 & 103.4 MHz

Bournemouth
BBC Radio Solent FM 96.1 MHz. MW 999 & 1359 kHz
2CR FM 97.2 & 102.3 MHz. MW 828 kHz

Bradford
Pennine Radio FM 97.5 MHz
Classic Gold MW 1278 kHz
Bradford City Radio FM 103.2 MHz

Brighton
BBC Radio Sussex FM 95.0, 95.1, 95.3, 104.0 & 104.5 MHz
MW 1161, 1368 & 1485 kHz
Southern Sound FM 103.5 and 96.9 MHz. MW 1323 kHz

Bristol
BBC Radio Bristol FM 94.9, 95.5 & 104.6 MHz. MW 1323 & 1548 kHz
GWR FM 96.3 MHz
Brunel MW 1206 kHz

Bury St Edmunds
Saxon Radio FM 96.4 MHz. MW 1251 kHz

Cambridge
BBC Radio Cambridgeshire FM 96.0 & 95.7 MHz. MW 1026 & 1449 kHz
CNFM FM 103.0 MHz

Canterbury
BBC Radio Kent FM 96.7 & 104.2 MHz. MW 774, 1035 & 1603 kHz
Invicta Radio FM 102.8 MHz

Cardiff
Red Dragon Radio FM 103.2 MHz. MW 1359 kHz

Carlisle
BBC Radio Cumbria/(R. Furness) FM 96.1, 95.2 & 104.2 MHz. MW 837 kHz

Chelmsford
BBC Essex FM 95.3 & 103.5 MHz. MW 729, 765 & 1530 kHz
Essex Radio FM 102.6 MHz
Breeze MW 1359 kHz

Colchester
Mellow 1557 MW 1557 kHz

Coventry
BBC CWR FM 94.8 & 103.7 MHz
Mercia Sound FM 97.0 & 102.9 MHz. MW 1359 kHz

Cumbria
BBC Radio Cumbria FM 95.6 MHz. MW 756 & 1458 kHz

Derby
BBC Radio Derby FM 94.2, 95.3 & 104.5 MHz. MW 1116 kHz
Radio Trent FM 102.8 MHz
Gem-AM MW 945 kHz

Dundee
Radio Tay FM 102.8 MHz. MW 1161 kHz

Eastbourne
Southern Sound FM 102.4 MHz

Edinburgh
Radio Forth FM 97.3 MHz. MW 1548 kHz

Exeter
BBC Radio Devon FM 94.8, 103.4, 96.0 & 95.8 MHz
MW 801, 855, 990 & 1458 kHz
Devon Air Radio FM 97.0 & 103.0 MHz. MW 666 kHz

Glasgow
Radio Clyde FM 102.5 MHz. MW 1152 kHz

Gloucester & Cheltenham
BBC Radio Gloucestershire FM 95.0 & 104.7 MHz
MW 603 kHz
Severn Sound FM 102.4 & 103.0 MHz. MW 774 kHz

Great Yarmouth
Radio Broadland FM 102.4 MHz. MW 1152 kHz

Guernsey
BBC Radio Guernsey FM 93.2 MHz. MW 1116 kHz

Guildford
BBC Radio Surrey FM 104.6 MHz
County Sound FM 96.4 & 97.1 MHz. MW 1476 kHz

Haslemere
Delta FM 97.1 MHz

Hastings
Southern Sound FM 97.5 MHz

Hereford
BBC Radio Hereford and Worcester FM 94.7 & 104 MHz.
MW 738 & 819 kHz
Radio Wyvern FM 97.6 MHz. MW 954 kHz

Huddersfield and Halifax
Pennine Radio FM 102.5 MHz
Classic Gold MW 1530 kHz

Hull
BBC Radio Humberside FM 95.9 MHz. MW 1485 kHz
Viking Radio FM 96.9 MHz
Classic Gold MW 1161 kHz

Inverness
Moray Firth Radio FM 97.4 MHz. MW 1107 kHz

Ipswich
BBC Radio Suffolk FM 95.5, 103.9 & 104.6 MHz
Radio Orwell FM 97.1 MHz. MW 1170 kHz

Jersey
BBC Radio Jersey FM 88.8 MHz. MW 1026 kHz

Kent
BBC Radio Kent FM 96.7 & 104.2 MHz. MW 774, 1034 & 1602 kHz
Invicta Radio FM 102.8, 96.1, 97.0, 95.9 & 103.1 MHz
Coast MW 603 & 1242 kHz

Kettering
KCBC MW 1530 kHz

Leeds
BBC Radio Leeds FM 92.4 & 95.3 MHz. MW 774 kHz
Radio Aire FM 96.3 MHz. MW 828 kHz
Magic 828 MW 828 kHz

Leicester
BBC Radio Leicester FM 104.9 MHz. MW 837 kHz
Leicester Sound FM 103.2 MHz
GEM-AM MW 1260 kHz

Lincoln
BBC Radio Lincolnshire FM 94.9 MHz. MW 1368 kHz

Liverpool
BBC Radio Merseyside FM 95.8 MHz. MW 1485 kHz
Radio City FM 96.7 kHz
City Talk MW 1548 kHz

London
Greater London Radio FM 94.9 Mhz. MW 1458 kHz
Capital FM 95.8 MHz
Capital Gold MW 1548 kHz
Choice FM 96.9 MHz
Jazz FM FM 102.2 MHz
Kiss FM FM 100.0 MHz
LBC Newstalk FM 97.3 MHz
London Greek FM 103.3 MHz
London Talkback MW 1152 kHz
Melody FM 104.9 MHz
RTM FM 103.8 MHz
Spectrum MW 558 kHz
Sunrise MW 1413 kHz
WNK FM 103.3 MHz

Luton
Supergold AM MW 828 kHz

Maidstone/Medway
BBC Radio Kent FM 96.7 & 104.2 MHz. MW 774, 1035 & 1602 kHz
Invicta Radio FM 95.9, 96.1, 97.0 & 103.1 MHz
Coast Classics MW 603 & 1242 kHz

Manchester
BBC Radio Manchester FM 95.1 MHz. MW 1458 kHz
Piccadilly Gold MW 1552 kHz
Piccadilly Key 103 FM 103.0 MHz
Sunset Radio FM 102.0 MHz

Milton Keynes
Horizon Radio FM 103.3 MHz

Newcastle
BBC Radio Newcastle FM 96.0 & 104.4 MHz. MW 1458 kHz
Metro Radio FM 97.1 & 103.0 MHz
Great North Radio MW 1152 kHz

Newport
Red Dragon Radio FM 97.4 MHz. MW 1305 kHz

Northampton
BBC Radio Northampton FM 104.2 & 103.6 MHz. MW 1107 kHz
Northants Radio FM 96.6 MHz
Supergold AM MW 1557 kHz

Norwich
BBC Radio Norfolk FM 95.1 & 104.4 MHz. MW 855 & 873 kHz
Radio Broadland FM 102.4 MHz. MW 1152 kHz

Nottingham
BBC Radio Nottingham FM 95.5 & 103.8 MHz. MW 1521 & 1584 kHz
Radio Trent FM 96.2 MHz
Gem-Am MW 999 kHz

Oxford
BBC Radio Oxford FM 95.2 MHz. MW 1485 kHz
Fox FM FM 97.4 & 102.6 MHz

Perth
Radio Tay FM 96.4 MHz. MW 1584 kHz

Peterborough
Hereward Radio FM 102.7 MHz. MW 1332 kHz

Plymouth
Plymouth Sound FM 97.0 & 96.6 MHz. MW 1152 kHz

Portsmouth
Ocean Sound FM 97.5 MHz. MW 1170 & 1557 kHz
Power FM FM 103.2 MHz

Preston/Blackpool
BBC Radio Lancashire FM 95.5 & 104.5. MW 855 & 1557 kHz
Red Rose Radio FM 97.4 MHz

Reading
BBC Radio Berkshire FM 94.6, 95.4 & 104.4 MHz
Radio 210 FM 97.0 MHz. MW 1431 kHz

Reigate & Crawley
Radio Mercury FM 97.5 & 102.7 MHz. MW 1521 kHz

Sheffield/Rotherham
BBC Radio Sheffield FM 104.1 & 88.6 MHz. MW 1035 kHz
Radio Hallam FM 97.4 & 96.1 MHz
Classic Gold MW 1548 kHz

Shrewsbury
BBC Radio Shropshire FM 96.0 & 95.0 MHz. MW 756 & 1584 kHz
Beacon Radio FM 103.1 MHz

Solway
BBC Radio Solway FM 94.7, 93.1 & 94.1 MHz. MW 585 kHz

Southampton
BBC Radio Solent FM 96.1 MHz. MW 999 & 1359 kHz
Ocean Sound FM 97.5 MHz. MW 11704 & 1557 kHz
Power FM FM 103.2 MHz

Southend
BBC Essex FM 95.3 & 103.5 MHz. MW 729, 765 & 1530 kHz
Essex Radio FM 96.3 MHz
Breeze MW 1431 kHz

Stafford
Echo 96 FM 96.4 MHz

Stockport
KFM Radio FM 104.9 MHz

Stoke-on-Trent
BBC Radio Stoke FM 94.6 MHz. MW 1503 kHz
Signal Radio FM 96.4, 96.9 & 102.6 MHz. MW 1170 kHz

Sunderland
Wear FM 103.4 MHz

Swansea
Swansea Sound FM 96.4 MHz. MW 1170 kHz

Swindon/Wilts
BBC Wiltshire Sound FM 103.5, 103.6 & 104.3 MHz
MW 1332 & 1368 kHz
GWR-Swindon FM 97.l2 MHz. MW 1161 kHz

Teesside
BBC Radio Cleveland FM 95.0 & 95.8 MHz. MW 1548 kHz
TFM Radio FM 96.6 MHz.
Great North Radio MW 1170 kHz

Torbay
Devon Air Radio FM96.4 MHz. MW 954 kHz

Truro
BBC Radio Cornwall FM 95.2, 96.0 & 103.9 MHz. MW 630 & 657 kHz

Tweed
BBC Radio Tweed FM 92.8, 93.5, 93.9 & 104.6 MHz

Woking
First Gold MW 1476 kHz
Premier FM 97.1 MHz

Wolverhampton
BBC Radio WM FM 95.6 MHz. MW 828 & 1458 kHz
Beacon Radio FM 97.2 MHz
WABC MW 990 kHz

Worcester
BBC Radio Hereford and Worcester FM 94.7 & 104.0 MHz
MW 738 & 819 kHz
Radio Wyvern FM 102.8 MHz. MW 1530 kHz

Wrexham & Deeside
Marcher Sound/Sain-Y-Gororav MW 1260 kHz
MFM FM 97.0 & 103.4 MHz

York
BBC Radio York FM 95.5, 103.7 & 104.3 MHz. MW 666 & 1260 kHz

Yeovil/Taunton
Orchard FM FM 102.6 MHz

Key to Map Symbols

- Motorways with Service Areas
- Primary Routes (Dual Carriageway)
- Primary Routes (Single Carriageway)
- 'A' Roads (Dual Carriageway)
- 'A' Roads (Single Carriageway)
- 'B' Roads
- Other Roads
- Motorways & roads under construction
- Motorway Interchanges & numbers
- Distances between symbols in Miles / Kilometres
- Car Ferries, Sea & Rivers
- Toll Roads & Bridges
- Hills 1 in 7 or steeper (Arrow points downhill). Main roads only
- Railways
- Navigable Rivers & Canals
- International Boundaries
- County Boundaries
- Spot heights in feet
- National Parks
- Designated Areas of Outstanding Natural Beauty
- Principal inland viewpoints
- ESHER Primary Route Towns
- Airports
- Castles
- Cathedrals and Abbeys
- Houses and Gardens open to the public
- N.T. National Trust Property open to the public
- Other places of interest
- AA and R.A.C. Telephone Boxes
- Youth Hostels
- Golf Courses
- Race Courses
- Motor Racing Circuits
- Coastal Yachting Centres
- Water Skiing Centres
- Country Parks
- Skiing Centres
- Rock Climbing Centres
- Pot-holing Centres
- Sand beaches
- Sand and Shingle beaches

Narrow Roads

- Primary Routes (trunk roads)
- Primary Routes
- "A" Roads

Narrow Roads with passing places

0 1 2 3 4 5 10 Miles
0 1 2 3 4 5 6 7 8 16 Kilometres

Motorway Interchanges

Because of limitations of scale it is not always possible to show the full details of complex interchanges.

The representation of a road on this map is no evidence of the existence of a right of way.

Based upon the Ordnance Survey map with the permission of the Controller of Her Majesty's Stationery Office.

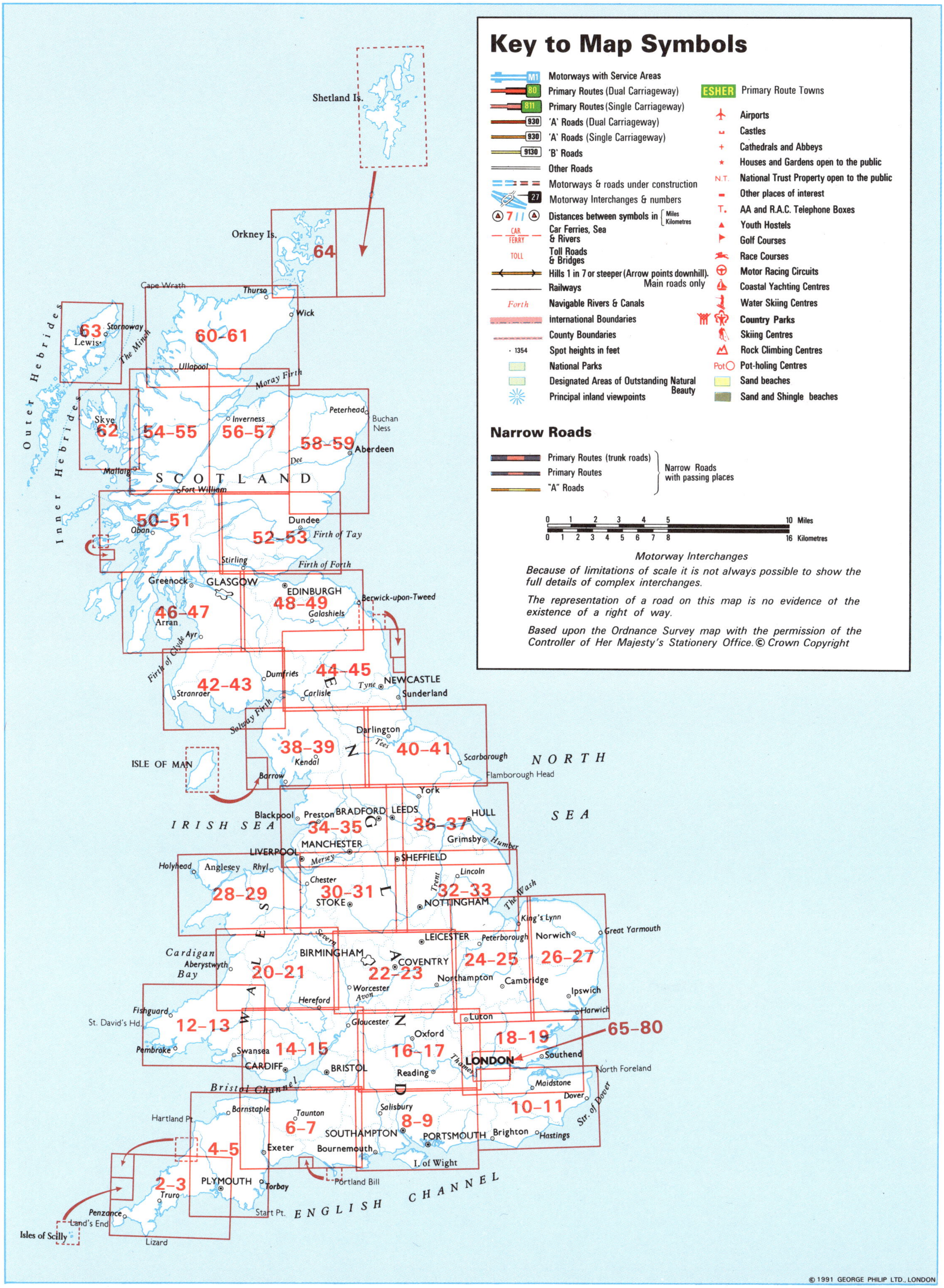

ATLANTIC OCEAN
ISLES OF SCILLY
CORNWALL
MOUNT'S BAY
PENWITH
WENDRON MOORS
THE LIZARD
Bude Bay
Bideford
Bude
Wadebridge
Boscastle
Tintagel
Padstow
NEWQUAY
Perranporth
St. Agnes
Portreath
Camborne
Redruth
TRURO
FALMOUTH
St. Mawes
Helston
Porthleven
Mullion
Lizard
Lizard Point
St. Ives
Hayle
PENZANCE
Newlyn
Mousehole
St. Just
Sennen
Lands End
Marazion
St. Michael's Mount
St. Mary's
Tresco
Bryher
St. Martin's
St. Agnes
Samson
Eastern Isles
Bishop Rock
SCILLY ISLES (ST. MARYS)
Penryn
Goonhilly Downs
Coverack
St. Keverne
Carrick Roads
Falmouth Bay
Watergate Bay
Ligger or Perran Bay
Whitesand Bay
Runnel Stone
The Manacles
Gerrans Bay
Tregony
Probus
St. Columb Major
Indian Queens
Chacewater
St. Day
Mevagissey

7 8 9 10 11 12

Bideford
Holsworthy
Okehampton
4
5
Newton Abbot
Exeter
Kingsbridge
A
B
C
D
E
F
G
H
C O R N W A L L
D E V O N
B O D M I N M O O R
E N G L I S H C H A N N E L
Boscastle
Tintagel
Camelford
Port Isaac
Wadebridge
Bodmin
St. Austell
Mevagissey
Lostwithiel
Fowey
Polperro
Looe
Liskeard
Launceston
Callington
Saltash
Torpoint
Tavistock
PLYMOUTH
Plympton
Plymstock
Devonport
Princetown
Lydford
Gunnislake
Calstock
Millbrook
Yelverton
Lifton
St. Austell Bay
Mevagissey Bay
Whitsand Bay
The Sound
Breakwater
Eddystone Rocks
Rame Head
Dodman Point
Bridestowe and Sourton Common
TO ROSCOFF, SANTANDER

7 8 9 10 11 12

A B C D E F

Bridgwater
Minehead
6
Taunton
Taunton
Taunton
Honiton
Wadebridge
BRISTOL CHANNEL
EXMOOR
SOMERSET
DEVON
BARNSTAPLE OR BIDEFORD BAY
Minehead
Lynton
Lynmouth
Combe Martin
Ilfracombe
Woolacombe
Braunton
BARNSTAPLE
BIDEFORD
Appledore
Westward Ho!
Clovelly
Hartland
Kilkhampton
Bude
Holsworthy
Great Torrington
Hatherleigh
OKEHAMPTON
North Tawton
Chulmleigh
South Molton
Dulverton
Tiverton
Crediton

1 2 3 4 5 6 7 8

A B C D E F

ENGLISH CHANNEL
CORNWALL
DARTMOOR
DARTMOOR FOREST
DARTMOOR NATIONAL PARK
BODMIN MOOR
SOUTH HAMS
EXETER
Exmouth
Dawlish
Teignmouth
Newton Abbot
Torbay
TORQUAY
PAIGNTON
Brixham
Dartmouth
Totnes
Kingsbridge
Salcombe
Ivybridge
Plympton
PLYMOUTH
Plymstock
DEVONPORT
Saltash
Tavistock
Launceston
Liskeard
Looe
Polperro
Ashburton
Buckfastleigh
Moretonhampstead
Chagford
Bovey Tracey
Princetown
Yelverton
Callington
Torpoint
Babbacombe Bay
Tor Bay
Start Bay
Bigbury Bay
Whitsand Bay
Eddystone Rocks
Brent Moor
Holne Moor
Bodmin
St. Austell
TO ROSCOFF, SANTANDER

14

BRISTOL CHANNEL
WARNING: Drivers of heavy vehicles are reminded of the steep hills on the A39 between Minehead and Lynmouth.
BRIDGWATER BAY
Lynmouth Bay
Porlock Bay
Blue Anchor Bay
EXMOOR
Brendon Hills
The Quantocks
VALE OF TAUNTON DEANE
Blackdown Hills
Culm Valley
SOMERSET
DEVON
Minehead
Watchet
Burnham-on-Sea
Highbridge
South Molton
Dulverton
Bampton
Wiveliscombe
Wellington
TAUNTON
Tiverton
Cullompton
Crediton
EXETER
Honiton
Sidmouth
Exmouth
Budleigh Salterton
Seaton
Dawlish
Moretonhampstead
Bovey Tracey
Barnstaple
Ilfracombe
Okehampton
Newton Abbot
Plymouth
Torquay

4

5

← Weston-super-Mare
Bristol
15
Bath
Devizes
Chippenham
7
MENDIP HILLS
Wells
Glastonbury
Shepton Mallet
Frome
Trowbridge
WARMINSTER
WILTSHIRE
Westbury
Street
Yeovil
Sherborne
Shaftesbury
Wincanton
Gillingham
Crewkerne
Chard
Ilminster
Bridport
Lyme Regis
LYME BAY
DORCHESTER
WEYMOUTH
Blandford Forum
Wareham
DORSET
NORTH DORSET DOWNS
SOUTH DORSET DOWNS
PURBECK HILLS
BLACKMORE VALE
Cranborne Chase
Isle of Portland
Chesil Beach
Weymouth Bay
Swanage
Salisbury
Andover
Ringwood
Poole
Bournemouth
COPYRIGHT, GEORGE PHILIP LTD.

W I L T S H I R E
S A L I S B U R Y
P L A I N
D O R S E T
H A M P S
N E W
F O R E S T
ISLE OF W
Vale of Wardour
Cranborne Chase
Isle of Purbeck
Purbeck Hills
SALISBURY
SOUTHAMPTON
WINCHESTER
ANDOVER
BOURNEMOUTH
POOLE
Ringwood
Blandford Forum
Christchurch
Lymington
Swanage
Wimborne Minster
Romsey
Eastleigh
Amesbury
Wilton
Fordingbridge
Wareham
Cowes
Newport
Yarmouth
Totland
Freshwater
New Milton
Lyndhurst
Hythe
Fawley
Poole Harbour
Poole Bay
Studland Bay
Swanage Bay
Christchurch Bay
Southampton Water
Danger Area
CAR FERRY
TO CHERBOURG, GUERNSEY, JERSEY
The Needles
Devizes
Marlborough
Newbury
Warminster
Wincanton
Sherborne
Dorchester
16
7

Newbury
Reading
Reading
Staines
London
17
7
8
9
10
11
12
A
B
C
D
E
F
G
H
Sevenoaks
Horsham
Horsham
Brighton
Brighton
10
BASINGSTOKE
Farnborough
Aldershot
GUILDFORD
FARNHAM
Alton
Godalming
Haslemere
Petersfield
Midhurst
Petworth
Cranleigh
Billingshurst
Pulborough
Storrington
Arundel
CHICHESTER
BOGNOR REGIS
Littlehampton
WORTHING
Havant
FAREHAM
Gosport
PORTSMOUTH
Portsea Island
Hayling Island
Selsey
Ryde
Bembridge
Sandown
Shanklin
Ventnor
S U R R E Y
W E S T
S U S S E X
South Downs
H I R E
I G H T
Waterlooville
Horndean
Cowplain
Fleet
Odiham
Hindhead
Liphook
Emsworth
Bosham
Middleton-on-Sea
Rustington
Angmering
Ferring
Goring-by-Sea
Fernhurst
Chiddingfold
Milford
Witley
Shalford
Gomshall
East Horsley
West Horsley
Fetcham
Ockham
Hog's Back
Chawton
Selborne
New Alresford
Wickham
Purbrook
Southsea
Lee-on-the-Solent
Stubbington
Alverstoke
Eastney
Wittering
East Wittering
West Wittering
Church Norton
Pagham
Aldwick
Felpham
Yapton
Walberton
Slindon
Singleton
Charlton
Cocking
Graffham
Duncton
Amberley
Washington
Findon
Steyning
Durrington
Salvington
Broadwater
Bury
Stopham
Fittleworth
Wisborough Green
Kirdford
Loxwood
Alfold
Dunsfold
Hambledon
Grayshott
Headley
Bordon
Whitehill
Liss
Rogate
Trotton
Harting
Buriton
Chalton
Clanfield
Hambledon
Soberton
Droxford
Meonstoke
West Meon
East Meon
Langrish
Bramdean
Cheriton
Ropley
Four Marks
Medstead
Bentworth
Binsted
Bentley
Crondall
Ewshot
Church Crookham
Hook
Hartley Wintney
Tongham
Ash
Puttenham
Compton
Elstead
Tilford
Frensham
Rowledge
Wrecclesham
Selsey Bill
Spithead
Stokes Bay
Osborne Bay
Chichester Harbour
Langstone Harbour
Portsmouth Harbour
Hayling Bay
Sandown Bay
Whitecliff Bay
Shanklin Chine
Luccombe Village
Bonchurch
St. Lawrence
Whitwell
Niton
Wroxall
Godshill
Apse Heath
Newchurch
Brading
St. Helens
Seaview
Nettlestone
Binstead
Fishbourne
Wootton Bridge
Havenstreet
Arreton
Horringford
Yaverland
Bridgemary
Rowner
Peel Common
Hill Head
Titchfield
Portchester
Cosham
Hilsea
Drayton
Bedhampton
Leigh Park
Rowland's Castle
Westbourne
Southbourne
Nutbourne
Fishbourne
Hunston
Donnington
Apuldram
Birdham
Earnley
Sidlesham
Highleigh
Somerley
North Mundham
Merston
Runcton
Oving
Tangmere
Westhampnett
Boxgrove
Halnaker
Eartham
Madehurst
Westergate
Eastergate
Barnham
Aldingbourne
Woodgate
Shripney
Flansham
Elmer
Climping
Ford
Lyminster
Poling
Patching
Clapham
Heyshott
Bepton
Didling
Treyford
Elsted
Chilgrove
West Dean
East Dean
Upwaltham
Compton
East Marden
North Marden
Up Marden
West Marden
Stoughton
Walderton
Funtington
West Ashling
East Ashling
Lavant
Mid Lavant
East Lavant
Summersdale
Stansted Park
Lordington
Forestside
Finchdean
Blendworth
Catherington
Lovedean
Denmead
Hambledon
COPYRIGHT, GEORGE PHILIP LTD.

1
2
3
4
5
6
London
18
19
A
B
C
D
E
F
G
H
17
9
Guildford
Chichester
Petworth
Salvington
Worthing
HOUNSLOW
Richmond
WANDSWORTH
LAMBETH
LEWISHAM
BEXLEY
Dartford
TILBURY
Gravesend
KINGSTON UPON THAMES
MERTON
BROMLEY
Swanley
Rochester
Chatham
CROYDON
Sutton
Epsom
Ewell
Orpington
Banstead
Leatherhead
Warlingham
Caterham
Redhill
Reigate
Dorking
Oxted
SEVENOAKS
MAIDSTONE
SURREY
Tonbridge
Edenbridge
Horley
GATWICK
EAST GRINSTEAD
TUNBRIDGE WELLS
Crowborough
CRAWLEY
HORSHAM
WEST SUSSEX
Ashdown Forest
Haywards Heath
Burgess Hill
Uckfield
EAST SUSSEX
Heathfield
Hailsham
LEWES
Newhaven
Seaford
Hove
BRIGHTON
Shoreham-by-Sea
EASTBOURNE
Bexhill
Pevensey Bay
Peacehaven
Beachy Head
M25
M20
M26
M23
M2

19
TO VLISSINGEN
Sheerness
Minster-on-Sea
Queenborough
Eastchurch
Warden
Leysdown-on-Sea
ISLE OF SHEPPEY
Elmley Island
Isle of Harty
The Swale
Medway
Gillingham
Rainham
Sittingbourne
Conyer
Teynham
Faversham
Whitstable
Seasalter
Herne Bay
Herne
Reculver
Birchington
Westgate on Sea
MARGATE
Cliftonville
Foreness Point
North Foreland
Broadstairs
Isle of Thanet
RAMSGATE
Minster
Manston
Monkton
Pegwell Bay
Sandwich Bay
Sandwich
Sandwich Flats
Stour
TO DUNKIRK
CANTERBURY
Sturry
Fordwich
Chartham
Bridge
Wingham
Ash
Eastry
Aylesham
Deal
Walmer
Kingsdown
St. Margaret's-at-Cliffe
St. Margaret's Bay
South Foreland
DOVER
TO ZEEBRUGGE, OSTEND
TO CALAIS, BOULOGNE
TO BOULOGNE
Whitfield
Temple Ewell
Buckland
Maxton
Farthingloe
Capel-le-Ferne
Hawkinge
FOLKESTONE
Cheriton
Sandgate
East Wear Bay
Hythe
Saltwood
Lympne
Elham
Lyminge
Lyminge Forest
Barham
Stelling Minnis
Petham
Wye
Chilham
Selling
Boughton Street
Charing
KENT
Lenham
Harrietsham
Hollingbourne
Bearsted
Headcorn
Pluckley
Egerton
ASHFORD
Kennington
Willesborough
Kingsnorth
Mersham
Smeeth
Aldington
Bilsington
Ham Street
Tenterden
Biddenden
Smarden
Bethersden
Woodchurch
Appledore
Snave
Brenzett
Romney Marsh
Dymchurch
St. Mary's Bay
New Romney
Old Romney
Littlestone-on-Sea
Greatstone-on-Sea
Romney Sands
Lydd
Lydd-on-Sea
Denge Marsh
Denge Beach
Dungeness
Walland Marsh
East Guldeford
Camber
Rye
Rye Harbour
Rye Bay
Winchelsea
Winchelsea Beach
Isle of Oxney
Rother Levels
Wittersham
Northiam
Peasmarsh
Udimore
Westfield
Pett
Cliff End
Fairlight
Fairlight Cove
Ore
HASTINGS
St. Leonards
West Road
East Road
STRAIT OF DOVER
Royal Military Canal
M2
M20
7
8
9
10
11
12
A
B
C
D
E
F
G
H

CARDIGAN BAY
CARMARTHEN BAY
ST. BRIDES BAY
Mynydd Preseli
DYFED
Cardigan
Fishguard
Haverfordwest
MILFORD HAVEN
Pembroke Dock
Pembroke
Tenby
St. Clears
Newcastle Emlyn
St. David's
Newport
Narberth
Whitland
Aberporth
Cardigan I.
Newport Bay
Fishguard Bay
Ramsey I.
Skomer I.
Skokholm I.
Gateholm I.
Sheep I.
Caldey I.
Green Scar
Ynysdeullyn
Broad Sound
Milford Haven
Freshwater West
Saundersfoot Bay
Pendine Sands
Laugharne Sands
Whitesand Bay or Porth-mawr
St. David's Head
Strumble Head
Dinas Head
Cemaes Head
St. Ann's Head
Linney Head
St. Govan's Head
Stackpole Head
Old Castle Head
Chapel Point
Monkstone Point
Ynys Lochdyn
TO ROSSLARE
Solva
Goodwick
Dinas
Crymych
Letterston
Johnston
Neyland
Saundersfoot
Kilgetty
Amroth
Pendine
Laugharne
Manorbier
Penally
Lamphey
Angle
Dale
Marloes
Roch
Newgale
Broad Haven
Little Haven
Llys-y-fran Res.
Scolton Manor
Picton Castle
Foel-cwmcerwyn 1760
Mynydd Carningli
487
477
40
4076
478

Aberystwyth
Aberystwyth
20
Aberaeron
New Quay
Lampeter
CAMBRIAN MOUNTAINS
POWYS
Llandovery
Builth Wells
Brecon
Brecon
Merthyr Tydfil
CARMARTHEN
Llandeilo
BRECON BEACONS NATIONAL PARK
FFOREST FAWR
Mynydd Du
Ammanford
Kidwelly
Burry Port
LLANELLI
WEST GLAMORGAN
Pontardulais
Pontardawe
Ystalyfera
Vale of Neath
NEATH
SWANSEA
PORT TALBOT
SWANSEA BAY
Maesteg
Hirwaun
Rhondda Valley
Cardiff
Pembrey Forest
Cefn Sidan Sands
Oxwich Bay
Llandovery
Usk Res.
Towy Forest
Mynydd Eppynt
Llyn Brianne Res.
Sennybridge
Trecastle
Vale of Tywi
Llanelli
Gorseinon
Morriston
Skewen
Glynneath
Forest of Brechfa
Gower
Rhossili Bay
14
14
COPYRIGHT, GEORGE PHILIP LTD.

Builth Wells
20
Builth Wells
Willersley
Llandovery
Llandeilo
Brecon
BLACK MOUNTAINS
POWYS
BRECON BEACONS NATIONAL PARK
Brecon Beacons
FFOREST FAWR
Mynydd Du
Crickhowell
Abergavenny
Talgarth
Hay Bluff
The Tumpa
Llanthony
Merthyr Tydfil
Tredegar
Ebbw Vale
Blaenavon
Abertillery
Pontypool
Cwmbran
Brynmawr
Aberdare
Mountain Ash
Rhondda
Pontypridd
Caerphilly
Blackwood
Bargoed
Risca
Newport
WEST GLAMORGAN
MID GLAMORGAN
SOUTH GLAMORGAN
Vale of Neath
Neath
Swansea
Port Talbot
Pontardawe
Ystalyfera
Maesteg
Bridgend
Porthcawl
Cowbridge
Llantrisant
Cardiff
Penarth
Barry
Barry Island
Cardiff Wales
Llantwit Major
Vale of Glamorgan
Ogmore-by-Sea
Nash Point
Sully I.
Flat Holm
Steep Holme
Weston-super-Mare
Bridgwater
Mouth of Severn
BRISTOL CHANNEL
13
6
Swansea

HEREFORD & WORCESTER
GLOUCESTER
AVON
WILTS
GWENT
FOREST OF DEAN
VALE OF BERKELEY
VALE OF GLOUCESTER
COTSWOLD HILLS
THE SEVERN
Hereford
Worcester
Birmingham
Evesham
Burford
Cirencester
Swindon
Marlborough
Devizes
Trowbridge
Warminster
Frome
Shepton Mallet
Bridgwater
CHELTENHAM
GLOUCESTER
ROSS-ON-WYE
MONMOUTH
Chepstow
Stroud
Tewkesbury
BRISTOL
Avonmouth
BATH
Chippenham
Clevedon
Portishead
Keynsham
Kingswood
Mangotsfield
Yate
Chipping Sodbury
Thornbury
Dursley
Tetbury
Malmesbury
Melksham
Bradford-on-Avon
Cinderford
Lydney
Ledbury
Sharpness
Berkeley
Wotton-under-Edge
Nailsworth
Painswick
M4
M5
M50
M32
7
8
9
10
11
12
21
22
16
A
B
C
D
E
F
G
H

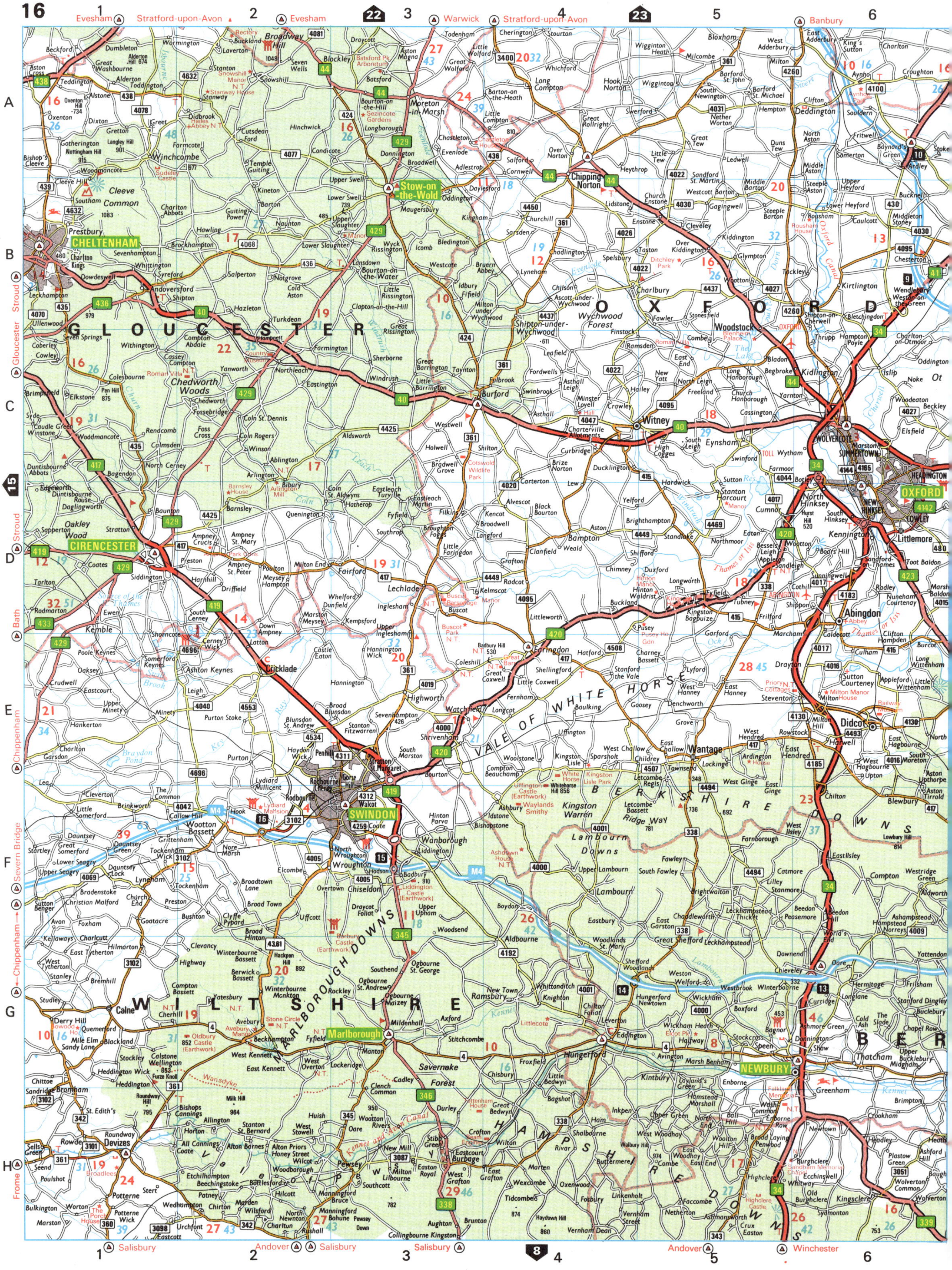
Evesham
Stratford-upon-Avon
Evesham
22
Warwick
Stratford-upon-Avon
23
Banbury
CHELTENHAM
Cleeve Common
GLOUCESTER
Stow-on-the-Wold
Moreton-in-Marsh
Chipping Norton
OXFORD
Wychwood Forest
Woodstock
Burford
Witney
Kidlington
OXFORD
CIRENCESTER
Chedworth Woods
Fairford
Lechlade
Faringdon
Abingdon
Didcot
Cricklade
VALE OF WHITE HORSE
Wantage
SWINDON
BERKSHIRE DOWNS
Lambourn Downs
MARLBOROUGH DOWNS
Marlborough
WILTSHIRE
Calne
Devizes
Hungerford
NEWBURY
Savernake Forest
HAMPSHIRE DOWNS
VALE OF PEWSEY
Salisbury
Andover
Salisbury
Salisbury
8
Andover
Winchester
Gloucester
Stroud
Bath
Chippenham
Severn Bridge
Chippenham
Frome
15

Towcester
Towcester
Towcester
23
Northampton
Bedford
25
7
8
9
10
11
12
A
B
C
D
E
F
G
H
MILTON KEYNES
Bletchley
Buckingham
BEDFORD
Leighton Buzzard
DUNSTABLE
LUTON
Letchworth
Hitchin
Bicester
Harpenden
Baldock
Stevenage
Hertford
B U C K S
AYLESBURY
HERTFORD
Berkhamsted
ST. ALBANS
Hemel Hempstead
Tring
The Three Hundreds of Aylesbury
Thame
Princes Risborough
Chesham
Amersham
WATFORD
Borehamwood
Rickmansworth
HIGH WYCOMBE
Beaconsfield
HARROW
CHILTERN
Marlow
Henley-on-Thames
MAIDENHEAD
Slough
HILLINGDON
EALING
HEATHROW
HOUNSLOW
RICHMOND
Windsor
READING
BRACKNELL
Wokingham
STAINES
KINGSTON UPON THAMES
Chertsey
Walton-on-Thames
Esher
Weybridge
Camberley
Woking
SURREY
Leatherhead
Epsom
London
Wallingford
Basingstoke
Basingstoke
Basingstoke
Alton
Guildford
9
18
10

1
Bedford
2
St. Neots
3
25
Royston
4
Stump Cross
5
Stump Cross
6
A
B
C
D
E
F
G
H
Northampton
Towcester
Aylesbury
17
High Wycombe
Slough
Guildford
Letchworth
Baldock
Hitchin
STEVENAGE
LUTON
HERTFORD
Harpenden
Welwyn Garden City
HERTFORD
Ware
Hoddesdon
HARLOW
BISHOP'S STORTFORD
ST. ALBANS
HATFIELD
Hemel Hempstead
Potters Bar
Cheshunt
Waltham Abbey
Epping
Ongar
WATFORD
Borehamwood
Rickmansworth
ENFIELD
BARNET
Chigwell
Brentwood
HARROW
HARINGEY
WALTHAM FOREST
REDBRIDGE
HAVERING
ROMFORD
ISLINGTON
HACKNEY
CAMDEN
BRENT
BARKING
Dagenham
NEWHAM
HILLINGDON
EALING
LONDON
City
HAMMERSMITH
KENSINGTON
WESTMINSTER
CHELSEA
SOUTHWARK
TOWER HAMLETS
GREENWICH
Ferry
Kew Br.
HEATHROW
HOUNSLOW
Richmond
WANDSWORTH
LAMBETH
LEWISHAM
BEXLEY
Dartford Tunnel
Grays
TILBURY
Gravesend
Dartford
Swanley
STAINES
KINGSTON UPON THAMES
MERTON
BROMLEY
Orpington
Sunbury on Thames
Walton-on-Thames
Chertsey
Weybridge
Esher
Epsom
Ewell
Sutton
CROYDON
Leatherhead
Banstead
Caterham
Warlingham
SEVENOAKS
SURREY
9
Horsham
Crawley
East Grinstead
Guildford
10
Tonbridge
Tonbridge

25
27
7
8
9
10
11
12
A
B
C
D
E
F
G
H
Haverhill
Sudbury
Ipswich
FELIXSTOWE
HARWICH
Halstead
Braintree
Coggeshall
COLCHESTER
Wivenhoe
Brightlingsea
Mersea Island
West Mersea
Tiptree
Witham
Maldon
HELMSFORD
CLACTON ON SEA
Walton on the Naze
Frinton-on-Sea
Holland-on-Sea
St. Osyth
Blackwater
Dengie Flat
Buxey Sand
Burnham-on-Crouch
Foulness Sands
Foulness Island
Maplin Sands
Rochford
Rayleigh
Billericay
Wickford
BASILDON
SOUTHEND ON SEA
Canvey Island
Thames
Blyth Sands
Sheerness
Queenborough
Minster-on-Sea
ISLE OF SHEPPEY
Rochester
Gillingham
Chatham
Sittingbourne
Faversham
Whitstable
Herne Bay
CANTERBURY
MAIDSTONE
Margate
Ramsgate
Ashford
Dover
TO VLISSINGEN
S E X
K E N T

Penrhyndeudraeth
Betws-y-coed
Corwen
28
29
13
14
Carmarthen
Llanwrda
Llandovery
Aberaeron
Cardigan
Barmouth
Barmouth Bay
Fairbourne
Dolgellau
Cader Idris
Mynydd Ceiswyn
Mynydd Dolgoed
Dyfi Forest
Dinas Mawddwy
Mallwyd
Llangadfan
Llanfair Caereinion
Corris
Towyn
Aberdyfi
Machynlleth
Aberystwyth
Borth
Talybont
Plynlimon
Llanidloes
Llangurig
Rhayader
Caersws
Carno
Llandrindod Wells
Builth Wells
Llanwrtyd Wells
Tregaron
Lampeter
Llanrhystyd
Devil's Bridge
Pontrhydfendigaid
Strata Florida
Nant-y-moch Res.
Claerwen Res.
Caban Coch Res.
Craig Goch Res.
Penygarreg Res.
Garreg-ddu Res.
Llyn Brianne Res.
Llyn Clywedog
Tywi Forest
Hafren Forest
Mynydd Eppynt
DYFED
POWYS
CAMBRIAN MOUNTAINS

7 Oswestry 8 9 Pentre 10 Overton Whitchurch 11 30 Whitchurch 12 Whitchurch

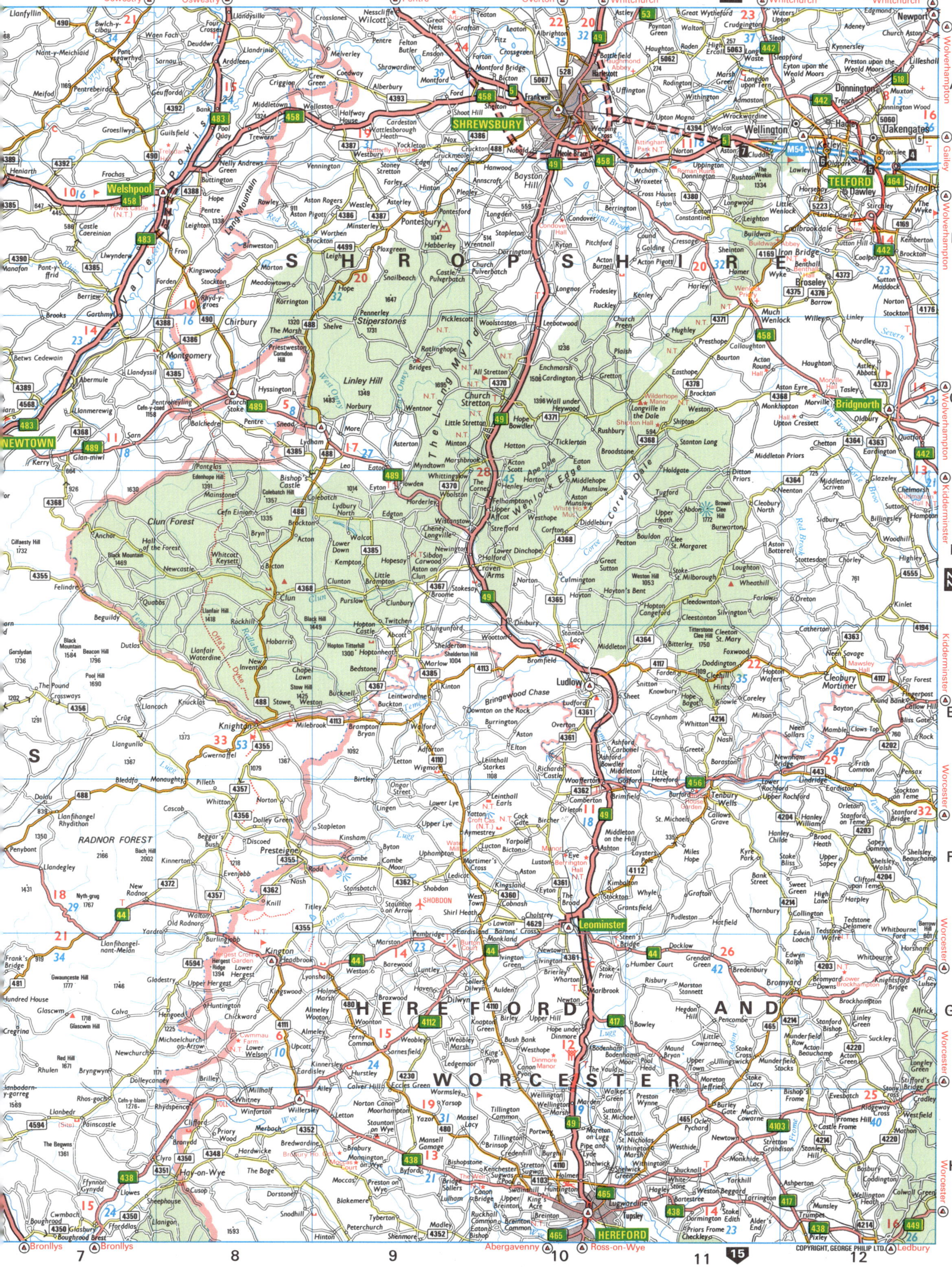

7 Bronllys 8 9 Abergavenny 10 Ross-on-Wye 11 15 12 Ledbury

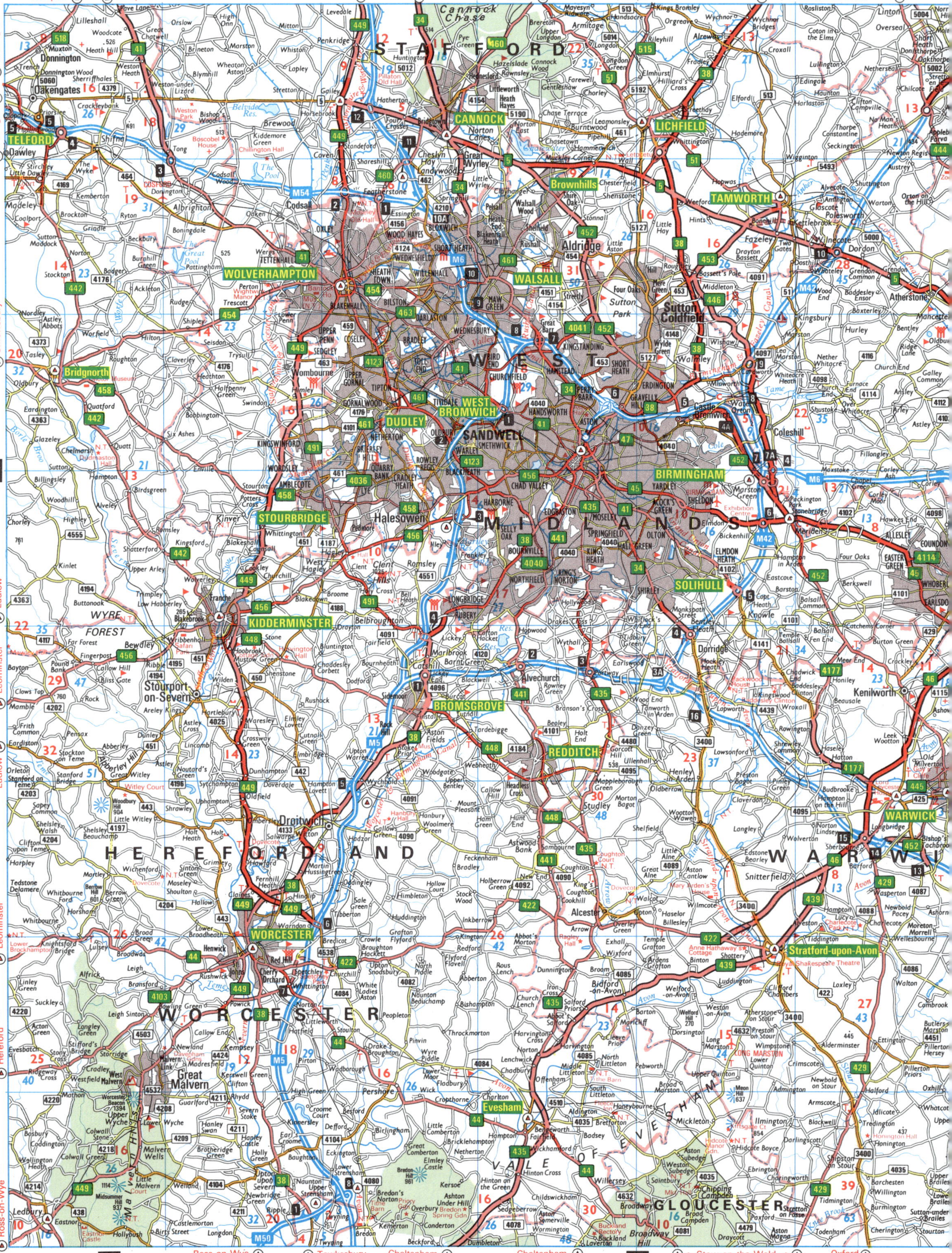

Newport
Newport
Stafford
Stafford
Stone
31
Burton-on-Trent
Wellington
Shrewsbury
Ludlow
Leominster
Hereford
Ross-on-Wye
21
Cannock Chase
STAFFORD
WEST
MIDLANDS
HEREFORD AND
WORCESTER
WARWICK
GLOUCESTER
VALE OF EVESHAM
WYRE FOREST
TELFORD
Donnington
Oakengates
Dawley
Madeley
CANNOCK
LICHFIELD
Brownhills
TAMWORTH
WOLVERHAMPTON
WALSALL
Aldridge
Sutton Coldfield
Bridgnorth
WEST BROMWICH
DUDLEY
SANDWELL
BIRMINGHAM
Halesowen
STOURBRIDGE
Kidderminster
SOLIHULL
Stourport-on-Severn
Bewdley
Kinver
BROMSGROVE
REDDITCH
Alvechurch
Droitwich
WORCESTER
Great Malvern
Alcester
Stratford-upon-Avon
Warwick
Kenilworth
Evesham
Pershore
Chipping Campden
Atherstone
Coleshill
M6
M5
M42
M54
M50
Ledbury
Upton upon Severn
Tewkesbury

Nottingham
Derby
Newark
Melton Mowbray
Grantham
Stamford
Peterborough
Bedford
Luton
Oxford
Baynard's Green
Buckingham
St. Albans
LEICESTER
NORTHANTS
BUCKS
OXFORD
LEICESTER
Coalville
Loughborough
Hinckley
NUNEATON
Bedworth
COVENTRY
LEAMINGTON SPA
Rugby
Lutterworth
Market Harborough
Oakham
CORBY
KETTERING
WELLINGBOROUGH
Rushden
NORTHAMPTON
Daventry
Towcester
BANBURY
MILTON KEYNES
Wigston
Oadby
Syston
Uppingham
Desborough
Rothwell
Burton Latimer
Irthlingborough
Long Buckby
Southam
Brackley
Stony Stratford
Wolverton
Newport Pagnell
Olney
Rutland Water
Vale of Catmose
Rockingham Forest
Whittlewood Forest
Yardley Chase
Charnwood Forest
M1
M6
M45
M69
M40
COPYRIGHT, GEORGE PHILIP LTD.

32
24
25
17

Cromer
Fakenham
Fakenham
26
Swaffham
Swaffham
Thetford
Skegness
Louth
Horncastle
Lincoln
Newark
Grantham
Grantham
32
Grantham
Melton Mowbray
Leicester
23
Kettering
33
Brancaster Bay
THE WASH
Seal Sand
Peter Black Sand
Bull Dog Sand
Breast Sand
Hunstanton
Heacham
KINGS LYNN
WISBECH
BOSTON
SPALDING
PETERBOROUGH
Downham Market
Sleaford
Stamford
Holbeach
Bourne
March
Whittlesey
Long Sutton
Sutton Bridge
Crowland
Market Deeping
N O R F O L K
L I N C O L N
L E I C E S T E R
THE FENS
ISLE OF ELY
BEDFORD LEVEL
NORTH LEVEL
BEDFORD MIDDLE LEVEL
Terrington Marsh
Gedney Marsh
Holbeach Marsh
Lutton Marsh
Marshland
Marshland Fen
Great Ouse

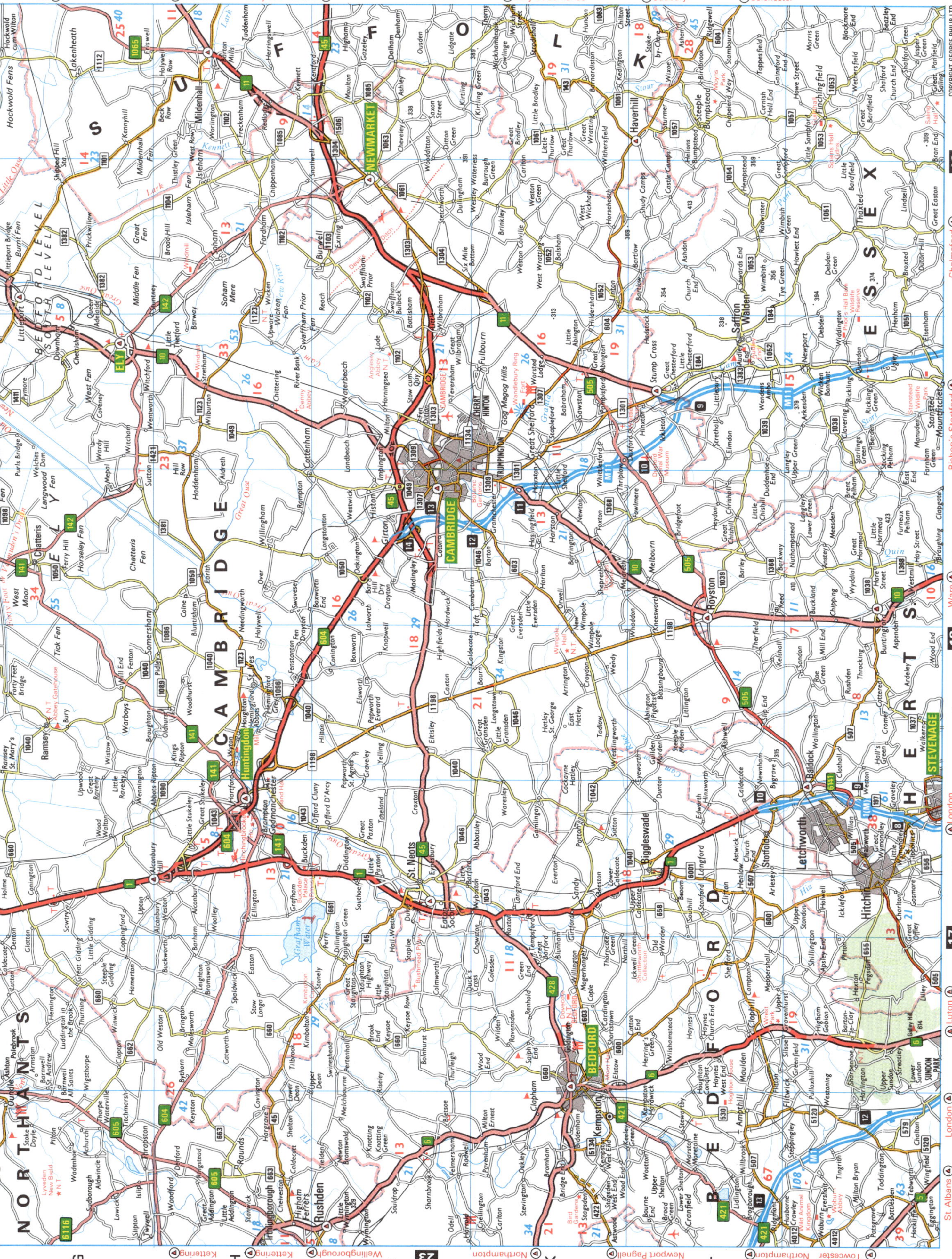
Swaffham
Thetford
Bury St.Edmunds
Sudbury
Colchester
Chelmsford
Bishop's Stortford
Ware
London
Luton
St. Albans
Towcester
Northampton
Newport Pagnell
Wellingborough
Kettering
NEWMARKET
CAMBRIDGE
ELY
Huntingdon
BEDFORD
STEVENAGE
Letchworth
Hitchin
Royston
Haverhill
Saffron Walden
St. Neots
Biggleswade
St. Ives
Ramsey
Chatteris
Mildenhall
Soham
Sandy
Ampthill
Kempston
Rushden
Baldock
NORTHANTS
CAMBRIDGE
BEDFORD
HERTS
ESSEX
SUFFOLK
ELY
Grafham Water

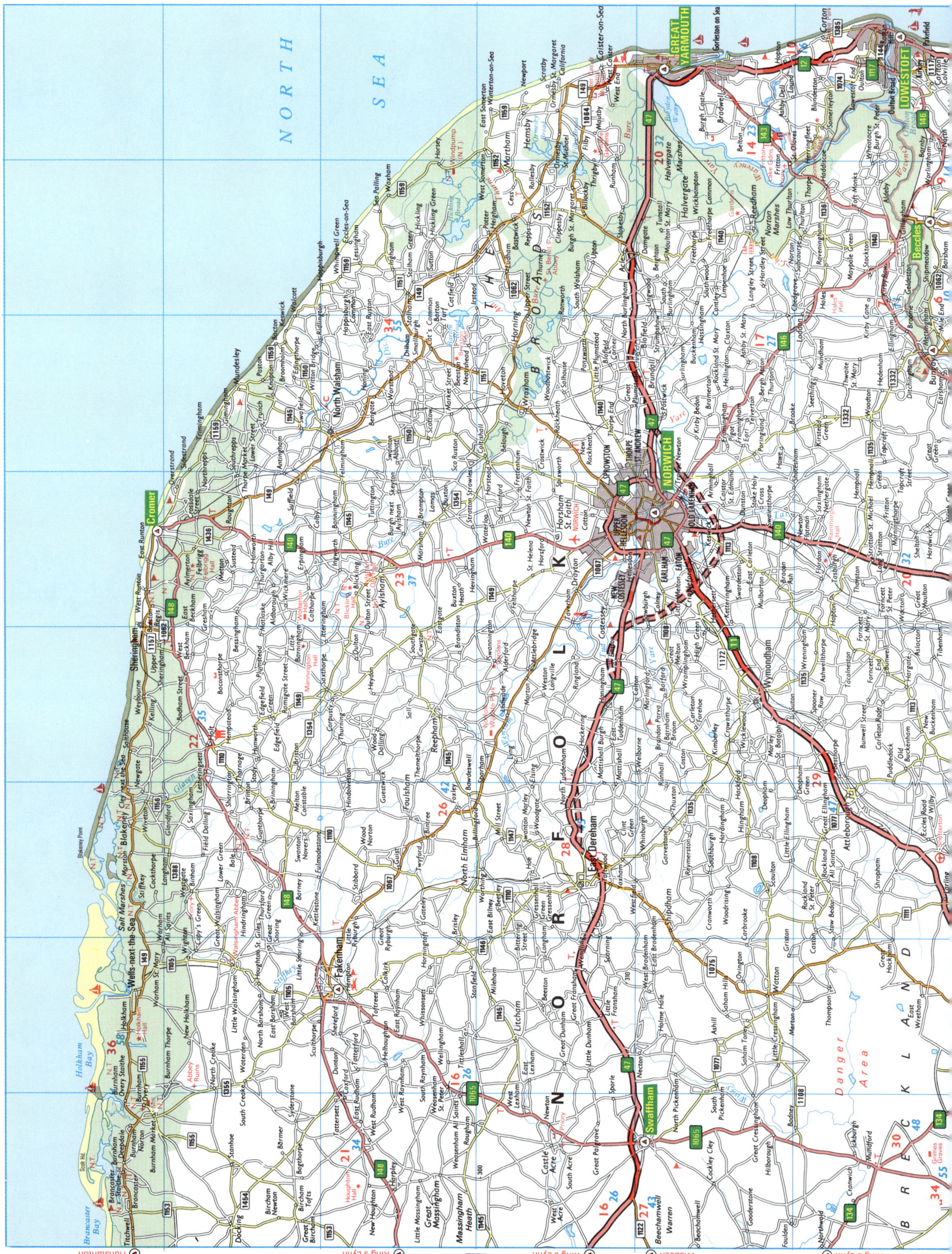
NORTH SEA
Cromer
Sheringham
Wells-next-the-Sea
Fakenham
North Walsham
Aylsham
Reepham
East Dereham
Swaffham
NORWICH
GREAT YARMOUTH
LOWESTOFT
Beccles
Wymondham
Attleborough
Holt
Blakeney
Hunstanton
King's Lynn
Wisbech
N O R F O L K
T H E   B R O A D S
B R E C K L A N D
Danger Area
Holkham Bay
Brancaster Bay
Salt Marshes
Halvergate Marshes
Acle
Mundesley
Happisburgh
Stalham
Wroxham
Hoveton
Horning
Hickling
Martham
Caister-on-Sea
Reedham
Watton
Shipdham
Litcham
Massingham Heath
Dersingham
Docking
Thetford
Mundford
Hingham
Loddon
Bungay
Harleston
Diss

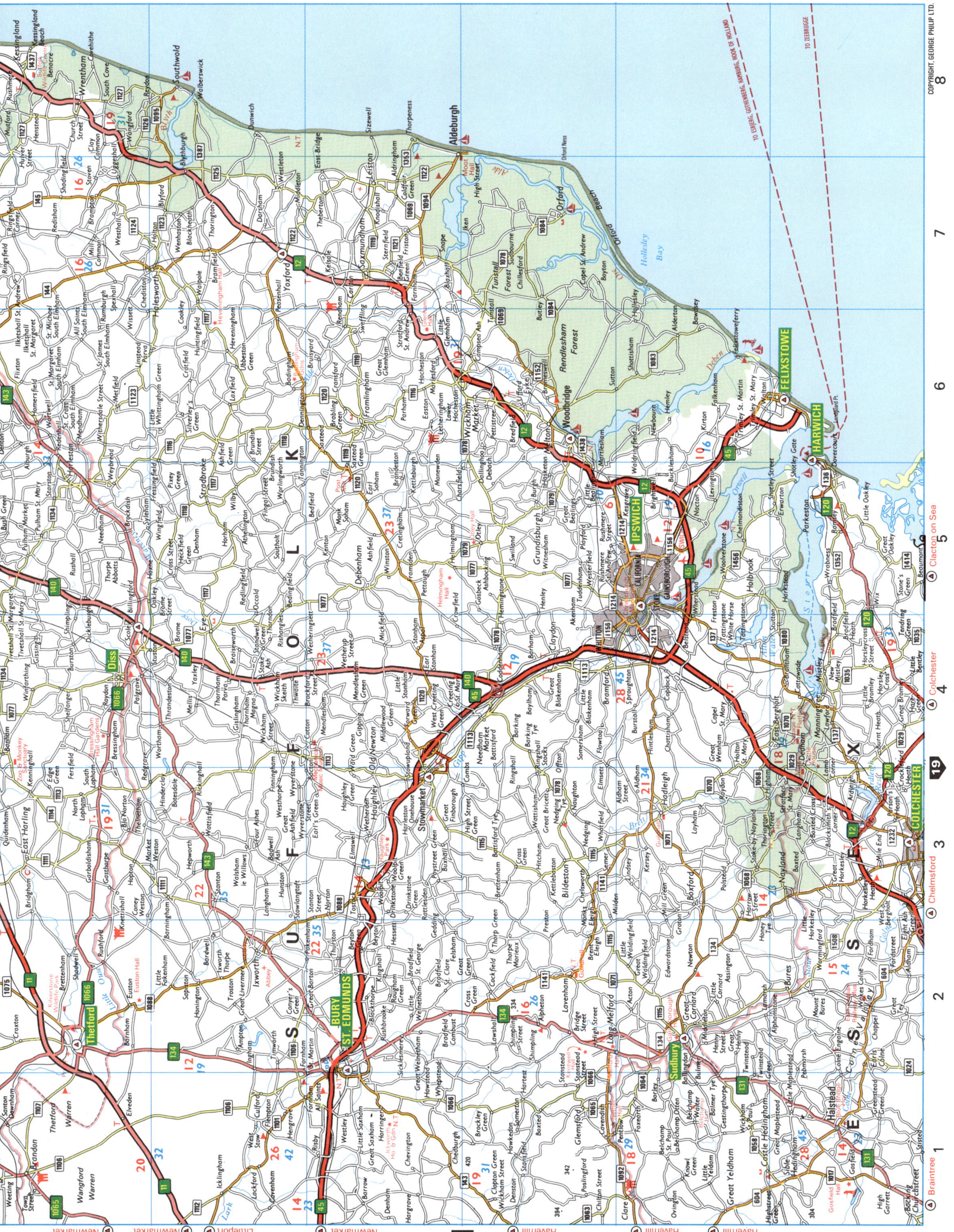
G
H
J
K
L
M
1
2
3
4
5
6
7
8
Southwold
Aldeburgh
Orford
Woodbridge
IPSWICH
FELIXSTOWE
HARWICH
COLCHESTER
Stowmarket
BURY ST. EDMUNDS
Thetford
Diss
Eye
Halesworth
Framlingham
Saxmundham
Leiston
Debenham
Hadleigh
Sudbury
Halstead
Long Melford
Lavenham
Clare
Haverhill
Newmarket
Chelmsford
Braintree
Colchester
Clacton on Sea
Brandon
Rendlesham Forest
Hollesley Bay
Orford Ness
Wrentham
Kessingland
Yoxford
Wickham Market
Needham Market
Ixworth
Nayland
Dedham
Manningtree
Mistley
Walton
Saxtead Green
Harleston
Stradbroke
East Harling
COPYRIGHT, GEORGE PHILIP LTD.
TO ESBJERG, GOTHENBURG, HAMBURG, HOOK OF HOLLAND
TO ZEEBRUGGE

1
2
3
4
5
6
A
B
C
D
E
F
G
H
The Skerries
Carmel Head
Dinas Gynfor
Cemlyn Bay
Cemaes Bay
Llanbadrig
Bull Bay
Amlwch
Amlwch Port
Point Lynas
Llaneilian
Penrhyn
Burwen
Tregele
Cemaes
Llanfechell
Bodewryd
Pentre-felin
Parys Mountain
Penysarn
Nebo
Dulas
Ynys Dulas
Dulas Bay
Llanfairynghornwy
Llanrhyddlad
Rhosgoch
Carreglefn
Llanfflewyn
Rhosybol
Church Bay
Holyhead Bay
Rhydwyn
Llanfaethlu
Llanbabo
Llyn Alaw
Capel Parc
City Dulas
Brynrefail
Din Lligwy Ancient Village
Moelfre
Llanallgo
Marianglas
Llandyfrydog
Maenaddwyn
Llanddeusant
Elim
Gwredog
Llantrisant
Llanerchymedd
Bachau
Llanfwrog
TO DUN LAOGHAIRE DUBLIN CAR FERRY
North Stack
South Stack
Llaingoch
HOLYHEAD
Kingsland
Porthdafarch
Penrhyn Mawr
Trearddur Bay
Llanfachraeth
Llanfigael
Llanynghenedl
Pen-llyn
Llyn Llywenan
Carmel
Tyn-y-gongl
Benllech
Red Wharf Bay
Red Wharf
Mariandyrys
Penmon
Penmon Priory
Puffin Island
Conwy Bay
Capel-coch
Llanbedrgoch
Tregaian
Glan-yr-Afon
Llanddona
Llangoed
Valley
Caergeiliog
Bodedern
Trefor
Four Mile Bridge
Llanfair-yn-Neubwll
Rhoscolyn
Bryngwran
Llynfaes
Llanddyfnan
Pentraeth
Rhos-meirch
Llanfihangel yn Nhowyn
VALLEY
Tywyn Trewan
Capel-gwyn
Gwalchmai
Bodffordd
Heneglwys
Talwrn
Llangefni
Pen-y-garnedd
Llansadwrn
Llanfaes
Beaumaris
Lavan Sands
Llanfairfechan
Penmaenmawr
Dwygyfylchi
Garizim
Penmaenan
Nant-y-pandy
Cymyran Bay
Rhosneigr
Pencarnisiog
Cerrigceinwen
Llangristiolus
Penmynydd
Llandegfan
Menai Bridge
Bangor
Penrhyn Castle
Aber
Gorddinog
Tal-y-fan
Ty-croes
Llanfaelog
Llyn Coron
Pentre Berw
Gaerwen
Llanfairpwllgwyngyll (Llanddaniel Fab)
Bryn-celli-ddu
Tal-y-bont
Llandegai
Penrhos-garnedd
Malltraeth Marsh
Llangwyfan
Bethel
Trefdraeth
Llangadwaladr
Aberffraw
Barclodiad Y Gawres Burial Chamber
Hermon
Malltraeth
Llangaffo
Bryn-Siencyn
Port Dinorwic
Plas Newydd
Glasinfryn
Llanllechid
Rachub
Moel Wnion
Aber Falls
Drum
Foel-fras
Bethesda
Gerlan
Bodorgan
Malltraeth Sands
Llangeinwen
Newborough
Dwyran
Anglesey Sea Zoo
Llanddeiniolen
Pentir
Tregarth
Sling
Rhiwlas
Douglas Hill
Malltraeth Bay
Newborough Warren
Caernarfon
Segontium
Abermenai Point
Bethel
Saron
Penisarwaun
Llanrug
Deiniolen
Brynrefail
Clwt-y-bont
Dinorwic
Carnedd Llewelyn
Carnedd Dafydd
Pen Llithrig-y-wrach
Llyn Eigiau Res.
Pont-rug
Cwm-y-glo
Ceunant
Fachwen
Llanberis
Llyn Padarn
Dinorwic Slate Museum
Llyn Peris
Nant Ffrancon
Llyn Ogwen
Pont Pen-y-benglog
Pont Rhyd-goch
Crafnant
CAERNARFON BAY
The Bar
Caeathrow
Bontnewydd
Waunfawr
Llanfaglan
Gwyrfai
Rhostryfan
Hafoty House
Betws Garmon
Nant Peris
Pass of Llanberis
Glyder Fach
Glyder Fawr
Llugwy
Capel Curig
Dinas Dinlle
Llandwrog
Llanwnda
Rhosgadfan
Salem
Moel Tryfan
Pen-y-Gwryd
Pont Cyfyng
Groeslon
Glynllifon Park
Carmel
Fron
Snowdon
Llyn Cwellyn
Llyn Llydaw Res.
Moel-siabod
Dolwyddelan Castle
BAY
Penygroes
Talysarn
Nantlle
Rhyd-Ddu
Y Cribau
Blaenau-Dolwyddelan
Yr Arddu
Pont-llyfni
Trwyn Maen Dylan
Aberdesach
Llanllyfni
Llyfni
Tal'r-lon
Nebo
Nasareth
Yr Aran
Bethania
Llyn Gwynant
Nantgwynant
Glanaber
Moel Penamnen
Clynnog-fawr
Capel-uchaf
Bwlch Mawr
Garnedd-goch
Pant-glas
GWYNEDD
Beddgelert
Pass of Aberglaslyn
Nantmor
Lechwedd Quarries
Trwyn y Tal
Gurn Ddu
Upper Clynnog
Dwyfach
Moel Hebog
Cnicht
Rhiwbryfdir
Blaenau Ffestiniog
Trwyn y Gorlech
Trevor
Yr Eifl
Llanaelhaearn
Bryncir
Garn-Dolbenmaen
Llanfihangel-y-pennant
Moel-ddu
Croesor
Tan-y-grisiau
Moelwyn Mawr
Bethania
Congl-y-wal
Lithfaen
Pistyll
Glan-Dwyfach
Golan
Llyn Cwmystradllyn
Dolbenmaen
Rhos-lan
Prenteg
Garreg
Tan-lan
Rhyd
Rhyd-y-sarn
Tan-y-bwlch
Ffestiniog
Bont Newydd
Carreg Ddu
Morfa Nefyn
Nefyn
Groesffordd
Edern
Fron
Pencaenewydd
Llangybi
Yffor
Llanarmon
Chwilog
Llanystumdwy
Wern
Pentrefelin
Tremadog
Penmorfa
Llanfrothen
Penrhyndeudraeth
Maentwrog
Gellilydan
Rhos-y-llan
Tudweiliog
Tan-y-graig
Bodfuan
Efailnewydd
Llannor
Abererch
Criccieth
Porthmadog
Morfa Bychan
Borth-y-gest
Portmeirion
Minffordd
Trawsfynydd
Llyn Trawsfynydd Res.
Porth Colmon
Dinas
Garn
Rhydyclafdy
Pwllheli
West End
South Beach
Carreg yr Imbill
Pen-ychain
Tremadog Bay
Harlech Point
Llanfihangel-y-traethau
Glan-y-Wern
Morfa Harlech
Moel Ysgyfarnogod
Talsarnau
Fron-oleu
Llangwnnadl
Meillteyrn
Llaniestyn
Sarn
Penhros
Windmill
Penrhyn Mawr
Ty-Hen
Pen-y-groeslon
Bryncroes
Botwnnog
Mynytho
Llanbedrog
Trwyn Llanbedrog
Methlem
Rhydlios
Harlech
Bronaber
Capel Carmel
Rhoshirwaun
Llangian
St. Tudwal's Road
Abersoch
Llandanwg
Llanfair
Rhinog Fawr
Braich Anelog
Aberdaron
Rhiw
Plas-yn-Rhiw
Llanfaelrhys
Llanengan
Porth Neigwl or Hell's Mouth
Pentre Gwynfryn
Rhinog Fach
Eden
Pwlldefaid
Braich y Pwll
Uwchmynydd
Aberdaron Bay
Trwyn Talfarach
Sarn-bach
Machros
Bwlchtocyn
St. Tudwal's Islands
Llanbedr
Y Llethr
Gamlan
Bardsey Sound
Pen y Cil
Ynys Gwylan-fawr
Trwyn yr Wylfa
Trwyn Cilan
Morfa Dyffryn
Moelfre
Llyn Bodlyn
Diffwys
Ganllwyd
Abbey Ruins
Bardsey Island
Coed Ystumgwern
Dyffryn-Ardudwy
Llanenddwyn
Ysgethin
Tal-y-bont
Llawlech
Y Garn
Dolmelynllyn
Cymmer Abbey
CARDIGAN BAY
Uwch-mynydd
Bontddu
Llanelltyd
Llanaber
Caerdeon
Penmaenpool
Aber-Gwynant
Dolgellau
Barmouth
Aberdyfi

7 8 9 10 11 34 12

Southport
Preston
Manchester Warrington
Chester
Warrington
Chester
Nantwich
Whitchurch
Overton
Whitchurch
Shrewsbury
A
B
C
D
E
F
G
H
30
BOOTLE
LIVERPOOL
WALLASEY
Hoylake
West Kirby
MERSEYSIDE
BIRKENHEAD
Bebington
Heswall
Neston
CHES.
Flint
Connah's Quay
Queensferry
Mold
Buckley
LANDUDNO
Conwy
Colwyn Bay
Abergele
Rhyl
Prestatyn
St. Asaph
Holywell
Denbigh
Ruthin
Llanrwst
Betws-y-Coed
CLWYD
Clocaenog Forest
Mynydd Hiraethog
CAMBRIAN MOUNTAINS
WREXHAM
Llangollen
Corwen
Bala
OSWESTRY
POWYS
Berwyn
GWYNEDD
Migneint
Cerrigydrudion
Llyn Tegid or Bala Lake
Lake Vyrnwy
Welshpool
Machynlleth
Mallwyd

7 8 20 9 10 21 11 12

Southport
Preston
Preston
34
Wigan
Manchester
Manchester
MERSEYSIDE
BOOTLE
ST. HELENS
Knowsley
WALLASEY
LIVERPOOL
Haydock
Newton-Le-Willows
Hoylake
West Kirby
BIRKENHEAD
Prescot
Whiston
Huyton
WARRINGTON
TRAFFORD PARK
SALFORD
Urmston
Irlam
Chat Moss
Culcheth
Altrincham
Hale
Bebington
Heswall
Garston
Speke
WIDNES
Runcorn
Eastham Sands
Ellesmere Port
Frodsham
Helsby
Neston
Knutsford
Northwich
Winsford
Middlewich
Flint
St. Asaph
St. Asaph
Queensferry
CHESTER
Mold
Buckley
Ruthin
CHESHIRE
Sandbach
Crewe
Nantwich
29
WREXHAM
CLWYD
Llangollen
Corwen
Whitchurch
Market Drayton
Ellesmere
OSWESTRY
SHROPSHIRE
POWYS
Newport
Neuadd
Welshpool
Shrewsbury
Shrewsbury
Shrewsbury
21
Wellington
Wellington
Wolverh'ton

7 Manchester 8 Flouch Inn 9 35 10 Flouch Inn 11 Barnsley Leeds 12

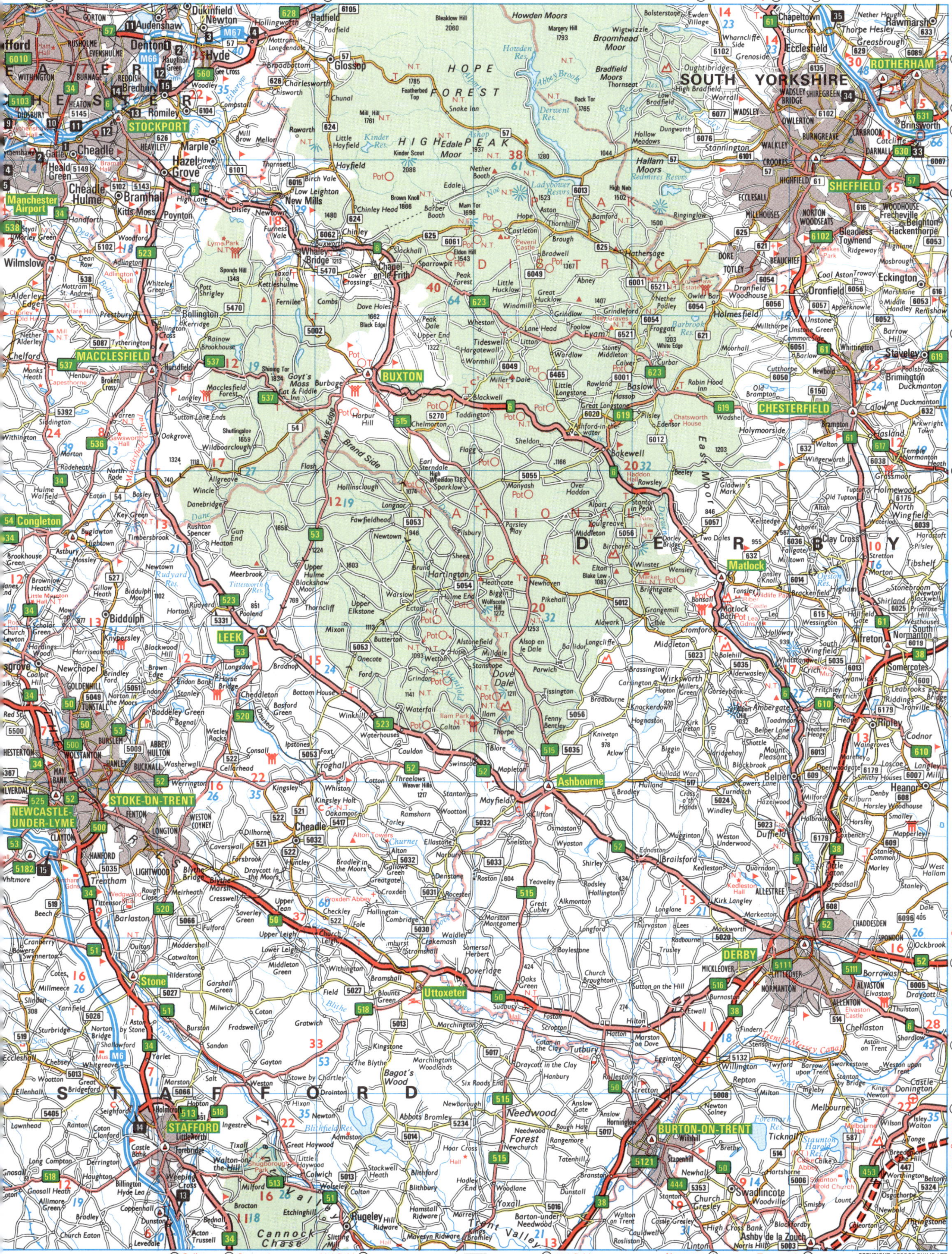

Doncaster Bawtry Nottingham Lincoln Worksop Mansfield 32 Nottingham Leicester Nottingham

7 Gailey 8 Cannock Lichfield 9 22 10 Lichfield Nuneaton 11 Tamworth 12

SOUTH YORKSHIRE
NOTTINGHAM
DERBY
LEICESTER
SHERWOOD FOREST
SHEFFIELD
ROTHERHAM
CHESTERFIELD
WORKSOP
MANSFIELD
NEWARK
NOTTINGHAM
DERBY
GAINSBOROUGH
GRANTHAM
LOUGHBOROUGH
MELTON MOWBRAY
East Retford
Sutton in Ashfield
Kirkby in Ashfield
Hucknall
Arnold
Carlton
West Bridgford
Beeston
Stapleford
Long Eaton
Ilkeston
Eastwood
Heanor
Ripley
Alfreton
Belper
Bolsover
Clowne
Staveley
Dronfield
Maltby
Bawtry
Blyth
Tuxford
Southwell
Bingham
Radcliffe on Trent
Shepshed
Castle Donington
Melbourne
Ashby de la Zouch
Leeds
Doncaster
Thorne
Goole
Scunthorpe
Manchester
Flouch Inn
Chapel-en-le-Frith
Buxton
Ashbourne
Burton-on-Trent
Tamworth
Leicester
Stamford

Brigg
Grimsby
37
Grimsby
Market Rasen
Binbrook
Louth
Mablethorpe
Sutton on Sea
Alford
THE WOLDS
LINCOLN
Horncastle
Woodhall Spa
L I N C O L N
Coningsby
Tattershall
Skegness
Wainfleet All Saints
Gibraltar Point
East Fen
West Fen
BOSTON
Skirbeck
Sleaford
THE WASH
Kirton
Algarkirk
Gosberton
Holbeach
Holbeach Marsh
Gedney Marsh
Terrington Marsh
SPALDING
Bourne
Sutton Bridge
Terrington St. Clement
Deeping Fen
Peterborough
Stamford
Peterborough
24
Wisbech
Wisbech
King's Lynn
A
B
C
D
E
F
G
H
7
8
9
10
11
12

Isle of Walney
Biggar
Roa Island
Rampside
Foulney Island
Piel Island
Sheep Island
South End
TO DOUGLAS
TO DOUGLAS (Summer only)
MORECAMBE
HEYSHAM
LANCASTER
Kendal
Settle
Halton
Caton
Caton Moor
Claughton
Tatham Fells
Burn Moor
Goodber Common
Littledale
Clougha
Quernmore
Mallowdale Fell
Ward's Stone
FOREST OF BOWLAND
Croasdale Fell
Gisburn Forest
Tosside
Slaidburn
Newton
Easington Fell
Holden
Dunsop Bridge
Sykes Fell
Hareden
Marshaw
Hawthornthwaite Fell
Abbeystead
Tarnbrook
Fell Top
Bleasdale Moors
Oakenclough
Fair Snape Fell
Whitewell
Grindleton
West Bradford
Waddington
Chipping
Walker Fold
Longridge Fell
Clitheroe
Pendleton
Whalley
Wiswell
Billington
Great Mitton
Knowle Green
Hurst Green
Longridge
Ribchester
Grimsargh
Goosnargh
Inglewhite
Hesketh Lane
Calder Vale
Beacon Fell
White Chapel
Bilsborrow
Garstang
Bowgreave
Catterall
Nateby
Churchtown
St. Michael's on Wyre
Great Eccleston
Sunderland
Overton
Middleton
Heaton
Glasson
Conder Green
Galgate
Thurnham
Cockerham
Cockerham Sands
Shoulder of Lune
Braides
Forton
Pilling
Pilling Lane
Preesall
Stalmine
Stake Pool
Winmarleigh
Eagland Hill
Hambleton
Out Rawcliffe
FLEETWOOD
Cleveleys
Thornton
BISPHAM
Poulton-le-Fylde
BLACKPOOL
NORTH SHORE
SOUTH SHORE
Marton
Staining
Singleton
Elswick
Inskip
Kirkham
Wesham
Treales
Wharton
Great Plumpton
Weeton
Lytham St. Anne's
St. Anne's
Warton
Freckleton
Newton
Clifton
Lea Town
Woodplumpton
Broughton
Fulwood
PRESTON
Penwortham
Higher Penwortham
Walton-le-Dale
Bamber Bridge
Samlesbury
BLACKBURN
Darwen
Great Harwood
Clayton-le-Moors
Rishton
Oswaldtwistle
Church
Haslingden
LANCASHIRE
Hoghton
Longton
Hesketh Bank
Much Hoole
Tarleton
Leyland
Euxton
Chorley
Anglezarke Moor
Turton Moor
Withnell
Abbey Village
Whittle-le-Woods
Clayton-le-Woods
Croston
Eccleston
Mawdesley
Rufford
Banks
Crossens
Churchtown
SOUTHPORT
Birkdale
Birkdale Sands
Ainsdale
Formby
Formby Hills
Freshfield
Woodvale
Halsall
Scarisbrick
Burscough
Ormskirk
Aughton
Maghull
Lydiate
Skelmersdale
Up Holland
Orrell
Standish
Shevington
Horwich
Adlington
Rivington
Blackrod
WIGAN
Hindley
Westhoughton
Ince-in-Makerfield
Ashton-in-Makerfield
Golborne
Abram
Atherton
Tyldesley
Farnworth
BOLTON
Kearsley
Walkden
Little Hulton
LEIGH
Astley
Worsley
Eccles
Chat Moss
Irlam
Urmston
Partington
Cadishead
MANCHESTER
GREATER
Crosby
LIVERPOOL BAY
BOOTLE
Litherland
Kirkby
MERSEYSIDE
WALLASEY
NEW BRIGHTON
LIVERPOOL
BIRKENHEAD
Hoylake
West Kirby
Greasby
Moreton
Prescot
ST. HELENS
Haydock
Newton-le-Willows
Rainford
Billinge
Knowsley
Huyton
Roby
Whiston
Rainhill
WARRINGTON
Culcheth
Penketh
Widnes
Chester
Stoke-on-Trent
Altrincham

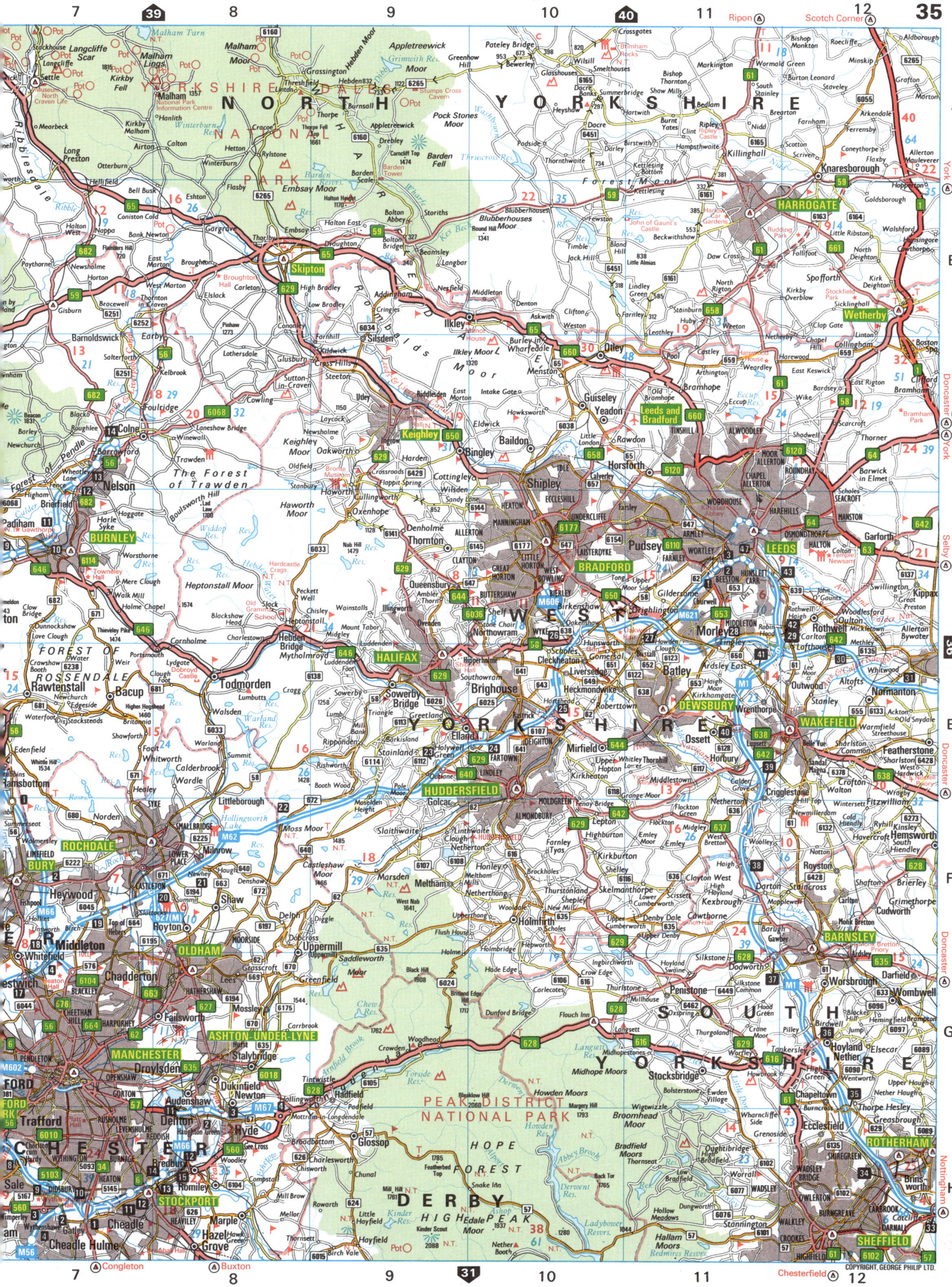
NORTH YORKSHIRE
YORKSHIRE DALES NATIONAL PARK
Skipton
Harrogate
Knaresborough
Wetherby
Keighley
Ilkley
Otley
Leeds and Bradford
Bingley
Shipley
Bradford
Leeds
Pudsey
Morley
Halifax
Brighouse
Dewsbury
Batley
Wakefield
Huddersfield
Todmorden
Burnley
Nelson
Colne
Rawtenstall
Bacup
Rochdale
Bury
Heywood
Middleton
Oldham
Manchester
Ashton-under-Lyne
Stockport
Sheffield
Rotherham
Barnsley
Penistone
Glossop
Hyde
WEST YORKSHIRE
SOUTH YORKSHIRE
PEAK DISTRICT NATIONAL PARK
DERBY
HIGH PEAK
HOPE FOREST
The Forest of Trawden
FOREST OF ROSSENDALE
Ripon
Scotch Corner
York
Doncaster
Selby
Nottingham
Chesterfield
Congleton
Buxton
COPYRIGHT, GEORGE PHILIP LTD.

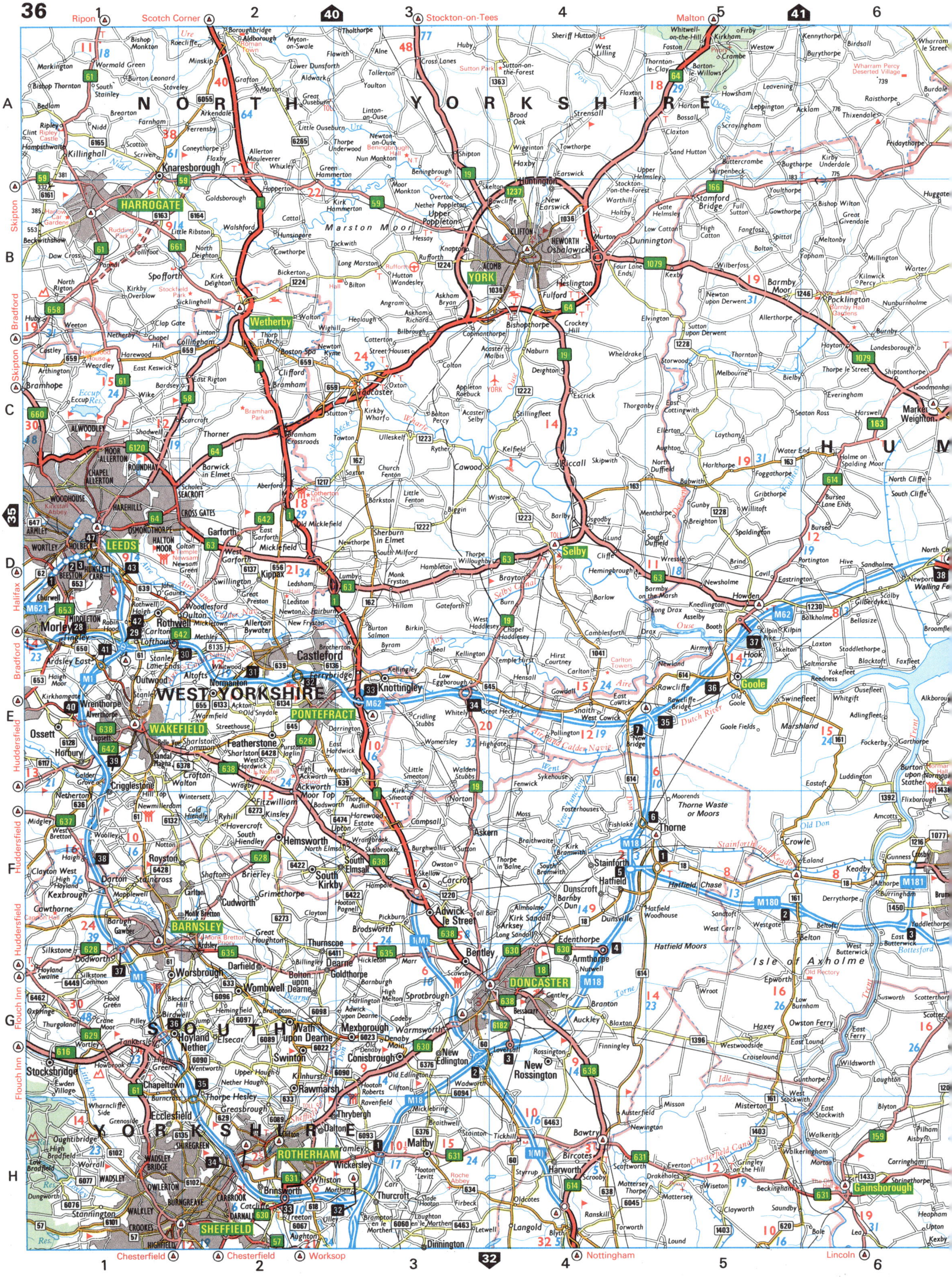
Ripon
Scotch Corner
40
Stockton-on-Tees
Malton
41
1
2
3
4
5
6
A
B
C
D
E
F
G
H
NORTH YORKSHIRE
WEST YORKSHIRE
SOUTH YORKSHIRE
HUM
Skipton
Bradford
Halifax
Huddersfield
Flouch Inn
35
38
Harrogate
Knaresborough
Wetherby
York
Leeds
Morley
Wakefield
Pontefract
Castleford
Knottingley
Selby
Goole
Howden
Barnsley
Doncaster
Rotherham
Sheffield
Stocksbridge
Thorne
Gainsborough
Pocklington
Market Weighton
Stamford Bridge
Tadcaster
Sherburn in Elmet
Hemsworth
South Kirkby
Adwick le Street
Bentley
Conisbrough
Mexborough
Wath upon Dearne
Wombwell
Rawmarsh
Maltby
Bawtry
Harworth
Thorne Waste or Moors
Hatfield Chase
Hatfield Moors
Isle of Axholme
Marston Moor
Ossett
Horbury
Rothwell
Garforth
Featherstone
Normanton
Tickhill
New Rossington
Edenthorpe
Armthorpe
Stainforth
Epworth
Crowle
Snaith
Rawcliffe
Askern
Cawood
M1
M18
M180
M181
M62
M621
1(M)
Chesterfield
Worksop
32
Nottingham
Lincoln

41
Scarborough
BRIDLINGTON
Hilderthorpe
Bridlington Bay
Langtoft
Sledmere
Sledmere House
Kilham
Burton Agnes Hall
Burton Agnes
Norman Manor
Haisthorpe
Thornholme
Carnaby
Bessingby
Fraisthorpe
Ruston Parva
Harpham
Lowthorpe
Nafferton
Little Kelk
Gransmoor
Great Kelk
Lisset
Barmston
Garton-on-the-Wolds
Wetwang
Elmswell
Little Driffield
Driffield
Gembling
Ulrome
Foston on the Wolds
Wansford
Skipsea Castle
Skipsea
Skipsea Brough
Tibthorpe
Kirkburn
Eastburn
Southburn
Skerne
Brigham
North Frodingham
Beeford
North Dalton
Cranswick
Hutton
Bainton
Dunnington
Atwick
Middleton-on-the-Wolds
Watton
Kilnwick
Rotsea
Hempholme
Bewholme
Lund
Beswick
Lockington
Burshill
Brandesburton
Hornsea
Thorpe
Holme on the Wolds
South Dalton
Scorborough
Aike
Leven
Catwick
Seaton
Hornsea Mere
Hornsea Bridge
Rolston
Sigglesthorne
Goxhill
Mappleton
Etton
Arram
Leven Canal
Little Hatfield
Great Cowden
Gardham
Cherry Burton
Leconfield
Routh
Tickton
Long Riston
Rise
Great Hatfield
Withernwick
Bishop Burton
Molescroft
Beverley
Arnold
South Skirlaugh
New Ellerby
Marton
Aldbrough
NORTH SEA
Sancton
Weel
Woodmansey
Old Ellerby
West Newton
North Newbald
South Newbald
Walkington
Bentley
Wawne
Thearne
Swine
Burton Constable
Flinton
Garton
Grimston
High Hunsley
Skidby
Dunswell
Coniston
Fitling
Hilston
Rowley
Little Weighton
Windmill
Cottingham
Ganstead
Sproatley
Humbleton
Lelley
Bilton
Elstronwick
Owstwick
Tunstall
Everthorpe
Riplingham
NEWLAND
SUTTON-ON-HULL
STONEFERRY
SCULCOATES
Burton Pidsea
North End
Roos
Waxholme
West End
South Cave
Wauldby
Willerby
Kirk Ella
West Ella
Brantingham
Swanland
Anlaby
MARFLEET
Hedon
Preston
Rimswell
Withernsea
Ellerker
Elloughton
Welton
Melton
KINGSTON UPON HULL
Wilberforce House
Burstwick
Halsham
East End
Brough
North Ferriby
HULL (BROUGH)
Hessle
Paull
Thorngumbald
Camerton
Ryhill
Keyingham
Ottringham
Hollym
Humber Br.
Goxhill Haven
New Holland
Thorney Crofts
Winestead
Whitton
Humber
Read's I.
Winteringham
West Halton
Barton-upon-Humber
Barrow Haven
Barrow upon Humber
East Halton Skitter
Patrington
Holmpton
Goxhill
Foulholme Sands
Partington Haven
Welwick
Out Newton
Coleby
Winterton
South Ferriby
South End
East Halton
Sunk Island
Skeffling
Easington
Thealby
Horkstow
Thornton Abbey
Thornton Curtis
North Killingholme
MOUTH OF THE HUMBER
Old Hall
Roxby
Saxby All Saints
Burnham
Wootton
South Killingholme
Immingham Dock
Sunk Island Sands
Kilnsea
Risby
Appleby
Bonby
Worlaby
Ulceby
Ulceby Skitter
Immingham
Habrough
Low Santon
Land Drain
Croxton
Kirmington
Brocklesby
Stallingborough
Elsham Hall
Elsham
Frodingham
SCUNTHORPE
New Ancholme
Weir Dyke
M180
Melton Ross
HUMBERSIDE
Barnetby le Wold
Great Limber
Keelby
Healing
Great Coates
GRIMSBY
West Marsh
Old Clee
Cleethorpes
Spurn Head
Thrunscoe
Ashby
Bottesford
Broughton
Wrawby
Brigg
Bigby
Riby Cross Roads
Riby
Aylesby
Laceby
Bradley
Nunsthorpe
Holme
Manton Warren
Scawby Brook
Scawby
Somerby
Searby
Owmby
Grasby
Clixby
Scartho
Humberston
TO ROTTERDAM, ZEEBRUGGE
Messingham
Sturton
Howsham
Irby upon Humber
Barnoldby le Beck
Waltham
New Waltham
Manton
Hibaldstow
Cadney
North Kelsey Beck
North Kelsey
Caistor
Cabourne
Swallow
Beelsby
Brigsley
Holton le Clay
Tetney Lock
Nettleton
Cuxwold
Hatcliffe
Ashby cum Fenby
Tetney
North Coates
Danger Area
Kirton in Lindsey
Redbourne
Rothwell
East Ravendale
Grainsby
North Thoresby
Marsh Chapel
Eskham
Northorpe
South Kelsey
Brandy Wharf
Moortown
Croxby
Thorganby
West End
Wragholme
Meals
Grayingham
Waddingham
Holton le Moor
Thoresway
Swinhope
Wold Newton
Fulstow
Grainthorpe
Ludney
North Somercotes
Church End
Thornton le Moor
Snitterby
Normanby le Wold
Ludborough
Covenham St. Bartholomew
Conisholme
Blyborough
North Owersby
Claxby
Stainton le Vale
Covenham St. Mary
Austen Fen
South Somercotes
Saltfleet
Willoughton
South Owersby
Kingerby
Usselby
Binbrook
Utterby
Yarburgh
Canal
Yawthorpe
Osgodby
Bishop Norton
Kirkby
Walesby
Bully Hill
Kirmond le Mire
North Ormsby
Fotherby
Skidbrooke
Saltfleetby St. Clements
Hemswell
Spital in the Street
Bishopbridge
LINCOLN
Tealby
Great Tows
Kelstern
North Elkington
Little Grimsby
Alvingham
North Cockerington
Saltfleetby All Saints
Harpswell
Glentham
West Rasen
Market Rasen
Ludford
South Elkington
South Cockerington
Saltfleetby St. Peter
Theddlethorpe St. Helen
Caenby Corner
Caenby
Normanby by Spital
Middle Rasen
North Willingham
Keddington
Grimoldby
Glentworth
Owmby by Spital
Toft next Newton
Newton by Toft
Linwood
Sixhills
Burgh on Bain
Welton le Wold
Stewton
Theddlethorpe All Saints
Saxby
Res.
Louth
Manby
Fillingham
Legsby
Gayton le Wold
Meers Bridge
Lincoln
Lincoln
33
Boston
COPYRIGHT, GEORGE PHILIP LTD.
7
8
9
10
11
12
A
B
C
D
E
F
G
H

ISLE OF MAN
REFERENCE
T.T. Course
First Class Roads
Second Class Roads
Other Roads
Roads in the Isle of Man are not classified by the D.O.T.
Miles 10
Kilometres 16
SOLWAY FIRTH
IRISH SEA
Allonby Bay
Saltom Bay
Maryport
WORKINGTON
WHITEHAVEN
Cockermouth
Aspatria
Keswick
Ambleside
Ulverston
Millom
Egremont
Cleator Moor
Dalton-in-Furness
BARROW-IN-FURNESS
Broughton in Furness
Coniston
Grasmere
Flimby
Harrington
Distington
Seascale
Ravenglass
Silecroft
Haverigg
Askam in Furness
Skiddaw Forest
Thornthwaite Forest
Copeland Forest
Blengdale Forest
Grizedale Forest
Furness Fells
Ennerdale Fell
Ennerdale Water
Loweswater Fell
Derwent Fells
Wythburn Fells
Rydal Fell
Harter Fell
Ulpha Fell
Thwaites Fell
Bootle Fell
Black Combe
Birker Fell
Caw Fell
Sca Fell
Scafell Pikes
Hard Knott Pass
Wrynose Pass
Honister Pass
Whinlatter Pass
Kirkstone Pass
Duddon Sands
Morecambe Bay
LAKE DISTRICT
NATIONAL PARK
CUMBRIAN MOUNTAINS
Carlisle
AYRE
MICHAEL
GARFF
GLENFABA
MIDDLE
RUSHEN
Ramsey
Peel
Douglas
Castletown
Port Erin
Calf of Man
Douglas Bay
Laxey Bay
Ramsey Bay
Niarbyl Bay
Fleshwick Bay
TO HEYSHAM
TO LIVERPOOL
TO BELFAST
CAR FERRY

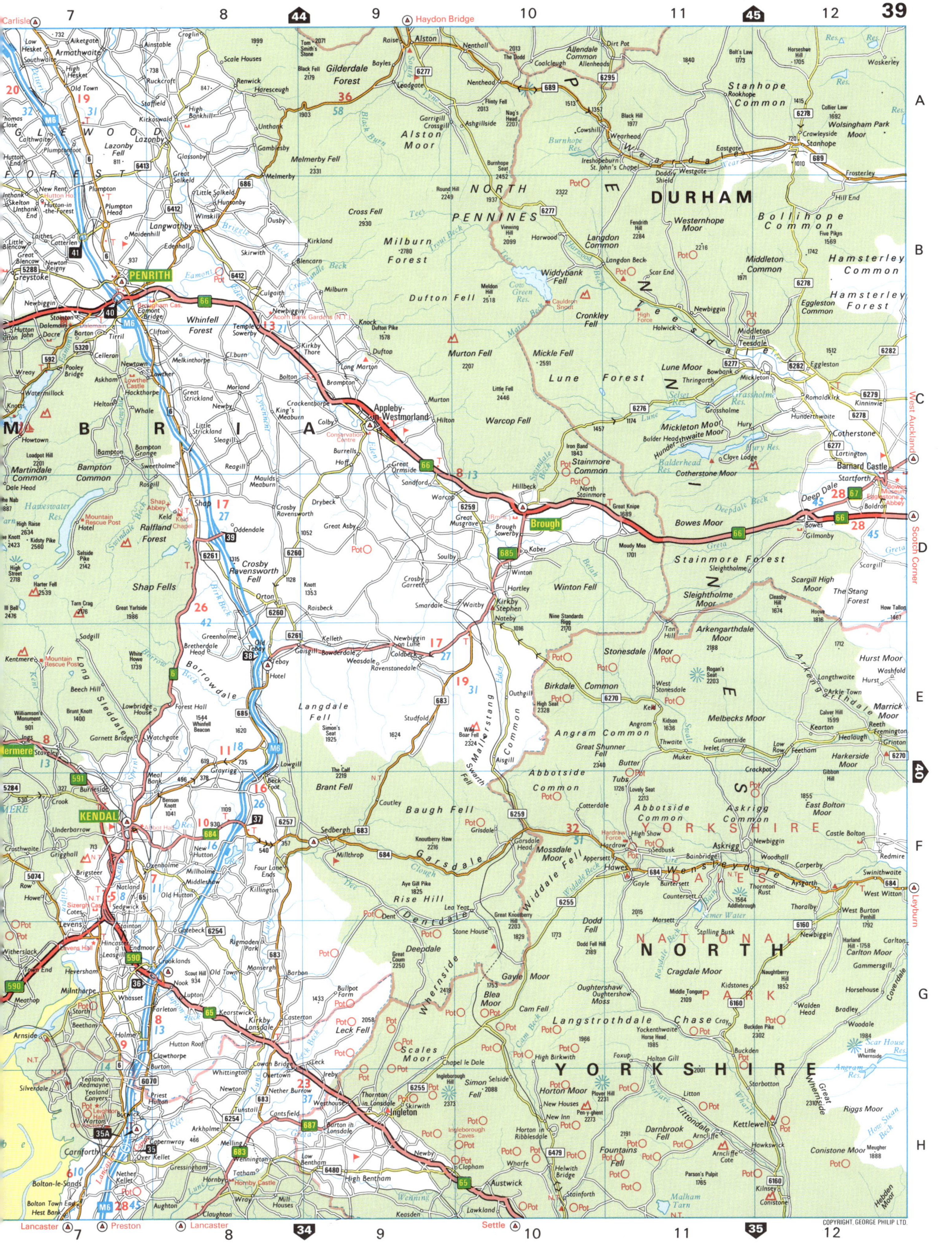
7
8
44
9
10
11
45
12
A
B
C
D
E
F
G
H
40
7
8
34
9
10
11
35
12
Carlisle
Haydon Bridge
Lancaster
Preston
Lancaster
Settle
West Auckland
Scotch Corner
Leyburn
PENRITH
KENDAL
Brough
Appleby-in-Westmorland
Alston
Sedbergh
Kirkby Stephen
Kirkby Lonsdale
Ingleton
Barnard Castle
Middleton-in-Teesdale
Stanhope
Hawes
Askrigg
Kettlewell
Shap
Tebay
Orton
Carnforth
Milnthorpe
Burneside
Staveley
Windermere
Armathwaite
Kirkoswald
Lazonby
Greystoke
Dacre
Pooley Bridge
Askham
Lowther
Clifton
Temple Sowerby
Kirkby Thore
Long Marton
Dufton
Murton
Hilton
Warcop
Kaber
Winton
Nateby
Ravenstonedale
Newbiggin on Lune
Garsdale
Dent
Dentdale
Deepdale
Cowan Bridge
High Bentham
Low Bentham
Clapham
Austwick
Horton in Ribblesdale
Malham Tarn
Kilnsey
Conistone
Arncliffe
Buckden
Hubberholme
Bainbridge
Gayle
Thoralby
Aysgarth
Carperby
West Witton
Cotherstone
Romaldkirk
Eggleston
Bowes
Langdon Beck
St. John's Chapel
Westgate
Eastgate
Ireshopeburn
Cowshill
Allenheads
Nenthead
Garrigill
Gilderdale Forest
Melmerby Fell
Cross Fell
Milburn Forest
Dufton Fell
Murton Fell
Mickle Fell
Warcop Fell
Lune Forest
Cronkley Fell
Widdybank Fell
Stainmore Forest
Stainmore Common
Winton Fell
Baugh Fell
Langdale Fell
Brant Fell
Wild Boar Fell
Mallerstang Common
Rise Hill
Whernside
Blea Moor
Gayle Moor
Dodd Fell
Langstrothdale Chase
Simon Fell
Leck Fell
Scales Moor
Crosby Ravensworth Fell
Shap Fells
Ralfland Forest
Bampton Common
Martindale Common
Whinfell Forest
Borrowdale
Long Sleddale
Birkdale Common
Stonesdale Moor
Angram Common
Abbotside Common
Askrigg Common
Melbecks Moor
Arkengarthdale Moor
Sleightholme Moor
Bowes Moor
Cotherstone Moor
Lune Moor
Mickleton Moor
Eggleston Common
Middleton Common
Hamsterley Common
Hamsterley Forest
Bollihope Common
Westernhope Moor
Stanhope Common
Wolsingham Park Moor
Weardale
Teesdale
Wensleydale
Garsdale
Swaledale
Arkengarthdale
NORTH PENNINES
DURHAM
CUMBRIA
NORTH YORKSHIRE
YORKSHIRE DALES NATIONAL PARK
M6
A66
A6
A683
A684
A685
A686
A689
A65
A590
A591
A6
COPYRIGHT, GEORGE PHILIP LTD.

Castleside
Newcastle upon Tyne
Sunderland
45
Carlisle
Brough
Kendal
39
Harrogate
Wetherby
York
35
36
DURHAM
D U R H A M
HARTLEPOOL
BISHOP AUCKLAND
DARLINGTON
STOCKTON-ON-TEES
MIDDLESBROUGH
C L E V E L A N D
N O R T H
Y O R K S H I R E
Redcar
Billingham
Thornaby-on-Tees
Guisborough
Eston
Newton Aycliffe
Spennymoor
Shildon
Crook
Wolsingham
Sedgefield
Peterlee
Horden
Seaton Carew
Barnard Castle
Scotch Corner
Richmond
Catterick
Catterick Camp
Leyburn
Bedale
Northallerton
Thirsk
Masham
Ripon
Topcliffe
Yarm
Stokesley
Great Ayton
Helmsley
Hamsterley Forest
Hamsterley Common
Wensleydale
Coverdale
Nidderdale
Hambleton Hills
Cleveland Hills
Bilsdale West Moor
Tees Bay
Hartlepool Bay
Masham Moor
Stean Moor
Riggs Moor
Middlesmoor
Sutton-under-Whitestonecliffe
Kirkby Malzeard
Boroughbridge
Easingwold
A1(M)
66(M)

7
8
9
10
11
12
A
B
C
D
E
F
G
H
NORTH
SEA
Saltburn-by-the-Sea
Brotton
Skinningrove
Boulby
Carlin How
Kilton
North Skelton
Loftus
Easington
Dalehouse
Staithes
Port Mulgrave
Hinderwell
Runswick
Kettleness
Goldsborough
Lythe
Sandsend
Lingdale
Stanghow
Liverton
Moorsholm
Roxby
Newton Mulgrave
Ellerby
Scaling
Mickleby
West Barnby
East Barnby
WHITBY
Saltwick Bay
Abbey
Dunsley
Newholm
Ugthorpe
Danby
Commondale
Castleton
Ainthorpe
Lealholm
Egton
Aislaby
Ruswarp
Briggswath
Sneaton
Stainsacre
High Hawsker
Sleights
Ugglebarnby
Egton Bridge
Grosmont
Littlebeck
Sneaton Thorpe
Raw
Robin Hood's Bay
Fylingthorpe
Ness Point or North Cheek
Old Peak or South Cheek
Ravenscar
Westerdale
Church House
Glaisdale
Beck Hole
Goathland
Goathland Moor
Fylingdales Moor
Staintondale
Danby High Moor
Glaisdale Moor
Egton High Moor
Rosedale Moor
Hunt Ho.
Wheeldale Moor
NORTH YORK MOORS
NATIONAL PARK
Hill Cottages
Thorgill
Rosedale Abbey
Harwood Dale
Cloughton Newlands
Cloughton
Cloughton Wyke
Burniston
Cromer Point
Allerston High Moor
Langdale Forest
Broxa Forest
Spaunton Moor
Stape
Newton Dale
Kelda Castle
Levisham
Lockton
Newton-on-Rawcliffe
Stain dale
Dalby Forest
Low Dalby
Silpho
Broxa
Langdale End
Suffield
Hackness
Scalby
Newby
Barrowcliff
SCARBOROUGH
Falsgrave
Wykeham Forest
Everley
Lastingham
Gillamoor
Fadmoor
Hutton-le-Hole
Spaunton
Cropton
Cawthorne
Appleton-le-Moors
Kirkbymoorside
Keldholme
Sinnington
Wrelton
Aislaby
Kirkby Mills
Middleton
Pickering
Thornton-Dale
Welburn
Great Edstone
Nawton
Marton
Wilton
Allerston
Ebberston
Ebberston Hall
Snainton
Brompton
Sawdon
West Ayton
East Ayton
Hutton Buscel
Ruston
Wykeham
Irton
Seamer
Eastfield
Osgodby
Cayton Bay
Cayton
Lebberston
Gristhorpe
Filey Brigg
Filey
Filey Bay
Primrose Valley
Muston
Folkton
Flixton
Hunmanby
Reighton Gap
Reighton
Speeton
Buckton
Bempton
North Moor
Flamborough
Flamborough Head
Sewerby Hall
Sewerby
BRIDLINGTON
Bessingby
Boynton
Rudston
Grindale
Burton Fleming
Gypsey Race
Wold Newton
Fordon
Thwing
Octon
Langtoft
HUMBERSIDE
VALE OF PICKERING
Hertford
Willerby
Staxton
Ganton
Potter Brompton
Sherburn
East Heslerton
West Heslerton
East Knapton
West Knapton
Scampston
Yedingham
Rillington
Thorpe Bassett
Wintringham
Place Newton
Scagglethorpe
Settrington
Rookdale
Weaverthorpe
Butterwick
Foxholes
Helperthorpe
East Lutton
West Lutton
High Mowthorpe
Kirby Grindalythe
Duggleby
Wharram le Street
North Grimston
Normanby
Salton
Little Barugh
Great Barugh
Kirby Misperton
Flamingo Land Zoo Fun Park
High Marishes
Low Marishes
Brawby
Butterwick
Habton
Ryton
Wykeham
Old Malton Moor
Broughton
Old Malton
Malton
Norton
Roman Museum
Amotherby
Swinton
Appleton-le-Street
Barton-le-Street
Slingsby
Hovingham
Fryton
South Holme
East Ness
West Ness
Nunnington
Nunnington Hall
Stonegrave
Muscoates
South Field
Howardian Hills
Terrington
Ganthorpe
Coneysthorpe
Castle Howard
Welburn
Bulmer
Whitwell-on-the-Hill
High Hutton
Low Hutton
Firby
Langton
Kennythorpe
York
Kingston upon Hull
COPYRIGHT, GEORGE PHILIP LTD.

STRATHCLYDE
DUMFRIES
THE MACHARS
THE RHINS
CARRICK
GALLOWAY
CARRICK FOREST
Ailsa Craig
Ayr
Culzean Castle N.T.
Maidenhead Bay
Souter Johnnie's Cottage
Maidens
Morriston
Turnberry
Turnberry Bay
Kirkoswald
Maybole
Crossraguel Abbey
Pennyglen
Whitefaulds
Ballochbroe
Kirkmichael
Crosshill
Straiton
Patna
Dalmellington
Waterside
Doonbank
Loch Doon
Girvan
Girvan Mains
Dunepark
Woodland Bay
Dailly
Old Dailly
Penkill
Killochan Castle
Barr
Pinmore
Pinwherry
Colmonell
Knockdolian Castle
Ballantrae
Ballantrae Bay
Glenapp Castle & Gardens
Lendalfoot
Carleton Castle
Barrhill
Glentrool Forest
Glentrool Village
Loch Trool
Glen of Trool
Merrick 2770
Balloch Plantation
Tairlaw Plantation
Changue Forest
Kirroughtree Forest
Penninghame Forest
Newton Stewart
Minnigaff
Creebridge
Cairnsmore of Fleet
Clatteringshaws
Galloway Deer Museum
Bruce's Stone
Murray's Monument
Carsphairn
Dundeugh Forest
Loch Grannoch
Clints of Dromore
Creetown
Carsluith
Cardoness Castle
Cairn Holy
Kirkdale House
Fleet Bay
Islands of Fleet
Wigtown Bay
Wigtown
Wigtown Sands
Baldoon Sands
Bladnoch
Kirkinner
Whauphill
Sorbie
Garlieston
Galloway House Gardens
Eggerness Point
Whithorn
Isle of Whithorn
St. Ninian's Chapel
St. Ninian's Cave
Port Castle Bay
Burrow Head
Glasserton
Monreith
Port William
Monreith Bay
Mochrum
Elrig
Kirkcowan
Shennanton
Glenluce
Castle of Park
Dunragit
Castle Kennedy
Lochinch Castle
Castle Kennedy Gdns.
Soulseat Loch
Luce Bay
Luce Sands
Torrs Warren
Sandhead
Sandhead Bay
Stranraer
Cairnryan
Innermessan
Loch Ryan
Kirkcolm
Leswalt
Lochnaw Castle
Portpatrick
Dunskey Castle
Port of Spittal Bay
Stoneykirk
Ardwell
Ardwell House
Chapel Rossan Bay
Logan Botanic Gdns.
Port Logan
Port Logan Bay
Port Nessock or Port Logan Bay
Clanyard Bay
Kirkmaiden
Drummore
Maryport
Maryport Bay
Port Kemin
Mull of Galloway
Corsewall Point
Milleur Point
Finnarts Bay
Car Ferry to Larne
Water of App
Main Water of Luce
Cross Water of Luce
Penwhirn Res.
New Luce
Auchenmalg
Auchenmalg Bay
Chapel Finian
Alticry
Port of Spittal
Water of Minnoch
Drumlamford Loch
Loch Maberry
Loch Ochiltree
Glenwhilly
Old Place of Mochrum
Mochrum Loch
Castle Loch
Dernaglar Loch
Whitefield Loch
Knock Moss

47

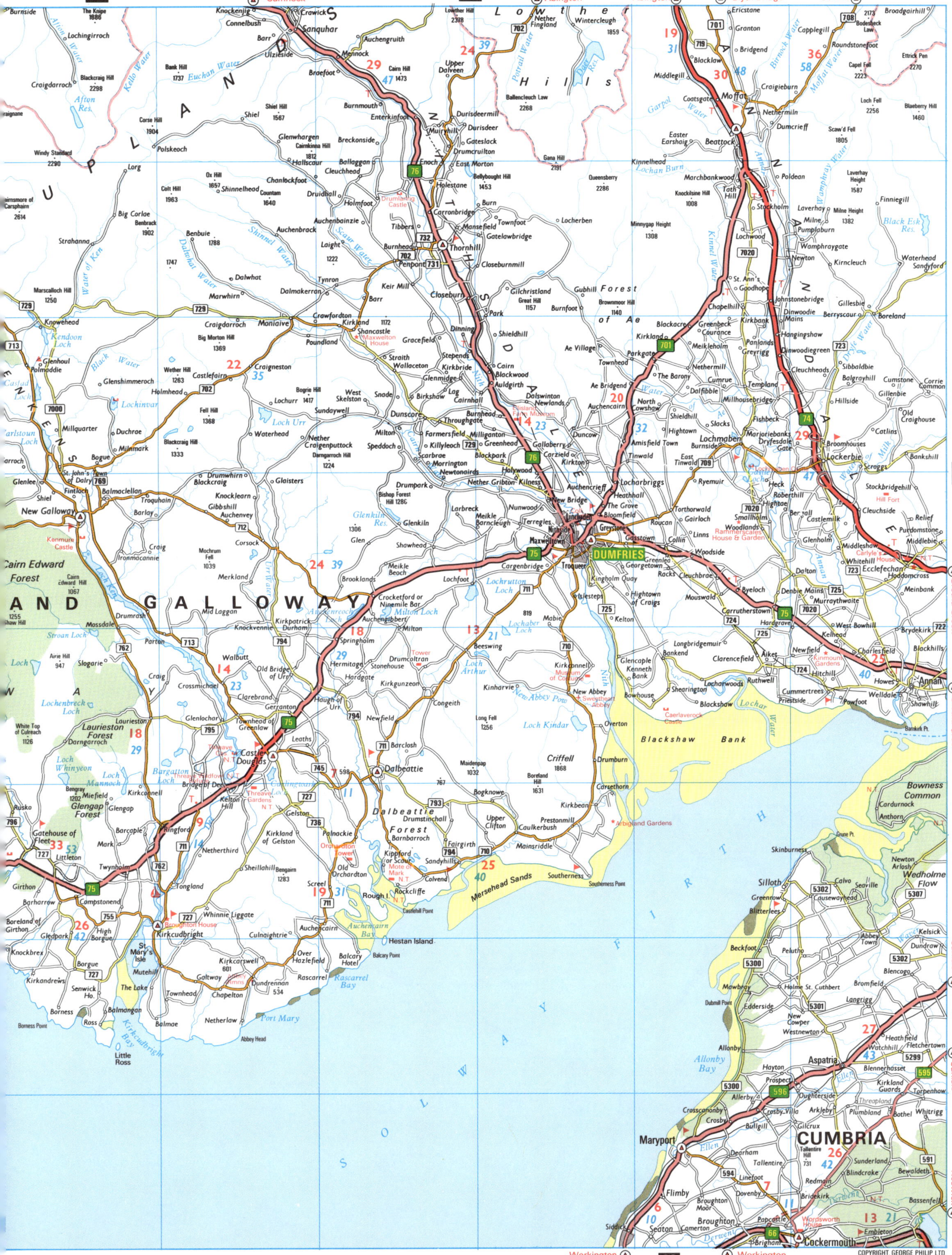

7
47
8
Cumnock
9
48
10
Abington
Abington
11
Blyth Bridge
Selkirk
12
A
B
C
D
E
F
G
H
44
Gretna Green
Gretna Green
Carlisle
Carlisle
Keswick
Workington
38
Workington
Keswick
COPYRIGHT GEORGE PHILIP LTD.
UPLANDS
LOWTHER HILLS
NITHSDALE
ANNANDALE
GALLOWAY
SOLWAY FIRTH
Forest of Ae
Dalbeattie Forest
Cairn Edward Forest
Laurieston Forest
Glengap Forest
Gatehouse of Fleet
Sanquhar
Kirkconnel
Crawick
Mennock
Wanlockhead
Moffat
Beattock
Thornhill
Penpont
Moniaive
Closeburn
Dumfries
Lincluden
Maxwelltown
Troqueer
New Galloway
Castle Douglas
Dalbeattie
Kirkcudbright
Lochmaben
Lockerbie
Annan
Ecclefechan
Carrutherstown
Kirkpatrick Durham
Crocketford or Ninemile Bar
New Abbey
Kippford or Scaur
Rockcliffe
Auchencairn
Hestan Island
Mersehead Sands
Southerness
Arbigland Gardens
Blackshaw Bank
Caerlaverock Castle
Bowness Common
Silloth
Skinburness
Abbey Town
Beckfoot
Allonby
Allonby Bay
Aspatria
Maryport
Cockermouth
Dearham
Flimby
CUMBRIA
Threave Gardens
Threave Castle
Drumlanrig Castle
Maxwelton House
Sweetheart Abbey
Kenmure Castle
Rammerscales House & Garden
Broughton House
Wordsworth House
Loch Ken
Loch Urr
Loch Arthur
Loch Kindar
Lochrutton Loch
Milton Loch
Auchenreoch Loch
Carlingwark Loch
Criffell
Kirkcudbright Bay
Rascarrel Bay
Auchencairn Bay
Port Mary
Little Ross
Balcary Point
Castlehill Point
Southerness Point

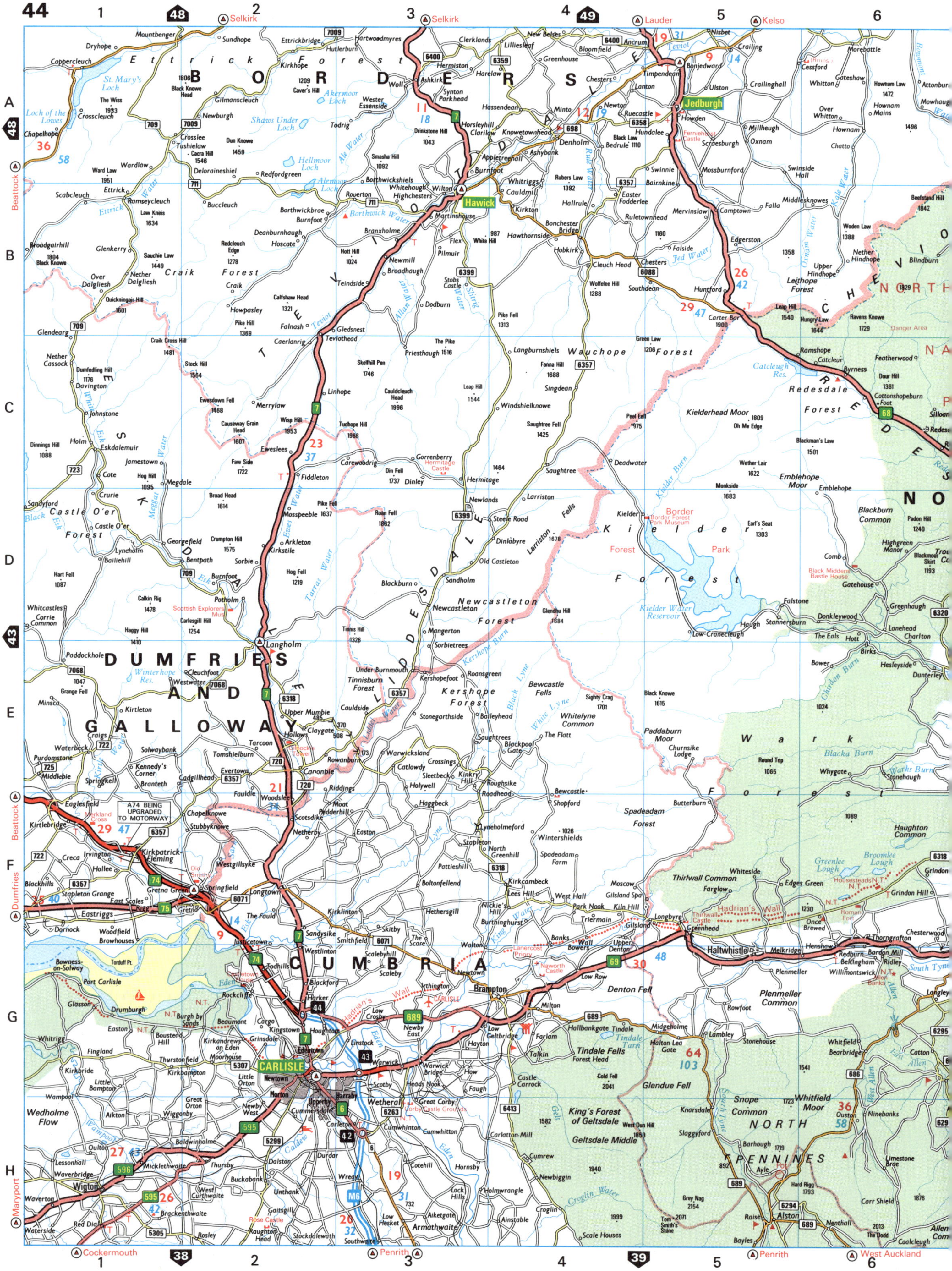

Selkirk
Lauder
Kelso
Beattock
Dumfries
Maryport
Cockermouth
Penrith
West Auckland
BORDERS
Ettrick Forest
St. Mary's Loch
Loch of the Lowes
Tushielaw
Ettrick
Buccleuch
Craik Forest
Ashkirk
Hawick
Jedburgh
Denholm
Minto
Wilton
Teviothead
TEVIOTDALE
ESKDALE
Langholm
Canonbie
Newcastleton
Newcastleton Forest
LIDDESDALE
Hermitage Castle
Wauchope Forest
Kielder
Kielder Forest
Kielder Water Reservoir
Border Forest Park Museum
Redesdale Forest
Catcleugh Res.
Carter Bar
Byrness
Wark Forest
Spadeadam Forest
DUMFRIES AND GALLOWAY
Gretna Green
Gretna
Springfield
Longtown
Annan
A74 BEING UPGRADED TO MOTORWAY
CUMBRIA
CARLISLE
Brampton
Dalston
Wigton
Bowness-on-Solway
Port Carlisle
Burgh by Sands
Haltwhistle
Greenhead
Hadrian's Wall
Gilsland
Bewcastle
Bewcastle Fells
Kershope Forest
Tindale Fells
Geltsdale Middle
King's Forest of Geltsdale
NORTH PENNINES
Alston
Thirlwall Common
Haughton Common
Plenmeller Common
Whitfield Moor
Armathwaite
Wetheral
Scotby
Cumwhinton
Rose Castle
Lanercost Priory
Naworth Castle
Cross Fell
Castle O'er Forest
Eskdalemuir
Border
Forest
Park

Wooler
Berwick-upon-Tweed
Cockburnspath
Continuation North
BERWICK-UPON-TWEED
HOLY I.
Continuation East
Farne Is.
Alnwick
Amble
Morpeth
ASHINGTON
Newbiggin-by-the-Sea
Bedlington
Blyth
Whitley Bay
TYNEMOUTH
SOUTH SHIELDS
NEWCASTLE UPON TYNE
GATESHEAD
SUNDERLAND
Seaham
Hexham
Corbridge
CONSETT
Stanley
Chester-le-Street
Washington
Houghton-le-Spring
Wallsend
Jarrow
Hebburn
NORTHUMBERLAND
Harwood Forest
Kidland Forest
Holystone Common
Simonside Hills
Rothbury
Slaley Forest
Blanchland Moor
Hexhamshire Common
TYNE AND WEAR
DURHAM
West Auckland
Durham
Darlington
Stockton-on-Tees

JURA
SOUND OF JURA
I. of Danna
Lochgilphead
Oban
Inveraray
Strachur
KNAPDALE
Tarbert
West Tarbert
GIGHA
KINTYRE
Campbeltown
MACHRIHANISH
Carradale
Skipness
Claonaig
KILBRANNAN SOUND
ARRAN
Goat Fell
Brodick
Lamlash
Holy Island
Lochranza
Blackwaterfoot
Pladda
Inchmarnock
BUTE
Rothesay
Port Bannatyne
Kames
Tighnabruaich
Portavadie
Sound of Bute
STRATH
GREAT CUMBRAE ISLAND
Little Cumbrae I.
Millport
Dunoon
Toward
Mull of Kintyre
Southend
Carradale Forest
Achaglachgach Forest
Glendaruel Forest
Loch Fyne
Loch Sween
Loch Caolisport
Kyles of Bute
Otter Ferry
Ardrishaig
Crinan
CAR FERRY TO ISLAY-PORT ELLEN
TO PORT ASKAIG

7
8
51
9
10
11
52
12
Tarbet
Stirling
A
B
C
D
E
F
G
H
LOCH LOMOND
CENTRAL
HILLS
LENNOX
Campsie Fells
Carron Valley Forest
CLYDE
Helensburgh
Alexandria
Jamestown
Bonhill
Dumbarton
Gourock
GREENOCK
Port Glasgow
Kilmacolm
Erskine Br.
Clydebank
Bearsden
Milngavie
Bishopbriggs
Kirkintilloch
Kilsyth
Cumbernauld
Stepps
Coatbridge
Airdrie
GLASGOW
Renfrew
PAISLEY
Johnstone
Barrhead
Rutherglen
Cambuslang
Uddingston
Bellshill
Motherwell
Wishaw
Hamilton
Blantyre
East Kilbride
Strathaven
Larkhall
Busby
Newton Mearns
Clarkston
Thornliebank
Eaglesham
Skelmorlie
Largs
Fairlie
West Kilbride
Ardrossan
Saltcoats
Stevenston
Kilwinning
Dalry
Beith
Kilbirnie
Lochwinnoch
Dunlop
Stewarton
Kilmaurs
IRVINE
Irvine Bay
KILMARNOCK
Hurlford
Galston
Newmilns
Darvel
Troon
Prestwick
New Prestwick
AYR
Mauchline
Catrine
Auchinleck
Cumnock
New Cumnock
Muirkirk
Kirkconnel
Sanquhar
Dalmellington
Patna
Maybole
Culzean Bay
Girvan
New Galloway
Kincardine
Edinburgh
Newmains
Lanark
Abington
Uddington
Thornhill
48
42
43
Girvan
COPYRIGHT, GEORGE PHILIP LTD.

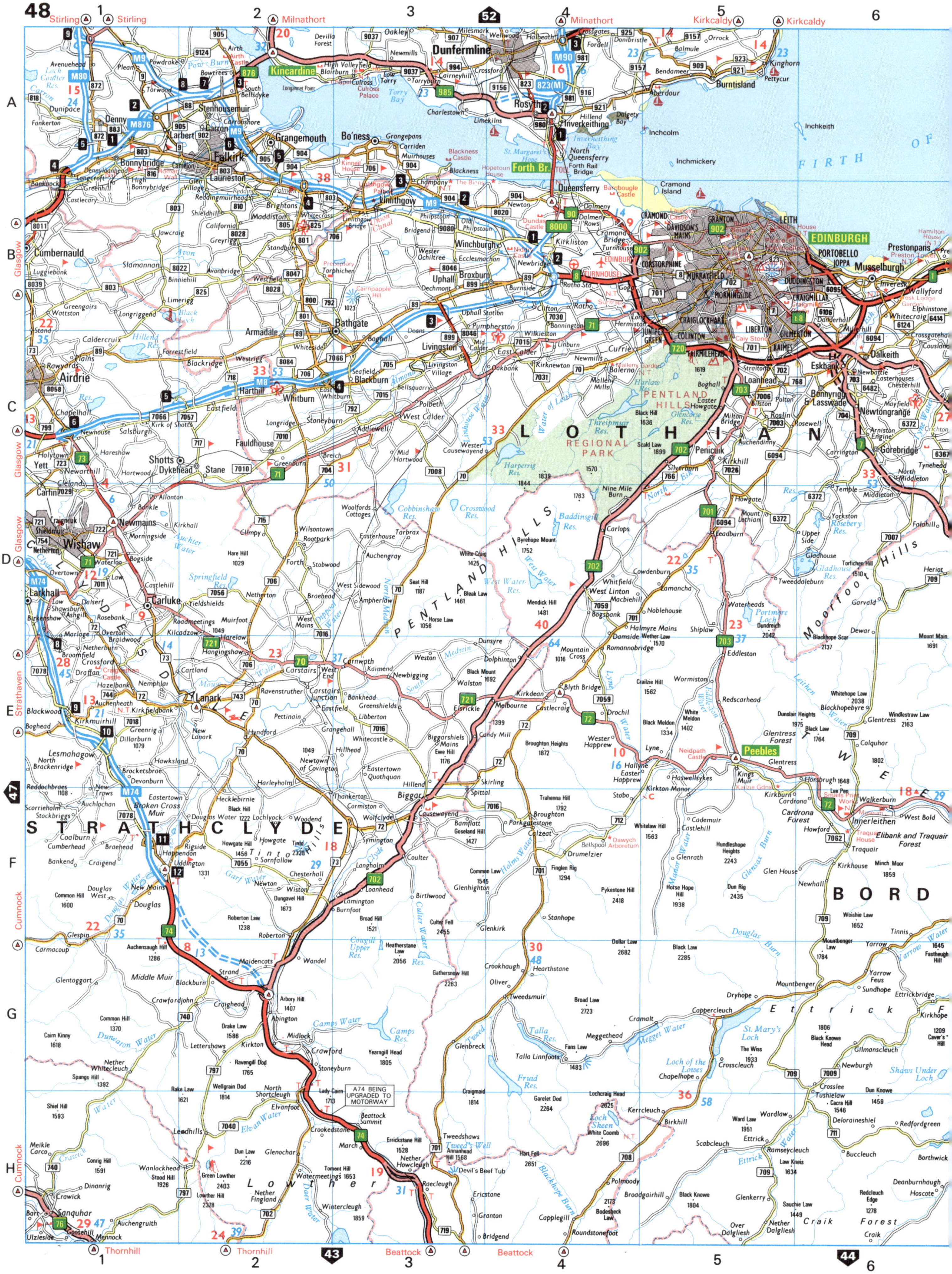
Stirling
Milnathort
Kirkcaldy
52
Dunfermline
Kincardine
Rosyth
Inverkeithing
North Queensferry
Forth Rail Bridge
Forth Br
Queensferry
Burntisland
Kinghorn
Pettycur
Aberdour
Inchcolm
Inchkeith
Inchmickery
Cramond Island
FIRTH OF
EDINBURGH
LEITH
PORTOBELLO
JOPPA
Musselburgh
Prestonpans
Dalkeith
Grangemouth
Bo'ness
Falkirk
Stenhousemuir
Larbert
Denny
Bonnybridge
Linlithgow
Cumbernauld
Airdrie
Bathgate
Livingston
Broxburn
Uphall
Winchburgh
Kirkliston
Armadale
Whitburn
Harthill
Shotts
Wishaw
Carluke
Lanark
Larkhall
Lesmahagow
Biggar
Penicuik
Loanhead
Bonnyrigg & Lasswade
Gorebridge
Peebles
Innerleithen
Walkerburn
West Linton
Carnwath
Carstairs
Abington
Crawford
Leadhills
Sanquhar
Tweedsmuir
PENTLAND HILLS
PENTLAND HILLS REGIONAL PARK
LOTHIAN
STRATHCLYDE
BORD
Moorfoot Hills
Tinto Hills
Lowther
Ettrick
Craik Forest
St. Mary's Loch
Talla Res.
Fruid Res.
A74 BEING UPGRADED TO MOTORWAY
Glasgow
Strathaven
Cumnock
Thornhill
Beattock
43
44
47

FORTH
Fidra
Craigleith
Bass Rock
North Berwick
Tantallon Castle
Auldhame
Scoughall
New Mains
Whitekirk
St. Baldred's Cradle
Gullane Bay
Gullane Point
Gullane
Dirleton
Dirleton Castle N.T.
Kingston
Aberlady Bay
Aberlady
Fenton Barns
Luffness House
Drem
East Fortune
Gosford Bay
Gosford Ho.
Ballencrieff
Athelstaneford
Markle
Preston Mill N.T.
Preston
Tyninghame
Belhaven
Dunbar
West Barns
Broxburn
Barns Ness
East Barns
Spittal
Longniddry
Hopetoun Monument
East Linton
Traprain
Hailes Castle
Pitcox
Spott
Meikle Pinkerton
Skateraw
Thorntonloch
Gladsmuir
Macmerry
Haddington
Lennoxlove
Stevenson House
Luggate Burn
Stenton
The Chesters Fort
Dry Burn
Innerwick
Halls
Penston
Cockles
Papple
New Winton
Samuelston
Bolton
Woodhall
Cocklaw Hill 1046
Cockburnspath
Ormiston
Garvald
Bransly Hill 1301
Oldhamstocks
Winton House
Pencaitland
Easter Pencaitland
Western Pencaitland
Carfrae
Dunbar Common 1307
Monynut Edge
Meikle Black Law 803
Ecclow
Telegraph Hill
St. Abb's Head
West Byres
Peaston Bank
West Saltoun
East Saltoun
Gifford
Danskine
Spartleton Edge
Bothwell Water
Heart Law 1283
Lumsdaine
Coldingham Moor
Northfield
St. Abbs
Coldingham Bay
Coldingham
Priory (Rmns.)
Marvingston
Longyester
Gamelshiel
Grantshouse
Houndwood
Eye Water
Eyemouth
Cairncross
Humbie
Blegbie
Lammer Law 1730
West Hopes
Meikle Says Law 1755
Lammermuir
Hopes Res.
Whiteadder Res.
Cranshaws Hill 1245
Cranshaws
Quixwood
Abbey St. Bathans
Horseley Hill 859
Reston
Ayton
Burnmouth
Auchencrow
Fala
Soutra Mains
Crib Law 1670
Ellemford
Edinshall Fort
Marygold
Fala Moor
Hunt Law 1625
Dye Water
Primrosehill
Lintlaw
Watch Water Res.
Longformacus
Cumledge
Preston
Chirnsidebridge
Edrom
East Blanerne
Chirnside
Nunlands
Mordington Mains
Clappers
Cumberland Bower
Gilston
Nether Brotherstone
Hartside Hill
Crookston North Mains
Hillhouse
Hogs Law 1470
Longcroft
Rawburn
Stobswood
Dirrington Great Law
The Hardens
Duns
Manderston Ho.
Buxley
Kelloe Mains
Allanton
Edington
Foulden
Hutton
Conundrum
Highfields
Berwick-upon-Tweed
Oxton
Netherhowden
Addinston
Braidshawrig
Clockmill
Reedy Loch
Broomdykes
Blackadder Bank
Paxton
Threeburnford
Lylestone
Wedderlie
Kettelshiel
Gavinton
Cheeklaw
Whitelaw
West Blackadder
Sunwick
Dykegatehead
East Ord
Tweedmouth
Spittal
Collie Law 1253
Blackburn
Edgehope
Newbigging
Forest
Blythe
Westruther
Bedshiel
Choicelee
Kyles Hill 935
Ladyflat
Polwarth
Middlefield
Sinclair's Hill
Rayelaw
Whitsome
Hilton
Fishwick
Horncliffe
Loanend
Prior Park
Burnhouse Mains
Lauder
Thirlestane Castle
Spottiswoode
Halliburton
Cothill
Bogend
Mount Pleasant
Whitsomehill
Horndean
Middle Ord
Unthank
Borewell
Scremerston
Torquhan
Lauder Common
Thirlestane
Whiteburn
Thornydykes
Hexpath
Sisterpath
Fogo
Fogorig
Ryslaw
Swinton Quarter
Ladykirk
Thorntonpark
Thornton
Murton
Norham
Newbiggin
Cheswick
Cathpair
Woodheads
High Cross
Houndslow
Greenlaw
Whinkerstones
Printonan
Swintonmill
Swinton
Little Swinton
Ladykirk Home Farm
Shoreswood
Shoresdean
West Allerdean
Killochyett
Stow
Sell Moor
Boon
Bassendean
Fawside
Rumbletonlaw
Eccles Tofts
Simprim
Grindon
Ancroft Northmoor
Ancroft
Stagehall
Lugate
Corsbie
Greenknowe
Gordon
East Gordon
Middlethird
Ploughlands
Leitholm
Ruthven
Shellacres
Grindonrigg
Felkington
Berringtonlaw
Threepwood
Wooplaw
Nether Blainslie
Legerwood
Birkhill
Huntlywood
Greenknowe Tower
Byrewalls
Easter Howlaws
Lambden
Crosshall
Orange Lane
Oxenrig
St. Cuthberts
Greenlaw Walls
Duddo
Berrington
Bowsden
New Haggerston
Old Dryburn
Bow
Caitha Bowland 1314
William Law
Chapel Mains
Kedslie
West Morriston
Fans
Fallsidehill
Hume
Caldside
Eccles
Hatchednize
Harper Ridge
Castle Heaton
Woodside
Barmoor Castle
Langshaw
Mosshouses
Purvishaugh
Sweethope
Homebyres
Hassington
Bartlehill
Coldstream
Homebank
Lennel
Cornhill-on-Tweed
Crookham Westfield
Etal
Slainsfield
Lowick
Knowes Hill 1222
Buckholm
Glendearg
Earlston
Mellerstain House
Harpertoun
Eden Hall
Stichill
Birgham
Carham
Redden
Shidlaw
Wark
West Learmouth
Coldstream
Crookham
Ford
Barmoor Ridge
Brownridge
Clovenfords
Galashiels
Easter Langlee
Wester Housebyres
Gattonside
Redpath
Brotherstone
West Third
Smailholm
Nenthorn
Houndridge
Ednam
Ferneyhill
Hadden
Kerchesters
Sprouston
East Learmouth
Branxton
Branxtonmoor
Blinkbonny
Pressen
Flodden
Kimmerston
Linthaugh
Fentonhill
Hetton Steads
Caddonfoot
Yair Hill Forest
Fairnilee
Abbotsford House
Darnick
Melrose
Abbey
Dingleton
Newstead
Leaderfoot
Bemersyde
Smailholm Tower
Charterhouse
Hayhount
Floors Castle
Kelso
Maxwellheugh
Windywalls
Eastfield of Lempitlaw
Hoselaw
Howburn
Downham
Howtel
Thornington
Milfield
Wrangham
Fenton Town
Hetton Law
Boleside
Eildon
Eildon Hills 1385
Newton St. Boswells
Clintmains
Dryburgh
Dryburgh Abbey (Rmns.)
Manorhill
Trows
Lempitlaw
Mindrummill
Mindrum
Pawston
Kilham
Marleyknowe
Galewood
Nesbit
Doddington
Lindean
White Law 1059
Bowden
Whitelee
St. Boswells
Roxburgh Newtown
Kersmains
Huntershall
Easter Softlaw
Blakelaw
Graden
Shotton
Yetholm Mains
Westnewton
Kirknewton
Yeavering
Yeavering Bell
Lanton
Coupland
Newtown
Akeld Steads
East Horton
West Horton
Weetwoodhill
Broadmeadows
Ovenscloss
Bridgelands
Newark Castle
Bowhill House
Bowhill
Selkirk
Philiphaugh
Carterhaugh
Clarilawmoor
Thornielaw
Longnewton
Maxton
Rutherford
Heiton
Roxburgh
Pirnie
Upper Nisbet
Kalemouth
Frogden
Linton Hill 926
Town Yetholm
Kirk Yetholm
Cherrytrees
Coldsmouth Hill 1363
Hethpool
Newton Tors 1762
Akeld
Humbleton
Turvelaws
Wooler
Hartwoodburn
Oakwood
Midlem
Toftbarns
Bewlie
Sandystones
Greenend
Waterloo Monument
Harrietsfield
New Belses
Nisbet
Eckford
Crookhouse
Linton
Primsidemill
Fredden Hill 1140
Middleton Hall
Earle
Haugh Head
Lilburn Hill
Hutlerburn
Hartwoodmyres
Clerklands
Lilliesleaf
Bloomfield
Ancrum
Monteviot House
Teviot
Crailing
Morebattle
Cessford
Southernknowe
Preston Hill 1724
Cold Law 1484
North Middleton
South Middleton
Lilburn Tower
Hermiston
Greenhouse
Harelaw
Chesters
Bonjedward
Timpendean
Ulston
Crailinghall
Whitton
Gateshaw
Hownam Law 1472
Attonburn
The Schil 1985
Langleeford
Ilderton
Roseden
Wollrig
Ashkirk
Synton Parkhead
Akermoor Loch
Wester Essenside
Hassendean
Minto
Lanton
Newton
Ruecastle
Jedburgh
Howden
Over Whitton
Hownam Mains
Mowhaugh
Sourhope
The Cheviot 2676
Hedgehope Hill 2343
Dunmoor Hill 1860
Roddam
Calder
Roddam Rigg
Todrig
Drinkstone Hill 1043
Horsleyhill
Clarilaw
Knowetownhead
Denholm
Bedrule 1110
Hundalee
Millheugh
Oxnam
Hownam
Chatto
1496
Cocklawfoot
Cock Law 1223
Kings Seat 1743
2419
NORTHUMBERLAND NATIONAL PARK
Linhope
Reaveley
Ale Water
Smasha Hill 1092
Ashybank
Appletreehall
Black Law
Rule Water
Scraesburgh
Ferniehirst Castle
Swinnie
Mossburnford
Swinside Hall
Kale Water
Breamish
Greensidehill
Ingram
Fawdon
Borthwickshiels
Whitehaugh
Highchesters
Roberton
Alemoor Loch
Burnfoot
Hawick
Wilton
Whitriggs
Rubers Law 1392
Bairnkine
6357
Easter Fodderlee
Hallrule
Middlesknowes
Falla
Windy Gyle 2032
Beefstand Hill 1842
Bloodybush Edge 2001
Cushat Law 2020
High Knowes 1294
Great Ryle
Borthwick Water
Burnfoot
Branxholme
Martinshouse
Kirkton
Bonchester Bridge
Hawthornside
Ruletownhead
Mervinslaw
Camptown
Woden Law 1388
Usway Burn
Kidland Forest
Wether Cairn 1846
Prendwick
Hott Hill 1024
Newmill
White Hill 987
Flex
Pilmuir
Hobkirk
1160
Falside
Jed Water
Edgerston
1358
Oxnam Water
Nether Hindhope
Blindburn
Bell Hill 1612
CHEVIOT HILLS
Barrowburn
Shillhope Law 1644
Alnham
Little Ryle
Teindside
Broadhaugh
Stobs Castle
Cleuch Head
Chesters
Wolfelee Hill 1288
Southdean
Huntford
Upper Hindhope
Leithope Forest
1829
Scrainwood
Biddlestone
Ellilaw
Yetlington
Langholm
Elishaw
Alnwick
Newcastle upon Tyne
LAUDERDALE
TEVIOTDALE
ETTRICK FOREST
TWEED
MERSE
Tweed
Leet Water
Blackadder Water
Whiteadder Water
Eden Water
Gala Water
Leader Water
Till
Glen
College Burn
Bowmont Water
Harthope Burn
Coquet
Biel Water
Peffer Burn
Tyne
Birns Water
Whiteadder Water
Soonhope Burn

Lochailort
55
Sanna Point
Sanna
Sanna Bay
Fascadale
Achateny
Kilmory
Ockle
Point of Ardnamurchan
Portuairk
Achnaha
Achosnich
Meall nan Con 1433
Ardnamurchan
Bheinn Bhreac 1171
Leac Shoilleir 1434
Loch Mudle
Beinn na Seilg 1123
Ormsaigmore
Ormsaigbeg
Kilchoan
Mingary Castle
Kilchoan Bay
Ben Hiant 1731
8007
Glenmore
Glenbeg
Glenborrodale
Ardslignish
Macleans Nose
Meall nan Each 1607
Ben Laga 1679
Ardtoe
Newton of Ardtoe
Shielfoot
Kentra Bay
8044
Blain
Dalnabreck
Mingarrypark
Acharacle
Moss
Ardshealach
Salen
Resipole
Loch Shiel
Dalelia
Polloch
Loch Doilet
Glenhurich
Glen Hurich
Kinlochan
Sunart
Beinn Resipol 2775
Scotstown
Ariundle
Strontian
Anaheilt
Ardery
Ardnastang
Camuschoirk
Loch Sunart
Laga
Eilean Mòr
Oronsay
Risga
Carna
Glencripesdale
Meall an Damhain 1693
Laudale Ho.
Liddesdale
Beinn Mhеadhoin 2579
Sgurr Dhomhnuill 2914
Garbh Bheinn 2903
Acharacle
Achnalea
Glen Tarbert
Carnoch
Tarbert
Ardmore Bay
Ardmore Point
Bloody Bay
Auliston Point
Rubha nan Gall
Quinish Point
Glengorm Castle
Meall an Inbhire 868
Tobermory
Folk Museum
Calve Island
Mishnish
Rubha an 'Ard
Quinish Ho.
Quinish
S Airde Beinn 959
Caliach Point
Sunipol
Mornish
Penmore Mill
Dervaig
Achnadrish
Loch Peallach
Upper Druimfin
Calgary
Calgary Bay
Ardow
Drimnin
Bonnavoulin
Torraneidhinn
Morvern
Beinn Bhuidhe 1480
Glenmorven Cottage
Rhemore
Sithean na Raplaich 1806
Beinn Iadain 1873
Beinn na h-Uamha 1521
Gleann Dubh
Beinn nam Beathrach 1869
Beinn Chlaonleud 1569
Loch Uisge
Lochuisge
Beach
Fuar Bheinn 2511
Creach Bheinn 2800
Kilmalieu
Kingairloch Ho.
North Corry
Camasnacroise
Beinn Mheadhoin 2423
Kingairloch
Loch a' Choire
Treshnish Point
Ensay
Càrn Mòr 1122
Haunn
Reudle
Rubh' a' Chaoil
Burg
Kilninian
Tostarie
Achleck
Gnoc an da Chinn 1280
Fanmore
Ballygowan
Speinne Mòr 1456
Aros
Lettermore
Ardnacross
Achnacraig
Salen Forest
Loch Frisa
Sound of Mull
Killundine
Fiunary
Savary
Fiunary Forest
Larachbeg
Acharn
Claggan
Achranich
Loch Arienas
Loch Teàrnait
Beinn a' Chaisil 1431
Loch nan Clach
Glensanda
Rannoch
Loch Aline
Lochaline
Ardtornish Castle
Glais Bheinn 1570
An Sleaghach 1685
Eignaig
Aros Mains
Aros Castle
Cranach
Clenaros Ho.
Salen
Rubha Mòr
Pennygown
Killbeg
Fishnish Point
Corrynachenchy
Garmony
Ardtornish Point
Inninmore Bay
Loch Tuath
Gometra
Gometra Ho. 503
Beinn Chreagach 1025
Bearnus
Ulva
Ulva House
Laggan Bay
Lagganulva
Oskamull
Killiemor
Kellan
Killiechronan
Gruline Ho.
Beinn Bhuidhe 1352
Goodhail
Beinn Chreagach Mhor 1903
Salen Forest
Scallastle Bay
Scallastle
Rubha an Ridire
Bernera Island
Achadun
Loch Fiart
Kilcheran
Eilean Dubh
Achnacroish
Lismore
Saileán
Clachan
Eriska
North Shian
Balure
Barcaldine Castle
Baravullin
Kiel Crofts
Ferlochan
Benderloch
Ledaig
Shuna
Appin House
Appin Wildlife Museum
Castle Stalker
Portnacroish
Tynribbie
Port Appin
Port Ramsay
Little Colonsay
Staffa
Fingal's Cave N.T.
Inch Kenneth
Eorsa
Loch na Keal
Knock
Beinn a' Ghràig 1939
Loch Ba
Glen Cannel
Dùn da Ghaoithe 2512
Craignure
Torosay Castle
Duart Bay
Duart Point
Duart Castle
Eilean Musdile
Rubha Garbh-aird
Ardmucknish Bay
Dunstaffnage Castle
Connel
Dunbeg
Black Lochs
Derryguaig
Gribun
Erisgeir
Balmeanach
Coirc Bheinn 1837
Ben More 3171
Corra-bheinn 2311
MULL
Beinn Talaidh 2496
Sgùrr Dearg 2429
Lochdon
Ganavan
Dunollie
Oban
Soroba Fm.
Altnacraig
Strontoiller
Clenamacrie
Beinn na Sréine 1704
Ishriff
Lussa
Strathcoil
Ardura
Ardachoil
Grass Point
Ardmeanach
Rubha na h Uamha
Bearraich 1416 N.T.
Kilfinichen
Ardvergnish
Glen More
Loch Airdeglais
Creach Beinn 2289
Kinlochspelve
Loch Spelve
Carn Ban 811
Croggan
Rubha na Faoilinn
Kerrera
Bach Island
Dubh Sgeir
Ardmore
Carn Breugach 617
Gallanachmore
Gallanach
Ariogan
Kilbride
Cleigh
Kilmore
Kilbride
Lerags
Rubha Seanach
Loch Nell
Loch Scridain
Pennyghael
Killunaig
Beinn na Croise 1649
Loch Fuaron
Ben Buie 2354
Creach Bheinn Lodge
Lochbuie
Moy Castle
Loch Uisg
Barachandroman
Maol Bàn 1106
Ardentallan Ho.
Minard Point
Rubha nan Cearc
Kintra
Ardchrishnish
Torrans
Loch Pottie na h-I
Aridhglas
Tirghoil
Eorabus
Ardtun
Lee
Fionnphort
Bunessan
Ross of Mull
Loch Assopol
Brolass
Beinn Chreagach 1235
Carsaig
Leidle
Loch Buie
Druim Fada 1329
Laggan Deer Forest
Cruachan Min 1232
Ardalanish
Uisken
Scoor
Carsaig Bay
Rubha Dubh
Frank Lockwood's Island
Eilean Dùin
Beinn Mhor 635
Kilninver
An Creachan 1167
A'Chruach 1208
Kilbride
Clachan Bridge
Barrachrail
World in Miniature
Glen Euchar
Braglenbeg
Carn Dearg 1436
Beinn a' Chaol-achaidh 411
Ardchiavaig
Ardalanish Bay
Carsaig Arches 1082
Malcolm's Point
Rubha nam Bràithrean
Eilean a' Chalmain
Eilean Mòr
Rubh' Ardalanish
Insh Island
Ardencaple Ho.
An Cala Gdn
Clachan
Clachan-Seil
Seil
Easdale
Folk Museum
Balvicar
Cruach Rarey 876
Blaran
Braes of Lorn
Loch Tralaig
Narrachan
Firth of Lorn
Dubh fheith
Car Ferry
8003
Torsa
Kilchoan
Melfort
Ardanstur
Kilmelford
Cruach Maolachy 1239
Maolachy
Glenmore
Garbh Eileach
Belnahua
Cullipool
Ardlarach
Ardinamar
Luing
Achafolla
Garvellachs
Eilean Dubh Mòr
Eileach an Naoimh
Loch Melfort
Arduaine Gardens
Rubh a' Chnaip
Arduaine
Kames
Tom Soilleir 1199
Lagalochan
Carn Duchara 1608
Lunga
Guirasdeal
Toberonochy
Sound of Luing
Shuna Sound
Shuna
Shuna Point
Barravullin
Lunga (Hotel)
Barbreck House
Cruach an Eachlaich 1148
Kintraw
Rubha nam Faoilean
Cruach Scarba 1470
Scarba
Rubh Ard Luing
Ardfern
8002
Eilean Mhic Chrion
Creag Mhor 745
Eilean Righ
Ford
Fincharn
Loch Ederline
Whirlpool
Rubha Righinn
Gulf of Corryvreckan
Rèisa Mhic Phaidean
Aird
Loch Craignish
Carnasserie Castle
Loch Gaineamhach
Sith Mor 1339
Reisa t-Sruith
Island Macaskin
Kilmartin
Craignish Point
Garbh Rèisa
Kinuachdrach
Kinuachdrach Harbour
Cruach na Seilcheig 967
Loch a' Chonaire
Glengarrisdale Bay
Slockavullin
Cairns
Kilmichael Forest
Loch Leathan
Dun Dubh 758
Glendebadel Bay
Rubh' a' Bhacain
Rubha Garbh ard
Ballymeanoch
Ben Garrisdale 1194
Loch a' Gheoidh
Ardnoe Point
Loch Crinan
Crinan
8025
Dunadd Fort
Kilmichael Glassary
Loch Glashan
Kilmahumaig
Bridgend
Ruadh Sgeir
Rubha nam Barr
Bellanoch
Crinan Canal
841
Jura
Corpach Bay
Beinn Bhreac 1527
Lussa
Sound of Jura
Gallchoille
Cairnbaan
816
Lochgilphead
Asknish Forest
Lochgair
Kiloran Bay
Carnan Eoin 470
Rubh' a' Geodha
Beinn Bhreac 456
Kiloran
Kilchattan
An Rubha
871
Loch Fada 445
Colonsay
870
Scalasaig
Machrins
Milbuie
869
Balarumindubh
Chladaich
Garvard
Rubha Dubh
Rèidh Eilean
Eilean Annraidh
Baile Mòr 332
Iona
St Mary's Abbey
Stac an Aoineidh
N.T.
Fidden
Sound of Iona
Erraid 246
Soa Island
Eilean nam Muc
Continuation West
To Coll & Tiree
To Castlebay
Lochboisdale
46
Strath

7
8
9
10
11
12
Drimsallie
Lochy Bridge
55
57
A
B
C
D
E
F
G
H
H
L
A
N
D
GRAMPIAN MOUNTAINS
TAYSIDE
CENTRAL
STRATHCLYDE
ARGYLL
Scaddle
Ardgour
Conaglen Ho.
Aryhoulan
Inverscaddle Bay
Coruanan Lodge
Blarmachfoldach
Glen Nevis
Water of Nevis
Achriabhach
Mullach nan Coirean 3077
Sgurr a' Mhàim 3601
Mamore Forest
Binnein Mor 3700
Am Bodach 3382
Loch Eilde Beag
Loch Eilde Mòr
Creaguaineach Lodge
L. Treig
Luibeilt
Amhainn Rath
Corrour Shooting Lodge
Loch Ossian
Corrour Forest
Sgor Gaibhre 3124
Càrn Dearg 3080
Rannoch Forest
Talla Bheith Forest
Loch Ericht
Stob an Aonaich Mhoir 2805
Lubnaclach
Leum Uilleim 2971
Glas Bheinn 2587
Corran
Clovulin
Sallachan
Onich
Glenrigh Forest
Lundavra
Lairigmor
Mam na Gualainn 2603
Kinlochmore
Kinlochleven
Loch Leven
North Ballachulish
South Ballachulish
Callert Ho.
Blackwater Reservoir
Ciaran Water
Allt na Caim
Sròn Bheag 1631
Glencoe
Folk Museum
Visitor Centre
Pap of Glencoe 2430
Ballachulish
Glen Coe
Achnacon
Ossian's Cave
Meall Mor
Altnafeadh
Beinn a' Chrulaiste 2811
Meall nan Ruadhag 2120
Black Corries
Stob na Cruaiche 2423
Rannoch Sta.
Hotel
Dunan
Bridge of Ericht
Killichonan
Loch Rannoch
Finnart
Bridge of Gaur
Camghouran
Loch Eigheach
Kentallen
Glenduror Forest
Achindarroch
Beinn a' Bheithir
Duror
Cuil Bay
Keil
Bidean nam Bian 3766
Kingshouse Hotel
Royal Forest
Buachaille Etive Mor
3345
Rannoch Moor
Lochan Gaineamhach
Sgor na h-Ulaidh 3258
Dalness
Alltchaorunn
Meall à Bhuiridh 3636
Ski-lift
Loch Bà
Fraochaidh 2883
Salachail
Glen Creran
Glen Etive
Stob Dubh 2897
Aonach Mor
Clach Leathad 3602
Lochan na h-Achlaise
Water of Tulla
Meall Buidhe 3054
Meall a' Mhuic 2444
Carn Chreag 2823
Meall Cruinn 2717
Eas Daimh
Bridge of Balgie
Meggernie Castle
Beinn Fhionnlaidh 3139
Invercharnan
Glen Ure
Elleric
Invercreran
Glasdrum
Creagan
Appin
Druimavuic
Gualachulain
Kinlochetive
Stob Coir'an Albannaich 3425
Stob Ghabhar 3565
Achallader
Beinn a' Chreachain 3540
Meall Buidhe 2976
Stuchd an Lochain 3144
Glen Lyon
Gallin
Beinn Sgulaird
Beinn Trilleachan 2752
Ben Starav 3541
Loch Dochard
Forest Lodge
Black Mount
Loch Tulla
Beinn Mhanach 3125
Pubil
Cashlie
Stronuich
Stronuich Res.
South Creagan
Barcaldine
Sea Life Centre
Barcaldine Forest
Creach Bheinn 2657
Inveroran Hotel
Beinn an Dòthaidh 3267
Loch Lyon
Meall Ghaordie 3410
Barrs
Loch Etive
Glen Kinglass
Beinn Suidhe 2215
Bridge of Orchy
Beinn Inverveigh 2087
Beinn Dòrain 3524
Beinn Heasgarnich 3530
Ardmaddy
Beinn nan Lus 2327
Meall Garbh 2283
Cadderlie
Inveresragan
Ardchattan Priory
Glen Lochay
Tullich
Kenknock
Innischoarach
Creag Mhor 3387
Forest of Mamlorn
Aberfeldy
Bonawe Quarries
Auchnacloich Pier
Glen Liever
Beinn Mhic-Mhonaidh 2602
Glen Orchy
Arichastlich
Beinn Udlaidh 2759
Beinn Bhreac-liath 2633
Beinn Odhar 2948
Breadalbane
Creag Mhor 2359
Fish Lift
Boreland
Falls of Lochay
Hotel
Killin
Fearnoch Forest
Taynuilt
Glen Noe
Beinn Eunaich 3242
Beinn Donachain 2127
Arrivain
Clifton
Tyndrum
Ben Challum 3354
Beinn Cheathaich 3076
Meall a' Churain 3007
Beinn nan Imirean 2769
Dochart
Bridge of Awe
Ben Cruachan 3689
Cruachan Resvr.
Pass of Brander
Kilchurn Castle
Glen Strae
Beinn a' Bhùiridh 2941
Achnafalnich
Beinn na Sròine 2085
Strath Fillan
Auchtertyre
Auchlyne
Ardchyle
Beinn Leabhainn 2312
Barguillean Farm
Glen Nant
Lochawe
Stronmilchan
Strath of Orchy
Inverlochy
Lower Kinchrackine
Dalmally
Cononish
Auchrioch
Lochdochart House
Glen Dochart
Luib Hotel
Ledcharrie 1946
Loch Iubhair
Loch Tromlee
Innis Chonain
Inishail
Ardanaiseig
Ardanaiseig Garden
Achlian
Teatle Water
Eas a' Ghaill
Ben Lui 3708
Ben Oss 3374
Beinn Dubhchraig 3204
Fiarach
Inverherive
Crianlarich
Portnellan
Loch Dochart
Ben More 3843
Lochearnhead
Loch Nant
Kilchrenan
Annat
Instrynich
Taychreggan
(North Port)
Cladich
Allt Fearna
Allt an Stacain
Beinn Bhalgairean 2085
Meall nan Tighearn 2423
Glen Falloch
Stob Binnein 3821
3140
Monachyle Glen
Meall an t-Seallaidh 2793
Auchachenna
Coillaig
South Port
Upper Sonachan
Lochan Shira
Dubh Eas
Falls of Falloch
Braes of Balquhidder
Rob Roy's Grave
Balquhidder
Auchtoo
Kingshouse
Inverinan
Inverinan Forest
Ballimeanoch
Taynafead
Lochan Stron Mor
Beinn Bhuidhe 3106
Glenfalloch Farm
Inverarnan
Troisgeach 2407
Ben Glas Burn
Beinn Tulaichean 3099
Monachylemore
Beinn a' Chroin 3104
Loch Voil
Loch Doine
Inverlochlarig
Ballimore
Strathyre
Beinn Ghlas 1804
Rob Roy's House
Brannie Burn
Allt na Lairige
Glen Fyne
Glenfyne Lodge
Maol Breac 2115
Ardlui
Stuckindroin
Meall Mor 2451
Stob a' Choin 2839
Forestry Exhibition
Laggan
Barnaline
Blarghour
Dalavich
Tullich
Drimfern
Cruach Mhòr 1932
Glen Aray
Elrigbeog
Glen Shira
Clachan Hill 2159
Kilblaan Burn
Beinn a' Choin 2524
Glengyle
Portnellan
Cruinn Bheinn 1787
Beinn Bhreac 2242
Benvane 2685
Runacraig
Callander
Ardchonnell
Portinnisherrich
Clachan
Drishaig
Cairndow
Binnein an Fhidhleir 2660
Ben Vorlich 3092
Ardvorlich
Strath Gartney
Meall Cala 2203
Glen Finglas
Glen Finglas Res.
Loch Lubnaig
Beinn Bhreac 1723
Malt Land
Dubh Loch
Strone Gardens
Glen Kinglas
Ben Vane 3004
Inveruglas
Rob Roy's Cave
Stronachlachar
Loch Katrine
Ben Ledi 2873
Eredine
Inveraray Castle
Bell Tower
Inveraray
Ardno
Beinn an Lochain 2992
Ben Ime 3318
Rest and be thankful
Ben Narnain 3036
2785
Inversnaid Hotel
L. Arklet
Cruachan 1762
1962
French
Goblin's Cave
The Trossachs
Trossachs Hotel
Brig o' Turk
Lendrick Lo.
An Suidhe 1687
Douglas Water
Wildlife Park
St. Catherines
Stob an Eas 2402
Hells Glen
Dalchenna
Creag a' Phuill
Cruach nan Capull 1854
Monevechadan
Ben Arthur (The Cobbler) 2891
Succoth
1362
Tarbet
Craig Rostan
Cruinn a' Bheinn 2077
Ben Venue 2386
Loch Chon
Duncraggan
Loch Achray
Loch Venachar
Beinn Dearg 1575
Open Air Museum
Auchindrain
Mullach Coire a' Chuir 2098
Ben Donich 2771
Ardgoil Estate
Glen Croe
Ardgartan
Arrochar
Beinn Dubh 1675
Achray Forest
Loch Drunkie
Menteith Hills
Stirling
Loch Leacann
Dùn Leacainn
Kenmore
Brenochoille
Furnace
Creggans
Strachur
Drimsynie
Lochgoilhead
Cnoc Coinnich 2497
Ardmay
Stuckgowan
Ben Lomond 3192
Kinlochard
Altskeith
Loch Ard
Milton
Aberfoyle
Sanahole
Beinn Ghlas 1377
Tigh-na-criche
Glensluain
Argyll National Forest Park
Beinn Lochain 2306
Corrow
2075
Ptarmigan Lodge
Ardess
Duchray Water
Braeval
Malling
Lake of Menteith
Craroe
Crarae Lodge
Minard
Invernoaden
Beinn Bheula 2556
Glenbranter
Glenbranter Forest
Cormonachan
Ardgoil Forest
1704
Craggan
Glen Douglas
Inverbeg Hotel
Beinn Bhreac 2233
Rowardennan Hotel
Beinn Uird 1957
Loch Ard Forest
Cobleland
Gartmore
Queen Elizabeth National Forest Park
Garbhallt
Eilean Aoghainn
Tullochgorm
Barnacarry
Castle Lachlan
Leanach
Cruach nan Capull 1578
Doune Hill 2408
1922
Rowardennan Forest
Kelty Water
Dalmary
Flanders Moss
Strathlachlan Forest
Lephinmore
Cruach an Lochain 1658
Carrick
Carrick Castle
Loch Eck
Loch Goil
1435
Beinn a' Mhanaich 2328
Ardarroch
Beinn Eich 2302
Edentaggart
Glen Luss
Inchlonaig
Gualann 1514
Gartacholl
Lephinchapel
Dunans
Beinn Bheag 2029
Cruach a' Bhuic 2084
Portincaple
Garelochhead
Beinn Chaorach 2340
Luss
Beinn Ruisg 2036
Aldochlay
Conic Hill 1175
Moor Park
Creachan Mòr 2156
Beinn Mhòr 2433
Sligrachan
Strone
Balmaha
Buchanan Smithy
Garadhban Forest
Loch Long
Loch Lomond
Loch Fyne
Loch Awe
Ardentraive
46
Dunoon
Dumbarton
47
Dumbarton
Dumbarton
82
828
861
863
846
8005
8074
8077
85
845
840
819
815
839
828
83
886
814
8000
837
835
811
875
829
821
81
Stirling
Callander
Lochearnhead

Dalwhinnie
57
Braemar
Crianlarich
51
Aberfoyle
Dumbarton
Glasgow
47
Edinburgh
48
Rosyth
TAYSIDE
CENTRAL
TUMMEL FOREST PARK
Glen Errochty
Loch Rannoch
Loch Tummel
Blair Atholl
Killiecrankie
Pitlochry
Moulin
Ballinluig
Strathardle
Kirkmichael
Aberfeldy
Appin of Dull
Glen Lyon
Fortingall
Kenmore
Drummond Hill
Loch Tay
Killin
Lawers
Ardtalnaig
Glen Quaich
Strathbraan
Dunkeld
Birnam
Craigvinean Forest
Blairgowrie
Kinclaven
Stanley
Glen Almond
Logiealmond
Amulree
Bankfoot
Methven
Luncarty
PERTH
Scone Palace
Lochearnhead
Loch Earn
St. Fillans
Comrie
Crieff
Strathearn
Muthill
Auchterarder
Gleneagles Hotel
Blackford
Glen Devon
Ochil Hills
Strathallan
Glen Artney
Forest of Glenartney
Strathyre
Strathyre Forest
Loch Lubnaig
Ben Ledi
Pass of Leny
Kilmahog
Callander
Braes of Doune
Doune
Dunblane
Bridge of Allan
STIRLING
Cambuskenneth
Bannockburn
Alloa
Clackmannan
Tullibody
Alva
Menstrie
Tillicoultry
Dollar
Kincardine
Dunfermline
Kinross
Loch Leven
Milnathort
Kelty
Blairadam Forest
Cleish Hills
Port of Menteith
Lake of Menteith
Flanders Moss
Carse of Forth
Kippen
Gargunnock
Gargunnock Hills
Touch Hills
Fintry
Fintry Hills
Carron Valley
Bridge of Earn
Forteviot
Dunning
Glenfarg
Forgandenny
M9
M90
M80
M85

Stonehaven
Montrose
Brechin
Kirriemuir
Forfar
Arbroath
Carnoustie
Monifieth
Broughty Ferry
Dundee
Tay Br.
Newport-on-Tay
Tayport
Tentsmuir Forest
Firth of Tay
Eden Mouth
St. Andrews Bay
St. Andrews
Cupar
Glenrothes
Leven
Methil
Buckhaven
Kirkcaldy
Largo Bay
Isle of May
Crail
Anstruther Easter
Anstruther Wester
Pittenweem
St. Monance
Elie
Fife Ness
Carr Brigs
Bass Rock
Fidra
Craigleith
Braes of Angus
Strathmore
Sidlaw Hills
Lunan Bay
Montrose Basin
Carse of Gowrie
Lomond Hills
Fife Regional Park
Howe of Fife
Coupar Angus
Alyth
Glamis
Letham
Auchtermuchty
Falkland
Newburgh
Leuchars
Lochgelly
Burntisland
Kinghorn
Rosyth

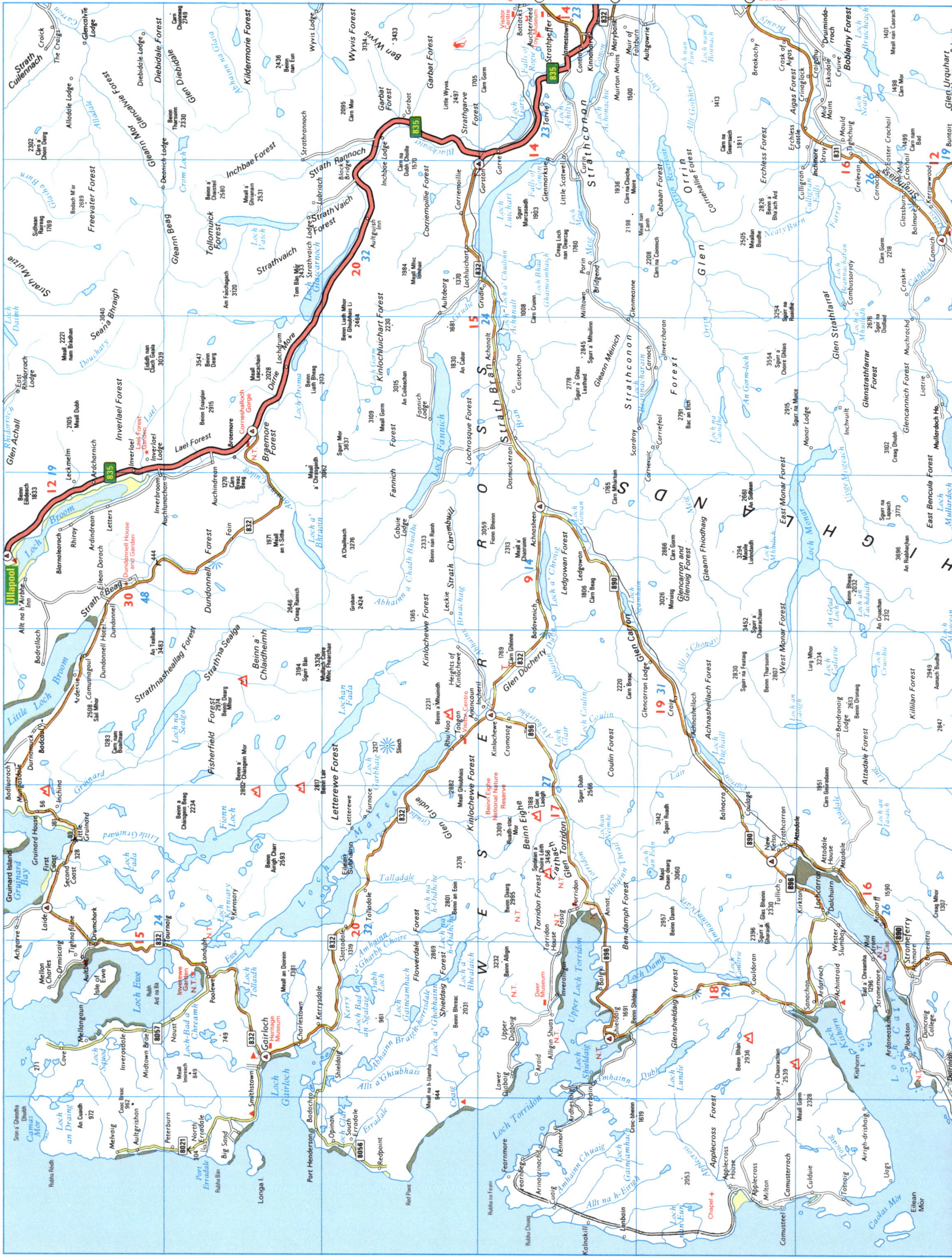
Ullapool
Loch Broom
Little Loch Broom
Dingwall
Muir of Ord
Balblair
Strathpeffer
Garve
Gorstan
Achnasheen
Kinlochewe
Loch Maree
Gairloch
Poolewe
Loch Ewe
Isle of Ewe
Gruinard Bay
Gruinard Island
Laide
Aultbea
Dundonnell
Braemore
Corrieshalloch Gorge
Inverlael
Loch Glascarnoch
Aultguish Inn
Strath Bran
Glen Docherty
Glen Carron
Achnashellach
Lochcarron
Loch Carron
Stromeferry
Plockton
Kishorn
Applecross
Shieldaig
Torridon
Loch Torridon
Upper Loch Torridon
Beinn Eighe
Liathach
Loch Fannich
Strathconon
Glen Orrin
Strathfarrar
Glen Strathfarrar
Loch Monar
Wyvis Forest
Ben Wyvis
Fisherfield Forest
Letterewe Forest
Flowerdale Forest
Coulin Forest
Inverewe Garden
Redpoint
Port Henderson
Badachro
Opinan
Melvaig
Cove
Inverasdale
Loch Luichart
Contin
Marybank
Tarvie
Loch Achilty
Strath Vaich
Strath Rannoch
Strathvaich
Inchbae Forest
Kildermorie Forest
Freevater Forest
Inverlael Forest
Dundonnell Forest
Strathnasheallag Forest
Kinlochewe Forest
Kinlochluichart Forest
Torridon Forest
Ben-damph Forest
Glenshieldaig Forest
Applecross Forest
Attadale Forest
West Monar Forest
East Monar Forest
Killilan Forest
Strathcarron
Craig
Achnasheen
Ledgowan Forest
Corriemoillie Forest
Garbat Forest
Strathgarve Forest
Glen Achall
Strath Cuileannach
Loch Damh
Beinn Alligin
Diabaig
Kenmore
Fearnmore
Arinacrinachd
Sanachan
Ardarroch
Ardaneaskan
Duncraig College
Achmore
Dornie
Erchless Forest
Aigas Forest
Kilmorack
Struy
Cannich
Glen Urquhart
Balblair
Glen Cannich
Mullardoch Ho.

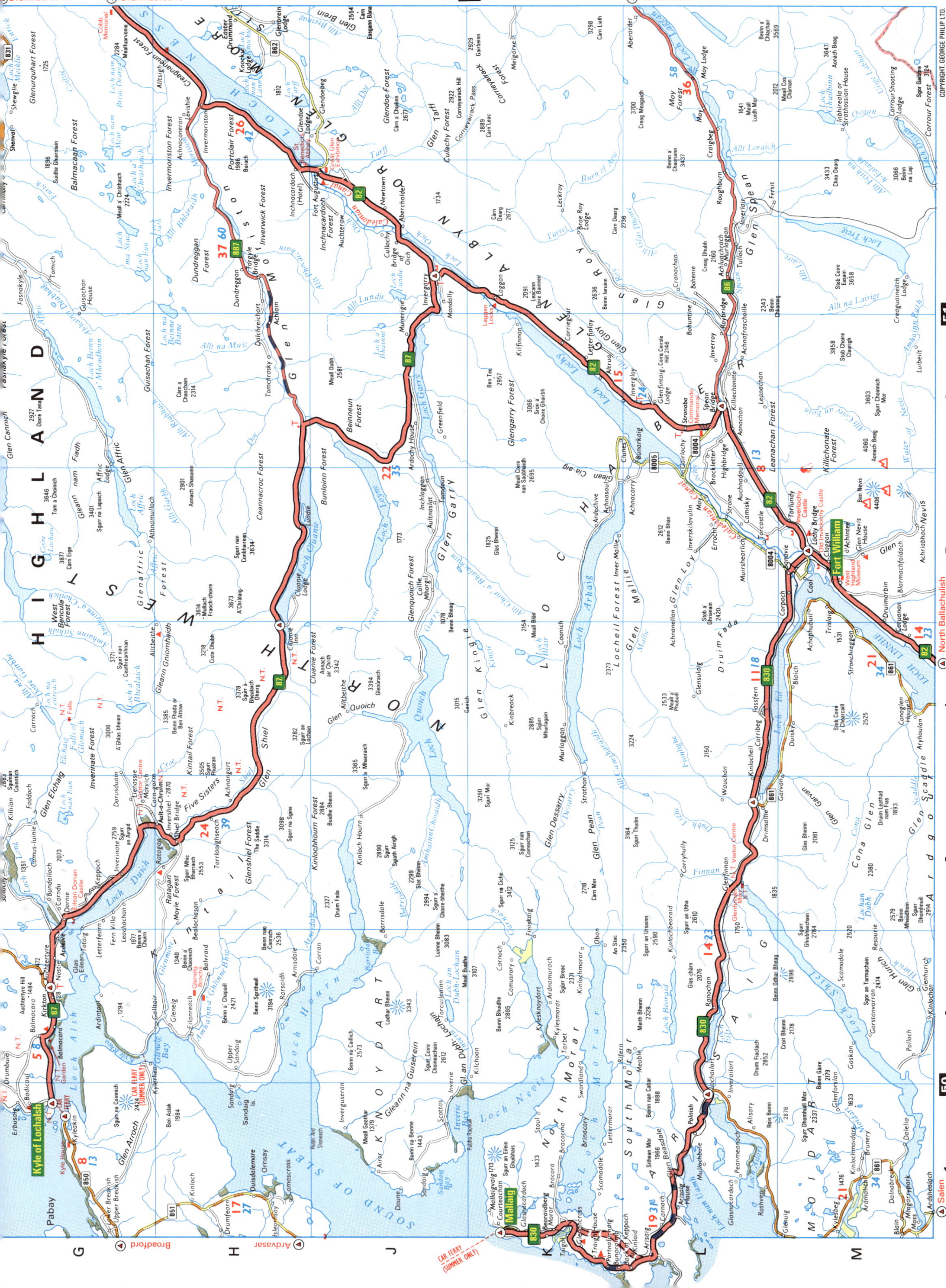

Drumnadrochit
Newtonmore
57
HIGHLAND
LOCH NESS
GLEN MORE
Fort Augustus
Invermoriston
Glenmoriston
Glen Affric
Glen Shiel
Five Sisters
Kintail Forest
Loch Duich
Eilean Donan Castle
Kyle of Lochalsh
Kyleakin
Broadford
Ardvasar
Glenelg
Loch Hourn
Knoydart
Loch Nevis
Mallaig
CAR FERRY (SUMMER ONLY)
Loch Morar
North Morar
South Morar
Arisaig
Loch nan Uamh
Moidart
Glenfinnan
Loch Eil
Loch Arkaig
Loch Lochy
Loch Garry
Loch Quoich
Loch Loyne
Invergarry
Spean Bridge
Commando Memorial
Glen Spean
Glen Roy
Roybridge
Fort William
Ben Nevis
4406
West Highland Museum
Corpach
Caledonian Canal
LOCH LINNHE
North Ballachulish
Salen
Ardgour
Loch Laggan
Loch Treig
Corrour Forest
Moy
Tulloch
Loch Shiel
SOUND OF SLEAT
Pabay
COPYRIGHT, GEORGE PHILIP LTD.

NORTH SEA
MORAY FIRTH
GRAMPIAN
Inverness
Nairn
Forres
Elgin
Lossiemouth
Burghead
Dingwall
Cromarty
Invergordon
Dornoch
Tain
Beauly
Fortrose
Rosemarkie
Portmahomack
Findhorn
Rothes
BLACK ISLE
EASTER ROSS
Beauly Firth
Cromarty Firth
Dornoch Firth
Burghead Bay
Nigg Bay
Munlochy Bay
Keith
Rhynie
Lairg
The Mound
Gorstan
Cannich
Strathdearn Forest
Culloden Forest
The Bar
Tarbat Ness
Lossie Forest
Coversea Skerries
Halliman Skerries
Glen Glass
Strath Rusdale

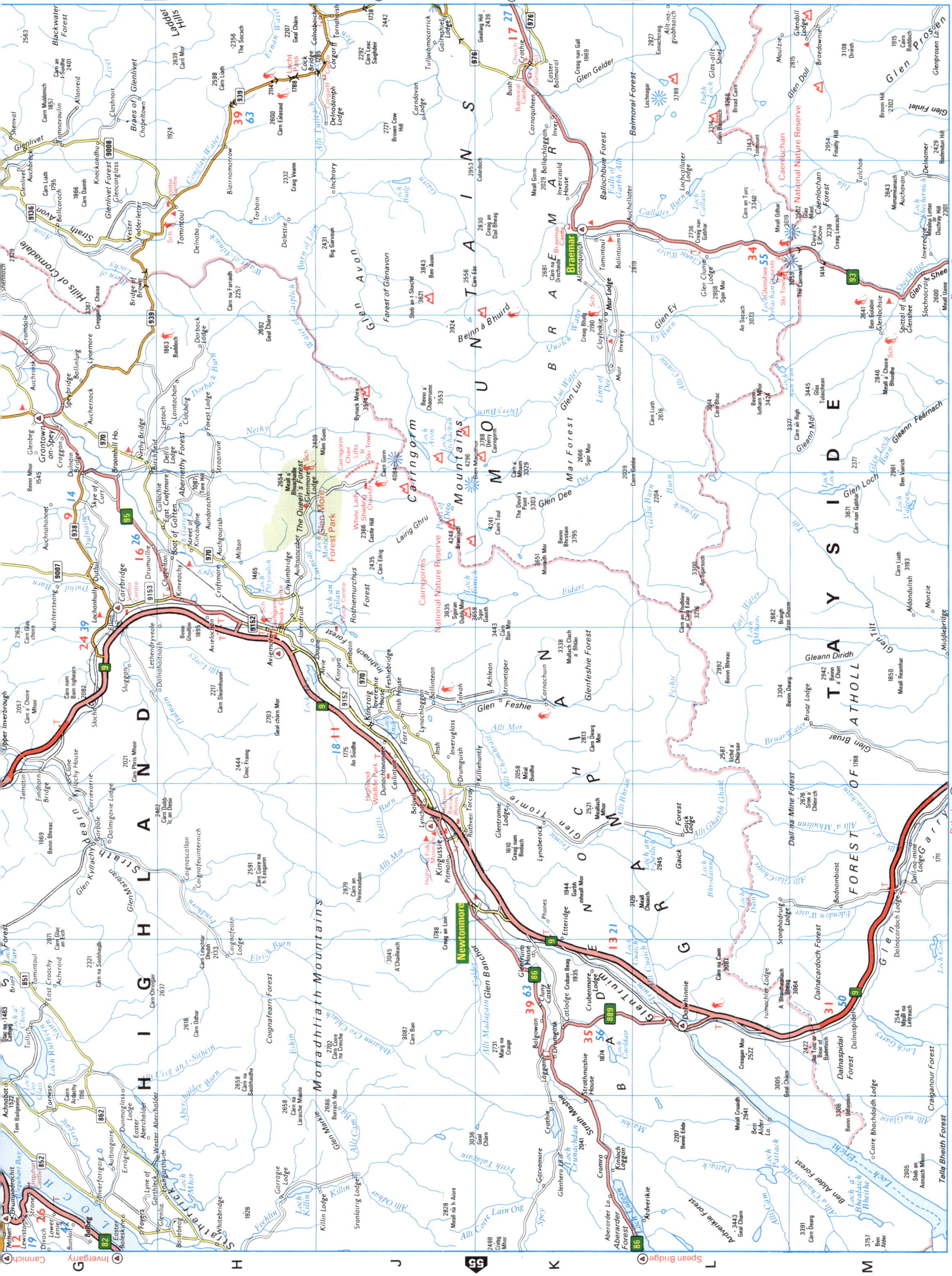

HIGHLAND
GRAMPIAN MOUNTAINS
CAIRNGORM MOUNTAINS
Monadhliath Mountains
TAYSIDE
FOREST OF ATHOLL
Aviemore
Kingussie
Newtonmore
Grantown-on-Spey
Carrbridge
Braemar
Tomintoul
Dalwhinnie
Glen More Forest Park
Cairngorms National Nature Reserve
Caenlochan National Nature Reserve
Balmoral Forest
Mar Forest
Glenfeshie Forest
Gaick Forest
Ben Alder Forest
Rothiemurchus Forest
Abernethy Forest
Glenlivet
Hills of Cromdale
Loch Ericht
Loch Laggan
Glen Feshie
Glen Tromie
Glen Truim
Glen Dee
Glen Ey
Glen Shee
Glen Clova
Strath Mashie
Strathspey
Ladder Hills
Ben Macdhui
Cairn Gorm
Beinn a' Bhuird
Ballater
Pitlochry
Spean Bridge
Invergarry
Cannich
Rattray

COPYRIGHT, GEORGE PHILIP LTD.

Fraserburgh
Peterhead
Macduff
Banff
Portsoy
Cullen
Buckie
Keith
Huntly
Turriff
Ellon
Inverurie
Oldmeldrum
Kintore
Alford
Dufftown
Rhynie
Insch
Fyvie
Maud
Mintlaw
New Deer
New Pitsligo
Strichen
Rosehearty
Aberchirder
Spey Bay
Boyne Bay
Cruden Bay
Bay of Cruden
Newburgh
Dyce
ABERDEEN
Bridge of Don
BUCHAN
FORMARTIN
GARIOCH
STRATHDON
GRAMPIAN
Correen Hills
Clashindarroch
Forest of Deer
Bennachie
CAR FERRY TO LERWICK & STROMNESS
Elgin
Craigellachie
56
57

ABERDEEN
Stonehaven
Montrose
Brechin
FORFAR
Kirriemuir
Ballater
Banchory
Laurencekirk
Inverbervie
Johnshaven
Aboyne
Tarland
DEESIDE
TAYSIDE
Braes of Angus
Howe of the Mearns
Glen Esk
Glen Mark
Glen Lee
Glen Clova
Glen Muick
Glen Tanar
Forest of Glentanar
Forest of Birse
Blackhall Forest
Durris Forest
Fetteresso Forest
Drumtochty Forest
Midmar Forest
Montreathmont Forest
Lunan Bay
Montrose Basin
Nigg Bay
Cove Bay
Bervie Bay
Dunnottar Castle
Crathes Castle
Glamis Castle
Edzell Castle & Gardens
Coupar Angus
Dundee
Arbroath
Rattray
Crathie
Grantown-on-Spey

NORTH MINCH
Cape Wrath
Clais Chornach
Kearvaig
Faraid Head
Durness
Balnakeil
Sangomore
Keoldale
Cave of Smoo
Leirinmore
Eilean Hoan
Whiten Head
Rispond
Inshore
Achiemore
Sandwood Loch
Strath Shinary
Loch Eriboll
Portnancon
Heilam
Hope
Moin House
Tongue
Tongue Bay
Kyle of Tongue
Talmine
West Strathan
Strathan
Portvasgo
Rabbit Is.
Midtown
Skullomie
Achuvoldrach
Rhiconich
Kinlochbervie
Badcall
Achriesgill
Oldshore More
Blairmore
Sheigra
Balchrick
Eilean an Roin Mor
Carbreck
Gualin House
Strath Dionard
Strath Beag
Polla
Eriboll
Loch Hope
Ben Hope
Strath More
Rhiconich
Achlyness
Foinaven
Loch Dionard
Skerricha
Fanagmore
Tarbet
Handa Island
Foindle
Laxford Bridge
Badnabay
Claisfearn
Scourie More
Scourie
Lower Badcall
Upper Badcall
Arkle
Loch Stack
Lochstack Lodge
Lone
Airdachuillinn
REAY FOREST
Loch More
Achfary
Lochmore Lodge
Loch Crocach
Eddrachillis Bay
Calva Mor
Calva Beg
Geisgeil
Duartmore Forest
Kylestrome
Kylesku
Unapool
Glendhu Forest
Loch Glendhu
Gleann Dubh
Kinloch
Point of Stoer
Oldany Island
Culkein
Culkein Drumbeg
Drumbeg
Achnacarnin
Oldany
Raffin
Clashnessie
Nedd
Balchladich
Rienachait
Stoer
Clachtoll
Loch Poll
Gleann Leireag
Quinag
Loch Glencoul
Glen Coul
Newton
Loch an Eircill
Loch Merkland
Merkland Lodge
Loch Fiag
Fiag Lodge
Glen Fiag
Achmelvich
Rhicarn
Brackloch
Baddidarach
Lochinver
Glencanisp Lodge
Little Assynt
Lochassynt Lodge
Loch Assynt
Skiag Bridge
Ardvreck Castle
Inchnadamph
Inchnadamph Forest
Corriekinloch
Overscraig Hotel
Fiag Bridge
Crask Inn
Soyea Island
Inverkirkaig
Strathan
Glencanisp Forest
Suilven
Canisp
Enard Bay
Rhegreanoch
Stronchrubie
Loch Awe
Cam Loch
Ledmore
Benmore Forest
Duchally
Glen Cassley
Loch Shin
Allt Car
HIGHLAND
WEST
Shinness
Strath Tirry
Rubha Mor
Reiff
Achnahaird
Altandhu
Isle Ristol
Polbain
Badnagyle
Loch Sionascaig
Inverpolly Lodge
Inverpolly Forest
Stac Polly
Drumrunie Forest
Cul Mor
Elphin
Knockan
Knockanrock
Loch Urigill
Altnacealgach Hotel
Benmore Lodge
Glen Oykel
Badintagairt
Achnairn
Dalmichy
Colaboll
Dalchork
Dalchork Wood
Sallachy
Saval
Lairg
Lairg Muir
Eilean Mullagrach
Glas-leac Mor
Summer Isles
Tanera Beg
Tanera More
Achiltibuie
Polglass
Achavraie
Horse Island
Horse Sound
Eilean Dubh
Culnacraig
Ben More Coigach
COIGACH
Loch Lurgainn
Linneraineach
Cul Beag
Drumrunie
Cromalt Hills
Rappach
Strath nan Lon
Glencassley Castle
Glenrossal
Oykel Forest
Strath Oykel
Oykel Bridge
Invercassley
Shin Forest
Achany
Torrobole
Gruids
Priest Island
STORNOWAY CAR FERRY
Strathkanaird
Blughasary
Isle Martin
Ardmair
Rhue
Morefield
Rhidorroch
Loch Achall
Glen Achall
Rhidorroch Forest
Rappach Water
Craggan
Glen Einig
Duag Bridge
Lubcroy
Langwell
Doune
Newton of Ochtow
Altass
Linsidemore
Achnahannat
Balblair Forest
Carbisdale Castle
Culrain
Invershin
Greenstone Point
Opinan
Mellon Udrigle
Static Point
Scoraig
Annat Bay
Little Loch Broom
Loch Broom
Ullapool
Gruinard Island
Gruinard Bay
Achgarve
Mellon Charles
Ormiscaig
Laide
Badluarach
Mungasdale
Durnamuck
Badcaul
Allt na h'Airbhe
Badralloch
Corriemulzie Lodge
Strath Mulzie
Lubachoinnich
Strath Cuileannach
Croick
Craigs Forest
Strathcarron
Gruinard House
First Coast
Second Coast
Tighnafiline
Aultbea
Isle of Ewe
Drumchork
Loch Ewe
Inchina
Little Gruinard
Ardessie
Camusnagaul
Dundonnell Hotel
Dundonnell
Eilean Darach
Strath Beag
Ardindrean
Leckmelm
Ardcharnich
Letters
Inverlael Forest
Inverlael
Inverlael Lodge
Inverbroom
Auchlunachan
Seana Bhraigh
Freevater Forest
Glencalvie Forest
Gleann Mor
Diebidale Lodge
Diebidale Forest
Glen Diebidale
Glencalvie Lodge
Alladale Lodge
The Craigs
Western Greenyards
Ardgay
Kincardine
Gledfield
Dounie
Ardchronie
Poolewe
Tournaig
Londubh
Inverewe Gardens (N.T.)
Loch Kernsary
Kernsary
Loch Tollaidh
Gairloch
Fionn Loch
Fisherfield Forest
Strathnasheallag Forest
Strath na Sealga
Loch na Sealga
An Teallach
Dundonnell Forest
Fain
Auchindrean
Lael Forest
Braemore
Corrieshalloch Gorge
Braemore Forest
Dirrie More
Lochdrum
Gorstan
Gleann Beag
Deanich Lodge
Crom Loch
Tollomuick Forest
Inchbae Forest
Loch Vaich
Kildermorie Forest
Kildermorie Lodge
EASTER
Strath Rusdale
Braeantra
Dalmore
Beinn a' Chlaidheimh
Beinn Dearg
NORTH

Island of Stroma
Uppertown
Dunnet Head
St. John's Point
Boars of Duncansby
Duncansby Head
Castle of Mey Gardens
Gills Bay
Huna
Dunnet Hill
Brough
Scarfskerry
Rattar
Mey
Gills
Kirkstyle
Canisbay
John o' Groats
Hunspow
St. John's Loch
Dunnet
Corsback
Barrock
Inkstack
Brims Ness
Holborn Head
CAR FERRY TO STROMNESS
Scrabster
Thurso Bay
Crosskirk
Dunnet Bay
Loch Heilen
Brabstermire
Tofts
Skirza
Lochend
Freswick Bay
Freswick
Bridge of Forss
Thurso
Thurso East
Murkle
Greenland
Castletown
Slickly
Strathy Point
Totegan
Lower Dounreay
Sandside Bay
Achrear
Upper Dounreay
Newlands of Geise
Tain
Reaster
Weydale
Bowermadden
Aultiphurst
Strathy Inn
Baligill
Portskerra
Fresgoe
Sandside Ho.
Isauld
Reay
Shebster
Westfield
Lyth
Sortat
Auckingill
Howe
Keiss
Eilean nan Ron
Neave or Coomb Is.
Armadale
Lednagullin
Strathy
Melvich
Farr
Kirtomy
Swordly
Skerray
Achtoty
Bettyhill
Achina
Strathnaver Museum
Airdtorrisdale
Invernaver
Borgie
Leckfurin
Golval
Sordale
Knockdee
Bowertower
Hastigrow
Mireland
Calder Mains
Halkirk
Loch Calder
Roadside
Halcro
Burn of Lyth
Loch Meadie
Strathy Forest
Bowside Lodge
834 Beinn Ruadh
Loch Buidhe Mor
Loch na Seilge
Broubster
Georgemas Junc. Sta.
Loch Scarmclate
Gillock
North Watten
Kirk
Loch of Wester
Myrelandhorn
Borgie Forest
Achiemore
Craigtown
Brawlbin
Spital Hill 577
Loch Watten
Killimster
Sinclair's Bay
Girnigoe Castle
Skelpick
Loch Mor na Caorach
Shurrery Lodge
952 Beinn nam Bad Mor
Loch Scye
Scotscalder Sta.
Loch Shurrery
Dorrery
Strathcoul
Noss Head
Castle Sinclair
Achagary
Dalhalvaig
Loch nan Clach
Trantlemore
797
Loch Tuim Ghlais
Spittal
Mybster
Watten
Loch of Toftingall
Reiss
Winless
Ackergill Tower
Ackergill
WICK
Staxigoe
Bylbster
Acharole
Loch Caluim
Westerdale
1728 Beinn Stumanadh
Loch Loyal
Carnachy
Rhifail
Lochstrathy
Strath Halladale
Forsinain
Stirkoke House
Milton
Broadhaven
Wick Bay
Wick
Newton
Castle of Old Wick
Loch Strathy
Loch nam Breac
Skail
Lochan Dubh nan Geodh
Loch Eileanach
Strathmore Lodge
Badlipster
Tannach
Loch Hempriggs
Langdale
Strathnaver
919 Sletill Hill
Altnabreac Sta.
Sleach Water
Loch More
Thrumster
Loch Syre
Syre
Dalvina Lodge
Loch Crocach
Forsinard
Lochdhu Hotel
Loch Ruard
Grey Cairns of Camster
Loch of Yarrows
Sarclet
Loch Druim a' Chliabhain
Forsinard Station
Achavanich
Camster
Mains of Ulbster
965 Pole Hill
1321 Beinn a' Mhadaidh
1903 Ben Griam Beg
Rumsdale Water
Dalnawillan Lodge
Loch Rangag
Ulbster
Ceann-na-coille
Rimsdale
Bruan
Roster
1936 Ben Griam More
Achentoul Forest
1142 Ben Alisky
Loch Breac
Rumster Forest
Oscaig
Upper Lybster
Mid Clyth
Loch nan Clar
Loch Rimsdale
Loch an Ruathair
Lochside
Glutt Lodge
Loch Dubh
867 Cnocan Conachreag
Braehungie
Badanloch Forest
Loch Badanloch
Loch Arichlinie
Achentoul
Knockfin Heights
1415
Houstry
Swiney
Lybster
West Clyth
Forse
Invershore
Loch an Alltain Fhearna
Truderscaig
Badanloch Lodge
Kinbrace
Dunbeath Water
Smerral
Latheron
Latheronwheel
Loch Choire Lodge
Meall nan Aighean
2287 Ben Armine
Creag a' Choire Ghlais 2311
1423 Cnoc an Liath-bhaid Mhoir
Kinbrace Burn
Braemore
Berriedale Water
Dunbeath
1907
Borrobol Forest
Altanduin
1194 Cnoc na Breun-choille
2313 Morven
1698 Cnoc an Eireannaich
Ramscraigs
2054 Scaraben
Borgue
Newport
Borrobol Lodge
Suisgill
Langwell Forest
2338 Creag Mhor
Gorm-loch Mor
1273 Creag nam Fiadh
1819 Creag Scalabsdale
Berriedale
Langwell Water
Ben Armine Forest
1163 Cnoc Tuarie
Kildonan Lodge
Kildonan Burn
Strath of Kildonan
Ben Armine Lodge
Tuarie Burn
Craggie Burn
Ousdale
Glas-loch Mor
Strath na Seilge
1516 Meallan Liath Mor
Kilphedir
Helmsdale
Marrel
Navidale
West Helmsdale
Gartymore
Helmsdale
Dalnessie
Loch Beannach
Black Water
1512 Meallan Liath Beag
2060 Beinn Dhorain
Portgower
Glen Loth
Lothmore
Kilmote
Crakaig
Lothbeg
Balnacoil
1767 Col-bheinn
Gordonbush
Achnaluachrach
Grumby Rock 978
Sciberscross
Strath Brora
West Langwell
Dalreavoch
Loch Brora
Knockarthur
Ben Horn 1706
Loch Horn
Loch Craggie
East Langwell
Achrimsdale
East Clyne
West Clyne
Clynelish
Dalchalm
Brora
Doll
Muie
Rovie Lodge
Rovie Lodge Gardens
Rogart
Strath Fleet
Ardochu
Pittentrail
1104 An Stoc-bheinn
Rogart Halt
1239 Cagar Feosaig
Coire Beinn Lunndaidh 1464
Golspie Burn
Backies
Uppat
Mains
Morvich Lodge
Mon.
Dunrobin Castle
Culmaily
Golspie
Loch Buidhe
Dalnamain
The Mound
Loch Fleet
Littleferry
Reidhbreac
Beinn Donuill 1144
Loch an Lagain
Achvaich
Clashcoig
Skelbo
Rearquhar
Embo
Migdale
Loch Migdale
Kyloag
Bardnabeinne
Evelix
Clashmore Wood
Spinningdale
Whiteface
Dornoch
Clashmore
Skibo Castle
Lonemore
Dornoch Sands
Dornoch Firth
Tarbat Ness
Wilkhaven
Easter Fearn
Ardmore
Ferry Point
Cambuscurrie Bay
Whiteness Sands
Danger Area
Struie 1218
Edderton
Portmahomack
Bindal
Meikle Gluich
Rockfield
1792 Cnoc Muigh-bhlàraidh
Aultnamain Inn
Tain
Balnagall
Inver
Aldie
Hilton
Loch Eye
Toulvaddie
Cnoc an t-Sabhail 1243
Rhynie
Lamington
Newfield
Hill of Fearn
Balmuchy
Fearn
Hilton of Cadboll
Scotsburn
Logie Hill
Torran
Balintore
NORTH SEA
ROSS
CAITHNESS
0 1 2 3 4 5 10 15 Miles
0 1 2 3 4 5 6 7 8 16 24 Kilometres
A B C D E F G H

Dingwall 56 Dingwall

1
2
3
4
5
6
A
B
C
D
E
F
G
H
CAR FERRY TO TARBERT
CAR FERRY TO LOCHMADDY
Rubha Hunish
Duntulm
Kilmaluag
Balmacquien
Lùb Score
Monument to Flora MacDonald
Flodigarry Hotel
Eilean Flodigarry
Borneskitaig
Kilmuir
Hungladder
Kilvaxter
Meall na Suiramach 1281
Digg
Glashvin
Staffin Bay
Staffin I.
Stenscholl
Staffin
Brogaig
Balgown
Linicro
Bioda Buidhe 1523
Kilt Rock
Elishader
Totscore
Kilbride Point
Idrigil
Uig
Uig Bay
Conon
Balnaknock
Beinn Edra 2006
Marishader
Valtos
Garros
32
51
Breckrey
Culnaknock
Lealt
Lower Tote
Upper Tote
Earlish
Peinlich
Peinaha
Creag a' Lain 1995
Ascrib Is.
LOCH SNIZORT
VATERNISH
TROTTERNISH
Ben Geary 931
Geary
Trumpan
Upper Halistra
Knockbreck
Lower Halistra
Gillen
Hallin
Ard Beag
Ardmore Point
Isay I.
Mingay
Beinn Charnach Bheag 877
Stein
Lusta
Dunvegan Head
Lyndale Point
Greshornish Point
Lynedale House
Beinn a' Sgà 1480
Kingsburgh
15
24
Romesdal
Eyre
The Storr 2358
Old Man of Storr
RONA
Eilean Garbh
Eilean Tigh
Garbh Eilean
An Cool
Biod an Athair 1025
Galtrigill
Boreraig
Uig
Husabost
Piers
Totaig
Claigan
Beinn Bhreac 1074
Greshornish
Flashader
Breabost
Treaslane
The Aird
Kensaleyre
Rhenetra
Beinn a' Chearcaill 1812
Loch Leathan
Loch Fada
Prince Charles Cave
Holm I.
Eilean Fladday
Torran
Arnish
Umachan
Brochel
Lower Milovaig
Upper Milovaig
Ferinquarrie
Glasphein 438
Lephin
Colbost
Black House Folk Museum
Holmisdal
Glen Dale
Garbh Eilean
Dunvegan Castle
Skinidin
Dunvegan
Kilmuir
Lonmore
22
35
Edinbain
Blackhill
Ben Uigshader 804
Bernisdale
Prabost
Tote
Peinmore
Carbost
Borve
Drumuie
Glen Bernisdale
Skeabost
Uigshader
Achachork
Torvaig
Kalnakill
Lonbain
Applecross House
Applecross
Milton
Camusteel
Camusterrach
Culduie
Toscaig
Fearnmore
Cuaig
Moonen Bay
Ramasaig
Healabhal Mhor 1538
Macleod's Tables
Healabhal Bheag 1601
Hoe Point
The Hoe 759
Ben Connan 799
Beinn na Boineid 1207
Roag
Orbost
Harlosh
Balmore
Harlosh I.
Tarner I.
Roskhill
Vatten
Caroy
Ose
24
39
Bracadale
Struan
Ullinish
Coillore
Cruachan Beinn a' Chearcaill
Ben Aketil 872
Beinn a' Ghlinne Bhig 682
HIGHLAND
Glengrasco
Salisbaderbeg
Portree
Penifiler
Ben Tianavaig 1355
Heatherfield
Beinn na Greine 1367
Glenmore
Stroc-bheinn 1300
Mugeary
Ben Duagrich 996
Loch Duagrich
Camastianavaig
9
14
Tianavaig Bay
RAASAY
Oskaig
Raasay House (Hotel)
Clachan
E. Suisnish
Dun Caan 1456
Glame 1242
Holoman Bay
North Fearns
Eilean na Bà
Crowlin Is.
Eilean Mòr
Uags
Loch Bracadale
Wiay
Oronsay
Geodha Mor
Idrigill Point
Portnalong
Fiskavaig
Fernilea
Carbost
Arnaval 1210
Drynoch
Merkadale
Talisker
Talisker Bay
Stockval 1365
Roineval 1442
SKYE
Glen Varragill
Lower Ollach
Upper Ollach
Gedintailor
The Braes
Ben Lee 1456
Peinchorran
Scalpay
SCALPAY
Longay
Mullach nan Carn 1298
Scalpay House
Sconser
Sligachan Hotel
Glamaig 2542
Glen Sligachan
Glen Brittle Forest
Eynort
Beinn Bhreac 1468
Beinn a' Bhràghad 1489
MINGINISH
Sgurr nan Gillean 3167
Marsco 2414
Dunan
Luib
Old Skye Crofter's House
18
29
Red Hills
Glas Bheinn Mhor 1852
Guillamon I.
Pabay
Corry
Broadford Bay
Broadford
Waterloo
Harrapool
Lower Breakish
Upper Breakish
Skulamus
Kyleakin
8
13
Beinn na Caillich 2400
Garbh-Bheinn 2649
Bla Bheinn (Blaven) 3042
An Cruachan 1428
Sgurr a' Ghreadaidh 3197
Cuillin Hills
Glenbrittle House
Bualintur
Sgurr Alasdair 3257
Sgurr nan Eag 3037
Loch Coruisk
Loch Brittle
Ceann na Beinn 736
Sgurr na Stri 1623
Strathaird
Camasunary
Kirkibost
Kilmarie
Ben Meabost 1128
14
23
Torrin
Kilbride
Loch Slapin
Beinn nan Càrn 983
Heast
Kinloch
Rubh' an Dunain
Soay Sound
Loch Scavaig
Mol-chlach
Soay
Elgol
Glasnakille
Rubha na h-Easgainne
Rubha Suisnish
Loch Eishort
Drumfearn
17
27
Ord
Sgorach Breac 980
Duisdalemore
Ornsay
Isleornsay
Camuscross
Dunsgiath Castle
Tokavaig
Tarskavaig Point
Tarskavaig
Sgurr na h-Iolaire 959
Achnacloich
Teangue
Knock
Knock Bay
SLEAT
Ferrindonald
Kilmore
Kilbeg
818
CANNA
690
Carn a' Ghaill
An Coroghon
A' Chill
Canna Harbour
Garrisdale Point
N.T.
Sanday
Rubha Shamhnan Insir
Sound of Canna
Kilmory Glen
913
Mullach Mòr 996
Sgor Mhòr 1273
A' Bhrideanach
Kinloch Glen
Orval 1872
Kinloch Castle
RHUM
Rubha Port na Caranean
PASSENGER FERRY TO EIGG
Oigh-sgeir
Rubha Chàrn nan Cearc
Gleann Meadhonach
Clandonald Centre
Armadale Gardens
Armadale Castle
Armadale Bay
Ardvasar
Calligarry
Sgurr nan Caorach 918
Aird of Sleat
Ard Thurinish
Point of Sleat
CAR FERRY TO CASTLEBAY
PASSENGER FERRY TO EIGG
CAR FERRY
Mallaigvaig
Mallaig
Sgurr an Eilein Ghuibhais 1713
Courteachan
Lochailort
Airor
Doune
Sandaig
Sandaig Bay
Redpoint
Red Point
SEA OF THE HEBRIDES
SOUND OF RAASAY
INNER SOUND
SOUND OF SLEAT
54
55
850
851
853
855
856
863
883
884
885
886
8009
8036
8083

1
2
3
4
5
6
A
B
C
D
E
F
G
H
Butt of Lewis
Europie
Five Penny Ness
Port of Ness
Lionel
Habost
Swainbost
Cross
North Dell
South Dell
Skigersta
Ness
Cuiashader
Cellar Head
North Galson
South Galson
Melbost Borve
Five Penny Borve
Lower Shader
Shader
Upper Shader
Ballantrushal
Aird Barvas
Loch Mor Barvas
Upper Barvas
Barvas
Brue
Arnol
Black House Museum
Bragar
Labost
North Shawbost
South Shawbost
Museum
New Shawbost
Dalbeg
Dalmore
Garenin
Carloway
Broch Dun Carloway
Kirivick
Tolsta Chaolais
Campay
Little Bernera
Floday
West Loch Roag
Gallan Head
Aird Uig
Forsnaval 670
Valtos
Cliff
Miavaig
Reef
Pabay Mor
Vacsay
Tobson
Croir
Breaclete
GREAT BERNERA
Hacklete
Kirkibost
Barraglom
Breasclete
Callanish
Standing Stones
Linshader
Crulivig
Vuia Mor
Vuia Beag
Floday
Loch Roag
Crowlista
Timsgarry
Caryshader
Uig
Ardroil
Geshader
Cornish
Ard More Mangersta
Mangersta
Suainaval 1404
Loch Suainaval
Islivig
Mealisval 1885
Aird Brenish
Brenish
Laival a Tuath 1625
Loch Chaolartan
Beinn Mheadhonach 1303
Enaclete
Gisla
Loch Grunavat
Little Loch Roag
Loch Smuaisaval
Teahaval 839
Loch Tungavat
Garynahine
Eitshal 733
Achmore
Loch Ouraval
Greeta or Creed
Lews Castle
Stornoway
Sandwick
Holm
Melbost
Aignish
Eye Peninsula
Garrabost
Seisiader
Sulaisiader
Aird
Port Mholair
Fleisirin
Portnaguiran
Rubha an Tampan
Pabail Uarach
Pabail Iarach
An Cnoc
Bayble Hill 290
Suardail
Bagh Phabail
Gob na Cnoige
CAR FERRY TO ULLAPOOL
STORNOWAY
Broad Bay or Loch a Tuath
Tung
Aird Tunga
Upper Coll
Col
Bac
Vatisker Point
Griais
New Tolsta
North Tolsta
Tolsta Head
Muirneag 813
Diaval 520
Gleann Mòr Barvas
Glen Bhruthadail
Glen Bragar
Beinn Bragar 857
Beinn Mholach 955
Loch Mor an Stairr
Loch nan Stearnag
Laxdale
Newmarket
New Valley
Arnish Moor
Loch Orasay
Loch Thota Bridein
Loch nam Falcag
Leurbost
Grimshader
Ben Casgro
Soval Lodge
Crossbost
Ranish Point
Barkin Is.
Tabhaidh Mhor
Eilean Chaluim Chille
Eilean Orasaidh
Cromore
Eilean Thoraidh
Marvig
Calbost
Keose
Laxay
Balallan
Loch Erisort
Garyvard
Caversta
Kershader
Habost
Shiltenish
Loch Trealaval
Trealaval 396
Roineval 923
Loch Airigh na h-Airde
LOCHS
LEWIS
WESTERN
ISLES
Mealasta I.
Kearstay
Scarp
Strone Romul 1011
Braighe Mor
Loch Tealasavay
Loch Bodavat
Loch Benisval
Loch Resort
Taran Mor 996
Morsgail Forest
Loch Morsgail
Beinn a' Bhoth 1008
Loch Langavat
Loch Strandavat
Arivruaich
Seaforth Head
Loch Sgibacleit
Glenside
Gravir
Loch Odhairn
Kebock Head
Loch Shannadabhat
PARK
Eishken
Orosay
Lemreway
Loch Shell or Loch Sealg
Eilean Iubhard
Hushinish
Hushinish Point
Hushinish Bay
Loch a' Ghlinne
Tirga Mor 2227
Oreval 2165
Forest of Harris
Amhuinnsuidhe
Cliasamol
Uisgnaval Mor 2392
Stulaval 1899
Liuthaid 1611
Aline Lodge
Seaforth I.
Ardvourlie
Beinn Mhor 1874
Clisham 2622
North Harris
Maaruig
Loch Seaforth
Loch Claidh
Caiteshal 1473
Uisenis 1217
1542
Soay Beag
Soay Mor
Tolmachan
West Loch Tarbert
Bunavoneader
Sgaoth Ard 1829
Ardhasaig
Gillaval Glas 1547
Isay
Taddun 1733
Rhenigidale
Loch Trollamarig
Laxadale Lochs
TARANSAY
Ben Raah 875
Paible
Rudha Sgeirigin
Beinn Dhubh 1661
Luskentyre
Ben Luskentyre 1532
Tarbert
Urgha Beag
Carragreich
Kyles Scalpay
Carnach
Scalpay
SCALPAY
Sound of Shiant
Shiant Is.
Eilean Mhuire
Eilean an Tighe
South Harris Forest
Sound of Taransay
Horgabost
Seilebost
Borve Lodge
Borve
Toe Head
Scotasay
Meavag
East Loch Tarbert
Kennavay
Drinishader
South Harris
Scarastavore
Chaipaval 1201
An Coileach 1267
Ardvey
Grosebay
Lockaleе
Kyles Stockinish
Stockinish
Cluer
Plocropool Point
Plocropool
Scadabay
Rhuba Bhocaig
Loch Grosebay
Bleaval 1305
Geocrab
Beacravik
Ardslave
Manish
Flodabay
Loch Langavat
Northton
Greaval 922
Loch Steisevat
Leverburgh
Finsbay
Roineabhal 1506
Loch Flodabay
Loch Finsbay
Stockinish I.
CAR FERRY TO LOCHMADDY
CAR FERRY TO UIG
Ensay
Carminish
Killegray
Strond
Lingarabay I.
Rodel
St Clements Church
Vallay
Renish Point

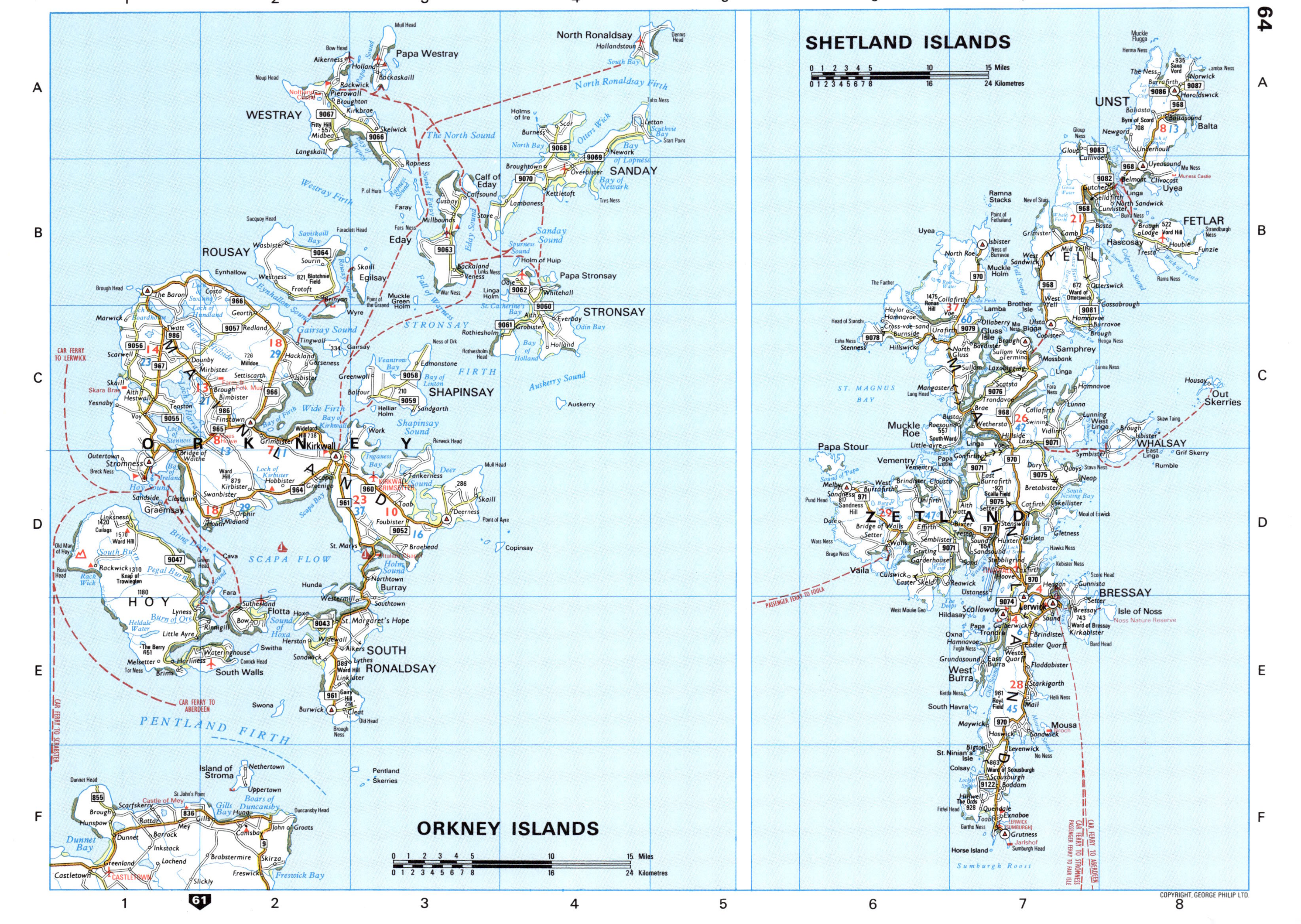
SHETLAND ISLANDS
ORKNEY ISLANDS
0 1 2 3 4 5 10 15 Miles
0 1 2 3 4 5 6 7 8 16 24 Kilometres
ZETLAND
ORKNEY
UNST
YELL
FETLAR
WHALSAY
BRESSAY
Isle of Noss
Noss Nature Reserve
Out Skerries
Papa Stour
Muckle Roe
Vementry
Samphrey
Mousa
Vaila
West Burra
Horse Island
Sumburgh Roost
Lerwick
Scalloway
ST. MAGNUS BAY
PASSENGER FERRY TO FOULA
CAR FERRY TO ABERDEEN
CAR FERRY TO STROMNESS
PASSENGER FERRY TO FAIR ISLE
North Ronaldsay
North Ronaldsay Firth
Papa Westray
WESTRAY
Westray Firth
The North Sound
SANDAY
Eday
Calf of Eday
ROUSAY
Egilsay
Papa Stronsay
STRONSAY
STRONSAY FIRTH
SHAPINSAY
Auskerry
Kirkwall
Stromness
HOY
SCAPA FLOW
Flotta
SOUTH RONALDSAY
South Walls
Copinsay
Pentland Skerries
PENTLAND FIRTH
Island of Stroma
Dunnet Bay
John o' Groats
Castletown
CAR FERRY TO LERWICK
CAR FERRY TO ABERDEEN
CAR FERRY TO SCRABSTER

Birmingham 96 miles
Key to Map Symbols
Motorway with Access Point
Primary Route
Other 'A' Road
Primary Route
Other 'A' Road
Dual Carriageway
'B' Road
Other Road
County Boundary
Railway and Station
Underground Station
STAINES
Primary Route Town
Canal
Built-up Area
Woodland
Park
Airport
Motor Racing Circuit
Golf Course
Greyhound Track
RAC/AA Telephone Box
Scale 3/4 inch to 1 mile
© Crown Copyright
High Wycombe 8 miles
Central Slough 1 mile
WATFORD
Croxley Green
Colney Butts
Bushey
Oxhey
Watford Heath
Merry Hill
Bushey Heath
RICKMANSWORTH
Batchworth
Batchworth Heath
Carpenders Park
South Oxhey
Eastbury
Northwood
Royston Park
Hatch End
Woodridings
Hill End
Chalfont St. Peter
Harefield
Pinner Green
Pinner
Headstone
Ruislip Lido
Ruislip Common
Gerrards Cross
Denham
Eastcote
West Harrow
Tatling End
Rayners Lane
Ruislip
Ickenham
South Harrow
Roxeth
Fulmer
Willowbank
Wood End
Northolt Park
Uxbridge
New Denham
Northolt
Greenford Green
Iver Heath
HILLINGDON
Hillingdon
Hillingdon Heath
Greenford
Cowley
Yeading
Colham Green
Hayes End
Wood End
Iver
Mount Pleasant
Yiewsley
Hayes
Southall
SLOUGH
West Drayton
Richings Park
Langley
Southall Green
Norwood Green
North Hyde
Harlington
Harmondsworth
Sipson
Heston
Datchet
The Queen Mother Reservoir
Colnbrook
Cranford
Longford
Heathrow Airport
Hounslow
Poyle
Horton
Hatton

St. Albans 7 miles
Peterborough 69 miles
Hatfield 8 miles
Elstree Aerodrome
Hilfield Reservoir
Aldenham Park
Aldenham Reservoir
Tykes Water Lake
Borehamwood
Elstree
Rowley Bank
Arkley
Barnet Gate
Totteridge
Cockfosters
New Barnet
East Barnet
Oakleigh Park
Whetstone
Friern Barnet
Bushey Heath
Scratchwood
Scratchwood Service Area
Moat Mount
Brockley Hill
Highwood Hill
BARNET
Stanmore
Stone Grove
Canons Park
Edgware
Mill Hill
North Finchley
New Southgate
Colney Hatch
Palmer's Green
Finchley
Harrow Weald
Belmont
Hatch End
Burnt Oak
HARROW
Church End
Holders Hill
Queensbury
Colindale
Wealdstone
The Hyde
Hendon
East Finchley
Muswell Hill
Alexandra Palace
Headstone
Kingsbury
Harrow
Greenhill
Kenton
Kingsbury Green
Golders Green
Hornsey
Crouch End
West Harrow
Harrow on the Hill
Preston
BRENT
Brent Reservoir (Welsh Harp)
Highgate
Hampstead Heath
Roxeth
Neasden
Cricklewood
Hampstead
Wembley
Wembley Stadium
Wood End
Kentish Town
Greenford Green
Willesden Green
Willesden
Brondesbury
CAMDEN
Camden Town
Alperton
Harlesden
Perivale
Brondesbury Park
Kilburn
Kensal Rise
Kensal Green
St. John's Wood
Maida Vale
Regent's Park
Somers Town
Greenford
Park Royal
Hanger Hill
Paddington
Marylebone
Bloomsbury
Elthorne Heights
EALING
Drayton Green
Ealing
Acton
East Acton
Notting Hill
Bayswater
Soho
Hanwell
Shepherd's Bush
Kensington
Hyde Park
Mayfair
Westminster
KENSINGTON AND CHELSEA
HAMMERSMITH
Brook Green
Brompton
Belgravia
Little Ealing
Brentford
Gunnersbury Park
Gunnersbury
Chiswick
Kew Bridge
Pimlico
Osterley Park
Osterley
Spring Grove
HOUNSLOW
Royal Botanic Gardens
Kew
FULHAM
Battersea Park
Battersea
Barnes
Lampton
Hounslow
Isleworth
Old Deer Park
Mortlake
River Thames
Clapham
1 2 3 4 5 6
A B C D E F G H
65
69
70

ORTH)
7
8
9
10
11
12
A
B
C
D
E
F
G
H
Cambridge 40 miles
Ongar 7 miles
Enfield
Bush Hill Park
Winchmore Hill
Ponders End
Lower Edmonton
Upper Edmonton
Sewardstonebury
King George Reservoir
William Girling Reservoir
Chingford
Chingford Hatch
Highams Park
Hale End
Loughton
Buckhurst Hill
Woodford Wells
Woodford Green
Woodford Bridge
Woodford
Chigwell
Chigwell Row
Lambourne End
Abridge
Hainault
Grange Hill
Hainault Estate
Epping Forest
Waltham Forest
Chapel End
Higham Hill
Tottenham
Tottenham Hale
West Green
Noel Park
Upper Walthamstow
Walthamstow
Snaresbrook
Redbridge
Clayhall
Barkingside
Aldborough Hatch
Padnall Corner
Chadwell Heath
Newbury Park
Seven Kings
Goodmayes
Ilford
Barking
Upney
Wanstead
Aldersbrook
Leyton
Lea Bridge
Upper Clapton
Stamford Hill
Stoke Newington
Highbury
Hackney
Dalston
Canonbury
Kingsland
Homerton
Hackney Wick
Stratford
Stratford New Town
Forest Gate
Manor Park
Upton
East Ham
Plaistow
West Ham
Newham
Beckton
Creekmouth
Thamesmead
Canning Town
Bow
Bromley
Bow Common
Poplar
Tower Hamlets
Bethnal Green
Shoreditch
Hoxton
Finsbury
Spitalfields
Whitechapel
Stepney
Limehouse
Wapping
Rotherhithe
Millwall
Isle of Dogs
Blackwall
Blackwall Tunnel
Silvertown
North Woolwich
Woolwich Ferry
Woolwich
Plumstead
Abbey Wood
West Heath
East Wickham
Welling
Shooters Hill
Charlton
New Charlton
Greenwich
Kidbrooke
Blackheath
Lewisham
Deptford
Bermondsey
Southwark
Walworth
Camberwell
Peckham
Nunhead
Brixton
Royal Albert Dock
Royal Victoria Dock
King George V Dock
River Thames
M11
A102(M)
71
68

LONDON APPROACHES (NORTH-EAST)

Chelmsford 9 miles
Tilbury 9 miles
Southend-on-Sea 18 miles
Southend-on-Sea 18 miles
Abridge
Stapleford Abbotts
Bournebridge
Lambourne End
Havering -atte-Bower
Noak Hill
Pilgrims Hatch
South Weald
Shenfield
BRENTWOOD
Ingrave Green
Ingrave
Harold Hill
Havering Park
Collier Row
Marks Gate
Gidea Park
Hare Street
Harold Wood
Great Warley
Padnall Corner
Squirrels Heath
Ardleigh Green
Romford
Chadwell Heath
Heath Park
Emerson Park
Cranham
Hornchurch
HAVERING
Beacontree Heath
Rush Green
Goodmayes
Becontree
Upminster
Elm Park
LONDON
BARKING
North Ockendon
Corbets Tey
DAGENHAM
South Hornchurch
Rainham
South Ockendon
Wennington
Thamesmead
Danger Area
Aveley
Stifford
Belvedere
Abbey Wood
Lessness Heath
Erith
Purfleet
West Thurrock
West Heath
RIVER THAMES
Northumberland Heath
North End
Slade Green
South Stifford
GRAYS
Welling
Barnehurst
Bexleyheath
Crayford
Dartford Tunnel
KENT
BEXLEY
M25
71
72
67

Windsor 3 miles
Basingstoke 27 miles
Chobham 1 mile
Portsmouth 46 miles
Heathrow Airport
STAINES
ESHER
WALTON UPON THAMES
WOKING
Harmondsworth
Sipson
Harlington
Cranford
Heston
Osterley
Spring Grove
Lampton
Hounslow
Whitton
Twickenham
Colnbrook
Longford
Poyle
Horton
Stanwell
Stanwell Moor
Wraysbury
Wraysbury Reservoir
The Queen Mother Reservoir
King George VI. Res.
Staines Reservoirs
West Bedfont
East Bedfont
Hatton
Feltham
Lower Feltham
Hanworth
Feltham Hill
Hounslow Heath
Hythe End
Runnymede
River Thames
EGHAM
Hythe
Knowle Green
Ashford
Queen Mary Reservoir
Laleham
Littleton
Sunbury
Hampton
BUSHY PARK
Stroude
Thorpe
Thorpe Park
Chertsey
Shepperton
East Molesey
West Molesey
Queen Elizabeth II Reservoir
Pyrcroft
Eastworth
Botleys
Bretlands
Addlestone
Ottershaw
Weybridge
Oatlands Park
Ashley Park
Hersham
Lower Green
Weston Green
Thistlecroft
West End
Row Town
New Haw
Woodham
Byfleet
West Byfleet
Whiteley Village
Esher Common
Fairmile
Cobham
Oxshott
Wisley
Wisley Common
Ockham Common
Pyrford
Mayburg
Kingfieldgreen
Ripley
Ockham Park
Hatchford Park
Downside
Stoke D'Abernon
Woodland Park
Leatherhead Common
Great Bookham Common
SURREY
LONDON
M4
M25
M3
COPYRIGHT. GEORGE PHILIP. LTD.

66
69
Chiswick
Kew Bridge
Osterley
Spring Grove
Kew
ROYAL BOTANIC GARDENS
Barnes
RIVER THAMES
Putney
Fulham
Battersea
BATTERSEA PARK
Pimlico
Kennington
Brixton
Clapham
CLAPHAM COMMON
LAMBETH
Isleworth
Mortlake
East Sheen
RICHMOND
St. Margarets
Twickenham Park
Cambridge Park
Cole Park
Twickenham
River Thames
RICHMOND PARK
Petersham
RICHMOND UPON THAMES
Roehampton
WANDSWORTH
Balham
Brockwell Park
Ham
Ham Common
Kingston Vale
WIMBLEDON COMMON
Wimbledon Park
Wimbledon
Streatham
Tooting Graveney
Teddington
BUSHY PARK
Hampton Wick
KINGSTON
Norbiton
Cottenham Park
Collier's Wood
Norbury
New Malden
Raynes Park
MERTON
Mitcham
Thornton Heath
HAMPTON COURT PARK
KINGSTON UPON THAMES
Surbiton
Thames Ditton
Motspur Park
Morden
Malden
Morden Park
St. Helier
Beddington Corner
Hackbridge
Weston Green
Long Ditton
Southborough
Tolworth
North Cheam
The Wrythe
Worcester Park
Carshalton
Waddon
Hinchley Wood
Hook
Cheam
Beddington
Chessington
West Ewell
Nonsuch Park
SUTTON
Wallington
Roundshaw
Claygate
Carshalton on the Hill
EWELL
East Ewell
Horton
Howell Hill
Malden Rushett
PRINCES COVERTS
BANSTEAD DOWNS
Little Woodcote
Purley
EPSOM
EPSOM COMMON
Woodmansterne
ASHTEAD COMMON
Banstead
Coulsdon
Ashtead
Lower Ashtead
Leatherhead Common
Langley Vale
SURREY
Burgh Heath
Furze Hill
Ashtead Park
Chipstead
Old Coulsdon
WALTON DOWNS
Horsham 17 miles
Reigate 4 miles
Brighton 38 miles

Walworth
SOUTHWARK
Camberwell
Peckham
Nunhead
East Dulwich
Dulwich
Deptford
Greenwich
Blackheath
Kidbrooke
Lewisham
LEWISHAM
Hither Green
Catford
Lee
Forest Hill
Upper Sydenham
Sydenham
Lower Sydenham
Bellingham
Southend
Downham Estate
Grove Park
Mottingham
Charlton
GREENWICH
Plumstead
Abbey Wood
West Heath
East Wickham
Shooters Hill
Welling
Bexleyheath
BEXLEY
Eltham
South End
New Eltham
Blackfen
Longlands
Sidcup
Foots Cray
North Cray
Elmstead
Chislehurst West
Chislehurst
Crystal Palace
Norwood
Penge
New Beckenham
Beckenham
Bromley
Shortlands
Parklangley
Elmers End
South Norwood
Grangewood
Woodside
Upper Elmers End
Eden Park
BROMLEY
Bickley
Southborough
Petts Wood
St. Paul's Cray
St. Mary Cray
Derry Downs
ORPINGTON
CROYDON
Addiscombe
Shirley
West Wickham
Hayes
Hayes Common
Bromley Common
Keston Mark
Keston
Locksbottom
Farnborough
Green Street Green
Chelsfield Village
Addington
Nash
New Addington
CROYDON
Selsdon
Sanderstead
Farleigh
Fickleshole
Leaves Green
Downe
Hazel Wood
Pratt's Bottom
Knockholt Pound
Biggin Hill
Cudham
Horns Green
Knockholt
CHEVENING PARK
Scott's Lodge
Hamsey Green
Warlingham
Chelsham
Whyteleafe
Tatsfield
BIGGIN HILL AIRPORT

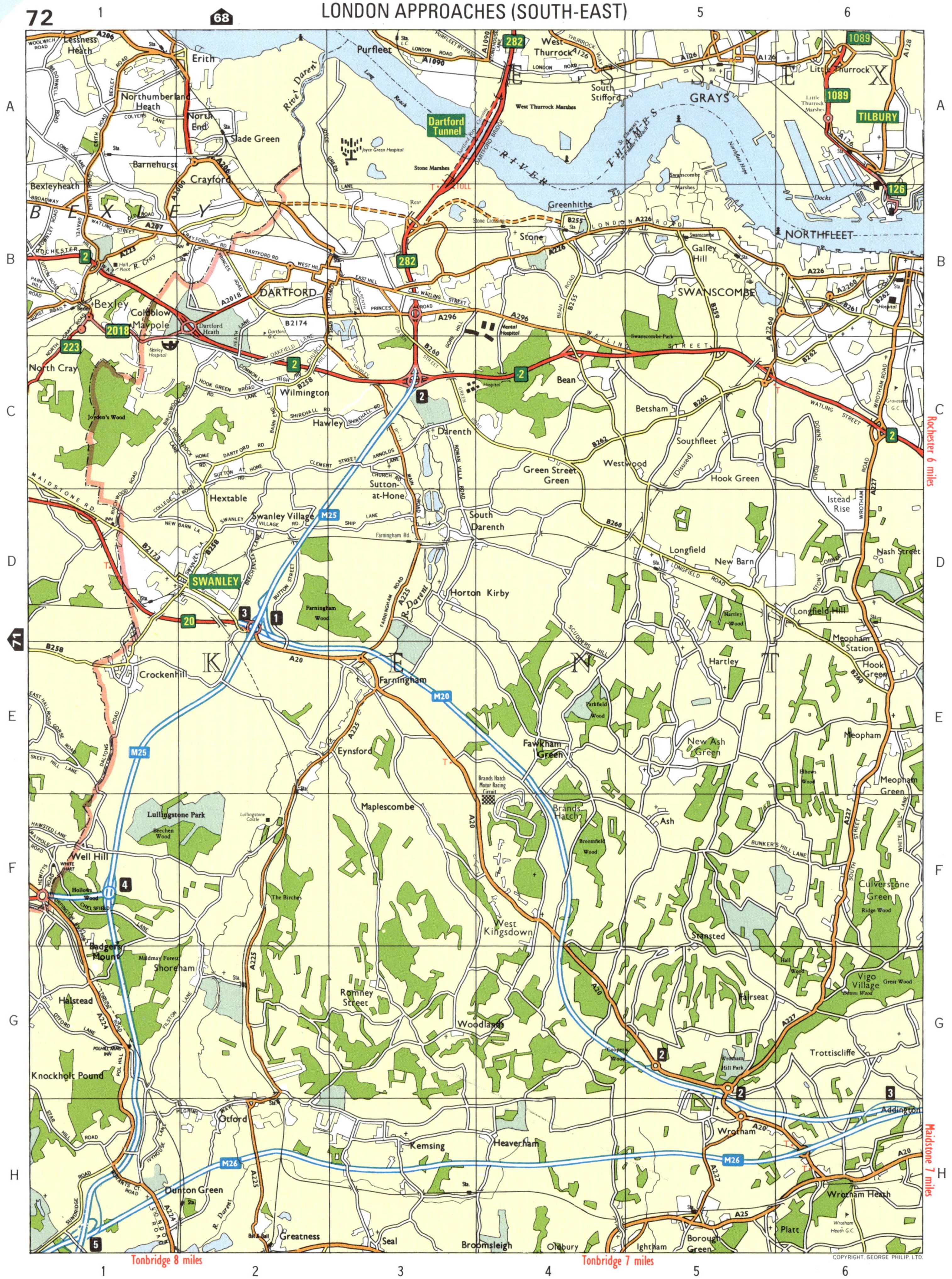

68
71
1
2
3
4
5
6
A
B
C
D
E
F
G
H
Lessness Heath
Erith
Purfleet
West Thurrock
Little Thurrock
Northumberland Heath
North End
Slade Green
South Stifford
GRAYS
TILBURY
Dartford Tunnel
Joyce Green Hospital
Stone Marshes
West Thurrock Marshes
RIVER THAMES
Barnehurst
Crayford
Bexleyheath
BEXLEY
Greenhithe
Swanscombe Marshes
Stone
NORTHFLEET
Galley Hill
Docks
DARTFORD
SWANSCOMBE
Bexley
Coldblow
Maypole
Dartford Heath
Swanscombe Park
North Cray
Joyden's Wood
Wilmington
Hawley
Darenth
Bean
Betsham
Southfleet
Westwood
Green Street Green
Hook Green
Sutton-at-Hone
Hextable
Swanley Village
South Darenth
Istead Rise
Nash Street
Longfield
New Barn
SWANLEY
Horton Kirby
Farningham Wood
Hartley Wood
Longfield Hill
Meopham Station
Crockenhill
Farningham
Hartley
Hook Green
Parkfield Wood
New Ash Green
Meopham
Fawkham Green
Eynsford
Brands Hatch Motor Racing Circuit
Meopham Green
Maplescombe
Lullingstone Park
Beechen Wood
Lullingstone Castle
Brands Hatch
Broomfield Wood
Ash
Well Hill
Hollows Wood
The Birches
Culverstone Green
Ridge Wood
West Kingsdown
Stansted
Badgers Mount
Mildmay Forest
Shoreham
Romney Street
Fairseat
Vigo Village
Great Wood
Halstead
Woodlands
Trottiscliffe
Knockholt Pound
Coopers Wood
Wrotham Hill Park
Addington
Otford
Kemsing
Heaverham
Wrotham
Dunton Green
Wrotham Heath
Greatness
Seal
Bromsleigh
Oldbury
Ightham
Borough Green
Platt
Wrotham Heath G.C.
M25
M20
M26
A20
A225
A227
A2
Rochester 6 miles
Maidstone 7 miles

Tonbridge 8 miles   Tonbridge 7 miles

1 2 5 6 7

Key to Map Symbols
A4209 'A' Road Number
Road with Periods of Restricted Access
Public Building
Park
Railway and Station
Underground Railway and Station
Footpath
Built-up Area
Scale 5 inches to 1 mile
0
¼
½ mile
© Crown Copyright
A B C D E F G H J
1 2 3 4 5 6 7
PRINCESS ROAD
GRANVILLE ROAD
CARLTON VALE
STAFFORD ROAD
MALVERN ROAD
KILBURN PARK ROAD
Paddington Recreation Ground
Sports Arena
Bandstand
MORSHEAD ROAD
LAUDERDALE ROAD
SHIRLAND ROAD
ELGIN AVENUE
DELAWARE ROAD
B.B.C. Studios
Paddington Sports Club
CASTELLAIN ROAD
SUTHERLAND AVENUE
CHIPPENHAM ROAD
CHIPPENHAM MEWS
HARROW ROAD
Council Offices
Paddington General Hospital
Grand Union Canal
WARWICK ESTATE
ALFRED ROAD
A40(M)
BOURNE TERRACE
SENIOR ST.
ROWINGTON CL.
DELAMERE TERRACE
BLOMFIELD ROAD
Little Venice
WARWICK AVENUE
WARWICK CRESCENT
CLIFTON GARDENS
RANDOLPH AVENUE
MAIDA VALE
A5
Maida Vale Hospital
HAMILTON TERRACE
ABERCORN PLACE
ABBEY ROAD
CLIFTON HILL
BLENHEIM TERRACE
MARLBOROUGH PLACE
LOUDOUN ROAD
FINCHLEY RD.
WELLINGTON ROAD
A41
GROVE END ROAD
CIRCUS ROAD
ST. JOHN'S WOOD ROAD
A5205
Lord's Cricket Ground
PRINCE ALBERT ROAD
Grand Union Canal
OUTER CIRCLE
PARK ROAD
Winfield House
Mosque
LISSON GREEN ESTATE
BLANDFORD ESTATE
MARYLEBONE STATION
LISSON GROVE
EDGWARE ROAD
HARROW ROAD
MARYLEBONE FLYOVER
A404
A501
CHAPEL ST.
Paddington Basin
NORTH WHARF ROAD
SOUTH WHARF ROAD
PADDINGTON STATION
EASTBOURNE TERRACE
PRAED STREET
A4209
SUSSEX GARDENS
WESTBOURNE PARK VILLAS
WESTBOURNE PARK ROAD
CHEPSTOW ROAD
WESTBOURNE GROVE
BISHOP'S BRIDGE ROAD
A4206
HALLFIELD ESTATE
QUEENSWAY
INVERNESS TERRACE
PORCHESTER GARDENS
LEINSTER GARDENS
CRAVEN HILL
CRAVEN TERRACE
WESTBOURNE TERRACE
BAYSWATER ROAD
A40
THE RING
NORTH RIDE
HYDE PARK
Lancaster Gate
Marlborough Gate
Victoria Gate
Westbourne Gate
Black Lion Gate
Orme Square Gate
PEMBRIDGE VILLAS
PEMBRIDGE SQUARE
A4207
CONNAUGHT STREET
HYDE PARK SQUARE
Royal Toxophilite Soc. Ground

3 4 5 6 7

77

Primrose Hill
Reservoir
Grand Union Canal
REGENT'S PARK
Zoological Gardens
OUTER CIRCLE
INNER CIRCLE
Boating Lake
Queen Mary's Gardens
CHESTER ROAD
PARK CRESCENT
EUSTON STATION
EUSTON CENTRE
BLANDFORD ESTATE
PADDINGTON STREET
MARYLEBONE HIGH STREET
PORTMAN SQUARE
CAVENDISH SQUARE
HANOVER SQUARE
GROSVENOR SQUARE
OXFORD STREET
OXFORD CIRCUS
MARBLE ARCH
BAYSWATER RD
THE RING
PARK LANE
HYDE PARK
PICCADILLY CIRCUS
PICCADILLY
SOHO
1 2 3 4 5 6 7
A B C D E F G H J

73

78

9
10
11
12
13
A
B
C
D
E
F
G
H
J
8
9
10
11
12
13
14
76
79
Barnard Park
YORK WAY ESTATE
Grand Union Canal
(Regent's Canal)
Battlebridge Basin
Goods Depot
Gas Works
KING'S CROSS STATION
ST. PANCRAS STATION
PENTONVILLE ROAD
CITY ROAD
City Road Basin
Wenlock Basin
KING SQUARE ESTATE
BRUNSWICK CL. ESTATE
FINSBURY ESTATE
New River Head
Coram's Field Playground
Mount Pleasant Sorting Office
Royal Free Hospital
Gray's Inn Gardens
GOLDEN LANE ESTATE
BARBICAN
LONDON WALL
Charterhouse
Smithfield Central Markets
CHARTERHOUSE STREET
HOLBORN
HOLBORN VIADUCT
HIGH HOLBORN
NEW OXFORD STREET
Lincoln's Inn Fields
CHANCERY LANE
FLEET STREET
LUDGATE HILL
NEWGATE STREET
CHEAPSIDE
PATERNOSTER SQUARE
ST. PAUL'S CATHEDRAL
QUEEN VICTORIA STREET
UPPER THAMES STREET
Temple Gardens
VICTORIA EMBANKMENT
STRAND
ALDWYCH
KINGSWAY
SOUTHAMPTON ROW
RUSSELL SQUARE
BLOOMSBURY
BRITISH MUSEUM
UNIVERSITY OF LONDON
WOBURN PLACE
TAVISTOCK SQUARE
GUILFORD STREET
THEOBALDS ROAD
CLERKENWELL ROAD
FARRINGDON ROAD
FARRINGDON STREET
ALDERSGATE STREET
GOSWELL ROAD
ST. JOHN STREET
SHAFTESBURY AVENUE
CHARING CROSS ROAD
COVENT GARDEN
TRAFALGAR SQUARE
WATERLOO BRIDGE
BLACKFRIARS BRIDGE
RIVER THAMES
KING'S REACH
H.M.S. Chrysanthemum
H.M.S. President
Cleopatra's Needle
BANKSIDE

1 2 5 6 7

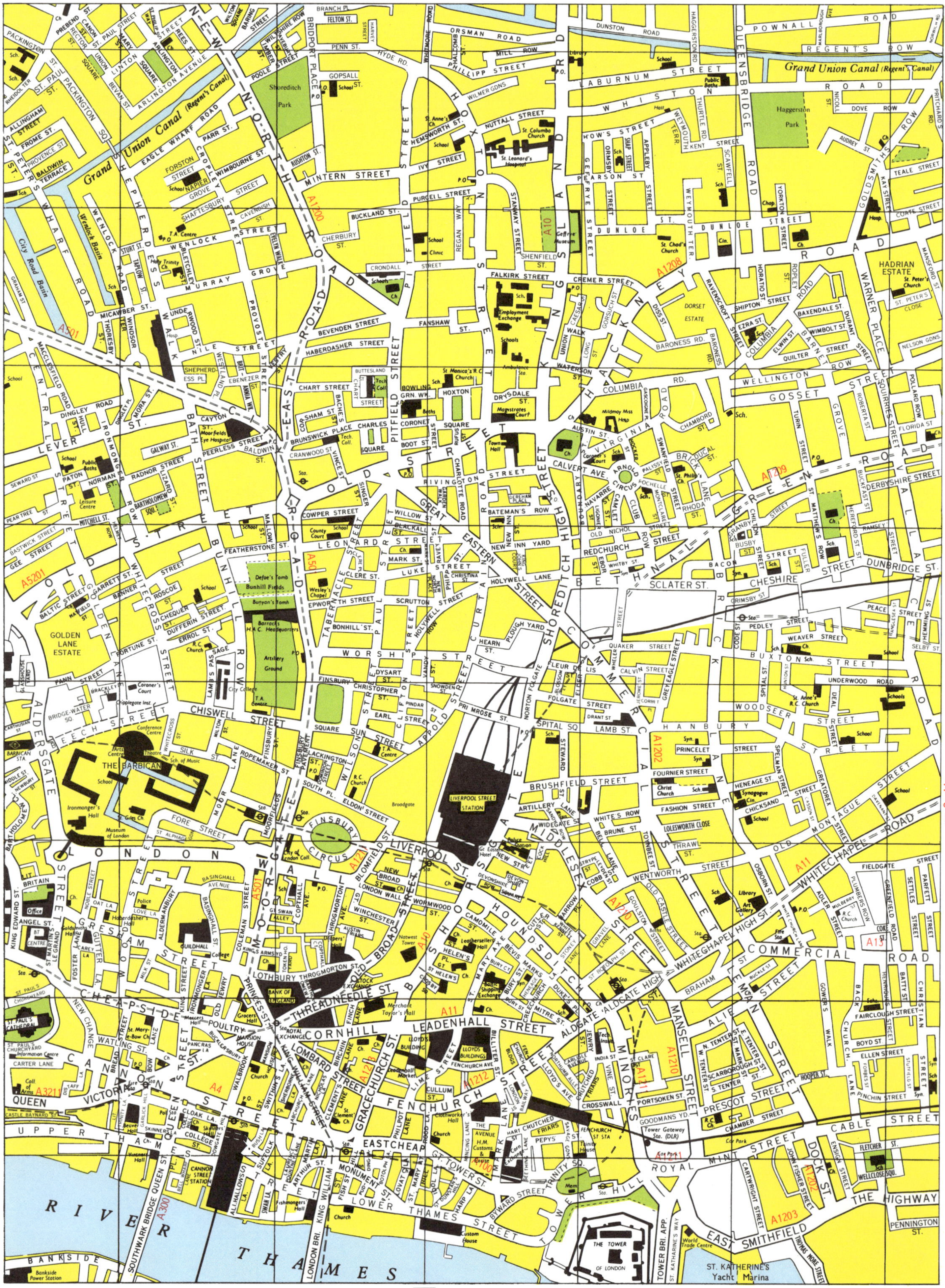
Grand Union Canal (Regent's Canal)
City Road Basin
Wenlock Basin
Shoreditch Park
Haggerston Park
NEW NORTH ROAD
EAST ROAD
CITY ROAD
OLD STREET
GREAT EASTERN STREET
SHOREDITCH HIGH STREET
KINGSLAND ROAD
HACKNEY ROAD
BETHNAL GREEN ROAD
COMMERCIAL STREET
COMMERCIAL ROAD
WHITECHAPEL ROAD
WHITECHAPEL HIGH ST.
LONDON WALL
MOORGATE
BISHOPSGATE
LIVERPOOL ST.
LIVERPOOL STREET STATION
FINSBURY CIRCUS
THE BARBICAN
GOLDEN LANE ESTATE
Bunhill Fields
Artillery Ground
CHEAPSIDE
THREADNEEDLE ST.
CORNHILL
LEADENHALL STREET
FENCHURCH STREET
CANNON STREET
QUEEN VICTORIA ST.
EASTCHEAP
GREAT TOWER ST.
LOWER THAMES STREET
UPPER THAMES ST.
ROYAL MINT STREET
CABLE STREET
THE HIGHWAY
EAST SMITHFIELD
TOWER HILL
THE TOWER OF LONDON
ST. KATHERINE'S Yacht Marina
RIVER THAMES
LONDON BRI.
SOUTHWARK BRIDGE
TOWER BRI. APP.
BANKSIDE
Bankside Power Station
BANK OF ENGLAND
ROYAL EXCHANGE
ST. PAUL'S CATHEDRAL
GUILDHALL
Epping A11
A1200
A10
A1208
A1209
A501
A5201
A50
A1202
A1210
A11
A13
A4
A3211
A1211
A1203
A300

75
80

A B C D E F G H J

1 2 3 4 5 6 7

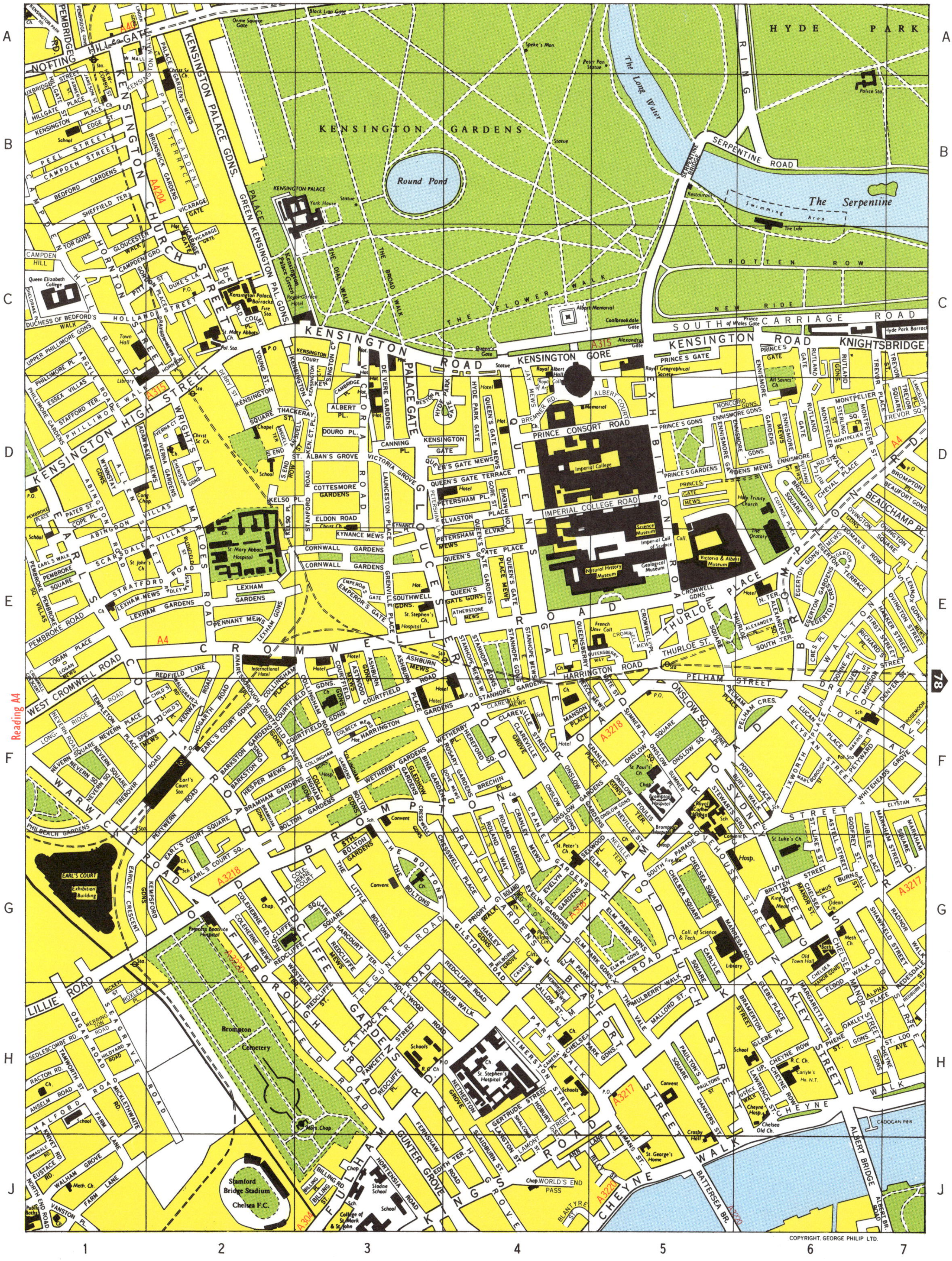
73
78
Reading A4
HYDE PARK
KENSINGTON GARDENS
Round Pond
The Long Water
The Serpentine
SERPENTINE ROAD
ROTTEN ROW
SOUTH CARRIAGE ROAD
KENSINGTON PALACE
KENSINGTON ROAD
KENSINGTON GORE
KNIGHTSBRIDGE
KENSINGTON HIGH STREET
KENSINGTON CHURCH STREET
KENSINGTON PALACE GDNS.
NOTTING HILL GATE
PRINCE CONSORT ROAD
IMPERIAL COLLEGE ROAD
EXHIBITION ROAD
QUEEN'S GATE
GLOUCESTER ROAD
CROMWELL ROAD
WEST CROMWELL ROAD
EARL'S COURT ROAD
EARL'S COURT Exhibition Building
OLD BROMPTON ROAD
BROMPTON ROAD
FULHAM ROAD
KING'S ROAD
CHEYNE WALK
LILLIE ROAD
REDCLIFFE GARDENS
FINBOROUGH ROAD
Brompton Cemetery
Stamford Bridge Stadium Chelsea F.C.
Natural History Museum
Science Museum
Victoria & Albert Museum
Imperial College
St. Mary Abbots Hospital
St. Stephen's Hospital
BATTERSEA BR.
ALBERT BRIDGE
A4
A315
A3218
A3217
A3220
A4204

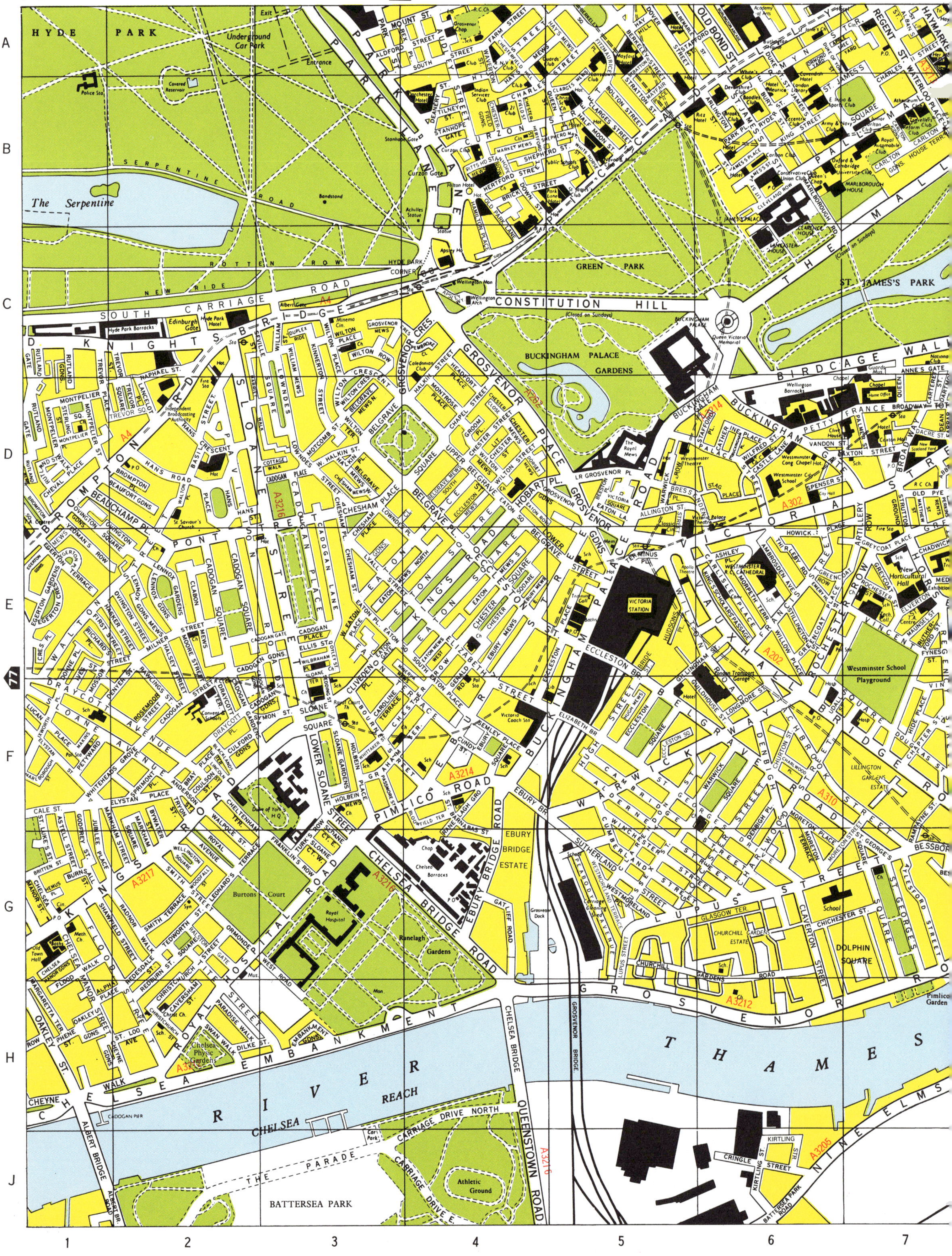
HYDE PARK
The Serpentine
SERPENTINE ROAD
ROTTEN ROW
SOUTH CARRIAGE ROAD
KNIGHTSBRIDGE
PARK LANE
GREEN PARK
CONSTITUTION HILL
ST. JAMES'S PARK
THE MALL
BUCKINGHAM PALACE GARDENS
BIRDCAGE WALK
GROSVENOR PLACE
BELGRAVE SQUARE
EATON SQUARE
SLOANE STREET
SLOANE SQUARE
CADOGAN SQUARE
PONT STREET
BROMPTON ROAD
BEAUCHAMP PL.
KING'S ROAD
VICTORIA STREET
VICTORIA STATION
BUCKINGHAM PALACE ROAD
VAUXHALL BRIDGE ROAD
BELGRAVE ROAD
WARWICK WAY
LUPUS STREET
GROSVENOR ROAD
PIMLICO ROAD
CHELSEA BRIDGE ROAD
CHELSEA EMBANKMENT
ROYAL HOSPITAL ROAD
Royal Hospital
Ranelagh Gardens
Burtons Court
EBURY BRIDGE ESTATE
CHELSEA BRIDGE
GROSVENOR BRIDGE
CHURCHILL GARDENS
DOLPHIN SQUARE
Westminster School Playground
RIVER THAMES
CHELSEA REACH
QUEENSTOWN ROAD
CARRIAGE DRIVE NORTH
THE PARADE
Athletic Ground
BATTERSEA PARK
NINE ELMS
ALBERT BRIDGE ROAD
CHEYNE WALK
Chelsea Physic Gardens
PALL MALL
PICCADILLY
CURZON
BUCKINGHAM GATE
A4
A3216
A3214
A302
A202
A3212
A3217
A3205
A310

A
B
C
D
E
F
G
H
J
80
TRAFALGAR SQUARE
STRAND
NORTHUMBERLAND AVE
WHITEHALL PLACE
HORSEGUARDS AVE
Ministry of Defence
HORSE GUARDS PARADE
WHITEHALL
Victoria Embankment Gardens
VICTORIA EMBANKMENT
DOWNING ST
RICHMOND TERR
Foreign & Commonwealth Office
KING CHARLES ST
Treasury
GREAT GEORGE ST
BRIDGE ST
WESTMINSTER BRIDGE
PARLIAMENT SQUARE
HOUSES OF PARLIAMENT
WESTMINSTER ABBEY
Victoria Tower Gardens
MILLBANK
LAMBETH BRIDGE
HORSEFERRY ROAD
TATE & CLORE GALLERIES
VAUXHALL BRIDGE ROAD
HUNGERFORD RAILWAY BRIDGE
RIVER THAMES
WATERLOO BRIDGE
Royal National Theatre
ROYAL FESTIVAL HALL
QUEEN ELIZABETH HALL & PURCELL ROOM
COUNTY HALL
WATERLOO STATION
YORK ROAD
STAMFORD STREET
UPPER GROUND
WATERLOO ROAD
THE CUT
BLACKFRIARS ROAD
SOUTHWARK STREET
UNION ST
BOROUGH ROAD
South Bank Polytechnic
ST. GEORGE'S CIRCUS
LONDON ROAD
WESTMINSTER BRIDGE ROAD
LAMBETH PALACE ROAD
Archbishop's Park
LAMBETH ROAD
LAMBETH PALACE
KENNINGTON ROAD
Geraldine Mary Harmsworth Park
Imperial War Museum
BROOK DRIVE
NEWINGTON CAUSEWAY
ELEPHANT AND CASTLE
NEW KENT RD.
NEWINGTON BUTTS
WALWORTH ROAD
KENNINGTON LANE
ALBERT EMBANKMENT
KENNINGTON PARK ROAD
VAUXHALL STATION
HARLEYFORD ROAD
The Oval Cricket Ground
KENNINGTON OVAL
Vauxhall Park
Kennington Park
BRANDON ESTATE
CAMBERWELL NEW ROAD
BRIXTON RD
CLAPHAM RD
SOUTH LAMBETH ROAD
WANDSWORTH ROAD
NEW COVENT GARDEN MARKET
FENTIMAN ROAD
A23
A3
A202
A3204
A3203
A302
A301
A3036
A3212
A3200
A201
A215

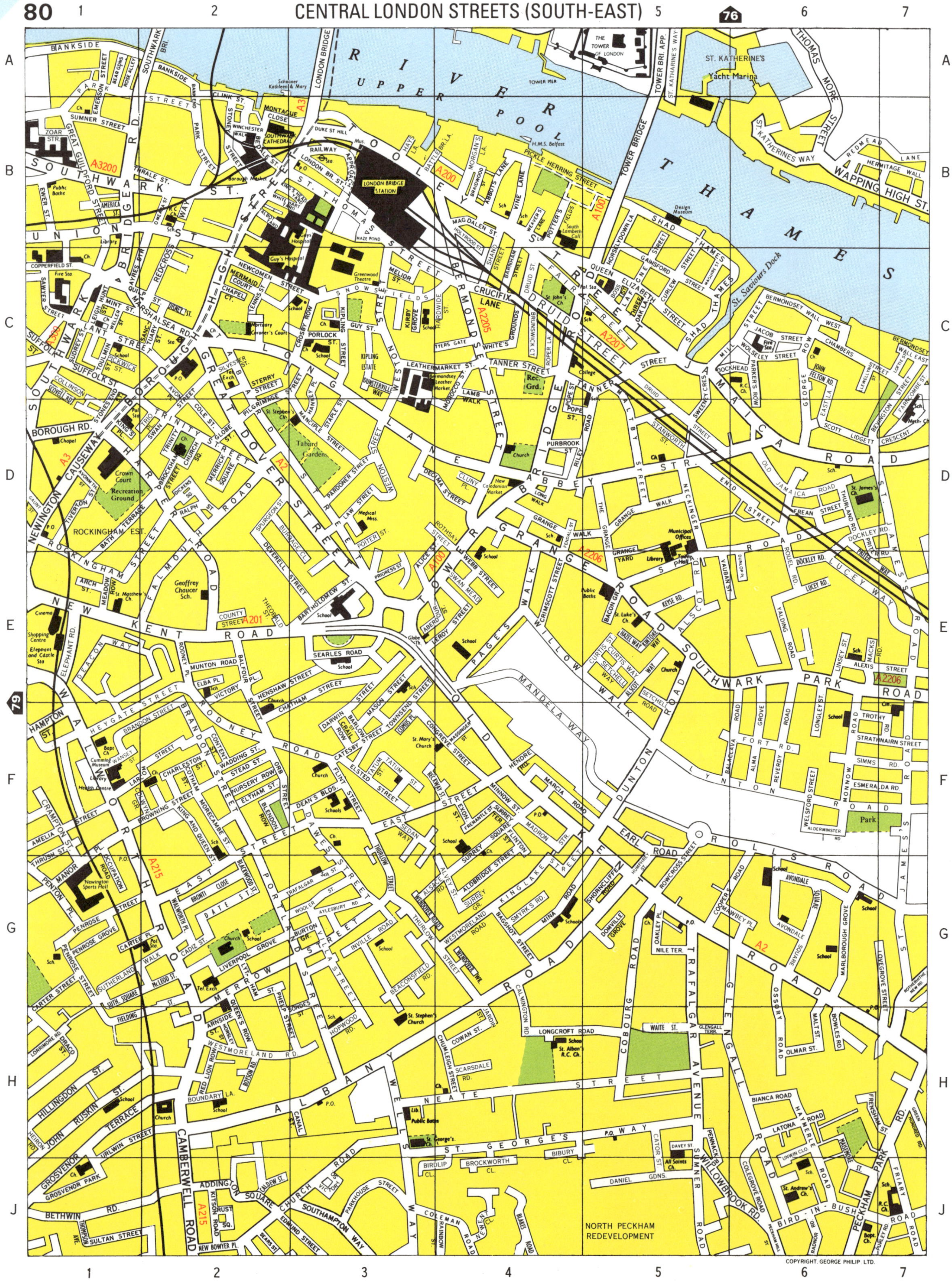
RIVER THAMES
UPPER POOL
THE TOWER OF LONDON
TOWER PIER
TOWER BRIDGE
ST. KATHERINE'S Yacht Marina
THOMAS MORE STREET
ST. KATHERINES WAY
WAPPING HIGH ST.
H.M.S. Belfast
LONDON BRIDGE
LONDON BRIDGE STATION
BANKSIDE
SOUTHWARK BRI.
SOUTHWARK CATHEDRAL
Borough Market
Guy's Hospital
TOOLEY STREET
ST. THOMAS STREET
BERMONDSEY STREET
CRUCIFIX LANE
DRUID STREET
SHAD THAMES
St. Saviours Dock
Design Museum
JAMAICA ROAD
SOUTHWARK STREET
SOUTHWARK BRIDGE RD.
UNION ST.
BOROUGH HIGH STREET
MARSHALSEA RD.
GREAT DOVER STREET
LONG LANE
BOROUGH RD.
NEWINGTON CAUSEWAY
Crown Court
Recreation Ground
ROCKINGHAM EST.
Tabard Gardens
Leathermarket
ABBEY STREET
GRANGE ROAD
TOWER BRIDGE ROAD
OLD KENT ROAD
NEW KENT ROAD
Shopping Centre
Elephant and Castle Sta.
Geoffrey Chaucer Sch.
MANDELA WAY
SOUTHWARK PARK ROAD
ROTHERHITHE NEW RD.
ROLLS ROAD
LYNTON ROAD
WALWORTH ROAD
EAST STREET
ALBANY ROAD
CAMBERWELL ROAD
Burgess Park
TRAFALGAR AVENUE
GLENGALL ROAD
COBOURG ROAD
ST. GEORGE'S WAY
NEATE STREET
WELLS WAY
PECKHAM PARK RD.
NORTH PECKHAM REDEVELOPMENT
SOUTHAMPTON WAY
A3
A2
A100
A200
A201
A202
A215
A2206
A3200
A2205

Key to Map Symbols

Town Maps / City Maps

- Through routes
- Inner ring roads
- Principal shopping streets
- Pedestrian precincts
- Limited access streets
- One-way streets
- Primary route destinations (A647 HALIFAX / A57 WARRINGTON)

Parking places · Police Station · Post Office · Theatre

Approach Maps

Motorways

M1 · Interchange (7) · Scratchwood Services · Service Area · Limited Interchange (8) · Access or exit only in direction of arrow

A3 Primary route	Road under construction
A423 Other A road	Dual carriageway
B4525 B road	Ring road
Minor road	Drive or track
Distance in miles	CRAWLEY DORKING Primary route destination
Toll Steep gradient, Toll	BATTLE Railway, Station & Level crossing
Car ferry	Passenger only ferry
Principal airport	Airfield
Beaches	County boundary
Picnic Area	LIGHTWATER Country Park
RAC/AA Telephone boxes	Caravan & camping sites

Places of Interest

Tourist Information Centre (All year/summer only)	Ancient monument
House (N.T. if National Trust)	Earthwork
Garden	Windmill/watermill
House & Garden	Other places of interest
Castle	Roman antiquity
Cathedral	Steam/miniature railway
Abbey/Priory	Historic ship
Church	Zoo
Museum	Safari park
Local museum	Farm park
Art collection	Aquarium/Dolphinarium
Art collection/museum	Bird Sanctuary/Aviary
Transport collection	Golf course
Military museum	BRANDS HATCH Race course
Maritime museum	JORDANS Youth hostel

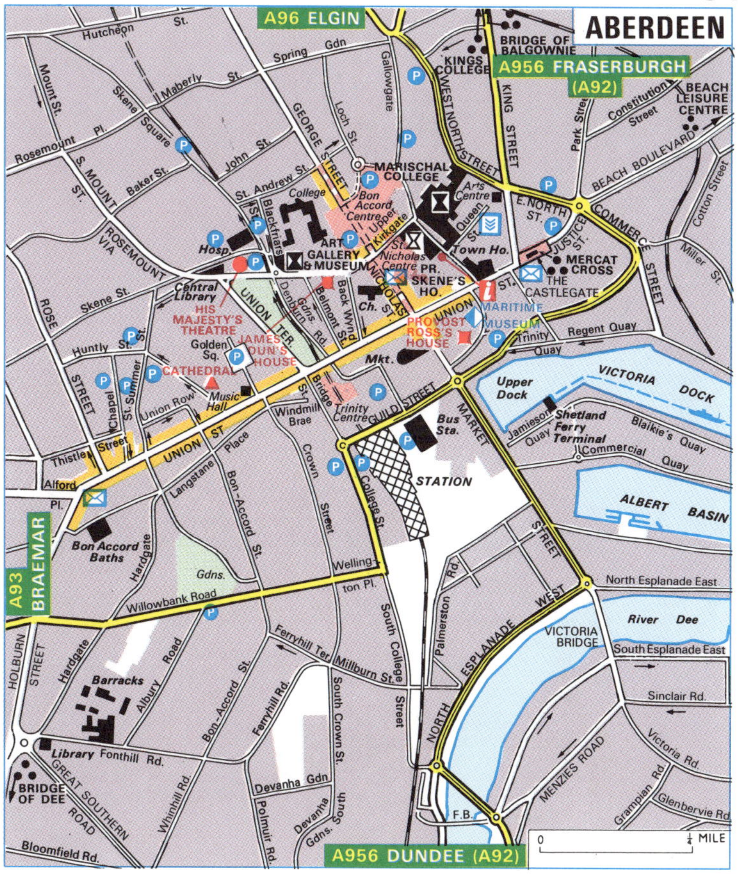

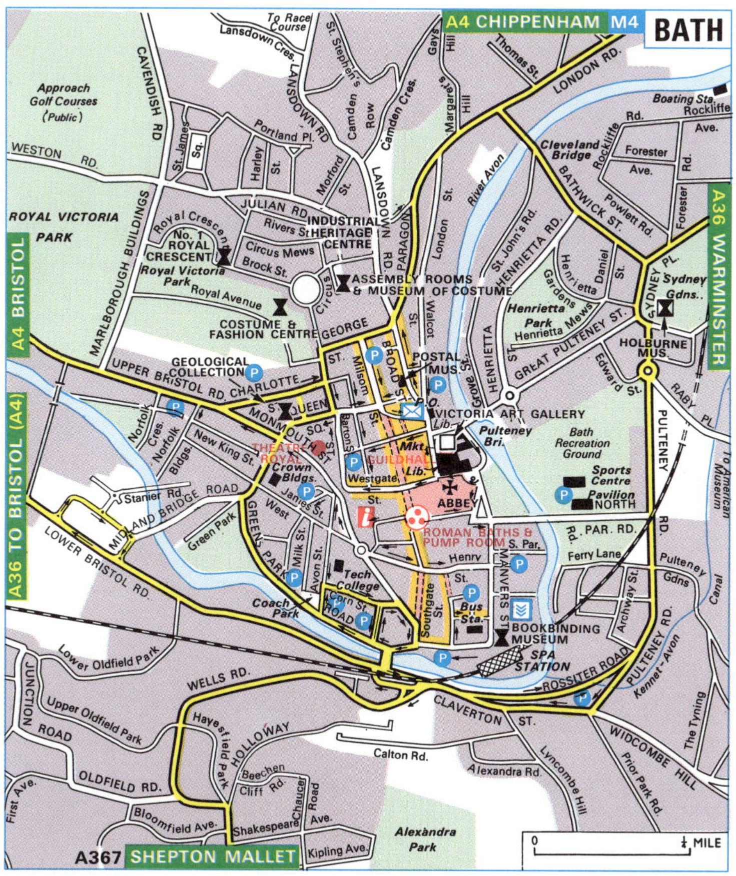

Codsall
Lane Green
Ford Houses
Essington
Little Bloxwich
Pelsall
Walsall Wood
Holly Bank
Oxley
Bushbury
Wallington Heath
High Heath
Vigo
Dam Mill
Wood Hayes
New Invention
Bloxwich
Blakenall Heath
Heath End
Shelfield
Palmers Cross
Wood End
Stubber's Green
Wergs
Perry Hall
Short Heath
Harden
Leighswood
Stockwell End
Dunstall
Wednesfield
Coal Pool
Rushall
Tettenhall
Daw End
Dunstall Hill
Park Village
Lane Head
Ashmore Lake
Sand Beds
Pool Green
Tettenhall Wood
Newbridge
Heath Town
Little Island
Bentley
Pouk Hill
Rushall Hall
Barr Common
Compton
WOLVERHAMPTON
WALSALL
Wightwick
WIGHTWICK MANOR (NT)
BANTOCK HOUSE MUSEUM
Moseley
Portobello
Willenhall
The Chuckery
Hayhead Fm.
Bradmore
Monmore Green
Priestfield
Bunkers Hill
Darlaston
Pleck
Daisy Bank
Merry Hill
Blakenhall
Bilston
The Lunt
Darlaston Green
Bescot
Palfrey
Maw Green
Goldthorn Park
Ettingshall
Fallings Heath
Beacon Fm.
Lower Penn
Parkfield
BILSTON MUSEUM & ART GALLERY
Woods Bank
King's Hill
Fullbrook
The Delves
Spring Hill
Penn
Colton Hills
Ettingshall Park
Lanesfield
Moxley
Wood Green
Wednesbury
Great Barr
Orton
Bradley
Coseley
Mesty Croft
Friar Park
Penn Common
WEDNESBURY ART GALLERY & MUSEUM
Sedgley
Cinder Hill
Wednesbury Oak
Stone Cross
Grove Vale
Netherby
Hurst Hill
Wallbrook
Ocker Hill
Balls Hill
Newton
Perry Beeches
The Wodehouse
Gospel End
Swan Village
Summer Hill
Golds Green
Hill Top
Bird End
Hamstead
The Foxhills
Woodsetton
Bloomfield
Toll End
Harvills Hawthorn
Hall End
Wombourne
Upper Gornal
Horseley Heath
Churchfield
Blakeley
Himley Park
Tipton
Tipton Green
Swan Village
WEST BROMWICH
Himley
Straits Green
Ruiton
Lower Gornal
Shaver's End
New Town
Guns Village
Brown's Green
Dudley Port
Tividale
Lambert's End
Gornalwood
London Fields
Eve Hill
Burnt Tree
Home Fm.
DUDLEY ZOO
Brades Village
Wall Heath
Oakfarm
Cooper's Bank
DUDLEY MUSEUM & ART GALLERY
DUDLEY
Oldbury
Handsworth
Shut End
Springs Mire
Oakham
The Village
Tansey Green
Tansley Hill
Darby's Hill
Sandwell
Dawley Brook
Tat Bank
Gib Heath
Kingswinford
Bromley
Pensnett
Woodside
Baptist End
Turner's Hill
Rood End
Winson Green
Ashwood
Springfield
Portway
Langley
Smethwick
Mount Pleasant
Brockmoor
Round Oak
Netherton
Bumble Hole
The Knowle
Whiteheath Gate
Londonderry
Darby End
Primrose Hill
Rowley Regis
Causeway Green
Summerfield Park
Wordsley
Buckpool
Brierley Hill
Bristnall Fields
Bearwood
Rotton Park Res.
Ladywood
Quarry Bank
Dudley Wood
Old Hill
Blackheath
Delph
Audnam
Cradley Heath
Hurst Green
Halfcot
Amblecote
Coalbournbrook
Coombeswood
Beech Lanes
Chad Valley
BIRMINGHAM BOTANICAL GARDEN
Hayden Cross
Holloway End
Stambermill
Overend
Harborne
Edgbaston
Stewponey
Lye
Cradley
The Hayes
Belle Vale
Short Cross
Quinton
Wollaston
Wollescote
Careless Green
Mucklow Hill
STOURBRIDGE
HALESOWEN
Ridgacre
BARBER INSTITUTE OF FINE ARTS
Old Swinford
Chawn Hill
Webb's Green
Lapal
Bourn Brook
Birmingham University
Whittington
Whittington Common
Lutley
Hasbury
Moor Fm.
California
Moor Street
Bournbrook
Pedmore
Wassell Gro. Fm.
Hodge Hill
Hayley Green
Abbey
HALESOWEN ABBEY
Woodgate
Weoley Castle
WEOLEY CASTLE
Selly Oak
Selly Park
Ten Acres
Sand Villas
Wychbury Hill
Illey
Bartley Green
Iverley Ho. Fm.
The Birches
Hagley
HAGLEY HALL
Hagley Park
Hagley Wood
Uffmoor Wood
Dove Ho. Fm.
Goodrest Fm.
Hunnington
Lower Illey
Woodcock Hill
Shenley Fields
Bartley Res.
Bournville
Stirchley
Five Ways
Chapel Fm.
Frankley Services
The Four Stones
Frankley Res.
Clent Grove
CLENT HILLS
Cotteridge
West Hagley
Lower Clent
Romsley
Egg Hill
Lifford
Churchill
Harborough Hall
Field Ho.
Clent
Ell Wood
Frankley Hill
Northfield
King's Norton
PATRICK COLLECTION
Whitenhall Fm.
Holy Cross
Frogmill Fm.
Blakedown
Wannerton Fm.
Broome
Walton Ho.
Calcot Hill
Gt. Farley Wood
Dayhouse Bank
Gannow Green
Turves Green
Walker's Heath
Red Hall
Breach Fm.
Hackman's Gate
Windmill Hill
Longbridge
Hosp.
Golf Co.
M5
M6
A449
A460
A41
A454
A4123
A461
A4148
A34
A4041
A4035
A4036
A491
A456
A458
A4040
A38
A441
A4540

APPROACHES TO BIRMINGHAM

Fazeley
DRAYTON MANOR PARK & ZOO
DRAYTON MANOR PARK MINIATURE RAILWAY
Drayton Bassett
Two Gates
Wilnecote
Glascote Heath
Belgrave
Birchmoor
Dosthill
Hockley
Freasley
Whateley
Edge Hill
Wood End
Kingsbury
Hurley Common
Hurley
Middleton
Hunts Green
Bodymoor Heath
Marston
Lea Marston
Whitacre Heath
Nether Whitacre
Over Whitacre
Hoggrill's End
Shustoke
Shustoke Res.
Church End
Coleshill
Maxstoke Castle
Maxstoke
Maxstoke Priory
Duke End
Curdworth
Minworth
Water Orton
Castle Bromwich
Wishaw
Grove End
Over Green
Walmley
Thimble End
SUTTON COLDFIELD
Maney
Reddicap Heath
Whitehouse Common
Four Oaks
Four Oaks Common
Four Oaks Park
Mere Green
Little Sutton
Roughley
Shenstone Woodend
Little Hay
Footherley
Little Aston
Streetly
Hardwick
Kingstanding
New Oscott
Boldmere
Wylde Green
Erdington
Perry Barr
Birchfield
Aston
Nechells
Bromford
Hodgehill
Washwood Heath
Ward End
Saltley
Vauxhall
Buckland End
Shard End
Kingshurst
Bacon's End
Tile Cross
Kitt's Green
Glebe Farm
Stechford
BIRMINGHAM
Bordesley Green
Little Bromwich
Small Heath
Yardley
Cockshut Hill
Garrett's Green
Lyndon Green
Gilbertstone
South Yardley
Hay Mills
Acock's Green
Tyseley
Sparkhill
Balsall Heath
Moseley
Wake Green
Springfield
Hall Green
Kineton Green
Olton
Ulverley Green
Sheldon
Wells Green
Marston Green
Coleshill Heath
Elmdon
Bickenhill
Middle Bickenhill
NATIONAL EXHIBITION CENTRE
BIRMINGHAM INTERNATIONAL
Stonebridge
Meriden
Little Packington
Packington Park
Great Pool
Hampton in Arden
Berkswell
Four Oaks
Flint's Green
Catherine de Barnes Heath
Elmdon Heath
Lode Heath
SOLIHULL
Shirley
Billesley
King's Heath
Yardley Wood
Warstock
Maypole
Shirley Heath
Solihull Lodge
Blossomfield
Santa Barbara
Copt Heath
Eastcote
Barston
Ravenshaw
GRAND UNION CANAL
BIRMINGHAM & FAZELEY CANAL
M6
M42
A38
A452
A446
A45
A5
A453
A4091
S T
D L A N D S
0 1 2 MILES

BIRMINGHAM
A34 WALSALL
A38(M) TO M6 Int. 6
GRAVELLY HILL
ASTON HALL
M5 Int. 1 WOLVERHAMPTON A41
A47 TO M6. Int. 5
A457 DUDLEY
A456 KIDDERMINSTER
A45 COVENTRY, BIRMINGHAM AIRPORT, NATIONAL EXHIBITION CENTRE M42
A41 WARWICK
A34 STRATFORD UPON-AVON
A38 WORCESTER
A441 REDDITCH
A435 EVESHAM
ASTON
A38(M)
ASTON EXPRESSWAY
NEW TOWN ROW
A4540
A34
A38
A47
SALTLEY RD.
DUDDESTON
VAUXHALL DUDDESTON
BROOKFIELDS
A457
NECHELLS PARKWAY
DARTMOUTH MIDDLEWAY
LAWLEY MIDDLEWAY
CORPORATION ST.
QUEENSWAY
JENNENS RD.
CURZON STREET
UNIVERSITY OF ASTON
LAW COURTS
General Hospital
METROPOLITAN CATHEDRAL
RAILWAY MOSAICS
MUSEUM OF SCIENCE & INDUSTRY
G.P.O. TOWER
ASSAY OFFICE
ST. PHILIP'S CATHEDRAL
MUSEUM & ART GALLERY
REPERTORY THEA.
NATIONAL INDOOR ARENA (U/C)
CONVENTION CENTRE
CENTRAL T.V.
TOWN HALL
Shopping Centre
NEW STREET
ROTUNDA
BULL RING
ST. MARTIN'S CIRCUS
ST. MARTIN'S CH.
DIGBETH HIGH ST.
DERITEND
OLD CROWN HO.
BORDESLEY
LADYWOOD
LADYWOOD MIDDLEWAY
BROAD STREET
ISLINGTON ROW
FIVE WAYS
LEE BANK ROAD
ACCIDENT HOSPITAL
BRISTOL STREET
BELGRAVE ROAD
M. Boulton Tech College
CAMP HILL
SANDY LANE
COVENTRY ROAD
SMALL HEATH HWY
STRATFORD ROAD
HIGHGATE MIDDLEWAY
SPARK BROOK
HIGHGATE ROAD
BALSALL HEATH
A4167
RAILWAY MUSEUM
EDGBASTON
CALTHORPE PARK
EDGBASTON GOLF COURSE
EDGBASTON POOL
Warwickshire County Cricket Grd
MOSELEY ROAD
St. Andrews Birmingham City F.C.
0 ¼ MILE

APPROACHES TO BLACKPOOL

Preesall Sands
North Wharf
DOUGLAS (SUMMER ONLY)
FLEETWOOD
Rossall Point
FLEETWOOD MUSEUM
A585
A587
Knott End-on-Sea
Pilling Lane
Muffy's Platt Fm.
Smithson's Fm.
Little Tongues
Parrox Hall
Preesall
Pointer Fm.
New Heys Fm.
Coat Walls Fm.
Preesall Moss Side
Preesall Park
Stalmine
Stalmine Moss
Moor End
Heads
Height o' th' Hill
Rossall School
Fleetwood Fm.
Burn Hall
Cleveleys
Burn Naze
RIVER WYRE
Cold Row
Sower Carr
Staynall
Brick Ho.
Crombleholme Fm.
Trunnah
Stanah
Thornton
Hambleton
Anchorsholme
Little Bispham
Little Thornton
Bank Fm.
Mill Fm.
Norbreck
Norcross
Shard Bri.
Moors Fm.
Churchtown
Toll
Liscoe
Four Lane Ends
Skippool
Mains Hall
Sch.
Carleton
Poulton-le-Fylde
A585
Golf Co.
Little Singleton
Warbreck
Little Carleton
Singleton
North Shore
Old Field Carr
Hardhorn
Main Dyke
A586
Queenstown
Little Layton
Avenham Hall
Summerer Fm.
Layton
Newton
Todderstaffe Hall
Weeton Camp
North Pier
Hosp.
Golf Course
Staining
Stanley Park
BLACKPOOL ZOOLOGICAL GARDENS
Hawes Ho.
Preese Hall
BLACKPOOL
Central Pier
BLACKPOOL COASTAL TRAMWAY
Great Marton
Marton Mere
Weeton
Mythop
A583
South Pier
Hawes Side
Mereside
Ream Hills
M55
South Shore
Marton Moss Side
Moss Ho Fm.
Peel Hill Fm.
Little Plumpton
Great Plumpton
Common Edge
A583
Squires Gate
Westby
Great Marton Moss
Peel
SQUIRES GATE
Holiday Camp
Lower Ballam
Golf Course
Convalescent Home
Lytham Moss
Higher Ballam
Moss Side
ST. ANNES-ON-THE-SEA
Moss Hall Fm.
Hey Houses
St. Anne's
Golf Course
Ansdell
Golf Course
Saltcoates
ART GALLERY
Salter's Bank
ANSDELL & FAIRHAVEN
Lytham Hall
Fairhaven
A584
LYTHAM ST. ANNE'S
Lytham
LYTHAM MOTIVE POWER MUSEUM
Fairhaven Lake
Church Scar
0 1 2 MILES

BLACKPOOL

A584 FLEETWOOD (A587)
A586 LANCASTER (A6)
North Station
NORTH PIER THEATRE
NORTH PIER
PROMENADE
GRUNDY ART GALL.
Talbot Sq.
CLIFTON
CHURCH
STREET
WINTER GDNS THEATRE & OPERA HOUSE
BLACKPOOL TOWER
AQUARIUM & ZOO
HORNBY ROAD
Leamington Road
Lincoln Rd.
Whitegate Drive
Newton Dr.
Bryan Rd.
Forest Gate
LANCASTER (A6)
B5266
Devonshire Rd.
London Rd.
Caunce Street
Granville
Park Road
Central Drive
Palatine
Read's Avenue
Manor Rd.
St. Albans Rd.
Gloucester Av.
Cumberland Ave.
Westmoreland Av.
LOUIS TUSSAUD'S WAXWORKS
CENTRAL PIER THEATRE
CENTRAL PIER
Chapel
Bonny St.
THE GOLDEN MILE
Princess St.
Blackpool Borough Rugby Grd.
Rigby Road
Coach Sta.
SEAFRONT TRAMWAY
SOUTH PIER THEATRE
SOUTH PIER
Recreation Ground
Blackpool F.C.
A583 PRESTON M55
A584 LYTHAM ST. ANNE'S
0 ¼ MILE

BOLTON

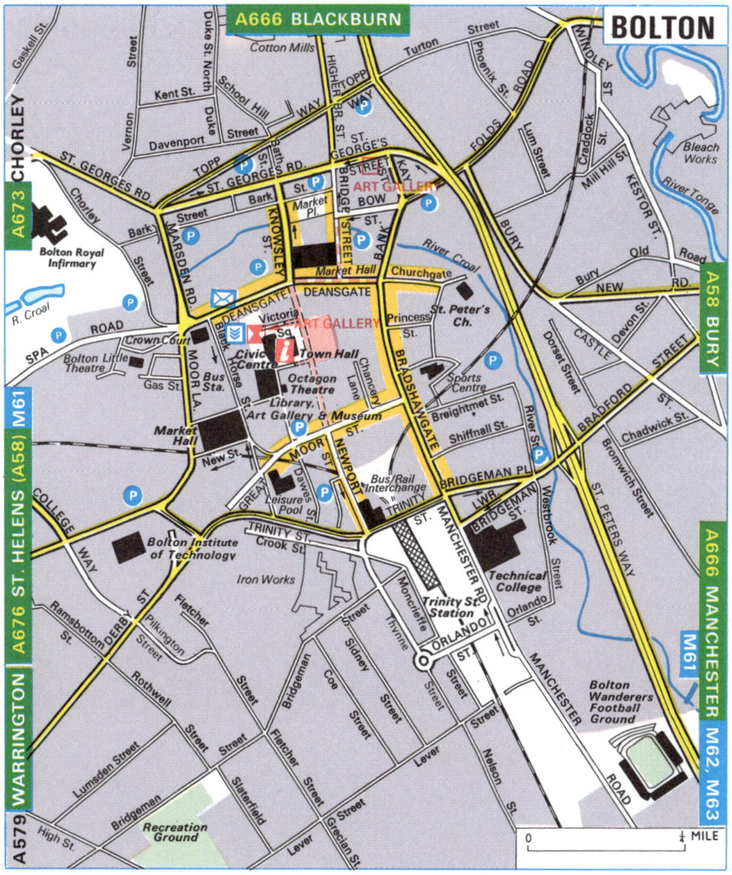
A666 BLACKBURN
Cotton Mills
Kent St.
Davenport Street
Turton Street
ST. GEORGES RD.
A673 CHORLEY
Bolton Royal Infirmary
R. Croal
ST. GEORGE'S RD.
ART GALLERY
Market Pl.
Market Hall
DEANSGATE
Churchgate
River Croal
St. Peter's Ch.
Bleach Works
River Tonge
A58 BURY
Crown Court
Civic Centre
Town Hall
Octagon Theatre
Library, Art Gallery & Museum
Bolton Little Theatre
Bus Sta.
Market Hall
Sports Centre
Breightmet St.
Shiffnall St.
Leisure Pool
Bus/Rail Interchange
BRIDGEMAN PL.
Bolton Institute of Technology
Iron Works
Trinity St. Station
Technical College
A676 ST. HELENS (A58) M61
A666 MANCHESTER
M61
Bolton Wanderers Football Ground
M62, M63
A579 WARRINGTON
Recreation Ground
0 ¼ MILE

APPROACHES TO BOURNEMOUTH

BOURNEMOUTH

APPROACHES TO BRADFORD

APPROACHES TO BRIGHTON
BRIGHTON
HOVE
LEWES
SHOREHAM by Sea
Portslade by Sea
Southwick
Kingston by Sea
Shoreham Beach
SHOREHAM HARBOUR & DOCKS
Fishergate
Portslade
Southern Cross
Mile Oak
Hangleton
West Blatchington
Tongdean
Aldrington
Red Hill
Patcham
Withdean
Preston
Hollingbury
Coldean
Stanmer
Stanmer Park
Moulsecoomb
North Moulsecoomb
Bevendean
Lower Bevendean
Kemp Town
Black Rock
Woodingdean
Ovingdean
Rottingdean
Saltdean
Telscombe
Telscombe Cliffs
Peacehaven
Falmer
Kingston near Lewes
Iford
Rodmell
Wallands Park
Offham
Hamsey
Cooksbridge
Plumpton
Westmeston
Clayton
Pyecombe
Poynings
Fulking
Edburton
Saddlescombe
Devil's Dyke
Brighton Marina
Palace Pier
VOLK'S ELECTRIC RAILWAY
SOUTH DOWNS WAY
University of Sussex
0 1 2 MILES

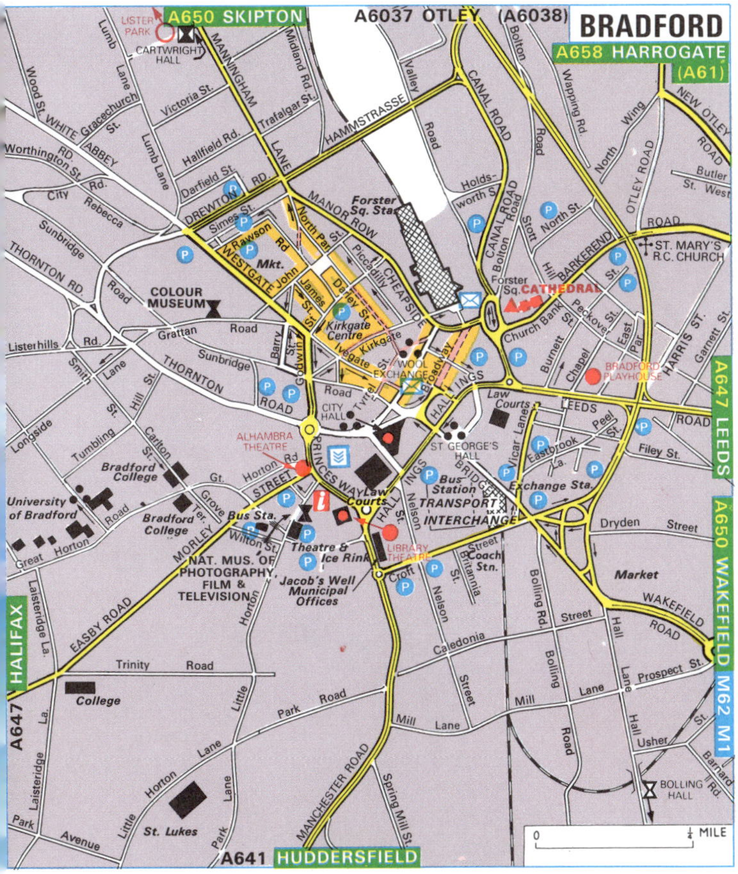
BRADFORD
A650 SKIPTON
A6037 OTLEY
(A6038)
A658 HARROGATE
(A61)
A647 LEEDS
A650 WAKEFIELD
M62 M1
A641 HUDDERSFIELD
A647 HALIFAX
CATHEDRAL
COLOUR MUSEUM
ALHAMBRA THEATRE
BRADFORD PLAYHOUSE
University of Bradford
Bradford College
NAT. MUS. OF PHOTOGRAPHY, FILM & TELEVISION
Jacob's Well Municipal Offices
TRANSPORT INTERCHANGE
Forster Sq. Sta.
ST. MARY'S R.C. CHURCH
CARTWRIGHT HALL
BOLLING HALL
CITY HALL
Law Courts
St. Lukes
College
0 ½ MILE

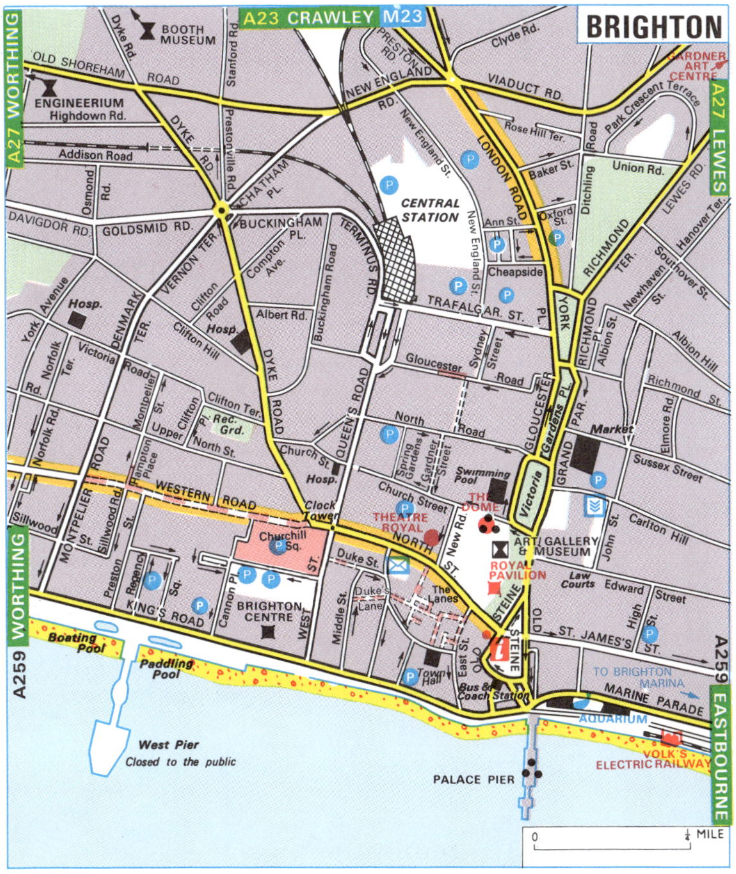
BRIGHTON
A23 CRAWLEY M23
A27 WORTHING
A27 LEWES
A259 WORTHING
A259 EASTBOURNE
BOOTH MUSEUM
ENGINEERIUM
CENTRAL STATION
Churchill Sq.
BRIGHTON CENTRE
THEATRE ROYAL
THE DOME
ART GALLERY & MUSEUM
ROYAL PAVILION
GARDNER ARTS CENTRE
West Pier
Closed to the public
PALACE PIER
AQUARIUM
VOLK'S ELECTRIC RAILWAY
TO BRIGHTON MARINA
MARINE PARADE
KING'S ROAD
WESTERN ROAD
Boating Pool
Paddling Pool
0 ½ MILE

APPROACHES TO BRISTOL

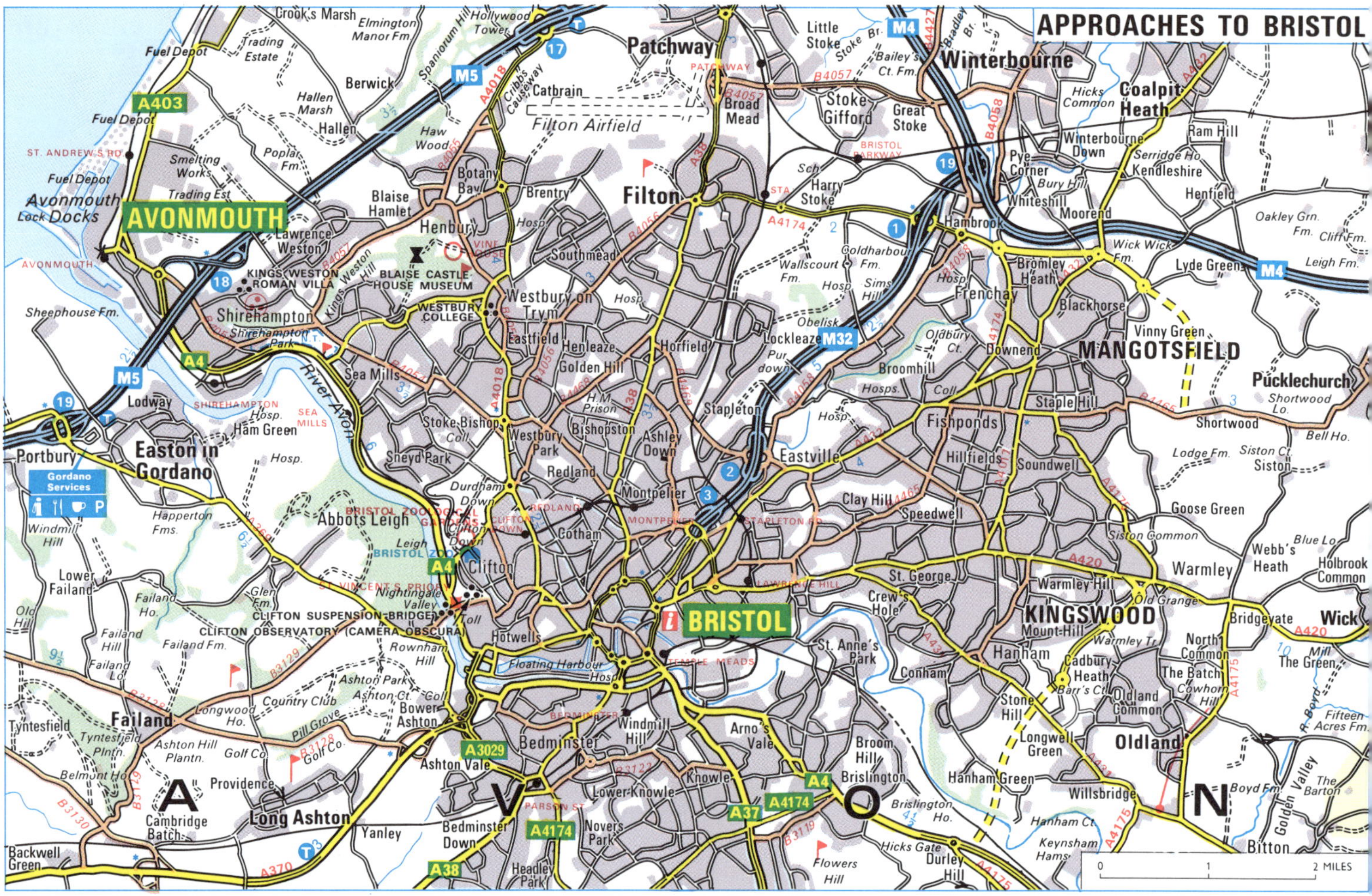
APPROACHES TO BRISTOL
AVONMOUTH
Avonmouth Lock Docks
Patchway
Winterbourne
Coalpit Heath
Filton
Filton Airfield
Henbury
Shirehampton
Westbury on Trym
Stoke Gifford
Frenchay
MANGOTSFIELD
Pucklechurch
Fishponds
Easton in Gordano
Portbury
Abbots Leigh
Clifton
BRISTOL
KINGSWOOD
Hanham
Oldland
Bedminster
Long Ashton
Failand
Brislington
Warmley
Wick
Keynsham
A V O N
River Avon
Floating Harbour
CLIFTON SUSPENSION BRIDGE
BLAISE CASTLE HOUSE MUSEUM
KINGSWESTON ROMAN VILLA
M5
M4
M32
A403
A4
A38
A37
A420
A4174
A3029
Gordano Services
0 1 2 MILES

BRISTOL

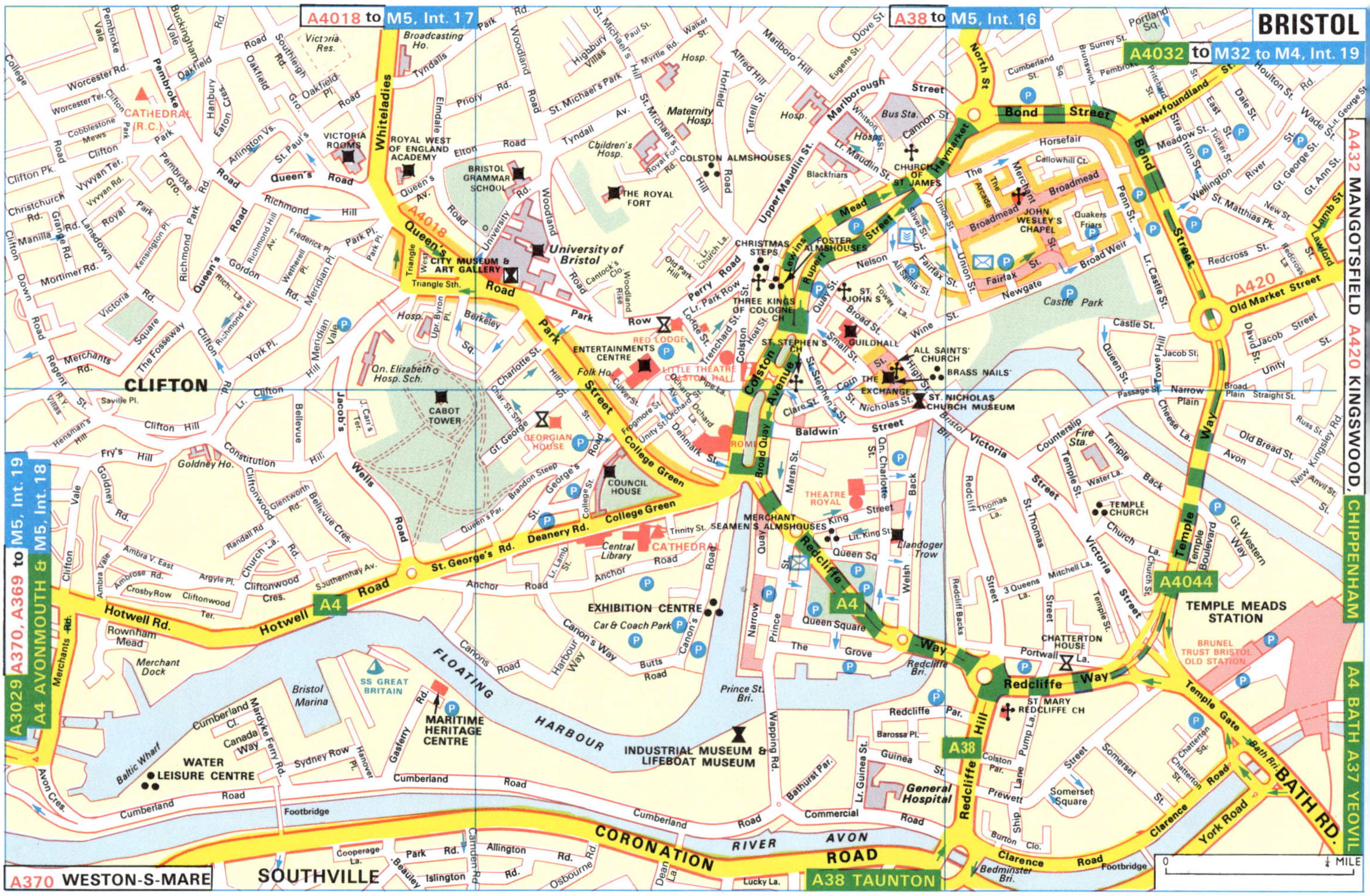
BRISTOL
A4018 to M5, Int. 17
A38 to M5, Int. 16
A4032 to M32 to M4, Int. 19
A432 MANGOTSFIELD A420 KINGSWOOD, CHIPPENHAM
A4 BATH A37 YEOVIL
A3029 A370, A369 to M5, Int. 19 A4 AVONMOUTH & M5, Int. 18
A370 WESTON-S-MARE
A38 TAUNTON
CLIFTON
SOUTHVILLE
CABOT TOWER
CITY MUSEUM & ART GALLERY
University of Bristol
THE ROYAL FORT
COLSTON ALMSHOUSES
CHRISTMAS STEPS
GEORGIAN HOUSE
COUNCIL HOUSE
CATHEDRAL
EXHIBITION CENTRE
SS GREAT BRITAIN
MARITIME HERITAGE CENTRE
INDUSTRIAL MUSEUM & LIFEBOAT MUSEUM
WATER LEISURE CENTRE
JOHN WESLEY'S CHAPEL
Broadmead
Castle Park
ST NICHOLAS CHURCH MUSEUM
THE EXCHANGE
ALL SAINTS' CHURCH
BRASS NAILS
GUILDHALL
THEATRE ROYAL
TEMPLE CHURCH
TEMPLE MEADS STATION
BRUNEL TRUST BRISTOL OLD STATION
ST MARY REDCLIFFE CH
CHATTERTON HOUSE
General Hospital
FLOATING HARBOUR
RIVER AVON
CORONATION ROAD
Hotwell Rd.
Park Street
Bond Street
Temple Way
Redcliffe Way
BATH RD.
0 1/4 MILE

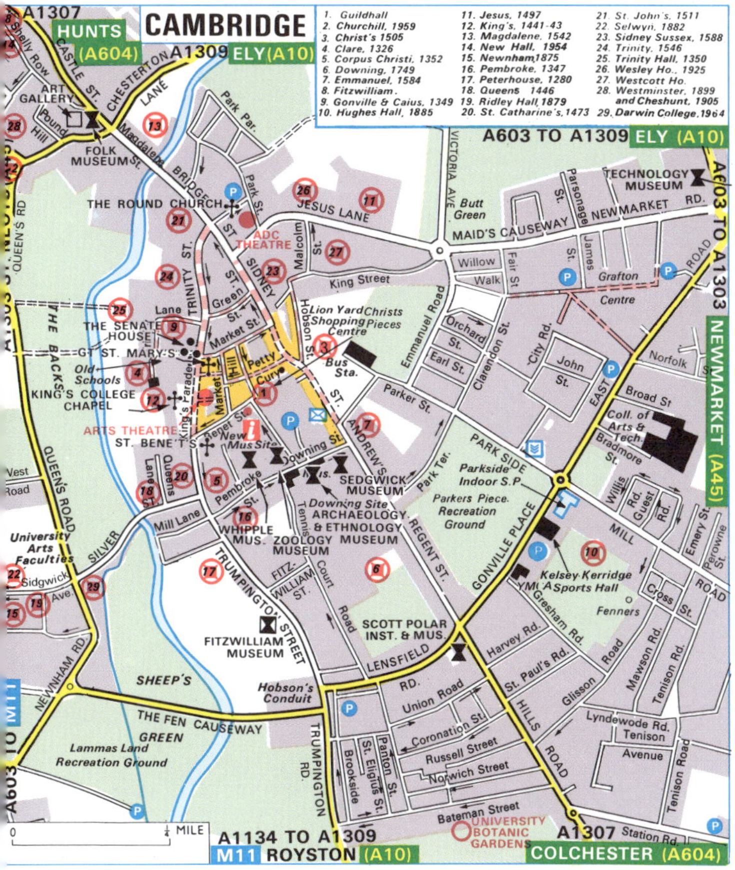
CAMBRIDGE
A1307
HUNTS (A604)
A1309 ELY (A10)
1. Guildhall
2. Churchill, 1959
3. Christ's 1505
4. Clare, 1326
5. Corpus Christi, 1352
6. Downing, 1749
7. Emmanuel, 1584
8. Fitzwilliam
9. Gonville & Caius, 1349
10. Hughes Hall, 1885
11. Jesus, 1497
12. King's, 1441-43
13. Magdalene, 1542
14. New Hall, 1954
15. Newnham 1875
16. Pembroke, 1347
17. Peterhouse, 1280
18. Queens 1446
19. Ridley Hall 1879
20. St. Catharine's 1473
21. St. John's, 1511
22. Selwyn, 1882
23. Sidney Sussex, 1588
24. Trinity, 1546
25. Trinity Hall, 1350
26. Wesley Ho., 1925
27. Westcott Ho.
28. Westminster, 1899 and Cheshunt, 1905
29. Darwin College, 1964
A603 TO A1309 ELY (A10)
A603 TO A1303 NEWMARKET (A45)
TECHNOLOGY MUSEUM
FOLK MUSEUM
THE ROUND CHURCH
ADC THEATRE
JESUS LANE
MAID'S CAUSEWAY
NEWMARKET RD.
King Street
Lion Yard Shopping Centre
Christs Pieces
THE SENATE HOUSE
GT. ST. MARY'S
Old Schools
KING'S COLLEGE CHAPEL
ARTS THEATRE
ST. BENET'S
Bus Sta.
Parker St.
PARK SIDE
Parkside Indoor S.P.
Parkers Piece Recreation Ground
Coll. of Arts & Tech.
SEDGWICK MUSEUM
Downing Site ARCHAEOLOGY & ETHNOLOGY MUSEUM
WHIPPLE MUS.
ZOOLOGY MUSEUM
SCOTT POLAR INST. & MUS.
Kelsey Kerridge Sports Hall
Fenners
University Arts Faculties
FITZWILLIAM MUSEUM
SHEEP'S GREEN
Hobson's Conduit
THE FEN CAUSEWAY
Lammas Land Recreation Ground
LENSFIELD RD.
TRUMPINGTON ST.
TRUMPINGTON RD.
UNIVERSITY BOTANIC GARDENS
A1134 TO A1309
M11 ROYSTON (A10)
A1307
COLCHESTER (A604)
A603 TO M11
0 ¼ MILE

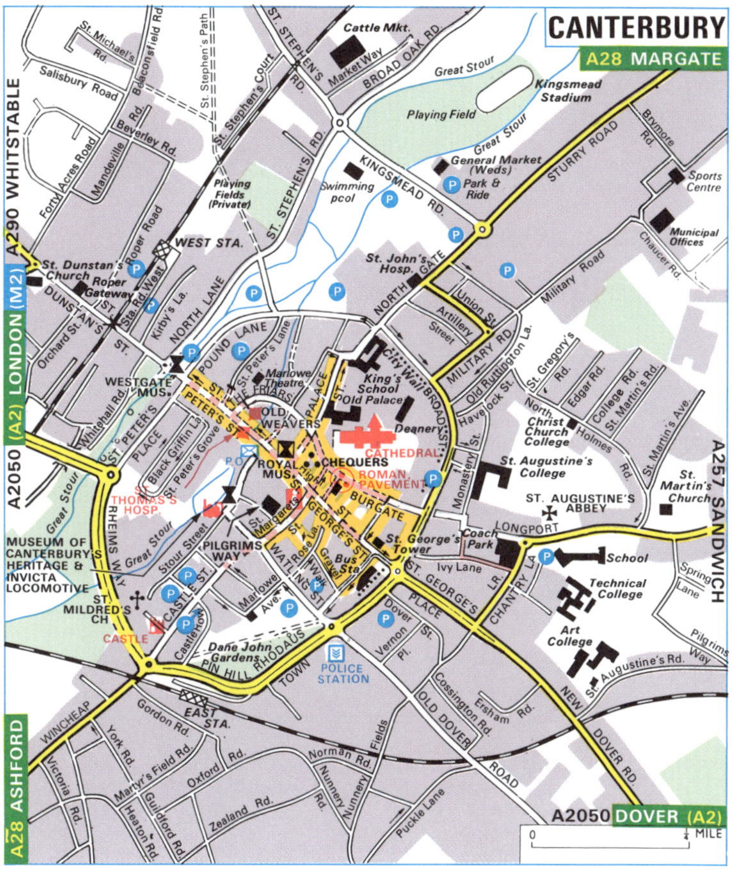
CANTERBURY
A28 MARGATE
A290 WHITSTABLE
A2050 (A2) LONDON (M2)
A28 ASHFORD
A2050 DOVER (A2)
A257 SANDWICH
Cattle Mkt.
Kingsmead Stadium
Playing Field
Great Stour
General Market (Weds)
Park & Ride
Sports Centre
Municipal Offices
Swimming pool
KINGSMEAD RD.
WEST STA.
St. Dunstan's Church
Roper Gateway
St. John's Hosp.
WESTGATE MUS.
Marlowe Theatre
King's School
Old Palace
Deanery
CATHEDRAL
OLD WEAVERS
ROYAL MUS.
CHEQUERS
ROMAN PAVEMENT
BURGATE
Christ Church College
St. Augustine's College
ST. AUGUSTINE'S ABBEY
St. Martin's Church
St. George's Tower
Coach Park
School
Technical College
Art College
MUSEUM OF CANTERBURY'S HERITAGE & INVICTA LOCOMOTIVE
THOMAS'S HOSP.
PILGRIMS WAY
ST. MILDRED'S CH.
CASTLE
Dane John Gardens
POLICE STATION
EAST STA.
OLD DOVER RD.
NEW DOVER RD.
0 ¼ MILE

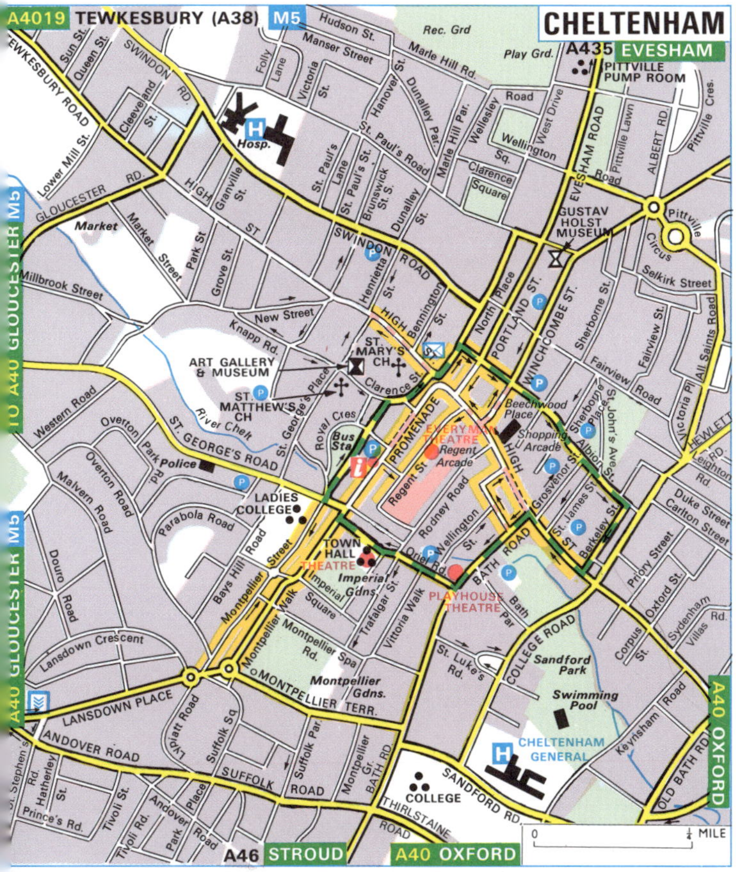
CHELTENHAM
A4019 TEWKESBURY (A38) M5
A435 EVESHAM
PITTVILLE PUMP ROOM
Hosp.
Market
GUSTAV HOLST MUSEUM
SWINDON ROAD
ART GALLERY & MUSEUM
ST. MARY'S CH.
ST. MATTHEW'S CH.
Police
LADIES COLLEGE
TOWN HALL
THEATRE
Imperial Gdns.
PROMENADE
EVERYMAN THEATRE
Regent Arcade
Beechwood Place
Shopping Arcade
PLAYHOUSE THEATRE
Montpellier Gdns.
MONTPELLIER TERR.
Sandford Park
Swimming Pool
CHELTENHAM GENERAL
COLLEGE
A40 GLOUCESTER M5
A40 OXFORD
A46 STROUD
A40 OXFORD
0 ¼ MILE

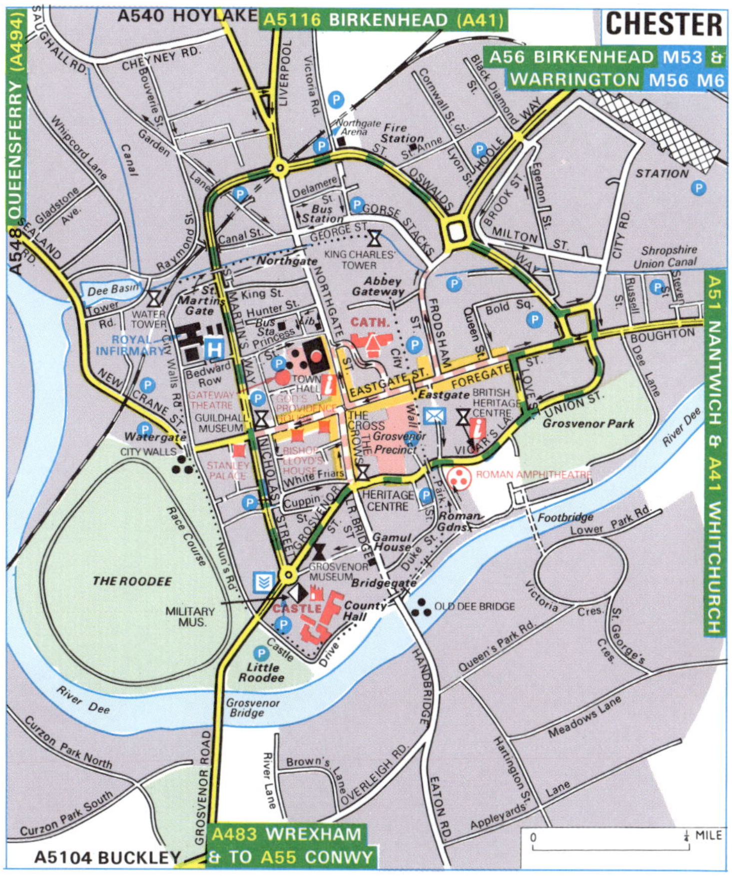
CHESTER
A540 HOYLAKE
A5116 BIRKENHEAD (A41)
A56 BIRKENHEAD M53 & WARRINGTON M56 M6
A548 QUEENSFERRY (A494)
A51 NANTWICH & A41 WHITCHURCH
Northgate Arena
Fire Station
STATION
Shropshire Union Canal
KING CHARLES' TOWER
Abbey Gateway
Dee Basin
WATER TOWER
ROYAL INFIRMARY
CATH.
GATEWAY THEATRE
GUILDHALL MUSEUM
TOWN HALL
EASTGATE ST.
FOREGATE
BRITISH HERITAGE CENTRE
Grosvenor Park
Grosvenor Precinct
Watergate
CITY WALLS
STANLEY PALACE
BISHOP LLOYD'S HOUSE
ROMAN AMPHITHEATRE
HERITAGE CENTRE
Roman Gdns.
Gamul House
GROSVENOR MUSEUM
Bridgegate
THE ROODEE
MILITARY MUS.
CASTLE
County Hall
OLD DEE BRIDGE
Little Roodee
River Dee
Grosvenor Bridge
A483 WREXHAM & TO A55 CONWY
A5104 BUCKLEY
0 ¼ MILE

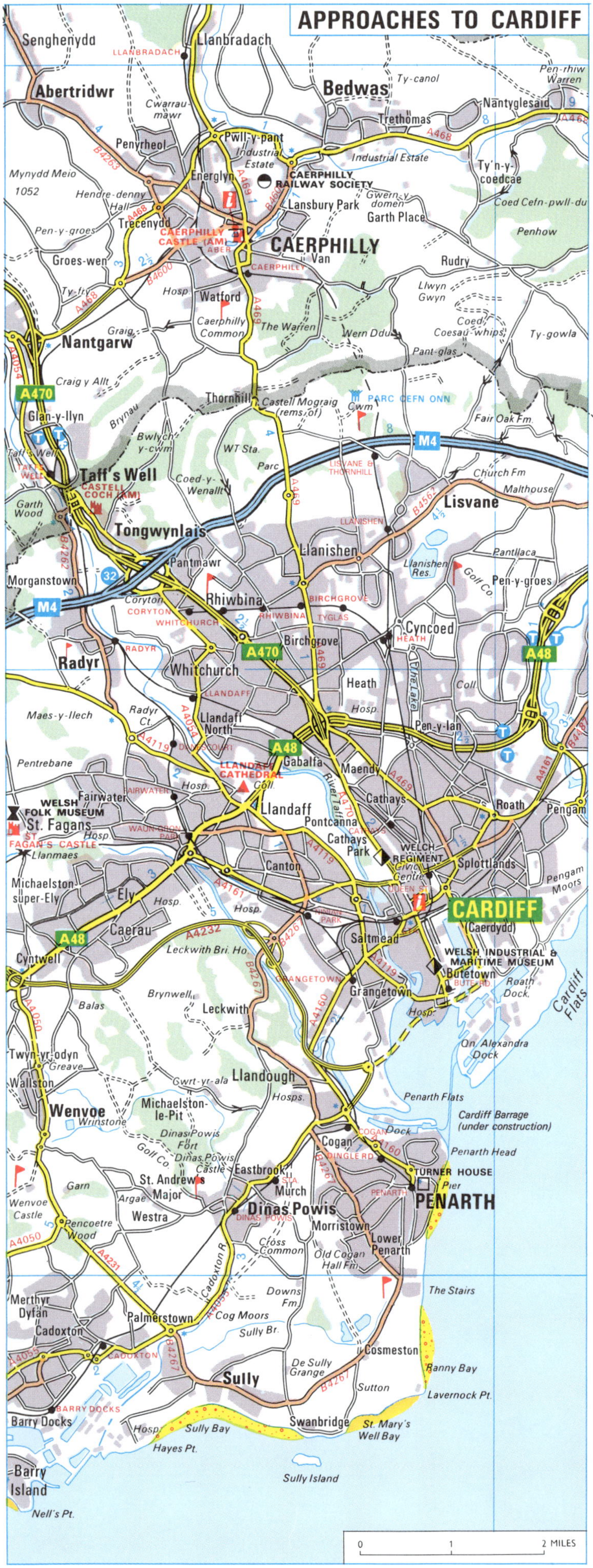
APPROACHES TO CARDIFF
Senghenydd
Llanbradach
Abertridwr
Bedwas
Trethomas
Nantyglesaid
Penyrheol
Pwll-y-pant
Energlyn
CAERPHILLY RAILWAY SOCIETY
Lansbury Park
Garth Place
Trecenydd
CAERPHILLY
Van
Rudry
Penhow
Groes-wen
Watford
The Warren
Nantgarw
Wern Ddu
Ty-gowla
Craig y Allt
Thornhill
Castell Mograig (rems. of)
PARC CEFN ONN
A470
Glan-y-llyn
Taff's Well
CASTELL COCH (AM)
Garth Wood
M4
Lisvane
Church Fm
Malthouse
Tongwynlais
Pantmawr
Llanishen
Llanishen Res.
Pantllaca
Pen-y-groes
Morganstown
Rhiwbina
Birchgrove
Cyncoed
Radyr
Whitchurch
A48
Heath
Maes-y-llech
Llandaff North
Pen-y-lan
Pentrebane
Gabalfa
Maendy
LLANDAFF CATHEDRAL
WELSH FOLK MUSEUM
St. Fagans
ST. FAGAN'S CASTLE
Fairwater
Llandaff
Pontcanna
Cathays
Cathays Park
Roath
Pengam
Michaelston-super-Ely
Ely
Canton
WELCH REGIMENT
Splottlands
Caerau
CARDIFF
(Caerdydd)
Cyntwell
Leckwith Bri. Ho.
Saltmead
WELSH INDUSTRIAL & MARITIME MUSEUM
Butetown
Grangetown
Roath Dock
Cardiff Flats
Balas
Brynwell
Leckwith
Twyn-yr-odyn
Walston
Llandough
Qn. Alexandra Dock
Wenvoe
Michaelston-le-Pit
Penarth Flats
Cardiff Barrage (under construction)
Dinas Powis Fort
Cogan
Penarth Head
Garn
St. Andrews Major
Eastbrook
TURNER HOUSE
PENARTH
Wenvoe Castle
Westra
Murch
Dinas Powis
Morristown
Pencoetre Wood
Cross Common
Old Cogan Hall Fm.
Lower Penarth
The Stairs
Merthyr Dyfan
Downs Fm.
Cadoxton
Palmerstown
Cog Moors
Sully Br.
Cosmeston
Sully
De Sully Grange
Ranny Bay
Sutton
Lavernock Pt.
Barry Docks
Sully Bay
Swanbridge
St. Mary's Well Bay
Hayes Pt.
Barry Island
Sully Island
Nell's Pt.
0
1
2 MILES

A469 CAERPHILLY
CARDIFF
A48
WHITCHURCH RD
CRWYS ROAD
Cemetery
Pleasure Gardens
MAENDY
Barracks
Maendy Stadium
A470 to M4, Int. 32 & MERTHYR TYDFIL
CATHAYS
A469 to A48 NEWPORT
BLACKWEIR
NORTH ROAD
Cathays Stn.
UNIVERSITY OF WALES COLLEGE OF CARDIFF
TEMPLE OF HEALTH & WELSH OFFICE
TEMPLE OF PEACE
NATIONAL WAR MEMORIAL
U.W.C.C.
SHERMAN THEATRE
CATHAYS PARK
NATIONAL MUSEUM OF WALES
A4119 LLANTRISANT
Glamorgan County Cricket Ground
NATIONAL SPORTS CENTRE
Sophia Gardens
COUNTY HALL
CITY HALL
UNIVERSITY REGISTRY
LAW COURTS
INVESTITURE FOUNTAIN
Castle Mews
A4161 to A48 NEWPORT
BLACKFRIARS PRIORY
MUNICIPAL BUILDINGS
NEW THEATRE
Queen St. Station
To St. David's Hosp.
CARDIFF CASTLE
Castle Grn.
Queens West Shopping Centre
PHOTOGRAPHIC GALLERY
CATHEDRAL ST. DAVID'S
Cardiff Bri.
Shopping Centre
ST. JOHN THE BAPTIST CH.
A4161 to A48 PORT TALBOT, SWANSEA & M4, Int. 38
Market
ST. DAVID'S HALL
Library
Mkt.
WORLD TRADE CENTRE
Cardiff Arms Park
(Nat. Rugby Football Grd.)
WALES INTERNATIONAL ICE RINK
Bus Station
WALES EMPIRE POOL
Cardiff Central Station
River Taff
Works
Sevenoaks Park
A4160 PENARTH BARRY
Grangetown Stn.
GRANGETOWN
(Afon Taf)
0
1 MILE

APPROACHES TO COVENTRY
A5
A444
Woodford Bri.
Purley Park
Monks Park Wood
Quarries
R. Anker
Caldecote
Lindley Lo.
Harper's Hill
White Hall Fm.
HARTSHILL HAYES
Ridge Lane
Oldbury
COVENTRY CANAL
Top Fm.
Hartshill
Weddington
B4114
Ansley Hall
Chapel End
Camp Hill
Church End
Plough Hill
Galley Common
A47
NUNEATON
Ansley
Whittleford
Abbey
NUNEATON MUSEUM & ART GALLERY
Nuneaton Fields
Mine
Stockingford
Robinson's End
B4112
B4102
Attleborough
Arley Ho. Fm.
Nuthurst Heath Fm.
Seeswood Pool
Chilvers Coton
Hill Fm.
Coton Lawn
Griff Hollow
Temple Ho.
Astley Castle
ARBURY HALL
The Lawn
White Stone
New Arley
Astley
Arbury Park
ASHBY CANAL
Griff
Cowley Wood
The South Fm.
Griff Lo. Fm.
Marston Jabbett
How Green
Collycroft
Wood End
Cow Lees
Bedworth Woodlands
High Ho. Farm
Taffs Fm.
Astley Ct.
BEDWORTH
Weston in Arden
The Grange
Corley Services
Market End
Bedworth Heath
Coalpit Field
Bulkington
Black Bank
Breach Brook
M6
Newland Fm.
Newland Hall
Keresley Newlands
Goodyers End
Hayes Green
Hollyhurst
Corley
Little Bayton
Barnacle
Ash Green
Neal's Green
Hawkesbury
Special School
Keresley Ho.
Wall Hill
Keresley
Rowley's Green
Longford
Foxford
Alderman's Green
M69
Hawkes End
Hosp
Holbrooks
Hall Green
Sherbourne Ho. Fm.
Brownshill Green
Whitmore Park
Little Heath
Foleshill
Wood End
Potter's Green
Coundon
Court House Green
Henley Green
A4600
Allesley
Radford
R. Sowe
Walsgrave on Sowe
R. Sherbourne
Great Heath
Stoke Heath
Wyken
A46
Castle
A4114
Church End
Spon End
Sowe Bri.
Coombe Pool
Lime Tree Park
Whoberly
Hearsall Common
Gosford Green
The Woodlands
A428
Stoke Binley Bri.
Binley
B4101
CANLEY
Earlsdon
WHITEFRIARS MUSEUM
COVENTRY
Ernesford Grange
Training College
Golf Co.
Stivichall Common
Cheylesmore
COVENTRY ZOO PARK
Whitley Common
Pinley
Piles Coppice
A45
Canley
Hosp
Kirby Corner
The University of Warwick
Stivichall
A444
Willenhall
The Leasowes
Finham
LUNT ROMAN FORT
Tollbar End
Ryton Bri.
Ryton-on-Dunsmore
Cryfield Grange
Castle
Baginton
COVENTRY
King's Hill
Golf Course
A423
Crackley
Westley Bri.
R. Sowe
A46
Finham Brook
Stoneleigh Grange
Bubbenhall Bri.
A445
Police College
Golf Course
Stoneleigh
Mill End
Sowe Mouth
Bubbenhall
Ryton Wood
STONELEIGH FARM & COUNTRY CENTRE
Cloud Bri.
Kenilworth
Castle End
National Agriculture Centre
Stare Bri.
Sch. of Farm Mechanization
Stretton Lo. Fm.
Windy Arbour
Abbey
STONELEIGH ABBEY
Stareton
Bubbenhall Ho.
A452
0
1
2 MILES

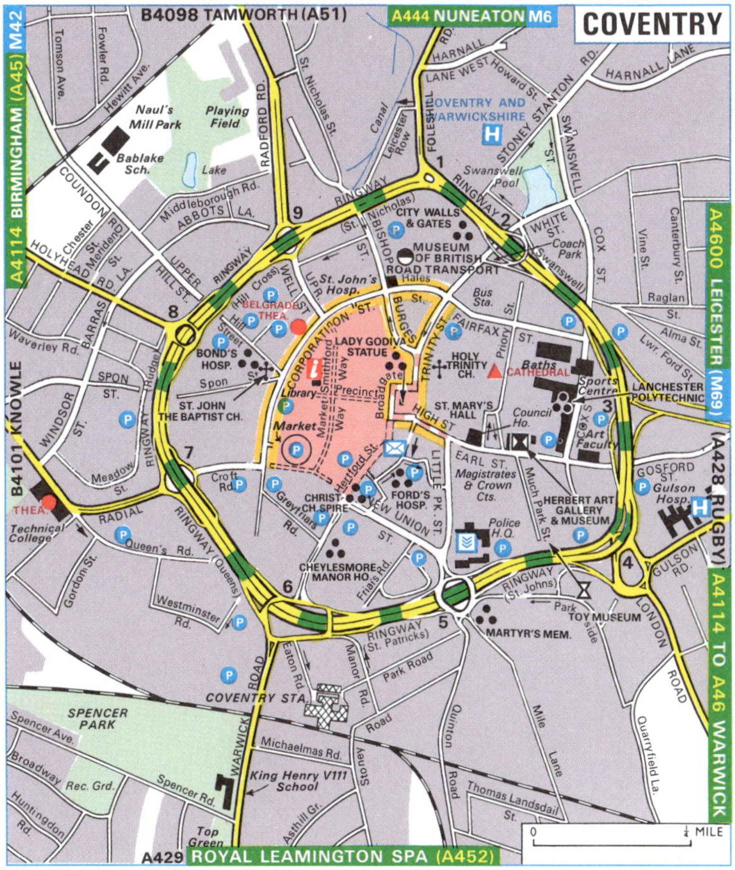

COVENTRY
B4098 TAMWORTH (A51)
A444 NUNEATON M6
M42
A4114 BIRMINGHAM (A45)
A4600 LEICESTER (M69)
A428 RUGBY)
A4114 TO A46 WARWICK
B4101 KNOWLE
A429 ROYAL LEAMINGTON SPA (A452)
Naul's Mill Park
Playing Field
Bablake Sch.
COVENTRY AND WARWICKSHIRE
Swanswell Pool
CITY WALLS & GATES
MUSEUM OF BRITISH ROAD TRANSPORT
BELGRADE THEA.
St. John's Hosp.
BOND'S HOSP.
LADY GODIVA STATUE
HOLY TRINITY CH.
CATHEDRAL
Sports Centre
LANCHESTER POLYTECHNIC
ST. JOHN THE BAPTIST CH.
Library
Precinct
ST. MARY'S HALL
Council Ho.
Art Faculty
Market
FORD'S HOSP.
CHRIST CH. SPIRE
Magistrates & Crown Cts.
HERBERT ART GALLERY & MUSEUM
Gulson Hosp.
Technical College
THEA.
Police H.Q.
CHEYLESMORE MANOR HO.
TOY MUSEUM
MARTYR'S MEM.
COVENTRY STA.
SPENCER PARK
King Henry VIII School
Top Green
RINGWAY
0
¼ MILE

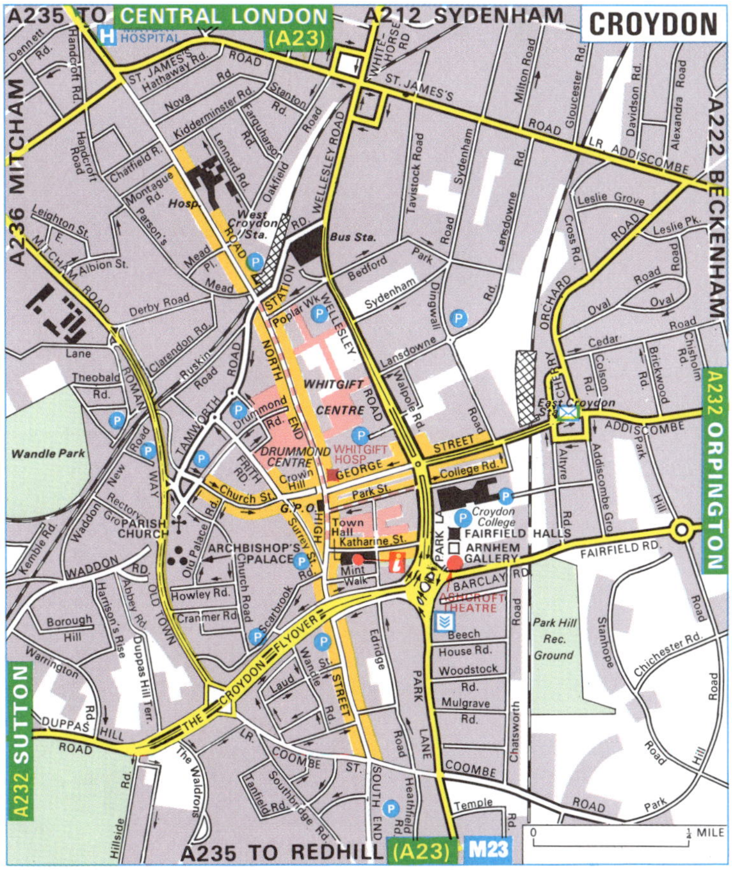

A235 TO CENTRAL LONDON (A23)
A212 SYDENHAM
CROYDON
HOSPITAL
A236 MITCHAM
A222 BECKENHAM
A232 ORPINGTON
A232 SUTTON
A235 TO REDHILL (A23)
M23
ST. JAMES'S ROAD
ADDISCOMBE
Hosp
West Croydon Sta.
Bus Sta.
WHITGIFT CENTRE
DRUMMOND CENTRE
WHITGIFT HOSP
Wandle Park
PARISH CHURCH
ARCHBISHOP'S PALACE
Town Hall
Croydon College
FAIRFIELD HALLS
ARNHEM GALLERY
ASHCROFT THEATRE
East Croydon
Park Hill Rec. Ground
THE CROYDON FLYOVER
DUPPAS HILL ROAD
0
¼ MILE

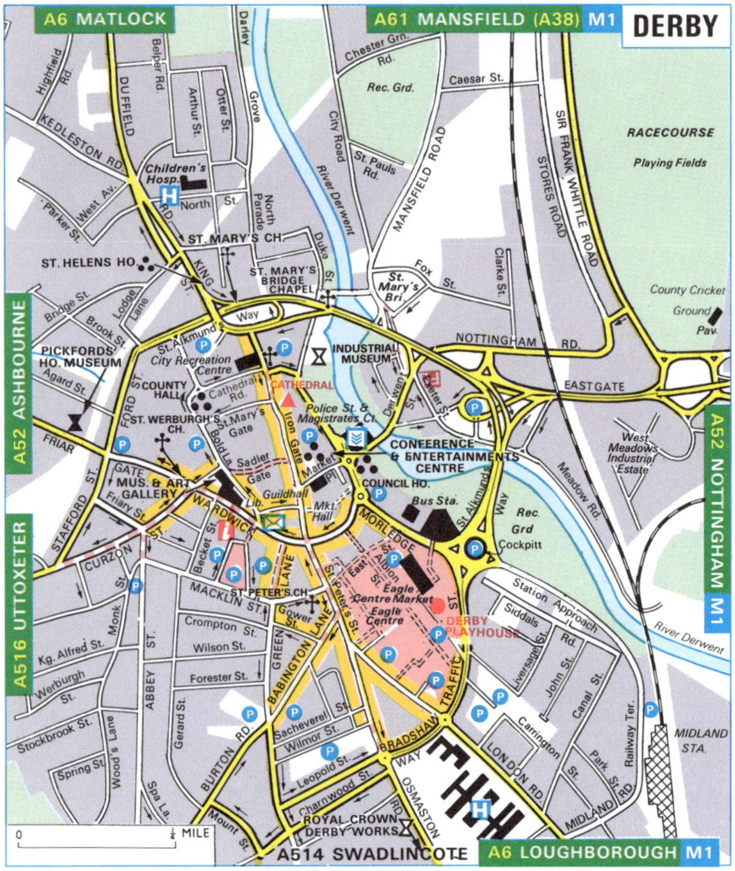
DERBY
A6 MATLOCK
A61 MANSFIELD (A38) M1
A52 NOTTINGHAM M1
A52 ASHBOURNE
A516 UTTOXETER
A514 SWADLINCOTE
A6 LOUGHBOROUGH M1
RACECOURSE
Playing Fields
County Cricket Ground
Children's Hosp.
ST. HELENS HO
ST. MARY'S CH
ST. MARY'S BRIDGE CHAPEL
PICKFORDS HO. MUSEUM
COUNTY HALL
ST. WERBURGH'S CH.
INDUSTRIAL MUSEUM
CATHEDRAL
CONFERENCE & ENTERTAINMENTS CENTRE
COUNCIL HO.
MUS. & ART GALLERY
Bus Sta.
Eagle Centre Market
DERBY PLAYHOUSE
ST. PETER'S CH.
MIDLAND STA.
ROYAL CROWN DERBY WORKS
River Derwent
West Meadows Industrial Estate
0 ¼ MILE

DUNDEE
FORFAR A929
A92 ABERDEEN
A923 COUPAR ANGUS
PERTH A85
EDINBURGH A914 (A92)
Royal Infirmary
DUDHOPE CASTLE
LITTLE THEATRE
STEPS THEATRE
CENTRAL MUSEUM & ART GALLERY
WISHART ARCH
BARRACK STREET MUSEUM
THE HOWFF
CITY CHURCHES
CAIRD HALL
ST. PAUL'S EPISCOPAL CATHEDRAL
RRS. DISCOVERY
HMS UNICORN
MERCAT CROSS
UNIVERSITY OF DUNDEE
ST. ANDREW'S R.C. CATHEDRAL
REPERTORY THEATRE
STATION
Swimming & Leisure Centre
TAY ROAD BRIDGE
FIRTH OF TAY
RIVERSIDE DRIVE
0 ¼ MILE

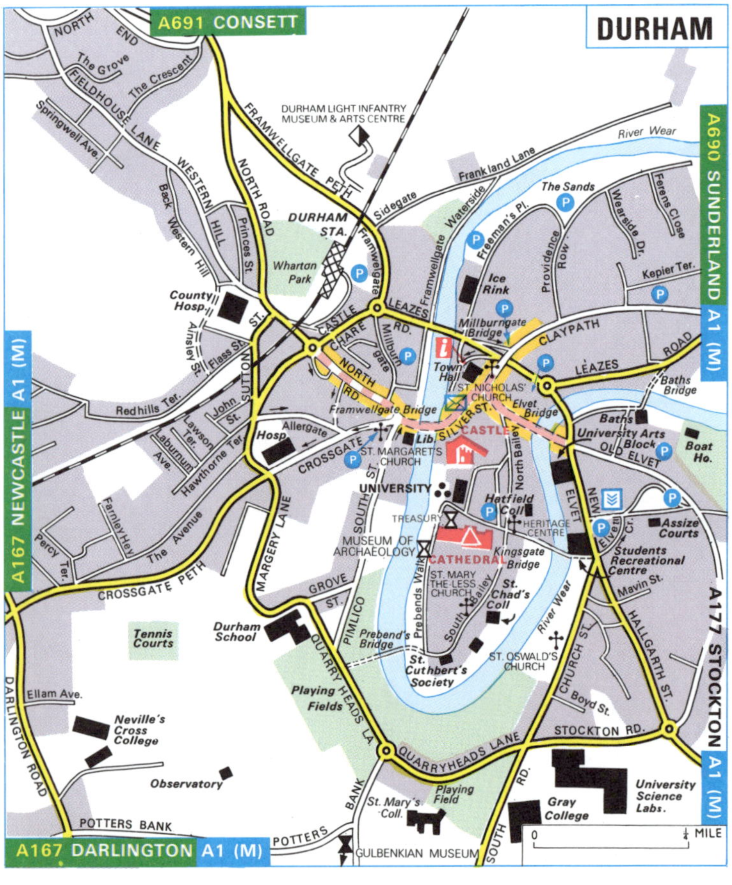
DURHAM
A691 CONSETT
A690 SUNDERLAND A1 (M)
A167 NEWCASTLE A1 (M)
A177 STOCKTON A1 (M)
A167 DARLINGTON A1 (M)
DURHAM LIGHT INFANTRY MUSEUM & ARTS CENTRE
DURHAM STA.
Wharton Park
County Hosp.
Ice Rink
Town Hall
ST. NICHOLAS' CHURCH
CASTLE
ST. MARGARET'S CHURCH
UNIVERSITY
CATHEDRAL
MUSEUM OF ARCHAEOLOGY
Hatfield Coll.
St. Chad's Coll.
University Arts Block
Students Recreational Centre
Assize Courts
Durham School
Tennis Courts
Playing Fields
Neville's Cross College
Observatory
St. Mary's Coll.
Gray College
University Science Labs.
GULBENKIAN MUSEUM
River Wear
0 ¼ MILE

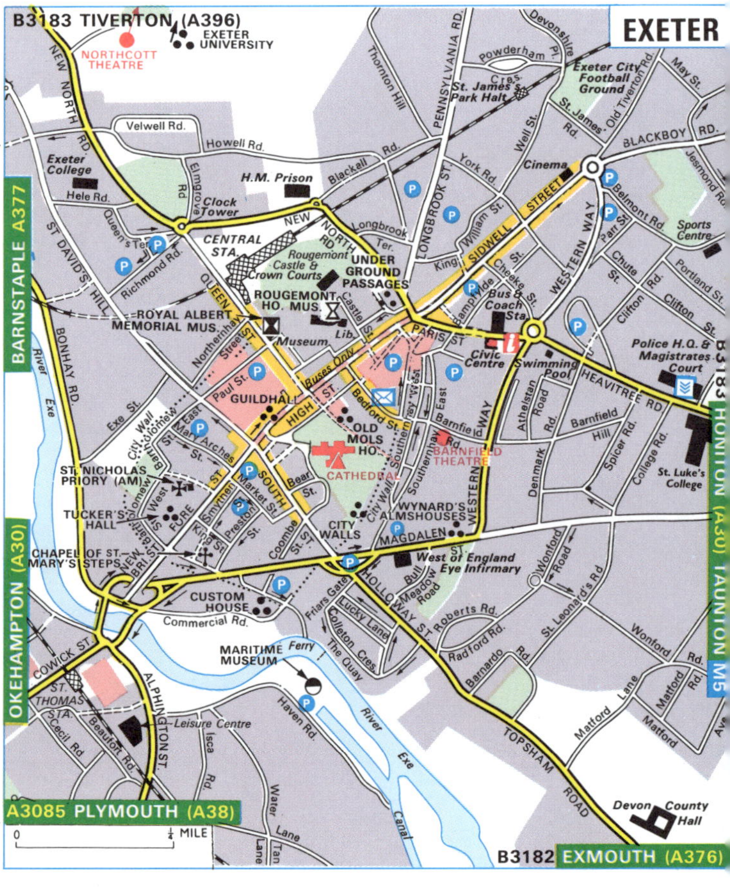
EXETER
B3183 TIVERTON (A396)
EXETER UNIVERSITY
NORTHCOTT THEATRE
BARNSTAPLE A377
OKEHAMPTON (A30)
B3183 HONITON (A30) TAUNTON M5
A3085 PLYMOUTH (A38)
B3182 EXMOUTH (A376)
Exeter College
H.M. Prison
Exeter City Football Ground
St. James' Park Halt
CENTRAL STA.
Clock Tower
Rougemont Castle & Crown Courts
ROUGEMONT HO. MUS.
UNDER GROUND PASSAGES
ROYAL ALBERT MEMORIAL MUS.
GUILDHALL
CATHEDRAL
OLD MOLS HO.
BARNFIELD THEATRE
Bus & Coach Sta.
Civic Centre
Swimming Pool
Police H.Q. & Magistrates Court
St. Luke's College
ST. NICHOLAS PRIORY (AM)
TUCKER'S HALL
CHAPEL OF ST. MARY'S STEPS
CITY WALLS
WYNARD'S ALMSHOUSES
MAGDALEN
West of England Eye Infirmary
CUSTOM HOUSE
MARITIME MUSEUM
Leisure Centre
St. Thomas Sta.
Devon County Hall
River Exe
0 ¼ MILE

APPROACHES TO EDINBURGH

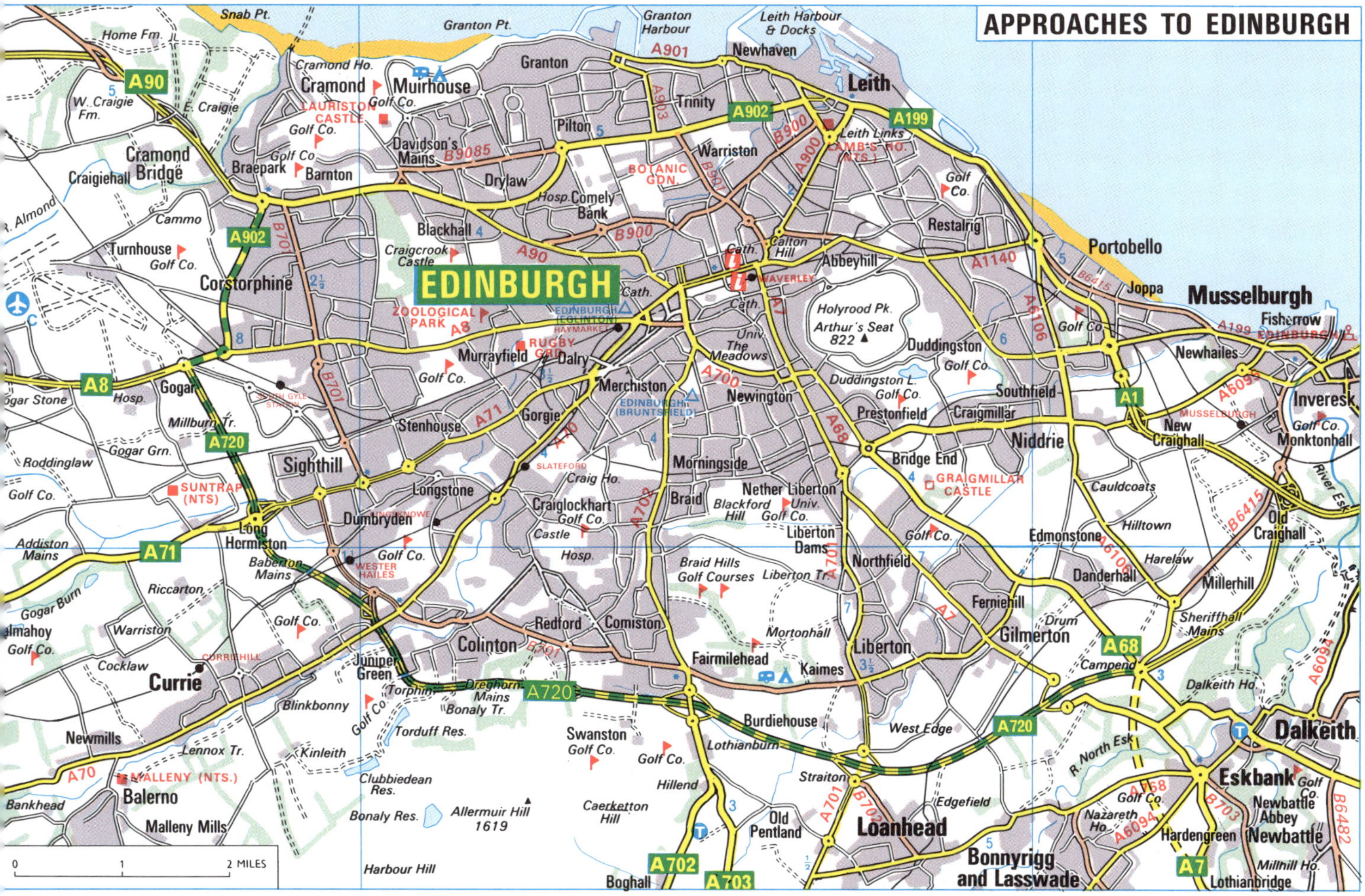

Snab Pt.
Granton Pt.
Granton Harbour
Leith Harbour & Docks
Home Fm.
Cramond Ho.
Cramond
Muirhouse
Granton
A901
Newhaven
Leith
A90
W. Craigie Fm.
E. Craigie
Lauriston Castle
Golf Co.
Pilton
Trinity
A902
A199
Leith Links
Lamb's Ho. (NTS)
Cramond Bridge
Craigiehall
Braepark
Barnton
Davidson's Mains
B9085
Drylaw
Warriston
Botanic Gdn.
Comely Bank
Restalrig
R. Almond
Cammo
Blackhall
B900
A1140
Portobello
Turnhouse Golf Co.
A902
Craigcrook Castle
A90
Calton Hill
Abbeyhill
Joppa
Musselburgh
Corstorphine
EDINBURGH
Cath.
Waverley
Holyrood Pk.
Arthur's Seat 822
Fisherrow
Zoological Park
Edinburgh (Haymarket)
A8
Univ.
The Meadows
Duddingston
Newhailes
Murrayfield
Rugby
Dalry
A700
Duddingston L.
Golf Co.
Southfield
Inveresk
A8
Gogar
Hosp.
Gogar Stone
Merchiston
Edinburgh (Bruntsfield)
Newington
Prestonfield
Craigmillar
A1
New Craighall
Golf Co.
Monktonhall
Millburn Tr.
Gogar Grn.
Stenhouse
A71
Gorgie
Niddrie
A720
Roddinglaw
Sighthill
Slateford
Morningside
Bridge End
Craigmillar Castle
Cauldcoats
River Esk
Golf Co.
Suntrap (NTS)
Longstone
Craig Ho.
Braid
Nether Liberton
Univ.
Hilltown
Old Craighall
Craiglockhart Golf Co.
Blackford Hill
Golf Co.
Dumbryden
Castle
Liberton Dams
Golf Co.
Edmonstone
Addiston Mains
A71
Long Hermiston
Golf Co.
Hosp.
Braid Hills Golf Courses
Liberton Tr.
Northfield
Harelaw
Danderhall
Millerhill
Baberton Mains
Wester Hailes
Riccarton
Ferniehill
Sheriffhall Mains
Gogar Burn
Golf Co.
Redford
Comiston
Mortonhall
Drum
Warriston
Gilmerton
Dalmahoy Golf Co.
Cocklaw
Colinton
Fairmilehead
Liberton
A68
Campend
Currie
Juniper Green
Kaimes
Dalkeith Ho.
Torphin
Dreghorn Mains
A720
Blinkbonny
Bonaly Tr.
Burdiehouse
West Edge
A720
Dalkeith
Newmills
Golf Co.
Torduff Res.
Swanston Golf Co.
Golf Co.
Lothianburn
R. North Esk
Lennox Tr.
Kinleith
Eskbank
A70
Malleny (NTS)
Clubbiedean Res.
Hillend
Straiton
Edgefield
Newbattle Abbey
Balerno
Golf Co.
Nazareth Ho.
A68
Bankhead
Allermuir Hill 1619
Caerketton Hill
Old Pentland
Loanhead
Newbattle
Malleny Mills
Bonaly Res.
Hardengreen
B6482
Harbour Hill
A702
A703
Bonnyrigg and Lasswade
A7
Millhill Ho.
Boghall
Lothianbridge
0 1 2 MILES

EDINBURGH

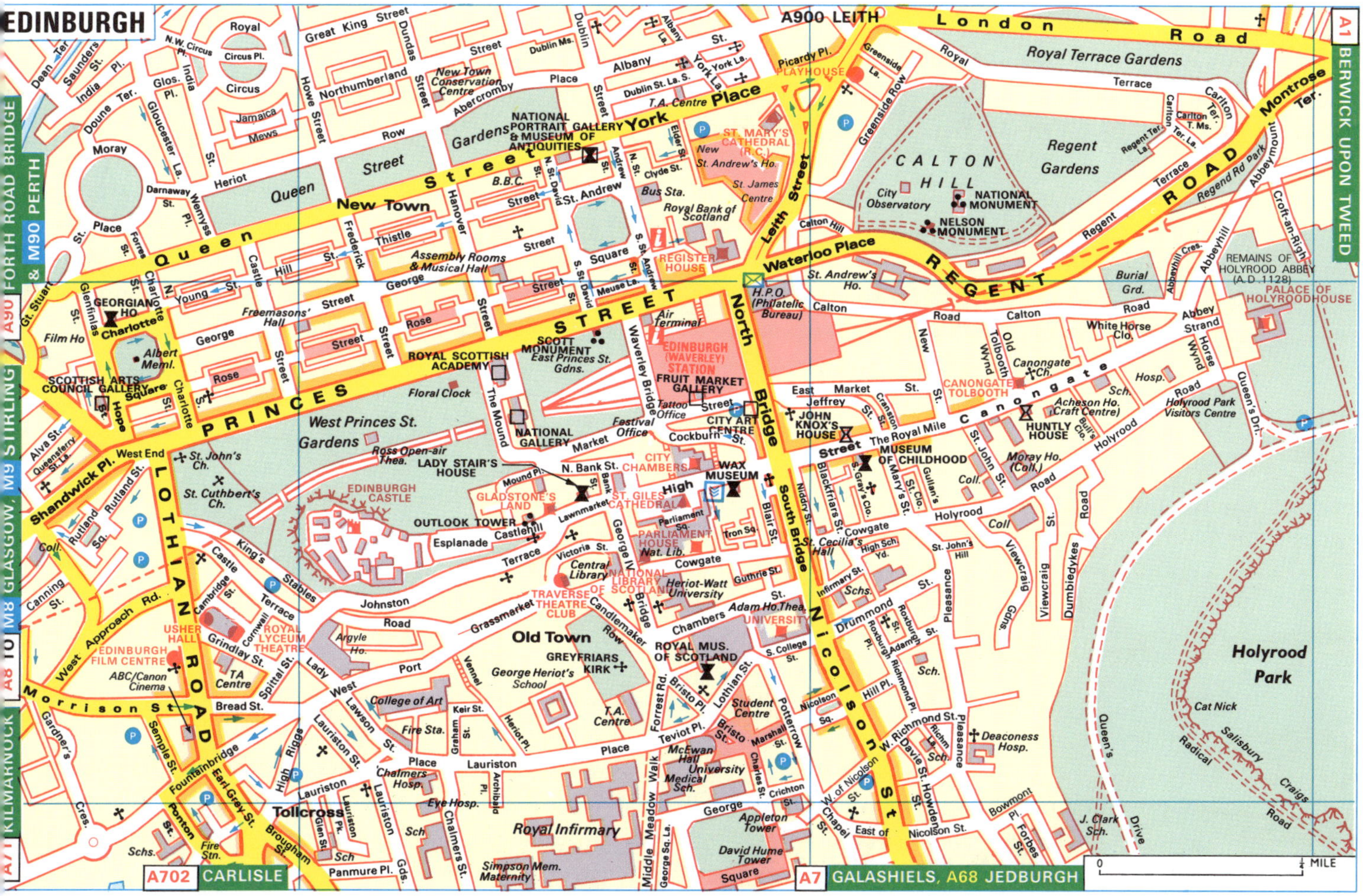

A900 LEITH
London Road
A1 BERWICK UPON TWEED
Royal Terrace Gardens
Royal Circus
Great King Street
Dundas Street
Dublin Street
Albany St.
York La.
Picardy Pl.
Playhouse
Greenside Row
Royal Terrace
Carlton Ter.
Dean Ter.
Saunders St.
N.W. Circus Pl.
Circus Pl.
Northumberland Street
New Town Conservation Centre
Abercromby Place
Dublin Ms.
Albany Street
Dublin St. La. S.
T.A. Centre
Place
India St.
Glos. Pl.
Circus
Howe Street
National Portrait Gallery & Museum of Antiquities
York Place
St. Mary's Cathedral
Calton Hill
Regent Gardens
Montrose Ter.
Doune Ter.
Moray
Jamaica Mews
Row
Gardens
Elder St.
New St. Andrew's Ho.
Leith Street
National Monument
City Observatory
Nelson Monument
Regent Ter.
Royal Terrace
Regent Road
Regent Rd. Park
Abbeymount
Croft-an-Righ
Gloucester La.
Heriot Row
Queen Street
B.B.C.
Clyde St.
Bus Sta.
St. James Centre
Royal Bank of Scotland
Darnaway St.
Wemyss Pl.
New Town
Hanover Street
St. Andrew Square
Frederick Street
Thistle St.
Assembly Rooms & Musical Hall
Register House
Waterloo Place
Regent Road
Remains of Holyrood Abbey (A.D. 1128)
Palace of Holyroodhouse
Burial Grd.
Queen Street
Castle Street
Hill St.
George Street
Meuse La.
H.P.O. (Philatelic Bureau)
St. Andrew's Ho.
Calton Road
Abbeyhill Cres.
Glenfinlas St.
Georgian Ho.
Charlotte Sq.
Young St.
Freemasons' Hall
Rose Street
Air Terminal
North Bridge
New Street
Tolbooth Wynd
Old
Calton
White Horse Clo.
Abbey Strand
Horse Wynd
Queen's Dr.
Film Ho.
Albert Meml.
Scott Monument
East Princes St. Gdns.
Edinburgh (Waverley) Station
Fruit Market Gallery
East Market St.
Jeffrey St.
Canongate Ch.
Canongate Tolbooth
Canongate
Sch.
Hosp.
Holyrood Park Visitors Centre
Scottish Arts Council Gallery
Princes Street
Royal Scottish Academy
Floral Clock
The Mound
Waverley Bridge
Tattoo Office
City Art Centre
John Knox's House
Cranston St.
Acheson Ho. (Craft Centre)
Huntly House
Holyrood
West Princes St. Gardens
Alva St.
Shandwick Pl.
West End
St. John's Ch.
Ross Open-air Thea.
National Gallery
Market St.
Festival Office
Cockburn St.
The Royal Mile
Museum of Childhood
Moray Ho. (Coll.)
Rutland St.
St. Cuthbert's Ch.
Lady Stair's House
Mound Pl.
N. Bank St.
City Chambers
High Street
Wax Museum
Blackfriars St.
Coll.
Edinburgh Castle
Gladstone's Land
Lawnmarket
St. Giles Cathedral
Parliament House
Tron Sq.
Niddry St.
Holyrood Road
Outlook Tower
Castlehill
Esplanade
Nat. Lib.
Cowgate
South Bridge
St. Cecilia's Hall
High Sch. Yd.
St. John's Hill
Viewcraig Gdns.
Dumbiedykes Road
Canning St.
King's Stables Road
Castle Terrace
Victoria St.
Central Library
National Library of Scotland
Heriot-Watt University
Guthrie St.
Infirmary St.
Schs.
Pleasance
Traverse Theatre Club
Candlemaker Row
Adam Ho. Thea.
University
Johnston Terrace
Grassmarket
George IV Bridge
Chambers St.
Drummond St.
West Approach Rd.
Usher Hall
Royal Lyceum Theatre
Cornwall St.
Grindlay St.
Cambridge St.
Old Town
Greyfriars Kirk
Royal Mus. of Scotland
S. College St.
Roxburgh Pl.
Sch.
Holyrood Park
Edinburgh Film Centre
ABC/Canon Cinema
T.A. Centre
Lady Lawson St.
Spittal St.
Argyle Ho.
West Port
George Heriot's School
Bristo Pl.
Lothian St.
Richmond Pl.
Nicolson Street
Morrison St.
Bread St.
College of Art
Keir St.
Forrest Rd.
Student Centre
Potterrow
Nicolson Sq.
Hill Pl.
W. Richmond St.
Pleasance
Cat Nick
Gardner's Cres.
Sempie St.
Lauriston St.
Fire Sta.
Graham St.
Heriot Pl.
T.A. Centre
Teviot Pl.
Bristo St.
Marshall St.
Deaconess Hosp.
Salisbury Craigs
Radical Road
Queen's Drive
Fountainbridge
Earl Grey St.
High Riggs
Chalmers Hosp.
Lauriston Place
McEwan Hall
University Medical Sch.
Crichton St.
Charles St.
W. of Nicolson St.
Davie St.
Howden St.
Bowmont Pl.
Forbes St.
J. Clark Sch.
Ponton St.
Tollcross
Lauriston Gdns.
Eye Hosp.
Archibald Pl.
Royal Infirmary
George Square
Appleton Tower
David Hume Tower
Chapel St.
East of Nicolson St.
Schs.
Fire Stn.
Brougham St.
Sch.
Chalmers St.
Simpson Mem. Maternity
Middle Meadow Walk
George Sq. La.
Panmure Pl.
A702 CARLISLE
A7 GALASHIELS, A68 JEDBURGH
A90 FORTH ROAD BRIDGE & M90 PERTH
M9 STIRLING
M8 GLASGOW
A8
A71 KILMARNOCK
0 ¼ MILE

APPROACHES TO GLASGOW
Old Kilpatrick
Parkhall
Hardgate
Mountblow
Radnor Park
Kilbowie
Dalmuir
Drumry
Drumchapel
Bearsden
Buchley
Cadder
Lenzie
Boghead
Auchinloch
Bishopbriggs
Lumloch
Stepps
CLYDEBANK
Garnieland
Whitecrook
Knightswood
Scotstounhill
Yoker
Scotstoun
Anniesland
Kelvindale
Maryhill
Lambhill
Milton
Crowhill
Auchinairn
Balornock
Barmulloch
Springburn
Possil Park
Kelvinside
Partick
Dowanhill
GLASGOW
Provanmill
Millerston
Garthamlock
Ruchazie
Garnoad
Dennistoun
Carntyne
Inchinnan
New Mains
Town of Inchinnan
Brownsfield
Renfrew
River Clyde
Whiteinch
CLYDE TUNNEL
Shieldhall
Hillington Industrial Estate
Victory Gardens
Middle Walkinshaw
Wester Walkinshaw
St. James Park
Shortroods
Ferguslie Park
Gallowhill
Oldhall
Hillington
Cardonald
Govan
Ibrox
SCOTTISH EXHIBITION CENTRE
Bellahouston
Bellahouston Park
Pollokshields
Gorbals
Hutchesontown
Bridgeton
Parkhead
Tollcross Park
Shettleston
Springboig
Mount Vernon
PAISLEY
Millarston
Castlehead
Blackhall
Crookston
Mosspark
Dumbreck
Oatlands
Dalmarnock
Braidfauld
Fullarton
Charleston
Brodie Park
Thornly Park
Glenburn
Pollok
Pollok Grounds
Crookston Home
Crossmyloof
Queen's Park
Govanhill
Polmadie
Shawlands
Langside
Battlefield
Mt. Florida
Rutherglen
Carmyle
Eastfield
Pollokshaws
Hurlet
Priesthill
Nitshill
Waterside
Mansewood
Newlands
Cathcart
King's Park
Croftfoot
High Crosshill
Burnside
Kennishead
Muirend
0 1 2 MILES
ANTONINE WALL
M8
M77
A82
A8
A80
A726
A737
A739
A74
A77

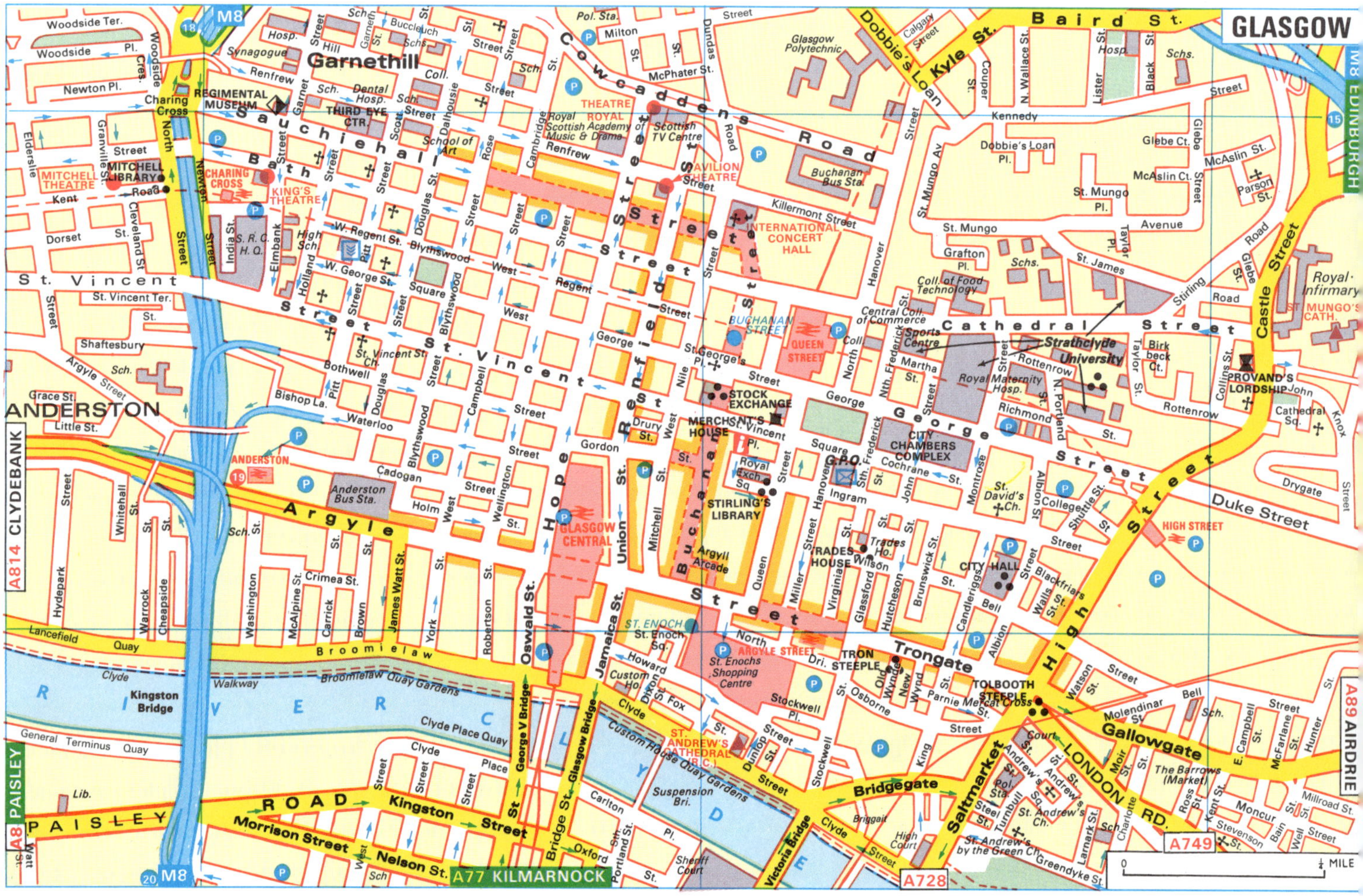
GLASGOW
Garnethill
Sauchiehall Street
Bath Street
Renfrew Street
Cowcaddens Road
Baird St.
Kyle St.
Dobbie's Loan
Glasgow Polytechnic
Buchanan Bus Sta.
THEATRE ROYAL
Royal Scottish Academy of Music & Drama
Scottish TV Centre
PAVILION THEATRE
INTERNATIONAL CONCERT HALL
CHARING CROSS
KING'S THEATRE
MITCHELL LIBRARY
MITCHELL THEATRE
REGIMENTAL MUSEUM
THIRD EYE CTR
School of Art
St. Vincent Street
West George St.
West Regent St.
ANDERSTON
Anderston Bus Sta.
Argyle Street
GLASGOW CENTRAL
QUEEN STREET
STOCK EXCHANGE
MERCHANTS' HOUSE
STIRLING'S LIBRARY
Argyll Arcade
Royal Exch. Sq.
G.P.O.
CITY CHAMBERS COMPLEX
Cathedral Street
Strathclyde University
Royal Infirmary
ST. MUNGO'S CATH.
PROVAND'S LORDSHIP
Castle Street
High Street
Duke Street
HIGH STREET
George Street
TRADES HOUSE
CITY HALL
TRON STEEPLE
Trongate
TOLBOOTH STEEPLE
Mercat Cross
Gallowgate
The Barrows (Market)
London Rd.
Saltmarket
Bridgegate
ST. ANDREW'S CATHEDRAL (R.C.)
St. Enochs Shopping Centre
ARGYLE STREET
ST. ENOCH
Broomielaw
Clyde Place Quay
Kingston Bridge
RIVER CLYDE
Glasgow Bridge
George V Bridge
Victoria Bridge
Kingston Street
Paisley Road
Morrison Street
Nelson St.
A77 KILMARNOCK
A8 PAISLEY
A814 CLYDEBANK
M8 EDINBURGH
A89 AIRDRIE
A728
A749
0 ¼ MILE

GLOUCESTER

A38 TEWKESBURY
A40 CHELTENHAM
M5
A417 CIRENCESTER
TO A38
A430 TO A38 BRISTOL M5
St. Oswald's Trading Estate
Cattle Mkt.
ST. OSWALDS RD.
KINGSHOLM ROAD
Sports Grd.
Rugby Football Grd.
ESTCOURT ROAD
Denmark Road
LONDON ROAD
WORCESTER ST.
CATHEDRAL
FOLK MUSEUM
BISHOP HOOPER'S STATUE
ST. MARY DE LODE CH.
ST. NICHOLAS'S CHURCH
WESTGATE ST.
NORTHGATE ST.
SHIRE HALL
GUILDHALL
NEW INN
TRANSPORT MUS
RAIKES HO.
Eastgate Centre
ST. MARY DE CRYPT CH.
CITY MUSEUM & ART GALLERY
REGIMENTAL MUSEUM
DOCKS
BLACKFRIARS
NATIONAL WATERWAYS MUSEUM
College of Art
OLYMPUS THEATRE
Leisure Centre
Bus Station
STATION
GLOUCESTERSHIRE ROYAL HOSPITAL
Horton Road Hospital
Great Western Road
METZ WAY
BARTON STREET
THE PARK
Spa Field
WESTON ROAD
River Severn
0 ½ MILE

HULL

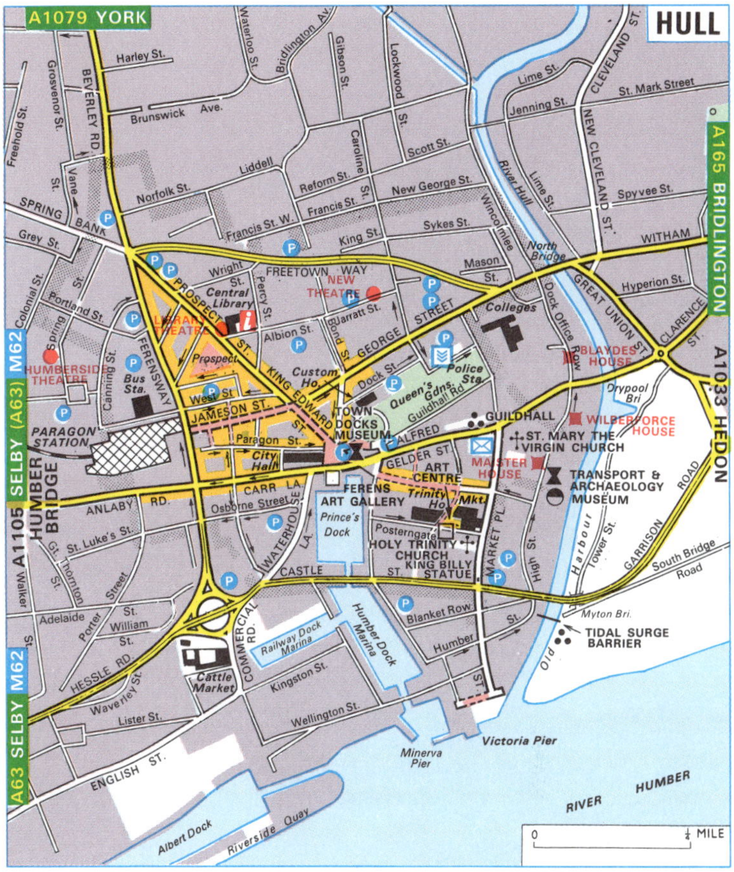
A1079 YORK
A165 BRIDLINGTON
A1033 HEDON
A63 SELBY M62
A1105 HUMBER BRIDGE
SELBY (A63) M62
BEVERLEY RD.
SPRING BANK
FREETOWN WAY
Central Library
NEW THEATRE
HUMBERSIDE THEATRE
PARAGON STATION
Bus Sta.
GEORGE STREET
Queen's Gdns.
Police Sta.
Colleges
GUILDHALL
TOWN DOCKS MUSEUM
City Hall
FERENS ART GALLERY
Prince's Dock
ST. MARY THE VIRGIN CHURCH
WILBERFORCE HOUSE
MAISTER HOUSE
TRANSPORT & ARCHAEOLOGY MUSEUM
ART CENTRE
HOLY TRINITY CHURCH
KING BILLY STATUE
BLAYDES HOUSE
Cattle Market
Railway Dock Marina
Humber Dock Marina
TIDAL SURGE BARRIER
Victoria Pier
Minerva Pier
Albert Dock
Riverside Quay
ENGLISH ST.
RIVER HUMBER
0 ½ MILE

APPROACHES TO HULL

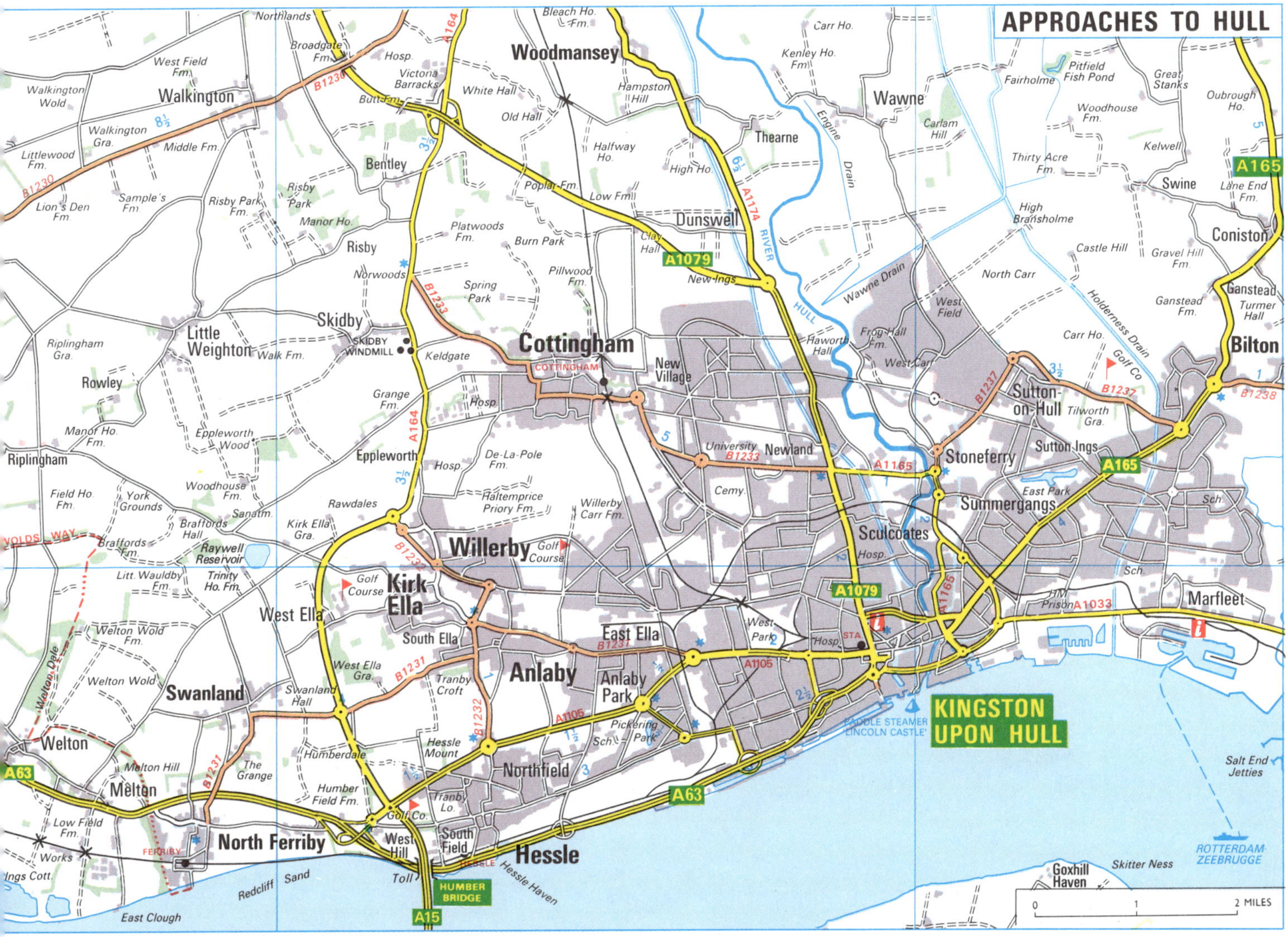
Woodmansey
Walkington
Bentley
Risby
Skidby
SKIDBY WINDMILL
Little Weighton
Rowley
Riplingham
Cottingham
New Village
Dunswell
Thearne
Wawne
Swine
Coniston
Bilton
Sutton-on-Hull
Stoneferry
Newland
Summergangs
Sculcoates
Marfleet
Willerby
Kirk Ella
West Ella
South Ella
Anlaby
Anlaby Park
Swanland
Welton
Melton
North Ferriby
Hessle
Northfield
KINGSTON UPON HULL
HUMBER BRIDGE
PADDLE STEAMER 'LINCOLN CASTLE'
ROTTERDAM ZEEBRUGGE
Goxhill Haven
Skitter Ness
Salt End Jetties
A1079
A165
A1033
A63
A15
A164
A1174
A1105
RIVER HULL
0 1 2 MILES

APPROACHES TO LEEDS

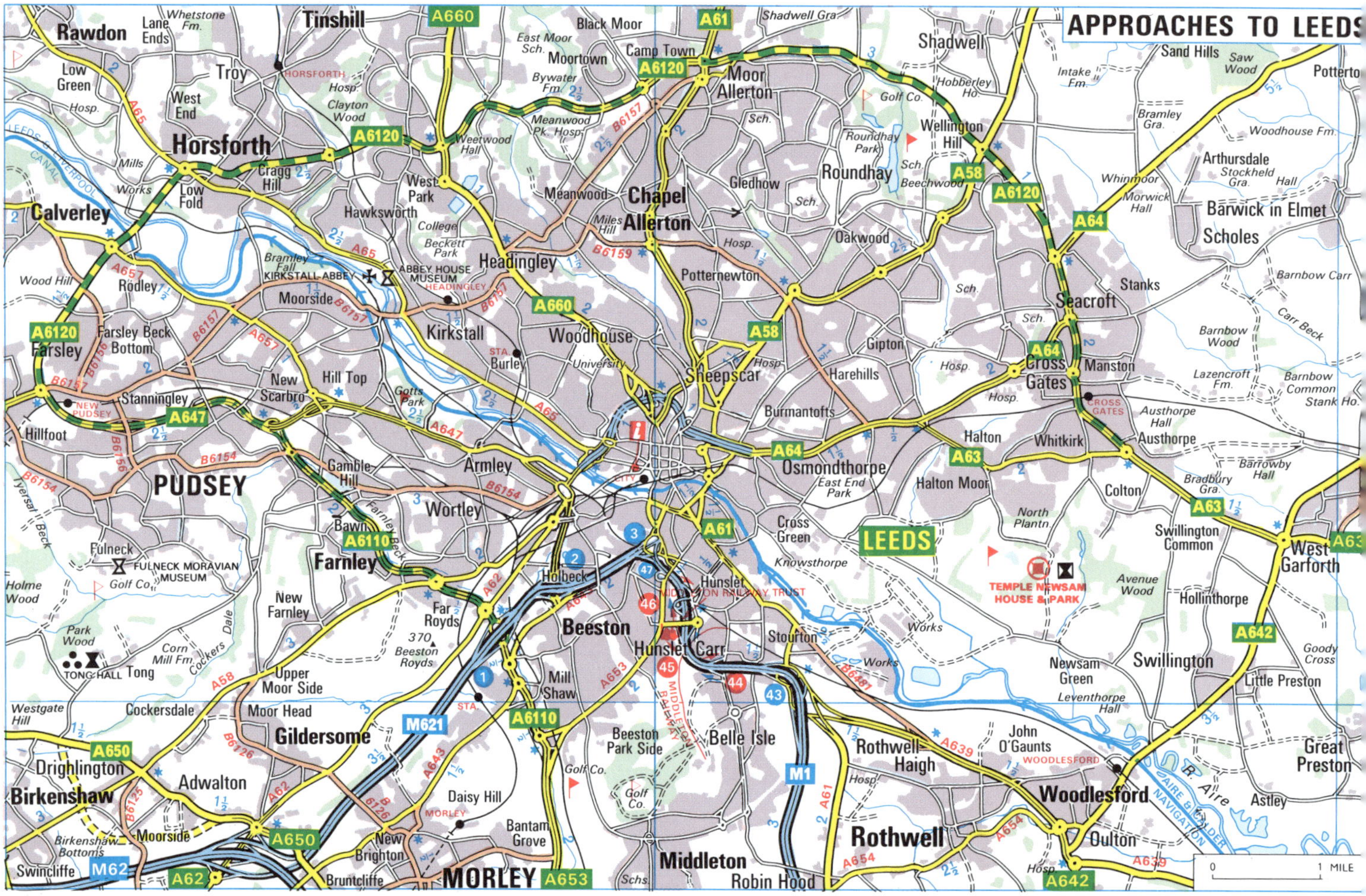
Rawdon
Lane Ends
Whetstone Fm.
Tinshill
A660
Black Moor
A61
Shadwell Gra.
Shadwell
Low Green
Troy
Horsforth Hosp.
Clayton Wood
East Moor Sch.
Moortown
Camp Town
A6120
Moor Allerton
Hobberley Ho.
Intake Fm.
Sand Hills
Saw Wood
Potterton
West End
Horsforth
A6120
Weetwood Hall
Meanwood Pk. Hosp.
Bywater Fm.
Golf Co.
Wellington Hill
Bramley Gra.
Woodhouse Fm.
Calverley
Mills
Works
Low Fold
Cragg Hill
West Park
Meanwood
Chapel Allerton
Gledhow
Roundhay Park
Roundhay
Beechwood
A58
A6120
Whinmoor
Morwick Hall
Arthursdale
Stockheld Gra.
Hall
Barwick in Elmet
Scholes
Hawksworth
College
Beckett Park
Miles Hill
A64
Wood Hill
Rodley
Bramley Fall
KIRKSTALL ABBEY
ABBEY HOUSE MUSEUM
HEADINGLEY
Headingley
Potternewton
Oakwood
Stanks
Barnbow Carr
Moorside
A660
Seacroft
A6120
Farsley
Farsley Beck Bottom
Kirkstall
Woodhouse
University
A58
Gipton
Barnbow Wood
Carr Beck
Burley
Manston
New Scarbro
Hill Top
Hosp.
Sheepscar
Harehills
Hosp.
A64
Cross Gates
Lazencroft Fm.
Barnbow Common
Stank Ho.
Stanningley
NEW PUDSEY
A647
Gotts Park
Burmantofts
CROSS GATES
Austhorpe Hall
Hillfoot
A647
Austhorpe
Halton
Whitkirk
Barrowby Hall
Gamble Hill
Armley
A64
Osmondthorpe
East End Park
PUDSEY
Halton Moor
A63
Bradbury Gra.
Colton
Wortley
A61
Cross Green
North Plantn
A63
Bawn
A6110
Swillington Common
West Garforth
A63
Fulneck
FULNECK MORAVIAN MUSEUM
Golf Co.
Farnley
Holbeck
Hunslet
MIDDLETON RAILWAY TRUST
Knowsthorpe
LEEDS
TEMPLE NEWSAM HOUSE & PARK
Avenue Wood
Holme Wood
New Farnley
Far Royds
Beeston
Hunslet Carr
Stourton
Works
Hollinthorpe
Park Wood
370 Beeston Royds
Works
A642
TONG HALL
Tong
Corn Mill Fm.
Cockers Dale
Upper Moor Side
Mill Shaw
A653
Newsam Green
Swillington
Goody Cross
Little Preston
Leventhorpe Hall
Westgate Hill
Cockersdale
Moor Head
M621
A6110
MIDDLETON RAILWAY
Belle Isle
A639
John O'Gaunts
Great Preston
Gildersome
A650
Drighlington
Beeston Park Side
Golf Co.
Rothwell Haigh
WOODLESFORD
Birkenshaw
Adwalton
Daisy Hill
MORLEY
Golf Co.
M1
Hosp.
Woodlesford
AIRE & CALDER NAVIGATION
R. Aire
Astley
Birkenshaw Bottoms
Moorside
A650
New Brighton
Bantam Grove
Rothwell
A654
Oulton
Swincliffe
M62
A62
Bruntcliffe
MORLEY
A653
Schs.
Middleton
Robin Hood
A654
Hosp.
A642
A639
0 1 MILE

LEEDS

A660 to A65 SKIPTON
A61 HARROGATE, A58 WETHERBY
School
University Road
Little London
Woodsley Rd.
Clarendon
Lyddon Ter.
Cromer Place
Clarendon Pl.
Lifton Pl.
Cromer St.
Cromer Terr.
Kelso Rd.
Kelso
Mount Preston Street
Springfield Mt.
Leeds University
Willow Terr.
WOODHOUSE LANE
BLENHEIM WALK
Carlton
Carlton Rise
Park
Oatland Dri.
Oatland Road
CLAY PIT LANE
SHEEPSCAR ST. SOUTH
ROSEVILLE RD.
Benson Street
Winfoun St.
Whitelock St.
CROSS STAMFORD ST.
Mushroom Street
Lovell Road
Skinner Lane
Grafton St.
Concord St.
LEEDS PLAYHOUSE
Leeds Polytechnic
INNER RING ROAD
Hyde Terrace
Clarendon Road
Kendal Lane
Fenton St.
Calverley St.
Portland Way
Clay Pit Lane
Merrion Way
Lane
Coll. of Further Education
Merrion Centre
Byron St.
Mabgate
A 58(M)
Little Woodhouse
Hanover Sq.
Hanover Way
Thoresby Place
Leeds General Infirmary
CIVIC HALL
Portland St.
Great George St.
Rossington St.
Wade Lane
Belgrave St.
North
Melbourne St.
Lower Brunswick St.
Nile St.
Trafalgar St.
Gower St.
Hope Rd.
REGENT STREET
Cromwell
St. Mary's St.
Burley St.
Park St.
Crown & County Cts.
Magistrates Court
TOWN HALL
Alexander St.
Centenary Sq.
Victoria Sq.
Cookridge St.
ST. ANNE'S CATHEDRAL (R.C.)
Merrion St.
ST. JOHNS CENTRE
Mark Lane
New Briggate
GRAND THEATRE
Templar St.
NEW YORK ROAD
Burmantofts Street
A64(M)
YORK RD.
Westgate
The Headrow
Park Sq. West
Park Sq. East
Park Cross St.
East Parade
South Pde.
Bedford St.
Greek St.
Russell St.
Upper Basinghall St.
King Charles St.
Land's Lane
CITY PALACE OF VARIETIES
Victoria Quarter
Vicar Lane
EASTGATE
ST. PETER'S ST.
Quarry Hill
WEST YORKSHIRE PLAYHOUSE
Shannon St.
St. Paul's St.
Park Place
York Place
Infirmary St.
Quebec St.
Albion Place
Albion St.
Bond St.
Commercial St.
King Edward St.
Kirkgate Market
George St.
Dyer St.
Bus Depot
DUKE STREET
Lane
Wellington
King Street
City Square
Boar Lane
Briggate
HOLY TRINITY
ARCADES
New York St.
CORN EXCHANGE
Kirkgate
Marsh Lane
Saxton Lane
Railway St.
East Field St.
Aire St.
Duncan St.
Call Lane
Municipal Buildings Calverley Street
CENTRAL LIBRARY
CITY ART GALLERY
CITY MUSEUM
CITY MUSEUM AQUARIUM
Whitehall Road
RIVER AIRE
City Station
New Station
Swinegate
Bridge End
Warehouse Hill
The Calls
ST. PETER'S CHURCH
Steander
A65 SKIPTON to LEEDS, BRADFORD AIRPORT
A647 BRADFORD, A58 HALIFAX, A62 HUDDERSFIELD
A64 YORK
M621 Int. 3, M1 Int. 46
A653 DEWSBURY
M1, M621 (M62)
M1 LONDON
A61 WAKEFIELD
0 ¼ MILE

APPROACHES TO LEICESTER
LOUGHBOROUGH
Cotes
Burton on the Wolds
Walton on the Wolds
Prestwold Hall
Home Fm.
The Old Park Fm.
Middle Fm.
North Fm.
Barrow Hill
Tithe Fm.
Fishpool Brook
Catsick Hill
Grand Union Canal
Shelthorpe
Woodthorpe
Park Grange
Barrow upon Soar
Quebec Ho.
Seagrave
Paudy Cross Rds.
Belle Isle
Park Hill
Quorndon
Quorn Hall
Netherfield
Quorn Ho.
Woodhouse
Buddon Wood
Great Central Railway
North End
South End
Sileby
College
Ratcliffe on the Wreake
Swithland Res.
Mountsorrel
Rothley Plain
Rothley Lo.
Swithland
Cossington
Swithland Wood
Lewin Bri.
Fosse Way
Rothley
Bradgate Park Swithland Woods
The Temple Golf Course
Thurcaston
Wanlip Hill
Syston
Cropston
Cropston Res.
Wanlip
Barkby Lo.
Birstall
Castle Hill
Packhorse Bridge
Astill Lo.
Thurmaston
Anstey
Mowmacre Hill
Golf Co.
Watermead
Park Pale
Beaumont Leys
Belgrave Hall
Groby
Hospital
LEICESTER
Glenfield
Hosp.
Museum of Technology
Manor Ho.
New Humberstone
New Parks
Abbey Park
Dominion Estate
Golf Course
Spinney Hills
Crown Hills
Western Park
North Evington
Leicester Forest East
Braunstone Park
Victoria Park
Coll.
Evington
Braunstone
Stoneygate
Golf Course
Leicester Forest East Services
Clarendon Park
University Botanic Gardens
Hastings House
R. Soar
Aylestone Park
Aylestone
South Knighton
Leicester
Oadby
The Park
Enderby
Gee's Lock
Glen Parva
South Wigston
Wigston
R. Sence
Highfield Ho.
Hosp.
Narborough
Whetstone
Blaby
Blaby Hill
Norwood Ho.
Kilby Bri. Fm.
Kilby Bri.
Littlethorpe
Hosp.
A6
A46
A47
A50
A60
A426
A563
A607
A5125
A5131
A6030
M1
M69
B676
B675
B5328
B674
B5330
B5327
B6046
B591
B5351
B673
B667
B5418
B582
B5366
B528
0 1 2 MILES

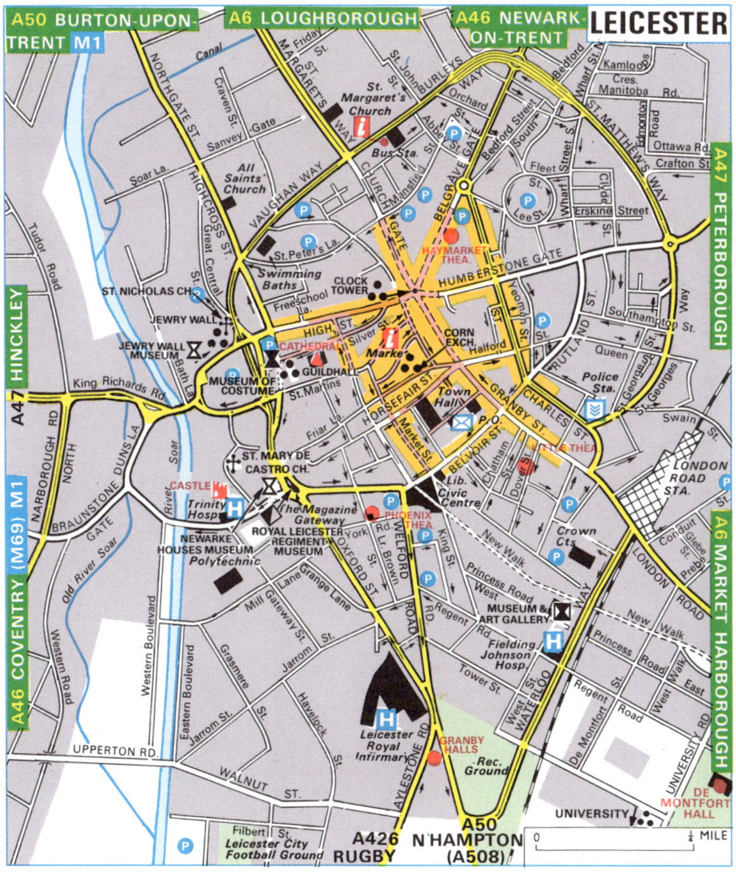
LEICESTER
A50 BURTON-UPON-TRENT M1
A6 LOUGHBOROUGH
A46 NEWARK-ON-TRENT
A47 PETERBOROUGH
A47 HINCKLEY
A46 COVENTRY (M69) M1
A6 MARKET HARBOROUGH
A426 RUGBY
A50 N'HAMPTON (A508)
Northgate St.
Canal
St. Margaret's Church
Bus Sta.
Belgrave Gate
Burleys Way
Sanvey Gate
All Saints Church
Soar La.
Vaughan Way
Haymarket Thea.
Humberstone Gate
St. Nicholas Ch.
Jewry Wall
Jewry Wall Museum
Swimming Baths
Clock Tower
High St.
Cathedral
Guildhall
Corn Exch.
Market
Museum of Costume
King Richards Rd.
Town Hall
P.O.
Charles St.
Police Sta.
Rutland St.
Granby St.
Little Thea.
St. Mary de Castro Ch.
Castle
Trinity Hosp.
The Magazine Gateway
Royal Leicester Regiment Museum
Newarke Houses Museum
Polytechnic
Phoenix Thea.
Lib.
Civic Centre
London Road Sta.
Crown Cts.
New Walk
Museum & Art Gallery
Fielding Johnson Hosp.
Oxford St.
Welford Road
Leicester Royal Infirmary
Granby Halls
Rec. Ground
Upperton Rd.
Walnut St.
Filbert St.
Leicester City Football Ground
University
De Montfort Hall
Western Road
Western Boulevard
Eastern Boulevard
Narborough Rd
Braunstone Gate
Tudor Road
0 ¼ MILE

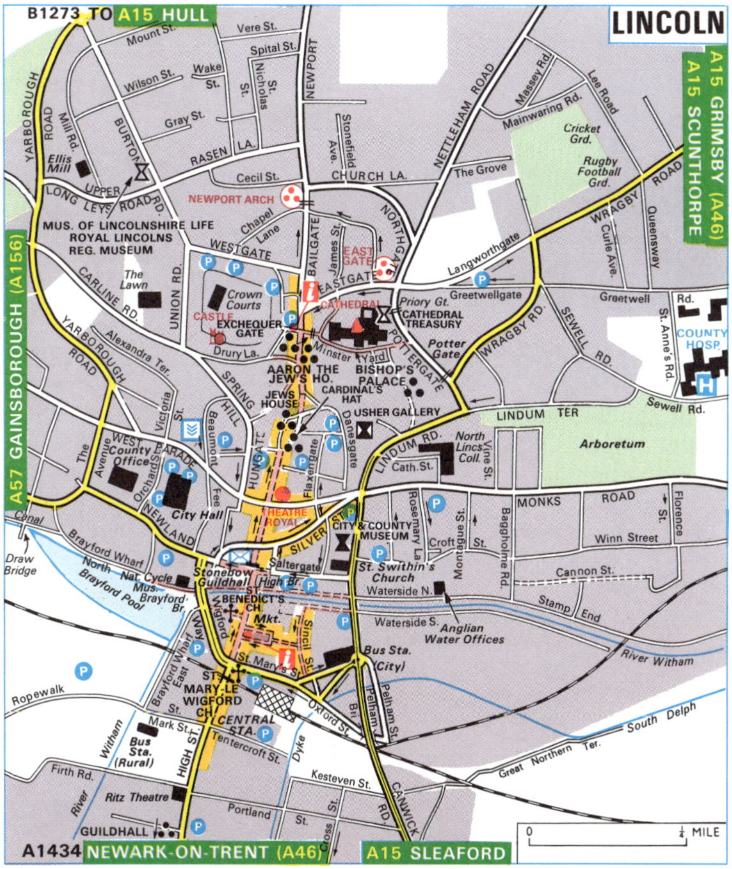
LINCOLN
B1273 TO A15 HULL
A15 GRIMSBY (A46)
A15 SCUNTHORPE
A57 GAINSBOROUGH (A156)
A1434 NEWARK-ON-TRENT (A46)
A15 SLEAFORD
Yarborough Road
Burton Rd.
Newport
Nettleham Road
Ellis Mill
Upper Long Leys Road
Newport Arch
Church La.
The Grove
Rugby Football Grd.
Cricket Grd.
Mus. of Lincolnshire Life
Royal Lincolns Reg. Museum
Westgate
Bailgate
East Gate
Eastgate
The Lawn
Crown Courts
Castle
Exchequer Gate
Cathedral
Cathedral Treasury
Potter Gate
County Hosp.
Aaron the Jew's Ho.
Jews House
Bishop's Palace
Cardinal's Hat
Usher Gallery
Lindum Ter.
Arboretum
County Offices
City Hall
North Lincs Coll.
Newland
Monks Road
Theatre Royal
City & County Museum
Brayford Wharf North
Nat. Cycle Mus.
Brayford Pool
Stonebow Guildhall
St. Swithin's Church
Waterside N.
St. Benedict's Ch.
Mkt.
Waterside S.
Anglian Water Offices
Bus Sta. (City)
River Witham
St. Mary-le-Wigford Ch.
Central Sta.
Ropewalk
Bus Sta. (Rural)
High St.
Ritz Theatre
Guildhall
Great Northern Ter.
South Delph
Canwick Rd.
0 ¼ MILE

LIVERPOOL
A59 PRESTON
A5047 MANCHESTER (M62)
A5047 WARRINGTON (M62)
A565 SOUTHPORT
BIRKENHEAD A5039 QUEENSWAY TUNNEL
A562 WIDNES
A561 WIDNES (A562)
LIME ST. STA.
St John's Precinct
R.C. CATHEDRAL
CATHEDRAL
Central Hall
Albert Dock
Tate Gallery Liverpool
Police H.Q.
Q.E.2 Crown Courts
SUDLEY ART GALLERY
¼ MILE
APPROACHES TO LIVERPOOL
ORMSKIRK
Halsall
Aughton
Maghull
Moss Side
Lydiate
Aintree
Waddicar
Melling
Northwood
KIRKBY
Kirkby Industrial Estate
Southdene
Knowsley
KNOWSLEY PARK
Bickerstaffe
Westhead
Scarth Hill
Blaguegate
Town Green
Holt Green
Bowker's Green
Royal Oak
Barrow Nook
Crosby
Waterloo
Seaforth
Seaforth Dock
Litherland
Orrell
Fazakerley
Walton on the Hill
Norris Green
Dog & Gun
Croxteth Park
BOOTLE
WALLASEY
New Brighton
Egremont
Liscard
Leasowe
Moreton
Bidston
Poulton
Seacombe
Kirkdale
Anfield
Everton
West Derby
Clubmoor
True Brook
LIVERPOOL
Old Swan
Fairfield
Knotty Ash
Dovecot
HUYTON-WITH-ROBY
Huyton Park
Page Moss
Woolfall Heath
Prescot
Whitfield Lane End
Broad Green
Court Hey
Bowring Park
Childwall
Gateacre
Edge Hill
Wavertree
BIRKENHEAD
Birkenhead Park
Claughton
Upton
Greasby
Arrowe Hill
Woodchurch
Arrowe Park
Landican
Prenton
Tranmere
Rock Ferry
Egerton Park
Woodhey
New Ferry
BEBINGTON
Port Sunlight
RIVER MERSEY
Dingle
Princes Park
Sefton Park
Mossley Hill
Aigburth
Allerton
Calderstones
Woolton
Halewood Green
Halewood
Hunt's Cross
Garston
Grassendale
Gaston Channel
Mockbeggar Wharf
DOUGLAS (Summer only)
Perch Rock
Road Tunnel
Rail Tunnel
M53
M57
M58
M62
A59
A580
A5058
A562
A561
A41
A5047
0 1 2 MILES

APPROACHES TO MANCHESTER

Tottington
Walmersley
Bury
Rochdale
Spotland Bridge
Milnrow
Heywood
Castleton
Radcliffe
Whitefield
Middleton
Royton
Shaw
Chadderton
Oldham
Prestwich
Pendlebury
Swinton
Kearsley
Little Lever
Walkden
Worsley
Eccles
Salford
Manchester
Failsworth
Droylsden
Ashton-under-Lyne
Audenshaw
Denton
Trafford Park
Stretford
Old Trafford
Hulme
Moss Side
Rusholme
Levenshulme
Gorton
Urmston
Davyhulme
Sale
Altrincham
Timperley
Baguley
Northenden
Didsbury
West Didsbury
Withington
Chorlton cum Hardy
Stockport
Bredbury
Reddish
Heaton Chapel
Gatley
Sharston
Cheadle Heath
Crumpsall
Blackley
Harpurhey
Moston
Newton Heath
Miles Platting
Ardwick
Longsight
Openshaw
Clayton
Cheetham Hill
Broughton Park
Higher Broughton
Lower Kersal
Ashton upon Mersey
Carrington
Partington
Irlam
Flixton
Heaton Park
Birch Services
Carr
Ainsworth
Breightmet
Harwood
Bradshaw
Lower Place
Buersil
Summit
Hollinwood
Hathershaw
0 1 2 MILES

MANCHESTER
A62 OLDHAM
A635 ASHTON under Lyne
A6 STOCKPORT
A34 CONGLETON
A664 ROCHDALE
A56 BURY & M62
A5103 to M56
A6144
A5066
A56 M63
A6 PRESTON & M6
M602 (M62 to LIVERPOOL)
A57 WARRINGTON &
Brunswick
University
HULME
St. Georges
SALFORD
PEEL PARK
Salford University
Playing Field
River Irwell
MANCUNIAN WAY
A57(M)
MANCHESTER SHIP CANAL
PICCADILLY STATION
VICTORIA STATION
SALFORD STATION
DEANSGATE STA.
OXFORD RD. STA.
Piccadilly Gardens
Arndale Shopping Centre
Granada Television Studios
GREATER MANCHESTER MUSEUM OF SCIENCE & INDUSTRY
Greater Manchester Exhibition Centre (GMEX)
St. George's Park
Pomona Docks
DEANSGATE
ROCHDALE ROAD
OLDHAM RD.
GREAT ANCOATS ST.
Swan Street
Miller Street
Piccadilly
London Road
Portland Street
Oxford Street
Oxford Road
Princess Street
Mosley Street
Whitworth Street
Medlock St.
PRINCESS RD.
UPPER BROOK ST.
Brook St.
CHORLTON RD.
CHESTER ROAD
Egerton St.
Dawson St.
Water Street
Liverpool Road
Quay Street
New Quay St.
Bridge Street
Irwell Street
CHAPEL STREET
Blackfriars Road
Blackfriars St.
Victoria St.
Corporation St.
Cannon Street
Market Street
Cross Street
John Dalton St.
Peter Street
Adelphi Street
Oldfield Road
REGENT ROAD
Ordsall Lane
CRESCENT
WINDSOR
Silk Street
Greengate
0 MILE

APPROACHES TO MIDDLESBROUGH

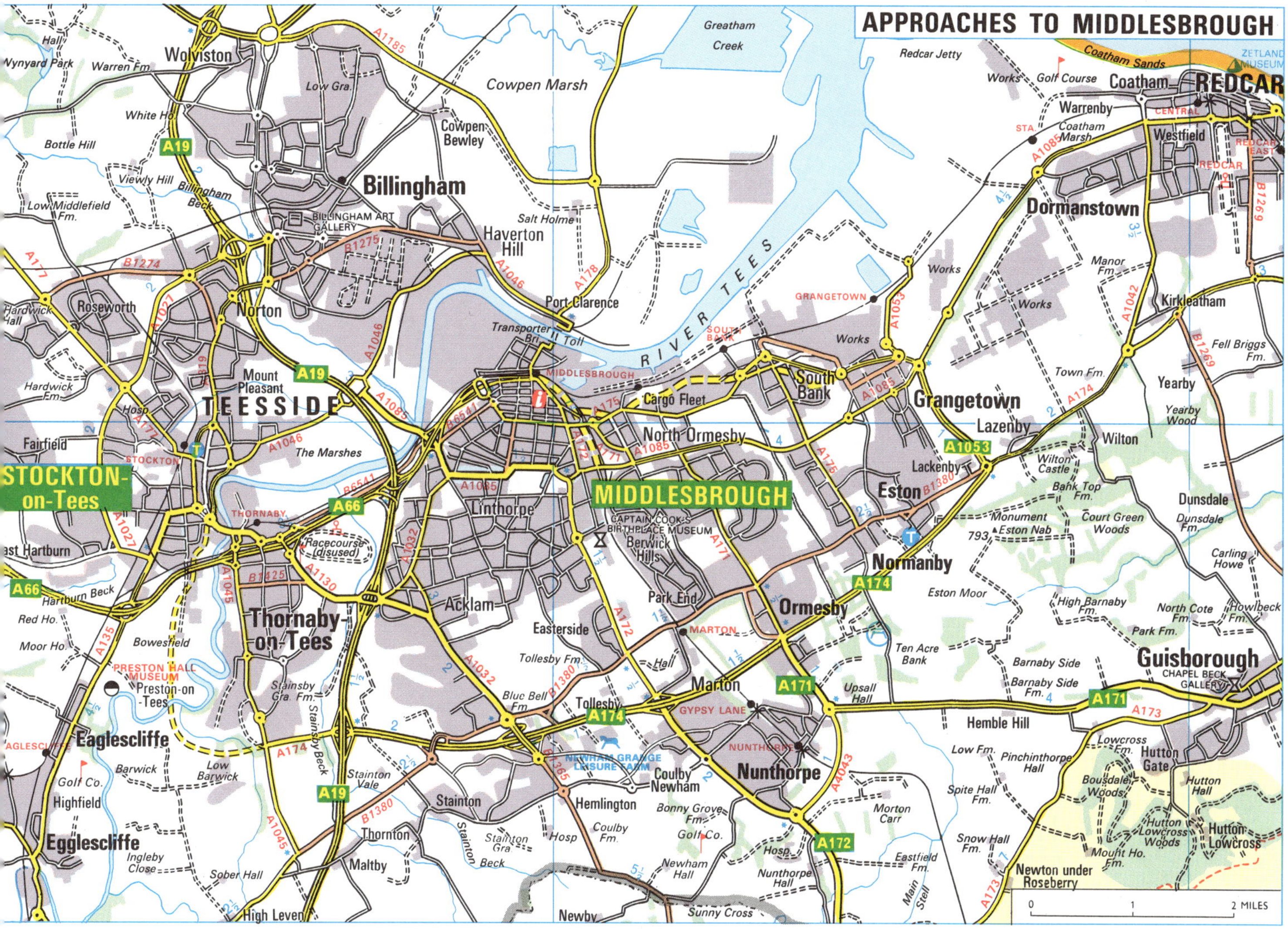

MIDDLESBROUGH

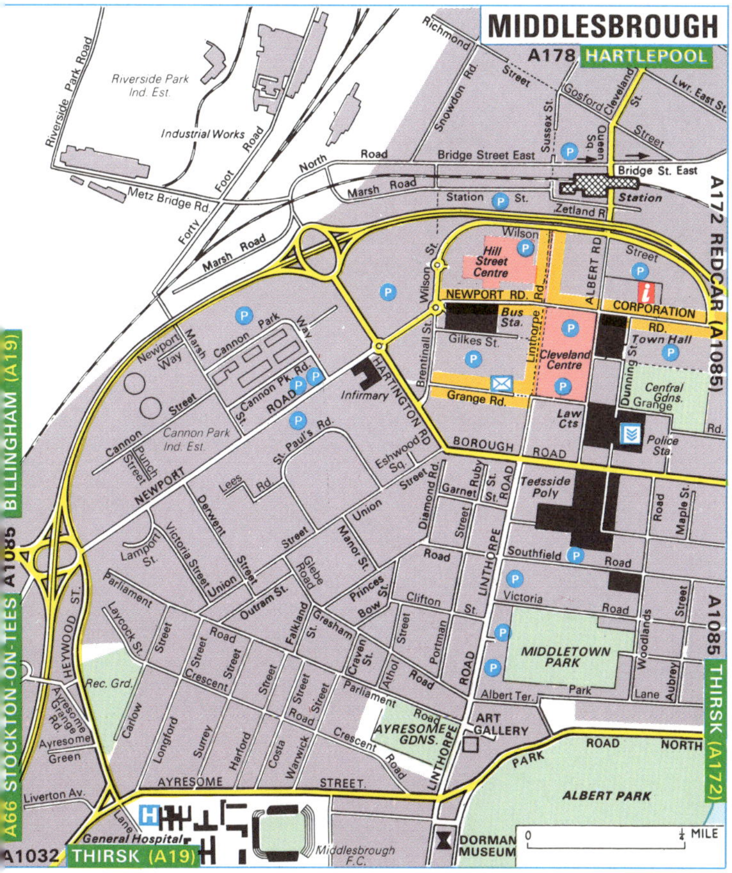

MILTON KEYNES

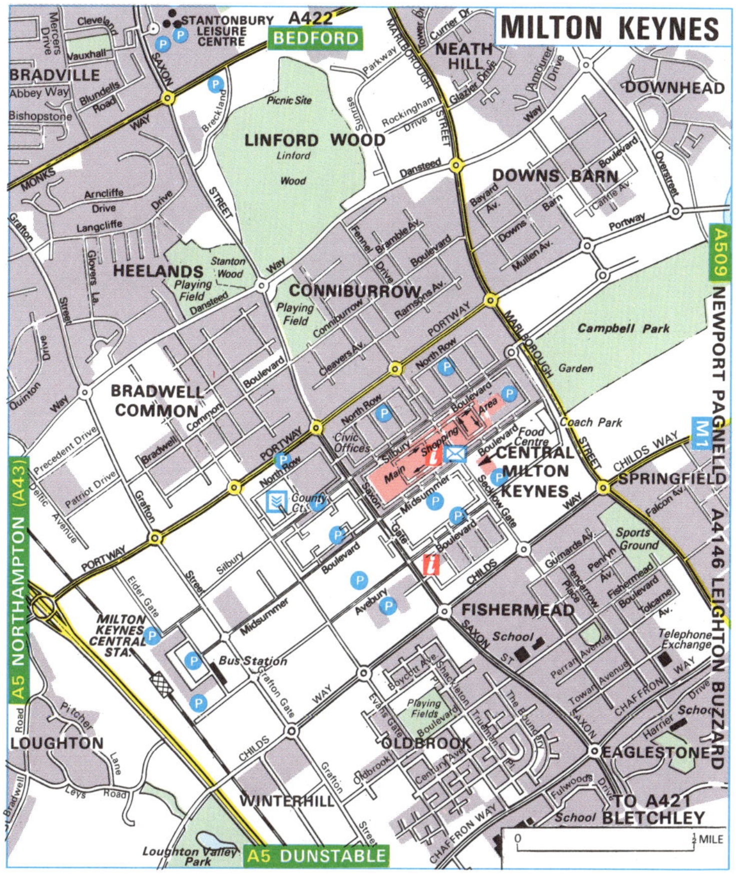

APPROACHES TO NEWCASTLE

NEWCASTLE upon Tyne
GATESHEAD
SUNDERLAND
SOUTH SHIELDS
TYNEMOUTH
Whitley Bay
Cullercoats
Marden
Monkseaton
Earsdon
Shiremoor
Backworth
Seaton Sluice
Hartley
Seaton Delaval
Seaton Terrace
Holywell
Seghill
Cramlington
East Cramlington
Nelson Village
Shankhouse
Seaton Burn
Annitsford
Dudley
Wide Open
Burradon
Camperdown
Killingworth
West Moor
Palmersville
Longbenton
Forest Hall
Gosforth
North Gosforth
Hazlerigg
North Brunton
Fawdon
Coxlodge
Kenton
South Gosforth
Jesmond
Heaton
Wallsend
Byker
Walker
Willington
Howdon
Willington Quay
Howdon Pans
North Shields
Chirton
West Chirton
Percy Main
Preston
Preston Grange
Billy Mill
New York
Murton
West Allotment
Jarrow
Hebburn
Monkton
Primrose
Simonside
Harton
West Harton
Westoe
Horsley Hill
Marsden
Marsden Bay
Cleadon
Cleadon Park
Whiteleas
Biddick Hall
Boldon
Boldon Colliery
East Boldon
New Town
Whitburn
Felling
Pelaw
Wardley
Heworth
High Felling
Carr Hill
Bill Quay
Fellgate
Fenham
Benwell
Elswick
Spital Tongues
Dunston
Low Team
Whickham Hill
Team Valley
Low Fell
Windy Nook
High Fell
Wrekenton
Eighton Banks
Springwell
Harlow Green
Low Eighton
Lamesley
Kibblesworth
Birtley
Usworth
Washington
New Washington
Albany
Hertburn
Sulgrave
Barmston
Washington Station
Castletown
Hylton Castle
Southwick
Monkwearmouth
Fulwell
Carley Hill
Pallion
South Hylton
North Hylton
Pennywell
Grindon
Hendon
Grangetown
Ryhope Colliery
Penshaw
North Biddick
Tunstall Hills
High Newport
Plains Farm
Thorney Close
Middle Herrington
Ouston
Whitelands
Barley Mow
Offerton
Cox Green
Downhill
Hylton Red House
Town End Farm
Mount Pleasant
Follingsby
Stephenson
RIVER TYNE
RIVER WEAR
TYNE TUNNEL
BERGEN STAVANGER GOTHENBERG ESBJERG KRISTIANSAND
WASHINGTON WILDFOWL REFUGE
Washington-Birtley Services
NORTH OF ENGLAND OPEN AIR MUSEUM
0 1 2 MILES
A1
A1(M)
A19
A184
A194
A194(M)
A167
A189
A1058
A1018
A1231
A1300
A690
A692

NEWCASTLE
A167 JEDBURGH (A696)
A189 ASHINGTON
A1058 TYNEMOUTH
Metro Station
ST JAMES
Royal Victoria Infirmary
Richardson Road
LEAZES PARK
JESMOND
HANCOCK MUSEUM
UNIVERSITY MUSEUM
UNIVERSITY THEATRE
UNIVERSITY
CIVIC CENTRE
SANDYFORD
Newcastle Upon Tyne Polytechnic
City Hall
Northumberland Road
Haymarket Bus Sta.
HAYMARKET
Newcastle United F.C.
BARRACK RD
Eldon Sq. Centre
MONUMENT
LAING ART GALLERY
NEW BRIDGE STREET
MANORS
GALLOWGATE
BLACKETT ST.
Market
CITY WALLS
THEATRE ROYAL
PLUMMER TOWER MUSEUM
Bus Sta.
MELBOURNE ST.
CITY ROAD
Old Assembly Rooms
JOHN GEORGE JOICEY MUSEUM
WESTGATE ROAD
CATHEDRAL
R.C. CATHEDRAL
TRINITY HOUSE
QUAYSIDE
RIVER TYNE
Quay
CENTRAL STATION
KEEP MUS
CASTLE
BLACK GATE
BAGPIPE MUSEUM
Marlborough Cres. Bus Sta.
GUILDHALL
Swing Bridge
Tyne Bridge
FORTH BANKS
High Level Bridge
Queen Elizabeth II Bridge
B1307 TO DURHAM (A167)
A167 TO SUNDERLAND (A184)
A6082 CONSETT (A692)
A695 BLAYDON
A6115 CORBRIDGE (A69)
A187 TYNEMOUTH
0 ¼ MILE

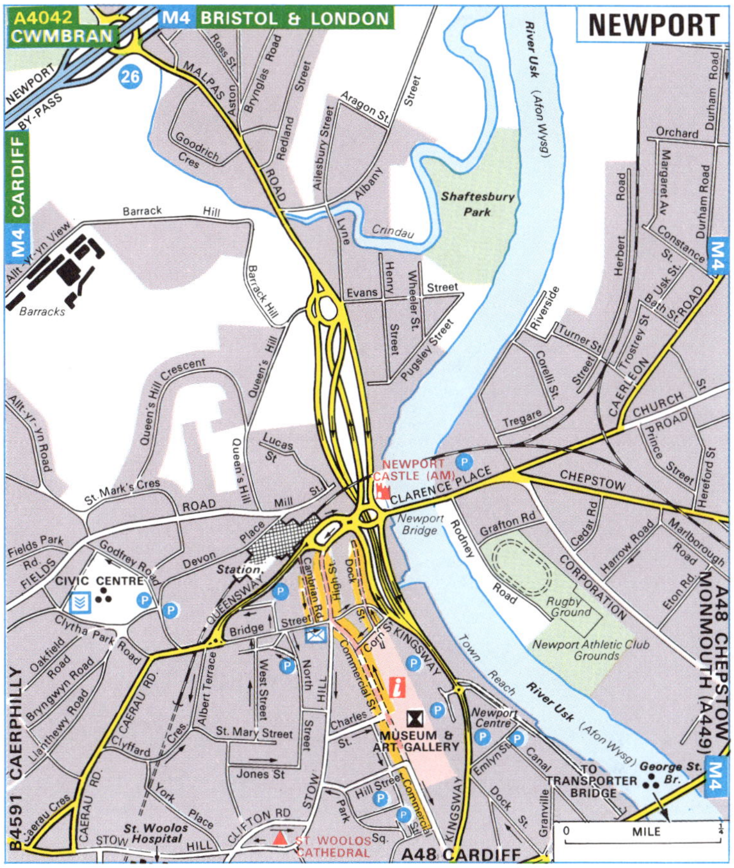
A4042 CWMBRAN
M4 BRISTOL & LONDON
NEWPORT
NEWPORT BY-PASS
26
M4 CARDIFF
Barracks
Barrack Hill
Shaftesbury Park
River Usk (Afon Wysg)
Crindau
Queen's Hill Crescent
Caerleon Road
CHURCH ROAD
Clarence Place
NEWPORT CASTLE (AM)
Newport Bridge
CHEPSTOW ROAD
CORPORATION ROAD
St. Mark's Cres
CIVIC CENTRE
Station
Rugby Ground
Newport Athletic Club Grounds
Bridge Street
MUSEUM & ART GALLERY
Newport Centre
St. Mary Street
KINGSWAY
TRANSPORTER BRIDGE
St. Woolos Hospital
ST. WOOLOS CATHEDRAL
A48 CARDIFF
B4591 CAERPHILLY
A48 CHEPSTOW MONMOUTH (A449)
M4
0 MILE

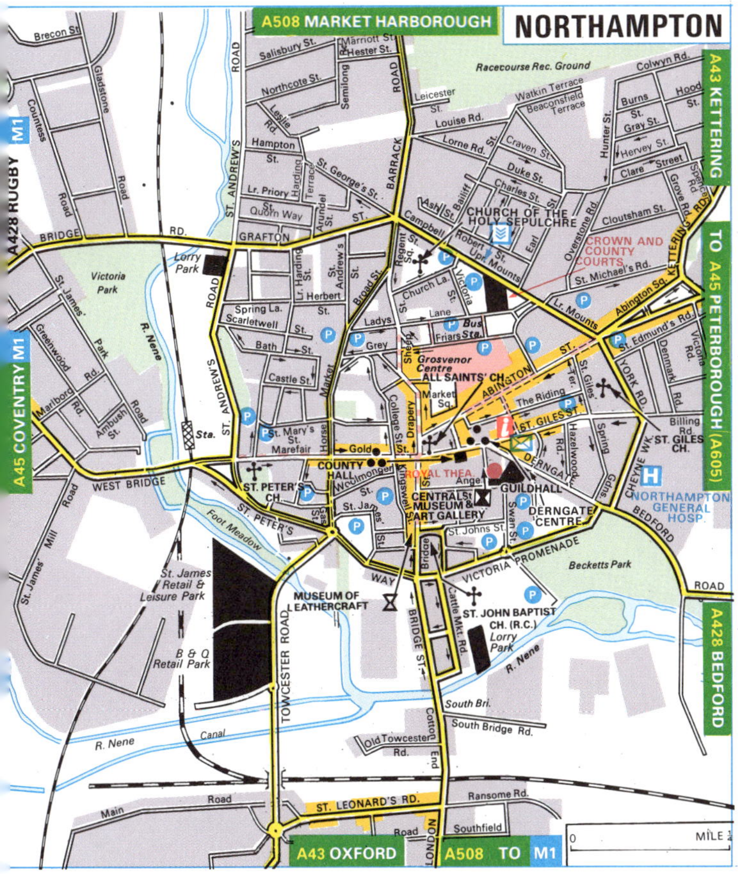
A508 MARKET HARBOROUGH
NORTHAMPTON
Racecourse Rec. Ground
A43 KETTERING
TO A45 PETERBOROUGH (A605)
M1
A428 RUGBY
A45 COVENTRY M1
Victoria Park
R. Nene
CHURCH OF THE HOLY SEPULCHRE
CROWN AND COUNTY COURTS
Grosvenor Centre
ALL SAINTS' CH.
Bus Sta.
Market Sq.
ST. GILES
ST. GILES CH.
NORTHAMPTON GENERAL HOSP.
ROYAL THEA.
GUILDHALL
CENTRAL MUSEUM ART GALLERY
DERNGATE CENTRE
COUNTY HALL
ST. PETER'S CH.
Sta.
WEST BRIDGE
Foot Meadow
Beckett's Park
St. James Retail & Leisure Park
B & Q Retail Park
MUSEUM OF LEATHERCRAFT
ST. JOHN BAPTIST CH. (R.C.)
VICTORIA PROMENADE
TOWCESTER ROAD
BRIDGE ST.
South Bridge Rd.
ST. LEONARD'S RD.
A43 OXFORD
A508 TO M1
A428 BEDFORD
0 ¼ MILE

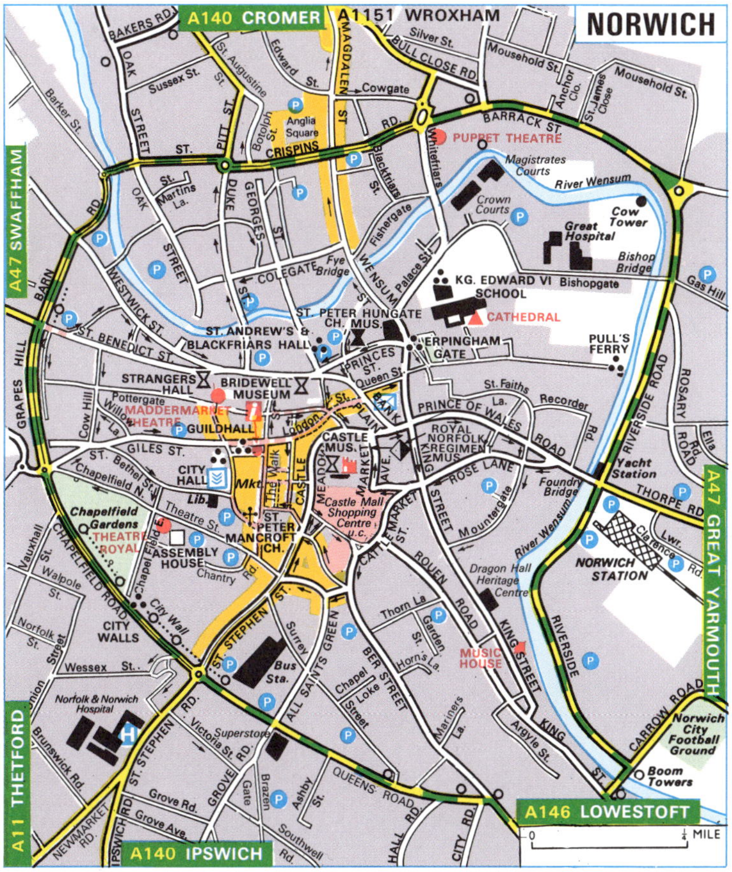
A140 CROMER
A1151 WROXHAM
NORWICH
BARRACK ST
PUPPET THEATRE
Magistrates Courts
Crown Courts
River Wensum
Cow Tower
Great Hospital
Bishop Bridge
Anglia Square
CRISPINS
KG. EDWARD VI SCHOOL
CATHEDRAL
Fye Bridge
ST. PETER HUNGATE CH. MUS.
ST. ANDREW'S & BLACKFRIARS HALL
ERPINGHAM GATE
PULL'S FERRY
STRANGERS HALL
BRIDEWELL MUSEUM
MADDERMARKET THEATRE
GUILDHALL
CASTLE MUS.
ROYAL NORFOLK REGIMENT MUS.
CITY HALL
Mkt
Castle Mall Shopping Centre
Chapelfield Gardens
THEATRE ROYAL
ASSEMBLY HOUSE
ST. PETER MANCROFT CH.
Yacht Station
NORWICH STATION
Dragon Hall Heritage Centre
MUSIC HOUSE
CITY WALLS
Bus Sta.
Norfolk & Norwich Hospital
ALL SAINTS GREEN
KING STREET
RIVERSIDE
Norwich City Football Ground
Boom Towers
A47 SWAFFHAM
A47 GREAT YARMOUTH
A146 LOWESTOFT
A11 THETFORD
A140 IPSWICH
0 ¼ MILE

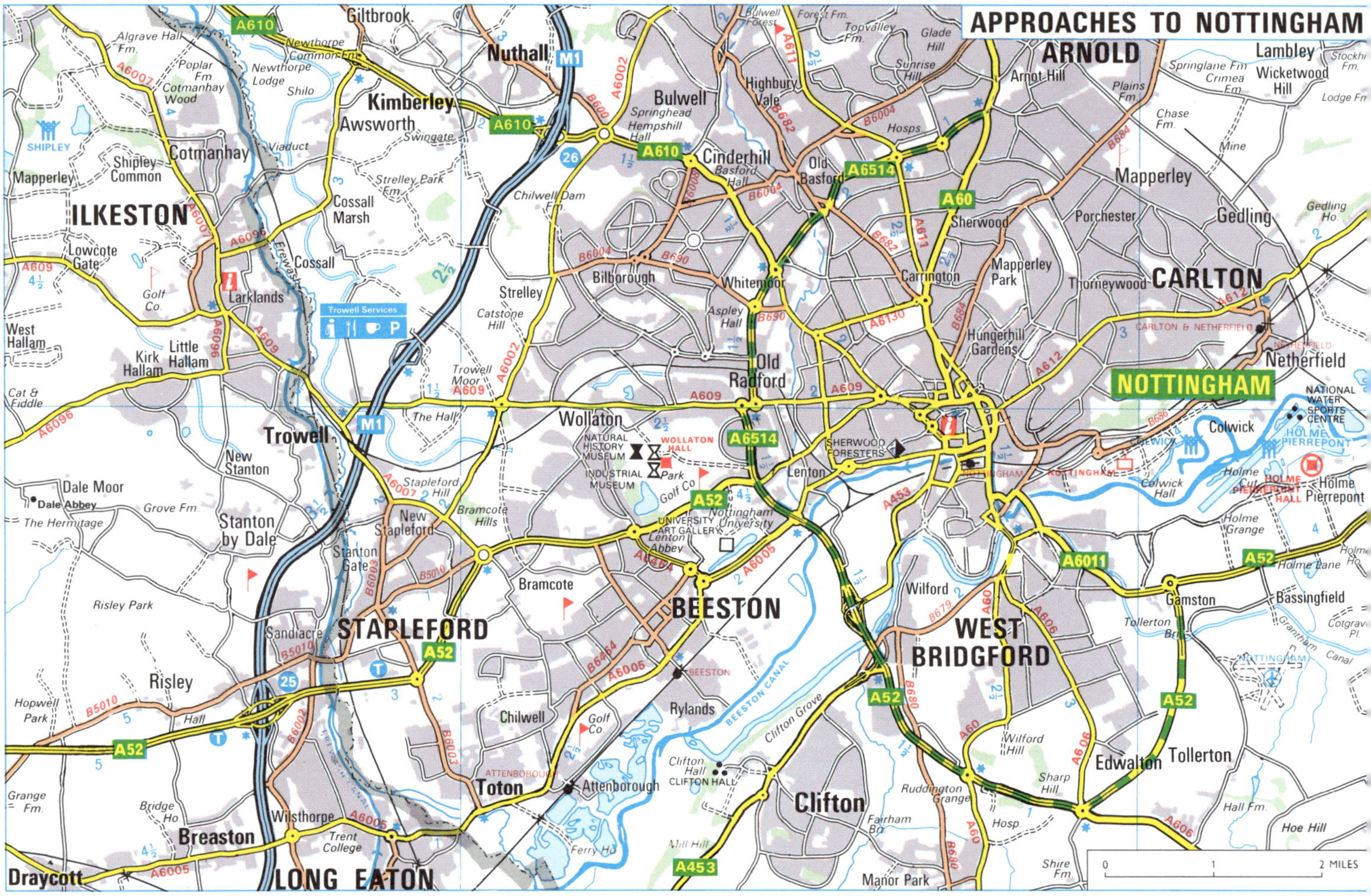
APPROACHES TO NOTTINGHAM
ARNOLD
Arnot Hill
Lambley
Wicketwood Hill
Giltbrook
Nuthall
M1
A610
Kimberley
Awsworth
Bulwell
Cinderhill
Old Basford
A6514
A60
Sherwood
Mapperley
Porchester
Gedling
Mapperley Park
Thorneywood
CARLTON
Netherfield
NOTTINGHAM
Carrington
Hungerhill Gardens
Cotmanhay
Shipley Common
Mapperley
ILKESTON
Larklands
Cossall
Cossall Marsh
Trowell Services
Strelley
Bilborough
Whitemoor
Aspley Hall
Old Radford
West Hallam
Little Hallam
Kirk Hallam
Trowell
New Stanton
Wollaton
Lenton
Sherwood Foresters
Colwick
Holme Pierrepont
Dale Moor
Dale Abbey
The Hermitage
Stanton by Dale
New Stapleford
Bramcote
Nottingham University
University Art Gallery
Lenton Abbey
BEESTON
Wilford
WEST BRIDGFORD
Gamston
Basingfield
Risley Park
Sandiacre
STAPLEFORD
A52
Risley
Hopwell Park
Chilwell
Rylands
Beeston Canal
Clifton Grove
Edwalton
Tollerton
Toton
Attenborough
Clifton Hall
Clifton
Ruddington Grange
Breaston
Wilsthorpe
Trent College
LONG EATON
Draycott
A453
Manor Park
Hoe Hill
0
1
2 MILES

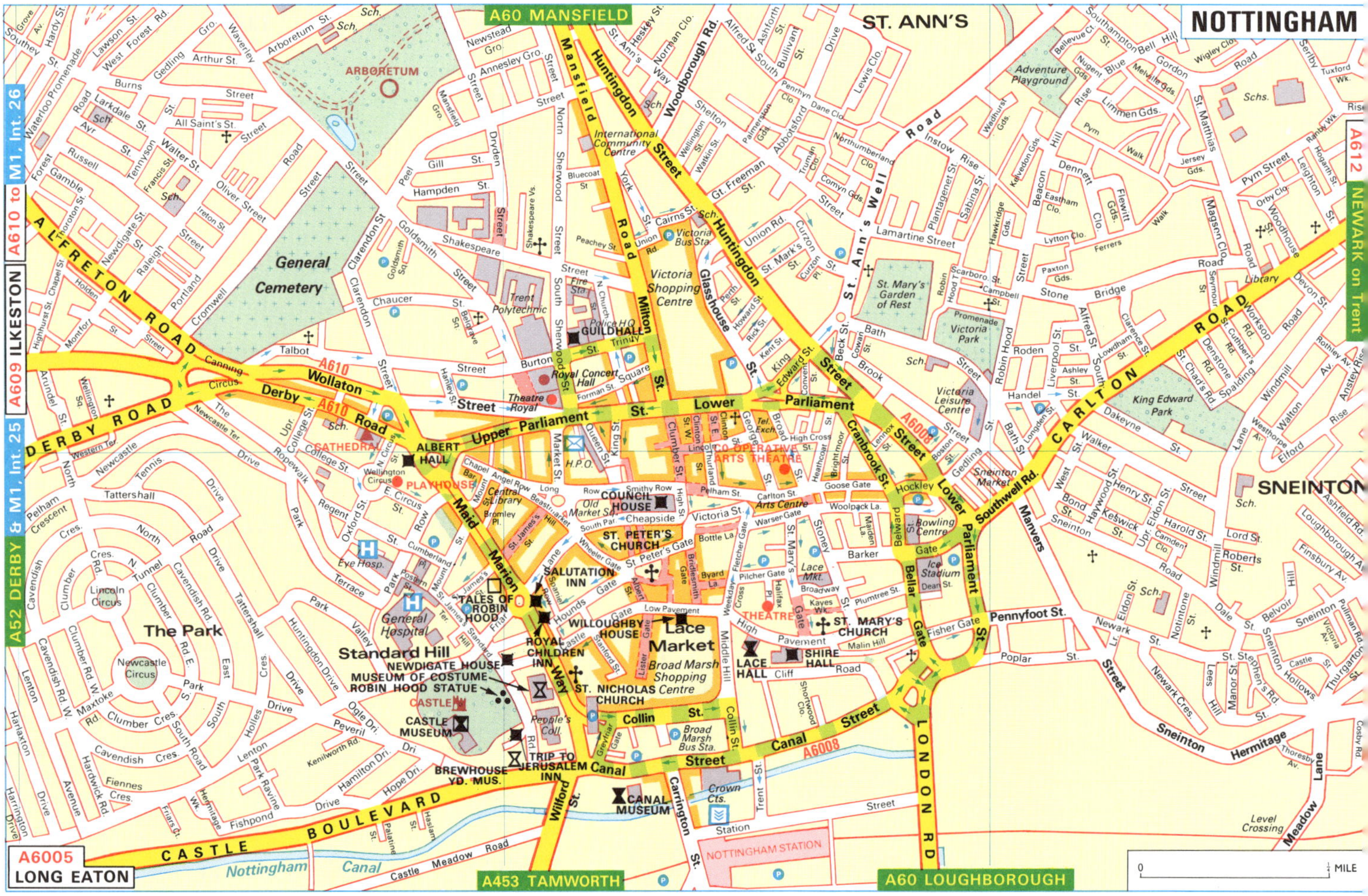
NOTTINGHAM
A60 MANSFIELD
ST. ANN'S
ARBORETUM
General Cemetery
Mansfield Road
Huntingdon Street
Alfreton Road
Derby Road
Wollaton Road
A609 ILKESTON
A610 to M1, Int. 26
A52 DERBY & M1, Int. 25
A612 NEWARK on Trent
International Community Centre
Victoria Shopping Centre
Victoria Bus Sta.
Trent Polytechnic
GUILDHALL
Royal Concert Hall
Theatre Royal
Upper Parliament St.
Lower Parliament
CATHEDRAL
ALBERT HALL
PLAYHOUSE
COUNCIL HOUSE
CO-OPERATIVE ARTS THEATRE
ST. PETER'S CHURCH
Central Library
SALUTATION INN
TALES OF ROBIN HOOD
WILLOUGHBY HOUSE
Lace Market
Broad Marsh Shopping Centre
ROYAL CHILDREN INN
NEWDIGATE HOUSE
MUSEUM OF COSTUME
ROBIN HOOD STATUE
CASTLE
CASTLE MUSEUM
ST. NICHOLAS CHURCH
BREWHOUSE YD. MUS.
TRIP TO JERUSALEM INN
LACE HALL
SHIRE HALL
ST. MARY'S CHURCH
THEATRE
Broad Marsh Bus Sta.
CANAL MUSEUM
Crown Cts.
Station
NOTTINGHAM STATION
Standard Hill
General Hospital
The Park
Newcastle Circus
Lincoln Circus
St. Mary's Garden of Rest
Victoria Park
Victoria Leisure Centre
King Edward Park
Sneinton Market
Ice Stadium
Bowling Centre
SNEINTON
Carlton Road
Southwell Rd.
Pennyfoot St.
London Rd
Canal Street
Castle Boulevard
Nottingham Canal
A6005 LONG EATON
A453 TAMWORTH
A60 LOUGHBOROUGH
0
MILE

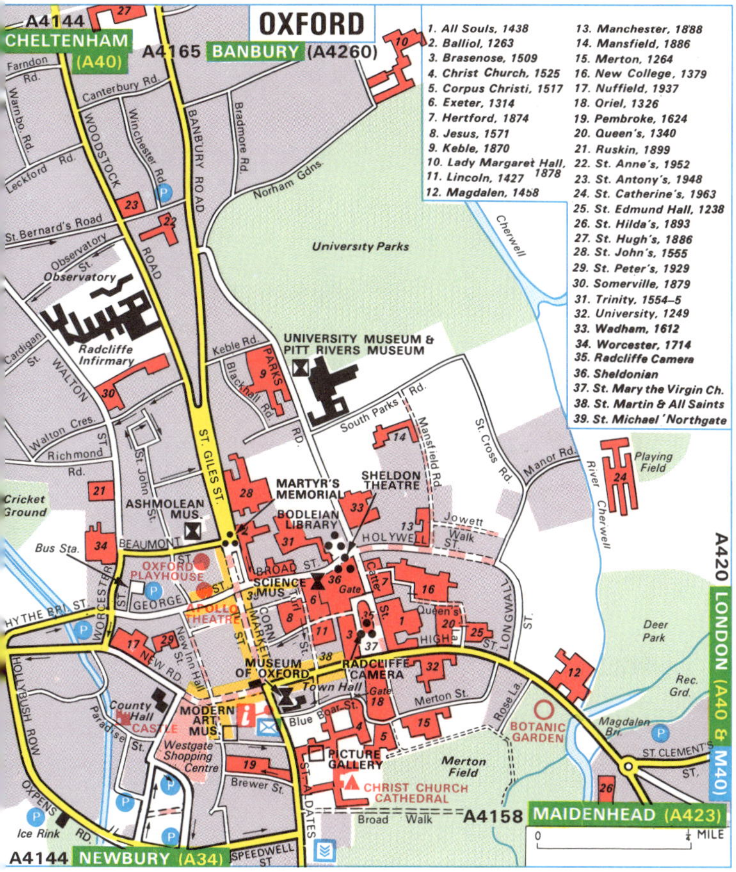
OXFORD
1. All Souls, 1438
2. Balliol, 1263
3. Brasenose, 1509
4. Christ Church, 1525
5. Corpus Christi, 1517
6. Exeter, 1314
7. Hertford, 1874
8. Jesus, 1571
9. Keble, 1870
10. Lady Margaret Hall, 1878
11. Lincoln, 1427
12. Magdalen, 1458
13. Manchester, 1888
14. Mansfield, 1886
15. Merton, 1264
16. New College, 1379
17. Nuffield, 1937
18. Oriel, 1326
19. Pembroke, 1624
20. Queen's, 1340
21. Ruskin, 1899
22. St. Anne's, 1952
23. St. Antony's, 1948
24. St. Catherine's, 1963
25. St. Edmund Hall, 1238
26. St. Hilda's, 1893
27. St. Hugh's, 1886
28. St. John's, 1555
29. St. Peter's, 1929
30. Somerville, 1879
31. Trinity, 1554–5
32. University, 1249
33. Wadham, 1612
34. Worcester, 1714
35. Radcliffe Camera
36. Sheldonian
37. St. Mary the Virgin Ch.
38. St. Martin & All Saints
39. St. Michael Northgate
A4144 CHELTENHAM (A40)
A4165 BANBURY (A4260)
University Parks
UNIVERSITY MUSEUM & PITT RIVERS MUSEUM
Radcliffe Infirmary
ASHMOLEAN MUS.
MARTYR'S MEMORIAL
SHELDON THEATRE
BODLEIAN LIBRARY
OXFORD PLAYHOUSE
APOLLO THEATRE
SCIENCE MUS.
RADCLIFFE CAMERA
MUSEUM OF OXFORD
Town Hall
MODERN ART MUS.
County Hall
CASTLE
Westgate Shopping Centre
PICTURE GALLERY
CHRIST CHURCH CATHEDRAL
Merton Field
BOTANIC GARDEN
Deer Park
Playing Field
Cricket Ground
Bus Sta.
Ice Rink
A420 LONDON (A40 & M40)
A4158 MAIDENHEAD (A423)
A4144 NEWBURY (A34)
0 ¼ MILE

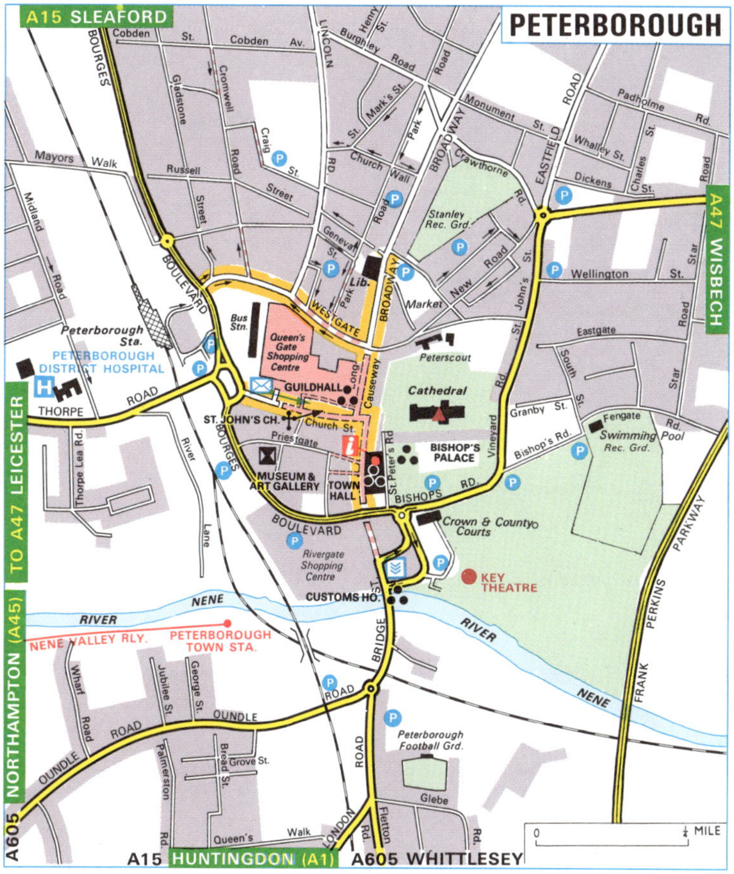
PETERBOROUGH
A15 SLEAFORD
A47 WISBECH
TO A47 LEICESTER
PETERBOROUGH DISTRICT HOSPITAL
Peterborough Sta.
THORPE
Queen's Gate Shopping Centre
GUILDHALL
ST. JOHN'S CH.
Cathedral
BISHOP'S PALACE
MUSEUM & ART GALLERY
TOWN HALL
Crown & County Courts
Rivergate Shopping Centre
CUSTOMS HO.
KEY THEATRE
RIVER NENE
NENE VALLEY RLY.
PETERBOROUGH TOWN STA.
Peterborough Football Grd.
Stanley Rec. Grd.
Swimming Pool
Fengate Rec. Grd.
A605 NORTHAMPTON (A45)
A15 HUNTINGDON (A1)
A605 WHITTLESEY
0 ¼ MILE

APPROACHES TO PLYMOUTH
Tamerton Foliot
Whitleigh
Ernesettle
Tamar Bridge
St. Budeaux
King's Tamerton
Honicknowle
Crownhill
Estover Industrial Estate
Plym Forest
Mainstone
Manadon
Leigham
Eggbuckland
Weston Mill
Ham
Pennycross
Hartley
Woodford
Devonport
Peverell
Efford
Longbridge
Crabtree
Mannamead
Compton
Laira
Ford
Stoke
Mutley
Underwood
SALTRAM HOUSE (NT)
Mount Gould
Hamoaze
Stonehouse
Barbican
Billacombe
Cattedown
Oreston
Pomphlett
Mount Wise
Cremyll
PLYMOUTH
Empacombe
MOUNT EDGCUMBE
Devil's Pt.
Mount Batten Pt.
Turnchapel
Plymstock
Elburton
Drake's Island
Hooe
Goosewell
The Sound
Staddon Heights
SOUTH DEVON COAST PATH
ROSCOFF SANTANDER
Breakwater
Cawsand Bay
Bovisand Bay
Staddiscombe
Down Thomas
Knighton
0 1 MILE

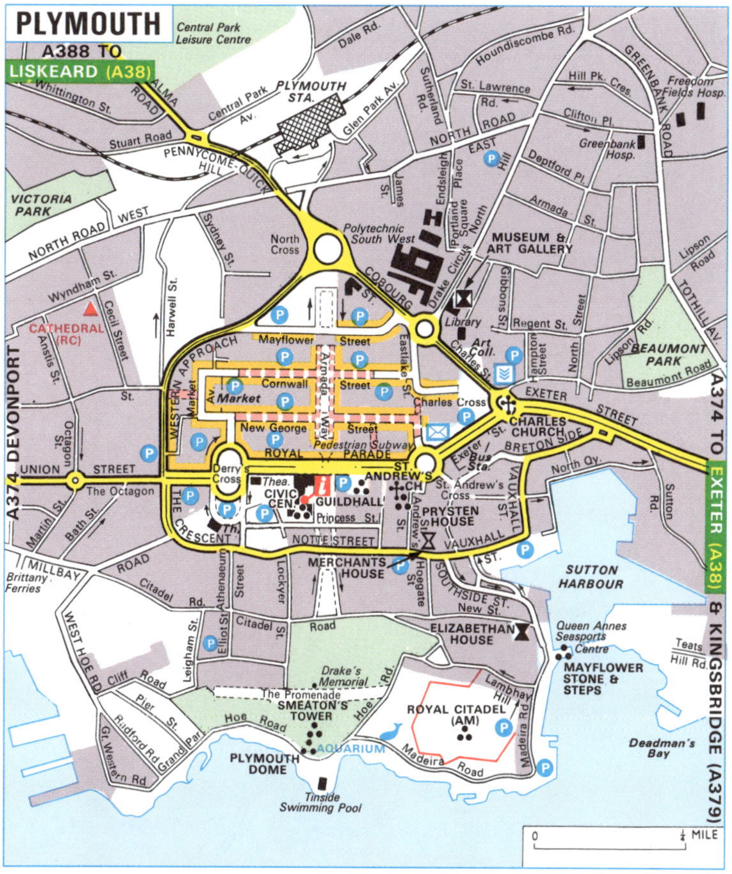
PLYMOUTH
A388 TO LISKEARD (A38)
Central Park Leisure Centre
PLYMOUTH STA.
VICTORIA PARK
North Cross
Polytechnic South West
MUSEUM & ART GALLERY
Library
Art Coll.
BEAUMONT PARK
CATHEDRAL (RC)
Market
CHARLES CHURCH
Pedestrian Subway
Bus Sta.
CIVIC CENTRE
GUILDHALL
ST. ANDREW'S CH.
PRYSTEN HOUSE
MERCHANTS HOUSE
SUTTON HARBOUR
ELIZABETHAN HOUSE
Queen Annes Seasports Centre
MAYFLOWER STONE & STEPS
Drake's Memorial
The Promenade
SMEATON'S TOWER
ROYAL CITADEL (AM)
AQUARIUM
PLYMOUTH DOME
Tinside Swimming Pool
Brittany Ferries
A374 DEVONPORT
A374 TO EXETER (A38) & KINGSBRIDGE (A379)
0 ¼ MILE

APPROACHES TO PORTSMOUTH

Waterlooville
Purbrook
Cosham
FAREHAM
Portchester
Bridgemary
GOSPORT
Alverstoke
PORTSMOUTH
Portsea
Southsea
PORTSMOUTH HARBOUR
PORTSEA ISLAND
LANGSTONE HARBOUR
HAVANT
Emsworth
Westbourne
Langstone
HAYLING ISLAND
South Hayling
Stokes Bay
Hayling Bay
Wallington
Drayton
Farlington
Hilsea
North End
Fratton
Milton
Eastney
Bedhampton
Stockheath
Warblington
Thorney Island
Southwick
Widley
Wymering
Paulsgrove
Privett
Anglesey
Elson
Rowner
Brockhurst
Lee on the Solent
DICKENS' BIRTHPLACE MUSEUM
PORTCHESTER CASTLE (AM)
SOUTHSEA CASTLE
D-DAY MUSEUM
ROYAL MARINES MUSEUM
CUMBERLAND HOUSE MUSEUM & AQUARIUM
SUBMARINE MUSEUM
GOSPORT MUSEUM
0 1 2 MILES

PORTSMOUTH

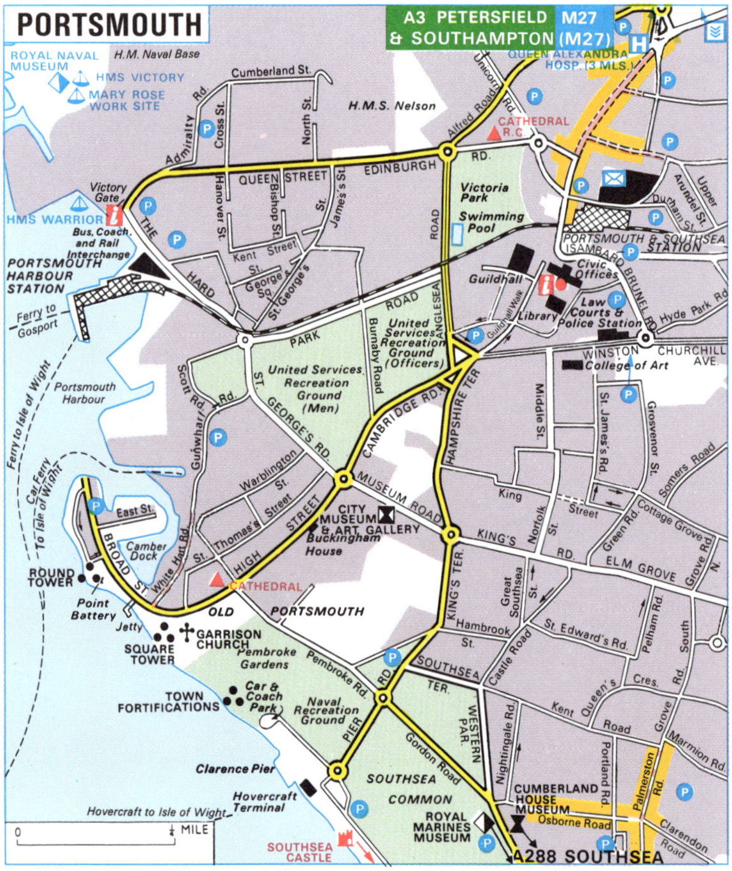
A3 PETERSFIELD & SOUTHAMPTON
M27 (M27)
ROYAL NAVAL MUSEUM
H.M. Naval Base
HMS VICTORY
MARY ROSE WORK SITE
HMS WARRIOR
Victory Gate
PORTSMOUTH HARBOUR STATION
Ferry to Gosport
QUEEN STREET
EDINBURGH RD.
CATHEDRAL R.C.
Victoria Park
Swimming Pool
PORTSMOUTH & SOUTHSEA STATION
Guildhall
Civic Offices
Law Courts & Police Station
Library
College of Art
United Services Recreation Ground (Officers)
United Services Recreation Ground (Men)
CITY MUSEUM & ART GALLERY
Buckingham House
CATHEDRAL
ROUND TOWER
Point Battery
SQUARE TOWER
GARRISON CHURCH
Pembroke Gardens
TOWN FORTIFICATIONS
Naval Recreation Ground
Clarence Pier
Hovercraft Terminal
Hovercraft to Isle of Wight
SOUTHSEA COMMON
ROYAL MARINES MUSEUM
CUMBERLAND HOUSE MUSEUM
SOUTHSEA CASTLE
A288 SOUTHSEA
QUEEN ALEXANDRA HOSP. (3 MLS.)
0 ¼ MILE

READING

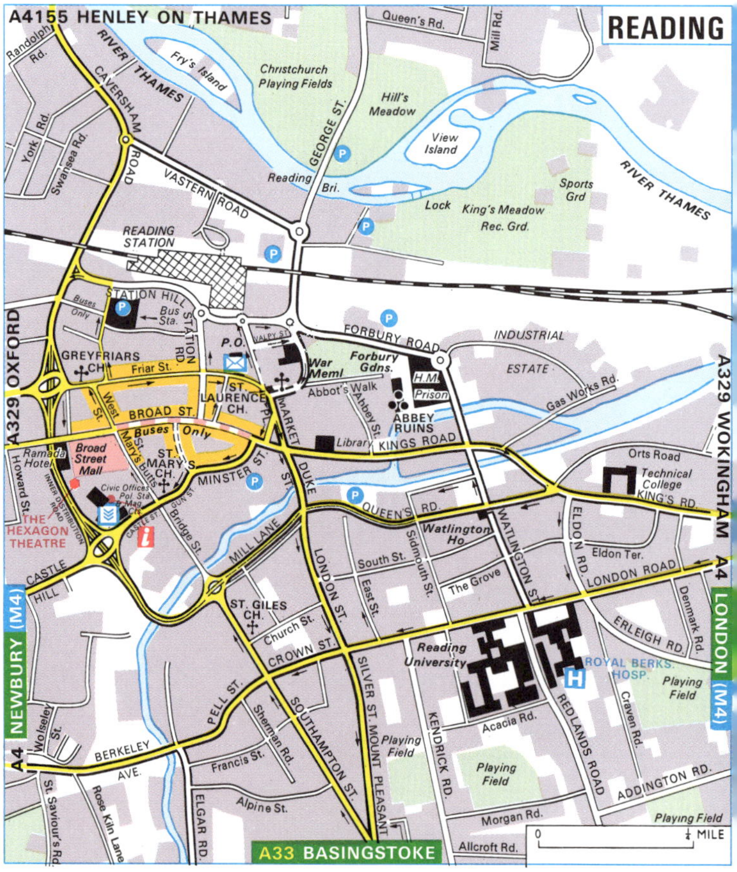
A4155 HENLEY ON THAMES
RIVER THAMES
Fry's Island
Christchurch Playing Fields
Hill's Meadow
View Island
King's Meadow Rec. Grd.
READING STATION
Reading Bri.
CAVERSHAM ROAD
VASTERN ROAD
GREYFRIARS CH.
Friar St.
BROAD ST.
ST. LAURENCE CH.
Broad Street Mall
ST. MARY'S CH.
THE HEXAGON THEATRE
FORBURY ROAD
Forbury Gdns.
H.M. Prison
ABBEY RUINS
KINGS ROAD
INDUSTRIAL ESTATE
Technical College
Watlington Ho.
Reading University
ROYAL BERKS HOSP.
A329 OXFORD
A329 WOKINGHAM
A4 LONDON (M4)
A4 NEWBURY (M4)
A33 BASINGSTOKE
LONDON ROAD
0 ¼ MILE

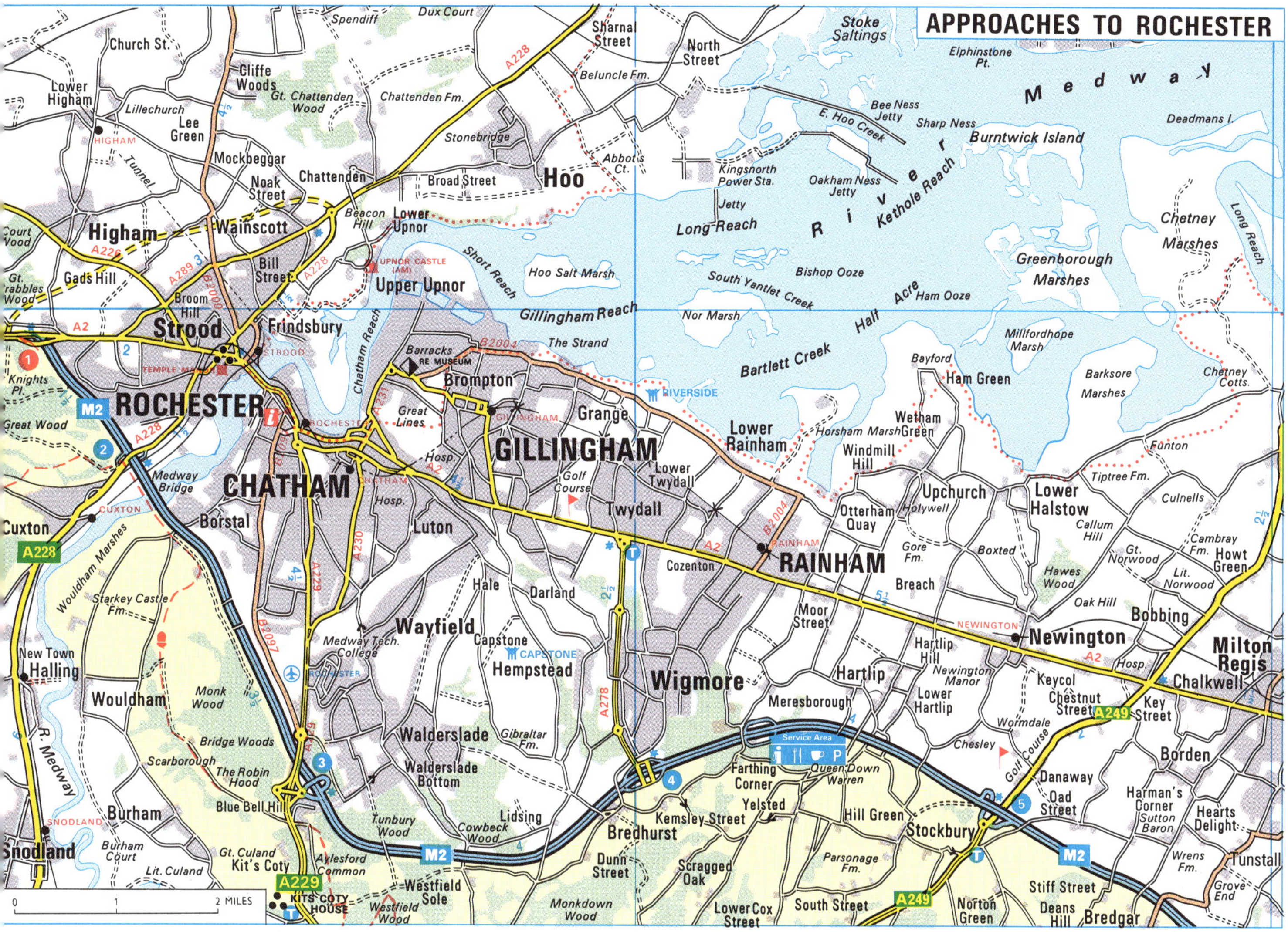
APPROACHES TO ROCHESTER
Spendiff
Dux Court
Sharnal Street
North Street
Stoke Saltings
Elphinstone Pt.
Church St.
Lower Higham
Cliffe Woods
Gt. Chattenden Wood
Chattenden Fm.
Beluncle Fm.
Lillechurch
Lee Green
HIGHAM
Stonebridge
Abbot's Ct.
Bee Ness Jetty
E. Hoo Creek
Sharp Ness
Burntwick Island
Medway
Deadmans I.
Tunnel
Mockbeggar
Noak Street
Chattenden
Broad Street
Hoo
Kingsnorth Power Sta.
Oakham Ness Jetty
River
Kethole Reach
Jetty
Long Reach
Chetney Marshes
Court Wood
Higham
Wainscott
Beacon Hill
Lower Upnor
Gt. Crabbles Wood
Gads Hill
Bill Street
UPNOR CASTLE (AM)
Upper Upnor
Short Reach
Hoo Salt Marsh
Bishop Ooze
South Yantlet Creek
Greenborough Marshes
Broom Hill
Strood
Frindsbury
STROOD
Gillingham Reach
Nor Marsh
Ham Ooze
Hall
Acre
Millfordhope Marsh
Bartlett Creek
The Strand
Chatham Reach
Barracks RE MUSEUM
B2004
Brompton
RIVERSIDE
Bayford
Ham Green
Barksore Marshes
Chetney Cotts.
Knights Pl.
TEMPLE MANOR
ROCHESTER
M2
Great Lines
GILLINGHAM
Grange
Lower Rainham
Horsham Marsh
Wetham Green
Great Wood
Hosp.
Windmill Hill
Funton
Medway Bridge
CHATHAM
CHATHAM
GILLINGHAM
Golf Course
Lower Twydall
Upchurch
Lower Halstow
Tiptree Fm.
Culnells
Cuxton
CUXTON
Borstal
Hosp.
Luton
Twydall
Otterham Quay
Holywell
Callum Hill
Cambray Fm.
Howt Green
A228
Wouldham Marshes
Cozenton
RAINHAM
RAINHAM
Gore Fm.
Boxted
Gt. Norwood
Lit. Norwood
Hale
Darland
Moor Street
Breach
Hawes Wood
Starkey Castle Fm.
Wayfield
Medway Tech. College
Capstone
CAPSTONE
Hempstead
Oak Hill
NEWINGTON
Newington
Bobbing
Milton Regis
New Town
Halling
ROCHESTER AIRPORT
Wigmore
Hartlip
Hartlip Hill
Newington Manor
Hosp.
Chalkwell
Keycol
Chestnut Street
Key Street
Wouldham
Monk Wood
Meresborough
Lower Hartlip
A249
Walderslade
Gibraltar Fm.
Service Area
Wormdale
R. Medway
Bridge Woods
Chesley
Golf Course
Borden
Scarborough
The Robin Hood
Walderslade Bottom
Farthing Corner
Queen Down Warren
Danaway
Blue Bell Hill
Yelsted
Oad Street
Harman's Corner
Sutton Baron
Hearts Delight
Burham
Tunbury Wood
Cowbeck Wood
Lidsing
Kemsley Street
Hill Green
Stockbury
SNODLAND
Bredhurst
Snodland
Burham Court
Gt. Culand
Kit's Coty
Aylesford Common
Dunn Street
Scragged Oak
Parsonage Fm.
Wrens Fm.
Tunstall
Lit. Culand
Westfield Sole
Stiff Street
Grove End
A229
KITS COTY HOUSE
Westfield Wood
Monkdown Wood
Lower Cox Street
South Street
Norton Green
Deans Hill
Bredgar
0
1
2 MILES

ROCHESTER
Grange Rd.
STATION RD.
STROOD STA.
Canal Rd.
River
Medway
Bridge Reach
Enterprise Close
Anthony's Way
Neptune Close
A2 LONDON
Rochester Bridge
Guildhall
Library
Castle Hill
CASTLE
Boley Hill
CATHEDRAL
The Precinct
High St.
CORPORATION
STREET
Limehouse
Reach
Blue Boar La.
MUSEUM
Vines Lane
East Row
ROCHESTER STA.
Esplanade
ST. MARGARET'S ST.
King Edward Rd.
Roebuck Rd.
WATTS AVE.
MAIDSTONE RD.
Union St.
King St.
Victoria St.
STAR HILL
HIGH ST.
A231 GILLINGHAM A2
Gordon Terr.
Ridley Rd.
South Ave.
John St.
James St.
Foord St.
Ross St.
Church St.
NEW ROAD
Hosp.
Gundulph Rd.
NEW RD AVE
CANTERBURY
Rochester Ave.
DELCE ROAD
CITY WAY
Coll.
FORT PITT HILL
CHATHAM STA.
Ethelbert Rd.
Castle Ave.
Sch.
Boundary Rd.
Fort Pitt St.
Ordnance St.
A229 MAIDSTONE
0
¼ MILE

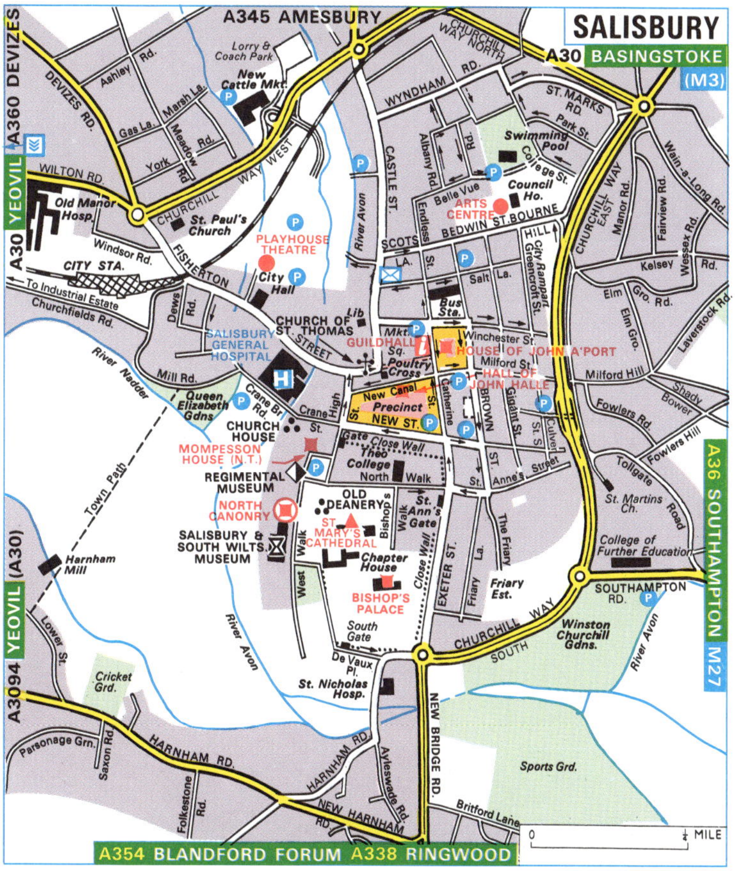
SALISBURY
A345 AMESBURY
CHURCHILL WAY NORTH
A30 BASINGSTOKE (M3)
A360 DEVIZES
Lorry & Coach Park
New Cattle Mkt.
Ashley Rd.
DEVIZES RD.
Gas La.
Marsh La.
Meadow Rd.
York Rd.
CHURCHILL WAY WEST
WYNDHAM RD.
ST. MARKS RD.
Park St.
Swimming Pool
College St.
A30 YEOVIL
WILTON RD.
Old Manor Hosp.
St. Paul's Church
FISHERTON
River Avon
CASTLE ST.
Albany Rd.
Endless St.
Belle Vue
ARTS CENTRE
Council Ho.
BEDWIN ST.
BOURNE HILL
CHURCHILL WAY EAST
Manor Rd.
Fairview Rd.
Wain-a-Long Rd.
Wessex Rd.
Windsor Rd.
CITY STA.
PLAYHOUSE THEATRE
City Hall
SCOTS LA.
Salt La.
City Rampart
Greencroft St.
Kelsey Rd.
To Industrial Estate
Churchfields Rd.
Dews Rd.
CHURCH OF ST. THOMAS
Lib.
Bus Sta.
Elm Gro. Rd.
Laverstock Rd.
SALISBURY GENERAL HOSPITAL
Mkt. Pl.
GUILDHALL
Sq.
Winchester St.
HOUSE OF JOHN A'PORT
Poultry Cross
Milford St.
HALL OF JOHN HALLE
Milford Hill
River Nadder
Mill Rd.
Queen Elizabeth Gdns.
Crane Br. Rd.
Crane St.
High St.
New Canal
Precinct
NEW ST.
Catherine St.
BROWN ST.
Gigant St.
St. St.
Culver St.
Fowlers Rd.
Shady Bower
Fowlers Hill
CHURCH HOUSE
MOMPESSON HOUSE (N.T.)
Close Wall
Theo. College
North Walk
St. Ann's Street
Town Path
REGIMENTAL MUSEUM
OLD DEANERY
Bishop's Walk
St. Ann's Gate
Tollgate Road
St. Martins Ch.
A36 SOUTHAMPTON M27
NORTH CANONRY
ST. MARY'S CATHEDRAL
SALISBURY & SOUTH WILTS. MUSEUM
West Walk
Chapter House
Close Wall Rd.
EXETER ST.
Friary La.
The Friary
Friary Est.
College of Further Education
SOUTHAMPTON RD.
Harnham Mill
A30 YEOVIL
BISHOP'S PALACE
South Gate
CHURCHILL WAY SOUTH
Winston Churchill Gdns.
River Avon
Lower St.
De Vaux Pl.
St. Nicholas Hosp.
A3094
Cricket Grd.
Parsonage Grn.
Saxon Rd.
River Avon
HARNHAM RD.
HARNHAM RD.
NEW BRIDGE RD.
Sports Grd.
Folkestone Rd.
NEW HARNHAM RD.
Aylesw Rd.
Britford Lane
A354 BLANDFORD FORUM
A338 RINGWOOD
0
¼ MILE

SCARBOROUGH
NORTH BAY
SOUTH BAY
North Sands
South Sands
A165 WHITBY (A171)
A64 YORK
A165 BRIDLINGTON
SCARBOROUGH ZOO & MARINELAND
NORTH CLIFF LIFT
Alexandra Gdns.
Alexandra Bowling Hall
MINIATURE RAILWAY
Peasholm Park
Castle Holms
Castle Keep
SCARBOROUGH CASTLE (A.M.)
ROMAN SIGNAL STATION
Queen's Tower Remains
Castle Walls
ST. MARY'S CHURCH
ST. THOMAS'S MUSEUM
Old Harbour
West Pier
East Pier
FUTURIST THEATRE
ST. NICHOLAS LIFT
CENTRAL TRAMWAY
ROTUNDA MUSEUM
CRESCENT ART GALLERY
WOOD END
CENTRAL STA
THEATRE IN THE ROUND
LONDESBOROUGH LODGE
ROYAL OPERA HOUSE
Town Hall
Lib.
Coach Park
Cricket Grd.
THE SPA
SPA THEATRE
SOUTH CLIFF TRAMWAY
0 ¼ MILE

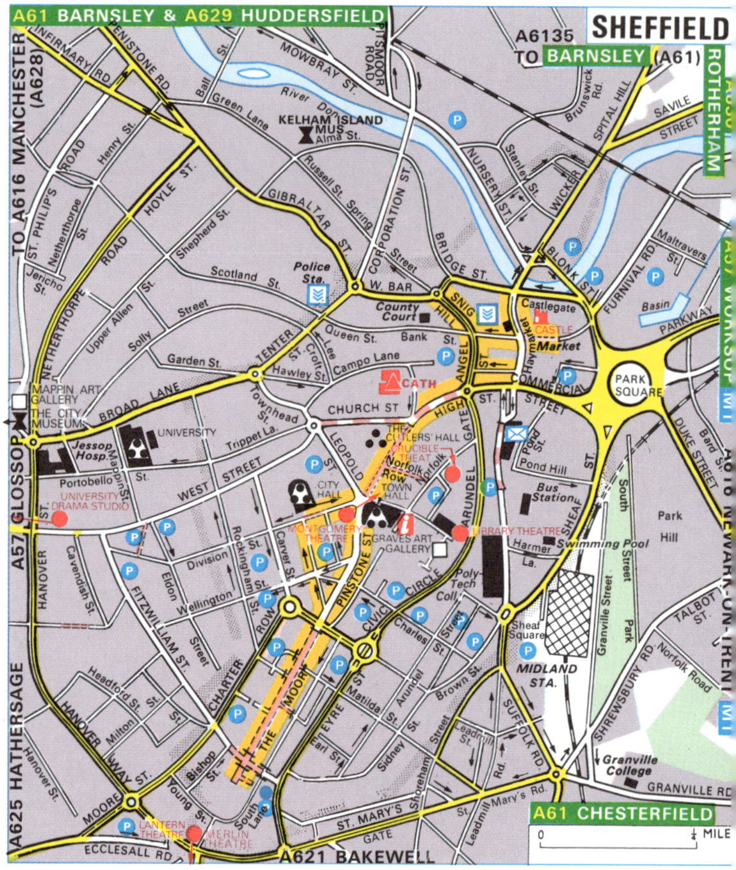
SHEFFIELD
A61 BARNSLEY & A629 HUDDERSFIELD
A6135 TO BARNSLEY (A61)
ROTHERHAM
TO A616 MANCHESTER (A628)
A57 GLOSSOP
A625 HATHERSAGE
A621 BAKEWELL
A61 CHESTERFIELD
KELHAM ISLAND MUS.
Police Sta.
County Court
CATH
Castlegate
Market
PARK SQUARE
MAPPIN ART GALLERY
THE CITY MUSEUM
UNIVERSITY
Jessop Hosp.
UNIVERSITY DRAMA STUDIO
CUTLERS' HALL
CRUCIBLE THEATRE
CITY HALL
TOWN HALL
GRAVES ART GALLERY
LYCEUM THEATRE
Swimming Pool
Poly. Tech. Coll.
Sheaf Square
MIDLAND STA.
Granville College
LANTERN THEATRE
MERLIN THEATRE
0 ¼ MILE

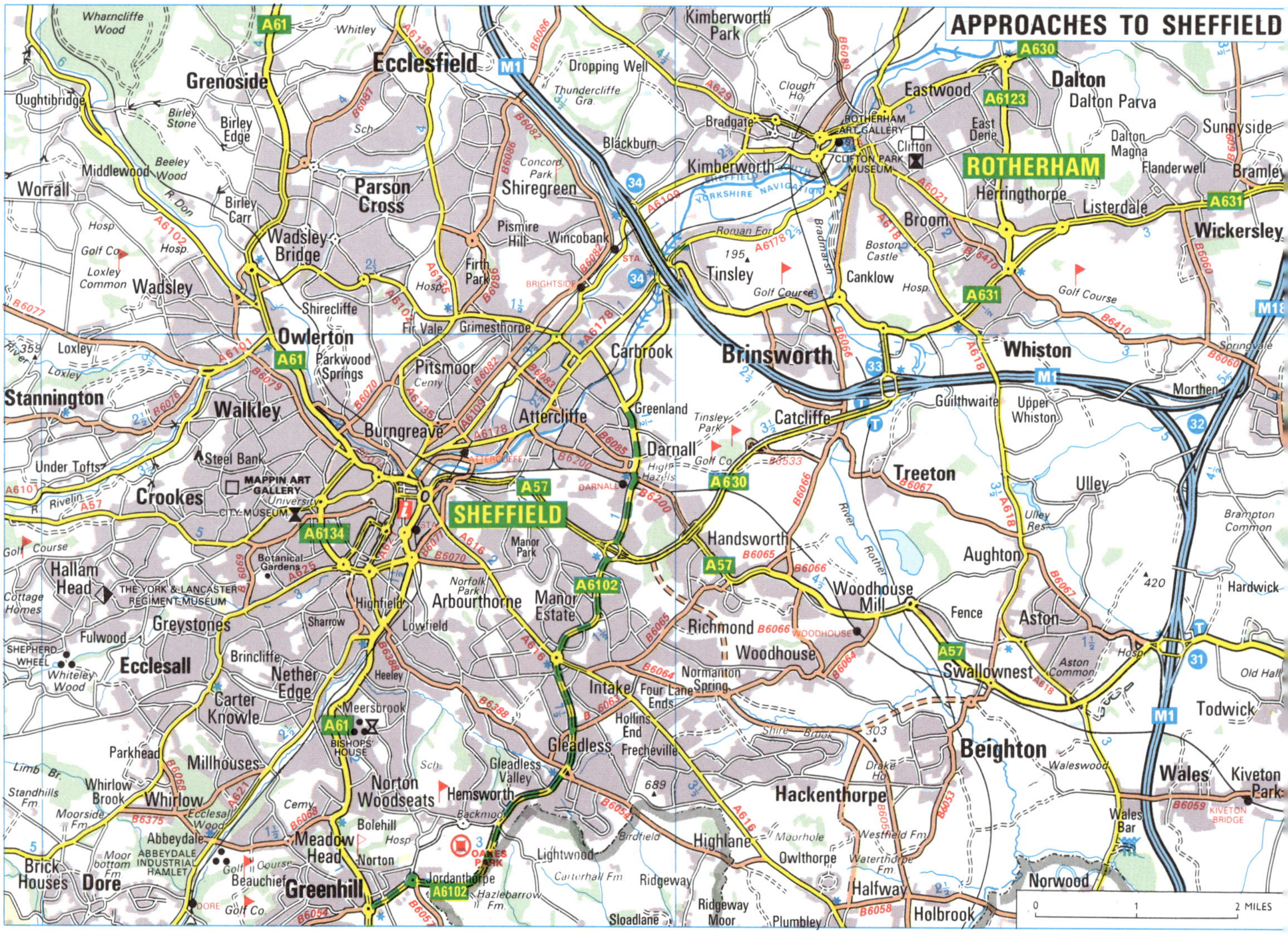
APPROACHES TO SHEFFIELD
SHEFFIELD
ROTHERHAM
Ecclesfield
Grenoside
Parson Cross
Shiregreen
Wadsley Bridge
Wadsley
Owlerton
Walkley
Stannington
Crookes
Burngreave
Attercliffe
Darnall
Brinsworth
Catcliffe
Treeton
Whiston
Wickersley
Dalton
Kimberworth
Tinsley
Handsworth
Woodhouse
Hallam Head
Ecclesall
Greystones
Nether Edge
Carter Knowle
Arbourthorne
Manor Estate
Intake
Gleadless
Norton Woodseats
Millhouses
Whirlow
Dore
Greenhill
Beighton
Hackenthorpe
Swallownest
Aughton
Ulley
Wales
Kiveton Park
Todwick
MAPPIN ART GALLERY
CITY MUSEUM
THE YORK & LANCASTER REGIMENT MUSEUM
ROTHERHAM ART GALLERY
CLIFTON PARK MUSEUM
SHEFFIELD & TINSLEY CANAL
0 1 2 MILES

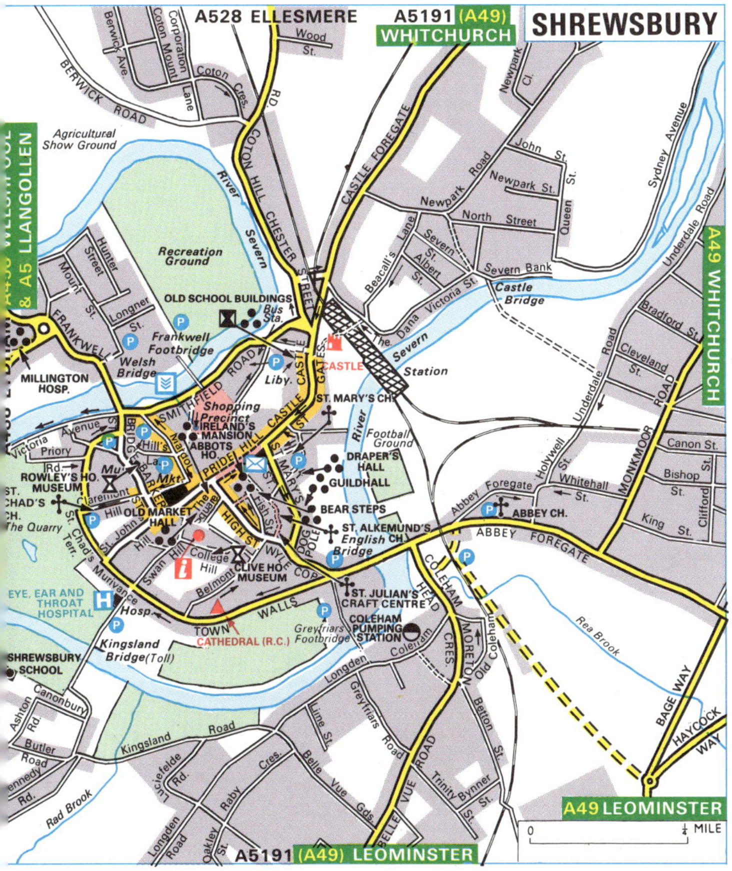
SHREWSBURY
A528 ELLESMERE
A5191 (A49) WHITCHURCH
A49 WHITCHURCH
A5 WELSHPOOL & A5 LLANGOLLEN
A49 LEOMINSTER
A5191 (A49) LEOMINSTER
Agricultural Show Ground
Recreation Ground
OLD SCHOOL BUILDINGS
Frankwell Footbridge
Welsh Bridge
MILLINGTON HOSP.
Shopping Precinct
IRELAND'S MANSION
ABBOTS HO
ROWLEY'S HO MUSEUM
OLD MARKET HALL
The Quarry
EYE, EAR AND THROAT HOSPITAL
SHREWSBURY SCHOOL
Kingsland Bridge (Toll)
TOWN WALLS
CATHEDRAL (R.C.)
CLIVE HO MUSEUM
College Hill
Castle Bridge
CASTLE
Station
ST. MARY'S CH
DRAPER'S HALL
GUILDHALL
BEAR STEPS
ST. ALKEMUND'S CH
English Bridge
ST. JULIAN'S CRAFT CENTRE
COLEHAM PUMPING STATION
Greyfriars Footbridge
ABBEY CH.
ABBEY FOREGATE
Football Ground
Liby.
Bus Sta.
CASTLE FOREGATE
Severn Bank
North Street
Newpark Road
Sydney Avenue
Underdale Road
MONKMOOR ROAD
Whitehall St.
Rea Brook
BAGE WAY
HAYCOCK WAY
Kingsland Road
Rad Brook
River Severn
0 ½ MILE

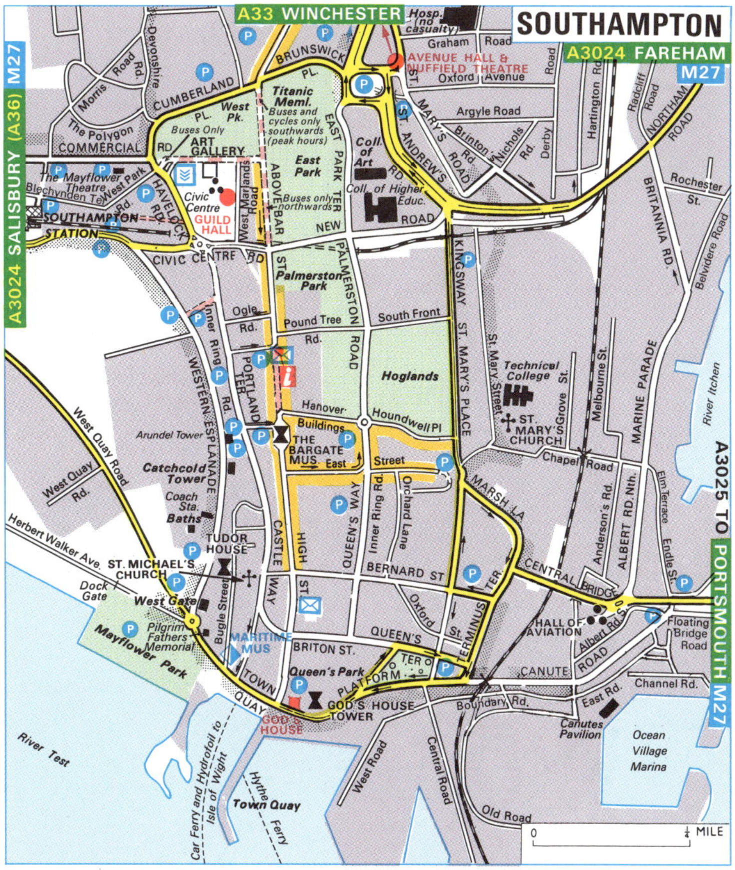
SOUTHAMPTON
A33 WINCHESTER
A3024 FAREHAM
M27
M27 A3024 SALISBURY (A36)
A3025 TO PORTSMOUTH M27
AVENUE HALL & NUFFIELD THEATRE
Hosp. (no casualty)
CUMBERLAND PL.
The Polygon
COMMERCIAL RD
Titanic Meml.
West Pk.
ART GALLERY
Civic Centre
GUILD HALL
The Mayflower Theatre
SOUTHAMPTON STATION
CIVIC CENTRE RD
East Park
Coll. of Art
Coll. of Higher Educ.
Palmerston Park
Hoglands
Technical College
ST. MARY'S CHURCH
Arundel Tower
Catchcold Tower
THE BARGATE
MUS
Coach Sta.
Baths
TUDOR HOUSE
ST. MICHAEL'S CHURCH
West Gate
Pilgrim Fathers Memorial
Mayflower Park
MARITIME MUS
Queen's Park
GOD'S HOUSE TOWER
GOD'S HOUSE
Town Quay
HALL OF AVIATION
Floating Bridge Road
Canutes Pavilion
Ocean Village Marina
River Itchen
River Test
Car Ferry and Hydrofoil to Isle of Wight
Hythe Ferry
WESTERN ESPLANADE
PORTLAND TER
ABOVE BAR
HIGH ST
QUEEN'S WAY
KINGSWAY
ST. MARY'S PLACE
MARSH LA
TERMINUS TER
BERNARD ST
BRITON ST.
CANUTE ROAD
PLATFORM RD
West Quay Rd.
Herbert Walker Ave.
Old Road
0 ½ MILE

APPROACHES TO SOUTHAMPTON
Romsey
ROMSEY ABBEY
Whitenap
North Baddesley
Chandler's Ford
Fryern Hill
Allbrook
A33 BEING UPGRADED TO MOTORWAY
EASTLEIGH
Bishopstoke
Fisher's Pond
Marwell Manor
MARWELL ZOOLOGICAL PARK
Fair Oak
Crowdhill
Lower Upham
Chilworth
Rownhams
Rownham Services
Nursling
Testwood
Totton
Redbridge
Netley Marsh
Ashurst
Calmore
Hillstreet
Lee
Ridge
Toot Hill
Bassett
Swaythling
SOUTHAMPTON PARKWAY
SOUTHAMPTON AIRPORT
Horton Heath
Durley
Hatch Bottom
Townhill Park
West End
Botley
Hedge End
Wildern
Broadoak
Bitterne
Bitterne Park
Midanbury
Harefield
Thornhill
Portswood
St. Denys
Highfield
Shirley
Millbrook
Freemantle
Wimpson
Aldermoor
Coxford
Maybush
SOUTHAMPTON
Eling
Marchwood
Hythe
Dibden
Applemore
Netley
Royal Victoria Hospital
Bursledon
Sholing
Woolston
Itchen
Peartree Green
Weston
Newtown
Lowford
Old Netley
Butlocks Heath
Hound
Sarisbury
Swanwick
Park Gate
Locks Heath
SOUTHAMPTON WATER
Ocean Terminal
Town Quay
HYTHE PIER RAILWAY
Colbury
Hounsdown
Foxhills
Ashurst Lo.
Deerleap Fm.
Langley Wood
Churchplace Inclosure
Longdown Inclosure
Pooksgreen
Cracknore Hard
Bury Fm.
Power Sta
St. Mary's Church
Brokenford
Hammond's Green
Testwood Ho.
Moorcourt
Nursling Ho.
Ashfield
Nightingale Wood
Golf Co
Upton
Lord's Wood
Lord's Hill
Chilworth Manor
Chilworth Common
Hut Wood
Nth. Stoneham Park
Sports Centre
Nutburn
Great Covert
Zionshill Fm.
Progress Fm.
Baddesley Common
Spursholt Ho.
Burnt Grove
Broadlands Ho.
Yewtree Copse
Skidmore
R. Test
Stoke Common
Stoke Park Fm
Stoke Park Wood
Lake Fm.
Knowle Hill
Hall Lands Ho.
Park Hills Wood
Stroudwood
Woolstreet Fm.
Greenwood Fm.
Job's Corner
Durley Street
Middle Fm.
Durley Manor Fm.
Brown Heath
Snakemoor
Stapleford Fm.
Durley Mill
Braxells Fm.
Long Common
Boorley Green
Berrywood Fm.
Moor Green
Moorgreen Fm.
Croft Ho
Chalcroft Fm.
Steeple Ct.
Fairthorne Manor
Manor Fm.
Hoe Moor Ho.
Burridge Fm.
Ridge Fm.
Burridge
Whiteley
Lower Swanwick
Netley Hill
Sholing Common
Weston Common
Hightown
Thornhill Park
Dibden Manor
Birchlands Fm.
Foxhill Fm.
New Fm.
Veal's Fm.
River Itchen
River Hamble
A27 A31 A36 A3057 A35 A3024 A3025 A33 A335 A334 A326 B3037 B3035 B3033 B3354 B3397 B3051 B2177
M27 M271
0 1 2 MILES

APPROACHES TO SOUTHEND
Runwell Hall
Battlesbridge
BATTLESBRIDGE
Highlands
Brandy Hole
Hullbridge
Malyons
Beckney Fm.
Lovedown
The Dome
Pudsey Hall
Canewdon
Lion Wharf
Grapnells
Beacon Hill
Lambourne Hall
Runwell
WICKFORD
Goose's Fm.
Walfords Fm.
Sch.
Ashingdon
Loftmans
Paglesham Pool
Rawreth Shot
Rawreth
Trenders Hall
Hockley Hall
Mink Fm.
Apton Hall
Scott's Hall
Ballards Gore
West Hall
Paglesham
The Wick
Shotgate
Rawreth Hall
Hockley
STA
Biggins Fm.
East Hall
Eastend
Dollymans Fm.
Hockley Ho.
Hawkwell
Brays
Doggetts
Great Stambridge
Hockley Woods
Barton Hall
Fanton Hall Fm.
A130
A127
Lit. Wheatley
RAYLEIGH CASTLE
New England
RAYLEIGH
Hosp.
Gt. Stambridge Hall
Stroud Green
Rochford
Barling Marsh
Nth. Benfleet Hall
The Lawn
ROCHFORD
Golf Course
North Benfleet
Flemings
Cherry Orchard
Mucking Hall
Barling Hall
Fleet Hall
Barling
SOUTHEND
New Thundersley
Daws Heath
Pound Wood
Sutton Hall
New Hall
High Ho.
Stonebridge
Little Wakering
Lt. Wakering Hall
B1464
Thundersley
West Wood
Bramble Hall
Eastwood
Shopland Hall
A13
Bowers Gifford
Great Tarpots
Claystreet
Barrow Hall
Great Wood
PRITTLEWELL PRIORY MUSEUM
Fox Hall
Bowers Hall
Jotman's Hall
SOUTH BENFLEET
Hadleigh
Golf Co.
PRITTLEWELL
Eton Ho
Nth. Shoebury Ho.
Great Wakering
Hope's Green
Hosp.
Prittlewell
Bournes Green
North Shoebury
Round Hill
Sandpit Hill
HADLEIGH CASTLE
Leigh on Sea
VICTORIA
Bowers Marshes
BENFLEET
Chalkwell
Southchurch
SOUTHCHURCH HALL
THORPE BAY
Hall
LEIGH ON SEA
Hadleigh Marsh
CHALKWELL
CENTRAL
Clifftown
Golf Co.
Thorpe Bay
East Haven Creek
Benfleet Creek
Two Tree I.
Leigh Marsh
Westcliff on Sea
Cambridge Town
SHOEBURYNESS
Winter Gardens
Hadleigh Ray
Marsh End Sand
SOUTHEND on Sea
Southend Flat
Shoeburyness
Northwick
CANVEY ISLAND
DUTCH COTTAGE MUSEUM
Ray Gut
Shoebury Common
Newlands
Canvey Pt.
Shoebury Ness
Holehaven Creek
Chapman Sands
Pier
Shellhaven Pt.
Leigh Beck
The Knock
Hole Haven
Thorney Bay
Shell Haven
Coryton Wharves
0 1 2 MILES

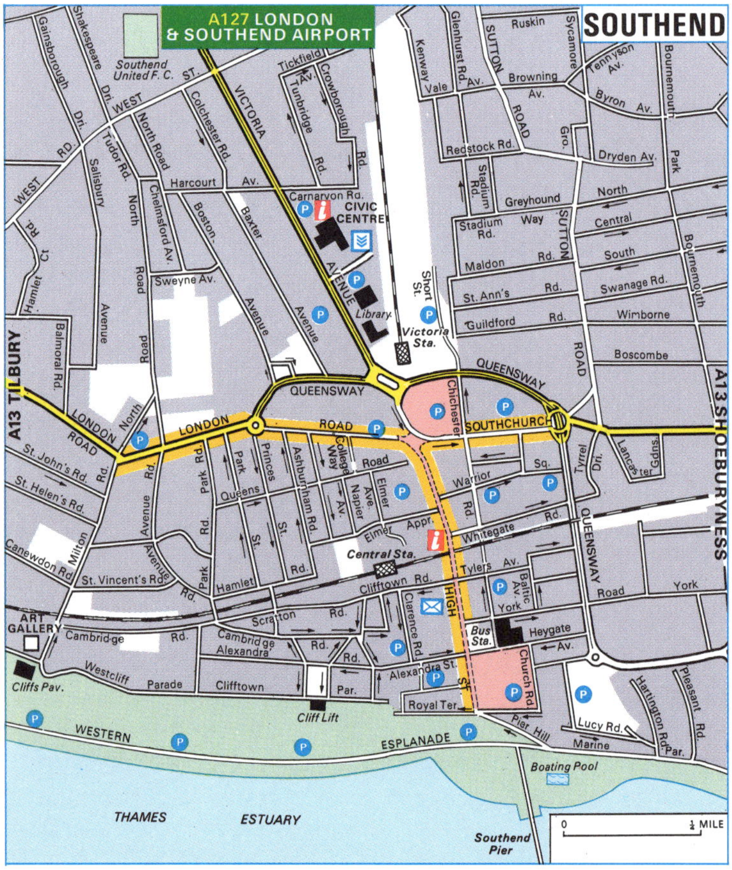

A127 LONDON & SOUTHEND AIRPORT
SOUTHEND
Southend United F.C.
Gainsborough Dr.
Shakespeare Dr.
WEST ST.
VICTORIA
Tickfield Av.
Crowborough Rd.
Tunbridge Rd.
Colchester Rd.
Kenway
Glenhurst Rd.
SUTTON ROAD
Ruskin Av.
Sycamore Gro.
Tennyson Av.
Byron Av.
Bournemouth Park Rd.
Browning Av.
Redstock Rd.
Dryden Av.
Harcourt Av.
Carnarvon Rd.
CIVIC CENTRE
Greyhound Way
Stadium Rd.
North
Central
South
Maldon Rd.
Swanage Rd.
St. Ann's Rd.
Wimborne
Guildford Rd.
Boscombe
Library
Short St.
Victoria Sta.
Sweyne Av.
QUEENSWAY
A13 TILBURY
LONDON ROAD
A13 SHOEBURYNESS
SOUTHCHURCH
Chichester Rd.
Warrior Sq.
Whitegate Rd.
Central Sta.
Clifftown Rd.
Tylers Av.
York Rd.
Heygate Av.
Bus Sta.
St. John's Rd.
St. Helen's Rd.
Canewdon Rd.
St. Vincent's Rd.
Hamlet
ART GALLERY
Cambridge Rd.
Scratton Rd.
Alexandra St.
Royal Ter.
Church Rd.
Westcliff Parade
Clifftown Par.
Cliffs Pav.
Cliff Lift
WESTERN ESPLANADE
Lucy Rd.
Marine Par.
Pier Hill
Boating Pool
THAMES ESTUARY
Southend Pier
0 ½ MILE

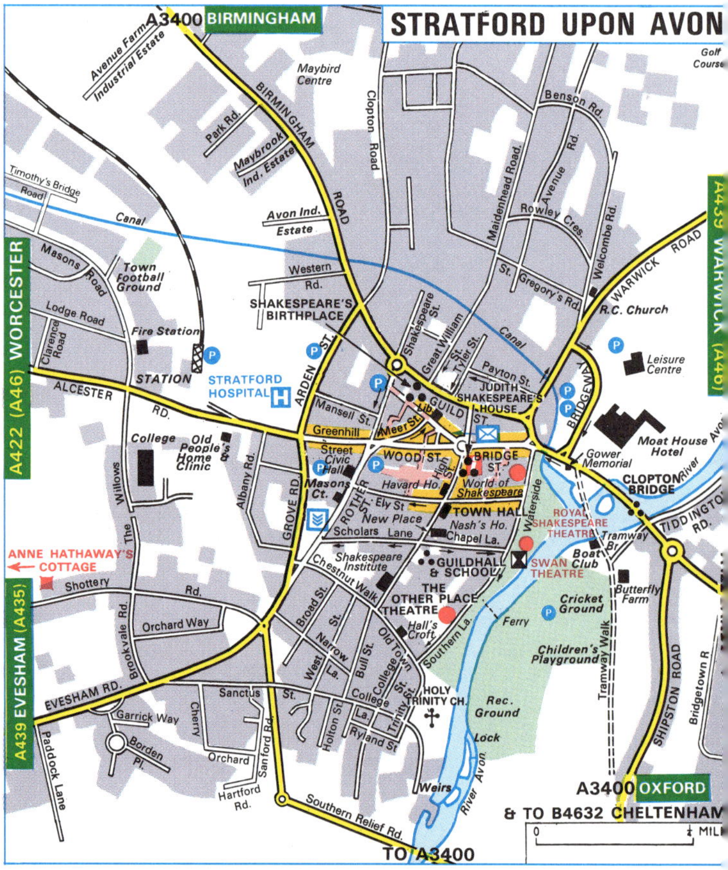

A3400 BIRMINGHAM
STRATFORD UPON AVON
Avenue Farm Industrial Estate
Maybird Centre
Golf Course
BIRMINGHAM ROAD
Clopton Road
Park Rd.
Maybrook Ind. Estate
Benson Rd.
Timothy's Bridge Road
Canal
Avon Ind. Estate
Maidenhead Road
Avenue Rd.
Welcombe Rd.
Rowley Cres.
A439 WARWICK (A46)
WARWICK ROAD
Masons Road
Town Football Ground
Western Rd.
SHAKESPEARE'S BIRTHPLACE
St. Gregory's Rd.
R.C. Church
Lodge Road
Fire Station
A422 (A46) WORCESTER
ALCESTER RD.
STATION
STRATFORD HOSPITAL
ARDEN ST.
Shakespeare St.
Great William St.
Payton St.
JUDITH SHAKESPEARE'S HOUSE
Leisure Centre
Mansell St.
GUILD ST.
BRIDGEWAY
Greenhill
Meer St.
College
Old People's Home
Clinic
Albany Rd.
WOOD ST.
BRIDGE ST.
Moat House Hotel
Gower Memorial
Havard Ho.
World of Shakespeare
CLOPTON BRIDGE
Civic Hall
Masons Ct.
Ely St.
New Place
TOWN HALL
Scholars Lane
Nash's Ho.
Chapel La.
ROYAL SHAKESPEARE THEATRE
Tramway Br.
TIDDINGTON RD.
ANNE HATHAWAY'S COTTAGE
Shottery
Shakespeare Institute
GUILDHALL & SCHOOL
SWAN THEATRE
Boat Club
Chestnut Walk
THE OTHER PLACE THEATRE
Cricket Ground
Butterfly Farm
Orchard Way
Hall's Croft
Ferry
Children's Playground
A439 EVESHAM (A435)
EVESHAM RD.
Sanctus St.
Garrick Way
HOLY TRINITY CH.
Rec. Ground
Tramway Walk
SHIPSTON ROAD
Borden Pl.
Lock
Orchard
Hartford Rd.
Weirs
River Avon
Paddock Lane
Southern Relief Rd.
A3400 OXFORD
& TO B4632 CHELTENHAM
TO A3400
0 ¼ MILE

STOKE ON TRENT
A50 CONGLETON (A34)
A52 ASHBOURNE
A5010 to A53 NEWCASTLE UNDER LYME
COBRIDGE RD.
HANLEY
Potteries Shopping Centre
ST. JOHN'S CHURCH
Market
Trinity St.
Etruria Road
THEATRE ROYAL
MITCHELL MEMORIAL THEATRE
CITY MUSEUM & ART GALLERY
LIBRARY
SPITFIRE MUSEUM
Bus Station
Civic Offices
Law Courts
Bicycle Race Track
Shelton Farm (Abattoir)
SHELTON
Hanley Park
Tennis Courts
Caldon Canal
Hanley Cemetery
Works
NORTH STAFFORDSHIRE POLYTECHNIC
STA.
WEDGWOOD MONUMENT
Trent & Mersey Canal
QUEENSWAY
LEEK ROAD
Sewage Works
Filter Beds
River Trent
Allotments
R.C. CHURCH
STOKE-ON-TRENT
TOWN HALL
SPODE LTD. WORKS
ST. PETER'S CHURCH
MINTON WORKS
Leisure Centre
Stoke City F.C. Victoria Ground
Steel Foundry
College
City Road
A500 to M6
A500 to M6 Int. 15
A5007
A5006
A50
A52
A5008
0 ¼ MILE

APPROACHES TO STOKE ON TRENT
Talke
A34
A500
A50
A527
A52
A53
A5006
M6
Tunstall
Burslem
Cobridge
Hanley
Northwood
Bucknall
Ubberley
Fenton
Longton
Dresden
Blurton
Hanford
Trentham
TRENTHAM GARDENS
Chesterton
Crackley
Wolstanton
Basford
Knutton
Silverdale
NEWCASTLE -under-Lyme
STOKE -on-Trent
Westlands
Clayton
Seabridge
Northwood
Butterton
Hanchurch
Acton
Whitmore
Alsagers Bank
Apedale
Keele Services
University
Norton in the Moors
Norton Green
Ball Green
Sandyford
Bradeley
Chell Heath
Etruria
Mount Pleasant
Hollybush
Hem Heath
Oak Hill
Trent Vale
Boothen
Dimsdale
May Bank
Bradwell
Red Street
Wood Lane
Boon Hill
Butters Green
Dunkirk
Newfield
Harecastle Tunnels
Fire Oaks
Swynnerton Old Park
King's Wood
Cocknage Fm.
Newpark Plantn.
0 1 MILE

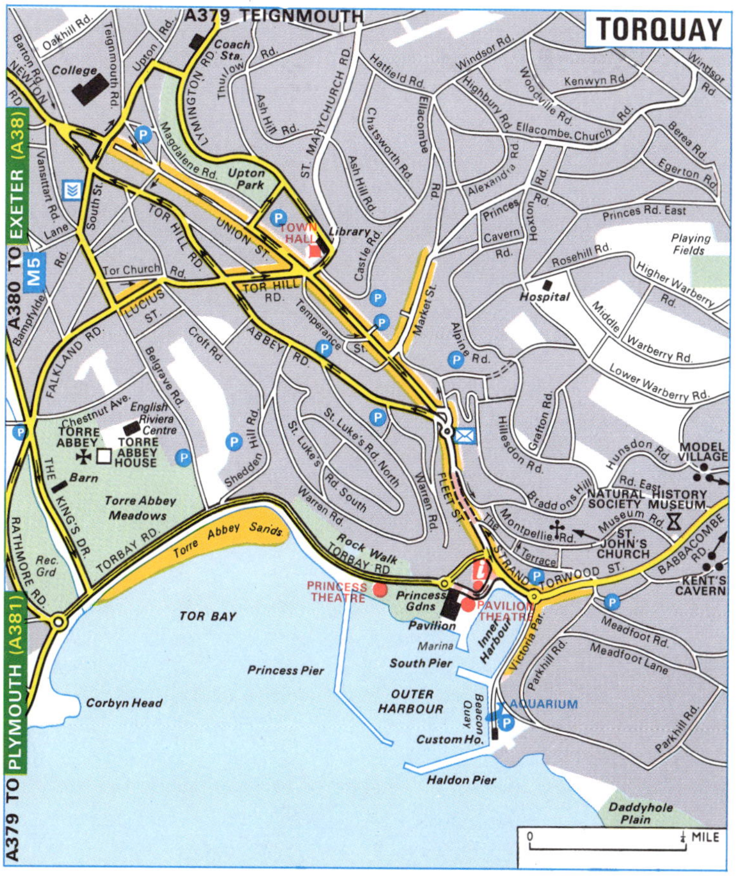
TORQUAY
A379 TEIGNMOUTH
A380 TO EXETER (A38)
M5
A379 TO PLYMOUTH (A381)
College
Coach Sta.
Upton Park
TOWN HALL
Library
Hospital
Playing Fields
UNION ST.
TOR HILL RD.
Tor Church
LUCIUS ST.
ABBEY RD
English Riviera Centre
TORRE ABBEY
TORRE ABBEY HOUSE
Barn
Torre Abbey Meadows
Rec. Grd
Torre Abbey Sands
TOR BAY
PRINCESS THEATRE
Princess Gdns
Pavilion
PAVILION THEATRE
Marina
Inner Harbour
South Pier
Princess Pier
OUTER HARBOUR
Beacon Quay
AQUARIUM
Custom Ho.
Haldon Pier
Corbyn Head
Daddyhole Plain
MODEL VILLAGE
NATURAL HISTORY SOCIETY MUSEUM
ST. JOHN'S CHURCH
KENT'S CAVERN
BABBACOMBE RD
TORWOOD ST
FLEET ST
THE STRAND
0 ¼ MILE

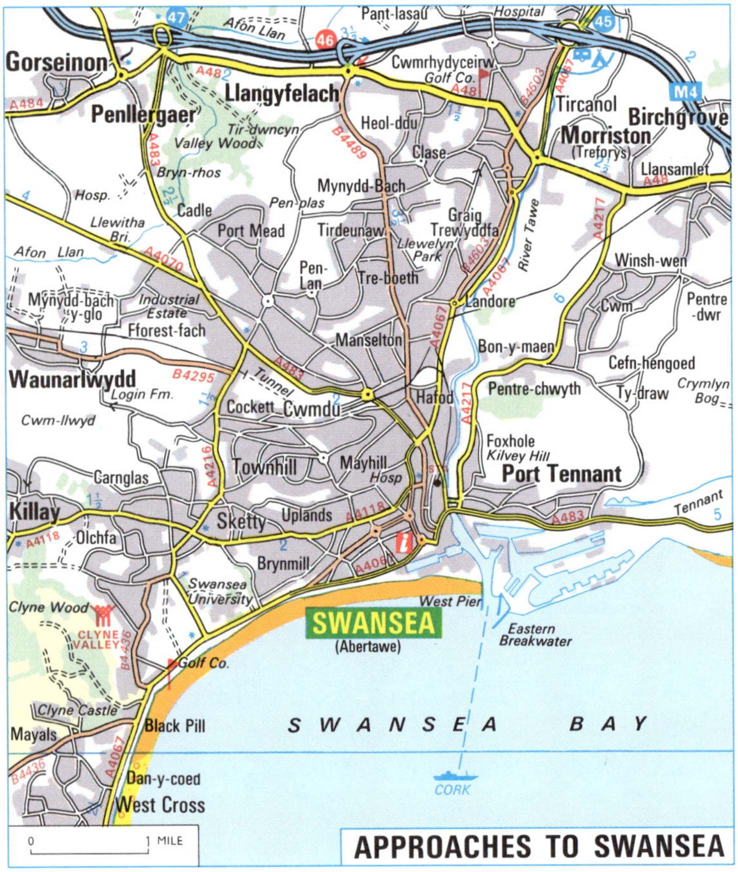
APPROACHES TO SWANSEA
Gorseinon
Penllergaer
Llangyfelach
Pant-lasau
Hospital
Cwmrhydyceirw
Golf Co.
Tircanol
Birchgrove
Morriston
(Treforys)
Llansamlet
Heol-ddu
Clase
Mynydd-Bach
Tir-dwncyn
Valley Wood
Bryn-rhos
Hosp.
Cadle
Pen-plas
Port Mead
Tirdeunaw
Graig
Trewyddfa
Llewelyn Park
Llewitha Bri.
Afon Llan
Mynydd-bach-y-glo
Industrial Estate
Fforest-fach
Pen-Lan
Tre-boeth
Landore
River Tawe
Winsh-wen
Pentre-dwr
Cwm
Manselton
Bon-y-maen
Cefn-hengoed
Waunarlwydd
Login Fm.
Tunnel
Cwm-Ilwyd
Cockett
Cwmdu
Hafod
Pentre-chwyth
Ty-draw
Crymlyn Bog
Townhill
Mayhill
Hosp
Foxhole
Kilvey Hill
Port Tennant
Carnglas
Killay
Sketty
Uplands
Tennant
Olchfa
Brynmill
Swansea University
West Pier
Clyne Wood
CLYNE VALLEY
SWANSEA
(Abertawe)
Eastern Breakwater
Golf Co.
Clyne Castle
Mayals
Black Pill
S W A N S E A   B A Y
Dan-y-coed
West Cross
CORK
0 1 MILE
A484
A48
A483
A4070
B4295
A4216
A4118
A4067
B4436
B4489
B4603
A4217
A4067
A48
A483
A4118
A4067
M4
47
46
45

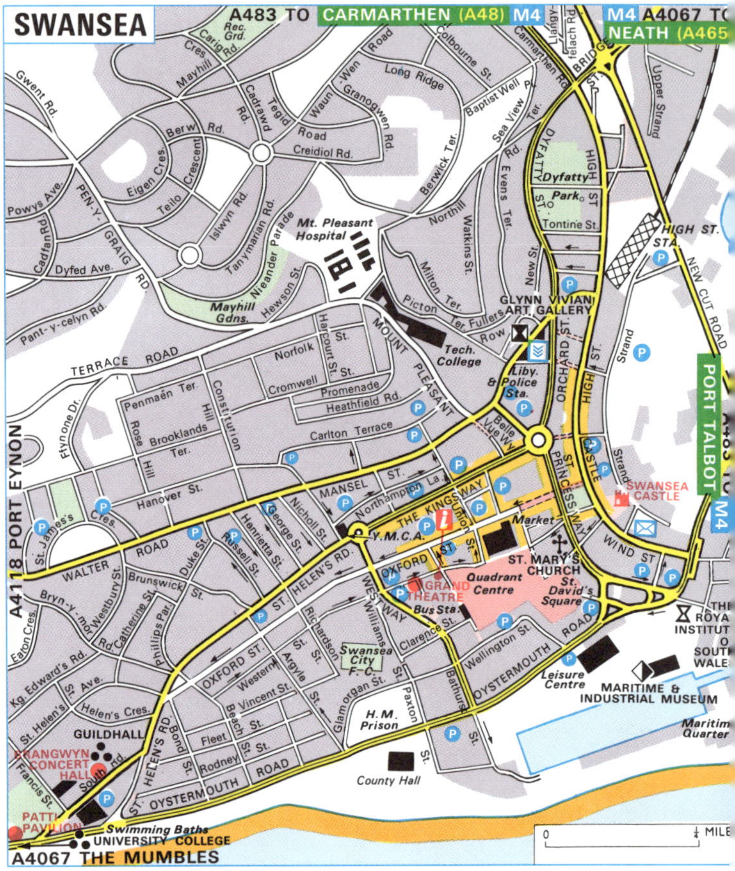
SWANSEA
A483 TO CARMARTHEN (A48) M4
M4 A4067 TO NEATH (A465)
Rec. Grd.
Gwent Rd.
Mayhill
Cadfan Rd.
Powys Ave.
Dyfed Ave.
Pant-y-celyn Rd.
PEN-Y-GRAIG RD
Eigen Cres.
Tello Crescent
Berw Rd.
Islwyn Rd.
Tanymarian Rd.
Cadrawd Rd.
Teilo Road
Waun Wen Road
Creidiol Rd.
Granogwen Rd.
Long Ridge
Colbourne St.
Baptist Well St.
Sea View Ter.
Mt. Pleasant Hospital
Mayhill Gdns.
Hewson St.
Neander Parade
Berwick Ter.
Northhill
Watkins St.
Evans Ter.
New St.
Dyfatty
Park St.
Tontine St.
HIGH ST.
HIGH ST. STA.
NEW CUT ROAD
Strand
TERRACE ROAD
Penmaen Ter.
Brooklands Ter.
Constitution Hill
Norfolk St.
Cromwell St.
Promenade
Heathfield Rd.
Carlton Terrace
Picton Ter.
MOUNT PLEASANT
Tech. College
GLYNN VIVIAN ART GALLERY
Liby. & Police Sta.
ORCHARD ST.
PORT TALBOT
Flynone Dr.
Rose Hill
Hanover St.
Nicholl St.
MANSEL ST.
Northampton La.
THE KINGSWAY
Y.M.C.A.
Market
PRINCESS WAY
CASTLE
SWANSEA CASTLE
A4118 PORT EYNON
St. James's Cres.
WALTER ROAD
Brunswick St.
Duke St.
Russell St.
George St.
ST. HELEN'S RD.
Oxford St.
GRAND THEATRE
Bus Sta.
Quadrant Centre
ST. MARY'S CHURCH
St. David's Square
WIND ST.
Bryn-y-mor Rd.
Westbury St.
Catherine St.
Phillips Pde.
Henrietta St.
Richardson St.
WESTWAY
Williams St.
Swansea City F.C.
Clarence St.
Wellington St.
OYSTERMOUTH ROAD
Leisure Centre
MARITIME & INDUSTRIAL MUSEUM
THE ROYAL INSTITUTE OF SOUTH WALES
Maritime Quarter
Eaton Cres.
Kg. Edward's Rd.
St. Helen's Ave.
Helen's Cres.
OXFORD ST.
Western St.
Vincent St.
Argyle St.
Glamorgan St.
Paxton St.
Bathurst St.
H.M. Prison
GUILDHALL
BRANGWYN CONCERT HALL
Francis St.
ST. HELEN'S RD.
Bond St.
Beach St.
Fleet St.
Rodney St.
OYSTERMOUTH ROAD
County Hall
PATTI PAVILION
Swimming Baths
UNIVERSITY COLLEGE
A4067 THE MUMBLES
0 ¼ MILE

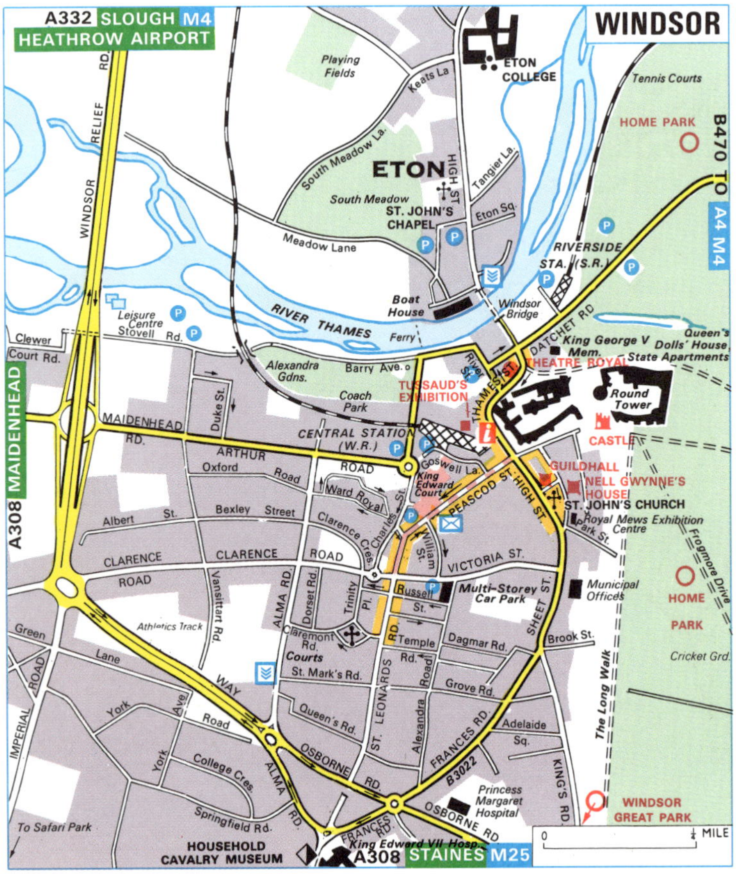
A332 SLOUGH M4
HEATHROW AIRPORT
WINDSOR
Playing Fields
Keats La.
ETON COLLEGE
Tennis Courts
HOME PARK
B470 TO A4 M4
South Meadow La.
ETON
HIGH ST.
Tangier La.
South Meadow
ST. JOHN'S CHAPEL
Eton Sq.
Meadow Lane
RIVERSIDE STA. (S.R.)
WINDSOR RELIEF RD.
Boat House
Windsor Bridge
RIVER THAMES
Ferry
Leisure Centre
Stovell Rd.
Clewer Court Rd.
DATCHET RD
King George V Mem.
THEATRE ROYAL
Queen's Dolls' House, State Apartments
Alexandra Gdns.
Barry Ave.
TUSSAUD'S EXHIBITION
Coach Park
Round Tower
A308 MAIDENHEAD
MAIDENHEAD RD.
CENTRAL STATION (W.R.)
CASTLE
ARTHUR ROAD
Oxford Road
Duke St.
King Edward Court
PEASCOD ST.
GUILDHALL
NELL GWYNNE'S HOUSE
ST. JOHN'S CHURCH
Bexley Street
Ward Royal
HIGH ST.
Royal Mews Exhibition Centre
Albert St.
Clarence Cres.
William St.
Park St.
Frogmore Drive
CLARENCE ROAD
CLARENCE ROAD
VICTORIA ST.
Vansittart Rd
ALMA RD
Dorset Rd.
Trinity Pl.
Russell St.
Multi-Storey Car Park
Municipal Offices
SHEET ST.
HOME PARK
Athletics Track
Claremont Rd.
Courts
Temple Rd.
Dagmar Rd.
Brook St.
Green Lane
St. Mark's Rd.
ST. LEONARDS RD.
Alexandra Road
Grove Rd.
Cricket Grd.
The Long Walk
IMPERIAL ROAD
York Road
Queen's Rd.
Adelaide Sq.
York Ave.
College Cres.
OSBORNE RD
FRANCES RD
KING'S RD.
Springfield Rd.
ALMA RD
B3022
Princess Margaret Hospital
WINDSOR GREAT PARK
To Safari Park
HOUSEHOLD CAVALRY MUSEUM
King Edward VII Hosp.
A308 STAINES M25
0 ¼ MILE

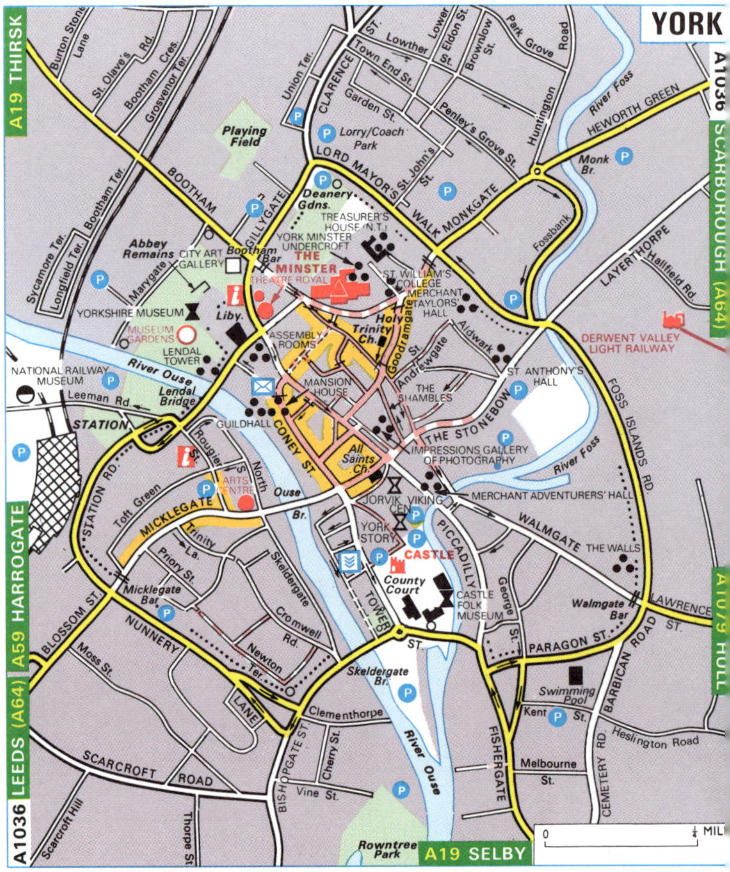
YORK
A19 THIRSK
Burton Stone Lane
St. Olave's Rd.
Bootham Cres.
Grosvenor Ter.
Union Ter.
CLARENCE ST.
Lowther St.
Town End St.
Garden St.
Eldon St.
Lower
Brownlow St.
Park Grove
Huntington Road
River Foss
HEWORTH GREEN
A1036 SCARBOROUGH (A64)
Playing Field
Lorry/Coach Park
LORD MAYOR'S WALK
St. John's St.
Penley's Grove St.
Monk Br.
BOOTHAM
Bootham Ter.
GILLYGATE
Deanery Gdns.
TREASURER'S HOUSE (N.T.)
YORK MINSTER UNDERCROFT
MONKGATE
Foss Bank
LAYERTHORPE
Hallfield Rd.
Sycamore Ter.
Longfield Ter.
Abbey Remains
CITY ART GALLERY
Bootham Bar
THE MINSTER
THEATRE ROYAL
ST. WILLIAM'S COLLEGE
MERCHANT TAYLORS HALL
Marygate
YORKSHIRE MUSEUM
MUSEUM GARDENS
Liby.
LENDAL TOWER
ASSEMBLY ROOMS
Holy Trinity Ch.
Goodramgate
Aldwark
DERWENT VALLEY LIGHT RAILWAY
NATIONAL RAILWAY MUSEUM
River Ouse
Lendal Bridge
MANSION HOUSE
THE SHAMBLES
ST. ANTHONY'S HALL
Leeman Rd.
STATION
GUILDHALL
CONEY ST.
All Saints Ch.
THE STONEBOW
IMPRESSIONS GALLERY OF PHOTOGRAPHY
River Foss
FOSS ISLANDS RD.
STATION RD.
Rougier St.
ARTS CENTRE
North St.
Ouse Br.
JORVIK VIKING CENTRE
MERCHANT ADVENTURERS' HALL
Toft Green
MICKLEGATE
YORK STORY
PICCADILLY
WALMGATE
THE WALLS
A59 HARROGATE
Trinity La.
Priory St.
Skeldergate
CASTLE
County Court
CASTLE FOLK MUSEUM
George St.
Walmgate Bar
LAWRENCE ST.
A1079 HULL
Micklegate Bar
BLOSSOM ST.
NUNNERY LANE
Cromwell Rd.
Newton Ter.
TOWER ST.
PARAGON ST.
BARBICAN ROAD
Moss St.
Skeldergate Br.
Clementhorpe
Swimming Pool
Kent St.
Heslington Road
A64 LEEDS (A64)
SCARCROFT ROAD
BISHOPGATE ST.
Cherry St.
River Ouse
FISHERGATE
CEMETERY RD
Melbourne St.
Vine St.
A1036
Scarcroft Hill
Thorpe St.
Rowntree Park
A19 SELBY
0 ¼ MILE

Index
to Road Maps

INDEX TO ROAD MAPS

ABBREVIATIONS

Beds	*Bedford*	**E Sussex**	*East Sussex*	**Hth.**	*Heath*	**Mersey**	*Merseyside*	**Som'set**	*Somerset*
Berks	*Berkshire*	**Glos**	*Gloucester*	**Humber**	*Humberside*	**Mid Glam**	*Mid Glamorgan*	**Staffs**	*Stafford*
Bri.	*Bridge*	**Gramp**	*Grampian*	**I of Man**	*Isle of Man*	**Northants**	*Northampton*	**S Yorks**	*South Yorkshire*
Bucks	*Buckinghamshire*	**Grn.**	*Green*	**I of Scilly**	*Isles of Scilly*	**Northum**	*Northumberland*	**Tyne/Wear**	*Tyne and Wear*
Cambs	*Cambridge*	**Gt.**	*Great*	**I of Wight**	*Isle of Wight*	**Notts**	*Nottingham*	**W Glam**	*West Glamorgan*
Chan Is	*Channel Islands*	**Gtr Man**	*Greater Manchester*	**Lancs**	*Lancashire*	**N Yorks**	*North Yorkshire*	**Wilts**	*Wiltshire*
Ches	*Cheshire*	**Gwyn**	*Gwynedd*	**Leics**	*Leicester*	**Oxon**	*Oxford*	**W Isles**	*Western Isles*
Clevl'd	*Cleveland*	**Hants**	*Hampshire*	**Lincs**	*Lincoln*	**S'clyde**	*Strathclyde*	**W Midlands**	*West Midlands*
Cornw'l	*Cornwall*	**Heref/Worcs**	*Hereford and Worcester*	**Lit.**	*Little*	**S Glam**	*South Glamorgan*	**W Sussex**	*West Sussex*
Cumb	*Cumbria*	**Herts**	*Hertford*	**Lo.**	*Lodge*	**Shetl'd**	*Shetland*	**W Yorks**	*West Yorkshire*
Dumf/Gal	*Dumfries and Galloway*	**H'land**	*Highland*	**Lr.**	*Lower*	**Shrops**	*Shropshire*		

Ab Kettleby *Leics* **32** H4
Abbas Combe *Som'set* **7** D10
Abberley *Heref/Worcs* **22** E1
Abberton *Essex* **19** B10
Abberton *Heref/Worcs* **22** G3
Abberwick *Northum* **45** B9
Abbess Roding *Essex* **18** C6
Abbey *Devon* **6** E5
Abbey Dore *Heref/Worcs* **15** A7
Abbey Hill *Som'set* **6** D6
Abbey Hulton *Staffs* **31** E7
Abbey St. Bathans *Borders* **49** C10
Abbey Town *Cumb* **43** G12
Abbey Village *Lancs* **34** E5
Abbeycwmhir *Powys* **20** E6
Abbeylands *I of Man* **38** G2
Abbeylands *Northum* **45** B10
Abbeystead *Lancs* **34** B4
Abbots Bickington *Devon* **4** E3
Abbots Bromley *Staffs* **31** H9
Abbots Langley *Herts* **17** D11
Abbot's Morton *Heref/Worcs* **22** G4
Abbots Ripton *Cambs* **25** G3
Abbot's Salford *Warwick* **22** G4
Abbotsbury *Dorset* **7** H9
Abbotsham *Devon* **4** C3
Abbotskerswell *Devon* **5** J7
Abbotsley *Cambs* **25** K3
Abbotswood *Hants* **8** D5
Abbotts Ann *Hants* **8** B5
Abcott *Shrops* **21** E9
Abdon *Shrops* **21** D11
Aber *Dyfed* **13** B8
Aber *Gwyn* **28** C6
Aber Gwydol *Powys* **20** B3
Aber Village *Powys* **14** B4
Aberaeron *Dyfed* **13** A8
Aberaman *Mid Glam* **14** D3
Aberangell *Powys* **20** A4
Aberarad *Dyfed* **12** C6
Aberarder *H'land* **55** L8
Aberarder Lo *H'land* **57** K1
Aberargie *Tayside* **52** F6
Aberarth *Dyfed* **13** A8
Aberavon *W Glam* **13** H11
Aber-banc *Dyfed* **13** C7
Aberbeeg *Gwent* **14** D5
Aberbran *Powys* **14** A3
Abercanaid *Mid Glam* **14** D4
Abercarn *Gwent* **14** E5
Abercastle *Dyfed* **12** D2
Abercegir *Powys* **20** B4
Aberchalder *H'land* **55** J7
Aberchirder *Gramp* **58** B4
Abercraf *Powys* **13** F11
Abercraf *Powys* **14** C2
Abercregan *W Glam* **14** E2
Abercwmboi *Mid Glam* **14** D3
Abercych *Dyfed* **12** C6
Abercynafon *Powys* **14** C4
Abercynon *Mid Glam* **14** E4
Aberdare *Mid Glam* **14** D3
Aberdaron *Gwyn* **28** H1
Aberdeen *Gramp* **59** G7
Aberdesach *Gwyn* **28** E4
Aberdour *Lothian* **48** A5
Aberdovey *Gwyn* **20** C2
Aberdulais *W Glam* **13** G11
Aberedw *Powys* **20** H6
Abereiddy *Dyfed* **12** D2
Abererch *Gwyn* **28** G3
Aberfan *Mid Glam* **14** D4
Aberfeldy *Tayside* **52** B3
Aberffraw *Gwyn* **28** C3
Aberffrwd *Dyfed* **20** E2
Aberford *W Yorks* **36** C2
Aberfoyle *Central* **51** G12
Abergavenny *Gwent* **14** C6
Abergele *Clwyd* **29** B9
Abergiar *Dyfed* **13** C8
Abergorlech *Dyfed* **13** D9
Abergwesyn *Powys* **20** G4
Abergwili *Dyfed* **13** E8
Aber-Gwynant *Gwyn* **28** H6
Abergwynfi *W Glam* **14** E2
Abergynolwyn *Gwyn* **20** B2
Aberhosan *Powys* **20** C4
Aberkenfig *Mid Glam* **14** F2
Aberlady *Lothian* **49** A7
Aberlemno *Tayside* **53** B10
Aberllefenni *Gwyn* **20** A3
Abermeurig *Dyfed* **20** G1
Abermule *Powys* **21** C7
Abernant *Dyfed* **13** E7
Aber-nant *Mid Glam* **14** D3
Abernethy *Tayside* **53** E7
Abernyte *Tayside* **53** D7
Aberporth *Dyfed* **12** B6
Abersoch *Gwyn* **28** G3
Abersychan *Gwent* **14** D6
Aberthin *S Glam* **14** G3
Abertillery *Gwent* **14** D5
Abertridwr *Mid Glam* **14** E4
Abertridwr *Powys* **29** H9
Abertysswg *Mid Glam* **14** D5
Aberuthven *Tayside* **52** F5
Aberyscir *Powys* **14** A3
Aberystwyth *Dyfed* **20** D2
Abingdon *Oxon* **16** D6
Abinger Common *Surrey* **9** B12
Abinger Hammer *Surrey* **9** A12
Abington *S'clyde* **48** G2
Abington Pigotts *Cambs* **25** L4
Ablington *Glos* **16** C2
Ablington *Wilts* **8** A3
Abney *Derby* **31** B10
Aboyne *Gramp* **59** H3
Abram *Gtr Man* **34** G5
Abriachan *H'land* **56** F1
Abridge *Essex* **18** D5
Abson *Avon* **15** G10
Abthorpe *Northants* **23** G10
Aby *Lincs* **33** B11
Acaster Malbis *N Yorks* **36** C4
Acaster Selby *N Yorks* **36** C3
Accott *Devon* **4** C5
Accrington *Lancs* **34** D6
Achachork *H'land* **62** D4
Achadun *H'land* **50** D5
Achafolla *S'clyde* **50** F5
Achahoish *S'clyde* **46** B3
Achallader *S'clyde* **51** C10
Achamore Farm *S'clyde* **46** E1
Achanalt *H'land* **54** D6
Achanamare *S'clyde* **46** A3
Achandunie *H'land* **56** C2
Achany *H'land* **60** F6
Achaphubuil *H'land* **55** M5
Acharacle *H'land* **50** A4
Acharn *H'land* **50** C4
Acharn *Tayside* **52** C2
Acharosson *S'clyde* **46** B4
Achateny *H'land* **50** A3
Achath *Gramp* **58** F5
Achavanich *H'land* **61** C11
Achavraat *H'land* **56** E5
Achavraie *H'land* **60** F2
Achddu *Dyfed* **13** G8
Achentoul *H'land* **61** D8
Achfary *H'land* **60** C4
Achgarve *H'land* **60** G1
Achiemore *H'land* **60** A4
Achiemore *H'land* **61** B9
A'Chill *H'land* **62** H2
Achiltibuie *H'land* **60** F2
Achina *H'land* **61** B7
Achindarroch *H'land* **51** B7
Achintee *H'land* **54** F3
Achintee *H'land* **55** M5
Achintraid *H'land* **54** F2
Achlain *H'land* **55** H6
Achlean *H'land* **57** K4
Achleck *H'land* **50** C1
Achleck *H'land* **50** C2
A'Chleit *S'clyde* **46** E2
Achlian *S'clyde* **51** E8
Achluachrach *H'land* **55** L7
Achlyness *H'land* **60** B4
Achmelvich *H'land* **60** E2
Achmore *Central* **52** D1
Achmore *H'land* **54** F2
Achmore *W Isles* **63** D4
Achnaba *S'clyde* **46** A4
Achnaba *S'clyde* **51** D7
Achnabat *H'land* **57** G2
Achnacarnin *H'land* **60** D2
Achnacarry *H'land* **55** L5
Achnacloich *H'land* **62** G5
Achnaconeran *H'land* **55** H8
Achnacraig *H'land* **50** C2
Achnacroish *H'land* **50** C6
Achnadrish *H'land* **50** B2
Achnafalnich *S'clyde* **51** E9
Achnafraschoille *H'land* **55** L6
Achnaggaron *H'land* **56** C2
Achnaha *H'land* **50** A2
Achnahanat *H'land* **60** G6
Achnairn *H'land* **60** F6
Achnalea *H'land* **50** A6
Achnaluachrach *H'land* **61** F7
Achnanellan *H'land* **55** L5
Achnangart *H'land* **55** H3
Achnasaul *H'land* **55** K5
Achnasheen *H'land* **54** D5
Achnashellach *H'land* **54** E4
Achosnich *H'land* **50** A2
Achranich *H'land* **50** C4
Achreamie *H'land* **61** A9
Achriabhach *H'land* **51** A8
Achriesgill *H'land* **60** B4
Achrimsdale *H'land* **61** F9
Achtoty *H'land* **61** B7
Achurch *Northants* **25** G1
Achuvoldrach *H'land* **60** B6
Achvaich *H'land* **61** G7
Achvraid *H'land* **56** F2
Achvraid *H'land* **57** G2
Ackergill *H'land* **61** B12
Acklam *Clevl'd* **40** C5
Acklam *N Yorks* **36** A5
Ackleton *Shrops* **22** B1
Acklington *Northum* **45** C10
Ackton *W Yorks* **36** E2
Ackworth Moor Top *W Yorks* **36** F2
Acle *Norfolk* **26** D7
Acock's Green *W Midlands* **22** D5
Acol *Kent* **11** A11
Acomb *N Yorks* **36** B4
Acomb *Northum* **45** F7
Aconbury *Heref/Worcs* **15** A8
Acre *Lancs* **34** E6
Acre Street *W Sussex* **9** F9
Acrefair *Clwyd* **29** F12
Acton *Ches* **30** E5
Acton *Clwyd* **30** E2
Acton *Dorset* **8** H1
Acton *London* **18** F2
Acton *Shrops* **21** D8
Acton *Suffolk* **27** L2
Acton Beauchamp *Heref/Worcs* **21** G12
Acton Bridge *Ches* **30** C4
Acton Burnell *Shrops* **21** B10
Acton Green *Heref/Worcs* **21** G12
Acton Pigott *Shrops* **21** B11
Acton Round *Shrops* **21** C11
Acton Scott *Shrops* **21** C10
Acton Trussell *Staffs* **31** H8
Acton Turville *Avon* **15** F11
Adbaston *Staffs* **30** G6
Adber *Dorset* **7** D9
Adderley *Shrops* **30** F5
Adderstone *Northum* **45** C12
Addiewell *Lothian* **48** C3
Addingham *W Yorks* **35** B9
Addington *Bucks* **17** A8
Addington *Kent* **10** B5
Addington *London* **18** G4
Addinston *Borders* **49** D8
Addlestone *Surrey* **17** H11
Addlethorpe *Lincs* **33** C12
Adeney *Shrops* **30** H5
Adfa *Powys* **20** B6
Adforton *Heref/Worcs* **21** E9
Adisham *Kent* **11** C11
Adlestrop *Glos* **16** A3
Adlingfleet *Humber* **36** E6
Adlington *Ches* **31** B7
Adlington *Lancs* **34** F5
Admaston *Shrops* **21** A11
Admaston *Staffs* **31** H9
Admington *Warwick* **22** G5
Adsborough *Som'set* **6** C6
Adstock *Bucks* **17** A8
Adstone *Northants* **23** G9
Adversane *W Sussex* **9** D12
Advie *H'land* **56** F7
Adwick le Street *S Yorks* **36** F3
Adwick upon Dearne *S Yorks* **36** G3
Adworthy *Devon* **4** D6
Ae Bridgend *Dumf/Gal* **43** C10
Ae Village *Dumf/Gal* **43** C10
Affeton Barton *Devon* **4** E6
Affleck *Gramp* **58** D3
Affleck *Gramp* **58** E6
Afflochie *Tayside* **53** A9
Afflochie *Tayside* **59** L2
Affpuddle *Dorset* **7** G11
Affric Lodge *H'land* **55** G5
Afonwen *Clwyd* **29** C10
Afton *Devon* **5** J7
Afton *I of Wight* **8** G5
Afton Bridgend *S'clyde* **47** H11
Agglethorpe *N Yorks* **40** F1
Agneash *I of Man* **38** G2
Aiginis *W Isles* **63** D6
Aike *Humber* **37** C8
Aikerness *Orkney* **64** A2
Aikers *Orkney* **64** E2
Aiket *Dumf/Gal* **43** E11
Aiketgate *Cumb* **39** A7
Aikton *Cumb* **44** H1
Ailey *Heref/Worcs* **21** G9
Ailsworth *Cambs* **24** F2
Ainderby Quernhow *N Yorks* **40** G4
Ainderby Steeple *N Yorks* **40** F4
Aingers Green *Essex* **19** B11
Ainsdale *Mersey* **34** F2
Ainstable *Cumb* **39** A7
Ainsworth *Gtr Man* **34** F6
Ainthorpe *N Yorks* **41** D7
Aintree *Mersey* **34** G3
Aird *Dumf/Gal* **42** F2
Aird *S'clyde* **50** G5
Aird *W Isles* **63** C6
Aird of Sleat *H'land* **62** H5
Aird Thunga *W Isles* **63** C6
Aird Uig *W Isles* **63** C2
Airdachuilinn *H'land* **60** C4
Airdrie *S'clyde* **47** C12
Airdsgreen *S'clyde* **47** F12
Airdvorrisdale *H'land* **61** B7
Airigh-drishaig *H'land* **54** F1
Airmyn *Humber* **36** E5
Airntully *Tayside* **52** D6
Airor *H'land* **55** J1
Airth *Central* **52** H4
Airton *N Yorks* **35** A8
Airyhassen *Dumf/Gal* **42** G4
Aisby *Lincs* **32** A6
Aisby *Lincs* **33** F7
Aisgill *Cumb* **39** E10
Aish *Devon* **5** K6
Aisholt *Som'set* **6** C5
Aiskew *N Yorks* **40** F3
Aislaby *N Yorks* **40** D4
Aislaby *N Yorks* **41** D8
Aislaby *N Yorks* **41** G8
Aisthorpe *Lincs* **32** B6
Aith *Orkney* **64** C4
Aith *Shetl'd* **64** D7
Aith Hestwall *Orkney* **64** C1
Aitkenhead *S'clyde* **42** A4
Aitnoch *Gramp* **56** F5
Akeld *Northum* **49** F12
Akeld Steads *Northum* **49** F12
Akeley *Bucks* **23** H10
Akenham *Suffolk* **27** K4
Albaston *Cornw'l* **3** C11
Alberbury *Shrops* **21** A9
Albert Town *Dyfed* **12** E3
Albourn *W Sussex* **10** F1
Albrighton *Shrops* **22** B2
Albrighton *Shrops* **30** H4
Alburgh *Norfolk* **27** G6
Albury *Herts* **18** B4
Albury *Surrey* **9** A12
Alby Hill *Norfolk* **26** B5
Alcaig *H'land* **56** D1
Alcester *Warwick* **22** F4
Alciston *E Sussex* **10** G4
Alcombe *Som'set* **6** B3
Alcombe *Wilts* **15** G11
Alconbury *Cambs* **25** H3
Alconbury Hill *Cambs* **25** G3
Alconbury Weston *Cambs* **25** H3
Aldandulish *Tayside* **57** M5
Aldborough *N Yorks* **35** A12
Aldborough *N Yorks* **40** H4
Aldborough *Norfolk* **26** B5
Aldbourne *Wilts* **16** G4
Aldbrough *Humber* **37** C10
Aldbrough St. John *N Yorks* **40** D2
Aldbury *Herts* **17** C10
Aldcharmaig *Tayside* **52** A3
Aldcliffe *Lancs* **34** A3
Aldclune *Tayside* **52** A4
Aldeburgh *Suffolk* **27** J8
Aldeby *Norfolk* **26** F7
Aldenham *Herts* **18** D1
Alderbury *Wilts* **8** C3
Alderford *Norfolk* **26** D4
Alderholt *Dorset* **8** E3
Alderley *Glos* **15** E11
Alderley Edge *Ches* **31** B7
Aldermaston *Berks* **17** H7
Aldermaston Wharf *Berks* **17** G7
Alderminster *Warwick* **22** G6
Alder's End *Heref/Worcs* **21** H11
Aldershot *Hants* **9** A10
Alderton *Glos* **16** A1
Alderton *Northants* **23** G10
Alderton *Shrops* **30** H4
Alderton *Suffolk* **27** L6
Alderton *Wilts* **15** F11
Alderwasley *Derby* **31** E11
Aldfield *N Yorks* **40** H3
Aldford *Ches* **30** D3
Aldham *Essex* **19** A9
Aldham *Suffolk* **27** L3
Aldham Street *Suffolk* **27** L3
Aldie *H'land* **56** B3
Aldingbourne *W Sussex* **9** F10
Aldingham *Cumb* **38** H5
Aldington *Heref/Worcs* **22** H4
Aldington *Kent* **11** D9
Aldington Corner *Kent* **11** D9
Aldochlay *S'clyde* **51** H10
Aldreth *Cambs* **25** H5
Aldridge *W Midlands* **22** B4
Aldringham *Suffolk* **27** J7
Aldsworth *Glos* **16** C3
Aldunie *Gramp* **58** E1
Aldwark *Derby* **31** D10
Aldwark *N Yorks* **36** A2
Aldwick *W Sussex* **9** F10
Aldwincle *Northants* **25** G1
Aldworth *Berks* **16** F6
Alexandria *S'clyde* **47** A9
Aley *Som'set* **6** B5
Alfardisworthy *Devon* **4** E2
Alfington *Devon* **6** F5
Alford *Gramp* **58** F3
Alford *Lincs* **33** C11
Alford *Som'set* **7** C9
Alford *Surrey* **9** C11
Alford Cross Ways *Surrey* **9** C11
Alfreton *Derby* **32** E1
Alfrick *Heref/Worcs* **22** G1
Alfriston *E Sussex* **10** H4
Algarkirk *Lincs* **24** B4
Alhampton *Som'set* **7** C9
Aline Lodge *W Isles* **63** F3
Alisary *H'land* **55** L1
Alkborough *Humber* **36** E6
Alkerton *Oxon* **23** H7
Alkham *Kent* **11** D11
Alkington *Shrops* **30** F4
Alkmonton *Derby* **31** F10
All Cannings *Wilts* **16** H1
All Saints South Elmham *Suffolk* **27** G6
All Stretton *Shrops* **21** C10
Alladale Lodge *H'land* **60** G5
Allaleigh *Devon* **5** K7
Allanaquoich *Gramp* **57** K7
Allanfearn *H'land* **56** E3
Allangrange Mains *H'land* **56** E2
Allanreid *Gramp* **57** G8
Allanton *Borders* **49** D11
Allbrook *Hants* **8** D6
Allendale Town *Northum* **45** G7
Allenheads *Northum* **39** A10
Allen's Green *Herts* **18** B4
Allensford *Durham* **45** H9
Allensmore *Heref/Worcs* **15** A8
Allenton *Derby* **31** G12
Allenton *S'clyde* **48** D1
Aller *Som'set* **7** C7
Allerby *Cumb* **43** H11
Allerdene *Northum* **45** C8
Allerford *Som'set* **6** B3
Allerston *N Yorks* **41** G9
Allerthorpe *Humber* **36** B5
Allerton *Mersey* **30** B3
Allerton *W Yorks* **35** D10
Allerton Bywater *W Yorks* **36** D2
Allerton Mauleverer *N Yorks* **36** A2
Allerwash *Northum* **45** F7
Allesley *W Midlands* **22** D6
Allestree *Derby* **31** F11
Allexton *Leics* **23** B11
Allgreave *Ches* **31** D8
Allhallows *Kent* **19** F8
Alligin Shuas *H'land* **54** D2
Allimore Green *Staffs* **31** H7
Allington *Hants* **8** B4
Allington *Lincs* **32** F6
Allington *Wilts* **16** H2
Allithwaite *Cumb* **38** G6
Allnabad *H'land* **60** C5
Alloa *Central* **52** H4
Allonby *Cumb* **43** G11
Alloway *S'clyde* **47** H8
Allowenshay *Som'set* **7** E7
Allt *Dyfed* **13** G9
Allt na h'Airbhe *H'land* **60** G3
Alltbeithe *H'land* **55** G4
Alltchaorunn *H'land* **51** B9
Alltmawr *Powys* **20** H6
Alltnacaillich *H'land* **60** C5
Allt-na-giubhsaich *Gramp* **57** L8
Alltneithe *H'land* **55** J4
Alltsigh *H'land* **55** H8
Alltwalis *Dyfed* **13** D8
Alltwen *W Glam* **13** G10
Alltyblacca *Dyfed* **13** B8
Allweston *Dorset* **7** E10
Alma Park Estate *Lincs* **32** F6
Almeley *Heref/Worcs* **21** G9
Almeley Wooton *Heref/Worcs* **21** G9
Almer *Dorset* **7** F12
Almholme *S Yorks* **36** F4
Almington *Staffs* **30** G5
Alminstone Cross *Devon* **4** D2
Almondbank *Tayside* **52** E5
Almondbury *W Yorks* **35** F10
Almondsbury *Avon* **15** F9
Alndyke *Northum* **45** B10
Alne *N Yorks* **36** A3
Alness *H'land* **56** C2
Alnham *Northum* **45** B8
Alnmouth *Northum* **45** B10
Alnwick *Northum* **45** B10
Alphamstone *Essex* **27** M2
Alpheton *Suffolk* **27** K2
Alphington *Devon* **5** G8
Alport *Derby* **31** D10
Alpraham *Ches* **30** D4
Alresford *Essex* **19** B10
Alrewas *Staffs* **22** A5
Alsager *Ches* **30** E6
Alsagers Bank *Staffs* **30** E6
Alsop en le Dale *Derby* **31** E10

Alston *Cumb* 44 H5
Alston *Devon* 6 F6
Alstone *Glos* 16 A1
Alstone *Som'set* 6 B6
Alstonefield *Staffs* 31 E9
Alswear *Devon* 4 D6
Altandhu *H'land* 60 F2
Altanduin *H'land* 61 E8
Altarnun *Cornw'l* 3 B9
Altass *H'land* 60 G6
Altgaltraig *S'clyde* 46 B5
Altham *Lancs* 34 D6
Althorne *Essex* 19 D9
Althorpe *Humber* 36 F6
Alticry *Dumf/Gal* 42 G4
Altnabreac Stn *H'land* 61 C9
Altnacardich *H'land* 56 E1
Altnacealgach Hot *H'land* 60 F4
Altnacraig *S'clyde* 50 E6
Altnafeadh *H'land* 51 B9
Altnaharra *H'land* 60 D6
Altofts *W Yorks* 35 E12
Alton *Derby* 32 D1
Alton *Hants* 9 B8
Alton *Staffs* 31 F9
Alton Barnes *Wilts* 16 H2
Alton Pancras *Dorset* 7 F10
Alton Priors *Wilts* 16 H2
Altonhill *S'clyde* 47 E9
Altrincham *Gtr Man* 30 A6
Altrua *H'land* 55 K6
Altskeith *Central* 51 G11
Alva *Central* 52 G4
Alvanlay *Ches* 30 C4
Alvaston *Derby* 31 G12
Alvechurch *Heref/Worcs* 22 E4
Alvecote *Warwick* 22 B6
Alvediston *Wilts* 8 D1
Alveley *Shrops* 22 D1
Alverdiscott *Devon* 4 C4
Alverstoke *Hants* 9 F7
Alverstone *I of Wight* 9 G7
Alverton *Notts* 32 F5
Alves *Gramp* 56 D7
Alvescot *Oxon* 16 D4
Alveston *Avon* 15 E9
Alveston *Warwick* 22 F6
Alvie *H'land* 57 J4
Alvingham *Lincs* 33 A10
Alvington *Glos* 15 D9
Alwalton *Cambs* 24 F2
Alwinton *Northum* 45 B7
Alwoodley *W Yorks* 35 C11
Alyth *Tayside* 53 B7
Amber Hill *Lincs* 33 E9
Ambergate *Derby* 31 E11
Amberley *Glos* 15 D11
Amberley *W Sussex* 9 E11
Amble *Northum* 45 C11
Amblecote *W Midlands* 22 D2
Ambler Thorn *W Yorks* 35 D9
Ambleside *Cumb* 38 E6
Ambleston *Dyfed* 12 D3
Ambrosden *Oxon* 17 B7
Amcotts *Humber* 36 F6
Americanmuir *Tayside* 53 D8
Amersham *Bucks* 17 D10
Amersham Common *Bucks* 17 D10
Amersidelaw *Northum* 45 C12
Amesbury *Wilts* 8 B3
Amhuinnsuidhe *W Isles* 63 F1
Amington *Staffs* 22 B6
Amisfield Town *Dumf/Gal* 43 C11
Amlwch *Gwyn* 28 A4
Amlwch Port *Gwyn* 28 A4
Ammanford *Dyfed* 13 F9
Amotherby *N Yorks* 41 H7
Ampfield *Hants* 8 D5
Ampherlaw *S'clyde* 48 D3
Ampleforth *N Yorks* 40 G6
Ampleforth College *N Yorks* 40 G6
Ampney Crucis *Glos* 16 D2
Ampney St. Mary *Glos* 16 D2
Ampney St. Peter *Glos* 16 D2
Amport *Hants* 8 B4
Ampthill *Beds* 25 L1
Ampton *Suffolk* 27 H2
Amroth *Dyfed* 12 F5
Amulree *Tayside* 52 C4
An Caol *H'land* 62 C5
An Choc *W Isles* 63 D6
An Coroghon *H'land* 62 H2
Anaheilt *H'land* 50 A5
Anancaun *H'land* 54 C4
Ancaster *Lincs* 33 F7
Anchor *Powys* 21 D7
Ancroft Northmoor *Northum* 49 E12
Ancrum *Borders* 49 G9
Anderby *Lincs* 33 C12
Anderson *Dorset* 7 F12
Anderton *Ches* 30 C5
Andover *Hants* 8 B5
Andover Down *Hants* 8 B5
Andoversford *Glos* 16 B1
Andreas *I of Man* 38 F2
Angansk *Tayside* 52 F6
Angarrak *Cornw'l* 2 F3
Angle *Dyfed* 12 G2
Anglers Hotel *Cumb* 38 D3
Angmering *W Sussex* 9 F12
Angmering-on-Sea *W Sussex* 9 F12
Angram *N Yorks* 36 B3
Angram *N Yorks* 39 E11
Anie *Central* 52 F1
Ankerville *H'land* 56 B4
Anlaby *Humber* 37 D8
Anmer *Norfolk* 24 C8
Anna Valley *Hants* 8 B5
Annan *Dumf/Gal* 43 E12
Annat *H'land* 54 D3
Annat *S'clyde* 51 E7
Annathill *S'clyde* 47 B12
Annbank *S'clyde* 47 G9
Annesley Woodhouse *Notts* 32 E2
Annfield *Gramp* 58 F3
Annfield Plain *Durham* 45 H10
Annitsford *Tyne/Wear* 45 F11
Annscroft *Shrops* 21 B10
Annstead *Northum* 45 D12
Ansford *Som'set* 7 C10
Ansley *Warwick* 22 C6
Anslow *Staffs* 31 H10
Anslow Gate *Staffs* 31 H10
Anstey *Hants* 9 B8
Anstey *Herts* 25 M5
Anstey *Leics* 23 A9
Anstruther Easter *Fife* 53 G10
Anstruther Wester *Fife* 53 G10
Ansty *W Sussex* 10 F2
Ansty *Warwick* 23 D7
Ansty *Wilts* 8 C1
Anthill Common *Hants* 9 E8
Anthorn *Cumb* 43 F12
Antingham *Norfolk* 26 B6
Antony *Cornw'l* 3 D11
Antrobus *Ches* 30 B5
Anvil Corner *Devon* 4 E2
Anwick *Lincs* 33 E8
Anwoth *Dumf/Gal* 42 F6
Aonachan *H'land* 55 L6
Apes Hall *Cambs* 24 F6
Apethorpe *Northants* 24 F1
Apley *Lincs* 33 C8
Apperknowle *Derby* 32 B1
Apperley *Glos* 15 B11
Appersett *N Yorks* 39 F10
Appin House *S'clyde* 50 C6
Appleby *Humber* 37 F7
Appleby Magna *Leics* 22 A6
Appleby Parva *Leics* 22 A6
Appleby-in-Westmoreland *Cumb* 39 C9
Applecross *H'land* 54 E1
Applecross House *H'land* 54 E1
Appledore *Devon* 4 C3
Appledore *Devon* 6 E4
Appledore *Kent* 11 E8
Appledore Heath *Kent* 11 E8
Appleford *Oxon* 16 E6
Appleshaw *Hants* 8 A4
Applethwaite *Cumb* 38 C5
Appleton *Oxon* 16 D5
Appleton Roebuck *N Yorks* 36 C3
Appleton Thorn *Ches* 30 B5
Appleton Wiske *N Yorks* 40 E4
Appleton-le-Moors *N Yorks* 41 F7
Appleton-le-Street *N Yorks* 41 H7
Appletreehall *Borders* 44 B3
Appletreewick *N Yorks* 35 A9
Appley *Som'set* 6 D4
Appley Bridge *Lancs* 34 F4
Apse Heath *I of Wight* 9 H7
Apsley End *Beds* 18 A1
Apuldram *W Sussex* 9 F9
Aquhythie *Gramp* 58 F5
Arabella *H'land* 56 B4
Araid *H'land* 54 D2
Arbeadie *Gramp* 59 H4
Arbirlot *Tayside* 53 C10
Arborfield *Berks* 17 G8
Arborfield Cross *Berks* 17 G8
Arbrack *Dumf/Gal* 42 H5
Arbroath *Tayside* 53 C11
Arbuthnott *Gramp* 59 K5
Archiestown *Gramp* 56 E8
Arclid Green *Ches* 30 D6
Ardachearanbeg *S'clyde* 46 A5
Ardachoil *H'land* 50 D4
Ardachuple *S'clyde* 46 A5
Ardachvie *H'land* 55 K5
Ardanaiseig *S'clyde* 51 E8
Ardaneaskan *H'land* 54 F2
Ardanstur *S'clyde* 50 F5
Ardarroch *H'land* 54 F2
Ardbeg *S'clyde* 46 C6
Ardcharnich *H'land* 60 G3
Ardchiavaig *S'clyde* 50 F1
Ardchonnell *S'clyde* 51 F7
Ardchrishnish *H'land* 50 E2
Ardchullarie More *Central* 52 F1
Ardchyle *Central* 51 E12
Ardcross *Fife* 53 G10
Arddarroch *S'clyde* 51 H9
Arddleen *Powys* 21 A8
Ardelanish *H'land* 50 F1
Ardeley *Herts* 18 A3
Ardelve *H'land* 55 G2
Arden *S'clyde* 47 A8
Arden Hall *N Yorks* 40 F5
Ardencaple Ho *S'clyde* 50 F5
Ardens Grafton *Warwick* 22 G5
Ardentallan Ho *S'clyde* 50 E5
Ardentraive *S'clyde* 46 B5
Ardeonaig *Central* 52 D2
Arderier *H'land* 56 D3
Ardery *H'land* 50 A5
Ardess *S'clyde* 51 H10
Ardessie *H'land* 60 G2
Ardfern *S'clyde* 50 G5
Ardgartan *S'clyde* 51 G10
Ardgay *H'land* 60 G6
Ardhasaig *W Isles* 63 G2
Ardheslaig *H'land* 54 D2
Ardinamar *S'clyde* 50 F5
Ardindrean *H'land* 60 G3
Ardingly *W Sussex* 10 E2
Ardington *Oxon* 16 E5
Ardintoul *H'land* 55 G2
Ardlair *Gramp* 58 E3
Ardlamont House *S'clyde* 46 C5
Ardlarach *S'clyde* 50 F5
Ardleigh *Essex* 27 M3
Ardler *Tayside* 53 C7
Ardley *Oxon* 16 A6
Ardlui *S'clyde* 51 F10
Ardlussa *S'clyde* 46 A2
Ardmaddy *S'clyde* 51 D8
Ardmair *H'land* 60 G3
Ardmaleish *S'clyde* 46 C6
Ardmay *S'clyde* 51 G10
Ardminish *S'clyde* 46 E2
Ardmolich *H'land* 55 M1
Ardmore *H'land* 61 H7
Ardmore *S'clyde* 47 B8
Ardmore *S'clyde* 50 E5
Ardnacross *H'land* 50 C3
Ardnadam *S'clyde* 47 A7
Ardnagrask *H'land* 56 E1
Ardnamurach *H'land* 55 K2
Ardnastang *H'land* 50 A5
Ardneil *S'clyde* 47 D7
Ardno *S'clyde* 51 G8
Ardo House *Gramp* 58 E7
Ardoch *Tayside* 52 C6
Ardochrig *S'clyde* 47 E11
Ardochu *H'land* 61 F7
Ardochy House *H'land* 55 J6
Ardow *H'land* 50 B2
Ardoyne *Gramp* 58 E4
Ardpatrick *S'clyde* 46 C3
Ardpatrick House *S'clyde* 46 C3
Ardpeaton *S'clyde* 47 A7
Ardrishaig *S'clyde* 46 A3
Ardroil *W Isles* 63 D1
Ardross *H'land* 56 B2
Ardrossan *S'clyde* 47 E7
Ardshealach *H'land* 50 A4
Ardslave *W Isles* 63 H2
Ardsley *S Yorks* 35 G12
Ardsley East *W Yorks* 35 E11
Ardslignish *H'land* 50 A3
Ardtalnaig *Tayside* 52 C2
Ardtaraig *S'clyde* 46 A5
Ardtoe *H'land* 50 A4
Ardtrostan *Tayside* 52 E2
Ardtun *H'land* 50 E1
Arduaine *S'clyde* 50 F5
Ardullie *H'land* 56 C1
Ardura *H'land* 50 E4
Ardvasar *H'land* 62 H5
Ardvergnish *H'land* 50 E3
Ardverikie *H'land* 57 L1
Ardvey, Loch Finsbay *W Isles* 63 H2
Ardvey, Loch Stockinish *W Isles* 63 H2
Ardvorlich *S'clyde* 51 F10
Ardvorlich *Tayside* 52 E1
Ardvourlie *W Isles* 63 F3
Ardwell *Dumf/Gal* 42 G2
Ardwell *S'clyde* 42 B3
Areley Kings *Heref/Worcs* 22 E2
Arford *Hants* 9 B9
Argaty *Central* 52 G2
Argoed *Gwent* 14 D5
Argoed Mill *Powys* 20 F5
Arichastlich *S'clyde* 51 D10
Aridhglas *H'land* 50 F1
Arinacrinachd *H'land* 54 D1
Ariogan *S'clyde* 50 E6
Arisaig *H'land* 55 L1
Arisaig House *H'land* 55 L1
Ariundle *H'land* 50 A5
Arivruaich *W Isles* 63 E3
Arkendale *N Yorks* 36 A2
Arkesden *Essex* 25 M6
Arkholme *Lancs* 39 H8
Arkle Town *N Yorks* 39 E12
Arkleby *Cumb* 43 H12
Arkleton *Dumf/Gal* 44 D2
Arkley *London* 18 D2
Arksey *S Yorks* 36 F4
Arkwright Town *Derby* 32 C2
Arle *Glos* 15 B12
Arlecdon *Cumb* 38 C3
Arlesey *Beds* 25 L3
Arleston *Shrops* 21 A12
Arley *Ches* 30 B5
Arley *Warwick* 22 C6
Arlingham *Glos* 15 C10
Arlington *Devon* 4 B5
Arlington *E Sussex* 10 G4
Arlington *Glos* 16 C2
Arlington Becott *Devon* 4 B5
Armadale *H'land* 61 B8
Armadale *Lothian* 48 C2
Armadale Castle *H'land* 62 H6
Armathwaite *Cumb* 39 A7
Arminghall *Norfolk* 26 E5
Armitage *Staffs* 22 A4
Armley *W Yorks* 35 D11
Armscote *Warwick* 22 H6
Armston *Northants* 25 G2
Armthorpe *S Yorks* 36 G4
Arncliffe *N Yorks* 39 H11
Arncliffe Cote *N Yorks* 39 H11
Arncroach *Fife* 53 G10
Arne *Dorset* 8 G1
Arnesby *Leics* 23 C9
Arnicle *S'clyde* 46 F2
Arnisdale *H'land* 55 H2
Arnish *H'land* 62 C5
Arniston Engine *Lothian* 48 C6
Arnol *W Isles* 63 B4
Arnold *Humber* 37 C9
Arnold *Notts* 32 F3
Arnprior *Central* 52 H1
Arnside *Cumb* 39 G7
Aros Mains *H'land* 50 C3
Arrad Foot *Cumb* 38 G5
Arrathorne *N Yorks* 40 F2
Arreton *I of Wight* 9 G7
Arrington *Cambs* 25 K4
Arrivain *S'clyde* 51 D10
Arrochar *S'clyde* 51 G10
Arrow *Warwick* 22 F4
Artafallie *H'land* 56 E2
Arthington *W Yorks* 35 C11
Arthingworth *Northants* 23 D11
Arthog *Gwyn* 20 A2
Arthrath *Gramp* 58 D7
Arundel *W Sussex* 9 E11
Aryhoulan *H'land* 51 A7
Asby *Cumb* 38 C3
Asby cum Fenby *Humber* 37 G10
Ascog *S'clyde* 46 C6
Ascot *Berks* 17 G10
Ascott under Wychwood *Oxon* 16 B4
Asenby *N Yorks* 40 H4
Asfordby *Leics* 32 H4
Asfordby Hill *Leics* 32 H4
Asgarby *Lincs* 24 A2
Asgarby *Lincs* 33 D10
Ash *Kent* 10 B5
Ash *Kent* 11 B11
Ash *Som'set* 7 D8
Ash *Surrey* 9 A10
Ash Bullayne *Devon* 4 E6
Ash Green *Warwick* 23 D7
Ash Magna *Devon* 4 D6
Ash Magna *Shrops* 30 F4
Ash Priors *Som'set* 6 C5
Ash Thomas *Devon* 6 E3
Ash Vale *Surrey* 9 A10
Ashampstead *Berks* 16 F6
Ashbocking *Suffolk* 27 K5
Ashbourne *Derby* 31 F10
Ashbrittle *Som'set* 6 D4
Ashburton *Devon* 5 J6
Ashbury *Devon* 4 F4
Ashbury *Oxon* 16 F4
Ashby *Humber* 37 F7
Ashby by Partney *Lincs* 33 D11
Ashby de la Launde *Lincs* 33 E7
Ashby de la Zouch *Leics* 31 H12
Ashby Dell *Suffolk* 26 E8
Ashby Folville *Leics* 23 A10
Ashby Magna *Leics* 23 C9
Ashby Parva *Leics* 23 C8
Ashby Puerorum *Lincs* 33 C10
Ashby St. Ledgers *Northants* 23 E9
Ashby St. Mary *Norfolk* 26 E6
Ashchurch *Glos* 15 A12
Ashcombe *Avon* 14 H6
Ashcombe *Devon* 6 H3
Ashcott *Som'set* 7 C8
Ashcroft *Berks* 17 F8
Ashdon *Essex* 25 L7
Ashe *Hants* 9 A7
Asheldham *Essex* 19 D9
Ashen *Essex* 25 L8
Ashendon *Bucks* 17 C8
Ashfield *Central* 52 G3
Ashfield *Dyfed* 13 D10
Ashfield *Suffolk* 27 J5
Ashfield Green *Suffolk* 27 H6
Ashford *Devon* 4 C4
Ashford *Hants* 8 E3
Ashford *Kent* 11 D9
Ashford *Surrey* 17 G11
Ashford Bowdler *Shrops* 21 E10
Ashford Carbonel *Shrops* 21 E10
Ashford Hill *Hants* 16 H6
Ashford in the water *Derby* 31 C10
Ashgbank *Borders* 44 B4
Ashgill *S'clyde* 47 D12
Ashgillside *Cumb* 39 A10
Ashill *Devon* 6 E4
Ashill *Norfolk* 26 E2
Ashill *Som'set* 6 D6
Ashingdon *Essex* 19 E8
Ashington *Northum* 45 D10
Ashington *Som'set* 7 D9
Ashington *W Sussex* 9 E12
Ashkirk *Borders* 49 G7
Ashlett *Hants* 8 F6
Ashleworth *Glos* 15 B11
Ashley *Cambs* 25 J8
Ashley *Ches* 30 B6
Ashley *Devon* 4 E5
Ashley *Glos* 15 E12
Ashley *Hants* 8 C5
Ashley *Hants* 8 G4
Ashley *Kent* 11 C11
Ashley *Northants* 23 C11
Ashley *Staffs* 30 F6
Ashley Green *Bucks* 17 D10
Ashley Heath *Dorset* 8 F3
Ashmansworth *Hants* 16 H5
Ashmansworthy *Devon* 4 D2
Ashmore *Dorset* 7 D12
Ashmore Green *Berks* 16 G6
Ashogle *Gramp* 58 B4
Ashorne *Warwick* 22 F6
Ashover *Derby* 32 D1
Ashow *Warwick* 22 E6
Ashperton *Heref/Worcs* 21 H11
Ashprington *Devon* 5 K7
Ashreigney *Devon* 4 E5
Ashstead *Surrey* 10 B1
Ashstton *Kent* 10 A6
Ashton *Ches* 30 C4
Ashton *Cornw'l* 2 G3
Ashton *Gtr Man* 35 G8
Ashton *Heref/Worcs* 21 F10
Ashton *Northants* 23 G11
Ashton *Northants* 25 G2
Ashton Common *Wilts* 15 H12
Ashton Keynes *Wilts* 16 E2
Ashton upon Mersey *Gtr Man* 34 H6
Ashton upon Mersey *Heref/Worcs* 22 H3
Ashurst *Hants* 8 E5
Ashurst *Kent* 10 D4
Ashurst *W Sussex* 10 F1
Ashurstwood *W Sussex* 10 D3
Ashwater *Devon* 4 F3
Ashwell *Herts* 25 L4
Ashwell *Leics* 23 A12
Ashwellthorpe *Norfolk* 26 F4
Ashwick *Som'set* 7 A9
Ashwicken *Norfolk* 24 D8
Askam in Furness *Cumb* 38 G4
Askern *S Yorks* 36 F3
Askerswell *Dorset* 7 G8
Askett *Bucks* 17 D9
Askham *Cumb* 39 C7
Askham *Notts* 32 C4
Askham Bryan *N Yorks* 36 B3
Askham Richard *N Yorks* 36 B3
Asknish *S'clyde* 50 H6
Askrigg *N Yorks* 39 F11
Askwith *N Yorks* 35 B10
Aslackby *Lincs* 24 C2
Aslacton *Norfolk* 26 F4
Aslockton *Notts* 32 F5
Asloun *Gramp* 58 F3
Aspatria *Cumb* 43 G12
Aspenden *Herts* 18 A4
Asperton *Lincs* 24 B4
Aspley Guise *Beds* 23 H12
Aspley Heath *Beds* 17 A10
Aspull *Gtr Man* 34 F5
Asselby *Humber* 36 D5
Asserby *Lincs* 33 B12
Assington *Suffolk* 27 L2
Astbury *Ches* 31 D7
Astcote *Northants* 23 G10
Asterley *Shrops* 21 B9
Asterton *Shrops* 21 C9
Asthall *Oxon* 16 C4
Asthall Leigh *Oxon* 16 C4
Astley *Gtr Man* 34 G6
Astley *Heref/Worcs* 22 E1
Astley *Shrops* 30 H4
Astley *Warwick* 22 C6
Astley Abbots *Shrops* 21 C12
Astley Bridge *Gtr Man* 34 F6
Astley Cross *Heref/Worcs* 22 E2
Astley Green *Gtr Man* 34 G6
Aston *Berks* 17 F9
Aston *Ches* 30 B4
Aston *Ches* 30 E5
Aston *Clwyd* 29 C12
Aston *Derby* 31 B10
Aston *Heref/Worcs* 21 E10
Aston *Heref/Worcs* 21 F10
Aston *Herts* 18 B3
Aston *Oxon* 16 D4
Aston *S Yorks* 32 B2
Aston *Shrops* 21 A11
Aston *Shrops* 30 G4
Aston *Staffs* 30 F6
Aston *W Midlands* 22 C4
Aston Abbotts *Bucks* 17 B9
Aston Botterell *Shrops* 21 D11
Aston by Stone *Staffs* 31 G7
Aston Cantlow *Warwick* 22 F5
Aston Clinton *Bucks* 17 C9
Aston Crews *Heref/Worcs* 15 B10
Aston Cross *Glos* 15 A12
Aston End *Herts* 18 B3
Aston Eyre *Shrops* 21 C12
Aston Fields *Heref/Worcs* 22 E3
Aston Flamville *Leics* 23 C8
Aston Ingham *Heref/Worcs* 15 B10
Aston Juxta Mondrum *Ches* 30 D5
Aston le Walls *Northants* 23 G8
Aston Magna *Glos* 16 A3
Aston on Clun *Shrops* 21 D9
Aston on Trent *Derby* 31 G12
Aston Pigott *Shrops* 21 B9
Aston Rogers *Shrops* 21 B9
Aston Rowant *Oxon* 17 D8
Aston Sandford *Bucks* 17 C8
Aston Somerville *Heref/Worcs* 22 H4
Aston Subedge *Glos* 22 H5
Aston Tirrold *Oxon* 16 F6
Aston Upthorpe *Oxon* 16 E6
Astwick *Beds* 25 L3
Astwood *Bucks* 25 K1
Astwood Bank *Heref/Worcs* 22 F4
Aswarby *Lincs* 24 B2
Aswardby *Lincs* 33 C10
Atcham *Shrops* 21 B11
Athelington *Suffolk* 27 H5
Athelney *Som'set* 7 C7
Athelstaneford *Lothian* 49 B8
Atherington *Devon* 4 D5
Atherington *W Sussex* 9 F11
Atherstone *Warwick* 22 B6
Atherstone on Stour *Warwick* 22 G5
Atherton *Gtr Man* 34 G5
Athnamulloch *H'land* 55 G5
Atley Hill *N Yorks* 40 E3
Atlow *Derby* 31 E10
Attadale *H'land* 54 F3
Attadale House *H'land* 54 F3
Attleborough *Norfolk* 26 F3
Attleborough *Warwick* 23 C7
Attlebridge *Norfolk* 26 D4
Atton *Tayside* 59 K1
Attonburn *Borders* 49 G10
Atwick *Humber* 37 B9
Atworth *Wilts* 15 H11
Aubourn *Lincs* 32 D6
Auchachenna *S'clyde* 51 E7
Auchagallon *S'clyde* 46 F4
Auchallater *Gramp* 57 K7
Auchalton *S'clyde* 42 A4
Aucharnie *Gramp* 58 D4
Auchavan *Tayside* 57 M7
Auchbreck *Gramp* 57 G8
Auchbroad *S'clyde* 46 A3
Aucheldy *Gramp* 58 D6
Auchenbainzie *Dumf/Gal* 43 B9
Auchenblae *Gramp* 59 J5
Auchenbrack *Dumf/Gal* 43 B8
Auchenbreck *S'clyde* 46 A5
Auchencairn *Dumf/Gal* 43 C10
Auchencairn *Dumf/Gal* 43 F9
Auchencarroch *S'clyde* 47 A9
Auchencheff *Dumf/Gal* 43 D10
Auchencrieff *Dumf/Gal* 43 D9
Auchencrosh *S'clyde* 42 D2

Auchencrow Borders 49 C11
Auchendinny Lothian 48 C5
Auchengary S'clyde 48 D3
Auchengibbert Dumf/Gal 43 D9
Auchengruith Dumf/Gal 43 A9
Auchenhairig Gramp 58 B1
Auchenheath S'clyde 48 E1
Auchenmalg Dumf/Gal 42 F3
Auchensoul S'clyde 42 B3
Auchentibbert Dumf/Gal 42 G2
Auchentiber S'clyde 47 E8
Auchenvennel S'clyde 47 A8
Auchenvey Dumf/Gal 43 D8
Auchernack H'land 57 G6
Auchgourish H'land 57 H5
Auchinadrain S'clyde 46 D2
Auchinderran Gramp 58 B2
Auchindram Central 51 G6
Auchindrean H'land 54 B6
Auchinhove Gramp 58 B2
Auchininna Gramp 58 C4
Auchinleck S'clyde 47 G10
Auchinloch S'clyde 47 B11
Auchinner Tayside 52 F2
Auchintender Gramp 58 D4
Auchintoul Gramp 58 F3
Auchintoul Gramp 59 G4
Auchiries Gramp 58 D8
Auchleven Gramp 58 E4
Auchlochan S'clyde 48 F1
Auchlossan Gramp 59 G3
Auchlunachan H'land 60 H3
Auchlunies Gramp 59 G6
Auchlyne Central 51 E12
Auchmacoy Gramp 58 D7
Auchmantle Dumf/Gal 42 E2
Auchmillan S'clyde 47 F10
Auchmithie Tayside 53 C11
Auchmuirbridge Fife 53 G7
Auchmull Tayside 59 K3
Auchnacloich Pier S'clyde 51 D7
Auchnacree Tayside 53 A9
Auchnacree Tayside 59 L2
Auchnadaull H'land 55 L5
Auchnagallin H'land 56 F6
Auchnagatt Gramp 58 C7
Auchnaha S'clyde 46 A4
Auchnahannet H'land 57 G5
Auchnahillin H'land 56 F3
Auchnotteroch Dumf/Gal 42 F1
Aucholzie Gramp 59 H1
Auchrioch Central 51 E10
Auchroisk H'land 57 G6
Auchronie Tayside 59 J2
Auchterarder Tayside 52 F4
Auchteraw H'land 55 J7
Auchterderran Fife 53 H7
Auchterhouse Tayside 53 C8
Auchtermuchty Fife 53 F7
Auchterneed H'land 54 D8
Auchterneed H'land 56 D1
Auchterteang H'land 57 G5
Auchtertool Fife 53 H7
Auchtertyre Central 51 E10
Auchtertyre Gramp 56 D7
Auchtertyre H'land 55 G2
Auchtoo Central 52 E1
Auckingill H'land 61 B12
Auckley S Yorks 36 G4
Auckmair Gramp 58 E1
Audenshaw Gtr Man 35 G8
Audlem Ches 30 F5
Audley Staffs 30 E6
Audley End Essex 25 L6
Auds Gramp 58 A4
Aughton Humber 36 C5
Aughton Lancs 34 G3
Aughton Lancs 39 H8
Aughton S Yorks 32 B2
Aughton Wilts 16 H3
Auldallan Tayside 53 A8
Auldearn H'land 56 D5
Aulden Heref/Worcs 21 G10
Auldgirth Dumf/Gal 43 C10
Auldhame Lothian 49 A8
Auldhouse S'clyde 47 D11
Auldtown Gramp 58 B3
Auldtown of Carnousie Gramp 58 C4
Aulich Tayside 52 A1
Ault Hucknall Derby 32 D2
Ault-a-chruinn H'land 55 H3
Aultanrynie H'land 60 D4
Aultbea H'land 60 G1
Aultdearg H'land 54 C7
Aultgowrie H'land 54 E8
Aultgrishan H'land 54 A1
Aultguish Inn H'land 54 C7
Aulthash Gramp 58 B1
Aultiphurst H'land 61 A8
Aultmore Gramp 58 B1
Aultnagoire H'land 57 G1
Aultnamain Inn H'land 56 B2
Aultnancaber H'land 57 H5
Aultnaslat H'land 55 J5
Aulton Gramp 58 E3
Aultonrea Gramp 59 H1
Aundorach H'land 57 H5
Aunk Devon 6 F4
Aunsby Lincs 24 B1
Aust Avon 15 E9
Austen Fen Lincs 37 H11
Austenwood Bucks 17 E10
Austerfield Notts 36 H4
Austrey Warwick 22 B6
Austwick N Yorks 39 H10
Authorpe Lincs 33 B11
Authorpe Row Lincs 33 C12
Avebury Wilts 16 G2
Aveley Essex 18 F6
Avening Glos 15 E12
Avenuehead Lothian 48 A1
Averham Notts 32 E5
Aveton Gifford Devon 5 L6
Avielochan H'land 57 H5
Aviemore H'land 57 H4
Avinagillan S'clyde 46 C3
Avington Berks 16 G5
Avington Hants 9 C7
Avoch H'land 56 D3
Avon Wilts 16 F1
Avon Co Avon 15 F9
Avon Dassett Warwick 23 G7
Avonbridge Lothian 48 B2
Avonmouth Avon 15 F8
Avonwick Devon 5 K6
Awbridge Hants 8 D5
Awhirk Dumf/Gal 42 F1
Awkley Avon 15 F9
Awliscombe Devon 6 F5
Awre Glos 15 D10
Awsworth Notts 32 F2
Axbridge Som'set 7 A8
Axford Hants 9 B7
Axford Wilts 16 G3
Axminster Devon 6 F6
Axmouth Devon 6 G6
Aycliffe Durham 40 C3
Aydon Northum 45 F8
Aylburton Glos 15 D9
Ayle Northum 44 H5
Aylesbeare Devon 6 G4
Aylesbury Bucks 17 C9
Aylesby Humber 37 F9
Aylescott Devon 4 D5
Aylesford Kent 10 B6
Aylestone Leics 23 B9
Aylmerton Norfolk 26 B5
Aylsham Kent 11 C11
Aylsham Norfolk 26 C5
Aylton Heref/Worcs 15 A9
Aymestrey Heref/Worcs 21 F9
Aynho Northants 16 A6
Ayot St. Lawrence Herts 18 B2
Ayot St. Peter Herts 18 B2
Ayr S'clyde 47 G8
Aysgarth N Yorks 39 F12
Ayshford Devon 6 E4
Ayside Cumb 38 G6
Ayston Leics 23 B12
Aythorpe Roding Essex 18 B6
Ayton Borders 49 C11
Azerley N Yorks 40 H3
Babbacombe Devon 5 J8
Babbinswood Shrops 30 G2
Babcary Som'set 7 C9
Babel Dyfed 13 C11
Babell Clwyd 29 C11
Babeny Devon 5 H5
Babraham Cambs 25 K6
Babworth Notts 32 B4
Bac W Isles 63 C6
Bachau Gwyn 28 B4
Back of Keppoch H'land 55 L1
Backaland Orkney 64 B3
Backaskaill Orkney 64 A3
Backbarrow Cumb 38 G6
Backe Dyfed 12 E6
Backford Ches 30 C3
Backford Cross Ches 30 C3
Backhill Gramp 58 D5
Backhill Gramp 58 F5
Backhill of Clackriach Gramp 58 C7
Backhill of Fortree Gramp 58 D7
Backhill of Trustach Gramp 59 H4
Backies H'land 61 F8
Backmuir of New Gilston Fife 53 F9
Backwell Avon 15 G8
Backworth Tyne/Wear 45 F11
Bacon End Essex 18 B6
Baconsthorpe Norfolk 26 B4
Bacton Heref/Worcs 15 A7
Bacton Norfolk 26 B6
Bacton Suffolk 27 J3
Bacup Lancs 35 E7
Badachro H'land 54 B2
Badanloch Lodge H'land 61 D8
Badavanich H'land 54 D5
Badbury Wilts 16 F3
Badby Northants 23 F9
Badcall H'land 60 B4
Badcaul H'land 60 G2
Baddeley Green Staffs 31 E8
Baddesley Clinton Warwick 22 E5
Baddesley Ensor Warwick 22 B6
Baddidarach H'land 60 E2
Baddington Glos 15 B12
Baddock H'land 56 D4
Badenyon Gramp 58 F1
Badger Shrops 22 B1
Badger's Mount Kent 10 B4
Badgeworth Glos 15 B12
Badgworth Som'set 7 A7
Badicaul H'land 55 G1
Badingham Suffolk 27 H6
Badintagairt H'land 60 F5
Badlesmere Kent 11 C9
Badlipster H'land 61 C11
Badluarach H'land 60 G2
Badnabay H'land 60 C3
Badnagyle H'land 60 F2
Badnambiast Tayside 57 M3
Badnonan Gramp 56 F5
Badrallach H'land 60 G2
Badsey Heref/Worcs 22 H4
Badshot Lea Surrey 9 A10
Badsworth W Yorks 36 F2
Badwell Ash Suffolk 27 H3
Bag Enderby Lincs 33 C10
Bagber Dorset 7 E11
Bagby N Yorks 40 G5
Bagendon Glos 16 C1
Bagillt Clwyd 29 C11
Baginton Warwick 23 E7
Baglan W Glam 13 H10
Bagley Shrops 30 G3
Bagnal Staffs 31 E8
Bagnor Berks 16 G5
Bagshot Surrey 17 H10
Bagshot Wilts 16 H4
Bagstone Avon 15 F10
Bagthorpe Norfolk 26 B1
Bagthorpe Notts 32 E2
Bagworth Leics 23 A8
Bagwy Llydiart Heref/Worcs 15 B8
Baildon W Yorks 35 C10
Baile Boidheach S'clyde 46 B2
Baile Mor H'land 50 F1
Bailebeag H'land 57 H1
Baileyhead Cumb 44 E3
Bailiehill Dumf/Gal 44 D1
Baillieston S'clyde 47 C11
Bailliesward Gramp 58 D2
Bainbridge N Yorks 39 F11
Bainshole Gramp 58 D4
Bainton Cambs 24 E2
Bainton Humber 37 B7
Bairnkine Borders 44 B5
Baker Street Essex 18 F6
Baker's End Herts 18 B4
Bakewell Derby 31 C10
Bala Gwyn 29 G8
Balado Tayside 52 G6
Balallan W Isles 63 E4
Balarumindubh H'land 50 H1
Balavil H'land 57 J3
Balbeg H'land 57 G1
Balbeggie Tayside 52 D6
Balbithan Gramp 58 F5
Balblair H'land 56 C3
Balblair H'land 56 E1
Balcary Hotel Dumf/Gal 43 G9
Balchedre Powys 21 C8
Balchladich H'land 60 D2
Balchraggan H'land 56 E1
Balchraggan H'land 56 F1
Balchrick H'land 60 B3
Balcombe W Sussex 10 E2
Balcurvie Fife 53 G8
Balder Head Durham 39 C11
Baldersby N Yorks 40 G4
Baldersby St. James N Yorks 40 G4
Balderstone Lancs 34 D5
Balderton Ches 30 D2
Balderton Notts 32 E5
Baldinnie Fife 53 F9
Baldock Herts 25 M3
Baldovie Tayside 53 D9
Baldrine I of Man 38 G2
Baldslow E Sussex 11 G7
Baldwin I of Man 38 G2
Baldwinholme Cumb 44 H2
Baldwin's Gate Staffs 30 F6
Bale Norfolk 26 B3
Balearn Gramp 58 B8
Balerno Lothian 48 C4
Balfarg Fife 53 G7
Balfeith Gramp 59 K5
Balfield Tayside 59 K3
Balfour Orkney 64 C3
Balfron Central 47 A10
Balgaveny Gramp 58 D4
Balgonar Fife 52 H5
Balgove Gramp 58 D6
Balgowan H'land 57 K2
Balgown H'land 62 A3
Balgrayhill Dumf/Gal 43 C12
Balgrochan S'clyde 47 B11
Balgy H'land 54 D2
Balhaldie Central 52 G3
Balhalgardy Gramp 58 E5
Balham London 18 G3
Balharry Tayside 53 C7
Baliasta Shetl'd 64 A8
Baligill H'land 61 A8
Balikinrain Castle Central 52 H1
Balintore H'land 56 B4
Balintore Tayside 53 A7
Balintraid H'land 56 C3
Balintuim Gramp 57 K7
Balintyre Tayside 52 B2
Balk N Yorks 40 G5
Balkeerie Tayside 53 C8
Balkholme Humber 36 D6
Balkissock S'clyde 42 C2
Ball Shrops 30 G2
Ball Hill Hants 16 H5
Ballabeg I of Man 38 H1
Ballacannel I of Man 38 G2
Ballacarnane Beg I of Man 38 G1
Ballachlaggan Gramp 57 K8
Ballachrock Gramp 59 H1
Ballachulish H'land 51 B8
Ballacraine I of Man 38 G1
Ballacuberagh I of Man 38 G2
Ballaggan Dumf/Gal 43 B9
Ballajora I of Man 38 G3
Ballakaigan I of Man 38 H1
Ballaleigh I of Man 38 G1
Ballantrae S'clyde 42 C2
Ballantrushal W Isles 63 B5
Ballards Gore Essex 19 E9
Ballasalla I of Man 38 F2
Ballasalla I of Man 38 H1
Ballater Gramp 59 H1
Ballaugh I of Man 38 G2
Ballcorach Gramp 57 G7
Ballencrieff Lothian 49 B7
Ballianlay S'clyde 46 C5
Ballidor Derby 31 E10
Balliemore S'clyde 50 E5
Ballig I of Man 38 G1
Ballimeanoch S'clyde 51 F7
Ballimore Central 51 F12
Ballindalloch Gramp 56 F7
Ballindean Tayside 53 D7
Ballingdon Suffolk 27 L2
Ballinger Common Bucks 17 D10
Ballingham Heref/Worcs 15 A9
Ballingry Tayside 52 G6
Ballinluig H'land 57 G6
Ballinluig Tayside 52 B5
Ballintean H'land 57 J4
Ballintuim Tayside 52 B6
Ballminnoch Dumf/Gal 42 E4
Balloan H'land 56 E2
Balloch H'land 56 E3
Balloch S'clyde 47 A9
Ballochan Gramp 59 H3
Ballochbroe S'clyde 42 A4
Ballochdoan S'clyde 42 D2
Ballochdowan S'clyde 42 D2
Ballochford Gramp 58 D1
Ballochgoy S'clyde 46 C6
Ballochmorrie S'clyde 42 C3
Ballochroy S'clyde 46 D2
Ballogie Gramp 59 H3
Balls Cross W Sussex 9 D11
Ball's Green E Sussex 10 D4
Ballygown H'land 50 C2
Ballymeanoch S'clyde 50 H5
Balmacara H'land 55 G2
Balmaclellan Dumf/Gal 43 D7
Balmacneil Tayside 52 B5
Balmacolm Fife 53 F8
Balmacquien H'land 62 A4
Balmae Dumf/Gal 43 G7
Balmaha Central 51 H11
Balmaneach H'land 50 D2
Balmangan Dumf/Gal 43 G7
Balmedie Gramp 58 F7
Balmerino Fife 53 E8
Balmerlawn Hants 8 F5
Balmore H'land 54 F7
Balmore H'land 62 D2
Balmore S'clyde 47 B11
Balmore Tayside 52 A4
Balmuchy H'land 56 B4
Balmule Fife 53 H7
Balmullo Fife 53 E9
Balmungie H'land 56 D3
Balnaboth Tayside 59 K1
Balnabruaich H'land 56 C3
Balnabual H'land 56 E3
Balnacoil H'land 61 F8
Balnacra H'land 54 E3
Balnacraig H'land 56 F1
Balnafoich H'land 56 F2
Balnagall H'land 56 B4
Balnageith Gramp 56 D6
Balnagowan Gramp 59 G2
Balnaguard Tayside 52 B4
Balnaguisich H'land 56 C2
Balnain H'land 55 G8
Balnakeil H'land 60 A5
Balnaknock H'land 62 B3
Balnapaling H'land 56 C4
Balquharn Tayside 59 L2
Balquhidder Central 51 E12
Balsall W Midlands 22 E6
Balsall Common W Midlands 22 D6
Balscote Oxon 23 H7
Balsham Cambs 25 K7
Baltasound Shetl'd 64 A8
Balterley Staffs 30 E6
Baltersan Dumf/Gal 42 E5
Balthangie Gramp 58 C6
Baltonsborough Som'set 7 C9
Balure S'clyde 50 C6
Balvack Gramp 58 F4
Balvaird H'land 56 D1
Balvenie Gramp 58 C1
Balvicar S'clyde 50 F5
Balvraid H'land 55 H2
Balvraid H'land 56 F4
Bamber Bridge Lancs 34 E4
Bamber's Green Essex 18 B6
Bamburgh Northum 45 D11
Bamburgh Northum 45 D12
Bamff Tayside 53 B7
Bamflatt Borders 48 F3
Bamford Derby 31 B10
Bamfurlong Gtr Man 34 G5
Bampton Cumb 39 C7
Bampton Devon 6 D3
Bampton Oxon 16 D4
Bampton Grange Cumb 39 C7
Banavie H'land 55 M5
Banbury Oxon 23 H8
Banc-c-ffordd Dyfed 13 C7
Bancffosfelen Dyfed 13 F8
Banchory Gramp 59 G7
Banchory Gramp 59 H4
Bancycapel Dyfed 13 E7
Bancycapel ross Inn Dyfed 13 D11
Bancyfelin Dyfed 12 E6
Bandirran House Tayside 53 D7
Banff Gramp 58 A4
Bangor Gwyn 28 C5
Bangor-Is-coed Clwyd 30 F3
Banham Norfolk 27 G4
Bank Hants 8 E4
Bank Powys 21 A8
Bank Newton N Yorks 35 B8
Bank Street Heref/Worcs 21 F11
Bankend Dumf/Gal 43 E11
Bankend S'clyde 48 F1
Bankfoot S'clyde 47 B7
Bankfoot Tayside 52 D5
Bankglen S'clyde 47 H11
Bankhead Gramp 58 F6
Bankhead Gramp 59 G4
Bankhead Northum 45 B8
Bankhead S'clyde 47 D8
Bankhead S'clyde 48 E3
Banknock S'clyde 47 B12
Banks Cumb 44 F4
Banks Lancs 34 E3
Bankshill Dumf/Gal 43 C12
Banningham Norfolk 26 C5
Bannister Green Essex 19 B7
Bannockburn Central 52 H3
Banstead Surrey 10 B1
Bantham Devon 5 L5
Banton S'clyde 47 B12
Banwell Avon 15 H7
Bapchild Kent 11 B8
Bar Hill Cambs 25 J5
Barachandroman H'land 50 E4
Barassie S'clyde 47 F8
Baravullin S'clyde 50 D6
Barbaraville H'land 56 C3
Barber Booth Derby 31 B9
Barbieston S'clyde 47 H9
Barbon Cumb 39 G8
Barbreck House S'clyde 50 G5
Barbridge Ches 30 E5
Barbrook Devon 4 A6
Barby Northants 23 E9
Barcaldine S'clyde 51 C7
Barcaple Dumf/Gal 43 F7
Barchesten Warwick 22 H6
Barclaugh S'clyde 47 G9
Barclosh Dumf/Gal 43 E9
Barcombe E Sussex 10 G3
Barcombe Cross E Sussex 10 F3
Barden N Yorks 40 F2
Barden Scale N Yorks 35 A9
Bardennoch Dumf/Gal 42 B6
Bardister Shetl'd 64 C7
Bardnabeinne H'land 61 G7
Bardney Lincs 33 C8
Bardon Leics 23 A8
Bardon Mill Northum 44 G6
Bardowie S'clyde 47 B10
Bardrainney S'clyde 47 B8
Bardsea Cumb 38 H5
Bardsey W Yorks 35 C12
Bardwell Suffolk 27 H2
Barelees Northum 49 F11
Barewood Heref/Worcs 21 G9
Barfad S'clyde 46 B4
Barford Norfolk 26 E4
Barford Warwick 22 F6
Barford St. John Oxon 16 A5
Barford St. Martin Wilts 8 C2
Barford St. Michael Oxon 16 A5
Barfrestone Kent 11 C11
Bargaly Dumf/Gal 42 E5
Bargoed Mid Glam 14 D5
Bargrennan S'clyde 42 D4
Barguillean Farm S'clyde 51 E7
Barham Cambs 25 H2
Barham Kent 11 C10
Barham Suffolk 27 K4
Barharrow Dumf/Gal 43 F7
Barholm Lincs 24 D2
Barhough Northum 44 H5
Barkby Leics 23 A9
Barkby Thorpe Leics 23 A9
Barkestone le Vale Leics 32 G5
Barkham Berks 17 G9
Barking London 18 E5
Barking Suffolk 27 K4
Barking Tye Suffolk 27 K4
Barkisland W Yorks 35 E9
Barkston Lincs 32 F6
Barkston N Yorks 36 D3
Barkway Herts 25 M5
Barlaston Staffs 31 F7
Barlay Dumf/Gal 43 D7
Barlborough Derby 32 C2
Barlby N Yorks 36 D4
Barlestone Leics 23 B8
Barley Herts 25 L5
Barley Lancs 35 C7
Barley Mow Tyne/Wear 45 H11
Barleyhill Northum 45 H8
Barleythorpe Leics 23 A11
Barling Essex 19 E9
Barlow Derby 32 C1
Barlow N Yorks 36 D4
Barlow Tyne/Wear 45 G9
Barmby Moor Humber 36 B5
Barmby on the Marsh Humber 36 D5
Barmer Norfolk 26 B1
Barmoor Castle Northum 49 E12
Barmoor Ridge Northum 49 E12
Barmouth Gwyn 20 A2
Barmpton Durham 40 C3
Barmston Humber 37 A9
Barnacarry S'clyde 51 H7
Barnack Cambs 24 E2
Barnacle Warwick 23 D7
Barnaline S'clyde 51 F7
Barnard Castle Durham 39 C12
Barnardiston Suffolk 25 K8
Barnbarroch Dumf/Gal 43 F9
Barnburgh S Yorks 36 G3
Barnby Suffolk 26 F8
Barnby Dun S Yorks 36 F4
Barnby in the Willows Notts 32 E6
Barnby Moor Notts 32 B4
Barncorkrie Dumf/Gal 42 H2
Barnes London 18 F2
Barnes Street Kent 10 C5
Barnet London 18 D3
Barnetby-le-Wold Humber 37 F8
Barney Norfolk 26 B3
Barnham Suffolk 27 G2
Barnham W Sussex 9 F11
Barnham Broom Norfolk 26 E4
Barnhead Tayside 59 L4
Barnhill Gramp 56 D7
Barnhill Tayside 53 D9
Barnhills Dumf/Gal 42 D1
Barningham Durham 40 D1
Barningham Suffolk 27 H3
Barnoldby le Beck Humber 37 G10
Barnoldswick Lancs 35 C7
Barns Green W Sussex 9 C12
Barnsley Glos 16 D2
Barnsley S Yorks 35 F12
Barnstaple Devon 4 C4
Barnston Essex 18 B6
Barnston Mersey 30 B1
Barnstone Notts 32 G4
Barnt Green Heref/Worcs 22 E4
Barnton Ches 30 C5
Barnwell All Saints Northants 25 G2

Barnwell St. Andrew *Northants* 25 G2
Barnwood *Glos* 15 C11
Barons Cross *Heref/Worcs* 21 G10
Barr *Dumf/Gal* 43 B9
Barr *Dumf/Gal* 47 H12
Barr *S'clyde* 42 B4
Barra Castle *Gramp* 58 E5
Barrachan *Dumf/Gal* 42 G4
Barrachrail *S'clyde* 50 E5
Barraglom *W Isles* 63 D3
Barrasford *Northum* 45 F7
Barravullin *S'clyde* 50 G5
Barregaroow *I of Man* 38 G2
Barrhead *S'clyde* 47 D10
Barrhill *S'clyde* 42 C3
Barrington *Cambs* 25 K5
Barrington *Som'set* 7 D7
Barripper *Cornw'l* 2 F3
Barrisdale *H'land* 55 J3
Barrmill *S'clyde* 47 D8
Barrock *H'land* 61 A11
Barrow *Lancs* 34 C6
Barrow *Leics* 23 A12
Barrow *Shrops* 21 B12
Barrow *Som'set* 7 C10
Barrow *Suffolk* 27 J1
Barrow Gurney *Avon* 15 G8
Barrow Haven *Humber* 37 E8
Barrow Hill *Derby* 32 C1
Barrow in Furness *Cumb* 38 H5
Barrow Nook *Lancs* 34 G3
Barrow Street *Wilts* 7 C11
Barrowburn *Northum* 45 B7
Barrowby *Lincs* 32 G6
Barrowcliff *N Yorks* 41 F10
Barrowden *Leics* 23 B12
Barrowford *Lancs* 35 C7
Barrows Green *Ches* 30 D5
Barrow-upon-Humber *Humber* 37 E8
Barrow-upon-Soar *Leics* 32 H3
Barrow-upon-Trent *Derby* 31 G12
Barrs *S'clyde* 51 D8
Barry *S Glam* 14 G4
Barry *Tayside* 53 D10
Barry Island *S Glam* 14 H4
Barsby *Leics* 23 A10
Barsham *Suffolk* 26 F7
Barston *W Midlands* 22 D5
Bartestree *Heref/Worcs* 21 H11
Barthol Chapel *Gramp* 58 D6
Barthomley *Ches* 30 E6
Bartle Hall *Lancs* 34 D4
Bartlehill *Borders* 49 E10
Bartlehill *Borders* 49 E9
Bartley *Hants* 8 E4
Bartlow *Cambs* 25 L7
Barton *Cambs* 25 K5
Barton *Ches* 30 E3
Barton *Cumb* 39 C7
Barton *Devon* 5 J8
Barton *Glos* 16 B2
Barton *Lancs* 34 C4
Barton *Lancs* 34 F2
Barton *N Yorks* 40 D3
Barton *Som'set* 7 A7
Barton *Warwick* 22 G4
Barton Bendish *Norfolk* 24 E8
Barton Common *Norfolk* 26 C7
Barton End *Glos* 15 E11
Barton Hartshorn *Bucks* 17 A7
Barton in Fabis *Notts* 32 G2
Barton Mills *Suffolk* 25 H8
Barton on Sea *Hants* 8 G4
Barton on the Heath *Warwick* 16 A4
Barton St. David *Som'set* 7 C9
Barton Seagrave *Northants* 23 D12
Barton Stacey *Hants* 8 B6
Barton Town *Devon* 4 B5
Barton Turf *Norfolk* 26 C6
Barton-in-the-Beans *Leics* 23 B7
Barton-le-Clay *Beds* 25 M2
Barton-le-Street *N Yorks* 41 H7
Barton-le-Willows *N Yorks* 36 A5
Barton-under-Needwood *Staffs* 31 H10
Barton-upon-Humber *Humber* 37 E8
Barugh *S Yorks* 35 F11
Barvas *W Isles* 63 B5
Barway *Cambs* 25 H6
Barwell *Leics* 23 B8
Barwick *Som'set* 7 E9
Barwick in Elmet *W Yorks* 36 C2
Baschurch *Shrops* 30 H3
Bascote *Warwick* 23 F7
Basford Green *Staffs* 31 E8
Bashall Eaves *Lancs* 34 C6
Bashley *Hants* 8 F4
Basildon *Essex* 19 E7
Basing *Hants* 9 A8
Basingstoke *Hants* 9 A7
Baslow *Derby* 31 C11
Bason Bridge *Som'set* 7 B7
Bassaleg *Gwent* 14 F6
Bassendean *Borders* 49 E9
Bassenfell *Cumb* 43 H12
Bassenthwaite *Cumb* 38 B5
Basset's Cross *Devon* 4 F4
Bassett *Hants* 8 D5
Bassett's Pole *Staffs* 22 B5
Bassingbourn *Cambs* 25 L4
Bassingfield *Notts* 32 F3
Bassingham *Lincs* 32 D6
Bassingthorpe *Lincs* 33 G7
Basta *Shetl'd* 64 B7
Baston *Lincs* 24 D2
Bastwick *Norfolk* 26 D7
Batchworth Heath *Herts* 18 E1
Batcombe *Dorset* 7 F9
Batcombe *Som'set* 7 B10
Bate Heath *Ches* 30 B5
Bath *Avon* 15 H10
Bathampton *Avon* 15 H11
Bathealton *Som'set* 6 D4
Batheaston *Avon* 15 G11
Bathford *Avon* 15 H11
Bathgate *Lothian* 48 B3
Bathley *Notts* 32 D5
Bathpool *Cornw'l* 3 B10
Bathpool *Som'set* 6 D6
Bathway *Som'set* 7 A9
Batley *W Yorks* 35 E11
Batsford *Glos* 16 A3
Battersby *N Yorks* 40 D6
Battersea *London* 18 F3
Battisford *Suffolk* 27 K4
Battisford Tye *Suffolk* 27 K3
Battle *E Sussex* 10 F6
Battle *Powys* 14 A3
Battleborough *Som'set* 7 A7
Battlefield *Shrops* 21 A10
Battlesbridge *Essex* 19 D8
Battlesden *Beds* 17 A10
Battleton *Som'set* 6 C3
Battramsley *Hants* 8 F5
Batt's Corner *Surrey* 9 B9
Bauds of Cullen *Gramp* 58 A2
Baughton *Heref/Worcs* 22 H2
Baughurst *Hants* 17 H7
Baulds *Gramp* 59 H4
Baulking *Oxon* 16 E4
Baumber *Lincs* 33 C9
Baunton *Glos* 16 D1
Baverstock *Wilts* 8 C2
Bawburgh *Norfolk* 26 E5
Bawdeswell *Norfolk* 26 C3
Bawdrip *Som'set* 7 B7
Bawdsey *Suffolk* 27 L6
Bawtry *S Yorks* 32 A4
Baxenden *Lancs* 34 E6
Baxterley *Warwick* 22 B6
Baybridge *Hants* 9 D7
Baycliffe *Cumb* 38 H5
Baydon *Wilts* 16 F4
Bayford *Herts* 18 C3
Bayford *Som'set* 7 C10
Bayles *Cumb* 39 A9
Baylham *Suffolk* 27 K4
Baynard's Green *Oxon* 16 A6
Bayston Hill *Shrops* 21 B10
Bayton *Heref/Worcs* 21 E12
Beach *Avon* 15 G10
Beach *H'land* 50 B5
Beach *S'clyde* 42 B4
Beachampton *Bucks* 23 H11
Beachamwell *Norfolk* 24 E8
Beachley *Glos* 15 E9
Beacon End *Essex* 19 A9
Beacon Hill *Dorset* 8 G1
Beacon Hill *Surrey* 9 B10
Beacon's Bottom *Bucks* 17 E9
Beaconsfield *Bucks* 17 E10
Beacravik *W Isles* 63 H2
Beadlam *N Yorks* 40 G6
Beadnell *Northum* 45 D12
Beaford *Devon* 4 D4
Beal *N Yorks* 36 E3
Beal *Northum* 45 B12
Bealachasan *H'land* 55 H3
Beamhurst *Staffs* 31 G9
Beaminster *Dorset* 7 F8
Beamish *Durham* 45 H10
Beamsley *N Yorks* 35 B9
Bean *Kent* 10 A5
Beanacre *Wilts* 15 H12
Beanley *Northum* 45 A9
Beara Moor *Devon* 4 D4
Bearbridge *Northum* 44 G6
Beare *Devon* 6 F3
Beare Green *Surrey* 10 D1
Bearl *Northum* 45 G9
Bearley *Warwick* 22 F5
Bearnus *H'land* 50 C1
Bearpark *Durham* 40 A3
Bearsden *S'clyde* 47 B10
Bearsted *Kent* 11 C7
Bearwood *Dorset* 8 F2
Beasley *Som'set* 6 B3
Beattock *Dumf/Gal* 43 A11
Beauchamp Roding *Essex* 18 C6
Beauchief *S Yorks* 32 B1
Beaufort *Gwent* 14 C5
Beaulieu *Hants* 8 F5
Beauly *H'land* 56 E1
Beaumaris *Gwyn* 28 C5
Beaumont *Cumb* 44 G2
Beaumont *Essex* 19 A11
Beaumont Hill *Durham* 40 C3
Beausale *Warwick* 22 E6
Beauworth *Hants* 9 C7
Beaworthy *Devon* 4 F3
Beazley End *Essex* 19 A7
Bebington *Mersey* 30 B2
Bebside *Northum* 45 E11
Beccles *Suffolk* 26 F7
Becconsall *Lancs* 34 E3
Beck Foot *Cumb* 39 F8
Beck Hole *N Yorks* 41 E8
Beck Row *Suffolk* 25 H8
Beck Side *Cumb* 38 G5
Beckbury *Shrops* 22 B1
Beckenham *London* 18 G4
Beckermet *Cumb* 38 D3
Beckfoot *Cumb* 43 G11
Beckford *Heref/Worcs* 16 A1
Beckhampton *Wilts* 16 G2
Beckingham *Lincs* 32 E6
Beckingham *Notts* 32 A5
Beckington *Som'set* 7 A11
Beckley *E Sussex* 11 F7
Beckley *Hants* 8 F4
Beckley *Oxon* 16 C6
Beckwithshaw *N Yorks* 35 B11
Becontree *London* 18 E5
Bedale *N Yorks* 40 F3
Bedburn *Durham* 40 B1
Bedchester *Dorset* 7 D12
Beddau *Mid Glam* 14 F4
Beddgelert *Gwyn* 28 E5
Beddingham *E Sussex* 10 G3
Beddington *London* 18 G3
Bedfield *Suffolk* 27 J5
Bedford *Beds* 25 K2
Bedfordshire Co *Beds* 25 K2
Bedhampton *Hants* 9 E8
Bedingfield *Suffolk* 27 H5
Bedlam *N Yorks* 35 A11
Bedlington *Northum* 45 E10
Bedlinog *Mid Glam* 14 D4
Bedminster *Avon* 15 G9
Bedmond *Herts* 17 D11
Bednall *Staffs* 31 H8
Bedrule *Borders* 44 A4
Bedshiel *Borders* 49 D9
Bedstone *Shrops* 21 E9
Bedwas *Mid Glam* 14 E5
Bedwellty *Gwent* 14 D5
Bedworth *Warwick* 23 C7
Beeby *Leics* 23 A10
Beech *Hants* 9 B8
Beech *Staffs* 31 F7
Beech Hill *Berks* 17 H8
Beech Hill *Cumb* 39 E7
Beech Hill *Gtr Man* 34 F4
Beechinstoke *Wilts* 16 H2
Beedon *Berks* 16 F6
Beedon Hill *Berks* 16 F6
Beeford *Humber* 37 B9
Beeley *Derby* 31 C11
Beelsby *Humber* 37 G9
Beenham *Berks* 17 G7
Beeny *Cornw'l* 2 B1
Beer *Devon* 6 G6
Beer *Som'set* 7 C7
Beer Crocombe *Som'set* 7 D7
Beer Hackett *Dorset* 7 E9
Beesands *Devon* 5 M7
Beesby *Lincs* 33 B11
Beeson *Devon* 5 L7
Beeston *Beds* 25 K3
Beeston *Ches* 30 D4
Beeston *Norfolk* 26 C6
Beeston *Norfolk* 26 D2
Beeston *Notts* 32 G3
Beeston *W Yorks* 35 D11
Beeston Regis *Norfolk* 26 A5
Beeswing *Dumf/Gal* 43 E10
Beetham *Cumb* 39 G7
Beetley *Norfolk* 26 D3
Began *S Glam* 14 F5
Begbroke *Oxon* 16 C5
Begdale *Cambs* 24 E6
Begelly *Dyfed* 12 F5
Beggar's Bush *Powys* 21 F8
Beguildy *Powys* 21 D7
Beighton *Norfolk* 26 E7
Beighton *S Yorks* 32 B2
Beith *S'clyde* 47 D8
Bekesbourne *Kent* 11 C10
Belaugh *Norfolk* 26 D6
Belbroughton *Heref/Worcs* 22 D3
Belchamp Otten *Essex* 27 L1
Belchamp St. Paul *Essex* 27 L1
Belchamp Walter *Essex* 27 L1
Belcherrie *Gramp* 58 D1
Belchers *Gramp* 58 B4
Belchford *Lincs* 33 C10
Belford *Northum* 45 C12
Belford Mains *Northum* 45 C12
Belhelvie *Gramp* 58 F7
Belhinnie *Gramp* 58 E2
Bell Bar *Herts* 18 C3
Bell Busk *N Yorks* 35 B7
Bell Heath *Heref/Worcs* 22 D3
Bellabeg *Gramp* 58 F1
Bellanoch *S'clyde* 50 H5
Bellasize *Humber* 36 D6
Belle Vue *W Yorks* 35 E12
Belleau *Lincs* 33 B11
Bellehiglash *Gramp* 56 F7
Bellerby *N Yorks* 40 F1
Bellever *Devon* 5 H5
Bellhaven *Lothian* 49 B9
Bellingdon *Bucks* 17 D10
Bellingham *Northum* 45 E7
Belloch *S'clyde* 46 F2
Bellochantuy *S'clyde* 46 F2
Bells Yew Green *E Sussex* 10 D5
Bellsbank *S'clyde* 42 A5
Bellshill *Northum* 45 C12
Bellshill *S'clyde* 47 C12
Bellspool *Borders* 48 F4
Bellsquarry *Lothian* 48 C3
Bellymore *S'clyde* 42 C3
Belmaduthy *H'land* 56 D2
Belmesthorpe *Leics* 24 D1
Belmont *Lancs* 34 F5
Belmont *S'clyde* 47 G8
Belmont *Shetl'd* 64 B8
Belmore *S'clyde* 47 A7
Belnacraig *Gramp* 58 F1
Belowda *Cornw'l* 3 D7
Belper *Derby* 31 E12
Belper Lane End *Derby* 31 E11
Belsay *Northum* 45 E9
Belstead *Suffolk* 27 L4
Belston *S'clyde* 47 G9
Belstone *Devon* 4 F5
Belstone Corner *Devon* 4 F5
Belthorn *Lancs* 34 E6
Beltinge *Kent* 11 A10
Beltingham *Northum* 44 G6
Beltoft *Humber* 36 F6
Belton *Humber* 36 F6
Belton *Leics* 23 B11
Belton *Leics* 32 H2
Belton *Lincs* 32 F6
Belton *Norfolk* 26 E8
Belvoir *Leics* 32 G5
Bembridge *I of Wight* 9 G8
Bemersyde *Borders* 49 F8
Bemerton *Wilts* 8 C3
Bempton *Humber* 41 H12
Ben Armine Lodge *H'land* 61 E7
Ben Casgro *W Isles* 63 D5
Benacre *Suffolk* 27 G8
Benalder Lodge *H'land* 57 L1
Benbruie *Dumf/Gal* 43 B8
Bendameer *Lothian* 48 A5
Benderloch *S'clyde* 50 D6
Bendronaig Lodge *H'land* 54 F4
Benenden *Kent* 11 E7
Benfield *Dumf/Gal* 42 E5
Benfield Green *Suffolk* 27 J7
Benfieldside *Durham* 45 H9
Bengall *Dumf/Gal* 43 D12
Bengate *Norfolk* 26 C6
Bengeworth *Heref/Worcs* 22 H4
Benholm *Gramp* 59 K5
Beningbrough *N Yorks* 36 A3
Benington *Herts* 18 B3
Benington *Lincs* 33 E11
Benington Sea End *Lincs* 33 F11
Benllech *Gwyn* 28 B4
Benmore Lodge *H'land* 60 F4
Bennacott *Cornw'l* 5 G2
Bennecarrigan *S'clyde* 46 G4
Benniworth *Lincs* 33 B9
Benover *Kent* 10 C6
Benson *Oxon* 17 E7
Benston *S'clyde* 47 H10
Bent *Gramp* 59 K4
Benthall *Northum* 45 D12
Benthall *Shrops* 21 B12
Bentham *Glos* 15 C12
Benthoul *Gramp* 59 G5
Bentick *Cambs* 24 F4
Bentley *Hants* 9 B9
Bentley *Humber* 37 D8
Bentley *S Yorks* 36 G3
Bentley *Warwick* 22 C6
Bentley Heath *W Midlands* 22 D5
Benton *Devon* 4 B5
Benton Polliwilline *S'clyde* 46 H2
Bentpath *Dumf/Gal* 44 D2
Bentwichen *Devon* 4 C6
Bentworth *Hants* 9 B8
Beoch *Dumf/Gal* 42 E2
Beoch *S'clyde* 42 B5
Beoley *Heref/Worcs* 22 E4
Beoraidbeg *H'land* 55 K1
Bepton *W Sussex* 9 D10
Berden *Essex* 18 A5
Bere Alston *Devon* 5 J3
Bere Ferrers *Cornw'l* 3 C11
Bere Ferrers *Devon* 5 J3
Bere Regis *Dorset* 7 G11
Berepper *Cornw'l* 2 G4
Bergh Apton *Norfolk* 26 E6
Berinsfield *Oxon* 17 E7
Berkeley *Glos* 15 D10
Berkhamsted *Herts* 17 C10
Berkley *Som'set* 7 A11
Berkswell *W Midlands* 22 D6
Bermondsey *London* 18 F3
Bernisdale *H'land* 62 C3
Berrick Salome *Oxon* 17 E7
Berriedale *H'land* 61 E10
Berrier *Cumb* 38 B6
Berriew *Powys* 21 B7
Berrington *Northum* 49 E12
Berrington *Shrops* 21 B10
Berringtonlaw *Northum* 49 E12
Berrow *Som'set* 6 A6
Berrow Green *Heref/Worcs* 22 F1
Berry Cross *Devon* 4 D3
Berry Down Cross *Devon* 4 B4
Berry Hill *Dyfed* 12 C4
Berry Hill *Glos* 15 C9
Berry Pomeroy *Devon* 5 K7
Berryhillock *Gramp* 58 B2
Berrynarbor *Devon* 4 A4
Berry's Green *London* 18 H4
Berryscour *Dumf/Gal* 43 B12
Berrysloch *Gramp* 59 H3
Bersham *Clwyd* 29 E12
Berthddu *Powys* 20 H4
Berwick *Dorset* 7 G8
Berwick *E Sussex* 10 H4
Berwick Bassett *Wilts* 16 G2
Berwick Hill *Northum* 45 E10
Berwick St. James *Wilts* 8 B2
Berwick St. John *Wilts* 8 D1
Berwick St. Leonard *Wilts* 7 C12
Berwick-upon-Tweed *Northum* 49 D12
Berwyn *Clwyd* 29 F11
Bescaby *Leics* 32 G5
Bescar *Lancs* 34 F3
Besford *Heref/Worcs* 22 H3
Bessacarr *S Yorks* 36 G4
Bessels Green *Kent* 10 C4
Bessels Leigh *Oxon* 16 D5
Bessingby *Humber* 37 A9
Bessingham *Norfolk* 26 B5
Best Beech Hill *E Sussex* 10 E5
Besthorpe *Norfolk* 26 F4
Besthorpe *Notts* 32 D5
Beswick *Humber* 37 B8
Betchworth *Surrey* 10 C1
Bethania *Dyfed* 20 F1
Bethania *Gwyn* 28 E5
Bethania *Gwyn* 28 F6
Bethel *Gwyn* 28 C3
Bethel *Gwyn* 28 D5
Bethel *Gwyn* 29 F9
Bethersden *Kent* 11 D8
Bethesda *Dyfed* 12 E4
Bethesda *Gwyn* 28 D6
Bethlehem *Dyfed* 13 D10
Bethnal Green *London* 18 F4
Betley *Staffs* 30 E6
Betsham *Kent* 10 A5
Betteshanger *Kent* 11 C11
Bettiscombe *Dorset* 7 F7
Bettisfield *Shrops* 30 G3
Betton *Shrops* 30 G5
Bettws Bledrws *Dyfed* 20 G2
Bettws Evan *Dyfed* 12 B6
Bettws Newydd *Gwent* 15 D7
Bettyhill *H'land* 61 B7
Betws *Dyfed* 13 F9
Betws *Mid Glam* 14 F2
Betws Cedewain *Powys* 21 C7
Betws Garmon *Gwyn* 28 D5
Betws Gwerfil Goch *Clwyd* 29 F9
Betws-y-coed *Gwyn* 29 E7
Betws-yn-Rhos *Clwyd* 29 C8
Beulah *Dyfed* 12 B6
Beulah *Powys* 20 G5
Bevercotes *Notts* 32 C4
Beverley *Humber* 37 C8
Beverstone *Glos* 15 E11
Bevington *Glos* 15 E10
Bewaldeth *Cumb* 38 B4
Bewcastle *Cumb* 44 F4
Bewdley *Heref/Worcs* 22 E1
Bewerley *N Yorks* 35 A10
Bewholme *Humber* 37 B9
Bewlie *Borders* 49 G8
Bexhill *E Sussex* 10 G6
Bexley *London* 18 F5
Bexleyheath *London* 18 F5
Bexwell *Norfolk* 24 E7
Beyton *Suffolk* 27 J2
Beyton Green *Suffolk* 27 J2
Bibury *Glos* 16 C2
Bicester *Oxon* 17 B7
Bickenhill *W Midlands* 22 D5
Bicker *Lincs* 24 B3
Bickerstaffe *Lancs* 34 G3
Bickerton *Ches* 30 E4
Bickerton *N Yorks* 36 B2
Bickerton *Northum* 45 C8
Bickingcott *Devon* 4 C6
Bickington *Devon* 4 C4
Bickington *Devon* 5 H7
Bickleigh *Devon* 5 J4
Bickleigh *Devon* 6 E3
Bickleton *Devon* 4 C4
Bickley Moss *Ches* 30 E4
Bicknacre *Essex* 19 D8
Bicknoller *Som'set* 6 B5
Bicknor *Kent* 11 B7
Bickton *Hants* 8 E3
Bicton *Heref/Worcs* 21 F10
Bicton *Shrops* 21 A10
Bicton *Shrops* 21 D8
Bidborough *Kent* 10 D4
Biddenden *Kent* 11 D7
Biddenden Green *Kent* 11 D7
Biddenham *Beds* 25 K1
Biddestone *Wilts* 15 G11
Biddisham *Som'set* 7 A7
Biddlesden *Bucks* 23 H9
Biddlestone *Northum* 45 B8
Biddulph *Staffs* 31 D7
Biddulph Moor *Staffs* 31 D7
Bideford *Devon* 4 C3
Bidford-on-Avon *Warwick* 22 G4
Bielby *Humber* 36 C5
Bieldside *Gramp* 59 G6
Bierley *I of Wight* 8 H6
Bierley *W Yorks* 35 D10
Bierton *Bucks* 17 C9
Big Corlae *Dumf/Gal* 43 B7
Big Sand *H'land* 54 B1
Bigbury *Devon* 5 L5
Bigbury-on-Sea *Devon* 5 L5
Bigby *Lincs* 37 F8
Biggar *Cumb* 34 A1
Biggar *S'clyde* 48 F3
Biggarshiels Mains *S'clyde* 48 E3
Biggin *Derby* 31 D10
Biggin *Derby* 31 E11
Biggin *N Yorks* 36 D3
Biggin Hill *London* 18 H4
Biggleswade *Beds* 25 L3
Bighton *Hants* 9 C7
Bignor *W Sussex* 9 E11
Bigton *Shetl'd* 64 F7
Bilberry *Cornw'l* 3 D7
Bilborough *Notts* 32 F3
Bilbrook *Som'set* 6 B4
Bilbrough *N Yorks* 36 C3
Bilby *Notts* 32 B4
Bildeston *Suffolk* 27 K3
Billacott *Cornw'l* 3 A9
Billericay *Essex* 19 D7
Billesdon *Leics* 23 B10
Billesley *Warwick* 22 F5
Billingborough *Lincs* 24 B2
Billinge *Mersey* 34 G4
Billingford *Norfolk* 26 C3
Billingford *Norfolk* 27 G5
Billingham *Clevl'd* 40 C5
Billinghay *Lincs* 33 E8
Billinghurst *W Sussex* 9 C12
Billingley *S Yorks* 36 G2
Billingsley *Shrops* 21 D12
Billington *Beds* 17 B10
Billington *Lancs* 34 D6
Billington *Staffs* 31 H7
Billockby *Norfolk* 26 D7
Billy Row *Durham* 40 A2
Bilsborrow *Lancs* 34 C4
Bilsby *Lincs* 33 C11
Bilsham *W Sussex* 9 F11
Bilsington *Kent* 11 E9
Bilson Green *Glos* 15 C9
Bilsthorpe *Notts* 32 D4
Bilston *Lothian* 48 C5
Bilston *W Midlands* 22 B3
Bilstone *Leics* 23 B7
Bilting *Kent* 11 C9
Bilton *Humber* 37 D9
Bilton *N Yorks* 36 B3
Bilton *Northum* 45 B10
Bilton *Warwick* 23 E8
Bimbister *Orkney* 64 C2
Binbrook *Lincs* 37 H10

Bincombe Dorset 7 H10
Bindal H'land 61 H9
Binegar Som'set 7 A9
Binfield Berks 17 G9
Binfield Heath Oxon 17 F8
Bingfield Northum 45 F8
Bingham Notts 32 F4
Bingham's Melcombe Dorset 7 F11
Bingley W Yorks 35 C10
Binham Norfolk 26 B3
Binley Hants 8 A6
Binniehill Lothian 48 B1
Binsoe N Yorks 40 G3
Binstead I of Wight 9 G7
Binsted Hants 9 B9
Binton Warwick 22 G5
Bintree Norfolk 26 C3
Binweston Shrops 21 B8
Birch Essex 19 B9
Birch Gtr Man 35 F7
Birch W Yorks 35 E12
Birch Green Essex 19 B9
Birch Vale Derby 31 B8
Bircham Newton Norfolk 26 B1
Bircham Tofts Norfolk 26 B1
Birchanger Essex 18 B5
Bircher Heref/Worcs 21 F10
Birchfield H'land 57 G6
Birchgrove W Glam 13 G10
Birchington Kent 11 A11
Birchover Derby 31 D10
Bircotes Notts 32 A3
Bird End W Midlands 22 C4
Birdbrook Essex 25 L8
Birdham W Sussex 9 F9
Birdingbury Warwick 23 E8
Birdlip Glos 15 C12
Birdsall N Yorks 36 A6
Birdsgreen Shrops 22 D1
Birdsmoor Gate Dorset 7 F7
Birdston S'clyde 47 B11
Birdwell S Yorks 35 G12
Birdwood Glos 15 B10
Birgham Borders 49 E10
Birkacre Lancs 34 F4
Birkby N Yorks 40 E3
Birkdale Mersey 34 F2
Birkenhead Mersey 30 A2
Birkenhills Gramp 58 C5
Birkenshaw S'clyde 47 D12
Birkenshaw W Yorks 35 D10
Birkhall Gramp 59 H1
Birkhill Borders 48 H5
Birkhill Borders 49 E8
Birkhill Tayside 53 D8
Birkin N Yorks 36 D3
Birks Northum 44 E6
Birkshaw Dumf/Gal 43 C9
Birley Heref/Worcs 21 G10
Birling Kent 10 B5
Birling Northum 45 B10
Birling Gap E Sussex 10 H4
Birlingham Heref/Worcs 22 H3
Birmingham W Midlands 22 D5
Birnam Tayside 52 C5
Birse Gramp 59 H3
Birsemore Gramp 59 H3
Birstall Leics 23 A9
Birstall W Yorks 35 E11
Birstwith N Yorks 35 A11
Birthorpe Lincs 24 B2
Birthwood S'clyde 48 F3
Birtley Heref/Worcs 21 E9
Birtley Northum 45 E7
Birtley Tyne/Wear 45 G11
Birts Street Heref/Worcs 15 A11
Bisbrooke Leics 23 B12
Bish Mill Devon 4 C6
Bisham Berks 17 F9
Bishampton Heref/Worcs 22 G3
Bishop Auckland Durham 40 B2
Bishop Burton Humber 37 C7
Bishop Middleham Durham 40 B3
Bishop Monkton N Yorks 40 H3
Bishop Norton Lincs 33 A7
Bishop Sutton Avon 15 H9
Bishop Thornton N Yorks 35 A11
Bishop Wilton Humber 36 B6
Bishopbridge Lincs 33 A7
Bishopbriggs S'clyde 47 B11
Bishopmill Gramp 56 C8
Bishops Cannings Wilts 16 H1
Bishop's Castle Shrops 21 D8
Bishop's Caundle Dorset 7 E10
Bishops Cleeve Glos 15 B12
Bishops Frome Heref/Worcs 21 G12
Bishop's Green Essex 18 B6
Bishop's Hull Som'set 6 D5
Bishop's Itchington Warwick 23 F7
Bishops Lydeard Som'set 6 C5
Bishop's Nympton Devon 4 D6
Bishop's Offley Staffs 30 G6
Bishop's Stortford Herts 18 B5
Bishops Sutton Hants 9 C7
Bishop's Tachbrook Warwick 22 F6
Bishop's Tawton Devon 4 C4
Bishop's Waltham Hants 9 D7
Bishop's Wood Staffs 22 A2
Bishopsbourne Kent 11 C10
Bishopsteignton Devon 5 H8
Bishopstoke Hants 8 D6
Bishopston W Glam 13 H9
Bishopstone Bucks 17 C9
Bishopstone E Sussex 10 H4
Bishopstone Heref/Worcs 21 H9
Bishopstone Wilts 16 F3
Bishopstone Wilts 8 C2
Bishopstrow Wilts 7 B12
Bishopswood Som'set 6 E6
Bishopsworth Avon 15 G9
Bishopthorpe N Yorks 36 B4
Bishopton Durham 40 C4
Bishopton N Yorks 40 H3
Bishopton S'clyde 47 B9
Bishpool Gwent 15 E7
Bishton Gwent 15 F7
Bisley Glos 15 D12
Bisley Surrey 17 H10
Bispham Lancs 34 C2
Bissoe Cornw'l 2 E5
Bisterne Close Hants 8 F4
Bitchfield Lincs 33 G7
Biteford Devon 4 D2
Bittadon Devon 4 B4
Bittaford Devon 5 K5
Bittering Street Norfolk 26 D2
Bitterley Shrops 21 E11
Bitterne Hants 8 E6
Bitteswell Leics 23 D8
Bitton Avon 15 G10
Bix Oxon 17 F8
Bixter Shetl'd 64 D7
Blaby Leics 23 B9
Black Bourton Oxon 16 D4
Black Bridge H'land 54 C7
Black Callerton Tyne/Wear 45 F10
Black Clauchrie S'clyde 42 C4
Black Corries H'land 51 B10
Black Croft S'clyde 50 D6
Black Dog Devon 4 E7
Black Heddon Northum 45 E9
Black Mount S'clyde 51 C10
Black Notley Essex 19 B7
Black Pill W Glam 13 H9
Black Torrington Devon 4 E3
Blackacre Dumf/Gal 43 C11
Blackadder Bank Borders 49 D11
Blackawton Devon 5 L7
Blackborough Devon 6 E4
Blackborough End Norfolk 24 D8
Blackboys E Sussex 10 F4
Blackbrook Derby 31 E11
Blackbrook Mersey 34 G4
Blackbrook Staffs 30 F6
Blackburn Borders 44 D3
Blackburn Borders 49 D8
Blackburn Gramp 58 D3
Blackburn Gramp 58 F6
Blackburn Lancs 34 D5
Blackburn Lothian 48 C3
Blackburn S'clyde 48 G2
Blackcraig Dumf/Gal 43 D8
Blackditch Cross Devon 4 E6
Blackdog Gramp 58 F7
Blackenhall W Midlands 22 B3
Blacker Hill S Yorks 35 G12
Blackfield Hants 8 F6
Blackford Cumb 44 G2
Blackford Som'set 7 A7
Blackford Som'set 7 D10
Blackford Tayside 52 F4
Blackfordby Leics 31 H11
Blackgang I of Wight 8 H6
Blackhall Colliery Durham 40 A5
Blackhall Mill Tyne/Wear 45 G9
Blackham E Sussex 10 D4
Blackhaugh Borders 49 E7
Blackheath Essex 19 B10
Blackheath Suffolk 27 H7
Blackheath Surrey 9 B11
Blackheath W Midlands 22 D3
Blackhill Gramp 58 B8
Blackhill Gramp 58 C8
Blackhill H'land 62 C3
Blackhillock Gramp 58 C1
Blackhills Dumf/Gal 44 F1
Blackhills Gramp 56 D8
Blackhopebyre Borders 48 E6
Blackhorse Avon 15 F10
Blackland Wilts 16 G1
Blacklaw Dumf/Gal 43 A11
Blackley Gtr Man 35 G7
Blacklunans Tayside 52 A6
Blackmarstone Heref/Worcs 21 H10
Blackmill Mid Glam 14 F3
Blackmoor Hants 9 C9
Blackmoor Gate Devon 4 B5
Blackmore Essex 18 D6
Blackmore End Essex 25 M8
Blackmore End Herts 18 B2
Blackness Lothian 48 A3
Blacknest Hants 9 B9
Blacko Lancs 35 C7
Blackpark Dumf/Gal 43 C10
Blackpool Lancs 34 C2
Blackpool Gate Cumb 44 E4
Blackridge Lothian 48 C2
Blackrock Gwent 14 C5
Blackrock Gwent 15 E8
Blackrod Gtr Man 34 F5
Blackshaw Dumf/Gal 43 E11
Blackshaw Head W Yorks 35 D8
Blackshaw Moor Staffs 31 D8
Blacksmith's Corner Essex 27 M3
Blackstone W Sussex 10 F1
Blackthorn Oxon 17 B7
Blackthorpe Suffolk 27 J2
Blacktoft Humber 36 E6
Blacktop Gramp 59 G6
Blackwater Cornw'l 2 E4
Blackwater Hants 17 H9
Blackwater I of Wight 8 G6
Blackwater Som'set 6 E6
Blackwaterfoot S'clyde 46 G4
Blackwell Derby 31 C10
Blackwell Derby 32 D2
Blackwell Durham 40 D3
Blackwell Heref/Worcs 22 E3
Blackwell Som'set 6 D4
Blackwell Warwick 22 H6
Blackwood Dumf/Gal 43 C10
Blackwood Gwent 14 E5
Blackwood S'clyde 47 E12
Blackwood Hill Staffs 31 E8
Blacon Ches 30 C2
Bladclaw Gramp 58 B4
Bladnoch Dumf/Gal 42 F5
Bladon Oxon 16 C5
Blaen Celyn Dyfed 13 B7
Blaen Dyryn Powys 14 A3
Blaenannerch Dyfed 12 B6
Blaenau Dolwyddelan Gwyn 28 E6
Blaenau Ffestiniog Gwyn 28 F6
Blaenavon Gwent 14 C6
Blaenawey Gwent 14 B6
Blaenffos Dyfed 12 C5
Blaengarw Mid Glam 14 E2
Blaengwrach W Glam 14 D2
Blaengwynfi W Glam 14 E2
Blaenhondda Mid Glam 14 D3
Blaenpennal Dyfed 20 F2
Blaenplwyf Dyfed 20 E1
Blaenporth Dyfed 12 B6
Blaenwaun Dyfed 12 D6
Blaen-y-Coed Dyfed 13 D7
Blagdon Avon 15 H8
Blagdon Hill Som'set 6 D5
Blaich H'land 55 M4
Blain H'land 50 A4
Blaina Gwent 14 D5
Blair Gramp 58 E6
Blair Atholl Tayside 52 A4
Blairadam Tayside 52 H6
Blairburn Lothian 48 A3
Blairdaff Gramp 58 F4
Blairgowrie Tayside 52 C6
Blairhall Fife 52 H5
Blairingone Tayside 52 G5
Blairlogie Central 52 G3
Blairmore H'land 60 B3
Blairmore S'clyde 47 A7
Blairnairn S'clyde 47 A8
Blairnmarrow Gramp 57 H8
Blairquhosh Central 47 A10
Blair's Ferry S'clyde 46 B5
Blairskaith S'clyde 47 B10
Blaisdon Glos 15 C10
Blakebrook Heref/Worcs 22 D2
Blakedown Heref/Worcs 22 D2
Blakelaw Borders 49 F10
Blakemere Heref/Worcs 21 H9
Blakeney Glos 15 D10
Blakeney Norfolk 26 A3
Blakenhall Ches 30 E6
Blakenhall Heath W Midlands 22 B4
Blakeshall Heref/Worcs 22 D2
Blakesley Northants 23 G9
Blanchland Northum 45 H8
Bland Hill N Yorks 35 B10
Blandford Forum Dorset 7 E12
Blandford St. Mary Dorset 7 F12
Blanefield Central 47 A10
Blankney Lincs 33 D8
Blar a Chaorainn H'land 51 A8
Blaran S'clyde 50 F6
Blarghour S'clyde 51 F7
Blarglas S'clyde 47 A8
Blarmachfoldach H'land 51 A8
Blarmachfoldach H'land 55 M5
Blarnalearoch H'land 60 G3
Blashford Hants 8 E3
Blaston Leics 23 C11
Blatherwycke Northants 24 F1
Blawith Cumb 38 F5
Blaxhall Suffolk 27 J7
Blaxton S Yorks 36 G4
Blaydon Tyne/Wear 45 G10
Bleadon Som'set 7 A7
Blean Kent 11 B10
Bleasby Lincs 33 B8
Bleasby Notts 32 E4
Blebocraigs Fife 53 F9
Bleddfa Powys 21 F7
Bledington Glos 16 B3
Bledlow Bucks 17 D8
Bledlow Ridge Bucks 17 D9
Blegberry Devon 4 C1
Blegbie Lothian 49 C7
Blencarn Cumb 39 B9
Blencogo Cumb 43 G12
Blendworth Hants 9 E8
Blennerhasset Cumb 43 G12
Bletchingdon Oxon 16 B6
Bletchingley Surrey 10 C2
Bletchley Bucks 17 A9
Bletchley Shrops 30 G5
Bletherston Dyfed 12 E4
Bletsoe Beds 25 J1
Blewbury Oxon 16 F6
Blickling Norfolk 26 C5
Blidworth Notts 32 E3
Blidworth Bottoms Notts 32 E3
Blindburn Northum 44 B6
Blindcrake Cumb 38 B4
Blindley Heath Surrey 10 C2
Blinkbonny Northum 49 F11
Blisland Cornw'l 3 B8
Bliss Gate Heref/Worcs 22 E1
Blissford Hants 8 E3
Blisworth Northants 23 G10
Blithbury Staffs 31 H9
Blithford Staffs 31 H9
Blitterlees Cumb 43 F11
Blo Norton Norfolk 27 G3
Blockley Glos 16 A3
Blofield Norfolk 26 E6
Blofield Corner Norfolk 26 D6
Bloomfield Borders 49 G8
Bloomfield Dumf/Gal 43 D10
Blore Staffs 31 E10
Blount's Green Staffs 31 G9
Bloxham Oxon 16 A5
Bloxholm Lincs 33 E8
Bloxwich W Midlands 22 B3
Bloxworth Dorset 7 G12
Blubberhouses N Yorks 35 B10
Blue Anchor Cornw'l 2 D6
Blue Anchor Som'set 6 B4
Blue Anchor W Glam 13 G9
Bluebell Hill Kent 10 B6
Blughasary H'land 60 F3
Blundellsands Mersey 34 G2
Blundeston Suffolk 26 F8
Blunham Beds 25 K3
Blunsdon St. Andrew Wilts 16 E2
Bluntington Heref/Worcs 22 E2
Bluntisham Cambs 25 H5
Blunts Cornw'l 3 C10
Blyborough Lincs 37 H7
Blyford Suffolk 27 H7
Blymhill Staffs 22 A2
Blyth Northum 45 E11
Blyth Notts 32 B3
Blyth Bridge Borders 48 E4
Blyth Marsh Staffs 31 F8
Blythburgh Suffolk 27 H7
Blythe Borders 49 D8
Blyton Lincs 36 H6
Boarhills Fife 53 F10
Boarhunt Hants 9 E7
Boars Hill Oxon 16 D6
Boarshead E Sussex 10 E4
Boarstall Bucks 17 C7
Boasley Cross Devon 4 F4
Boat of Garten H'land 57 H5
Boath H'land 56 B1
Bobbing Kent 11 B7
Bobbington Staffs 22 C2
Bobbingworth Essex 18 C5
Boblainy H'land 56 F1
Bocking Essex 19 B7
Bocking Churchstreet Essex 19 A7
Boconnoc Cornw'l 3 D8
Boddam Gramp 58 C8
Boddam Shetl'd 64 F7
Bodden Som'set 7 B10
Bodedern Gwyn 28 B3
Bodelwyddan Clwyd 29 C9
Bodenham Heref/Worcs 21 G10
Bodenham Wilts 8 D3
Bodenham Moor Heref/Worcs 21 G11
Bodewryd Gwyn 28 A3
Bodfari Clwyd 29 C10
Bodffordd Gwyn 28 C4
Bodfuan Gwyn 28 F3
Bodham Street Norfolk 26 B4
Bodiam E Sussex 10 E6
Bodicote Oxon 23 H8
Bodieve Cornw'l 3 B7
Bodinnick Cornw'l 3 D8
Bodle Street Green E Sussex 10 G5
Bodmin Cornw'l 3 C8
Bodnant Gwyn 29 C7
Bodney Norfolk 26 E1
Bodorgan Gwyn 28 C3
Bodsham Kent 11 D9
Bodwen Cornw'l 3 D7
Bogallan H'land 56 E2
Bogbrae Gramp 58 D8
Bogend Borders 49 D10
Bogend S'clyde 47 F9
Boghall Lothian 48 C3
Boghall Lothian 48 C5
Boghall S'clyde 47 H9
Boghead Gramp 58 E7
Boghead S'clyde 47 E12
Boghead S'clyde 47 F10
Bogknowe Dumf/Gal 43 F10
Bogmarsh Heref/Worcs 15 A8
Bogmuir Gramp 58 A1
Bogmuire Gramp 59 K4
Bogniebrae Gramp 58 C3
Bognor Regis W Sussex 9 F11
Bograxie Gramp 58 F4
Bogsbank Borders 48 D4
Bogside S'clyde 48 D1
Bogton Gramp 58 C4
Bogue Dumf/Gal 43 C7
Bohenie H'land 55 L7
Bohortha Cornw'l 2 F6
Bohuntine H'land 55 L7
Bokiddick Cornw'l 3 C7
Bolam Durham 40 C2
Bolam Northum 45 E9
Bolberry Devon 5 M6
Bold Heath Mersey 30 A4
Boldon Colliery Tyne/Wear 45 G11
Boldre Hants 8 F5
Boldron Durham 39 D12
Bole Notts 32 B5
Bolehill Derby 31 E11
Boleigh Cornw'l 2 G2
Boleside Borders 49 F7
Bolfracks Tayside 52 B3
Bolham Devon 6 E3
Bolham Water Devon 6 E5
Bolingey Cornw'l 2 D5
Bollington Ches 30 B6
Bollington Ches 31 B8
Bollington Cross Ches 31 C8
Bolney W Sussex 10 F1
Bolnhurst Beds 25 J2
Bolshan Tayside 53 B11
Bolsover Derby 32 C2
Bolsterstone S Yorks 35 G11
Bolstone Heref/Worcs 15 A8
Boltby N Yorks 40 F5
Bolter End Bucks 17 E9
Bolton Cumb 39 C8
Bolton Gtr Man 34 F6
Bolton Humber 36 B5
Bolton Lothian 49 B7
Bolton Northum 45 B9
Bolton Abbey N Yorks 35 B9
Bolton Bridge N Yorks 35 B9
Bolton by Bowland Lancs 34 B6
Bolton Low Houses Cumb 38 A5
Bolton Percy N Yorks 36 C3
Bolton Town End Lancs 39 H7
Boltonfellend Cumb 44 F3
Bolton-le-Sands Lancs 39 H7
Bolton-on-Dearne S Yorks 36 G2
Bolton-on-Swale N Yorks 40 E3
Bolventor Cornw'l 3 B9
Bomere Heath Shrops 30 H3
Bonar Bridge H'land 60 G6
Bonawe Quarries S'clyde 51 D7
Bonby Humber 37 F8
Boncath Dyfed 12 C5
Bonchester Bridge Borders 44 B4
Bonchurch I of Wight 9 H7
Bondleigh Devon 4 E5
Bonds Lancs 34 C4
Bonehill Staffs 22 B5
Bo'ness Lothian 48 A3
Bonhard Tayside 52 D6
Bonhill S'clyde 47 A9
Boningdale Shrops 22 B2
Bonjedward Borders 49 G9
Bonkle S'clyde 48 D1
Bonnavoulin H'land 50 B3
Bonnington Kent 11 D9
Bonnington Lothian 48 B4
Bonnybank Fife 53 G8
Bonnybridge Lothian 48 A1
Bonnykelly Gramp 58 B6
Bonnyrigg and Lasswade Lothian 48 C6
Bonnyton S'clyde 47 F9
Bonsall Derby 31 D11
Bont Gwent 15 B7
Bont Newydd Gwyn 28 F6
Bontddu Gwyn 28 H6
Bont-dolgadfan Powys 20 B4
Bontnewydd Dyfed 20 F2
Bont-newydd Gwyn 28 D4
Bontrhydgaled Powys 20 D4
Bontuchel Clwyd 29 D10
Bonvilston S Glam 14 G4
Bon-y-maen W Glam 13 G10
Boode Devon 4 B4
Booley Shrops 30 H4
Boon Borders 49 E8
Boosbeck Clevl'd 41 C7
Boot Cumb 38 E4
Booth Humber 36 D5
Booth Wood W Yorks 35 E9
Boothby Graffoe Lincs 33 D7
Boothby Pagnell Lincs 33 G7
Boothstown Gtr Man 34 G6
Bootle Cumb 38 F4
Bootle Mersey 34 H2
Boquhan Central 47 A10
Boraston Shrops 21 E11
Borden Hants 9 D9
Bordon Hants 9 C9
Boreham Essex 19 C7
Boreham Street E Sussex 10 G5
Boreland Central 52 D1
Boreland Dumf/Gal 43 B12
Boreland of Girthon Dumf/Gal 43 F7
Boreraig H'land 62 C1
Borewell Northum 49 D12
Borgie H'land 61 B7
Borgue Dumf/Gal 43 G7
Borgue H'land 61 E10
Borhamwood Herts 18 D2
Borley Essex 27 L1
Bornaskitaig H'land 62 A3
Borness Dumf/Gal 43 G7
Borough Green Kent 10 B5
Boroughbridge N Yorks 40 H4
Borras Head Clwyd 30 E2
Borrobol Lodge H'land 61 E8
Borrowash Derby 32 G1
Borrowby N Yorks 40 F4
Borrowdale Cumb 38 D5
Borrowfield Gramp 59 H6
Borth Dyfed 20 C2
Borthwickbrae Borders 44 B2
Borthwickshiels Borders 44 B3
Borth-y-Gest Gwyn 28 F5
Borve H'land 62 C4
Borve W Isles 63 G1
Borve Lodge W Isles 63 G1
Borwick Lancs 39 H7
Bosall N Yorks 36 A5
Bosbury Heref/Worcs 21 H12
Boscastle Cornw'l 3 A8
Boscombe Dorset 8 G3
Boscombe Wilts 8 B3
Boscoppa Cornw'l 3 D7
Bosham W Sussex 9 F9
Bosherston Dyfed 12 G3
Boskenna Cornw'l 2 G1
Bosley Ches 31 D7
Bossholes Gramp 59 H6
Bossiney Cornw'l 3 A8
Bossingham Kent 11 C10

Bossington *Som'set* 6 A3
Bostock Green *Ches* 30 C5
Boston *Lincs* 24 A4
Boston Long Hedges *Lincs* 33 E10
Boston Spa *W Yorks* 36 C2
Boswinger *Cornw'l* 3 F7
Botallack *Cornw'l* 2 F1
Botany Bay *London* 18 D3
Botary Mains *Gramp* 58 C2
Botcheston *Leics* 23 B8
Botesdale *Suffolk* 27 H3
Bothal *Northum* 45 D10
Bothamsall *Notts* 32 C4
Bothel *Cumb* 43 H12
Bothenhampton *Dorset* 7 G8
Bothwell *S'clyde* 47 D12
Botley *Bucks* 17 D10
Botley *Hants* 8 E6
Botley *Oxon* 16 C6
Botolph Claydon *Bucks* 17 B8
Botolphs *W Sussex* 10 G1
Bottacks *H'land* 54 D8
Bottesford *Humber* 37 F7
Bottesford *Leics* 32 F5
Bottisham *Cambs* 25 J6
Bottlesford *Wilts* 16 H2
Bottom House *Staffs* 31 E9
Bottom O'th'Moor *Gtr Man* 34 F5
Bottomcraig *Fife* 53 E8
Bottongate *Cumb* 38 A5
Bottreaux Mill *Devon* 4 C7
Botusfleming *Cornw'l* 3 D11
Botwnnog *Gwyn* 28 G2
Bough Beech *Kent* 10 C4
Boughrood *Powys* 21 H7
Boughrood Brest *Powys* 21 H7
Boughspring *Glos* 15 E9
Boughton *Norfolk* 24 E8
Boughton *Northants* 23 E11
Boughton *Notts* 32 C4
Boughton Aluph *Kent* 11 C9
Boughton Lees *Kent* 11 C9
Boughton Malherbe *Kent* 11 C7
Boughton Monchelsea *Kent* 10 C6
Boughton Street *Kent* 11 B9
Boulby *Clevl'd* 41 C8
Bouldon *Shrops* 21 D11
Boulmer *Northum* 45 B10
Boulston *Dyfed* 12 F3
Boultenstone *Gramp* 58 F2
Boultham *Lincs* 32 C6
Bourn *Cambs* 25 K4
Bourne *Lincs* 24 D2
Bourne End *Beds* 25 L1
Bourne End *Bucks* 17 E10
Bourne End *Herts* 17 D11
Bournebridge *Essex* 18 D5
Bournemouth *Dorset* 8 G3
Bournes Green *Essex* 19 E9
Bournes Green *Glos* 15 D12
Bournheath *Heref/Worcs* 22 E3
Bournmoor *Durham* 45 H11
Bournville *W Midlands* 22 D4
Bourton *Oxon* 16 E3
Bourton *Shrops* 21 C11
Bourton *Wilts* 7 C11
Bourton on Dunsmore *Warwick* 23 E8
Bourton-on-the-Hill *Glos* 16 A3
Bourton-on-the-Water *Glos* 16 B3
Boustead Hill *Cumb* 44 G1
Bouth *Cumb* 38 G6
Bouthwaite *N Yorks* 40 H2
Boveney *Bucks* 17 F10
Boverton *S Glam* 14 G3
Bovey Tracey *Devon* 5 H7
Bovingdon *Herts* 17 D11
Bovingdon Green *Bucks* 17 E9
Bovinger *Essex* 18 C5
Bow *Borders* 49 E7
Bow *Devon* 4 F6
Bow *Orkney* 64 E2
Bow Brickhill *Bucks* 17 A10
Bow of Fife *Fife* 53 F8
Bow Street *Dyfed* 20 D2
Bowbank *Durham* 39 C11
Bowburn *Durham* 40 A3
Bowcombe *I of Wight* 8 G6
Bowd *Devon* 6 G4
Bowden *Borders* 49 F8
Bowden *Devon* 5 L7
Bowden Hill *Wilts* 15 H12
Bowdon *Gtr Man* 30 B6
Bower *Northum* 44 E6
Bower Hinton *Som'set* 7 D8
Bowerchalke *Wilts* 8 D2
Bowerdale *Cumb* 39 E9
Bowerhill *Wilts* 15 H12
Bowermadden *H'land* 61 B11
Bowers *Staffs* 31 G7
Bowers Gifford *Essex* 19 E7
Bowershall *Fife* 52 H6
Bowertower *H'land* 61 B11
Bowes *Durham* 39 D12
Bowgreave *Lancs* 34 C4
Bowhill *Borders* 49 G7
Bowithick *Cornw'l* 3 A9
Bowker's Green *Lancs* 34 G3
Bowland Bridge *Cumb* 38 F6
Bowley *Heref/Worcs* 21 G11
Bowlhead Green *Surrey* 9 B10
Bowling *S'clyde* 47 B9
Bowling Bank *Clwyd* 30 E3
Bowling Green *Heref/Worcs* 22 G2
Bowmanstead *Cumb* 38 F5
Bowness-on-Solway *Cumb* 44 G1
Bowness-on-Windermere *Cumb* 38 E6
Bowouse *Dumf/Gal* 43 E11
Bowsden *Northum* 49 E12
Bowside Lodge *H'land* 61 B8
Bowtrees *Lothian* 48 A2
Box *Glos* 15 D11
Box *Wilts* 15 G11
Boxbush *Glos* 15 C10
Boxford *Berks* 16 G5
Boxford *Suffolk* 27 L3
Boxgrove *W Sussex* 9 E10
Boxley *Kent* 10 B6
Box's Shop *Cornw'l* 4 F1
Boxted *Essex* 27 M3
Boxted *Suffolk* 27 K1
Boxted Cross *Essex* 27 M3
Boxworth *Cambs* 25 J4
Boxworth End *Cambs* 25 H5
Boyden Gate *Kent* 11 B11
Boylestone *Derby* 31 G10
Boyndie *Gramp* 58 A4
Boynton *Humber* 41 H11
Boys Hill *Dorset* 7 E10
Boyton *Cornw'l* 5 G2
Boyton *Suffolk* 27 K7
Boyton *Wilts* 8 B1
Boyton Cross *Essex* 18 C6
Bozeat *Northants* 23 F12
Braaid *I of Man* 38 H2
Brabling Green *Suffolk* 27 J6
Brabourne *Kent* 11 D9
Brabourne Lees *Kent* 11 D9
Brabstermire *H'land* 61 A12
Bracadale *H'land* 62 D3
Braceborough *Lincs* 24 D2
Bracebridge Heath *Lincs* 33 C7
Braceby *Lincs* 33 G7
Bracewell *Lancs* 35 B7
Brackenfield *Derby* 32 D1
Brackenrigg *Gramp* 59 K5
Brackenthwaite *Cumb* 38 C4
Brackenthwaite *Cumb* 44 H1
Bracklesham *W Sussex* 9 F9
Brackletter *H'land* 55 L6
Brackley *Northants* 23 H9
Brackley *S'clyde* 46 E3
Brackloch *H'land* 60 E3
Bracknell *Berks* 17 G9
Braco *Tayside* 52 F3
Bracobrae *Gramp* 58 B3
Bracon Ash *Norfolk* 26 E5
Bracora *H'land* 55 K1
Bracorina *H'land* 55 K1
Bradbourne *Derby* 31 E10
Bradbury *Durham* 40 B3
Bradda *I of Man* 38 H1
Bradden *Northants* 23 G10
Bradenham *Bucks* 17 D9
Bradenstock *Wilts* 16 F1
Bradfield *Berks* 17 G7
Bradfield *Devon* 6 E4
Bradfield *Essex* 27 M4
Bradfield Combust *Suffolk* 27 J2
Bradfield Green *Ches* 30 D5
Bradfield Heath *Essex* 27 M4
Bradfield St. Clare *Suffolk* 27 J2
Bradfield St. George *Suffolk* 27 J2
Bradfield-on-the-Green *Northants* 23 F11
Bradford *Devon* 4 E3
Bradford *Northum* 45 D11
Bradford *W Yorks* 35 D10
Bradford Abbas *Dorset* 7 E9
Bradford Leigh *Wilts* 15 H11
Bradford Mill *Devon* 4 D7
Bradford Peverell *Dorset* 7 G10
Bradford-on-Avon *Wilts* 15 H11
Bradford-on-Tone *Som'set* 6 D5
Brading *I of Wight* 9 G7
Bradley *Clwyd* 30 E2
Bradley *Derby* 31 F10
Bradley *Hants* 9 B7
Bradley *Heref/Worcs* 22 F3
Bradley *Humber* 37 F10
Bradley *N Yorks* 39 G12
Bradley *Staffs* 31 H7
Bradley *W Midlands* 22 C3
Bradley Green *Ches* 30 F4
Bradley in the Moors *Staffs* 31 F9
Bradmore *Notts* 32 G3
Bradney *Som'set* 7 B7
Bradninch *Devon* 6 F3
Bradnop *Staffs* 31 E8
Bradpole *Dorset* 7 G8
Bradshaw *Gtr Man* 34 F6
Bradstone *Devon* 5 H3
Bradwall Green *Ches* 30 D6
Bradwell *Bucks* 23 H11
Bradwell *Derby* 31 B10
Bradwell *Essex* 19 B8
Bradwell *Norfolk* 26 E8
Bradwell Grove *Oxon* 16 C3
Bradwell Waterside *Essex* 19 C10
Bradwell-on-Sea *Essex* 19 C10
Bradworthy *Devon* 4 E2
Bradworthy Cross *Devon* 4 E2
Brae *Shetl'd* 64 C7
Brae Doune *H'land* 60 G5
Brae of Achnahaire *H'land* 60 E2
Brae Roy Lodge *H'land* 55 K7
Braeantra *H'land* 56 B1
Braedownie *Tayside* 57 M8
Braefoot *Dumf/Gal* 43 A9
Braehead *Dumf/Gal* 42 F5
Braehead *Gramp* 58 F7
Braehead *Orkney* 64 D3
Braehead *S'clyde* 48 D2
Braehead *S'clyde* 48 F1
Braehead *Tayside* 53 B11
Braehead of Lunan *Tayside* 59 M4
Braehungie *H'land* 61 D11
Braeintra *H'land* 54 F2
Braelangwell Lodge *H'land* 60 G6
Braemar *Gramp* 57 K7
Braemore *H'land* 54 B6
Braemore *H'land* 61 D10
Braeside *S'clyde* 47 B7
Braeval *Central* 51 G12
Brafferton *Durham* 40 C3
Bragar *W Isles* 63 B4
Bragbury End *Herts* 18 B3
Braglenbeg *S'clyde* 50 E6
Braides *Lancs* 34 B3
Braidshawrig *Borders* 49 D8
Braidwood *S'clyde* 48 E1
Brailsford *Derby* 31 F11
Brainshaugh *Northum* 45 C10
Braintree *Essex* 19 B7
Braiseworth *Suffolk* 27 H4
Braishfield *Hants* 8 D5
Braithwaite *Cumb* 38 C5
Braithwaite *S Yorks* 36 F4
Braithwell *S Yorks* 32 A3
Bramber *W Sussex* 10 G1
Bramcote *Notts* 32 F2
Bramdean *Hants* 9 C7
Bramerton *Norfolk* 26 E6
Bramfield *Herts* 18 B3
Bramfield *Suffolk* 27 H7
Bramford *Suffolk* 27 K4
Bramhall *Gtr Man* 31 B7
Bramham *W Yorks* 36 C2
Bramham Crossroads *N Yorks* 36 C2
Bramhope *W Yorks* 35 C11
Bramley *S Yorks* 32 A2
Bramley *Surrey* 9 B11
Bramley Green *Hants* 17 H7
Brampford Speke *Devon* 6 F3
Brampton *Cambs* 25 H3
Brampton *Cumb* 39 C9
Brampton *Cumb* 44 G4
Brampton *Heref/Worcs* 15 A7
Brampton *Lincs* 32 B6
Brampton *S Yorks* 36 G2
Brampton *Suffolk* 27 G7
Brampton Abbotts *Heref/Worcs* 15 B9
Brampton Ash *Northants* 23 C11
Brampton Bryan *Heref/Worcs* 21 E9
Brampton en le Morthen *S Yorks* 32 A2
Bramshall *Staffs* 31 G9
Bramshaw *Hants* 8 E4
Bramshott *Hants* 9 C9
Bran End *Essex* 18 A6
Brancaster *Norfolk* 26 A1
Brancaster Staithe *Norfolk* 26 A1
Brancepeth *Durham* 40 A2
Branchill *Gramp* 56 D6
Brand Green *Glos* 15 B10
Branderburgh *Gramp* 56 C8
Brandesburton *Humber* 37 B9
Brandeston *Suffolk* 27 J5
Brandingill *Cumb* 38 C4
Brandis Corner *Devon* 4 E3
Brandiston *Norfolk* 26 C4
Brandon *Durham* 40 A3
Brandon *Lincs* 32 E6
Brandon *Northum* 45 A8
Brandon *Suffolk* 27 G1
Brandon *Warwick* 23 D7
Brandon Creek *Norfolk* 24 F7
Brandon Parva *Norfolk* 26 E4
Brandsby *N Yorks* 40 H6
Brandy Wharf *Lincs* 37 G8
Brane *Cornw'l* 2 G1
Branksome *Dorset* 8 G2
Branksome Park *Dorset* 8 G2
Bransbury *Hants* 8 B6
Bransby *Lincs* 32 B6
Bransby *Lincs* 32 C6
Branscombe *Devon* 6 G5
Bransford *Heref/Worcs* 22 G1
Bransgore *Hants* 8 F3
Branson's Cross *Heref/Worcs* 22 E4
Branston *Leics* 32 G5
Branston *Lincs* 33 C7
Branston *Staffs* 31 H10
Branston Booths *Lincs* 33 C8
Branstone *I of Wight* 9 H7
Brant Broughton *Lincs* 32 E6
Branteth *Dumf/Gal* 44 E1
Brantham *Suffolk* 27 M4
Branthwaite *Cumb* 38 B5
Branthwaite *Cumb* 38 C3
Brantingham *Humber* 37 D7
Branton *Northum* 45 A8
Branton *S Yorks* 36 G4
Branxholme *Borders* 44 B3
Branxton *Northum* 49 F11
Branxtonmoor *Northum* 49 F11
Brassington *Derby* 31 E11
Brasted *Kent* 10 C3
Brasted Chart *Kent* 10 C3
Brathens *Gramp* 59 H4
Bratoft *Lincs* 33 D11
Brattleby *Lincs* 32 B6
Bratton *Som'set* 6 B3
Bratton *Wilts* 8 A1
Bratton Clovelly *Devon* 5 G3
Bratton Fleming *Devon* 4 B5
Bratton Seymour *Som'set* 7 C10
Braughing *Herts* 18 A4
Braunston *Leics* 23 A11
Braunston *Northants* 23 E9
Braunstone *Leics* 23 B9
Braunton *Devon* 4 B4
Braverton *N Yorks* 40 H4
Brawdy *N Yorks* 41 G7
Brawlbin *H'land* 61 B10
Bray *Berks* 17 F10
Bray Shop *Cornw'l* 3 B10
Bray Wick *Berks* 17 F9
Braybrooke *Northants* 23 D11
Brayford *Devon* 4 C6
Brayton *N Yorks* 36 D4
Brazacott *Cornw'l* 3 A9
Breabost *H'land* 62 C3
Breach *Kent* 11 B7
Breachwood Green *Herts* 18 B2
Breaclete *W Isles* 63 C2
Breadsall *Derby* 31 F12
Breadstone *Glos* 15 D10
Breafield *H'land* 54 F8
Breage *Cornw'l* 2 G3
Breakachy *H'land* 54 E8
Bream *Glos* 15 D9
Breamore *Hants* 8 D3
Brean *Som'set* 6 A6
Brearton *N Yorks* 35 A11
Breasclete *W Isles* 63 C3
Breaston *Derby* 32 G2
Brechfa *Dyfed* 13 D8
Brechin *Gramp* 59 L4
Breckonside *Dumf/Gal* 43 A9
Brecon *Powys* 14 A4
Bredbury *Gtr Man* 35 H8
Brede *E Sussex* 11 F7
Bredenbury *Heref/Worcs* 21 G11
Bredfield *Suffolk* 27 K6
Bredger *Kent* 11 B7
Bredhurst *Kent* 11 B7
Bredicot *Heref/Worcs* 22 G3
Bredon *Heref/Worcs* 15 A12
Bredon's Norton *Heref/Worcs* 22 H3
Bredwardine *Heref/Worcs* 21 H9
Breedon on the Hill *Leics* 32 H1
Breich *Lothian* 48 C2
Breighton *Humber* 36 D5
Breinton *Heref/Worcs* 21 H10
Breinton Common *Heref/Worcs* 21 H10
Brekery *H'land* 62 B4
Bremhill *Wilts* 16 G1
Brenachoille *S'clyde* 51 G7
Brenchley *Kent* 10 D5
Brendon *Devon* 4 A6
Brenfield *S'clyde* 46 A3
Brenish *W Isles* 63 D1
Brenkley *Tyne/Wear* 45 F10
Brent *London* 18 E2
Brent Eleigh *Suffolk* 27 K2
Brent Knoll *Som'set* 6 A6
Brent Pelham *Herts* 25 M5
Brentford *London* 18 F2
Brentwood *Essex* 18 E6
Brenzett *Kent* 11 E8
Brereton *Staffs* 22 A4
Brereton Green *Ches* 30 D6
Brereton Heath *Ches* 30 D6
Bressay *Shetl'd* 64 E7
Bressingham *Norfolk* 27 G4
Bretby *Derby* 31 H11
Bretford *Warwick* 23 D7
Bretforton *Heref/Worcs* 22 H4
Bretherdale Head *Cumb* 39 E8
Bretherton *Lancs* 34 E4
Brett *Som'set* 6 B4
Brettabister *Shetl'd* 64 D7
Brettenham *Norfolk* 27 G2
Brettenham *Suffolk* 27 K3
Bretton *Clwyd* 30 D2
Brewer Street *Surrey* 10 C2
Brewlands Bridge *Tayside* 53 A7
Brewood *Staffs* 22 A2
Briach *Gramp* 56 D6
Briantspuddle *Dorset* 7 G11
Brickenden *Herts* 18 C3
Bricket Wood *Herts* 18 D1
Bricklehampton *Heref/Worcs* 22 H3
Bride *I of Man* 38 F2
Bridekirk *Cumb* 38 B4
Bridell *Dyfed* 12 C5
Bridestowe *Devon* 5 G4
Brideswell *Gramp* 58 D3
Bridford *Devon* 5 G7
Bridge *Cornw'l* 2 E4
Bridge *Kent* 11 C10
Bridge End *Beds* 25 K1
Bridge End *Lincs* 24 B2
Bridge End *Northum* 45 B9
Bridge Hewick *N Yorks* 40 H4
Bridge of Alford *Gramp* 58 F3
Bridge of Allan *Central* 52 G3
Bridge of Avon *Gramp* 56 F7
Bridge of Awe *S'clyde* 51 E7
Bridge of Balgie *Tayside* 51 C12
Bridge of Balgie *Tayside* 52 A6
Bridge of Brown *Gramp* 57 G7
Bridge of Cally *Tayside* 52 B6
Bridge of Canny *Gramp* 59 H4
Bridge of Craigisla *Tayside* 53 B7
Bridge of Dee *Dumf/Gal* 43 F8
Bridge of Derrybeg *Gramp* 56 F8
Bridge of Don *Gramp* 58 F7
Bridge of Dun *Tayside* 59 L4
Bridge of Dye *Gramp* 59 J4
Bridge of Earn *Tayside* 52 E6
Bridge of Ericht *Tayside* 51 B12
Bridge of Feugh *Gramp* 59 H4
Bridge of Forss *H'land* 61 A10
Bridge of Gairn *Gramp* 59 H1
Bridge of Gaur *Tayside* 51 B12
Bridge of Murchalls *Gramp* 59 H6
Bridge of Oich *H'land* 55 J7
Bridge of Orchy *S'clyde* 51 D10
Bridge of Waith *Orkney* 64 D1
Bridge of Walls *Shetl'd* 64 D6
Bridge of Weir *S'clyde* 47 C9
Bridge Reeve *Devon* 4 E5
Bridge Sollars *Heref/Worcs* 21 H9
Bridge Street *Suffolk* 27 K2
Bridge Trafford *Ches* 30 C3
Bridgefoot *Cambs* 25 L5
Bridgefoot *Cumb* 38 B3
Bridgehampton *Som'set* 7 D9
Bridgelands *Borders* 49 F7
Bridgemary *Hants* 9 F7
Bridgend *Cornw'l* 3 D8
Bridgend *Cumb* 38 D6
Bridgend *Dumf/Gal* 43 A11
Bridgend *Dyfed* 12 B5
Bridgend *Fife* 53 F8
Bridgend *Gramp* 58 C5
Bridgend *Gramp* 58 D1
Bridgend *Gramp* 58 D3
Bridgend *Gramp* 58 E6
Bridgend *H'land* 54 D7
Bridgend *Lothian* 48 B3
Bridgend *Mid Glam* 14 F2
Bridgend *S'clyde* 50 H6
Bridgend *Tayside* 59 K3
Bridgend of Lintrathen *Tayside* 53 B7
Bridgerule *Devon* 4 F1
Bridges *Shrops* 21 C9
Bridgetown *Cornw'l* 3 A10
Bridgetown *Som'set* 6 C3
Bridgetown *Staffs* 22 A3
Bridgham *Norfolk* 27 G3
Bridgnorth *Shrops* 21 C12
Bridgwater *Som'set* 6 B6
Bridlington *Humber* 41 H12
Bridport *Dorset* 7 G8
Bridstow *Heref/Worcs* 15 B9
Brierfield *Lancs* 35 D7
Brierley Hill *W Midlands* 22 C3
Brierly *Glos* 15 C9
Brierly *Heref/Worcs* 21 G10
Brierly *S Yorks* 36 F2
Brierton *Clevl'd* 40 B5
Briery Hill *Gwent* 14 C5
Brig o'Turk *Central* 51 G12
Brigg *Humber* 37 F8
Briggs of Criggie *Gramp* 59 J6
Briggswath *N Yorks* 41 D9
Brigham *Cumb* 38 B3
Brigham *Humber* 37 B8
Brighouse *W Yorks* 35 E10
Brighstone *I of Wight* 8 H6
Brightgate *Derby* 31 D11
Brighthampton *Oxon* 16 D5
Brightling *E Sussex* 10 F5
Brightlingsea *Essex* 19 B10
Brighton *Cornw'l* 2 D6
Brighton *E Sussex* 10 H2
Brightons *Lothian* 48 B2
Brightwalton *Berks* 16 F5
Brightwell *Oxon* 17 E7
Brightwell *Suffolk* 27 L5
Brightwell Baldwin *Oxon* 17 E7
Brignall *Durham* 40 D1
Brigsley *Humber* 37 G10
Brigsteer *Cumb* 39 F7
Brigstock *Northants* 23 D12
Brigton *Gramp* 59 K4
Brill *Bucks* 17 C7
Brill *Cornw'l* 2 G4
Brilley *Heref/Worcs* 21 G8
Brimaston *Dyfed* 12 D3
Brimfield *Heref/Worcs* 21 F10
Brimington *Derby* 32 C1
Brimpsfield *Glos* 15 C12
Brimpton *Berks* 16 H6
Brims *Orkney* 64 D1
Brimscombe *Glos* 15 D11
Brimstage *Mersey* 30 B2
Brin *H'land* 57 G2
Brinacory *H'land* 55 K1
Brind *Humber* 36 D5
Brindister *Shetl'd* 64 D6
Brindister *Shetl'd* 64 E7
Brindle *Lancs* 34 E5
Brindley Ford *Staffs* 31 E7
Brineton *Staffs* 22 A2
Bringhurst *Leics* 23 C11
Brington *Cambs* 25 H2
Bringingham *Norfolk* 26 B3
Brinkhill *Lincs* 33 C10
Brinkley *Cambs* 25 K7
Brinklow *Warwick* 23 D8
Brinkworth *Wilts* 16 F1
Brinscall *Lancs* 34 E5
Brinsea *Avon* 15 H7
Brinsley *Notts* 32 E2
Brinsop *Heref/Worcs* 21 H10
Brinsworth *S Yorks* 32 A1
Brinton *Norfolk* 26 B3
Brinyan *Orkney* 64 B2
Brisley *Norfolk* 26 C3
Brislington *Avon* 15 G9
Brissenden Green *Kent* 11 D8
Bristol *Avon* 15 G9
Briston *Norfolk* 26 B4
Britford *Wilts* 8 C3
Brithdir *Gwyn* 29 H7
Brithdir *Mid Glam* 14 D5
Brithem Bottom *Devon* 6 E4
British Legion Village *Kent* 10 B6
Briton Ferry *W Glam* 13 G10
Britwell Salome *Oxon* 17 E7
Brixham *Devon* 5 K8
Brixton *Devon* 5 K4
Brixton Deverill *Wilts* 7 B12
Brixworth *Northants* 23 E10
Brize Norton *Oxon* 16 C4

Broad Blunsdon Wilts 16 E3
Broad Campden Glos 22 H5
Broad Chalke Wilts 8 C2
Broad Clyst Devon 6 F3
Broad Green Beds 25 L1
Broad Green Essex 19 B8
Broad Green Heref/Worcs 22 F1
Broad Haven Dyfed 12 F2
Broad Heath Heref/Worcs 21 F12
Broad Hill Cambs 25 H7
Broad Hinton Wilts 16 F2
Broad Laying Hants 16 H5
Broad Marston Heref/Worcs 22 G5
Broad Oak Cumb 38 F4
Broad Oak Dorset 7 E11
Broad Oak Dorset 7 G8
Broad Oak Dyfed 13 E9
Broad Oak E Sussex 11 F7
Broad Oak Heref/Worcs 15 B8
Broad Oak N Yorks 36 A4
Broad Street Kent 11 B7
Broad Street Green Essex 19 C8
Broad Town Wilts 16 F2
Broadbottom Gtr Man 35 H8
Broadbridge W Sussex 9 E9
Broadbridge Heath W Sussex 9 C12
Broadfield Dyfed 12 G5
Broadford H'land 62 F5
Broadford Bridge Hants 8 D12
Broadford Bridge W Sussex 9 D12
Broadgairhill Borders 48 H5
Broadhaugh Borders 44 B3
Broadhaven H'land 61 C12
Broadhembury Devon 6 F4
Broadhempston Devon 5 J7
Broadland Row E Sussex 11 F7
Broadlay Dyfed 13 F7
Broadley Gramp 58 B1
Broadley Common Essex 18 C4
Broadmayne Dorset 7 H10
Broadmeadows Borders 49 F7
Broadmere Hants 9 A7
Broadmoor Dyfed 12 F4
Broadnymett Devon 4 F6
Broadoak E Sussex 10 F5
Broadoak Kent 11 B10
Broadrashes Gramp 58 B2
Broadsea Gramp 58 E5
Broadstairs Kent 11 A12
Broadstone Dorset 8 F2
Broadstone Shrops 21 C11
Broadtown Lane Wilts 16 F2
Broadwas Heref/Worcs 22 G1
Broadwater Herts 18 B2
Broadwater W Sussex 9 F12
Broadway Dyfed 12 F2
Broadway Dyfed 12 F6
Broadway Heref/Worcs 22 H4
Broadway Som'set 6 E6
Broadwell Glos 15 C9
Broadwell Glos 16 A3
Broadwell Oxon 16 D3
Broadwell Warwick 23 F8
Broadwell House Northum 45 H7
Broadwey Dorset 7 H10
Broadwindsor Dorset 7 F8
Broadwood Kelly Devon 4 E5
Broadwoodwidger Devon 5 G3
Brobury Heref/Worcs 21 H9
Brobury Heref/Worcs 21 H8
Brochel H'land 62 D5
Brockbridge Hants 9 D7
Brockdam Northum 45 A9
Brockdish Norfolk 27 G5
Brockenhurst Hants 8 F4
Brockersbrae S'clyde 48 E1
Brockford Street Suffolk 27 J4
Brockhall Northants 23 F9
Brockham Surrey 10 C1
Brockhampton Glos 16 B1
Brockhampton Heref/Worcs 15 A9
Brockhampton Heref/Worcs 21 G12
Brockhampton Green Dorset 7 F10
Brockholes W Yorks 35 F10
Brockhurst Hants 9 F7
Brocklebank Cumb 38 A5
Brocklesby Lincs 37 F9
Brockley Avon 15 H8
Brockley Green Suffolk 27 K1
Brockton Shrops 21 B8
Brockton Shrops 21 C11
Brockton Shrops 21 D9
Brockton Shrops 22 B1
Brockweir Glos 15 D8
Brockwood Hants 9 D7
Brockworth Glos 15 C12
Brocton Staffs 31 H8
Brodick S'clyde 46 F5
Brodiesord Gramp 58 B3
Brodsworth S Yorks 36 F3
Brogaig H'land 62 A4
Brogborough Beds 25 L1
Broken Cross Ches 30 C5
Broken Cross Ches 31 C7
Brokenborough Wilts 15 E12
Bromborough Mersey 30 B2
Brome Suffolk 27 H4
Brome Street Suffolk 27 H5
Bromeswell Suffolk 27 K6
Bromfield Cumb 43 G12
Bromfield Shrops 21 E10
Bromham Beds 25 K1
Bromham Wilts 16 H1
Bromley London 18 G4
Bromley Green Kent 11 D8
Brompton Kent 10 A6
Brompton N Yorks 40 E4
Brompton N Yorks 41 G9
Brompton on Swale N Yorks 40 E2
Brompton Ralph Som'set 6 C4
Brompton Regis Som'set 6 C3
Bromsash Heref/Worcs 15 B9
Bromsberrow Glos 15 A10
Bromsgrove Heref/Worcs 22 E3
Bromyard Heref/Worcs 21 G12
Bromyard Downs Heref/Worcs 21 G12
Bronaber Gwyn 28 G6
Bronant Dyfed 20 F2
Brondwydd Arms Dyfed 12 C6
Brongest Shrops 30 F4
Bronington Clwyd 30 F3
Bronllys Dyfed 13 E7
Bronllys Powys 14 A5
Bronwydd Arms Dyfed 13 E7
Bronydd Powys 21 H8
Brook Dyfed 12 F6
Brook Hants 8 C5
Brook Hants 8 E4
Brook I of Wight 8 H5
Brook Kent 11 D9
Brook Surrey 9 B10
Brook Surrey 9 B12
Brook End Beds 25 J2
Brook Hill Hants 8 E4
Brook Street Essex 18 E6
Brook Street W Sussex 10 E2
Brooke Leics 23 B12
Brooke Norfolk 26 E6
Brookend Glos 15 D9
Brookfield S'clyde 47 C9
Brookhouse Ches 31 C8
Brookhouse Lancs 34 A4
Brookhouse Green Ches 31 D7
Brookland Kent 11 E8
Brooklands Dumf/Gal 43 D9
Brookmans Park Herts 18 D2
Brooks Powys 21 C7
Brookwood Surrey 17 H10
Broom Beds 25 L3
Broom Durham 40 A3
Broom Warwick 22 G4
Broom Hill Dorset 8 F2
Broom of Dalreoch Tayside 52 E5
Broomdykes Borders 49 D11
Broome Heref/Worcs 22 D3
Broome Norfolk 26 F6
Broome Shrops 21 D9
Broome Park Surrey 10 C1
Broomedge Ches 30 B5
Broomer's Corner W Sussex 9 D12
Broomfield Essex 19 C7
Broomfield Gramp 58 D7
Broomfield Kent 11 A10
Broomfield Kent 11 C7
Broomfield S'clyde 48 E1
Broomfield Som'set 6 C6
Broomfleet Humber 36 D6
Broomhall Surrey 17 G10
Broomhaugh Northum 45 G8
Broomhill H'land 56 C3
Broomhill Northum 45 C10
Broomhill House H'land 57 G6
Broomholm Norfolk 26 B6
Broomhouse Northum 45 C11
Broomhouses Dumf/Gal 43 C12
Broomley Northum 45 G8
Broom's Green Glos 15 A10
Broomsberrow Heath Glos 15 A10
Brora H'land 61 F9
Broseley Shrops 21 B12
Brotheridge Green Heref/Worcs 22 H2
Brotherstone Borders 49 F9
Brothertoft Lincs 33 F10
Brotherton W Yorks 36 E3
Brotherwick Northum 45 B10
Brotton Clevl'd 41 C7
Broubster H'land 61 B10
Brough Cumb 39 D10
Brough Derby 31 B10
Brough H'land 61 A11
Brough Humber 37 D7
Brough Notts 32 D5
Brough Orkney 64 C2
Brough, Mainland Shetl'd 64 C7
Brough, Yell Shetl'd 64 C7
Brough Shetl'd 64 C8
Brough Lodge Shetl'd 64 B8
Brough Sowerby Cumb 39 D10
Broughall Shrops 30 F4
Broughton Borders 48 F4
Broughton Bucks 23 H12
Broughton Cambs 25 G4
Broughton Clwyd 30 D2
Broughton Cumb 38 B3
Broughton Hants 8 C4
Broughton Humber 37 F7
Broughton Lancs 34 D4
Broughton Mid Glam 14 G3
Broughton N Yorks 35 B8
Broughton N Yorks 41 H8
Broughton Northants 23 E11
Broughton Orkney 64 A2
Broughton Oxon 23 H7
Broughton Astley Leics 23 C8
Broughton Beck Cumb 38 G5
Broughton Common Wilts 15 H12
Broughton Foggs Oxon 16 D3
Broughton Gifford Wilts 15 H12
Broughton Hackett Heref/Worcs 22 G3
Broughton in Furness Cumb 38 F5
Broughton Mills Cumb 38 F5
Broughton Moor Cumb 38 B3
Broughtown Orkney 64 B4
Broughty Ferry Tayside 53 D9
Browhouses Dumf/Gal 44 G1
Brown Candover Hants 9 B7
Brown Edge Staffs 31 E7
Brownhill Gramp 58 D6
Brownhill Shrops 30 H3
Brownhills Fife 53 F10
Brownhills W Midlands 22 B4
Brownlow Heath Ches 31 D7
Brownmuir Gramp 59 K5
Brownridge Northum 45 B11
Brown's Hill Glos 15 D12
Brownsover Warwick 23 D8
Brownston Devon 5 K6
Brownyside Northum 45 A9
Brox Surrey 17 H11
Broxa N Yorks 41 F9
Broxbourne Herts 18 C4
Broxburn Lothian 48 B4
Broxburn Lothian 49 B9
Broxted Essex 18 A6
Broxton Ches 30 E3
Broxwood Heref/Worcs 21 G9
Broyle Side E Sussex 10 G3
Bruan H'land 61 C12
Bruar Lodge Tayside 57 M4
Brue W Isles 63 B4
Bruera Ches 30 D3
Bruern Abbey Oxon 16 B4
Bruisyard Suffolk 27 J6
Bruisyard Street Suffolk 27 J6
Brumby Humber 36 F6
Brund Staffs 31 D9
Brundhall Norfolk 26 E6
Brundish Suffolk 27 H6
Brundish Street Suffolk 27 H6
Brunery H'land 55 M1
Brunswick Village Tyne/Wear 45 F10
Bruntingthorpe Leics 23 C9
Brunton Fife 53 E8
Brunton Northum 45 A10
Brunton Wilts 16 H3
Brushford Devon 4 E5
Brushford Som'set 6 D3
Bruton Som'set 7 C10
Bryanston Dorset 7 F12
Brydekirk Dumf/Gal 43 E12
Brymbo Clwyd 29 E12
Brympton Som'set 7 E8
Bryn Clwyd 29 F12
Bryn Dyfed 13 G9
Bryn Gtr Man 34 G4
Bryn Shrops 21 D8
Bryn W Glam 13 H11
Bryn Cae Mid Glam 14 F3
Bryn Golau Mid Glam 14 E3
Brynamman Dyfed 13 F10
Brynberian Dyfed 12 C4
Brynbryddan W Glam 13 H11
Bryncethin Mid Glam 14 F2
Bryncir Gwyn 28 F4
Bryn-coch W Glam 13 G10
Bryncroes Gwyn 28 G2
Bryncrug Gwyn 20 B2
Bryneglwys Clwyd 29 E10
Brynford Clwyd 29 C11
Bryngwran Gwyn 28 B3
Bryngwyn Gwent 15 C7
Bryngwyn Powys 21 G7
Bryn-henllan Dyfed 12 C4
Brynhoffnant Dyfed 13 B7
Bryning Lancs 34 D3
Brynmawr Gwent 14 C5
Brynmenyn Mid Glam 14 F2
Brynna Mid Glam 14 F3
Brynrefail Gwyn 28 B4
Brynrefail Gwyn 28 D5
Brynsadler Mid Glam 14 F4
Bryn-Siencyn Gwyn 28 D4
Bryn-teg Clwyd 29 E12
Brynteg Gwyn 28 B4
Bryn-y-gwenin Gwent 14 C6
Bryn-y-maen Clwyd 29 C7
Bualintur H'land 62 F3
Bubbenhall Warwick 23 E7
Buccleuch Borders 48 H6
Buchan Dumf/Gal 42 D5
Buchanan Castle Central 47 A9
Buchanan Smithy Central 51 H11
Buchanhaven Gramp 58 C8
Buchanty Tayside 52 D4
Buchlyvie Central 52 H1
Buchts Gramp 58 B7
Buckabank Cumb 44 H2
Buckden Cambs 25 H3
Buckden N Yorks 39 G11
Buckenham Norfolk 26 E6
Buckerell Devon 6 F5
Buckfast Devon 5 J6
Buckfastleigh Devon 5 J6
Buckhaven Fife 53 G8
Buckholm Borders 49 E7
Buckhorn Weston Dorset 7 D10
Buckhurst Hill London 18 E4
Buckie Gramp 58 A2
Buckingham Bucks 17 A8
Buckland Bucks 17 C9
Buckland Devon 5 L5
Buckland Glos 16 A2
Buckland Herts 25 M5
Buckland Kent 11 D11
Buckland Oxon 16 D4
Buckland Surrey 10 C1
Buckland Brewer Devon 4 D3
Buckland Common Bucks 17 C10
Buckland Dinham Som'set 7 A11
Buckland Filleigh Devon 4 E3
Buckland in the Moor Devon 5 H6
Buckland Manachorum Devon 5 J4
Buckland Newton Dorset 7 F10
Buckland St. Mary Som'set 6 E6
Bucklebury Berks 16 G6
Bucklegate Lincs 24 B4
Bucklerheads Tayside 53 D9
Bucklers Hard Hants 8 F5
Bucklesham Suffolk 27 L5
Buckley Clwyd 29 D12
Bucklow Hill Ches 30 B6
Buckminister Leics 32 H6
Bucknall Lincs 33 C9
Bucknall Staffs 31 E7
Bucknell Oxon 16 B6
Bucknell Shrops 21 E9
Buckpool Gramp 58 A2
Buck's Cross Devon 4 D2
Bucks Green W Sussex 9 C12
Bucks Horn Oak Hants 9 B9
Buck's Mills Devon 4 D2
Buckton Heref/Worcs 21 E9
Buckton Humber 41 H11
Buckton Northum 45 B12
Buckworth Cambs 25 H2
Budbrooke Warwick 22 F6
Budby Notts 32 C3
Budd's Titson Cornw'l 4 F1
Bude Cornw'l 4 E1
Budlake Devon 6 F3
Budle Northum 45 D12
Budleigh Salterton Devon 6 H4
Budock Water Cornw'l 2 F5
Budwith Humber 36 D5
Buerton Ches 30 F5
Bugbrooke Northants 23 F10
Buglawton Ches 31 D7
Bugle Cornw'l 3 D7
Bugthorpe Humber 36 A5
Buildwas Shrops 21 B11
Builstonend S'clyde 47 E9
Builth Road Powys 20 G6
Builth Wells Powys 20 G6
Bulbourne Bucks 17 C10
Bulby Lincs 24 C2
Bulcote Notts 32 F4
Bulford Wilts 8 B3
Bulkeley Ches 30 E4
Bulkington Warwick 23 D7
Bulkington Wilts 15 H12
Bulkworthy Devon 4 E3
Bull Bay Gwyn 28 A4
Bull Hill Hants 8 F5
Bullamore N Yorks 40 F4
Bullbrook Berks 17 G9
Bullers of Buchan Gramp 58 D8
Bulley Glos 15 B11
Bullgill Cumb 43 H11
Bullinghope Heref/Worcs 15 A8
Bullington Hants 8 B6
Bullington Lincs 33 B8
Bullpot Farm Cumb 39 G9
Bullwood S'clyde 46 B6
Bulmer Essex 27 L1
Bulmer N Yorks 41 H7
Bulmer Tye Essex 27 L1
Bulphan Essex 18 E6
Bulverhythe E Sussex 10 G6
Bulwark Gramp 58 C7
Bulwark Village Gwent 15 E8
Bulwell Notts 32 F3
Bulwick Northants 24 F1
Bumble's Green Essex 18 C4
Bunacaimb H'land 55 K1
Bunarkaig H'land 55 L6
Bunavopeadar W Isles 63 F2
Bunbury Ches 30 D4
Bunchrew H'land 56 E2
Buncton W Sussex 9 E12
Bundalloch H'land 55 G3
Bunessan H'land 50 E1
Bungalow Station I of Man 38 G2
Bungay Suffolk 26 F6
Bunloit H'land 57 G1
Bunny Notts 32 G3
Buntait H'land 54 F8
Buntingford Herts 18 A4
Bunwell Norfolk 26 F4
Bunwell Street Norfolk 26 F4
Burbage Derby 31 C9
Burbage Leics 23 C8
Burbage Wilts 16 H3
Burchett's Green Berks 17 F9
Burcombe Wilts 8 C2
Burcot Heref/Worcs 22 E3
Burcot Oxon 16 E6
Burcott Bucks 17 B9
Burdale N Yorks 36 A6
Bures Suffolk 27 M2
Burford Oxon 16 C4
Burford Shrops 21 F11
Burg H'land 50 C1
Burgess Hill W Sussex 10 F2
Burgh Suffolk 27 K5
Burgh by Sands Cumb 44 G2
Burgh Castle Norfolk 26 E8
Burgh Heath Surrey 10 B1
Burgh le Marsh Lincs 33 D12
Burgh Muir Gramp 58 E5
Burgh next Aylsham Norfolk 26 C5
Burgh on Bain Lincs 33 B9
Burgh St. Margaret Norfolk 26 D7
Burgh St. Peter Norfolk 26 F8
Burghclere Hants 16 H6
Burghead Gramp 56 C7
Burghfield Berks 17 G7
Burghfield Common Berks 17 G7
Burghill Heref/Worcs 21 H10
Burghwallis S Yorks 36 F3
Burham Kent 10 B6
Buriton Hants 9 D9
Burland Ches 30 E5
Burlawn Cornw'l 3 C7
Burlescombe Devon 6 E4
Burleston Dorset 7 G11
Burley Hants 8 F4
Burley Leics 23 A12
Burley Gate Heref/Worcs 21 H11
Burley in Wharfdale W Yorks 35 C10
Burley Lodge Hants 8 E4
Burley Street Hants 8 F3
Burleydam Ches 30 F5
Burlingjobb Powys 21 G8
Burlow E Sussex 10 F4
Burlton Shrops 30 H3
Burmarsh Kent 11 E9
Burmington Warwick 22 H6
Burn Devon 6 F3
Burn Dumf/Gal 43 B10
Burn N Yorks 36 D4
Burn Naze Lancs 34 C2
Burn of Cambus Central 52 G2
Burnage Gtr Man 35 H7
Burnaston Derby 31 G11
Burnbank S'clyde 47 D11
Burnbrae S'clyde 47 E12
Burnby Humber 36 C6
Burncross S Yorks 35 G12
Burneside Cumb 39 F7
Burness Orkney 64 A4
Burneston N Yorks 40 G3
Burnett Avon 15 H10
Burnfoot Borders 44 A3
Burnfoot Borders 44 B2
Burnfoot Dumf/Gal 43 B10
Burnfoot Dumf/Gal 44 D2
Burnfoot S'clyde 47 B11
Burngreave S Yorks 32 A1
Burnham Bucks 17 F10
Burnham Humber 37 E8
Burnham Deepdale Norfolk 26 A1
Burnham Green Herts 18 B3
Burnham Market Norfolk 26 A1
Burnham Norton Norfolk 26 A1
Burnham Overy Norfolk 26 A1
Burnham Overy Staithe Norfolk 26 A1
Burnham Thorpe Norfolk 26 B2
Burnham-on-Crouch Essex 19 D9
Burnham-on-Sea Som'set 6 A6
Burnhaven Gramp 58 C8
Burnhead Dumf/Gal 43 B9
Burnhead Dumf/Gal 43 C10
Burnhervie Gramp 58 F5
Burnhill Green Staffs 22 B1
Burnhope Durham 45 H10
Burnhouse S'clyde 47 D8
Burnhouse Main Borders 49 D7
Burniston N Yorks 41 F10
Burnley Lancs 35 D7
Burnmouth Borders 49 C12
Burnmouth Dumf/Gal 43 A9
Burnopfield Durham 45 G10
Burnroot Gramp 59 H2
Burnsall N Yorks 35 A9
Burnside Dumf/Gal 43 C11
Burnside H'land 56 F5
Burnside Lothian 48 B4
Burnside S'clyde 47 H10
Burnside Shetl'd 64 C6
Burnside Tayside 52 F6
Burnside Tayside 53 B9
Burnside of Dantrune Tayside 53 D9
Burnt Heath Essex 19 A10
Burnt Houses Durham 40 C2
Burnt Yates N Yorks 35 A11
Burnthouse Cornw'l 2 F5
Burntisland Lothian 48 A5
Burnton S'clyde 42 A6
Burnton S'clyde 47 H10
Burnton S'clyde 47 H8
Burntwood Staffs 22 A4
Burpham Surrey 9 A11
Burpham W Sussex 9 E11
Burradon Northum 45 B8
Burradon Tyne/Wear 45 F11
Burrafirth Shetl'd 64 A8
Burras Cornw'l 2 F4
Burravoe Shetl'd 64 C7
Burrells Cumb 39 C9
Burrelton Tayside 53 C7
Burridge Devon 4 C4
Burridge Hants 9 E7
Burrill N Yorks 40 F3
Burringham Humber 36 F6
Burrington Avon 15 H8
Burrington Devon 4 D5
Burrington Heref/Worcs 21 E10
Burrough Green Cambs 25 K7
Burrough on the Hill Leics 23 A10
Burrow Devon 6 G4
Burrow Som'set 6 B3
Burrow Bridge Som'set 7 C7
Burrowhill Surrey 17 H10
Burrows Cross Surrey 9 A12
Burry W Glam 13 H8
Burry Port Dyfed 13 G8
Burrygreen W Glam 13 H8
Burscough Lancs 34 F3

Burscough Bridge Lancs 34 F3
Bursea Humber 36 D6
Bursea Lane Ends Humber 36 D6
Burshill Humber 37 B8
Bursledon Hants 8 E6
Burslem Staffs 31 E7
Burstall Suffolk 27 L4
Burstock Dorset 7 F7
Burston Norfolk 27 G4
Burston Staffs 31 G8
Burstow Surrey 10 D2
Burstwick Humber 37 D10
Burtersett N Yorks 39 F11
Burthinghurst Cumb 44 F4
Burtle Som'set 7 B7
Burton Ches 30 C2
Burton Ches 30 D4
Burton Cumb 39 G8
Burton Dorset 8 G3
Burton Dyfed 12 F3
Burton Lincs 33 C7
Burton Northum 45 D12
Burton Som'set 6 B5
Burton Wilts 15 F11
Burton Agnes Humber 37 A9
Burton Bradstock Dorset 7 G8
Burton Coggles Lincs 33 H7
Burton Dassett Warwick 23 G7
Burton Fleming Humber 41 H11
Burton Green Clwyd 30 D2
Burton Green W Midlands 22 E6
Burton Hastings Warwick 23 C7
Burton in Lonsdale N Yorks 39 H9
Burton Joyce Notts 32 F4
Burton Latimer Northants 23 E12
Burton Lazers Leics 32 H5
Burton Leonard N Yorks 35 A12
Burton on the Wolds Leics 32 H3
Burton Overy Leics 23 B10
Burton Pedwardine Lincs 24 A2
Burton Pidsea Humber 37 D10
Burton Salmon N Yorks 36 D3
Burton upon Stather Humber 36 E6
Burton-on-Trent Staffs 31 H11
Burtonwood Ches 34 H4
Burwardsley Ches 30 D4
Burwarton Shrops 21 D11
Burwash E Sussex 10 F5
Burwash Common E Sussex 10 F5
Burwash Weald E Sussex 10 F5
Burwell Cambs 25 J7
Burwell Lincs 33 B10
Burwen Gwyn 28 A4
Burwick Orkney 64 E2
Bury Cambs 25 G4
Bury Gtr Man 35 F7
Bury Som'set 6 C3
Bury W Sussex 9 E11
Bury Green Herts 18 B4
Bury St. Edmunds Suffolk 27 J2
Burythorpe N Yorks 36 A6
Busby S'clyde 47 D10
Buscot Oxon 16 D3
Bush Gramp 57 K8
Bush Bank Heref/Worcs 21 G10
Bush Green Norfolk 27 G5
Bushey Herts 18 D1
Bushey Heath Herts 18 E2
Bushley Heref/Worcs 15 A11
Bushton Wilts 16 F2
Busta Shetl'd 64 C7
Buston Barns Northum 45 B10
Butcher's Pasture Essex 18 B6
Butcombe Avon 15 H8
Buteland Northum 45 E7
Butleigh Som'set 7 C8
Butleigh Wootton Som'set 7 C8
Butler's Cross Bucks 17 C9
Butlers Marston Warwick 22 G6
Butley Suffolk 27 K7
Butt Green Ches 30 E5
Butterburn Cumb 44 F5
Buttercrambe N Yorks 36 A5
Butterknowle Durham 40 C1
Butterleigh Devon 6 E3
Buttermere Cumb 38 D4
Buttermere Wilts 16 H4
Butters Green Staffs 30 E6
Buttershaw W Yorks 35 D10
Butterstone Tayside 52 C5
Butterton Staffs 31 E9
Butterwick Durham 40 B4
Butterwick Lincs 24 A5
Butterwick N Yorks 41 G7
Butterwick N Yorks 41 H10
Buttington Powys 21 B8
Buttock's Booth Northants 23 F11
Buttonoak Shrops 22 D1
Butt's Green Hants 8 C4
Buttsash Hants 8 E6
Buxhall Suffolk 27 J3
Buxley Borders 49 D10
Buxted E Sussex 10 F4
Buxton Derby 31 C9
Buxton Norfolk 26 C5
Buxton Heath Norfolk 26 C5
Buxworth Derby 31 B9
Bwlch Powys 14 B5
Bwlchgwyn Clwyd 29 E11
Bwlchllan Dyfed 20 F1
Bwlchtocyn Gwyn 28 H3
Bwlch-y-cibau Powys 29 H11
Bwlch-y-ddar Powys 29 H11
Bwlchyfadfa Dyfed 13 B8
Bwlch-y-ffridd Powys 20 C6
Bwlch-y-groes Dyfed 12 C6
Bwlch-y-sarnau Powys 20 E6
Byeloch Dumf/Gal 43 D11
Byers Green Durham 40 B2
Byfield Northants 23 G8
Byfleet Surrey 17 H11
Byford Heref/Worcs 21 H9
Bygrave Herts 25 L4
Bylbster H'land 61 B11
Bylchau Clwyd 29 D9
Byley Ches 30 C6
Bynea Dyfed 13 G9
Byram W Yorks 36 E3
Byrewalls Borders 49 E9
Byrness Northum 44 C6
Bythorn Cambs 25 H2
Byton Heref/Worcs 21 F9
Bywell Northum 45 G8
Byworth W Sussex 9 D11
Cablea Tayside 52 C4
Cabourne Lincs 37 G9
Cabrach Gramp 58 E1
Cabule Lodge H'land 54 C5
Cadbury Devon 6 F3
Cadbury Barton Devon 4 D6
Caddam Tayside 59 K1
Cadder S'clyde 47 B11
Cadderlie S'clyde 51 D7
Caddington Beds 17 B11
Caddonfoot Borders 49 F7
Cade Street E Sussex 10 F5
Cadeby Leics 23 B7
Cadeby S Yorks 36 G3
Cadeleigh Devon 6 E3
Cademuir Borders 48 F5
Cadgillhead Dumf/Gal 44 E1
Cadgwith Cornw'l 2 H4
Cadham Fife 53 G7
Cadishead Gtr Man 34 H6
Cadle W Glam 13 G9
Cadley Wilts 16 G3
Cadley Wilts 8 A4
Cadmore End Bucks 17 E8
Cadnam Hants 8 E5
Cadney Humber 37 G8
Cadole Clwyd 29 D11
Cadoxton-Juxta-Neath W Glam 13 G11
Caeathraw Gwyn 28 D4
Caehopkin Powys 14 C2
Caenby Lincs 33 A7
Caenby Corner Lincs 33 A7
Caeo Dyfed 13 C10
Caer Farchell Dyfed 12 D1
Caerau Mid Glam 14 E2
Cae'r-bryn Dyfed 13 F9
Caerdeon Gwyn 28 H6
Cae'r-geiliog Gwyn 28 B3
Caergwrle Clwyd 29 D12
Caerhun Castle Gwyn 29 C7
Caerlanrig Dumf/Gal 44 C2
Caerleon Gwent 14 E6
Caerlleon Dyfed 12 E6
Caernarfon Gwyn 28 D4
Caerphilly Mid Glam 14 F5
Caersws Powys 20 C6
Caerwedros Dyfed 13 A7
Caerwent Gwent 15 E8
Caerwys Clwyd 29 C10
Cairn Dumf/Gal 43 C10
Cairnargat Gramp 58 D2
Cairnbaan S'clyde 50 H5
Cairncross Borders 49 C11
Cairnderry S'clyde 42 D4
Cairness Gramp 58 B8
Cairneyhill Lothian 48 A3
Cairnfield Dumf/Gal 42 G5
Cairnfield House Gramp 58 B2
Cairngaan Dumf/Gal 42 H2
Cairngarroch Dumf/Gal 42 G1
Cairnhall Dumf/Gal 43 C10
Cairnhill Gramp 58 D4
Cairnie Gramp 58 C2
Cairnorrie Gramp 58 D6
Cairnryan Dumf/Gal 42 E2
Cairntable S'clyde 47 H9
Cairnwhin S'clyde 42 B3
Caiseachan H'land 54 D6
Caister-on-Sea Norfolk 26 D8
Caistor Lincs 37 G9
Caistor St. Edmund Norfolk 26 E5
Caistron Northum 45 C8
Caitha Bowland Borders 49 E7
Calbost W Isles 63 E5
Calbourne I of Wight 8 G6
Calceby Lincs 33 C11
Calchems Corner W Midlands 22 E6
Calcot Farm Glos 15 E11
Calcot Row Berks 17 G7
Calcott Kent 11 B10
Caldbeck Cumb 38 A6
Caldbergh N Yorks 40 G1
Caldecote Cambs 25 G2
Caldecote Cambs 25 K4
Caldecote Herts 25 L3
Caldecott Leics 23 C12
Caldecott Northants 25 H1
Calder Cumb 38 E3
Calder Northum 49 G12
Calder Bridge Cumb 38 E3
Calder Grove W Yorks 35 E11
Calder Mains H'land 61 B10
Calder Vale Lancs 34 C4
Calderbank S'clyde 47 C12
Calderbrook Gtr Man 35 E8
Caldercruix S'clyde 48 C1
Caldermill S'clyde 47 E11
Calderwood S'clyde 47 D11
Caldicot Gwent 15 E8
Caldside Borders 49 E9
Caldwell N Yorks 40 D2
Caldy Mersey 30 B1
Caledfwlch Dyfed 13 D10
Caledrhydiau Dyfed 13 B8
Calfsound Orkney 64 B3
Calgary H'land 50 B1
Califer Gramp 56 D6
California Lothian 48 B2
California Norfolk 26 D8
California Suffolk 27 L5
California Cross Devon 5 K6
Calke Derby 31 H12
Callaly Northum 45 B9
Callander Central 52 F1
Callanish W Isles 63 D3
Callaughton Shrops 21 C11
Callert House H'land 51 A8
Callestick Cornw'l 2 E5
Calligarry H'land 62 H5
Callington Cornw'l 3 C10
Callow Heref/Worcs 15 A8
Callow End Heref/Worcs 22 G2
Callow Hill Heref/Worcs 22 E1
Callow Hill Heref/Worcs 22 F4
Callow Hill Wilts 16 F1
Callowhill Berks 17 G11
Callows Grave Heref/Worcs 21 F11
Calmore Hants 8 E5
Calmsden Glos 16 C1
Calne Wilts 16 G1
Calow Derby 32 C1
Calshot Hants 8 F6
Calstock Cornw'l 3 C11
Calstone Wellington Wilts 16 G1
Calthorpe Norfolk 26 B5
Calthwaite Cumb 39 A7
Calton N Yorks 35 A8
Calton Staffs 31 E9
Calveley Ches 30 D4
Calver Derby 31 C11
Calver Hill Heref/Worcs 21 G9
Calverhall Shrops 30 F5
Calverleigh Devon 6 E3
Calverley W Yorks 35 C10
Calverton Bucks 23 H11
Calverton Notts 32 E3
Calvine Tayside 52 A3
Calvo Cumb 43 F12
Calzeat Borders 48 F4
Cam Glos 15 D10
Camascross H'land 62 G6
Camasnacroise H'land 50 B6
Camasterach H'land 54 E1
Camastianavaig H'land 62 D4
Camasunary H'land 62 F4
Camault Muir H'land 56 F1
Camb Shetl'd 64 B7
Camber E Sussex 11 F8
Camberley Surrey 17 H9
Camberwell London 18 F3
Camblesforth N Yorks 36 D4
Cambo Fife 53 F10
Cambo Northum 45 D8
Cambois Northum 45 E11
Camborne Cornw'l 2 F4
Cambridge Cambs 25 J5
Cambridge Glos 15 D10
Cambus Central 52 H3
Cambus o'May Gramp 59 G2
Cambusbarron Central 52 H3
Cambuskenneth Central 52 H3
Cambuslang S'clyde 47 C11
Cambussorray H'land 54 F7
Camden London 18 E3
Cameley Avon 15 H9
Camelford Cornw'l 3 A8
Camelon Lothian 48 A2
Camelsdale W Sussex 9 C10
Camerory H'land 56 F6
Camerton Avon 7 A10
Camerton Cumb 38 B3
Camerton Humber 37 D10
Camghouran Tayside 52 B1
Camisky H'land 55 L5
Cammachmore Gramp 59 H6
Cammeringham Lincs 32 B6
Campbeltown S'clyde 46 G2
Camperdown Tyne/Wear 45 F11
Campmuir Tayside 53 C7
Campsall S Yorks 36 F3
Campsea Ash Suffolk 27 K6
Campton Beds 25 L2
Camptown Borders 44 B5
Camrose Dyfed 12 E3
Camserney Tayside 52 B3
Camster H'land 61 C11
Camuschoirk H'land 50 A5
Camus-luinie H'land 55 G3
Camusnagoul H'land 60 G2
Camusteel H'land 54 E1
Camusvrachan Tayside 52 B1
Canada Hants 8 D4
Candacraig Gramp 59 G1
Candacraig House Gramp 58 F1
Candlesby Lincs 33 C11
Candy Gramp 59 J5
Candy Mill S'clyde 48 E3
Cane End Oxon 17 F8
Canewdon Essex 19 D9
Canfield End Essex 18 B6
Canford Bottom Dorset 8 F2
Canford Magna Dorset 8 F2
Canisbay H'land 61 A12
Cann Dorset 7 D12
Cann Common Dorset 7 D12
Cannard's Grave Som'set 7 B9
Cannich H'land 54 F7
Cannington Som'set 6 B6
Cannock Staffs 22 A3
Cannock Wood Staffs 22 A4
Cannop Glos 15 C9
Canon Bridge Heref/Worcs 21 H10
Canon Pyon Heref/Worcs 21 G10
Canonbie Dumf/Gal 44 E2
Canons Ashby Northants 23 G9
Canonstown Cornw'l 2 F2
Canterbury Kent 11 B10
Cantley Norfolk 26 E7
Cantley S Yorks 36 G4
Canton S Glam 14 G5
Cantraybruich H'land 56 E3
Cantraydoune H'land 56 E3
Cantraywood H'land 56 E3
Cantsfield Lancs 39 H8
Canvey Essex 19 F8
Canwick Lincs 33 C7
Canworthy Water Cornw'l 2 B2
Caol H'land 55 M5
Caonich H'land 55 K4
Capel Surrey 10 D1
Capel Betws Lleucu Dyfed 20 G2
Capel Carmel Gwyn 28 G1
Capel Curig Gwyn 28 D6
Capel Cynon Dyfed 13 B7
Capel Dewi Dyfed 13 C8
Capel Dewi Dyfed 13 E8
Capel Dewi Dyfed 20 D2
Capel Garmon Gwyn 29 E7
Capel Gwyn Dyfed 13 E8
Capel Gwynfe Dyfed 13 E10
Capel Hendre Dyfed 13 F9
Capel Isaac Dyfed 13 D9
Capel Iwan Dyfed 12 C6
Capel le Ferne Kent 11 D11
Capel Llanilterne Mid Glam 14 F4
Capel Parc Gwyn 28 B4
Capel St. Andrew Suffolk 27 K7
Capel St. Mary Suffolk 27 L4
Capel Seion Dyfed 20 D2
Capel Trisant Dyfed 20 E3
Capel Tygwydd Dyfed 12 C6
Capel Uchaf Gwyn 28 E4
Capel-Bangor Dyfed 20 D2
Capel-coch Gwyn 28 B4
Capel-gwyn Gwyn 28 C3
Capel-lago Dyfed 13 C9
Capelulo Gwyn 29 C7
Capel-y-ffin Powys 14 A6
Capenhurst Ches 30 C2
Capernwray Lancs 39 H8
Capheaton Northum 45 E8
Cappercleuch Borders 48 G5
Capplegill Dumf/Gal 48 H4
Capton Devon 5 K7
Capton Som'set 6 B4
Caputh Tayside 52 C6
Car Colston Notts 32 F4
Carbis Bay Cornw'l 2 F2
Carbost H'land 62 C4
Carbost H'land 62 E3
Carbreck H'land 60 B4
Carbrook S Yorks 32 A1
Carbrooke Norfolk 26 E2
Carburton Notts 32 C3
Carclaze Cornw'l 3 D7
Carcluie S'clyde 47 H8
Carcroft S Yorks 36 F3
Cardenden Fife 53 H7
Cardeston Shrops 21 A9
Cardiff S Glam 14 G5
Cardigan Dyfed 12 B5
Cardington Beds 25 K2
Cardington Shrops 21 C10
Cardinham Cornw'l 3 C8
Cardorcan Dumf/Gal 42 D5
Cardow Gramp 56 E7
Cardrona Borders 48 F6
Cardross S'clyde 47 B8
Cardurnock Cumb 43 F12
Careby Lincs 24 D1
Careston Tayside 59 L3
Carew Dyfed 12 G4
Carew Cheriton Dyfed 12 G4
Carew Newton Dyfed 12 F4
Carewoodrig Borders 44 C3
Carey Heref/Worcs 15 A9
Carfin S'clyde 47 D12
Carfrae Lothian 49 B8
Cargenbridge Dumf/Gal 43 D10
Cargill Tayside 52 C6
Cargo Cumb 44 G2
Cargreen Cornw'l 3 C11
Carham Northum 49 F10
Carhampton Som'set 6 B4
Carharrack Cornw'l 2 F4
Carie Tayside 52 A1
Carinbrogie Gramp 58 E6
Carisbrooke I of Wight 8 G6
Cark Cumb 38 G6
Carkeel Cornw'l 3 D11
Carlatton Mill Cumb 44 H4
Carlby Lincs 24 D2
Carlecotes S Yorks 35 G10
Carleen Cornw'l 2 G3
Carleton Cumb 44 H3
Carleton Dumf/Gal 42 H5
Carleton N Yorks 35 B8
Carleton Forehoe Norfolk 26 E4
Carleton Rode Norfolk 26 F4
Carlidnack Cornw'l 2 G5
Carlin How Clevl'd 41 C7
Carlingcott Avon 15 H10
Carlisle Cumb 44 G2
Carlops Borders 48 D4
Carloway W Isles 63 C3
Carlton Beds 25 K1
Carlton Cambs 25 K7
Carlton Clevl'd 40 C4
Carlton Leics 23 B7
Carlton N Yorks 40 F6
Carlton N Yorks 40 G1
Carlton Notts 32 F3
Carlton S Yorks 35 F12
Carlton S Yorks 36 E4
Carlton Suffolk 27 J7
Carlton W Yorks 36 D1
Carlton Colville Suffolk 26 F8
Carlton Curlieu Leics 23 B10
Carlton Husthwaite N Yorks 40 G5
Carlton in Cleveland N Yorks 40 E5
Carlton in Lindrick Notts 32 B3
Carlton Miniott N Yorks 40 G4
Carlton Scroop Lincs 32 F6
Carlton-le-Moorland Lincs 32 D6
Carlton-on-Trent Notts 32 D5
Carluke S'clyde 48 D1
Carlyon Bay Cornw'l 3 D7
Carmacoup S'clyde 48 G1
Carmarthen Dyfed 13 E7
Carmel Clwyd 29 C11
Carmel Dyfed 13 E9
Carmel Gwyn 28 B3
Carmel Gwyn 28 E4
Carmel Chapel Dyfed 13 D10
Carmel Fell Cumb 38 F6
Carminish W Isles 63 H1
Carmont Gramp 59 J5
Carmunnock S'clyde 47 D11
Carmyllie Tayside 53 C10
Carnaby Humber 37 A9
Carnach H'land 55 G4
Carnach H'land 55 L1
Carnach W Isles 63 G3
Carnachuin H'land 57 K4
Carnachy H'land 61 C7
Carnaquheen Gramp 57 K8
Carnbee Fife 53 F10
Carnbo Tayside 52 G5
Carndow S'clyde 51 F9
Carndu H'land 55 G3
Carnduff S'clyde 47 E11
Carne Cornw'l 2 F6
Carnell S'clyde 47 F9
Carnetown Mid Glam 14 E4
Carnforth Lancs 39 H7
Carn-gorm H'land 55 G3
Carnhedryn Uchaf Dyfed 12 D2
Carnhell Green Cornw'l 2 F3
Carnie Gramp 59 G5
Carnish W Isles 63 D1
Carnkie Cornw'l 2 F4
Carno Powys 20 C5
Carnoch H'land 54 E6
Carnoch H'land 54 F7
Carnoch H'land 55 K2
Carnock Fife 52 H5
Carnon Downs Cornw'l 2 F5
Carnoustie Tayside 53 D10
Carnwath S'clyde 48 E3
Carog Gwyn 29 E7
Caroy H'land 62 D2
Carperby N Yorks 39 F12
Carr S Yorks 32 A2
Carr Cross Lancs 34 F3
Carr Shield Northum 44 H6
Carr Vale Derby 32 C2
Carra Grich W Isles 63 G3
Carradale S'clyde 46 E3
Carrbridge H'land 57 G5
Carrbrook Gtr Man 35 G8
Carreglefn Gwyn 28 A3
Carregwen Dyfed 12 C6
Carrick Fife 53 E9
Carrick S'clyde 51 H9
Carriden Lothian 48 A3
Carrington Gtr Man 34 H6
Carrington Lincs 33 E10
Carrington Lothian 48 C6
Carrog Clwyd 29 F10
Carron Gramp 56 E8
Carron Lothian 48 A2
Carron Bridge Central 47 A12
Carronbridge Dumf/Gal 43 B9
Carronshore Lothian 48 A2
Carrot S'clyde 47 E10
Carrow Hill Gwent 15 E7
Carrutherstown Dumf/Gal 43 D11
Carrville Durham 40 A3
Carsaig H'land 50 E3
Carsaig S'clyde 46 A2
Carscreugh Dumf/Gal 42 F3
Carse House S'clyde 46 C2
Carsebuie Dumf/Gal 42 E4
Carsegowan Dumf/Gal 42 F5
Carseriggan Dumf/Gal 42 E4
Carsethorn Dumf/Gal 43 F10
Carshalton London 18 G3
Carsington Derby 31 E11
Carskiey S'clyde 46 H2
Carsluith Dumf/Gal 42 F6
Carsphairn Dumf/Gal 42 B6
Carstairs S'clyde 48 E2
Carstairs Junction S'clyde 48 E2
Carter Bar Borders 44 B5
Carterhaugh Borders 49 G7
Carter's Clay Hants 8 D4
Carterton Oxon 16 C4
Carterway Heads Northum 45 H8
Carthew Cornw'l 3 D7
Carthorpe N Yorks 40 G3
Cartington Northum 45 C8
Cartland S'clyde 48 E1
Cartmel Cumb 38 G6
Carway Dyfed 13 F8
Cary Fitzpaine Som'set 7 D9
Caryshader W Isles 63 D2
Carzield Dumf/Gal 43 C10
Cascob Powys 21 F8
Cashlie Tayside 51 C12
Cashmoor Dorset 8 E1
Cassey Compton Glos 16 C1
Cassington Oxon 16 C5
Cassington Som'set 7 B7
Cassop Durham 40 A4
Casswell's Bridge Lincs 24 C3
Castell-y-bwch Gwent 14 E6
Casterton Cumb 39 G8
Castle Acre Norfolk 26 D1

Castle Ashby *Northants* 23 F11
Castle Bank *Staffs* 31 H7
Castle Bolton *N Yorks* 39 F12
Castle Bromwich *W Midlands* 22 C5
Castle Bytham *Lincs* 24 D1
Castle Caereinion *Powys* 21 B7
Castle Camps *Cambs* 25 L7
Castle Carrock *Cumb* 44 G4
Castle Cary *Som'set* 7 C10
Castle Combe *Wilts* 15 F11
Castle Donnington *Leics* 32 G2
Castle Douglas *Dumf/Gal* 43 E8
Castle Eaton *Wilts* 16 E2
Castle Eden *Durham* 40 A4
Castle Forbes *Gramp* 58 F4
Castle Frome *Heref/Worcs* 21 H12
Castle Green *Surrey* 17 H10
Castle Gresley *Derby* 31 H11
Castle Heaton *Northum* 49 E11
Castle Hedingham *Essex* 27 L1
Castle Hill *Kent* 10 D6
Castle Howard *N Yorks* 41 H7
Castle Huntly *Tayside* 53 D8
Castle Kennedy *Dumf/Gal* 42 F2
Castle Morris *Dyfed* 12 D3
Castle O'er *Dumf/Gal* 44 D1
Castle Pulverbatch *Shrops* 21 B9
Castle Rising *Norfolk* 24 C8
Castle Stuart *H'land* 56 E3
Castlebythe *Dyfed* 12 D4
Castlecary *S'clyde* 47 B12
Castlecraig *Borders* 48 E4
Castlecraig *H'land* 56 C4
Castlefairn *Dumf/Gal* 43 C8
Castleford *W Yorks* 36 E2
Castlehill *Borders* 48 F5
Castlehill *S'clyde* 47 B9
Castlehill *S'clyde* 48 D1
Castlemaddy *Dumf/Gal* 42 C6
Castlemartin *Dyfed* 12 G3
Castlemilk *Dumf/Gal* 43 D12
Castlemorton *Heref/Worcs* 15 A11
Castleside *Durham* 45 H9
Castlethorpe *Bucks* 23 H11
Castleton *Derby* 31 B10
Castleton *Gtr Man* 35 F7
Castleton *Gwent* 14 F6
Castleton *N Yorks* 41 D7
Castleton *S'clyde* 46 A4
Castleton *Tayside* 53 C8
Castletown *Dorset* 7 H7
Castletown *H'land* 56 E3
Castletown *H'land* 61 A11
Castletown *I of Man* 38 H1
Castletown *Tyne/Wear* 45 G11
Castley *N Yorks* 35 C11
Caston *Norfolk* 26 F3
Castor *Cambs* 24 F2
Caswell *W Glam* 13 H9
Cat and Fiddle Inn *Ches* 31 C8
Catacol *S'clyde* 46 D4
Catbrain *Avon* 15 F9
Catbrook *Gwent* 15 D8
Catchall *Cornw'l* 2 G2
Catcleugh *Northum* 44 C6
Catcliffe *S Yorks* 32 A2
Catcott *Som'set* 7 B7
Caterham *Surrey* 10 C2
Catfield *Norfolk* 26 C7
Catfirth *Shetl'd* 64 D7
Catford *London* 18 G4
Catforth *Lancs* 34 D4
Cathays *S Glam* 14 F5
Cathcart *S'clyde* 47 C10
Cathedine *Powys* 14 B5
Catherington *Hants* 9 E8
Catherston Leweston *Dorset* 7 G7
Catherton *Shrops* 21 E12
Cathpair *Borders* 49 E7
Catlins *Dumf/Gal* 43 C12
Catlodge *H'land* 57 K2
Catlowdy *Cumb* 44 E3
Catmore *Berks* 16 F5
Caton *Lancs* 34 A4
Catour Court *Devon* 5 H5
Catrine *Dorset* 7 G10
Catrine *S'clyde* 47 G10
Cat's Ash *Gwent* 15 E7
Cat's Common *Norfolk* 26 C6
Catsfield *E Sussex* 10 G6
Catshill *Heref/Worcs* 22 E3
Cattal *N Yorks* 36 B2
Cattawade *Suffolk* 27 M4
Catterall *Lancs* 34 C4
Catterick *N Yorks* 40 E3
Catterick Bridge *N Yorks* 40 E3
Catterick Camp *N Yorks* 40 E2
Catterlen *Cumb* 39 B7
Catterline *Gramp* 59 J6
Catterton *N Yorks* 36 C3
Catteshall *Surrey* 9 B11
Catthorpe *Leics* 23 D9
Cattistock *Dorset* 7 F9
Catton *N Yorks* 40 G4
Catton *Norfolk* 26 D5
Catton *Northum* 44 G6
Catwick *Humber* 37 C9
Catworth *Cambs* 25 H2
Caulcott *Oxon* 16 B6
Cauldhame *Central* 52 H1
Cauldmill *Borders* 44 B4
Cauldon *Staffs* 31 E9
Cauldside *Dumf/Gal* 44 E3
Cauldwell *Derby* 31 H11
Cauldwells *Gramp* 58 B5
Caulkerbush *Dumf/Gal* 43 F10
Caundle Marsh *Dorset* 7 E10
Caunsall *Heref/Worcs* 22 D2
Caunton *Notts* 32 D5
Causeway End *Dumf/Gal* 42 F5
Causewayend *Gramp* 58 F7
Causewayend *S'clyde* 48 F3
Causewayhead *Central* 52 H3
Causewayhead *Cumb* 43 F12
Causey Park Bridge *Northum* 45 D10
Cautley *Cumb* 39 F9
Cavendish *Suffolk* 27 K1
Cavenham *Suffolk* 27 H1
Caversfield *Oxon* 17 B7
Caversham *Berks* 17 G8
Caversta *W Isles* 63 E5
Caverswall *Staffs* 31 F8
Cavil *Humber* 36 D5
Cawdor *H'land* 56 E4
Cawood *N Yorks* 36 C3
Cawsand *Cornw'l* 3 E11
Cawston *Norfolk* 26 C4
Cawthorne *N Yorks* 41 F8
Cawthorne *S Yorks* 35 F11
Cawthorpe *Lincs* 24 C2
Cawton *N Yorks* 40 G6
Caxton *Cambs* 25 J4
Caynham *Shrops* 21 E11
Caythorpe *Lincs* 32 E6
Caythorpe *Notts* 32 F4
Cayton *N Yorks* 41 G10
Ceann-na-coille *H'land* 61 C7
Cefn Coch *Powys* 29 G10
Cefn Cribbwr *Mid Glam* 14 F2
Cefn Cross *Mid Glam* 14 F2
Cefn Einion *Shrops* 21 D8
Cefn Fforest *Gwent* 14 D5
Cefn Llaithan *Gwent* 15 B7
Cefn Mawr *Clwyd* 29 F12
Cefn Rhigos *Mid Glam* 14 D2
Cefn-Berain *Clwyd* 29 C9
Cefn-brith *Clwyd* 29 E8
Cefn-bryn-brain *Dyfed* 13 F10
Cefn-Canol *Clwyd* 29 G11
Cefn-coed-y-cymmer *Mid Glam* 14 C4
Cefn-ddwysarn *Gwyn* 29 F9
Cefneithin *Dyfed* 13 F9
Cefngorwydd *Powys* 20 H5
Cefn-y-Bedd *Clwyd* 29 E12
Cefn-y-pant *Dyfed* 12 D5
Cellan *Dyfed* 13 B9
Cellarhead *Staffs* 31 E8
Celleron *Cumb* 39 C7
Cemaes *Gwyn* 28 A3
Cemmaes *Powys* 20 B4
Cemmaes Road *Powys* 20 B4
Cenarth *Dyfed* 12 C6
Ceres *Fife* 53 F9
Cerist *Dyfed* 20 D5
Cerne Abbas *Dorset* 7 F10
Cerney Wick *Glos* 16 E2
Cerrigceinwen *Gwyn* 28 C4
Cerrigydrudion *Clwyd* 29 E9
Cess *Norfolk* 26 D7
Cessford *Borders* 49 G10
Ceunant *Gwyn* 28 D5
Chaceley *Glos* 15 A11
Chacewater *Cornw'l* 2 E5
Chackmore *Bucks* 17 A8
Chacombe *Northants* 23 H8
Chad Valley *W Midlands* 22 D4
Chadbury *Heref/Worcs* 22 G4
Chadderton *Gtr Man* 35 G7
Chaddesden *Derby* 31 F12
Chaddesley Corbett *Heref/Worcs* 22 E2
Chaddleworth *Berks* 16 F5
Chadlington *Oxon* 16 B4
Chadshunt *Warwick* 23 G7
Chadwell *Leics* 32 H5
Chadwell St. Mary *Essex* 18 F6
Chadwick End *W Midlands* 22 E5
Chaffcombe *Som'set* 7 E7
Chagford *Devon* 5 G6
Chailey *E Sussex* 10 F3
Chainbridge *Cambs* 24 E5
Chainhurst *Kent* 10 C6
Chalbury *Dorset* 8 E2
Chalbury Common *Dorset* 8 E2
Chaldon *Surrey* 10 C2
Chaldon Herring or East Chaldon *Dorset* 7 H11
Chale *I of Wight* 8 H6
Chale Green *I of Wight* 8 H6
Chalfont St. Giles *Bucks* 17 E10
Chalfont St. Peter *Bucks* 17 E11
Chalford *Glos* 15 D12
Chalford Common *Bucks* 17 E11
Chalgrove *Oxon* 17 D7
Chalk *Kent* 10 A5
Challacombe *Devon* 4 B6
Challacombe *Devon* 4 D6
Challoch *Dumf/Gal* 42 E5
Challock Lees *Kent* 11 C8
Chalton *Beds* 17 B11
Chalton *Hants* 9 E8
Chalvey *Bucks* 17 F10
Chalvington *E Sussex* 10 G4
Champany *Lothian* 48 B3
Chancery *Dyfed* 20 E1
Chandler's Cross *Herts* 17 D11
Chandler's Ford *Hants* 8 D6
Chanlockfoot *Dumf/Gal* 43 B8
Chantry *Som'set* 7 B10
Chapel *Fife* 53 H7
Chapel Allerton *Som'set* 7 A7
Chapel Allerton *W Yorks* 35 C11
Chapel Amble *Cornw'l* 3 B7
Chapel Brampton *Northants* 23 E10
Chapel Chorlton *Staffs* 30 F6
Chapel End *Warwick* 23 C7
Chapel Green *Warwick* 22 D6
Chapel Haddlesey *N Yorks* 36 D4
Chapel Hill *Gramp* 58 D8
Chapel Hill *Gwent* 15 D8
Chapel Hill *Lincs* 33 E9
Chapel Hill *N Yorks* 35 C12
Chapel Lawn *Shrops* 21 E8
Chapel le Dale *N Yorks* 39 G9
Chapel Mains *Borders* 49 E8
Chapel of Barras *Gramp* 59 J6
Chapel of Garioch *Gramp* 58 E5
Chapel Rossan *Dumf/Gal* 42 G2
Chapel Row *Berks* 16 G6
Chapel Row *E Sussex* 10 G5
Chapel St. Leonards *Lincs* 33 C12
Chapel Stile *Cumb* 38 E5
Chapeldonan *S'clyde* 42 B3
Chapel-en-le-Frith *Derby* 31 B9
Chapelhall *S'clyde* 47 C12
Chapelhill *Dumf/Gal* 43 B11
Chapelhill *Tayside* 52 D5
Chapelhope *Borders* 48 G5
Chapelknowe *Dumf/Gal* 44 F2
Chapels *Cumb* 38 G5
Chapelton *Devon* 4 C5
Chapelton *Dumf/Gal* 43 G8
Chapelton *Gramp* 59 J5
Chapelton *H'land* 57 H5
Chapelton *S'clyde* 47 E11
Chapelton *Tayside* 53 B11
Chapeltown *Gramp* 57 G8
Chapeltown *Lancs* 34 F6
Chapeltown *S Yorks* 35 G12
Chapmanslade *Wilts* 7 B11
Chapmore End *Herts* 18 B3
Chappel *Essex* 19 A9
Chard *Som'set* 7 E7
Chardstock *Devon* 6 F6
Charfield *Avon* 15 E10
Charing *Kent* 11 C8
Charing Cross *Dorset* 8 E3
Charing Heath *Kent* 11 C8
Charingworth *Glos* 22 H5
Charlbury *Oxon* 16 B5
Charlcombe *Avon* 15 H10
Charlcutt *Wilts* 16 G1
Charlecote *Warwick* 22 F6
Charles *Devon* 4 C6
Charlesfield *Dumf/Gal* 43 E12
Charleston *Tayside* 53 C8
Charlestown *Cornw'l* 3 E7
Charlestown *Dorset* 7 H10
Charlestown *Gramp* 59 G7
Charlestown *H'land* 54 B2
Charlestown *H'land* 56 E2
Charlestown *Lothian* 48 A3
Charlestown *W Yorks* 35 D8
Charlestown of Aberlour *Gramp* 56 E8
Charlesworth *Derby* 35 H9
Charleton *Devon* 5 L6
Charlton *Clevl'd* 40 D6
Charlton *Hants* 8 A5
Charlton *Heref/Worcs* 22 H4
Charlton *Herts* 18 A2
Charlton *Northants* 16 A6
Charlton *Northum* 44 D6
Charlton *W Sussex* 9 E10
Charlton *Wilts* 16 E1
Charlton *Wilts* 16 H2
Charlton *Wilts* 7 D12
Charlton *Wilts* 8 A3
Charlton *Wilts* 8 D3
Charlton Abbots *Glos* 16 B1
Charlton Adam *Som'set* 7 C9
Charlton Horethorne *Som'set* 7 D10
Charlton Kings *Glos* 16 B1
Charlton Mackrell *Som'set* 7 C8
Charlton Marshall *Dorset* 7 F12
Charlton Mires *Northum* 45 A10
Charlton Musgrove *Som'set* 7 C10
Charlton on the Hill *Dorset* 7 F12
Charlton-on-Otmoor *Oxon* 16 C6
Charlwood *Hants* 9 C8
Charlwood *Surrey* 10 D1
Charlynch *Som'set* 6 B6
Charminster *Dorset* 7 G10
Charmouth *Dorset* 7 G7
Charndon *Bucks* 17 B7
Charney Bassett *Oxon* 16 E5
Charnock Richard *Lancs* 34 F4
Charsfield *Suffolk* 27 J5
Chart Sutton *Kent* 11 C7
Charter Alley *Hants* 17 H7
Charterhouse *Borders* 49 F9
Charterhouse *Som'set* 7 A8
Charterville Allotments *Oxon* 16 C4
Chartham *Kent* 11 C9
Chartham Hatch *Kent* 11 B9
Chartridge *Bucks* 17 D10
Charvil *Berks* 17 G8
Charwelton *Northants* 23 G8
Chase Terrace *Staffs* 22 A4
Chasetown *Staffs* 22 A4
Chastleton *Oxon* 16 A3
Chasty *Devon* 4 F2
Chatburn *Lancs* 34 C6
Chatcull *Staffs* 30 G6
Chatham *Kent* 10 B6
Chathill *Northum* 45 E12
Chattenden *Kent* 10 A6
Chatteris *Cambs* 25 G5
Chattisham *Suffolk* 27 L4
Chatto *Borders* 44 A6
Chatton *Northum* 45 C12
Chaul End *Beds* 17 B11
Chawleigh *Devon* 4 E6
Chawston *Beds* 25 K3
Chawton *Hants* 9 B8
Cheadle *Gtr Man* 31 A7
Cheadle *Staffs* 31 F8
Cheadle Hulme *Gtr Man* 31 B7
Cheam *London* 18 G2
Cheapside *Berks* 17 G10
Chearsley *Bucks* 17 C8
Chebsey *Staffs* 31 G7
Checkendon *Oxon* 17 F7
Checkley *Ches* 30 F6
Checkley *Heref/Worcs* 21 H11
Checkley *Staffs* 31 F9
Chedburgh *Suffolk* 27 J1
Cheddar *Som'set* 7 A8
Cheddington *Bucks* 17 B10
Cheddleton *Staffs* 31 E8
Cheddon Fitzpaine *Som'set* 6 C6
Chedgrave *Norfolk* 26 E7
Chedington *Dorset* 7 F8
Chediston *Suffolk* 27 G7
Chedworth *Glos* 16 C2
Chedzoy *Som'set* 7 B7
Cheeklaw *Borders* 49 D10
Cheetham Hill *Gtr Man* 35 G7
Cheglinch *Devon* 4 B4
Cheldon *Devon* 4 E6
Chelford *Ches* 31 C7
Chellaston *Derby* 31 G12
Chellington *Beds* 25 K1
Chelmarsh *Shrops* 22 C1
Chelmondiston *Suffolk* 27 L5
Chelmorton *Derby* 31 C9
Chelmsford *Essex* 19 C7
Chelsea *London* 18 F3
Chelsfield Village *London* 18 G5
Chelsworth *Suffolk* 27 K3
Cheltenham *Glos* 15 B12
Cheltenham *Gwent* 14 C5
Chelveston *Northants* 25 H1
Chelvey *Avon* 15 G8
Chelwood *Avon* 15 H9
Chelwood Common *E Sussex* 10 E3
Chelwood Gate *E Sussex* 10 E3
Cheney Longville *Shrops* 21 D9
Chenies *Bucks* 17 D11
Chepstow *Gwent* 15 E8
Cherhill *Wilts* 16 G1
Cherington *Glos* 15 D12
Cherington *Warwick* 22 H6
Cheriton *Devon* 4 A6
Cheriton *Hants* 9 C7
Cheriton *Kent* 11 D10
Cheriton *W Glam* 13 H8
Cheriton Bishop *Devon* 4 F6
Cheriton Cross *Devon* 5 G6
Cheriton Fitzpaine *Devon* 6 F2
Cheriton or Stackpole Elidor *Dyfed* 12 G3
Cherrington *Shrops* 30 H5
Cherry Burton *Humber* 37 C7
Cherry Hinton *Cambs* 25 K6
Cherry Orchard *Heref/Worcs* 22 G2
Cherrybank *Tayside* 52 E6
Cherrytrees *Borders* 49 F10
Chertsey *Surrey* 17 G11
Cheselbourne *Dorset* 7 F11
Chesham *Bucks* 17 D10
Chesham Bois *Bucks* 17 D10
Cheshunt *Herts* 18 D4
Cheslyn Hay *Staffs* 22 A3
Chessington *London* 18 H2
Chester *Ches* 30 D3
Chester Moor *Durham* 45 H11
Chesterblade *Som'set* 7 B10
Chesterfield *Derby* 32 C1
Chesterfield *Staffs* 22 B4
Chesterhall *S'clyde* 48 F2
Chesterhill *Lothian* 48 C6
Chester-le-Street *Durham* 45 H11
Chesters *Borders* 44 B5
Chesters *Borders* 49 G8
Chesterton *Cambs* 24 F2
Chesterton *Ches* 31 E7
Chesterton *Oxon* 16 B6
Chesterton *Warwick* 23 F7
Chesterwood *Northum* 44 F6
Chestfield *Kent* 11 B10
Cheswardine *Shrops* 30 G6
Cheswick *Northum* 45 A11
Cheswick Bldgs *Northum* 45 A11
Chetnole *Dorset* 7 E9
Chettiscombe *Devon* 6 E3
Chettisham *Cambs* 25 G6
Chettle *Dorset* 8 E1
Chetton *Shrops* 21 C12
Chetwynd Aston *Shrops* 30 H6
Chetwynd Park *Shrops* 30 H6
Cheveley *Cambs* 25 J8
Chevening *Kent* 10 B4
Chevington *Suffolk* 27 J1
Chevithorne *Devon* 6 E3
Chew Magna *Avon* 15 H9
Chew Stoke *Avon* 15 H9
Chewton Keynsham *Avon* 15 H9
Chewton Mendip *Som'set* 7 A9
Chicheley *Bucks* 23 G12
Chichester *W Sussex* 9 F10
Chickerell *Dorset* 7 H9
Chicklade *Wilts* 7 C12
Chickward *Heref/Worcs* 21 G8
Chidden *Hants* 9 D8
Chiddingfold *Surrey* 9 C11
Chiddingly *E Sussex* 10 G4
Chiddingstone *Kent* 10 D4
Chiddingstone Causeway *Kent* 10 C4
Chiddingstone Hoath *Kent* 10 D4
Chideock *Dorset* 7 G7
Chidham *W Sussex* 9 F9
Chieveley *Berks* 16 G5
Chignall St. James *Essex* 18 C6
Chignall Smealy *Essex* 18 C6
Chigwell *Essex* 18 E4
Chigwell Row *Essex* 18 E5
Chilbolton *Hants* 8 B5
Chilcomb *Hants* 8 C6
Chilcombe *Dorset* 7 G9
Chilcompton *Som'set* 7 A9
Chilcote *Leics* 22 A6
Child Okeford *Dorset* 7 E11
Childrey *Oxon* 16 E5
Child's Ercall *Shrops* 30 H5
Childswickham *Heref/Worcs* 22 H4
Childwall *Mersey* 30 A3
Childwick Green *Herts* 18 C1
Chilfrome *Dorset* 7 F9
Chilgrove *W Sussex* 9 E9
Chilham *Kent* 11 C9
Chilhampton *Wilts* 8 C3
Chilla *Devon* 4 F3
Chillaton *Devon* 5 H3
Chillenden *Kent* 11 C11
Chillerton *I of Wight* 8 H6
Chillesford *Suffolk* 27 K7
Chillingham *Northum* 45 C12
Chillington *Devon* 5 L7
Chillington *Som'set* 7 E7
Chilmark *Wilts* 8 C1
Chilson *Oxon* 16 B4
Chilsworthy *Cornw'l* 3 B11
Chilsworthy *Devon* 4 E2
Chilthorne Domer *Som'set* 7 D8
Chilton *Bucks* 17 C8
Chilton *Devon* 4 E7
Chilton *Durham* 40 B3
Chilton *Oxon* 16 F6
Chilton Candover *Hants* 9 B7
Chilton Cantelo *Som'set* 7 D9
Chilton Foliat *Wilts* 16 G4
Chilton Lane *Durham* 40 B3
Chilton Polden *Som'set* 7 B7
Chilton Street *Suffolk* 27 K1
Chilton Trinity *Som'set* 6 B6
Chilwell *Notts* 32 G2
Chilworth *Hants* 8 D5
Chilworth *Surrey* 9 A11
Chimney *Oxon* 16 D4
Chineham *Hants* 9 A8
Chingford *London* 18 E4
Chinley *Derby* 31 B9
Chinley Head *Derby* 31 B9
Chinnor *Oxon* 17 D8
Chipnall *Shrops* 30 G6
Chippenham *Cambs* 25 H8
Chippenham *Wilts* 15 G12
Chipperfield *Herts* 17 D11
Chipping *Herts* 25 M5
Chipping *Lancs* 34 C5
Chipping Campden *Glos* 22 H5
Chipping Norton *Oxon* 16 B4
Chipping Sodbury *Avon* 15 F10
Chipping Warden *Northants* 23 G8
Chipstable *Som'set* 6 D4
Chipstead *Kent* 10 B4
Chipstead *Surrey* 10 B2
Chirbury *Shrops* 21 C8
Chirk *Clwyd* 29 F12
Chirk Green *Clwyd* 29 F12
Chirmorie *S'clyde* 42 D3
Chirnside *Borders* 49 D11
Chirnsidebridge *Borders* 49 D11
Chirton *Wilts* 16 H2
Chisbury *Wilts* 16 G4
Chiselborough *Som'set* 7 E8
Chiseldon *Wilts* 16 F3
Chislehampton *Oxon* 17 D7
Chislehurst *London* 18 G4
Chislet *Kent* 11 B11
Chisley *W Yorks* 35 D9
Chiswell Green *Herts* 18 C1
Chiswick *London* 18 F2
Chisworth *Derby* 35 H8
Chitcombe *E Sussex* 11 F7
Chithurst *W Sussex* 9 D9
Chittering *Cambs* 25 H6
Chitterne *Wilts* 8 B2
Chittlehamholt *Devon* 4 D5
Chittlehampton *Devon* 4 C5
Chittoe *Wilts* 15 H12
Chivelstone *Devon* 5 M6
Chivenor *Devon* 4 C4
Chobham *Surrey* 17 H10
Choicelee *Borders* 49 D10
Cholderton *Wilts* 8 B4
Cholesbury *Bucks* 17 C10
Chollerford *Northum* 45 F7
Chollerton *Northum* 45 F7
Cholsey *Oxon* 17 E7
Cholstrey *Heref/Worcs* 21 F10
Chop Gate *N Yorks* 40 E6
Choppington *Northum* 45 E10
Chopwell *Tyne/Wear* 45 G9
Chorley *Ches* 30 E4
Chorley *Lancs* 34 E5
Chorley *Shrops* 21 D12
Chorley *Staffs* 22 A4
Chorleywood *Herts* 17 E11
Chorlton *Ches* 30 E6
Chorlton cum Hardy *Gtr Man* 35 H7
Chorlton Lane *Ches* 30 E3
Chrishall *Essex* 25 L5

Christchurch *Cambs* 24 F6
Christchurch *Dorset* 8 G3
Christchurch *Gwent* 15 E7
Christian Malford *Wilts* 16 F1
Christleton *Ches* 30 D3
Christmas Common *Oxon* 17 E8
Christon *Som'set* 7 A7
Christon Bank *Northum* 45 A10
Christow *Devon* 5 G7
Chryston *S'clyde* 47 B11
Chudleigh *Devon* 5 H7
Chudleigh Knighton *Devon* 5 H7
Chulmleigh *Devon* 4 E6
Chunal *Derby* 35 H9
Church *Lancs* 34 D6
Church Aston *Shrops* 30 H6
Church Brampton *Northants* 23 E10
Church Broughton *Derby* 31 G10
Church Cove *Cornw'l* 2 H4
Church Crookham *Hants* 9 A9
Church Eaton *Staffs* 31 H7
Church End *Beds* 25 L3
Church End *Essex* 19 A7
Church End *Essex* 25 L7
Church End *Glos* 15 A12
Church End *Hants* 17 H7
Church End *Herts* 17 C12
Church End *Lincs* 24 E5
Church End *Lincs* 37 G12
Church End *London* 18 E3
Church End *Warwick* 22 C6
Church End *Wilts* 16 F1
Church Enstone *Oxon* 16 B5
Church Fenton *N Yorks* 36 C3
Church Green *Devon* 6 G5
Church Gresley *Derby* 31 H11
Church Hanborough *Oxon* 16 C5
Church Hill *Ches* 30 D5
Church House *N Yorks* 41 E7
Church Knowle *Dorset* 8 H1
Church Laneham *Notts* 32 C5
Church Langton *Leics* 23 C10
Church Lawford *Warwick* 23 D8
Church Lawton *Ches* 31 E7
Church Leigh *Staffs* 31 G9
Church Lench *Heref/Worcs* 22 G4
Church Minshull *Ches* 30 D5
Church Preen *Shrops* 21 C11
Church Pulverbatch *Shrops* 21 B9
Church Stoke *Powys* 21 C8
Church Stowe *Northants* 23 F9
Church Street *Kent* 10 A6
Church Street *Suffolk* 27 G8
Church Stretton *Shrops* 21 C10
Church Village *Mid Glam* 14 F4
Church Warsop *Notts* 32 C3
Churcham *Glos* 15 B11
Churchdown *Glos* 15 B12
Churchend *Avon* 15 E10
Churchend *Essex* 18 B6
Churchend *Essex* 19 E10
Churchfield *W Midlands* 22 C4
Churchill *Avon* 15 H7
Churchill *Devon* 4 B5
Churchill *Devon* 6 F6
Churchill *Heref/Worcs* 22 D2
Churchill *Heref/Worcs* 22 G3
Churchill *Oxon* 16 B4
Churchinford *Som'set* 6 E5
Churchover *Warwick* 23 D8
Churchstanton *Som'set* 6 E5
Churchstow *Devon* 5 L6
Churchtown *Cumb* 38 A6
Churchtown *Devon* 4 F2
Churchtown *I of Man* 38 G2
Churchtown *Lancs* 34 C4
Churchtown *Mersey* 34 E3
Churnsike Lodge *Northum* 44 E5
Churston Ferrers *Devon* 5 K8
Churt *Surrey* 9 B10
Churton *Ches* 30 E3
Churwell *W Yorks* 35 D11
Chute Standen *Wilts* 8 A5
Chwilog *Gwyn* 28 F4
Cilcain *Clwyd* 29 D11
Cilcennin *Dyfed* 13 A8
Cilfrew *W Glam* 13 G11
Cilfynydd *Mid Glam* 14 E4
Cilgerran *Dyfed* 12 C5
Cilgwyn *Dyfed* 12 C4
Ciliau Aeron *Dyfed* 13 A8
Cilmaengwyn *W Glam* 13 F10
Cilmery *Powys* 20 G5
Cilrhedyn *Dyfed* 12 D6
Cilsan *Dyfed* 13 E9
Ciltalgarth *Gwyn* 29 F8
Cilwendeg *Dyfed* 12 C6
Cilycwm *Dyfed* 13 C11
Cinderford *Glos* 15 C10
Cippyn *Dyfed* 12 B5
Cirencester *Glos* 16 D1
Citadel *H'land* 56 E2
Citadilla *N Yorks* 40 E2
City Dulas *Gwyn* 28 B4
Clachaig *H'land* 57 H6
Clachaig *S'clyde* 46 A6
Clachan *H'land* 50 C6
Clachan *H'land* 62 E5
Clachan *S'clyde* 46 D3
Clachan *S'clyde* 50 F5
Clachan *S'clyde* 51 F9
Clachan of Campsie *Central* 47 A11
Clachan of Glendaruel *S'clyde* 46 A5
Clachan-Seil *S'clyde* 50 F5
Clachbreck *S'clyde* 46 B3
Clachnabrain *Tayside* 59 L1
Clachnaharry *H'land* 56 E2
Clachtoll *H'land* 60 D2
Clackmannan *Central* 52 H4
Clackmarras *Gramp* 56 D8
Clacton on Sea *Essex* 19 B11
Cladance *S'clyde* 47 E11
Cladich *S'clyde* 51 E8
Claggan *H'land* 50 C4
Claggan *H'land* 55 M5
Clagh Ougr *I of Man* 38 G2
Claigan *H'land* 62 C2
Claines *Heref/Worcs* 22 F2
Clais Charnach *H'land* 60 A4
Claisfearn *H'land* 60 C3
Clandown *Avon* 7 A10
Clanfield *Hants* 9 D8
Clanfield *Oxon* 16 D4
Clanville *Hants* 8 A5
Clanyard *Dumf/Gal* 42 H2
Claonaig *S'clyde* 46 D4
Clap Gate *N Yorks* 35 B12
Clap Hill *Kent* 11 D9
Clapgate *Dorset* 8 F2
Clapham *Beds* 25 K1
Clapham *Devon* 6 H2
Clapham *London* 18 F3
Clapham *N Yorks* 39 H9
Clapham *W Sussex* 9 E12
Clappers *Borders* 49 D12
Clappersgate *Cumb* 38 E6
Clapton *Som'set* 7 A10
Clapton *Som'set* 7 F7
Clapton on the Hill *Glos* 16 B3
Clapton-in-Gordano *Avon* 15 G8
Clapworthy *Devon* 4 D5
Clarach *Dyfed* 20 D2
Clarbeston *Dyfed* 12 E4
Clarbeston Road *Dyfed* 12 E4
Clarborough *Notts* 32 B4
Clare *Suffolk* 27 L1
Clarencefield *Dumf/Gal* 43 E11
Clarilaw *Borders* 49 G8
Clarilawmoor *Borders* 49 F8
Clarken Green *Hants* 9 A7
Clarkston *S'clyde* 47 D10
Clashandoran *H'land* 56 E1
Clashcoig *H'land* 61 G7
Clashindarroch *Gramp* 58 D2
Clashmore *H'land* 61 G7
Clashnessie *H'land* 60 D2
Clashnoir *Gramp* 57 G8
Clatebrand *Dumf/Gal* 43 E8
Clatt *Gramp* 58 E3
Clatter *Powys* 20 C5
Clatterford *I of Wight* 8 G6
Clattering Bridge *Gramp* 59 J4
Clatteringhawes *Dumf/Gal* 42 D6
Clatworthy *Som'set* 6 C4
Claughton *Lancs* 34 A4
Claughton *Lancs* 34 C4
Claughton *Mersey* 30 A2
Clavelshay *Som'set* 6 C6
Claverdon *Warwick* 22 F5
Claverham *Avon* 15 H8
Clavering *Essex* 25 M6
Claverley *Shrops* 22 C2
Claverton *Avon* 15 H11
Clawdd-coch *S Glam* 14 F4
Clawddnewydd *Clwyd* 29 E10
Claws Top *Shrops* 21 E12
Clawthorpe *Cumb* 39 G8
Clawton *Devon* 4 F2
Claxby *Lincs* 33 C11
Claxby *Lincs* 37 H9
Claxton *N Yorks* 36 A5
Claxton *Norfolk* 26 E6
Clay Common *Suffolk* 27 G8
Clay Coton *Northants* 23 D9
Clay Cross *Derby* 32 D1
Claybokie *Gramp* 57 K6
Claybrooke Magna *Leics* 23 C8
Claybrooke Parva *Leics* 23 C8
Claydon *Oxon* 23 G8
Claydon *Suffolk* 27 K4
Clayfolds *Gramp* 59 H6
Claygate *Dumf/Gal* 44 E2
Claygate *Kent* 10 D6
Claygate *Surrey* 17 H12
Clayhanger *Devon* 6 D4
Clayhanger *W Midlands* 22 B4
Clayhidon *Devon* 6 E5
Clayhill *E Sussex* 11 F7
Clayhill *Hants* 8 E5
Claymires *Gramp* 58 E7
Claypole *Lincs* 32 E6
Clayton *S Yorks* 36 F2
Clayton *Staffs* 31 F7
Clayton *W Sussex* 10 G2
Clayton *W Yorks* 35 D10
Clayton Green *Lancs* 34 E5
Clayton West *W Yorks* 35 F11
Clayton-le-Moors *Lancs* 34 D6
Clayton-le-Woods *Lancs* 34 E4
Clayworth *Notts* 32 A4
Cleadon *Tyne/Wear* 45 G12
Clearbrook *Devon* 5 J4
Clearwell *Glos* 15 D9
Cleasby *N Yorks* 40 D3
Cleat *Orkney* 64 E2
Cleatlam *Durham* 40 C1
Cleator *Cumb* 38 D3
Cleator Moor *Cumb* 38 D3
Cleckheaton *W Yorks* 35 E10
Clecuhhead *Dumf/Gal* 43 B9
Clee St. Margaret *Shrops* 21 D11
Cleedownton *Shrops* 21 D11
Cleehill *Shrops* 21 E11
Cleestanton *Shrops* 21 D11
Cleethorpes *Humber* 37 F10
Cleeton St. Mary *Shrops* 21 E11
Cleeve *Avon* 15 H8
Cleeve *Oxon* 17 F7
Cleeve Hill *Glos* 16 A1
Cleeve Prior *Heref/Worcs* 22 G4
Clehonger *Heref/Worcs* 15 A8
Cleigh *S'clyde* 50 E6
Cleish *Tayside* 52 G6
Cleland *S'clyde* 48 D1
Clenamacrie *S'clyde* 50 E6
Clenaros House *H'land* 50 C2
Clench Common *Wilts* 16 H3
Clenchwarton *Norfolk* 24 C7
Clennell *Northum* 45 B7
Clent *Heref/Worcs* 22 D3
Cleobury Mortimer *Shrops* 21 E12
Cleobury North *Shrops* 21 D11
Clephanton *H'land* 56 E4
Clerkland *S'clyde* 47 E9
Clerklands *Borders* 49 G7
Clestran *Orkney* 64 D1
Cleuch Head *Borders* 44 B4
Cleuchbrae *Dumf/Gal* 43 D11
Cleuchfoot *Dumf/Gal* 44 E2
Cleuchheads *Dumf/Gal* 43 C12
Cleuchside *Dumf/Gal* 43 D12
Clevancy *Wilts* 16 G2
Clevedon *Avon* 15 G7
Cleveland Common *Clevl'd* 40 C5
Cleveland Tontine Inn *N Yorks* 40 E5
Cleveley *Oxon* 16 B5
Cleveleys *Lancs* 34 C2
Cleverton *Wilts* 16 F1
Clewer *Som'set* 7 A8
Cley-next-the-Sea *Norfolk* 26 A3
Cliasamol *W Isles* 63 F2
Cliburn *Cumb* 39 C8
Cliddesden *Hants* 9 A7
Cliff *H'land* 50 A4
Cliff *W Isles* 63 C2
Cliff End *E Sussex* 11 G7
Cliff Woods *Kent* 10 A6
Cliffburn *Tayside* 53 C11
Cliffe *Kent* 19 F7
Cliffe *N Yorks* 36 D4
Cliffe *N Yorks* 40 D2
Clifford *Devon* 4 D2
Clifford *Heref/Worcs* 21 H8
Clifford *W Yorks* 36 C2
Clifford Chambers *Warwick* 22 G5
Clifford's Mesne *Glos* 15 B10
Cliffsend *Kent* 11 B12
Clifton *Avon* 15 G9
Clifton *Beds* 25 L3
Clifton *Central* 51 D10
Clifton *Cumb* 39 C8
Clifton *Derby* 31 F10
Clifton *Heref/Worcs* 22 G2
Clifton *Lancs* 34 D3
Clifton *Lothian* 48 B4
Clifton *N Yorks* 35 B10
Clifton *N Yorks* 36 B4
Clifton *Northum* 45 E10
Clifton *Notts* 32 G3
Clifton *Oxon* 16 A6
Clifton *S Yorks* 36 G3
Clifton Campville *Staffs* 22 A6
Clifton Hampden *Oxon* 16 E6
Clifton Reynes *Bucks* 23 G12
Clifton upon Dunsmore *Warwick* 23 D8
Clifton upon Teme *Heref/Worcs* 21 F12
Cliftonville *Kent* 11 A12
Climping *W Sussex* 9 F11
Climpy *S'clyde* 48 D2
Clink *Som'set* 7 A11
Clint *N Yorks* 35 A11
Clint Green *Norfolk* 26 D3
Clintmains *Borders* 49 F8
Clippesby *Norfolk* 26 D7
Clipsham *Leics* 24 D1
Clipston *Northants* 23 D10
Clipston *Notts* 32 G4
Clipstone *Notts* 32 D3
Cliston *Devon* 4 F5
Clitheroe *Lancs* 34 C6
Clive *Shrops* 30 H4
Clivocast *Shetl'd* 64 B8
Clixby *Lincs* 37 G8
Clocaenog *Clwyd* 29 E10
Clochan *Gramp* 58 B1
Clochyrie *Dyfed* 13 F8
Clock Face *Mersey* 30 A4
Clockmill *Borders* 49 D10
Clodock *Heref/Worcs* 14 B6
Cloford *Som'set* 7 B10
Cloigyn *Dyfed* 13 F8
Clola *Gramp* 58 C7
Clophill *Beds* 25 L2
Clopton *Northants* 25 G2
Clopton Green *Suffolk* 27 K1
Close Clark *I of Man* 38 H1
Closeburn *Dumf/Gal* 43 B9
Closeburnmill *Dumf/Gal* 43 B10
Closworth *Som'set* 7 E9
Clothall *Herts* 25 M4
Clotton *Ches* 30 D4
Clough *W Yorks* 35 F9
Clough Foot *W Yorks* 35 E8
Cloughton *N Yorks* 41 F10
Cloughton Newlands *N Yorks* 41 F10
Clouster *Shetl'd* 64 D6
Clova *Gramp* 58 E2
Clova *Tayside* 59 K1
Clove Lodge *Durham* 39 C11
Clovelly *Devon* 4 D2
Clovenfords *Borders* 49 F7
Clovenstone *Gramp* 58 F5
Clovulin *H'land* 51 A7
Clow Bridge *Lancs* 35 D7
Clowne *Derby* 32 C2
Cluanie Inn *H'land* 55 H4
Cluanie Lodge *H'land* 55 H5
Cluddley *Shrops* 21 A11
Cluer *W Isles* 63 H2
Clun *Shrops* 21 D8
Clunbury *Shrops* 21 D9
Clune *Gramp* 56 E7
Clunes *H'land* 55 K6
Clungunford *Shrops* 21 E9
Clunie *Gramp* 58 C4
Clunie *Tayside* 52 C6
Clunton *Shrops* 21 D9
Cluny *Fife* 53 H7
Cluny Castle *H'land* 57 K2
Clutton *Avon* 15 H9
Clutton *Ches* 30 E3
Clydach *Gwent* 14 C5
Clydach *W Glam* 13 G10
Clydach Vale *Mid Glam* 14 E3
Clydebank *S'clyde* 47 B10
Clydey *Dyfed* 12 C6
Clyffe Pypard *Wilts* 16 F2
Clynder *S'clyde* 47 A7
Clynderwen *Dyfed* 12 E5
Clyne *W Glam* 13 G11
Clynelish *H'land* 61 F8
Clynnog-fawr *Gwyn* 28 E4
Clyro *Powys* 21 H7
Clyst Honiton *Devon* 6 G3
Clyst Hydon *Devon* 6 F4
Clyst St. George *Devon* 6 G3
Clyst St. Lawrence *Devon* 6 F4
Clyst St. Mary *Devon* 6 G3
Clywt-y-bont *Gwyn* 28 D5
Cnwch Coch *Dyfed* 20 E2
Coachford *Gramp* 58 C2
Coad's Green *Cornw'l* 3 B10
Coal Aston *Derby* 32 B1
Coalbrookdale *Shrops* 21 B12
Coalbrookvale *Gwent* 14 C5
Coalburn *S'clyde* 48 F1
Coalburns *Tyne/Wear* 45 G9
Coalcleugh *Northum* 39 A10
Coaley *Glos* 15 D11
Coalford *Gramp* 59 G6
Coalhall *S'clyde* 47 G9
Coalhill *Essex* 19 D7
Coalpit Heath *Avon* 15 F10
Coalpit Hill *Staffs* 31 E7
Coalport *Shrops* 21 B12
Coalsnaughton *Central* 52 H4
Coaltown of Balgonie *Fife* 53 G8
Coaltown of Wemyss *Fife* 53 H8
Coalville *Leics* 23 A8
Coalway *Glos* 15 C9
Coat *Som'set* 7 D8
Coatbridge *S'clyde* 47 C12
Coatdyke *S'clyde* 47 C12
Coate *Wilts* 16 F3
Coate *Wilts* 16 H2
Coates *Cambs* 24 F4
Coates *Glos* 16 D1
Coates *W Sussex* 9 D11
Coatham *Clevl'd* 40 C6
Coatham Mundeville *Durham* 40 C3
Coatsgate *Dumf/Gal* 43 A11
Cobbaton *Devon* 4 C5
Coberley *Glos* 15 C12
Cobham *Kent* 10 A5
Cobham *Surrey* 17 H11
Cobleland *Central* 51 H12
Cobnash *Heref/Worcs* 21 F10
Coburty *Gramp* 58 A7
Cock Bridge *Gramp* 57 H8
Cock Clarks *Essex* 19 D8
Cock Gate *Heref/Worcs* 21 F10
Cockayne *N Yorks* 40 E6
Cockayne Hatley *Beds* 25 K4
Cockburnspath *Lothian* 49 B10
Cockenzie and Port Seton *Lothian* 49 B7
Cockerham *Lancs* 34 B3
Cockermouth *Cumb* 38 B4
Cockernhoe *Herts* 18 B1
Cockfield *Durham* 40 C2
Cockfield *Suffolk* 27 K2
Cocking *W Sussex* 9 D10
Cockington *Devon* 5 J8
Cocklake *Som'set* 7 A8
Cocklaw *Northum* 45 F7
Cocklawfoot *Borders* 49 G11
Cockles *Lothian* 49 B8
Cockley Clet *Norfolk* 26 E1
Cockmuir *Gramp* 58 D4
Cockpole Green *Berks* 17 F9
Cockshutt *Shrops* 30 G3
Cockthorpe *Norfolk* 26 A3
Cockwood *Devon* 6 H3
Cockyard *Heref/Worcs* 15 A7
Codda *Cornw'l* 3 B9
Coddenham *Suffolk* 27 K4
Coddington *Ches* 30 E3
Coddington *Heref/Worcs* 21 H12
Coddington *Notts* 32 E5
Codford St. Mary *Wilts* 8 B1
Codford St. Peter *Wilts* 8 B1
Codicote *Herts* 18 B2
Codmore Hill *W Sussex* 9 D12
Codnor *Derby* 32 E1
Codrington *Avon* 15 F10
Codsall *Staffs* 22 B2
Codsall Wood *Staffs* 22 B2
Coed Morgan *Gwent* 15 C7
Coed Ystumgwern *Gwyn* 28 H5
Coedely *Mid Glam* 14 F4
Coedkernew *Gwent* 14 F6
Coedpoeth *Clwyd* 29 E12
Coedway *Powys* 21 A9
Coed-y-bryn *Dyfed* 13 C7
Coed-y-fedw *Gwent* 15 C7
Coed-yr-ynys *Powys* 14 B5
Coelbren *Powys* 14 C2
Coffinswell *Devon* 5 J8
Cofton *Devon* 6 H3
Cofton Hacket *Heref/Worcs* 22 E3
Cogan *S Glam* 14 G5
Cogenhoe *Northants* 23 F11
Coggeshall *Essex* 19 B8
Coggeshall Hamlet *Essex* 19 B8
Coignafearn Lo *H'land* 57 H2
Coignafeuinternich *H'land* 57 H3
Coignascallan *H'land* 57 H3
Coilacreich *Gramp* 59 H1
Coilintuie *H'land* 57 J4
Coillaig *S'clyde* 51 E7
Coille Mhorgil *H'land* 55 J5
Coillore *H'land* 62 D3
Coire Bhachdaidh *Tayside* 57 M1
Coity *Mid Glam* 14 F3
Col *W Isles* 63 C6
Colaboll *H'land* 60 F6
Colan *Cornw'l* 2 D6
Colaton Raleigh *Devon* 6 G4
Colbost *H'land* 62 C1
Colburn *N Yorks* 40 E2
Colbury *Hants* 8 E5
Colby *Cumb* 39 C9
Colby *I of Man* 38 H1
Colby *Norfolk* 26 B5
Colchester *Essex* 19 A10
Cold Ash *Berks* 16 G6
Cold Ashby *Northants* 23 D10
Cold Ashton *Avon* 15 G10
Cold Aston *Glos* 16 B2
Cold Blow *Dyfed* 12 F5
Cold Brayfield *Bucks* 23 G12
Cold Hanworth *Lincs* 33 B7
Cold Hatton *Shrops* 30 H5
Cold Hesledon *Durham* 45 H12
Cold Hiendley *W Yorks* 35 F12
Cold Higham *Northants* 23 G10
Cold Kirby *N Yorks* 40 G5
Cold Northcott *Cornw'l* 3 A9
Cold Norton *Essex* 19 D8
Cold Overton *Leics* 23 A11
Coldbackie *H'land* 60 B6
Coldbeck *Cumb* 39 E9
Coldean *E Sussex* 10 G2
Coldeast *Devon* 5 H7
Colden Common *Hants* 8 D6
Coldfair Green *Suffolk* 27 J7
Coldham *Cambs* 24 E5
Coldharbour *Glos* 15 D8
Coldharbour *Kent* 10 C4
Coldharbour *Surrey* 9 B12
Coldhome *Gramp* 58 C3
Coldingham *Borders* 49 C11
Coldrain *Tayside* 52 G6
Coldred *Kent* 11 C11
Coldridge *Devon* 4 E6
Coldstream *Borders* 49 E11
Coldwaltham *W Sussex* 9 D11
Coldwells Croft *Gramp* 58 E3
Cole *Som'set* 7 C10
Cole Green *Herts* 18 C3
Cole Henley *Hants* 8 A6
Colebatch *Shrops* 21 D8
Colebrook *Devon* 6 F3
Colebrooke *Devon* 4 F6
Coleburn *Gramp* 56 D8
Coleby *Humber* 37 E7
Coleby *Lincs* 33 D7
Coleford *Devon* 4 F6
Coleford *Glos* 15 C9
Coleford *Som'set* 7 A10
Colehill *Dorset* 8 F2
Coleman's Hatch *E Sussex* 10 E3
Colemere *Shrops* 30 G3
Colemore *Hants* 9 C8
Coleorton *Leics* 32 H1
Colerne *Wilts* 15 G11
Colesbourne *Glos* 16 C1
Colesden *Beds* 25 K2
Coleshill *Bucks* 17 E10
Coleshill *Oxon* 16 E3
Coleshill *Warwick* 22 C5
Colestocks *Devon* 6 F4
Colgate *W Sussex* 10 E1
Colgrain *S'clyde* 47 A8
Colinsburgh *Fife* 53 G9
Colinton *Lothian* 48 C5
Colintraive *S'clyde* 46 B5
Colkirk *Norfolk* 26 C2
Collace *Tayside* 53 D7
Collafirth *Shetl'd* 64 C7
Collamoor Head *Cornw'l* 2 B2
Collaton *Devon* 5 L4
Collaton St. Mary *Devon* 5 K7
Collenan *S'clyde* 47 F8
Collessie *Fife* 53 F7
Colleton Mills *Devon* 4 D5
Collier Row *London* 18 E5
Collier Street *Kent* 10 C6
Collieston *Gramp* 58 E8
Collin *Dumf/Gal* 43 D11
Collingbourne Ducis *Wilts* 8 A4
Collingbourne Kingston *Wilts* 8 A4
Collingham *W Yorks* 35 C12
Collington *Heref/Worcs* 21 F12
Collingtree *Northants* 23 G11
Collins Green *Ches* 34 H4
Colliston *Tayside* 53 C10
Colliton *Devon* 6 F4
Collmuir *Gramp* 59 G3
Collynie *Gramp* 58 D6
Collyweston *Northants* 24 E1
Colmonell *S'clyde* 42 C2

Colmworth *Beds* 25 J2
Coln Rogers *Glos* 16 C2
Coln St. Aldwyns *Glos* 16 D2
Coln St. Dennis *Glos* 16 C2
Colnabaichin *Gramp* 57 H8
Colnbrook *London* 17 F11
Colne *Cambs* 25 H5
Colne *Lancs* 35 C7
Colne Engaine *Essex* 27 M2
Colney *Norfolk* 26 E5
Colney Heath *Herts* 18 C2
Colney Street *Herts* 18 D2
Colpitts Grange *Northum* 45 G8
Colpy *Gramp* 58 D4
Colquhar *Borders* 48 E6
Colscott *Devon* 4 D2
Colsterdale *N Yorks* 40 G2
Colsterworth *Lincs* 32 H6
Colston Bassett *Notts* 32 G4
Coltfield *Gramp* 56 C7
Coltishall *Norfolk* 26 D6
Colton *Cumb* 38 G5
Colton *N Yorks* 36 C3
Colton *Norfolk* 26 D4
Colton *Staffs* 31 H9
Colton *W Yorks* 35 D12
Colva *Powys* 21 G7
Colvend *Dumf/Gal* 43 F9
Colwall Green *Heref/Worcs* 22 H1
Colwall Stone *Heref/Worcs* 22 H1
Colwell *Northum* 45 E8
Colwich *Staffs* 31 H8
Colwinston *S Glam* 14 G3
Colwith *Cumb* 38 E5
Colwith *Cumb* 38 E6
Colworth *W Sussex* 9 F10
Colwyn Bay *Clwyd* 29 B8
Colyford *Devon* 6 G6
Colyton *Devon* 6 G6
Comb *Northum* 44 D6
Combe *Berks* 16 H5
Combe *Heref/Worcs* 21 F9
Combe *Oxon* 16 C5
Combe Common *Surrey* 9 B11
Combe Florey *Som'set* 6 C5
Combe Martin *Devon* 4 A5
Combe Moor *Heref/Worcs* 21 F9
Combe Raleigh *Devon* 6 F5
Combe St. Nicholas *Som'set* 6 E6
Combebow *Devon* 5 G4
Combeinteignhead *Devon* 5 J8
Comberbach *Ches* 30 C5
Comberton *Cambs* 25 K5
Comberton *Heref/Worcs* 21 F10
Combpyne *Devon* 6 G6
Combridge *Staffs* 31 F9
Combrook *Warwick* 22 G6
Combs *Derby* 31 B9
Combs *Suffolk* 27 K3
Combwich *Som'set* 6 B6
Comers *Gramp* 59 G4
Comin Capel Betws *Dyfed* 20 G2
Comins-coch *Dyfed* 20 D2
Comins-coch *Powys* 20 B4
Comisty *Gramp* 58 C3
Common Moor *Cornw'l* 3 C9
Common Side *Derby* 32 C1
Commondale *N Yorks* 41 D7
Compstall *Gtr Man* 31 A8
Compstonend *Dumf/Gal* 43 F7
Compton *Berks* 16 F6
Compton *Devon* 5 J7
Compton *Hants* 8 C6
Compton *Surrey* 9 A11
Compton *W Sussex* 9 E9
Compton *Wilts* 8 A3
Compton Abbas *Dorset* 7 D12
Compton Abdale *Glos* 16 C2
Compton Bassett *Wilts* 16 G1
Compton Beauchamp *Oxon* 16 E4
Compton Bishop *Som'set* 7 A7
Compton Chamberlayne *Wilts* 8 C2
Compton Dando *Avon* 15 H9
Compton Dundon *Som'set* 7 C8
Compton Greenfield *Avon* 15 F9
Compton Martin *Som'set* 7 A8
Compton Pauncefoot *Som'set* 7 D10
Compton Valance *Dorset* 7 G9
Comrie *Fife* 52 H5
Comrie *Tayside* 52 E3
Conaglen House *H'land* 51 A7
Conchra *S'clyde* 46 A5
Conder Green *Lancs* 34 B3
Condicote *Glos* 16 A3
Condorrat *S'clyde* 47 B12
Condover *Shrops* 21 B10
Coney Weston *Suffolk* 27 G3
Coneyhurst Common *W Sussex* 9 D12
Coneysthorpe *N Yorks* 41 H7
Coneythorpe *N Yorks* 35 A12
Coneythorpe *N Yorks* 36 A2
Confunderland *Gramp* 58 F3
Congdon's Shop *Cornw'l* 3 B10
Congeith *Dumf/Gal* 43 E9
Congerstone *Leics* 23 B7
Congham *Norfolk* 24 C8
Congleton *Ches* 31 D7
Congl-y-wal *Gwyn* 28 F6
Congresbury *Avon* 15 H7
Conicavel *Gramp* 56 D5
Coningsby *Lincs* 33 D9
Conington *Cambs* 25 G3
Conington *Cambs* 25 J4
Conisbrough *S Yorks* 36 G3
Conisholme *Lincs* 37 H11
Coniston *Cumb* 38 E5
Coniston *Humber* 37 D9
Coniston Cold *N Yorks* 35 B7
Conistone *N Yorks* 39 H12
Connah's Quay *Clwyd* 29 C12
Connel *S'clyde* 50 D6
Connel Park *S'clyde* 47 H11
Connelbush *Dumf/Gal* 47 H12
Connor Downs *Cornw'l* 2 F3
Cononbridge *H'land* 56 D1
Cononley *N Yorks* 35 B8
Cononsyth *Tayside* 53 C10
Consall *Staffs* 31 E8
Consett *Durham* 45 H9
Constable Burton *N Yorks* 40 F2
Constantine *Cornw'l* 2 G4
Constantine Bay *Cornw'l* 2 B6
Contin *H'land* 54 D8
Conundrum *Northum* 49 D12
Conveth Mains *Gramp* 59 K5
Convinth *H'land* 56 F1
Conwy *Gwyn* 29 B7
Conyer *Kent* 11 B8
Conyer's Green *Suffolk* 27 H2
Cooden *E Sussex* 10 G6
Cookbury *Devon* 4 E3
Cookham *Berks* 17 F10
Cookham Dean *Berks* 17 F9
Cookham Rise *Berks* 17 F9
Cookhill *Heref/Worcs* 22 F4
Cookley *Heref/Worcs* 22 D2
Cookley *Suffolk* 27 H6
Cookley Green *Oxon* 17 E8
Cookney *Gramp* 59 H6
Cooksbridge *E Sussex* 10 G3
Cooksmill Green *Essex* 18 C6
Coolham *W Sussex* 9 D12
Cooling *Kent* 10 A6
Cooling *Kent* 19 F7
Cooling Street *Kent* 10 A6
Coombe *Cornw'l* 2 D6
Coombe *Cornw'l* 3 C9
Coombe *Cornw'l* 4 E1
Coombe *Devon* 6 D4
Coombe *Wilts* 8 A3
Coombe Bissett *Wilts* 8 C3
Coombe Down *Avon* 15 H11
Coombe Hay *Avon* 15 H10
Coombe Hill *Glos* 15 B12
Coombe Keynes *Dorset* 7 H11
Coombes *W Sussex* 10 G1
Coombs *Dyfed* 12 F3
Cooper's Corner *Kent* 10 C4
Cooper's Green *E Sussex* 10 F4
Coopersale Common *Essex* 18 D5
Cootham *W Sussex* 9 E12
Copdock *Suffolk* 27 L4
Copford Green *Essex* 19 B9
Copister *Shetl'd* 64 C7
Cople *Beds* 25 K2
Copley *Durham* 40 C1
Copmanthorpe *N Yorks* 36 B3
Coppathorne *Cornw'l* 2 A2
Coppenhall *Staffs* 31 H7
Copperhouse *Cornw'l* 2 F3
Coppingford *Cambs* 25 G3
Coppleridge *Dorset* 7 D11
Copplestone *Devon* 4 F6
Coppull *Lancs* 34 F4
Coppull Moor *Lancs* 34 F4
Copsale *W Sussex* 10 F1
Copster Green *Lancs* 34 D5
Copt Heath *W Midlands* 22 D5
Copt Hewick *N Yorks* 40 H4
Copt Oak *Leics* 23 A8
Copthorne *W Sussex* 10 D2
Copy's Green *Norfolk* 26 B2
Copythorne *Hants* 8 E5
Corbridge *Northum* 45 G8
Corby *Northants* 23 C12
Corby Glen *Lincs* 33 H7
Coreley *Shrops* 21 E11
Cores End *Bucks* 17 E10
Corfe *Som'set* 6 D6
Corfe Castle *Dorset* 8 H1
Corfe Mullen *Dorset* 8 F1
Corfton *Shrops* 21 D10
Corgariff *Gramp* 57 J8
Corhampton *Hants* 9 D7
Corley *Warwick* 22 D6
Corley Ash *Warwick* 22 C6
Corley Moor *Warwick* 22 D6
Cormiston *S'clyde* 48 F3
Cormonachan *S'clyde* 51 H9
Cormuir *Tayside* 53 A8
Corndavon Lodge *Gramp* 57 J8
Cornforth *Durham* 40 B3
Cornhill *Gramp* 58 B3
Cornhill-on-Tweed *Northum* 49 E11
Cornhills *Northum* 45 E8
Cornholme *W Yorks* 35 E8
Cornish Hall End *Essex* 25 L8
Cornsay *Durham* 40 A2
Cornsay Colliery *Durham* 40 A2
Corntown *H'land* 56 D1
Corntown *S Glam* 14 G3
Cornulloch *Gramp* 59 H2
Cornwell *Oxon* 16 A4
Cornwood *Devon* 5 K5
Cornworthy *Devon* 5 K7
Corpach *H'land* 55 M5
Corpusty *Norfolk* 26 C4
Corran *H'land* 51 A7
Corran *H'land* 55 J2
Corranbuie *S'clyde* 46 C3
Corrany *I of Man* 38 G2
Corribeg *H'land* 55 L4
Corrie *S'clyde* 46 E5
Corrie Common *Dumf/Gal* 43 C12
Corriecravie *S'clyde* 46 G4
Corriefeol *H'land* 54 E6
Corriegour *H'land* 55 K6
Corriemoillie *H'land* 54 C7
Corriemulzie Lo *H'land* 60 G4
Corrieviue *H'land* 54 E6
Corrievorrie *H'land* 57 G3
Corrimony *H'land* 55 G7
Corringham *Essex* 19 F7
Corringham *Lincs* 32 A6
Corris *Gwyn* 20 B3
Corrour Shooting Lodge *H'land* 51 A11
Corrow *S'clyde* 51 G9
Corry *H'land* 62 F6
Corry of Ardnagrask *H'land* 56 E1
Corrygills *S'clyde* 46 F5
Corryhully *H'land* 55 L3
Corrykinloch *H'land* 60 E5
Corrymuckloch *Tayside* 52 D4
Corrynachenchy *H'land* 50 C4
Corsback *H'land* 61 A11
Corsbie *Borders* 49 E8
Corscombe *Dorset* 7 F8
Corse *Gramp* 58 B7
Corse *Gramp* 58 D3
Corse of Kinnoir *Gramp* 58 C3
Corsebauld *Gramp* 59 J5
Corsehill *Gramp* 58 B7
Corsemalzie *Dumf/Gal* 42 F4
Corsham *Wilts* 15 G11
Corsindae *Gramp* 59 G4
Corsley *Wilts* 7 B11
Corsley Heath *Wilts* 7 B11
Corsliehill *S'clyde* 47 C9
Corsock *Dumf/Gal* 43 D8
Corston *Avon* 15 H10
Corston *Wilts* 15 F12
Corstorphine *Lothian* 48 B5
Cortachy *Tayside* 59 L1
Corton *Suffolk* 26 F8
Corton *Wilts* 8 B1
Corton Denham *Som'set* 7 D9
Coruanan Lo *H'land* 51 A8
Corwen *Clwyd* 29 F10
Coryates *Dorset* 7 H9
Coryton *Devon* 5 G3
Coryton *Essex* 19 F7
Cosby *Leics* 23 C9
Coseley *W Midlands* 22 C3
Cosford *Warwick* 23 D8
Cosgrove *Northants* 23 H11
Cosham *Hants* 9 F8
Cosheston *Dyfed* 12 G3
Coshieville *Tayside* 52 B3
Cossall *Notts* 32 F2
Cossington *Leics* 23 A9
Costa *Orkney* 64 B2
Costessey *Norfolk* 26 D5
Costock *Notts* 32 H3
Coston *Leics* 32 H6
Coston *Norfolk* 26 E4
Cote *Dumf/Gal* 44 C1
Cotebrook *Ches* 30 D4
Cotehill *Cumb* 44 H3
Cotes *Staffs* 31 G7
Cotesbach *Leics* 23 D8
Cotgrave *Notts* 32 G4
Cothall *Gramp* 58 F6
Cotham *Notts* 32 E5
Cothelstone *Som'set* 6 C5
Cotherstone *Durham* 39 C12
Cothill *Borders* 49 D10
Cothill *Oxon* 16 D6
Cotleigh *Devon* 6 F5
Cotmanhay *Derby* 32 F2
Coton *Cambs* 25 J5
Coton *Northants* 23 E10
Coton *Staffs* 31 G8
Coton *Staffs* 31 H7
Coton Clanford *Staffs* 31 H7
Coton in the Clay *Staffs* 31 G10
Coton in the Elms *Derby* 22 A6
Cott *Devon* 5 K6
Cottam *Lancs* 34 D4
Cottam *Notts* 32 B5
Cottenham *Cambs* 25 H5
Cotterdale *N Yorks* 39 F10
Cottered *Herts* 18 A3
Cotterstock *Northants* 24 F1
Cottertown *H'land* 56 F6
Cottesbrooke *Northants* 23 E10
Cottesmore *Leics* 23 A12
Cotteylands *Devon* 6 E3
Cottingham *Humber* 37 D8
Cottingham *Northants* 23 C11
Cottingley *W Yorks* 35 C9
Cottisford *Oxon* 17 A7
Cotton *Staffs* 31 F9
Cotton *Suffolk* 27 J4
Cotton End *Beds* 25 L2
Cottonshopeburn Foot *Northum* 44 C6
Cot-town *Gramp* 58 D6
Cot-town *Gramp* 58 E2
Cotwalton *Staffs* 31 G8
Cotwells *Gramp* 58 B5
Couchsmill *Cornw'l* 3 D8
Coughton *Heref/Worcs* 15 B9
Coughton *Warwick* 22 F4
Coulaghailtro *S'clyde* 46 C2
* Coulags *H'land* 54 E3
Couldoran *H'land* 54 E2
Coull *Gramp* 59 G3
Coulport *S'clyde* 47 A7
Coulsdon *London* 18 H3
Coulston *Wilts* 8 A1
Coulter *S'clyde* 48 F3
Coulton *N Yorks* 40 H6
Cound *Shrops* 21 B11
Coundon *Durham* 40 B3
Coundon *W Midlands* 22 D6
Coundon Grange *Durham* 40 B2
Countersett *N Yorks* 39 F11
Countess *Wilts* 8 B3
Countess Wear *Devon* 6 G3
Countesthorpe *Leics* 23 C9
Countisbury *Devon* 4 A6
Coupar Angus *Tayside* 53 C7
Coupland *Northum* 49 F12
Couple Cross *Som'set* 6 B3
Cour *S'clyde* 46 E3
Courance *Dumf/Gal* 43 C11
Court Corner *Hants* 17 H7
Court Henry *Dyfed* 13 E9
Courteachan *H'land* 55 K1
Courteenhall *Northants* 23 G11
Courtsend *Essex* 19 E10
Courtway *Som'set* 6 C5
Cousland *Lothian* 48 C6
Cousley Wood *E Sussex* 10 E5
Coustonn *S'clyde* 46 B6
Cove *Devon* 6 D3
Cove *H'land* 54 A2
Cove *Hants* 9 A10
Cove *S'clyde* 47 A7
Cove Bay *Gramp* 59 G7
Covehithe *Suffolk* 27 G8
Coven *Staffs* 22 A3
Coveney *Cambs* 25 G6
Covenham St. Bartholomew *Lincs* 37 H11
Covenham St. Mary *Lincs* 37 H11
Coventry *W Midlands* 23 D7
Coverack *Cornw'l* 2 H5
Coverham *N Yorks* 40 F1
Covington *Cambs* 25 H2
Cowan Bridge *Lancs* 39 G8
Cowbeech *E Sussex* 10 G5
Cowbit *Lincs* 24 D4
* Coulby Newham *Clevl'd* 40 D5
Cowbridge *S Glam* 14 G3
Cowbridge *Som'set* 6 B3
Cowden *Kent* 10 D3
Cowden *Northum* 45 E7
Cowdenbeath *Fife* 52 H6
Cowdenburn *Borders* 48 D5
Cowers Lane *Derby* 31 E11
Cowes *I of Wight* 8 F6
Cowesby *N Yorks* 40 F5
Cowfold *W Sussex* 10 F1
Cowie *Central* 52 H3
Cowie *Gramp* 59 J6
Cowley *Devon* 6 G3
Cowley *Glos* 15 C12
Cowley *London* 18 F1
Cowley *Oxon* 16 D6
Cowling *N Yorks* 35 C8
Cowling *N Yorks* 40 F3
Cowlinge *Suffolk* 25 K8
Cowpen *Northum* 45 E11
Cowpen Bewley *Clevl'd* 40 C5
Cowplain *Hants* 9 E8
Cowshill *Durham* 39 A10
Cowstrandburn *Fife* 52 H5
Cowthorpe *N Yorks* 36 B2
Cox Green *Berks* 17 F9
Coxbank *Ches* 30 F5
Coxbench *Derby* 31 F12
Coxford *Norfolk* 26 C1
Coxheath *Kent* 10 C6
Coxhill *Kent* 11 C11
Coxhoe *Durham* 40 B3
Coxley *Som'set* 7 B8
Coxtie Green *Essex* 18 D5
Coxwold *N Yorks* 40 G5
Coychurch *Mid Glam* 14 F3
Coylton *S'clyde* 47 G9
Coylumbridge *H'land* 57 H5
Coynach *Gramp* 59 G2
Coynachie *Gramp* 58 D2
Coytrahen *Mid Glam* 14 F2
Cozae Lodge *H'land* 54 F6
Crabtree *W Sussex* 10 F1
Crackaig *H'land* 61 F9
Crackenthorpe *Cumb* 39 C9
Crackington Haven *Cornw'l* 2 B2
Crackley *Warwick* 22 E6
Crackley Bank *Shrops* 22 A1
Crackpot *N Yorks* 39 E12
Cracoe *N Yorks* 35 A8
Craddock *Devon* 6 E4
Cradley *Heref/Worcs* 22 G1
Cradley Heath *W Midlands* 22 D3
Cradoc *Powys* 14 A3
Crafthole *Cornw'l* 3 D10
Cragend *Northum* 45 C9
Cragg *W Yorks* 35 E8
Craggan *H'land* 57 G6
Craggan *H'land* 60 G4
Craggan *S'clyde* 51 H10
Craggiemore *H'land* 56 F3
Craghead *Durham* 45 H10
Craibstone *Gramp* 58 B2
Craibstone *Gramp* 58 F6
Craichie *Tayside* 53 B10
Craig *Clwyd* 29 C10
Craig *Dumf/Gal* 43 D7
Craig *Dumf/Gal* 43 E8
Craig *H'land* 54 E4
Craig *S'clyde* 42 A5
Craig Lodge *S'clyde* 46 B5
Craig Trebanos *W Glam* 13 G10
Craiganour Lodge *Tayside* 52 A1
Craigbeg *H'land* 55 L8
Craigcaffie *Dumf/Gal* 42 E2
Craig-cefn-parc *W Glam* 13 G10
Craigdam *Gramp* 58 E6
Craigdarroch *Dumf/Gal* 43 C8
Craigdarroch *S'clyde* 43 A7
Craigdews *Dumf/Gal* 42 D6
Craigdhu *H'land* 54 F8
Craigearn *Gramp* 58 F5
Craigellachie *Gramp* 56 E8
Craigencallie *Dumf/Gal* 42 D6
Craigencross *Dumf/Gal* 42 E1
Craigend *S'clyde* 48 F1
Craigend *Tayside* 52 E6
Craigendoran *S'clyde* 47 A8
Craigengillan *S'clyde* 42 A5
Craigenrae *S'clyde* 42 C4
Craigens *S'clyde* 47 G10
Craiggiecat *Gramp* 59 H6
Craighead *Gramp* 56 F8
Craighead *S'clyde* 48 G2
Craigie *Gramp* 58 F6
Craigie *S'clyde* 47 F9
Craigie *Tayside* 52 C6
Craigieburn *Dumf/Gal* 43 A11
Craiglockhart *Lothian* 48 B5
Craigmaud *Gramp* 58 B6
Craigmore *S'clyde* 46 C6
Craigmoston *Gramp* 59 K4
Craignant *Shrops* 30 G1
Craigneil *S'clyde* 42 C2
Craigneston *Dumf/Gal* 43 C8
Craigneuk *S'clyde* 47 D12
Craignure *H'land* 50 D4
Craigo *Gramp* 59 L4
Craigow *Tayside* 52 F6
Craigrothie *Fife* 53 F8
Craigs *Fife* 53 G7
Craigton *Gramp* 59 G6
Craigton *H'land* 56 E2
Craigton *S'clyde* 47 D10
Craigton *Tayside* 53 B8
Craigton *Tayside* 53 C10
Craigtown *H'land* 61 B9
Craig-y-Duke *W Glam* 13 G10
Craig-y-nos *Powys* 13 E11
Craig-y-nos *Powys* 14 C2
Craik *Borders* 44 B2
Crail *Fife* 53 F10
Crailing *Borders* 49 G9
Crailinghall *Borders* 49 G9
Craimalloch *S'clyde* 42 B5
Craiselound *Humber* 36 G5
Crakemarsh *Staffs* 31 G9
Cramalt *Borders* 48 G5
Crambe *N Yorks* 36 A5
Cramlington *Northum* 45 E11
Cramond *Lothian* 48 B5
Cramond Bridge *Lothian* 48 B4
Cranachan *H'land* 55 L7
Cranage *Ches* 30 C6
Cranberry *Staffs* 31 G7
Cranborne *Dorset* 8 E2
Cranbourne *Berks* 17 G10
Cranbrook *Kent* 10 D6
Cranbrook Common *Kent* 10 D6
Crane Moor *S Yorks* 35 G11
Cranfield *Beds* 25 L1
Cranford *London* 18 F1
Cranford St. Andrew *Northants* 23 D12
Cranford St. John *Northants* 23 D12
Cranham *Glos* 15 C12
Cranham *London* 18 E6
Crank *Mersey* 34 G4
Cranleigh *Surrey* 9 B12
Cranmore *I of Wight* 8 G5
Cranna *Gramp* 58 B4
Crannach *Gramp* 58 B2
Crannich *H'land* 50 C2
Cranoe *Leics* 23 C11
Cransford *Suffolk* 27 J6
Cranshaws *Borders* 49 C9
Cranstal *I of Man* 38 F2
Cranswick *Humber* 37 B8
Crantock *Cornw'l* 2 D5
Cranwell *Lincs* 33 E7
Cranwich *Norfolk* 26 F1
Cranworth *Norfolk* 26 E3
Crapstone *Devon* 5 J4
Crarae *S'clyde* 51 H7
Crask Inn *H'land* 60 E6
Crask of Aigas *H'land* 54 E8
Craskie *H'land* 54 F7
Craskins *Gramp* 59 G3
Craster *Northum* 45 A10
Cratfield *Suffolk* 27 H6
Crathes *Gramp* 59 H5
Crathie *Gramp* 57 K8
Crathie *H'land* 57 K1
Crathorne *N Yorks* 40 D5
Craven Arms *Shrops* 21 D10
Crawcrook *Tyne/Wear* 45 G9
Crawford *S'clyde* 48 G2
Crawfordjohn *S'clyde* 48 G2
Crawfordton *Dumf/Gal* 43 B9
Crawick *Dumf/Gal* 47 H12
Crawley *Hants* 8 C6
Crawley *Oxon* 16 C4
Crawley *W Sussex* 10 D1
Crawley Down *W Sussex* 10 D2
Crawleyside *Durham* 39 A12
Crawshaw Booth *Lancs* 35 E7
Crawton *Gramp* 59 J6
Cray *N Yorks* 39 G11
Cray *Powys* 14 B2
Cray *Tayside* 52 A6
Crayford *London* 18 F5
Crayke *N Yorks* 40 H6
Crays Hill *Essex* 19 E7
Cray's Pond *Oxon* 17 F7
Crazies Hill *Berks* 17 F9
Creach Bheinn Lodge *H'land* 50 E4
Creacombe *Devon* 4 D7
Creag a Phuill *S'clyde* 51 G8
Creagan *S'clyde* 51 C7
Creagan Beag *S'clyde* 46 A3
Creaguaineach Lo *H'land* 51 A10
Creaton *Northants* 23 E10
Creca *Dumf/Gal* 44 F1
Credenhill *Heref/Worcs* 21 H10
Crediton *Devon* 4 F7
Creebank *S'clyde* 42 D4
Creebridge *Dumf/Gal* 42 E5

Creech Heathfield Som'set 6 D6
Creech St. Michael Som'set 6 D6
Creed Cornw'l 2 E6
Creekmouth London 18 F5
Creeside S'clyde 42 C4
Creeting St. Mary Suffolk 27 J4
Creeton Lincs 24 D1
Creetown Dumf/Gal 42 F6
Cregerina Powys 21 G7
Creggans S'clyde 51 G8
Cregneish I of Man 38 H1
Creg-ny-Baa I of Man 38 G2
Creich Fife 53 E8
Creigiau Mid Glam 14 F4
Crelevan H'land 54 F7
Cremyll Cornw'l 3 D11
Cressage Shrops 21 B11
Cresselly Dyfed 12 F4
Cressex Bucks 17 E9
Cressing Essex 19 B8
Cresswell Dyfed 12 F4
Cresswell Northum 45 D11
Cresswell Staffs 31 F8
Creswell Derby 32 C2
Cretingham Suffolk 27 J5
Cretshengan S'clyde 46 C2
Crew Green Powys 21 A8
Crewe Ches 30 E3
Crewe Ches 30 E6
Crewkerne Som'set 7 E8
Cribyn Dyfed 13 B8
Criccieth Gwyn 28 F4
Crich Derby 32 E1
Crichton Lothian 48 C6
Crick Gwent 15 E8
Crick Northants 23 E9
Crickadarn Powys 20 H6
Cricket Malherbie Som'set 7 E7
Cricket St. Thomas Som'set 7 E7
Crickheath Shrops 30 H2
Crickhowell Powys 14 B5
Cricklade Wilts 16 E2
Cridling Stubbs N Yorks 36 E3
Crieff Tayside 52 E3
Criggian Powys 21 A8
Crigglestone W Yorks 35 E11
Crimond Gramp 58 B8
Crimonmogate Gramp 58 B8
Crimplesham Norfolk 24 E7
Crinaglack H'land 54 F8
Crinan S'clyde 50 H5
Cringleford Norfolk 26 E3
Cringles W Yorks 35 B9
Crinow Dyfed 12 F5
Cripplestyle Dorset 8 E3
Cripp's Corner E Sussex 10 F6
Croasdale Cumb 38 C3
Crock Street Som'set 7 E7
Crockenhill Kent 10 A4
Crockernwell Devon 5 G6
Crockerton Wilts 7 B12
Crocket or Ninemile Bar Dumf/Gal 43 D9
Crockey Hill N Yorks 36 B4
Crockham Hill Kent 10 C3
Crockhurst Street Kent 10 D5
Crockleford Heath Essex 19 A10
Croeserw W Glam 14 E2
Croesgoch Dyfed 12 D2
Croes-Hywel Gwent 14 C6
Croes-lan Dyfed 13 C7
Croesor Gwyn 28 F6
Croesyceiliog Dyfed 13 E7
Croes-y-ceiliog Gwent 14 E6
Croes-y-mwyalch Gwent 14 E6
Croft Ches 34 H5
Croft Dyfed 12 C5
Croft Leics 23 C8
Croft Lincs 33 D12
Croft N Yorks 40 D3
Croftamie S'clyde 47 A9
Crofthead S'clyde 47 E12
Croftmill Tayside 52 C3
Croftmore H'land 57 H5
Croftnacriech H'land 56 E2
Crofton W Yorks 35 E12
Crofton Wilts 16 H4
Crofts of Haddo Gramp 58 D6
Crofts of Hillbrae Gramp 58 C3
Crofts of Meikle Ardo Gramp 58 D6
Crofty W Glam 13 G8
Croggan H'land 50 E4
Croglin Cumb 44 H4
Croick H'land 60 G5
Croir W Isles 63 C2
Cromarty H'land 56 C3
Cromasag H'land 54 D4
Cromblet Gramp 58 D5
Cromdale H'land 57 G6
Cromer Norfolk 26 A5
Cromford Derby 31 E11
Cromhall Avon 15 E10
Cromhall Common Avon 15 E10
Cromore W Isles 63 E5
Cromra H'land 57 K1
Cromwell Notts 32 D5
Cronberry S'clyde 47 G11
Crondall Hants 9 A9
Cronk-y-Voddy I of Man 38 G2
Cronton Mersey 30 A4
Crook Cumb 39 F7
Crook Durham 40 B2
Crook of Devon Tayside 52 G5
Crooke Gtr Man 34 F4
Crookedholm S'clyde 47 F9
Crookedstane S'clyde 48 H2
Crookes S Yorks 32 B1
Crookham Berks 16 H6
Crookham Northum 49 F11
Crookham Village Hants 9 A9
Crookham Westfield Northum 49 F11
Crookhaugh Borders 48 G4
Crookhouse Borders 49 G10
Crooklands Cumb 39 G8
Crookston S'clyde 47 C10
Crookston North Mains Borders 49 D7
Croome Court Heref/Worcs 22 H2
Cropredy Oxon 23 G8
Cropston Leics 23 A9
Cropthorne Heref/Worcs 22 H3
Cropton N Yorks 41 F8
Cropwell Bishop Notts 32 G4
Cropwell Butler Notts 32 F4
Crosbie S'clyde 47 D7
Crosby Cumb 43 H11
Crosby Humber 36 F6
Crosby I of Man 38 G2
Crosby Mersey 34 G2
Crosby Court N Yorks 40 F4
Crosby Garrett Cumb 39 D9
Crosby Ravensworth Cumb 39 D8
Crosby Villa Cumb 43 H11
Croscombe Som'set 7 B9
Cross Som'set 7 A7
Cross W Isles 63 A6
Cross Ash Gwent 15 B7
Cross Foxes Gwyn 20 A3
Cross Gates W Yorks 36 D2
Cross Green Suffolk 27 K2
Cross Green Suffolk 27 K3
Cross Hands Dyfed 12 F4
Cross Hands Dyfed 13 F9
Cross Hills N Yorks 35 C9
Cross Houses Shrops 21 B11
Cross in Hand E Sussex 10 F4
Cross in Hand Kent 10 C6
Cross Inn Dyfed 13 A7
Cross Inn Dyfed 13 A9
Cross Inn Dyfed 13 D11
Cross Inn Mid Glam 14 F4
Cross Keys Kent 10 C4
Cross Keys Wilts 15 G11
Cross Lanes Clwyd 30 F2
Cross Lanes Cornw'l 2 G4
Cross Lanes Dorset 7 F11
Cross Lanes N Yorks 36 A3
Cross Oak Powys 14 B4
Cross of Jackson Gramp 58 D5
Cross o'th Hands Derby 31 F11
Cross Street Suffolk 27 H5
Crossaig S'clyde 46 D3
Crossbost W Isles 63 D5
Crosscanonby Cumb 43 H11
Crossdale Street Norfolk 26 B5
Crossens Mersey 34 E3
Crossford Lothian 48 A3
Crossford S'clyde 48 E1
Crossgate Lincs 24 C3
Crossgatehall Lothian 48 C6
Crossgates Fife 52 H6
Crossgates N Yorks 35 A10
Crossgates N Yorks 40 H2
Crossgates Powys 20 F6
Crossgill Cumb 39 A9
Crossgill Lancs 34 A4
Crossgreen Devon 5 G3
Crossgreen Shrops 21 A10
Crosshall Borders 49 E10
Crosshands Dyfed 12 E5
Crosshands S'clyde 47 F9
Crosshill S'clyde 42 A4
Crosshill S'clyde 47 G9
Crosshill Tayside 52 G6
Crosshouse S'clyde 47 F9
Crossings Cumb 44 E3
Crosske S'clyde 47 C9
Crosskeys Gwent 14 E5
Crosskirk H'land 61 A10
Crosslands Cumb 38 F6
Crosslanes Shrops 30 H2
Crosslee Borders 48 G6
Crosslees S'clyde 47 D10
Crossleuch Borders 48 G5
Crossmichael Dumf/Gal 43 E8
Crossmoor Lancs 34 C3
Crosspost W Sussex 10 F1
Crossroads Gramp 59 H5
Crossroads S'clyde 47 F9
Crossroads W Yorks 35 C9
Cross-voe-sand Shetl'd 64 C6
Crossway Gwent 15 B8
Crossway Heref/Worcs 15 A9
Crossway Powys 20 G6
Crossway Green Heref/Worcs 22 E2
Crossways Dorset 7 G11
Crosswell Dyfed 12 C5
Crossword Dyfed 20 E2
Crosthwaite Cumb 39 F7
Croston Lancs 34 E4
Crostwick Norfolk 26 D6
Crouch Kent 10 C5
Crouch Hill Dorset 7 E10
Croucheston Wilts 8 D2
Croughton Northants 16 A6
Crovie Gramp 58 A5
Crow Hants 8 F3
Crow Edge S Yorks 35 G10
Crow Hill Heref/Worcs 15 B9
Crowan Cornw'l 2 F4
Crowborough E Sussex 10 E4
Crowcombe Som'set 6 C5
Crowden Derby 35 G9
Crowell Oxon 17 D8
Crowfield Northants 23 H9
Crowfield Suffolk 27 J4
Crowhurst E Sussex 10 G6
Crowhurst Surrey 10 C3
Crowhurst Lane End Surrey 10 C3
Crowland Lincs 24 D3
Crowlas Cornw'l 2 F2
Crowle Heref/Worcs 22 G3
Crowle Humber 36 F5
Crowlista W Isles 63 D1
Crowmarsh Gifford Oxon 17 E7
Crown Town Cornw'l 2 G3
Crownhill Devon 5 K4
Crownthorpe Norfolk 26 E4
Crows Dumf/Gal 42 F4
Crows-an-wra Cornw'l 2 G1
Crowthorne Berks 17 H9
Crowton Ches 30 C4
Croxall Staffs 22 A5
Croxby Lincs 37 G9
Croxdale Durham 40 B3
Croxden Staffs 31 F9
Croxley Green Herts 17 E11
Croxton Cambs 25 J3
Croxton Humber 37 F8
Croxton Norfolk 27 G2
Croxton Staffs 30 G6
Croxton Kerrial Leics 32 G5
Croy H'land 56 E3
Croy S'clyde 47 B12
Croyde Devon 4 B3
Croyde Bay Devon 4 B3
Croydon Cambs 25 K4
Croydon London 18 G3
Crubenmore Lo H'land 57 K2
Cruckmeole Shrops 21 A9
Cruckton Shrops 21 A9
Cruden Bay Gramp 58 D8
Crudgington Shrops 30 H5
Crudwell Wilts 16 E1
Crug Powys 21 E7
Crugmeer Cornw'l 2 B6
Cruive H'land 54 F8
Crulivig W Isles 63 D3
Crumlin Gwent 14 D5
Crumplehorn Cornw'l 3 E9
Crundale Dyfed 12 E3
Crundale Kent 11 C9
Crurie Dumf/Gal 44 D1
Crux Easton Hants 16 H5
Crwbin Dyfed 13 F8
Cryers Hill Bucks 17 D9
Crymych Dyfed 12 D5
Crynant Powys 13 F11
Cuaig H'land 54 D1
Cubbington Warwick 23 E7
Cubert Cornw'l 2 D5
Cublington Bucks 17 B9
Cuckfield W Sussex 10 F2
Cucklington Som'set 7 D11
Cuckney Notts 32 C3
Cuddesdon Oxon 17 D7
Cuddington Bucks 17 C8
Cuddington Ches 30 C4
Cuddington Heath Ches 30 F3
Cuddy Hill Lancs 34 C4
Cudham London 18 H4
Cudiptown Devon 5 H4
Cudworth S Yorks 36 F2
Cudworth Som'set 7 E7
Cuffern Dyfed 12 E2
Cuffley Herts 18 D3
Cuiashader W Isles 63 A6
Culbo H'land 56 D2
Culbokie H'land 56 D2
Culburnie H'land 56 E1
Culcabock H'land 56 E2
Culcairn H'land 56 C2
Culcharry H'land 56 E4
Culcheth Ches 34 H5
Culdrain Gramp 58 D3
Culduie H'land 54 F1
Culford Suffolk 27 H1
Culgaith Cumb 39 B8
Culham Oxon 16 E6
Culinlongart S'clyde 46 H2
Culkein H'land 60 D2
Culkein Drumbeg H'land 60 D3
Culkerton Glos 15 E12
Cullachie H'land 57 G5
Cullen Gramp 58 A3
Cullercoats Tyne/Wear 45 F12
Cullicudden H'land 56 C2
Culligran H'land 54 F7
Cullingworth W Yorks 35 D9
Cullipool S'clyde 50 F5
Cullivoe Shetl'd 64 B8
Culloch Tayside 52 E3
Cullochy H'land 55 J7
Culloden H'land 56 E3
Cullompton Devon 6 E4
Culm Davy Devon 6 E5
Culmaily H'land 61 G8
Culmalzie Dumf/Gal 42 F5
Culmington Shrops 21 D10
Culmstock Devon 6 E4
Culnacraig H'land 60 F2
Culnaightrie Dumf/Gal 43 F8
Culnaknock H'land 62 B4
Culquhirk Dumf/Gal 42 F5
Culrain H'land 60 G6
Culross Lothian 48 A3
Culroy S'clyde 47 H8
Culscadden Dumf/Gal 42 G5
Culsh Gramp 59 H1
Culshabbin Dumf/Gal 42 F4
Culswick Shetl'd 64 D6
Cultercullen Gramp 58 E7
Cults Dumf/Gal 42 G5
Cults Gramp 58 D3
Cults Gramp 59 G6
Cultybraggan Tayside 52 E3
Culverstone Green Kent 10 B5
Culverthorpe Lincs 33 F7
Culworth Northants 23 G9
Cumberhead S'clyde 47 F12
Cumberland Bower Northum 49 D12
Cumbernauld S'clyde 47 B12
Cumberworth Lincs 33 C12
Cuminestown Gramp 58 C5
Cumledge Borders 49 D10
Cummersdale Cumb 44 H2
Cummertrees Dumf/Gal 43 E12
Cummingstown Gramp 56 C7
Cumnock S'clyde 47 G10
Cumnor Oxon 16 D5
Cumrew Cumb 44 H4
Cumrue Dumf/Gal 43 C11
Cumstone Dumf/Gal 43 C12
Cumwhinton Cumb 44 H3
Cumwhitton Cumb 44 H3
Cundall N Yorks 40 H4
Cunninghamhead S'clyde 47 E8
Cunnister Shetl'd 64 B7
Cupar Fife 53 F8
Cupar Muir Fife 53 F8
Cupernham Hants 8 D5
Curbar Derby 31 C11
Curbridge Hants 9 E7
Curbridge Oxon 16 C4
Curdbridge Hants 9 E7
Curdworth Warwick 22 C5
Curin H'land 54 D7
Curland Som'set 6 E6
Currarie S'clyde 42 B2
Curridge Berks 16 G6
Currie Lothian 48 C4
Curry Mallet Som'set 7 D7
Curry Rivel Som'set 7 D7
Curtisden Green Kent 10 D6
Cury Cornw'l 2 G4
Cushnie Gramp 58 B5
Cushuish Som'set 6 C5
Cusop Heref/Worcs 21 H8
Cutcloy Dumf/Gal 42 H5
Cutcombe Som'set 6 B3
Cutnall Green Heref/Worcs 22 E2
Cutsdean Glos 16 A2
Cutthorpe Derby 31 C11
Cuxham Oxon 17 E7
Cuxton Kent 10 A6
Cuxwold Lincs 37 G9
Cwm Clwyd 29 C10
Cwm Gwent 14 D5
Cwm Cych Dyfed 12 C6
Cwm Ffrwd Oer Gwent 14 D6
Cwm Irfon Powys 20 G4
Cwm Penmachno Gwyn 29 E7
Cwmafon W Glam 13 H11
Cwmaman Mid Glam 14 D3
Cwmann Dyfed 13 B9
Cwmbach Dyfed 12 D6
Cwm-bach Mid Glam 14 D4
Cwm-bach Powys 20 G6
Cwm-bach Powys 21 H7
Cwmbelan Dyfed 20 D5
Cwmbran Gwent 14 E6
Cwmbrwyno Dyfed 20 D3
Cwmby Lincs 37 G8
Cwmcarn Gwent 14 E5
Cwmcarvan Gwent 15 D8
Cwm-Cewydd Gwyn 20 A4
Cwmcoy Dyfed 12 C6
Cwmdare Mid Glam 14 D3
Cwmdu Dyfed 13 D9
Cwm-du Powys 14 B5
Cwm-Duad Dyfed 13 D7
Cwmfelin Mid Glam 14 D4
Cwmfelin Mid Glam 14 E2
Cwmfelin Boeth Dyfed 12 E5
Cwmfelinfach Gwent 14 E5
Cwmfelin-Mynach Dyfed 12 E6
Cwmffrwd Dyfed 13 E7
Cwmgiedd Powys 14 C1
Cwmgors W Glam 13 F10
Cwmgwili Dyfed 13 F9
Cwmifor Dyfed 13 D10
Cwmisfael Dyfed 13 E8
Cwm-Llinau Powys 20 B4
Cwmllyfri Dyfed 13 F7
Cwmllynfell W Glam 13 F10
Cwm-Mawr Dyfed 13 F8
Cwmmiles Dyfed 12 E5
Cwm-Morgan Dyfed 12 D6
Cwmparc Mid Glam 14 E3
Cwmpengraig Dyfed 13 C7
Cwm-rhos Powys 14 B5
Cwmsychpant Dyfed 13 B8
Cwmtillery Gwent 14 D5
Cwmtwrch Isaf Powys 13 F11
Cwmtwrch Uchaf Powys 13 F11
Cwmwysg Powys 14 A2
Cwmyglo Gwyn 28 D5
Cwmyoy Gwent 14 B6
Cwmystwyth Dyfed 20 E3
Cwrt Gwyn 20 B2
Cwrtnewydd Dyfed 13 B8
Cwrt-y-Cadno Dyfed 13 C10
Cwrt-y-defaid W Glam 14 F1
Cwrt-y-gollen Gwent 14 C6
Cyffylliog Clwyd 29 D10
Cymau Clwyd 29 E12
Cymer W Glam 14 E2
Cymmer Mid Glam 14 E3
Cyncoed S Glam 14 F5
Cynghordy Dyfed 13 C11
Cynghordy W Glam 13 G10
Cynheidre Dyfed 13 F8
Cynonville W Glam 14 E2
Cynwyd Clwyd 29 F10
Cynwyl Elfed Dyfed 13 D7
Dacre Banks N Yorks 35 A10
Daddry Sheild Durham 39 A11
Dadford Bucks 23 H10
Dadlington Leics 23 B7
Dafen Dyfed 13 G8
Dagenham London 18 F5
Daglingworth Glos 16 D1
Dagnall Bucks 17 C10
Dail S'clyde 51 D8
Dail-na-mine Lo Tayside 57 M3
Dairsie or Osnaburgh Fife 53 E9
Dairymple S'clyde 47 H8
Daisy Hill Gtr Man 34 G5
Dalavich S'clyde 51 F7
Dalbeattie Dumf/Gal 43 E9
Dalbeg W Isles 63 B3
Dalblair S'clyde 47 G11
Dalbog Tayside 59 K3
Dalby I of Man 38 H1
Dalchalm H'land 61 F9
Dalchenna S'clyde 51 G8
Dalchonzie Tayside 52 E2
Dalchork H'land 60 F6
Dalchreichart H'land 55 H7
Dalchruin Tayside 52 E2
Dalchurin H'land 54 F3
Dalderby Lincs 33 D9
Dale Derby 32 F2
Dale Dyfed 12 F2
Dale Shetl'd 64 D6
Dale Head Cumb 39 D7
Dalebank Derby 32 D1
Dalehouse N Yorks 41 C8
Dalelia H'land 50 A5
Dalestie Gramp 57 H7
Dalfibble Dumf/Gal 43 C11
Dalfram S'clyde 47 G11
Dalgarven S'clyde 47 E8
Dalgety Bay Lothian 48 A4
Dalgig S'clyde 47 H10
Dalginross Tayside 52 E3
Dalguise Tayside 52 B5
Dalhalvaig H'land 61 B9
Dalham Suffolk 25 J8
Dalinlongart S'clyde 46 A6
Dalkeith Lothian 48 C6
Dallas Gramp 56 D7
Dalleagles S'clyde 47 H10
Dallinghoo Suffolk 27 K5
Dallington E Sussex 10 F5
Dallington Northants 23 F10
Dalmain Dacre Cumb 39 C7
Dalmakerran Dumf/Gal 43 B8
Dalmally S'clyde 51 E9
Dalmary Central 51 H12
Dalmellington S'clyde 42 A6
Dalmeny Lothian 48 B4
Dalmeny Rows Lothian 48 B4
Dalmichy H'land 60 F6
Dalmigavie Lodge H'land 57 G3
Dalmore H'land 56 B1
Dalmore H'land 56 C2
Dalmore W Isles 63 B3
Dalmuir S'clyde 47 B10
Dalmunach Gramp 56 E8
Dalnabreck H'land 50 A4
Dalnacardoch Lodge Tayside 57 M3
Dalnacorn Tayside 52 A4
Dalnahaitnach H'land 57 H4
Dalnamain H'land 61 G7
Dalnaspidal Tayside 57 M2
Dalnawillan Lo H'land 61 C10
Dalness H'land 51 B9
Dalnessie H'land 61 E7
Daloist Tayside 52 A3
Dalqueich Tayside 52 G6
Dalquhairn S'clyde 42 B4
Dalreavoch H'land 61 F7
Dalriach Tayside 52 A2
Dalry S'clyde 47 D8
Dalserf S'clyde 48 D1
Dalston Cumb 44 H2
Dalswinton Dumf/Gal 43 C10
Dalton Dumf/Gal 43 D12
Dalton Lancs 34 F4
Dalton N Yorks 40 D1
Dalton N Yorks 40 G4
Dalton Northum 45 F9
Dalton Northum 45 G7
Dalton S Yorks 32 A2
Dalton Piercy Clevl'd 40 B5
Dalton-in-Furness Cumb 38 H5
Dalton-le-Dale Durham 45 H12
Dalton-on-Tees N Yorks 40 D3
Daltot S'clyde 46 A3
Dalvadie Dumf/Gal 42 F2
Dalveich Central 52 E1
Dalvennan S'clyde 47 H9
Dalvina Lodge H'land 61 C7
Dalwhat Dumf/Gal 43 B8
Dalwhinnie H'land 57 L2
Dalwood Devon 6 F6
Damerham Hants 8 D3
Damgate Norfolk 26 E7
Damnaglaur Dumf/Gal 42 H2
Damside Borders 48 D4
Danaway Border Kent 11 B7
Danbury Essex 19 C8
Danby N Yorks 41 D7
Danby Wiske N Yorks 40 E3
Dandaleith Gramp 56 E8
Danderhall Lothian 48 B6
Dane End Herts 18 B3
Dane Hills Leics 23 B9
Danebridge Ches 31 D8
Danehill E Sussex 10 E3
Dangerous Corner Gtr Man 34 F4
Dan's Castle Durham 40 A1
Danskine Lothian 49 C8
Danzey Green Warwick 22 E5
Daren-felen Gwent 14 C5
Darenth Kent 10 A4
Daresbury Ches 30 B4
Darfield S Yorks 36 G2
Dargate Kent 11 B9
Dargues Northum 45 D7
Darite Cornw'l 3 C9
Darlaston W Midlands 22 C3
Darley N Yorks 35 A10
Darley Bridge Derby 31 D11
Darlingscott Warwick 22 H6
Darlington Durham 40 D3
Darliston Shrops 30 G4
Darlton Notts 32 C5
Darnall S Yorks 32 A1
Darnaway Castle Gramp 56 D5
Darnconner S'clyde 47 G10
Darngarroch Dumf/Gal 43 E7
Darnick Borders 49 F8
Darowen Powys 20 B4
Darra Gramp 58 C5
Darracott Devon 4 B3

Darracott *Devon* **4** D1
Darras Hall *Northum* **45** F9
Darrington *W Yorks* **36** E3
Darsham *Suffolk* **27** H7
Dartford *Kent* **10** A4
Dartington *Devon* **5** J6
Dartmeet *Devon* **5** H5
Dartmouth *Devon* **5** K7
Darton *S Yorks* **35** F11
Darvel *S'clyde* **47** F10
Darwen *Lancs* **34** E6
Datchet *Berks* **17** F10
Datchworth *Herts* **18** B3
Datchworth Green *Herts* **18** B3
Daubill *Gtr Man* **34** F6
Dauntsey *Wilts* **16** F1
Dauntsey Green *Wilts* **16** F1
Dauntsey Lock *Wilts* **16** F1
Davenham *Ches* **30** C5
Daventry *Northants* **23** F9
David's Well *Powys* **20** E6
Davidson's Mains *Lothian* **48** B5
Davidston *H'land* **56** C3
Davidstow *Cornw'l* **3** A8
Davington *Dumf/Gal* **44** C1
Daviot *Gramp* **58** E5
Daviot *H'land* **56** F3
Davis Street *Berks* **17** G9
Davoch of Grange *Gramp* **58** C2
Daw Cross *N Yorks* **35** B11
Dawesgreen *Surrey* **10** C1
Dawley *Shrops* **21** B12
Dawlish *Devon* **5** H8
Dawlish Wake *Som'set* **7** E7
Dawlish Warren *Devon* **6** H3
Dawn *Clwyd* **29** C8
Daws Heath *Essex* **19** E8
Daw's House *Cornw'l* **3** A10
Dawsmere *Lincs* **24** C5
Daylesford *Glos* **16** B3
Ddol *Clwyd* **29** C10
Deadwater *Northum* **44** C4
Deadwaters *S'clyde* **47** E12
Deal *Kent* **11** C12
Dean *Cumb* **38** C3
Dean *Devon* **4** B4
Dean *Devon* **4** B5
Dean *Devon* **5** J6
Dean *Dorset* **8** D1
Dean *Hants* **9** D7
Dean *Som'set* **7** B10
Dean Prior *Devon* **5** J6
Dean Row *Ches* **31** B7
Dean Street *Kent* **10** C6
Deanburnhaugh *Borders* **44** B2
Deane *Gtr Man* **34** F6
Deane *Hants* **9** A7
Deanich Lodge *H'land* **60** H5
Deanland *Dorset* **8** D2
Deans *Lothian* **48** C3
Deanscales *Cumb* **38** C3
Deanshanger *Northants* **23** H11
Deanston *Central* **52** G2
Dearham *Cumb* **38** B3
Dearne *S Yorks* **36** G2
Debach *Suffolk* **27** K5
Debden *Essex* **25** M7
Debden Estate *Essex* **18** D4
Debden Green *Essex* **25** M7
Debenham *Suffolk* **27** J5
Dechmont *Lothian* **48** B3
Deddington *Oxon* **16** A6
Dedham *Essex* **27** M4
Deebank *Gramp* **59** H4
Deecastle *Gramp* **59** H2
Deene *Northants* **23** C12
Deenethorpe *Northants* **24** F1
Deepcut *Surrey* **17** H10
Deeping Gate *Lincs* **24** E3
Deeping St. James *Lincs* **24** E3
Deeping St. Nicholas *Lincs* **24** D3
Deerhill *Gramp* **58** B2
Deerhurst *Glos* **15** A11
Deerness *Orkney* **64** D3
Defford *Heref/Worcs* **22** H3
Defynnog *Powys* **14** B3
Deganwy *Gwyn* **29** B7
Dehewid *Dyfed* **13** A7
Deighton *N Yorks* **36** C4
Deighton *N Yorks* **40** E4
Deighton *W Yorks* **35** E10
Deiniolen *Gwyn* **28** D5
Delabole *Cornw'l* **3** A8
Delamere *Ches* **30** C4
Delamford *S'clyde* **42** B4
Delchirach *Gramp* **56** F7
Delfrigs *Gramp* **58** E7
Dell Lodge *H'land* **57** H6
Delliefure *H'land* **56** F6
Delnabo *Gramp* **57** H7
Delnadamph Lo *Gramp* **57** J8
Delnamer *Tayside* **57** M7
Deloraineshiel *Borders* **48** H6
Delph *Gtr Man* **35** F8
Delves *Durham* **45** H9
Dembleby *Lincs* **24** B1
Denaby Main *S Yorks* **36** G3
Denbie Mains *Dumf/Gal* **43** D11
Denbigh *Clwyd* **29** D10
Denbury *Devon* **5** J7
Denby *Derby* **32** F1
Denby Dale *W Yorks* **35** F11
Denchworth *Oxon* **16** E5
Denend *Gramp* **58** D3
Denford *Northants* **25** H1
Dengie *Essex* **19** D9
Denham *Bucks* **17** E11
Denham *Suffolk* **27** H5
Denham *Suffolk* **27** J1
Denhead *Fife* **53** F9
Denhead *Gramp* **58** B7
Denhead *Gramp* **58** E7
Denholm *Borders* **49** G8
Denholme *W Yorks* **35** D9
Denmead *Hants* **9** E8
Dennington *Suffolk* **27** H6
Denny *Lothian* **48** A1
Denny Bottom *Kent* **10** D4
Denny Lodge *Hants* **8** E5
Dennyloanhead *Lothian* **48** A1
Denshaw *Gtr Man* **35** F8
Denside *Gramp* **59** H5
Denston *Suffolk* **27** K1
Denstone *Staffs* **31** F9
Dent *Cumb* **39** F9
Denton *Cambs* **25** G2
Denton *Durham* **40** C2
Denton *E Sussex* **10** H3
Denton *Gtr Man* **35** H8
Denton *Kent* **11** C11
Denton *Lincs* **32** G6
Denton *N Yorks* **35** B10
Denton *Norfolk* **27** G6
Denton *Northants* **23** F11
Denton *Oxon* **17** D7
Denver *Norfolk* **24** E7
Denwick *Northum* **45** B10
Denwick Lane End *Northum* **45** A10
Deopham *Norfolk* **26** E3
Deopham Green *Norfolk* **26** F3
Deptford *Devon* **4** D1
Deptford *Devon* **4** D5
Deptford *London* **18** F4
Deptford *Wilts* **8** B2
Derby *Derby* **31** G11
Derbyhaven *I of Man* **38** H1
Derculich *Tayside* **52** B4
Deri *Mid Glam* **14** D5
Deri-Odwyn *Dyfed* **20** F2
Derringstone *Kent* **11** C10
Derrington *Staffs* **31** H7
Derry *Central* **52** E1
Derry Hill *Wilts* **15** G12
Derryguaig *H'land* **50** D2
Derrythorpe *Humber* **36** F6
Dersingham *Norfolk* **24** C8
Dervaig *H'land* **50** B2
Derwen *Clwyd* **29** E10
Derwlwyn *Dyfed* **13** C9
Desborough *Northants* **23** D11
Desford *Leics* **23** B8
Detchant *Northum* **45** B12
Detling *Kent* **11** B7
Deuddwr *Powys* **29** H11
Devauden *Gwent* **15** D8
Devenick *Gramp* **59** G7
Devil's Bridge *Dyfed* **20** E3
Devizes *Wilts* **16** H1
Devonburn *S'clyde* **48** E1
Devonport *Devon* **3** D11
Devonside *Central* **52** G4
Devoran *Cornw'l* **2** F5
Dewar *Borders* **48** D6
Dewlish *Dorset* **7** F11
Dewsall Court *Heref/Worcs* **15** A8
Dewsbury *W Yorks* **35** E11
Dhoon *I of Man* **38** G2
Dhoor *I of Man* **38** F2
Dhowin *I of Man* **38** F2
Dial Post *W Sussex* **9** D12
Dibden *Hants* **8** E5
Dibden Purlieu *Hants* **8** E5
Dickleburgh *Norfolk* **27** G5
Didbrook *Glos* **16** A2
Didcot *Oxon* **16** E6
Diddington *Cambs* **25** J3
Diddlebury *Shrops* **21** D10
Didley *Heref/Worcs* **15** A7
Didling *W Sussex* **9** D10
Didmarton *Glos* **15** F11
Didsbury *S Yorks* **35** G12
Didworthy *Devon* **5** J5
Diebidale Lodge *H'land* **60** H5
Digby *Lincs* **33** E8
Digg *H'land* **62** A4
Diggle *Gtr Man* **35** F9
Digmoor *Lancs* **34** G4
Digswell Water *Herts* **18** B3
Dihewid *N Yorks* **34** A8
Dikeneuk *S'clyde* **47** D11
Dilham *Norfolk* **26** C6
Dilhorne *Staffs* **31** F8
Dillarburn *S'clyde* **48** E1
Dillington *Cambs* **25** J2
Dilston *Northum* **45** G8
Dilton Marsh *Wilts* **7** A11
Dilwyn *Heref/Worcs* **21** G9
Dinanrig *S'clyde* **48** H1
Dinas *Dyfed* **12** C4
Dinas *Dyfed* **12** D6
Dinas *Gwyn* **28** G2
Dinas Dinlle *Gwyn* **28** D4
Dinas Mawddwy *Gwyn* **20** A4
Dinas Powis *S Glam* **14** G5
Dinasbach *Dyfed* **13** C11
Dinder *Som'set* **7** B9
Dinedor *Heref/Worcs* **15** A8
Dinedor Cross *Heref/Worcs* **15** A8
Dingestow *Gwent* **15** C8
Dingle *Mersey* **30** B2
Dingleton *Borders* **49** F8
Dingley *Northants* **23** C11
Dingwall *H'land* **56** D1
Dinlabyre *Borders* **44** D4
Dinley *Dumf/Gal* **44** C3
Dinmael *Gwyn* **29** F9
Dinnet *Gramp* **59** H2
Dinning *Dumf/Gal* **43** C9
Dinnington *Northum* **45** F10
Dinnington *S Yorks* **32** B3
Dinnington *Som'set* **7** E7
Dinorwic *Gwyn* **28** D5
Dinsdale Station *Durham* **40** D4
Dinton *Bucks* **17** C8
Dinton *Wilts* **8** C2
Dinvin *Dumf/Gal* **42** F1
Dinwoodie Mains *Dumf/Gal* **43** C11
Dinwoodiegreen *Dumf/Gal* **43** C11
Dinworthy *Devon* **4** D2
Dippen *S'clyde* **46** F3
Dippen *S'clyde* **46** G5
Dippenhall *Hants* **9** A9
Dipple *Gramp* **58** B1
Dipple *S'clyde* **42** A3
Diptford *Devon* **5** K6
Dipton *Durham* **45** H9
Dirleton *Lothian* **49** A8
Discoed *Powys* **21** F8
Diseworth *Leics* **32** H2
Dishforth *N Yorks* **40** H4
Disley *Ches* **31** B8
Diss *Norfolk* **27** G4
Disserth *Powys* **20** G6
Distington *Cumb* **38** C2
Ditchampton *Wilts* **8** C2
Ditcheat *Som'set* **7** C9
Ditchingham *Norfolk* **26** F6
Ditchling *E Sussex* **10** F2
Ditteridge *Wilts* **15** G11
Dittisham *Devon* **5** K7
Ditton *Ches* **30** B3
Ditton *Kent* **10** B6
Ditton Green *Cambs* **25** J8
Ditton Priors *Shrops* **21** D11
Divach *H'land* **57** G1
Divlyn *Dyfed* **13** C11
Dixton *Glos* **16** A1
Dixton *Gwent* **15** C8
Dobcross *Gtr Man* **35** F8
Dobwalls *Cornw'l* **3** C9
Doccombe *Devon* **5** G6
Dochfour House *H'land* **56** F2
Dochgarroch *H'land* **56** F2
Docking *Norfolk* **26** B1
Docklow *Heref/Worcs* **21** G11
Dockray *Cumb* **38** C6
Dodburn *Borders* **44** B3
Doddinghurst *Essex* **18** D6
Doddington *Cambs* **24** F5
Doddington *Kent* **11** B8
Doddington *Lincs* **32** C6
Doddington *Northum* **49** F12
Doddington *Shrops* **21** E11
Doddiscombsleigh *Devon* **6** H2
Dodford *Heref/Worcs* **22** E3
Dodford *Northants* **23** F9
Dodington *Avon* **15** F10
Dodington *Som'set* **6** B5
Dodleston *Ches* **30** D2
Dodworth *S Yorks* **35** G11
Doe Lea *Derby* **32** D2
Dog Village *Devon* **6** G3
Dogdyke *Lincs* **33** E9
Dogmersfield *Hants* **9** A9
Dolanog *Powys* **20** A6
Dolau *Mid Glam* **14** F3
Dolau *Powys* **21** F7
Dolbenmaen *Gwyn* **28** F4
Dolfach *Powys* **20** E5
Dol-ffanog *Gwyn* **20** A3
Dol-for *Powys* **20** B4
Dol-for *Powys* **20** D6
Dolgarrog *Gwyn* **29** C7
Dolgellau *Gwyn* **28** H6
Dolgerdd *Dyfed* **13** B7
Dol-goch *Gwyn* **20** B2
Dol-gran *Dyfed* **13** D8
Dolhelfa *Powys* **20** E5
Doll *H'land* **61** F8
Dollar *Central* **52** G4
Dollarbeg *Central* **52** G4
Dolley Green *Powys* **21** F8
Dolleycanney *Powys* **21** G7
Dolphinholme *Lancs* **34** B4
Dolphinton *S'clyde* **48** E4
Dolton *Devon* **4** E4
Dolwen *Clwyd* **29** C8
Dolwen *Powys* **20** B5
Dolwyd *Gwyn* **29** B7
Dolwyddelan *Gwyn* **29** E7
Dol-y-Bont *Dyfed* **20** D2
Dolypandy *Dyfed* **20** D2
Doncaster *S Yorks* **36** G4
Donhead St. Andrew *Wilts* **8** D1
Donhead St. Mary *Wilts* **7** D12
Donibristle *Fife* **52** H6
Doniford *Som'set* **6** B4
Donington *Lincs* **24** B3
Donington *Shrops* **22** B2
Donington on Bain *Lincs* **33** B9
Donington South Ing *Lincs* **24** B3
Donisthorpe *Leics* **22** A6
Donkey Town *Surrey* **17** H10
Donkleywood *Northum* **44** D6
Donnington *Berks* **16** G6
Donnington *Glos* **16** A3
Donnington *Heref/Worcs* **15** A10
Donnington *Shrops* **21** A12
Donnington *Shrops* **21** B11
Donnington *W Sussex* **9** F10
Donnington Wood *Shrops* **21** A12
Donyatt *Som'set* **7** E7
Doonbank *S'clyde* **47** H9
Doonfoot *S'clyde* **47** G8
Doonholm *S'clyde* **47** H8
Dorback Lodge *H'land* **57** H6
Dorchester *Dorset* **7** G10
Dorchester *Oxon* **17** E7
Dordon *Warwick* **22** B6
Dore *S Yorks* **31** B11
Dores *H'land* **56** F2
Dorket Head *Notts* **32** E3
Dorking *Surrey* **10** C1
Dormansland *Surrey* **10** D3
Dormanstown *Clevl'd* **40** C6
Dormington *Heref/Worcs* **21** H11
Dornal *S'clyde* **42** D4
Dorney *Bucks* **17** F10
Dornie *H'land* **55** G3
Dornoch *H'land* **61** G8
Dornock *Dumf/Gal* **44** F1
Dorrery *H'land* **61** B10
Dorridge *W Midlands* **22** E5
Dorrington *Lincs* **33** E8
Dorrington *Shrops* **21** B10
Dorsington *Warwick* **22** G5
Dorstone *Heref/Worcs* **21** H8
Dorton *Bucks* **17** C7
Dorusduain *H'land* **55** G3
Dosmuckeran *H'land* **54** D6
Dosthill *Staffs* **22** B6
Dottery *Dorset* **7** G8
Doublebois *Cornw'l* **3** C9
Dougarie *S'clyde* **46** F4
Doughton *Glos* **15** E12
Douglas *I of Man* **38** H2
Douglas *S'clyde* **48** F1
Douglas & Angus *Tayside* **53** D9
Douglas Hill *Gwyn* **28** D5
Douglas Water *S'clyde* **48** F2
Douglas West *S'clyde* **48** F1
Douglastown *Tayside* **53** B9
Doulting *Som'set* **7** B10
Dounby *Orkney* **64** C1
Doune *Central* **52** G2
Doune *H'land* **55** J1
Doune *H'land* **57** J4
Doune *H'land* **60** F5
Doune of Relugas *Gramp* **56** E5
Doune Park *Gramp* **58** B4
Dounepark *S'clyde* **42** B3
Douneside *Gramp* **59** G2
Dounie *H'land* **60** G6
Doura *S'clyde* **47** F9
Dousland *Devon* **5** J4
Dove Holes *Derby* **31** B9
Dovenby *Cumb* **38** B3
Dover *Kent* **11** D12
Dovercourt *Essex* **27** M5
Doverdale *Heref/Worcs* **22** F2
Doveridge *Derby* **31** G9
Dowally *Tayside* **52** B5
Dowbridge *Lancs* **34** D3
Dowdeswell *Glos* **16** B1
Dowhill *S'clyde* **42** A3
Dowlais *Mid Glam* **14** D4
Dowland *Devon* **4** E4
Down Ampney *Glos* **16** D2
Down Hatherley *Glos* **15** B11
Down St. Mary *Devon* **4** E6
Down Thomas *Devon* **5** L4
Downan *Gramp* **56** F7
Downan *S'clyde* **42** C2
Downderry *Cornw'l* **3** D10
Downe *London* **18** H4
Downend *Avon* **15** G9
Downend *Berks* **16** G6
Downend *I of Wight* **9** G7
Downfield *Tayside* **53** D8
Downgate *Cornw'l* **3** B10
Downham *Cambs* **25** G6
Downham *Essex* **19** D7
Downham *Lancs* **34** C6
Downham *Northum* **49** F11
Downham Market *Norfolk* **24** E7
Downhead *Som'set* **7** B10
Downhead *Som'set* **7** D9
Downhill *Tayside* **52** D6
Downholland Cross *Lancs* **34** F2
Downholme *N Yorks* **40** E1
Downies *Gramp* **59** H7
Downley *Bucks* **17** E9
Downside *Avon* **15** H8
Downside *Som'set* **7** A10
Downside *Som'set* **7** B9
Downside *Surrey* **17** H12
Downton *Hants* **8** G4
Downton *Wilts* **8** D3
Downton on the Rock *Heref/Worcs* **21** E9
Dowsby *Lincs* **24** C2
Doxford *Northum* **45** A10
Doynton *Avon* **15** G10
Draethen *Mid Glam* **14** F5
Draffan *S'clyde* **48** E1
Dragons Green *W Sussex* **9** D12
Drakeholes *Notts* **32** A4
Drakeholes *Notts* **36** H5
Drakeland Corner *Devon* **5** K4
Drakemyre *S'clyde* **47** D8
Drake's Broughton *Heref/Worcs* **22** G3
Drakes Cross *Heref/Worcs* **22** D4
Drakewalls *Cornw'l* **3** C11
Draughton *N Yorks* **35** B9
Draughton *Northants* **23** D11
Drax *N Yorks* **36** D5
Draycot Foliat *Wilts* **16** F3
Draycote *Warwick* **23** E8
Draycott *Derby* **32** G2
Draycott *Glos* **16** A3
Draycott *Som'set* **7** A8
Draycott in the Clay *Staffs* **31** G10
Draycott in the Moors *Staffs* **31** F8
Drayford *Devon* **4** E6
Drayton *Hants* **9** E8
Drayton *Heref/Worcs* **22** E3
Drayton *Leics* **23** C11
Drayton *Lincs* **24** B3
Drayton *Norfolk* **26** D5
Drayton *Oxon* **16** E6
Drayton *Oxon* **23** H8
Drayton *Som'set* **7** D7
Drayton Bassett *Staffs* **22** B5
Drayton Beauchamp *Bucks* **17** C10
Drayton Parslow *Bucks* **17** A9
Drayton St. Leonard *Oxon* **17** D7
Drebley *N Yorks* **35** A9
Dreenhill *Dyfed* **12** F3
Dre-fach *Dyfed* **13** B8
Drefach *Dyfed* **13** C7
Drefach *Dyfed* **13** F8
Dreghorn *S'clyde* **47** F8
Drellingore *Kent* **11** D11
Drem *Lothian* **49** A8
Drewsteignton *Devon* **5** G6
Driby *Lincs* **33** C11
Driffield *Glos* **16** D2
Driffield *Humber* **37** A8
Drigg *Cumb* **38** E3
Drighlington *W Yorks* **35** D11
Drimfern *S'clyde* **51** F8
Drimmies *Gramp* **58** E5
Drimnin *H'land* **50** B3
Drimpton *Dorset* **7** F7
Drimsallie *H'land* **55** L3
Drimsynie *S'clyde* **51** G9
Drinishader *W Isles* **63** G3
Drinkstone *Suffolk* **27** J3
Drinkstone Green *Suffolk* **27** J3
Drishaig *S'clyde* **51** F8
Drochil *Borders* **48** E4
Drointon *Staffs* **31** G9
Droitwich *Heref/Worcs* **22** F2
Dron *Tayside* **52** F6
Dronfield *Derby* **32** B1
Dronfield Woodhouse *Derby* **31** B11
Drongan *S'clyde* **47** G9
Dronley *Tayside* **53** D8
Drope *S Glam* **14** G4
Droxford *Hants* **9** D7
Droylsden *Gtr Man* **35** G8
Druid *Clwyd* **29** F9
Druidhall *Dumf/Gal* **43** B9
Druidston *Dyfed* **12** E2
Druimarbin *H'land* **55** M5
Druimavuic *S'clyde* **51** C7
Druimyeon More *S'clyde* **46** D2
Drum *H'land* **56** D2
Drum *S'clyde* **46** B4
Drum *Tayside* **52** G5
Drumbeg *H'land* **60** D3
Drumblade *Gramp* **58** D3
Drumblair House *Gramp* **58** C4
Drumbuie *Dumf/Gal* **42** C6
Drumbuie *H'land* **55** G2
Drumburgh *Cumb* **44** G1
Drumburn *Dumf/Gal* **43** E10
Drumchapel *S'clyde* **47** B10
Drumchardine *H'land* **56** E1
Drumclog *S'clyde* **47** E11
Drumcoltran *Dumf/Gal* **43** E9
Drumcroy *H'land* **56** F1
Drumcruilton *Dumf/Gal* **43** A9
Drumdaig *Gramp* **58** F3
Drumdrishaig *S'clyde* **46** B2
Drumdyre *H'land* **56** D2
Drumeldrie *Fife* **53** G9
Drumelzier *Borders* **48** F4
Drumfearn *H'land* **62** G6
Drumfork *S'clyde* **47** G10
Drumgask *H'land* **57** K2
Drumgley *Tayside* **53** B9
Drumguish *H'land* **56** F6
Drumguish *H'land* **57** J4
Drumhead *Gramp* **58** F7
Drumindarroch *H'land* **54** F8
Drumjohn *Dumf/Gal* **42** B6
Drumlanrig Castle *Dumf/Gal* **43** B9
Drumlasie *Gramp* **59** G4
Drumlemble *S'clyde* **46** G2
Drumligair *Gramp* **58** F6
Drumlithie *Gramp* **59** J5
Drummoddie *Dumf/Gal* **42** G5
Drummond *H'land* **56** C2
Drummore *Dumf/Gal* **42** H2
Drummuir *Gramp* **58** C1
Drumnadrochit *H'land* **57** G1
Drumnagair *Gramp* **59** K4
Drumnagorrach *Gramp* **58** B3
Drumnahoy *Gramp* **58** F4
Drumnunie *H'land* **60** F3
Drumonk *Gramp* **59** H5
Drumpail *Dumf/Gal* **42** E3
Drumpark *Dumf/Gal* **43** D9
Drumrae *Dumf/Gal* **42** G5
Drumrash *Dumf/Gal* **43** D7
Drums *Gramp* **58** E7
Drumshang *S'clyde* **47** H7
Drumstinchall *Dumf/Gal* **43** F9
Drumstudy *Tayside* **53** D9
Drumtochty Castle *Gramp* **59** J4
Drumuie *H'land* **62** D4
Drumuillie *H'land* **57** G5
Drumvaich *Central* **52** G2
Drumwalt *Dumf/Gal* **42** F4
Drumwhindle *Gramp* **58** D7
Drumwhirn *Dumf/Gal* **43** D8
Drury *Clwyd* **29** D12
Dry Doddington *Lincs* **32** F6
Dry Drayton *Cambs* **25** J5
Dry Street *Essex* **19** E7
Drybeck *Cumb* **39** D9
Drybridge *Gramp* **58** A2
Drybridge *S'clyde* **47** F8
Drybrook *Glos* **15** C9
Dryburgh *Borders* **49** F8
Dryfesdale Gate *Dumf/Gal* **43** C11
Dryhope *Borders* **48** G5
Drymen *Central* **47** A9
Drymuir *Gramp* **58** C6
Drynoch *H'land* **62** E3
Dryslwyn *Dyfed* **13** E9
Duag Bridge *H'land* **60** G4
Dubford *Gramp* **58** A5
Dubford *Gramp* **58** C5
Dubiton *Gramp* **58** C4
Duchally *H'land* **60** E5
Duchrae *Dumf/Gal* **43** C7
Duck Street *Hants* **8** A5
Duckington *Ches* **30** E4
Ducklington *Oxon* **16** C4
Duckmanton *Derby* **32** C2
Duckpool *Cornw'l* **4** E1
Duck's Cross *Beds* **25** K2
Duddenhoe End *Essex* **25** L6
Duddingston *Lothian* **48** B6
Duddington *Northants* **24** E1
Duddleswell *E Sussex* **10** E3

Duddo Northum 49 E12
Duddon Ches 30 D4
Duddon Bridge Cumb 38 F4
Dudlees Northum 45 B12
Dudlees Northum 45 C7
Dudleston Shrops 30 F2
Dudleston Heath Shrops 30 F2
Dudley Tyne/Wear 45 F10
Dudley W Midlands 22 C3
Dudwells Dyfed 12 E3
Duffield Derby 31 F11
Duffryn W Glam 14 E2
Dufftown Gramp 58 D1
Duffus Gramp 56 C7
Dufton Cumb 39 C9
Duggleby N Yorks 41 H9
Duisdalemore H'land 62 G6
Duisky H'land 55 M4
Dukestown Gwent 14 C5
Dukinfield Gtr Man 35 G8
Dularich H'land 56 F1
Dulas Gwyn 28 A4
Dulax Gramp 58 F1
Dulcote Som'set 7 B9
Dulford Devon 6 F4
Dull Tayside 52 B3
Dullatur S'clyde 47 B12
Dullingham Cambs 25 J7
Dulnain Bridge H'land 57 G5
Duloe Beds 25 J3
Duloe Cornw'l 3 D9
Dulsie H'land 56 E5
Dulverton Som'set 6 C3
Dulwich London 18 G3
Dumbarton S'clyde 47 B9
Dumbleton Glos 16 A1
Dumcrieff Dumf/Gal 43 A11
Dumeath Gramp 58 D2
Dumfries Dumf/Gal 43 D10
Dumgoyne Central 47 A10
Dummer Hants 9 B7
Dun Gramp 59 L4
Dun Carloway W Isles 63 C3
Dunachtonmore H'land 57 J4
Dunain House H'land 56 E2
Dunalastair Tayside 52 A2
Dunan H'land 62 E5
Dunan S'clyde 46 B6
Dunan Tayside 51 B11
Dunan Tayside 52 D2
Dunans S'clyde 51 H7
Dunbar Lothian 49 B9
Dunbeath H'land 61 D11
Dunbeg S'clyde 50 D6
Dunblane Central 52 G3
Dunbog Fife 53 E7
Dunboll Som'set 6 B6
Dunbridge Hants 8 C5
Duncansby Head H'land 61 A12
Duncanston Gramp 58 E3
Duncanston H'land 56 D2
Dunchideock Devon 6 G2
Dunchurch Warwick 23 E8
Duncote Northants 23 G10
Duncow Dumf/Gal 43 C10
Duncraggan Central 51 G12
Duncraig College H'land 54 F2
Duncrievie Tayside 52 F6
Duncton W Sussex 9 D11
Dundee Tayside 53 D9
Dundon Som'set 7 C8
Dundonald Fife 53 H7
Dundonald S'clyde 47 F8
Dundonnell H'land 60 H3
Dundonnell Hotel H'land 60 H2
Dundraw Cumb 43 G12
Dundreggan H'land 55 H7
Dundrennan Dumf/Gal 43 G8
Dundry Avon 15 H9
Dunduff Fife 52 H6
Dunecht Gramp 59 G5
Dunfermline Lothian 48 A4
Dunfield Glos 16 D2
Dunford Bridge S Yorks 35 G10
Dunge Wilts 7 A12
Dungworth S Yorks 36 H1
Dunham Notts 32 C5
Dunham on the Hill Ches 30 C3
Dunham Town Gtr Man 30 B6
Dunhampton Heref/Worcs 22 E2
Dunholme Lincs 33 B7
Dunie Tayside 52 D4
Dunino Fife 53 F10
Dunipace Lothian 48 A1
Dunira Tayside 52 E2
Dunkeld Tayside 52 C5
Dunkerton Avon 15 H10
Dunkeswell Devon 6 E5
Dunkirk Kent 11 B9
Dunk's Green Kent 10 C5
Dunlappie Tayside 59 K3
Dunley Heref/Worcs 22 E1
Dunlichity Lodge H'land 56 F2
Dunlop S'clyde 47 D9
Dunmaglass Lodge H'land 57 G2
Dunmere Cornw'l 3 C7
Dunmore Central 52 H4
Dunmore S'clyde 46 C3
Dunn Street Kent 11 B7
Dunnet H'land 61 A11
Dunnichen Tayside 53 B10
Dunninald Tayside 53 B11
Dunning Tayside 52 F5
Dunnington Humber 37 B9
Dunnington N Yorks 36 B4
Dunnington Warwick 22 G4
Dunnockshaw Lancs 35 D7
Dunnottar Mains Gramp 59 J6
Dunollie S'clyde 50 D6
Dunoon S'clyde 46 B6
Dunragit Dumf/Gal 42 F2
Dunrostan S'clyde 46 A2
Duns Borders 49 D10
Duns Tew Oxon 16 A5
Dunsby Lincs 24 C2
Dunscore Dumf/Gal 43 C9
Dunscroft S Yorks 36 F4
Dunsdale Clevl'd 40 C6
Dunsden Green Oxon 17 F8
Dunsfold Surrey 9 B11
Dunsford Devon 5 G7
Dunshelt Fife 53 F7
Dunsley N Yorks 41 D8
Dunsmore Bucks 17 D9
Dunsop Bridge Lancs 34 B5
Dunstable Beds 17 B11
Dunstall Staffs 31 H10
Dunster Som'set 6 B3
Dunston Lincs 33 D8
Dunston Norfolk 26 E5
Dunston Northum 45 A10
Dunston Staffs 31 H8
Dunston Tyne/Wear 45 G10
Dunstone Devon 5 H6
Dunsville S Yorks 36 F4
Dunswell Humber 37 D8
Dunsyre S'clyde 48 E3
Dunterley Northum 44 E6
Dunterton Devon 5 H2
Duntisborne Abbots Glos 16 C1
Duntisbourne Rouse Glos 16 D1
Duntish Dorset 7 F10
Duntocher S'clyde 47 B9
Dunton Beds 25 L3
Dunton Bucks 17 B9
Dunton Norfolk 26 C2
Dunton Bassett Leics 23 C9
Dunton Green Kent 10 B4
Dunton Wayletts Essex 18 E6
Duntulm H'land 62 A3
Dunure S'clyde 47 H7
Dunure Mains S'clyde 47 H7
Dunvant W Glam 13 H9
Dunvegan H'land 62 C2
Dunwich Suffolk 27 H8
Dunydeer Gramp 58 E4
Dupplin Castle Tayside 52 E5
Durdar Cumb 44 H2
Durham Durham 40 A3
Durisdeer Dumf/Gal 43 A10
Durisdeermill Dumf/Gal 43 A9
Durleigh Som'set 6 C6
Durley Hants 8 D6
Durley Wilts 16 H3
Durnamuck H'land 60 G2
Durness H'land 60 A5
Durno Gramp 58 E5
Durrington W Sussex 9 F12
Durrington Wilts 8 B3
Dursley Glos 15 D10
Durston Som'set 6 C6
Durweston Dorset 7 E11
Dury Shetl'd 64 D7
Duston Northants 23 F10
Duthil H'land 57 G5
Dutlas Powys 21 E7
Duton Hill Essex 18 A6
Dutson Cornw'l 3 A10
Dutton Ches 30 B4
Duxford Cambs 25 L6
Dwyran Gwyn 28 D4
Dyce Gramp 58 F6
Dye House Northum 45 G7
Dyffryn Dyfed 12 C3
Dyffryn Dyfed 12 E6
Dyffryn Mid Glam 14 E2
Dyffryn Mid Glam 14 F4
Dyffryn S Glam 14 G4
Dyffryn Ardudwy Gwyn 28 H5
Dyffryn Castell Dyfed 20 D3
Dyffryn Cellwen Powys 14 C2
Dyke Gramp 56 D5
Dyke Lincs 24 C2
Dykegatehead Borders 49 D11
Dykehead Central 52 G1
Dykehead S'clyde 48 C2
Dykehead Tayside 59 L1
Dykelands Gramp 59 K5
Dykends Tayside 53 A7
Dykeside Gramp 58 C5
Dylife Powys 20 C4
Dymchurch Kent 11 E9
Dymock Glos 15 A10
Dyrham Avon 15 G10
Dysart Fife 53 H8
Dyserth Clwyd 29 B10
Eachwick Northum 45 F9
Eagland Hill Lancs 34 C3
Eagle Lincs 32 D6
Eaglescliffe Clevl'd 40 D4
Eaglesfield Cumb 38 B3
Eaglesfield Dumf/Gal 44 F1
Eaglesham S'clyde 47 D10
Eaglethorpe Northants 24 F2
Eairy I of Man 38 H1
Eakley Lanes Bucks 23 G11
Eakring Notts 32 D4
Ealand Humber 36 F6
Ealing London 18 F2
Eamont Bridge Cumb 39 B7
Earby Lancs 35 C8
Earcroft Lancs 34 E5
Eardington Shrops 21 C12
Eardisland Heref/Worcs 21 F9
Eardisley Heref/Worcs 21 G8
Eardiston Heref/Worcs 21 F12
Eardiston Shrops 30 H2
Earith Cambs 25 H5
Earl Shilton Leics 23 B8
Earl Soham Suffolk 27 J5
Earl Sterndale Derby 31 C9
Earl Stonham Suffolk 27 J4
Earle Northum 49 G12
Earley Berks 17 G8
Earlham Norfolk 26 E5
Earlish H'land 62 B3
Earls Barton Northants 23 F12
Earls Colne Essex 19 A8
Earl's Croome Heref/Worcs 22 H2
Earl's Green Suffolk 27 J3
Earlsdon W Midlands 22 D6
Earlsferry Fife 53 G9
Earlsford Gramp 58 D6
Earlston Borders 49 F8
Earlston S'clyde 47 F9
Earlswood Gwent 15 E8
Earlswood W Midlands 22 E5
Earnley W Sussex 9 F9
Earsdon Northum 45 D10
Earsdon Tyne/Wear 45 F11
Earsham Norfolk 26 F6
Earswick N Yorks 36 A4
Eartham W Sussex 9 E10
Earystane I of Man 38 H1
Easby N Yorks 40 D6
Easby N Yorks 40 E2
Easdale S'clyde 50 F5
Easebourne W Sussex 9 D10
Easenhall Warwick 23 D8
Eashing Surrey 9 B11
Easington Bucks 17 C8
Easington Clevl'd 41 C7
Easington Durham 40 A4
Easington Humber 37 E11
Easington Northum 45 C12
Easington Oxon 17 D7
Easington Colliery Durham 40 A4
Easington Grange Northum 45 B12
Easington Lane Tyne/Wear 45 H12
Easingwold N Yorks 40 H5
Easole Street Kent 11 C11
Eassie & Nevay Tayside 53 C8
East Aberthaw S Glam 14 H4
East Adderbury Oxon 16 A6
East Allington Devon 5 L6
East Ancroft Northum 45 A11
East Anstey Devon 4 C7
East Appleton N Yorks 40 F3
East Ashling W Sussex 9 E9
East Auchronie Gramp 58 F6
East Ayton N Yorks 41 G10
East Bank Gwent 14 D5
East Barkwith Lincs 33 B9
East Barming Kent 10 C6
East Barnby N Yorks 41 D8
East Barnet London 18 D3
East Barns Lothian 49 B9
East Barsham Norfolk 26 B2
East Beckham Norfolk 26 B5
East Bedfont London 18 F1
East Bennan S'clyde 46 G5
East Bergholt Suffolk 27 M4
East Bilney Norfolk 26 D3
East Blanerne Borders 49 D11
East Blatchington E Sussex 10 H4
East Bloxworth Dorset 7 G12
East Boldre Hants 8 F5
East Brackenridge S'clyde 47 E11
East Bradenham Norfolk 26 E2
East Brent Som'set 7 A7
East Bridge Suffolk 27 J7
East Bridgford Notts 32 F4
East Brunton Tyne/Wear 45 F10
East Buckland Devon 4 C5
East Budleigh Devon 6 H4
East Burrafirth Shetl'd 64 D7
East Burton Dorset 7 G11
East Butsfield Durham 40 A1
East Butterwick Humber 36 G6
East Cairnbeg Gramp 59 K5
East Calder Lothian 48 C4
East Carleton Norfolk 26 E5
East Carlton Northants 23 C11
East Challow Oxon 16 E5
East Chelborough Dorset 7 F9
East Chiltington E Sussex 10 G3
East Chinnock Som'set 7 E8
East Chisenbury Wilts 8 A3
East Clandon Surrey 9 A12
East Claydon Bucks 17 B8
East Claydon Bucks 17 C8
East Clyne H'land 61 F9
East Coker Som'set 7 E9
East Combe Som'set 6 C5
East Compton Som'set 7 B9
East Cottingwith Humber 36 C5
East Cowes I of Wight 8 F6
East Cowick Humber 36 E4
East Cowton N Yorks 40 E3
East Cramlington Northum 45 E11
East Cranmore Som'set 7 B10
East Creech Dorset 8 H1
East Croachy H'land 57 G2
East Croftmore H'land 57 H5
East Darlochan S'clyde 46 G2
East Dean Hants 8 C4
East Dean W Sussex 9 E10
East Dereham Norfolk 26 D3
East Ditchburn Northum 45 A9
East Down Devon 4 B5
East Drayton Notts 32 C5
East Dundry Avon 15 H9
East Edington Northum 45 E10
East End Dorset 8 F2
East End Hants 16 H5
East End Hants 8 F5
East End Hants 9 D8
East End Herts 18 A4
East End Humber 37 D10
East End Kent 11 E7
East End Norfolk 26 D8
East End Oxon 16 C5
East Farleigh Kent 10 C6
East Farndon Northants 23 D10
East Ferry Lincs 36 G6
East Fleetham Northum 45 D12
East Flisk Fife 53 E8
East Fortune Lothian 49 A8
East Garforth W Yorks 36 D2
East Garston Berks 16 F5
East Ginge Oxon 16 E5
East Gordon Borders 49 E9
East Grafton Wilts 16 H4
East Grimstead Wilts 8 C4
East Grinstead W Sussex 10 D3
East Guldeford E Sussex 11 F8
East Haddon Northants 23 E10
East Hagbourne Oxon 16 E6
East Halton Humber 37 E9
East Halton Skitter Humber 37 E9
East Ham London 18 F4
East Hanney Oxon 16 E5
East Hanningfield Essex 19 D7
East Hardwick W Yorks 36 E2
East Harling Norfolk 27 G3
East Harlsey N Yorks 40 E4
East Harnham Wilts 8 C3
East Harptree Avon 7 A9
East Hartford Northum 45 E11
East Harting W Sussex 9 D9
East Hatch Wilts 7 C12
East Hatley Cambs 25 K4
East Haugh Tayside 52 B4
East Hauxwell N Yorks 40 F2
East Haven Tayside 53 D10
East Heckington Lincs 24 A3
East Hedleyhope Durham 40 A2
East Hendred Oxon 16 E5
East Heslerton N Yorks 41 G9
East Hoathley E Sussex 10 F4
East Horrington Som'set 7 B9
East Horsley Surrey 9 A12
East Horton Northum 45 C11
East Huntspill Som'set 7 B7
East Hyde Beds 17 B12
East Ilkerton Devon 4 A6
East Ilsley Berks 16 F6
East Keal Lincs 33 D11
East Kennett Wilts 16 G2
East Keswick W Yorks 35 C12
East Kilbride S'clyde 47 D11
East Kinharrachie Gramp 58 D7
East Kirkby Lincs 33 D10
East Knapton N Yorks 41 G9
East Knighton Dorset 7 H11
East Knowstone Devon 4 D7
East Knoyle Wilts 7 C12
East Kyloe Northum 45 B12
East Lambrook Som'set 7 D7
East Langdon Kent 11 C12
East Langton Leics 23 C10
East Langwell H'land 61 F7
East Lavant W Sussex 9 E10
East Layton N Yorks 40 D2
East Leake Notts 32 H3
East Learmouth Northum 49 F11
East Leigh Devon 4 E6
East Lexham Norfolk 26 D2
East Lilburn Northum 45 A8
East Linton Lothian 49 B8
East Liss Hants 9 C9
East Lockhead S'clyde 47 D8
East Looe Cornw'l 3 D9
East Lound Humber 36 G6
East Lovington W Sussex 9 E10
East Lulworth Dorset 7 H12
East Lutton N Yorks 41 H9
East Lydford Som'set 7 C9
East Mains Gramp 59 H4
East Malling Kent 10 B6
East Marden W Sussex 9 E9
East Markham Notts 32 C5
East Marton N Yorks 35 B8
East Meon Hants 9 D8
East Mere Devon 6 E3
East Mersea Essex 19 C10
East Molesey Surrey 17 G12
East Morden Dorset 7 G12
East Morton Dumf/Gal 43 B9
East Morton W Yorks 35 C9
East Muntloch Dumf/Gal 42 H2
East Ness N Yorks 41 G7
East Norton Leics 23 B11
East Nynehead Som'set 6 D5
East Oakley Hants 9 A7
East Ogwell Devon 5 J7
East Orchard Dorset 7 D11
East Ord Northum 49 D12
East Panson Devon 5 G2
East Peckham Kent 10 C5
East Pennard Som'set 7 C9
East Portlemouth Devon 5 M6
East Prawle Devon 5 M6
East Preston W Sussex 9 F12
East Quantoxhead Som'set 6 B5
East Rainton Tyne/Wear 45 H11
East Ravendale Humber 37 G10
East Raynham Norfolk 26 C2
East Retford Notts 32 B4
East Rigton W Yorks 35 C12
East Rounton N Yorks 40 E4
East Rudham Norfolk 26 C1
East Runton Norfolk 26 A5
East Ruston Norfolk 26 C6
East Saltoun Lothian 49 C7
East Scales Dumf/Gal 44 F1
East Shefford Berks 16 G5
East Sleekburn Northum 45 E11
East Somerton Norfolk 26 D8
East Stockwith Lincs 36 H6
East Stoke Dorset 7 H12
East Stoke Notts 32 E5
East Stour Dorset 7 D11
East Stourmouth Kent 11 B11
East Stowford Devon 4 C5
East Stratton Hants 9 B7
East Studdal Kent 11 C11
East Suisnish H'land 62 E5
East Taphouse Cornw'l 3 C9
East Tilbury Essex 19 F7
East Tinwald Dumf/Gal 43 C11
East Tisted Hants 9 C8
East Torrington Lincs 33 B8
East Town Gramp 59 J5
East Tuddenham Norfolk 26 D4
East Tytherley Hants 8 C4
East Tytherton Wilts 16 G1
East Village Devon 4 E7
East Walton Norfolk 24 D8
East Warlington Devon 4 E6
East Week Devon 5 G5
East Wellow Hants 8 D5
East Wemyss Fife 53 G8
East Whitburn Lothian 48 C2
East Wick Essex 19 D10
East Williamston Dyfed 12 F4
East Winch Norfolk 24 D8
East Wittering W Sussex 9 F9
East Witton N Yorks 40 G2
East Woodburn Northum 45 D7
East Woodhay Hants 16 H5
East Worldham Hants 9 B9
East Wretham Norfolk 26 F2
East Youlstone Devon 4 D1
Eastbourne E Sussex 10 H5
Eastburn Humber 37 B7
Eastbury Berks 16 F4
Eastbury Herts 18 E1
Eastchurch Kent 11 A8
Eastcombe Glos 15 D12
Eastcote London 18 E1
Eastcote Northants 23 G10
Eastcote W Midlands 22 D5
Eastcott Devon 4 D1
Eastcott Wilts 8 A2
Eastcourt Wilts 16 E1
Eastcourt Wilts 16 H3
Eastdean E Sussex 10 H4
Eastend Essex 19 E9
Easter Aberchalder H'land 57 G1
Easter Ardross H'land 56 B2
Easter Balcroy H'land 56 E4
Easter Balmoral Gramp 57 K8
Easter Boleskine H'land 57 G1
Easter Brae H'land 56 C2
Easter Compton Avon 15 F9
Easter Crochail H'land 54 F8
Easter Culbo H'land 56 D2
Easter Davoch Gramp 59 G2
Easter Drummond H'land 55 H8
Easter Dullater Central 52 F1
Easter Earshaig Dumf/Gal 43 A11
Easter Fearn H'land 61 H7
Easter Fodderlee Borders 44 B4
Easter Galcantray H'land 56 E4
Easter Green W Midlands 22 D6
Easter Happrew Borders 48 E4
Easter Howgate Lothian 48 C5
Easter Howlaws Borders 49 E10
Easter Kinkell H'land 56 D1
Easter Langlee Borders 49 F8
Easter Lednathie Tayside 53 A8
Easter Milton H'land 56 D5
Easter Moniack H'land 56 E1
Easter Muckovie H'land 56 E3
Easter Ogil Tayside 53 A9
Easter Ogil Tayside 59 L2
Easter Ord Gramp 59 G6
Easter Pencaitland Lothian 49 B7
Easter Quarff Shetl'd 64 E7
Easter Silverford Gramp 58 A5
Easter Skeld Shetl'd 64 D6
Easter Softlaw Borders 49 F10
Easter Tillygarmond Gramp 59 H4
Easter Tulloch Gramp 59 K5
Eastergate W Sussex 9 F11
Easterhouse S'clyde 47 C11
Easterhouse S'clyde 48 D3
Easterhouses Lothian 48 C6
Easterton Wilts 8 A2
Eastertown Gramp 58 D1
Eastertown S'clyde 48 E3
Eastertown S'clyde 48 F2
Eastertown Som'set 7 A7
Eastertown of Auchleuchries Gramp 58 D8
Eastfield Gramp 59 H1
Eastfield N Yorks 41 G10

Eastfield S'clyde 48 C2
Eastfield S'clyde 48 E2
Eastfield Hall Northum 45 B10
Eastfield of Lempitlaw Borders 49 F10
Eastgate Durham 39 A11
Eastgate Norfolk 26 C4
Eastham Mersey 30 B2
Easthampstead Berks 17 G9
Eastheath Berks 17 G9
Easthope Shrops 21 C11
Easthorpe Essex 19 B9
Easthorpe Notts 32 E4
Eastington Devon 4 E6
Eastington Glos 15 D11
Eastington Glos 16 C2
Eastleach Martin Glos 16 D3
Eastleach Turville Glos 16 D3
Eastleigh Devon 4 C4
Eastleigh Hants 8 D6
Eastling Kent 11 B8
Eastnook Northum 45 D8
Eastoft Humber 36 E6
Eastoke Hants 9 F8
Easton Cambs 25 H2
Easton Cumb 44 F3
Easton Cumb 44 G1
Easton Devon 5 G6
Easton Dorset 7 H7
Easton Hants 8 C6
Easton I of Wight 8 G5
Easton Lincs 32 G6
Easton Norfolk 26 D4
Easton Som'set 7 A8
Easton Suffolk 27 J6
Easton Wilts 15 G12
Easton Grey Wilts 15 E12
Easton Maudit Northants 23 F12
Easton on the Hill Northants 24 E1
Easton Royal Wilts 16 H3
Easton-in-Gordano Avon 15 G8
Eastrea Cambs 24 F4
Eastriggs Dumf/Gal 44 F1
Eastrington Humber 36 D6
Eastry Kent 11 C11
East-the-Water Devon 4 C3
Eastville Lincs 33 E11
Eastwell Leics 32 G5
Eastwick Herts 18 C4
Eastwood Essex 19 E8
Eastwood Notts 32 F2
Eathorpe Warwick 23 E7
Eaton Ches 30 D4
Eaton Ches 31 D7
Eaton Leics 32 G5
Eaton Norfolk 26 E5
Eaton Notts 32 B4
Eaton Oxon 16 D5
Eaton Shrops 21 C10
Eaton Shrops 21 C9
Eaton Bishop Heref/Worcs 21 H10
Eaton Bray Beds 17 B10
Eaton Constantine Shrops 21 B11
Eaton Green Beds 17 B10
Eaton Socon Cambs 25 J3
Eaton upon Tern Shrops 30 H5
Ebberston N Yorks 41 G9
Ebbesbourne Wake Wilts 8 D2
Ebbw Vale Gwent 14 C5
Ebchester Durham 45 G9
Ebdon Avon 15 H7
Ebford Devon 6 G3
Ebley Glos 15 D11
Ebrington Glos 22 H5
Ecchinswell Hants 16 H6
Ecclaw Borders 49 C10
Ecclefechan Dumf/Gal 43 D12
Eccles Borders 49 E10
Eccles Gtr Man 34 G6
Eccles Kent 10 B6
Eccles Green Heref/Worcs 21 H9
Eccles Road Norfolk 26 F3
Eccles Tofts Borders 49 E10
Ecclesall S Yorks 32 B1
Ecclesfield S Yorks 35 H12
Ecclesgreig Gramp 59 L5
Eccleshall Staffs 31 G7
Eccleshill W Yorks 35 D10
Ecclesmachan Lothian 48 B3
Eccles-on-Sea Norfolk 26 C7
Eccleston Ches 30 D3
Eccleston Lancs 34 E4
Eccleston Mersey 34 H4
Eccup W Yorks 35 C11
Echt Gramp 59 G5
Eckford Borders 49 G9
Eckington Heref/Worcs 22 H3
Eckington S Yorks 32 B2
Ecton Northants 23 F11
Ecton Staffs 31 D9
Edale Derby 31 B9
Edburton W Sussex 10 G1
Edderside Cumb 43 G11
Edderton H'land 61 H7
Eddington Berks 16 G4
Eddington Kent 11 A10
Eddistone Devon 4 D1
Eddleston Borders 48 E5
Eddlewood S'clyde 47 D12
Eden Hall Borders 49 F10
Edenbridge Kent 10 C3
Edenfield Lancs 35 E7
Edenhall Cumb 39 B8
Edenham Lincs 24 C2
Edensor Derby 31 C11
Edentaggart S'clyde 51 H10
Edenthorpe S Yorks 36 F4
Edentown Cumb 44 G2
Edern Gwyn 28 F2
Edgarley Som'set 7 C8
Edgbaston W Midlands 22 D4
Edgcott Bucks 17 B8
Edgcott Som'set 6 B2
Edge Shrops 21 B9
Edge End Glos 15 C9
Edge Green Ches 30 E3
Edge Green Norfolk 27 G3
Edge Hill Mersey 30 A2
Edgebolton Shrops 30 H4
Edgefield Norfolk 26 B4
Edgemond Shrops 30 H6
Edgerston Borders 44 B5
Edges Green Cumb 44 F5
Edgeside Lancs 35 E7
Edgeworth Glos 15 D12
Edgeworthy Devon 4 E7
Edgmond Shrops 30 H6
Edgmond Marsh Shrops 30 H6
Edgton Shrops 21 D9
Edgware London 18 E2
Edgworth Lancs 34 E6
Edinample Central 52 E1
Edinbain H'land 62 C3
Edinburgh Lothian 48 B5
Edinchip Central 52 E1
Edingale Staffs 22 A6
Edingley Notts 32 E4
Edingthorpe Norfolk 26 B6
Edington Borders 49 D11
Edington Som'set 7 B7
Edington Wilts 8 A1
Edingworth Som'set 7 A7
Edintore Gramp 58 C2
Edith Weston Leics 23 B12
Edithmead Som'set 6 A6
Edlesborough Bucks 17 B10
Edlingham Heref/Worcs 15 B9
Edlingham Northum 45 B9
Edlington Lincs 33 C9
Edmondsham Dorset 8 E2
Edmondsley Durham 45 H10
Edmondthorpe Leics 32 H6
Edmonstone Orkney 64 C3
Edmonton London 18 E3
Edmundbyers Durham 45 H8
Ednam Borders 49 F10
Ednaston Derby 31 F11
Edra Central 51 F11
Edrom Borders 49 D11
Edstaston Shrops 30 G4
Edstone Warwick 22 F5
Edvin Loach Heref/Worcs 21 G12
Edwalton Notts 32 G3
Edwardstone Suffolk 27 L2
Edwinsford Dyfed 13 D9
Edwinstowe Notts 32 D3
Edworth Beds 25 L3
Edwyn Ralph Heref/Worcs 21 G12
Edzell Tayside 59 K3
Efail Isaf Mid Glam 14 F4
Efailnewydd Gwyn 28 G3
Efail-rhyd Clwyd 29 H11
Efailwen Dyfed 12 D5
Efenechtyd Clwyd 29 E10
Effingham Surrey 9 A12
Effirth Shetl'd 64 D6
Efford Devon 4 F8
Egerton Gtr Man 34 F6
Egerton Kent 11 C8
Eggesford Barton Devon 4 E6
Eggington Beds 17 B10
Egginton Derby 31 G11
Egglescliffe Clevl'd 40 D4
Eggleston Durham 39 C12
Egham Surrey 17 G11
Egleton Leics 23 A12
Eglingham Northum 45 A9
Egloshayle Cornw'l 3 C7
Egloskerry Cornw'l 3 A9
Eglwysbach Gwyn 29 C7
Eglwys-Brewis S Glam 14 G3
Eglwysfach Dyfed 20 C3
Eglwyswrw Dyfed 12 C5
Egmanton Notts 32 C4
Egremont Cumb 38 D3
Egremont Mersey 30 A2
Egton N Yorks 41 D8
Egton Bridge N Yorks 41 E8
Egypt Bucks 17 F10
Eight Ash Green Essex 19 A9
Eignaig H'land 50 C5
Eilanreach H'land 55 H2
Eildon Borders 49 F8
Eilean Datach H'land 60 H3
Eileanach Lodge H'land 56 C1
Eishken W Isles 63 F4
Elan Village Powys 20 F5
Elberton Avon 15 E9
Elburton Devon 5 K4
Elcho Tayside 52 E6
Elcombe Wilts 16 F2
Eldernell Cambs 24 F4
Eldersfield Heref/Worcs 15 A11
Eldon Durham 40 B3
Eldrick S'clyde 42 C4
Eldroth N Yorks 34 A6
Eldwick W Yorks 35 C10
Elerch Dyfed 20 D2
Elfhill Gramp 59 J5
Elford Northum 45 D12
Elford Staffs 22 A5
Elgin Grampn 56 C8
Elgol H'land 62 G4
Elham Kent 11 D10
Elie Fife 53 G9
Elilaw Northum 45 B8
Elim Gwyn 28 B3
Eling Hants 8 E5
Elishader H'land 62 B4
Elishaw Northum 45 D7
Elkesley Notts 32 C4
Elkstone Glos 16 C1
Ellan H'land 57 G5
Elland W Yorks 35 E10
Ellary S'clyde 46 B2
Ellastone Staffs 31 F9
Ellel Lancs 34 B4
Ellemford Borders 49 C10
Ellenhall Staffs 31 G7
Ellen's Green Surrey 9 C12
Ellerbeck N Yorks 40 E4
Ellerby N Yorks 41 D8
Ellerdine Heath Shrops 30 H5
Ellerhayes Devon 6 F3
Elleric S'clyde 51 C7
Ellerker Humber 37 D7
Ellerton Humber 36 C5
Ellerton N Yorks 40 E3
Ellerton Shrops 30 H6
Ellesborough Bucks 17 C9
Ellesmere Shrops 30 G3
Ellesmere Port Ches 30 C3
Ellingham Hants 8 E3
Ellingham Norfolk 26 F6
Ellingham Northum 45 E12
Ellingstring N Yorks 40 G2
Ellington Cambs 25 H3
Ellington Northum 45 D11
Ellisfield Hants 9 B8
Ellistown Leics 23 A8
Ellon Gramp 58 D7
Ellonby Cumb 38 B6
Elloughton Humber 37 D7
Ellwood Glos 15 C9
Ellwood Glos 15 D9
Elm Cambs 24 E6
Elm Park London 18 E5
Elmbridge Heref/Worcs 22 E2
Elmdon Essex 25 L6
Elmdon W Midlands 22 D5
Elmdon Heath W Midlands 22 D5
Elmers End London 18 G4
Elmesthorpe Leics 23 C8
Elmfield I of Wight 9 G7
Elmhurst Staffs 22 A5
Elmley Castle Heref/Worcs 22 H3
Elmley Lovett Heref/Worcs 22 E2
Elmore Glos 15 C11
Elmore Back Glos 15 C10
Elmscott Devon 4 D1
Elmsett Suffolk 27 K3
Elmstead Market Essex 19 B10
Elmstone Kent 11 B11
Elmstone Hardwicke Glos 15 B12
Elmswell Humber 37 A7
Elmswell Suffolk 27 J3
Elmton Derby 32 C2
Elphin H'land 60 F3
Elphinstone Lothian 48 B6
Elrig Dumf/Gal 42 G4
Elrigbeag S'clyde 51 F8
Elrik Gramp 59 G6
Elsdon Northum 45 D7
Elsecar S Yorks 35 G12
Elsenham Essex 18 A5
Elsfield Oxon 16 C6
Elsham Humber 37 F8
Elsing Norfolk 26 D4
Elslack N Yorks 35 B8
Elson Shrops 30 G2
Elsrickle S'clyde 48 E3
Elstead Surrey 9 B10
Elsted W Sussex 9 D9
Elston Notts 32 E5
Elston Wilts 8 B2
Elstone Devon 4 D5
Elstow Beds 25 K2
Elstree Herts 18 D2
Elstronwick Humber 37 D10
Elswick Lancs 34 C3
Elsworth Cambs 25 J4
Elterwater Cumb 38 E6
Eltham London 18 F4
Eltisley Cambs 25 J4
Elton Cambs 24 F2
Elton Ches 30 C3
Elton Clevl'd 40 C4
Elton Derby 31 D10
Elton Glos 15 C10
Elton Gtr Man 34 F6
Elton Heref/Worcs 21 E10
Elton Notts 32 F5
Elvanfoot S'clyde 48 H2
Elvaston Derby 31 G12
Elveden Suffolk 27 G1
Elvington Kent 11 C11
Elvington N Yorks 36 B5
Elwartlaw Borders 49 E10
Elwick Clevl'd 40 B5
Elwick Northum 45 B12
Elworth Ches 30 D6
Elworthy Som'set 6 C4
Ely Cambs 25 G6
Ely S Glam 14 G5
Emberton Bucks 23 G12
Emblehope Northum 44 D6
Embleton Cumb 38 B4
Embleton Durham 40 B4
Embleton Northum 45 A10
Embo H'land 61 G8
Emborough Som'set 7 A9
Embsay N Yorks 35 B8
Emery Down Hants 8 E4
Emley W Yorks 35 F11
Emley Moor W Yorks 35 F11
Emmbrook Berks 17 G9
Emmington Oxon 17 D8
Emneth Norfolk 24 E6
Emneth Hungate Norfolk 24 E6
Empingham Leics 23 A12
Empshott Hants 9 C9
Emsworth Hants 9 E9
Enaclete W Isles 63 D2
Enborne Berks 16 G5
Enborne Row Berks 16 H5
Enchmarsh Shrops 21 C10
Enderby Leics 23 B8
Endmoor Cumb 39 G7
Endon Staffs 31 E8
Endon Bank Staffs 31 E8
Enfield London 18 D3
Enford Wilts 8 A3
Engine Common Avon 15 F10
Englefield Berks 17 G7
Englefield Green Surrey 17 G10
English Bicknor Glos 15 C9
English Frankton Shrops 30 G3
Englishcombe Avon 15 H10
Enham Alamein Hants 8 A5
Enmore Som'set 6 C6
Ennerdale Bridge Cumb 38 D3
Enoch Dumf/Gal 43 B9
Enochdu Tayside 52 A5
Ensay H'land 50 C1
Ensbury Dorset 8 F2
Ensdon Shrops 21 A9
Ensis Devon 4 C4
Enstone Oxon 16 B5
Enterkinfoot Dumf/Gal 43 A9
Enterpen N Yorks 40 E5
Enville Staffs 22 C2
Eorabus H'land 50 E1
Eoropie W Isles 63 A6
Epney Glos 15 C11
Epperstone Notts 32 E4
Epping Essex 18 D4
Epping Green Essex 18 C4
Epping Green Herts 18 C3
Epping Upland Essex 18 C4
Eppleby N Yorks 40 D2
Epsom Surrey 10 B1
Epwell Oxon 23 H7
Epworth Humber 36 G5
Erbistock Clwyd 29 F12
Erbusaig H'land 55 G1
Erchless Castle H'land 54 E8
Erdington W Midlands 22 C7
Eredine Central 51 G5
Eribol H'land 60 B5
Ericstane Dumf/Gal 48 H3
Eridge Green E Sussex 10 E4
Erines S'clyde 46 B4
Eriswell Suffolk 25 G8
Erith London 18 F5
Erlestoke Wilts 8 A1
Ermine Lincs 33 C7
Ermington Devon 5 K5
Erpingham Norfolk 26 B5
Errocht H'land 55 L5
Errogie H'land 57 G1
Errol Fife 53 E7
Erskine S'clyde 47 B9
Ervie Dumf/Gal 42 E1
Erwarton Suffolk 27 M5
Erwood Powys 20 H6
Eryholme N Yorks 40 D3
Eryrys Clwyd 29 D11
Escart S'clyde 46 C3
Escomb Durham 40 B2
Escrick N Yorks 36 C4
Esgair Dyfed 13 D7
Esgairgeiliog Powys 20 B3
Esgerdawe Dyfed 13 C9
Esh Durham 40 A2
Esh Winning Durham 40 A2
Esher Surrey 17 H12
Eshott Northum 45 C10
Eshton N Yorks 35 B8
Eskadale H'land 54 F8
Eskbank Lothian 48 C6
Eskdale Green Cumb 38 E4
Eskdalemuir Dumf/Gal 44 C1
Eskham Lincs 37 G11
Esprick Lancs 34 D3
Essendine Leics 24 D1
Essendon Herts 18 C3
Essich H'land 56 F2
Essington Staffs 22 B3
Eston Clevl'd 40 C6
Etal Northum 49 E11
Etchilhampton Wilts 16 H2
Etchingham E Sussex 10 E6
Etchinghill Kent 11 D10
Etchinghill Staffs 31 H8
Ethie Mains Tayside 53 B11
Eton Berks 17 F10
Eton Wick Berks 17 F10
Etteridge H'land 57 K3
Ettington Warwick 22 G6
Etton Cambs 24 E2
Etton Humber 37 C7
Ettrick Borders 48 H5
Ettrickbridge Borders 48 G6
Etwall Derby 31 G11
Euston Suffolk 27 G2
Euximoor Drove Cambs 24 F6
Euxton Lancs 34 E4
Evanstown Mid Glam 14 E3
Evanton H'land 56 C2
Evedon Lincs 33 E8
Evelix H'land 61 G7
Evenjobb Powys 21 F8
Evenley Northants 17 A7
Evenlode Glos 16 A3
Evenwood Durham 40 C2
Evenwood Gate Durham 40 C2
Everbay Orkney 64 C4
Evercreech Som'set 7 B10
Everdon Northants 23 F9
Everingham Humber 36 C6
Everleigh Wilts 8 A3
Everley N Yorks 41 F10
Eversholt Beds 25 M1
Evershot Dorset 7 F9
Eversley Hants 17 H8
Eversley Cross Hants 17 H9
Everthorpe Humber 37 D7
Everton Beds 25 K3
Everton Hants 8 G4
Everton Mersey 30 A2
Everton Notts 32 A4
Evertown Dumf/Gal 44 E2
Evesbatch Heref/Worcs 21 H12
Evesham Heref/Worcs 22 H4
Evington Leics 23 B10
Ewden Village S Yorks 35 G11
Ewell Surrey 10 B1
Ewell Minnis Kent 11 D11
Ewelme Oxon 17 E7
Ewen Glos 16 D1
Ewenny Mid Glam 14 G2
Ewerby Lincs 33 E8
Eweslees Borders 44 C2
Ewhurst Surrey 9 B12
Ewhurst Green E Sussex 11 F7
Ewhurst Green Surrey 9 B12
Ewloe Clwyd 29 D12
Eworthy Devon 4 F3
Ewshot Hants 9 A9
Ewyas Harold Heref/Worcs 15 B7
Exbourne Devon 4 F5
Exbury Hants 8 F6
Exebridge Som'set 6 D3
Exelby N Yorks 40 F3
Exeter Devon 6 G3
Exford Som'set 6 B2
Exhall Warwick 22 G4
Exlade Street Oxon 17 F7
Exminster Devon 6 G3
Exmouth Devon 6 H4
Exnaboe Shetl'd 64 F7
Exning Suffolk 25 J7
Exton Devon 6 H3
Exton Hants 9 D7
Exton Leics 23 A12
Exton Som'set 6 C3
Exwick Devon 6 G3
Eyam Derby 31 C10
Eydon Northants 23 G9
Eye Cambs 24 E3
Eye Heref/Worcs 21 F10
Eye Suffolk 27 H4
Eyemouth Borders 49 C12
Eyeworth Beds 25 L4
Eyhorne Street Kent 11 C7
Eyke Suffolk 27 K6
Eynesbury Cambs 25 J3
Eynesford Kent 10 B4
Eynort H'land 62 E3
Eynsham Oxon 16 C5
Eype Dorset 7 G8
Eyre H'land 62 C3
Eythorne Kent 11 C11
Eyton Clwyd 29 F12
Eyton Heref/Worcs 21 F10
Eyton Shrops 21 B11
Eyton Shrops 21 D9
Eyton Shrops 30 H3
Eyton upon the Weald Moors Shrops 21 A12
Faccombe Hants 16 H5
Faceby N Yorks 40 E5
Fachwen Gwyn 28 D5
Facit Lancs 35 E7
Faddiley Ches 30 E4
Faddoch H'land 55 G3
Fadmoor N Yorks 41 F7
Fagwyr W Glam 13 G10
Fail S'clyde 47 F9
Failand Avon 15 G8
Failford S'clyde 47 G9
Failsworth Gtr Man 35 G8
Fain H'land 54 B5
Fair Oak Devon 6 D4
Fair Oak Hants 8 D6
Fair Oak Green Hants 17 H7
Fairbourne Gwyn 20 A2
Fairburn N Yorks 36 D2
Fairfield Heref/Worcs 22 E3
Fairfield Heref/Worcs 22 H4
Fairford Glos 16 D3
Fairgirth Dumf/Gal 43 F9
Fairlie S'clyde 47 D7
Fairlight E Sussex 11 G7
Fairlight Cove E Sussex 11 G7
Fairmile Devon 6 F4
Fairmilehead Lothian 48 C5
Fairnilee Borders 49 F7
Fairoak Staffs 30 G6
Fairseat Kent 10 B5
Fairstead Essex 19 B7
Fairwarp E Sussex 10 E3
Fairy Cross Devon 4 D3
Fakenham Norfolk 26 C2
Fala Lothian 49 C7
Falahill Borders 48 D6
Falcon Inn N Yorks 41 E10
Faldingworth Lincs 33 B8
Falfield Avon 15 E10
Falkenham Suffolk 27 L6
Falkirk Lothian 48 A2
Falkland Fife 53 F7
Falla Borders 44 B5
Fallgate Derby 32 D1
Fallin Central 52 H3
Fallsidehill Borders 49 E9
Falmer E Sussex 10 G2
Falmouth Cornw'l 2 F5
Falnash Borders 44 B2
Falsgrave N Yorks 41 F10
Falside Borders 44 B5
Falstone Northum 44 D5
Fanagmore H'land 60 C3
Fangdale Beck N Yorks 40 F6
Fangfoss Humber 36 B5
Fankerton Central 47 A11
Fankerton Central 47 A12
Fanmore H'land 50 C2
Fannich Lodge H'land 54 C6
Fans Borders 49 E9
Far Bletchley Bucks 17 A9
Far Coton Northants 23 F11
Far Forest Heref/Worcs 22 E1
Far Sawrey Cumb 38 F6
Farcet Cambs 24 F3
Farden Shrops 21 E11
Fareham Hants 9 F7
Farewell Staffs 22 A4
Farforth Lincs 33 B10
Farglow Northum 44 F5
Faringdon Oxon 16 E4
Farington Lancs 34 E4
Farlam Cumb 44 G4
Farleigh Avon 15 G8
Farleigh Surrey 10 B3
Farleigh Hungerford Som'set 7 A11
Farleigh Wallop Hants 9 A8
Farleigh Wick Wilts 15 H11
Farlesthorpe Lincs 33 C11
Farleton Cumb 39 G8
Farley Avon 15 G7
Farley Shrops 21 B9
Farley Staffs 31 F9

Farley *Wilts* **8** C4
Farley Green *Surrey* **9** B12
Farley Hill *Berks* **17** H8
Farleys End *Glos* **15** C11
Farlington *N Yorks* **40** H6
Farlow *Shrops* **21** D11
Farmborough *Avon* **15** H10
Farmcote *Glos* **16** A2
Farmers *Dyfed* **13** C10
Farmersfield *Dumf/Gal* **43** C9
Farmington *Glos* **16** C2
Farmoor *Oxon* **16** C5
Farmtown *Gramp* **58** C3
Farnborough *Berks* **16** F5
Farnborough *Hants* **9** A10
Farnborough *London* **18** G4
Farnborough *Warwick* **23** G8
Farnborough Green *Hants* **17** H9
Farncombe *Surrey* **9** B11
Farndon *Ches* **30** E3
Farndon *Notts* **32** E5
Farnell *Tayside* **53** B11
Farnham *Dorset* **8** E1
Farnham *Essex* **18** A5
Farnham *N Yorks* **35** A12
Farnham *Suffolk* **27** J7
Farnham *Surrey* **9** B9
Farnham Common *Bucks* **17** F10
Farnham Green *Essex* **18** A5
Farnham Royal *Bucks* **17** F10
Farnhill *N Yorks* **35** C9
Farningham *Kent* **10** A4
Farnley *N Yorks* **35** B11
Farnley *W Yorks* **35** D11
Farnley Tyas *W Yorks* **35** F10
Farnsfield *Notts* **32** D4
Farnworth *Ches* **30** B4
Farnworth *Gtr Man* **34** G6
Farr *H'land* **56** F2
Farr *H'land* **57** J4
Farr *H'land* **61** B7
Farr House *H'land* **56** F2
Farringdon *Devon* **6** G4
Farrington Gurney *Avon* **7** A9
Farsley *W Yorks* **35** D10
Farthinghoe *Northants* **23** H8
Farthingloe *Kent* **11** D11
Farthingstone *Northants* **23** G9
Fartown *W Yorks* **35** E10
Farway *Devon* **6** G5
Fasag *H'land* **54** D3
Fascadale *H'land* **50** A2
Fasnakyle *H'land* **55** G7
Fasque *Gramp* **59** K4
Fassfern *H'land* **55** L4
Fatfield *Tyne/Wear* **45** H11
Fattahead *Gramp* **58** B4
Faugh *Cumb* **44** G3
Fauldhouse *Lothian* **48** C2
Fauldie *Dumf/Gal* **44** F2
Faulkbourn *Essex* **19** B8
Faulkland *Som'set* **7** A10
Faulsgreen *Shrops* **30** G4
Faversham *Kent* **11** B9
Favillar *Gramp* **56** F8
Fawdon *Northum* **45** A8
Fawdon *Northum* **45** B8
Fawfieldhead *Staffs* **31** D9
Fawkham Green *Kent* **10** B5
Fawler *Oxon* **16** B5
Fawley *Berks* **16** F5
Fawley *Bucks* **17** E8
Fawley *Hants* **8** F6
Fawley Chapel *Heref/Worcs* **15** A9
Fawside *Borders* **49** E9
Faxfleet *Humber* **36** E6
Faygate *W Sussex* **10** E1
Fazeley *Staffs* **22** B5
Fearby *N Yorks* **40** G2
Fearn *H'land* **56** B4
Fearn Lodge *H'land* **60** H6
Fearnan *Tayside* **52** C2
Fearnbeg *H'land* **54** D1
Fearnhead *Ches* **30** A5
Fearnmore *H'land* **54** D1
Featherstone *Staffs* **22** B3
Featherstone *W Yorks* **36** E2
Featherwood *Northum* **44** C6
Feckenham *Heref/Worcs* **22** F4
Feddan *H'land* **56** D5
Feering *Essex* **19** B8
Feetham *N Yorks* **39** E12
Felbridge *Surrey* **10** D3
Felbrigg *Norfolk* **26** B5
Felcourt *Surrey* **10** D3
Felden *Herts* **17** D11
Felhampton *Shrops* **21** D10
Felin gwn Isaf *Dyfed* **13** E8
Felindre *Dyfed* **13** D10
Felindre *Dyfed* **13** E9
Felindre *Dyfed* **20** G1
Felindre *Powys* **14** B5
Felindre *Powys* **21** D7
Felindre *W Glam* **13** G9
Felin-fach *Dyfed* **13** A8
Felinfach *Powys* **14** A4
Felinfoel *Dyfed* **13** G8
Felingwm Uchaf *Dyfed* **13** E8
Felin-Wnda *Dyfed* **12** B6
Felixkirk *N Yorks* **40** G5
Felixstowe *Suffolk* **27** M6
Felixstoweferry *Suffolk* **27** L6
Felkington *Northum* **49** E12
Felldownhead *Devon* **5** H2
Felling *Tyne/Wear* **45** G11
Fellside *Cumb* **38** B5
Felmersham *Beds* **25** J1
Felmingham *Norfolk* **26** C6
Felpham *W Sussex* **9** F11
Felsham *Suffolk* **27** J2
Felstead *Essex* **19** B7
Feltham *London* **18** G1
Felthorpe *Norfolk* **26** D5
Felton *Avon* **15** H8
Felton *Heref/Worcs* **21** G11
Felton *Northum* **45** C10
Felton Butler *Shrops* **21** A9
Feltwell *Norfolk* **24** F8
Fen Ditton *Cambs* **25** J6
Fen Drayton *Cambs* **25** H4
Fen End *W Midlands* **22** E6
Fenay Bridge *W Yorks* **35** F10
Fence *Lancs* **35** C7
Fence Houses *Tyne/Wear* **45** H11
Fendike Corner *Lincs* **33** D11
Fengate *Cambs* **24** F3
Fenham *Northum* **45** B12
Fenhamhill *Northum* **45** B12
Feniscowles *Lancs* **34** E5
Feniton *Devon* **6** F4
Fenny Bentley *Derby* **31** E10
Fenny Compton *Warwick* **23** G7
Fenny Drayton *Leics* **23** B7
Fenny Stratford *Bucks* **17** A10
Fenrother *Northum* **45** D10
Fenstanton *Cambs* **25** H4
Fenton *Cambs* **25** G4
Fenton *Lincs* **32** C6
Fenton *Lincs* **32** E6
Fenton *Staffs* **31** F7
Fenton Barns *Lothian* **49** A8
Fenton Town *Northum* **49** F12
Fentonhill *Northum* **49** F12
Fenwick *Northum* **45** B12
Fenwick *Northum* **45** F9
Fenwick *S Yorks* **36** E4
Fenwick *S'clyde* **47** E9
Feochaig *S'clyde* **46** H3
Feock *Cornw'l* **2** F5
Feriniquarrie *H'land* **62** C1
Ferlochan *S'clyde* **50** D6
Fern *Tayside* **59** L2
Fern Villa *H'land* **55** G3
Ferndale *Mid Glam* **14** E3
Ferndown *Dorset* **8** F2
Ferness *H'land* **56** E5
Ferneyhill *Borders* **49** F10
Fernham *Oxon* **16** E4
Fernhill *W Sussex* **10** D2
Fernhill Heath *Heref/Worcs* **22** F2
Fernhurst *W Sussex* **9** C10
Fernie *Fife* **53** F8
Fernilea *H'land* **62** E3
Fernilee *Derby* **31** B8
Ferny Common *Heref/Worcs* **21** G9
Ferrensby *N Yorks* **35** A12
Ferrensby *N Yorks* **36** A2
Ferrindonald *H'land* **62** G6
Ferring *W Sussex* **9** F12
Ferry Hill *Cambs* **25** G5
Ferry Point *H'land* **61** H7
Ferrybridge *W Yorks* **36** E3
Ferryden *Tayside* **53** B12
Ferryhill *Durham* **40** B3
Ferryhill *Gramp* **59** G7
Ferryhill Station *Durham* **40** B3
Ferryside *Dyfed* **13** F7
Fersfield *Norfolk* **27** G4
Fersit *H'land* **55** L7
Feshiebridge *H'land* **57** J4
Fetcham *Surrey* **17** H12
Fetterangus *Gramp* **58** C7
Fettercairn *Gramp* **59** K4
Fewston *N Yorks* **35** B10
Ffaid-y-brenin *Dyfed* **13** C9
Ffairfach *Dyfed* **13** E9
Ffair-rhos *Dyfed* **20** F3
Ffawyddog *Powys* **14** B5
Ffestiniog *Gwyn* **28** F6
Fforddlas *Powys* **21** H7
Fforest *Dyfed* **13** G9
Fforest Fach *W Glam* **13** G9
Fforest Goch *W Glam* **13** G10
Ffostrasol *Dyfed* **13** B7
Ffos-y-ffin *Dyfed* **13** A8
Ffrith *Clwyd* **29** E12
Ffynnon Gynydd *Powys* **21** H7
Ffynnon-ddrain *Dyfed* **13** E7
Ffynnongroew *Clwyd* **29** B10
Fiag Bridge *H'land* **60** E5
Fiag Lodge *H'land* **60** D5
Fidden *H'land* **50** G1
Fiddington *Glos* **15** A12
Fiddington *Som'set* **6** B5
Fiddleford *Dorset* **7** E11
Fiddlers Hamlet *Essex* **18** D5
Fiddleton *Borders* **44** C2
Field *Staffs* **31** G9
Field Broughton *Cumb* **38** G6
Field Dalling *Norfolk* **26** B3
Field Head *Leics* **23** A8
Fife of Keith *Gramp* **58** C2
Fifehead Magdalen *Dorset* **7** D11
Fifehead Neville *Dorset* **7** E11
Fifehead St. Quintin *Dorset* **7** E11
Fifield *Berks* **17** F10
Fifield *Oxon* **16** B3
Fifield *Wilts* **8** A3
Fifield Bavant *Wilts* **8** D2
Figheldean *Wilts* **8** A3
Fighting Cocks *Durham* **40** D4
Filby *Norfolk* **26** D8
Filey *N Yorks* **41** G11
Filgrave *Bucks* **23** G12
Filkins *Oxon* **16** D3
Filleigh *Devon* **4** C5
Filleigh *Devon* **4** E6
Fillingham *Lincs* **32** B6
Fillongley *Warwick* **22** C6
Filton *Avon* **15** F9
Fimber *Humber* **37** A7
Finavon *Tayside* **59** L2
Fincham *Norfolk* **24** E8
Finchampstead *Berks* **17** H9
Fincharn *S'clyde* **50** G6
Finchdean *Hants* **9** E9
Finchingfield *Essex* **25** M8
Finchley *London* **18** E3
Fincraigs *Fife* **53** E8
Findern *Derby* **31** G11
Findhorn *Gramp* **56** C6
Findhorn Bridge *H'land* **57** G4
Findochty *Gramp* **58** A2
Findon *Gramp* **59** H7
Findon *W Sussex* **9** E12
Findon Mains *H'land* **56** D2
Findrack House *Gramp* **59** G3
Finedon *Northants* **23** E12
Fingal Street *Suffolk* **27** H5
Fingask *Gramp* **58** E4
Fingask *Tayside* **52** E6
Fingerpost *Heref/Worcs* **22** E1
Fingest *Bucks* **17** E8
Finghall *N Yorks* **40** F2
Fingland *Cumb* **44** G1
Fingland *Dumf/Gal* **47** H12
Finglesham *Kent* **11** C12
Fingringhoe *Essex* **19** B10
Finiskaig *H'land* **55** K2
Finlarig *Central* **52** D1
Finmere *Oxon* **17** A7
Finnart *Tayside* **51** B12
Finniegill *Dumf/Gal* **43** B12
Finningham *Suffolk* **27** H3
Finningley *S Yorks* **36** G4
Finnygaud *Gramp* **58** B3
Finsbay *W Isles* **63** H2
Finsbury *London* **18** F3
Finstall *Heref/Worcs* **22** E3
Finsthwaite *Cumb* **38** F6
Finstock *Oxon* **16** C4
Finstown *Orkney* **64** C2
Fintloch *Dumf/Gal* **43** D7
Fintry *Central* **47** A11
Fintry *Gramp* **58** B5
Fintry *Tayside* **53** D9
Finzean *Gramp* **59** H3
Fionnphort *H'land* **50** F1
Fir Tree *Durham* **40** B2
Firbeck *S Yorks* **32** A3
Firby *N Yorks* **40** G3
Firby *N Yorks* **41** H7
Firsby *Lincs* **33** D11
First Coast *H'land* **60** G1
Fishbeck *Dumf/Gal* **43** C11
Fishbourne *I of Wight* **9** G7
Fishbourne *W Sussex* **9** F10
Fishburn *Durham* **40** B4
Fishcross *Central* **52** H4
Fisherford *Gramp* **58** D4
Fisher's Pond *Hants* **8** D6
Fisherstreet *W Sussex* **9** C11
Fisherton *H'land* **56** E3
Fisherton *S'clyde* **47** H7
Fisherton de la Mere *Wilts* **8** B2
Fishguard *Dyfed* **12** C3
Fishlake *S Yorks* **36** F4
Fishponds *Avon* **15** G9
Fishpool *Gtr Man* **35** F7
Fishtoft *Lincs* **24** A5
Fishtoft Drove *Lincs* **33** E10
Fishtown of Usan *Tayside* **53** B12
Fishwick *Borders* **49** D11
Fiskavaig *H'land* **62** E2
Fiskerton *Lincs* **33** C7
Fiskerton *Notts* **32** E4
Fitling *Humber* **37** D10
Fitten End *Cambs* **24** D5
Fittleton *Wilts* **8** A3
Fittleworth *W Sussex* **9** D11
Fitz *Shrops* **30** H3
Fitzhead *Som'set* **6** C5
Fitzwilliam *W Yorks* **36** F2
Fiunary *H'land* **50** C3
Five Acres *Glos* **15** C9
Five Ashes *E Sussex* **10** F4
Five Lane Ends *Lancs* **34** B4
Five Lanes *Cornw'l* **3** B9
Five Oak Green *Kent* **10** D5
Five Oaks *W Sussex* **9** C12
Five Penny Borve *W Isles* **63** A5
Five Penny Ness *W Isles* **63** A6
Five Roads *Dyfed* **13** F8
Fivecrosses *Ches* **30** C4
Fivehead *Som'set* **7** D7
Flack's Green *Essex* **19** B7
Flackwell Heath *Bucks* **17** E9
Fladbury *Heref/Worcs* **22** G3
Fladdabister *Shetl'd* **64** E7
Flagg *Derby* **31** C10
Flamstead *Herts* **17** C11
Flansham *W Sussex* **9** F11
Flappit Spring *W Yorks* **35** C9
Flasbader *H'land* **62** C3
Flash *Staffs* **31** C8
Flashby *N Yorks* **35** B8
Flaunden *Herts* **17** D11
Flawborough *Notts* **32** F5
Flawith *N Yorks* **36** A3
Flax Bourton *Avon* **15** G8
Flaxby *N Yorks* **35** A12
Flaxby *N Yorks* **36** A2
Flaxley *Glos* **15** C10
Flaxpool *Som'set* **6** C5
Flaxton *N Yorks* **36** A4
Fleckney *Leics* **23** C10
Flecknoe *Warwick* **23** F8
Fledborough *Notts* **32** C5
Fleet *Dorset* **7** H9
Fleet *Hants* **9** A9
Fleet *Hants* **9** F8
Fleet *Lincs* **24** C5
Fleet Hargate *Lincs* **24** C5
Fleetham *Northum* **45** E12
Fleetwood *Lancs* **34** B2
Fleisirin *W Isles* **63** C6
Flemingston *S Glam* **14** G3
Flemington *S'clyde* **47** C11
Flemington *S'clyde* **47** E12
Flempton *Suffolk* **27** H1
Fletchertown *Cumb* **38** A4
Fletching *E Sussex* **10** F3
Flex *Borders* **44** B3
Flexbury *Cornw'l* **4** E1
Flexford *Hants* **9** A10
Flimby *Cumb* **38** B3
Flimwell *E Sussex* **10** E6
Flint *Clwyd* **29** C11
Flint Mountain *Clwyd* **29** C11
Flintham *Notts* **32** F5
Flinton *Humber* **37** D10
Flitcham *Norfolk* **24** C8
Flitton *Beds* **25** L2
Flitton Barton *Devon* **4** C6
Flitwick *Beds* **25** M1
Flixborough *Humber* **36** F6
Flixton *Gtr Man* **34** H6
Flixton *N Yorks* **41** G10
Flixton *Suffolk* **27** G6
Flockton *W Yorks* **35** F11
Flockton Green *W Yorks* **35** F11
Flodabay *W Isles* **63** H2
Flodden *Northum* **49** F11
Flodigarry Hotel *H'land* **62** A4
Flood's Ferry *Cambs* **24** F5
Flookburgh *Cumb* **38** H6
Flordon *Norfolk* **26** F5
Flore *Northants* **23** F9
Flotterton *Northum* **45** C8
Flouch Inn *S Yorks* **35** G10
Flowton *Suffolk* **27** K4
Flushing *Cornw'l* **2** F5
Flushing *Gramp* **58** C8
Fluxton *Devon* **6** G4
Flyford Flavell *Heref/Worcs* **22** G3
Fobbing *Essex* **19** E7
Fochabers *Gramp* **58** B1
Fochriw *Mid Glam* **14** D4
Fockerby *Humber* **36** E6
Fodderty *H'land* **56** D1
Foddington *Som'set* **7** C9
Foel *Powys* **20** A5
Foelgastell *Dyfed* **13** E9
Foffarty *Tayside* **53** C9
Foggathorpe *Humber* **36** C5
Fogo *Borders* **49** D10
Fogorig *Borders* **49** E10
Foindle *H'land* **60** C3
Folda *Tayside* **53** A7
Fole *Staffs* **31** F9
Foleshill *W Midlands* **23** D7
Folke *Dorset* **7** E10
Folkestone *Kent* **11** E11
Folkingham *Lincs* **24** B2
Folkington *E Sussex* **10** H4
Folksworth *Cambs* **24** F2
Folkton *N Yorks* **41** G10
Folla Rule *Gramp* **58** D5
Follifoot *N Yorks* **35** B12
Folly Gate *Devon* **4** F4
Fonmon *S Glam* **14** G4
Fonthill Bishop *Wilts* **8** C1
Fonthill Gifford *Wilts* **7** C12
Fontmell Magna *Dorset* **7** E12
Fontwell *W Sussex* **9** E10
Foolow *Derby* **31** C10
Foots Cray *London* **18** G5
Forbestown *Gramp* **58** F1
Forcett *N Yorks* **40** D2
Forches Corner *Som'set* **6** D5
Ford *Bucks* **17** C8
Ford *Devon* **4** D3
Ford *Devon* **5** L7
Ford *Glos* **16** A2
Ford *Northum* **49** F12
Ford *S'clyde* **50** G6
Ford *Shrops* **21** A9
Ford *Som'set* **6** C4
Ford *Staffs* **31** E9
Ford *W Sussex* **9** F11
Ford *Wilts* **15** G11
Ford Barton *Devon* **6** D3
Ford End *Essex* **19** B7
Ford Street *Som'set* **6** D5
Fordcombe *Kent* **10** D4
Fordel *Tayside* **52** F6
Fordell *Fife* **52** H6
Forden *Powys* **21** B8
Fordham *Cambs* **25** H7
Fordham *Essex* **19** A9
Fordham *Norfolk* **24** E7
Fordingbridge *Hants* **8** E3
Fordon *Humber* **41** H10
Fordoun *Gramp* **59** K5
Fordstreet *Essex* **19** A9
Fordwells *Oxon* **16** C4
Fordwich *Kent* **11** B10
Fordyce *Gramp* **58** A3
Forebridge *Staffs* **31** H8
Forest Green *Surrey* **9** B12
Forest Hall *Cumb* **39** E8
Forest Head *Cumb* **44** G4
Forest Hill *Oxon* **17** C7
Forest Lo *H'land* **57** H6
Forest Lo *S'clyde* **51** C10
Forest Mill *Central* **52** H4
Forest Row *E Sussex* **10** D3
Forest Town *Notts* **32** D3
Forestburn Gate *Northum* **45** C9
Foresterseat *Gramp* **56** D7
Forestside *W Sussex* **9** E9
Forfar *Tayside* **53** B9
Forgandenny *Tayside* **52** E6
Forge Hammer *Gwent* **14** E6
Forge Side *Gwent* **14** D6
Forgie *Gramp* **58** B1
Forgieside *Gramp* **58** B1
Forglen House *Gramp* **58** B4
Formby *Mersey* **34** F2
Forncett End *Norfolk* **26** F4
Forncett St. Mary *Norfolk* **26** F5
Forncett St. Peter *Norfolk* **26** F5
Forneth *Tayside* **52** C6
Fornham All Saints *Suffolk* **27** J1
Fornham St. Martin *Suffolk* **27** H2
Forres *Gramp* **56** D6
Forrestfield *S'clyde* **48** C1
Forsbrook *Staffs* **31** F8
Forse *H'land* **61** D11
Forsinain Farm *H'land* **61** C9
Forsinard *H'land* **61** C9
Forsinard Station *H'land* **61** C8
Forston *Dorset* **7** G10
Fort Augustus *H'land* **55** J7
Fort George *H'land* **56** D3
Fort William *H'land* **55** M5
Fortacres *S'clyde* **47** F9
Forteviot *Tayside* **52** E5
Forth *S'clyde* **48** D2
Forthampton *Glos* **15** A11
Fortingall *Tayside* **52** B2
Forton *Hants* **8** B6
Forton *Lancs* **34** B4
Forton *Shrops* **21** A9
Forton *Som'set* **7** E7
Forton *Staffs* **30** H6
Fortrie *Gramp* **58** C4
Fortrose *H'land* **56** D3
Fortuneswell *Dorset* **7** H7
Forty Feet Bridge *Cambs* **25** G4
Forty Green *Bucks* **17** E10
Forward Green *Suffolk* **27** J4
Fosbury *Wilts* **16** H4
Fosdyke *Lincs* **24** B4
Fosdyke Bridge *Lincs* **24** B4
Foss *Tayside* **52** A3
Foss Cross *Glos* **16** C2
Fossebridge *Glos* **16** C2
Foster Street *Essex* **18** C5
Fosterhouses *S Yorks* **36** F4
Foston *Derby* **31** G10
Foston *Lincs* **32** F6
Foston *N Yorks* **36** A5
Foston on the Wolds *Humber* **37** B8
Fotherby *Lincs* **33** A10
Fotheringhay *Northants* **24** F2
Foubister *Orkney* **64** D3
Foul Mile *E Sussex* **10** F5
Foulden *Borders* **49** D11
Foulden *Norfolk* **26** E1
Foulis Castle *H'land* **56** C1
Foulridge *Lancs* **35** C7
Foulsham *Norfolk* **26** C3
Fountainbleau *Gramp* **58** D8
Fountainbleau *Gramp* **58** E7
Fountainhall *Borders* **49** D7
Four Ashes *Suffolk* **27** H3
Four Crosses *Powys* **20** B6
Four Crosses *Powys* **29** H12
Four Crosses *Staffs* **22** A3
Four Elms *Kent* **10** C3
Four Forks *Som'set* **6** C6
Four Gates *Cambs* **24** D5
Four Gates *Gtr Man* **34** F5
Four Lane Ends *Ches* **30** D4
Four Lane Ends *Cumb* **39** F8
Four Lane Ends *Lancs* **34** B4
Four Lane Ends *Lancs* **34** C2
Four Lane Ends *N Yorks* **36** B4
Four Lanes *Cornw'l* **2** F4
Four Marks *Hants* **9** C8
Four Mile Bridge *Gwyn* **28** B2
Four Oaks *E Sussex* **11** F7
Four Oaks *Glos* **15** B10
Four Oaks *W Midlands* **22** B4
Four Oaks *W Midlands* **22** D6
Four Roads *Dyfed* **13** F8
Four Roads *I of Man* **38** H1
Four Throws *Kent* **10** E6
Fourlanes End *Ches* **30** D6
Fourlaws *Northum* **45** E7
Fourstones *Northum* **45** F7
Fovant *Wilts* **8** C2
Foveran *Gramp* **58** E7
Fowey *Cornw'l* **3** D8
Fowlershill *Gramp* **58** F7
Fowlis *Tayside* **53** D8
Fowlis Wester *Tayside* **52** E4
Fowlmere *Cambs* **25** L5
Fownhope *Heref/Worcs* **15** A9
Fox Corner *Surrey* **9** A11
Fox Lane *Hants* **17** H9
Foxcote *Avon* **7** A10
Foxdale *I of Man* **38** H1
Foxearth *Essex* **27** L1
Foxfield *Cumb* **38** G5
Foxham *Wilts* **16** F1
Foxhole *Cornw'l* **3** D7
Foxholes *N Yorks* **41** H10
Foxhunt Green *E Sussex* **10** F4
Foxley *Norfolk* **26** C3
Foxley *Wilts* **15** F12
Foxt *Staffs* **31** E9
Foxton *Cambs* **25** K5
Foxton *Durham* **40** C4
Foxton *Leics* **23** C10
Foxup *N Yorks* **39** G11
Foxwist Green *Ches* **30** C5
Foxwood *Shrops* **21** E11
Foy *Heref/Worcs* **15** A9
Foyers *H'land* **57** G1
Foys *Dorset* **7** E9
Fraddam *Cornw'l* **2** F3
Fraddon *Cornw'l* **2** D6
Fradley *Staffs* **22** A5
Fradswell *Staffs* **31** G8
Fraisthorpe *Humber* **37** A9
Framfield *E Sussex* **10** F4
Framingham Earl *Norfolk* **26** E6
Framingham Pigot *Norfolk* **26** E6
Framlingham *Suffolk* **27** J6
Frampton *Dorset* **7** G9
Frampton *Lincs* **24** B4
Frampton Cotterell *Avon* **15** F9
Frampton Mansell *Glos* **15** D12
Frampton on Severn *Glos* **15** D10
Frampton West End *Lincs* **24** B4
Framsden *Suffolk* **27** J5
Framwellgate Moor *Durham* **40** A3
Franche *Heref/Worcs* **22** D2
Frandley *Ches* **30** B5

Frankby *Mersey* **30** B 1
Frankley *Heref/Worcs* **22** D 3
Frank's Bridge *Powys* **21** G 7
Frankton *Warwick* **23** E 7
Frankwell *Shrops* **21** A10
Frant *E Sussex* **10** E 5
Fraserburgh *Gramp* **58** A 7
Frating *Essex* **19** B10
Frating Green *Essex* **19** B10
Freathy *Cornw'l* **3** D11
Frecheville *S Yorks* **32** B 1
Freckenham *Suffolk* **25** H 8
Freckleton *Lancs* **34** D 3
Freeby *Leics* **32** H 5
Freeland *Oxon* **16** C 5
Freethorpe *Norfolk* **26** E 7
Freethorpe Com *Norfolk* **26** E 7
Freiston *Lincs* **24** A 5
Fremington *Devon* **4** C 4
Fremington *N Yorks* **40** E 1
Frenchay *Avon* **15** F 9
Frenchbeer *Devon* **5** G 5
Frenich *Central* **51** G11
Frenich *Tayside* **52** A 3
Frensham *Surrey* **9** B 9
Fresgoe *H'land* **61** A 9
Freshfield *Mersey* **34** F 2
Freshford *Wilts* **15** H11
Freshwater *I of Wight* **8** G 5
Freshwater Bay *I of Wight* **8** G 5
Freshwater East *Dyfed* **12** G 4
Fressingfield *Suffolk* **27** H 5
Freston *Suffolk* **27** L 6
Freswick *H'land* **61** A12
Fretherne *Glos* **15** C10
Frettenham *Norfolk* **26** D 5
Freuchie *Fife* **53** F 7
Freystrop Cross *Dyfed* **12** F 3
Friar Waddon *Dorset* **7** H10
Friarton *Tayside* **52** E 6
Friday Bridge *Cambs* **24** E 6
Friday Street *E Sussex* **10** H 5
Fridaythorpe *Humber* **36** A 6
Friern Barnet *London* **18** E 3
Friesthorpe *Lincs* **33** B 8
Frieston *Lincs* **32** E 6
Frieth *Bucks* **17** E 9
Frilford *Oxon* **16** D 5
Frilsham *Berks* **16** G 6
Frimley *Surrey* **17** H 9
Frimley Green *Surrey* **17** H10
Frindsbury *Kent* **10** A 6
Fring *Norfolk* **24** B 8
Fringford *Oxon* **17** A 7
Frinsted *Kent* **11** B 7
Frinton-on-Sea *Essex* **19** B12
Friockheim *Tayside* **53** B10
Friog *Gwyn* **20** A 2
Frisby on the Wreake *Leics* **32** H 4
Friskney *Lincs* **33** E11
Friston *E Sussex* **10** H 4
Friston *Suffolk* **27** J 7
Fritchley *Derby* **32** E 1
Frith Bank *Lincs* **33** E10
Frith Common *Heref/Worcs* **21** E12
Fritham *Hants* **8** E 4
Frithelstock *Devon* **4** D 3
Frithelstock Stone *Devon* **4** D 3
Frithsden *Herts* **17** C11
Frithville *Lincs* **33** E10
Frittenden *Kent* **11** D 7
Fritton *Norfolk* **26** E 8
Fritton *Norfolk* **26** F 5
Fritwell *Oxon* **16** A 6
Frizington *Cumb* **38** D 3
Frocester *Glos* **15** D11
Frochas *Powys* **21** B 7
Frodesley *Shrops* **21** B10
Frodingham *Humber* **37** F 7
Frodsham *Ches* **30** B 4
Frogden *Borders* **49** G10
Froggatt *Derby* **31** C11
Froghall *Staffs* **31** E 9
Frogland Cross *Avon* **15** F 9
Frogmore *Devon* **5** L 6
Frogmore *Hants* **17** H 9
Frolesworth *Leics* **23** C 8
Frome *Som'set* **7** B11
Frome St. Quintin *Dorset* **7** F 9
Fromes Hill *Heref/Worcs* **21** H12
Fron *Clwyd* **29** D10
Fron *Dyfed* **13** D11
Fron *Gwyn* **28** E 4
Fron *Gwyn* **28** F 3
Fron *Powys* **20** F 6
Fron *Powys* **21** B 8
Fron Isaf *Clwyd* **29** F12
Froncysyllte *Clwyd* **29** F12
Fron-deg *Clwyd* **29** E12
Frongoch *Gwyn* **29** F 8
Fron-oleu *Gwyn* **28** G 6
Frosterley *Durham* **39** A12
Frotoft *Orkney* **64** B 2
Froxfield *Wilts* **16** G 4
Froxfield Green *Hants* **9** D 8
Froyle *Hants* **9** B 9
Fryerning *Essex* **18** D 6
Fryton *N Yorks* **41** H 7
Fulbeck *Lincs* **32** E 6
Fulbourn *Cambs* **25** K 6
Fulbrook *Oxon* **16** C 4
Fulford *N Yorks* **36** B 4
Fulford *Som'set* **6** C 5
Fulford *Staffs* **31** F 8
Fulham *London* **18** F 2
Fulking *W Sussex* **10** G 1
Full Sutton *Humber* **36** B 5
Fullaford *Devon* **4** B 6
Fullarton *S'clyde* **47** F 8
Fuller Street *Essex* **19** B 7
Fuller's Moor *Ches* **30** E 4
Fullerton *Hants* **8** B 5
Fulletby *Lincs* **33** C10
Fullwood *S'clyde* **47** D 9
Fulmer *Bucks* **17** F10
Fulmodestone *Norfolk* **26** B 3
Fulnetby *Lincs* **33** B 8
Fulstow *Lincs* **37** G11
Fulwood *Lancs* **34** D 4
Fulwood *Som'set* **6** D 5
Funtington *W Sussex* **9** E 9
Funtley *Hants* **9** E 7
Funtullich *Tayside* **52** D 2
Funzie *Shetl'd* **64** B 8
Furley *Devon* **6** F 6
Furnace *H'land* **54** C 3
Furnace *S'clyde* **51** G 7
Furnace End *Warwick* **22** C 6
Furner's Green *E Sussex* **10** E 3
Furness Vale *Derby* **31** B 8
Furneux Pelham *Herts* **18** A 4
Furze Platt *Berks* **17** F 9
Furzebrook *Dorset* **7** H12
Furzehill *Devon* **4** B 6
Fyfett *Som'set* **6** E 6
Fyfield *Essex* **18** C 6
Fyfield *Glos* **16** D 3
Fyfield *Hants* **8** A 4
Fyfield *Oxon* **16** D 5
Fyfield *Wilts* **16** G 2
Fylingthorpe *N Yorks* **41** E 9
Fyvie *Gramp* **58** D 5
Gabroe Hill *S'clyde* **47** D 9
Gaddesby *Leics* **23** A10
Gadgirth *S'clyde* **47** G 9
Gaer *Powys* **14** B 5
Gaerwen *Gwyn* **28** C 4
Gagingwell *Oxon* **16** B 5
Gaick Lodge *H'land* **57** L 3
Gailes *S'clyde* **47** F 8
Gailey *Staffs* **22** A 3
Gainford *Durham* **40** C 2
Gainsborough *Lincs* **32** A 5
Gainsborough *Suffolk* **27** L 5
Gainsford End *Essex* **25** L 8
Gairloch *Dumf/Gal* **43** D11
Gairloch *Gramp* **59** G 5
Gairloch *H'land* **54** B 2
Gairlochy *H'land* **55** L 6
Gairney Bank *Tayside* **52** G 6
Gairnsheil Lodge *Gramp* **57** J 8
Gaisgill *Cumb* **39** E 8
Gaitsgill *Cumb* **44** H 2
Galashiels *Borders* **49** F 7
Galby *Leics* **23** B10
Galdenoch *Dumf/Gal* **42** E 3
Galewood *Northum* **49** F12
Galgate *Lancs* **34** B 4
Galhampton *Som'set* **7** C 9
Gallaberry *Dumf/Gal* **43** C10
Gallanach *S'clyde* **50** E 5
Gallanachmore *S'clyde* **50** E 5
Gallatown *Fife* **53** H 7
Gallchoille *S'clyde* **50** H 5
Galley Common *Warwick* **22** C 6
Galleyend *Essex* **19** D 7
Galleywood *Essex* **19** D 7
Gallin *Tayside* **51** C12
Gallowfauld *Tayside* **53** C 9
Gallows Green *Heref/Worcs* **22** F 3
Gallows Green *Staffs* **31** F 9
Gallowstree Common *Oxon* **17** F 8
Galltair *H'land* **55** G 2
Galmpton *Devon* **5** K 7
Galmpton *Devon* **5** M 6
Galphay *N Yorks* **40** H 3
Galston *S'clyde* **47** F10
Galtrigill *H'land* **62** C 1
Galtway *Dumf/Gal* **43** G 8
Gamblesby *Cumb* **39** A 8
Gamelshiel *Lothian* **49** C 9
Gamlingay *Cambs* **25** K 3
Gammaton Moor *Devon* **4** D 4
Gammersgill *N Yorks* **40** G 1
Gamrie *Gramp* **58** A 5
Gamston *Notts* **32** C 4
Gamston *Notts* **32** F 3
Ganarew *Heref/Worcs* **15** C 8
Ganavan *S'clyde* **50** D 6
Ganllwyd *Gwyn* **28** H 6
Gannachy *Gramp* **59** K 3
Gannochy *Tayside* **52** E 6
Gannow Hill *Shrops* **30** G 2
Ganstead *Humber* **37** D 9
Ganthorpe *N Yorks* **41** H 7
Ganton *N Yorks* **41** G10
Gaodhail *H'land* **50** D 3
Garbat *H'land* **54** C 8
Garbhallt *S'clyde* **51** H 7
Garboldisham *Norfolk* **27** G 3
Garden City *Clwyd* **29** C12
Gardenstown *Gramp* **58** A 5
Garderhouse *Shetl'd* **64** D 7
Gardham *Humber* **37** C 7
Gare Hill *Som'set* **7** B11
Garelochhead *S'clyde* **51** H 9
Garenin *W Isles* **63** C 3
Garford *Oxon* **16** E 5
Garforth *W Yorks* **36** D 2
Gargrave *N Yorks* **35** B 8
Gargunnock *Central* **52** H 2
Garizim *Gwyn* **28** C 6
Garlandhayes *Devon* **6** E 5
Garlieston *Dumf/Gal* **42** G 5
Garlinge Green *Kent* **11** C 9
Garlogie *Gramp* **59** G 5
Garmond *Gramp* **58** B 5
Garmony *H'land* **50** D 4
Garmouth *Gramp* **58** A 1
Garn *Gwyn* **28** G 2
Garnant *Dyfed* **13** F10
Garndiffaith *Gwent* **14** D 6
Garn-Dolbenmaen *Gwyn* **28** F 4
Garnett Bridge *Cumb* **39** E 7
Garnkirk *S'clyde* **47** C11
Garnlydan *Gwent* **14** C 5
Garnswllt *W Glam* **13** F 9
Garn-yr-erw *Gwent* **14** C 5
Garrabost *W Isles* **63** D 6
Garragie Lo *H'land* **57** H 1
Garras *Cornw'l* **2** G 4
Garreg *Gwyn* **28** F 5
Garrick *Tayside* **52** F 3
Garrigill *Cumb* **39** A 9
Garriston *N Yorks* **40** F 2
Garroch *Dumf/Gal* **43** C 7
Garrochtrie *Dumf/Gal* **42** H 2
Garros *H'land* **62** B 4
Garrow *Tayside* **52** C 3
Garryhorn *S'clyde* **47** H 8
Garsdale Head *Cumb* **39** F10
Garsdon *Wilts* **16** E 1
Garshall Green *Staffs* **31** G 8
Garsington *Oxon* **17** D 7
Garstang *Lancs* **34** C 4
Garston *Mersey* **30** B 3
Garswood *Mersey* **34** G 4
Gartachoil *Central* **51** H12
Gartcosh *S'clyde* **47** C11
Garth *Clwyd* **29** F11
Garth *I of Man* **38** H 2
Garth *Mid Glam* **14** E 2
Garth *Powys* **20** G 5
Garth House *Tayside* **52** B 2
Garth Place *Mid Glam* **14** E 5
Garthamlock *S'clyde* **47** C11
Garthbrengy *Powys* **14** A 4
Garthdee *Gramp* **59** G 7
Garthmyl *Powys* **21** C 7
Garthorpe *Humber* **36** E 6
Garthorpe *Leics* **32** H 5
Gartly *Gramp* **58** D 3
Gartmore *Central* **51** H12
Gartnagrenach *S'clyde* **46** C 3
Gartness *Central* **47** A10
Gartocharn *S'clyde* **47** A 9
Garton *Humber* **37** D10
Garton-on-the-Wolds *Humber* **37** A 7
Gartymore *H'land* **61** E 9
Garvald *Borders* **48** D 6
Garvald *Lothian* **49** B 8
Garvamore *H'land* **57** K 1
Garvan *H'land* **55** M 3
Garvard *H'land* **50** H 1
Garve *H'land* **54** D 8
Garvestone *Norfolk* **26** E 3
Garvock *Gramp* **59** K 5
Garvock *S'clyde* **47** B 7
Garway *Heref/Worcs* **15** B 8
Garynahine *W Isles* **63** D 3
Garyvard *W Isles* **63** E 5
Gaskan *H'land* **55** M 2
Gaspar *Wilts* **7** C11
Gass *S'clyde* **42** A 5
Gasstown *Dumf/Gal* **43** D10
Gasswater *S'clyde* **47** G11
Gastard *Wilts* **15** G12
Gasthorpe *Norfolk* **27** G 3
Gatcombe *I of Wight* **8** H 6
Gate Helmsley *N Yorks* **36** B 5
Gateacre *Mersey* **30** A 3
Gatebeck *Cumb* **39** G 8
Gateforth *N Yorks* **36** D 3
Gatehead *S'clyde* **47** F 9
Gatehouse *Northum* **44** D 6
Gatehouse *Tayside* **52** B 4
Gatehouse of Fleet *Dumf/Gal* **43** F 7
Gatelawbridge *Dumf/Gal* **43** B10
Gateley *Norfolk* **26** C 3
Gatenby *N Yorks* **40** F 3
Gatesgarth *Cumb* **38** D 4
Gateshaw *Borders* **49** G10
Gateshead *Tyne/Wear* **45** G10
Gatesheath *Ches* **30** D 3
Gateside *Gramp* **56** D 7
Gateside *S'clyde* **47** B 8
Gateside *S'clyde* **47** D 8
Gateside *Tayside* **52** F 6
Gateside *Tayside* **53** C 9
Gateslack *Dumf/Gal* **43** A10
Gathurst *Gtr Man* **34** F 4
Gatley *Gtr Man* **31** A 7
Gattonside *Borders* **49** F 8
Gaufron *Powys* **20** F 5
Gauldry *Fife* **53** E 8
Gaultree *Norfolk* **24** E 6
Gaunt's Common *Dorset* **8** F 2
Gautby *Lincs* **33** C 9
Gavinton *Borders* **49** D10
Gawanhill *Gramp* **58** A 8
Gawber *S Yorks* **35** F11
Gawcott *Bucks* **17** A 8
Gawthwaite *Cumb* **38** G 5
Gaydon *Warwick* **23** G 7
Gayhurst *Bucks* **23** G11
Gayle *N Yorks* **39** F11
Gayles *N Yorks* **40** D 1
Gayton *Mersey* **30** B 1
Gayton *Norfolk* **24** D 8
Gayton *Northants* **23** G10
Gayton *Staffs* **31** G 8
Gayton le Marsh *Lincs* **33** B11
Gayton le Wold *Lincs* **33** B 9
Gayton Thorpe *Norfolk* **24** D 8
Gaywood *Norfolk* **24** C 7
Gazeley *Suffolk* **25** J 8
Geary *H'land* **62** B 2
Geddes House *H'land* **56** D 4
Gedding *Suffolk* **27** J 2
Geddington *Northants* **23** D12
Gedintailor *H'land* **62** E 4
Gedney *Lincs* **24** C 5
Gedney Broadgate *Lincs* **24** C 5
Gedney Drove End *Lincs* **24** C 6
Gedney Dyke *Lincs* **24** C 5
Gedney Hill *Lincs* **24** D 4
Gee Cross *Gtr Man* **35** H 8
Geisgeil *H'land* **60** C 3
Geldeston *Norfolk* **26** F 7
Gell *Clwyd* **29** C 8
Gelli *Mid Glam* **14** E 3
Gellideg *Mid Glam* **14** D 4
Gelligaer *Mid Glam* **14** E 5
Gellilydan *Gwyn* **28** F 6
Gellinudd *W Glam* **13** G10
Gellioedd *Clwyd* **29** F 8
Gelly *Dyfed* **12** E 4
Gellyburn *Tayside* **52** C 6
Gellywen *Dyfed* **12** E 6
Gelston *Dumf/Gal* **43** F 8
Gelston *Lincs* **32** F 6
Gembling *Humber* **37** A 9
Genoch Square *Dumf/Gal* **42** F 2
Gentleshaw *Staffs* **22** A 4
Geocrab *W Isles* **63** H 2
George Nympton *Devon* **4** D 6
Georgefield *Dumf/Gal* **44** D 1
Georgeham *Devon* **4** B 3
Georgetown *Dumf/Gal* **43** D10
Georgetown *Gwent* **14** C 5
Georgetown *S'clyde* **47** C 9
Georgmas Junction Station *H'land* **61** B11
Georth *Orkney* **64** C 2
Gerlan *Gwyn* **28** D 6
Germansweek *Devon* **4** F 3
Germoe *Cornw'l* **2** G 3
Gerrans *Cornw'l* **2** F 6
Gerranton *Dumf/Gal* **43** E 8
Gerrard's Cross *Bucks* **17** E11
Geshader *W Isles* **63** D 2
Gestingthorpe *Essex* **27** L 1
Geuffordd *Powys* **21** A 7
Gibbshill *Dumf/Gal* **43** D 8
Gibraltar *Lincs* **33** D12
Giddeahall *Wilts* **15** G11
Gidea Park *London* **18** E 5
Gidleigh *Devon* **5** G 5
Gifford *Lothian* **49** C 8
Giffordtown *Fife* **53** F 7
Giggleswick *N Yorks* **35** A 7
Gilberdyke *Humber* **36** D 6
Gilchristland *Dumf/Gal* **43** B10
Gilcrux *Cumb* **43** H12
Gildersome *W Yorks* **35** D11
Gildingwells *S Yorks* **32** B 3
Gilesgate Moor *Durham* **40** A 3
Gilfach *Mid Glam* **14** D 5
Gilfach Goch *Mid Glam* **14** E 3
Gilfachrheda *Dyfed* **13** A 7
Gillamoor *N Yorks* **41** F 7
Gillen *H'land* **62** B 2
Gillenbie *Dumf/Gal* **43** C12
Gillesbie *Dumf/Gal* **43** B12
Gilling East *N Yorks* **40** G 6
Gilling West *N Yorks* **40** E 2
Gillingham *Dorset* **7** D11
Gillingham *Kent* **11** A 7
Gillingham *Norfolk* **26** F 7
Gillock *H'land* **61** B11
Gillow Heath *Staffs* **31** D 7
Gill's Green *Kent* **10** E 6
Gills Kirkstyle *H'land* **61** A12
Gilmanscleuch *Borders* **48** G 6
Gilmerton *Lothian* **48** C 5
Gilmerton *Tayside* **52** E 4
Gilmonby *Durham* **39** D12
Gilmorton *Leics* **23** C 9
Gilsland *Northum* **44** F 5
Gilsland Spa *Cumb* **44** F 5
Gilston *Lothian* **49** D 7
Gilwern *Gwent* **14** C 6
Gimingham *Norfolk* **26** B 6
Gipping *Suffolk* **27** J 4
Gipsey Bridge *Lincs* **33** E10
Girdle Toll *S'clyde* **47** E 8
Girlsta *Shetl'd* **64** D 7
Girsby *N Yorks* **40** D 4
Girtford *Beds* **25** K 3
Girthill *S'clyde* **47** E 7
Girthon *Dumf/Gal* **43** F 7
Girton *Cambs* **25** J 5
Girton *Notts* **32** D 5
Girvan *S'clyde* **42** B 3
Girvan Mains *S'clyde* **42** B 3
Gisburn *Lancs* **35** B 7
Gisla *W Isles* **63** D 2
Gisleham *Suffolk* **26** F 8
Gislingham *Suffolk* **27** H 4
Gissing *Norfolk* **27** G 4
Gittisham *Devon* **6** F 5
Givons Grove *Surrey* **10** C 1
Glack *Tayside* **52** D 5
Glackbea *H'land* **56** F 1
Gladestry *Powys* **21** G 8
Gladhouse *Lothian* **48** D 6
Gladsmuir *Lothian* **49** B 7
Gladwin's Mark *Derby* **31** D11
Glais *W Glam* **13** G10
Glaisdale *N Yorks* **41** E 8
Glaisters *Dumf/Gal* **43** D 8
Glame *H'land* **62** D 5
Glamis *Tayside* **53** B 8
Glan Duar *Dyfed* **13** C 8
Glanaber *Gwyn* **28** E 6
Glanaman *Dyfed* **13** F10
Glandford *Norfolk* **26** B 3
Glandwr *Dyfed* **12** D 5
Glan-Dwyfach *Gwyn* **28** F 4
Glandyfi *Dyfed* **20** C 3
Glangrwyne *Powys* **14** C 5
Glanmile *Powys* **21** C 7
Glan-rhyd *Powys* **14** C 1
Glanryd *Dyfed* **12** C 5
Glanton *Northum* **45** B 9
Glanton Pike *Northum* **45** B 9
Glanvilles Wootton *Dorset* **7** E10
Glan-y-don *Clwyd* **29** B11
Glan-y-nant *Dyfed* **20** D 5
Glanyrafon *Gwyn* **29** F 9
Glan-y-wern *Gwyn* **28** G 5
Glapthorn *Northants* **24** F 1
Glapwell *Derby* **32** D 2
Glas-allt Shiel *Gramp* **57** L 8
Glasbury *Powys* **21** H 7
Glaschoil *H'land* **56** F 6
Glascoe *I of Man* **38** F 2
Glascoed *Clwyd* **29** C 9
Glascoforest *Gramp* **58** F 5
Glascote *Staffs* **22** B 6
Glascwm *Powys* **21** G 7
Glasdrum *S'clyde* **51** C 7
Glasfryn *Clwyd* **29** E 8
Glasgow *S'clyde* **47** C10
Glashvin *H'land* **62** A 4
Glasinfryn *Gwyn* **28** C 5
Glaslaw *Gramp* **59** J 6
Glasnacardoch *H'land* **55** K 1
Glasnacardoch *H'land* **55** L 1
Glasnakille *H'land* **62** G 5
Glasphein *H'land* **62** C 1
Glaspwll *Powys* **20** C 3
Glassburn *H'land* **54** F 7
Glasserton *Dumf/Gal* **42** H 5
Glassford *S'clyde* **47** E12
Glasshouse Hill *Glos* **15** B10
Glasshouses *N Yorks* **35** A10
Glasslie *Fife* **53** G 7
Glassoch *Dumf/Gal* **42** E 4
Glasson *Cumb* **44** G 1
Glasson *Lancs* **34** B 3
Glassonby *Cumb* **39** A 8
Glasterlaw *Tayside* **53** B10
Glaston *Leics* **23** B12
Glastonbury *Som'set* **7** B 8
Glastron *S'clyde* **47** H 8
Glatton *Cambs* **25** G 2
Glazebury *Ches* **34** G 5
Glazeley *Shrops* **21** D12
Gleadless Townend *S Yorks* **32** B 1
Gleaston *Cumb* **38** H 5
Glecknabae *S'clyde* **46** C 5
Gledpark *Dumf/Gal* **43** F 7
Gledsnest *Borders* **44** B 3
Glemanuilt *S'clyde* **46** H 1
Glemsford *Suffolk* **27** K 1
Glen *Dumf/Gal* **42** F 6
Glen *Dumf/Gal* **43** D 9
Glen *Tayside* **52** E 6
Glen Auldyn *I of Man* **38** G 2
Glen Barry *Gramp* **58** B 3
Glen Bernisdale *H'land* **62** C 3
Glen Clunie Lodge *Gramp* **57** L 7
Glen Dronoch *Gramp* **58** C 4
Glen House *Borders* **48** F 6
Glen Mona *I of Man* **38** G 2
Glen Nevis House *H'land* **55** M5
Glen Parva *Leics* **23** B 9
Glen Tanar House *Gramp* **59** H 2
Glen Village *Lothian* **48** B 2
Glen Vine *I of Man* **38** G 2
Glenancross *H'land* **55** K 1
Glenbarr *S'clyde* **46** F 2
Glenbeg *H'land* **50** A 3
Glenbeg *H'land* **57** G 6
Glenbervie *Gramp* **59** J 5
Glenboig *S'clyde* **47** C12
Glenborrodale *H'land* **50** A 3
Glenbranter *S'clyde* **51** H 8
Glenbreck *Borders* **48** G 3
Glenbrein Lo *H'land* **55** H 8
Glenbrittle House *H'land* **62** F 3
Glenbuchat Lodge *Gramp* **58** F 1
Glenbuck *S'clyde* **47** F12
Glenburn *S'clyde* **47** C 9
Glencally *Tayside* **59** L 1
Glencalvie Lodge *H'land* **60** G 5
Glencanisp Lodge *H'land* **60** E 3
Glencaple *Dumf/Gal* **43** E10
Glencarron Lodge *H'land* **54** E 4
Glencarse *Fife* **53** E 7
Glencassley Castle *H'land* **60** F 5
Glencloy *S'clyde* **46** F 5
Glencoe *H'land* **51** B 8
Glenconglass *Gramp* **57** G 7
Glencraig *Fife* **52** H 6
Glencripesdale *H'land* **50** B 4
Glencuie *Gramp* **58** F 2
Glendavan House *Gramp* **59** G 2
Glendearg *Borders* **49** F 8
Glendearg *Dumf/Gal* **44** C 1
Glendevon *Tayside* **52** G 5
Glendoe Lodge *H'land* **55** H 8
Glendoebeg *H'land* **55** J 8
Glendoik *Fife* **53** E 7
Glendoll Lo *Tayside* **57** M8
Glenduckie *Fife* **53** E 7
Glendye Lodge *Gramp* **59** J 4
Gleneagles Hotel *Tayside* **52** F 4
Gleneig *H'land* **55** H 2
Glenernie *Gramp* **56** E 6
Glenfalloch Farm *Central* **51** F10
Glenfarg *Tayside* **52** F 6
Glenfenzie *Gramp* **59** G 1
Glenferness House *H'land* **56** E 5
Glenfiddich Lodge *Gramp* **58** D 1
Glenfield *Leics* **23** B 9
Glenfinart House *S'clyde* **47** A 7
Glenfinnan *H'land* **55** L 3
Glenfintaig Lodge *H'land* **55** L 6
Glenfoot *Tayside* **52** F 6
Glenforslan *H'land* **55** M1
Glenfyne Lodge *S'clyde* **51** F 9
Glengap *Dumf/Gal* **43** F 7
Glengarnock *S'clyde* **47** D 8
Glengorm Castle *H'land* **50** B 2
Glengoulandie *Tayside* **52** B 3
Glengrasco *H'land* **62** D 4
Glengyle *Central* **51** F11
Glengyre *Dumf/Gal* **42** E 1
Glenhead *Tayside* **52** G 4
Glenhead Farm *Tayside* **53** A 7
Glenhighton *Borders* **48** F 4
Glenhoise *Dumf/Gal* **42** E 5
Glenholm *Dumf/Gal* **43** D12
Glenhoul *Dumf/Gal* **43** C 7
Glenhurich *H'land* **50** A 5
Glenkerry *Borders* **48** H 5
Glenkiln *Dumf/Gal* **43** D 9
Glenkindie *Gramp* **58** F 2
Glenkirk *Borders* **48** F 3
Glenlatterach *Gramp* **56** D 7

Glenlee Dumf/Gal 43 D7
Glenlia H'land 57 H1
Glenlivet Gramp 57 G7
Glenlochar Dumf/Gal 43 E8
Glenlochsie Tayside 57 M6
Glenloig S'clyde 46 F4
Glenluce Dumf/Gal 42 F3
Glenmarksie H'land 54 D7
Glenmarvis S'clyde 47 C12
Glenmassan S'clyde 46 A6
Glenmaye I of Man 38 G1
Glenmeanne H'land 54 D7
Glenmidge Dumf/Gal 43 C9
Glenmooar I of Man 38 G2
Glenmore H'land 50 A3
Glenmore S'clyde 50 F6
Glenmore Lodge H'land 57 H5
Glenmorven Cott H'land 50 B3
Glenmoy Tayside 53 A9
Glenmoy Tayside 59 L2
Glenmuck S'clyde 42 A6
Glenochar S'clyde 48 H2
Glenogil Tayside 59 L2
Glenprosen Village Tayside 53 A8
Glenproser Lo Tayside 57 M8
Glenquiech Tayside 59 L2
Glenrath Borders 48 F5
Glenridding Cumb 38 D6
Glenrisdell S'clyde 46 D4
Glenrossal H'land 60 F5
Glenrothes Fife 53 G7
Glenruther Dumf/Gal 42 D4
Glensanda H'land 50 C5
Glensaugh Gramp 59 J4
Glenshee Tayside 52 D5
Glenshero Lo H'land 57 K1
Glenshimmeroch Dumf/Gal 43 C7
Glenside S'clyde 47 D7
Glenside W Isles 63 E5
Glensluain S'clyde 51 H8
Glenstodcdale Dumf/Gal 42 E1
Glenstriven S'clyde 46 B6
Glensulaig H'land 55 L4
Glentaggart S'clyde 48 G1
Glentham Lincs 33 A7
Glentress Borders 48 E5
Glentress Borders 48 E6
Glentromie Lo H'land 57 K3
Glentrool Village Dumf/Gal 42 D4
Glentruan I of Man 38 F2
Glentruim House H'land 57 K2
Glentworth Lincs 32 A6
Glenuig H'land 55 M1
Glenurquhart H'land 56 C3
Glenwhargen Dumf/Gal 43 A8
Glenwhilly Dumf/Gal 42 D3
Glespin S'clyde 48 G1
Gletness Shetl'd 64 D7
Glewstone Heref/Worcs 15 B9
Glinton Cambs 24 E3
Glithno Gramp 59 H6
Glooston Leics 23 C11
Glossop Derby 35 H9
Gloster Hill Northum 45 C10
Gloucester Glos 15 C11
Gloup Shetl'd 64 A7
Gloweth Cornw'l 2 E5
Glusburn N Yorks 35 C8
Glutt Lodge H'land 61 D9
Gluvian Cornw'l 2 C6
Glympton Oxon 16 B5
Glyn Gwyn 29 D7
Glyn Ceiriog Clwyd 29 F11
Glynarthen Dyfed 12 B6
Glynbrochan Dyfed 20 D5
Glyncoch Mid Glam 14 E4
Glyncorrwg W Glam 14 D2
Glynde E Sussex 10 G3
Glyndebourne E Sussex 10 G3
Glyndyfrdwy Clwyd 29 F10
Glynllifon Park Gwyn 28 E4
Glynneath W Glam 14 D2
Glynogwr Mid Glam 14 F3
Glyntaff Mid Glam 14 E4
Glynteg Dyfed 13 C7
Gnosall Staffs 31 H7
Gnosall Heath Staffs 31 H7
Goadby Leics 23 B11
Goadby Marwood Leics 32 H5
Goat Lees Kent 11 C9
Goatacre Wilts 16 F1
Goathill Dorset 7 E10
Goathland N Yorks 41 E8
Goathurst Som'set 6 C6
Goathurst Common Kent 10 C4
Gobowen Shrops 30 G2
Godalming Surrey 9 B11
Goddard's Green Kent 11 E7
Godden Green Kent 10 C4
Godford Cross Devon 6 F5
Godmanchester Cambs 25 H3
Godmanston Dorset 7 F10
Godmersham Kent 11 C9
Godney Som'set 7 B8
Godolphin Cross Cornw'l 2 F3
Godre'r-graig W Glam 13 F11
Godshill Hants 8 E3
Godshill I of Wight 9 H7
Godstone Surrey 10 C2
Godwinscroft Hants 8 F3
Goetre Gwent 14 D6
Goff's Oak Herts 18 D3
Gogar Lothian 48 B4
Gogman Dyfed 20 D2
Golan Gwyn 28 F5
Golant Cornw'l 3 D8
Golberdon Cornw'l 3 C10
Golborne Gtr Man 34 G5
Golcar W Yorks 35 E9
Gold Hill Cambs 24 F6
Gold Hill Dorset 7 E11
Goldcliff Gwent 15 F7
Golden Balls Oxon 16 D6
Golden Cross E Sussex 10 G4
Golden Green Kent 10 C5
Golden Grove Dyfed 13 E9
Golden Hill Dyfed 12 G3
Golden Hill Hants 8 F4
Golden Pot Hants 9 B8
Golden Valley Glos 15 B12
Goldenhill Staffs 31 E7
Golders Green London 18 E3
Goldhanger Essex 19 C9
Golding Shrops 21 B11
Goldington Beds 25 K2
Goldsborough N Yorks 36 B2
Goldsborough N Yorks 41 D8
Goldsithney Cornw'l 2 G3
Goldstone Shrops 30 G6
Goldthorpe S Yorks 36 G3
Goldworthy Devon 4 D3
Gollanfield H'land 56 D4
Gollinglith Foot N Yorks 40 G2
Golsoncott Som'set 6 B4
Golspie H'land 61 G8
Golval H'land 61 B9
Gomeldon Wilts 8 C3
Gomersal W Yorks 35 E10
Gometra House H'land 50 C1
Gomshall Surrey 9 A12
Gonalston Notts 32 E4
Gonfirth Shetl'd 64 D7
Good Easter Essex 18 C6
Gooderstone Norfolk 26 E1
Goodhope Dumf/Gal 43 B11
Goodleigh Devon 4 C5
Goodmanham Humber 36 C6
Goodnestone Kent 11 B9
Goodnestone Kent 11 C11
Goodrich Heref/Worcs 15 B9
Goodrington Devon 5 K8
Goodwick Dyfed 12 C3
Goodworth Clatford Hants 8 B5
Goodyers End Warwick 23 D7
Goole Humber 36 E5
Goole Fields Humber 36 E5
Goonbell Cornw'l 2 E4
Goonhavern Cornw'l 2 D5
Goonrea Cornw'l 2 E4
Goose Green Kent 10 C5
Goosecruives Gramp 59 J5
Gooseham Cornw'l 4 D1
Goosewell Devon 5 K4
Goosey Oxon 16 E4
Goosnargh Lancs 34 C4
Goostrey Ches 30 C6
Gorcott Hill Heref/Worcs 22 E4
Gorddinog Gwyn 28 C6
Gordon Borders 49 E9
Gordonbush H'land 61 F8
Gordonstown Gramp 58 B3
Gordonstown Gramp 58 D5
Gore Cross Wilts 8 A2
Gorebridge Lothian 48 C6
Gorefield Cambs 24 D5
Goring Oxon 17 F7
Goring by Sea W Sussex 9 F12
Goring Heath Oxon 17 F7
Gorleston on Sea Norfolk 26 E8
Gornalwood W Midlands 22 C3
Gorran Churchtown Cornw'l 3 E7
Gorran Haven Cornw'l 3 E7
Gorrenberry Dumf/Gal 44 C3
Gors Dyfed 20 E2
Gorse Hill Wilts 16 E3
Gorsedd Clwyd 29 C10
Gorseinon W Glam 13 G9
Gorseness Orkney 64 C2
Gorseybank Derby 31 E11
Gorsgoch Dyfed 13 B8
Gorslas Dyfed 13 F9
Gorsley Glos 15 B10
Gorstan H'land 54 D7
Gorstanvorran H'land 55 M2
Gorstella Ches 30 D2
Gorsty Common Heref/Worcs 15 A8
Gorton Gtr Man 35 G7
Gosbeck Suffolk 27 K5
Gosberton Lincs 24 B3
Gosberton Clough Lincs 24 C3
Gosfield Essex 27 M1
Gosford Heref/Worcs 21 F10
Gosford House Lothian 49 B7
Gosforth Cumb 38 E3
Gosforth Tyne/Wear 45 F10
Gosmore Herts 18 A2
Gosport Hants 9 F7
Gossabrough Shetl'd 64 C8
Goswick Northum 45 B12
Gotham Notts 32 G3
Gotherington Glos 16 A1
Goudhurst Kent 10 D6
Goulceby Lincs 33 B9
Gourdon Gramp 59 K6
Gourock S'clyde 47 B7
Govan S'clyde 47 C10
Goverton Notts 32 E4
Goveton Devon 5 L6
Govilon Gwent 14 C6
Gowdall Humber 36 E4
Gowerton W Glam 13 G9
Gowkhall Fife 52 H5
Gowthorpe Humber 36 B5
Goxhill Humber 37 C9
Goxhill Humber 37 E9
Goxhill Haven Humber 37 E9
Goytre W Glam 13 H11
Gracefield Dumf/Gal 43 C9
Graden Borders 49 F10
Graffham W Sussex 9 D10
Grafham Cambs 25 H3
Grafham Surrey 9 B11
Grafton Heref/Worcs 15 A8
Grafton Heref/Worcs 21 F11
Grafton N Yorks 36 A2
Grafton Oxon 16 D4
Grafton Shrops 30 H3
Grafton Flyford Heref/Worcs 22 G3
Grafton Regis Northants 23 G11
Grafton Underwood Northants 23 D12
Grafty Green Kent 11 C7
Graianrhyd Clwyd 29 E11
Graig Gwyn 29 C7
Graig Penllyn S Glam 14 F3
Graig-fechan Clwyd 29 E10
Graigmillar Lothian 48 B6
Grain Kent 19 F9
Grainsby Lincs 37 G10
Grainthorpe Lincs 37 G11
Grampound Cornw'l 2 E6
Grampound Road Cornw'l 2 E6
Granborough Bucks 17 B8
Granby Notts 32 G5
Grandborough Warwick 23 E8
Grandtully Tayside 52 B4
Grane Lancs 34 E6
Grange Cumb 38 C5
Grange Fife 53 E7
Grange Mersey 30 B1
Grange N Yorks 40 F6
Grange S'clyde 47 F9
Grange Crossroads Gramp 58 B2
Grange Hall Gramp 56 D6
Grange Moor W Yorks 35 E11
Grange of Lindores Fife 53 E7
Grange Villa Durham 45 H10
Grangehall S'clyde 48 E2
Grangemill Derby 31 D11
Grangemouth Lothian 48 A2
Grange-over-Sands Cumb 38 G6
Grangepans Lothian 48 A3
Grangetown Clevl'd 40 C6
Grangetown S Glam 14 G5
Gransmoor Humber 37 A9
Granston Dyfed 12 D2
Grantchester Cambs 25 K5
Grantham Lincs 32 G6
Grantlodge Gramp 58 F5
Granton Dumf/Gal 48 H3
Granton Lothian 48 B5
Granton-on-Spey H'land 57 G6
Grantsfield Heref/Worcs 21 F10
Grantshouse Borders 49 C10
Grappenhall Ches 30 B5
Grasby Lincs 37 G8
Grasmere Cumb 38 D6
Grasscroft Gtr Man 35 G8
Grassendale Mersey 30 B3
Grassholme Durham 39 C11
Grassington N Yorks 35 A9
Grasslees Northum 45 C8
Grassmoor Derby 32 D1
Grassthorpe Notts 32 C5
Grateley Hants 8 B4
Gratwich Staffs 31 G9
Graveley Cambs 25 J4
Graveley Herts 18 A2
Gravelly Hill W Midlands 22 C5
Graveney Kent 11 B9
Gravesend Kent 10 A5
Gravir W Isles 63 E5
Grayingham Lincs 37 G7
Grayrigg Cumb 39 E8
Grays Essex 18 F6
Grayshott Hants 9 C10
Grayswood Surrey 9 C10
Graythorp Clevl'd 40 B5
Grazeley Berks 17 G8
Greasborough S Yorks 36 H2
Greasby Mersey 30 B1
Greasley Notts 32 E2
Great Abington Cambs 25 K6
Great Addington Northants 25 H1
Great Alne Warwick 22 F5
Great Altcar Lancs 34 F2
Great Amwell Herts 18 C4
Great Asby Cumb 39 D9
Great Ashfield Suffolk 27 H3
Great Ayton N Yorks 40 D6
Great Baddow Essex 19 C7
Great Badminton Avon 15 F11
Great Bardfield Essex 25 M8
Great Barford Beds 25 K2
Great Barr W Midlands 22 C4
Great Barrington Glos 16 C3
Great Barrow Ches 30 C3
Great Barton Suffolk 27 J2
Great Barugh N Yorks 41 G7
Great Bavington Northum 45 E8
Great Bealings Suffolk 27 K5
Great Bedwyn Wilts 16 H4
Great Bentley Essex 19 B11
Great Billing Northants 23 F11
Great Bircham Norfolk 26 B1
Great Blakenham Suffolk 27 K4
Great Blencow Cumb 39 B7
Great Bolas Shrops 30 H5
Great Bookham Surrey 9 A12
Great Bourton Oxon 23 H8
Great Bowden Leics 23 C10
Great Bradley Suffolk 25 K8
Great Bricett Suffolk 27 K3
Great Brickhill Bucks 17 A10
Great Bridgeford Staffs 31 G7
Great Brington Northants 23 F10
Great Bromley Essex 19 A10
Great Broughton N Yorks 40 E6
Great Budworth Ches 30 B5
Great Burdon N Yorks 40 D3
Great Burstead Essex 19 E7
Great Bushby N Yorks 40 E5
Great Canfield Essex 18 B6
Great Carlton Lincs 33 B11
Great Casterton Leics 24 E1
Great Chalfield Wilts 15 H11
Great Chart Kent 11 D8
Great Chatwell Staffs 22 A1
Great Chesterford Essex 25 L6
Great Cheverell Wilts 8 A1
Great Chishill Cambs 25 L5
Great Clacton Essex 19 B11
Great Clifton Cumb 38 B3
Great Coate Humber 37 F10
Great Comberton Heref/Worcs 22 H3
Great Corby Cumb 44 H3
Great Cornard Suffolk 27 L2
Great Cowden Humber 37 C10
Great Coxwell Oxon 16 E4
Great Crakehall N Yorks 40 F3
Great Cransley Northants 23 D11
Great Cressingham Norfolk 26 E1
Great Crosby Mersey 34 G2
Great Cubley Derby 31 F10
Great Dalby Leics 23 A10
Great Doddington Northants 23 F12
Great Dorweeke Devon 6 F3
Great Doward Heref/Worcs 15 C9
Great Dunham Norfolk 26 D2
Great Dunmow Essex 18 B6
Great Durnford Wilts 8 B3
Great Easton Essex 18 A6
Great Easton Leics 23 C11
Great Eccleston Lancs 34 C3
Great Edstone N Yorks 41 G7
Great Ellingham Norfolk 26 F3
Great Elm Som'set 7 A10
Great Eversden Cambs 25 K5
Great Fencote N Yorks 40 F3
Great Finborough Suffolk 27 J3
Great Fransham Norfolk 26 D2
Great Gaddesden Herts 17 C11
Great Gidding Cambs 25 G2
Great Givendale Humber 36 B6
Great Glemham Suffolk 27 J6
Great Glen Leics 23 B10
Great Gonerby Lincs 32 F6
Great Gransden Cambs 25 K4
Great Green Norfolk 26 F6
Great Green Suffolk 27 K2
Great Habton N Yorks 41 G8
Great Hale Lincs 24 A2
Great Hallingbury Essex 18 B5
Great Hameldon Lancs 34 D6
Great Harrowden Northants 23 E12
Great Harwood Lancs 34 D6
Great Haseley Oxon 17 D7
Great Hatfield Humber 37 C9
Great Haywood Staffs 31 H8
Great Heath W Midlands 23 D7
Great Heck N Yorks 36 E4
Great Henny Essex 27 L2
Great Hinton Wilts 15 H12
Great Hockham Norfolk 26 F2
Great Holland Essex 19 B12
Great Horkesley Essex 27 M3
Great Hormead Herts 25 M5
Great Horton W Yorks 35 D10
Great Horwood Bucks 17 A8
Great Houghton Northants 23 F11
Great Houghton S Yorks 36 F2
Great Hucklow Derby 31 B10
Great Kelk Humber 37 A8
Great Kimble Bucks 17 D9
Great Kingshill Bucks 17 D9
Great Langton N Yorks 40 F3
Great Leighs Essex 19 B7
Great Limber Lincs 37 F9
Great Linford Bucks 23 H12
Great Livermere Suffolk 27 H2
Great Longstone Derby 31 C10
Great Lumley Durham 45 H11
Great Malvern Heref/Worcs 22 G2
Great Maplestead Essex 27 M1
Great Marton Lancs 34 D2
Great Massingham Norfolk 26 C1
Great Melton Norfolk 26 E4
Great Milton Oxon 17 D7
Great Missenden Bucks 17 D10
Great Mitton Lancs 34 C6
Great Mongeham Kent 11 C12
Great Moulton Norfolk 26 F5
Great Munden Herts 18 B4
Great Musgrave Cumb 39 D10
Great Ness Shrops 30 H3
Great Oakley Essex 19 A11
Great Oakley Northants 23 D12
Great Offley Herts 18 A1
Great Ormside Cumb 39 C9
Great Orton Cumb 44 H2
Great Ouseburn N Yorks 36 A2
Great Oxendon Northants 23 D10
Great Oxney Green Essex 18 C6
Great Palgrave Norfolk 26 D1
Great Parndon Essex 18 C4
Great Paxton Cambs 25 J3
Great Plumpton Lancs 34 D3
Great Plumstead Norfolk 26 D6
Great Ponton Lincs 32 G6
Great Preston W Yorks 36 D2
Great Raveley Cambs 25 G4
Great Rissington Glos 16 B3
Great Rollright Oxon 16 A4
Great Ryburgh Norfolk 26 C3
Great Ryle Northum 45 B8
Great Saling Essex 19 A7
Great Salkeld Cumb 39 B8
Great Sampford Essex 25 L7
Great Sankey Ches 30 A4
Great Saxham Suffolk 27 J1
Great Shefford Berks 16 G5
Great Shelford Cambs 25 K6
Great Smeaton N Yorks 40 E4
Great Snoring Norfolk 26 B2
Great Somerford Wilts 16 F1
Great Stainton Durham 40 C3
Great Stambridge Essex 19 E9
Great Staughton Cambs 25 J2
Great Steeping Lincs 33 D11
Great Stonar Kent 11 B12
Great Strickland Cumb 39 C8
Great Stukeley Cambs 25 H3
Great Sturton Lincs 33 C9
Great Sutton Ches 30 C2
Great Sutton Shrops 21 D10
Great Swinburne Northum 45 E7
Great Tarpots Essex 19 E7
Great Tew Oxon 16 A5
Great Tey Essex 19 A9
Great Thurlow Suffolk 25 K8
Great Torrington Devon 4 D4
Great Tosson Northum 45 C8
Great Totham Essex 19 C8
Great Tows Lincs 37 H10
Great Urswick Cumb 38 H5
Great Wakering Essex 19 E9
Great Waldingfield Suffolk 27 L2
Great Walsingham Norfolk 26 B2
Great Waltham Essex 19 C7
Great Warley Essex 18 E6
Great Washbourne Glos 16 A1
Great Welnetham Suffolk 27 J2
Great Wenham Suffolk 27 L4
Great Whigborough Essex 19 B9
Great Whittington Northum 45 F8
Great Wilbraham Cambs 25 J6
Great Wishford Wilts 8 C2
Great Witcombe Glos 15 C12
Great Witley Heref/Worcs 22 E1
Great Wolford Oxon 16 A3
Great Wratting Suffolk 25 K8
Great Wymondley Herts 18 A2
Great Wyrley Staffs 22 A3
Great Wytheford Shrops 30 H4
Great Yarmouth Norfolk 26 E8
Great Yeldham Essex 27 L1
Greatford Lincs 24 D2
Greatgate Staffs 31 F9
Greatham Clevl'd 40 B5
Greatham Hants 9 C9
Greatstone-on-Sea Kent 11 F9
Greatworth Northants 23 H9
Green End Beds 25 K2
Green Hammerton N Yorks 36 A2
Green Moorland Som'set 7 C7
Green Ore Som'set 7 A9
Green Street Green Kent 10 A5
Green Street Green London 10 B2
Green Tye Herts 18 B4
Greenbeck Dumf/Gal 43 C11
Greenburn Lothian 48 C2
Greendale Cumb 38 E4
Greendown Som'set 7 A9
Greendykes Northum 45 C10
Greenend Borders 49 G8
Greenfield Beds 25 M2
Greenfield Clwyd 29 B11
Greenfield Gtr Man 35 G8
Greenfield H'land 55 J6
Greenfield Oxon 17 E8
Greenford London 18 F1
Greengairs Lothian 48 B1
Greenhalgh Lancs 34 D3
Greenham Berks 16 H6
Greenham Som'set 6 D4
Greenhaugh Northum 44 D6
Greenhead Dumf/Gal 43 C10
Greenhead Northum 44 F5
Greenhead S'clyde 47 E9
Greenhill Kent 11 A10
Greenhill Lothian 48 B1
Greenhills S'clyde 47 D8
Greenhithe Kent 10 A5
Greenholm S'clyde 47 F10

Greenholme *Cumb* 39 E8
Greenhouse *Borders* 49 G8
Greenhow Hill *N Yorks* 35 A9
Greenigo *Orkney* 64 D2
Greenknowe *Borders* 49 E9
Greenland *H'land* 61 A11
Greenlands *Bucks* 17 F8
Greenlaw *Borders* 49 E9
Greenlaw *Gramp* 58 B4
Greenlaw Walls *Northum* 49 E12
Greenlea *Dumf/Gal* 43 D11
Greenlea *S'clyde* 47 A7
Greenloaning *Tayside* 52 F3
Greenock *S'clyde* 47 B8
Greenodd *Cumb* 38 G5
Greenrig *S'clyde* 48 E1
Greenrow *Cumb* 43 F11
Greens Norton *Northants* 23 G10
Greenscares *Tayside* 52 F3
Greenshields *S'clyde* 48 E3
Greenside *Tyne/Wear* 45 G9
Greensidehill *Northum* 45 A8
Greenstead Green *Essex* 19 A8
Greensted Green *Essex* 18 D5
Greenwall *Orkney* 64 C3
Greenway *Dyfed* 12 D4
Greenway *S Glam* 14 G4
Greenwich *London* 18 F4
Greet *Glos* 16 A1
Greete *Shrops* 21 E11
Greetham *Leics* 23 A12
Greetham *Lincs* 33 C10
Greetland *W Yorks* 35 E9
Greinton *Som'set* 7 C7
Grendon *Northants* 23 F12
Grendon *Warwick* 22 B6
Grendon Common *Warwick* 22 B6
Grendon Green *Heref/Worcs* 21 G11
Grendon Underwood *Bucks* 17 B8
Grenofen *Devon* 5 J4
Grenoside *S Yorks* 35 H12
Gresford *Clwyd* 30 E2
Gresham *Norfolk* 26 B5
Greshornish *H'land* 62 C3
Gress *W Isles* 63 C6
Gressenhall *Norfolk* 26 D3
Gressenhall Grn *Norfolk* 26 D3
Gressingham *Lancs* 39 H8
Greta Bridge *Durham* 40 D1
Gretna *Dumf/Gal* 44 F2
Gretna Green *Dumf/Gal* 44 F2
Gretton *Glos* 16 A1
Gretton *Northants* 23 C12
Gretton *Shrops* 21 C10
Grewelthorpe *N Yorks* 40 G2
Grey Stone *Gramp* 58 E6
Greygarth *N Yorks* 40 H2
Greynor *Dyfed* 13 F9
Greyrigg *Dumf/Gal* 43 C11
Greyrigg *Lothian* 48 B2
Greysouthen *Cumb* 38 B3
Greystoke *Cumb* 39 B7
Greystoke *Tayside* 53 C10
Greystone *Dumf/Gal* 43 D10
Greywell *Hants* 9 A8
Gribbleford Bridge *Devon* 4 F4
Gribthorpe *Humber* 36 D5
Gribun *H'land* 50 D2
Griff *Warwick* 23 C7
Griffithstown *Gwent* 14 D6
Grigghall *Cumb* 39 F7
Grimbister *Orkney* 64 C2
Grimeford Village *Lancs* 34 F5
Grimethorpe *S Yorks* 36 F2
Grimister *Shetl'd* 64 B7
Grimley *Heref/Worcs* 22 F2
Grimmet *S'clyde* 47 H8
Grimoldby *Lincs* 33 A11
Grimsargh *Lancs* 34 D5
Grimsby *Humber* 37 F10
Grimscote *Northants* 23 G10
Grimscott *Cornw'l* 4 E1
Grimshader *W Isles* 63 D5
Grimsthorpe *Lincs* 24 C2
Grimston *Humber* 37 D10
Grimston *Leics* 32 H4
Grimston *Norfolk* 24 C8
Grimstone *Dorset* 7 G9
Grinacombe Moor *Devon* 5 G3
Grindale *Humber* 41 H11
Grindle *Shrops* 22 B1
Grindleford *Derby* 31 B11
Grindleton *Lancs* 34 C6
Grindley Brook *Shrops* 30 F4
Grindlow *Derby* 31 B10
Grindon *Clevl'd* 40 C4
Grindon *Northum* 44 F6
Grindon *Northum* 49 E11
Grindon *Staffs* 31 E9
Grindon Hill *Northum* 44 F6
Grindonrigg *Northum* 49 E11
Gringley on the Hill *Notts* 32 A4
Grinsdale *Cumb* 39 F10
Grinsdale *Cumb* 44 G2
Grinshill *Shrops* 30 H4
Grinton *N Yorks* 40 E1
Gristhorpe *N Yorks* 41 G11
Griston *Norfolk* 26 E2
Grittenham *Wilts* 16 F1
Grittleton *Wilts* 15 F11
Grizebeck *Cumb* 38 G5
Grizedale *Cumb* 38 F6
Grobister *Orkney* 64 C4
Groby *Leics* 23 A8
Groes *Clwyd* 29 D9
Groes *W Glam* 13 H11
Groesfaen *Mid Glam* 14 F4
Groesffordd *Gwyn* 28 F2
Groesffordd *Gwyn* 29 C7
Groesffordd Marli *Clwyd* 29 C9
Groesllwyd *Powys* 21 A7
Groeslon *Gwyn* 28 E4
Grogport *S'clyde* 46 E3
Gronant *Clwyd* 29 B10
Groombridge *E Sussex* 10 D4
Grosebay *W Isles* 63 H2
Grosmont *Gwent* 15 B7
Grosmont *N Yorks* 41 E8
Groton *Suffolk* 27 L2
Grove *Dorset* 7 H7
Grove *Notts* 32 B4
Grove *Oxon* 16 E5
Grovesend *W Glam* 13 G9
Grudie *H'land* 54 D7
Gruids *H'land* 60 F6
Gruinard House *H'land* 60 G1
Gruline House *H'land* 50 D3
Grumbla *Cornw'l* 2 G1
Grundasound *Shetl'd* 64 E7
Grundisburgh *Suffolk* 27 K5
Gruting *Shetl'd* 64 D6
Grutness *Shetl'd* 64 F7
Grwedog *Gwyn* 28 B3
Gualachulain *H'land* 51 C8
Gualin House *H'land* 60 B4
Guard Bridge *Fife* 53 E9
Guarlford *Heref/Worcs* 22 H2
Guay *Tayside* 52 B5
Gubhill *Dumf/Gal* 43 B10
Guestling Green *E Sussex* 11 G7
Guestling Thorn *E Sussex* 11 F7
Guestwick *Norfolk* 26 C3
Guide *Lancs* 34 E6
Guide Post *Northum* 45 E10
Guilden Morden *Cambs* 25 L4
Guilden Sutton *Ches* 30 C3
Guildford *Surrey* 9 A11
Guildtown *Tayside* 52 D6
Guilsborough *Northants* 23 E10
Guilsfield *Powys* 21 A8
Guilton *Kent* 11 B11
Guiltreehill *S'clyde* 47 H8
Guineaford *Devon* 4 B4
Guisachan House *H'land* 55 G7
Guisborough *Clevl'd* 40 D6
Guiseley *W Yorks* 35 C10
Guist *Norfolk* 26 C3
Guiting Power *Glos* 16 B2
Gulberwick *Shetl'd* 64 E7
Gullane *Lothian* 49 A7
Gulval *Cornw'l* 2 F2
Gulworthy *Devon* 5 H3
Gumfreston *Dyfed* 12 G4
Gumley *Leics* 23 C10
Gummow's Shop *Cornw'l* 2 D6
Gun End *Staffs* 31 D8
Gunby *Humber* 36 D5
Gunby *Lincs* 32 H6
Gundleton *Hants* 9 C7
Gunn *Devon* 4 C5
Gunnerside *N Yorks* 39 E11
Gunnerton *Northum* 45 F7
Gunnerton Fell *Northum* 45 E7
Gunness *Humber* 36 F6
Gunnislake *Cornw'l* 3 C11
Gunnista *Shetl'd* 64 D7
Gunthorpe *Lincs* 36 G6
Gunthorpe *Norfolk* 26 B3
Gunthorpe *Notts* 32 F4
Gunville *I of Wight* 8 G6
Gupworthy *Som'set* 6 C3
Gurnard *I of Wight* 8 F6
Gurney Slade *Som'set* 7 A9
Gurnos *Powys* 14 C1
Gussage All Saints *Dorset* 8 E2
Gussage St. Andrew *Dorset* 8 E1
Gussage St. Michael *Dorset* 8 E1
Guston *Kent* 11 D11
Gutcher *Shetl'd* 64 B8
Guthrie *Tayside* 53 B10
Guyhirn *Cambs* 24 E5
Guy's Head *Lincs* 24 C6
Guy's Marsh *Dorset* 7 D11
Guyzance *Northum* 45 C10
Gwaelod-y-garth *Mid Glam* 14 F4
Gwaenysgor *Clwyd* 29 B10
Gwalchmai *Gwyn* 28 C3
Gwastad *Dyfed* 12 D4
Gwaun-Cae-Gurwen *W Glam* 13 F10
Gwbert-on-Sea *Dyfed* 12 B5
Gweek *Cornw'l* 2 G4
Gwehelog Com *Gwent* 15 D7
Gwenddwr *Powys* 20 H6
Gwennap *Cornw'l* 2 F4
Gwenter *Cornw'l* 2 H4
Gwernaffel *Powys* 21 E8
Gwernaffield *Clwyd* 29 D11
Gwernesney *Gwent* 15 D7
Gwernogle *Dyfed* 13 D8
Gwernymynydd *Clwyd* 29 D11
Gwern-y-Steeple *S Glam* 14 G4
Gwersyllt *Clwyd* 30 E2
Gwespyr *Clwyd* 29 B10
Gwinear *Cornw'l* 2 F3
Gwithian *Cornw'l* 2 F3
Gwyddelwern *Clwyd* 29 F10
Gwyddgrug *Dyfed* 13 C8
Gwynfryn *Clwyd* 29 E11
Gwystre *Powys* 20 F6
Gwytherin *Clwyd* 29 D8
Gyfelia *Clwyd* 29 F12
Gyffin *Gwyn* 29 C7
Gyffylliog *Clwyd* 29 D10
Habberley *Shrops* 21 B9
Habost *W Isles* 63 A6
Habost *W Isles* 63 E4
Habrough *Humber* 37 F9
Haceby *Lincs* 24 B1
Hacheston *Suffolk* 27 J6
Hackenthorpe *S Yorks* 32 B1
Hackford *Norfolk* 26 E3
Hackforth *N Yorks* 40 F3
Hackland *Orkney* 64 C2
Hacklete *W Isles* 63 C2
Hackleton *Northants* 23 G11
Hackness *N Yorks* 41 F10
Hackney *London* 18 E4
Hackthorn *Lincs* 33 B7
Hackthorpe *Cumb* 39 C7
Haconby *Lincs* 24 C2
Hacton *London* 18 E5
Hadden *Borders* 49 F10
Haddenham *Bucks* 17 C8
Haddenham *Cambs* 25 H6
Haddington *Lincs* 32 D6
Haddington *Lothian* 49 B8
Haddiscoe *Norfolk* 26 F7
Haddoch *Gramp* 58 C3
Haddon *Cambs* 24 F2
Hade Edge *W Yorks* 35 G10
Hademore *Staffs* 22 A5
Hadfield *Derby* 35 G9
Hadham Cross *Herts* 18 B4
Hadham Ford *Herts* 18 B4
Hadleigh *Essex* 19 E8
Hadleigh *Suffolk* 27 L3
Hadley *Shrops* 21 A12
Hadley End *Staffs* 31 H10
Hadley Wood *London* 18 D3
Hadlow *Kent* 10 C5
Hadlow Down *E Sussex* 10 F4
Hadnall *Shrops* 30 H4
Hadstock *Essex* 25 L7
Hadwin's Close *Northum* 45 B10
Hadzor *Heref/Worcs* 22 F3
Haffenden Quarter *Kent* 11 D7
Hafod-Dinbych *Clwyd* 29 E8
Hafod-Peris *Dyfed* 20 F1
Haggate *Lancs* 35 D7
Haggbeck *Cumb* 44 F3
Haggerston *Northum* 45 B11
Hagley *Heref/Worcs* 21 H11
Hagley *Heref/Worcs* 22 D3
Hagworthingham *Lincs* 33 C10
Haigh *Gtr Man* 34 F5
Haigh *S Yorks* 35 F11
Haigh Moor *W Yorks* 35 E11
Haighton Green *Lancs* 34 D4
Hail Weston *Cambs* 25 J3
Haile *Cumb* 38 D3
Hailey *Herts* 18 C4
Hailey *Oxon* 16 C4
Hailsham *E Sussex* 10 G5
Hainault *London* 18 E4
Hainford *Norfolk* 26 D5
Hainton *Lincs* 33 B9
Haisthorpe *Humber* 37 A9
Halam *Notts* 32 E4
Halbeath *Fife* 52 H6
Halberton *Devon* 6 E3
Halcro *H'land* 61 B11
Hale *Ches* 30 B3
Hale *Gtr Man* 30 B6
Hale *Hants* 8 D3
Hale *Hants* 9 A10
Hale Cliff *Mersey* 30 B3
Hale Street *Kent* 10 C5
Halebarns *Gtr Man* 30 B6
Hales *Norfolk* 26 F7
Hales *Staffs* 30 G6
Halesowen *W Midlands* 22 D3
Halesworth *Suffolk* 27 H7
Halewood *Mersey* 30 B3
Halford *Shrops* 21 D10
Halford *Warwick* 22 H6
Halfpenny Furze *Dyfed* 12 F6
Halfpenny Green *Staffs* 22 C2
Halfway *Berks* 16 G5
Halfway *Dyfed* 13 D10
Halfway *Dyfed* 13 D11
Halfway House *Cornw'l* 3 C8
Halfway House *Devon* 6 G4
Halfway House *Dumf/Gal* 42 E4
Halfway House *Shrops* 21 A9
Halfway Houses *Kent* 11 A8
Halifax *W Yorks* 35 E9
Halket *S'clyde* 47 D9
Halkirk *H'land* 61 B10
Halkyn *Clwyd* 29 C11
Hall Dunnerdale *Cumb* 38 F5
Hall Green *W Midlands* 22 D5
Hall of the Forest *Shrops* 21 D7
Hall Waberthwaite *Cumb* 38 F3
Halland *E Sussex* 10 F4
Hallaton *Leics* 23 B11
Hallatrow *Avon* 7 A10
Hallbankgate *Cumb* 44 G4
Hallen *Avon* 15 F8
Hallfield Gate *Derby* 32 D1
Halliburton *Borders* 49 D9
Hallin *H'land* 62 B2
Halling *Kent* 10 B6
Hallington *Lincs* 33 B10
Hallington *Northum* 45 E8
Halliwell *Gtr Man* 34 F6
Halloughton *Notts* 32 E4
Hallow *Heref/Worcs* 22 F2
Hallrule *Borders* 44 B4
Halls *Lothian* 49 B9
Hall's Green *Herts* 18 A3
Hallsands *Devon* 5 M7
Hallscaur *Dumf/Gal* 43 B8
Halltoft End *Lincs* 24 A5
Halltree *Borders* 49 D7
Hallworthy *Cornw'l* 3 A9
Hallyne *Borders* 48 E5
Halmer End *Staffs* 30 E6
Halmore *Glos* 15 D10
Halmyre Mains *Borders* 48 D4
Halnaker *W Sussex* 9 E10
Halsall *Lancs* 34 F3
Halse *Northants* 23 H9
Halse *Som'set* 6 C5
Halsetown *Cornw'l* 2 F2
Halsham *Humber* 37 D10
Halsinger *Devon* 4 B4
Halstead *Essex* 27 M1
Halstead *Kent* 10 B4
Halstead *Leics* 23 B11
Halstock *Som'set* 7 E9
Haltcliff Bridge *Cumb* 38 B6
Haltham *Lincs* 33 D9
Halton *Bucks* 17 C9
Halton *Ches* 30 B4
Halton *Clwyd* 29 F12
Halton *Lancs* 34 A4
Halton *W Yorks* 35 D12
Halton East *N Yorks* 35 B9
Halton Gill *N Yorks* 39 G11
Halton Holegate *Lincs* 33 D11
Halton Lea Gate *Northum* 44 G5
Halton Park *Lancs* 34 A4
Halton Shields *Northum* 45 F8
Halton West *N Yorks* 35 B7
Haltwhistle *Northum* 44 G5
Halvergate *Norfolk* 26 E7
Halwell *Devon* 5 K6
Halwill *Devon* 4 F3
Halwill Junction *Devon* 4 F3
Ham *Devon* 6 F6
Ham *Glos* 15 D10
Ham *Kent* 11 C12
Ham *London* 18 G2
Ham *Wilts* 16 H4
Ham Green *Avon* 15 G8
Ham Green *Heref/Worcs* 22 F4
Ham Green *Kent* 11 A7
Ham Hill *Kent* 10 B6
Ham Street *Kent* 11 E8
Ham Street *Som'set* 7 C9
Hamble *Hants* 8 E6
Hambledon *Bucks* 17 E8
Hambledon *Hants* 9 E8
Hambledon *Surrey* 9 B11
Hambleton *Lancs* 34 C3
Hambleton *N Yorks* 36 D3
Hambridge *Som'set* 7 D7
Hambrook *W Sussex* 9 E9
Hameringham *Lincs* 33 C10
Hamerton *Cambs* 25 G2
Hamilton *S'clyde* 47 D12
Hammer *W Sussex* 9 C10
Hammerpot *W Sussex* 9 F12
Hammersmith *London* 18 F2
Hammerwich *Staffs* 22 A4
Hammond Street *Herts* 18 C3
Hammoon *Dorset* 7 E11
Hamnavoe *Shetl'd* 64 C6
Hamnavoe, Mainland *Shetl'd* 64 C7
Hamnavoe, Yell *Shetl'd* 64 C7
Hamnavoe *Shetl'd* 64 E7
Hampden *E Sussex* 10 H5
Hampden Row *Bucks* 17 D9
Hampnett *Glos* 16 C2
Hampole *S Yorks* 36 F3
Hampreston *Dorset* 8 F2
Hampstead *London* 18 E3
Hampstead Norris *Berks* 16 F6
Hampsthwaite *N Yorks* 35 A11
Hampton *Heref/Worcs* 22 H4
Hampton *London* 18 G1
Hampton *Shrops* 22 D1
Hampton Bishop *Heref/Worcs* 15 A9
Hampton Heath *Ches* 30 E4
Hampton in Arden *W Midlands* 22 D5
Hampton Lovett *Heref/Worcs* 22 F2
Hampton Lucy *Warwick* 22 F6
Hampton on the Hill *Warwick* 22 F6
Hampton Poyle *Oxon* 16 C6
Hamstall Ridware *Staffs* 31 H9
Hamstead *I of Wight* 8 G5
Hamstead *W Midlands* 22 C4
Hamstead Marshall *Berks* 16 H5
Hamsteels *Durham* 40 A2
Hamsterley *Durham* 40 B1
Hamsterley *Durham* 45 G9
Hamworthy *Dorset* 8 G1
Hanbury *Heref/Worcs* 22 F3
Hanbury *Staffs* 31 G10
Handbridge *Ches* 30 D3
Handcross *W Sussex* 10 E2
Handforth *Ches* 31 B7
Handley *Ches* 30 D3
Handsacre *Staffs* 22 A4
Handsworth *W Midlands* 22 C4
Handy Cross *Bucks* 17 E9
Handy Cross *Devon* 4 C3
Hanford *Staffs* 31 F7
Hanging Langford *Wilts* 8 B2
Hangingshaw *Dumf/Gal* 43 C11
Hangingshaw *S'clyde* 48 E2
Hankelow *Ches* 30 F5
Hankerton *Wilts* 16 E1
Hankham *E Sussex* 10 G5
Hanley *Staffs* 31 E7
Hanley Castle *Heref/Worcs* 22 H2
Hanley Childe *Heref/Worcs* 21 F12
Hanley Swan *Heref/Worcs* 22 H2
Hanley William *Heref/Worcs* 21 F12
Hanlith *N Yorks* 35 A8
Hanmer *Clwyd* 30 F3
Hannah *Lincs* 33 B12
Hannington *Hants* 9 A7
Hannington *Northants* 23 E11
Hannington *Wilts* 16 E3
Hannington Wick *Wilts* 16 E3
Hanslope *Bucks* 23 G11
Hanthorpe *Lincs* 24 C2
Hanwell *London* 18 F2
Hanwell *Oxon* 23 H8
Hanwood *Shrops* 21 B10
Hanworth *London* 18 G1
Hanworth *Norfolk* 26 B5
Happendon *S'clyde* 48 F1
Happisburgh *Norfolk* 26 B7
Happisburgh Common *Norfolk* 26 C7
Hapsford *Ches* 30 C3
Hapton *Lancs* 34 D6
Hapton *Norfolk* 26 F5
Harberton *Devon* 5 K6
Harbertonford *Devon* 5 K6
Harbledown *Kent* 11 B10
Harborne *W Midlands* 22 D4
Harborough Magna *Warwick* 23 D8
Harbottle *Northum* 45 C7
Harbourneford *Devon* 5 J6
Harbury *Warwick* 23 F7
Harby *Leics* 32 G5
Harby *Notts* 32 C6
Harcombe *Devon* 6 G5
Harcombe *Devon* 6 H2
Harcourt *Cornw'l* 2 F5
Hard Horn *Lancs* 34 C2
Harden *W Yorks* 35 C9
Hardenhuish *Wilts* 15 G12
Hardgate *Dumf/Gal* 43 E9
Hardgate *Gramp* 59 G5
Hardham *W Sussex* 9 D11
Hardingham *Norfolk* 26 E3
Hardings Wood *Ches* 31 E7
Hardingstone *Northants* 23 F11
Hardington *Som'set* 7 A10
Hardington Mandeville *Som'set* 7 E8
Hardington Marsh *Som'set* 7 E8
Hardisworthy *Devon* 4 D1
Hardley *Hants* 8 F6
Hardley Street *Norfolk* 26 E7
Hardmonsworth *London* 18 F1
Hardrow *N Yorks* 39 F11
Hardstoft *Derby* 32 D2
Hardway *Som'set* 7 C10
Hardwick *Bucks* 17 B9
Hardwick *Cambs* 25 J5
Hardwick *Lincs* 32 C6
Hardwick *Norfolk* 26 F5
Hardwick *Northants* 23 E11
Hardwick *Oxon* 16 D5
Hardwick *Oxon* 17 A7
Hardwick Grange *Notts* 32 C4
Hardwicke *Glos* 15 B12
Hardwicke *Glos* 15 C11
Hardwicke *Heref/Worcs* 21 H8
Hardy's Green *Essex* 19 B9
Hare Green *Essex* 19 A10
Hare Hatch *Berks* 17 F9
Hare Street *Essex* 18 C4
Hare Street *Herts* 18 A4
Harebeating *E Sussex* 10 G5
Hareby *Lincs* 33 D10
Hareden *Lancs* 34 B5
Harefield *Herts* 17 E11
Harefield *Herts* 18 E1
Harehills *W Yorks* 35 D11
Harehope *Northum* 45 A9
Harelaw *Borders* 49 G8
Harelaw *S'clyde* 47 D9
Harelaw *S'clyde* 48 E2
Haremuir *Gramp* 59 K5
Harescеugh *Cumb* 39 A8
Harescombe *Glos* 15 C11
Haresfield *Glos* 15 C11
Hareshaw *S'clyde* 48 C1
Hareshaw Head *Northum* 45 D7
Harewood *W Yorks* 35 C12
Harewood End *Heref/Worcs* 15 B8
Harewood Estate *W Yorks* 36 F3
Harford *Devon* 4 F7
Harford *Devon* 5 K5
Hargabost *W Isles* 63 G1
Hargate *Norfolk* 26 F4
Hargatewall *Derby* 31 C9
Hargrave *Ches* 30 D3
Hargrave *Northants* 25 H1
Hargrave *Suffolk* 27 J1
Haringey *London* 18 E3
Harker *Cumb* 44 G2
Harkstead *Suffolk* 27 M5
Harlaston *Staffs* 22 A5
Harlaxton *Lincs* 32 G6
Harle Syke *Lancs* 35 D7
Harlech *Gwyn* 28 G5
Harlescott *Shrops* 21 A10
Harlesden *London* 18 F2
Harleston *Norfolk* 27 G5
Harleston *Suffolk* 27 J3
Harlestone *Northants* 23 F10
Harley *Shrops* 21 B11
Harleyholm *S'clyde* 48 F2
Harlington *Beds* 25 M1
Harlington *London* 18 F1
Harlington *S Yorks* 36 G3
Harlosh *H'land* 62 D2
Harlow *Essex* 18 C5
Harlow Hill *Northum* 45 F9
Harlthorpe *Humber* 36 C5
Harlton *Cambs* 25 K5
Harman's Cross *Dorset* 8 H1
Harmby *N Yorks* 40 F2
Harmer Green *Herts* 18 B3
Harmerhill *Shrops* 30 H3
Harmston *Lincs* 33 D7
Harnhill *Glos* 16 D2
Harold Hill *London* 18 E5
Haroldston West *Dyfed* 12 E2
Haroldswick *Shetl'd* 64 A8
Harome *N Yorks* 40 G6
Harpenden *Herts* 17 C12

Harper Ridge Northum 49 E11
Harpertoun Borders 49 E10
Harpford Devon 6 G4
Harpham Humber 37 A8
Harpley Heref/Worcs 21 F12
Harpley Norfolk 26 C1
Harpole Northants 23 F10
Harpsden Oxon 17 F8
Harpswell Lincs 32 A6
Harpur Hill Derby 31 C9
Harpurhey Gtr Man 35 G7
Harraby Cumb 44 H3
Harracott Devon 4 C4
Harrapool H'land 62 F6
Harrietfield Tayside 52 D5
Harrietsfield Borders 49 G9
Harrietsham Kent 11 C7
Harrington Cumb 38 C2
Harrington Lincs 33 C10
Harrington Northants 23 D11
Harringworth Northants 23 B12
Harriseahead Staffs 31 E7
Harrogate N Yorks 35 B12
Harrold Beds 23 F12
Harrow London 18 E2
Harrow Street Suffolk 27 L3
Harrow Weald London 18 E2
Harrowbarrow Cornw'l 3 C11
Harrowbridge Cornw'l 3 B9
Harrowgate Village Durham 40 C3
Harston Cambs 25 K5
Harston Leics 32 G5
Harswell Humber 36 C6
Hart Clevl'd 40 B5
Hart Loch Northum 45 B10
Hartburn Northum 45 D9
Hartest Suffolk 27 K1
Hartfield E Sussex 10 E4
Hartford Cambs 25 H4
Hartford Ches 30 C5
Hartford End Essex 19 B7
Hartfordbridge Hants 17 H8
Harthill Ches 30 E4
Harthill Derby 32 B2
Harthill S'clyde 48 C2
Hartington Derby 31 D9
Hartland Devon 4 D1
Hartlebury Heref/Worcs 22 E2
Hartlepool Clevl'd 40 B5
Hartley Cumb 39 D10
Hartley Kent 10 A5
Hartley Kent 10 E6
Hartley Northum 45 E11
Hartley Green Kent 10 A5
Hartley Wespall Hants 17 H8
Hartley Wintney Hants 17 H8
Hartlip Kent 11 B7
Harton N Yorks 36 A5
Harton Shrops 21 D10
Harton Tyne/Wear 45 G12
Hartpury Glos 15 B11
Hartshead W Yorks 35 E10
Hartshill Warwick 23 C7
Hartshorne Derby 31 H11
Hartsop Cumb 38 D6
Hartwell Bucks 17 C9
Hartwell Northants 23 G11
Hartwith N Yorks 35 A11
Hartwood S'clyde 48 C1
Hartwoodburn Borders 49 G7
Hartwoodmyres Borders 49 G7
Harvel Kent 10 B5
Harvington Heref/Worcs 22 G4
Harvington Cross Heref/Worcs 22 G4
Harwell Oxon 16 E6
Harwich Essex 27 M6
Harwood Durham 39 B10
Harwood Gtr Man 34 F6
Harwood Northum 45 D8
Harwood Dale N Yorks 41 F9
Harworth Notts 32 A3
Hascombe Surrey 9 B11
Haselbech Northants 23 D10
Haselbury Plucknett Som'set 7 E8
Haseley Warwick 22 E6
Haselor Warwick 22 F5
Hasfield Glos 15 B11
Hasguard Dyfed 12 F2
Hasguard Cross Dyfed 12 F2
Haskayne Lancs 34 F2
Hasketon Suffolk 27 K5
Hasland Derby 32 C1
Haslemere Surrey 9 C10
Haslingden Lancs 34 E6
Haslingfield Cambs 25 K5
Haslington Ches 30 E6
Hassall Ches 30 D6
Hassall Green Ches 30 D6
Hassell Street Kent 11 C9
Hassendean Borders 49 G8
Hassingham Norfolk 26 E7
Hassington Borders 49 E10
Hassocks W Sussex 10 F2
Hassop Derby 31 C10
Hastigrow H'land 61 B11
Hastingleigh Kent 11 D9
Hastings E Sussex 11 G7
Hastingwood Essex 18 C5
Hastoe Herts 17 C10
Haswell Durham 40 A4
Haswell Plough Durham 40 A4
Haswellsykes Borders 48 E5
Hatch Hants 9 A8
Hatch Beauchamp Som'set 6 D6
Hatch End London 18 E1
Hatch Green Som'set 6 D6
Hatchednze Borders 49 E10
Hatchet Gate Hants 8 F5
Hatchmere Ches 30 C4
Hatcliffe Humber 37 G10
Hatfield Heref/Worcs 21 F11
Hatfield Heref/Worcs 22 G2
Hatfield Herts 18 C2
Hatfield S Yorks 36 F4
Hatfield Broad Oak Essex 18 B5
Hatfield Heath Essex 18 B5
Hatfield Peverel Essex 19 C8
Hatfield Woodhouse S Yorks 36 F5
Hatford Oxon 16 E4
Hatherden Hants 8 A5
Hatherleigh Devon 4 E4
Hathern Leics 32 H2
Hatherop Glos 16 D3
Hathersage Derby 31 B10
Hathershaw Gtr Man 35 G8
Hatherton Ches 30 E5
Hatherton Staffs 22 A3
Hatley St. George Cambs 25 K4
Hatt Cornw'l 3 C11
Hattingley Hants 9 B8
Hatton Ches 30 B4
Hatton Derby 31 G10
Hatton Gramp 58 D8
Hatton Lincs 33 C9
Hatton London 18 F1
Hatton Shrops 21 C10
Hatton Warwick 22 E6
Hatton Fintray Gramp 58 F6
Hatton Heath Ches 30 D3
Hattoncrook Gramp 58 E6
Haugh Gtr Man 35 F8
Haugh S'clyde 47 G10
Haugh Head Northum 49 G12
Haugh of Glass Gramp 58 D2
Haugh of Urr Dumf/Gal 43 E9
Haugham Lincs 33 B10
Haughhead S'clyde 47 B11
Haughley Suffolk 27 J3
Haughley Green Suffolk 27 J3
Haughs of Clinterty Gramp 58 F6
Haughterslaw Northum 45 A9
Haughton Notts 32 C4
Haughton Shrops 21 A11
Haughton Shrops 21 C12
Haughton Shrops 30 G2
Haughton Staffs 31 H7
Haughton Castle Northum 45 F7
Haughton Green Gtr Man 35 H8
Haughton Moss Ches 30 E4
Haultwick Herts 18 B3
Haunn H'land 50 C1
Hauxley Northum 45 C11
Hauxton Cambs 25 K5
Havant Hants 9 F8
Haven Heref/Worcs 21 G9
Haven Street I of Wight 9 G7
Havercroft W Yorks 36 F2
Haverfordwest Dyfed 12 E3
Haverhill Suffolk 25 L8
Haverigg Cumb 38 G4
Havering London 18 E5
Havering-atte-Bower London 18 E5
Haversham Bucks 23 H11
Haverthwaite Cumb 38 G6
Haverton Hill Clevl'd 40 C5
Hawarden Clwyd 29 D12
Hawbush Green Essex 19 B8
Hawen Dyfed 13 B7
Hawes N Yorks 39 F11
Hawford Heref/Worcs 22 F2
Hawick Borders 44 B3
Hawk Green Gtr Man 31 B8
Hawkchurch Devon 7 F7
Hawkedon Suffolk 27 K1
Hawkenbury Kent 10 D5
Hawkeridge Wilts 7 A12
Hawkes End W Midlands 22 D6
Hawkesbury Avon 15 F10
Hawkesbury Upton Avon 15 F11
Hawkhill Northum 45 B10
Hawkhurst Kent 10 E6
Hawkinge Kent 11 D10
Hawkley Hants 9 C9
Hawkridge Som'set 6 C2
Hawkshaw Lane Gtr Man 34 F6
Hawkshead Cumb 38 E6
Hawkshead Hill Cumb 38 E6
Hawksland S'clyde 48 E1
Hawkswick N Yorks 39 H12
Hawksworth Notts 32 F5
Hawksworth W Yorks 35 C10
Hawkwell Essex 19 E8
Hawley Hants 17 H9
Hawley Kent 10 A4
Hawling Glos 16 B2
Hawnby N Yorks 40 F5
Haworth W Yorks 35 D9
Hawstead Suffolk 27 J1
Hawthorn Durham 40 A4
Hawthorn Wilts 15 G11
Hawthornside Borders 44 B4
Hawthorpe Lincs 24 C2
Hawton Notts 32 E5
Haxby N Yorks 36 A4
Haxey Humber 36 G5
Haxted Surrey 10 D3
Hay on Wye Powys 21 H8
Hay Street Herts 18 A4
Haycastle Dyfed 12 D2
Haycastle Cross Dyfed 12 D3
Haydock Mersey 34 G4
Haydon Dorset 7 E10
Haydon Northum 45 F7
Haydon Bridge Northum 45 G7
Haydon Wick Wilts 16 E2
Haye Cornw'l 3 C10
Hayes London 18 F1
Hayes London 18 G4
Hayfield Derby 31 B9
Hayfield Fife 53 H7
Hayhill S'clyde 47 H9
Hayle Cornw'l 2 F3
Hayling Island Hants 9 F8
Haymount Borders 49 F9
Hayne Devon 6 F2
Haynes Beds 25 L2
Haynes West End Beds 25 L2
Haysden Kent 10 D4
Hayshead Tayside 53 C11
Hayton Cumb 43 G11
Hayton Cumb 44 G3
Hayton Gramp 59 G7
Hayton Humber 36 C6
Hayton Notts 32 B4
Hayton Shrops 21 D10
Hayton's Bent Shrops 21 D10
Haytor Vale Devon 5 H6
Hayward's Heath W Sussex 10 F2
Haywood Oaks Notts 32 E3
Hazel Grove Gtr Man 31 B8
Hazel Street Kent 10 D6
Hazelbank S'clyde 48 E1
Hazelbury Bryan Dorset 7 E10
Hazeley Hants 17 H8
Hazelmere Bucks 17 E10
Hazelslade Staffs 22 A4
Hazelton Walls Fife 53 E8
Hazelwood Derby 31 F11
Hazlerigg Tyne/Wear 45 F10
Hazleton Glos 16 B2
Hazon Northum 45 C10
Heacham Norfolk 24 B8
Headbourne Worthy Hants 8 C6
Headbrook Heref/Worcs 21 G8
Headcorn Kent 11 D7
Headington Oxon 16 C6
Headlam Durham 40 C2
Headless Cross Heref/Worcs 22 F4
Headley Hants 16 H6
Headley Hants 9 C9
Headley Surrey 10 C1
Headley Down Hants 9 B10
Headon Notts 32 C5
Heads S'clyde 47 E12
Heads Nook Cumb 44 G3
Heagan Shetl'd 64 D7
Heage Derby 32 E1
Healaugh N Yorks 36 B3
Healaugh N Yorks 39 E12
Heald Green Gtr Man 31 B7
Heale Devon 4 A5
Heale Som'set 7 B10
Healey Lancs 35 E7
Healey N Yorks 40 G2
Healey Northum 45 G8
Healey Cote Northum 45 C9
Healeyfield Durham 45 H9
Healing Humber 37 F10
Heamoor Cornw'l 2 G2
Heanor Derby 32 F2
Heanton Punchardon Devon 4 B4
Heapham Lincs 32 A6
Hearthstane Borders 48 G4
Heasley Mill Devon 4 C6
Heast H'land 62 F6
Heath Derby 32 C2
Heath and Reach Beds 17 A10
Heath Cross Devon 4 F7
Heath End Hants 17 H7
Heath End Surrey 9 A10
Heath End W Midlands 22 B4
Heath Hayes Staffs 22 A4
Heath Hill Shrops 22 A1
Heath House Som'set 7 B7
Heath Pault Cross Som'set 6 C3
Heath Town W Midlands 22 B3
Heathcote Derby 31 D10
Heathcross Devon 4 F6
Heather Leics 23 A7
Heatherfield H'land 62 D4
Heatheryhaugh Tayside 52 B6
Heathfield Cumb 43 G12
Heathfield Devon 5 H7
Heathfield E Sussex 10 F4
Heathfield S'clyde 47 C8
Heathfield Som'set 6 D5
Heathhall Dumf/Gal 43 D10
Heathton Shrops 22 C2
Heatley Ches 30 A5
Heaton Gtr Man 35 H7
Heaton Lancs 34 A3
Heaton Staffs 31 D8
Heaton W Yorks 35 D10
Heaton's Bridge Lancs 34 F3
Heaverham Kent 10 B4
Heavitree Devon 6 G3
Hebburn Tyne/Wear 45 G11
Hebden N Yorks 35 A9
Hebden Bridge W Yorks 35 D8
Hebden Green Ches 30 D5
Hebron Dyfed 12 D5
Hebron Northum 45 D10
Heck Dumf/Gal 43 D11
Heckfield Hants 17 H8
Heckfield Green Suffolk 27 H5
Heckington Lincs 24 A2
Hecklebirnie S'clyde 48 F2
Heckmondwike W Yorks 35 E10
Heddington Wilts 16 G1
Heddington Wick Wilts 16 G1
Heddon Devon 4 C5
Heddon on the Wall Northum 45 F9
Hedenham Norfolk 26 F6
Hedge Cross Devon 5 G4
Hedge End Hants 8 E6
Hedgerley Bucks 17 E10
Hedging Som'set 6 C6
Hedgon Hill Heref/Worcs 21 G11
Hedley on the Hill Northum 45 G9
Hednesford Staffs 22 A3
Hedon Humber 37 D9
Hedsor Bucks 17 E10
Heiferlaw Bank Northum 45 A10
Heighington Durham 40 C3
Heighington Lincs 33 C7
Heights of Brae H'land 56 D1
Heights of Kinlochewe H'land 54 C4
Heilam H'land 60 B5
Heiton Borders 49 F9
Hele Devon 4 A4
Hele Devon 5 G2
Hele Devon 6 F3
Hele Som'set 6 D5
Helensburgh S'clyde 47 A8
Helentongate S'clyde 47 F9
Helford Cornw'l 2 G5
Helford Passage Cornw'l 2 G5
Helhoughton Norfolk 26 C2
Helions Bumpstead Essex 25 L7
Helland Cornw'l 3 C8
Hellandbridge Cornw'l 3 C8
Hellesdon Norfolk 26 D5
Hellidon Northants 23 F8
Hellifield N Yorks 35 B7
Helling E Sussex 10 G4
Hellington Norfolk 26 E6
Helm Northum 45 C10
Helmdon Northants 23 H9
Helmingham Suffolk 27 J5
Helmington Row Durham 40 B2
Helmsdale H'land 61 E10
Helmshore Lancs 34 E6
Helmsley N Yorks 40 G6
Helperby N Yorks 40 H5
Helperthorpe N Yorks 41 H9
Helpringham Lincs 24 B2
Helpston Cambs 24 E2
Helsby Ches 30 C3
Helston Cornw'l 2 G4
Helstone Cornw'l 3 B8
Helton Cumb 39 C7
Helwith Bridge N Yorks 39 H10
Hemel Hempstead Herts 17 D11
Hemingbrough N Yorks 36 D4
Hemingby Lincs 33 C9
Hemingford Abbots Cambs 25 H4
Hemingford Grey Cambs 25 H4
Hemingstone Suffolk 27 K5
Hemington Leics 32 G2
Hemington Northants 25 G2
Hemington Som'set 7 A10
Hemley Suffolk 27 L6
Hemlington Clevl'd 40 D5
Hemngfield S Yorks 36 G2
Hempholme Humber 37 B8
Hempnall Norfolk 26 F5
Hempnall Green Norfolk 26 F5
Hempstead Essex 25 L7
Hempstead Kent 10 B6
Hempstead Norfolk 26 B4
Hempsted Glos 15 C11
Hempton Norfolk 26 C2
Hempton Oxon 16 A5
Hemsby Norfolk 26 D8
Hemswell Lincs 32 A6
Hemsworth W Yorks 36 F2
Hemyock Devon 6 E5
Henbury Avon 15 F9
Henbury Ches 31 C7
Henderbarrow Corner Devon 4 F3
Hendon London 18 E2
Hendon Tyne/Wear 45 G12
Hendre Clwyd 29 D11
Hendreforgan Mid Glam 14 E3
Hendre-wen Dyfed 12 D3
Hendy Dyfed 13 G9
Heneglwys Gwyn 28 C4
Hen-feddau Dyfed 12 D6
Henfield Avon 15 F10
Henfield W Sussex 10 F1
Hengherst Kent 11 D8
Hengoed Mid Glam 14 E5
Hengoed Powys 21 G8
Hengoed Shrops 30 G2
Hengrave Suffolk 27 H1
Henham Essex 18 A5
Henhill Northum 45 E12
Heniarth Powys 21 B7
Henlade Som'set 6 D6
Henlaw Northum 45 C11
Henley Dorset 7 F10
Henley Shrops 21 D10
Henley Som'set 7 C8
Henley Suffolk 27 K5
Henley W Sussex 9 D10
Henley Street Kent 10 A5
Henley-in-Arden Warwick 22 E5
Henley-on-Thames Oxon 17 F8
Henllan Clwyd 29 C9
Henllan Dyfed 13 C7
Henllan Amgoed Dyfed 12 E5
Henllys Gwent 14 E6
Henlow Beds 25 L3
Hennock Devon 5 H7
Henny Street Essex 27 L2
Henryd Gwyn 29 C7
Henry's Moat Dyfed 12 D4
Hensall N Yorks 36 E4
Henshaw Northum 44 G6
Hensingham Cumb 38 D2
Henstead Suffolk 27 G8
Henstridge Som'set 7 D10
Henstridge Ash Som'set 7 D10
Henstridge Bowden Som'set 7 D10
Henton Oxon 17 D8
Henton Som'set 7 B8
Henwick Heref/Worcs 22 G2
Henwood Cornw'l 3 B9
Heol Senni Powys 14 B3
Heol-y-Cyw Mid Glam 14 F3
Hepburn Northum 45 A9
Hepple Northum 45 C8
Hepple Whitefield Northum 45 C8
Hepscott Northum 45 E10
Hepstoonstall W Yorks 35 D8
Hepworth Suffolk 27 H3
Hepworth W Yorks 35 F10
Herbrandston Dyfed 12 F2
Hereford Heref/Worcs 21 H10
Heriot Borders 48 D6
Hermiston Borders 49 G8
Hermitage Berks 16 G6
Hermitage Borders 44 C3
Hermitage Dorset 7 F10
Hermitage Dumf/Gal 43 E9
Hermitage W Sussex 9 F9
Hermon Dyfed 12 D5
Hermon Dyfed 13 D10
Hermon Gwyn 28 C3
Herne Kent 11 B10
Herne Bay Kent 11 A10
Herner Devon 4 C5
Hernhill Kent 11 B9
Herodsfoot Cornw'l 3 D9
Heronden Kent 11 C11
Herongate Essex 18 E6
Heronsford S'clyde 42 C2
Heronsgate Herts 17 E11
Herriard Hants 9 B8
Herringfleet Suffolk 26 F8
Herring's Green Beds 25 L2
Herringswell Suffolk 25 H8
Herrington Tyne/Wear 45 H11
Hersden Kent 11 B10
Hersham Surrey 17 H12
Herstmonceux E Sussex 10 G5
Herston Dorset 8 H2
Herston Orkney 64 E2
Hertford Herts 18 C3
Hertford Heath Herts 18 C3
Hertingfordbury Herts 18 C3
Hesket Newmarket Cumb 38 A6
Hesketh Bank Lancs 34 E3
Hesketh Lane Lancs 34 C5
Heskin Green Lancs 34 F4
Hesleden Durham 40 A4
Hesleyside Northum 44 E6
Heslington N Yorks 36 B4
Hessay N Yorks 36 B3
Hessenford Cornw'l 3 D10
Hessett Suffolk 27 J2
Hessilhead S'clyde 47 D9
Hessle Humber 37 E8
Hest Bank Lancs 34 A3
Heston London 18 F1
Heswall Mersey 30 B1
Hethe Oxon 17 A7
Hethersett Norfolk 26 E5
Hethersgill Cumb 44 F3
Hethpool Northum 49 G11
Hett Durham 40 B3
Hetton N Yorks 35 A8
Hetton Downs Tyne/Wear 45 H11
Hetton Law Northum 45 C11
Hetton Steads Northum 45 B11
Hetton-le-Hole Tyne/Wear 45 H11
Heugh Northum 45 F9
Heugh-head Gramp 58 F1
Heveningham Suffolk 27 H6
Hever Kent 10 D4
Heversham Cumb 39 G7
Hevingham Norfolk 26 C5
Hewelsfield Glos 15 D9
Hewish Avon 15 H7
Hewish Som'set 7 E7
Heworth N Yorks 36 B4
Hexham Northum 45 G7
Hexpath Borders 49 E9
Hextable Kent 10 A4
Hexworthy Devon 5 H5
Heybridge Essex 18 D6
Heybridge Essex 19 C8
Heybridge Basin Essex 19 C8
Heybrook Bay Devon 5 L4
Heydon Cambs 25 L5
Heydon Norfolk 26 C4
Heydour Lincs 33 F7
Heylor Shetl'd 64 C6
Heysham Lancs 34 A3
Heyshaw N Yorks 35 A10
Heyshott W Sussex 9 D10
Heytesbury Wilts 8 B1
Heythrop Oxon 16 A4
Heywood Gtr Man 35 F7
Heywood Wilts 7 A12
Hibaldstow Humber 37 G7
Hickleton S Yorks 36 G3
Hickling Norfolk 26 C7
Hickling Notts 32 G4
Hickling Green Norfolk 26 C7
Hickstead E Sussex 10 F2
Hidcote Boyce Glos 22 H5
High Ackworth W Yorks 36 E2
High Angerton Northum 45 E9
High Bankhill Cumb 39 A8
High Beach Essex 18 D4
High Bentham N Yorks 39 H9
High Bickington Devon 4 D5
High Birkwith N Yorks 39 G10
High Blantyre S'clyde 47 D11
High Bonnybridge Lothian 48 B1
High Borgue Dumf/Gal 43 F7
High Bradfield S Yorks 35 H11
High Bradley N Yorks 35 B9
High Bray Devon 4 C6
High Brooms Kent 10 D5
High Bullen Devon 4 D4
High Burton N Yorks 40 G2

High Buston *Northum* **45** B10
High Callerton *Northum* **45** F10
High Catton *Humber* **36** B5
High Church *Northum* **45** E10
High Cleughearn *S'clyde* **47** E11
High Cogges *Oxon* **16** C5
High Coniscliffe *Durham* **40** D3
High Cross *Borders* **49** E8
High Cross *Hants* **9** C8
High Cross *Herts* **18** B4
High Cross Bank *Derby* **31** H11
High Duncryne *S'clyde* **47** A9
High Easter *Essex* **18** B6
High Ellington *N Yorks* **40** G2
High Entercommon *N Yorks* **40** E4
High Ercall *Shrops* **21** A11
High Etherley *Durham* **40** B2
High Garrett *Essex* **19** A7
High Grange *Durham* **40** B2
High Grantley *N Yorks* **40** H3
High Green *Heref/Worcs* **22** H2
High Green *Norfolk* **26** E4
High Green *S Yorks* **35** G12
High Halden *Kent* **11** D8
High Halstow *Kent* **10** A6
High Ham *Som'set* **7** C8
High Harrington *Cumb* **38** C3
High Haswell *Durham* **40** A4
High Hatton *Shrops* **30** H5
High Hawsker *N Yorks* **41** D9
High Hesket *Cumb* **39** A7
High Hesleden *Durham* **40** A5
High Hoyland *S Yorks* **35** F11
High Hunsley *Humber* **37** D7
High Hurstwood *E Sussex* **10** E4
High Hutton *N Yorks* **41** H8
High Ireby *Cumb* **38** B5
High Kilburn *N Yorks* **40** G5
High Lane *Gtr Man* **31** B8
High Lane *Heref/Worcs* **21** F12
High Laver *Essex* **18** C5
High Legh *Ches* **30** B5
High Leven *Clevl'd* **40** D5
High Littleton *Avon* **15** H9
High Lorton *Cumb* **38** C4
High Marishes *N Yorks* **41** G8
High Marnham *Notts* **32** C5
High Melton *S Yorks* **36** G3
High Mickley *Northum* **45** G9
High Mindork *Dumf/Gal* **42** F4
High Mowthorpe *N Yorks* **41** H9
High Newton *Cumb* **38** G6
High Newton-by-the-Sea *Northum* **45** E12
High Nibthwaite *Cumb* **38** F5
High Offley *Staffs* **30** H6
High Ongar *Essex* **18** D5
High Onn *Staffs* **22** A2
High Pennyvenie *S'clyde* **42** A6
High Roding *Essex* **18** B6
High Row *Cumb* **38** B6
High Shaw *N Yorks* **39** F11
High Skelding *N Yorks* **40** H2
High Spen *Tyne/Wear* **45** G9
High Stoop *Durham* **40** A1
High Street *Cornw'l* **3** D7
High Street *Suffolk* **27** K2
High Street *Suffolk* **27** K7
High Street Green *Suffolk* **27** K3
High Throston *Clevl'd* **40** B5
High Toynton *Lincs* **33** C10
High Trewhitt *Northum* **45** B8
High Valleyfield *Lothian* **48** A3
High Warden *Northum* **45** F7
High Wray *Cumb* **38** E6
High Wych *Herts* **18** C5
High Wycombe *Bucks* **17** E9
Higham *Derby* **32** D1
Higham *Kent* **10** A6
Higham *Lancs* **35** D7
Higham *Suffolk* **25** J8
Higham *Suffolk* **27** L3
Higham Dykes *Northum* **45** E9
Higham Ferrers *Northants* **25** H1
Higham Gobion *Beds* **25** M2
Higham on the Hill *Leics* **23** C7
Higham Wood *Kent* **10** C5
Highampton *Devon* **4** E4
Highbridge *H'land* **55** L6
Highbridge *Som'set* **6** B6
Highbrook *W Sussex* **10** E2
Highburton *W Yorks* **35** F10
Highbury *Som'set* **7** A10
Highchesters *Borders* **44** B3
Highclere *Hants* **16** H5
Highcliffe *Dorset* **8** G4
Higher Alham *Som'set* **7** B10
Higher Ansty *Dorset* **7** F11
Higher Ashton *Devon* **6** H2
Higher Ballam *Lancs* **34** D2
Higher Boscaswell *Cornw'l* **2** F1
Higher Combe *Som'set* **6** C3
Higher Heath *Shrops* **30** G4
Higher Kinnerton *Clwyd* **29** D12
Higher Nyland *Dorset* **7** D10
Higher Penwortham *Lancs* **34** D4
Higher Town *I of Scilly* **2** C2
Higher Walton *Ches* **30** B4
Higher Walton *Lancs* **34** D4
Higher Whatcombe *Dorset* **7** F11
Higher Whitley *Ches* **30** B5
Higher Wych *Ches* **30** F3
Highfield *S Yorks* **32** B1
Highfield *S'clyde* **47** D8
Highfield *Tyne/Wear* **45** G9
Highfields *Cambs* **25** J5
Highfields *Northum* **49** D12
Highgate *London* **18** E3
Highgate *N Yorks* **36** E4
Highgreen Manor *Northum* **44** D6
Highlands *Durham* **40** C2
Highlands *Gramp* **58** F6
Highlane *Derby* **32** B1
Highleadon *Glos* **15** B11
Highleigh *W Sussex* **9** F10
Highley *Shrops* **22** D1
Highmoor Cross *Oxon* **17** F8
Highmoor Hill *Gwent* **15** E8
Highnam Green *Glos* **15** B11
Highridge *Devon* **4** D6
Highsted *Kent* **11** B8
Highstreet Green *Essex* **27** M1
Hightae *Dumf/Gal* **43** D11
Hightown *Ches* **31** D7
Hightown *Dumf/Gal* **43** C11
Hightown *Mersey* **34** G2
Hightown of Craigs *Dumf/Gal* **43** D11
Highway *Cornw'l* **2** E4
Highway *Wilts* **16** G2
Highweek *Devon* **5** J7
Highworth *Wilts* **16** E3
Hilborough *Norfolk* **26** E1
Hilcote *Derby* **32** D2
Hilcott *Wilts* **16** H2
Hilden Park *Kent* **10** C4
Hildenborough *Kent* **10** C4
Hildersham *Cambs* **25** K6
Hilderstone *Staffs* **31** G8
Hilderthorpe *Humber* **37** A9
Hilfield *Dorset* **7** F9
Hilgay *Norfolk* **24** F7
Hill *Avon* **15** E9
Hill *Devon* **4** C6
Hill *W Midlands* **22** B5
Hill Brow *W Sussex* **9** D9
Hill Cottages *N Yorks* **41** E7
Hill Dale *Lancs* **34** F4
Hill Dyke *Lincs* **33** E10
Hill End *Durham* **39** B12
Hill End *Fife* **52** H5
Hill Gate *Heref/Worcs* **15** B8
Hill Head *Hants* **9** F7
Hill Head *Northum* **45** F7
Hill Mountain *Dyfed* **12** F3
Hill of Beath *Fife* **52** H6
Hill of Fearn *H'land* **56** B4
Hill of Mountblairy *Gramp* **58** B4
Hill Ridware *Staffs* **31** H9
Hill Row *Cambs* **25** H5
Hill Top *Hants* **8** F5
Hill Top *W Yorks* **35** F12
Hill View *Dorset* **8** F1
Hillam *N Yorks* **36** D3
Hillbeck *Cumb* **39** D10
Hillberry *I of Man* **38** G2
Hillborough *Kent* **11** A10
Hillbourne *Dorset* **8** G2
Hillbrae *Gramp* **58** E5
Hillbutts *Dorset* **8** F1
Hillcairnie *Fife* **53** E8
Hillcommon *Som'set* **6** D5
Hillend *Lothian* **48** A4
Hillend *S'clyde* **48** E3
Hillersland *Glos* **15** C9
Hillesden *Bucks* **17** A8
Hillesley *Avon* **15** E11
Hillfarrance *Som'set* **6** D5
Hillhead *Devon* **5** K8
Hillhead *Gramp* **58** D3
Hillhead *Gramp* **58** E5
Hillhead *Northum* **45** B9
Hillhead *S'clyde* **47** F10
Hillhead *S'clyde* **47** G9
Hillhead *S'clyde* **48** E3
Hillhead of Auchentumb *Gramp* **58** B7
Hillhead of Cocklaw *Gramp* **58** C8
Hillhouse *Borders* **49** D7
Hilliard's Cross *Staffs* **22** A5
Hillingdon *London* **18** F1
Hillington *Norfolk* **24** C8
Hillmorton *Warwick* **23** E8
Hillockhead *Gramp* **58** F2
Hillockhead *Gramp* **59** G1
Hillpound *Hants* **9** D7
Hillside *Dumf/Gal* **43** C12
Hillside *Gramp* **58** B5
Hillside *Gramp* **59** H7
Hillside *Shetl'd* **64** C7
Hillside *Tayside* **59** L4
Hillstreet *Hants* **8** D5
Hillswick *Shetl'd* **64** C6
Hillway *I of Wight* **9** G8
Hillwell *Shetl'd* **64** F7
Hilmarton *Wilts* **16** G1
Hilperton *Wilts* **15** H12
Hilperton Marsh *Wilts* **15** H11
Hilsea *Hants* **9** F8
Hilston *Humber* **37** D10
Hilton *Borders* **49** D11
Hilton *Cambs* **25** J4
Hilton *Clevl'd* **40** D5
Hilton *Cumb* **39** C9
Hilton *Derby* **31** G11
Hilton *Dorset* **7** F11
Hilton *Durham* **40** C2
Hilton *Gramp* **58** D7
Hilton *H'land* **61** H8
Hilton *Shrops* **22** C1
Hilton of Cadboll *H'land* **56** B4
Himbleton *Heref/Worcs* **22** F3
Himley *Staffs* **22** C2
Hincaster *Cumb* **39** G7
Hinchwick *Glos* **16** A2
Hinckley *Leics* **23** C7
Hinderclay *Suffolk* **27** H3
Hinderwell *N Yorks* **41** D8
Hindford *Shrops* **30** G2
Hindhead *Surrey* **9** C10
Hindley *Gtr Man* **34** G5
Hindley *Northum* **45** G8
Hindley Green *Gtr Man* **34** G5
Hindlip *Heref/Worcs* **22** F2
Hindolveston *Norfolk* **26** C3
Hindon *Wilts* **7** C12
Hindringham *Norfolk* **26** B3
Hingham *Norfolk* **26** E3
Hinstock *Shrops* **30** H5
Hintlesham *Suffolk* **27** L4
Hinton *Avon* **15** G10
Hinton *Hants* **8** G4
Hinton *Heref/Worcs* **21** H9
Hinton *Northants* **23** G8
Hinton *Shrops* **21** B9
Hinton Ampner *Hants* **9** C7
Hinton Blewett *Avon* **7** A9
Hinton Charterhouse *Avon* **15** H11
Hinton Cross *Heref/Worcs* **22** H4
Hinton Martell *Dorset* **8** E2
Hinton on the Green *Heref/Worcs* **22** H4
Hinton Parva *Wilts* **16** F3
Hinton St. George *Som'set* **7** E7
Hinton St. Mary *Dorset* **7** E11
Hinton Waldrist *Oxon* **16** D5
Hinton-in-the-Hedge *Northants* **23** H9
Hints *Shrops* **21** E11
Hints *Staffs* **22** B5
Hinwick *Beds* **23** F12
Hinxhill *Kent* **11** D9
Hinxton *Cambs* **25** L6
Hinxworth *Herts* **25** L3
Hipperholme *W Yorks* **35** E10
Hipswell *N Yorks* **40** E2
Hiraeth *Dyfed* **12** E5
Hirn *Gramp* **59** G5
Hirnant *Powys* **20** E4
Hirnant *Powys* **29** H10
Hirst *Northum* **45** D11
Hirst Courtney *N Yorks* **36** E4
Hirwaen *Clwyd* **29** D10
Hirwaun *Mid Glam* **14** D3
Hiscott *Devon* **4** C4
Histon *Cambs* **25** J5
Hitcham *Suffolk* **27** K3
Hitchill *Dumf/Gal* **43** E12
Hitchin *Herts* **18** A2
Hither Green *London* **18** F4
Hittisleigh Cross *Devon* **4** F6
Hive *Humber* **36** D6
Hixon *Staffs* **31** H8
Hoaden *Kent* **11** B11
Hoaldalbert *Gwent* **15** B7
Hoar Cross *Staffs* **31** H10
Hoarwithy *Heref/Worcs* **15** A8
Hoath *Kent* **11** B10
Hobarris *Shrops* **21** E8
Hobbister *Orkney* **64** D2
Hobbs Cross *Essex* **18** D5
Hobkirk *Borders* **44** B4
Hobston *Durham* **45** G10
Hoby *Leics* **32** H4
Hockering *Norfolk* **26** D4
Hockerton *Notts* **32** E4
Hockley *Essex* **19** E8
Hockley Heath *W Midlands* **22** E5
Hockliffe *Beds* **17** A10
Hockwold cum Wilton *Norfolk* **25** G8
Hockworthy *Devon* **6** D4
Hoddesdon *Herts* **18** C4
Hoddlesden *Lancs* **34** E6
Hoddomcross *Dumf/Gal* **43** D12
Hodgeston *Dyfed* **12** G4
Hodnet *Shrops* **30** G5
Hodsall Street *Kent* **10** B5
Hodson *Wilts* **16** F3
Hodthorpe *Derby* **32** C3
Hoe *Hants* **9** D7
Hoe *Norfolk* **26** D3
Hoe Gate *Hants* **9** E8
Hoff *Cumb* **39** C9
Hog Patch *Hants* **9** A9
Hoggeston *Bucks* **17** B9
Hoghton *Lancs* **34** E5
Hognaston *Derby* **31** E11
Hogsthorpe *Lincs* **33** C12
Holbeach *Lincs* **24** C5
Holbeach Bank *Lincs* **24** C5
Holbeach Clough *Lincs* **24** C4
Holbeach Drove *Lincs* **24** D4
Holbeach Hurn *Lincs* **24** C5
Holbeach St. Johns *Lincs* **24** D4
Holbeach St. Marks *Lincs* **24** C5
Holbeach St. Matthew *Lincs* **24** B5
Holbeck *Notts* **32** C3
Holbeck *W Yorks* **35** D11
Holberrow Green *Heref/Worcs* **22** F4
Holbeton *Devon* **5** L5
Holborough *Kent* **10** B6
Holbrook *Derby* **31** F12
Holbrook *Suffolk* **27** L5
Holburn *Northum* **45** B10
Holburn *Northum* **45** B11
Holbury *Hants* **8** F6
Holcombe *Devon* **5** H8
Holcombe *Gtr Man* **34** E6
Holcombe *Som'set* **7** A10
Holcombe Brook *Gtr Man* **34** F6
Holcombe Rogus *Devon* **6** D4
Holcot *Northants* **23** E11
Holden *Lancs* **34** B6
Holdenby *Northants* **23** E10
Holdenhurst *Dorset* **8** G3
Holdgate *Shrops* **21** C11
Holdingham *Lincs* **33** E7
Holditch *Dorset* **7** F7
Holefield *Borders* **49** F10
Holehouse *S'clyde* **47** D8
Hole-in-the-Wall *Heref/Worcs* **15** A9
Holestane *Dumf/Gal* **43** B9
Holford *Som'set* **6** B5
Holker *Cumb* **38** G6
Holkham *Norfolk* **26** A2
Hollacombe *Devon* **4** F2
Holland Fen *Lincs* **33** E9
Holland, Papa Westray *Orkney* **64** A3
Holland, Stronsay *Orkney* **64** C4
Holland-on-Sea *Essex* **19** B11
Hollandstoun *Orkney* **64** A4
Hollee *Dumf/Gal* **44** F1
Hollesley *Suffolk* **27** L6
Hollingbourne *Kent* **11** C7
Hollingfare *Ches* **34** H6
Hollingrove *E Sussex* **10** F6
Hollington *Derby* **31** F10
Hollington *E Sussex* **10** G6
Hollington *Staffs* **31** F9
Hollingworth *Gtr Man* **35** G8
Hollins *Gtr Man* **35** F7
Hollins Lane *Lancs* **34** B4
Hollinsclough *Staffs* **31** D9
Hollocombe *Devon* **4** E5
Hollow Court *Heref/Worcs* **22** F3
Hollow Meadows *S Yorks* **31** A11
Holloway *Derby* **31** E11
Hollowell *Northants* **23** E10
Hollows *Dumf/Gal* **44** E2
Holly Bush *Clwyd* **30** F3
Holly End *Norfolk* **24** E6
Holly Green *Heref/Worcs* **22** H2
Hollybush *Heref/Worcs* **15** A10
Hollybush *S'clyde* **47** H9
Hollym *Humber* **37** E11
Hollywood *Heref/Worcs* **22** D4
Holm *Dumf/Gal* **44** C1
Holm *W Isles* **63** D5
Holmacott *Devon* **4** C4
Holmbridge *W Yorks* **35** F10
Holmbury St. Mary *Surrey* **9** B12
Holmbush *Cornw'l* **3** D7
Holmcroft *Staffs* **31** H8
Holme *Cambs* **25** G3
Holme *Cumb* **39** G7
Holme *Humber* **37** F7
Holme *N Yorks* **40** G4
Holme *Notts* **32** D5
Holme *W Yorks* **35** G9
Holme Chapel *Lancs* **35** D7
Holme Hale *Norfolk* **26** E2
Holme Lacy *Heref/Worcs* **15** A9
Holme Marsh *Heref/Worcs* **21** G9
Holme next the Sea *Norfolk* **24** A8
Holme Pierrepont *Notts* **32** F3
Holme St. Cuthbert *Cumb* **38** A3
Holme-on-Spalding-Moor *Humber* **36** C6
Holme-on-the-Wolds *Humber* **37** C7
Holmer *Heref/Worcs* **21** H10
Holmer Green *Bucks* **17** D10
Holmes Chapel *Ches* **30** C6
Holmesfield *Derby* **31** B11
Holmeswood *Lancs* **34** E3
Holmewood *Derby* **32** D2
Holmfirth *W Yorks* **35** F10
Holmfoot *Dumf/Gal* **43** B9
Holmhead *S'clyde* **47** G10
Holmisdal *H'land* **62** C1
Holmpton *Humber* **37** E11
Holmrook *Cumb* **38** E3
Holmside *Durham* **45** H10
Holmwrangle *Cumb* **44** H4
Holne *Devon* **5** J6
Holsworthy *Devon* **4** F2
Holsworthy Beacon *Devon* **4** E2
Holt *Clwyd* **30** E3
Holt *Dorset* **8** F2
Holt *Heref/Worcs* **22** F2
Holt *Norfolk* **26** B4
Holt *Wilts* **15** H11
Holt End *Hants* **9** B8
Holt End *Heref/Worcs* **22** E4
Holt Heath *Heref/Worcs* **22** F2
Holt Wood *Dorset* **8** E2
Holtby *N Yorks* **36** B4
Holton *Berks* **17** G7
Holton *Lincs* **33** B8
Holton *Som'set* **7** D10
Holton *Suffolk* **27** H7
Holton Heath *Dorset* **8** G1
Holton le Clay *Lincs* **37** G10
Holton le Moor *Lincs* **37** G8
Holton St. Mary *Suffolk* **27** L4
Holtye *E Sussex* **10** D3
Holwell *Dorset* **7** E10
Holwell *Herts* **18** A2
Holwell *Leics* **32** H5
Holwell *Oxon* **16** C3
Holwick *Durham* **39** C11
Holworth *Dorset* **7** H11
Holy Cross *Heref/Worcs* **22** D3
Holy Island *Northum* **45** B12
Holybourne *Hants* **9** B9
Holyhead *Gwyn* **28** B2
Holymoorside *Derby* **31** C11
Holyport *Berks* **17** F10
Holystone *Northum* **45** C8
Holytown *S'clyde* **47** C12
Holywell *Cambs* **25** H4
Holywell *Clwyd* **29** C11
Holywell *Cornw'l* **2** D5
Holywell *Cumb* **44** E3
Holywell *Dorset* **7** F9
Holywell *Tyne/Wear* **45** F11
Holywell Green *W Yorks* **35** E9
Holywell Lake *Som'set* **6** D5
Holywell Row *Suffolk* **25** H8
Holywood *Dumf/Gal* **43** C10
Hom Green *Heref/Worcs* **15** B9
Homebank *Borders* **49** E10
Homebyres *Borders* **49** E9
Homer *Shrops* **21** B11
Homersfield *Suffolk* **27** G6
Homington *Wilts* **8** D3
Honey Hill *Kent* **11** B10
Honey Street *Wilts* **16** H2
Honey Tye *Suffolk* **27** L2
Honeyborough *Dyfed* **12** F3
Honeybourne *Heref/Worcs* **22** H5
Honeychurch *Devon* **4** F5
Honiley *Warwick* **22** E6
Honing *Norfolk* **26** C6
Honingham *Norfolk* **26** D4
Honington *Lincs* **32** F6
Honington *Suffolk* **27** H2
Honington *Warwick* **22** H6
Honiton *Devon* **6** F5
Honley *W Yorks* **35** F10
Hoo *Kent* **10** A6
Hoobrook *Heref/Worcs* **22** E2
Hood Green *S Yorks* **35** G11
Hooe *Devon* **5** K4
Hooe *E Sussex* **10** G6
Hooe Common *E Sussex* **10** G6
Hook *Dyfed* **12** F3
Hook *Hants* **8** F6
Hook *Hants* **9** A8
Hook *Humber* **36** E5
Hook *London* **18** G2
Hook *Wilts* **16** F2
Hook Green *Kent* **10** A5
Hook Green *Kent* **10** D5
Hook Norton *Oxon* **16** A4
Hooke *Dorset* **7** F9
Hookgate *Staffs* **30** G6
Hookway *Devon* **4** F7
Hookwood *Surrey* **10** D2
Hoole *Ches* **30** C3
Hooley *Surrey* **10** B2
Hooton *Ches* **30** B2
Hooton Levitt *S Yorks* **32** A2
Hooton Pagnell *S Yorks* **36** F3
Hooton Roberts *S Yorks* **36** G3
Hoove *Shetl'd* **64** D7
Hop Pole *Lincs* **24** D3
Hope *Clwyd* **29** D12
Hope *Derby* **31** B10
Hope *Devon* **5** M5
Hope *H'land* **60** B5
Hope *Powys* **21** B8
Hope *Shrops* **21** B9
Hope *Staffs* **31** E9
Hope Bagot *Shrops* **21** E11
Hope Bowdler *Shrops* **21** C10
Hope Mansell *Heref/Worcs* **15** B9
Hope under Dinmore *Heref/Worcs* **21** G10
Hopeman *Gramp* **56** C7
Hopesay *Shrops* **21** D9
Hopperton *N Yorks* **36** B2
Hopton *Derby* **31** E11
Hopton *Norfolk* **26** E8
Hopton *Shrops* **30** G4
Hopton *Staffs* **31** H8
Hopton *Suffolk* **27** G3
Hopton Cangeford *Shrops* **21** D11
Hopton Castle *Shrops* **21** E9
Hopton Wafers *Shrops* **21** E11
Hoptonheath *Shrops* **21** E9
Hopwas *Staffs* **22** B5
Hopwood *Heref/Worcs* **22** E4
Horam *E Sussex* **10** F4
Horbling *Lincs* **24** B2
Horbury *W Yorks* **35** E11
Horden *Durham* **40** A5
Horderley *Shrops* **21** D9
Hordle *Hants* **8** F4
Hordley *Shrops* **30** G2
Horeb *Dyfed* **13** C7
Horeb *Dyfed* **13** D8
Horfield *Avon* **15** F9
Horham *Suffolk* **27** H5
Horkesley Heath *Essex* **19** A9
Horkstow *Humber* **37** E7
Horley *Oxon* **23** H7
Horley *Surrey* **10** D2
Hornblotton Green *Som'set* **7** C9
Hornby *Lancs* **39** H8
Hornby *N Yorks* **40** E4
Hornby *N Yorks* **40** F2
Horncastle *Lincs* **33** C9
Hornchurch *London* **18** E5
Horncliffe *Northum* **49** D11
Horndean *Borders* **49** D11
Horndean *Hants* **9** E8
Horndon *Devon* **5** H4
Horndon-on-the-Hill *Essex* **18** F6
Horne *Surrey* **10** D2
Horner *Som'set* **6** B3
Horning *Norfolk* **26** D6
Horninghold *Leics* **23** B11
Horninglow *Staffs* **31** H10
Horningsea *Cambs* **25** J6
Horningsham *Wilts* **7** B11
Horningtoft *Norfolk* **26** C2
Horningtops *Cornw'l* **3** D9
Horns Cross *Devon* **4** D3
Horns Cross *E Sussex* **11** F7
Hornsby *Cumb* **44** H3
Hornsea *Humber* **37** B9
Hornsea Bridge *Humber* **37** B9

Hornsey *London* 18 E3
Hornton *Oxon* 23 H7
Horrabridge *Devon* 5 J4
Horringer *Suffolk* 27 J1
Horringford *I of Wight* 9 H7
Horsburgh *Borders* 48 E6
Horse Bridge *Staffs* 31 E8
Horsebridge *Hants* 8 C5
Horsebrook *Staffs* 22 A2
Horsecastle *Avon* 15 H7
Horsehay *Shrops* 21 B12
Horseheath *Cambs* 25 K7
Horsehouse *N Yorks* 39 G12
Horsell *Surrey* 17 H10
Horseman's Green *Clwyd* 30 F3
Horsendon *Bucks* 17 D9
Horsey *Norfolk* 26 C8
Horsford *Norfolk* 26 D5
Horsforth *W Yorks* 35 C11
Horsham *Heref/Worcs* 22 F1
Horsham *W Sussex* 10 E1
Horsham St. Faith *Norfolk* 26 D5
Horsington *Lincs* 33 C9
Horsington *Som'set* 7 D10
Horsley *Derby* 32 F1
Horsley *Glos* 15 E11
Horsley *Northum* 45 C7
Horsley *Northum* 45 F9
Horsley Cross *Essex* 19 A11
Horsley Woodhouse *Derby* 32 F1
Horsleycross Street *Essex* 19 A11
Horsleyhill *Borders* 49 G8
Horsmonden *Kent* 10 D6
Horspath *Oxon* 17 D7
Horstead *Norfolk* 26 D5
Horsted Keynes *W Sussex* 10 E3
Horton *Avon* 15 F10
Horton *Bucks* 17 B10
Horton *Dorset* 8 E2
Horton *Lancs* 35 B7
Horton *London* 17 F12
Horton *Northants* 23 G11
Horton *Som'set* 6 E6
Horton *Staffs* 31 D8
Horton *W Glam* 13 H8
Horton *Wilts* 16 H2
Horton Cross *Som'set* 7 E7
Horton Green *Ches* 30 E3
Horton Heath *Hants* 8 D6
Horton in Ribblesdale *N Yorks* 39 H10
Horton Kirby *Kent* 10 A4
Horwich *Gtr Man* 34 F5
Horwood *Devon* 4 C4
Hoscote *Borders* 44 B2
Hose *Leics* 32 G5
Hoselaw *Borders* 49 F10
Hoses *Cumb* 38 F5
Hosh *Tayside* 52 E4
Hoswick *Shetl'd* 64 E7
Hotel *Cumb* 39 E8
Hotel *I of Man* 38 G2
Hotham *Humber* 37 D7
Hothfield *Kent* 11 D8
Hoton *Leics* 32 H3
Hott *Northum* 44 D6
Houbie *Shetl'd* 64 B8
Hough *Ches* 30 E6
Hough Green *Mersey* 30 B3
Hougham *Lincs* 32 F6
Hough-on-the-Hill *Lincs* 32 F6
Houghton *Cambs* 25 H4
Houghton *Cumb* 44 G2
Houghton *Dyfed* 12 F3
Houghton *Hants* 8 C5
Houghton *W Sussex* 9 E11
Houghton Conquest *Beds* 25 L2
Houghton Green *Ches* 30 A5
Houghton Regis *Beds* 17 B11
Houghton St. Giles *Norfolk* 26 B2
Houghton-on-the-Hill *Leics* 23 B10
Houlsyke *N Yorks* 41 D7
Hound *Hants* 8 E6
Hound Green *Hants* 17 H8
Houndridge *Borders* 49 F10
Houndslow *Borders* 49 E9
Houndsmoor *Som'set* 6 D5
Houndwood *Borders* 49 C11
Hounsdown *Hants* 8 E5
Hounslow *London* 18 F2
Housay *Shetl'd* 64 C8
House of Glenmuick *Gramp* 59 H1
Housieside *Gramp* 58 E6
Houston *S'clyde* 47 C9
Houstry *H'land* 61 D10
Hove *E Sussex* 10 H2
Hoveringham *Notts* 32 E4
Hoveton *Norfolk* 26 D6
Hovingham *N Yorks* 41 H7
How *Cumb* 44 G3
How Caple *Heref/Worcs* 15 A9
How Green *Kent* 10 C4
How Head *Cumb* 38 E6
Howbrook *S Yorks* 35 G11
Howburn *Borders* 49 F10
Howden *Borders* 49 G9
Howden *Humber* 36 D5
Howden Clough *W Yorks* 35 D11
Howden-le-Wear *Durham* 40 B2
Howe *Cumb* 39 F7
Howe *H'land* 61 B12
Howe *Norfolk* 26 E6
Howe Green *Essex* 19 D7
Howe of Teucher *Gramp* 58 C5
Howe Street *Essex* 19 B7
Howe Street *Essex* 25 M8
Howell *Lincs* 33 F8
Howes *Dumf/Gal* 43 E12
Howey *Powys* 20 F6
Howford *Borders* 48 F6
Howgate *Lothian* 48 D5
Howgate *S'clyde* 48 F2
Howick *Northum* 45 A10
Howle *Shrops* 30 H5
Howle Hill *Heref/Worcs* 15 B9
Howlett End *Essex* 25 M7
Howley *Som'set* 6 E6
Howliston *Lothian* 49 D7
Hownam *Borders* 49 G10
Hownam Mains *Borders* 49 G10
Howpasley *Borders* 44 B2
Howsham *Humber* 37 G8
Howsham *N Yorks* 36 A5
Howtel *Northum* 49 F11
Howth *Orkney* 64 D2
Howton *Heref/Worcs* 15 A7
Howtown *Cumb* 39 C7
Howwood *S'clyde* 47 C9
Hoxa *Orkney* 64 E2
Hoxne *Suffolk* 27 G5
Hoylake *Mersey* 30 A1
Hoyland Nether *S Yorks* 35 G12
Hoyland Swaine *S Yorks* 35 G11
Hubberston *Dyfed* 12 F2
Hubbert's Bridge *Lincs* 24 A4
Huby *N Yorks* 35 B11
Huby *N Yorks* 36 A3
Hucclecote *Glos* 15 C12
Hucking *Kent* 11 B7
Hucknall *Notts* 32 E3
Huddersfield *W Yorks* 35 E10
Huddington *Heref/Worcs* 22 F3
Hudswell *N Yorks* 40 E2
Huggate *Humber* 36 B6
Hugh Town *I of Scilly* 2 D2
Hughenden Valley *Bucks* 17 D9
Hughley *Shrops* 21 C11
Huish *Devon* 4 E4
Huish *Wilts* 16 H2
Huish Barton *Som'set* 6 B4
Huish Champflower *Som'set* 6 C4
Huish Episcopi *Som'set* 7 D8
Hulcott *Bucks* 17 B9
Hulland *Derby* 31 F11
Hulland Ward *Derby* 31 E11
Hullavington *Wilts* 15 F12
Hullbridge *Essex* 19 D8
Hulme End *Staffs* 31 D9
Hulme Walfield *Ches* 31 D7
Hulver Street *Suffolk* 27 G8
Hulverstone *I of Wight* 8 H5
Humber Court *Heref/Worcs* 21 G11
Humberston *Humber* 37 G10
Humberstone *Leics* 23 B10
Humbie *Lothian* 49 C7
Humbleton *Humber* 37 D10
Humbleton *Northum* 49 G12
Humby *Lincs* 33 G7
Hume *Borders* 49 E9
Humeston *S'clyde* 47 H7
Humshaugh *Northum* 45 F7
Huna *H'land* 61 A12
Huncoat *Lancs* 34 D6
Huncote *Leics* 23 B8
Hundalee *Borders* 49 G9
Hunderthwaite *Durham* 39 C12
Hundleby *Lincs* 33 D11
Hundleton *Dyfed* 12 G3
Hundon *Suffolk* 25 K8
Hundred Acres *Hants* 9 E7
Hundred End *Lancs* 34 E3
Hundred House *Powys* 21 G7
Hungarton *Leics* 23 A10
Hungerford *Berks* 16 G4
Hungerford Newton *Wilts* 16 G4
Hungerton *Lincs* 32 G6
Hunglader *H'land* 62 A3
Hunmanby *N Yorks* 41 G11
Hunningham *Warwick* 23 E7
Hunny Hill *I of Wight* 8 G6
Hunsdon *Herts* 18 C4
Hunsingore *N Yorks* 36 B2
Hunslett Carr *W Yorks* 35 D11
Hunsonby *Cumb* 39 B8
Hunspow *H'land* 61 A11
Hunstanton *Norfolk* 24 B8
Hunstanworth *Durham* 45 H8
Hunston *Suffolk* 27 H3
Hunston *W Sussex* 9 F10
Hunstrete *Avon* 15 H9
Hunsworth *W Yorks* 35 D10
Hunt End *Heref/Worcs* 22 F4
Hunt Ho *N Yorks* 41 E8
Hunter's Quay *S'clyde* 47 B7
Huntershall *Borders* 49 F10
Hunterston Works *S'clyde* 47 D7
Huntford *Borders* 44 B5
Hunthill Lodge *Tayside* 59 K2
Huntingdon *Cambs* 25 H3
Huntingfield *Suffolk* 27 H6
Huntington *Heref/Worcs* 21 G8
Huntington *Heref/Worcs* 21 H10
Huntington *N Yorks* 36 B4
Huntington *Staffs* 22 A3
Huntingtower Haugh *Tayside* 52 E5
Huntley *Glos* 15 B10
Huntley *Staffs* 31 F8
Huntly *Gramp* 58 D3
Huntlywood *Borders* 49 E9
Hunton *Kent* 10 C6
Hunton *N Yorks* 40 F2
Hunton Bridge *Herts* 17 D11
Hunt's Cross *Mersey* 30 B3
Huntscott *Som'set* 6 B3
Huntsham *Devon* 6 D3
Huntspill *Som'set* 6 B6
Huntworth *Som'set* 7 C7
Hunwick *Durham* 40 B2
Hunworth *Norfolk* 26 B4
Hurcott *Som'set* 7 E7
Hurdcott *Wilts* 8 C3
Hurley *Berks* 17 F9
Hurley *W Midlands* 22 C9
Hurley *Warwick* 22 C6
Hurlford *S'clyde* 47 F9
Hurliness *Orkney* 64 D1
Hurn *Dorset* 8 F3
Hursdfield *Ches* 31 C8
Hursley *Hants* 8 D6
Hurst *Berks* 17 G9
Hurst *Gtr Man* 35 G8
Hurst *N Yorks* 40 E1
Hurst *Som'set* 7 D8
Hurst Green *E Sussex* 10 E6
Hurst Green *Lancs* 34 C6
Hurst Green *Surrey* 10 C3
Hurst Wickham *W Sussex* 10 F2
Hurstbourne Priors *Hants* 8 A6
Hurstbourne Tarrant *Hants* 8 A5
Hurstley *Heref/Worcs* 21 G9
Hurstpierpoint *W Sussex* 10 F2
Hurtmore *Surrey* 9 B11
Hurworth on Tees *Durham* 40 D3
Hury *Durham* 39 C11
Husabost Piers *H'land* 62 C1
Husbands Bosworth *Leics* 23 D10
Husborne Crawley *Beds* 25 L1
Hushinish *W Isles* 63 F1
Husthwaite *N Yorks* 40 H5
Huthwaite *Notts* 32 D2
Huttoft *Lincs* 33 C12
Hutton *Avon* 15 H7
Hutton *Borders* 49 D11
Hutton *Cumb* 39 C7
Hutton *Essex* 18 D6
Hutton *Humber* 37 B8
Hutton *Lancs* 34 D4
Hutton Buscel *N Yorks* 41 G9
Hutton Conyers *N Yorks* 40 H3
Hutton End *Cumb* 39 A7
Hutton Hang *N Yorks* 40 F2
Hutton Henry *Durham* 40 B4
Hutton John *Cumb* 39 C7
Hutton Magna *Durham* 40 D2
Hutton Roof *Cumb* 38 B6
Hutton Roof *Cumb* 39 G8
Hutton Rudby *N Yorks* 40 E5
Hutton Sessay *N Yorks* 40 H5
Hutton Village *Clevl'd* 40 D6
Hutton Wandesley *N Yorks* 36 B3
Hutton-in-the-Forest *Cumb* 39 B7
Hutton-le-Hole *N Yorks* 41 F7
Huxham *Devon* 6 F3
Huxley *Ches* 30 D4
Huxter *Shetl'd* 64 D7
Huyton *Mersey* 30 A3
Hycemoor *Cumb* 38 F3
Hyde *Glos* 15 D12
Hyde *Gtr Man* 35 H8
Hyde *Hants* 8 E3
Hyde Heath *Bucks* 17 D10
Hyde Lea *Staffs* 31 H7
Hydestile *Surrey* 9 B11
Hyndford *S'clyde* 48 E2
Hyssington *Powys* 21 C8
Hythe *Hants* 8 E6
Hythe *Kent* 11 E10
Hythe *Som'set* 7 A8
Hythe End *Berks* 17 G11
Hythie *Gramp* 58 C7
Ianstown *Gramp* 58 A2
Ibberton *Dorset* 7 E11
Ible *Derby* 31 D11
Ibsley *Hants* 8 E3
Ibstock *Leics* 23 A7
Ibstone *Bucks* 17 E8
Ibthorpe *Hants* 8 A5
Ibworth *Hants* 9 A7
Icelton *Avon* 15 H7
Ickburgh *Norfolk* 26 F1
Ickenham *London* 18 E1
Ickford *Oxon* 17 C7
Ickham *Kent* 11 B11
Ickleford *Herts* 18 A2
Icklesham *E Sussex* 11 F7
Ickleton *Cambs* 25 L6
Icklingham *Suffolk* 27 H1
Ickwell Green *Beds* 25 L3
Icomb *Glos* 16 B3
Idbury *Oxon* 16 B3
Iddesleigh *Devon* 4 E4
Ide *Devon* 6 G2
Ide Hill *Kent* 10 C4
Ideford *Devon* 5 H8
Iden *E Sussex* 11 F8
Iden Green *Kent* 10 D6
Iden Green *Kent* 11 E7
Idle *W Yorks* 35 C10
Idlicote *Warwick* 22 H6
Idmiston *Wilts* 8 B3
Idole *Dyfed* 13 E7
Idridgehay *Derby* 31 E11
Idrigil *H'land* 62 B3
Idstone *Oxon* 16 F4
Idvies *Tayside* 53 B10
Ifield *W Sussex* 10 D1
Ifold *W Sussex* 9 C11
Iford *E Sussex* 10 G3
Ifton *Gwent* 15 E8
Ifton Heath *Shrops* 30 G2
Ightfield *Shrops* 30 F5
Ightham *Kent* 10 B5
Iken *Suffolk* 27 K7
Ilam *Staffs* 31 E10
Ilchester *Som'set* 7 D8
Ilderton *Northum* 49 G12
Ilford *London* 18 E4
Ilfracombe *Devon* 4 A4
Ilkeston *Derby* 32 F2
Ilketshall St. Andrew *Suffolk* 27 G6
Ilketshall St. Margaret *Suffolk* 27 G6
Ilkley *W Yorks* 35 B9
Illey *W Midlands* 22 D2
Illingworth *W Yorks* 35 D9
Illogan *Cornw'l* 2 E4
Illogan Highway *Cornw'l* 2 E4
Illston on the Hill *Leics* 23 B10
Ilmer *Bucks* 17 D8
Ilmington *Warwick* 22 H5
Ilminster *Som'set* 7 E7
Ilsington *Devon* 5 H6
Ilston *W Glam* 13 H9
Ilton *N Yorks* 40 G2
Ilton *Som'set* 7 D7
Imacher *S'clyde* 46 E4
Immingham *Humber* 37 F9
Immingham Dock *Humber* 37 E9
Impington *Cambs* 25 J5
Inbhireala or Strathossian Ho *H'land* 55 M8
Ince *Ches* 30 C3
Ince Blundell *Mersey* 34 G2
Ince-in-Makerfield *Gtr Man* 34 G5
Inch of Arnholl *Gramp* 59 K4
Inchbae Lodge *H'land* 54 C8
Inchbare *Tayside* 59 L3
Inchberry *Gramp* 58 B1
Incheoch *Tayside* 53 B7
Incheril *H'land* 54 C4
Inchina *H'land* 60 G2
Inchinnan *S'clyde* 47 B9
Inchkinloch *H'land* 60 C6
Inchlaggan *H'land* 55 J5
Inchlumpie *H'land* 56 B1
Inchmore *H'land* 54 F8
Inchnabobart *Gramp* 59 J1
Inchnacardoch *H'land* 55 H7
Inchnadamph *H'land* 60 E4
Inchrory *Gramp* 57 J7
Inchture *Tayside* 53 D7
Inchvuilt *H'land* 54 F6
Inchyra *Tayside* 52 E6
Indian Queens *Cornw'l* 2 D6
Indicott *Devon* 4 B4
Ingatestone *Essex* 18 D6
Ingbirchworth *S Yorks* 35 G10
Ingestre *Staffs* 31 H8
Ingham *Lincs* 32 B6
Ingham *Norfolk* 26 C7
Ingham *Suffolk* 27 H2
Ingleborough *N Yorks* 39 H10
Ingleborough *Norfolk* 24 D6
Ingleby *Derby* 31 G12
Ingleby Arncliffe *N Yorks* 40 E5
Ingleby Cross *N Yorks* 40 E5
Ingleby Greenhow *N Yorks* 40 E6
Inglesbatch *Avon* 15 H10
Inglesham *Wilts* 16 D3
Ingleton *Durham* 40 C2
Ingleton *N Yorks* 39 H9
Inglewhite *Lancs* 34 C4
Ingoe *Northum* 45 F8
Ingoldmells *Lincs* 33 C12
Ingoldsby *Lincs* 33 G7
Ingoldsthorpe *Norfolk* 24 B8
Ingram *Northum* 45 A8
Ingrave *Essex* 18 E6
Ingrow *W Yorks* 35 C9
Ings *Cumb* 39 E7
Ingst *Avon* 15 E9
Ingworth *Norfolk* 26 C5
Inistrynich *S'clyde* 51 E8
Injebreck *I of Man* 38 G2
Inkberrow *Heref/Worcs* 22 F4
Inkpen *Berks* 16 H4
Inkstack *H'land* 61 A11
Inn *Cumb* 38 D6
Innellan *S'clyde* 46 B6
Innerleithen *Borders* 48 F6
Innerleven *Fife* 53 G8
Innermessan *Dumf/Gal* 42 E2
Innerwell Fishery *Dumf/Gal* 42 G6
Innerwick *Lothian* 49 B10
Innerwick *Tayside* 52 B1
Innis Chonain *S'clyde* 51 E8
Innischoarach *Central* 51 D12
Insch *Gramp* 58 E4
Inschtammack *Gramp* 58 C2
Insh *H'land* 57 J4
Insh House *H'land* 57 J4
Inshaig *H'land* 51 B7
Inshore *H'land* 60 A4
Inskip *Lancs* 34 C3
Instow *Devon* 4 C3
Intake Gate *W Yorks* 35 C10
Inver *Gramp* 57 K8
Inver *H'land* 56 B4
Inver *Tayside* 52 C5
Inver Mallie *H'land* 55 K5
Inverailort *H'land* 55 L1
Inveralligin *H'land* 54 D2
Inveran *H'land* 60 G6
Inverarity *Tayside* 53 C9
Inverarnan *S'clyde* 51 F10
Inverary *S'clyde* 51 G8
Inverasdale *H'land* 54 A2
Inverbain *H'land* 54 D2
Inverbeg Hotel *S'clyde* 51 H10
Inverbervie *Gramp* 59 K6
Inverboyndie *Gramp* 58 A4
Inverbroom *H'land* 60 H3
Invercassley *H'land* 60 F5
Invercauld House *Gramp* 57 K7
Inverchapel *S'clyde* 46 A6
Inverchoran *H'land* 54 E6
Invercreran *S'clyde* 51 C7
Inverdruie *H'land* 57 H5
Inverebrie *Gramp* 58 D7
Inveredrie *Tayside* 57 M7
Invererie *Gramp* 58 E5
Invereshie House *H'land* 57 J4
Inveresk *Lothian* 48 B6
Inveresragan *S'clyde* 51 D7
Inverey *Gramp* 57 K6
Inverfarigaig *H'land* 57 G1
Invergarry *H'land* 55 J7
Invergeldie *Tayside* 52 D2
Invergloy *H'land* 55 L6
Invergordon *H'land* 56 C3
Invergowrie *Tayside* 53 D8
Inverguseran *H'land* 55 J1
Inverhadden *Tayside* 52 A2
Inverherive *Central* 51 E10
Inverie *H'land* 55 J1
Inverinan *S'clyde* 51 F7
Inverinate *H'land* 55 G3
Inverkeilor *Tayside* 53 B11
Inverkeithing *Lothian* 48 A4
Inverkeithny *Gramp* 58 C4
Inverkip *S'clyde* 47 B7
Inverkirkaig *H'land* 60 E2
Inverlael *H'land* 60 H3
Inverlael Lodge *H'land* 60 H3
Inverlair *H'land* 55 L7
Inverllochy *Gramp* 58 A8
Inverlochlarig *Central* 51 F11
Inverlochy *S'clyde* 51 E9
Invermark Lodge *Tayside* 59 J2
Invermoriston *H'land* 55 H8
Invernam House *Gramp* 58 F1
Invernaver *H'land* 61 B7
Inverness *H'land* 56 E2
Invernettie *Gramp* 58 C8
Invernoaden *S'clyde* 51 H8
Inveroran Hotel *S'clyde* 51 C10
Inverpolly Lodge *H'land* 60 E2
Inverquhomery *Gramp* 58 C8
Inverroy *H'land* 55 L6
Invershiel *H'land* 55 H3
Invershin *H'land* 60 G6
Invershore *H'land* 61 D11
Inverskilavulin *H'land* 55 L5
Inversnaid Hotel *Central* 51 G10
Inverugie *Gramp* 56 C7
Inverugie *Gramp* 58 C8
Inveruglas *S'clyde* 51 G10
Inveruglass *H'land* 57 J4
Invervar *Tayside* 52 B2
Invery House *Gramp* 59 H4
Inverythan *Gramp* 58 C5
Inwardleigh *Devon* 4 F4
Inworth *Essex* 19 B8
Inyercharnan *H'land* 51 C8
Iping *W Sussex* 9 D10
Ipplepen *Devon* 5 J7
Ipsden *Oxon* 17 F7
Ipstones *Staffs* 31 E8
Ipswich *Suffolk* 27 L5
Irby *Mersey* 30 B1
Irby in the Marsh *Lincs* 33 D11
Irby Upon Humber *Humber* 37 G9
Irchester *Northants* 23 E12
Ireby *Lancs* 39 H9
Ireleth *Cumb* 38 G5
Ireshopeburn *Durham* 39 A11
Irlam *Gtr Man* 34 H6
Irnham *Lincs* 33 G7
Iron Acton *Avon* 15 F10
Iron Bridge *Shrops* 21 B12
Iron Cross *Warwick* 22 G4
Ironmacannie *Dumf/Gal* 43 D7
Ironville *Derby* 32 E2
Irstead *Norfolk* 26 C7
Irthlingborough *Northants* 23 E12
Irthlington *Cumb* 44 G3
Irton *N Yorks* 41 G10
Irvine *S'clyde* 47 E8
Irvington *Dumf/Gal* 44 F1
Isauld *H'land* 61 A9
Isbister *Orkney* 64 C2
Isbister *Shetl'd* 64 B7
Isbister *Shetl'd* 64 C8
Isfield *E Sussex* 10 F3
Isham *Northants* 23 E12
Ishriff *H'land* 50 D4
Isle Abbotts *Som'set* 7 D7
Isle Brewers *Som'set* 7 D7
Isle of Dogs *London* 18 F4
Isle of Whithorn *Dumf/Gal* 42 H6
Isleham *Cambs* 25 H7
Isleornsay *H'land* 62 G6
Islesteps *Dumf/Gal* 43 D10
Isleworth *London* 18 F2
Isley Walton *Leics* 32 H2
Islington *London* 18 E3
Islip *Northants* 25 G1
Islip *Oxon* 16 C6
Islivig *W Isles* 63 D1
Istead Rise *Kent* 18 G6
Itchen *Hants* 8 E6
Itchen Stoke *Hants* 9 C7
Itchingfield *W Sussex* 9 C12
Itchington *Avon* 15 F10
Itteringham *Norfolk* 26 C4
Itton Common *Gwent* 15 E8
Ivegill *Cumb* 38 A6
Ivelet *N Yorks* 39 E11
Iver *Bucks* 17 F11
Iver Heath *Bucks* 17 F11
Iveston *Durham* 45 H9
Ivinghoe *Bucks* 17 B10
Ivinghoe Aston *Bucks* 17 B10
Ivington *Heref/Worcs* 21 G10
Ivington Green *Heref/Worcs* 21 G10
Ivy Hatch *Kent* 10 C5
Ivybridge *Devon* 5 K5
Ivychurch *Kent* 11 E9
Iwade *Kent* 11 A7
Iwerne Courtney or Shroton *Dorset* 7 E12
Iwerne Minster *Dorset* 7 E12
Ixworth *Suffolk* 27 H2
Ixworth Thorpe *Suffolk* 27 H2
Jack Hill *N Yorks* 35 B10
Jacksdale *Notts* 32 E2

Jackstown Gramp 58 D5
Jacobstow Cornw'l 2 B2
Jacobstowe Devon 4 F5
Jacobswell Surrey 9 A11
Jameston Dyfed 12 G4
Jamestown Dumf/Gal 44 C1
Jamestown H'land 54 D8
Jamestown S'clyde 47 A9
Jarrow Tyne/Wear 45 F11
Jarvis Brook E Sussex 10 E4
Jasper's Green Essex 19 A7
Jawcraig Lothian 48 B1
Jaywick Essex 19 C11
Jealott's Hill Berks 17 G9
Jeater Houses N Yorks 40 F4
Jedburgh Borders 49 G9
Jeffreyston Dyfed 12 F4
Jemimaville H'land 56 C3
Jersey Marine W Glam 13 H10
Jessiefield Gramp 59 G6
Jevington E Sussex 10 H4
Jockey End Herts 17 C11
Jodrell Bank Ches 30 C6
John O'Graunts W Yorks 35 D12
John o'Groats H'land 61 A12
Johnby Cumb 38 B6
John's Cross E Sussex 10 F6
Johnshaven Gramp 59 K6
Johnston Dyfed 12 F3
Johnstone Dumf/Gal 44 C1
Johnstone S'clyde 47 C9
Johnstonebridge Dumf/Gal 43 B11
Johnstown Clwyd 29 F12
Johnstown Dyfed 13 E7
Joppa Dyfed 20 F1
Joppa Lothian 48 B6
Jordans Bucks 17 E10
Jordanston Dyfed 12 D3
Jump S Yorks 35 G12
Jumpers Green Dorset 8 G3
Juniper Green Lothian 48 B5
Jurby East I of Man 38 F2
Jurby West I of Man 38 F2
Justicetown Cumb 44 G2
Kaber Cumb 39 D10
Kaimend S'clyde 48 E3
Kaimes Lothian 48 C5
Kalemouth Borders 49 G9
Kalnakill H'land 54 D1
Kames S'clyde 46 B5
Kames S'clyde 47 G11
Kames S'clyde 50 F5
Keadby Humber 36 F6
Keal Cotes Lincs 33 D10
Kearsley Gtr Man 34 G6
Kearstwick Cumb 39 G8
Kearton N Yorks 39 E12
Kearvaig H'land 60 A4
Keasden N Yorks 39 H9
Keddington Lincs 33 A10
Kedington Suffolk 25 K8
Kedleston Derby 31 F11
Kedslie Borders 49 E8
Keelby Lincs 37 F9
Keeley Green Beds 25 L1
Keepershield Northum 45 F7
Keeston Dyfed 12 E3
Keevil Wilts 15 H12
Kegworth Leics 32 G2
Kehelland Cornw'l 2 F3
Keig Gramp 58 F3
Keighley W Yorks 35 C9
Keil H'land 51 B7
Keilarsbrae Central 52 H4
Keilhill Gramp 58 B5
Keillmore S'clyde 46 A2
Keillour Tayside 52 E5
Keinton Mandeville Som'set 7 C9
Keir House Central 52 G3
Keir Mill Dumf/Gal 43 B9
Keisby Lincs 24 C1
Keiss H'land 61 B12
Keith Gramp 58 C2
Keithen Gramp 58 C5
Kelbrook Lancs 35 C8
Kelby Lincs 33 F7
Keld Cumb 39 D8
Keld N Yorks 39 E11
Keldholme N Yorks 41 F7
Keldy Castle N Yorks 41 F8
Kelfield N Yorks 36 C4
Kelham Notts 32 E5
Kelhead Dumf/Gal 43 E12
Kellan H'land 50 C3
Kellas Gramp 56 D7
Kellas Tayside 53 D9
Kellaton Devon 5 M7
Kellaways Wilts 16 G1
Kelleth Cumb 39 E9
Kelling Norfolk 26 A4
Kellingley N Yorks 36 E3
Kellington N Yorks 36 E3
Kelloe Durham 40 B4
Kelloe Mains Borders 49 D11
Kelly Devon 5 H3
Kelly Bray Cornw'l 3 C10
Kelmarsh Northants 23 D10
Kelmscot Oxon 16 D3
Kelsale Suffolk 27 J7
Kelsall Ches 30 C4
Kelsall Hill Ches 30 C4
Kelshall Herts 25 L4
Kelsick Cumb 43 F12
Kelso Borders 49 F10
Kelstedge Derby 31 D11
Kelstern Lincs 33 A9
Kelsterton Clwyd 29 C12
Kelston Avon 15 H10
Kelton Dumf/Gal 43 D10
Kelton Hill Dumf/Gal 43 F8
Keltreyburn Tayside 52 B3
Kelty Fife 52 H6
Kelvedon Essex 19 B8
Kelvedon Hatch Essex 18 D6
Kelynack Cornw'l 2 G1
Kemback Fife 53 F9
Kemberton Shrops 22 B1
Kemble Glos 16 D1
Kemerton Heref/Worcs 22 H3
Kemeys Commander Gwent 15 D7
Kemnay Gramp 58 F5
Kemp Town E Sussex 10 H2
Kempie H'land 60 B5
Kempley Glos 15 A10
Kempsey Heref/Worcs 22 G2
Kempsford Glos 16 D3
Kempshott Hants 9 A7
Kempston Beds 25 K1
Kempston Hardwick Beds 25 L1
Kempston West End Beds 25 K1
Kempton Shrops 21 D9
Kemsing Kent 10 B4
Kemsley Kent 11 A8
Kenardington Kent 11 E8
Kenchester Sugwas Heref/Worcs 21 H10
Kencot Oxon 16 D4
Kendal Cumb 39 F7
Kenderchurch Heref/Worcs 15 A7
Kenfig Mid Glam 14 F1
Kenfig Hill Mid Glam 14 F2
Kenilworth Warwick 22 E6
Kenknock Central 51 D11
Kenley Shrops 21 B11
Kenmore H'land 54 D1
Kenmore S'clyde 51 G8
Kenmore Tayside 52 C3
Kenn Avon 15 G7
Kenn Devon 6 H3
Kennacraig S'clyde 46 C3
Kennards House Cornw'l 3 A10
Kennavog W Isles 63 G3
Kennedy's Corner Dumf/Gal 44 E1
Kenneggy Downs Cornw'l 2 G3
Kennerleigh Devon 4 E7
Kennet Cambs 25 H8
Kenneth Bank Dumf/Gal 43 E10
Kennethmont Gramp 58 E3
Kennett Central 52 H4
Kennford Devon 6 G3
Kenninghall Norfolk 27 G3
Kennington Kent 11 D9
Kennington London 18 F3
Kennington Oxon 16 D6
Kennoway Fife 53 G8
Kennox S'clyde 47 E8
Kennyhill Suffolk 25 G8
Kennythorpe N Yorks 36 A6
Kensaleyre H'land 62 C3
Kensington London 18 F3
Kensworth Beds 17 B11
Kensworth Com Beds 17 B11
Kent Street Kent 10 C5
Kentallen H'land 51 B7
Kentchurch Heref/Worcs 15 B7
Kentford Suffolk 25 J8
Kentisbeare Devon 6 E4
Kentisbury Devon 4 B5
Kentisburyford Devon 4 B5
Kentmere Cumb 39 E7
Kenton Devon 6 H3
Kenton London 18 E2
Kenton Suffolk 27 J5
Kenton Bank Foot Tyne/Wear 45 F10
Kentra H'land 50 A4
Kents Bank Cumb 38 H6
Kent's Green Glos 15 B10
Kent's Oak Hants 8 D5
Kentstone Northum 45 B11
Kenwick Shrops 30 G3
Kenwyn Cornw'l 2 E5
Keoldale H'land 60 A5
Keose W Isles 63 E5
Keppeoh H'land 55 G3
Keprigan S'clyde 46 H2
Kepwick N Yorks 40 F5
Kerchesters Borders 49 F10
Keresley W Midlands 23 D7
Kerne Bridge Heref/Worcs 15 B9
Kernsary H'land 54 B3
Kerrcleuch Borders 48 H5
Kerridge Ches 31 C8
Kerris Cornw'l 2 G2
Kerrowwood H'land 54 F7
Kerry Powys 21 C7
Kerrycroy S'clyde 46 C6
Kerrylamont S'clyde 46 D6
Kerry's Gate Heref/Worcs 15 A7
Kerrysdale H'land 54 B2
Kerrytonlia S'clyde 46 D6
Kersall Notts 32 D4
Kersbrooke Devon 6 H4
Kerscott Devon 4 C5
Kerse S'clyde 47 D8
Kersey Suffolk 27 L3
Kershader W Isles 63 E4
Kershopefoot Cumb 44 E3
Kersmains Borders 49 F9
Kersoe Heref/Worcs 22 H3
Kerswell Devon 6 F4
Kerswell Green Heref/Worcs 22 G2
Kesgrave Suffolk 27 L5
Keskadale Cumb 38 C4
Kessingland Suffolk 27 G8
Kessingland Beach Suffolk 27 G8
Kestle Mill Cornw'l 2 D5
Keston London 18 G4
Keswick Cumb 38 C5
Keswick Norfolk 26 B6
Keswick Norfolk 26 E5
Ketley Shrops 21 A12
Kettelshiel Borders 49 D9
Kettering Northants 23 D12
Ketteringham Norfolk 26 E5
Kettins Tayside 53 C7
Kettlebaston Suffolk 27 K3
Kettlebridge Fife 53 F8
Kettlebrook Staffs 22 B6
Kettleburgh Suffolk 27 J5
Kettlehill Fife 53 F8
Kettleness N Yorks 41 D8
Kettleshulme Ches 31 B8
Kettlesing N Yorks 35 B11
Kettlesing Bottom N Yorks 35 A11
Kettlestone Norfolk 26 B3
Kettlethorpe Lincs 32 C6
Kettletoft Orkney 64 B4
Kettlewell N Yorks 39 H11
Ketton Leics 24 E1
Kew London 18 F2
Kewstoke Avon 14 H6
Kexbrough S Yorks 35 F11
Kexby Lincs 32 B6
Kexby N Yorks 36 B5
Key Green Ches 31 D7
Key Street Kent 11 B7
Keyham Leics 23 B10
Keyhaven Hants 8 G5
Keyingham Humber 37 E10
Keymer W Sussex 10 F2
Keynsham Avon 15 G9
Key's Toft Lincs 33 D12
Keysoe Beds 25 J2
Keysoe Row Beds 25 J2
Keyston Cambs 25 H1
Keyworth Notts 32 G3
Kibblesworth Tyne/Wear 45 G10
Kibworth Beauchamp Leics 23 C10
Kibworth Harcourt Leics 23 C10
Kidbrooke London 18 F4
Kiddemore Green Staffs 22 A2
Kidderminster Heref/Worcs 22 D2
Kiddington Oxon 16 B5
Kidlington Oxon 16 C6
Kidmore End Oxon 17 F8
Kidnal Ches 30 E3
Kidrummy Gramp 58 F2
Kidsgrove Staffs 31 E7
Kidstones N Yorks 39 G11
Kidwelly Dyfed 13 F7
Kiel Crofts S'clyde 50 D6
Kielder Northum 44 D4
Kilbagie Central 52 H4
Kilbarchan S'clyde 47 C9
Kilbeg H'land 62 H6
Kilberry S'clyde 46 C2
Kilbirnie S'clyde 47 D8
Kilbride H'land 62 F5
Kilbride S'clyde 50 E6
Kilburn Derby 32 F1
Kilburn N Yorks 40 G5
Kilburn Northum 49 G5
Kilburn Tayside 59 K1
Kilby Leics 23 C9
Kilcadzow S'clyde 48 D2
Kilchattan H'land 50 H1
Kilchattan S'clyde 46 D6
Kilchenzie S'clyde 46 G2
Kilcheran H'land 50 D5
Kilchoan H'land 50 A2
Kilchoan H'land 55 K2
Kilchoan S'clyde 50 F5
Kilchrenan S'clyde 51 E7
Kilconquhar Fife 53 G9
Kilcot Glos 15 B10
Kilcoy H'land 56 E1
Kilcreggan S'clyde 47 A7
Kildale N Yorks 40 D6
Kildalloig S'clyde 46 G3
Kildary H'land 56 B3
Kildavanan S'clyde 46 C5
Kildermorie Lodge H'land 56 B1
Kildonan S'clyde 46 G5
Kildonan Lodge H'land 61 E9
Kildwick W Yorks 35 C9
Kilfinan S'clyde 46 B4
Kilfinichen H'land 50 E2
Kilfinnan H'land 55 K6
Kilgetty Dyfed 12 F5
Kilham Humber 37 A8
Kilham Northum 49 F11
Kilkerran S'clyde 42 A4
Kilkhampton Cornw'l 4 E1
Killamarsh Derby 32 B2
Killay W Glam 13 H9
Killbeg H'land 50 C3
Killchianaig S'clyde 46 A1
Killean S'clyde 46 E2
Killearn Central 47 A10
Killellan S'clyde 46 H2
Killen H'land 56 D2
Killerby Durham 40 C2
Killern Dumf/Gal 42 F6
Killichonan Tayside 51 B12
Killiechonate H'land 55 L6
Killiechronan H'land 50 C3
Killiecrankie Tayside 52 A4
Killiehuntly H'land 57 K4
Killiemor H'land 50 D2
Killilan H'land 55 G3
Killimster H'land 61 B12
Killin Central 52 D1
Killin Lodge H'land 57 J1
Killinghall N Yorks 35 A11
Killington Cumb 39 F8
Killochyett Borders 49 E7
Killunaig H'land 50 E2
Killundine H'land 50 C3
Killyleoch Dumf/Gal 43 C9
Kilmacolm S'clyde 47 B8
Kilmahog Central 52 F1
Kilmahumaig S'clyde 50 H5
Kilmalieu H'land 50 B6
Kilmaluag H'land 62 A4
Kilmany Fife 53 E8
Kilmarie H'land 62 F5
Kilmarnock S'clyde 47 F9
Kilmaron Castle Fife 53 E8
Kilmartin S'clyde 50 H5
Kilmaurs S'clyde 47 E9
Kilmelford S'clyde 50 F6
Kilmersdon Som'set 7 A10
Kilmeston Hants 9 D7
Kilmichael S'clyde 46 G2
Kilmichael Glassary S'clyde 50 H6
Kilmichael of Inverlussa S'clyde 46 A3
Kilmington Devon 6 F6
Kilmington Wilts 7 C11
Kilmington Street Wilts 7 C11
Kilmorack H'land 56 E1
Kilmore H'land 62 G6
Kilmore S'clyde 50 E6
Kilmory H'land 50 A3
Kilmory S'clyde 46 B2
Kilmory S'clyde 46 G4
Kilmote H'land 61 F9
Kilmuir H'land 56 B3
Kilmuir H'land 56 E2
Kilmuir H'land 62 A3
Kilmuir H'land 62 C2
Kilmun S'clyde 46 A6
Kiln Green Berks 17 F9
Kiln Hill Cumb 44 F4
Kiln Pit Hill Northum 45 H8
Kilndown Kent 10 E6
Kilness Dumf/Gal 43 D10
Kilnford S'clyde 47 F8
Kilnhurst S Yorks 36 G2
Kilninian H'land 50 C1
Kilninver S'clyde 50 E5
Kilnsea Humber 37 F11
Kilnsey N Yorks 39 H12
Kilnwick Humber 37 B7
Kilnwick Percy Humber 36 B6
Kiloran H'land 50 H1
Kilpatrick S'clyde 46 G4
Kilpeck Heref/Worcs 15 A7
Kilpheder H'land 61 E9
Kilpin Humber 36 D5
Kilpin Pike Humber 36 D5
Kilrenny Fife 53 G10
Kilsby Northants 23 E9
Kilspindie Fife 53 E7
Kilsyth S'clyde 47 B12
Kilton Clevl'd 41 C7
Kilton Som'set 6 B5
Kilvaxter H'land 62 A3
Kilve Som'set 6 B5
Kilvington Notts 32 F5
Kilwinning S'clyde 47 E8
Kimberley Norfolk 26 E4
Kimberley Notts 32 F2
Kimble Wick Bucks 17 C9
Kimblesworth Durham 45 H11
Kimbolton Cambs 25 H2
Kimbolton Heref/Worcs 21 F10
Kimcote Leics 23 C9
Kimmeridge Dorset 7 H12
Kimmerston Northum 49 F12
Kimpton Hants 8 A4
Kimpton Herts 18 B2
Kinalty Tayside 53 A9
Kinbrace H'land 61 D8
Kinbreack H'land 55 K4
Kinbuck Central 52 G3
Kincaidston S'clyde 47 G8
Kincaple Fife 53 E9
Kincardine Fife 52 H4
Kincardine H'land 60 G6
Kincardine O'Neil Gramp 59 G3
Kinclaven Tayside 52 C6
Kincoed Gwent 15 D7
Kincorth Gramp 59 G7
Kincorth House Gramp 56 D6
Kincraig H'land 57 J4
Kindallachan Tayside 52 B5
Kindrummond H'land 56 F2
Kinerarach S'clyde 46 D2
Kineton Glos 16 B2
Kineton Warwick 23 G7
Kinfauns Tayside 52 E6
King Stanley Glos 15 D11
Kingairloch Ho H'land 50 B6
Kingarth S'clyde 46 D6
Kingasbarns Fife 53 F10
Kingerby Lincs 33 A7
Kingford Devon 4 D5
Kingham Oxon 16 B3
Kingholm Quay Dumf/Gal 43 D10
Kinghorn Lothian 48 A5
Kinghouse Hotel H'land 51 B10
Kinglassie Fife 53 G7
Kingoodie Tayside 53 D8
King's Acre Heref/Worcs 21 H10
Kings Bromley Staffs 31 H9
Kings Caple Heref/Worcs 15 A9
King's Cliffe Northants 24 F1
King's Coughton Warwick 22 F4
Kings Heath W Midlands 22 D4
Kings Langley Herts 17 D11
King's Lynn Norfolk 24 D7
King's Meaburn Cumb 39 C8
Kings Muir Borders 48 E5
Kings Newnham Warwick 23 D8
Kings Newton Derby 31 H12
King's Norton Leics 23 B10
King's Norton W Midlands 22 D4
King's Nympton Devon 4 D6
King's Pyon Heref/Worcs 21 G10
Kings Ripton Cambs 25 H4
King's Somborne Hants 8 C5
King's Stag Dorset 7 E10
King's Sutton Northants 16 A6
King's Walden Herts 18 B2
Kings Wood Kent 11 C7
Kings Worth Hants 8 C6
Kingsand Cornw'l 3 E11
Kingsbridge Devon 5 L6
Kingsbridge Som'set 6 C3
Kingsburgh H'land 62 C3
Kingsbury London 18 E2
Kingsbury Warwick 22 C6
Kingsbury Episcopi Som'set 7 D8
Kingsclere Hants 16 H6
Kingscote Glos 15 E11
Kingscott Devon 4 D4
Kingscross S'clyde 46 G5
Kingsdon Som'set 7 D8
Kingsdown Kent 11 C12
Kingseat Fife 52 H6
Kingsey Bucks 17 C8
Kingsfold W Sussex 10 D1
Kingsford Gramp 59 G6
Kingsford Heref/Worcs 22 D2
Kingsford S'clyde 47 E9
Kingshall Suffolk 27 J2
Kingsheanton Devon 4 B4
Kingshouse Central 52 E1
Kingskerswell Devon 5 J7
Kingskettle Fife 53 F8
Kingsland Gwyn 28 B2
Kingsland Heref/Worcs 21 F10
Kingsley Ches 30 C4
Kingsley Hants 9 B9
Kingsley Staffs 31 F8
Kingsley Green W Sussex 9 C10
Kingsley Holt Staffs 31 F9
Kingsmuir Tayside 53 B9
Kingsnorth Kent 11 D9
Kingstanding W Midlands 22 C4
Kingsteignton Devon 5 H7
Kingsthorn Heref/Worcs 15 A8
Kingsthorpe Northants 23 F11
Kingston Cambs 25 K4
Kingston Devon 5 L5
Kingston Dorset 7 E11
Kingston Dorset 8 H1
Kingston Gramp 58 A1
Kingston Hants 8 F3
Kingston I of Wight 8 H6
Kingston Kent 11 C10
Kingston Lothian 49 A8
Kingston W Sussex 9 F12
Kingston Bagpuize Oxon 16 D5
Kingston Blount Oxon 17 D8
Kingston by Sea W Sussex 10 H1
Kingston Deverill Wilts 7 C11
Kingston Lisle Oxon 16 E4
Kingston near Lewes E Sussex 10 G3
Kingston on Soar Notts 32 G2
Kingston Russell Dorset 7 G9
Kingston St. Mary Som'set 6 C6
Kingston Seymour Avon 15 H7
Kingston upon Hull Humber 37 D8
Kingston upon Thames London 18 G2
Kingston Vale London 18 G2
Kingstone Heref/Worcs 15 A7
kingstone Som'set 7 E7
Kingstone Staffs 31 G9
Kingstown Cumb 44 G2
Kingswear Devon 5 K7
Kingswinford W Midlands 22 C2
Kingswood Avon 15 G9
Kingswood Bucks 17 B8
Kingswood Glos 15 E10
Kingswood Heref/Worcs 21 G8
Kingswood Powys 21 B8
Kingswood Surrey 10 B1
Kingswood Warwick 22 E5
Kington Heref/Worcs 21 G8
Kington Heref/Worcs 22 G3
Kington Langley Wilts 15 G12
Kington Magna Dorset 7 D11
Kington St. Michael Wilts 15 F12
Kingussie H'land 57 J3
Kingweston Som'set 7 C8
Kinharvie Dumf/Gal 43 E10
Kinkell Bridge Tayside 52 E4
Kinknockie Gramp 58 C7
Kinknockie Gramp 58 E7
Kinkry Hill Cumb 44 E3
Kinlet Shrops 22 D1
Kinloch Fife 53 F7
Kinloch H'land 60 D4
Kinloch H'land 62 F6
Kinloch Tayside 52 C6
Kinloch Tayside 53 C7
Kinloch Castle H'land 62 H3
Kinloch Hourn H'land 55 J3
Kinloch Laggan H'land 57 K1
Kinloch Lodge H'land 60 B6
Kinloch Rannoch Tayside 52 A2
Kinlochan H'land 50 A5
Kinlochard Central 51 G11
Kinlochbeoraid H'land 55 L2
Kinlochbervie H'land 60 B3
Kinlocheil H'land 55 L4
Kinlochetive H'land 51 C8
Kinlochewe H'land 54 D4
Kinlochleven H'land 51 A9
Kinlochmoidart H'land 55 M1
Kinlochmorar H'land 55 K2
Kinlochmore H'land 51 A9
Kinlochspelve H'land 50 E4
Kinloid H'land 55 L1
Kinloss Gramp 56 D6
Kinmel Bay Clwyd 29 B9
Kinmuck Gramp 58 F6
Kinmundy Gramp 58 F6
Kinnadie Gramp 58 C7
Kinnahaird H'land 54 D8
Kinnaid Castle Tayside 59 L4
Kinnaird Tayside 53 D7
Kinnaird Castle Tayside 53 B11
Kinneff Gramp 59 K6
Kinnelhead Dumf/Gal 43 B11
Kinnell Tayside 53 B10

Kinnerley *Shrops* **30** H2
Kinnersley *Heref/Worcs* **21** G9
Kinnersley *Heref/Worcs* **22** H2
Kinnerton *Powys* **21** F8
Kinnesswood *Tayside* **52** G6
Kinninvie *Durham* **40** C1
Kinnordy *Tayside* **53** B8
Kinoulton *Notts* **32** G4
Kinrara *H'land* **57** J4
Kinross *Tayside* **52** G6
Kinrossie *Tayside* **53** D7
Kinsham *Heref/Worcs* **21** F9
Kinsley *W Yorks* **36** F2
Kinson *Dorset* **8** F2
Kintaravie *W Isles* **63** E3
Kintbury *Berks* **16** G5
Kintessack *Gramp* **56** D6
Kintillo *Tayside* **52** E6
Kintocher *Gramp* **59** G3
Kinton *Heref/Worcs* **21** E9
Kinton *Shrops* **30** H2
Kintore *Gramp* **58** F5
Kintra *H'land* **50** F1
Kintrae *Gramp* **56** C7
Kintraw *S'clyde* **50** G5
Kinuachdrach *H'land* **50** H4
Kinveachy *H'land* **57** H5
Kinver *Staffs* **22** D2
Kippax *W Yorks* **36** D2
Kippen *Central* **52** H1
Kippford or Scaur *Dumf/Gal* **43** F9
Kipping's Cross *Kent* **10** D5
Kirbister *Orkney* **64** D2
Kirby *I of Man* **38** H2
Kirby Bedon *Norfolk* **26** E6
Kirby Bellars *Leics* **32** H4
Kirby Cane *Norfolk* **26** F7
Kirby Cross *Essex* **19** B12
Kirby Grindalythe *N Yorks* **41** H9
Kirby Hill *N Yorks* **40** E2
Kirby Hill *N Yorks* **40** H4
Kirby Knowle *N Yorks* **40** F5
Kirby le Soken *Essex* **19** B12
Kirby Misperton *N Yorks* **41** G8
Kirby Muxloe *Leics* **23** B8
Kirby Overblow *N Yorks* **35** B12
Kirby Row *Norfolk* **26** F7
Kirby Sigston *N Yorks* **40** F4
Kirby Underdale *Humber* **36** A6
Kirby Wiske *N Yorks* **40** G4
Kirdford *W Sussex* **9** C11
Kirivik *W Isles* **63** C3
Kirk *H'land* **61** B11
Kirk Bramwith *S Yorks* **36** F4
Kirk Deighton *N Yorks* **35** B12
Kirk Ella *Humber* **37** D8
Kirk Hallam *Derby* **32** F2
Kirk Hammerton *N Yorks* **36** B3
Kirk Ireton *Derby* **31** E11
Kirk Langley *Derby* **31** F11
Kirk Merrington *Durham* **40** B3
Kirk Michael *I of Man* **38** G1
Kirk of Shotts *S'clyde* **48** C1
Kirk Sandall *S Yorks* **36** F4
Kirk Smeaton *N Yorks* **36** E3
Kirk Yetholm *Borders* **49** G11
Kirkabister *Shetl'd* **64** E7
Kirkandrews *Dumf/Gal* **43** G7
Kirkandrews on Eden *Cumb* **44** G2
Kirkbampton *Cumb* **44** G1
Kirkbank *Dumf/Gal* **43** C11
Kirkbean *Dumf/Gal* **43** F10
Kirkbrae *Orkney* **64** A2
Kirkbride *Cumb* **44** G1
Kirkbride *Dumf/Gal* **43** C9
Kirkbuddo *Tayside* **53** C9
Kirkburn *Borders* **48** F5
Kirkburn *Humber* **37** B7
Kirkburton *W Yorks* **35** F10
Kirkby *Lincs* **33** A8
Kirkby *Mersey* **34** G3
Kirkby *N Yorks* **40** E5
Kirkby Fleetham *N Yorks* **40** F3
Kirkby Green *Lincs* **33** D8
Kirkby in Ashfield *Notts* **32** E2
Kirkby la Thorpe *Lincs* **24** A2
Kirkby Lonsdale *Cumb* **39** G8
Kirkby Malham *N Yorks* **35** A7
Kirkby Mallory *Leics* **23** B8
Kirkby Malzeard *N Yorks* **40** H2
Kirkby Mills *N Yorks* **41** G7
Kirkby on Bain *Lincs* **33** D9
Kirkby Stephen *Cumb* **39** D10
Kirkby Thore *Cumb* **39** C9
Kirkby Underwood *Lincs* **24** C2
Kirkby Wharf *N Yorks* **36** C3
Kirkby-in-Furness *Cumb* **38** G5
Kirkbymoorside *N Yorks* **41** F7
Kirkcaldy *Fife* **53** H7
Kirkcambeck *Cumb* **44** F4
Kirkcarswell *Dumf/Gal* **43** G8
Kirkcolm *Dumf/Gal* **42** E1
Kirkconnel *Dumf/Gal* **47** H12
Kirkconnell *Dumf/Gal* **43** E10
Kirkconnell *Dumf/Gal* **43** F7
Kirkcowan *Dumf/Gal* **42** E4
Kirkcudbright *Dumf/Gal* **43** F8
Kirkdale *Mersey* **30** A2
Kirkdale House *Dumf/Gal* **42** F6
Kirkdean *Borders* **48** E4
Kirkfieldbank *S'clyde* **48** E1
Kirkgunzeon *Dumf/Gal* **43** E9
Kirkham *Lancs* **34** D3
Kirkham *N Yorks* **36** A5
Kirkhamgate *W Yorks* **35** E11
Kirkharle *Northum* **45** E8
Kirkheaton *Northum* **45** E8
Kirkheaton *W Yorks* **35** E10
Kirkhill *Gramp* **56** F8
Kirkhill *H'land* **56** E1
Kirkhill *Lothian* **48** C5
Kirkhill *Tayside* **59** L4
Kirkhope *Borders* **48** G6
Kirkhouse *Borders* **48** F6
Kirkibost *H'land* **62** F5
Kirkibost *W Isles* **63** C3
Kirkinch *Tayside* **53** C8
Kirkinner *Dumf/Gal* **42** F5
Kirkintilloch *S'clyde* **47** B11
Kirkland *Cumb* **38** C3
Kirkland *Cumb* **39** B9
Kirkland *Dumf/Gal* **42** G5
Kirkland *Dumf/Gal* **43** C11
Kirkland *Dumf/Gal* **43** B7
Kirkland *Dumf/Gal* **43** C9
Kirkland *Dumf/Gal* **47** H12
Kirkland Guards *Cumb* **43** G12
Kirkland of Gelston *Dumf/Gal* **43** F8
Kirkleatham *Clevl'd* **40** C6
Kirklevington *Clevl'd* **40** D4
Kirkley *Suffolk* **26** F8
Kirkley March *Northum* **45** E9
Kirklington *N Yorks* **40** G3
Kirklington *Notts* **32** D4
Kirklinton *Cumb* **44** F3
Kirkliston *Lothian* **48** B4
Kirkmaiden *Dumf/Gal* **42** H2
Kirkmichael *S'clyde* **42** A4
Kirkmichael *Tayside* **52** A6
Kirkmuirhill *S'clyde* **47** E12
Kirknewton *Lothian* **48** C4
Kirknewton *Northum* **49** F11
Kirkney *Gramp* **58** D3
Kirkoswald *Cumb* **39** A8
Kirkoswald *S'clyde* **42** A3
Kirkpatrick *Dumf/Gal* **43** D8
Kirkpatrick-Fleming *Dumf/Gal* **44** F1
Kirksanton *Cumb* **38** G4
Kirkstead *Lincs* **33** D9
Kirkstile *Dumf/Gal* **44** D2
Kirkstile *Gramp* **58** D3
Kirkston of Culsalmond *Gramp* **58** D4
Kirkton *Borders* **44** B4
Kirkton *Dumf/Gal* **43** C10
Kirkton *Fife* **53** E8
Kirkton *Gramp* **58** C4
Kirkton *Gramp* **58** E4
Kirkton *Gramp* **58** F6
*Kirkton *H'land* **54** F3
Kirkton *H'land* **56** C3
Kirkton *H'land* **56** F2
Kirkton *S'clyde* **48** G2
Kirkton *Tayside* **52** E4
Kirkton *Tayside* **53** C9
Kirkton *Tayside* **59** J2
Kirkton of Airlie *Tayside* **53** B8
Kirkton of Auchterhouse *Tayside* **53** C8
Kirkton of Balfour *Gramp* **59** K3
Kirkton of Barevan *H'land* **56** E4
Kirkton of Collace *Tayside* **53** D7
Kirkton of Craig *Tayside* **53** B11
Kirkton of Durris *Gramp* **59** H5
Kirkton of Glenbuchat *Gramp* **58** F1
Kirkton of Glenisla *Tayside* **53** A7
Kirkton of Kingoldrum *Tayside* **53** B8
Kirkton of Largo *Fife* **53** G9
Kirkton of Lethendy *Tayside* **52** C6
Kirkton of Logie Buchan *Gramp* **58** E7
*Kirkton *Highland* **55** G2
Kirkton of Maryculter *Gramp* **59** G6
Kirkton of Menmuir *Tayside* **59** L3
Kirkton of Monikie *Tayside* **53** C10
Kirkton of Oyne *Gramp* **58** E4
Kirkton of Skene *Gramp* **59** G5
Kirkton of Strathmartine *Tayside* **53** D8
Kirkton of Tealing *Tayside* **53** C9
Kirkton of Tough *Gramp* **58** F4
Kirktonbarns *Fife* **53** D9
Kirktown *Gramp* **58** B8
Kirktown of Alvah *Gramp* **58** B4
Kirktown of Auchterless *Gramp* **58** C5
Kirktown of Bourtie *Gramp* **58** E5
Kirktown of Deskford *Gramp* **58** B2
Kirktown of Fetteresso *Gramp* **59** J6
Kirktown of Mortlach *Gramp* **58** D1
Kirktown of Rayne *Gramp* **58** E4
Kirktown of Slains *Gramp* **58** E8
Kirkwall *Orkney* **64** D2
Kirkwhelpington *Northum* **45** E8
Kirmington *Humber* **37** F9
Kirmond le Mire *Lincs* **33** A9
Kirn *S'clyde* **47** B7
Kirncleuch *Dumf/Gal* **43** B12
Kirriemuir *Tayside* **53** B8
Kirstead Green *Norfolk* **26** F6
Kirtlebridge *Dumf/Gal* **44** F1
Kirtleton *Dumf/Gal* **44** E1
Kirtling *Cambs* **25** J8
Kirtling Green *Cambs* **25** K8
Kirtlington *Oxon* **16** B6
Kirtomy *H'land* **61** B7
Kirton *H'land* **56** D3
Kirton *Lincs* **24** B4
Kirton *Notts* **32** C4
Kirton *Suffolk* **27** L6
Kirton End *Lincs* **24** B4
Kirton Holme *Lincs* **24** A4
Kirton in Lindsey *Humber* **37** G7
Kislingbury *Northants* **23** F10
Kites Hardwick *Warwick* **23** E8
Kittisford *Som'set* **6** D4
Kittle *W Glam* **13** H9
Kitt's Moss *Gtr Man* **31** B7
Kittybrewster *Gramp* **59** G7
Kitwood *Hants* **9** C8
Kiverley *Devon* **4** D4
Kivernoll *Heref/Worcs* **15** A8
Kiveton Park *S Yorks* **32** B2
Klibreck *H'land* **60** D6
Knaith *Lincs* **32** B5
Knaith Park *Lincs* **32** B5
Knaphill *Surrey* **17** H10
Knapp *Som'set* **6** D6
Knapp *Tayside* **53** D7
Knapton *N Yorks* **36** B3
Knapton *Norfolk* **26** B6
Knapton Green *Heref/Worcs* **21** G10
Knapwell *Cambs* **25** J4
Knaresborough *N Yorks* **35** A12
Knarsdale *Northum* **44** H5
Knauchland *Gramp* **58** C3
Knaven *Gramp* **58** C6
Knayton *N Yorks* **40** F4
Knebworth *Herts* **18** B3
Knedlington *Humber* **36** D5
Kneesall *Notts* **32** D4
Kneesworth *Cambs* **25** L4
Kneeton *Notts* **32** F4
Knelston *W Glam* **13** H8
Knettishall *Suffolk* **27** G3
Knightacott *Devon* **4** B5
Knightcote *Warwick* **23** G7
Knighton *Devon* **5** L4
Knighton *Dorset* **7** E9
Knighton *Leics* **23** B9
Knighton *Powys* **21** E8
Knighton *Staffs* **30** F6
Knighton *Staffs* **30** G6
Knighton *Wilts* **16** G4
Knightsford Bridge *Heref/Worcs* **22** G1
Knill *Heref/Worcs* **21** F8
Knipton *Leics* **32** G5
Knitsley *Durham* **45** H9
Kniveton *Derby* **31** E10
Knock *Cumb* **39** B9
Knock *Gramp* **58** B3
Knock *H'land* **50** D3
Knock *H'land* **62** G6
Knockan *H'land* **60** F3
Knockandhu *Gramp* **57** G8
Knockando *Gramp* **56** E7
Knockanrock *H'land* **60** F3
Knockarthur *H'land* **61** F7
Knockbain *H'land* **56** D2
Knockbreck *H'land* **62** B2
Knockbrex *Dumf/Gal* **43** G7
Knockdee *H'land* **61** B11
Knockdolian Castle *S'clyde* **42** C2
Knockdon *S'clyde* **42** B5
Knockendon *S'clyde* **47** D7
Knockenkelly *S'clyde* **46** G5
Knockentiber *S'clyde* **47** E9
Knockespock Ho *Gramp* **58** E3
Knockgardner *S'clyde* **42** A4
Knockglass *Dumf/Gal* **42** F1
Knockholt *Kent* **10** B4
Knockie Lodge *H'land* **55** H8
Knockin *Shrops* **30** H2
Knockinlaw *S'clyde* **47** E9
Knocklaugh *S'clyde* **42** B3
Knocklearn *Dumf/Gal* **43** D8
Knocknain *Dumf/Gal* **42** E1
Knockrome *S'clyde* **46** B1
Knockshannoch *Tayside* **53** A7
Knocksharry *I of Man* **38** G1
Knocksheen *Dumf/Gal* **42** C6
Knockvennie *Dumf/Gal* **43** D8
Knockycoid *S'clyde* **42** D3
Knodishall *Suffolk* **27** J7
Knole *Som'set* **7** D8
Knole Park *Avon* **15** F9
Knolls Green *Ches* **30** B6
Knolton *Clwyd* **30** F2
Knook *Wilts* **8** B1
Knossington *Leics* **23** A11
Knott End-on-Sea *Lancs* **34** B2
Knotting *Beds* **25** J1
Knotting Green *Beds* **25** J1
Knottingley *W Yorks* **36** E3
Knotts *Cumb* **39** C7
Knotty Ash *Mersey* **30** A3
Knotty Green *Bucks* **17** E10
Knowbury *Shrops* **21** E11
Knowe *Dumf/Gal* **42** D4
Knowes of Elride *Gramp* **58** B3
Knowesgate *Northum* **45** D8
Knoweside *S'clyde* **47** H7
Knowetownhead *Borders* **49** G8
Knowhead *Dumf/Gal* **43** C7
Knowhead *Gramp* **58** F2
Knowl Green *Essex* **27** L1
Knowl Hill *Berks* **17** F9
Knowle *Avon* **15** G9
Knowle *Devon* **4** B4
Knowle *Devon* **4** F6
Knowle *Devon* **6** H4
Knowle *Shrops* **21** E11
Knowle *Som'set* **7** B7
Knowle *W Midlands* **22** D5
Knowle Green *Lancs* **34** C5
Knowlton *Dorset* **8** E2
Knowlton *Kent* **11** C11
Knowsie *Gramp* **58** B8
Knowsley *Mersey* **34** H3
Knowstone *Devon* **4** D7
Knox Bridge *Kent* **10** D6
Knucklas *Powys* **21** E8
Knutsford *Ches* **30** B6
Knypersley *Staffs* **31** E7
Kuggar *Cornw'l* **2** H4
Kyle of Lochalsh *H'land* **55** G1
Kyleakin *H'land* **55** G1
Kylerhea *H'land* **55** G2
Kyles Scalpay *W Isles* **63** G3
Kyles Stockinish *W Isles* **63** H2
Kylesbeg *H'land* **55** M1
Kylesknoydart *H'land* **55** K2
Kylesku *H'land* **60** D3
Kylesmorar *H'land* **55** K2
Kylestrome *H'land* **60** D4
Kyllachy House *H'land* **57** G3
Kyloag *H'land* **61** G7
Kymin *Gwent* **15** C8
Kynaston *Heref/Worcs* **15** B8
Kynnersley *Shrops* **21** A12
Kyre Park *Heref/Worcs* **21** F11
Labost *W Isles* **63** B4
Laceby *Humber* **37** F10
Lacey Green *Bucks* **17** D9
Lach Dennis *Ches* **30** C5
Lackalee *W Isles* **63** H2
Lackenby *Clevl'd* **40** C6
Lackford *Suffolk* **27** H1
Lacock *Wilts* **15** G12
Ladbroke *Warwick* **23** F7
Ladcok *Cornw'l* **2** E6
Laddingford *Kent* **10** C6
Lade Bank *Lincs* **33** E11
Ladybank *Fife* **53** F8
Ladybank *S'clyde* **42** A3
Ladycross *Cornw'l* **3** A10
Ladyflat *Borders* **49** D10
Ladykirk *Borders* **49** E11
Ladyleys *Gramp* **58** E6
Ladysford *Gramp* **58** B6
Lag *Dumf/Gal* **43** C9
Laga *H'land* **50** B4
Lagalochan *S'clyde* **50** F6
Lagg *S'clyde* **46** B1
Lagg *S'clyde* **46** G4
Laggan *Central* **52** F1
Laggan *Gramp* **58** D1
Laggan *H'land* **55** K7
Laggan *H'land* **57** K2
Laggan *S'clyde* **42** C2
Laggan *S'clyde* **42** C3
Lagganlia *H'land* **57** J4
Lagganmullan *Dumf/Gal* **42** F6
Lagganulva *H'land* **50** C2
Laid *H'land* **60** B5
Laide *H'land* **60** G1
Laigh Braidley *S'clyde* **47** E10
Laigh Brocklar *S'clyde* **47** G10
Laigh Cleughearn *S'clyde* **47** D11
Laigh Fenwick *S'clyde* **47** E9
Laighmuir *S'clyde* **47** E9
Laighstonehall *S'clyde* **47** D12
Laight *Dumf/Gal* **43** B9
Laindon *Essex* **19** E7
Laintachan *H'land* **57** H6
Lairg *H'land* **60** F6
Lairg Muir *H'land* **60** F6
Lairigmor *H'land* **51** A8
Laisterdyke *W Yorks* **35** D10
Laithes *Cumb* **39** B7
Lake *Wilts* **8** B3
Lake of Moy *Gramp* **56** D6
Lake Side *Cumb* **38** F6
Lakenheath *Suffolk* **25** G8
Lakesend *Norfolk* **24** F6
Laleham *Surrey* **17** G11
Laleston *Mid Glam* **14** F2
Lamancha *Borders* **48** D5
Lamarsh *Essex* **27** L2
Lamas *Norfolk* **26** C5
Lamb Corner *Essex* **27** M3
Lambaness *Orkney* **64** B4
Lambden *Borders* **49** E10
Lamberhurst *Kent* **10** D5
Lamberhurst Quarter *Kent* **10** D5
Lambeth *London* **18** F3
Lambley *Northum* **44** G5
Lambley *Notts* **32** F3
Lambourn *Berks* **16** F4
Lambourne End *Essex* **18** D5
Lambs Green *W Sussex* **10** D1
Lambston *Dyfed* **12** E3
Lamerton *Devon* **5** H3
Lamesley *Tyne/Wear* **45** G10
Lamford *Dumf/Gal* **42** B6
Lamington *H'land* **56** B3
Lamington *S'clyde* **48** F3
Lamlash *S'clyde* **46** F5
Lamloch *Dumf/Gal* **42** B6
Lamonby *Cumb* **38** B6
Lamorna *Cornw'l* **2** G2
Lamorran *Cornw'l* **2** E6
Lampeter *Dyfed* **13** B9
Lampeter Velfrey *Dyfed* **12** F5
Lamphey *Dyfed* **12** G4
Lamplugh *Cumb* **38** C3
Lamport *Northants* **23** E11
Lamyatt *Som'set* **7** C10
Lana *Devon* **4** E2
Lana *Devon* **4** F2
Lanark *S'clyde* **48** E2
Lancaster *Lancs* **34** A4
Lanchester *Durham* **45** H10
Landacre *Som'set* **6** C2
Landbeach *Cambs* **25** J6
Landcross *Devon* **4** D3
Landerberry *Gramp* **59** G5
Landewednack *Cornw'l* **2** H4
Landford *Wilts* **8** D4
Landford Manor *Wilts* **8** D4
Landimore *W Glam* **13** H8
Landkey *Devon* **4** C5
Landore *W Glam* **13** G10
Landrake *Cornw'l* **3** D10
Landrake *Devon* **6** D3
Landshipping *Dyfed* **12** F4
Landulph *Cornw'l* **3** D11
Landwith Junc *Derby* **32** C3
Landywood *Staffs* **22** B3
Lane *Cornw'l* **2** D5
Lane End *Bucks* **17** E9
Lane End *Cumb* **38** F3
Lane End *Hants* **9** D7
Lane End *I of Wight* **9** G8
Lane End *Kent* **10** A4
Lane Ends *Durham* **40** B2
Lane Head *Derby* **31** C10
Lane Head *Durham* **40** D1
Lane Head *Gtr Man* **34** G5
Laneast *Cornw'l* **3** A9
Lanehad *Northum* **44** D6
Laneham *Notts* **32** C5
Laneshawbridge *Lancs* **35** C8
Langar *Notts* **32** G4
Langbank *S'clyde* **47** B8
Langbar *N Yorks* **35** B9
Langburnshiels *Borders* **44** C4
Langcliffe *N Yorks* **35** A7
Langdale *H'land* **61** C7
Langdale End *N Yorks* **41** F9
Langdon *Cornw'l* **2** B2
Langdon *Cornw'l* **3** A10
Langdon Beck *Durham* **39** B11
Langdon Hills *Essex* **19** E7
Langdyke *Fife* **53** G8
Langenhoe *Essex* **19** B10
Langford *Beds* **25** L3
Langford *Devon* **6** F4
Langford *Essex* **19** C8
Langford *Notts* **32** D5
Langford *Oxon* **16** D3
Langford Budville *Som'set* **6** D4
Langford End *Beds* **25** K3
Langham *Devon* **4** E4
Langham *Essex* **27** M3
Langham *Leics* **23** A11
Langham *Norfolk* **26** B3
Langham *Suffolk* **27** H3
Langho *Lancs* **34** D6
Langholm *Dumf/Gal* **44** E2
Langholm *S'clyde* **48** F3
Langleeford *Northum* **49** G12
Langley *Berks* **17** F11
Langley *Ches* **31** C8
Langley *Hants* **8** F6
Langley *Herts* **18** B2
Langley *Kent* **11** C7
Langley *Northum* **44** G6
Langley *W Sussex* **9** C9
Langley *Warwick* **22** F5
Langley Burrell *Wilts* **15** G12
Langley Green *W Sussex* **10** D1
Langley Heath *Kent* **11** C7
Langley Lower Green *Essex* **25** M5
Langley Marsh *Som'set* **6** C4
Langley Mill *Derby* **32** E2
Langley Moor *Durham* **40** A3
Langley Park *Durham* **40** A2
Langley Street *Norfolk* **26** E7
Langley Upper Green *Essex* **25** M5
Langney Park *E Sussex* **10** H5
Langold *Notts* **32** B3
Langore *Cornw'l* **3** A10
Langport *Som'set* **7** D7
Langrick *Lincs* **33** E9
Langridge *Avon* **15** G10
Langridge Ford *Devon* **4** D4
Langrigg *Cumb* **43** G12
Langrish *Hants* **9** D8
Langriville *Lincs* **33** E10
Langsett *S Yorks* **35** G10
Langshaw *Borders* **49** E8
Langside *Tayside* **52** F3
Langskaill *Orkney* **64** A2
Langstone *Hants* **9** F8
Langthorne *N Yorks* **40** F3
Langthorpe *N Yorks* **40** H4
Langthwaite *N Yorks* **39** E12
Langtoft *Humber* **41** H10
Langtoft *Lincs* **24** D2
Langton *Durham* **40** C2
Langton *Lincs* **33** C11
Langton *Lincs* **33** C9
Langton *N Yorks* **41** H8
Langton by Wragby *Lincs* **33** C8
Langton Green *Kent* **10** D4
Langton Herring *Dorset* **7** H9
Langton Matravers *Dorset* **8** H2
Langtree *Devon* **4** D3
Langwathby *Cumb* **39** B8
Langwell *H'land* **60** G5
Langworth *Lincs* **33** C8
Lanivet *Cornw'l* **3** C7
Lank *Cornw'l* **3** B8
Lanlivery *Cornw'l* **3** D8
Lanner *Cornw'l* **2** F4
Lanreath *Cornw'l* **3** D9
Lansallos *Cornw'l* **3** E9
Lansdown *Avon* **15** G10
Lansdown *Glos* **16** B3
Lanteglos Highway *Cornw'l* **3** D8
Lanton *Borders* **49** G9
Lanton *Northum* **49** F11
Lapford *Devon* **4** E6
Lapley *Staffs* **22** A2
Lapworth *Warwick* **22** E5
Larachbeg *H'land* **50** C4
Larbet *Lothian* **48** A1
Larbreck *Dumf/Gal* **43** D9
Larden Green *Ches* **30** E5

Largie *Gramp* **58** D4
Largiemore *S'clyde* **46** A4
Largoward *Fife* **53** F9
Largs *S'clyde* **47** C7
Largue *Gramp* **58** D4
Largymore *S'clyde* **46** G5
Larkfield *Kent* **10** B6
Larkfield *S'clyde* **47** B7
Larkhall *S'clyde* **47** D12
Larkhill *Wilts* **8** B3
Larling *Norfolk* **26** F3
Larriston *Borders* **44** D4
Lartington *Durham* **39** C12
Lary *Gramp* **59** G1
Lasham *Hants* **9** B8
Laskill *N Yorks* **40** F6
Lassington *Glos* **15** B11
Lastingham *N Yorks* **41** F7
Latchford *Herts* **18** B4
Latchingdon *Essex* **19** D8
Latchley *Cornw'l* **3** B11
Latchmeregreen *Hants* **17** H7
Lately Common *Gtr Man* **34** G5
Lathbury *Bucks* **23** H12
Latheron *H'land* **61** D11
Latheronwheel *H'land* **61** D11
Lathockar *Fife* **53** F9
Lathones *Fife* **53** F9
Latimer *Bucks* **17** D10
Latterhead *Cumb* **38** C4
Latteridge *Avon* **15** F10
Lattiford *Som'set* **7** D10
Latton *Wilts* **16** E2
Lauchintilly *Gramp* **58** F5
Laudale House *H'land* **50** B5
Lauder *Borders* **49** E8
Laugharne *Dyfed* **12** F6
Laugherton *Lincs* **32** C5
Laughton *E Sussex* **10** G4
Laughton *Leics* **23** C10
Laughton *Lincs* **36** G6
Laughton en le Morthen *S Yorks* **32** A2
Launcells *Cornw'l* **4** E1
Launceston *Cornw'l* **3** A10
Launcherley *Som'set* **7** B9
Launton *Oxon* **17** B7
Laurel Bank *I of Man* **38** G1
Laurencekirk *Gramp* **59** K5
Laurieston *Dumf/Gal* **43** E7
Laurieston *Lothian* **48** A2
Lavendon *Bucks* **23** G12
Lavenham *Suffolk* **27** K2
Laverhay *Dumf/Gal* **43** B12
Lavernock *S Glam* **14** G5
Laverstock *Wilts* **8** C3
Laverstoke *Hants* **8** A6
Laverton *Glos* **16** A2
Laverton *N Yorks* **40** H2
Laverton *Som'set* **7** A11
Lavister *Clwyd* **30** D2
Law *S'clyde* **48** D1
Lawers *Tayside* **52** C2
Lawers *Tayside* **52** E3
Lawford *Essex* **27** M4
Lawhitton *Cornw'l* **3** A10
Lawkland *N Yorks* **39** H10
Lawley *Shrops* **21** B12
Lawnhead *Staffs* **31** H7
Lawrenny *Dyfed* **12** F4
Lawshall *Suffolk* **27** K2
Lawton *Heref/Worcs* **21** F10
Laxay *W Isles* **63** E4
Laxdale *W Isles* **63** C5
Laxey *I of Man* **38** G2
Laxfield *Suffolk* **27** H6
Laxfirth *Shetl'd* **64** D7
Laxford Bridge *H'land* **60** C4
Laxo *Shetl'd* **64** C7
Laxobigging *Shetl'd* **64** C7
Laxton *Humber* **36** E6
Laxton *Northants* **24** F1
Laxton *Notts* **32** D4
Laycock *W Yorks* **35** C9
Layer Breton *Essex* **19** B9
Layer Marney *Essex* **19** B9
Layer-de-la-Haye *Essex* **19** B9
Layham *Suffolk* **27** L3
Layland's Green *Berks* **16** G5
Laymore *Dorset* **7** F7
Laysters Pole *Heref/Worcs* **21** F11
Laytham *Humber* **36** C5
Lazenby *Clevl'd* **40** C6
Lazonby *Cumb* **39** A8
Lea *Derby* **31** D11
Lea *Heref/Worcs* **15** B10
Lea *Lincs* **32** B5
Lea *Shrops* **21** B9
Lea *Shrops* **21** C9
Lea *Wilts* **15** F12
Lea Marston *Warwick* **22** C5
Lea Town *Lancs* **34** D4
Lea Yeat *Cumb* **39** F10
Leabrooks *Derby* **32** E1
Leachachan *H'land* **55** G3
Leachkin *H'land* **56** E2
Leadburn *Lothian* **48** D5
Leaden Roding *Essex* **18** C6
Leadenham *Lincs* **33** E7
Leaderfoot *Borders* **49** F8
Leadgate *Cumb* **39** A9
Leadgate *Durham* **45** H9
Leadgate *Northum* **45** G9
Leadhills *S'clyde* **48** H2
Leafield *Oxon* **16** C4
Leagrave *Beds* **17** B11
Leake *N Yorks* **40** F4
Leake Common Side *Lincs* **33** E11
Leake Hurn's End *Lincs* **33** E11
Lealholm *N Yorks* **41** D8
Leamington Hastings *Warwick* **23** E8
Leamington Spa *Warwick* **23** F7
Leamonsley *Staffs* **22** A4
Leamside *Durham* **45** H11
Leanach *S'clyde* **51** H7
Leanachan *H'land* **55** L6
Leanaig *H'land* **56** D1
Leargybreck *S'clyde* **46** B1
Leasgill *Cumb* **39** G7
Leasingham *Lincs* **33** E7
Leasingthorne *Durham* **40** B3
Leatherhead *Surrey* **17** H12
Leathley *N Yorks* **35** B11
Leaths *Dumf/Gal* **43** E8
Leaton *Shrops* **30** H3
Leatt *H'land* **62** B4
Leaveland *Kent* **11** C8
Leavening *N Yorks* **36** A5
Leaves Green *London* **18** H4
Leavesden Green *Herts* **18** D1
Leazes *Durham* **45** G10
Lebberston *N Yorks* **41** G10
Lechlade *Glos* **16** D3
Leck *Lancs* **39** G9
Leckford *Hants* **8** B5
Leckfurin *H'land* **61** B7
Leckhampstead *Berks* **16** F5
Leckhampstead *Berks* **16** G5
Leckhampstead *Bucks* **23** H10
Leckhampstead Thicket *Berks* **16** F5
Leckhampton *Glos* **15** B12
Leckie *H'land* **54** C5
Leckmelm *H'land* **60** G3
Leckroy *H'land* **55** K7
Leckwith *S Glam* **14** G5
Leconfield *Humber* **37** C8
Ledaig *S'clyde* **50** D6
Ledburn *Bucks* **17** B10
Ledbury *Heref/Worcs* **15** A10
Ledcharrie *Central* **51** E12
Ledgemoor *Heref/Worcs* **21** G9
Ledgowan *H'land* **54** D5
Ledicot *Heref/Worcs* **21** F9
Ledmore *H'land* **60** F4
Lednagullin *H'land* **61** B8
Ledsham *Ches* **30** C2
Ledsham *W Yorks* **36** D2
Ledston *W Yorks* **36** D2
Ledwell *Oxon* **16** A5
Lee *Devon* **4** A4
Lee *H'land* **50** E1
Lee *Hants* **8** D5
Lee *Lancs* **34** B4
Lee *Shrops* **30** G3
Lee Brockhurst *Shrops* **30** G4
Lee Clump *Bucks* **17** D10
Lee Mill Bridge *Devon* **5** K5
Lee Moor *Devon* **5** J4
Leebotwood *Shrops* **21** C10
Leece *Cumb* **38** H5
Leeds *Kent* **11** C7
Leeds *W Yorks* **35** D11
Leedstown *Cornw'l* **2** F3
Leek *Staffs* **31** E8
Leek Wootton *Warwick* **22** E6
Leeming *N Yorks* **40** F3
Leeming Bar *N Yorks* **40** F3
Lee-on-the-Solent *Hants* **9** F7
Lees *Derby* **31** F11
Lees *Gtr Man* **35** G8
Lees Hill *Cumb* **44** F4
Leeswood *Clwyd* **29** D12
Leftwich *Ches* **30** C5
Legbourne *Lincs* **33** B10
Legerwood *Borders* **49** E8
Legsby *Leics* **23** B9
Legsby *Lincs* **33** B8
Leicester *Leics* **23** B9
Leicester Forest East *Leics* **23** B8
Leigh *Dorset* **7** E9
Leigh *Glos* **15** B11
Leigh *Gtr Man* **34** G5
Leigh *Heref/Worcs* **22** G1
Leigh *Kent* **10** C4
Leigh *Shrops* **21** B9
Leigh *Surrey* **10** C1
Leigh *Wilts* **16** E2
Leigh Beck *Essex* **19** F8
Leigh Delamere *Wilts* **15** F12
Leigh Green *Kent* **11** E8
Leigh Park *Hants* **9** E8
Leigh Sinton *Heref/Worcs* **22** G1
Leigh upon Mendip *Som'set* **7** B10
Leighland Chapel *Som'set* **6** C4
Leigh-on-Sea *Essex* **19** E8
Leighterton *Glos* **15** E11
Leighton *N Yorks* **40** G2
Leighton *Powys* **21** B8
Leighton *Shrops* **21** B11
Leighton *Som'set* **7** B10
Leighton Bromswold *Cambs* **25** H2
Leighton Buzzard *Beds* **17** B10
Leightonhill *Tayside* **59** L4
Leighwoods *Avon* **15** G9
Leinthall Earls *Heref/Worcs* **21** F10
Leinthall Starkes *Heref/Worcs* **21** E10
Leintwardine *Heref/Worcs* **21** E9
Leire *Leics* **23** C8
Leirinmore *H'land* **60** A5
Leiston *Suffolk* **27** J7
Leitfie *Tayside* **53** C7
Leith *Lothian* **48** B5
Leitholm *Borders* **49** E10
Lelant *Cornw'l* **2** F3
Lelley *Humber* **37** D10
Lemlair *H'land* **56** D1
Lemmington Hall *Northum* **45** B9
Lempitlaw *Borders* **49** F10
Lemreway *W Isles* **63** F5
Lemsford *Herts* **18** C2
Lenabo *Gramp* **58** C8
Lenchwick *Heref/Worcs* **22** G4
Lendalfoot *S'clyde* **42** C2
Lendrick Lodge *Central* **51** G12
Lenham *Kent* **11** C7
Lenham Heath *Kent* **11** C8
Lenmes *Dumf/Gal* **42** F5
Lennel *Borders* **49** E11
Lennoxtown *S'clyde* **47** B11
Lent Rise *Berks* **17** F10
Lenton *Lincs* **24** C1
Lenwade *Norfolk* **26** D4
Lenzie *S'clyde* **47** B11
Leochel Cushnie *Gramp* **58** F3
Leominster *Heref/Worcs* **21** F10
Leonard Stanley *Glos* **15** D11
Lepe *Hants* **8** F6
Lephin *H'land* **62** C1
Lephinchapel *S'clyde* **51** H7
Lephinmore *S'clyde* **51** H7
Leppington *N Yorks* **36** A5
Lepton *W Yorks* **35** F10
Lerags *S'clyde* **50** E6
Lerwick *Shetl'd* **64** E7
Lesbury *Northum* **45** B10
Leslie *Fife* **53** G7
Leslie *Gramp* **58** E3
Lesmahagow *S'clyde* **48** E1
Lesnewth *Cornw'l* **2** B2
Lessingham *Norfolk* **26** C7
Lessonhall *Cumb* **44** H1
Leswalt *Dumf/Gal* **42** E1
Letchmore Heath *Herts* **18** D2
Letchworth *Herts* **25** M3
Letcombe Bassett *Oxon* **16** F5
Letcombe Regis *Oxon* **16** E5
Letham *Fife* **53** F8
Letham *Tayside* **52** E6
Letham *Tayside* **53** B10
Letham Grange *Tayside* **53** C11
Lethen House *H'land* **56** D5
Lethendryvcole *H'land* **57** H5
Lethenty *Gramp* **58** D5
Lethenty *Gramp* **58** E5
Letheringham *Suffolk* **27** J6
Letheringsett *Norfolk* **26** B4
Lettaford *Devon* **5** G6
Lettan *Orkney* **64** A4
Letterewe *H'land* **54** C3
Letterfearn *H'land* **55** G3
Letterfinlay *H'land* **55** K6
Lettermorar *H'land* **55** K1
Lettermore *H'land* **50** C2
Lettermore *H'land* **60** C6
Letters *H'land* **60** H3
Lettershaws *S'clyde* **48** G2
Letterston *Dyfed* **12** D3
Lettoch *H'land* **56** F6
Lettoch *H'land* **57** H6
Letton *Heref/Worcs* **21** E9
Letton *Heref/Worcs* **21** H9
Letty Green *Herts* **18** C3
Letwell *S Yorks* **32** B3
Leuchars *Fife* **53** E9
Leuchars House *Gramp* **56** C8
Leurbost *W Isles* **63** D5
Levedale *Staffs* **22** A3
Leven *Fife* **53** G8
Leven *Humber* **37** C8
Levencorroch *S'clyde* **46** G5
Levens *Cumb* **39** G7
Levenshulme *Gtr Man* **35** H7
Levenwick *Shetl'd* **64** F7
Leverburgh *W Isles* **63** H1
Leverington *Cambs* **24** D5
Leverton *Berks* **16** G4
Leverton *Lincs* **33** E11
Leverton Outgate *Lincs* **33** E11
Levington *Suffolk* **27** L5
Levisham *N Yorks* **41** F8
Levishie *H'land* **55** H8
Lew *Oxon* **16** D4
Lewannick *Cornw'l* **3** B9
Lewdown *Devon* **5** G3
Lewes *E Sussex* **10** G3
Leweston *Dyfed* **12** E3
Lewisham *London* **18** G3
Lewiston *H'land* **57** G1
Lewistown *Mid Glam* **14** E3
Lewknor *Oxon* **17** D8
Leworthy *Devon* **4** B5
Lews Castle *W Isles* **63** D5
Lewson Street *Kent* **11** B8
Lewtrenchard *Devon* **5** G3
Ley *Cornw'l* **3** C9
Ley *Gramp* **58** F3
Leybourne *Kent* **10** B5
Leyburn *N Yorks* **40** F1
Leycett *Staffs* **30** E6
Leygreen *Herts* **18** B2
Leyhill *Bucks* **17** D10
Leyland *Lancs* **34** E4
Leylodge *Gramp* **58** F5
Leys *Gramp* **58** B7
Leys Castle *H'land* **56** F2
Leys of Cossans *Tayside* **53** B8
Leys of Drummuies *Gramp* **58** D3
Leysdown-on-Sea *Kent* **11** A9
Leysmill *Tayside* **53** B10
Leyton *London* **18** E4
Leytonstone *London* **18** E4
Lezant *Cornw'l* **3** B10
Liatrie *H'land* **54** F6
Libanus *Powys* **14** B3
Libberton *S'clyde* **48** E3
Liberton *Lothian* **48** B5
Lichfield *Staffs* **22** A5
Lickey *Heref/Worcs* **22** E3
Lickey End *Heref/Worcs* **22** E3
Lickfold *W Sussex* **9** D10
Liddesdale *H'land* **50** B5
Liddington *Wilts* **16** F3
Lidgate *Suffolk* **25** J8
Lidlington *Beds* **25** L1
Lidstone *Oxon* **16** B4
Lienassie *H'land* **55** G3
Liff *Tayside* **53** D8
Lifton *Devon* **5** G3
Liftondown *Devon* **5** G2
Lighthorne *Warwick* **23** G7
Lightwater *Surrey* **17** H10
Lightwood *Staffs* **31** F7
Lightwood Green *Ches* **30** F5
Lilbourne *Northants* **23** D9
Lilburn Hill *Northum* **49** G12
Lilburn Tower *Northum* **45** A8
Lilleshall *Shrops* **22** A1
Lilley *Berks* **16** F5
Lilley *Herts* **18** A1
Lilliesleaf *Borders* **49** G8
Lillingstone Dayrell *Bucks* **23** H10
Lillingstone Lovell *Bucks* **23** H10
Lillington *Dorset* **7** E9
Lillington *Warwick* **23** E7
Lilliput *Dorset* **8** G2
Lilstock *Som'set* **6** B5
Lily Bank *S'clyde* **47** B8
Limbrick *Lancs* **34** F5
Limefield *Gtr Man* **35** F7
Limekilnburn *S'clyde* **47** D12
Limekilns *Lothian* **48** A3
Limerigg *Lothian* **48** B1
Limestone *I of Wight* **8** H6
Limestone Brae *Northum* **44** H6
Limington *Som'set* **7** D8
Limpenhoe *Norfolk* **26** E7
Limpley Stoke *Wilts* **15** H11
Limpsfield *Surrey* **10** C3
Limpsfield Chart *Surrey* **10** C3
Linburn *Lothian* **48** C4
Linby *Notts* **32** E3
Linchmere *W Sussex* **9** C10
Lincluden *Dumf/Gal* **43** D10
Lincoln *Lincs* **33** C7
Lincomb *Heref/Worcs* **22** E2
Lincro *H'land* **62** B3
Lindal in Furness *Cumb* **38** H5
Lindale *Cumb* **38** G6
Lindean *Borders* **49** F7
Lindfield *W Sussex* **10** E2
Lindford *Hants* **9** C9
Lindifferon *Fife* **53** F8
Lindley *W Yorks* **35** E10
Lindley Green *N Yorks* **35** B11
Lindores *Fife* **53** E7
Lindridge *Heref/Worcs* **21** E12
Lindsell *Essex* **18** A6
Lindsey *Suffolk* **27** L3
Linefoot *Cumb* **38** B3
Linford *Essex* **19** F7
Linford *Hants* **8** E3
Lingague *I of Man* **38** H1
Lingdale *N Yorks* **41** D7
Lingen *Heref/Worcs* **21** F9
Lingfield *Surrey* **10** D3
Lingfield Common *Surrey* **10** D3
Lingwood *Norfolk* **26** E7
Linhope *Dumf/Gal* **44** C2
Linhope *Northum* **45** A8
Linkenholt *Hants* **16** H5
Linkinhorne *Cornw'l* **3** B10
Linklater *Orkney* **64** E2
Linktown *Fife* **53** H7
Linley *Shrops* **21** C12
Linley Green *Heref/Worcs* **21** G12
Linlithgow *Lothian* **48** B3
Linlithgow Bridge *Lothian* **48** B3
Linneraineach *H'land* **60** F3
Linney *Dyfed* **12** G2
Linns *Dumf/Gal* **43** D11
Linshader *W Isles* **63** D3
Linshiels *Northum* **45** B7
Linsidemore *H'land* **60** G6
Linslade *Beds* **17** B10
Linstead Parva *Suffolk* **27** G6
Linstock *Cumb* **44** G3
Linthaugh *Northum* **49** F12
Linthwaite *W Yorks* **35** F9
Lintlaw *Borders* **49** D11
Lintmill *Gramp* **58** A3
Linton *Borders* **49** G10
Linton *Cambs* **25** K7
Linton *Derby* **22** A6
Linton *Heref/Worcs* **15** B9
Linton *Kent* **10** C6
Linton *N Yorks* **35** A8
Linton *W Yorks* **35** B12
Linton-on-Ouse *N Yorks* **36** A3
Linwood *Hants* **8** E3
Linwood *Lincs* **33** B8
Linwood *S'clyde* **47** C9
Lionel *W Isles* **63** A6
Liphook *Hants* **9** C9
Liscombe *Som'set* **6** C2
Liskeard *Cornw'l* **3** C9
Liss *Hants* **9** C9
Liss Forest *Hants* **9** C9
Lissett *Humber* **37** A9
Lissington *Lincs* **33** B8
Lisvane *S Glam* **14** F5
Liswerry *Gwent* **15** F7
Litcham *Norfolk* **26** D2
Litchborough *Northants* **23** G9
Litchfield *Hants* **8** A6
Litherland *Mersey* **34** G2
Litlington *Cambs* **25** L4
Litlington *E Sussex* **10** H4
Little Abington *Cambs* **25** K6
Little Addington *Northants* **25** H1
Little Alne *Warwick* **22** F5
Little Assynt *H'land* **60** E3
Little Aston *Staffs* **22** B4
Little Atherfield *I of Wight* **8** H6
Little Ayre *Orkney* **64** D1
Little Ayton *N Yorks* **40** D6
Little Baddow *Essex* **19** C7
Little Badminton *Avon* **15** F11
Little Ballinluig *Tayside* **52** B4
Little Bampton *Cumb* **44** G1
Little Bardfield *Essex* **25** M8
Little Barford *Beds* **25** J3
Little Barningham *Norfolk* **26** B4
Little Barrington *Glos* **16** C3
Little Barrow *Ches* **30** C3
Little Barugh *N Yorks* **41** G8
Little Bavington *Northum* **45** E8
Little Bealings *Suffolk* **27** K5
Little Bedwyn *Wilts* **16** G4
Little Bentley *Essex* **19** A11
Little Berkhamstead *Herts* **18** C3
Little Billing *Northants* **23** F11
Little Birch *Heref/Worcs* **15** A8
Little Blakenham *Suffolk* **27** K4
Little Blencow *Cumb* **39** B7
Little Bookham *Surrey* **9** A12
Little Bowden *Leics* **23** C11
Little Bradley *Suffolk* **25** K8
Little Brampton *Shrops* **21** D9
Little Braxted *Essex* **19** B8
Little Brechin *Tayside* **59** L3
Little Brickhill *Bucks* **17** A10
Little Brington *Northants* **23** F10
Little Bromley *Essex* **19** A10
Little Budworth *Ches* **30** D5
Little Burstead *Essex* **18** E6
Little Bytham *Lincs* **24** D1
Little Cairnbrock *Dumf/Gal* **42** E1
Little Carlton *Lincs* **33** B11
Little Carlton *Notts* **32** D5
Little Casterton *Leics* **24** E1
Little Cawthorpe *Lincs* **33** B10
Little Chalfont *Bucks* **17** D11
Little Chart *Kent* **11** D8
Little Cheney *Dorset* **7** G9
Little Chesterford *Essex* **25** L6
Little Cheverell *Wilts* **8** A2
Little Chishill *Cambs* **25** L5
Little Clacton *Essex* **19** B11
Little Clifton *Cumb* **38** B3
Little Colp *Gramp* **58** C5
Little Comberton *Heref/Worcs* **22** H3
Little Compton *Warwick* **16** A4
Little Cornard *Suffolk* **27** L2
Little Cowarne *Heref/Worcs* **21** G11
Little Coxwell *Oxon* **16** E4
Little Crakehall *N Yorks* **40** F3
Little Cressingham *Norfolk* **26** E2
Little Crosby *Mersey* **34** G2
Little Dalby *Leics* **23** A11
Little Dawley *Shrops* **21** B12
Little Dewchurch *Heref/Worcs* **15** A8
Little Driffield *Humber* **37** A8
Little Dunham *Norfolk* **26** D2
Little Dunkeld *Tayside* **52** C5
Little Dunmow *Essex* **18** B6
Little Easton *Essex* **18** B6
Little Eaton *Derby* **31** F12
Little Ellingham *Norfolk* **26** E3
Little Elm *Som'set* **7** B10
Little End *Essex* **18** D5
Little Eversden *Cambs* **25** K5
Little Fakenham *Suffolk* **27** H2
Little Faringdon *Oxon* **16** D3
Little Fencote *N Yorks* **40** F3
Little Fenton *N Yorks* **36** D3
Little Fransham *Norfolk* **26** D2
Little Gaddesden *Herts* **17** C10
Little Gidding *Cambs* **25** G2
Little Glemham *Suffolk* **27** J6
Little Gransden *Cambs* **25** K4
Little Green *Som'set* **7** A10
Little Grimsby *Lincs* **33** A10
Little Gruinard *H'land* **60** G1
Little Hadham *Herts* **18** B4
Little Hale *Lincs* **24** B2
Little Hallingbury *Essex* **18** B5
Little Hampden *Bucks* **17** D9
Little Harrowden *Northants* **23** E12
Little Haseley *Oxon* **17** D7
Little Hatfield *Humber* **37** C9
Little Haven *Dyfed* **12** F2
Little Hay *Staffs* **22** B5
Little Hayfield *Derby* **31** A9
Little Haywood *Staffs* **31** H8
Little Hereford *Heref/Worcs* **21** F11
Little Horkesley *Essex* **27** M2
Little Hormead *Herts* **18** A4
Little Horsted *E Sussex* **10** F3
Little Horton *W Yorks* **35** D10
Little Horwood *Bucks* **17** A9
Little Houghton *Northants* **23** F10
Little Houghton *Northants* **23** F11
Little Hucklow *Derby* **31** B10
Little Hulton *Gtr Man* **34** G6
Little Irchester *Northants* **23** E12
Little Kelk *Humber* **37** A8
Little Kimble *Bucks* **17** C9
Little Kingshill *Bucks* **17** D10
Little Langdale *Cumb* **38** E5
Little Langford *Wilts* **8** C2
Little Ledikin *Gramp* **58** E4
Little Leigh *Ches* **30** C5
Little Leighs *Essex* **19** B7
Little Lever *Gtr Man* **34** F6
Little Linford *Bucks* **23** H11

Little London E Sussex 10 F4
Little London Hants 17 H7
Little London Hants 8 A5
Little London Lincs 24 C5
Little London W Yorks 35 C10
Little Longstone Derby 31 C10
Little Lynturk Gramp 58 F3
Little Malvern Heref/Worcs 22 H1
Little Maplestead Essex 27 M1
Little Marcle Heref/Worcs 15 A10
Little Marlow Bucks 17 E9
Little Massingham Norfolk 26 C1
Little Melton Norfolk 26 E5
Little Milford Dyfed 12 F3
Little Mill Gwent 14 D6
Little Milton Oxon 17 D7
Little Missenden Bucks 17 D10
Little Ness Shrops 30 H3
Little Neston Ches 30 C2
Little Newcastle Dyfed 12 D3
Little Newsham Durham 40 C1
Little Oakley Essex 19 A12
Little Oakley Northants 23 D12
Little Orton Cumb 44 G2
Little Ouseburn N Yorks 36 A2
Little Paxton Cambs 25 J3
Little Petherick Cornw'l 2 B6
Little Pinmore S'clyde 42 C3
Little Plumstead Norfolk 26 D6
Little Ponton Lincs 32 G6
Little Potheridge Devon 4 E4
Little Raveley Cambs 25 G4
Little Ribston N Yorks 35 B12
Little Rissington Glos 16 B3
Little Ryburgh Norfolk 26 C3
Little Ryle Northum 45 B8
Little Salkeld Cumb 39 B8
Little Sampford Essex 25 M7
Little Sandhurst Berks 17 H9
Little Saxham Suffolk 27 J1
Little Scatwell H'land 54 D7
Little Shelford Cambs 25 K5
Little Silver Devon 4 F7
Little Silver Devon 6 E3
Little Singleton Lancs 34 C3
Little Skillymarn Gramp 58 B7
Little Smeaton N Yorks 36 E3
Little Snoring Norfolk 26 B2
Little Sodbury Avon 15 F10
Little Somborne Hants 8 C5
Little Somerford Wilts 16 F1
Little Stainton Durham 40 C4
Little Stanney Ches 30 C3
Little Staughton Beds 25 J2
Little Steeping Lincs 33 D11
Little Stonham Suffolk 27 J4
Little Stretton Leics 23 B10
Little Stretton Shrops 21 C10
Little Strickland Cumb 39 C8
Little Stukeley Cambs 25 H3
Little Swinburne Northum 45 E8
Little Swinton Borders 49 E11
Little Tew Oxon 16 A5
Little Thetford Cambs 25 H6
Little Thurlow Suffolk 25 K8
Little Thurrock Essex 18 F6
Little Torhouse Dumf/Gal 42 F5
Little Torrington Devon 4 D4
Little Tosson Northum 45 C8
Little Totham Essex 19 C9
Little Town Cumb 38 C5
Little Urchany H'land 56 E4
Little Urswick Cumb 38 H5
Little Wakering Essex 19 E9
Little Waldingfield Suffolk 27 L2
Little Walsingham Norfolk 26 B2
Little Waltham Essex 19 C7
Little Warley Essex 18 E6
Little Weighton Humber 37 D7
Little Welnetham Suffolk 27 J2
Little Wenlock Shrops 21 B12
Little Whittingham Green Suffolk 27 H6
Little Whittington Northum 45 F8
Little Wilbraham Cambs 25 J6
Little Wishford Wilts 8 B2
Little Witley Heref/Worcs 22 F1
Little Wittenham Oxon 16 E6
Little Wolford Oxon 16 A4
Little Wymington Beds 25 J1
Little Wymondley Herts 18 A2
Little Wyrley Staffs 22 B4
Little Yeldham Essex 27 L1
Little-ayre Shetl'd 64 C6
Littlebeck N Yorks 41 E9
Littleborough Gtr Man 35 F8
Littleborough Notts 32 B5
Littlebourne Kent 11 B10
Littlebredy Dorset 7 G9
Littlebury Essex 25 L6
Littledale Lancs 34 A4
Littledean Glos 15 C10
Littleferry H'land 61 G8
Littleham Devon 4 D3
Littleham Devon 6 H4
Littlehampton W Sussex 9 F11
Littlehempston Devon 5 J7
Littlehoughton Northum 45 A10
Littlemill Gramp 59 H1
Littlemill H'land 56 E5
Littlemill Northum 45 A10
Littlemill S'clyde 47 H9
Littlemore Oxon 16 D6
Littleover Derby 31 G11
Littleport Cambs 25 G7
Littleport Bridge Cambs 25 G7
Littlestone-on-Sea Kent 11 F9
Littlethorpe N Yorks 40 H3
Littleton Ches 30 D3
Littleton Dumf/Gal 43 F7
Littleton Hants 8 C6
Littleton Som'set 7 C8
Littleton Surrey 17 G11
Littleton Surrey 9 A11
Littleton Tayside 53 D7
Littleton Drew Wilts 15 F11
Littleton Panell Wilts 8 A2
Littleton upon Severn Avon 15 E9
Littletown Durham 40 A4
Littlewick Green Berks 17 F9
Littleworth Glos 15 D11
Littleworth Heref/Worcs 22 G2
Littleworth Oxon 16 D4
Littleworth Staffs 22 A4
Littleworth Staffs 31 H8
Littleworth W Sussex 10 F1
Litton Derby 31 C10
Litton N Yorks 39 H11
Litton Som'set 7 A9
Liverpool Mersey 30 A2
Liversedge W Yorks 35 E10
Liverton Devon 5 H7
Liverton N Yorks 41 D7
Livingston Lothian 48 C3
Lixwm Clwyd 29 C11
Lizard Cornw'l 2 H4
Llaingoch Gwyn 28 B2
Llaithddu Powys 20 D6
Llan Powys 20 B4
Llanaber Gwyn 28 H5
Llanaelhaearn Gwyn 28 F3
Llanaeron Dyfed 13 A8
Llanafan Dyfed 20 E2
Llanafan-fawr Powys 20 G5
Llanafan-fechan Powys 20 G5
Llanallgo Gwyn 28 B4
Llanarmon Gwyn 28 F4
Llanarmon Dyffryn Ceiriog Clwyd 29 G10
Llanarmon-yn-lal Clwyd 29 E11
Llanarth Dyfed 13 A7
Llanarth Gwent 15 C7
Llanarthney Dyfed 13 E8
Llanasa Clwyd 29 B10
Llanbabo Gwyn 28 B3
Llanbadarn Fawr Dyfed 20 D2
Llanbadarn Fynydd Powys 20 E6
Llanbadarn-y-garreg Powys 21 G7
Llanbadoc Gwent 15 D7
Llanbadrig Gwyn 28 A3
Llanbeder Gwent 15 E7
Llanbedr Gwyn 28 H5
Llanbedr Gwyn 29 C7
Llanbedr Powys 14 B6
Llanbedr Powys 21 H7
Llanbedr-Dyffryn-Clwyd Clwyd 29 D10
Llanbedrog Gwyn 28 G3
Llanberis Gwyn 28 D5
Llanbethery S Glam 14 G4
Llanbister Powys 20 E6
Llanblethian S Glam 14 G3
Llanboidy Dyfed 12 E5
Llanbradach Mid Glam 14 E5
Llanbryde Gramp 56 D8
Llanbrynmair Powys 20 B5
Llancadle S Glam 14 G4
Llancarfan S Glam 14 G4
Llancayo Gwent 15 D7
Llancloudy Heref/Worcs 15 B8
Llancoch Powys 21 E7
Llandaf S Glam 14 F5
Llandanwg Gwyn 28 G5
Llandarcy W Glam 13 G10
Llandawke Dyfed 12 F6
Llanddaniel Fab Gwyn 28 C4
Llanddarog Dyfed 13 E8
Llanddeiniol Dyfed 20 E1
Llanddeiniolen Gwyn 28 D5
Llandderfel Gwyn 29 F9
Llanddeusant Dyfed 13 E11
Llanddeusant Gwyn 28 B3
Llanddew Powys 14 A4
Llanddewi W Glam 13 H8
Llanddewi Rhydderch Gwent 15 C7
Llanddewi-Brefi Dyfed 20 G2
Llanddewi'r-Cwm Powys 20 G6
Llanddoget Gwyn 29 D7
Llanddona Gwyn 28 B5
Llanddowror Dyfed 12 F6
Llanddulas Clwyd 29 B8
Llanddyfan Gwyn 28 B4
Llandedrgoch Gwyn 28 B4
Llandefaelog Fach Powys 14 A4
Llandefaelog ter-graig Powys 14 A4
Llandefalle Powys 14 A4
Llandegai Gwyn 28 C5
Llandegfan Gwyn 28 C5
Llandegfedd Gwent 15 E7
Llandegla Clwyd 29 E11
Llandegley Powys 21 F7
Llandeilo'r-Fan Powys 14 A2
Llandeilo Dyfed 13 E9
Llandeilo Graban Powys 20 H6
Llandeloy Dyfed 12 D2
Llandenny Gwent 15 D7
Llandevenny Gwent 15 F7
Llandewi Velfrey Dyfed 12 E5
Llandewi Ystradenny Powys 20 E6
Llandilo Dyfed 12 D4
Llandinabo Heref/Worcs 15 A8
Llandinam Powys 20 D6
Llandissilio Dyfed 12 E5
Llandllawddog Dyfed 13 D8
Llandogo Gwent 15 D8
Llandough S Glam 14 G3
Llandough S Glam 14 G5
Llandovery Dyfed 13 D11
Llandow S Glam 14 G3
Llandre Dyfed 13 C10
Llandre Dyfed 20 D2
Llandrillo Clwyd 29 F9
Llandrillo-yn-Rhos Clwyd 29 B7
Llandrindod Wells Powys 20 F6
Llandrinio Powys 21 A8
Llandudno Gwyn 29 B7
Llandudno Junction Gwyn 29 B7
Llandwrog Gwyn 28 E4
Llandybie Dyfed 13 E9
Llandyfaelog Dyfed 13 F7
Llandyfan Dyfed 13 E9
Llandyfriog Dyfed 13 C7
Llandyfrydog Gwyn 28 B4
Llandygwydd Dyfed 12 C6
Llandyrnog Clwyd 29 D10
Llandysilio Powys 29 H12
Llandyssil Powys 21 C7
Llandysul Dyfed 13 C7
Llanedeyrn S Glam 14 F5
Llaneglwys Powys 20 H6
Llanegryn Gwyn 20 B2
Llanegwad Dyfed 13 E8
Llaneilian Gwyn 28 A4
Llanelian-yn-Rhos Clwyd 29 C8
Llanelidan Clwyd 29 E10
Llanelieu Powys 14 A5
Llanellen Gwent 14 C6
Llanelli Dyfed 13 G8
Llanelli Gwent 14 C5
Llanelltyd Gwyn 28 H6
Llanelwedd Powys 20 G6
Llanenddwyn Gwyn 28 H5
Llanengan Gwyn 28 G2
Llanerchymedd Gwyn 28 B4
Llanerfyl Powys 20 A6
Llanfachraeth Gwyn 28 B3
Llanfachreth Gwyn 29 H7
Llanfaelog Gwyn 28 C3
Llanfaelrhys Gwyn 28 G2
Llanfaenor Gwent 15 C7
Llanfaes Gwyn 28 C5
Llanfaes Powys 14 B4
Llanfaethlu Gwyn 28 B3
Llanfagan Gwyn 28 D4
Llanfair Gwyn 28 G5
Llanfair Dyfryn Clwyd Clwyd 29 E10
Llanfair Talhaiarn Clwyd 29 C8
Llanfair Waterdine Shrops 21 E8
Llanfair-Caereinion Powys 20 B6
Llanfair-Clydogau Dyfed 20 G2
Llanfairfechan Gwyn 28 C6
LLanfair-Nant-Gwyn Dyfed 12 C5
Llanfairpwllgwyngyll Gwyn 28 C5
Llanfairynghornwy Gwyn 28 A3
Llanfair-yn-Neubwll Gwyn 28 C2
Llanfallteg Dyfed 12 E5
Llanfaredd Powys 20 G6
Llanfarian Dyfed 20 E2
Llanfechain Powys 29 H11
Llanfechell Gwyn 28 A3
Llanfendigaid Gwyn 20 B1
Llanferres Clwyd 29 D11
Llanfflewyn Gwyn 28 A3
Llanfigael Gwyn 28 B3
Llanfihangel Powys 20 A6
Llanfihangel Crucorney Gwent 14 B6
Llanfihangel Glyn Myfyr Clwyd 29 E9
Llanfihangel Nant Bran Powys 14 A3
Llanfihangel Rhydithon Powys 21 F7
Llanfihangel Rogiet Gwent 15 F8
Llanfihangel Tal-y-llyn Powys 14 A4
Llanfihangel yn Nhowyn Gwyn 28 C3
Llanfihangel-ar-arth Dyfed 13 C8
Llanfihangel-nant-Melan Powys 21 G7
Llanfihangel-uwch-Gwili Dyfed 13 E8
Llanfihangel-y-Creuddyn Dyfed 20 E2
Llanfihangel-y-Pennant Gwyn 20 B2
Llanfihangel-y-pennant Gwyn 28 F5
Llanfihangel-y-traethau Gwyn 28 G5
Llanfilo Powys 14 A4
Llanfoist Gwent 14 C6
Llanfor Gwyn 29 G8
Llanfrechfa Gwent 14 E6
Llanfrothen Gwyn 28 F5
Llanfrynach Powys 14 B4
Llanfwrog Clwyd 29 D10
Llanfwrog Gwyn 28 B2
Llanfyllin Powys 29 H10
Llanfynydd Clwyd 29 E12
Llanfynydd Dyfed 13 D9
Llanfyrnach Dyfed 12 D6
Llangadfan Powys 20 A6
Llangadog Dyfed 13 D10
Llangadog Dyfed 13 F7
Llangadwaladr Clwyd 29 G11
Llangadwaladr Gwyn 28 C3
Llangaffo Gwyn 28 C4
Llangain Dyfed 13 E7
Llangammarch Wells Powys 20 H5
Llangan S Glam 14 G3
Llangarron Heref/Worcs 15 B8
Llangasty-Tal-y-llyn Powys 14 B5
Llangathen Dyfed 13 E9
Llangattock Powys 14 C5
Llangattock Lingoed Gwent 15 B7
Llangattock Vibon-Avel Gwent 15 C8
Llangedwyn Clwyd 29 H11
Llangefni Gwyn 28 C4
Llangeinor Mid Glam 14 F2
Llangeinwen Gwyn 28 D4
Llangeitho Dyfed 20 F2
Llangeler Dyfed 13 C7
Llangelynin Gwyn 20 B1
Llangendeirne Dyfed 13 F8
Llangennech Dyfed 13 G9
Llangennith W Glam 13 H7
Llangenny Powys 14 C6
Llangernyw Clwyd 29 C8
Llangian Gwyn 28 G2
Llangiwg W Glam 13 F10
Llangloffan Dyfed 12 D3
Llanglydwen Dyfed 12 D5
Llangoed Gwyn 28 B5
Llangoedmor Dyfed 12 B5
Llangollen Clwyd 29 F11
Llangolman Dyfed 12 D5
Llangorse Powys 14 B4
Llangoven Gwent 15 D8
Llangower Gwyn 29 G8
Llangranog Dyfed 12 B6
Llangristiolus Gwyn 28 C4
Llangrove Heref/Worcs 15 B8
Llangua Gwent 15 B7
Llangunllo Powys 21 E7
Llangunnor Dyfed 13 E8
Llangurig Dyfed 20 D5
Llangwm Clwyd 29 F9
Llangwm Dyfed 12 F3
Llangwm Gwent 15 D7
Llangwyfan Clwyd 29 D10
Llangwyfanisaf Gwyn 28 C3
Llangwynnadl Gwyn 28 G2
Llangwyryfon Dyfed 20 E2
Llangybi Dyfed 20 G2
Llangybi Gwent 15 E7
Llangybi Gwyn 28 F4
Llangynfelyn Dyfed 20 C2
Llangynhafal Clwyd 29 D10
Llangynidr Powys 14 B5
Llangynin Dyfed 12 E6
Llangynllo Dyfed 13 C7
Llangynog Dyfed 13 E7
Llangynog Powys 29 H9
Llangynwyd Mid Glam 14 E2
Llanhamlach Powys 14 B4
Llanharan Mid Glam 14 F3
Llanharry Mid Glam 14 F3
Llanhennock Gwent 15 E7
Llanhilleth Gwent 14 D5
Llanidloes Dyfed 20 D5
Llaniestyn Gwyn 28 G2
Llanigan Powys 21 H7
Llanilar Dyfed 20 E2
Llanilid Mid Glam 14 F3
Llanishen Gwent 15 D8
Llanishen S Glam 14 F5
Llanllechid Gwyn 28 C5
Llanllugan Powys 20 B6
Llanllwch Dyfed 13 E7
Llanllwchaiarn Powys 21 C7
Llanllyfni Gwyn 28 E4
Llanllywel Gwent 15 D7
Llanmadoc W Glam 13 H8
Llanmaes S Glam 14 G3
Llanmartin Gwent 15 E7
Llanmerewig Powys 21 C7
Llanmihangel S Glam 14 G3
Llanmiloe Dyfed 12 F6
Llanmorlais W Glam 13 G8
Llannefydd Clwyd 29 C9
Llannon Dyfed 13 F9
Llannor Gwyn 28 F3
Llanon Dyfed 20 F1
Llanpumsaint Dyfed 13 D7
Llanreithan Dyfed 12 D2
Llanrhaeadr Clwyd 29 D10
Llanrhaeadr-ym-Mochnant Clwyd 29 H10
Llanrhidian W Glam 13 H8
Llanrhos Gwyn 29 B7
Llanrhyddlad Gwyn 28 A3
Llanrhystyd Dyfed 20 E1
Llanrian Dyfed 12 D2
Llanrug Gwyn 28 D5
Llan-Rumney S Glam 14 F5
Llanrwst Gwyn 29 D7
Llansadurnen Dyfed 12 F6
Llansadwrn Dyfed 13 D10
Llansadwrn Gwyn 28 C5
Llansaint Dyfed 13 F7
Llansamlet W Glam 13 G10
Llansannan Clwyd 29 D8
Llansannor S Glam 14 G3
Llansantffraed Powys 14 B5
Llansantffraed-Cwmdeuddwr Powys 20 F5
Llansantffraed-in-Elvel Powys 20 G6
Llansantffraid Dyfed 20 F1
Llansantffraid Glan Conway Gwyn 29 C7
Llansantffraid-ym-Mechain Powys 29 H11
Llansawel Dyfed 13 C9
Llansilin Clwyd 29 G11
Llansoy Gwent 15 D7
Llanspyddid Powys 14 B3
Llanstadwell Dyfed 12 F3
Llanstephan Dyfed 13 F7
Llanteg Dyfed 12 F5
Llanthony Gwent 14 B6
Llantilio Crossenny Gwent 15 C7
Llantilio Pertholey Gwent 14 C6
Llantood Dyfed 12 C5
Llantrisant Gwent 15 E7
Llantrisant Gwyn 28 B3
Llantrisant Mid Glam 14 F4
Llantrithyd S Glam 14 G4
Llantwit Fardre Mid Glam 14 F4
Llantwit-Major S Glam 14 G3
Llanuwchllyn Gwyn 29 G8
Llanvaches Gwent 15 E7
Llanvair Discoed Gwent 15 E8
Llanvapley Gwent 15 C7
Llanvetherine Gwent 15 C7
Llanveynoe Heref/Worcs 14 A6
Llanvihangel Pontymoel Gwent 14 D6
Llanvihangel Ystern-Llewern Gwent 15 C7
Llanwarne Heref/Worcs 15 B8
Llanwddyn Powys 29 H9
Llanwenarth Gwent 14 C6
Llanwenog Dyfed 13 B8
Llanwern Gwent 15 E7
Llanwinio Dyfed 12 D6
Llanwnda Dyfed 12 C3
Llanwnda Gwyn 28 D4
Llanwnen Dyfed 13 B8
Llanwnog Powys 20 C6
Llanwrda Dyfed 13 D10
Llanwrin Powys 20 B3
Llanwrthwl Powys 20 F5
Llanwrtyd Powys 20 H4
Llanwrtyd Wells Powys 20 H4
Llanwyddelan Powys 20 B6
Llanyblodwel Shrops 30 H1
Llanybri Dyfed 13 F7
Llanybydder Dyfed 13 C8
Llanycefn Dyfed 12 E4
Llanychaer Dyfed 12 C3
Llanycil Gwyn 29 G8
Llanymawddwy Gwyn 29 H8
Llanymynech Shrops 30 H1
Llanynghenedl Gwyn 28 B3
Llanynys Clwyd 29 D10
Llan-y-pwll Clwyd 30 E2
Llanyre Powys 20 F6
Llanystumdwy Gwyn 28 F4
Llanywern Powys 14 A4
Llawhaden Dyfed 12 E4
Llawnt Shrops 30 G1
Llawr-y-glyn Powys 20 C5
Llay Clwyd 30 E2
Llechfaen Powys 14 A4
Llechryd Dyfed 12 C5
Llechryd Mid Glam 14 C4
Llechrydau Clwyd 29 G11
Lledrod Dyfed 20 E2
Llethr Dyfed 12 D5
Llethrid W Glam 13 H8
Llidiadnenog Dyfed 13 C9
Llidiardau Gwyn 29 F8
Llidiart-y-parc Clwyd 29 F10
Llithfaen Gwyn 28 F3
Lloc Clwyd 29 C10
Llong Clwyd 29 D12
Llowes Powys 21 H7
Llundain-fach Dyfed 20 G1
Llwydcoed Mid Glam 14 D3
Llwyn Dafydd Dyfed 13 B7
Llwyncelyn Dyfed 13 A8
Llwynderw Dyfed 20 D5
Llwynderw Powys 21 B7
Llwyn-drain Dyfed 12 D6
Llwyngwril Gwyn 20 A2
Llwyn-mawr Clwyd 29 G11
Llwyn-on Mid Glam 14 C3
Llwyn-y-groes Dyfed 20 G2
Llwyn-y-pia Mid Glam 14 E3
Llynclys Shrops 30 H1
Llynfaes Gwyn 28 B3
Llysdinam Powys 20 F6
Llysfaen Clwyd 29 C8
Llyswen Powys 14 A5
Llysworney S Glam 14 G3
Llys-y-fran Dyfed 12 E4
Llywel Powys 14 A2
Llywernog Dyfed 20 D3
Loadwater Bucks 17 E10
Loanend Northum 49 D12
Loanhead Lothian 48 C5
Loanhead S'clyde 47 D9
Loanhead S'clyde 48 F3
Loanhead of Fedderate Gramp 58 C6
Loans S'clyde 47 F8
Loans of Tullich H'land 56 B4
Loansdean Northum 45 E10
Lobb Devon 4 B3
Loch Choire Lodge H'land 61 D7
Loch Head Dumf/Gal 42 G4
Loch Loyal Lo H'land 60 C6
Lochailort H'land 55 L2
Lochaline H'land 50 C4
Lochanhully H'land 57 G5
Locharbriggs Dumf/Gal 43 D10
Locharwoods Dumf/Gal 43 E11
Lochassynt Lodge H'land 60 D3
Lochawe S'clyde 51 E8
Lochbuie H'land 50 E3
Lochcallater Lo Gramp 57 L7
Lochcarron H'land 54 F3
Lochdhu Hotel H'land 61 C9
Lochdochart Ho Central 51 E11
Lochdon H'land 50 D5
Lochdrum H'land 54 B6
Lochead S'clyde 46 A5
Lochead S'clyde 46 B3
Lochearnhead Central 52 E1
Lochee Tayside 53 D8
Lochend Fife 52 H6

Lochend *H'land* **56** F 2
Lochend *H'land* **61** A11
Locherben *Dumf/Gal* **43** B10
Lochfoot *Dumf/Gal* **43** D9
Lochgair *S'clyde* **50** H6
Lochgarthside *H'land* **57** H1
Lochgate *S'clyde* **47** F11
Lochgelly *Fife* **53** H7
Lochgilphead *S'clyde* **46** A4
Lochgoilhead *S'clyde* **51** G9
Loch-hill *Gramp* **56** C8
Lochhill *S'clyde* **47** H11
Lochindorb Lo *H'land* **56** F5
Lochingirrcoh *S'clyde* **47** H11
Lochinver *H'land* **60** E3
Lochluichart *H'land* **54** C7
Lochlycoch *S'clyde* **48** F2
Lochmaben *Dumf/Gal* **43** C11
Lochmore Lodge *H'land* **60** D4
Lochore *Tayside* **52** G6
Lochranza *S'clyde* **46** D4
Lochridge *S'clyde* **47** E9
Lochs Crofts *Gramp* **58** B1
Lochside *Gramp* **59** L5
Lochside *H'land* **56** D4
Lochside *H'land* **61** D8
Lochstack Lodge *H'land* **60** C4
Lochstrathy *H'land* **61** C8
Lochton *Gramp* **59** H5
Lochton of Leys *Gramp* **59** H4
Lochty *Fife* **53** F10
Lochty *Tayside* **59** L3
Lochuisge *H'land* **50** B5
Lochurr *Dumf/Gal* **43** C8
Lochwinnoch *S'clyde* **47** C8
Lochwood *Dumf/Gal* **43** B11
Lochy Bridge *H'land* **55** M5
Lockengate *Cornw'l* **3** D7
Lockerbie *Dumf/Gal* **43** C12
Lockeridge *Wilts* **16** G3
Lockerley *Hants* **8** C4
Locking *Avon* **15** H7
Lockinge *Oxon* **16** E5
Lockington *Humber* **37** B7
Lockington *Leics* **32** G2
Lockleywood *Shrops* **30** G5
Lock's Heath *Hants* **8** E6
Lockton *N Yorks* **41** F8
Loddington *Leics* **23** B11
Loddington *Northants* **23** D11
Loddiswell *Devon* **5** L6
Loddon *Norfolk* **26** F6
Lode *Cambs* **25** J6
Loders *Dorset* **7** G8
Lodges *Gramp* **59** G5
Lodsworth *W Sussex* **9** D10
Lofthouse *N Yorks* **40** H1
Lofthouse *W Yorks* **35** E12
Loftus *Clevl'd* **41** C7
Logan *S'clyde* **47** G10
Logan Mains *Dumf/Gal* **42** G2
Loggerheads *Staffs* **30** G6
Logie *Fife* **53** E7
Logie *Fife* **53** E9
Logie Coldstone *Gramp* **59** G2
Logie Hill *H'land* **56** B3
Logie Newton *Gramp* **58** D4
Logie Pert *Gramp* **59** L4
Logiealmond Lo *Tayside* **52** D4
Logierait *Tayside* **52** B5
Login *Dyfed* **12** E5
Lohans *Dumf/Gal* **42** F2
Lolworth *Cambs* **25** J5
Lonbain *H'land* **54** D1
Londesborough *Humber* **36** C6
London *London* **18** F3
London Apprentice *Cornw'l* **3** E7
London Colney *Herts* **18** D2
Londonderry *N Yorks* **40** F3
Londonthorpe *Lincs* **33** F7
Londubh *H'land* **54** B2
Lone *H'land* **60** C4
Long Ashton *Avon* **15** G9
Long Bennington *Lincs* **32** F5
Long Bredy *Dorset* **7** G9
Long Buckby *Northants* **23** E9
Long Clawson *Leics* **32** G4
Long Common *Hants* **8** E6
Long Compton *Staffs* **31** H7
Long Compton *Warwick* **16** A4
Long Crendon *Bucks* **17** C8
Long Crichel *Dorset* **8** E1
Long Ditton *Surrey* **17** G12
Long Drax *N Yorks* **36** D5
Long Duckmanton *Derby* **32** C2
Long Eaton *Derby* **32** G2
Long Green *Ches* **30** C3
Long Hanborough *Oxon* **16** C5
Long Hermiston *Lothian* **48** B4
Long Itchington *Warwick* **23** F7
Long Lawford *Warwick* **23** D8
Long Load *Som'set* **7** D8
Long Marston *Herts* **17** C9
Long Marston *N Yorks* **36** B3
Long Marston *Warwick* **22** G5
Long Marton *Cumb* **39** C9
Long Melford *Suffolk* **27** K2
Long Newnton *Glos* **15** E12
Long Newton *Clevl'd* **40** D4
Long Preston *N Yorks* **35** A7
Long Riston *Humber* **37** C9
Long Sandall *S Yorks* **36** F4
Long Stanton *Cambs* **25** J5
Long Stratton *Norfolk* **26** F5
Long Street *Bucks* **23** G11
Long Sutton *Hants* **9** A9
Long Sutton *Lincs* **24** C5
Long Sutton *Som'set* **7** D8
Long Waste *Shrops* **21** A11
Long Whatton *Leics* **32** H2
Long Wittenham *Oxon* **16** E6
Longbar *S'clyde* **47** D8
Longbenton *Tyne/Wear* **45** F11
Longborough *Glos* **16** A3
Longbridge *W Midlands* **22** D3
Longbridge *Warwick* **22** F6
Longbridge Deverill *Wilts* **7** B12
Longbridgemuir *Dumf/Gal* **43** E11
Longbridgemuir *H'land* **54** E11
Longburton *Dorset* **7** E10
Longbyre *Northum* **44** F5
Longcastle *Dumf/Gal* **42** G5
Longcliffe *Derby* **31** E10
Longcot *Oxon* **16** E4
Longcroft *Borders* **49** D8
Longcroft *Lothian* **48** A1
Longcross *Surrey* **17** H10
Longden *Shrops* **21** B10
Longdon *Heref/Worcs* **15** A11
Longdon *Staffs* **22** A4
Longdon Green *Staffs* **22** A4
Longdon upon Tern *Shrops* **21** A11
Longdown *Devon* **6** G2
Longdowns *Cornw'l* **2** F4
Longdyke *Northum* **45** B10
Longfield *Kent* **10** A5
Longfield Hill *Kent* **10** A5
Longford *Derby* **31** F10
Longford *Glos* **15** B11
Longford *London* **18** F1
Longford *Shrops* **30** G5
Longford *W Midlands* **23** D7
Longforgan *Tayside* **53** D8
Longformacus *Borders* **49** D9
Longframlington *Northum* **45** C9
Longham *Dorset* **8** F2
Longham *Norfolk* **26** D2
Longhaven *Gramp* **58** D8
Longhill *Gramp* **58** B7
Longhirst *Northum* **45** D10
Longhope *Glos* **15** B10
Longhorsley *Northum* **45** D9
Longhoughton *Northum* **45** B10
Longlands *Cumb* **38** B5
Longlane *Berks* **16** G6
Longlane *Derby* **31** F11
Longlevens *Glos* **15** B11
Longley Green *Heref/Worcs* **22** G1
Longmanhill *Gramp* **58** A5
Longmoor Camp *Hants* **9** C9
Longmorn *Gramp* **56** D8
Longnewton *Borders* **49** G8
Longney *Glos* **15** C11
Longniddry *Lothian* **49** B7
Longnor *Shrops* **21** B10
Longnor *Staffs* **31** D9
Longparish *Hants* **8** B6
Longridge *Lancs* **34** C5
Longridge *Lancs* **34** D5
Longridge *Lothian* **48** C2
Longriggend *Lothian* **48** B1
Longsdon *Staffs* **31** E8
Longshaw *Gtr Man* **34** G4
Longside *Gramp* **58** C8
Longslow *Shrops* **30** G5
Longstock *Hants* **8** B5
Longstone *Cornw'l* **3** B7
Longstowe *Cambs* **25** K4
Longthorpe *Cambs* **24** F3
Longton *Lancs* **34** E4
Longton *Staffs* **31** F7
Longtown *Cumb* **44** F2
Longtown *Heref/Worcs* **14** A6
Longville in the Dale *Shrops* **21** C11
Longwell Green *Avon* **15** G10
Longwick *Bucks* **17** D8
Longwitton *Northum* **45** D9
Longwood *Shrops* **21** B11
Longworth *Oxon* **16** D5
Longyester *Lothian* **49** C8
Lonmore *H'land* **62** D2
Loose *Kent* **10** C6
Loosley Row *Bucks* **17** D9
Lopcombe Corner *Wilts* **8** C4
Lopen *Som'set* **7** E8
Loppington *Shrops* **30** G3
Lorbottle *Northum* **45** B8
Lorbottle Hall *Northum* **45** B8
Lordington *W Sussex* **9** E9
Lorg *Dumf/Gal* **43** B7
Loscoe *Derby* **32** E2
Lossiemouth *Gramp* **56** C8
Lostock Gralam *Ches* **30** C5
Lostock Green *Ches* **30** C5
Lostock Junction *Gtr Man* **34** F5
Lostwithiel *Cornw'l* **3** D8
Lothbeg *H'land* **61** F9
Lothersdale *N Yorks* **35** C8
Lothmore *H'land* **61** F9
Lottisham *Som'set* **7** C9
Loughborough *Leics* **32** H3
Loughor *W Glam* **13** G9
Loughton *Bucks* **23** H11
Loughton *Essex* **18** D4
Loughton *Shrops* **21** D11
Lound *Lincs* **24** D2
Lound *Notts* **32** B4
Lound *Suffolk* **26** E8
Lount *Leics* **31** H12
Louth *Lincs* **33** B10
Love Clough *Lancs* **35** D7
Lovedean *Hants* **9** E8
Lover *Wilts* **8** D4
Loversall *S Yorks* **36** G4
Loves Green *Essex* **18** C6
Lovesome Hill *N Yorks* **40** E4
Loveston *Dyfed* **12** F4
Lovington *Som'set* **7** C9
Low Ardwell *Dumf/Gal* **42** G2
Low Bentham *N Yorks* **39** H9
Low Bradfield *S Yorks* **35** H11
Low Bradley *N Yorks* **35** B9
Low Braithwaite *Cumb* **38** A6
Low Brunton *Northum* **45** F7
Low Burnham *Humber* **36** G5
Low Burton *N Yorks* **40** G3
Low Buston *Northum* **45** B10
Low Catton *Humber* **36** B5
Low Coniscliffe *N Yorks* **40** D3
Low Craighead *S'clyde* **42** A3
Low Cranecleugh *Northum* **44** D5
Low Crosby *Cumb* **44** G3
Low Dalby *N Yorks* **41** F8
Low Dinsdale *Durham* **40** D4
Low Eggborough *N Yorks* **36** E3
Low Ellington *N Yorks* **40** G2
Low Etherley *Durham* **40** B2
Low Geltbridge *Cumb* **44** G4
Low Grange *S'clyde* **47** H8
Low Habberley *Heref/Worcs* **22** D2
Low Ham *Som'set* **7** C8
Low Hedgeley *Northum* **45** A9
Low Hesket *Cumb* **39** A7
Low Hesleyhurst *Northum* **45** C9
Low Hutton *N Yorks* **41** H8
Low Knockbrex *Dumf/Gal* **42** E5
Low Leighton *Derby* **31** B8
Low Lorton *Cumb* **38** C4
Low Malzie *Dumf/Gal* **42** F4
Low Marishes *N Yorks* **41** G8
Low Marnham *Notts* **32** C5
Low Mill *N Yorks* **41** F7
Low Moor *Lancs* **34** C6
Low Morsley *Tyne/Wear* **45** H11
Low Newton-by-the-Sea *Northum* **45** A10
Low Row *Cumb* **38** B6
Low Row *Cumb* **44** G4
Low Row *N Yorks* **39** E12
Low Salchrie *Dumf/Gal* **42** E1
Low Santon *Humber* **37** F7
Low Shawsburn *S'clyde* **47** D12
Low Thurlton *Norfolk* **26** E7
Low Torry *Lothian* **48** A3
Low Town *Northum* **45** C9
Low Worsall *N Yorks* **40** D4
Low Wray *Cumb* **38** E6
Lowca *Cumb* **38** C2
Lowdham *Notts* **32** F4
Lowe *Shrops* **30** G4
Lower Airsholt *Som'set* **6** C5
Lower Ansty *Dorset* **7** F11
Lower Ashton *Devon* **6** H2
Lower Assendon *Oxon* **17** F8
Lower Badcall *H'land* **60** C3
Lower Basildon *Berks* **17** F7
Lower Bayble *W Isles* **63** D6
Lower Beeding *W Sussex* **10** E1
Lower Benefield *Northants* **24** F1
Lower Bockhampton *Dorset* **7** G10
Lower Boddington *Northants* **23** G8
Lower Boscaswell *Cornw'l* **2** F1
Lower Bourne *Surrey* **9** B10
Lower Brailes *Warwick* **22** H6
Lower Breakish *H'land* **62** F6
Lower Broadheath *Heref/Worcs* **22** F2
Lower Bullingham *Heref/Worcs* **15** A8
Lower Caldecote *Beds* **25** K3
Lower Cam *Glos* **15** D10
Lower Chapel *Powys* **14** A4
Lower Chicksgrove *Wilts* **8** C1
Lower Chute *Wilts* **8** A4
Lower Cokeham *W Sussex* **10** H1
Lower Crossings *Derby* **31** B9
Lower Cumberworth *W Yorks* **35** F11
Lower Darwen *Lancs* **34** E6
Lower Dean *Beds* **25** H2
Lower Diabaig *H'land* **54** D2
Lower Dicker *E Sussex* **10** G4
Lower Dinchope *Shrops* **21** D10
Lower Dounreay *H'land* **61** A9
Lower Down *Shrops* **21** D9
Lower Drift *Cornw'l* **2** G2
Lower Dunsforth *N Yorks* **36** A2
Lower Everleigh *Wilts* **8** A3
Lower Failand *Avon* **15** G8
Lower Farringdon *Hants* **9** C8
Lower Foxdale *I of Man* **38** G1
Lower Freystrop *Dyfed* **12** F3
Lower Froyle *Hants* **9** B9
Lower Gledfield *H'land* **60** G6
Lower Green *Kent* **10** D5
Lower Green *Norfolk* **26** B3
Lower Hacheston *Suffolk* **27** J6
Lower Halistra *H'land* **62** B2
Lower Halstow *Kent* **11** A7
Lower Hardres *Kent* **11** C10
Lower Hempriggs *Gramp* **56** C7
Lower Hergest *Heref/Worcs* **21** G8
Lower Heyford *Oxon* **16** B6
Lower Higham *Kent* **10** A6
Lower Hordley *Shrops* **30** G3
Lower Horsebridge *E Sussex* **10** G4
Lower Kinchrackine *S'clyde* **51** E8
Lower Kingcombe *Dorset* **7** F9
Lower Kingswood *Surrey* **10** C1
Lower Kinnerton *Ches* **30** D2
Lower Langford *Avon* **15** H8
Lower Largo *Fife* **53** G9
Lower Lavacott *Devon* **4** C4
Lower Leigh *Staffs* **31** G8
Lower Lenie *H'land* **57** G1
Lower Llanfadog *Powys* **20** F5
Lower Loxhore *Devon* **4** B5
Lower Lydbrook *Glos* **15** C9
Lower Lye *Heref/Worcs* **21** F9
Lower Machen *Gwent* **14** E5
Lower Maes-coed *Heref/Worcs* **15** A7
Lower Mayland *Essex* **19** D9
Lower Milovaig *H'land* **62** C1
Lower Moor *Heref/Worcs* **22** G3
Lower Nazeing *Essex* **18** C4
Lower Oakfield *Fife* **52** H6
Lower Ollach *H'land* **62** D4
Lower Penn *Staffs* **22** C2
Lower Pennington *Hants* **8** G5
Lower Peover *Ches* **30** C6
Lower Place *Gtr Man* **35** F8
Lower Quinton *Warwick* **22** G5
Lower Rochford *Heref/Worcs* **21** F11
Lower Seagry *Wilts* **16** F1
Lower Shader *W Isles* **63** A5
Lower Shelton *Beds* **25** L1
Lower Shiplake *Oxon* **17** F8
Lower Shuckburgh *Warwick* **23** F8
Lower Slaughter *Glos* **16** B3
Lower Stanton St. Quintin *Wilts* **15** F12
Lower Stoke *Kent* **11** A7
Lower Street *Norfolk* **26** B6
Lower Strensham *Heref/Worcs* **22** H3
Lower Sundon *Beds* **17** A11
Lower Swanwick *Hants* **8** E6
Lower Swell *Glos* **16** B3
Lower Tote *H'land* **62** B4
Lower Town *Dyfed* **12** C3
Lower Tysoe *Warwick* **23** H7
Lower Upham *Hants* **9** D7
Lower Vexford *Som'set* **6** C5
Lower Walton *Ches* **30** B5
Lower Walton *Ches* **34** H5
Lower Waterston *Dorset* **7** G10
Lower Weare *Som'set* **7** A7
Lower Welson *Heref/Worcs* **21** G8
Lower Whitley *Ches* **30** B5
Lower Wield *Hants* **9** B8
Lower Winchendon *Bucks* **17** C8
Lower Woodend *Bucks* **17** E9
Lower Woodford *Wilts* **8** C3
Lower Wyche *Heref/Worcs* **22** H1
Lowesby *Leics* **23** A10
Lowestoft *Suffolk* **26** F8
Lowestoft End *Suffolk* **26** F8
Loweswater *Cumb* **38** C4
Lowfield Heath *W Sussex* **10** D2
Lowgill *Cumb* **39** E8
Lowgill *Lancs* **34** A5
Lowick *Northants* **25** G1
Lowick *Northum* **45** B11
Lowick Green *Cumb* **38** G5
Lowlands *Gwent* **14** E6
Lownie Moor *Tayside* **59** M2
Lowsonford *Warwick* **22** E5
Lowther *Cumb* **39** C8
Lowthorpe *Humber* **37** A8
Lowton *Gtr Man* **34** G5
Lowton *Som'set* **6** D5
Lowton Common *Gtr Man* **34** G5
Loxbeare *Devon* **6** E3
Loxhill *Surrey* **9** B11
Loxhore *Devon* **4** B5
Loxley *Warwick* **22** G6
Loxton *Som'set* **7** A7
Loxwood *W Sussex* **9** C11
Lubachoinnich *H'land* **60** G5
Lubcroy *H'land* **60** F4
Lubenham *Leics* **23** C10
Lubnaclach *H'land* **51** A11
Lubriach *H'land* **54** B7
Luccombe *Som'set* **6** B3
Luccombe Village *I of Wight* **9** H7
Lucker *Northum* **45** D11
Luckett *Cornw'l* **3** B11
Luckington *Wilts* **15** F11
Lucklawhill *Fife* **53** E9
Luckwell Bridge *Som'set* **6** B2
Lucton *Heref/Worcs* **21** F10
Ludborough *Lincs* **37** H10
Ludchurch *Dyfed* **12** F5
Luddenden *W Yorks* **35** E9
Luddenden Foot *W Yorks* **35** E9
Luddesdown *Kent* **10** B5
Luddington *Humber* **36** E6
Luddington *Warwick* **22** G5
Luddington in the Brook *Northants* **25** G2
Ludford *Lincs* **33** A9
Ludford *Shrops* **21** E10
Ludgershall *Bucks* **17** B7
Ludgershall *Wilts* **8** A4
Ludgvan *Cornw'l* **2** F2
Ludham *Norfolk* **26** D7
Ludlow *Shrops* **21** E10
Ludney *Lincs* **37** G11
Ludwell *Wilts* **7** D12
Ludworth *Durham* **40** A4
Luffincott *Devon* **4** F2
Lugar *S'clyde* **47** G10
Lugate *Borders* **49** E7
Luggate Burn *Lothian* **49** B8
Luggiebank *S'clyde* **47** B12
Lugton *S'clyde* **47** D9
Lugwardine *Heref/Worcs* **21** H11
Luib *H'land* **62** E5
Luib Hotel *Central* **51** E12
Luibeilt *H'land* **51** A9
Lulham *Heref/Worcs* **21** H9
Lullington *Derby* **22** A6
Lullington *Som'set* **7** A11
Lulsey *Heref/Worcs* **22** G1
Lulsgate Bottom *Avon* **15** H8
Lumb *W Yorks* **35** E9
Lumbutts *W Yorks* **35** E8
Lumby *N Yorks* **36** D3
Lumloch *S'clyde* **47** B11
Lumphanan *Gramp* **59** G3
Lumphinnans *Fife* **52** H6
Lumsdaine *Borders* **49** B11
Lumsden *Gramp* **58** E2
Lunan *Tayside* **53** B11
Lunanhead *Tayside* **53** B9
Luncarty *Tayside* **52** D6
Lund *Humber* **37** B7
Lund *N Yorks* **36** D4
Lundavra *H'land* **51** A8
Lunderton *Gramp* **58** C8
Lundie *H'land* **55** H5
Lundie *Tayside* **53** D8
Lundin Links *Fife* **53** G9
Lungar *S'clyde* **50** G5
Lunna *Shetl'd* **64** C7
Lunning *Shetl'd* **64** C7
Lunnon *W Glam* **13** H9
Lunsford *Kent* **10** B6
Lunsford's Cross *E Sussex* **10** G6
Lunt *Mersey* **34** G2
Luntley *Heref/Worcs* **21** G9
Luppitt *Devon* **6** F5
Lupset *W Yorks* **35** E11
Lupton *Cumb* **39** G8
Lurgashall *W Sussex* **9** C10
Lurgmore *H'land* **56** F1
Lusby *Lincs* **33** C10
Luskentyre *W Isles* **63** G2
Luss *S'clyde* **51** H10
Lusta *H'land* **62** C2
Lustleigh *Devon* **5** H6
Luston *Heref/Worcs* **21** F10
Luthermuir *Gramp* **59** K4
Luthrie *Fife* **53** E8
Luton *Beds* **17** B12
Luton *Devon* **5** H8
Luton *Kent* **10** A6
Lutterworth *Leics* **23** D9
Lutton *Devon* **5** K5
Lutton *Lincs* **24** C5
Lutton *Northants* **25** G2
Luxborough *Som'set* **6** B3
Luxulyan *Cornw'l* **3** D7
Lybster *H'land* **61** D11
Lydbury North *Shrops* **21** D9
Lydd *Kent* **11** F9
Lydden *Kent* **11** D11
Lyddington *Leics* **23** B12
Lydd-on-Sea *Kent* **11** F9
Lyde Green *Hants* **17** H8
Lydeard St. Lawrence *Som'set* **6** C5
Lydford *Devon* **5** G4
Lydgate *W Yorks* **35** E8
Lydham *Shrops* **21** C9
Lydiard Millicent *Wilts* **16** F2
Lydiate *Mersey* **34** G2
Lydlinch *Dorset* **7** E10
Lydney *Glos* **15** D9
Lydstep *Dyfed* **12** G4
Lye *W Midlands* **22** D3
Lye Cross *Avon* **15** H8
Lye Green *Bucks* **17** D10
Lye Green *E Sussex* **10** E4
Lyford *Oxon* **16** E5
Lylestone *Borders* **49** D8
Lylestone *S'clyde* **47** E8
Lymbridge Green *Kent* **11** D10
Lyme Regis *Dorset* **7** G7
Lyminge *Kent* **11** D10
Lymington *Hants* **8** F5
Lyminster *W Sussex* **9** F11
Lymm *Ches* **30** B5
Lymore *Hants* **8** G4
Lympne *Kent* **11** E10
Lympsham *Som'set* **7** A7
Lympstone *Devon* **6** H3
Lynaberack *H'land* **57** K3
Lynchat *H'land* **57** J3
Lyndhurst *Hants* **8** E4
Lyndon *Leics* **23** B12
Lyne *Borders* **48** E5
Lyne *Surrey* **17** G11
Lyne Down *Heref/Worcs* **15** A9
Lyne of Garthledc *H'land* **57** G1
Lyne of Skene *Gramp* **58** F5
Lyneal *Shrops* **30** G3
Lynedale House *H'land* **62** C3
Lyneham *Oxon* **16** B4
Lyneham *Wilts* **16** F1
Lyneholm *Dumf/Gal* **44** D1
Lyneholmeford *Cumb* **44** F2
Lynemore *H'land* **57** G6
Lynemouth *Northum* **45** D11
Lyness *Orkney* **64** D1
Lyng *Norfolk* **26** D4
Lyng *Som'set* **7** C7
Lynmouth *Devon* **4** A6
Lynsted *Kent* **11** B8
Lynton *Devon* **4** A6
Lyon's Gate *Dorset* **7** F10
Lyonshall *Heref/Worcs* **21** G9

Lytchett Matravers *Dorset* 8 G1
Lytchett Minster *Dorset* 8 G1
Lyth *H'land* 61 B11
Lytham *Lancs* 34 D3
Lytham St. Anne's *Lancs* 34 D2
Lythe *N Yorks* 41 D8
Lythes *Orkney* 64 E3
Maaruig *W Isles* 63 F3
Mabe Burnthouse *Cornw'l* 2 F5
Mabie *Dumf/Gal* 43 D10
Mablethorpe *Lincs* 33 B12
Macbiehill *Borders* 48 D4
Macclesfield *Ches* 31 C7
Macclesfield Forest *Ches* 31 C8
Macduff *Gramp* 58 A4
Machen *Mid Glam* 14 E5
Machrihanish *S'clyde* 46 G1
Machrins *H'land* 50 H1
Machynlleth *Powys* 20 B3
Mackworth *Derby* 31 F11
Macmerry *Lothian* 49 B7
Madderty *Tayside* 52 E4
Maddiston *Lothian* 48 B2
Madehurst *W Sussex* 9 E11
Madeley *Staffs* 30 F6
Madeley Heath *Staffs* 30 F6
Madingley *Cambs* 25 J5
Madley *Heref/Worcs* 21 H9
Madresfield *Heref/Worcs* 22 G2
Madron *Cornw'l* 2 F2
Maenaddwyn *Gwyn* 28 B4
Maenclochog *Dyfed* 12 D4
Maendy *S Glam* 14 G3
Maentwrog *Gwyn* 28 F6
Maen-y-groes *Dyfed* 13 A7
Maer *Staffs* 30 F6
Maerdy *Clwyd* 29 F9
Maerdy *Dyfed* 13 D10
Maerdy *Mid Glam* 14 D3
Maesbrook *Shrops* 30 H2
Maesbury *Shrops* 30 H2
Maesbury Marsh *Shrops* 30 H2
Maesgwynne *Dyfed* 12 E5
Maeshafn *Clwyd* 29 D11
Maesllyn *Dyfed* 13 C7
Maesmynis *Powys* 20 H6
Maesteg *Mid Glam* 14 E2
Maestir *Dyfed* 13 B9
Maestwynog *Dyfed* 13 C10
Maesybont *Dyfed* 13 E9
Maesycrugiau *Dyfed* 13 C8
Maes-y-cwmmer *Mid Glam* 14 E5
Maesymeillon *Dyfed* 13 B7
Magdalen Laver *Essex* 18 C5
Maggieknockater *Gramp* 58 C1
Magham Down *E Sussex* 10 G5
Maghull *Mersey* 34 G3
Magor *Gwent* 15 F7
Maiden Bradley *Wilts* 7 B11
Maiden Law *Durham* 45 H10
Maiden Newton *Dorset* 7 F9
Maiden Wells *Dyfed* 12 G3
Maidencombe *Devon* 5 J8
Maidencotes *S'clyde* 48 G2
Maidenhead *Berks* 17 F10
Maidenhill *Cumb* 39 B7
Maidens *S'clyde* 42 A3
Maiden's Green *Berks* 17 G9
Maidenwell *Lincs* 33 B10
Maidford *Northants* 23 G9
Maid's Moreton *Bucks* 17 A8
Maidstone *Kent* 10 C6
Maidwell *Northants* 23 D10
Mail *Shetl'd* 64 E7
Maindee *Gwent* 14 E6
Mains *H'land* 61 F8
Mains *S'clyde* 47 D11
Mains *Tayside* 52 B6
Mains of Airies *Dumf/Gal* 42 E1
Mains of Allardice *Gramp* 59 K6
Mains of Altries *Gramp* 59 H6
Mains of Annochie *Gramp* 58 C7
Mains of Ardestie *Tayside* 53 D10
Mains of Arnage *Gramp* 58 D7
Mains of Auchindachy *Gramp* 58 C2
Mains of Auchmedden *Gramp* 58 A6
Mains of Balgavis *Tayside* 53 B10
Mains of Ballindarg *Tayside* 53 B9
Mains of Balnakettle *Gramp* 59 K4
Mains of Birness *Gramp* 58 D7
Mains of Bunachton *H'land* 56 F2
Mains of Cairnborrow *Gramp* 58 D2
Mains of Cardno *Gramp* 58 A7
Mains of Crichie *Gramp* 58 C7
Mains of Dalvey *H'land* 56 F7
Mains of Drum *Gramp* 59 G5
Mains of Drummuir *Gramp* 58 C2
Mains of Drynie *H'land* 56 E2
Mains of Edingight *Gramp* 58 B3
Mains of Esslemont *Gramp* 58 E7
Mains of Fedderate *Gramp* 58 C6
Mains of Glenfarquhar *Gramp* 59 J5
Mains of Haulkerton *Gramp* 59 K5
Mains of Inkhorn *Gramp* 58 D7
Mains of Keithfield *Gramp* 58 D6
Mains of Kirkhall *Gramp* 58 F6
Mains of Logie *Gramp* 58 B8
Mains of Melgund *Tayside* 53 B10
Mains of Melgund *Tayside* 59 L3
Mains of Newhall *H'land* 56 C3
Mains of Thornton *Gramp* 59 K4
Mains of Throsk *Central* 52 H3
Mains of Tore *H'land* 56 D2
Mains of Towie *Gramp* 58 C5
Mains of Ulbster *H'land* 61 C12
Mains of Usan *Tayside* 53 B12
Mainsforth *Durham* 40 B3
Mainsriddle *Dumf/Gal* 43 F10
Mainstone *Shrops* 21 D8
Maisemore *Glos* 15 B11
Malborough *Devon* 5 M6
Malden Rushett *London* 18 H2
Maldon *Essex* 19 C8
Malham *N Yorks* 35 A8
Mallaig *H'land* 55 K1
Mallaigvaig *H'land* 55 K1
Malleny Mills *Lothian* 48 C4
Malling *Central* 52 G1
Malltraeth *Gwyn* 28 C3
Mallwyd *Gwyn* 20 A4
Malmesbury *Wilts* 15 F12
Malmsmead *Devon* 4 A7
Malpas *Ches* 30 E3
Malpas *Cornw'l* 2 E5
Malpas *Gwent* 14 E6
Malt Land *S'clyde* 51 F8
Maltby *Clevl'd* 40 D5
Maltby *S Yorks* 32 A3
Maltby le Marsh *Lincs* 33 B11
Maltman's Hill *Kent* 11 D8
Malton *N Yorks* 41 H8
Malvern Link *Heref/Worcs* 22 G1
Malvern Wells *Heref/Worcs* 22 H1
Mamble *Heref/Worcs* 21 E12
Mamhilad *Gwent* 14 D6
Manaccan *Cornw'l* 2 G5
Manafon *Powys* 21 B7
Manaton *Devon* 5 H6
Manby *Lincs* 33 B11
Mancetter *Warwick* 22 C6
Manchester *Gtr Man* 35 G7
Mancot *Clwyd* 29 D12
Mandally *H'land* 55 J7
Manea *Cambs* 24 F6
Maneight *S'clyde* 42 A6
Manfield *N Yorks* 40 D2
Mangaster *Shetl'd* 64 C7
Mangersta *W Isles* 63 D1
Mangertton *Borders* 44 D3
Mangotsfield *Avon* 15 G10
Manish *W Isles* 63 H2
Manley *Ches* 30 C4
Manmoel *Gwent* 14 D5
Mannian Fawr *Dyfed* 12 B5
Manningford Bohune *Wilts* 16 H2
Manningford Bruce *Wilts* 16 H2
Manningham *W Yorks* 35 D10
Mannings Heath *W Sussex* 10 E1
Mannington *Dorset* 8 F2
Manningtree *Essex* 27 M4
Mannofield *Gramp* 59 G6
Manorbier *Dyfed* 12 G4
Manorbier Newton *Dyfed* 12 G4
Manorhill *Borders* 49 F9
Manorowen *Dyfed* 12 C3
Mansel Lacy *Heref/Worcs* 21 H9
Manselfield *W Glam* 13 H9
Mansell Gamage *Heref/Worcs* 21 H9
Mansergh *Cumb* 39 G8
Mansfield *Dumf/Gal* 43 B9
Mansfield *Notts* 32 D3
Mansfield *S'clyde* 47 H11
Mansfield Woodhouse *Notts* 32 D3
Mansriggs *Cumb* 38 G5
Manston *Dorset* 7 E11
Manston *Kent* 11 B12
Manswood *Dorset* 8 E2
Manthorpe *Lincs* 24 D2
Manthorpe *Lincs* 32 F6
Manton *Humber* 37 G7
Manton *Leics* 23 B12
Manton *Wilts* 16 G3
Manton Warren *Humber* 37 G7
Manuden *Essex* 18 A5
Maolachy *S'clyde* 50 F6
Maperton *Som'set* 7 D10
Maple Cross *Herts* 17 E11
Maplebeck *Notts* 32 D4
Mapledurham *Oxon* 17 F7
Mapledurwell *Hants* 9 A8
Maplehurst *W Sussex* 10 F1
Maplescombe *Kent* 10 B4
Mapleton *Derby* 31 E10
Mapperley *Derby* 32 F2
Mapperley Park *Notts* 32 F3
Mapperton *Dorset* 7 F12
Mapperton *Dorset* 7 F8
Mappleborough Green *Warwick* 22 E4
Mappleton *Humber* 37 C10
Mapplewell *S Yorks* 35 F12
Mappowder *Dorset* 7 F10
Mar Lodge *Gramp* 57 K7
Marazion *Cornw'l* 2 G2
Marbury *Ches* 30 F4
March *Cambs* 24 F5
March *S'clyde* 48 H3
Marcham *Oxon* 16 D5
Marchamley *Shrops* 30 G4
Marchbankwood *Dumf/Gal* 43 B11
Marchburn *Dumf/Gal* 47 H11
Marchington *Staffs* 31 G9
Marchington Woodlands *Staffs* 31 G9
Marchros *Gwyn* 28 H3
Marchwiel *Clwyd* 30 E2
Marchwood *Hants* 8 E5
Marcross *S Glam* 14 G3
Marden *Heref/Worcs* 21 H10
Marden *Kent* 10 D6
Marden *Wilts* 16 H2
Marden Ash *Essex* 18 D5
Marden Beech *Kent* 10 D6
Marden Thorn *Kent* 10 D6
Mardy *Gwent* 14 C6
Marefield *Bucks* 17 E9
Marefield *Leics* 23 A11
Mareham le Fen *Lincs* 33 D10
Mareham on the Hill *Lincs* 33 C10
Marehey *Derby* 32 E1
Maresfield *E Sussex* 10 F3
Marfleet *Humber* 37 D9
Marford *Clwyd* 30 E2
Margam *W Glam* 13 H11
Margaret Marsh *Dorset* 7 D11
Margaret Roding *Essex* 18 C6
Margaretting *Essex* 18 D6
Margate *Kent* 11 A12
Margnaheglish *S'clyde* 46 F5
Marham *Norfolk* 24 D8
Marhamchurch *Cornw'l* 4 F1
Marholm *Cambs* 24 E2
Mariage *S'clyde* 47 E12
Mariandyrys *Gwyn* 28 B5
Marianglas *Gwyn* 28 B4
Mariansleigh *Devon* 4 D6
Marionburgh *Gramp* 59 G5
Marishader *H'land* 62 B4
Marjoriebanks *Dumf/Gal* 43 C11
Mark *Dumf/Gal* 43 F7
Mark *S'clyde* 42 D2
Mark *Som'set* 7 A7
Mark Causeway *Som'set* 7 B7
Mark Cross *E Sussex* 10 E5
Markbeech *Kent* 10 D4
Markby *Lincs* 33 B12
Markeaton *Derby* 31 F11
Market Bosworth *Leics* 23 B7
Market Deeping *Lincs* 24 E2
Market Drayton *Shrops* 30 G5
Market Harborough *Leics* 23 C10
Market Lavington *Wilts* 8 A2
Market Overton *Leics* 23 A12
Market Rasen *Lincs* 33 A8
Market Stainton *Lincs* 33 B9
Market Street *Norfolk* 26 C6
Market Weighton *Humber* 36 C6
Market Weston *Suffolk* 27 G3
Markfield *Leics* 23 A8
Markham *Gwent* 14 D5
Markham Moor *Notts* 32 C4
Markinch *Fife* 53 G8
Markington *N Yorks* 35 A11
Markle *Lothian* 49 B8
Marks Tey *Essex* 19 B9
Marksbury *Avon* 15 H10
Markyate *Herts* 17 C11
Marlage *S'clyde* 48 D1
Marlborough *Wilts* 16 G3
Marlbrook *Heref/Worcs* 21 G10
Marlbrook *Heref/Worcs* 22 E3
Marlcliff *Warwick* 22 G4
Marldon *Devon* 5 J7
Marlesford *Suffolk* 27 J6
Marley Green *Ches* 30 F4
Marley Hill *Tyne/Wear* 45 G10
Marley Mount *Hants* 8 F4
Marleyknowe *Northum* 49 F12
Marlingford *Norfolk* 26 E4
Marloes *Dyfed* 12 F1
Marlow *Bucks* 17 E9
Marlow *Heref/Worcs* 21 E9
Marlow Bottom *Bucks* 17 E9
Marlpit Hill *Kent* 10 C3
Marlpool *Derby* 32 F2
Marnach *Gramp* 58 C3
Marnhull *Dorset* 7 D11
Marple *Gtr Man* 31 A8
Marr *S Yorks* 36 G3
Marrel *H'land* 61 E9
Marrick *N Yorks* 40 E1
Marros *Dyfed* 12 F5
Marsden *Tyne/Wear* 45 G12
Marsden *W Yorks* 35 F9
Marsett *N Yorks* 39 F11
Marsh *Devon* 6 E6
Marsh *Som'set* 6 C4
Marsh Baldon *Oxon* 16 D6
Marsh Benham *Berks* 16 G5
Marsh Gibbon *Bucks* 17 B7
Marsh Green *Devon* 6 G4
Marsh Green *Kent* 10 D3
Marsh Green *Shrops* 21 A11
Marsh Street *Som'set* 6 B3
Marshall's Heath *Herts* 18 B2
Marsham *Norfolk* 26 C5
Marshaw *Lancs* 34 B5
Marshborough *Kent* 11 B11
Marshbrook *Shrops* 21 C10
Marshchapel *Lincs* 37 G11
Marshfield *Avon* 15 G11
Marshfield *Gwent* 14 F6
Marshgate *Cornw'l* 2 B2
Marshland *Derby* 32 B1
Marshland *Humber* 36 E6
Marshside *Mersey* 34 E2
Marshwood *Dorset* 7 F7
Marske *N Yorks* 40 E1
Marske-by-the-Sea *Clevl'd* 40 C6
Marston *Ches* 30 C5
Marston *Heref/Worcs* 21 G9
Marston *Lincs* 32 F6
Marston *Oxon* 16 C6
Marston *Staffs* 22 A2
Marston *Staffs* 31 G8
Marston *Warwick* 21 C5
Marston *Warwick* 22 C5
Marston *Wilts* 16 H1
Marston Green *W Midlands* 22 D5
Marston Magna *Som'set* 7 D9
Marston Meysey *Wilts* 16 D2
Marston Montgomery *Derby* 31 F10
Marston Moretaine *Beds* 25 L1
Marston on Dove *Derby* 31 G11
Marston St. Lawrence *Northants* 23 H8
Marston Stannett *Heref/Worcs* 21 G11
Marston Trussell *Northants* 23 D10
Marstow *Heref/Worcs* 15 B9
Marsworth *Bucks* 17 C10
Marten *Wilts* 16 H4
Marthall *Ches* 30 C6
Martham *Norfolk* 26 D7
Martin *Hants* 8 D2
Martin *Kent* 11 C12
Martin *Lincs* 33 D8
Martin Drove End *Hants* 8 D2
Martin Hussingtree *Heref/Worcs* 22 F2
Martinhoe *Devon* 4 A5
Martinhoe Cross *Devon* 4 A6
Martinscroft *Ches* 30 A5
Martinshouse *Borders* 44 B3
Martinstown *Dorset* 7 G10
Martlesham *Suffolk* 27 K5
Martletwy *Dyfed* 12 F4
Martley *Heref/Worcs* 22 F1
Martock *Som'set* 7 D8
Marton *Ches* 31 C7
Marton *Clevl'd* 40 D5
Marton *Humber* 37 C9
Marton *Lincs* 32 B5
Marton *N Yorks* 35 A12
Marton *N Yorks* 36 A2
Marton *N Yorks* 41 G7
Marton *Shrops* 21 B8
Marton *Warwick* 23 E7
Marton le Moor *N Yorks* 40 H4
Marton-in-the-Forest *N Yorks* 40 H6
Martyr Worthy *Hants* 8 C6
Martyr's Green *Surrey* 17 H11
Marvig *W Isles* 63 E5
Marvingstone *Lothian* 49 C8
Marwhirn *Dumf/Gal* 43 B8
Marwick *Orkney* 64 C1
Marwood *Devon* 4 B4
Mary Tavy *Devon* 5 H4
Marybank *H'land* 54 D8
Maryburgh *H'land* 56 D1
Marygold *Borders* 49 C10
Maryhill *Gramp* 58 C6
Maryhill *S'clyde* 47 B10
Marykirk *Gramp* 59 L4
Marypark *Gramp* 56 F7
Maryport *Cumb* 38 B3
Maryport *Dumf/Gal* 42 H2
Marystow *Devon* 5 G3
Maryton *Tayside* 53 B11
Maryton *Tayside* 53 B8
Marywell *Gramp* 59 G7
Marywell *Gramp* 59 H3
Marywell *Tayside* 53 C11
Masham *N Yorks* 40 G2
Mason *Tyne/Wear* 45 F10
Mastin Moor *Derby* 32 C2
Mastrick *Gramp* 59 G6
Matching *Essex* 18 C5
Matching Green *Essex* 18 C5
Matching Tye *Essex* 18 C5
Matfen *Northum* 45 F8
Matfield *Kent* 10 D5
Mathern *Gwent* 15 E8
Mathon *Heref/Worcs* 22 H1
Mathry *Dyfed* 12 D2
Matlaske *Norfolk* 26 B5
Matlock *Derby* 31 D11
Matlock Bath *Derby* 31 D11
Matson *Glos* 15 C11
Matterdale End *Cumb* 38 C6
Mattersey *Notts* 32 A4
Mattersey Thorpe *Notts* 32 A4
Mattingley *Hants* 17 H8
Mattishall *Norfolk* 26 D4
Mattishall Burgh *Norfolk* 26 D4
Mattocks *Tayside* 53 C9
Mauchline *S'clyde* 47 G10
Maud *Gramp* 58 C7
Maudsland *Dyfed* 13 D7
Maugersbury *Glos* 16 B3
Maughold *I of Man* 38 G3
Mauld *H'land* 54 F8
Maulden *Beds* 25 L2
Maulds Meaburn *Cumb* 39 D8
Maunby *N Yorks* 40 F4
Maund Bryan *Heref/Worcs* 21 G11
Maundown *Som'set* 6 C4
Mautby *Norfolk* 26 D8
Mavesyn Ridware *Staffs* 22 A4
Mavis Enderby *Lincs* 33 D10
Maw Green *W Midlands* 22 B4
Mawbray *Cumb* 43 G11
Mawcarse *Tayside* 52 G6
Mawdesley *Lancs* 34 F4
Mawdlam *Mid Glam* 14 F1
Mawgan *Cornw'l* 2 G4
Mawla *Cornw'l* 2 E4
Mawnan *Cornw'l* 2 G5
Mawnan Smith *Cornw'l* 2 G5
Maxey *Cambs* 24 E2
Maxstroke *Warwick* 22 C6
Maxton *Borders* 49 F8
Maxton *Kent* 11 D11
Maxwellheugh *Borders* 49 F10
Maxwellston *S'clyde* 42 B4
Maxwelltown *Dumf/Gal* 43 D10
Maxworthy *Cornw'l* 5 G1
May Bank *Staffs* 31 E7
Mayals *W Glam* 13 H9
Maybole *S'clyde* 47 H8
Maybury *Surrey* 17 H11
Mayfield *E Sussex* 10 E5
Mayfield *Lothian* 48 C6
Mayfield *Staffs* 31 F10
Mayford *Surrey* 17 H10
Mayland *Essex* 19 D9
Maynard's Green *E Sussex* 10 F5
Maypole *Gwent* 15 C8
Maypole *I of Scilly* 2 D2
Maypole Green *Norfolk* 26 F7
Maywick *Shetl'd* 64 E7
Mead *Devon* 4 D1
Meadgate *Avon* 15 H10
Meadle *Bucks* 17 D9
Meadowfoot *S'clyde* 47 E11
Meadowtown *Shrops* 21 B8
Meal Bank *Cumb* 39 F8
Meals *Lincs* 37 G11
Mealsgate *Cumb* 38 A4
Mearbeck *N Yorks* 35 A7
Meare *Som'set* 7 B8
Meare Green *Som'set* 6 D6
Mearns *S'clyde* 47 D10
Mears Ashby *Northants* 23 E11
Measham *Leics* 23 A7
Meath Green *Surrey* 10 D2
Meathop *Cumb* 39 G7
Meavag *W Isles* 63 G3
Meavy *Devon* 5 J4
Medbourne *Leics* 23 C11
Medburn *Northum* 45 F9
Meddon *Devon* 4 D2
Meden Valley *Notts* 32 C3
Medmenham *Bucks* 17 F9
Medomsley *Durham* 45 H9
Medstead *Hants* 9 B8
Meer End *W Midlands* 22 E6
Meerbrook *Staffs* 31 D8
Meersbridge *Lincs* 33 B12
Meesden *Herts* 25 M5
Meeth *Devon* 4 E4
Megdale *Dumf/Gal* 44 C1
Meggethead *Borders* 48 G4
Meidrim *Dyfed* 12 E6
Meifod *Powys* 21 A7
Meigle *Tayside* 53 C7
Meikle Barncleugh *Dumf/Gal* 43 D10
Meikle Beoch *Dumf/Gal* 43 D9
Meikle Carco *Dumf/Gal* 47 H12
Meikle Earnock *S'clyde* 47 D12
Meikle Fiddes *Gramp* 59 J5
Meikle Forter *Tayside* 52 A6
Meikle Gluich *H'land* 61 H7
Meikle Grenach *S'clyde* 46 C6
Meikle Hareshaw *S'clyde* 47 E11
Meikle Ittington *S'clyde* 47 E7
Meikle Kildrummie *H'land* 56 D4
Meikle Pinkerton *Lothian* 49 B9
Meikle Strath *Gramp* 59 K4
Meikle Tarty *Gramp* 58 E7
Meikle Wartle *Gramp* 58 D5
Meikleholm *Dumf/Gal* 43 C11
Meiklelaught *S'clyde* 47 E7
Meikleour *Tayside* 52 C6
Meikleton *Gramp* 58 C3
Meillteyrn *Gwyn* 28 G2
Meinbank *Dumf/Gal* 43 D12
Meinciau *Dyfed* 13 F8
Meir Heath *Staffs* 31 F8
Melbost *W Isles* 63 D6
Melbost Borve *W Isles* 63 A5
Melbourn *Cambs* 25 L5
Melbourne *Derby* 31 H12
Melbourne *Humber* 36 C5
Melbourne *S'clyde* 48 E4
Melbury Abbas *Dorset* 7 D12
Melbury Bubb *Dorset* 7 F9
Melbury Osmond *Dorset* 7 E9
Melbury Sampford *Dorset* 7 F9
Melby *Shetl'd* 64 D6
Melchbourne *Beds* 25 J1
Melcombe Bingham *Dorset* 7 F11
Melcombe Regis *Dorset* 7 H10
Meldon *Devon* 5 G4
Meldon *Northum* 45 E9
Meldreth *Cambs* 25 L5
Meldrum House *Gramp* 58 E6
Melfort *S'clyde* 50 F5
Melgrave *H'land* 55 K8
Meliden *Clwyd* 29 B10
Melin Court *W Glam* 14 D2
Melin-byrhedin *Powys* 20 C4
Melin-y-coed *Gwyn* 29 D7
Melin-y-grug *Powys* 20 B6
Melin-y-wig *Clwyd* 29 E8
Melkinthorpe *Cumb* 39 C8
Melkridge *Northum* 44 G5

Melksham *Wilts* 15 H12
Mellanguan *H'land* 54 A2
Melldalloch *S'clyde* 46 B4
Melling *Lancs* 39 H8
Melling *Mersey* 34 G3
Melling Mount *Mersey* 34 G3
Mellis *Suffolk* 27 H4
Mellon Charles *H'land* 60 G1
Mellon Udrigle *H'land* 60 G1
Mellor *Gtr Man* 31 A8
Mellor *Lancs* 34 D5
Mellor Brook *Lancs* 34 D5
Mells *Som'set* 7 A10
Melmerby *Cumb* 39 B8
Melmerby *N Yorks* 40 G1
Melmerby *N Yorks* 40 G4
Melplash *Dorset* 7 F8
Melrose *Borders* 49 F8
Melsetter *Orkney* 64 D1
Melsonby *N Yorks* 40 D2
Meltham *W Yorks* 35 F9
Meltham Mills *W Yorks* 35 F9
Melton *Humber* 37 D7
Melton *Suffolk* 27 K6
Melton Constable *Norfolk* 26 B3
Melton Mowbray *Leics* 32 H5
Melton Ross *Humber* 37 F8
Meltonby *Humber* 36 B6
Melvaig *H'land* 54 A1
Melverley *Shrops* 21 A9
Melvich *H'land* 61 B8
Membury *Devon* 6 F6
Memsie *Gramp* 58 A7
Memus *Tayside* 59 L2
Menabilly *Cornw'l* 3 E8
Menai Bridge *Gwyn* 28 C5
Mendham *Suffolk* 27 G6
Mendlesham *Suffolk* 27 J4
Mendlesham Green *Suffolk* 27 J4
Menheniot *Cornw'l* 3 C10
Mennock *Dumf/Gal* 43 A9
Menston *W Yorks* 35 C10
Menstrie *Central* 52 G3
Menthorpe *N Yorks* 36 D5
Mentmore *Bucks* 17 B10
Meoble *H'land* 55 L2
Meole Brace *Shrops* 21 A10
Meonstoke *Hants* 9 D7
Meopham *Kent* 10 B5
Meopham Green *Kent* 10 B5
Meopham Station *Kent* 10 A5
Mepal *Cambs* 25 G5
Meppershall *Beds* 25 L2
Merbach *Heref/Worcs* 21 H8
Mere *Ches* 30 B6
Mere *Wilts* 7 C11
Mere Brow *Lancs* 34 E3
Mereclough *Lancs* 35 D7
Meresborough *Kent* 11 B7
Mereside *Lancs* 34 D2
Meretown *Staffs* 30 H6
Mereworth *Kent* 10 C5
Mergie *Gramp* 59 H5
Meriden *W Midlands* 22 D6
Merkadale *H'land* 62 E3
Merkland *Dumf/Gal* 43 D8
Merkland Lodge *H'land* 60 D5
Merlin's Bridge *Dyfed* 12 F3
Merrington *Shrops* 30 H3
Merrion *Dyfed* 12 G3
Merriott *Som'set* 7 E8
Merrivale *Devon* 5 H4
Merrow *Surrey* 9 A11
Merrylaw *Dumf/Gal* 44 C2
Merrymeet *Cornw'l* 3 C10
Mersham *Kent* 11 D9
Merstham *Surrey* 10 C2
Merston *W Sussex* 9 F10
Merstone *I of Wight* 8 H6
Merther *Cornw'l* 2 E6
Merthyr *Dyfed* 13 E7
Merthyr Cynog *Powys* 14 A3
Merthyr Mawr *Mid Glam* 14 F2
Merthyr Tydfil *Mid Glam* 14 D4
Merthyr Vale *Mid Glam* 14 D4
Merton *Devon* 4 E4
Merton *London* 18 G3
Merton *Norfolk* 26 F2
Merton *Oxon* 17 B7
Mervinslaw *Borders* 44 B5
Meshaw *Devon* 4 D6
Messing *Essex* 19 B9
Messingham *Humber* 37 G7
Metfield *Suffolk* 27 G6
Metheringham *Lincs* 33 D8
Methil *Fife* 53 G8
Methlem *Gwyn* 28 G1
Methley *W Yorks* 35 D12
Methlick *Gramp* 58 D6
Methven *Tayside* 52 E5
Methwold *Norfolk* 24 F8
Methwold Hythe *Norfolk* 24 F8
Mettingham *Suffolk* 26 F6
Metton *Norfolk* 26 B5
Mevagissey *Cornw'l* 3 E7
Mexborough *S Yorks* 36 G3
Mey *H'land* 61 A12
Meysey Hampton *Glos* 16 D2
Miavaig *W Isles* 63 C2
Michaelchurch *Heref/Worcs* 15 B8
Michaelchurch Escley *Heref/Worcs* 14 A6
Michaelchurch-on-Arrow *Powys* 21 G8
Michaelston-le-pit *S Glam* 14 G5
Michaelston-super-Ely *S Glam* 14 G4
Michaelston-y-Fedw *Gwent* 14 F6
Michaelstow *Cornw'l* 3 B8
Michelmersh *Hants* 8 C5
Mickfield *Suffolk* 27 J4
Mickle Trafford *Ches* 30 C3
Micklebring *S Yorks* 36 H3
Mickleby *N Yorks* 41 D8
Micklefield *W Yorks* 36 D2
Mickleham *Surrey* 10 C1
Mickleover *Derby* 31 G11
Micklethwaite *Cumb* 44 H1
Mickleton *Durham* 39 C12
Mickleton *Glos* 22 H5
Mickletown *W Yorks* 35 D12
Mickley *N Yorks* 40 G3
Mickley Square *Northum* 45 G9
Mid Ardlaw *Gramp* 58 A7
Mid Beltie *Gramp* 59 G4
Mid Cairncross *Tayside* 59 J2
Mid Calder *Lothian* 48 C3
Mid Cloch Forbie *Gramp* 58 B5
Mid Clyth *H'land* 61 D11
Mid Cowbog *Gramp* 58 B6
Mid Crochail *H'land* 54 F7
Mid Drumloch *S'clyde* 47 D11
Mid Hartwood *Lothian* 48 C3
Mid Laggan *Dumf/Gal* 43 D8
Mid Lavant *W Sussex* 9 E10
Mid Mains *H'land* 54 F8
Mid Sannox *S'clyde* 46 E5
Mid Storm *H'land* 54 F2
Mid Thundergay *S'clyde* 46 E4
Mid Yell *Shetl'd* 64 B7
Midbea *Orkney* 64 A2
Middle Assendon *Oxon* 17 F8
Middle Aston *Oxon* 16 A6
Middle Barton *Oxon* 16 B5
Middle Chinnock *Som'set* 7 E8
Middle Claydon *Bucks* 17 B8
Middle Crackington *Cornw'l* 2 B2
Middle Drums *Tayside* 59 L3
Middle Handley *Derby* 32 B1
Middle Littleton *Heref/Worcs* 22 G4
Middle Mill *Dyfed* 12 D2
Middle Ord *Northum* 49 D12
Middle Rasen *Lincs* 33 A8
Middle Rigg *Tayside* 52 F5
Middle Street *Glos* 15 D11
Middle Tysoe *Warwick* 23 H7
Middle Wallop *Hants* 8 B4
Middle Winterslow *Wilts* 8 C4
Middle Woodford *Wilts* 8 C3
Middlebie *Dumf/Gal* 43 D12
Middlebridge *Tayside* 57 M4
Middlefield *Borders* 49 D10
Middlegill *Dumf/Gal* 43 A11
Middleham *N Yorks* 40 F2
Middlehope *Shrops* 21 D10
Middlemarsh *Dorset* 7 E10
Middlemuir House *Gramp* 58 E7
Middlesbrough *Clevl'd* 40 C5
Middleshaw *Cumb* 39 F8
Middleshaw *Dumf/Gal* 43 D12
Middlesknowes *Borders* 44 B6
Middlesmoor *N Yorks* 40 H1
Middlestone *Durham* 40 B3
Middlestone Moor *Durham* 40 B3
Middlestown *W Yorks* 35 E11
Middlethird *Borders* 49 E9
Middleton *Derby* 31 D10
Middleton *Derby* 31 E11
Middleton *Essex* 27 L2
Middleton *Gramp* 58 E6
Middleton *Gtr Man* 35 F7
Middleton *Hants* 8 B6
Middleton *Heref/Worcs* 21 E11
Middleton *Lancs* 34 A3
Middleton *Lothian* 48 D6
Middleton *N Yorks* 35 B10
Middleton *N Yorks* 41 G8
Middleton *Norfolk* 24 D8
Middleton *Norfolk* 25 C11
Middleton *Northants* 23 C11
Middleton *Northum* 45 B12
Middleton *Northum* 45 E9
Middleton *S'clyde* 47 E8
Middleton *Shrops* 21 E11
Middleton *Shrops* 30 G2
Middleton *Suffolk* 27 H7
Middleton *Tayside* 52 B6
Middleton *Tayside* 52 F6
Middleton *W Glam* 13 H7
Middleton *W Yorks* 35 D11
Middleton *Warwick* 22 B5
Middleton Cheney *Northants* 23 H8
Middleton Green *Staffs* 31 G8
Middleton Hall *Northum* 49 G12
Middleton in Teesdale *Durham* 39 C11
Middleton of Rora *Gramp* 58 C8
Middleton on the Hill *Heref/Worcs* 21 F11
Middleton One Row *Durham* 40 D4
Middleton Priors *Shrops* 21 C11
Middleton Quernhow *N Yorks* 40 G3
Middleton St. George *Durham* 40 D4
Middleton Scriven *Shrops* 21 D12
Middleton Stoney *Oxon* 16 B6
Middleton Tyas *N Yorks* 40 E3
Middleton-in-Leven *Clevl'd* 40 D5
Middleton-on-Sea *W Sussex* 9 F11
Middleton-on-the-Wolds *Humber* 37 B7
Middletown *Powys* 21 A8
Middlewich *Ches* 30 D6
Middlewood Green *Suffolk* 27 J4
Middleyard *S'clyde* 47 F10
Middlezoy *Som'set* 7 C7
Middridge *Durham* 40 C3
Midford *Avon* 15 H10
Midge Hall *Lancs* 34 E4
Midgeholme *Cumb* 44 G5
Midgeley *W Yorks* 35 F11
Midgham *Berks* 16 G6
Midgley *W Yorks* 35 D9
Midhopestones *S Yorks* 35 G11
Midhurst *W Sussex* 9 D10
Midlem *Borders* 49 G8
Midlock *S'clyde* 48 G2
Midsomer Norton *Avon* 7 A10
Midtown *H'land* 60 B6
Midtown Brae *H'land* 54 A2
Midtown of Buchromb *Gramp* 58 C1
Midville *Lincs* 33 E11
Miefield *Dumf/Gal* 43 F7
Migdale *H'land* 61 G7
Migvie *Gramp* 59 G2
Milborne Port *Som'set* 7 D10
Milborne St. Andrew *Dorset* 7 F11
Milborne Wick *Som'set* 7 D10
Milbourne *Northum* 45 E9
Milbuie *H'land* 50 H1
Milburn *Cumb* 39 B9
Milbury Heath *Avon* 15 E10
Milby *N Yorks* 40 H4
Milcombe *Oxon* 16 A5
Milden *Suffolk* 27 K3
Mildenhall *Suffolk* 25 H8
Mildenhall *Wilts* 16 G3
Mile Elm *Wilts* 16 G1
Mile End *Essex* 19 A9
Mile End *Suffolk* 26 F6
Milebrook *Powys* 21 E8
Mileham *Norfolk* 26 D2
Miles End *Glos* 15 C9
Miles Green *Staffs* 30 E6
Miles Hope *Heref/Worcs* 21 F11
Milesmark *Fife* 52 H5
Milfield *Northum* 49 F12
Milford *Derby* 31 F12
Milford *Devon* 4 D1
Milford *Staffs* 31 H8
Milford *Surrey* 9 B11
Milford *Wilts* 8 C3
Milford Haven *Dyfed* 12 F3
Milford on Sea *Hants* 8 G4
Milhall *S'clyde* 47 D10
Milkwall *Glos* 15 C9
Milkwell *Wilts* 8 D1
Mill Bank *W Yorks* 35 E9
Mill Brow *Gtr Man* 31 A8
Mill Common *Suffolk* 27 G7
Mill End *Bucks* 17 F9
Mill End *Cambs* 25 G4
Mill End *Herts* 17 E11
Mill End *Herts* 25 M4
Mill Green *Essex* 18 D6
Mill Green *Suffolk* 27 L3
Mill Hill *London* 18 E2
Mill Houses *Lancs* 39 H8
Mill Lane *Hants* 9 A9
Mill of Ardo *Gramp* 58 D6
Mill of Ardo *Gramp* 58 E7
Mill of Carden *Gramp* 58 E4
Mill of Culfork *Gramp* 58 F2
Mill of Gellan *Gramp* 59 G3
Mill of Kingoochie *Gramp* 58 E6
Mill of Monquich *Gramp* 59 H6
Mill of Muiresk *Gramp* 58 C4
Mill of Pot *Gramp* 58 C5
Mill of Uras *Gramp* 59 J6
Mill Street *Norfolk* 26 D3
Millbeck *Cumb* 38 C5
Millbounds *Orkney* 64 B3
Millbreck *Gramp* 58 C7
Millbridge *Surrey* 9 B10
Millbrook *Beds* 25 L1
Millbrook *Cornw'l* 3 D11
Millbrook *Devon* 4 C6
Millbrook *Hants* 8 E5
Millburn *S'clyde* 47 F9
Millcombe *Devon* 5 L7
Millcorner *E Sussex* 11 F7
Milldale *Staffs* 31 E10
Millden Lodge *Tayside* 59 J3
Milldens *Tayside* 53 B10
Millerhill *Lothian* 48 B6
Miller's Dale *Derby* 31 C10
Millers Green *Derby* 31 E11
Millerston *S'clyde* 47 C11
Millfield *Gramp* 59 H2
Millgreen *Shrops* 30 G5
Millhalf *Heref/Worcs* 21 H8
Millhayes *Devon* 6 E5
Millheugh *Borders* 49 G9
Millheugh *S'clyde* 47 D12
Millholme *Cumb* 39 F8
Millhouse *Cumb* 38 B6
Millhouse *S Yorks* 35 G11
Millhouse *S'clyde* 46 B4
Millhousebridge *Dumf/Gal* 43 C11
Millhouses *S Yorks* 32 B1
Milliganton *Dumf/Gal* 43 C10
Millikenpark *S'clyde* 47 C9
Millington *Humber* 36 B6
Millmeece *Staffs* 31 G7
Millom *Cumb* 38 G4
Millpool *Cornw'l* 3 C8
Millport *S'clyde* 46 D6
Millquarter *Dumf/Gal* 43 C7
Millthorpe *Derby* 31 C11
Millthrop *Cumb* 39 F9
Milltimber *Gramp* 59 G6
Millton *Gramp* 59 G4
Millton *Tayside* 53 C8
Milltown *Derby* 32 D1
Milltown *Devon* 4 B4
Milltown *Gramp* 58 C3
Milltown *Gramp* 58 F2
Milltown *Gramp* 59 K5
Milltown *H'land* 54 D7
Milltown of Aberdalgie *Tayside* 52 E5
Milltown of Auchindoun *Gramp* 58 D1
Milltown of Campfield *Gramp* 59 G4
Milltown of Minnes *Gramp* 58 E7
Milltown of Towie *Gramp* 58 F2
Millwell *S'clyde* 47 D11
Milnacraig *Tayside* 53 B7
Milnathort *Tayside* 52 G6
Milne *Dumf/Gal* 43 B12
Milngavie *S'clyde* 47 B10
Milnmark *Dumf/Gal* 43 C7
Milnrow *Gtr Man* 35 F8
Milnthorpe *Cumb* 39 G7
Milson *Shrops* 21 E11
Milstead *Kent* 11 B7
Milston *Wilts* 8 B3
Milton *Avon* 14 H6
Milton *Cambs* 25 J6
Milton *Central* 51 G12
Milton *Cumb* 44 G4
Milton *Derby* 31 G11
Milton *Dumf/Gal* 42 F3
Milton *Dumf/Gal* 43 C9
Milton *Dumf/Gal* 43 D9
Milton *Dyfed* 12 G4
Milton *Gramp* 58 A3
Milton *H'land* 54 E1
Milton *H'land* 56 B3
Milton *H'land* 56 D2
Milton *H'land* 56 E1
Milton *H'land* 57 G1
Milton *H'land* 57 H5
Milton *H'land* 61 C12
Milton *Oxon* 16 A5
Milton *Oxon* 16 E6
Milton *S'clyde* 42 A3
Milton *S'clyde* 42 B4
Milton *S'clyde* 47 B9
Milton *Som'set* 7 D8
Milton *Tayside* 52 A6
Milton *Tayside* 59 J2
Milton Abbas *Dorset* 7 F11
Milton Abbot *Devon* 5 H3
Milton Bridge *Lothian* 48 C5
Milton Bryan *Beds* 25 M1
Milton Clevedon *Som'set* 7 C10
Milton Coldwells *Gramp* 58 D7
Milton Damerel *Devon* 4 E3
Milton End *Glos* 16 D2
Milton Ernest *Beds* 25 K1
Milton Green *Ches* 30 D3
Milton Hill *Oxon* 16 E6
Milton Keynes *Bucks* 23 H12
Milton Lilbourne *Wilts* 16 H3
Milton Malsor *Northants* 23 G10
Milton Morenish *Central* 52 D1
Milton of Ardlethen *Gramp* 58 D6
Milton of Auchinhove *Gramp* 59 G3
Milton of Balgonie *Fife* 53 G8
Milton of Campsie *S'clyde* 47 B11
Milton of Cushnie *Gramp* 58 F3
Milton of Dillavaird *Gramp* 59 J5
Milton of Farr *H'land* 56 F2
Milton of Fishrie *Gramp* 58 B5
Milton of Gollanfield *H'land* 56 D3
Milton of Lesmore *Gramp* 58 E2
Milton of Logie *Gramp* 59 G2
Milton of Murtle *Gramp* 59 G6
Milton of Noth *Gramp* 58 E2
Milton of Smerby *S'clyde* 46 G2
Milton of Tullich *Gramp* 59 H1
Milton on Stour *Dorset* 7 C11
Milton Regis *Kent* 11 B7
Milton under Wychwood *Oxon* 16 B4
Miltoncombe *Devon* 5 J4
Miltonduff *Gramp* 56 D7
Miltonise *Dumf/Gal* 42 D3
Miltown of Craigston *Gramp* 58 B5
Miltown of Edinvillie *Gramp* 56 F8
Milverton *Som'set* 6 D4
Milwich *Staffs* 31 G8
Minard *S'clyde* 51 H7
Minchinhampton *Glos* 15 D12
Mindrum *Northum* 49 F11
Mindrummill *Northum* 49 F11
Minehead *Som'set* 6 B3
Minera *Clwyd* 29 E12
Minety *Wilts* 16 E1
Minffordd *Gwyn* 28 F5
Mingarrypark *H'land* 50 A4
Miningsby *Lincs* 33 D10
Minions *Cornw'l* 3 C9
Minishant *S'clyde* 47 H8
Minnigaff *Dumf/Gal* 42 E5
Minnonie *Gramp* 58 B5
Minorca *I of Man* 38 G2
Minsca *Dumf/Gal* 44 E1
Minskip *N Yorks* 35 A12
Minstead *Hants* 8 E4
Minster *Kent* 11 B11
Minster Lovell *Oxon* 16 C4
Minster on Sea *Kent* 11 A8
Minsteracres *Northum* 45 G8
Minsterley *Shrops* 21 B9
Minsterworth *Glos* 15 C11
Minterne Magna *Dorset* 7 F10
Minting *Lincs* 33 C9
Mintlaw *Gramp* 58 C7
Minto *Borders* 49 G8
Minton *Shrops* 21 C9
Minwear *Dyfed* 12 F4
Minworth *W Midlands* 22 C5
Mirbister *Orkney* 64 C1
Mirehouse *Cumb* 38 D2
Mireland *H'land* 61 B12
Mirfield *W Yorks* 35 E10
Miserden *Glos* 15 C12
Miskin *Mid Glam* 14 D4
Miskin *Mid Glam* 14 F4
Misson *Notts* 36 H5
Misterton *Leics* 23 D9
Misterton *Notts* 36 H5
Misterton *Som'set* 7 E8
Mistley *Essex* 27 M4
Mitcham *London* 18 G3
Mitchel Troy *Gwent* 15 C8
Mitcheldean *Glos* 15 B10
Micheldever *Hants* 8 B6
Mitchell *Cornw'l* 2 D6
Mitcheltroy Common *Gwent* 15 C8
Mitford *Northum* 45 D10
Mithian *Cornw'l* 2 E4
Mitton *Staffs* 22 A2
Mixbury *Oxon* 17 A7
Mixon *Staffs* 31 D9
Moanzie *Fife* 53 E8
Moat *Cumb* 44 F3
Mobberley *Ches* 30 B6
Moccas *Heref/Worcs* 21 H9
Mochdre *Clwyd* 29 B7
Mochdre *Powys* 20 D6
Mochrum *Dumf/Gal* 42 G4
Mockbeggar *Hants* 8 E3
Mockbeggar *Kent* 10 A6
Mockbeggar *Kent* 10 C6
Mockerkin *Cumb* 38 C3
Modbury *Devon* 5 K5
Moddershall *Staffs* 31 G8
Modsarie *H'land* 61 B7
Moelfre *Clwyd* 29 G11
Moelfre *Gwyn* 28 B4
Moffat *Dumf/Gal* 43 A11
Moggerhanger *Beds* 25 K2
Moin House *H'land* 60 B6
Moira *Leics* 22 A6
Molash *Kent* 11 C9
Mol-chlach *H'land* 62 G4
Mold *Clwyd* 29 D11
Moldgreen *W Yorks* 35 F10
Molehill Green *Essex* 18 A5
Molescroft *Humber* 37 C8
Molesden *Northum* 45 E9
Molesworth *Cambs* 25 H2
Molland *Devon* 4 C7
Molland Cross *Devon* 4 C6
Mollington *Ches* 30 C2
Mollington *Oxon* 23 G8
Mollinsburn *S'clyde* 47 B12
Molting Green *Essex* 19 B9
Monachty *Dyfed* 13 A8
Monachylemore *Central* 51 F11
Monamore Bridge *S'clyde* 46 F5
Monar Lodge *H'land* 54 F6
Monaughty *Powys* 21 F8
Monboddo House *Gramp* 59 J5
Monevechadan *S'clyde* 51 G9
Monewden *Suffolk* 27 J5
Moneydie *Tayside* 52 D5
Moniaive *Dumf/Gal* 43 C8
Monifieth *Tayside* 53 D9
Monikie *Tayside* 53 C9
Monimail *Fife* 53 F8
Monington *Dyfed* 12 C5
Monk Bretton *S Yorks* 35 F12
Monk Fryston *N Yorks* 36 D3
Monk Sherborne *Hants* 17 H7
Monk Soham *Suffolk* 27 J5
Monkhide *Heref/Worcs* 21 H11
Monkhopton *Shrops* 21 C11
Monkland *Heref/Worcs* 21 G10
Monkleigh *Devon* 4 D3
Monknash *S Glam* 14 G3
Monkokehampton *Devon* 4 E5
Monkridge *Northum* 45 D7
Monks Eleigh *Suffolk* 27 K3
Monk's Gate *W Sussex* 10 E1
Monks' Heath *Ches* 31 C7
Monks Kirby *Warwick* 23 D8
Monks Risborough *Bucks* 17 D9
Monkshill *Gramp* 58 D5
Monksilver *Som'set* 6 C4
Monkspath Street *W Midlands* 22 D5
Monkswood *Gwent* 15 D7
Monkton *Devon* 6 F5
Monkton *Dyfed* 12 G3
Monkton *Kent* 11 B11
Monkton *S'clyde* 47 G8
Monkton Coombe *Avon* 15 H11
Monkton Deverill *Wilts* 7 B12
Monkton Farleigh *Wilts* 15 H11
Monkton Heathfield *Som'set* 6 D6
Monkton Up Wimborne *Dorset* 8 E2
Monkton Wyld *Dorset* 7 F7
Monktonhill *S'clyde* 47 F8
Monk-Wearmouth *Tyne/Wear* 45 G12
Monkwood *Hants* 9 C8
Monmouth *Gwent* 15 C8
Monmouth Cap *Gwent* 15 B7
Monnington on Wye *Heref/Worcs* 21 H9
Monorgan *Tayside* 53 D8
Monreith *Dumf/Gal* 42 G4
Monreith Mains *Dumf/Gal* 42 G4

Montacute *Som'set* 7 E8
Montcoffer House *Gramp* 58 B4
Montford *S'clyde* 46 C6
Montford *Shrops* 21 A9
Montford Bridge *Shrops* 21 A9
Montgarrie *Gramp* 58 F3
Montgomery *Powys* 21 C8
Montgreenan *S'clyde* 47 E8
Montrave *Fife* 53 F8
Montrose *Tayside* 59 L5
Monxton *Hants* 8 B5
Monyash *Derby* 31 D10
Monymusk *Gramp* 58 F4
Monzie *Tayside* 52 E4
Monzie *Tayside* 57 M5
Moodiesburn *S'clyde* 47 B11
Moor Allerton *W Yorks* 35 C11
Moor Crichel *Dorset* 8 E2
Moor Monkton *N Yorks* 36 B3
Moor of Granary *Gramp* 56 D6
Moor Row *Cumb* 38 D3
Moor Street *Kent* 11 B7
Moorby *Lincs* 33 D10
Moordown *Dorset* 8 G3
Moore *Ches* 30 B4
Moorend *Glos* 15 D10
Moorends *S Yorks* 36 F5
Moorgreen *Hants* 8 E6
Moorhall *Derby* 31 C11
Moorhampton *Heref/Worcs* 21 H9
Moorhouse *Cumb* 44 G2
Moorhouse *Notts* 32 D5
Moorlinch *Som'set* 7 C7
Moorsholm *N Yorks* 41 D7
Moorshop *Devon* 5 H4
Moorside *Gtr Man* 35 F8
Moorside *Lincs* 33 D9
Moortown *Hants* 8 F3
Moortown *I of Wight* 8 H6
Moortown *Lincs* 37 G8
Morar *H'land* 55 K1
Morborne *Cambs* 24 F2
Morchard Bishop *Devon* 4 E6
Morcott *Leics* 23 B12
Morda *Shrops* 30 G2
Morden *Dorset* 7 G12
Morden *London* 18 G2
Mordiford *Heref/Worcs* 15 A9
Mordington Mains *Borders* 49 D12
Mordon *Durham* 40 C3
More *Shrops* 21 C9
Morebath *Som'set* 6 D3
Morebattle *Borders* 49 G10
Morecambe *Lancs* 34 A3
Morecombelake *Dorset* 7 G7
Morefield *H'land* 60 G3
Moreland *Cumb* 39 C8
Moreleigh *Devon* 5 K6
Morenish *Central* 52 D1
Moresby *Cumb* 38 C2
Morestead *Hants* 8 D6
Moreton *Dorset* 7 G11
Moreton *Essex* 18 C5
Moreton *Mersey* 30 A1
Moreton *Oxon* 17 D8
Moreton Corbet *Shrops* 30 H4
Moreton Jeffries *Heref/Worcs* 21 G11
Moreton Morrell *Warwick* 22 F6
Moreton on Lugg *Heref/Worcs* 21 H10
Moreton Pinkney *Northants* 23 G9
Moreton Say *Shrops* 30 G5
Moreton Valence *Glos* 15 C11
Moretonhampstead *Devon* 5 G6
Moreton-in-Marsh *Glos* 16 A3
Morfa *Dyfed* 13 F9
Morfa Bychan *Gwyn* 28 F5
Morfa Glas *W Glam* 14 D2
Morfa-Nefyn *Gwyn* 28 F2
Morgan's Vale *Wilts* 8 D4
Morley *Derby* 32 F1
Morley *Durham* 40 B2
Morley *Durham* 40 B3
Morley *W Yorks* 35 D11
Morley Green *Ches* 31 B7
Morley St. Botolph *Norfolk* 26 E4
Morningside *Lothian* 48 B5
Morningside *S'clyde* 48 D1
Morningthorpe *Norfolk* 26 F5
Morpeth *Northum* 45 D10
Morrey *Staffs* 31 H10
Morrington *Dumf/Gal* 43 C9
Morris Green *Essex* 25 M8
Morriston *S'clyde* 42 A3
Morriston *W Glam* 13 G10
Morston *Norfolk* 26 A3
Mortehoe *Devon* 4 B3
Morthen *S Yorks* 32 A2
Mortimer *Berks* 17 H7
Mortimer West End *Hants* 17 H7
Mortimer's Cross *Heref/Worcs* 21 F9
Mortlake *London* 18 F2
Morton *Avon* 15 E9
Morton *Cumb* 44 H2
Morton *Derby* 32 D1
Morton *Lincs* 24 C2
Morton *Lincs* 32 A5
Morton *Norfolk* 26 D4
Morton *Notts* 32 E4
Morton *Shrops* 30 H2
Morton Bagot *Warwick* 22 F4
Morton Tinmouth *Durham* 40 C2
Morton-on-Swale *N Yorks* 40 F3
Morvah *Cornw'l* 2 F1
Morval *Cornw'l* 3 D9
Morvich *H'land* 55 G3
Morvich Lodge *H'land* 61 F8
Morville *Shrops* 21 C12
Morwenstow *Cornw'l* 4 D1
Mosbrough *S Yorks* 32 B2
Moscow *Cumb* 44 F4
Moscow *S'clyde* 47 E9
Mosedale *Cumb* 38 B6
Moselden Height *W Yorks* 35 F9
Moseley *Heref/Worcs* 22 F2
Moseley *W Midlands* 22 D4
Moss *Clwyd* 29 E12
Moss *H'land* 50 A4
Moss *S Yorks* 36 F4
Moss Bank *Mersey* 34 G4
Moss End *Berks* 17 G9
Moss of Barmuckity *Gramp* 56 D8
Mossat *Gramp* 58 F2
Mossbank *Shetl'd* 64 C7
Mossblown *S'clyde* 47 G9
Mossburnford *Borders* 44 A5
Mossdale *Dumf/Gal* 43 D7
Mossend *S'clyde* 47 C12
Mosser *Cumb* 38 C4
Mossgiel *S'clyde* 47 F9
Mosshouses *Borders* 49 E8
Mossley *Ches* 31 D7
Mossley *Gtr Man* 35 G8
Mossley Hill *Mersey* 30 B3
Mosspeeble *Dumf/Gal* 44 D2
Moss-side *H'land* 56 D4
Mosstodloch *Gramp* 58 B1
Mosterton *Dorset* 7 F8
Mostyn *Clwyd* 29 B11
Motcombe *Dorset* 7 D11
Mothecombe *Devon* 5 L5
Motherwell *S'clyde* 47 D12
Mottingham *London* 18 G4
Mottisfont *Hants* 8 C5
Mottistone *I of Wight* 8 H5
Mottram in Longdendale *Gtr Man* 35 H8
Mottram St. Andrew *Ches* 31 B7
Mouldsworth *Ches* 30 C4
Moulin *Tayside* 52 A4
Moulinearn *Tayside* 52 B4
Moulsford *Oxon* 17 F7
Moulsoe *Bucks* 23 H12
Moulton *Ches* 30 C5
Moulton *Lincs* 24 C4
Moulton *N Yorks* 40 E3
Moulton *Norfolk* 26 E7
Moulton *Northants* 23 E11
Moulton *S Glam* 14 G4
Moulton *Suffolk* 25 J8
Moulton Chapel *Lincs* 24 D4
Moulton St. Michael *Norfolk* 25 F5
Moulton Seas End *Lincs* 24 C4
Moulzie *Tayside* 57 L8
Mounie Castle *Gramp* 58 E5
Mount *Cornw'l* 3 C8
Mount Ambrose *Cornw'l* 2 E4
Mount Bures *Essex* 27 M2
Mount Hawke *Cornw'l* 2 E4
Mount Lothian *Lothian* 48 D5
Mount Pleasant *Borders* 49 D10
Mount Pleasant *Derby* 31 E11
Mount Pleasant *Hants* 17 H7
Mount Pleasant *Hants* 8 F4
Mount Pleasant *Heref/Worcs* 22 F3
Mount Pleasant *Mid Glam* 14 D4
Mount Sorrel *Wilts* 8 D2
Mount Tabor *W Yorks* 35 D9
Mountain *Northum* 45 B8
Mountain Ash *Mid Glam* 14 D4
Mountain Cross *Borders* 48 E4
Mountain Water *Dyfed* 12 E3
Mountbenger *Borders* 48 G6
Mountblairy *Gramp* 58 B4
Mountfield *E Sussex* 10 F6
Mountgerald *H'land* 56 D1
Mountjoy *Cornw'l* 2 D6
Mountnessing *Essex* 18 D6
Mounton *Gwent* 15 E8
Mountsolie *Gramp* 58 B7
Mountsorrel *Leics* 23 A9
Mousehole *Cornw'l* 2 G2
Mouswald *Dumf/Gal* 43 D11
Mow Cop *Ches* 31 D7
Mowhaugh *Borders* 49 G10
Mowsley *Leics* 23 C10
Mowtie *Gramp* 59 H6
Moy *H'land* 55 L5
Moy *H'land* 55 L8
Moy *H'land* 56 F3
Moy Hall *H'land* 56 F3
Moy House *Gramp* 56 D6
Moy Lodge *H'land* 55 L8
Moylgrove *Dyfed* 12 C5
Mt Cansp *H'land* 56 C4
Muasdale *S'clyde* 46 E2
Much Birch *Heref/Worcs* 15 A8
Much Cowarne *Heref/Worcs* 21 H11
Much Dewchurch *Heref/Worcs* 15 A8
Much Hadham *Herts* 18 B4
Much Hoole *Lancs* 34 E3
Much Marcle *Heref/Worcs* 15 A10
Much Wenlock *Shrops* 21 B11
Muchalls *Gramp* 59 H6
Muchelney *Som'set* 7 D8
Muchlarnick *Cornw'l* 3 D9
Muchrachd *H'land* 54 F6
Muckernich *H'land* 56 D2
Muckfoot *S'clyde* 42 C3
Mucking *Essex* 19 F7
Muckleford *Dorset* 7 G9
Mucklestone *Staffs* 30 F6
Muckleton *Shrops* 30 H4
Muckletown *Gramp* 58 E3
Muckley Corner *Staffs* 22 B4
Muckton *Lincs* 33 B10
Mudale *H'land* 60 D6
Muddiford *Devon* 4 B4
Muddles Green *E Sussex* 10 G4
Mudeford *Dorset* 8 G3
Mudford *Som'set* 7 D9
Mudgley *Som'set* 7 B8
Mugdock *Central* 47 B10
Mugeary *H'land* 62 D4
Mugginton *Derby* 31 F11
Muggleswick *Durham* 45 H9
Muie *H'land* 61 F7
Muir *Gramp* 57 K6
Muir of Fairburn *H'land* 54 D8
Muir of Fowlis *Gramp* 58 F3
Muir of Lochs *Gramp* 56 C8
Muir of Ord *H'land* 56 E1
Muirden *Gramp* 58 B4
Muirfoot *S'clyde* 48 D2
Muirhead *Fife* 53 E9
Muirhead *Fife* 53 G7
Muirhead *Gramp* 59 L5
Muirhead *S'clyde* 47 B11
Muirhead *Tayside* 53 D8
Muirhouses *Lothian* 48 A3
Muirkirk *S'clyde* 47 G11
Muirmill *Central* 47 A12
Muirsdrum *Tayside* 53 C10
Muirshearlich *H'land* 55 L5
Muirskie *Gramp* 59 H6
Muirtack *Gramp* 58 C5
Muirtack *Gramp* 58 D7
Muirton *H'land* 56 C3
Muirton *Tayside* 52 E6
Muirton *Tayside* 59 L4
Muirton Mains *H'land* 54 D8
Muirton of Ardblair *Tayside* 52 C6
Muirtown *Tayside* 52 F4
Muiryfold *Gramp* 58 C5
Muiryhill *Dumf/Gal* 43 A9
Muker *N Yorks* 39 E11
Mulbarton *Norfolk* 26 E5
Mulben *Gramp* 58 C1
Mullardoch House *H'land* 54 F6
Mullion *Cornw'l* 2 H4
Mullion Cove *Cornw'l* 2 H4
Mullochbuie *H'land* 55 L1
Mumbles *W Glam* 13 H9
Mumby *Lincs* 33 C12
Munderfield Row *Heref/Worcs* 21 G12
Munderfield Stocks *Heref/Worcs* 21 G12
Mundesley *Norfolk* 26 B6
Mundford *Norfolk* 26 F1
Mundham *Norfolk* 26 F6
Mundon Hill *Essex* 19 D8
Munerigie *H'land* 55 J6
Mungasdale *H'land* 60 G2
Munlochy *H'land* 56 D2
Munnoch *S'clyde* 47 E7
Munsgrisdale *Cumb* 38 B6
Munsley *Heref/Worcs* 21 H12
Munslow *Shrops* 21 D10
Munslow Aston *Shrops* 21 D10
Murchington *Devon* 5 G6
Murcott *Bucks* 17 C7
Murkle *H'land* 61 A11
Murlaggan *H'land* 55 K4
Murlaggan *H'land* 55 L7
Murrayfield *Lothian* 48 B5
Murrayfield *Tayside* 52 D5
Murraythwaite *Dumf/Gal* 43 D12
Murrow *Cambs* 24 E5
Mursley *Bucks* 17 A9
Murthil *Tayside* 59 L2
Murthill *Tayside* 53 A9
Murthly *Tayside* 52 C6
Murthly Castle *Tayside* 52 C5
Murton *Cumb* 39 C9
Murton *Durham* 45 H12
Murton *N Yorks* 36 B4
Murton *Northum* 49 E12
Murton Grange *N Yorks* 40 F5
Musbury *Devon* 6 G6
Muscoates *N Yorks* 41 G7
Musselburgh *Lothian* 48 B6
Muston *Leics* 32 F5
Muston *N Yorks* 41 G11
Mustow Green *Heref/Worcs* 22 E2
Mutehill *Dumf/Gal* 43 G7
Mutford *Suffolk* 27 G8
Muthill *Tayside* 52 E4
Mutterton *Devon* 6 F4
Muxton *Shrops* 21 A12
Mybster *H'land* 61 B11
Myddfai *Dyfed* 13 D11
Myddle *Shrops* 30 H3
Mydroilyn *Dyfed* 13 B8
Mylor Bridge *Cornw'l* 2 F5
Mynachlog-ddu *Dyfed* 12 D5
Myndtown *Shrops* 21 C9
Mynydd-bach *Dyfed* 20 E3
Mynydd-bach *Gwent* 15 E8
Mynyddygarreg *Dyfed* 13 F7
Mynytho *Gwyn* 28 G3
Myre of Bedlam *Gramp* 58 C6
Myrebird *Gramp* 59 G5
Myrelandhorn *H'land* 61 B12
Mytchett *Surrey* 9 A10
Mytholmroyd *W Yorks* 35 E9
Mythop *Lancs* 34 D2
Myton-on Swale *N Yorks* 40 H4
Naburn *N Yorks* 36 C4
Nackington *Kent* 11 C10
Nacton *Suffolk* 27 L5
Nafferton *Humber* 37 A8
Nailbridge *Glos* 15 C9
Nailsea *Avon* 15 G8
Nailstone *Leics* 23 A7
Nailsworth *Glos* 15 D11
Nairn *H'land* 56 D4
Nalderswood *Surrey* 10 D1
Nancegollan *Cornw'l* 2 F3
Nancledra *Cornw'l* 2 F2
Nanhurst *Surrey* 9 B11
Nannerch *Clwyd* 29 C11
Nanpantan *Leics* 32 H2
Nanpean *Cornw'l* 3 D7
Nanstallon *Cornw'l* 3 C7
Nant Peris *Gwyn* 28 D5
Nant-ddu *Powys* 14 C3
Nanternis *Dyfed* 13 A7
Nantgaredig *Dyfed* 13 E8
Nantgarw *Mid Glam* 14 F4
Nant-glas *Powys* 20 F5
Nantglyn *Clwyd* 29 D9
Nantgwyn *Powys* 20 E5
Nantile *Gwyn* 28 E4
Nantmawr *Shrops* 30 H1
Nantmel *Powys* 20 F6
Nantmor *Gwyn* 28 F5
Nantwich *Ches* 30 E5
Nantybai *Dyfed* 13 C11
Nant-y-Bwch *Gwent* 14 C5
Nant-y-cafn *W Glam* 14 D2
Nant-y-ffin *Dyfed* 13 D9
Nantyffyllon *Mid Glam* 14 E2
Nantyglo *Gwent* 14 C5
Nant-y-Meichiaid *Powys* 21 A7
Nant-y-moel *Mid Glam* 14 E3
Nant-y-pandy *Gwyn* 28 C6
Naphill *Bucks* 17 D9
Nappa *N Yorks* 35 B7
Napton on the Hill *Warwick* 23 F8
Narberth *Dyfed* 12 E4
Narborough *Leics* 23 B8
Narborough *Norfolk* 24 D8
Narkurs *Cornw'l* 3 D10
Narrachan *S'clyde* 50 F6
Nasareth *Gwyn* 28 E4
Naseby *Northants* 23 D10
Nash *Bucks* 17 A8
Nash *Gwent* 15 F7
Nash *Heref/Worcs* 21 F8
Nash *Shrops* 21 E11
Nassington *Northants* 24 F2
Nasty *Herts* 18 B4
Natcott *Devon* 4 D2
Nateby *Cumb* 39 D10
Nateby *Lancs* 34 C3
Natland *Cumb* 39 F7
Naughton *Suffolk* 27 K3
Naunton *Glos* 16 B2
Naunton *Heref/Worcs* 22 H2
Naunton Beauchamp *Heref/Worcs* 22 G3
Naust *H'land* 54 B2
Navenby *Lincs* 33 D7
Navestock *Essex* 18 D5
Navestock Side *Essex* 18 D5
Navidale *H'land* 61 E10
Nawton *N Yorks* 41 G7
Nayland *Suffolk* 27 M3
Naze Park *Essex* 19 B12
Nazeing *Essex* 18 C4
Neacroft *Hants* 8 F3
Neap *Shetl'd* 64 D7
Near Sawrey *Cumb* 38 F6
Neasham *Durham* 40 D4
Neath *W Glam* 13 G11
Neath Abbey *W Glam* 13 G10
Neather Heage *Derby* 31 E12
Neatishead *Norfolk* 26 C6
Nebo *Dyfed* 20 F1
Nebo *Gwyn* 28 E4
Nebo *Gwyn* 29 E7
Necton *Norfolk* 26 E2
Nedd *H'land* 60 D3
Nedging *Suffolk* 27 K3
Nedging Tye *Suffolk* 27 K3
Needham *Norfolk* 27 G5
Needham Market *Suffolk* 27 K4
Needingworth *Cambs* 25 H4
Needlewood *Staffs* 31 H10
Neen Savage *Shrops* 21 E12
Neen Sollars *Shrops* 21 E12
Neenton *Shrops* 21 D11
Nefyn *Gwyn* 28 F3
Neilston *S'clyde* 47 D9
Neithrop *Oxon* 23 H8
Nelly Andrews Green *Powys* 21 A8
Nelson *Lancs* 35 C7
Nelson *Mid Glam* 14 E4
Nelson Village *Northum* 45 E10
Nemphlar *S'clyde* 48 E1
Nempnett Thrubwell *Avon* 15 H8
Nenthall *Cumb* 39 A10
Nenthead *Cumb* 39 A10
Nenthorn *Borders* 49 F9
Nercwys *Clwyd* 29 D11
Nerston *S'clyde* 47 D11
Nesbit *Northum* 49 F12
Nesfield *N Yorks* 35 B9
Ness *Ches* 30 C2
Nesscliff *Shrops* 30 H3
Neston *Ches* 30 B2
Neston *Wilts* 15 G11
Nether Alderley *Ches* 31 C7
Nether Blainslie *Borders* 49 E8
Nether Booth *Derby* 31 B10
Nether Brotherstone *Borders* 49 D7
Nether Broughton *Leics* 32 H4
Nether Burrow *Lancs* 39 H8
Nether Cassock *Dumf/Gal* 44 C1
Nether Cerne *Dorset* 7 F10
Nether Compton *Wilts* 7 D9
Nether Contlaw *Gramp* 59 G6
Nether Craigenputtock *Dumf/Gal* 43 C9
Nether Crimond *Gramp* 58 E6
Nether Dalgliesh *Borders* 48 H5
Nether Dallachy *Gramp* 58 A1
Nether Exe *Devon* 6 F3
Nether Fingland *S'clyde* 48 H2
Nether Glasslaw *Gramp* 58 B6
Nether Gribton *Dumf/Gal* 43 D10
Nether Handwick *Tayside* 53 C8
Nether Haugh *S Yorks* 36 G2
Nether Heyford *Northants* 23 F10
Nether Hindhope *Borders* 44 B6
Nether Howcleugh *S'clyde* 48 H3
Nether Kellet *Lancs* 39 H7
Nether Kinmundy *Gramp* 58 C8
Nether Kirkton *S'clyde* 47 D9
Nether Langwith *Derby* 32 C3
Nether Leask *Gramp* 58 D8
Nether Newton *S'clyde* 47 E10
Nether Padley *Derby* 31 B11
Nether Park *Gramp* 58 B7
Nether Pitforthie *Gramp* 59 J6
Nether Poppleton *N Yorks* 36 B3
Nether Silton *N Yorks* 40 F5
Nether Stowey *Som'set* 6 B5
Nether Thaineston *Gramp* 59 K4
Nether Urquhart *Fife* 53 F7
Nether Wallop *Hants* 8 B5
Nether Whitacre *Warwick* 22 C6
Nether Whitecleuch *S'clyde* 48 G1
Nether Worton *Oxon* 16 A5
Netheravon *Wilts* 8 A3
Netherbrae *Gramp* 58 B5
Netherburn *S'clyde* 48 E1
Netherbury *Dorset* 7 F8
Netherby *Cumb* 44 F2
Netherby *N Yorks* 35 C11
Nethercott *Devon* 4 B4
Netherend *Glos* 15 D9
Netherfield *E Sussex* 10 F6
Netherhampton *Wilts* 8 C3
Netherhowden *Borders* 49 D7
Netherlaw *Dumf/Gal* 43 G8
Netherley *Gramp* 59 H6
Nethermill *Dumf/Gal* 43 C11
Nethermill *Gramp* 58 D8
Nethermiln *Dumf/Gal* 43 A11
Nethermuir *Gramp* 58 C7
Netherplace *S'clyde* 47 D10
Netherseal *Derby* 22 A6
Netherthird *Dumf/Gal* 43 F8
Netherthird *S'clyde* 47 G10
Netherthong *W Yorks* 35 F10
Netherton *Central* 47 A10
Netherton *Devon* 5 J8
Netherton *Hants* 16 H5
Netherton *Heref/Worcs* 22 H3
Netherton *Mersey* 34 G2
Netherton *Northum* 45 B8
Netherton *S'clyde* 47 D12
Netherton *S'clyde* 48 D2
Netherton *Tayside* 52 B6
Netherton *Tayside* 59 L3
Netherton *W Midlands* 22 C3
Netherton *W Yorks* 35 E11
Netherton *W Yorks* 35 F10
Netherton *W Yorks* 35 F11
Netherton Burnfoot *Northum* 45 B8
Nethertown *Cumb* 38 D2
Nether Wasdale *Cumb* 38 E4
Netherwitton *Northum* 45 D9
Netherwood *S'clyde* 47 F11
Nethy Bridge *H'land* 57 G6
Netley *Hants* 8 E6
Netley Marsh *Hants* 8 E5
Nettlebed *Oxon* 17 E8
Nettlebridge *Som'set* 7 A10
Nettlecombe *Dorset* 7 G8
Nettlecombe *I of Wight* 9 H7
Nettleden *Herts* 17 C11
Nettleham *Lincs* 33 C7
Nettlestead *Kent* 10 C6
Nettlestead Green *Kent* 10 C5
Nettlestone *I of Wight* 9 G8
Nettlesworth *Durham* 45 H10
Nettleton *Lincs* 37 G9
Nettleton *Wilts* 15 F11
Netton *Devon* 5 L4
Netton *Wilts* 8 B3
Neuadd *Powys* 20 B6
Neuadd-ddu *Powys* 20 E5
Nevendon *Essex* 19 E7
Nevern *Dyfed* 12 C4
New Abbey *Dumf/Gal* 43 E10
New Aberdour *Gramp* 58 A6
New Addington *London* 18 H4
New Alresford *Hants* 9 C7
New Alyth *Tayside* 53 B7
New Annesley *Notts* 32 E2
New Ash Green *Kent* 10 B5
New Barnet *London* 18 D3
New Base *Kent* 18 G6
New Belses *Borders* 49 G8
New Berwick *Northum* 45 A9
New Bilton *Warwick* 23 E8
New Bolingbroke *Lincs* 33 D10
New Bradwell *Bucks* 23 H11
New Brampton *Derby* 32 C1
New Brancepath *Durham* 40 A2
New Bridge *Dumf/Gal* 43 D10
New Bridge *Humber* 36 E4
New Brighton *Clwyd* 29 D11
New Brighton *Mersey* 30 A2
New Brinsley *Notts* 32 E2

New Buckenham *Norfolk* **26** F 4
New Byth *Gramp* **58** B 6
New Cheriton *Hants* **9** C 7
New Clipstone *Notts* **32** D 3
New Costessey *Norfolk* **26** D 5
New Cowper *Cumb* **43** G12
New Cross *Dyfed* **20** E 2
New Cummock *S'clyde* **47** H11
New Deer *Gramp* **58** C 6
New Delaval *Northum* **45** E11
New Denham *Bucks* **17** F11
New Duston *Northants* **23** F10
New Earswick *N Yorks* **36** B 4
New Edlington *S Yorks* **36** G 3
New Elgin *Gramp* **56** D 8
New Ellerby *Humber* **37** C 9
New End *Heref/Worcs* **22** F 4
New Ferry *Mersey* **30** B 2
New Fryston *W Yorks* **36** D 2
New Galloway *Dumf/Gal* **43** D 7
New Grimsby *I of Scilly* **2** D 2
New Haggerston *Northum* **45** B11
New Hartley *Northum* **45** E11
New Haw *Surrey* **17** H11
New Hedges *Dyfed* **12** G 5
New Herrington *Tyne/Wear* **45** H11
New Hey *Gtr Man* **35** F 8
New Hinksey *Oxon* **16** D 6
New Holkham *Norfolk* **26** B 2
New Holland *Humber* **37** E 8
New Horton Grange *Tyne/Wear* **45** E10
New Hotel *Cumb* **38** E 5
New Houghton *Derby* **32** D 2
New Houghton *Norfolk* **26** C 1
New Houses *N Yorks* **39** H10
New Hutton *Cumb* **39** F 8
New Hythe *Kent* **10** B 6
New Inn *Dyfed* **13** C 8
New Inn *Gwent* **14** D 6
New Inn *Gwent* **15** D 8
New Inn *N Yorks* **39** H10
New Invention *Shrops* **21** E 8
New Kelso *H'land* **54** E 3
New Kendal *Gramp* **58** E 6
New Lambton *Tyne/Wear* **45** H11
New Lanark *S'clyde* **48** E 2
New Lane *Lancs* **34** F 3
New Leake *Lincs* **33** D11
New Leeds *Gramp* **58** B 7
New Lonton *Lancs* **34** E 4
New Luce *Dumf/Gal* **42** E 3
New Mains *Lothian* **49** A 8
New Mains *S'clyde* **48** F 1
New Mains of Ury *Gramp* **59** J 6
New Malden *London* **18** G 2
New Marske *Clevl'd* **40** C 6
New Marton *Shrops* **30** G 2
New Mill *W Yorks* **35** F10
New Mill *Wilts* **16** H 3
New Mills *Cornw'l* **2** D 6
New Mills *Derby* **31** B 8
New Mills *Powys* **20** B 6
New Milton *Hants* **8** F 4
New Mistley *Essex* **27** M4
New Moat *Dyfed* **12** D 4
New Ollerton *Notts* **32** C 4
New Pitsligo *Gramp* **58** B 6
New Polzeath *Cornw'l* **2** B 6
New Prestwick *S'clyde* **47** G 8
New Quay *Dyfed* **13** A 7
New Rackheath *Norfolk* **26** D 6
New Radnor *Powys* **21** F 7
New Rent *Cumb* **39** B 7
New Romney *Kent* **11** F 9
New Rossington *S Yorks* **36** G 4
New Row *Dyfed* **20** E 3
New Sarum *Wilts* **8** C 3
New Sauchie *Central* **52** H 4
New Scone *Tayside* **52** E 6
New Shawbost *W Isles* **63** B 4
New Shoreston *Northum* **45** D12
New Stevenston *S'clyde* **47** C12
New Swanage *Dorset* **8** H 2
New Tolsta *W Isles* **63** B 6
New Town *Berks* **17** G 7
New Town *Berks* **17** H 7
New Town *Dorset* **7** D11
New Town *Dorset* **8** D 2
New Town *E Sussex* **10** F 3
New Town *Lothian* **49** B 7
New Town *Wilts* **16** G 4
New Tredegar *Mid Glam* **14** D 5
New Valley *W Isles* **63** C 5
New Waltham *Humber* **37** G10
New Wimpole *Cambs* **25** K 4
New Winton *Lothian* **49** B 7
New Yatt *Oxon* **16** C 5
New York *Lincs* **33** E 9
New York *Tyne/Wear* **45** F11
Newark *Cambs* **24** E 3
Newark *Notts* **32** E 5
Newark *Orkney* **64** A 4
Newarthill *S'clyde* **48** C 1
Newbattle *Lothian* **48** C 6
Newbiggin *Cumb* **38** H 5
Newbiggin *Cumb* **39** B 7
Newbiggin *Cumb* **39** B 8
Newbiggin *Cumb* **44** H 4
Newbiggin *Durham* **39** B11
Newbiggin *Durham* **45** H 9
Newbiggin *N Yorks* **39** F11
Newbiggin *N Yorks* **39** G12
Newbiggin *Northum* **45** G 8
Newbiggin on Lune *Cumb* **39** E 9
Newbiggin-by-the-Sea *Northum* **45** D11
Newbigging *Borders* **49** D 8
Newbigging *S'clyde* **48** E 3
Newbigging *Tayside* **53** D 9
Newbigging *Tayside* **59** K 1
Newbold *Derby* **32** C 1
Newbold *Leics* **32** H 1
Newbold on Avon *Warwick* **23** D 8
Newbold on Stour *Warwick* **22** G 6
Newbold Pacey *Warwick* **22** F 6
Newbold Verdon *Leics* **23** B 8
Newborough *Cambs* **24** E 3
Newborough *Gwyn* **28** D 4
Newborough *Staffs* **31** H10
Newbottle *Northants* **23** H 8
Newbourne *Suffolk* **27** L 6
Newbridge *Clwyd* **29** F12
Newbridge *Cornw'l* **2** F 1
Newbridge *Cornw'l* **3** C10
Newbridge *Dyfed* **12** D 3
Newbridge *Gwent* **14** E 5
Newbridge *Hants* **8** E 4
Newbridge *I of Wight* **8** G 6
Newbridge *Lothian* **48** B 4
Newbridge on Wye *Powys* **20** F 6
Newbridge-on-Usk *Gwent* **15** E 7
Newbrough *Northum* **45** F 7
Newburgh *Borders* **48** G 6
Newburgh *Fife* **53** E 7
Newburgh *Gramp* **58** B 7
Newburgh *Gramp* **58** E 7
Newburgh Priory *N Yorks* **40** G 5
Newburn *Northum* **49** E11
Newburn *Tyne/Wear* **45** G10
Newbury *Berks* **16** G 5
Newby *Cumb* **39** C 8
Newby *N Yorks* **39** H 9
Newby *N Yorks* **40** D 5
Newby *N Yorks* **41** F10
Newby Bridge *Cumb* **38** G 6
Newby East *Cumb* **44** G 3
Newby West *Cumb* **44** H 2
Newby Wiske *N Yorks* **40** F 4
Newcastle *Gwent* **15** C 7
Newcastle *Shrops* **21** D 8
Newcastle Emlyn *Dyfed* **12** C 6
Newcastle upon Tyne *Tyne/Wear* **45** F10
Newcastleton *Borders* **44** D 3
Newcastle-under-Lyme *Staffs* **31** F 7
Newchapel *Dyfed* **12** C 6
Newchapel *Staffs* **31** E 7
Newchapel *Surrey* **10** D 2
Newchurch *Dyfed* **13** E 7
Newchurch *Gwent* **15** E 8
Newchurch *I of Wight* **9** H 7
Newchurch *Kent* **11** E 9
Newchurch *Lancs* **35** C 7
Newchurch *Lancs* **35** E 7
Newchurch *Powys* **21** G 7
Newchurch *Staffs* **31** H10
Newcott *Devon* **6** E 6
Newdigate *Surrey* **10** D 1
Newell Green *Berks* **17** G 9
Newenden *Kent* **11** E 7
Newent *Glos* **15** B10
Newerne *Glos* **15** D 9
Newfield *Dumf/Gal* **43** E12
Newfield *Dumf/Gal* **43** E 9
Newfield *Durham* **40** B 2
Newfield *Durham* **45** H10
Newfield *H'land* **56** B 3
Newfound *Hants* **9** A 7
Newgale *Dyfed* **12** E 2
Newgate *Norfolk* **26** A 3
Newgate Street *Herts* **18** C 3
Newgord *Shetl'd* **64** A 8
Newhall *Borders* **48** F 6
Newhall *Ches* **30** F 5
Newhall *Derby* **31** H11
Newhallpoint *H'land* **56** C 3
Newham *London* **18** F 4
Newham *Northum* **45** E12
Newham Hall *Northum* **45** D12
Newhaven *Derby* **31** D10
Newhaven *E Sussex* **10** H 3
Newholm *N Yorks* **41** D 8
Newhouse *S'clyde* **48** C 1
Newhouses *Northum* **45** E 8
Newick *E Sussex* **10** F 3
Newingreen *Kent* **11** D10
Newington *Kent* **11** B 7
Newington *Kent* **11** D10
Newington *Notts* **32** A 4
Newington *Oxon* **17** D 7
Newington *Shrops* **21** D 9
Newland *Glos* **15** C 9
Newland *Heref/Worcs* **22** G 2
Newland *Humber* **37** D 8
Newland *N Yorks* **36** E 5
Newlandhead *Tayside* **53** C 9
Newlands *Borders* **44** D 3
Newlands *Dumf/Gal* **43** C10
Newlands *Gramp* **56** E 8
Newlands *H'land* **56** E 3
Newlands *Northum* **45** G 9
Newlands of Geise *H'land* **61** A10
Newlyn *Cornw'l* **2** G 2
Newmachar *Gramp* **58** F 6
Newmains *S'clyde* **48** D 1
Newmarket *Suffolk* **25** J 7
Newmarket *W Isles* **63** C 5
Newmill *Borders* **44** B 3
Newmill *Cornw'l* **2** F 2
Newmill *Gramp* **58** B 2
Newmill of Inshewan *Tayside* **59** L 2
Newmillerdam *W Yorks* **35** F12
Newmills *Gwent* **15** D 8
Newmills *H'land* **56** C 2
Newmills *Lothian* **48** A 3
Newmills *Lothian* **48** C 4
Newmills of Boyne *Gramp* **58** B 3
Newmiln *Tayside* **52** D 6
Newmilns *S'clyde* **47** F10
Newnham *Glos* **15** C10
Newnham *Hants* **9** A 8
Newnham *Herts* **25** L 3
Newnham *Kent* **11** B 8
Newnham *Northants* **23** F 9
Newnham Bridge *Heref/Worcs* **21** E11
Newpark *Fife* **53** F 9
Newport *Devon* **4** C 4
Newport *Dyfed* **12** C 4
Newport *Essex* **25** M6
Newport *Glos* **15** E10
Newport *Gwent* **14** F 6
Newport *H'land* **61** E10
Newport *Humber* **36** D 6
Newport *I of Wight* **8** G 6
Newport *Norfolk* **26** D 8
Newport *Shrops* **30** H 6
Newport Pagnell *Bucks* **23** H12
Newport Sands *Dyfed* **12** C 4
Newport-on-Tay *Fife* **53** D 9
Newpound Common *W Sussex* **9** C12
Newquay *Cornw'l* **2** D 5
Newrow *Fife* **52** H 4
Newsam Green *W Yorks* **36** D 2
Newseat *Gramp* **58** D 4
Newsham *Lancs* **34** D 4
Newsham *N Yorks* **40** D 1
Newsham *N Yorks* **40** G 4
Newsholme *Humber* **36** D 5
Newsholme *Lancs* **35** B 7
Newsholme *W Yorks* **35** C 9
Newstead *Borders* **49** F 8
Newstead *Notts* **32** E 2
Newthorpe *N Yorks* **36** D 3
Newton *Borders* **49** G 8
Newton *Cambs* **24** D 5
Newton *Cambs* **25** K 5
Newton *Ches* **30** C 3
Newton *Ches* **30** C 4
Newton *Ches* **30** D 4
Newton *Clevl'd* **40** D 6
Newton *Cumb* **38** H 5
Newton *Derby* **32** D 2
Newton *Dorset* **7** E11
Newton *Dumf/Gal* **43** B12
Newton *Gramp* **56** C 7
Newton *Gramp* **58** C 8
Newton *Gtr Man* **35** G 8
Newton *Gwent* **14** F 6
Newton *H'land* **56** C 3
Newton *H'land* **56** E 1
Newton *H'land* **56** E 3
Newton *H'land* **60** D 4
Newton *H'land* **61** C12
Newton *Heref/Worcs* **15** A 7
Newton *Heref/Worcs* **21** G10
Newton *Lancs* **34** B 6
Newton *Lancs* **34** D 2
Newton *Lancs* **34** D 3
Newton *Lancs* **39** H 8
Newton *Lincs* **24** B 1
Newton *Lothian* **48** B 4
Newton *Mid Glam* **14** G 2
Newton *Norfolk* **26** D 1
Newton *Northants* **23** D12
Newton *Northum* **45** B 8
Newton *Northum* **45** G 8
Newton *Notts* **32** F 4
Newton *S'clyde* **48** F 2
Newton *Som'set* **6** B 5
Newton *Staffs* **31** H 9
Newton *Suffolk* **27** L 2
Newton *Tayside* **52** D 4
Newton *W Glam* **13** H 9
Newton *W Yorks* **36** D 2
Newton *Warwick* **23** D 8
Newton *Wilts* **8** D 4
Newton Abbot *Devon* **5** J 7
Newton Arlosh *Cumb* **43** F12
Newton Aycliffe *Durham* **40** C 3
Newton Bewley *Clevl'd* **40** C 5
Newton Blossomville *Bucks* **23** G12
Newton Bromswold *Northants* **25** J 1
Newton Burgoland *Leics* **23** A 7
Newton by Toft *Lincs* **33** B 7
Newton Ferrers *Devon* **5** L 4
Newton Flotman *Norfolk* **26** F 5
Newton Harcourt *Leics* **23** B 9
Newton Hill *Gramp* **59** H 7
Newton House *Gramp* **58** E 4
Newton Kyme *N Yorks* **36** C 2
Newton Longville *Bucks* **17** A 9
Newton Mearns *S'clyde* **47** D10
Newton Morrell *Durham* **40** D 3
Newton Mountain *Dyfed* **12** F 3
Newton Mulgrave *N Yorks* **41** D 8
Newton of Ardtoe *H'land* **50** A 4
Newton of Balcanquhal *Tayside* **52** F 6
Newton of Falkland *Fife* **53** F 7
Newton of Murcar *Gramp* **58** F 7
Newton of Ochtow *H'land* **60** G 5
Newton of Pitcairns *Tayside* **52** F 5
Newton on Trent *Lincs* **32** C 5
Newton Poppleford *Devon* **6** G 4
Newton Purcell *Oxon* **17** A 7
Newton Regis *Warwick* **22** A 6
Newton Reigny *Cumb* **39** B 7
Newton St. Boswells *Borders* **49** F 8
Newton St. Cyres *Devon* **4** F 7
Newton St. Faith *Norfolk* **26** D 5
Newton St. Loe *Avon* **15** H10
Newton St. Petrock *Devon* **4** E 3
Newton Solney *Derby* **31** H11
Newton Stacey *Hants* **8** B 6
Newton Stewart *Dumf/Gal* **42** E 5
Newton Toney *Wilts* **8** B 4
Newton Tracey *Devon* **4** C 4
Newton upon Ayr *S'clyde* **47** G 8
Newton upon Derwent *Humber* **36** B 5
Newton Valence *Hants* **9** C 8
Newtonairds *Dumf/Gal* **43** D 9
Newtongrange *Lothian* **48** C 6
Newtonhill *H'land* **56** E 2
Newton-le-Willows *Mersey* **34** H 4
Newton-le-Willows *N Yorks* **40** F 2
Newtonmill *Tayside* **59** L 3
Newtonmore *H'land* **57** J 3
Newton-on-Ouse *N Yorks* **36** A 3
Newton-on-Rawcliffe *N Yorks* **41** F 8
Newton-on-the-Moor *Northum* **45** C10
Newtown *Ches* **30** E 5
Newtown *Ches* **31** B 8
Newtown *Cornw'l* **2** G 4
Newtown *Cumb* **39** C 7
Newtown *Cumb* **44** G 2
Newtown *Cumb* **44** G 3
Newtown *Devon* **4** C 6
Newtown *Dorset* **8** G 2
Newtown *Glos* **15** A12
Newtown *Glos* **15** D10
Newtown *H'land* **55** J 7
Newtown *Hants* **16** H 6
Newtown *Hants* **8** D 4
Newtown *Hants* **8** E 4
Newtown *Hants* **9** D 7
Newtown *Hants* **9** E 7
Newtown *Heref/Worcs* **21** G10
Newtown *Heref/Worcs* **21** H11
Newtown *I of Man* **38** H 2
Newtown *I of Wight* **8** G 6
Newtown *Lancs* **34** E 4
Newtown *Northum* **45** A 8
Newtown *Northum* **45** C 8
Newtown *Northum* **49** F12
Newtown *Powys* **21** C 7
Newtown *Shrops* **30** G 3
Newtown *Staffs* **31** D 7
Newtown *Staffs* **31** D 9
Newtown *Wilts* **7** C12
Newtown Linford *Leics* **23** A 8
Newtown of Covington *S'clyde* **48** E 3
Newtown of Melrose *Gramp* **58** A 5
Newtyle *Tayside* **53** C 8
Neyland *Dyfed* **12** F 3
Nibley *Avon* **15** F10
Nicholashayne *Devon* **6** E 4
Nicholaston *W Glam* **13** H 8
Nickie's Hill *Cumb* **44** F 4
Nidd *N Yorks* **35** A11
Nigg *Gramp* **59** G 7
Nigg *H'land* **56** C 4
Nightcott *Som'set* **6** D 2
Nine Ashes *Essex* **18** D 6
Nine Mile Burn *Borders* **48** D 4
Ninebanks *Northum* **44** H 6
Ninfield *E Sussex* **10** G 6
Ningwood *I of Wight* **8** G 5
Nisbet *Borders* **49** G 9
Nithside *Dumf/Gal* **43** D10
Niton *I of Wight* **8** H 6
No Man's Heath *Ches* **30** E 4
No Man's Heath *Warwick* **22** A 6
No Man's Land *Devon* **4** E 7
Noak Hill *London* **18** E 5
Noblehouse *Borders* **48** D 5
Nobold *Shrops* **21** A10
Nobottle *Northants* **23** F10
Nocton *Lincs* **33** D 8
Noke *Oxon* **16** C 6
Nolton *Dyfed* **12** E 2
Nolton Haven *Dyfed* **12** E 2
Noneley *Shrops* **30** G 3
Nonington *Kent* **11** C11
Nook *Cumb* **39** G 8
Norbury *Ches* **30** E 4
Norbury *Derby* **31** F 9
Norbury *Shrops* **21** C 9
Norbury *Staffs* **30** H 6
Nordelph *Norfolk* **24** E 7
Norden *Gtr Man* **35** F 7
Norden Heath *Dorset* **8** H 1
Nordley *Shrops* **21** C12
Nore Marsh *Wilts* **16** F 2
Norham *Northum* **49** E11
Norley *Ches* **30** C 4
Norleywood *Hants* **8** F 5
Norman Cross *Cambs* **24** F 3
Normanby *Humber* **36** E 6
Normanby *N Yorks* **41** G 7
Normanby le Wold *Lincs* **37** H 9
Normanby-by-Spital *Lincs* **33** A 7
Normandy *Surrey* **9** A10
Norman's Bay *E Sussex* **10** G 6
Norman's Green *Devon* **6** F 4
Normansland *Wilts* **8** D 4
Normanton *Derby* **31** G11
* Normanton *Leics* **32** F 5
Normanton *Lincs* **32** F 6
Normanton *Notts* **32** E 4
Normanton *W Yorks* **36** E 2
Normanton le Heath *Leics* **23** A 7
Normanton on Soar *Notts* **32** H 2
Normanton on the Wolds *Notts* **32** G 3
Normanton on Trent *Notts* **32** C 5
Normos *Lancs* **34** C 2
Norney *Surrey* **9** B10
Norrington Common *Wilts* **15** H12
Norris Hill *Leics* **31** H11
North Anston *S Yorks* **32** B 2
North Aston *Oxon* **16** A 6
North Atrochie *Gramp* **58** D 7
North Baddesley *Hants* **8** D 5
North Ballachulish *H'land* **51** B 8
North Barrow *Som'set* **7** C 9
North Barrule *I of Man* **38** G 2
North Barsham *Norfolk* **26** B 2
North Benfleet *Essex* **19** E 7
*Normanton *Leics* **23** B 1
North Bersted *W Sussex* **9** F10
North Berwick *Lothian* **49** A 8
North Boarhunt *Hants* **9** E 7
North Bovey *Devon* **5** G 6
North Brackenridge *S'clyde* **47** E12
North Bradley *Wilts* **7** A12
North Brentor *Devon* **5** H 4
North Brewham *Som'set* **7** C10
North Buckland *Devon* **4** B 4
North Burlingham *Norfolk* **26** D 7
North Cadbury *Som'set* **7** D 9
North Carlton *Lincs* **32** B 6
North Carlton *Notts* **32** B 3
North Carrine *S'clyde* **46** H 2
North Cave *Humber* **36** D 6
North Cerney *Glos* **16** C 1
North Chapel *W Sussex* **9** C11
North Charford *Hants* **8** D 3
North Charlton *Northum* **45** A10
North Cheriton *Som'set* **7** D10
North Chideock *Dorset* **7** G 8
North Cliffe *Humber* **36** C 6
North Clifton *Notts* **32** C 5
North Coates *Lincs* **37** G11
North Cockerington *Lincs* **33** A10
North Coker *Som'set* **7** E 9
North Collingham *Notts* **32** D 5
North Common *E Sussex* **10** F 3
North Cornelly *Mid Glam* **14** F 2
North Corry *H'land* **50** B 5
North Cottown *Gramp* **58** F 5
North Cove *Suffolk* **26** F 8
North Cowshaw *Dumf/Gal* **43** C11
North Cowton *N Yorks* **40** E 3
North Crawley *Bucks* **23** H12
North Cray *London* **18** G 5
North Creake *Norfolk* **26** B 2
North Curry *Som'set* **7** D 7
North Dalton *Humber* **37** B 7
North Darley *Cornw'l* **3** B10
North Deighton *N Yorks* **35** B12
North Dell *W Isles* **63** A 6
North Drumboy *S'clyde* **47** D10
North Duffield *N Yorks* **36** C 5
North Elkington *Lincs* **33** A10
North Elmham *Norfolk* **26** C 3
North Elmsall *W Yorks* **36** F 3
North End *Avon* **15** G11
North End *Avon* **15** H 7
North End *Bucks* **17** A 9
North End *Bucks* **17** E 8
North End *Dorset* **7** D11
North End *Essex* **18** B 6
North End *Hants* **16** H 5
North End *Hants* **9** F 8
North End *Humber* **37** D10
North End *Lincs* **24** B 3
North End *Northum* **45** C 9
North End *Som'set* **6** D 6
North End *W Sussex* **9** E12
North Erradale *H'land* **54** B 1
North Esworthy *Devon* **6** D 2
North Fambridge *Essex* **19** D 8
North Fearns *H'land* **62** F 5
North Feorline *S'clyde* **46** F 4
North Ferriby *Humber* **37** E 7
North Frodingham *Humber* **37** B 8
North Galson *W Isles* **63** A 5
North Gluss *Shetl'd* **64** C 7
North Gorley *Hants* **8** E 3
North Gorrachie *Gramp* **58** B 5
North Green *Norfolk* **26** F 5
North Greenhill *Cumb* **44** F 3
North Grimston *N Yorks* **41** H 8
North Halling *Kent* **10** B 6
North Halls *S'clyde* **47** F11
North Hayling *Hants* **9** F 9
North Hazelrigg *Northum* **45** C12
North Heath *W Sussex* **9** D12
North Hill *Cornw'l* **3** B 9
North Hinksey *Oxon* **16** D 6
North Holmwood *Surrey* **10** C 1
North Hourat *S'clyde* **47** D 8
North Huish *Devon* **5** K 6
North Hykeham *Lincs* **32** D 6
North Johnson *Dyfed* **12** F 3
North Kelsey *Lincs* **37** G 8
North Kessock *H'land* **56** E 2
North Killingholme *Humber* **37** E 9

North Kilvington N Yorks 40 G4
North Kilworth Leics 23 D9
North Kinmundy Gramp 58 F6
North Kirkton Gramp 58 C8
North Kyme Lincs 33 E8
North Lancing W Sussex 10 G1
North Lee Bucks 17 C9
North Lees N Yorks 40 H3
North Leigh Oxon 16 C5
North Leverton with Habblesthorpe Notts 32 B5
North Littleton Heref/Worcs 22 G4
North Lopham Norfolk 27 G3
North Luffenham Leics 23 B12
North Lyham Northum 45 C12
North Marden W Sussex 9 D9
North Marston Bucks 17 B8
North Middleton Lothian 48 C6
North Middleton Northum 49 G12
North Molton Devon 4 C6
North Moor Humber 41 H12
North Moreton Oxon 16 E6
North Mundham W Sussex 9 F10
North Muskham Notts 32 D5
North Newbald Humber 37 C7
North Newington Oxon 23 H7
North Newnton Wilts 16 H2
North Newton Som'set 6 C6
North Nibley Glos 15 E10
North Oakley Hants 9 A7
North Ockendon London 18 E6
North Ormesby Clevl'd 40 C5
North Ormsby Lincs 33 A10
North Otterington N Yorks 40 F4
North Owersby Lincs 37 H8
North Perrott Som'set 7 E8
North Petherton Som'set 6 C6
North Petherwin Cornw'l 3 A10
North Pickenham Norfolk 26 E2
North Piddle Heref/Worcs 22 G3
North Poorton Dorset 7 F8
North Quarme Som'set 6 C3
North Queensferry Lothian 48 A4
North Radworthy Devon 4 C6
North Rauceby Lincs 33 F7
North Rigton N Yorks 35 B11
North Rode Ches 31 D7
North Roe Shetl'd 64 B7
North Runcton Norfolk 24 D7
North Sandwick Shetl'd 64 B8
North Scale Cumb 38 H4
North Scarle Lincs 32 D6
North Shawbost W Isles 63 B4
North Shian S'clyde 50 C6
North Shields Tyne/Wear 45 F11
North Shoebury Essex 19 E9
North Shore Lancs 34 D2
North Shortcleugh S'clyde 48 H2
North Side Cambs 24 E4
North Side Cumb 38 B2
North Skelton Clevl'd 41 C7
North Somercoates Lincs 37 G12
North Stainley N Yorks 40 G3
North Stainmore Cumb 39 D10
North Stoke Avon 15 G10
North Stoke Oxon 17 F7
North Stoke W Sussex 9 E11
North Street Berks 17 G7
North Street Hants 9 C8
North Sunderland Northum 45 D12
North Tamerton Cornw'l 4 F2
North Tawton Devon 4 F5
North Thoresby Lincs 37 G10
North Tidworth Wilts 8 A4
North Togston Northum 45 C10
North Tolsta W Isles 63 B6
North Tuddenham Norfolk 26 D3
North Walbottle Tyne/Wear 45 F10
North Walsham Norfolk 26 C6
North Waltham Hants 9 B7
North Warnborough Hants 9 A9
North Water Bridge Gramp 59 L4
North Watten H'land 61 B11
North Weald Bassett Essex 18 D5
North Wheatley Notts 32 B5
North Whilborough Devon 5 J7
North Wick Avon 15 H9
North Willingham Lincs 33 A8
North Wingfield Derby 32 D1
North Witham Lincs 32 H6
North Wootton Dorset 7 E10
North Wootton Norfolk 24 C7
North Wootton Som'set 7 B9
North Wraxall Wilts 15 G11
North Wroughton Wilts 16 F3
North Yardhope Northum 45 C7
Northallerton N Yorks 40 F4
Northam Devon 4 C3
Northam Hants 8 E6
Northampton Northants 23 F11
Northaw Herts 18 D3
Northborough Cambs 24 E3
Northbourne Kent 11 C12
Northbrook Hants 8 B6
Northchurch Herts 17 C10
Northcott Devon 5 G2
Northend Mersey 34 G2
Northend Warwick 23 G7
Northfield Borders 49 C11
Northfield Gramp 59 G6
Northfield W Midlands 22 D4
Northfleet Kent 10 A5
Northiam E Sussex 11 F7
Northill Beds 25 K3
Northington Hants 9 B7
Northlands Lincs 33 E10
Northleach Glos 16 C2
Northleigh Devon 6 G5
Northlew Devon 4 F4
Northmoor Oxon 16 D5
Northmoor Green or Moorland Som'set 7 C7
Northmuir Tayside 53 B8
Northney Hants 9 F9
Northolt London 18 E1
Northop Clwyd 29 C11
Northophall Clwyd 29 C12
Northorpe Lincs 24 B3
Northorpe Lincs 24 D2
Northorpe Lincs 37 G7
Northover Som'set 7 B8
Northover Som'set 7 D8
Northowram W Yorks 35 D10
Northport Dorset 8 G1
Northrepps Norfolk 26 B5
Northton W Isles 63 H1
Northtown Orkney 64 D3
Northway Glos 15 A12
Northway Som'set 6 C5
Northwich Ches 30 C5
Northwick Avon 15 F9
Northwold Norfolk 24 F8
Northwood I of Wight 8 G6
Northwood London 18 E1
Northwood Shrops 30 G3
Northwood Green Glos 15 C10
Norton Ches 30 B4
Norton Clevl'd 40 C5
Norton Glos 15 B11
Norton Gwent 15 B7
Norton Heref/Worcs 22 G2
Norton Heref/Worcs 22 G4
Norton I of Wight 8 G5
Norton N Yorks 41 H8
Norton Northants 23 F9
Norton Notts 32 C3
Norton Powys 21 F8
Norton S Yorks 36 F3
Norton Shrops 21 A11
Norton Shrops 21 D10
Norton Shrops 22 B1
Norton Suffolk 27 J3
Norton Wilts 15 F12
Norton Bavant Wilts 8 B1
Norton Bridge Staffs 31 G7
Norton Canes Staffs 22 A4
Norton Canon Heref/Worcs 21 H9
Norton Disney Lincs 32 D6
Norton East Staffs 22 A4
Norton Ferris Wilts 7 C11
Norton Fitzwarren Som'set 6 D5
Norton Green I of Wight 8 G5
Norton Hawkfield Avon 15 H9
Norton Heath Essex 18 D6
Norton in Hales Shrops 30 F5
Norton in the Moors Staffs 31 E7
Norton Juxta Twycross Leics 23 A7
Norton Lindsey Warwick 22 F6
Norton Malreward Avon 15 H9
Norton St. Philip Som'set 7 A11
Norton sub Hamdon Som'set 7 E8
Norton Subcourse Norfolk 26 F7
Norton Woodseats S Yorks 32 B1
Norton-le-Clay N Yorks 40 H4
Norwell Notts 32 D5
Norwell Woodhouse Notts 32 D5
Norwich Norfolk 26 E5
Norwick Shetl'd 64 A8
Norwood Derby 32 B2
Norwood Hill Surrey 10 D1
Noseley Leics 23 B10
Noss Mayo Devon 5 L4
Nosterfield N Yorks 40 G3
Nostie H'land 55 G2
Notgrove Glos 16 B2
Nottage Mid Glam 14 F2
Nottingham Notts 32 F3
Notton W Yorks 35 F12
Notton Wilts 15 G12
Nounsley Essex 19 C8
Noutard's Green Heref/Worcs 22 E2
Nox Shrops 21 A9
Nuffield Oxon 17 E7
Nun Monkton N Yorks 36 A3
Nunburnholme Humber 36 B6
Nuncargate Notts 32 E2
Nuneaton Warwick 23 C7
Nuneham Courtenay Oxon 16 D6
Nunlands Northum 49 D12
Nunnery Howe I of Man 38 H2
Nunney Som'set 7 B10
Nunnington N Yorks 41 G7
Nunnykirk Northum 45 D9
Nunsthorpe Humber 37 F10
Nunthorpe Clevl'd 40 D5
Nunton Wilts 8 C3
Nunwick N Yorks 40 H3
Nunwood Dumf/Gal 43 D10
Nursling Hants 8 D5
Nutbourne W Sussex 9 D12
Nutbourne W Sussex 9 F9
Nutfield Surrey 10 C2
Nuthall Notts 32 F2
Nuthampstead Herts 25 M5
Nuthurst W Sussex 10 E1
Nutley E Sussex 10 E3
Nutley Hants 9 B7
Nutwell S Yorks 36 G4
Nyetimber W Sussex 9 F10
Nyewood W Sussex 9 D9
Nymet Rowland Devon 4 E6
Nymet Tracey Devon 4 F6
Nympsfield Glos 15 D11
Nynehead Som'set 6 D5
Nythe Som'set 7 C7
Nyton W Sussex 9 E10
Oad Street Kent 11 B7
Oadby Leics 23 B9
Oakamoor Staffs 31 F9
Oakbank Lothian 48 C4
Oakdale Gwent 14 D5
Oake Som'set 6 D5
Oaken Staffs 22 B2
Oakenclough Lancs 34 B4
Oakengates Shrops 21 A12
Oakenholt Clwyd 29 C12
Oakenshaw Durham 40 A2
Oakenshaw W Yorks 35 D10
Oakfield Gwent 14 E6
Oakford Devon 6 D3
Oakford Dyfed 13 A8
Oakfordbridge Devon 6 D3
Oakgrove Ches 31 C8
Oakhanger Hants 9 C9
Oakhill Som'set 7 B9
Oakington Cambs 25 J5
Oaklands Gwyn 29 D7
Oakle Street Glos 15 C10
Oakley Beds 25 K1
Oakley Bucks 17 C7
Oakley Dorset 8 F2
Oakley Fife 52 H5
Oakley Hants 9 A7
Oakley Oxon 17 D8
Oakley Suffolk 27 H5
Oakley Green Berks 17 F10
Oakleypark Dyfed 20 D5
Oakridge Glos 15 D12
Oaksey Wilts 16 E1
Oakthorpe Leics 22 A6
Oaktree Hill N Yorks 40 E4
Oakwood Borders 49 G7
Oakwood Northum 45 F8
Oakwoodhill Surrey 9 B12
Oakworth W Yorks 35 C9
Oare Berks 16 G6
Oare Kent 11 B9
Oare Som'set 6 B2
Oare Wilts 16 H3
Oareford Som'set 6 B2
Oasby Lincs 33 F7
Oathlaw Tayside 53 B9
Oathlaw Tayside 59 M2
Oban H'land 55 K2
Oban S'clyde 50 E6
Obliston Gramp 58 B1
Oborne Dorset 7 D10
Obsdale H'land 56 C2
Occlestone Green Ches 30 D5
Occold Suffolk 27 H5
Ochil Hills Hosp Tayside 52 F6
Ochiltree S'clyde 47 G10
Ochtermuthill Tayside 52 E3
Ochtrelure Dumf/Gal 42 F2
Ockbrook Derby 32 G2
Ockham Surrey 17 H11
Ockle H'land 50 A3
Ockley Surrey 9 B12
Ocle Pychard Heref/Worcs 21 H11
Octon Humber 41 H10
Odcombe Som'set 7 E8
Odd Down Avon 15 H10
Oddendale Cumb 39 D8
Oddingley Heref/Worcs 22 F3
Oddington Glos 16 B3
Oddington Oxon 16 C6
Odell Beds 25 J1
Odie Orkney 64 B4
Odiham Hants 9 A9
Odstock Wilts 8 C3
Odstone Leics 23 A7
Offchurch Warwick 23 F7
Offenham Heref/Worcs 22 G4
Offerton Tyne/Wear 45 G11
Offham E Sussex 10 G3
Offham Kent 10 B5
Offord Cluny Cambs 25 J3
Offord D'Arcy Cambs 25 J3
Offton Suffolk 27 K4
Offwell Devon 6 F5
Ogbourne Maizey Wilts 16 G3
Ogbourne St. Andrew Wilts 16 G3
Ogbourne St. George Wilts 16 G3
Ogle Northum 45 E9
Ogmore Mid Glam 14 G2
Ogmore Vale Mid Glam 14 E3
Ogmore-by-Sea Mid Glam 14 G2
Okeford Fitzpaine Dorset 7 E11
Okehampton Devon 4 F5
Old Northants 23 E11
Old Aberdeen Gramp 59 G7
Old Alresford Hants 9 C7
Old Balkello Tayside 53 C8
Old Berwick Northum 45 A9
Old Blair Tayside 52 A4
Old Bolingbroke Lincs 33 D10
Old Bramhope N Yorks 35 C11
Old Brampton Derby 31 C11
Old Bridge of Urr Dumf/Gal 43 E8
Old Buckenham Norfolk 26 F4
Old Burghclere Hants 16 H6
Old Byland N Yorks 40 G6
Old Castleton Borders 44 D3
Old Clee Humber 37 F10
Old Cleeve Som'set 6 B4
Old Colwyn Clwyd 29 B8
Old Craighouse Dumf/Gal 43 C12
Old Dailly S'clyde 42 B3
Old Dalby Leics 32 H4
Old Deer Gramp 58 C7
Old Denaby S Yorks 36 G3
Old Dryburn Northum 49 E12
Old Edlington S Yorks 36 G3
Old Eldon Durham 40 B3
Old Ellerby Humber 37 C9
Old Fletton Cambs 24 F3
Old Goole Humber 36 E5
Old Hall Humber 37 E10
Old Heath Essex 19 B10
Old Heathfield E Sussex 10 F5
Old Hurst Cambs 25 H4
Old Hutton Cumb 39 F8
Old Kea Cornw'l 2 E5
Old Kilpatrick S'clyde 47 B9
Old Knebworth Herts 18 B2
Old Lakenham Norfolk 26 E5
Old Laxey I of Man 38 G2
Old Leake Lincs 33 E11
Old Lyham Northum 45 C12
Old Malton N Yorks 41 H8
Old Micklefield W Yorks 36 D2
Old Milton Hants 8 G4
Old Milverton Warwick 22 E6
Old Monkland S'clyde 47 C12
Old Montsale Essex 19 D10
Old Mousen Northum 45 C12
Old Netley Hants 8 E6
Old Newton Suffolk 27 J3
Old Orchardton Dumf/Gal 43 F9
Old Philpstoun Lothian 48 B3
Old Quarrington Durham 40 A3
Old Radford Notts 32 F3
Old Radnor Powys 21 F8
Old Rayne Gramp 58 E4
Old Romney Kent 11 E9
Old Scone Tayside 52 D6
Old Snydale W Yorks 36 E2
Old Sodbury Avon 15 F10
Old Somerby Lincs 33 G7
Old Stratford Northants 23 H11
Old Swan Mersey 30 A3
Old Tebay Cumb 39 E8
Old Thirsk N Yorks 40 G4
Old Town Cumb 39 A7
Old Town Cumb 39 G8
Old Town I of Scilly 2 D2
Old Town Northum 45 D7
Old Tupton Derby 32 D1
Old Warden Beds 25 L2
Old Weston Cambs 25 H2
Old Windsor Berks 17 G10
Old Wives Lees Kent 11 C9
Old Woking Surrey 17 H11
Oldany H'land 60 D3
Oldberrow Warwick 22 F5
Oldborough Devon 4 E6
Oldbury Shrops 21 C12
Oldbury W Midlands 22 C3
Oldbury Warwick 22 C6
Oldbury on the Hill Glos 15 E11
Oldbury-upon-Severn Avon 15 E9
Oldcastle Gwent 14 B6
Oldcastle Mid Glam 14 F2
Oldcotes Notts 32 A3
Oldfield Heref/Worcs 22 F2
Oldfield W Yorks 35 C8
Oldford Som'set 7 A11
Oldham Gtr Man 35 G8
Oldhamstocks Lothian 49 B10
Oldland Avon 15 G10
Oldmeldrum Gramp 58 E6
Oldnoth Gramp 58 D3
Oldpark Shrops 21 A12
Oldshore Beg H'land 60 B3
Oldshore More H'land 60 B3
Oldstead N Yorks 40 G5
Oldtown of Ord Gramp 58 B4
Oldway W Glam 13 H9
Oldways End Devon 4 D7
Oldwhat Gramp 58 C6
Oliver Borders 48 G4
Oliver's Battery Hants 8 C6
Ollaberry Shetl'd 64 C7
Ollerton Ches 30 C6
Ollerton Notts 32 C4
Ollerton Shrops 30 H5
Olmarch Dyfed 20 G2
Olney Bucks 23 G12
Olton W Midlands 22 D5
Olveston Avon 15 F9
Ombersley Heref/Worcs 22 F2
Ompton Notts 32 D4
Once Brewed Northum 44 F6
Onchan I of Man 38 H2
Onecote Staffs 31 E9
Onen Gwent 15 C7
Ongar Essex 18 D5
Ongar Street Heref/Worcs 21 F9
Onger Hill Norfolk 24 C7
Onibury Shrops 21 D10
Onich H'land 51 A7
Onllwyn W Glam 14 C2
Onneley Staffs 30 F6
Onslow Village Surrey 9 A11
Onthank S'clyde 47 E9
Openshaw Gtr Man 35 G7
Openwoodgate Derby 32 E1
Opinan H'land 54 C1
Opinan H'land 60 G1
Orange Lane Borders 49 E10
Orbost H'land 62 D2
Orby Lincs 33 C12
Orchard Hill Devon 4 C3
Orchard Portman Som'set 6 D6
Orcheston Wilts 8 B2
Orcop Heref/Worcs 15 B8
Orcop Hill Heref/Worcs 15 A8
Ord H'land 62 G5
Ordale Shetl'd 64 A8
Ordens Gramp 58 B4
Ordhead Gramp 58 F4
Ordie Gramp 59 G2
Ordiequish Gramp 58 B1
Ordsall Notts 32 B4
Ore E Sussex 11 G7
Oreton Shrops 21 D12
Orford Ches 30 A5
Orford Suffolk 27 K7
Organford Dorset 8 G1
Orgill Orkney 64 D1
Orgreave Staffs 22 A5
Orlestone Kent 11 E8
Orleton Heref/Worcs 21 F10
Orleton Heref/Worcs 21 F12
Orlingbury Northants 23 E12
Ormely Hall I of Man 38 F2
Ormesby Clevl'd 40 C5
Ormesby St. Margaret Norfolk 26 D8
Ormesby St. Michael Norfolk 26 D8
Ormiscaig H'land 60 G1
Ormiston Lothian 49 B7
Ormsaigbeg H'land 50 A2
Ormsaigmore H'land 50 A2
Ormsary House S'clyde 46 B2
Ormskirk Lancs 34 F3
Orosay W Isles 63 F5
Orphir Orkney 64 D2
Orpington London 18 G5
Orrell Gtr Man 34 G4
Orrell Mersey 34 G2
Orrell Post Gtr Man 34 G4
Orrock Fife 53 H7
Orsett Essex 18 F6
Orsett Heath Essex 18 F6
Orslow Staffs 22 A2
Orston Notts 32 F5
Orthwaite Cumb 38 B5
Orton Cumb 39 D8
Orton Northants 23 D11
Orton Longueville Cambs 24 F3
Orton on the Hill Leics 22 B6
Orton Waterville Cambs 24 F3
Orwell Cambs 25 K5
Osbaldeston Lancs 34 D5
Osbaldwick N Yorks 36 B4
Osbaston Leics 23 B7
Osbournby Lincs 24 B2
Osclay H'land 61 D11
Oscroft Ches 30 D4
Ose H'land 62 D2
Osgathorpe Leics 32 H2
Osgodby Lincs 33 A8
Osgodby N Yorks 36 D4
Osgodby N Yorks 41 G10
Oskaig H'land 62 D5
Oskamuil H'land 50 D2
Osmaston Derby 31 F10
Osmington Dorset 7 H10
Osmington Mills Dorset 7 H10
Osmondthorpe W Yorks 35 D12
Osmotherley N Yorks 40 E5
Ospringe Kent 11 B8
Ossett W Yorks 35 E11
Ossington Notts 32 D5
Ostend Essex 19 D9
Oswaldkirk N Yorks 40 G6
Oswaldtwistle Lancs 34 D6
Oswestry Shrops 30 G2
Otford Kent 10 B4
Otham Kent 11 C7
Othery Som'set 7 C7
Otley Suffolk 27 K5
Otley W Yorks 35 C10
Otter Ferry S'clyde 46 A4
Otterbourne Hants 8 D6
Otterburn N Yorks 35 A7
Otterburn Northum 45 D7
Otterburn Camp Northum 45 C7
Otterham Cornw'l 2 B2
Otterhampton Som'set 6 B6
Ottershaw Surrey 17 H11
Otterswick Shetl'd 64 B7
Otterton Devon 6 H4
Ottery St. Mary Devon 6 G4
Ottinge Kent 11 D10
Ottingham Humber 37 E10
Oughtershaw N Yorks 39 G11
Oughterside Cumb 43 H12
Oughtibridge S Yorks 35 H11
Oulston N Yorks 40 H6
Oulton Cumb 44 H1
Oulton Norfolk 26 C4
Oulton Staffs 31 G7
Oulton Suffolk 26 F8
Oulton W Yorks 35 D12
Oulton Broad Suffolk 26 F8
Oulton Street Norfolk 26 C5
Oundle Northants 25 G1
Ousby Cumb 39 B8
Ousdale H'land 61 E10
Ousden Suffolk 25 J8
Ousefleet Humber 36 E6
Ouston Durham 45 H10
Ouston Northum 44 H6

Ouston Northum 45 F9
Out Gate Cumb 38 E6
Out Newton Humber 37 E11
Out Rawcliffe Lancs 34 C3
Outchester Northum 45 C12
Outertown Orkney 64 D1
Outhgill Cumb 39 E10
Outlane W Yorks 35 E9
Outwell Norfolk 24 E6
Outwick Hants 8 D3
Outwood Surrey 10 D2
Outwood W Yorks 35 E12
Ovenden W Yorks 35 D9
Ovenscloss Borders 49 F7
Over Avon 15 F9
Over Cambs 25 H5
Over Ches 30 D5
Over Compton Dorset 7 E9
Over Dalgleish Borders 48 H5
Over Haddon Derby 31 D10
Over Hazlefield Dumf/Gal 43 G8
Over Kellet Lancs 39 H7
Over Kiddlington Oxon 16 B5
Over Norton Oxon 16 A4
Over Silton N Yorks 40 F5
Over Stowey Som'set 6 B5
Over Stratton Som'set 7 E8
Over Tabley Ches 30 B6
Over Wallop Hants 8 B4
Over Whitacre Warwick 22 C6
Over Whitton Borders 49 G10
Over Woodhouse Derby 32 C2
Overbister Orkney 64 B4
Overbury Heref/Worcs 22 H3
Overhall Gramp 58 C5
Overleigh Som'set 7 C8
Overley Green Warwick 22 F4
Overpool Ches 30 C3
Overscraig Hotel H'land 60 E5
Overseal Derby 22 A6
Overside Gramp 58 B8
Oversland Kent 11 B9
Overstone Northants 23 E11
Overstrand Norfolk 26 B5
Overthorpe Northants 23 H8
Overton Ches 30 C4
Overton Clwyd 30 F2
Overton Dumf/Gal 43 E10
Overton Gramp 58 D7
Overton Gramp 58 F6
Overton Hants 8 A6
Overton Lancs 34 A3
Overton N Yorks 36 B3
Overton S'clyde 47 D8
Overton W Glam 13 H8
Overton Bridge Clwyd 29 F12
Overtown Gramp 58 B7
Overtown Lancs 39 H8
Overtown S'clyde 48 D1
Overtown Wilts 16 F3
Oving Bucks 17 B8
Oving W Sussex 9 F10
Ovingdean E Sussex 10 H2
Ovingham Northum 45 G9
Ovington Durham 40 D2
Ovington Essex 27 L1
Ovington Hants 9 C7
Ovington Norfolk 26 E2
Ovington Northum 45 G9
Ower Hants 8 D5
Owermoigne Dorset 7 H11
Owler Bar Derby 31 B11
Owlerton S Yorks 32 A1
Owlswick Bucks 17 C8
Owmby Lincs 37 G8
Owmby-by-Spital Lincs 33 B7
Owslebury Hants 8 D6
Owston Leics 23 A11
Owston S Yorks 36 F3
Owston Ferry Humber 36 G6
Owstwick Humber 37 D10
Owthorpe Notts 32 G4
Oxborough Norfolk 24 E8
Oxcombe Lincs 33 C10
Oxen Park Cumb 38 F5
Oxenholme Cumb 39 F8
Oxenhope W Yorks 35 D9
Oxenrig Borders 49 E11
Oxenton Glos 16 A1
Oxenwood Wilts 16 H4
Oxford Oxon 16 D6
Oxford Cross Devon 4 B3
Oxhey Herts 18 D1
Oxhill Warwick 22 G6
Oxley W Midlands 22 B2
Oxley Green Essex 19 C9
Oxnam Borders 49 G9
Oxshott Surrey 17 H12
Oxspring S Yorks 35 G11
Oxted Surrey 10 C3
Oxton Borders 49 D7
Oxton N Yorks 36 C3
Oxton Notts 32 E3
Oxwich W Glam 13 H8
Oxwich Green W Glam 13 H8
Oykel Bridge H'land 60 G5
Oyne Gramp 58 E4
Oystermouth W Glam 13 H9
Ozleworth Glos 15 E11
Pabail Larach W Isles 63 D6
Pabail Uarach W Isles 63 D6
Packers Hill Dorset 7 E10
Packington Leics 23 A7
Packington Park W Midlands 22 D5
Padanaram Tayside 53 B9
Padbury Bucks 17 A8
Paddington London 18 F3
Paddlesworth Kent 11 D10
Paddock Wood Kent 10 D5
Paddockhaugh Gramp 56 D8
Paddockhole Dumf/Gal 44 E1
Paddolgreen Shrops 30 G4
Padfield Derby 35 G9
Padgate Ches 30 A5
Padiham Lancs 35 D7
Padog Gwyn 29 E8
Padside N Yorks 35 A10
Padstow Cornw'l 2 B6
Padworth Berks 17 G7
Page Bank Durham 40 B3
Pagham W Sussex 9 F10
Paglesham Essex 19 E9
Paible W Isles 63 G1
Paignton Devon 5 K8
Pailton Warwick 23 D8
Painscastle Powys 21 H7
Painshawfield Northum 45 G9
Painswick Glos 15 C12
Painter's Forstal Kent 11 B8
Paisley S'clyde 47 C9
Paithnick Gramp 58 B2
Pakefield Suffolk 26 F8
Pakenham Suffolk 27 J2
Pale Gwyn 29 G9
Palehouse Common E Sussex 10 F4
Palestine Hants 8 B4
Paley Street Berks 17 G9
Palgowan Dumf/Gal 42 C5
Palgrave Suffolk 27 G4
Palmarsh Kent 11 E10
Palmers Green London 18 E3
Palnackie Dumf/Gal 43 F9
Palnure Dumf/Gal 42 E5
Palterton Derby 32 C2
Pamber End Hants 17 H7
Pamber Green Hants 17 H7
Pamber Heath Hants 17 H7
Pamphill Dorset 8 F1
Pampisford Cambs 25 K6
Panborough Som'set 7 B8
Panbride Tayside 53 D10
Pancrasweek Devon 4 E2
Pandy Clwyd 29 G11
Pandy Gwent 15 B7
Pandy Gwyn 20 B2
Pandy Powys 20 B5
Pandy Tudur Clwyd 29 D8
Panfield Essex 19 A7
Pangbourne Berks 17 F7
Panlands Dumf/Gal 43 C11
Pannal N Yorks 35 B11
Pannancih Gramp 59 H1
Pant Shrops 30 H1
Pant Mawr Powys 20 D4
Pant y Goitre Gwent 15 C7
Pant-glas Gwyn 28 E4
Pantglas Shrops 21 C8
Pantgwyn Dyfed 12 B6
Pantgwyn Dyfed 13 D9
Pant-lasau W Glam 13 G10
Panton Lincs 33 B9
Pant-perthog Gwyn 20 B3
Pant-y-dwr Powys 20 E5
Pant-y-ffrid Powys 21 B7
Pantyffynnon Dyfed 13 F9
Pantygasseg Gwent 14 D6
Pantymenyn Dyfed 12 D5
Pantymwyn Clwyd 29 D11
Pant-yr-awel Mid Glam 14 E3
Panxworth Norfolk 26 D6
Papcastle Cumb 38 B3
Papple Lothian 49 B8
Papplewick Notts 32 E3
Papworth Everard Cambs 25 J4
Papworth St. Agnes Cambs 25 J4
Par Cornw'l 3 D8
Parbold Lancs 34 F4
Parbrook Som'set 7 C9
Parc Gwyn 29 G8
Parcllyn Dyfed 12 B6
Pardshaw Cumb 38 C3
Parham Suffolk 27 J6
Park Dumf/Gal 43 B10
Park Gramp 59 G5
Park S'clyde 50 C6
Park Corner E Sussex 10 D4
Park Corner Oxon 17 E8
Park End Clevl'd 40 C5
Park End Northum 45 E7
Park Gate Hants 9 E7
Park Nook Cumb 44 F4
Parkdargue Gramp 58 C4
Parkend Cumb 38 A5
Parkend Glos 15 D9
Parkeston Essex 27 M5
Parkgate Ches 30 B1
Parkgate Dumf/Gal 43 C11
Parkgate Surrey 10 D1
Parkgatestone Borders 48 F4
Parkham Devon 4 D3
Parkham Ash Devon 4 D2
Parkhead Gramp 56 F8
Parkhill House Gramp 58 F6
Parkhouse Gwent 15 D8
Parkhurst I of Wight 8 G6
Parkmill W Glam 13 H9
Parkneuk Gramp 59 K5
Parkside Clwyd 30 E3
Parkstone Dorset 8 G2
Parley Cross Dorset 8 F2
Parracombe Devon 4 B5
Parrah Green Ches 30 F6
Parrog Dyfed 12 C4
Parsley Hay Derby 31 D10
Parson Drove Cambs 24 E5
Parson's Heath Essex 19 A10
Partick S'clyde 47 C10
Partington Gtr Man 34 H6
Partington Haven Humber 37 E10
Partney Lincs 33 C11
Parton Cumb 38 C2
Parton Dumf/Gal 43 E8
Parton Glos 15 B12
Partridge Green W Sussex 10 F1
Parwich Derby 31 E10
Passenham Northants 23 H11
Passfield Hants 9 C9
Paston Norfolk 26 B6
Patchacott Devon 4 F3
Patcham E Sussex 10 G2
Patching W Sussex 9 E12
Patchole Devon 4 B5
Patchway Avon 15 F9
Pateley Bridge N Yorks 35 A10
Paternoster Heath Essex 19 B9
Path of Condie Tayside 52 F5
Pathe Som'set 7 C7
Pathead Fife 53 H8
Pathead Lothian 48 C6
Pathhead S'clyde 47 H11
Pathstruie Tayside 52 F5
Patna S'clyde 47 H9
Patney Wilts 16 H2
Patrick I of Man 38 G1
Patrick Brompton N Yorks 40 F2
Patricroft Gtr Man 34 G6
Patrington Humber 37 E10
Patrixbourne Kent 11 C10
Patterdale Cumb 38 D6
Pattieshill Cumb 44 F3
Pattingham Staffs 22 B2
Pattishall Northants 23 G10
Pattiswick Green Essex 19 B8
Paul Cornw'l 2 G2
Paulerspury Northants 23 G10
Paull Humber 37 E9
Paulton Avon 7 A10
Pauperhaugh Northum 45 C9
Pavenham Beds 25 K1
Pawlett Som'set 6 B6
Pawston Northum 49 F11
Paxford Glos 22 H5
Paxton Borders 49 D12
Payhembury Devon 6 F4
Paythorne Lancs 35 B7
Peacehaven E Sussex 10 H3
Peak Dale Derby 31 C9
Peak Forest Derby 31 B9
Peakirk Cambs 24 E3
Peanmeanach H'land 55 L1
Pearsie Tayside 59 L1
Pearsons Green Kent 10 D6
Pease Pottage W Sussex 10 E1
Peasedown St. John Avon 7 A10
Peasemore Berks 16 F5
Peasenhall Suffolk 27 H6
Peaslake Surrey 9 B12
Peasley Cross Mersey 34 H4
Peasmarsh E Sussex 11 F7
Peaston Lothian 49 C7
Peaston Bank Lothian 49 C7
Peat Inn Fife 53 F9
Peathill Gramp 58 A7
Peatling Magna Leics 23 C9
Peatling Parva Leics 23 C9
Peaton Shrops 21 D10
Pebmarsh Essex 27 M2
Pebworth Heref/Worcs 22 G5
Peckett Well W Yorks 35 D8
Peckforton Ches 30 E4
Peckham London 18 F3
Peckleton Leics 23 B8
Pedderhill Cumb 44 F3
Pedlinge Kent 11 E10
Pedmore W Midlands 22 D3
Pedwell Hants 8 C8
Pedwell Som'set 7 C7
Peebles Borders 48 E5
Peel I of Man 38 G1
Peel Common Hants 9 F7
Peening Quarter Kent 11 E7
Pegsdon Beds 25 M2
Pegswood Northum 45 D10
Peinaha H'land 62 B3
Peinchorran H'land 62 E4
Peinlich H'land 62 B3
Peinmore H'land 62 C4
Pelcomb Cross Dyfed 12 E3
Peldon Essex 19 B9
Pelsall W Midlands 22 B4
Pelton Durham 45 H10
Pelton Fell Durham 45 H10
Pelutho Cumb 43 G12
Pelynt Cornw'l 3 D9
Pemberton Dyfed 13 G8
Pemberton Gtr Man 34 G4
Pembrey Dyfed 13 G7
Pembridge Heref/Worcs 21 G9
Pembroke Dyfed 12 G3
Pembroke Dock Dyfed 12 G3
Pembury Kent 10 D5
Pen Rhiwfawr W Glam 13 F10
Penally Dyfed 12 G5
Penalt Gwent 15 C8
Penalt Heref/Worcs 15 A9
Penare Cornw'l 3 F7
Penarth S Glam 14 G5
Pen-bont-rhyd-y-beddau Dyfed 20 D2
Penbryn Dyfed 12 B6
Pencader Dyfed 13 C8
Pen-cae Dyfed 13 A7
Pencaenewydd Gwyn 28 F3
Pencarnisiog Gwyn 28 C3
Pencarreg Dyfed 13 C8
Pencelli Powys 14 B4
Penclawdd W Glam 13 G9
Pencoed Mid Glam 14 F3
Pencombe Heref/Worcs 21 G11
Pencoyd Heref/Worcs 15 B8
Pencraig Heref/Worcs 15 B9
Pencraig Powys 29 G9
Pendeen Cornw'l 2 F1
Penderyn Mid Glam 14 C3
Pendine Dyfed 12 F6
Pendlebury Gtr Man 34 G6
Pendleton Gtr Man 35 G7
Pendleton Lancs 34 C6
Pendock Heref/Worcs 15 A11
Pendogett Cornw'l 3 B7
Pendomer Som'set 7 E8
Pendoylan S Glam 14 G4
Pendre Mid Glam 14 F2
Penegoes Powys 20 B3
Penfeidir Dyfed 12 D2
Pen-ffordd Dyfed 12 E4
Pen-ffordd Dyfed 13 C8
Pengam Gwent 14 E5
Penge London 18 G3
Pengelly Cornw'l 3 A8
Pengenffordd Powys 14 A5
Pengover Green Cornw'l 3 C10
Pen-groes oped Gwent 14 D6
Penhale Cornw'l 2 H4
Penhalurick Cornw'l 2 F4
Penhill Wilts 16 E2
Penhow Gwent 15 E7
Penhurst E Sussex 10 F6
Peniarth Gwyn 20 B2
Penicuik Lothian 48 C5
Peniel Dyfed 13 E8
Penifiler H'land 62 D4
Peninver S'clyde 46 G3
Penisar-waun Gwyn 28 D5
Penistone S Yorks 35 G11
Penketh Ches 30 A4
Penkill S'clyde 42 B3
Penkiln Dumf/Gal 42 G6
Penkridge Staffs 22 A3
Penley Clwyd 30 F3
Penllergaer W Glam 13 G9
Pen-llyn Gwyn 28 B3
Penllyn S Glam 14 G3
Penmachno Gwyn 29 E7
Penmaen W Glam 13 H8
Penmaenen Gwyn 28 C6
Penmaenmawr Gwyn 28 C6
Penmaenpool Gwyn 28 H6
Penmaenrhos Clwyd 29 B8
Penmark S Glam 14 G4
Penmon Gwyn 28 B6
Penmore Mill H'land 50 B1
Penmorfa Gwyn 28 F5
Penmynydd Gwyn 28 C4
Penn Bucks 17 E10
Penn Street Bucks 17 E10
Pennal Gwyn 20 B3
Pennan Gramp 58 A6
Pennant Clwyd 29 G9
Pennant Dyfed 13 A8
Pennant Gwyn 29 D7
Pennant Powys 20 C4
Pennant-Melangell Powys 29 H9
Pennard W Glam 13 H9
Pennerley Shrops 21 C9
Pennington Cumb 38 G5
Pennington Hants 8 G5
Penorth Powys 14 B4
Penny Bridge Cumb 38 G5
Penny Hill Lincs 24 C5
Pennyghael H'land 50 E3
Pennyglen S'clyde 47 H7
Pennygown H'land 50 C3
Pennymoor Devon 4 E7
Pennywell Tyne/Wear 45 G11
Penparc Dyfed 12 B5
Penparc Dyfed 12 D2
Penparcau Dyfed 20 D2
Penpelleni Gwent 14 D6
Penpillick Cornw'l 3 D8
Penpoint Cornw'l 3 B8
Penpol Cornw'l 2 F5
Penpont Dumf/Gal 43 B9
Penpont Powys 14 A3
Penrherber Dyfed 12 C6
Penrhiw Dyfed 12 C6
Penrhiwceiber Mid Glam 14 E4
Penrhiw-goch Dyfed 13 E9
Penrhiwllan Dyfed 13 C7
Penrhiwpal Dyfed 13 B7
Penrhos Gwent 15 C7
Penrhos Gwyn 28 G3
Penrhos Powys 14 C1
Penrhos-garnedd Gwyn 28 C5
Penrhyn Gwyn 28 A3
Penrhyn Bay Gwyn 29 B7
Penrhyn-coch Dyfed 20 D2
Penrhyndeudraeth Gwyn 28 F5
Penrhynside Gwyn 29 B7
Penrice W Glam 13 H8
Penrieth Dyfed 12 C6
Penrith Cumb 39 B7
Penrose Cornw'l 2 C6
Penruddock Cumb 38 B6
Penryn Cornw'l 2 F5
Pensarn Clwyd 29 B9
Pen-Sarn Dyfed 13 E7
Pensax Heref/Worcs 22 E1
Pensby Mersey 30 B1
Penselwood Som'set 7 C11
Pensford Avon 15 H9
Penshaw Tyne/Wear 45 H11
Penshurst Kent 10 D4
Pensilva Cornw'l 3 C10
Penston Lothian 49 B7
Pentewan Cornw'l 3 E7
Pentir Gwyn 28 D5
Pentire Cornw'l 2 D5
Pentire Mid Glam 14 E3
Pentireg Cornw'l 2 B6
Pentlepoir Dyfed 12 F5
Pentlow Essex 27 L1
Pentney Norfolk 24 D8
Penton Mewsey Hants 8 A5
Pentraeth Gwyn 28 B5
Pentre Clwyd 29 D10
Pentre Clwyd 29 F12
Pentre Powys 20 D6
Pentre Powys 21 B8
Pentre Powys 21 C8
Pentre Shrops 21 A9
Pentre Berw Gwyn 28 C4
Pentre Dolau-Honddu Powys 20 H5
Pentre Gwenlais Dyfed 13 E9
Pentre Gwynfryn Gwyn 28 G5
Pentre Halkyn Clwyd 29 C11
Pentre llwyn-llwyd Powys 20 G5
Pentre Meyrick S Glam 14 G3
Pentre Saron Clwyd 29 D9
Pentrebach Dyfed 13 B9
Pentrebach Mid Glam 14 D4
Pentre-bach Powys 14 A2
Pentrebach W Glam 13 F9
Pentrebeiridd Powys 21 A7
Pentre-bont Gwyn 29 E7
Pentre-cagal Dyfed 13 C7
Pentre-celyn Clwyd 29 E10
Pentre-cwrt Dyfed 13 C7
Pentre-dwfr Clwyd 29 F11
Pentre-dwr W Glam 13 G10
Pentrefelin Dyfed 13 E9
Pentrefelin Gwyn 28 A4
Pentrefelin Gwyn 29 C7
Pentrefoelas Clwyd 29 E8
Pentre-galar Dyfed 12 D5
Pentregat Dyfed 13 B7
Pentreheyling Shrops 21 C8
Pentre-Isaf Clwyd 29 C8
Pentre-poeth Gwent 14 F6
Pentre'r felin Gwyn 28 F5
Pentre'r-felin Dyfed 13 B9
Pentre'r-felin Powys 14 A3
Pentre-tafarn-y-fedw Gwyn 29 D7
Pentre-ty-gwyn Dyfed 13 C11
Pentre-uchaf Clwyd 29 C10
Pentrich Derby 32 E1
Pentridge Dorset 8 D2
Pent-twyn Gwent 15 C8
Pentwyn Mid Glam 14 D4
Pentyrch Mid Glam 14 F4
Penuchadre Mid Glam 14 G2
Penuwch Dyfed 20 F2
Penwithick Cornw'l 3 D7
Penwood Hants 16 H5
Penwyllt Powys 14 C2
Penybanc Dyfed 13 E9
Pen-y-banc Dyfed 13 F9
Pen-y-bont Clwyd 29 H11
Penybont Powys 21 F7
Pen-y-bont-fawr Powys 29 H10
Pen-y-bryn Dyfed 12 C5
Pen-y-cae Clwyd 29 F12
Pen-y-cae Powys 14 C2
Pen-y-cae-mawr Gwent 15 E7
Pen-y-clwdd Gwent 15 D7
Pen-y-coedcae Mid Glam 14 F4
Penycwm Dyfed 12 E2
Pen-y-fai Mid Glam 14 F2
Penyffordd Clwyd 29 D12
Pen-y-gamedd Gwyn 28 C5
Pen-y-garnedd Powys 29 H10
Penygraig Mid Glam 14 E3
Penygroes Dyfed 12 C5
Penygroes Dyfed 13 F9
Penygroes Gwyn 28 E4
Pen-y-groes S Glam 14 F5
Pen-y-groeslon Gwyn 28 G2
Pen-y-Gwyrd Gwyn 28 E6
Penyrheol Gwent 14 E5
Pen-yr-Heolgerrig Mid Glam 14 D4
Penyrynys Powys 14 B2
Penysarn Gwyn 28 A4
Pen-y-stryt Clwyd 29 E11
Penywaun Mid Glam 14 D3
Penzance Cornw'l 2 G2
Peopleton Heref/Worcs 22 G3
Peover Heath Ches 30 C6
Peper Harow Surrey 9 B10
Peplow Shrops 30 H5
Peppermoor Northum 45 B10
Perceton S'clyde 47 E8
Percie Gramp 59 H3
Percyhorner Gramp 58 A7
Perkinsville Durham 45 H10
Perranarworthal Cornw'l 2 F5
Perranporth Cornw'l 2 D5
Perranuthnoe Cornw'l 2 G3
Perranwell Cornw'l 2 F5
Perranwell Station Cornw'l 2 F5
Perranzabuloe Cornw'l 2 D5
Perry Cambs 25 J2
Perry Barr W Midlands 22 C4
Perry Green Herts 18 B4
Perry Street Kent 10 A5
Pershore Heref/Worcs 22 G3
Pertenhall Beds 25 J2
Perth Tayside 52 E6
Perton Staffs 22 B2
Pertwood Wilts 7 C12
Peter Tavy Devon 5 H4
Peterborough Cambs 24 F3
Peterburn H'land 54 B1
Peterchurch Heref/Worcs 21 H9
Petercutter Gramp 59 G6
Peterhead Gramp 58 C8
Peterlee Durham 40 A4
Peter's Green Herts 18 B2
Peters Marland Devon 4 E3
Petersfield Hants 9 D9
Peterstone Wentlooge Gwent 14 F6
Peterston-super-Ely S Glam 14 G4
Peterstow Heref/Worcs 15 B9
Petham Kent 11 C10
Petrockstowe Devon 4 E4
Pett E Sussex 11 G7
Pettaugh Suffolk 27 J5
Petterden Tayside 53 C9
Pettinain S'clyde 48 E2
Pettistree Suffolk 27 K6
Petton Devon 6 D4
Petton Shrops 30 G3
Petts Wood London 18 G4
Petty Gramp 58 D5
Pettycur Fife 48 A5
Pettymuck Gramp 58 E6
Petworth W Sussex 9 D11
Pevensey E Sussex 10 H5
Pevensey Bay E Sussex 10 H5
Pewsey Wilts 16 H3
Pheasants Bucks 17 E9

Pheasant's Hill Bucks 17 E9
Philham Devon 4 D1
Philiphaugh Borders 49 G7
Phillack Cornw'l 2 F3
Philleigh Cornw'l 2 F6
Phil-stoun Lothian 48 B3
Phocle Green Heref/Worcs 15 B9
Phoenix Green Hants 17 H8
Phones H'land 57 K3
Phort Mholain W Isles 63 C6
Phurt I of Man 38 F2
Pica Cumb 38 C3
Piccott's End Herts 17 C11
Pickburn S Yorks 36 F3
Pickering N Yorks 41 G8
Picket Piece Hants 8 A5
Picket Post Hants 8 E3
Pickhill N Yorks 40 G4
Picklescott Shrops 21 B10
Pickletillem Fife 53 E9
Pickmere Ches 30 C5
Pickney Som'set 6 C5
Pickwell Devon 4 B3
Pickwell Leics 23 A11
Pickworth Leics 24 D1
Pickworth Lincs 24 B1
Picton Ches 30 C3
Picton N Yorks 40 D4
Piddinghoe E Sussex 10 H3
Piddington Bucks 17 E9
Piddington Northants 23 G11
Piddington Oxon 17 B7
Piddlehinton Dorset 7 F10
Piddletrenthide Dorset 7 F10
Pidley Cambs 25 H4
Piercebridge Durham 40 D2
Pierowall Orkney 64 A2
Pigdon Northum 45 D9
Pikehall Derby 31 D10
Pilgrims Hatch Essex 18 D6
Pilham Lincs 32 A6
Pill Avon 15 G8
Pillaton Cornw'l 3 C10
Pillerton Hersey Warwick 22 G6
Pillerton Priors Warwick 22 G6
Pilleth Powys 21 F8
Pilley Hants 8 F5
Pilley S Yorks 35 G12
Pillhead Devon 4 C3
Pilling Lancs 34 B3
Pilling Lane Lancs 34 B3
Pillowell Glos 15 D9
Pillwell Dorset 7 D11
Pilmuir Borders 44 B3
Pilmuir Gramp 59 H5
Pilning Avon 15 F9
Pilsbury Derby 31 D9
Pilsdon Dorset 7 F7
Pilsley Derby 31 C11
Pilsley Derby 32 D2
Pilton Leics 23 B12
Pilton Northants 25 G1
Pilton Som'set 7 B9
Pilton Green W Glam 13 H8
Pimperne Dorset 7 E12
Pinchbeck Lincs 24 C3
Pinchbeck Bars Lincs 24 C3
Pinchbeck West Lincs 24 C3
Pinclanty S'clyde 42 B3
Pinfold Lancs 34 F3
Pinhoe Devon 6 G3
Pinkneys Green Berks 17 F9
Pinley Green Warwick 22 E5
Pinminnoch S'clyde 42 B3
Pinmore S'clyde 42 B3
Pinmore Mains S'clyde 42 C3
Pinn Devon 6 G4
Pinner London 18 E1
Pinvin Heref/Worcs 22 G3
Pinwherry S'clyde 42 C3
Pinxton Derby 32 E2
Pipe and Lyde Heref/Worcs 21 H10
Pipe Gate Shrops 30 F6
Pipehill Staffs 22 A4
Piperhill H'land 56 E4
Pipers Pool Cornw'l 3 A9
Pipewell Northants 23 D11
Pippacott Devon 4 B4
Pipton Powys 14 A5
Pirbright Surrey 17 H10
Pirnie Borders 49 G9
Pirnmill S'clyde 46 E4
Pirton Heref/Worcs 22 G2
Pirton Herts 18 A2
Pishill Oxon 17 E8
Pistyll Gwyn 28 F3
Pitagowan Tayside 52 A3
Pitblae Gramp 58 A7
Pitcairlie Farm Fife 53 F7
Pitcairn Tayside 52 B4
Pitcairngreen Tayside 52 D5
Pitcaple Gramp 58 E5
Pitch Green Bucks 17 D8
Pitch Place Surrey 9 A11
Pitchcombe Glos 15 D11
Pitchcott Bucks 17 B8
Pitchford Shrops 21 B10
Pitcombe Som'set 7 C10
Pitcorthie Fife 53 F10
Pitcox Lothian 49 B9
Pitdrichie Gramp 59 J5
Pitfichie Gramp 58 F4
Pitfour Castle Fife 53 E7
Pitkevy Fife 53 G7
Pitlessie Fife 53 F8
Pitlochry Tayside 52 A4
Pitmachie Gramp 58 E4
Pitmain H'land 57 J3
Pitmedden Gramp 58 E6
Pitminster Som'set 6 D6
Pitmuies Tayside 53 B10
Pitmunie Gramp 58 F4
Pitnacree Tayside 52 B4
Pitney Som'set 7 C8
Pitroddie Fife 53 E7
Pitscottie Fife 53 F9
Pitsea Essex 19 E7
Pitsford Northants 23 E11
Pitstone Bucks 17 C10
Pitstone Green Bucks 17 C10
Pittarrow Gramp 59 K5
Pittendreich Gramp 56 D7
Pittenraill H'land 61 F7
Pittenweem Fife 53 G10
Pittington Durham 40 A3
Pittodrie Gramp 58 E4
Pitton Wilts 8 C4
Pittswood Kent 10 C5
Pittulie Gramp 58 A7
Pity Me Durham 40 A3
Pity Me Northum 45 E7
Pixey Green Suffolk 27 H5
Pixham Surrey 10 C1
Pixley Heref/Worcs 21 H12
Place Fell Cumb 38 D6
Place Newton N Yorks 41 H9
Plaidy Gramp 58 B5
Plain Dealings Dyfed 12 E4
Plains S'clyde 48 C1
Plainsfield Som'set 6 C5
Plaish Shrops 21 C10
Plaistow W Sussex 9 C11
Plaistow Street Surrey 10 D3
Plaitford Hants 8 D4
Plas Newydd Clwyd 29 F11
Plastow Green Hants 16 H6
Plas-yn-Cefn Clwyd 29 C9
Platt Kent 10 B5
Platt Bridge Gtr Man 34 G5
Platt's Heath Kent 11 C7
Plawsworth Durham 45 H11
Plaxtol Kent 10 C5
Play Hatch Oxon 17 F8
Playden E Sussex 11 F8
Playford Suffolk 27 K5
Playing Place Cornw'l 2 E5
Playley Green Glos 15 A10
Plealey Shrops 21 B9
Plean Central 52 H3
Pleasance Fife 53 F7
Pleasington Lancs 34 E5
Pleasley Derby 32 D2
Plenmeller Northum 44 G5
Pleshey Essex 18 B6
Plockton H'land 54 F2
Plocrapool W Isles 63 H2
Ploughlands Borders 49 E10
Plowden Shrops 21 D9
Ploxgreen Shrops 21 B9
Pluckley Kent 11 D8
Pluckley Thorne Kent 11 D8
Plumbland Cumb 43 H12
Plumley Ches 30 C6
Plumpton Cumb 39 B7
Plumpton E Sussex 10 G2
Plumpton Green E Sussex 10 F2
Plumpton Head Cumb 39 B7
Plumptonfoot Cumb 39 A7
Plumstead Norfolk 26 B4
Plumtree Notts 32 G3
Plush Dorset 7 F10
Plwmp Dyfed 13 B7
Plymouth Devon 5 K4
Plympton Devon 5 K4
Plymstock Devon 5 K4
Plymtree Devon 6 F4
Pockley N Yorks 40 G6
Pocklington Humber 36 B6
Pode Hole Lincs 24 C3
Podimore Som'set 7 D9
Podington Beds 23 F12
Podmoor Staffs 30 G6
Pointon Lincs 24 B2
Pokesdown Dorset 8 G3
Polbae Dumf/Gal 42 D4
Polbain H'land 60 F2
Polbathic Cornw'l 3 D10
Polbeth Lothian 48 C3
Poldean Dumf/Gal 43 B11
Polduillie Bridge Gramp 58 F1
Pole Moor W Yorks 35 E9
Polebrook Northants 25 G2
Polegate E Sussex 10 G5
Polesworth Warwick 22 B6
Polglass H'land 60 F2
Polgooth Cornw'l 3 E7
Poling W Sussex 9 F11
Poling Corner W Sussex 9 E11
Polkerris Cornw'l 3 D8
Polla H'land 60 B5
Pollington Humber 36 E4
Polloch H'land 50 A5
Pollockshaws S'clyde 47 C10
Pollokshields S'clyde 47 C10
Polmaddie Dumf/Gal 43 C7
Polmaily H'land 54 F8
Polmassick Cornw'l 3 E7
Polmont Lothian 48 B2
Polmoody Dumf/Gal 48 H4
Polnessan S'clyde 47 H9
Polnish H'land 55 L1
Polperro Cornw'l 3 E9
Polruan Cornw'l 3 E8
Polsham Som'set 7 B8
Polskeoch Dumf/Gal 43 A8
Polstead Suffolk 27 L3
Poltimore Devon 6 G3
Polton Lothian 48 C5
Polwarth Borders 49 D10
Polyphant Cornw'l 3 B9
Polzeath Cornw'l 2 B6
Pondersbridge Cambs 24 F4
Pondtail Hants 9 A9
Ponsanooth Cornw'l 2 F5
Ponsworthy Devon 5 H6
Pont ar Hydfer Powys 14 B2
Pont Hentry Dyfed 13 F8
Pont Hirwaun Dyfed 12 B6
Pont Llanrhaiadr Gwyn 29 H7
Pont Llogel Powys 20 A6
Pont Pen-y-benglog Gwyn 28 D6
Pont Rhyd-goch Gwyn 28 D6
Pont y Clogwyn Clwyd 29 E8
Pont Yates Dyfed 13 F8
Pontamman Dyfed 13 F9
Pont-Antwn Dyfed 13 F8
Pontardawe W Glam 13 G10
Pontardulais W Glam 13 G9
Pontargothi Dyfed 13 E8
Pont-ar-llechau Dyfed 13 E10
Pontarsais Dyfed 13 D8
Pontblyddyn Clwyd 29 D12
Pontbren Llwyd Mid Glam 14 D3
Pontefract W Yorks 36 E2
Ponteland Northum 45 F10
Ponterwyd Dyfed 20 D3
Pontesbury Shrops 21 B9
Pontesford Shrops 21 B9
Pontfadog Clwyd 29 F11
Pontfaen Dyfed 12 D4
Pont-faen Powys 14 A3
Pontgarreg Dyfed 13 B7
Ponthir Gwent 14 E6
Pont-llan-fraith Gwent 14 E5
Pontlliw W Glam 13 G9
Pontlottyn Mid Glam 14 D4
Pontlyfni Gwyn 28 E4
Pontneddfechan W Glam 14 D2
Pontnewydd Gwent 14 E6
Pontrhydfendigaid Dyfed 20 F3
Pontrhydyfen W Glam 13 G11
Pontrhydygroes Dyfed 20 E3
Pontrhydyrun Gwent 14 E6
Pontrilas Heref/Worcs 15 B7
Pont-Robert Powys 20 A6
Pont-rug Gwyn 28 D4
Ponts Green E Sussex 10 F5
Pontshaen Dyfed 13 B8
Pontshill Heref/Worcs 15 B9
Pontsticill Mid Glam 14 C4
Pont-tywely Dyfed 13 C7
Pontyberem Dyfed 13 F8
Pont-y-bodkin Clwyd 29 D12
Pontyclun Mid Glam 14 F4
Pontycymer Mid Glam 14 E2
Pontyglazier Dyfed 12 C5
Pont-y-gwaith Mid Glam 14 E3
Pont-y-pant Gwyn 29 E7
Pontypool Gwent 14 D6
Pontypridd Mid Glam 14 E4
Pont-yr-hafod Dyfed 12 D3
Pont-ysgawrhyd Powys 21 A7
Pontywaun Gwent 14 E5
Pooksgreen Hants 8 E5
Pool Cornw'l 2 E4
Pool Heref/Worcs 21 H10
Pool W Yorks 35 C11
Pool Head Heref/Worcs 21 G11
Pool Hey Lancs 34 F2
Pool of Muckhart Central 52 G5
Pool Quay Powys 21 A8
Poole Dorset 8 G2
Poole Green Ches 30 E5
Poole Keynes Glos 16 E1
Poolend Staffs 31 D8
Poolewe H'land 54 B2
Pooley Bridge Cumb 39 C7
Poolhill Glos 15 A10
Poolsbrook Derby 32 C2
Poortown I of Man 38 G1
Pootings Kent 10 C3
Popeswood Berks 17 G9
Popham Hants 9 B7
Poplar London 18 F4
Porchfield I of Wight 8 G6
Porin H'land 54 D7
Poringland Norfolk 26 E6
Porkellis Cornw'l 2 F4
Porlock Som'set 6 B2
Porlock Weir Som'set 6 B2
Port Allen Fife 53 E7
Port an Eilein S'clyde 46 B5
Port Appin S'clyde 50 C6
Port Bannatyne S'clyde 46 C6
Port Carlisle Cumb 44 G1
Port Clarence Clevl'd 40 C5
Port Dinorwic Gwyn 28 C5
Port Driseach S'clyde 46 B5
Port e Vullen I of Man 38 G3
Port Elphinstone Gramp 58 F5
Port Erin I of Man 38 H1
Port Erroll Gramp 58 D8
Port Eynon W Glam 13 H8
Port Glasgow S'clyde 47 B8
Port Henderson H'land 54 B1
Port Isaac Cornw'l 3 B7
Port Lamont S'clyde 46 B6
Port Logan Dumf/Gal 42 H2
Port Mulgrave N Yorks 41 C8
Port of Menteith Central 52 G1
Port of Ness W Isles 63 A6
Port Quin Cornw'l 3 B7
Port Ramsay S'clyde 50 C6
Port St. Mary I of Man 38 H1
Port Sunlight Mersey 30 B2
Port Talbot W Glam 13 H10
Port Tennant W Glam 13 H10
Port William Dumf/Gal 42 G4
Portachoillan S'clyde 46 D3
Portavadie S'clyde 46 B4
Portbury Avon 15 G8
Portchester Hants 9 F7
Portencross S'clyde 47 D7
Portesham Dorset 7 H9
Portessie Gramp 58 A2
Portfield Gate Dyfed 12 E3
Portgate Devon 5 G3
Portgordon Gramp 58 A1
Portgower H'land 61 E9
Porth Cornw'l 2 C5
Porth Mid Glam 14 E4
Porth Navas Cornw'l 2 G5
Porthallow Cornw'l 2 G5
Porthallow Cornw'l 3 D9
Porthcawl Mid Glam 14 G2
Porthcurno Cornw'l 2 G1
Porthdafarch Gwyn 28 B2
Porthgain Dyfed 12 D2
Porthilly Cornw'l 2 B6
Porthkerry S Glam 14 H4
Porthleven Cornw'l 2 G3
Porthmadog Gwyn 28 F5
Porthmeor Cornw'l 2 F2
Porthoustock Cornw'l 2 G5
Porthpean Cornw'l 3 D7
Porthtowann Cornw'l 2 E4
Porthyrhyd Dyfed 13 C10
Porthyrhyd Dyfed 13 E8
Portincaple S'clyde 51 H9
Portington Humber 36 D6
Portinnisherrich S'clyde 51 F7
Portinscale Cumb 38 C5
Portishead Avon 15 G8
Portknockie Gramp 58 A2
Portlethen Village Gramp 59 H7
Portleven Gramp 59 H7
Portloe Cornw'l 2 F6
Portmahomack H'land 61 H9
Portmeirion Gwyn 28 F5
Portmellon Cornw'l 3 E7
Portmore Hants 8 F5
Portnaguiran W Isles 63 C6
Portnalong H'land 62 E3
Portnaluchaig H'land 55 K1
Portnancon H'land 60 B5
Portnellan Central 51 E11
Portnellan Central 51 F11
Portnocroish S'clyde 50 C6
Portobello Lothian 48 B6
Porton Wilts 8 B3
Portpatrick Dumf/Gal 42 F1
Portreath Cornw'l 2 E4
Portree H'land 62 D4
Portrye S'clyde 47 D7
Portscatho Cornw'l 2 F6
Portsea Hants 9 F8
Portskerra H'land 61 A8
Portskewett Gwent 15 E8
Portslade E Sussex 10 G1
Portsmouth Hants 9 F8
Portsmouth Lancs 35 E7
Portsoy Gramp 58 A3
Portswood Hants 8 E6
Portuairk H'land 50 A2
Portvasgo H'land 60 A6
Portway Heref/Worcs 15 A8
Portway Heref/Worcs 21 H10
Portway Warwick 22 E4
Portwrinkle Cornw'l 3 D10
Portyerrock Dumf/Gal 42 H5
Poslingford Suffolk 27 K1
Postbridge Cornw'l 2 H5
Postbridge Devon 5 H5
Postcombe Oxon 17 D8
Postling Kent 11 D10
Postwick Norfolk 26 E6
Potarch Gramp 59 H3
Potholm Dumf/Gal 44 D2
Potsgrove Beds 17 A10
Pott Row Norfolk 24 C8
Pott Shrigley Ches 31 B8
Potten End Herts 17 C11
Potter Brompton N Yorks 41 G10
Potter Heigham Norfolk 26 D7
Potter Street Essex 18 C5
Potterhanworth Lincs 33 D7
Potterhanworth Booths Lincs 33 C8
Potterne Wilts 16 H1
Potterne Wick Wilts 16 H1
Potters Bar Herts 18 D3
Potters Cross Staffs 22 D2
Potterspury Bucks 23 H11
Potterton Gramp 58 F7
Potto N Yorks 40 E5
Potton Beds 25 K3
Poughill Cornw'l 4 E1
Poughill Devon 4 E7
Poulshot Wilts 16 H1
Poulton Ches 30 D3
Poulton Glos 16 D2
Poulton-le-Fylde Lancs 34 C2
Pound Bank Heref/Worcs 22 E1
Pound Green E Sussex 10 F4
Pound Green I of Wight 8 G5
Pound Hill W Sussex 10 D2
Poundland Dumf/Gal 43 C8
Poundland S'clyde 42 C3
Poundon Bucks 17 B7
Poundsbridge Kent 10 D4
Poundsgate Devon 5 J6
Poundstock Cornw'l 2 A2
Pourie Tayside 53 D9
Powburn Northum 45 A9
Powderham Devon 6 H3
Powdrake Central 52 H3
Powerstock Dorset 7 G8
Powfoot Dumf/Gal 43 E12
Powgavie Fife 53 E7
Powick Heref/Worcs 22 G2
Powler's Piece Devon 4 D2
Powmill Tayside 52 G5
Poxwell Dorset 7 H11
Poynings W Sussex 10 G1
Poyntington Dorset 7 D10
Poynton Ches 31 B8
Poynton Green Shrops 30 H4
Poyston Cross Dyfed 12 E3
Poystreet Green Suffolk 27 J3
Praa Sands Cornw'l 2 G3
Prabost H'land 62 C3
Pratt's Bottom London 18 H5
Praze Cornw'l 2 F3
Praze-an-Beeble Cornw'l 2 F3
Predannack Wollas Cornw'l 2 H4
Prees Shrops 30 G4
Prees Heath Shrops 30 F4
Preesall Lancs 34 B2
Preesall Park Lancs 34 C3
Prendergast Dyfed 12 E3
Prendwick Northum 45 B8
Pren-gwyn Dyfed 13 C7
Prenteg Gwyn 28 F5
Prenton Mersey 30 B2
Prescot Mersey 30 A3
Prescott Shrops 30 H3
Pressen Northum 49 F11
Pressgreen Shrops 30 G4
Prestatyn Clwyd 29 B10
Prestbury Ches 31 C7
Prestbury Glos 15 B12
Presteigne Powys 21 F8
Presthope Shrops 21 C11
Prestleigh Som'set 7 B9
Preston Borders 49 D10
Preston Devon 5 H7
Preston Dorset 7 H10
Preston E Sussex 10 G2
Preston Glos 15 A10
Preston Glos 16 D2
Preston Herts 18 A2
Preston Humber 37 D9
Preston Kent 11 B11
Preston Kent 11 B9
Preston Leics 23 B12
Preston Lothian 48 B6
Preston Lothian 49 B8
Preston Northum 45 E12
Preston Suffolk 27 K2
Preston Wilts 16 F1
Preston Bagot Warwick 22 E5
Preston Bissett Bucks 17 A7
Preston Bowyer Som'set 6 D5
Preston Brockhurst Shrops 30 H4
Preston Brook Ches 30 B4
Preston Candover Hants 9 B7
Preston Capes Northants 23 G9
Preston Crowmarsh Oxon 17 E7
Preston Gubbals Shrops 30 H4
Preston on Stour Warwick 22 G5
Preston on the Hill Ches 30 B4
Preston on Wye Heref/Worcs 21 H9
Preston Plucknett Som'set 7 E9
Preston upon the Weald Moors Shrops 21 A12
Preston Wynne Heref/Worcs 21 H11
Prestonmill Dumf/Gal 43 F10
Prestonpans Lothian 48 B6
Preston-under-Scar N Yorks 40 F1
Prestwich Gtr Man 35 G7
Prestwick Northum 45 F10
Prestwick S'clyde 47 G8
Prestwood Bucks 17 D9
Price Town Mid Glam 14 E3
Prickwillow Cambs 25 G7
Priddy Som'set 7 A8
Priest Hutton Lancs 39 H7
Priesthaugh Dumf/Gal 44 C3
Priesthill S'clyde 47 C10
Priestland S'clyde 47 F10
Priestweston Shrops 21 C8
Primethorpe Leics 23 C8
Primrose Hill Cambs 24 F5
Primrose Hill Derby 32 D2
Primrose Valley N Yorks 41 G11
Primrosehill Borders 49 D10
Primrosehill Herts 17 D11
Primsidemill Borders 49 G10
Prince Charles Cove H'land 62 C4
Princes Gate Dyfed 12 F5
Princes Risborough Bucks 17 D9
Princethorpe Warwick 23 E7
Princetown Devon 5 H5
Princetown Mid Glam 14 C4
Printonan Borders 49 E10
Prion Clwyd 29 D10
Prior Park Borders 49 D12
Prior's Frome Heref/Worcs 21 H11
Priors Hardwick Warwick 23 G8
Priors Marston Warwick 23 F8
Priorslee Shrops 21 A12
Priory Wood Heref/Worcs 21 H8
Priston Avon 15 H10
Prittlewell Essex 19 E8
Privett Hants 9 C8
Prixford Devon 4 B4
Probus Cornw'l 2 E6
Prospect Cumb 43 G12
Protstonhill Gramp 58 A6
Prudhoe Northum 45 G9
Ptarmigan Lodge Central 51 G10
Pubil Tayside 51 C11
Publow Avon 15 H9
Puckeridge Herts 18 B4
Puckington Som'set 7 D7
Pucklechurch Avon 15 G10
Pucknall Hants 8 D5
Puddington Ches 30 C2
Puddington Devon 4 E7
Puddledock Norfolk 26 F4
Puddletown Dorset 7 G11
Pudleston Heref/Worcs 21 F11
Pudsey W Yorks 35 D11
Pulborough W Sussex 9 D12
Puleston Shrops 30 H6
Pulford Ches 30 D2
Pulham Dorset 7 E10
Pulham Market Norfolk 27 G5
Pulham St. Mary Norfolk 27 G5
Pulloxhill Beds 25 M2
Pumpherston Lothian 48 B3
Pumplaburn Dumf/Gal 43 B12
Pumpsaint Dyfed 13 C10
Puncheston Dyfed 12 D3
Puncknowle Dorset 7 G9
Punnett's Town E Sussex 10 F5

Purbrook Hants 9 E8
Purdomstone Dumf/Gal 44 E1
Purewell Dorset 8 G3
Purfleet Essex 18 F5
Puriton Som'set 7 B7
Purleigh Essex 19 D8
Purley Berks 17 F7
Purley London 18 H3
Purls Bridge Cambs 25 G6
Purse Caundle Dorset 7 D10
Purslow Shrops 21 D9
Purston Jaglin W Yorks 36 E2
Purtington Som'set 7 E7
Purton Glos 15 D10
Purton Wilts 16 E2
Purton Stoke Wilts 16 E2
Purvishaugh Borders 49 E8
Pury End Northants 23 H10
Pusey Oxon 16 D4
Putford Devon 4 D2
Putley Heref/Worcs 15 A9
Putney London 18 F2
Putsborough Devon 4 B3
Puttenham Bucks 17 C9
Puttenham Surrey 9 A10
Putts Corner Devon 6 G5
Puxton Avon 15 H7
Pwll Dyfed 13 G8
Pwllcrochan Dyfed 12 G3
Pwlldefaid Gwyn 28 H1
Pwllgloyw Powys 14 A4
Pwllheli Gwyn 28 G3
Pwllmeyric Gwent 15 E8
Pwlltrap Dyfed 12 E6
Pwll-y-glaw W Glam 13 H11
Pye Bridge Derby 32 E2
Pye Corner Gwent 15 F7
Pye Corner Herts 18 C4
Pye Green Staffs 22 A3
Pyecombe W Sussex 10 G2
Pyle I of Wight 8 H6
Pyle Mid Glam 14 F2
Pylle Som'set 7 B9
Pymore Cambs 25 G6
Pyrford Surrey 17 H11
Pyrgad Powys 14 C4
Pyrton Oxon 17 E8
Pytchley Northants 23 E12
Pyworthy Devon 4 F2
Quabbs Shrops 21 D7
Quadring Lincs 24 B3
Quainton Bucks 17 B8
Quarley Hants 8 B4
Quarndon Derby 31 F11
Quarndon Leics 23 A9
Quarrier's Homes S'clyde 47 C8
Quarrington Lincs 24 A2
Quarrington Hill Durham 40 A4
Quarry Bank W Midlands 22 C3
Quarrybank Ches 30 D4
Quarrywood Gramp 56 C7
Quarter S'clyde 47 D12
Quat Shrops 22 C1
Quatford Shrops 22 C1
Quebec Durham 40 A2
Quedgeley Glos 15 C11
Queen Adelaide Cambs 25 G7
Queen Charlton Avon 15 H9
Queen Dart Devon 4 D7
Queen Oak Dorset 7 C11
Queen Street Kent 10 D6
Queenborough Kent 11 A8
Queens Camel Som'set 7 D9
Queens Head Shrops 30 G2
Queensbury W Yorks 35 D9
Queensferry Clwyd 29 C12
Queensferry Lothian 48 B4
Queenstown Lancs 34 D2
Queenzieburn S'clyde 47 B11
Quemerford Wilts 16 G1
Quendale Shetl'd 64 F7
Quendon Essex 25 M6
Queniborough Leics 23 A10
Quenington Glos 16 D2
Quernmore Lancs 34 A4
Quethiock Cornw'l 3 C10
Quidenham Norfolk 27 G3
Quidhampton Hants 8 A6
Quidhampton Wilts 8 C3
Quilquox Gramp 58 D6
Quine's Hill I of Man 38 H2
Quinish House H'land 50 B2
Quinton Northants 23 G11
Quintrel Downs Cornw'l 2 D5
Quiog Tayside 52 E3
Quixwood Borders 49 C10
Quoditch Devon 4 F3
Quothquan S'clyde 48 E3
Quoys Shetl'd 64 D7
Rabscott Devon 4 C6
Raby Mersey 30 B2
Rachub Gwyn 28 C5
Rackenford Devon 4 D7
Rackham W Sussex 9 E11
Rackheath Norfolk 26 D6
Racks Dumf/Gal 43 D11
Rackwick Orkney 64 A2
Rackwick Orkney 64 D1
Radbourne Derby 31 G11
Radcliffe Gtr Man 34 F6
Radcliffe Northum 45 C11
Radcliffe on Trent Notts 32 F4
Radclive Bucks 17 A7
Radcot Oxon 16 D4
Raddery H'land 56 D3
Radford Semele Warwick 23 F7
Radipole Dorset 7 H10
Radlett Herts 18 D2
Radley Oxon 16 D6
Radnage Bucks 17 D8
Radstock Dorset 7 A10
Radstone Northants 23 H9
Radway Warwick 23 G7
Radway Green Ches 30 E6
Radwell Beds 25 J1
Radwinter Essex 25 L7
Radyr S Glam 14 F5
Raecleugh Dumf/Gal 48 H3
Raecloch Gramp 58 C4
Raffin H'land 60 D2
Rafford Gramp 56 D6
Ragdale Leics 32 H4
Ragfield Fife 53 F10
Raglan Gwent 15 D7
Ragnall Notts 32 C5
Rainford Mersey 34 G4
Rainham Kent 11 B7
Rainham Kent 18 F5
Rainhill Mersey 30 A4
Rainhill Stoops Mersey 30 A4
Rainow Ches 31 C8
Rainton N Yorks 40 H4
Rainworth Notts 32 D3
Raisbeck Cumb 39 D9
Raise Cumb 44 H5
Raisthorpe N Yorks 36 A6
Rait Tayside 53 D7
Raithby Lincs 33 B10
Raithby Lincs 33 C10
Rake W Sussex 9 C9
Ram Lane Kent 11 C8
Ramasaig H'land 62 D1
Rame Cornw'l 2 F4
Rame Cornw'l 3 E11
Rampisham Dorset 7 F9
Rampside Cumb 34 A1
Rampton Cambs 25 H5
Rampton Notts 32 B5
Ramsay Cambs 25 G4
Ramsay Island Essex 19 C9
Ramsay St. Mary's Cambs 25 G4
Ramsbottom Gtr Man 35 E7
Ramsbury Wilts 16 G4
Ramscraigs H'land 61 D10
Ramsdean Hants 9 D8
Ramsdell Hants 17 H7
Ramsden Oxon 16 C4
Ramsden Bellhouse Essex 19 E7
Ramsden Heath Essex 19 D7
Ramsey Essex 27 M5
Ramsey I of Man 38 G2
Ramseycleuch Borders 48 H5
Ramsgate Kent 11 B12
Ramsgate Street Norfolk 26 B4
Ramsgill N Yorks 40 H1
Ramshaw Durham 45 H8
Ramshope Northum 44 C6
Ramshorn Staffs 31 F9
Ramsley Devon 5 G5
Ramsnest Common Surrey 9 C11
Ranby Notts 32 B4
Rand Lincs 33 B8
Randwick Glos 15 D11
Ranfurly S'clyde 47 C9
Rangemore Staffs 31 H10
Rangeworthy Avon 15 F10
Ranish W Isles 63 D5
Rankinston S'clyde 47 H9
Ranmore Common Surrey 9 A12
Rann Lancs 34 E6
*Rannerdale Cumb 38 C4
*Rannoch Station Tayside 51 B11
Ranochan H'land 55 L2
Ranscombe Som'set 6 B3
Ranskill Notts 32 A4
Ranton Staffs 31 H7
Ranworth Norfolk 26 D7
Rapness Orkney 64 B3
Rarsaidh H'land 55 H2
Rascarrel Dumf/Gal 43 G9
Rashfield S'clyde 46 A6
Rashiereive Gramp 58 E7
Raskelf N Yorks 40 H5
Rassau Gwent 14 C5
Rassay House H'land 62 D5
Rastrick W Yorks 35 E10
Ratagan H'land 55 H3
Ratby Leics 23 B8
Ratcliffe Culey Leics 23 B7
Ratcliffe on the Wreake Leics 23 A9
Ratcliffe on Soar Notts 32 G2
Rathen Gramp 58 B7
Rathillet Fife 53 E8
Rathmell N Yorks 35 A7
Ratho Lothian 48 B4
Ratho Station Lothian 48 B4
Rathven Gramp 58 A2
Ratley Warwick 23 G7
Ratlinghope Shrops 21 C9
Rattar H'land 61 A11
Rattery Devon 5 K6
Rattlesden Suffolk 27 J3
Rattray Tayside 53 C7
Raughton Head Cumb 38 A6
Raunds Northants 25 H1
Ravelaw Borders 49 D11
Ravenfield S Yorks 36 H3
Ravenglass Cumb 38 F3
Raveningham Norfolk 26 F7
Ravenscar N Yorks 41 E10
Ravenscraig S'clyde 47 B7
Ravensdale I of Man 38 G2
Ravensden Beds 25 K2
Ravenshead Notts 32 E3
Ravensmoor Ches 30 E5
Ravensthorpe Northants 23 E10
Ravenstone Bucks 23 G11
Ravenstone Leics 23 A7
Ravenstonedale Cumb 39 E9
Ravenstruther S'clyde 48 E2
Ravensworth N Yorks 40 D2
Raw N Yorks 41 E9
Rawburn Borders 49 D9
Rawcliffe Humber 36 E5
Rawcliffe N Yorks 36 B4
Rawcliffe Br Humber 36 E5
Rawdon W Yorks 35 C10
Rawmarsh S Yorks 36 G2
Rawnsley Staffs 22 A4
Rawreth Essex 19 E8
Rawridge Devon 6 F5
Raws S'clyde 47 E9
Rawtenstall Lancs 35 E7
Rawyards S'clyde 47 C12
Raxton Gramp 58 D6
Raydon Suffolk 27 L3
Raylees Northum 45 D7
Rayleigh Essex 19 E8
Raymond's Hill Dorset 7 F7
Rayne Essex 19 B7
Reach Cambs 25 J7
Read Lancs 34 D6
Reading Berks 17 G8
Reading Street Kent 11 E8
Reagill Cumb 39 C8
Rearquhar H'land 61 G7
Rearsby Leics 23 A10
Reaster H'land 61 A11
Reaveley Northum 45 A8
Reawick Shetl'd 64 D7
Reay H'land 61 B9
Reculver Kent 11 A11
Red Ball Devon 6 E4
Red Dial Cumb 44 H1
Red Hill Heref/Worcs 22 G2
Red Post Devon 5 J7
Red Rock Gtr Man 34 F5
Red Roses Dyfed 12 F5
Red Row Northum 45 C10
Red Street Staffs 31 E7
Red Wharf Gwyn 28 B5
Redberth Dyfed 12 G4
Redbourn Herts 17 C12
Redbourne Humber 37 G7
Redbridge London 18 E4
Redbrook Clwyd 30 F4
Redbrook Glos 15 C8
Redburn H'land 56 C1
Redburn H'land 56 E5
Redburn Northum 44 G6
Redcar Clevl'd 40 C8
Redcastle H'land 56 E1
Redcastle Tayside 53 B11
Redcliffe Bay Avon 15 G7
Redcraig S'clyde 47 G9
Redden Borders 49 F10
Redding Lothian 48 B2
Reddingmuirhead Lothian 48 B2
Reddish Gtr Man 35 H8
Redditch Heref/Worcs 22 E4
Reddochbraes S'clyde 47 F12
Redenhall Norfolk 27 G6
Redesdale Camp Northum 44 C6
Redesmouth Northum 45 E7
Redford Gramp 59 K5
Redford Tayside 53 C10
Redfordgreen Borders 48 H6
Redgrave Suffolk 27 G3
Redhill Avon 15 H8
Redhill Gramp 58 D4
Redhill Gramp 59 G5
Redhill Surrey 10 C2
Redhouse S'clyde 46 C3
Redisham Suffolk 27 G7
Redland Avon 15 G9
Redland Orkney 64 C2
Redlingfield Suffolk 27 H5
Redlodge Suffolk 25 H8
Redlynch Som'set 7 C10
Redlynch Wilts 8 D4
Redmain Cumb 38 B4
Redmarley D'Abitot Glos 15 A10
Redmarshall Clevl'd 40 C4
Redmile Leics 32 G5
Redmire N Yorks 40 F1
Redmoor Cornw'l 3 D8
Redmyre Gramp 59 K5
Rednal Shrops 30 G2
Redpath Borders 49 F8
Redpoint H'land 54 C1
Redruth Cornw'l 2 E4
Redscarhead Borders 48 E5
Redwick Avon 15 F8
Redwick Gwent 15 F7
Redworth Durham 40 C3
Reed Herts 25 L5
Reedham Norfolk 26 E7
Reedness Humber 36 E6
Reedy Loch Borders 49 D11
Reef W Isles 63 C2
Reepham Lincs 33 C7
Reepham Norfolk 26 C4
Reeth N Yorks 40 E1
Regaby I of Man 38 F2
Regoul H'land 56 E4
Rehaurie H'land 56 E5
Reidhbreac H'land 61 G7
Reiff H'land 60 E2
Reigate Surrey 10 C1
Reighton N Yorks 41 H11
Reighton Gap N Yorks 41 G11
Reiss H'land 61 B12
Rejerrah Cornw'l 2 D5
Releath Cornw'l 2 F4
Relief Dumf/Gal 43 D12
Relubbus Cornw'l 2 F3
Remenham Berks 17 F8
Remenham Hill Berks 17 F8
Rempstone Notts 32 H3
Rendcomb Glos 16 C1
Rendham Suffolk 27 J6
Renfrew S'clyde 47 C10
Renhold Beds 25 K2
Renishaw Derby 32 B2
Rennington Northum 45 A10
Renton S'clyde 47 B9
Renwick Cumb 39 A8
Repps Norfolk 26 D7
Repton Derby 31 G11
Reraig H'land 55 G2
Rescobie Tayside 53 B10
Resipole H'land 50 A4
Resolis H'land 56 C2
Resolven W Glam 14 D2
Resourie H'land 55 M2
Reston Borders 49 C11
Rettendon Essex 19 D7
Rettendon Place Essex 19 D7
Retyn Cornw'l 2 D6
Reudle H'land 50 C1
Revesby Lincs 33 D10
Rew Street I of Wight 8 G6
Rewe Devon 6 F3
Reydon Suffolk 27 G8
Reymerston Norfolk 26 E3
Reynalton Dyfed 12 F4
Reynoldston W Glam 13 H8
Rezare Cornw'l 3 B10
Rhadyr Gwent 15 D7
Rhandirmwyn Dyfed 13 C11
Rhayader Powys 20 F5
Rhegreanoch H'land 60 E3
Rheindown H'land 56 E1
Rhemore H'land 50 C3
Rhenetra H'land 62 C3
Rhenigidale W Isles 63 G3
Rhewl Clwyd 29 D10
Rhewl Clwyd 29 F11
Rhicarn H'land 60 E2
Rhiconich H'land 60 B4
Rhicullen H'land 56 C3
Rhidorroch H'land 60 G3
Rhid-y-sarn Gwyn 28 F6
Rhifail H'land 61 C7
Rhigos Mid Glam 14 D3
Rhimichie H'land 60 B4
Rhinduie H'land 56 E1
Rhiw Gwyn 28 G2
Rhiwbryfdir Gwyn 28 F6
Rhiwderyn Gwent 14 F6
Rhiwlas Clwyd 29 G11
Rhiwlas Gwyn 29 F8
Rhode Som'set 6 C6
Rhodes Minnis Kent 11 D10
Rhodesia Notts 32 B3
Rhodiad Dyfed 12 D1
Rhoose S Glam 14 H4
Rhos Dyfed 13 C7
Rhos W Glam 13 G10
Rhosamman Dyfed 13 F10
Rhoscolyn Gwyn 28 C2
Rhoscrowther Dyfed 12 G3
Rhosesmor Clwyd 29 C11
Rhosfach Dyfed 12 D5
Rhosgadfan Gwyn 28 D4
Rhosgoch Gwyn 28 A3
Rhosgoch Powys 21 H7
Rhos-hill Dyfed 12 C5
Rhoshirwaun Gwyn 28 G1
Rhos-lan Gwyn 28 F4
Rhoslefain Gwyn 20 B1
Rhosllanerchrugog Clwyd 29 F12
Rhosmaen Dyfed 13 E9
Rhos-meirch Gwyn 28 B4
Rhosneigr Gwyn 28 C3
Rhos-on-Sea Clwyd 29 B8
Rhossili W Glam 13 H7
Rhosson Dyfed 12 D1
Rhostryfan Gwyn 28 D4
Rhostyllen Clwyd 30 E2
Rhosybol Gwyn 28 A4
Rhos-y-gwaliau Gwyn 29 G9
Rhos-y-llan Gwyn 28 F2
Rhu S'clyde 46 C3
Rhu S'clyde 47 A7
Rhu Noa H'land 54 C4
Rhualt Clwyd 29 C10
Rhubodach S'clyde 46 B5
Rhuddall Heath Ches 30 D4
Rhuddlan Clwyd 29 B9
Rhude Cross Cornw'l 4 E1
Rhue H'land 60 G2
Rhulen Powys 21 G7
Rhunahaorine S'clyde 46 E2
Rhyd Gwyn 28 F6
Rhyd Powys 20 B5
Rhydargaeau Dyfed 13 D8
Rhydberry Powys 14 A3
Rhydcymerau Dyfed 13 C9
Rhydd Heref/Worcs 22 H2
Rhyd-Ddu Gwyn 28 E5
Rhydding W Glam 13 G10
Rhyddlan Dyfed 13 C8
Rhyd-leos Clwyd 29 G11
Rhydlewis Dyfed 13 B7
Rhydlios Gwyn 28 G1
Rhyd-Lydan Clwyd 29 E8
Rhydlydan Powys 20 C6
Rhydowen Dyfed 13 C8
Rhydspence Heref/Worcs 21 H8
Rhydtalog Clwyd 29 E11
Rhydwyn Gwyn 28 A3
Rhyd-y-croesau Shrops 29 G11
Rhydyeclafdy Gwyn 28 G3
Rhydyfelin Dyfed 20 D2
Rhydyfelin Mid Glam 14 E4
Rhydyfro W Glam 13 F10
Rhyd-y-groes Powys 21 B8
Rhydymain Gwyn 29 H7
Rhyd-y-meirch Gwent 14 D6
Rhydymwyn Clwyd 29 D11
Rhyd-yr-onmen Gwyn 20 B2
Rhyfuhr Dyfed 20 F2
Rhyl Clwyd 29 B9
Rhymney Mid Glam 14 D4
Rhynd Fife 53 E9
Rhynd Tayside 52 E6
Rhynie Gramp 58 E2
Ribble Heref/Worcs 22 E1
Ribbleton Lancs 34 D4
Ribby Lancs 34 D3
Ribchester Lancs 34 D5
Ribigill H'land 60 B6
Riby Lincs 37 F9
Riby Cross Roads Lincs 37 F9
Riccall N Yorks 36 C4
Riccarton S'clyde 47 F9
Richards Castle Heref/Worcs 21 E10
Richings Park London 17 F11
Richmond London 18 F2
Richmond N Yorks 40 E2
Rickinghall Suffolk 27 H3
Rickling Essex 25 M6
Rickling Green Essex 18 A5
Rickmansworth Herts 17 E11
Riddings Cumb 44 E3
Riddings Derby 32 E2
Riddlecombe Devon 4 E5
Riddlesden W Yorks 35 C9
Ridge Dorset 8 G1
Ridge Hants 8 D5
Ridge Herts 18 D2
Ridge Wilts 8 C1
Ridge Green Surrey 10 C2
Ridge Lane Warwick 22 C6
Ridgebourne Powys 20 F6
Ridgehill Avon 15 H8
Ridgeway Derby 32 B1
Ridgeway Cross Heref/Worcs 21 H12
Ridgewell Essex 25 L8
Ridgewood E Sussex 10 F3
Ridgmont Beds 25 L1
Riding Mill Northum 45 G8
Ridley Kent 10 B5
Ridley Northum 44 G6
Ridley Green Ches 30 E4
Ridlington Leics 23 B11
Ridlington Norfolk 26 B6
Ridsdale Northum 45 E7
Riechip Tayside 52 B5
Riemore Tayside 52 B5
Rienachait H'land 60 D2
Rievaulx N Yorks 40 G6
Rifern H'land 55 K2
Rigfoot S'clyde 47 D9
Rigg Dumf/Gal 44 F1
Riggend S'clyde 47 B12
Righead S'clyde 47 F10
Rigmaden Park Cumb 39 G8
Rigsby Lincs 33 C11
Rigside S'clyde 48 F2
Rileyhill Staffs 22 A5
Rilla Mill Cornw'l 3 B10
Rillington N Yorks 41 H8
Rimington Lancs 35 C7
Rimpton Dorset 7 D9
Rimsdale H'land 61 C7
Rimswell Humber 37 D10
Rinaston Dyfed 12 D3
Ringford Dumf/Gal 43 F8
Ringinglow S Yorks 31 B11
Ringland Norfolk 26 D4
Ringles Cross E Sussex 10 F3
Ringmer E Sussex 10 G3
Ringmore Devon 5 J8
Ringmore Devon 5 L5
Ringmore Gramp 58 F2
Ringorm Gramp 56 E8
Ring's End Cambs 24 E5
Ringsfield Suffolk 27 G7
Ringsfield Corner Suffolk 27 G7
Ringshall Bucks 17 C10
Ringshall Suffolk 27 K3
Ringshall Stocks Suffolk 27 K3
Ringstead Norfolk 24 B8
Ringstead Northants 25 H1
Ringwood Hants 8 F3
Ringwould Kent 11 C12
Rinnigill Orkney 64 E2
Rinsey Cornw'l 2 G3
Ripe E Sussex 10 G4
Ripley Derby 32 E1
Ripley Hants 8 F3
Ripley N Yorks 35 A11
Ripley Surrey 17 H11
Riplingham Humber 37 D7
Ripon N Yorks 40 H3
Rippingale Lincs 24 C2
Ripple Heref/Worcs 22 H2
Ripple Kent 11 C12
Ripponden W Yorks 35 E9
Risbury Heref/Worcs 21 G11
Risby Humber 37 F7
Risby Suffolk 27 J1
Risca Gwent 14 E6
Rise Humber 37 C9
Risegate Lincs 24 C3
Riseholme Lincs 33 C7
Riseley Beds 25 J1
Riseley Berks 17 H8
Rishangles Suffolk 27 H4
Rishton Lancs 34 D6
Rishworth W Yorks 35 E9
Risley Derby 32 G2
Risplith N Yorks 40 H3
Rispond H'land 60 A5
Rivar Wilts 16 H4
Rivenhall End Essex 19 B8
River Bank Cambs 25 H6
Riverhead Kent 10 B4
Rivington Lancs 34 F5
Roachill Devon 4 D7
Roade Northants 23 G11
Roadhead Cumb 44 F3
Roadmeetings S'clyde 48 D1
Roadside H'land 61 B11
Roadside S'clyde 47 H10
Roadside of Catterline Gramp 59 J6
Roadside of Kinneff Gramp 59 K6
Roadwater Som'set 6 B4
Roag H'land 62 D2
Roan of Craigoch S'clyde 42 A4
Roansgreen Cumb 44 E3
Roath S Glam 14 F5
Roberthill Dumf/Gal 43 D12
Roberton Borders 44 B3
Roberton S'clyde 48 F2
Robertsbridge E Sussex 10 F6
Roberttown W Yorks 35 E10
Robeston Cross Dyfed 12 F2
Robeston Wathen Dyfed 12 E4
Robin Hood W Yorks 35 D11
Robin Hood Inn Derby 31 C11
Robin Hood's Bay N Yorks 41 E9
Roborough Devon 4 D4
Roborough Devon 5 J4
Roby Mersey 30 A3
Roby Mill Lancs 34 F4
Rocester Staffs 31 F9
Roch Dyfed 12 E2
Roch Gate Dyfed 12 E2
Rochdale Gtr Man 35 F7
Roche Cornw'l 3 D7

*Rannoch School Tayside 52 B1

Rochester *Kent* 10 A6
Rochester *Northum* 44 C6
Rochford *Essex* 19 E8
Rock *Cornw'l* 2 B6
Rock *Heref/Worcs* 22 E1
Rock *Northum* 45 A10
Rock *W Sussex* 9 E12
Rock Ferry *Mersey* 30 B2
Rock Hill *Heref/Worcs* 22 E3
Rockbeare *Devon* 6 G4
Rockcliffe *Cumb* 44 G2
Rockcliffe *Dumf/Gal* 43 F9
Rockfield *Gwent* 15 C8
Rockfield *H'land* 61 H9
Rockford *Hants* 8 E3
Rockhampton *Avon* 15 E9
Rockhill *Shrops* 21 D8
Rockingham *Northants* 23 C12
Rockland All Saints *Norfolk* 26 F3
Rockland St. Mary *Norfolk* 26 E6
Rockland St. Peter *Norfolk* 26 F3
Rockley *Wilts* 16 G3
Rockwell End *Bucks* 17 E9
Rockwell Green *Som'set* 6 D5
Rodborough *Glos* 15 D11
Rodbourne *Wilts* 15 F12
Rodbourne *Wilts* 16 F2
Rodbourne Cheney *Wilts* 16 E2
Rodd *Heref/Worcs* 21 F8
Roddam *Northum* 49 G12
Roddam Rigg *Northum* 49 G12
Rodden *Dorset* 7 H9
Rode *Som'set* 7 A11
Rode Heath *Ches* 30 D6
Rodeheath *Ches* 31 C7
Rodel *W Isles* 63 H1
Roden *Shrops* 21 A11
Rodhuish *Som'set* 6 B4
Rodington *Shrops* 21 A11
Rodley *Glos* 15 C10
Rodmarton *Glos* 15 D12
Rodmell *E Sussex* 10 G3
Rodmersham *Kent* 11 B8
Rodney Stoke *Som'set* 7 A8
Rodsley *Derby* 31 F10
Rodway *Som'set* 6 B6
Rodwell *Dorset* 7 H7
Roe Green *Herts* 25 M4
Roecliff *N Yorks* 35 A12
Roecliffe *N Yorks* 36 A2
Roehampton *London* 18 G2
Roesound *Shetl'd* 64 C7
Roffey *W Sussex* 10 E1
Rogart *H'land* 61 F7
Rogart Halt *H'land* 61 F7
Rogate *W Sussex* 9 D9
Rogerstone *Gwent* 14 E6
Rogerton *S'clyde* 47 D11
Rogiet *Gwent* 15 E8
Rollesby *Norfolk* 26 D7
Rolleston *Leics* 23 B10
Rolleston *Notts* 32 E5
Rolleston *Staffs* 31 G10
Rolston *Humber* 37 C10
Rolvenden *Kent* 11 E7
Rolvenden Layne *Kent* 11 E7
Romaldkirk *Durham* 39 C12
Roman Hill *Suffolk* 26 F8
Romanby *N Yorks* 40 F4
Romannobridge *Borders* 48 E4
Romansleigh *Devon* 4 D6
Romesdal *H'land* 62 C3
Romford *London* 18 E5
Romiley *Gtr Man* 31 A8
Romsey *Hants* 8 D5
Romsley *Heref/Worcs* 22 D3
Romsley *Shrops* 22 D1
Ronague *I of Man* 38 H1
Rookdale *N Yorks* 41 H9
Rookhope *Durham* 39 A11
Rookley *I of Wight* 8 H6
Rooks Bridge *Som'set* 7 A7
Rook's Nest *Som'set* 6 C4
Roos *Humber* 37 D10
Rootpark *S'clyde* 48 D2
Ropley *Hants* 9 C8
Ropley Dean *Hants* 9 C7
Ropsley *Lincs* 33 G7
Rora *Gramp* 58 C8
Rorandle *Gramp* 58 F4
Rorrington *Shrops* 21 B8
Rose *Cornw'l* 2 D5
Rose Ash *Devon* 4 D7
Rose Hill *E Sussex* 10 F3
Roseacre *Kent* 10 C6
Roseacre *Lancs* 34 C3
Rosebank *S'clyde* 48 D1
Rosebrough *Northum* 45 C12
Rosebush *Dyfed* 12 D4
Rosecare *Cornw'l* 2 B2
Rosedale Abbey *N Yorks* 41 F7
Roseden *Northum* 45 A8
Rosehaugh House *H'land* 56 D2
Rosehearty *Gramp* 58 A7
Rosehill *Shrops* 30 G5
Roseisle *Gramp* 56 C7
Rosemarket *Dyfed* 12 F3
Rosemarkie *H'land* 56 D3
Rosemary Lane *Devon* 6 E5
Rosemount *Tayside* 53 C7
Rosewarne *Cornw'l* 2 F3
Rosewell *Lothian* 48 C5
Roseworth *Clevl'd* 40 C4
Roseworthy *Cornw'l* 2 F3
Rosgill *Cumb* 39 D8
Roshven *H'land* 55 L1
Roskhill *H'land* 62 D2
Rosley *Cumb* 38 A6
Roslin *Lothian* 48 C5
Rosliston *Derby* 31 H11
Rosneath *S'clyde* 47 A7
Ross *Dumf/Gal* 43 G7
Ross *Northum* 45 B12
Rossett *Clwyd* 30 D2
Rossie Ochill *Tayside* 52 F6
Rossington *S Yorks* 36 G4
Rosskeen *H'land* 56 C2
Rossland *S'clyde* 47 B9
Ross-on-Wye *Heref/Worcs* 15 B9
Roster *H'land* 61 C11
Rostherne *Ches* 30 B6
Rosthwaite *Cumb* 38 D5
Roston *Derby* 31 F10
Rosudgeon *Cornw'l* 2 G3
Rosyth *Lothian* 48 A4
Rothbury *Northum* 45 C9
Rotherby *Leics* 23 A10
Rotherfield *E Sussex* 10 E4
Rotherfield Greys *Oxon* 17 F8
Rotherfield Peppard *Oxon* 17 F8
Rotherham *S Yorks* 32 A2
Rothersthorpe *Northants* 23 F10
Rotherwick *Hants* 17 H8
Rothes *Gramp* 56 E8
Rothesay *S'clyde* 46 C6
Rothiebrisbane *Gramp* 58 D5
Rothienorman *Gramp* 58 D5
Rothiesholm *Orkney* 64 C4
Rothill *Northum* 45 B9
Rothley *Leics* 23 A9
Rothmaise *Gramp* 58 D4
Rothwell *Lincs* 37 G9
Rothwell *Northants* 23 D11
Rothwell *W Yorks* 35 D12
Rothwell haigh *W Yorks* 35 D12
Rotsea *Humber* 37 B8
Rottal *Tayside* 59 K1
Rottingdean *E Sussex* 10 H3
Rottington *Cumb* 38 D2
Roucan *Dumf/Gal* 43 D11
Roud *I of Wight* 8 H6
Rough Close *Staffs* 31 F8
Rough Common *Kent* 11 B10
Rough Hay *Staffs* 31 H10
Rougham *Norfolk* 26 C1
Rougham Green *Suffolk* 27 J2
Roughburn *H'land* 55 L7
Roughlee *Lancs* 35 C7
Roughley *W Midlands* 22 B5
Roughsike *Cumb* 44 E3
Roughton *Lincs* 33 D9
Roughton *Norfolk* 26 B5
Roughton *Shrops* 22 C1
Roughwood *S'clyde* 47 D8
Round Oak *Berks* 17 H7
Roundham *Som'set* 7 E7
Roundhay *W Yorks* 35 C12
Roundstonefoot *Dumf/Gal* 43 A12
Roundstreet Common *W Sussex* 9 C12
Roundway *Wilts* 16 H1
Roundyhill *Tayside* 59 M1
Rous Lench *Heref/Worcs* 22 G4
Rousdon *Devon* 6 G6
Rousham *Oxon* 16 B6
Routdaneburn *S'clyde* 47 D7
Routenburn *S'clyde* 47 C7
Routh *Humber* 37 C8
Rovie Lodge *H'land* 61 F7
Row *Cornw'l* 3 B8
Row *Cumb* 39 F7
Row Green *Essex* 19 B7
Rowanburn *Dumf/Gal* 44 E2
Rowardennan Hotel *S'clyde* 51 H10
Rowarth *Derby* 31 A8
Rowde *Wilts* 16 H1
Ro-wen *Gwyn* 29 C7
Rowfoot *Northum* 44 G5
Rowhedge *Essex* 19 B10
Rowhook *W Sussex* 9 C12
Rowington *Warwick* 22 E5
Rowland *Derby* 31 C10
Rowland's Castle *Hants* 9 E9
Rowland's Gill *Tyne/Wear* 45 G10
Rowledge *Surrey* 9 B9
Rowley *Humber* 37 D7
Rowley *Shrops* 21 B8
Rowley Regis *W Midlands* 22 C3
Rowlstone *Heref/Worcs* 15 B7
Rowly *Surrey* 9 B11
Rowney Green *Heref/Worcs* 22 E4
Rownhams *Hants* 8 D5
Rowsham *Bucks* 17 B9
Rowsley *Derby* 31 D11
Rowston *Lincs* 33 E8
Rowton *Ches* 30 D3
Rowton *Shrops* 30 H5
Roxburgh *Borders* 49 F9
Roxburgh Newtown *Borders* 49 F9
Roxby *Humber* 37 E7
Roxby *N Yorks* 41 D7
Roxton *Beds* 25 K3
Roxwell *Essex* 18 C6
Royal Oak *Durham* 40 C2
Royal Oak *Lancs* 34 G3
Roybridge *H'land* 55 L6
Roydon *Essex* 18 C4
Roydon *Norfolk* 24 C8
Roydon *Norfolk* 27 G4
Royston *Herts* 25 L5
Royston *S Yorks* 35 F12
Royton *Gtr Man* 35 F8
Ruabon *Clwyd* 29 F12
Ruan High Lanes *Cornw'l* 2 F6
Ruan Lanihorne *Cornw'l* 2 E6
Ruan Minor *Cornw'l* 2 H4
Ruardean *Glos* 15 C9
Ruardean Woodside *Glos* 15 C9
Rubery *W Midlands* 22 D3
Ruckcroft *Cumb* 39 A8
Ruckhall Common *Heref/Worcs* 21 H10
Ruckinge *Kent* 11 E9
Ruckland *Lincs* 33 B10
Ruckley *Shrops* 21 B10
Rudbaxton *Dyfed* 12 E3
Rudby *N Yorks* 40 D5
Rudchester *Northum* 45 F9
Ruddington *Notts* 32 G3
Rudford *Glos* 15 B11
Rudge *Shrops* 22 B2
Rudge *Som'set* 7 A11
Rudgeway *Avon* 15 F9
Rudgwick *W Sussex* 9 C12
Rudhall *Heref/Worcs* 15 B9
Rudry *Mid Glam* 14 F5
Rudston *Humber* 41 H11
Rudyard *Staffs* 31 D8
Ruecastle *Borders* 49 G8
Rufford *Lancs* 34 F3
Rufforth *N Yorks* 36 B3
Ruffside *Durham* 45 H8
Rugby *Warwick* 23 E8
Rugeley *Staffs* 31 H9
Ruilick *H'land* 56 E1
Ruishton *Som'set* 6 D6
Ruislip *London* 18 E1
Ruislip Common *London* 18 E1
Ruletownhead *Borders* 44 B4
Rumbletonlaw *Borders* 49 E9
Rumblingbridge *Central* 52 G5
Rumburgh *Suffolk* 27 G6
Rumford *Cornw'l* 2 C6
Rumney *S Glam* 14 F5
Runacraig *Central* 52 F1
Runcorn *Ches* 30 B4
Runcton *W Sussex* 9 F10
Runcton Holme *Norfolk* 24 E7
Rundlestone *Devon* 5 H4
Runfold *Surrey* 9 A10
Runhall *Norfolk* 26 E4
Runham *Norfolk* 26 D7
Runnington *Som'set* 6 D5
Runsell Green *Essex* 19 C8
Runswick *N Yorks* 41 D8
Runtaleave *Tayside* 57 M8
Runwell *Essex* 19 D7
Ruscombe *Berks* 17 F9
Rush Green *Essex* 19 B11
Rushall *Heref/Worcs* 15 A9
Rushall *Norfolk* 27 G5
Rushall *W Midlands* 22 B4
Rushall *Wilts* 8 A3
Rushbrooke *Suffolk* 27 J2
Rushbury *Shrops* 21 C10
Rushden *Herts* 25 M4
Rushden *Northants* 25 J1
Rushford *Suffolk* 27 G2
Rushlake Green *E Sussex* 10 F5
Rushmere *Suffolk* 27 G8
Rushmere St. Andrew *Suffolk* 27 K5
Rushmere Street *Suffolk* 27 K5
Rushmoor *Surrey* 9 B10
Rushmoor *Wilts* 8 D1
Rushock *Heref/Worcs* 22 E2
Rusholm *Gtr Man* 35 H7
Rushton *Ches* 30 D4
Rushton *Northants* 23 D11
Rushton *Shrops* 21 B11
Rushton Spencer *Staffs* 31 D8
Rushwick *Heref/Worcs* 22 G2
Rushyford *Durham* 40 B3
Ruskie *Central* 52 G1
Ruskington *Lincs* 33 E8
Rusko *Dumf/Gal* 43 F7
Rusland *Cumb* 38 F6
Rusper *W Sussex* 10 D1
Ruspidge *Glos* 15 C9
Russell's Green *E Sussex* 10 G6
Russell's Water *Oxon* 17 E8
Rustington *W Sussex* 9 F11
Ruston *N Yorks* 41 G9
Ruston Parva *Humber* 37 A8
Ruswarp *N Yorks* 41 D9
Rutherford *Borders* 49 F9
Rutherglen *S'clyde* 47 C11
Ruthernbridge *Cornw'l* 3 C7
Ruthin *Clwyd* 29 D10
Ruthrieston *Gramp* 59 G7
Ruthven *Borders* 49 E10
Ruthven *Gramp* 58 C3
Ruthven *H'land* 56 F4
Ruthven *H'land* 57 J3
Ruthven *Tayside* 53 B7
Ruthven House *Tayside* 53 B8
Ruthvoes *Cornw'l* 2 D6
Ruthwell *Dumf/Gal* 43 E11
Ruxton Green *Heref/Worcs* 15 B8
Ruyton Eleven Towns *Shrops* 30 H3
Ryal *Northum* 45 F8
Ryall *Dorset* 7 G7
Rydal *Cumb* 38 E6
Ryde *I of Wight* 9 G7
Rydon *Devon* 4 F2
Rye *E Sussex* 11 F8
Rye Foreign *E Sussex* 11 F7
Rye Harbour *E Sussex* 11 F8
Ryemuir *Dumf/Gal* 43 D11
Ryhall *Leics* 24 D1
Ryhill *Humber* 37 E10
Ryhill *W Yorks* 36 F2
Ryhope *Tyne/Wear* 45 H12
Ryland *Lincs* 33 B7
Rylstone *N Yorks* 35 A8
Ryme Intrinseca *Dorset* 7 E9
Ryslaw *Borders* 49 E10
Ryther *N Yorks* 36 C3
Ryton *Glos* 15 A10
Ryton *N Yorks* 41 H8
Ryton *Shrops* 21 B10
Ryton *Shrops* 22 B1
Ryton *Tyne/Wear* 45 G9
Ryton-on-Dunsmore *Warwick* 23 E7
Sabden *Lancs* 34 C6
Sacombe *Herts* 18 B3
Sacriston *Durham* 45 H10
Sadberge *Durham* 40 C4
Saddell *S'clyde* 46 F3
Saddington *Leics* 23 C10
Saddle Bow *Norfolk* 24 D7
Sadgill *Cumb* 39 E7
Saffron Walden *Essex* 25 L6
Sageston *Dyfed* 12 G4
Saham Hills *Norfolk* 26 E2
Saham Toney *Norfolk* 26 E2
Saighton *Ches* 30 D3
Sailean *S'clyde* 50 C6
St. Abbs *Borders* 49 C11
St. Agnes *Cornw'l* 2 E4
St. Agnes *I of Scilly* 2 D2
St. Albans *Herts* 18 C2
St. Allen *Cornw'l* 2 E5
St. Andrews *Fife* 53 E10
St. Andrew's Major *S Glam* 14 G5
St. Anne's *Lancs* 34 D2
St. Ann's *Dumf/Gal* 43 B11
St. Ann's Chapel *Cornw'l* 3 C11
St. Ann's Chapel *Devon* 5 L5
St. Anthony *Cornw'l* 2 G5
St. Anthony's Hill *E Sussex* 10 H5
St. Arvans *Gwent* 15 E8
St. Asaph *Clwyd* 29 C9
St. Athan *S Glam* 14 G3
St. Austell *Cornw'l* 3 D7
St. Bartholomew's Hill *Wilts* 7 D12
St. Bees *Cumb* 38 D2
St. Blazey *Cornw'l* 3 D8
St. Blazey Gate *Cornw'l* 3 D7
St. Boswells *Borders* 49 F8
St. Breock *Cornw'l* 3 C7
St. Breward *Cornw'l* 3 B8
St. Briavels *Glos* 15 D9
St. Brides *Dyfed* 12 F2
St. Brides Major *Mid Glam* 14 G2
St. Brides Netherwent *Gwent* 15 E7
St. Bride's Wentlooge *Gwent* 14 F6
St. Bride's-super-Ely *S Glam* 14 G4
St. Budeaux *Devon* 5 K3
St. Buryan *Cornw'l* 2 G1
St. Catherine *Avon* 15 G11
St. Catherines *S'clyde* 51 G8
St. Clears *Dyfed* 12 E6
St. Cleer *Cornw'l* 3 C9
St. Clement *Cornw'l* 2 E5
St. Clether *Cornw'l* 3 A9
St. Colmac *S'clyde* 46 C5
St. Columb Major *Cornw'l* 2 C6
St. Columb Minor *Cornw'l* 2 C5
St. Columb Road *Cornw'l* 2 D6
St. Combs *Gramp* 58 A8
St. Cross South Elmham *Suffolk* 27 G6
St. Cuthberts *Northum* 49 E11
St. Cyrus *Tayside* 53 A12
St. David's *Dyfed* 12 D1
St. David's *Tayside* 52 E4
St. Day *Cornw'l* 2 E4
St. Decumans *Som'set* 6 B4
St. Dennis *Cornw'l* 2 D6
St. Devereux *Heref/Worcs* 15 A7
St. Dogmaels *Dyfed* 12 B5
St. Dogwells *Dyfed* 12 D3
St. Dominick *Cornw'l* 3 C11
St. Donats *S Glam* 14 G3
St. Edith's *Wilts* 16 H1
St. Endellion *Cornw'l* 3 B7
St. Enoder *Cornw'l* 2 D6
St. Erme *Cornw'l* 2 E5
St. Erney *Cornw'l* 3 D10
St. Erth *Cornw'l* 2 F3
St. Ervan *Cornw'l* 2 C6
St. Ewe *Cornw'l* 3 E7
St. Faggans *S Glam* 14 F4
St. Fergus *Gramp* 58 B8
St. Fillans *Tayside* 52 E2
St. Florence *Dyfed* 12 G4
St. Gennys *Cornw'l* 2 B2
St. George *Clwyd* 29 C9
St. George's *Avon* 15 H7
St. George's *S Glam* 14 G4
St. Germans *Cornw'l* 3 D10
St. Giles in the Wood *Devon* 4 D4
St. Giles on the Heath *Devon* 5 G2
St. Harmon *Powys* 20 E5
St. Helen Auckland *Durham* 40 C2
St. Helena *Norfolk* 26 D5
St. Helens *I of Wight* 9 G7
St. Helens *Mersey* 34 G4
St. Hilary *Cornw'l* 2 F3
St. Hilary *S Glam* 14 G3
St. Hill *E Sussex* 10 D3
St. Illtyd *Gwent* 14 D5
St. Ishmael's *Dyfed* 12 F2
St. Issey *Cornw'l* 2 C6
St. Ive *Cornw'l* 3 C10
St. Ive Cross *Cornw'l* 3 C10
St. Ives *Cambs* 25 H4
St. Ives. *Cornw'l* 2 F2
St. Ives *Dorset* 8 F3
St. James South Elmham *Suffolk* 27 G6
St. John *Cornw'l* 3 D11
St. John's *Heref/Worcs* 22 G2
St. John's *I of Man* 38 G1
St. John's Chapel *Devon* 4 C4
St. John's Chapel *Durham* 39 A11
St. John's Fen End *Norfolk* 24 D6
St. John's Highway *Norfolk* 24 D6
St. John's Town of Dalry *Dumf/Gal* 43 C7
St. Judas *I of Man* 38 F2
St. Just *Cornw'l* 2 G1
St. Just in Roseland *Cornw'l* 2 F5
St. Katherines *Gramp* 58 D5
St. Keverne *Cornw'l* 2 H5
St. Kew *Cornw'l* 3 B7
St. Kew Highway *Cornw'l* 3 B7
St. Keyne *Cornw'l* 3 D9
St. Lawrence *Cornw'l* 3 C7
St. Lawrence *Essex* 19 C9
St. Lawrence *I of Wight* 9 H7
St. Leonards *Bucks* 17 C10
St. Leonards *Dorset* 8 F3
St. Leonards *E Sussex* 11 G7
St. Levan *Cornw'l* 2 G1
St. Lythans *S Glam* 14 G4
St. Mabyn *Cornw'l* 3 B7
St. Margaret South Elmham *Suffolk* 27 G6
St. Margarets *Heref/Worcs* 15 A7
St. Margarets *Herts* 18 C4
St. Margaret's at Cliffe *Kent* 11 D12
St. Margaret's Hope *Orkney* 64 E2
St. Mark's *I of Man* 38 H1
St. Martin *Cornw'l* 3 D9
St. Martin's *Cornw'l* 2 G4
St. Martin's *Shrops* 30 G2
St. Martin's *Tayside* 52 D6
St. Mary Bourne *Hants* 8 A6
St. Mary Church *S Glam* 14 G3
St. Mary Cray *London* 18 G5
St. Mary in the Marsh *Kent* 11 E9
St. Marylebone *London* 18 F3
St. Mary's *Orkney* 64 D3
St. Mary's Bay *Kent* 11 E9
St. Mary's Grove *Avon* 15 G8
St. Mary's Hoo *Kent* 19 F8
St. Maughans *Gwent* 15 C8
St. Mawes *Cornw'l* 2 F5
St. Mawgan *Cornw'l* 2 C6
St. Mellion *Cornw'l* 3 C11
St. Mellons *S Glam* 14 F6
St. Merryn *Cornw'l* 2 B6
St. Mewan *Cornw'l* 3 E7
St. Michael Caerhays *Cornw'l* 3 E7
St. Michael Penkevil *Cornw'l* 2 E6
St. Michael South Elmham *Suffolk* 27 G6
St. Michael's *Heref/Worcs* 21 F11
St. Michaels *Kent* 11 E7
St. Michaels on Wyre *Lancs* 34 C3
St. Minver *Cornw'l* 3 B7
St. Monance *Fife* 53 G10
St. Neot *Cornw'l* 3 C9
St. Neots *Cambs* 25 J3
St. Newlyn East *Cornw'l* 2 D5
St. Nicholas *Dyfed* 12 C2
St. Nicholas *S Glam* 14 G4
St. Nicholas at Wade *Kent* 11 A11
St. Ninians *Central* 52 H3
St. Olaves *Norfolk* 26 E8
St. Osyth *Essex* 19 B11
St. Osyth Heath *Essex* 19 B11
St. Owen's Cross *Heref/Worcs* 15 B8
St. Pancras *London* 18 F3
St. Paul's Cray *London* 18 G5
St. Paul's Walden *Herts* 18 B2
St. Peters *Kent* 11 A12
St. Petrox *Dyfed* 12 G3
St. Quivox *S'clyde* 47 G8
St. Stephen *Cornw'l* 2 D6
St. Stephen's *Cornw'l* 3 A10
St. Stephen's *Cornw'l* 3 D11
St. Teath *Cornw'l* 3 B7
St. Tudy *Cornw'l* 3 B8
St. Twynnells *Dyfed* 12 G3
St. Veep *Cornw'l* 3 D8
St. Vigeans *Tayside* 53 C11
St. Wenn *Cornw'l* 3 C7
St. Weonards *Heref/Worcs* 15 B8
St. Winnow *Cornw'l* 3 D8
Saintbury *Glos* 22 H5
Salachail *S'clyde* 51 B8
Salcombe *Devon* 5 M6
Salcombe Regis *Devon* 6 G5
Salcott *Essex* 19 C9
Sale *Gtr Man* 35 H7
Sale Green *Heref/Worcs* 22 F3
Saleby *Lincs* 33 B11
Salehurst *E Sussex* 10 F6
Salem *Dyfed* 13 D9
Salem *Dyfed* 20 D2
Salem *Gwyn* 28 E5
Salen *H'land* 50 A4
Salen *H'land* 50 C3
Salesbury *Lancs* 34 D5
Salford *Beds* 23 H12
Salford *Gtr Man* 35 G7
Salford *Oxon* 16 A4
Salford Priors *Warwick* 22 G4
Salfords *Surrey* 10 C2
Salhouse *Norfolk* 26 D6
Saline *Fife* 52 H5
Salisbury *Wilts* 8 C3
Sall *Norfolk* 26 C4

Sallachan *H'land* **51** A7
Sallachy *H'land* **55** G3
Sallachy *H'land* **60** F6
Salmonby *Lincs* **33** C10
Salmonds Muir *Tayside* **53** C10
Salperton *Glos* **16** B2
Salph End *Beds* **25** K2
Salsburgh *S'clyde* **48** C1
Salt *Staffs* **31** G8
Saltash *Cornw'l* **3** D11
Saltburn *H'land* **56** C3
Saltburn-by-the-Sea *Clevl'd* **41** C7
Saltby *Leics* **32** H6
Saltcoats *S'clyde* **47** E7
Salterforth *Lancs* **35** C7
Salters Lode *Norfolk* **24** E7
Saltfleet *Lincs* **33** A11
Saltfleetby All Saints *Lincs* **33** A11
Saltfleetby St. Clements *Lincs* **33** A11
Saltfleetby St. Peter *Lincs* **33** A11
Saltford *Avon* **15** G10
Salthouse *Norfolk* **26** A4
Saltmarshe *Humber* **36** E6
Saltney *Ches* **30** D3
Salton *N Yorks* **41** G7
Saltrens *Devon* **4** D3
Saltwick *Northum* **45** E10
Saltwood *Kent* **11** D10
Salvington *W Sussex* **9** F12
Salwarpe *Heref/Worcs* **22** F2
Salway Ash *Dorset* **7** F8
Sambourne *Warwick* **22** F4
Sambrook *Shrops* **30** H6
Samlesbury *Lancs* **34** D5
Samlesbury Bottoms *Lancs* **34** D5
Sampford *Som'set* **6** B4
Sampford Arundel *Som'set* **6** D5
Sampford Courtenay *Devon* **4** F5
Sampford Peverell *Devon* **6** E4
Sampford Spiney *Devon* **5** H4
Samuel's Corner *Essex* **19** E9
Samuelston *Lothian* **49** B7
Sanachan *H'land* **54** F2
Sanahole *S'clyde* **51** G7
Sancreed *Cornw'l* **2** G1
Sancton *Humber* **37** C7
Sand Hutton *N Yorks* **36** A5
Sandaig *H'land* **55** H1
Sandaig *H'land* **55** J1
Sandal Magna *W Yorks* **35** E12
Sandale *Cumb* **38** A5
Sandbach *Ches* **30** D6
Sandbank *S'clyde* **46** A6
Sandbanks *Dorset* **8** G2
Sandend *Gramp* **58** A3
Sanderstead *London* **18** H3
Sandford *Avon* **15** H7
Sandford *Cumb* **39** D9
Sandford *Devon* **4** F7
Sandford *Dorset* **8** G1
Sandford *I of Wight* **9** H7
Sandford *S'clyde* **47** E12
Sandford *Shrops* **30** H2
Sandford on Thames *Oxon* **16** D6
Sandford Orcas *Dorset* **7** D9
Sandford St. Martin *Oxon* **16** B5
Sandfordhill *Gramp* **58** C8
Sandgarth *Orkney* **64** C3
Sandgate *Kent* **11** E10
Sandhaven *Gramp* **58** A7
Sandhead *Dumf/Gal* **42** G2
Sandhill *S'clyde* **47** H9
Sandhoe *Northum* **45** F8
Sandholm *Borders* **44** D3
Sandholme *Humber* **36** D6
Sandholme *Lincs* **24** B4
Sandhurst *Berks* **17** H9
Sandhurst *Glos* **15** B11
Sandhurst *Kent* **11** E7
Sandhurst Cross *Kent* **10** E6
Sandhutton *N Yorks* **40** G4
Sandiacre *Derby* **32** G2
Sandilands *Lincs* **33** B12
Sandiway *Ches* **30** C5
Sandle Heath *Hants* **8** E3
Sandleigh *Oxon* **16** D6
Sandling *Kent* **10** B6
Sandness *Shetl'd* **64** D6
Sandon *Essex* **19** C7
Sandon *Herts* **25** M4
Sandon *Staffs* **31** G8
Sandown *I of Wight* **9** H7
Sandplace *Cornw'l* **3** D9
Sandridge *Herts* **18** C2
Sandridge *Wilts* **15** H12
Sandsend *N Yorks* **41** D8
Sandside *Orkney* **64** D1
Sandside Hotel *H'land* **61** A9
Sandsound *Shetl'd* **64** D7
Sandtoft *Humber* **36** F5
Sandway *Kent* **11** C7
Sandway Cross *Som'set* **6** C2
Sandwell *W Midlands* **22** C4
Sandwich *Kent* **11** B12
Sandwick *Cumb* **38** C6
Sandwick *Orkney* **64** E2
Sandwick *Shetl'd* **64** E7
Sandwick *W Isles* **63** D5
Sandwith *Cumb* **38** D2
Sandy *Beds* **25** K3
Sandy Bank *Shrops* **30** G4
Sandy Haven *Dyfed* **12** F2
Sandy Lane *W Yorks* **35** D9
Sandy Lane *Wilts* **16** G1
Sandycroft *Clwyd* **29** D12
Sandyford *Dumf/Gal* **43** B12
Sandyford *S'clyde* **47** G9
Sandygate *I of Man* **38** F2
Sandyhills *Dumf/Gal* **43** F9
Sandylands *Lancs* **34** A3
Sandymoor Cross *Devon* **4** F3
Sandypark *Devon* **5** G6
Sandysike *Cumb* **44** F2
Sandystones *Borders* **49** G8
Sandyway *Heref/Worcs* **15** B8
Sangomore *H'land* **60** A5
Sanna *H'land* **50** A2
Sanquhar *Dumf/Gal* **47** H12
Santon Bridge *Cumb* **38** E4
Santon Downham *Suffolk* **27** G1
Sapcote *Leics* **23** C8
Sapey Common *Heref/Worcs* **21** F12
Sapiston *Suffolk* **27** H2
Sapperton *Glos* **15** D12
Sapperton *Lincs* **33** G7
Saracen's Head *Lincs* **24** C4
Sarclet *H'land* **61** C12
Sardis *Dyfed* **12** F3
Sardis Mountain *Dyfed* **12** F5
Sarisbury *Hants* **8** E6
Sarn *Gwyn* **28** G2
Sarn *Mid Glam* **14** F2
Sarn *Powys* **21** C7
Sarnau *Dyfed* **12** B6
Sarnau *Dyfed* **13** D8
Sarnau *Gwyn* **29** F9
Sarnau *Powys* **14** A3
Sarnau *Powys* **21** A8
Sarn-bach *Gwyn* **28** H2
Sarnesfield *Heref/Worcs* **21** G9
Saron *Dyfed* **13** C7
Saron *Dyfed* **13** F9
Saron *Gwyn* **28** D5
Sarratt *Herts* **17** D11
Sarre *Kent* **11** B11
Sarsden *Oxon* **16** B4
Sarson *Hants* **8** B4
Sartfield *I of Man* **38** F2
Satley *Durham* **40** A1
Satterleigh *Devon* **4** D5
Satterswall *Ches* **30** D5
Satterthwaite *Cumb* **38** F6
Satwell *Oxon* **17** F8
Sauchen *Gramp* **58** F4
Saucher *Tayside* **53** D7
Sauchieburn *Gramp* **59** K4
Sauchrie *S'clyde* **47** H8
Saughall *Ches* **30** C2
Saughtree *Borders* **44** C4
Saughtrees *Cumb* **44** E3
Saul *Glos* **15** C10
Saundby *Notts* **32** A5
Saundersfoot *Dyfed* **12** F5
Saunderton *Bucks* **17** D9
Saunderton Lee *Bucks* **17** D9
Saunton *Devon* **4** B3
Sausthorpe *Lincs* **33** C11
Saval *H'land* **60** F6
Saverley Green *Staffs* **31** F8
Savory *H'land* **50** C4
Sawbridge *Warwick* **23** F8
Sawbridgeworth *Herts* **18** B5
Sawdon *N Yorks* **41** G9
Sawley *Derby* **32** G2
Sawley *Lancs* **34** C6
Sawston *Cambs* **25** K6
Sawtry *Cambs* **25** G3
Saxby *Leics* **32** H5
Saxby *Lincs* **33** B7
Saxby All Saints *Humber* **37** E7
Saxelbye *Leics* **32** H4
Saxilby *Lincs* **32** C6
Saxlingham *Norfolk* **26** B3
Saxlingham Nethergate *Norfolk* **26** F5
Saxmundham *Suffolk* **27** J7
Saxon Street *Cambs* **25** J8
Saxondale *Notts* **32** F4
Saxstead *Suffolk* **27** J6
Saxstead Green *Suffolk* **27** J6
Saxthorpe *Norfolk* **26** C4
Saxton *N Yorks* **36** C3
Sayers Common *W Sussex* **10** F2
Scabcleuch *Borders* **48** H5
Scackleton *N Yorks* **40** H6
Scadabay *W Isles* **63** H3
Scaftworth *Lincs* **32** A6
Scagglethorpe *N Yorks* **41** H8
Scalasaig *H'land* **50** H1
Scalby *Humber* **36** D6
Scalby *N Yorks* **41** F10
Scaldwell *Northants* **23** E11
Scaleby *Cumb* **44** G3
Scalebyhill *Cumb* **44** G3
Scales *Cumb* **38** C6
Scales *Cumb* **38** H5
Scales *Lancs* **34** D3
Scales House *Cumb* **39** A8
Scalford *Leics* **32** H5
Scaling *N Yorks* **41** D7
Scallastle *H'land* **50** D4
Scalloway *Shetl'd* **64** E7
Scalpay *W Isles* **63** G3
Scalpay House *H'land* **62** E5
Scamadale *H'land* **55** K1
Scamodale *H'land* **55** M2
Scampston *N Yorks* **41** H8
Scampton *Lincs* **33** B7
Scaniport *H'land* **56** F2
Scapa *Orkney* **64** D2
Scar *Orkney* **64** A4
Scar End *Durham* **39** B11
Scarastavore *W Isles* **63** H1
Scarborough *N Yorks* **41** F10
Scarbrae *Dumf/Gal* **43** C9
Scarcliffe *Derby* **32** C2
Scarcroft *W Yorks* **35** C12
Scardroy *H'land* **54** D6
Scarfskerry *H'land* **61** A11
Scargill *Durham* **40** D1
Scarisbrick *Lancs* **34** F3
Scarning *Norfolk* **26** D2
Scarrington *Notts* **32** F4
Scarth Hill *Lancs* **34** F3
Scartho *Humber* **37** G10
Scarwell *Orkney* **64** C1
Scatraig *H'land* **56** F3
Scatsta *Shetl'd* **64** C7
Scawby *Humber* **37** G7
Scawby Brook *Humber* **37** F7
Scawsby *S Yorks* **36** G3
Scawton *N Yorks* **40** G6
Scayne's Hill *W Sussex* **10** F3
Scethrog *Powys* **14** B4
Schaw *S'clyde* **47** G9
Scholar Green *Ches* **31** E7
Scholes *W Yorks* **35** E10
Scholes *W Yorks* **35** F10
Scholes *W Yorks* **36** D2
School Aycliffe *Durham* **40** C3
Scissett *W Yorks* **35** F11
Scleddau *Dyfed* **12** D3
Sco Ruston *Norfolk* **26** C6
Scole *Norfolk* **27** G4
Scolly's Cross *Gramp* **59** J4
Scolton *Dyfed* **12** E3
Sconser *H'land* **62** E4
Scoonie *Fife* **53** G8
Scoor *H'land* **50** F2
Scopwick *Lincs* **33** D8
Scoraig *H'land* **60** G2
Scorborough *Humber* **37** C8
Scorrieholm *S'clyde* **47** F12
Scorrier *Cornw'l* **2** E4
Scorriton *Devon* **5** J6
Scorton *N Yorks* **40** E3
Scot Lane End *Gtr Man* **34** F5
Scotby *Cumb* **44** G3
Scotch Corner *N Yorks* **40** E2
Scotforth *Lancs* **34** A4
Scothern *Lincs* **33** B7
Scots' Gap *Northum* **45** D8
Scotsburn *H'land* **56** B3
Scotscalder Sta *H'land* **61** B10
Scotscraig *Fife* **53** D9
Scotsdike *Cumb* **44** F2
Scotston *Gramp* **59** K5
Scotston *Tayside* **52** C4
Scotstown *H'land* **50** A5
Scotswood *Tyne/Wear* **45** G10
Scottas *H'land* **55** J1
Scotter *Lincs* **36** G6
Scotterthorpe *Lincs* **36** G6
Scotton *Lincs* **37** G7
Scotton *N Yorks* **35** A12
Scotton *N Yorks* **40** F2
Scottow *Norfolk* **26** C6
Scoughall *Lothian* **49** A8
Scoulay *S'clyde* **46** D6
Scoulton *Norfolk* **26** E3
Scourie *H'land* **60** C3
Scourie More *H'land* **60** C3
Scousburgh *Shetl'd* **64** F7
Scrabster *H'land* **61** A10
Scraesburgh *Borders* **49** G9
Scrafield *Lincs* **33** C10
Scrainwood *Northum* **45** B8
Scramblesby *Lincs* **33** B10
Scrane End *Lincs* **24** A5
Scraptoft *Leics* **23** B10
Scratby *Norfolk* **26** D8
Scrayingham *N Yorks* **36** A5
Scredington *Lincs* **24** B2
Screedy *Som'set* **6** D4
Screel *Dumf/Gal* **43** F9
Scremby *Lincs* **33** C11
Scremerston *Northum* **49** D12
Screveton *Notts* **32** F4
Scriberscross *H'land* **61** F8
Scrivelsby *Lincs* **33** D9
Scriven *N Yorks* **35** A12
Scroggs *Dumf/Gal* **43** C12
Scrooby *Notts* **32** A4
Scropton *Derby* **31** G10
Scrub Hill *Lincs* **33** E9
Scruton *N Yorks* **40** F3
Sculcoates *Humber* **37** D8
Sculthorpe *Norfolk* **26** B2
Scunthorpe *Humber* **37** F7
Scurlage *W Glam* **13** H8
Sea Palling *Norfolk* **26** C7
Seaborough *Dorset* **7** F8
Seacombe *Mersey* **30** A2
Seacroft *Lincs* **33** D12
Seacroft *W Yorks* **35** D12
Seafield *Lothian* **48** C3
Seafield *S'clyde* **47** G8
Seaford *E Sussex* **10** H4
Seaforth *Mersey* **34** G2
Seaforth Head *W Isles* **63** E4
Seaham *Durham* **45** H12
Seahouses *Northum* **45** D12
Seal *Kent* **10** B4
Sealand *Clwyd* **30** C2
Seale *Surrey* **9** A10
Seamer *N Yorks* **40** D5
Seamer *N Yorks* **41** G10
Seamill *S'clyde* **47** E7
Searby *Lincs* **37** G8
Seasalter *Kent* **11** B9
Seascale *Cumb* **38** E3
Seathorne *Lincs* **33** D12
Seathwaite *Cumb* **38** D5
Seathwaite *Cumb* **38** F5
Seatoller *Cumb* **38** D5
Seaton *Cornw'l* **3** D10
Seaton *Cumb* **38** B3
Seaton *Devon* **6** G6
Seaton *Durham* **45** H12
Seaton *Humber* **37** B9
Seaton *Leics* **23** B12
Seaton *Northum* **45** E11
Seaton Burn *Tyne/Wear* **45** F10
Seaton Carew *Clevl'd* **40** B5
Seaton Delaval *Northum* **45** E11
Seaton Ross *N Yorks* **36** C5
Seaton Sluice *Northum* **45** E11
Seatown *Dorset* **7** G7
Seatown *Gramp* **58** A2
Seatown *Gramp* **58** A3
Seave Green *N Yorks* **40** E6
Seaview *I of Wight* **9** G8
Seaville *Cumb* **43** F12
Seavington St. Mary *Som'set* **7** E7
Seavington St. Michael *Som'set* **7** E7
Seawick Sands *Essex* **19** C12
Sebastopol *Gwent* **14** E6
Sebergham *Cumb* **38** A6
Seckington *Warwick* **22** A6
Second Coast *H'land* **60** G1
Sedbergh *Cumb* **39** F9
Sedbury *Glos* **15** E9
Sedbusk *N Yorks* **39** F11
Sedgeberrow *Heref/Worcs* **22** H4
Sedgebrook *Lincs* **32** F6
Sedgefield *Durham* **40** B4
Sedgeford *Norfolk* **24** B8
Sedgehill *Wilts* **7** C12
Sedgley *W Midlands* **22** C3
Sedgwick *Cumb* **39** F7
Sedlescombe *E Sussex* **10** F6
Seend *Wilts* **15** H12
Seend Cleeve *Wilts* **15** H12
Seer Green *Bucks* **17** E10
Seething *Norfolk* **26** F6
Sefton *Mersey* **34** G2
Seghill *Northum* **45** F11
Seighford *Staffs* **31** H7
Seilebost *W Isles* **63** G2
Seisdon *Staffs* **22** C2
Seisiader *W Isles* **63** C6
Selattyn *Shrops* **30** G1
Selborne *Hants* **9** C9
Selby *N Yorks* **36** D4
Selham *W Sussex* **9** D10
Selkirk *Borders* **49** G7
Sellack *Heref/Worcs* **15** B9
Sellafield Station *Cumb* **38** E3
Sellafirth *Shetl'd* **64** B7
Sellindge *Kent* **11** D9
Sellindge Lees *Kent* **11** D9
Selling *Kent* **11** B9
Sells Green *Wilts* **15** H12
Selly Oak *W Midlands* **22** D4
Selmeston *E Sussex* **10** G4
Selsdon *London* **18** H4
Selsey *Glos* **15** D11
Selsfield Common *W Sussex* **10** E2
Selside *N Yorks* **39** H10
Selstead *Kent* **11** D10
Selston *Notts* **32** E2
Selworthy *Som'set* **6** B3
Semblister *Shetl'd* **64** D7
Semer *Suffolk* **27** K3
Semington *Wilts* **15** H12
Semley *Wilts* **7** D12
Send *Surrey* **9** A11
Sendmarsh *Surrey* **9** A11
Senghenydd *Mid Glam* **14** E4
Sennen *Cornw'l* **2** G1
Sennen Cove *Cornw'l* **2** G1
Sennybridge *Powys* **14** B3
Senwick Ho *Dumf/Gal* **43** G7
Sessay *N Yorks* **40** H5
Setchey *Norfolk* **24** D7
Setley *Hants* **8** F5
Settascarth *Orkney* **64** C2
Setter *Shetl'd* **64** D6
Setter *Shetl'd* **64** D7
Setter *Shetl'd* **64** E7
Settle *N Yorks* **35** A7
Settlingstones *Northum* **45** F7
Settrington *N Yorks* **41** H8
Seven Ash *Som'set* **6** C5
Seven Kings *London* **18** E4
Seven Sisters *W Glam* **14** C2
Seven Springs *Glos* **16** B1
Seven Wells *Glos* **16** A2
Sevenhampton *Glos* **16** B1
Sevenhampton *Wilts* **16** E3
Sevenoaks *Kent* **10** C4
Sevenoaks Weald *Kent* **10** C4
Severn Beach *Avon* **15** F8
Severn Stoke *Heref/Worcs* **22** H2
Sevington *Kent* **11** D9
Sevington *Wilts* **15** F11
Sewards End *Essex* **25** L7
Sewerby *Humber* **41** H12
Seworgan *Cornw'l* **2** G4
Sewstern *Leics* **32** H6
Shabbington *Bucks* **17** C7
Shackerstone *Leics* **23** A7
Shackleford *Surrey* **9** B10
Shader *W Isles* **63** B5
Shadforth *Durham* **40** A4
Shadingfield *Suffolk* **27** G7
Shadoxhurst *Kent* **11** D8
Shadwell *Norfolk* **27** G2
Shadwell *W Yorks* **35** C12
Shaftesbury *Dorset* **7** D12
Shafton *S Yorks* **36** F2
Shalbourne *Wilts* **16** H4
Shalcombe *I of Wight* **8** G5
Shalden *Hants* **9** B8
Shaldon *Devon* **5** J8
Shalfleet *I of Wight* **8** G5
Shalford *Essex* **19** A7
Shalford *Surrey* **9** A11
Shalford Green *Essex* **19** A7
Shallowford *Devon* **4** B6
Shalmsford Street *Kent* **11** C9
Shalstone *Bucks* **23** H9
Shalunt *S'clyde* **46** B5
Shamley Green *Surrey* **9** B11
Shancastle *Dumf/Gal* **43** C9
Shandon *S'clyde* **47** A7
Shandwick *H'land* **56** B4
Shangton *Leics* **23** C10
Shankhouse *Northum* **45** E11
Shanklin *I of Wight* **9** H7
Shannochie *S'clyde* **46** G5
Shanzie *Tayside* **53** B7
Shap *Cumb* **39** D8
Shapwick *Dorset* **8** F1
Shapwick *Som'set* **7** B7
Shardlow *Derby* **32** G2
Shareshill *Staffs* **22** B3
Sharlston *W Yorks* **36** E2
Sharlston Common *W Yorks* **36** E2
Sharnal Street *Kent* **11** A7
Sharnbrook *Beds* **25** J1
Sharnford *Leics* **23** C8
Sharoe Green *Lancs* **34** D4
Sharow *N Yorks* **40** H3
Sharpenhoe *Beds* **25** M2
Sharperton *Northum* **45** C8
Sharpness *Glos* **15** D10
Sharpthorne *W Sussex* **10** E3
Sharrington *Norfolk* **26** B3
Shatterford *Heref/Worcs* **22** D1
Shaugh Prior *Devon* **5** J4
Shave Cross *Dorset* **7** F7
Shavington *Ches* **30** E5
Shaw *Berks* **16** G6
Shaw *Gtr Man* **35** F8
Shaw *Wilts* **15** H12
Shaw Green *Lancs* **34** E4
Shaw Mills *N Yorks* **35** A11
Shawbury *Shrops* **30** H4
Shawdon Hill *Northum* **45** B9
Shawell *Leics* **23** D9
Shawford *Hants* **8** D6
Shawforth *Lancs* **35** E7
Shawhead *Dumf/Gal* **43** D9
Shawhill *Dumf/Gal* **43** E12
Shawton *S'clyde* **47** D11
Shawwood *S'clyde* **47** G10
Shearington *Dumf/Gal* **43** E11
Shearsby *Leics* **23** C9
Shebbear *Devon* **4** E3
Shebdon *Staffs* **30** H6
Shebster *H'land* **61** B9
Shedfield *Hants* **9** E7
Sheen *Staffs* **31** D9
Sheephouse *Powys* **21** H7
Sheepscombe *Glos* **15** C12
Sheepstor *Devon* **5** J4
Sheepwash *Devon* **4** C7
Sheepwash *Devon* **4** E4
Sheepwash *Northum* **45** D10
Sheepway *Avon* **15** G8
Sheepy Magna *Leics* **23** B7
Sheepy Parva *Leics* **23** B7
Sheering *Essex* **18** C5
Sheerness *Kent* **11** A8
Sheet *Hants* **9** D9
Sheet *Shrops* **21** E10
Sheffield *S Yorks* **32** B1
Shefford *Beds* **25** L2
Shefford Woodlands *Berks* **16** G4
Sheigra *H'land* **60** B3
Sheildaig *H'land* **54** D2
Sheillahill *Dumf/Gal* **43** F8
Sheinton *Shrops* **21** B11
Shelderton *Shrops* **21** E9
Sheldon *Derby* **31** C10
Sheldon *Devon* **6** E5
Sheldon *W Midlands* **22** D5
Sheldwich *Kent* **11** B9
Shelf *W Yorks* **35** D10
Shelfanger *Norfolk* **27** G4
Shelfield *W Midlands* **22** B4
Shelfield *Warwick* **22** F5
Shelford *Notts* **32** F4
Shellacres *Northum* **49** E11
Shelley *Essex* **18** C5
Shelley *W Yorks* **35** F10
Shellingford *Oxon* **16** E4
Shellow Bowells *Essex* **18** C6
Shelsley Beauchamp *Heref/Worcs* **22** F1
Shelsley Walsh *Heref/Worcs* **21** F12
Shelthorpe *Leics* **32** H3
Shelton *Beds* **25** H1
Shelton *Norfolk* **26** F5
Shelton *Notts* **32** F5
Shelton *Shrops* **21** A10
Shelve *Shrops* **21** C9
Shelwick *Heref/Worcs* **21** H10
Shelwick Green *Heref/Worcs* **21** H10
Shenachie *H'land* **56** F4
Shenfield *Essex* **18** D6
Shenington *Oxon* **23** H7
Shenley *Herts* **18** D2
Shenley Brook End *Bucks* **17** A9
Shenley Church End *Bucks* **23** H11
Shenmore *Heref/Worcs* **15** A7
Shennach *H'land* **57** G7
Shennanton *Dumf/Gal* **42** E4
Shenstone *Heref/Worcs* **22** E2
Shenstone *Staffs* **22** B4
Shenton *Leics* **23** B7
Shenval *Gramp* **57** G8
Shenval *H'land* **55** G8
Shepeu Stow *Lincs* **24** D4
Shephall *Herts* **18** B3
Shepherd's Bush *London* **18** F2
Shepherd's Green *Oxon* **17** F8
Shepherdswell *Kent* **11** C11
Shepley *W Yorks* **35** F10
Shepperdine *Avon* **15** E9
Shepperton *Surrey* **17** G11
Shepperton Green *Surrey* **17** G11
Shepreth *Cambs* **25** K5
Shepshed *Leics* **32** H2
Shepton Beauchamp *Som'set* **7** D7
Shepton Mallet *Som'set* **7** B9
Shepton Montague *Som'set* **7** C10
Shepway *Kent* **10** C6
Sheraton *Durham* **40** B5
Sherborne *Dorset* **7** E9

Sherborne *Glos* **16** C3
Sherborne St. John *Hants* **9** A8
Sherbourne *Warwick* **22** F6
Sherburn *Durham* **40** A3
Sherburn *N Yorks* **41** G9
Sherburn Hill *Durham* **40** A4
Sherburn in Elmet *N Yorks* **36** D3
Shere *Surrey* **9** A12
Shereford *Norfolk* **26** C2
Sherfield English *Hants* **8** D4
Sherfield on Loddon *Hants* **17** H7
Sherford *Devon* **5** L6
Sheriff Hutton *N Yorks* **36** A4
Sheriffhales *Shrops* **22** A11
Sheringham *Norfolk* **26** A4
Sherington *Bucks* **23** G12
Shernborne *Norfolk* **24** B8
Sherrington *Wilts* **8** B1
Sherston *Wilts* **15** F11
Sherwood Green *Devon* **4** D4
Shettleston *S'clyde* **47** C11
Shevington *Gtr Man* **34** F4
Shevington Moor *Gtr Man* **34** F4
Sheviock *Cornw'l* **3** D10
Shewglie *H'land* **55** G8
Shian *Tayside* **52** C3
Shidlaw *Northum* **49** F10
Shiel *Dumf/Gal* **43** A8
Shiel *Dumf/Gal* **43** D7
Shiel Bridge *H'land* **55** H3
Shiel Dykes *Northum* **45** B9
Shieldaig *H'land* **54** C2
Shieldhill *Dumf/Gal* **43** C10
Shieldhill *Dumf/Gal* **43** C11
Shieldhill *Lothian* **48** B2
Shieldmuir *S'clyde* **47** D12
Shielfoot *H'land* **50** A4
Shielhill *Gramp* **58** B8
Shielhill *Tayside* **59** L2
Shieloans *S'clyde* **47** F11
Shifford *Oxon* **16** D5
Shifnal *Shrops* **22** A1
Shilbottle *Northum* **45** B10
Shildon *Durham* **40** C3
Shillford *S'clyde* **47** D9
Shillingford *Devon* **6** D3
Shillingford *Oxon* **17** E7
Shillingford Abbot *Devon* **6** G2
Shillingford St. George *Devon* **6** G2
Shillingstone *Dorset* **7** E11
Shillington *Beds* **25** M2
Shillmoor *Northum* **45** B7
Shiltenish *W Isles* **63** E4
Shilton *Oxon* **16** C4
Shilton *Warwick* **23** D7
Shilvinghampton *Dorset* **7** H9
Shimpling *Norfolk* **27** G4
Shimpling *Suffolk* **27** K2
Shimpling Street *Suffolk* **27** K2
Shincliffe *Durham* **40** A3
Shincliffe Colliery *Durham* **40** A3
Shiney Row *Tyne/Wear* **45** H11
Shinfield *Berks* **17** G8
Shinfur *Tayside* **59** J2
Shinnelhead *Dumf/Gal* **43** B8
Shinness *H'land* **60** E6
Shipbourne *Kent* **10** C5
Shipdham *Norfolk* **26** E3
Shipham *Som'set* **7** A8
Shiphay *Devon* **5** J8
Shiplake *Oxon* **17** F8
Shiplaw *Borders* **48** D5
Shipley *Northum* **45** A9
Shipley *Shrops* **22** C2
Shipley *W Sussex* **9** D12
Shipley *W Yorks* **35** C10
Shipley Bridge *Surrey* **10** D2
Shipmeadow *Suffolk* **26** F7
Shippea Hill Sta *Cambs* **25** G7
Shippon *Oxon* **16** D6
Shipston on Stour *Warwick* **22** H6
Shipton *Glos* **16** B1
Shipton *N Yorks* **36** A3
Shipton *Shrops* **21** C11
Shipton Bellinger *Hants* **8** B4
Shipton Gorge *Dorset* **7** G8
Shipton Green *W Sussex* **9** F9
Shipton Moyne *Glos* **15** E12
Shipton-on-Cherwell *Oxon* **16** B6
Shiptonthorpe *Humber* **36** C6
Shipton-under-Wychwood *Oxon* **16** B4
Shirburn *Oxon* **17** E8
Shirdley Hill *Lancs* **34** F2
Shire Oak *W Midlands* **22** B4
Shirebrook *Derby* **32** C3
Shiregreen *S Yorks* **32** A1
Shirehampton *Avon* **15** F8
Shiremoor *Tyne/Wear* **45** F11
Shirenewton *Gwent* **15** E8
Shireoaks *Notts* **32** B3
Shirewell Cross *Devon* **4** B5
Shirl Heath *Heref/Worcs* **21** F10
Shirland *Derby* **32** D1
Shirley *Derby* **31** F10
Shirley *Hants* **8** E5
Shirley *W Midlands* **22** D5
Shiroak *Kent* **11** D8
Shirrell Heath *Hants* **9** E7
Shirwell *Devon* **4** B5
Shishkine *S'clyde* **46** F4
Shobdon *Heref/Worcs* **21** F9
Shobrooke *Devon* **4** F7
Shocklach *Ches* **30** E3
Shoeburyness *Essex* **19** E9
Sholden *Kent* **11** C12
Sholing *Hants* **8** E6
Shoot Hill *Shrops* **21** A9
Shop *Cornw'l* **2** B6
Shop *Cornw'l* **4** D1
Shopford *Cumb* **44** F4
Shoreditch *London* **18** F3
Shoreham *Kent* **10** B4
Shoreham-by-Sea *W Sussex* **10** G1
Shoremill *H'land* **56** C3
Shoresdean *Northum* **49** E12
Shoreswood *Northum* **49** E12
Shoretown *H'land* **56** D2
Shorncote *Glos* **16** E1
Shorne Ridgeway *Kent* **10** A6
Short Heath *W Midlands* **22** B3
Short Heath *W Midlands* **22** C4
Shortacombe *Devon* **5** G4
Shortgate *E Sussex* **10** G4
Shortlandsend *Cornw'l* **2** E5
Shortlees *S'clyde* **47** F9
Shortstown *Beds* **25** K2
Shortwood *Avon* **15** G10
Shorwell *I of Wight* **8** H6
Shoscombe *Avon* **7** A10
Shotatton *Shrops* **30** H2
Shotesham *Norfolk* **26** F5
Shotgate *Essex* **19** E7
Shotley Bridge *Northum* **45** H9
Shotley Gate *Suffolk* **27** M5
Shotley Street *Suffolk* **27** M5
Shotleyfield *Northum* **45** H9
Shottenden *Kent* **11** C9
Shottermill *Surrey* **9** C10
Shottery *Warwick* **22** G5
Shotteswell *Oxon* **23** H8
Shottisham *Suffolk* **27** L6
Shottle *Derby* **31** E11
Shotton *Clwyd* **29** C12
Shotton *Durham* **40** A4
Shotton *Northum* **49** F11
Shotton Colliery *Durham* **40** A4
Shotts *S'clyde* **48** C1
Shotwick *Ches* **30** C2
Shoughlaige-e-Caine *I of Man* **38** G1
Shougle *Gramp* **56** D8
Shouldham *Norfolk* **24** E8
Shouldham Thorpe *Norfolk* **24** E8
Shoulton *Heref/Worcs* **22** F2
Shover's Green *E Sussex* **10** E5
Shrathellie *Gramp* **58** B8
Shrawardine *Shrops* **21** A9
Shrawley *Heref/Worcs* **22** F2
Shreding Green *Bucks* **17** F11
Shrewley Common *Warwick* **22** E5
Shrewsbury *Shrops* **21** A10
Shrewton *Wilts* **8** B2
Shripney *W Sussex* **9** F10
Shrivenham *Oxon* **16** E3
Shropham *Norfolk* **26** F3
Shrub End *Essex* **19** B9
Shucknall *Heref/Worcs* **21** H11
Shudy Camps *Cambs* **25** L7
Shundraw *Cumb* **38** C5
Shurdington *Glos* **15** B12
Shurlock Row *Berks* **17** G9
Shurrery Lodge *H'land* **61** B10
Shurton *Som'set* **6** B5
Shustoke *Warwick* **22** C6
Shute *Devon* **4** F8
Shute *Devon* **6** F6
Shutford *Oxon* **23** H7
Shuthonger *Glos* **15** A12
Shutlanger *Northants* **23** G10
Shuttington *Warwick* **22** B6
Shuttlewood *Derby* **32** C2
Sibbaldbie *Dumf/Gal* **43** C12
Sibbertoft *Northants* **23** D10
Sibdon Carwood *Shrops* **21** D9
Sibford Ferris *Oxon* **23** H7
Sibford Gower *Oxon* **23** H7
Sible Hedingham *Essex* **27** M1
Sibsey *Lincs* **33** E10
Sibson *Cambs* **24** F2
Sibson *Leics* **23** B7
Sibthorpe *Notts* **32** F5
Sicklesmere *Suffolk* **27** J2
Sicklinghall *N Yorks* **35** B12
Sid *Devon* **6** G5
Sidbury *Devon* **6** G5
Sidbury *Shrops* **21** D12
Sidcup *London* **18** G5
Siddick *Cumb* **38** B2
Siddington *Ches* **31** C7
Siddington *Glos* **16** D1
Sidemoor *Heref/Worcs* **22** E3
Sidestrand *Norfolk* **26** B6
Sidford *Devon* **6** G5
Sidlesham *W Sussex* **9** F10
Sidley *E Sussex* **10** G6
Sidlowbridge *Surrey* **10** C1
Sidmouth *Devon* **6** G5
Sigford *Devon* **5** H6
Siggingston *S Glam* **14** G3
Sigglesthorne *Humber* **37** C9
Silchester *Hants* **17** H7
Sileby *Leics* **23** A9
Silecroft *Cumb* **38** G4
Silian *Dyfed* **20** G1
Silk Willoughby *Lincs* **24** A2
Silkstone *S Yorks* **35** G11
Silkstone Common *S Yorks* **35** G11
Silloans *Northum* **44** C6
Silloth *Cumb* **43** F11
Sillyearn *Gramp* **58** B3
Siloh *Dyfed* **13** C10
Silpho *N Yorks* **41** F9
Silsden *W Yorks* **35** C9
Silsoe *Beds* **25** M2
Silver End *Essex* **19** B8
Silver Street *Kent* **11** B7
Silverburn *Lothian* **48** C5
Silverdale *Lancs* **39** H7
Silverdale *Staffs* **31** F7
Silverley's Green *Suffolk* **27** H6
Silverstone *Northants* **23** H10
Silverton *Devon* **6** F3
Silvington *Shrops* **21** D11
Simonburn *Northum* **45** F7
Simonsbath *Som'set* **6** B1
Simonstone *Lancs* **34** D6
Simprim *Borders* **49** E11
Simpson *Bucks* **23** H12
Simpson *Dyfed* **12** E2
Sinclair's Hill *Borders* **49** D10
Sinclairston *S'clyde* **47** H9
Sinderby *N Yorks* **40** G4
Sinderhope *Northum* **45** H7
Sindlesham *Berks* **17** G8
Singdean *Borders* **44** C4
Singleborough *Bucks* **17** A8
Singleton *Lancs* **34** C3
Singleton *W Sussex* **9** E10
Singlewell or Ifield *Kent* **10** A5
Singret *Clwyd* **30** E2
Sinnahard *Gramp* **58** F2
Sinnington *N Yorks* **41** G7
Sinton Green *Heref/Worcs* **22** F2
Sipson *London* **18** F1
Sirhowy *Gwent* **14** C5
Sissinghurst *Kent* **11** D7
Sisterpath *Borders* **49** E10
Siston *Avon* **15** G10
Sithney *Cornw'l* **2** G3
Sittingbourne *Kent* **11** B8
Sittyton *Gramp* **58** E6
Six Ashes *Staffs* **22** C2
Six Hills *Leics* **32** H4
Six Mile Bottom *Cambs* **25** J7
Six Roads End *Staffs* **31** G10
Sixhills *Lincs* **33** B9
Sixpenny handley *Dorset* **8** D2
Sizewell *Suffolk* **27** J8
Skail *H'land* **61** C7
Skail *Orkney* **64** B3
Skaill *Orkney* **64** C1
Skaill *Orkney* **64** D3
Skares *S'clyde* **47** H10
Skateraw *Lothian* **49** B10
Skeabost *H'land* **62** C3
Skeeby *N Yorks* **40** E2
Skeffington *Leics* **23** B11
Skeffling *Humber* **37** E11
Skegby *Notts* **32** D2
Skegness *Lincs* **33** D12
Skelbo *H'land* **61** G8
Skelbrooke *S Yorks* **36** F3
Skeldyke *Lincs* **24** B4
Skellingthorpe *Lincs* **32** C6
Skellister *Shetl'd* **64** D7
Skellow *S Yorks* **36** F3
Skelmanthorpe *W Yorks* **35** F11
Skelmersdale *Lancs* **34** G3
Skelmonae *Gramp* **58** D6
Skelmorlie *S'clyde* **47** C7
Skelmuir *Gramp* **58** C7
Skelpick *H'land* **61** B7
Skelton *Clevl'd* **40** C6
Skelton *Cumb* **39** B7
Skelton *Humber* **36** E5
Skelton *N Yorks* **36** B3
Skelton *N Yorks* **40** E1
Skelton *N Yorks* **40** H4
Skelwick *Orkney* **64** A3
Skelwirth Bridge *Cumb* **38** E6
Skendleby *Lincs* **33** C11
Skene House *Gramp* **58** F5
Skenfrith *Gwent* **15** B8
Skerne *Humber* **37** B8
Skeroblingarry *S'clyde* **46** G2
Skerray *H'land* **61** B7
Skerricha *H'land* **60** C4
Skerton *Lancs* **34** A4
Sketchley *Leics* **23** C7
Sketty *W Glam* **13** H9
Skewen *W Glam* **13** G10
Skewsby *N Yorks* **40** H6
Skeyton *Norfolk* **26** C5
Skiag Bridge *H'land* **60** E4
Skidbrooke *Lincs* **33** A11
Skidby *Humber* **37** D8
Skigersta *W Isles* **63** A6
Skilgate *Som'set* **6** D3
Skillington *Lincs* **32** H6
Skinburness *Cumb* **43** F12
Skinidin *H'land* **62** C1
Skinningrove *Clevl'd* **41** C7
Skipness *S'clyde* **46** D4
Skipsea *Humber* **37** B9
Skipsea Brough *Humber* **37** B9
Skipton-on-Swale *N Yorks* **40** G4
Skipwith *N Yorks* **36** C4
Skirbeck *Lincs* **24** A4
Skirling *S'clyde* **48** E3
Skirmett *Bucks* **17** E8
Skirpenbeck *Humber* **36** A5
Skirwith *Cumb* **39** B8
Skirwith *N Yorks* **39** H9
Skirza *H'land* **61** A12
Skitby *Cumb* **44** F3
Skulamus *H'land* **62** F6
Skullomie *H'land* **60** B6
Skye of Curr *H'land* **57** G5
Slack *W Yorks* **35** D8
Slackhall *Derby* **31** B9
Slackhead *Gramp* **58** A2
Slacks *Dumf/Gal* **43** C11
Slad *Glos* **15** D12
Slade *Devon* **4** B4
Slade Green *London* **18** F5
Slade Hooton *S Yorks* **36** H3
Sladesbridge *Cornw'l* **3** C7
Slaggyford *Northum* **44** H5
Slaidburn *Lancs* **34** B6
Slains Park *Gramp* **59** K6
Slainsfield *Northum* **49** E12
Slaithwaite *W Yorks* **35** F9
Slaley *Northum* **45** G8
Slamannan *S'clyde* **48** B1
Slapton *Bucks* **17** B10
Slapton *Devon* **5** L7
Slapton *Northants* **23** G9
Slattadale *H'land* **54** C3
Slattocks *Gtr Man* **35** F7
Slaugham *W Sussex* **10** E1
Slaughter Hill *Ches* **30** E6
Slaughterbridge *Cornw'l* **3** A8
Slaughterford *Wilts* **15** G11
Slawston *Leics* **23** C11
Sleaford *Hants* **9** B9
Sleaford *Lincs* **24** A2
Sleagill *Cumb* **39** C8
Sleap *Shrops* **21** A11
Sleapford *Shrops* **21** A11
Sledge Green *Heref/Worcs* **15** A11
Sledmere *Humber* **37** A7
Sleetbeck *Cumb* **44** E3
Sleightholme *Durham* **39** D11
Sleights *N Yorks* **41** D8
Slepe *Dorset* **8** G1
Slerra *Devon* **4** D2
Slickly *H'land* **61** A12
Sliddery *S'clyde* **46** G4
Sligachan Hotel *H'land* **62** E4
Sligrachan *S'clyde* **51** H9
Slimbridge *Glos* **15** D10
Slindon *Staffs* **31** G7
Slindon *W Sussex* **9** E11
Slinfold *W Sussex* **9** C12
Sling *Gwyn* **28** D5
Slingsby *N Yorks* **41** H7
Slioch *Gramp* **58** D3
Slip End *Beds* **17** B11
Slip End *Herts* **25** L4
Slipper's Bottom *Norfolk* **26** D6
Slipton *Northants* **23** D12
Slitting Mill *Staffs* **31** H9
Slochd *H'land* **57** G4
Slochnacraig *Tayside* **57** M7
Slockavullin *S'clyde* **50** H5
Slogarie *Dumf/Gal* **43** E7
Sloothby *Lincs* **33** C12
Slough *Berks* **17** F10
Slough Green *Som'set* **6** D6
Sluggan *H'land* **57** G4
Slyne *Lancs* **34** A4
Smailholm *Borders* **49** F9
Small Dole *W Sussex* **10** G1
Small Hythe *Kent* **11** E7
Smallbridge *Gtr Man* **35** F8
Smallburgh *Norfolk* **26** C6
Smallburn *Gramp* **58** D8
Smallburn *S'clyde* **47** G11
Smalley *Derby* **32** F1
Smallfield *Surrey* **10** D2
Smallford *Herts* **18** C2
Smallholm *Dumf/Gal* **43** D11
Smallridge *Devon* **6** F6
Smannell *Hants* **8** A5
Smardale *Cumb* **39** D9
Smarden *Kent* **11** D7
Smeatharpe *Devon* **6** E5
Smeeth *Kent* **11** D9
Smeeth *Norfolk* **24** E6
Smeeton Westerby *Leics* **23** C10
Smelthouses *N Yorks* **35** A10
Smerral *H'land* **61** D11
Smethwick *W Midlands* **22** C4
Smisby *Derby* **31** H12
Smith Green *Lancs* **34** B4
Smithfield *Cumb* **44** F3
Smithincott *Devon* **6** E4
Smith's Green *Essex* **18** B6
Smithstown *H'land* **54** B2
Smithtown *H'land* **56** E3
Smithwaite *Cumb* **38** C5
Smithy Houses *Derby* **32** E1
Snableazes *Northum* **45** B10
Snade *Dumf/Gal* **43** C9
Snailbeach *Shrops* **21** B9
Snailwell *Suffolk* **25** H7
Snainton *N Yorks* **41** G9
Snaith *Humber* **36** E4
Snake Inn *Derby* **31** A9
Snape *N Yorks* **40** G3
Snape *Suffolk* **27** J7
Snape Green *Lancs* **34** F3
Snarestone *Leics* **23** A7
Snarford *Lincs* **33** B7
Snargate *Kent* **11** E8
Snave *Kent* **11** E9
Snead *Powys* **21** C8
Sneaton *N Yorks* **41** D9
Sneatonthorpe *N Yorks* **41** E9
Snelland *Lincs* **33** B8
Snelston *Derby* **31** F10
Snettisham *Norfolk* **24** B8
Snitter *Northum* **45** C8
Snitterby *Lincs* **33** A7
Snitterfield *Warwick* **22** F5
Snodhill *Heref/Worcs* **21** H8
Snodland *Kent* **10** B6
Snowdown *Kent* **11** C11
Snowshill *Glos* **16** A2
Soar *Devon* **5** M6
Soar *Dyfed* **13** D9
Soar *Powys* **14** A3
Soberton *Hants* **9** D7
Soberton Heath *Hants* **9** E7
Sockburn *Durham* **40** D4
Soham *Cambs* **25** H7
Solbury *Dyfed* **12** F2
Soldon Cross *Devon* **4** E2
Soldridge *Hants* **9** C8
Sole Street *Kent* **10** A5
Solestreet *Kent* **11** C9
Solihull *W Midlands* **22** D5
Sollers Dilwyn *Heref/Worcs* **21** G9
Sollers Hope *Heref/Worcs* **15** A9
Sollom *Lancs* **34** E3
Solva *Dyfed* **12** E2
Solwayash *Dorset* **7** F8
Solwaybank *Dumf/Gal* **44** E1
Somerby *Leics* **23** A11
Somerby *Lincs* **37** F8
Somercotes *Derby* **32** E2
Somerford *Dorset* **8** G3
Somerford Keynes *Glos* **16** E1
Somerley *W Sussex* **9** F9
Somerleyton *Suffolk* **26** F8
Somersal Herbert *Derby* **31** G10
Somersby *Lincs* **33** C10
Somersham *Cambs* **25** H5
Somersham *Suffolk* **27** K4
Somerton *Oxon* **16** A6
Somerton *Som'set* **7** C8
Somerton *Suffolk* **27** K1
Sompting *W Sussex* **10** G1
Sonning *Berks* **17** G8
Sonning Common *Oxon* **17** F8
Sonning Eye *Oxon* **17** F8
Sootywells *Gramp* **59** K5
Sopley *Hants* **8** F3
Sopworth *Wilts* **15** F11
Sorbie *Dumf/Gal* **42** G5
Sorbie *Dumf/Gal* **44** D2
Sorbietrees *Borders* **44** E3
Sordale *H'land* **61** B10
Sorn *S'clyde* **47** G10
Sornbeg *S'clyde* **47** F10
Sornfallow *S'clyde* **48** F2
Sornhill *S'clyde* **47** F10
Soroba Farm *S'clyde* **50** E6
Sortat *H'land* **61** B12
Sotby *Lincs* **33** B9
Sots Hole *Lincs* **33** D8
Sotwell *Oxon* **17** E7
Soudley *Shrops* **30** G6
Soughton *Clwyd* **29** D11
Soulbury *Bucks* **17** A9
Soulby *Cumb* **39** D9
Souldern *Oxon* **16** A6
Souldrop *Beds* **25** J1
Sound *Shetl'd* **64** D7
Sound *Shetl'd* **64** E7
Sourhope *Borders* **49** G11
Sourin *Orkney* **64** B2
Sourton *Devon* **5** G4
Soutergate *Cumb* **38** G5
South Acre *Norfolk* **26** D1
South Alkham *Kent* **11** D11
South Allington *Devon* **5** M7
South Alloa *Central* **52** H4
South Ambersham *W Sussex* **9** D10
South Anston *S Yorks* **32** B2
South Ascot *Berks* **17** G10
South Baddelsley *Hants* **8** F5
South Ballachulish *H'land* **51** A7
South Balloch *S'clyde* **42** B4
South Barrow *Som'set* **7** C9
South Beach *Gwyn* **28** G3
South Bellsdyke *Lothian* **48** A2
South Benfleet *Essex* **19** E7
South Bersted *W Sussex* **9** F10
South Bramwith *S Yorks* **36** F4
South Brent *Devon* **5** K6
South Brewham *Som'set* **7** C10
South Bridge-end *Tayside* **52** E3
South Broomhill *Northum* **45** C10
South Burlingham *Norfolk* **26** E7
South Cadbury *Som'set* **7** D9
South Cairn *Dumf/Gal* **42** E1
South Carlton *Lincs* **33** C7
South Carrine *S'clyde* **46** H2
South Cave *Humber* **37** D7
South Cerney *Glos* **16** D2
South Chard *Som'set* **7** F7
South Charlton *Northum* **45** A9
South Cheriton *Som'set* **7** D10
South Cliffe *Humber* **36** D6
South Clifton *Notts* **32** C5
South Cockerington *Lincs* **33** A11
South Collingham *Notts* **32** D5
South Cornelly *Mid Glam* **14** F2
South Cove *Suffolk* **27** G8
South Creagan *S'clyde* **51** C7
South Creake *Norfolk* **26** B2
South Croxton *Leics* **23** A10
South Dalton *Humber* **37** C7
South Darenth *Kent* **10** A4
South Dell *W Isles* **63** A6
South Denmore *Gramp* **58** F7
South Druimachro *S'clyde* **46** E2
South Duffield *N Yorks* **36** D5
South Elkington *Lincs* **33** A10
South Elmsall *W Yorks* **36** F3
South End *Berks* **17** G7
South End *Bucks* **17** B9
South End *Cumb* **34** A1
South End *Humber* **37** E9
South Erradale *H'land* **54** C1
South Fambridge *Essex* **19** D8
South Fawley *Berks* **16** F5
South Feorline *S'clyde* **46** G4
South Ferriby *Humber* **37** E7
South Fornet *Gramp* **58** F5
South Galson *W Isles* **63** A5
South Garrachie *Gramp* **58** B5
South Garrochty *S'clyde* **46** D6
South Godstone *Surrey* **10** C2
South Gorley *Hants* **8** E3
South Green *Essex* **19** E7
South Green *Kent* **11** B7

South Hall S'clyde 46 B5
South Hanningfield Essex 19 D7
South Harting W Sussex 9 D9
South Hayling Hants 9 F8
South Hazelrigg Northum 45 C11
South Heath Bucks 17 D10
South Heighton E Sussex 10 H3
South Hetton Durham 40 A4
South Hiendley W Yorks 36 F2
South Hill Cornw'l 3 B10
South Hill Som'set 7 D8
South Hinksey Oxon 16 D6
South Hole Devon 4 D1
South Holme N Yorks 41 G7
South Holmwood Surrey 10 D1
South Hornchurch London 18 F5
South Hourat S'clyde 47 D8
South Hykeham Lincs 32 D6
South Hylton Tyne/Wear 45 G11
South Kelsey Lincs 37 G8
South Killingholme Humber 37 F9
South Kilrusken S'clyde 47 D7
South Kilvington N Yorks 40 G4
South Kilworth Leics 23 D9
South Kirkby W Yorks 36 F2
South Kirktown Gramp 59 G5
South Kiscadale S'clyde 46 G5
South Kyme Lincs 33 E9
South Lancing W Sussex 10 H1
South Leigh Oxon 16 C5
South Leverton Notts 32 B5
South Limmerhaugh S'clyde 47 G11
South Littleton Heref/Worcs 22 G4
South Lopham Norfolk 27 G3
South Luffenham Leics 23 B12
South Malling E Sussex 10 G3
South Marston Wilts 16 E3
South Middleton Northum 49 G12
South Milford N Yorks 36 D3
South Millbrex Gramp 58 C6
South Milton Devon 5 L6
South Mimms Herts 18 D2
South Molton Devon 4 C6
South Moreton Oxon 16 E6
South Mundham W Sussex 9 F10
South Muskham Notts 32 E5
South Newbald Humber 37 D7
South Newington Oxon 16 A5
South Newton Wilts 8 C2
South Normanton Derby 32 E2
South Norwood London 18 G3
South Nutfield Surrey 10 C2
South Ockendon Essex 18 F6
South Ormsby Lincs 33 C10
South Otterington N Yorks 40 F4
South Owersby Lincs 33 A8
South Oxhey Herts 18 E1
South Perrot Dorset 7 F8
South Petherton Som'set 7 D8
South Petherwin Cornw'l 3 B10
South Pickenham Norfolk 26 E1
South Pool Devon 5 M6
South Port S'clyde 51 E8
South Radworthy Devon 4 C6
South Rauceby Lincs 33 F7
South Raynham Norfolk 26 C2
South Reston Lincs 33 B11
South Runcton Norfolk 24 E7
South Scarle Notts 32 D6
South Shawbost W Isles 63 B3
South Shields Tyne/Wear 45 F12
South Shore Lancs 34 D2
South Skirlaugh Humber 37 C9
South Somercotes Lincs 33 A11
South Stainley N Yorks 35 A11
South Stifford Essex 18 F6
South Stoke Avon 15 H10
South Stoke Oxon 17 F7
South Stoke W Sussex 9 E11
South Street E Sussex 10 F3
South Street Kent 11 B9
South Street London 18 H4
South Tawton Devon 4 F5
South Thoresby Lincs 33 C11
South Tidworth Hants 8 A4
South Town Hants 9 B8
South Walsham Norfolk 26 D7
South Warnborough Hants 9 A8
South Weald Essex 18 E6
South Weston Oxon 17 D8
South Wheatley Cornw'l 5 G1
South Wheatley Notts 32 B5
South Widcombe Avon 7 A9
South Wigston Leics 23 B9
South Willingham Lincs 33 B9
South Wingfield Derby 32 E1
South Witham Lincs 32 H6
South Wonston Hants 8 B6
South Woodham Ferrers Essex 19 D8
South Wootton Norfolk 24 C7
South Wraxall Wilts 15 H11
South Zeal Devon 4 F5
Southall London 18 F1
Southam Glos 16 B1
Southam Warwick 23 F7
Southampton Hants 8 E5
Southborough E Sussex 10 D5
Southbourne Dorset 8 G3
Southbourne W Sussex 9 E9
Southburgh Norfolk 26 E3
Southburn Humber 37 B7
Southchurch Essex 19 E9
Southcott Devon 4 D3
Southcott Wilts 16 H3
Southdean Borders 44 B5
Southease E Sussex 10 H3
Southend S'clyde 46 H2
Southend Wilts 16 G3
Southend on Sea Essex 19 E8
Southerndown Mid Glam 14 G2
Southerness Dumf/Gal 43 F10
Southernknowe Northum 49 G11
Southery Norfolk 24 F7
Southfield N Yorks 41 G7
Southfleet Kent 10 A5
Southgate London 18 E3
Southgate Norfolk 24 B8
Southgate Norfolk 26 C4
Southgate W Glam 13 H9
Southill Beds 25 L3
Southleigh Devon 6 G5
Southminster Essex 19 D9
Southmoor Northum 45 B10
Southoe Cambs 25 J3
Southolt Suffolk 27 H5
Southorpe Cambs 24 E2
Southowram W Yorks 35 E10
Southport Mersey 34 E2
Southrepps Norfolk 26 B6
Southrey Lincs 33 D8
Southrop Glos 16 D3
Southrope Hants 9 B8
Southsea Hants 9 F8
Southtown Orkney 64 D3
Southwaite Cumb 39 A7
Southwark London 18 F3
Southwater W Sussex 9 D12
Southway Som'set 7 B8
Southwell Dorset 7 H7
Southwell Notts 32 E4
Southwick Hants 9 E8
Southwick Northants 24 F1
Southwick Tyne/Wear 45 G12
Southwick W Sussex 10 G1
Southwick Wilts 7 A11
Southwold Suffolk 27 H8
Southwood Norfolk 26 E7
Southwood Som'set 7 C9
Soutra Mains Lothian 49 C7
Soval Lodge W Isles 63 D4
Sowerby N Yorks 40 G4
Sowerby W Yorks 35 E9
Sowerby Bridge W Yorks 35 E9
Sowerby Row Cumb 38 A6
Sowton Devon 6 G3
Spadeadam Farm Cumb 44 F4
Spalding Lincs 24 C3
Spaldington Humber 36 D5
Spaldwick Cambs 25 H2
Spalefield Fife 53 F10
Spalford Notts 32 C5
Spanby Lincs 24 B2
Sparham Norfolk 26 D4
Spark Bridge Cumb 38 G5
Sparkford Som'set 7 D9
Sparklow Derby 31 D9
Sparkwell Devon 5 K4
Sparrowpit Derby 31 B9
Sparsholt Hants 8 C6
Sparsholt Oxon 16 E4
Spartylea Northum 45 H7
Spaunton N Yorks 41 F7
Spaxton Som'set 6 C6
Spean Bridge H'land 55 L6
Spearywell Hants 8 C5
Speddoch Dumf/Gal 43 C9
Speen Berks 16 G5
Speen Bucks 17 D9
Speeton N Yorks 41 H11
Speke Mersey 30 B3
Speldhurst Kent 10 D4
Spellbrook Herts 18 B5
Spelsbury Oxon 16 B4
Spelter Mid Glam 14 E2
Spencer's Wood Berks 17 G8
Spennithorne N Yorks 40 F2
Spennymoor Durham 40 B3
Spetchley Heref/Worcs 22 G2
Spetisbury Dorset 7 F12
Spexhall Suffolk 27 G7
Spey Bay Gramp 58 A1
Speybridge H'land 57 G6
Speyview Gramp 56 E8
Spilsby Lincs 33 D11
Spindlestone Northum 45 D11
Spinkhill Derby 32 B2
Spinney Hills Leics 23 B9
Spinningdale H'land 61 G7
Spital in the Street Lincs 33 A7
Spitalford Northum 45 A10
Spithurst E Sussex 10 F3
Spittal Dumf/Gal 42 E5
Spittal Dumf/Gal 42 F4
Spittal Dyfed 12 E3
Spittal H'land 61 B10
Spittal Humber 36 B5
Spittal Lothian 49 B7
Spittal Northum 49 D12
Spittal S'clyde 48 F3
Spittal of Glenmuick Gramp 59 J1
Spittal of Glenshee Tayside 57 M7
Spittalburn Gramp 59 J4
Spittalfield Tayside 52 C6
Spixworth Norfolk 26 D5
Splatt Cornw'l 3 A9
Splayne's Green E Sussex 10 F3
Spofforth N Yorks 35 B12
Spon Green Clwyd 29 D12
Spondon Derby 32 G1
Spooner Row Norfolk 26 F4
Sporle Norfolk 26 D2
Spotbrough S Yorks 36 G3
Spott Lothian 49 B9
Spottiswoode Borders 49 D8
Spratton Northants 23 E10
Spreakley Surrey 9 B9
Spreyton Devon 4 F6
Spridlington Lincs 33 B7
Spring Valley I of Man 38 H2
Springburn S'clyde 47 C10
Springfield Dumf/Gal 44 F2
Springfield Essex 19 C7
Springfield Fife 53 F8
Springfield Gramp 56 D6
Springfield W Midlands 22 D4
Springhill Staffs 22 B3
Springholm Dumf/Gal 43 E9
Springkell Dumf/Gal 44 E1
Springside S'clyde 47 E8
Springwell Tyne/Wear 45 G11
Sproatley Humber 37 D9
Sproston Green Ches 30 C6
Sproughton Suffolk 27 L4
Sprouston Borders 49 F10
Sprowston Norfolk 26 D6
Sproxton Leics 32 H6
Sproxton N Yorks 40 G6
Spurstow Ches 30 E4
Sronlairig Lodge H'land 57 J1
Sronpadruig Lo Tayside 57 L3
Stackhouse N Yorks 35 A7
Stackpole Dyfed 12 G3
Stacksteads Lancs 35 E7
Staddiscombe Devon 5 K4
Staddlethorpe Humber 36 E6
Stadhampton Oxon 17 D7
Staffield Cumb 39 A8
Staffin H'land 62 A4
Stafford Staffs 31 H8
Stagehall Borders 49 E7
Stag's Holt Cambs 24 E5
Stagsden Beds 25 K1
Stagsden West End Beds 25 K1
Stainburn N Yorks 35 B11
Stainby Lincs 32 H6
Staincross S Yorks 35 F12
Staindrop Durham 40 C2
Staines Surrey 17 G11
Stainfield Lincs 24 C2
Stainfield Lincs 33 C8
Stainforth N Yorks 39 H10
Stainforth S Yorks 36 F4
Staining Lancs 34 D2
Stainland W Yorks 35 E9
Stainsacre N Yorks 41 D9
Stainton Clevl'd 40 D5
Stainton Cumb 39 B7
Stainton Cumb 39 G7
Stainton Durham 40 C1
Stainton N Yorks 40 F1
Stainton S Yorks 32 A3
Stainton by Langworth Lincs 33 B8
Stainton le Vale Lincs 37 H9
Stainton with Adgarley Cumb 38 H5
Staintondale N Yorks 41 E10
Stair Cumb 38 C5
Stair S'clyde 47 G9
Staithes N Yorks 41 C8
Stake Pool Lancs 34 B3
Stakeford Northum 45 D11
Stalbridge Dorset 7 D10
Stalbridge Weston Dorset 7 E10
Stalham Norfolk 26 C7
Stalham Green Norfolk 26 C7
Stalisfield Green Kent 11 C8
Stalling Busk N Yorks 39 G11
Stallingborough Humber 37 F9
Stalmine Lancs 34 C3
Stalybridge Gtr Man 35 G8
Stambourne Essex 25 L8
Stamford Lincs 24 E1
Stamford Northum 45 A10
Stamford Bridge Humber 36 B5
Stamfordham Northum 45 F9
Stanah Cumb 38 C6
Stanborough Herts 18 C2
Stanbridge Beds 17 B10
Stanbridge Dorset 8 F2
Stanbury W Yorks 35 C9
Stand S'clyde 47 C12
Standburn Lothian 48 B2
Standeford Staffs 22 A3
Standen Kent 11 D7
Standerwick Som'set 7 A11
Standford Hants 9 C9
Standish Gtr Man 34 F4
Standlake Oxon 16 D5
Standon Hants 8 C6
Standon Herts 18 B4
Standon Staffs 30 G6
Standon Massey Essex 18 D6
Standwell Green Suffolk 27 H4
Stane S'clyde 48 C2
Stanfield Norfolk 26 C2
Stanford Beds 25 L3
Stanford Kent 11 D10
Stanford Bishop Heref/Worcs 21 G12
Stanford Bridge Heref/Worcs 22 F1
Stanford Dingley Berks 16 G6
Stanford le Hope Essex 19 F7
Stanford on Avon Northants 23 D9
Stanford on Soar Notts 32 H3
Stanford on Teme Heref/Worcs 21 F12
Stanford Rivers Essex 18 D5
Stanford the Vale Oxon 16 E4
Stanford's End Kent 10 D3
Stanground Cambs 24 F3
Stanhoe Norfolk 26 B1
Stanhope Borders 48 F4
Stanhope Durham 39 A12
Stanion Northants 23 C12
Stank Central 52 F1
Stanley Derby 32 F1
Stanley Durham 45 H10
Stanley Staffs 31 E8
Stanley Tayside 52 D6
Stanley W Yorks 35 E12
Stanley Wilts 16 G1
Stanley Common Derby 32 F1
Stanley Hill Heref/Worcs 21 H12
Stanmer E Sussex 10 G2
Stanmore Berks 16 F6
Stanmore Hants 8 C6
Stanmore London 18 E2
Stannersburn Northum 44 D5
Stannington Northum 45 E10
Stannington S Yorks 31 A11
Stansbatch Heref/Worcs 21 F9
Stansfield Suffolk 27 K1
Stanshope Staffs 31 E9
Stanstead Suffolk 27 K1
Stanstead Abbots Herts 18 C4
Stanstead Street Suffolk 27 K1
Stansted Kent 10 B5
Stansted Mountfichet Essex 18 A5
Stanton Derby 31 H11
Stanton Glos 16 A2
Stanton Gwent 14 B6
Stanton Northum 45 D9
Stanton Staffs 31 F9
Stanton Suffolk 27 H3
Stanton by Bridge Derby 31 G12
Stanton Drew Avon 15 H9
Stanton Fitzwarren Wilts 16 E3
Stanton Harcourt Oxon 16 D5
Stanton Hill Notts 32 D2
Stanton in Peak Derby 31 D11
Stanton Lacy Shrops 21 E10
Stanton Long Shrops 21 C11
Stanton on the Wolds Notts 32 G3
Stanton Prior Avon 15 H10
Stanton St. Bernard Wilts 16 H2
Stanton St. John Oxon 17 C7
Stanton St. Quintin Wilts 15 F12
Stanton Street Suffolk 27 J3
Stanton under Bardon Leics 23 A8
Stanton upon Hine Heath Shrops 30 H4
Stanton Wick Avon 15 H9
Stanwardine in the Fields Shrops 30 H3
Stanway Essex 19 B9
Stanway Glos 16 A2
Stanwell Surrey 17 G11
Stanwell Moor Surrey 17 G11
Stanwick Northants 25 H1
Stape N Yorks 41 F8
Stapehill Dorset 8 F2
Stapeley Ches 30 E5
Stapenhill Staffs 31 H11
Staple Kent 11 B11
Staple Som'set 6 B4
Staple Cross Devon 6 D4
Staple Cross E Sussex 10 F6
Staple Fitzpaine Som'set 6 D6
Staple Hill Avon 15 G9
Staplefield W Sussex 10 E2
Stapleford Cambs 25 K6
Stapleford Herts 18 B3
Stapleford Leics 32 H5
Stapleford Lincs 32 D6
Stapleford Notts 32 F2
Stapleford Wilts 8 B2
Stapleford Abbotts Essex 18 D5
Stapleford Tawney Essex 18 D5
Staplegrove Som'set 6 D6
Staplehay Som'set 6 D5
Staplehurst Kent 10 D6
Staplers I of Wight 8 G6
Stapleton Cumb 44 F3
Stapleton Heref/Worcs 21 F9
Stapleton Leics 23 B8
Stapleton N Yorks 40 D3
Stapleton Shrops 21 B10
Stapleton Som'set 7 D8
Stapleton Grange Dumf/Gal 44 F1
Stapley Som'set 6 E5
Staploe Beds 25 J2
Star Dyfed 12 C6
Star Fife 53 G8
Star Som'set 15 H7
Starbotton N Yorks 39 H11
Starcross Devon 6 H3
Starforth Durham 39 D12
Starkigarth Shetl'd 64 E7
Starlings Green Essex 25 M6
Starston Norfolk 27 G5
Starthvaich Lo H'land 54 B7
Startley Wilts 15 F12
Stathe Som'set 7 C7
Stathern Leics 32 G5
Station Town Durham 40 B4
Staughton Green Cambs 25 J2
Staughton Highway Cambs 25 J2
Staunton Glos 15 A11
Staunton Glos 15 C9
Staunton in the Vale Notts 32 F5
Staunton on Arrow Heref/Worcs 21 F9
Staunton on Wye Heref/Worcs 21 H9
Staveley Cumb 38 G6
Staveley Cumb 39 E7
Staveley N Yorks 35 A12
Stavely Derby 32 C2
Staverton Devon 5 J7
Staverton Glos 15 B12
Staverton Northants 23 F9
Staverton Wilts 15 H11
Staverton Bridge Glos 15 B12
Stawell Som'set 7 B7
Stawford Devon 5 G3
Stawley Som'set 6 D4
Staxigoe H'land 61 B12
Staxton N Yorks 41 G10
Staylittle Powys 20 C4
Staynall Lancs 34 C2
Staythorpe Notts 32 E5
Stean N Yorks 40 H1
Stearsby N Yorks 40 H6
Steart Som'set 6 B6
Stebbing Essex 18 B6
Stebbligrind Shetl'd 64 D7
Stedham W Sussex 9 D10
Steel Rigg Northum 45 E8
Steele Road Borders 44 D4
Steen's Bridge Heref/Worcs 21 G11
Steep Hants 9 D9
Steep Marsh Hants 9 C9
Steeple Dorset 7 H12
Steeple Essex 19 D9
Steeple Ashton Wilts 7 A12
Steeple Aston Oxon 16 B6
Steeple Barton Oxon 16 B5
Steeple Bumpstead Essex 25 L8
Steeple Claydon Bucks 17 A8
Steeple Gidding Cambs 25 G2
Steeple Langford Wilts 8 B2
Steeple Morden Cambs 25 L4
Steeton W Yorks 35 C9
Stein H'land 62 C2
Steinmanhill Gramp 58 C5
Stelling Hall Northum 45 F8
Stelling Minnis Kent 11 C10
Stenalees Cornw'l 3 D7
Stenhousemuir Lothian 48 A2
Stenness Shetl'd 64 C6
Stenscholl H'land 62 A4
Stenson Staffs 31 G11
Stenswall Shetl'd 64 D7
Stenton Lothian 49 B9
Stepaside Dyfed 12 F5
Stepends Dumf/Gal 43 C9
Stepney London 18 F4
Steppingley Beds 25 M1
Stepps S'clyde 47 C11
Sternfield Suffolk 27 J7
Stert Wilts 16 H1
Stetchworth Cambs 25 J7
Stevenage Herts 18 A2
Stevenston S'clyde 47 E7
Steventon Hants 9 A7
Steventon Oxon 16 E5
Stevington Beds 25 K1
Stewartby Beds 25 L1
Stewarton S'clyde 46 G2
Stewarton S'clyde 47 E9
Stewkley Bucks 17 B9
Stewton Lincs 33 B10
Steyning W Sussex 10 G1
Steynton Dyfed 12 F3
Stibb Cornw'l 4 E1
Stibb Cross Devon 4 D3
Stibb Green Wilts 16 H3
Stibbard Norfolk 26 C3
Stibbington Cambs 24 F2
Stichill Borders 49 F9
Sticker Cornw'l 3 E7
Stickford Lincs 33 D10
Sticklepath Devon 4 F5
Sticklepath Som'set 6 C4
Sticklepath Som'set 6 E6
Stickney Lincs 33 D10
Stiffkey Norfolk 26 A3
Stifford Essex 18 F6
Stifford's Bridge Heref/Worcs 22 G1
Stile Bridge Kent 10 C6
Stillingfleet N Yorks 36 C4
Stillington Durham 40 C4
Stillington N Yorks 40 H6
Stilton Cambs 24 F3
Stinchcombe Glos 15 D10
Stinsford Dorset 7 G10
Stippollits Herts 18 A2
Stirchley Shrops 21 B12
Stirkoke House H'land 61 C12
Stirling Central 52 H3
Stirling Gramp 58 C8
Stisted Essex 19 A8
Stitchcombe Wilts 16 G3
Stithians Cornw'l 2 F4
Stittenham H'land 56 B2
Stivichall W Midlands 23 D7
Stixwould Lincs 33 D9
Stoak Ches 30 C3
Stobo Borders 48 F4
Stoborough Dorset 7 H12
Stoborough Green Dorset 7 H12
Stobs Castle Borders 44 B3

Stobswood *Borders* 49 D9
Stobswood *Northum* 45 D10
Stobwood *S'clyde* 48 D2
Stock *Essex* 19 D7
Stock Well Heath *Staffs* 31 H9
Stock Wood *Heref/Worcs* 22 F3
Stockbridge *Gramp* 58 C8
Stockbridge *Hants* 8 C5
Stockbridgehill *Dumf/Gal* 43 D12
Stockbriggs *S'clyde* 47 F12
Stockbury *Kent* 11 B7
Stockcross *Berks* 16 G5
Stockdale Wath *Cumb* 38 A6
Stockerston *Leics* 23 B11
Stockheath *Hants* 9 E8
Stockholm *Dumf/Gal* 43 B11
Stockiemuir *Central* 47 A10
Stocking Pelham *Herts* 18 A4
Stockingford *Warwick* 23 C7
Stockland *Devon* 6 F6
Stockland Bristol *Som'set* 6 B6
Stockleigh English *Devon* 4 E7
Stockleigh Pomeroy *Devon* 4 F7
Stockley *Wilts* 16 G1
Stocklinch *Som'set* 7 E7
Stockport *Gtr Man* 31 A7
Stocksbridge *S Yorks* 35 G11
Stocksfield *Northum* 45 G9
Stockton *Heref/Worcs* 21 F10
Stockton *Norfolk* 26 F7
Stockton *Shrops* 21 B8
Stockton *Shrops* 22 B1
Stockton *Warwick* 23 F8
Stockton *Wilts* 8 B1
Stockton Heath *Ches* 30 B5
Stockton on Teme *Heref/Worcs* 22 E1
Stockton-on-Tees *Clevl'd* 40 C4
Stockton-on-the-Forest *N Yorks* 36 B4
Stodmarsh *Kent* 11 B11
Stody *Norfolk* 26 B4
Stoer *H'land* 60 D2
Stoford *Som'set* 7 E9
Stoford *Wilts* 8 C2
Stogumber *Som'set* 6 C4
Stogursey *Som'set* 6 B5
Stoke *Devon* 4 D1
Stoke *Hants* 8 A5
Stoke *Hants* 9 F8
Stoke *Kent* 11 A7
Stoke *Suffolk* 27 L5
Stoke Abbott *Dorset* 7 F8
Stoke Albany *Northants* 23 C11
Stoke Ash *Suffolk* 27 H4
Stoke Bardolph *Notts* 32 F4
Stoke Bliss *Heref/Worcs* 21 F12
Stoke Bruerne *Northants* 23 G10
Stoke Canon *Devon* 6 F3
Stoke Charity *Hants* 8 B6
Stoke Climsland *Cornw'l* 3 B10
Stoke Cross *Heref/Worcs* 21 G11
Stoke D'Abernon *Surrey* 17 H12
Stoke Doyle *Northants* 25 G1
Stoke Dry *Leics* 23 B12
Stoke Edith *Heref/Worcs* 21 H11
Stoke Farthing *Wilts* 8 D2
Stoke Ferry *Norfolk* 24 E8
Stoke Fleming *Devon* 5 L7
Stoke Gabriel *Devon* 5 K7
Stoke Gifford *Avon* 15 F9
Stoke Golding *Leics* 23 B7
Stoke Goldington *Bucks* 23 G11
Stoke Green *Bucks* 17 F10
Stoke Hammond *Bucks* 17 A9
Stoke Holy Cross *Norfolk* 26 E5
Stoke Lacy *Heref/Worcs* 21 G11
Stoke Lyne *Oxon* 16 A6
Stoke Mandeville *Bucks* 17 C9
Stoke Newington *London* 18 E3
Stoke Orchard *Glos* 15 A12
Stoke Pero *Som'set* 6 B2
Stoke Poges *Bucks* 17 F10
Stoke Prior *Heref/Worcs* 21 G10
Stoke Prior *Heref/Worcs* 22 E3
Stoke Rivers *Devon* 4 C5
Stoke Rochford *Lincs* 32 G6
Stoke Row *Oxon* 17 F8
Stoke St. Gregory *Som'set* 7 D7
Stoke St. Mary *Som'set* 6 D6
Stoke St. Michael *Som'set* 7 B10
Stoke St. Milborough *Shrops* 21 D11
Stoke sub Hamdon *Som'set* 7 D8
Stoke Talmage *Oxon* 17 D7
Stoke Trister *Som'set* 7 C10
Stoke upon Tern *Shrops* 30 G5
Stoke Wake *Dorset* 7 F11
Stoke-by-Clare *Suffolk* 25 L8
Stoke-by-Neyland *Suffolk* 27 L3
Stokeford *Dorset* 7 G12
Stokeham *Notts* 32 C5
Stokeinteignhead *Devon* 5 J8
Stokenchurch *Bucks* 17 D8
Stokenham *Devon* 5 L7
Stoke-on-Trent *Staffs* 31 F7
Stokesay *Shrops* 21 D10
Stokesby *Norfolk* 26 D7
Stokesley *N Yorks* 40 D5
Stolford *Som'set* 6 B5
Ston Easton *Som'set* 7 A9
Stone *Bucks* 17 C8
Stone *E Sussex* 11 G7
Stone *Glos* 15 E10
Stone *Heref/Worcs* 22 E2
Stone *Kent* 10 A4
Stone *Kent* 11 E8
Stone *S Yorks* 32 A3
Stone Allerton *Som'set* 7 A7
Stone Bridge Corner *Cambs* 24 E4
Stone Chair *W Yorks* 35 D10
Stone Cross *Devon* 4 C5
Stone Cross *E Sussex* 10 H5
Stone Cross *Kent* 11 D9
Stone House *Cumb* 39 G10
Stone Street *Kent* 10 C4
Stonebridge *W Midlands* 22 D5
Stonebroom *Derby* 32 D1
Stonecrouch *Kent* 10 E6
Stone-edge-Batch *Avon* 15 G8
Stoneferry *Humber* 37 D8
Stonefield *S'clyde* 47 D11
Stonefield Castle Hotel *S'clyde* 46 B4
Stonegarthside *Cumb* 44 E3
Stonegate *E Sussex* 10 E5
Stonegate *N Yorks* 41 D8
Stonegrave *N Yorks* 41 G7
Stonehaugh *Northum* 44 E6
Stonehaven *Gramp* 59 J6
Stonehouse *Devon* 5 K3
Stonehouse *Dumf/Gal* 43 E9
Stonehouse *Glos* 15 D11
Stonehouse *Northum* 44 G5
Stonehouse *S'clyde* 47 E12
Stoneleigh *Warwick* 23 E7
Stonely *Cambs* 25 J2
Stone's Green *Essex* 19 A11
Stonesby *Leics* 32 H5
Stonesfield *Oxon* 16 B5
Stonethwaite *Cumb* 38 D5
Stoney Cross *Hants* 8 E4
Stoney Middleton *Derby* 31 C10
Stoney Stanton *Leics* 23 C8
Stoney Stoke *Som'set* 7 C10
Stoney Stratton *Som'set* 7 B10
Stoney Stretton *Shrops* 21 A9
Stoneyburn *S'clyde* 48 G2
Stoneyburn *Lothian* 48 C2
Stoneygate *Leics* 23 B9
Stoneyhills *Essex* 19 D9
Stoneykirk *Dumf/Gal* 42 F2
Stoneywood *Gramp* 58 F6
Stonham Aspal *Suffolk* 27 J4
Stonor *Oxon* 17 E8
Stonton Wyville *Leics* 23 C10
Stony Cross *Devon* 4 C4
Stony Cross *Heref/Worcs* 22 G1
Stony Stratford *Bucks* 23 H11
Stoodleigh *Devon* 4 C5
Stoodleigh *Devon* 6 D3
Stopham *W Sussex* 9 D11
Stopsley *Beds* 17 B12
Storeton *Mersey* 30 B2
Storiths *N Yorks* 35 B9
Stornoway *W Isles* 63 D5
Storridge *Heref/Worcs* 22 G1
Storrington *W Sussex* 9 E12
Storth *Cumb* 39 G7
Storwood *Humber* 36 C5
Stotfield *Gramp* 56 C8
Stotfold *Beds* 25 L3
Stotford *Som'set* 6 B6
Stottesdon *Shrops* 21 D12
Stoughton *Leics* 23 B9
Stoughton *Surrey* 9 A11
Stoughton *W Sussex* 9 E9
Stoul *H'land* 55 K1
Stour Provost *Dorset* 7 D11
Stour Row *Dorset* 7 D11
Stourbridge *W Midlands* 22 D2
Stourlton *Heref/Worcs* 22 G3
Stourpaine *Dorset* 7 E12
Stourport-on-Severn *Heref/Worcs* 22 E2
Stourton *Staffs* 22 D2
Stourton *Warwick* 22 H6
Stourton *Wilts* 7 C11
Stourton Caundle *Dorset* 7 E10
Stove *Orkney* 64 B3
Stoven *Suffolk* 27 G7
Stow *Borders* 49 E7
Stow *Lincs* 32 B6
Stow Bardolph *Norfolk* 24 E7
Stow Bedon *Norfolk* 26 F3
Stow cum Quy *Cambs* 25 J6
Stow Longa *Cambs* 25 H2
Stow Maries *Essex* 19 D8
Stowbridge *Norfolk* 24 E7
Stowe *Shrops* 21 E8
Stowe by Chartley *Staffs* 31 G8
Stowe Green *Glos* 15 D9
Stowell *Som'set* 7 D10
Stowlangtoft *Suffolk* 27 H3
Stowmarket *Suffolk* 27 J3
Stow-on-the-Wold *Glos* 16 B3
Stowting *Kent* 11 D10
Stowupland *Suffolk* 27 J4
Straad *S'clyde* 46 C5
Straanruie *H'land* 57 H6
Strachan *Gramp* 59 H4
Strachur *S'clyde* 51 G8
Stradbroke *Suffolk* 27 H5
Stradishall *Suffolk* 25 K8
Stradsett *Norfolk* 24 E8
Stragglethorpe *Lincs* 32 E6
Strahanna *Dumf/Gal* 43 B7
Straid *S'clyde* 42 C2
Straith *Dumf/Gal* 43 C9
Straiton *Lothian* 48 C5
Straiton *S'clyde* 42 A5
Straloch *Tayside* 52 A5
Stralock *Gramp* 58 E6
Stramshall *Staffs* 31 G9
Strand *S'clyde* 48 G2
Strandhead *S'clyde* 47 G9
Strang *I of Man* 38 H2
Stranghow *N Yorks* 41 D7
Stranog *Gramp* 59 H6
Stranraer *Dumf/Gal* 42 E1
Strata Florida *Dyfed* 20 F3
Stratfield Mortimer *Berks* 17 H7
Stratfield Saye *Hants* 17 H8
Stratfield Turgis *Hants* 17 H8
Stratford *London* 18 F4
Stratford St. Andrew *Suffolk* 27 J6
Stratford St. Mary *Suffolk* 27 M3
Stratford sub Castle *Wilts* 8 C3
Stratford Tony *Wilts* 8 C2
Stratford-upon-Avon *Warwick* 22 G5
Strathan *H'land* 55 K3
Strathan *H'land* 60 A6
Strathan *H'land* 60 E2
Strathaven *S'clyde* 47 E12
Strathblane *Central* 47 B10
Strathcarron *H'land* 54 E3
Strathcoil *H'land* 50 D4
Strathcoul *H'land* 61 B10
Strathdon *Gramp* 58 F1
Strathkanaird *H'land* 60 F3
Strathkinness *Fife* 53 F9
Strathmashie Ho *H'land* 57 K2
Strathmiglo *Fife* 53 F7
Strathmore Lodge *H'land* 61 C10
Strathpeffer *H'land* 54 D8
Strathrannoch *H'land* 54 B8
Strathy *H'land* 61 A8
Strathy Inn *H'land* 61 A8
Strathyre *Central* 52 E1
Stratton *Cornw'l* 4 E1
Stratton *Dorset* 7 G10
Stratton *Glos* 16 D1
Stratton Audley *Oxon* 17 B7
Stratton St. Margaret *Wilts* 16 E3
Stratton St. Michael *Norfolk* 26 F5
Stratton Strawless *Norfolk* 26 C5
Stratton-on-the-Fosse *Som'set* 7 A10
Stravithie *Fife* 53 F10
Streat *E Sussex* 10 F2
Streatham *London* 18 G3
Streatley *Beds* 17 A11
Streatley *Berks* 17 F7
Street *N Yorks* 41 E7
Street *Som'set* 7 C8
Street Dinas *Shrops* 30 F2
Street End *Kent* 11 C10
Street End *W Sussex* 9 F10
Street Houses *N Yorks* 36 C3
Street of Kincardine *H'land* 57 H5
Streethay *Staffs* 22 A5
Streethouse *W Yorks* 36 E2
Streetlam *N Yorks* 40 E3
Streetly *W Midlands* 22 B4
Strefford *Shrops* 21 D10
Strelley *Notts* 32 F2
Strensall *N Yorks* 36 A4
Stretcholt *Som'set* 6 B6
Strete *Devon* 5 L7
Strethall *Essex* 25 L6
Stretham *Cambs* 25 H6
Stretton *Ches* 30 B5
Stretton *Ches* 30 E3
Stretton *Derby* 32 D1
Stretton *Leics* 23 A12
Stretton *Staffs* 22 A2
Stretton *Staffs* 31 G11
Stretton en le Field *Leics* 22 A6
Stretton Grandison *Heref/Worcs* 21 H11
Stretton on Fosse *Warwick* 22 H6
Stretton Sugwas *Heref/Worcs* 21 H10
Stretton-on-Dunsmore *Warwick* 23 E7
Stretton-under-Fosse *Warwick* 23 D8
Strichen *Gramp* 58 B7
Stringston *Som'set* 6 B5
Strixton *Northants* 23 F12
Stroat *Glos* 15 E9
Stromeferry *H'land* 54 F2
Stromemore *H'land* 54 F2
Stromness *Orkney* 64 D1
Stronaba *H'land* 55 L6
Stronachlacher *Central* 51 F11
Stronchreggan *H'land* 55 M4
Stronchrubie *H'land* 60 E4
Strond *W Isles* 63 H1
Strone *H'land* 55 L5
Strone *H'land* 57 G1
Strone *S'clyde* 47 A7
Strone *S'clyde* 51 H10
Stronetoper *H'land* 57 K4
Stronmilchan *S'clyde* 51 E8
Strontian *H'land* 50 A5
Strontoiller *S'clyde* 50 E6
Stronuich *Tayside* 51 C12
Strood *Kent* 10 A6
Strood Green *Surrey* 10 C1
Stroud *Glos* 15 D11
Stroud *Hants* 9 D8
Stroud Green *Essex* 19 E8
Stroude *Surrey* 17 G11
Stroxton *Lincs* 32 G6
Struan *H'land* 62 D3
Struan *Tayside* 52 A3
Strubby *Lincs* 33 B11
Strumpshaw *Norfolk* 26 E6
Struy *H'land* 54 F8
Stuartfield *Gramp* 58 C7
Stubbington *Hants* 9 F7
Stubbins *Lancs* 35 E7
Stubbs Cross *Kent* 11 D8
Stubby knowe *Dumf/Gal* 44 F2
Stubhampton *Dorset* 8 E1
Stubshaw Cross *Gtr Man* 34 G5
Stubton *Lincs* 32 E6
Stuckgowan *S'clyde* 51 G10
Stuckindroin *S'clyde* 51 F10
Stuckton *Hants* 8 E3
Stud Green *Berks* 17 F9
Studdon *Northum* 45 H7
Studfold *Cumb* 39 E9
Studham *Bucks* 17 C11
Studland *Dorset* 8 H2
Studley *Oxon* 17 C7
Studley *Warwick* 22 F4
Studley *Wilts* 16 G1
Studley Roger *N Yorks* 40 H3
Stump Cross *Essex* 25 L6
Stuntney *Cambs* 25 G7
Stunts Green *E Sussex* 10 G5
Sturbridge *Staffs* 31 G7
Sturmer *Essex* 25 L8
Sturminster Marshall *Dorset* 8 F1
Sturminster Newton *Dorset* 7 E11
Sturry *Kent* 11 B10
Sturton *Humber* 37 G7
Sturton by Stow *Lincs* 32 B6
Sturton le Steeple *Notts* 32 B5
Stuston *Suffolk* 27 H4
Stutton *N Yorks* 36 C3
Stutton *Suffolk* 27 M4
Styal *Ches* 31 B7
Styrrup *Notts* 32 A3
Succoth *Gramp* 58 D2
Succoth *S'clyde* 51 G10
Suckley *Heref/Worcs* 21 G12
Sudborough *Northants* 25 G1
Sudbourne *Suffolk* 27 K7
Sudbrook *Gwent* 15 F8
Sudbrook *Lincs* 33 F7
Sudbrooke *Lincs* 33 C7
Sudbury *Derby* 31 G10
Sudbury *London* 18 E2
Sudbury *Suffolk* 27 L2
Suddie *H'land* 56 D2
Sudgrove *Glos* 15 D12
Suffield *N Yorks* 41 F10
Suffield *Norfolk* 26 B5
Sugnall *Staffs* 30 G6
Suisgill *H'land* 61 E9
Sulaisiader *W Isles* 63 C6
Sulby *I of Man* 38 G2
Sulgrave *Northants* 23 H9
Sulham *Berks* 17 G7
Sulhamstead *Berks* 17 G7
Sulhamstead Abbots *Berks* 17 G7
Sulishaderbeg *H'land* 62 D4
Sullington *W Sussex* 9 E12
Sullom *Shetl'd* 64 C7
Sully *S Glam* 14 G5
Summer Hill *Clwyd* 29 E12
Summerbridge *N Yorks* 35 A10
Summercourt *Cornw'l* 2 D6
Summerdale *W Sussex* 9 E10
Summerhouse *Durham* 40 C2
Summerleaze *Gwent* 15 F7
Summerseat *Gtr Man* 35 F7
Summertown *Oxon* 16 C6
Summit *Gtr Man* 35 E8
Summit *Gtr Man* 35 F8
Sunbury on Thames *Surrey* 17 G11
Sundaywell *Dumf/Gal* 43 C9
Sunderland *Cumb* 38 B4
Sunderland *Lancs* 34 B3
Sunderland *Tyne/Wear* 45 G12
Sunderland Bridge *Durham* 40 A3
Sundhope *Borders* 48 G6
Sundon Park *Beds* 17 B11
Sundridge *Kent* 10 C4
Sunipol *H'land* 50 B1
Sunk Island *Humber* 37 E10
Sunningdale *Berks* 17 G10
Sunninghill *Berks* 17 G10
Sunningwell *Oxon* 16 D6
Sunniside *Durham* 40 A2
Sunniside *Tyne/Wear* 45 G10
Sunny Bank *Cumb* 38 F5
Sunnyhillock *H'land* 56 D4
Sunnylaw *Central* 52 G3
Sunnyside *W Sussex* 10 D3
Sunton *Wilts* 8 A4
Sunwick *Borders* 49 D11
Surbiton *London* 18 G2
Surby *I of Man* 38 H1
Surfleet *Lincs* 24 C3
Surfleet Seas End *Lincs* 24 C4
Surlingham *Norfolk* 26 E6
Sustead *Norfolk* 26 B5
Susworth *Lincs* 36 G6
Sutcombe *Devon* 4 E2
Sutherland *Orkney* 64 E2
Suton *Norfolk* 26 E4
Sutors of Cromarty *H'land* 56 C4
Sutterby *Lincs* 33 C11
Sutterton *Lincs* 24 B4
Sutton *Beds* 25 K3
Sutton *Bucks* 17 F11
Sutton *Cambs* 24 F2
Sutton *Cambs* 25 G5
Sutton *Dyfed* 12 E3
Sutton *Kent* 11 C12
Sutton *London* 10 B1
Sutton *London* 18 H3
Sutton *Mersey* 34 H4
Sutton *Norfolk* 26 C7
Sutton *Notts* 32 B4
Sutton *Notts* 32 F5
Sutton *Oxon* 16 C5
Sutton *S Yorks* 36 F3
Sutton *Shrops* 22 C1
Sutton *Shrops* 30 G5
Sutton *Som'set* 7 C9
Sutton *Staffs* 30 H6
Sutton *Suffolk* 27 K6
Sutton *Surrey* 9 B12
Sutton *W Sussex* 9 E11
Sutton at Hone *Kent* 10 A4
Sutton Bassett *Northants* 23 C11
Sutton Benger *Wilts* 15 F12
Sutton Bonington *Notts* 32 H2
Sutton Bridge *Lincs* 24 C6
Sutton Cheney *Leics* 23 B7
Sutton Coldfield *W Midlands* 22 B5
Sutton Courteney *Oxon* 16 E6
Sutton Crosses *Lincs* 24 C5
Sutton Grange *N Yorks* 40 H3
Sutton Green *Surrey* 9 A11
Sutton Hill *Shrops* 21 B12
Sutton Howgrave *N Yorks* 40 G3
Sutton in Ashfield *Notts* 32 D2
Sutton in the Elms *Leics* 23 C8
Sutton Lane Ends *Ches* 31 C8
Sutton Maddock *Shrops* 21 B12
Sutton Mallet *Som'set* 7 C7
Sutton Mandeville *Wilts* 8 C1
Sutton Montis *Som'set* 7 D9
Sutton on Sea *Lincs* 33 B12
Sutton on the Hill *Derby* 31 G11
Sutton on Trent *Notts* 32 D5
Sutton St. Edmund *Lincs* 24 D5
Sutton St. James *Lincs* 24 D5
Sutton St. Michael *Heref/Worcs* 21 H10
Sutton St. Nicholas *Heref/Worcs* 21 H10
Sutton Scotney *Hants* 8 B6
Sutton upon Derwent *Humber* 36 B5
Sutton Valence *Kent* 11 C7
Sutton Veny *Wilts* 7 B12
Sutton Waldron *Dorset* 7 E12
Sutton Weaver *Ches* 30 B4
Sutton Wick *Avon* 15 H9
Sutton-in-Craven *N Yorks* 35 C8
Sutton-on-Hull *Humber* 37 D9
Sutton-on-the-Forest *N Yorks* 36 A4
Sutton-under-Brailes *Warwick* 22 H6
Sutton-under-Whitestonecliffe *N Yorks* 40 G5
Swaby *Lincs* 33 B11
Swadlincote *Derby* 31 H11
Swaffham *Norfolk* 26 E1
Swaffham Bulbeck *Cambs* 25 J7
Swaffham Prior *Cambs* 25 J7
Swafield *Norfolk* 26 B6
Swainby *N Yorks* 40 E5
Swainshill *Heref/Worcs* 21 H10
Swainsthorpe *Norfolk* 26 E5
Swainswick *Avon* 15 G10
Swalcliffe *Oxon* 23 H7
Swalecliffe *Kent* 11 A10
Swallow *Lincs* 37 G9
Swallowcliffe *Wilts* 8 C1
Swallowfield *Berks* 17 H8
Swallownest *S Yorks* 32 B2
Swalwell *Tyne/Wear* 45 G10
Swan Green *Ches* 30 C6
Swanage *Dorset* 8 H2
Swanbister *Orkney* 64 D2
Swanbourne *Bucks* 17 A9
Swanibost *W Isles* 63 A6
Swanland *Humber* 37 D7
Swanley *Kent* 10 A4
Swanley Village *Kent* 10 A4
Swanmore *Hants* 9 D7
Swannington *Leics* 23 A7
Swannington *Norfolk* 26 D4
Swanscombe *Kent* 10 A5
Swansea *W Glam* 13 H10
Swanton Abbot *Norfolk* 26 C6
Swanton Morley *Norfolk* 26 D3
Swanton Novers *Norfolk* 26 B3
Swanwick *Derby* 32 E1
Swarby *Lincs* 24 B1
Swardail *W Isles* 63 D6
Swardeston *Norfolk* 26 E5
Swarkestone *Derby* 31 G12
Swarland *Northum* 45 C10
Swarland Estate *Northum* 45 C10
Swarraton *Hants* 9 B7
Swaton *Lincs* 24 B2
Swavesey *Cambs* 25 H5
Sway *Hants* 8 F4
Swayfield *Lincs* 33 H7
Swaythling *Hants* 8 D6
Sweet Green *Heref/Worcs* 21 F12
Sweetham *Devon* 4 F7
Sweetholme *Cumb* 39 C8

Sweethope Borders 49 E9
Sweethouse Cornw'l 3 C8
Sweffling Suffolk 27 J6
Swepstone Leics 23 A7
Swerford Oxon 16 A5
Swettenham Ches 30 C6
Swetton N Yorks 40 H2
Swilland Suffolk 27 K5
Swillington W Yorks 36 D2
Swimbridge Devon 4 C5
Swimbridge Newland Devon 4 C5
Swinbrook Oxon 16 C4
Swinderley Lincs 32 D6
Swindon Glos 15 B12
Swindon Staffs 22 C2
Swindon Wilts 16 F3
Swine Humber 37 D9
Swinefleet Humber 36 E5
Swineford Avon 15 G10
Swineshead Beds 25 J2
Swineshead Lincs 24 B3
Swineshead Bridge Lincs 24 A3
Swiney H'land 61 D11
Swinford Leics 23 D9
Swinford Oxon 16 C5
Swingfield Minnis Kent 11 D10
Swingfield Street Kent 11 D11
Swinhoe Northum 45 E12
Swinhope Lincs 37 G9
Swining Shetl'd 64 C7
Swinithwaite N Yorks 40 F1
Swinnie Borders 44 A5
Swinscoe Staffs 31 E9
Swinside Hall Borders 44 A5
Swinstead Lincs 24 C1
Swinton Borders 49 E11
Swinton Gtr Man 34 G6
Swinton N Yorks 40 G2
Swinton N Yorks 41 H7
Swinton S Yorks 36 G2
Swinton Quarter Borders 49 E11
Swintonmill Borders 49 E10
Swithland Leics 23 A9
Swordale H'land 56 C1
Swordland H'land 55 K2
Swordly H'land 61 B7
Sworton Heath Ches 30 B5
Swydd-ffynnon Dyfed 20 F3
Swynnerton Staffs 31 G7
Swyre Dorset 7 G8
Sychnant Powys 20 E5
Sychtyn Powys 20 B5
Syde Glos 15 C12
Sydenham Oxon 17 D8
Sydenham Damerel Devon 5 H3
Syderstone Norfolk 26 B1
Sydling St. Nicholas Dorset 7 F9
Sydmonton Hants 16 H6
Syerston Notts 32 E5
Syke Gtr Man 35 F8
Sykehouse S Yorks 36 E4
Sykes Lancs 34 B5
Syleham Suffolk 27 G5
Symington S'clyde 47 F8
Symington S'clyde 48 F3
Symonds Yat Heref/Worcs 15 C9
Symondsbury Dorset 7 G8
Synod Inn Dyfed 13 B7
Synton Parkhead Borders 49 G7
Syre H'land 61 C7
Syreford Glos 16 B1
Syresham Northants 23 H9
Syston Leics 23 A9
Syston Lincs 32 F6
Sytchampton Heref/Worcs 22 F2
Sywell Northants 23 E11
Taagan H'land 54 C4
Tackhouse S'clyde 47 E11
Tackley Oxon 16 B6
Tacolneston Norfolk 26 F4
Tadcaster N Yorks 36 C3
Taddington Derby 31 C10
Taddiport Devon 4 D4
Tadley Hants 17 H7
Tadlow Cambs 25 K4
Tadmarton Oxon 23 H7
Tadwick Avon 15 G10
Tadworth Surrey 10 B1
Tafarnau-bach Gwent 14 C4
Tafarn-gelyn Clwyd 29 D11
Tafarn-y-bwlch Dyfed 12 D4
Taffs Well Mid Glam 14 F5
Tafolwern Powys 20 B4
Tai Gwyn 29 D7
Tai-bach Clwyd 29 G10
Taibach W Glam 13 H11
Tai-mawr Clwyd 29 F9
Tain H'land 56 B3
Tain H'land 61 A11
Tainant Clwyd 29 F12
Tairgwaith W Glam 13 F10
Tair-lon Gwyn 28 E4
Takeley Essex 18 B5
Takeley Street Essex 18 B5
Talachddu Powys 14 A4
Talacre Clwyd 29 B10
Talaton Devon 6 F4
Talbenny Dyfed 12 F2
Talbot Green Mid Glam 14 F4
Talbot Village Dorset 8 G2
Talerddig Powys 20 B5
Talgarreg Dyfed 13 B7
Talgarth Powys 14 A5
Taliesin Dyfed 20 C2
Talisker H'land 62 E3
Talke Staffs 31 E7
Talkin Cumb 44 G4
Talla Linnfoots Borders 48 G4
Talladale H'land 54 C3
Tallantire Cumb 38 B3
Tallardd Gwyn 29 G8
Tallarn Green Clwyd 30 F3
Talley Dyfed 13 D9
Tallington Lincs 24 E2
Talmine H'land 60 B6
Talog Dyfed 13 D7
Talsarn Dyfed 14 B1
Talsarn Dyfed 20 G1
Talsarnau Gwyn 28 G5
Talskiddy Cornw'l 2 C6
Talwrn Clwyd 29 E12
Talwrn Gwyn 28 C4
Talybont Dyfed 20 C2
Tal-y-bont Gwyn 28 C5
Tal-y-bont Gwyn 28 H5
Tal-y-bont Gwyn 29 C7
Talybont Powys 14 B4
Tal-y-cafn Gwyn 29 C7
Tal-y-coed Gwent 15 C7
Tal-y-garn Mid Glam 14 F4
Tal-y-llyn Gwyn 20 A3
Tal-y-llyn Powys 14 B4
Talysarn Gwyn 28 E4
Talywain Gwent 14 D6
Tal-y-wern Powys 20 B4
Tame Clevl'd 40 D5
Tamerton Foliot Devon 5 K3
Tamworth Staffs 22 B5
Tan Hill N Yorks 39 E11
Tancredston Dyfed 12 D2
Tanden Kent 11 D8
Tandlemuir S'clyde 47 C8
Tandridge Surrey 10 C3
Tanfield Durham 45 G10
Tanfield Lea Durham 45 H10
Tangley Hants 8 A5
Tangmere W Sussex 9 E10
Tankerness Orkney 64 D3
Tankersley S Yorks 35 G12
Tan-lan Gwyn 28 F5
Tannach H'land 61 C12
Tannachie Gramp 59 J5
Tannadice Tayside 59 L2
Tannington Suffolk 27 H5
Tansley Derby 31 D11
Tansley Knoll Derby 31 D11
Tansor Northants 24 F2
Tantobie Durham 45 H10
Tanton N Yorks 40 D5
Tanworth in Arden Warwick 22 E5
Tan-y-bwlch Gwyn 28 F6
Tan-y-fron Clwyd 29 D9
Tan-y-graig Dyfed 20 E3
Tan-y-graig Gwyn 28 F3
Tan-y-grisiau Gwyn 28 F6
Tan-y-groes Dyfed 12 B6
Tan-y-pistyll Clwyd 29 G10
Taplow Bucks 17 F10
Tarbert S'clyde 46 A1
Tarbert S'clyde 46 C4
Tarbert W Isles 63 G2
Tarbet H'land 55 K2
Tarbet H'land 60 C3
Tarbet S'clyde 51 G10
Tarbolton S'clyde 47 G9
Tarbrax S'clyde 48 D3
Tarbuck Green Mersey 30 A3
Tarcoon Dumf/Gal 44 E2
Tardebigge Heref/Worcs 22 E3
Tarfside Tayside 59 J2
Tarland Gramp 59 G2
Tarleton Lancs 34 E3
Tarlscough Lancs 34 F3
Tarlton Glos 15 D12
Tarnbrook Lancs 34 B5
Tarporley Ches 30 D4
Tarr Som'set 6 C4
Tarrant Crawford Dorset 8 F1
Tarrant Gunville Dorset 8 E1
Tarrant Hinton Dorset 8 E1
Tarrant Keyneston Dorset 8 F1
Tarrant Launceston Dorset 8 E1
Tarrant Monkton Dorset 8 E1
Tarrant Rawston Dorset 8 E1
Tarrant Rushton Dorset 8 E1
Tarring Neville E Sussex 10 H3
Tarrington Heref/Worcs 21 H11
Tarskavaig H'land 62 G5
Tarves Gramp 58 D6
Tarvie H'land 54 D8
Tarvin Ches 30 D4
Tasburgh Norfolk 26 F5
Tasley Shrops 21 C12
Taston Oxon 16 B5
Tatenhill Staffs 31 H10
Tath Hill Dumf/Gal 43 B11
Tatham Lancs 39 H8
Tathwell Lincs 33 B10
Tatling End Bucks 17 E11
Tatsfield Surrey 10 B3
Tattenhall Ches 30 D3
Tatterford Norfolk 26 C2
Tattersett Norfolk 26 C1
Tattershall Lincs 33 D9
Tattershall Bridge Lincs 33 E9
Tattershall Thorpe Lincs 33 D9
Tattingstone Suffolk 27 L4
Tattingstone Whitehorse Suffolk 27 L4
Tatworth Devon 6 F6
Tauchers Gramp 58 C1
Taunton Som'set 6 D6
Taverham Norfolk 26 D5
Tavernspite Dyfed 12 F5
Tavistock Devon 5 H3
Taw Green Devon 4 E5
Taw Green Devon 4 F5
Tawstock Devon 4 C4
Taxal Derby 31 B8
Tayburn S'clyde 47 E10
Taychreggan S'clyde 51 E7
Tayinloan S'clyde 46 E2
Taymouth Castle Tayside 52 C3
Taynafead S'clyde 51 F8
Taynton Glos 15 B10
Taynton Oxon 16 C3
Taynuilt S'clyde 51 D7
Tayport Fife 53 D9
Tayvallich S'clyde 46 A2
Tealby Lincs 33 A8
Tealing Tayside 53 C9
Teangue H'land 62 G6
Tebay Cumb 39 E8
Tebworth Beds 17 A10
Tedburn St. Mary Devon 4 F7
Teddington Glos 16 A1
Teddington London 18 G2
Tedstone Delamere Heref/Worcs 21 F12
Tedstone Wafre Heref/Worcs 21 F12
Teeton Northants 23 E10
Teffont Evias Wilts 8 C1
Teffont Magna Wilts 8 C2
Tegryn Dyfed 12 D6
Teigh Leics 23 A12
Teigngrace Devon 5 H7
Teignmouth Devon 5 H8
Teindland Gramp 56 D8
Teindside Borders 44 B3
Telford Shrops 21 B12
Telham E Sussex 10 G6
Tellisford Som'set 7 A11
Telscombe E Sussex 10 H3
Tempelton Bridge Devon 4 E7
Templand Dumf/Gal 43 C11
Temple Cornw'l 3 B8
Temple Lothian 48 D6
Temple Balsall W Midlands 22 E5
Temple Bar Dyfed 13 B8
Temple Bar Dyfed 13 E9
Temple Cloud Avon 7 A9
Temple Ewell Kent 11 D11
Temple Grafton Warwick 22 G5
Temple Guiting Glos 16 A2
Temple Herdewyke Warwick 23 G7
Temple Hirst N Yorks 36 E4
Temple Normanton Derby 32 C1
Temple Sowerby Cumb 39 C8
Templecombe Som'set 7 D10
Templehall Fife 53 H7
Templeton Devon 6 E2
Templeton Dyfed 12 F4
Tempsford Beds 25 K3
Ten Mile Bank Norfolk 24 F7
Tenbury Wells Heref/Worcs 21 F11
Tenby Dyfed 12 G5
Tendring Essex 19 B11
Tendring Green Essex 19 A11
Tenston Orkney 64 C1
Tenterden Kent 11 E7
Terally Dumf/Gal 42 G2
Terling Essex 19 B7
Ternhill Shrops 30 G5
Terras Cornw'l 2 D6
Terregles Dumf/Gal 43 D10
Terrick Bucks 17 C9
Terrington N Yorks 41 H7
Terrington St. Clement Norfolk 24 D6
Terrington St. John Norfolk 24 D6
Teston Kent 10 C6
Testwood Hants 8 E5
Tetbury Glos 15 E12
Tetbury Upton Glos 15 E12
Tetchill Shrops 30 G3
Tetcott Devon 4 F2
Tetford Lincs 33 C10
Tetney Lincs 37 G10
Tetney Lock Lincs 37 G11
Tetsworth Oxon 17 D8
Tettenhall W Midlands 22 B2
Teuchar Gramp 58 C5
Teuchatcroft Tayside 53 B9
Teversal Notts 32 D2
Teversham Cambs 25 J6
Teviothead Dumf/Gal 44 C2
Tewel Gramp 59 J6
Tewin Herts 18 B3
Tewkesbury Glos 15 A12
Teynham Kent 11 B8
Teynham Street Kent 11 B8
Thackley W Yorks 35 C10
Thackthwaite Cumb 38 C4
Thackthwaite Cumb 38 C6
Thakeham W Sussex 9 D12
Thame Oxon 17 D8
Thames Ditton Surrey 17 G12
Thamesmead London 18 F5
Thanington Kent 11 B10
Thankerton S'clyde 48 F2
Tharston Norfolk 26 F5
Thatcham Berks 16 G6
Thatto Heath Mersey 34 H4
Thaxted Essex 25 M7
The Aird H'land 62 C3
The Bage Heref/Worcs 21 H8
The Barony Dumf/Gal 43 C11
The Barony Orkney 64 B1
The Blythe Staffs 31 G9
The Braes H'land 62 E4
The Broad Heref/Worcs 21 F10
The Bryn Gwent 14 D6
The Camp Glos 15 C12
The City Bucks 17 D8
The Cleaver Heref/Worcs 15 A8
The Common Wilts 16 F1
The Common Wilts 8 C4
The Corner Shrops 21 D10
The Craigs H'land 60 G5
The Cronk I of Man 38 F2
The Den S'clyde 47 D8
The Eals Northum 44 D6
The Eaves Glos 15 D9
The Engine Cambs 24 E4
The Fauld Cumb 44 F2
The Flatt Cumb 44 E4
The Forstal Kent 11 C7
The Green Cumb 38 G4
The Green Wilts 7 C12
The Grove Dumf/Gal 43 D10
The Hardens Borders 49 D10
The Haven W Sussex 9 C12
The Hendre Gwent 15 C8
The Hermitage Surrey 10 C1
The Highlands Hotel S'clyde 46 A5
The Hill Cumb 38 G4
The Howe I of Man 38 H1
The Hythe Essex 19 B10
The Lake Dumf/Gal 43 G7
The Leacon Kent 11 E8
The Lee Bucks 17 D10
The Lhen I of Man 38 F2
The Marsh Powys 21 C8
The Middles Durham 45 H10
The Moor Kent 10 E6
The Mound H'land 61 G8
The Murray S'clyde 47 D11
The Ness Shetl'd 64 A8
The Neuk Gramp 59 H5
The Oval Avon 15 H10
The Pill Gwent 15 F8
The Pole of Itlaw Gramp 58 B4
The Pound Powys 21 E7
The Quarry Glos 15 D10
The Rhos Dyfed 12 F4
The Sands Surrey 9 B10
The Scare Cumb 44 F3
The Slade Berks 16 G6
The Stocks Kent 11 E8
The Stone Essex 19 C9
The Throat Berks 17 G9
The Towans Cornw'l 2 F3
The Vauld Heref/Worcs 21 G10
The Wyke Shrops 22 B1
Theakston N Yorks 40 G3
Thealby Humber 37 E7
Theale Berks 17 G7
Theale Som'set 7 B8
Thearne Humber 37 C8
Theberton Suffolk 27 J7
Theddingworth Leics 23 D10
Theddlethorpe All Saints Lincs 33 A11
Theddlethorpe St. Helen Lincs 33 A11
Thelbridge Cross Devon 4 E7
Thelnetham Suffolk 27 G3
Thelwall Ches 30 B5
Themelthorpe Norfolk 26 C4
Thenford Northants 23 H8
Therfield Herts 25 L4
Thetford Norfolk 27 G2
Theydon Bois Essex 18 D4
Thickwood Wilts 15 G11
Thimbleby Lincs 33 C9
Thimbleby N Yorks 40 F5
Thingwall Mersey 30 B1
Thirkleby N Yorks 40 G5
Thirlby N Yorks 40 G5
Thirlestane Borders 49 E8
Thirlspot Cumb 38 C5
Thirn N Yorks 40 G2
Thirsk N Yorks 40 G4
Thistlebottom Cumb 38 A5
Thistleton Lancs 34 C3
Thistleton Leics 32 H6
Thistley Green Suffolk 25 H8
Thixendale N Yorks 36 A6
Thockrington Northum 45 E8
Tholomas Drove Cambs 24 E5
Tholthorpe N Yorks 40 H5
Thomas Chapel Dyfed 12 F4
Thomas Close Cumb 39 A7
Thomastown Gramp 58 D3
Thompson Norfolk 26 F2
Thomshill Gramp 56 D8
Thong Kent 10 A5
Thoralby N Yorks 39 F12
Thorbedc Green Mersey 34 H3
Thoresby Notts 32 C4
Thoresway Lincs 37 G9
Thorganby Lincs 37 G9
Thorganby N Yorks 36 C5
Thorgill N Yorks 41 E7
Thorington Suffolk 27 H7
Thorington Street Suffolk 27 L3
Thorlby N Yorks 35 B8
Thorley Herts 18 B5
Thorley I of Wight 8 G5
Thorley Street Herts 18 B5
Thorley Street I of Wight 8 G5
Thormanby N Yorks 40 H5
Thornaby-on-Tees Clevl'd 40 C5
Thornage Norfolk 26 B4
Thornborough Bucks 17 A8
Thornborough N Yorks 40 G3
Thornbury Avon 15 E9
Thornbury Devon 4 E3
Thornbury Heref/Worcs 21 F11
Thornby Northants 23 E10
Thorncliff Staffs 31 D8
Thorncombe Dorset 7 F7
Thorncombe Street Surrey 9 B11
Thorncote Green Beds 25 K3
Thorncross I of Wight 8 H6
Thorndon Suffolk 27 H4
Thorndon Cross Devon 4 F4
Thorndykes Borders 49 E9
Thorne S Yorks 36 F5
Thorne St. Margaret Som'set 6 D4
Thorner W Yorks 35 C12
Thorney Cambs 24 E4
Thorney Notts 32 C6
Thorney Som'set 7 D7
Thorney Crofts Humber 37 E9
Thorney Hill Hants 8 F4
Thorneybank Gramp 58 D4
Thornfalcon Som'set 6 D6
Thornford Dorset 7 E9
Thorngrafton Northum 44 F6
Thorngrove Som'set 7 C7
Thorngumbald Humber 37 D9
Thornham Norfolk 24 A8
Thornham Magna Suffolk 27 H4
Thornham Parva Suffolk 27 H4
Thornhaugh Cambs 24 E2
Thornhill Central 52 G2
Thornhill Cumb 38 D3
Thornhill Derby 31 B10
Thornhill Dumf/Gal 43 B9
Thornhill Hants 8 E6
Thornhill Mid Glam 14 F5
Thornhill W Yorks 35 E11
Thornholme Humber 37 A9
Thornielaw Borders 49 F8
Thornington Northum 49 F11
Thornley Durham 40 A4
Thornley Durham 40 B1
Thornlibank S'clyde 47 D10
Thorns Suffolk 25 K8
Thornseat S Yorks 35 H11
Thornsett Derby 31 B8
Thornthwaite Cumb 38 C5
Thornthwaite N Yorks 35 A10
Thornton Bucks 17 A8
Thornton Clevl'd 40 D5
Thornton Dyfed 12 F2
Thornton Fife 53 G7
Thornton Humber 36 C5
Thornton Lancs 34 C2
Thornton Leics 23 A8
Thornton Lincs 33 C9
Thornton Mersey 34 G2
Thornton Northum 49 E12
Thornton Tayside 53 C9
Thornton W Yorks 35 D9
Thornton Curtis Humber 37 E8
Thornton Heath London 18 G3
Thornton Hough Mersey 30 B2
Thornton in Craven N Yorks 35 B8
Thornton in Lonsdale N Yorks 39 H9
Thornton le Moor Lincs 37 G8
Thornton Moor N Yorks 36 A4
Thornton Rust N Yorks 39 F12
Thornton Steward N Yorks 40 F2
Thornton Watlass N Yorks 40 G3
Thornton-a-Dale N Yorks 41 G8
Thorntonhall S'clyde 47 D10
Thornton-le-Beans N Yorks 40 F4
Thornton-le-Clay N Yorks 36 A5
Thornton-le-Moor N Yorks 40 F4
Thornton-le-Moors Ches 30 C3
Thornton-le-Street N Yorks 40 G4
Thorntonloch Lothian 49 B10
Thorntonpark Northum 49 E12
Thornwood Common Essex 18 C5
Thornythwaite Cumb 38 C6
Thoroton Notts 32 F5
Thorp Arch W Yorks 36 C2
Thorp Green Suffolk 27 K2
Thorpe Derby 31 E10
Thorpe Humber 37 B7
Thorpe Lincs 33 B12
Thorpe N Yorks 35 A9
Thorpe Norfolk 26 F7
Thorpe Notts 32 E5
Thorpe Surrey 17 G11
Thorpe Abbots Norfolk 27 G5
Thorpe Acre Leics 32 H2
Thorpe Arnold Leics 32 H5
Thorpe Audlin W Yorks 36 F3
Thorpe Bassett N Yorks 41 H8
Thorpe Bay Essex 19 E9
Thorpe by Water Leics 23 C12
Thorpe Constantine Staffs 22 A6
Thorpe End Norfolk 26 D6
Thorpe Hesley S Yorks 35 G12
Thorpe in Balne S Yorks 36 F4
Thorpe in the Fallows Lincs 32 B6
Thorpe Langton Leics 23 C10
Thorpe Larches Clevl'd 40 C4
Thorpe le Street Humber 36 C6
Thorpe Malsor Northants 23 D11
Thorpe Mandeville Northants 23 H9
Thorpe Market Norfolk 26 B5
Thorpe Morieux Suffolk 27 K2
Thorpe on the Hill Lincs 32 D6
Thorpe St. Andrew Norfolk 26 D6
Thorpe St. Peter Lincs 33 D11
Thorpe Salvin S Yorks 32 B2
Thorpe Satchville Leics 23 A10
Thorpe Thewles Clevl'd 40 C4
Thorpe Underwood N Yorks 36 A2
Thorpe Waterville Northants 25 G1

Thorpe Willoughby N Yorks 36 D4
Thorpe Willoughby Norfolk 26 D3
Thorpe-le-Soken Essex 19 B11
Thorpeness Suffolk 27 J8
Thorrington Essex 19 B11
Thorverton Dorset 7 F3
Thorverton Devon 6 F3
Thrandeston Suffolk 27 H4
Thrapston Northants 25 G1
Threapland Cumb 38 A4
Threapwood Clwyd 30 F3
Threave S'clyde 42 A4
Three Bridges W Sussex 10 D2
Three Burrows Cornw'l 2 E4
Three Chimneys Kent 11 D7
Three Cocks Powys 14 A5
Three Crosses W Glam 13 H9
Three Cups Corner E Sussex 10 F5
Three Gates Clevl'd 40 B5
Three Gates Dorset 7 E9
Three Holes Norfolk 24 E6
Three Legged Cross Dorset 8 E2
Three Oaks E Sussex 11 G7
Threeburnford Borders 49 D7
Threekingham Lincs 24 B2
Threelegged Cross E Sussex 10 E6
Threelows Staffs 31 E9
Threemile Cross Berks 17 G8
Threemilestone Cornw'l 2 E5
Threlkeld Cumb 38 C6
Threshfield N Yorks 35 A8
Thrigby Norfolk 26 D7
Thringarth Durham 39 C11
Thringstone Leics 32 H2
Thrintoft N Yorks 40 F3
Thriplow Cambs 25 K5
Throckenholt Lincs 24 E5
Throcking Herts 25 M4
Throckley Tyne/Wear 45 F9
Throckmorton Heref/Worcs 22 G3
Throphill Northum 45 D9
Thropton Northum 45 C8
Throughgate Dumf/Gal 43 C9
Throwleigh Devon 5 G5
Throwley Kent 11 C8
Throwley Forstal Kent 11 C8
Thrumpton Notts 32 G2
Thrumster H'land 61 C12
Thrunscoe Humber 37 F10
Thrunton Northum 45 B9
Thrupe Som'set 7 B9
Thrupp Glos 15 D11
Thrupp Oxon 16 C6
Thrushelton Devon 5 G3
Thrushesbush Essex 18 C5
Thrussington Leics 23 A10
Thruxton Hants 8 B4
Thruxton Heref/Worcs 15 A7
Thrybergh S Yorks 36 H3
Thundersley Essex 19 E8
Thundridge Herts 18 B4
Thurcaston Leics 23 A9
Thurcroft S Yorks 32 A2
Thurdon Cornw'l 4 E2
Thurgarton Notts 32 E4
Thurgaton Norfolk 26 B5
Thurgoland S Yorks 35 G11
Thurlaston Leics 23 B8
Thurlaston Warwick 23 E8
Thurlbear Som'set 6 D6
Thurlby Lincs 24 D2
Thurlby Lincs 32 D6
Thurleigh Beds 25 J2
Thurlestone Devon 5 L5
Thurloxton Som'set 6 C6
Thurlston Derby 32 G1
Thurlstone S Yorks 35 G11
Thurlton Norfolk 26 F7
Thurmaston Leics 23 A9
Thurnby Leics 23 B10
Thurne Norfolk 26 D7
Thurnham Kent 11 B7
Thurnham Lancs 34 B3
Thurning Norfolk 26 C4
Thurning Northants 25 G2
Thurnscoe S Yorks 36 G2
Thursby Cumb 44 H2
Thursford Green Norfolk 26 B3
Thursley Surrey 9 B10
Thurso H'land 61 A10
Thurso East H'land 61 A10
Thurstaston Mersey 30 B1
Thurston Suffolk 27 J2
Thurstonfield Cumb 44 G2
Thurstonland W Yorks 35 F10
Thurton Norfolk 26 E6
Thurvaston Derby 31 F11
Thuxton Norfolk 26 E3
Thwaite N Yorks 39 E11
Thwaite Suffolk 27 H4
Thwaite St. Mary Norfolk 26 F6
Thwing Humber 41 H10
Tibbermore Tayside 52 E5
Tibbers Dumf/Gal 43 B9
Tibberton Glos 15 B10
Tibberton Heref/Worcs 22 F3
Tibberton Shrops 30 H5
Tibenham Norfolk 26 F4
Tibshelf Derby 32 D2
Tibthorpe Humber 37 B7
Ticehurst E Sussex 10 E6
Tichborne Hants 9 C7
Tickencote Leics 24 E1
Tickenham Avon 15 G8
Tickhill S Yorks 32 A3
Ticklerton Shrops 21 C10
Ticknall Derby 31 H12
Tickton Humber 37 C8
Tidbury Green W Midlands 22 E4
Tidcombe Wilts 16 H4
Tiddington Oxon 17 D7
Tidebrook E Sussex 10 E5
Tideford Cornw'l 3 D10
Tideford Cross Cornw'l 3 D10
Tidenham Glos 15 E9
Tideswell Derby 31 C10
Tidington Warwick 22 F6
Tidmarsh Berks 17 G7
Tidmington Warwick 22 H6
Tidpit Hants 8 D2
Tiers Cross Dyfed 12 F3
Tiffield Northants 23 G10
Tifty Gramp 58 D5
Tigerton Tayside 59 L3
Tighchuig H'land 54 F8
Tighnablair Tayside 52 E3
Tighnabruaich S'clyde 46 B5
Tigh-na-criche S'clyde 51 G8
Tighnafiline H'land 60 G1
Tigley Devon 5 K6
Tilbrook Cambs 25 H2
Tilbury Essex 18 F6
Tilehurst Berks 17 G7
Tilford Surrey 9 B10
Tilgate W Sussex 10 E2
Tillathrowie Gramp 58 D2
Tilley Shrops 30 G4
Tillicoultry Central 52 G4
Tillingham Essex 19 D10
Tillington Heref/Worcs 21 H10
Tillington W Sussex 9 D11
Tillington Common Heref/Worcs 21 H10
Tillyarblet Tayside 59 L3
Tillybardine Tayside 59 K2
Tillycorthie Gramp 58 E7
Tillydrine House Gramp 59 H4
Tillyfar Gramp 58 E7
Tillyfourie Gramp 58 F4
Tillyminnate Gramp 58 D2
Tilmanstone Kent 11 C11
Tiln Notts 32 B4
Tilney All Saints Norfolk 24 D7
Tilney High End Norfolk 24 D7
Tilney St. Lawrence Norfolk 24 D6
Tilshead Wilts 8 A2
Tilstock Shrops 30 F4
Tilston Ches 30 E3
Tilstone Fearnall Ches 30 D4
Tilsworth Beds 17 B10
Tilton on the Hill Leics 23 B10
Tiltups End Glos 15 E11
Tilygreig Gramp 58 E6
Timberland Lincs 33 D8
Timbersbrook Ches 31 D7
Timberscombe Som'set 6 B3
Timble N Yorks 35 B10
Timpendean Borders 49 G9
Timperley Gtr Man 30 A6
Timsbury Avon 15 H10
Timsbury Hants 8 D5
Timsgarry W Isles 63 D2
Timworth Suffolk 27 H2
Tincleton Dorset 7 G11
Tindale Cumb 44 G4
Tingewick Bucks 17 A7
Tingley W Yorks 35 E11
Tingrith Beds 25 M1
Tinhay Devon 5 G3
Tinnis Borders 48 F6
Tinshill W Yorks 35 C11
Tintagel Cornw'l 3 A7
Tintern Parva Gwent 15 D8
Tintinhull Som'set 7 D8
Tintwhistle Derby 35 G9
Tinwald Dumf/Gal 43 C11
Tinwell Leics 24 E1
Tippacott Devon 4 A6
Tipperty Gramp 58 B4
Tipperty Gramp 58 E7
Tipp's End Norfolk 24 F6
Tiptoe Hants 8 F4
Tipton W Midlands 22 C3
Tipton St. John Devon 6 G4
Tiptree Essex 19 B9
Tirabad Powys 20 H4
Tirghoil H'land 50 E1
Tirley Glos 15 A11
Tirphil Mid Glam 14 D5
Tirril Cumb 39 C7
Tisbury Wilts 8 C1
Tisman's Common W Sussex 9 C12
Tissington Derby 31 E10
Titchberry Devon 4 C1
Titchfield Hants 9 F7
Titchmarsh Northants 25 G1
Titchwell Norfolk 26 A1
Tithby Notts 32 F4
Titley Heref/Worcs 21 F9
Titlington Northum 45 A9
Titlington Northum 45 B9
Titsey Surrey 10 C3
Tittensor Staffs 31 F7
Tittleshall Norfolk 26 C2
Tiverton Ches 30 D4
Tiverton Devon 6 E3
Tiverton Junction Devon 6 E4
Tivetshall St. Margaret Norfolk 27 G5
Tivetshall St. Mary Norfolk 27 G5
Tividale W Midlands 22 C3
Tivington Som'set 6 B3
Tixall Staffs 31 H8
Tixover Leics 24 E1
Toab Orkney 64 D3
Toab Shetl'd 64 F7
Toadmoor Derby 31 E12
Tobermory H'land 50 B2
Toberonochy S'clyde 50 G5
Tobson W Isles 63 C2
Tocher Gramp 58 D4
Tockenham Wilts 16 F2
Tockenham Wick Wilts 16 F1
Tockholes Lancs 34 E5
Tockington Avon 15 F9
Tockwith N Yorks 36 B3
Todber Dorset 7 D11
Toddington Beds 17 A11
Toddington Glos 16 A1
Todenham Glos 22 H6
Todhall Fife 53 E8
Todhills Cumb 44 G2
Todmorden W Yorks 35 E8
Todrig Borders 49 G7
Todwick S Yorks 32 B2
Toft Cambs 25 K5
Toft Lincs 24 D2
Toft Hill Durham 40 B2
Toft Monks Norfolk 26 F7
Toft Next Newton Lincs 33 A7
Toftbarns Borders 49 G8
Toftrees Norfolk 26 C2
Tofts H'land 61 A12
Toftwood Norfolk 26 D3
Togston Northum 45 C10
Toigal H'land 55 K1
Tokavaig H'land 62 G5
Tokers Green Oxon 17 F8
Toll Bar S Yorks 36 F3
Toll End W Midlands 22 C3
Toll of Birness Gramp 58 D7
Tolland Som'set 6 C4
Tollard Royal Wilts 8 D1
Toller Fratrum Dorset 7 F9
Toller Porcorum Dorset 7 F9
Tollerton N Yorks 36 A3
Tollerton Notts 32 G3
Tollesbury Essex 19 C9
Tolleshunt D'Arcy Essex 19 C9
Tolleshunt Major Essex 19 C9
Tollie H'land 56 D1
Tolmachan W Isles 63 F2
Tolpuddle Dorset 7 G11
Tolsta Chaolais W Isles 63 C3
Tolvah H'land 57 J4
Tolworth London 10 B1
Tomatin H'land 57 G4
Tombain H'land 57 J4
Tombreck H'land 56 F2
Tomchrasky H'land 55 H6
Tomdoun H'land 55 J5
Tomich H'land 55 G7
Tomich H'land 56 C3
Tomich H'land 56 E1
Tomich H'land 60 F6
Tomintoul Gramp 57 H7
Tomintoul H'land 57 G2
Tomishielburn Dumf/Gal 44 E2
Tomnaven Gramp 58 D2
Tomnavoulin Gramp 57 G8
Tomphibil Tayside 52 B3
Tonbridge Kent 10 C5
Tondu Mid Glam 14 F2
Tonfanau Gwyn 20 B1
Tong Shrops 22 A2
Tong W Yorks 35 D10
Tonge Leics 32 H2
Tongham Surrey 9 A10
Tongland Dumf/Gal 43 F8
Tongue H'land 60 B6
Tongue House H'land 60 B6
Tongwynlais S Glam 14 F5
Tonna W Glam 13 G11
Ton-Pentre Mid Glam 14 E3
Ton-teg Mid Glam 14 F4
Tonwell Herts 18 B3
Tonypandy Mid Glam 14 E3
Tonyrefail Mid Glam 14 E3
Toot Baldon Oxon 16 D6
Toothill Essex 18 D5
Top of Hebers Gtr Man 35 F7
Topcliffe N Yorks 40 H4
Topcroft Norfolk 26 F6
Topcroft Street Norfolk 26 F5
Toppesfield Essex 25 L8
Toppings Gtr Man 34 F6
Topsham Devon 6 G3
Torbain Gramp 57 H7
Torbay Devon 5 J8
Torbeg Gramp 59 G1
Torbeg S'clyde 46 F4
Torbreck H'land 56 F2
Torbryan Devon 5 J7
Torcastle H'land 55 L5
Torcross Devon 5 G7
Torcross Devon 5 L7
Torcroy H'land 57 J3
Tore H'land 56 D2
Torgyle Bridge H'land 55 H7
Torinturk S'clyde 46 C3
Torksey Lincs 32 B5
Torlundy H'land 55 M5
Tormarton Avon 15 F11
Tormitchell S'clyde 42 B3
Tormore S'clyde 46 F4
Tornagrain H'land 56 E3
Tornahaish Gramp 57 J8
Tornaveen Gramp 59 G4
Torness H'land 57 G1
Toronto Durham 40 B2
Torpenhow Cumb 38 A4
Torphichen Lothian 48 B2
Torphins Gramp 59 G4
Torpoint Cornw'l 3 D11
Torquay Devon 5 J8
Torquhan Borders 49 E7
Torran H'land 56 B3
Torran H'land 62 C5
Torrance S'clyde 47 B11
Torraneidhinn H'land 50 B3
Torrans H'land 50 E2
Torranyard S'clyde 47 E8
Torre Devon 5 J8
Torre Som'set 6 B4
Torridon H'land 54 D3
Torridon House H'land 54 D2
Torrin H'land 62 F5
Torrisholme Lancs 34 A3
Torrlaoighseach H'land 55 H3
Torrobole H'land 60 F6
Torry Gramp 58 D2
Torry Gramp 59 G7
Torryburn Lothian 48 A3
Torterston Gramp 58 C8
Torthorwald Dumf/Gal 43 D11
Tortington W Sussex 9 F11
Torvaig H'land 62 D4
Torver Cumb 38 F5
Torwood Lothian 48 A1
Torworth Notts 32 B4
Tosberry Devon 4 D1
Toscaig H'land 54 F1
Toseland Cambs 25 J3
Tosside Lancs 34 B6
Tostarie H'land 50 C1
Tostock Suffolk 27 J3
Totaig H'land 55 G2
Totaig H'land 62 C1
Tote H'land 62 C3
Totegan H'land 61 A8
Totland I of Wight 8 G5
Totley S Yorks 31 B11
Totnell Dorset 7 E9
Totnes Devon 5 K7
Totscore H'land 62 B3
Tottenham London 18 E3
Tottenhill Norfolk 24 D7
Totteridge London 18 E2
Totternhoe Beds 17 B10
Tottington Gtr Man 34 F6
Totton Hants 8 E5
Touchen-end Berks 17 F9
Toulton Som'set 6 C5
Toulvaddie H'land 56 B4
Tournaig H'land 54 B2
Toux Gramp 58 C7
Tow Law Durham 40 A1
Toward S'clyde 46 C6
Toward Quay S'clyde 46 C6
Towcester Northants 23 G10
Towednack Cornw'l 2 F2
Tower Hamlets London 18 F4
Tower Hill W Sussex 10 E1
Towersey Oxon 17 D8
Towie Gramp 58 F2
Towiemore Gramp 58 C1
Town End Cumb 39 G7
Town Green Lancs 34 G3
Town Row E Sussex 10 E4
Town Street Glos 15 A11
Town Street Suffolk 27 G1
Town Yetholm Borders 49 F10
Townfoot Dumf/Gal 43 B10
Townhead Dumf/Gal 43 C10
Townhead Dumf/Gal 43 G8
Townhead Gramp 59 K5
Townhead Northum 45 F7
Townhead S'clyde 42 A3
Townhead of Gree S'clyde 47 E9
Townhead of Grenlaw Dumf/Gal 43 E8
Townhill Fife 52 H6
Townsend Oxon 16 E5
Townsend Som'set 7 A8
Townshend Cornw'l 2 F3
Towthorpe N Yorks 36 A4
Towton N Yorks 36 C3
Towyn Clwyd 29 B9
Toynton All Saints Lincs 33 D11
Toynton Fen Side Lincs 33 D11
Toynton St. Peter Lincs 33 D11
Toy's Hill Kent 10 C3
Trabboch S'clyde 47 G9
Trabboch Mains S'clyde 47 G9
Trabbochburn S'clyde 47 G9
Traboe Cornw'l 2 G4
Tradespark H'land 56 D4
Trafford Park Gtr Man 35 H7
Traigh House H'land 55 K1
Trallong Powys 14 A3
Tranent Lothian 49 B7
Tranmere Mersey 30 A2
Trantlemore H'land 61 B8
Tranwell Northum 45 E10
Trapp Dyfed 13 E10
Traprain Lothian 49 B8
Traquair Borders 48 F6
Traveller's Rest Bucks 17 B10
Trawden Lancs 35 C8
Trawscoed Powys 14 A4
Trawsfynydd Gwyn 28 G6
Treales Lancs 34 D3
Trearddur Bay Gwyn 28 B2
Treaslane H'land 62 C3
Trebanog Mid Glam 14 E3
Trebartha Cornw'l 3 B9
Trebarwith Cornw'l 3 A7
Trebetherick Cornw'l 2 B6
Treborough Som'set 6 C4
Trebudannon Cornw'l 2 D6
Trebullet Cornw'l 3 B10
Treburley Cornw'l 3 B10
Trebyan Cornw'l 3 C8
Trecastle Powys 14 A2
Trecenydd Mid Glam 14 F5
Trecwn Dyfed 12 D3
Trecynon Mid Glam 14 D3
Tredaule Cornw'l 3 B9
Tre-ddiog Dyfed 12 D2
Tredegar Gwent 14 C5
Tredington Glos 15 A12
Tredington Warwick 22 H6
Tredizzick Cornw'l 2 B6
Tredomen Powys 14 A4
Tredrissi Dyfed 12 C4
Tredustan Powys 14 A5
Treen Cornw'l 2 G1
Treeton S Yorks 32 A2
Trefasser Dyfed 12 C2
Trefdraeth Gwyn 28 C3
Trefecca Powys 14 A5
Trefeglwys Powys 20 C5
Trefenter Dyfed 20 E2
Treffgarne Dyfed 12 E3
Treffgarne Owen Dyfed 12 D2
Treffynnon Dyfed 12 D2
Trefil Gwent 14 C4
Trefilan Dyfed 20 G1
Trefnant Clwyd 29 C10
Trefonen Shrops 30 G1
Trefor Gwyn 28 B3
Treforest Industrial Estate Mid Glam 14 F4
Trefriw Gwyn 29 D7
Tref-y-nant Clwyd 29 F11
Tref-y-nant Gwyn 29 G8
Tregadillet Cornw'l 3 A10
Tregaian Gwyn 28 B4
Tregare Gwent 15 C7
Tregaron Dyfed 20 F2
Tregarth Gwyn 28 C5
Tregeare Cornw'l 3 A9
Tregeiriog Clwyd 29 G11
Tregele Gwyn 28 A3
Tregeseal Cornw'l 2 F1
Treglemais Dyfed 12 D2
Tregonetha Cornw'l 2 C6
Tregony Cornw'l 2 E6
Tregoss Cornw'l 3 D7
Tregowris Cornw'l 2 G5
Tregoyd Powys 14 A5
Tre-groes Dyfed 13 C7
Tregurrian Cornw'l 2 C5
Tregynon Powys 20 C6
Trehafod Mid Glam 14 E4
Treharris Mid Glam 14 E4
Treherbert Mid Glam 14 D3
Trekenner Cornw'l 3 B10
Treknow Cornw'l 3 A7
Trelach Dyfed 12 D6
Trelash Cornw'l 3 A9
Trelaw Mid Glam 14 E3
Trelawnyd Clwyd 29 B10
Tre-lech-a'r-Betws Dyfed 12 D6
Treleddyd fawr Dyfed 12 D1
Trelewis Mid Glam 14 E4
Treligga Cornw'l 3 A7
Trelights Cornw'l 3 B7
Trelill Cornw'l 3 B7
Trelissick Cornw'l 2 F5
Trelleck Gwent 15 D8
Trelleck Grange Gwent 15 D8
Trelogan Clwyd 29 B10
Tremadog Gwyn 28 F5
Tremail Cornw'l 3 A8
Tremain Dyfed 12 B6
Tremaine Cornw'l 3 A9
Tremar Cornw'l 3 C9
Trematon Cornw'l 3 D11
Tremeirchion Clwyd 29 C10
Tremore Cornw'l 3 C7
Trenance Cornw'l 2 C5
Trenance Cornw'l 2 C6
Trenance Cornw'l 2 H4
Trenarren Cornw'l 3 E7
Trench Shrops 21 A12
Trenear Cornw'l 2 F4
Treneglos Cornw'l 3 A9
Trenewan Cornw'l 3 D9
Trengune Cornw'l 2 B2
Trent Som'set 7 D9
Trentham Staffs 31 F7
Trentishoe Devon 4 A5
Treoes S Glam 14 F3
Treorchy Mid Glam 14 E3
Trequite Cornw'l 3 B7
Tre'r-ddol Dyfed 20 C2
Trerule Foot Cornw'l 3 D10
Tresaith Dyfed 12 B6
Tresayes Cornw'l 3 D7
Trescott Staffs 22 B2
Trescowe Cornw'l 2 G3
Tresham Avon 15 E11
Tresillian Cornw'l 2 E6
Tresinwen Dyfed 12 C2
Treskinnick Cross Cornw'l 2 A2
Tresmear Cornw'l 3 A9
Tresparret Cornw'l 2 B2
Tresparret Posts Cornw'l 2 B2
Tressait Tayside 52 A3
Tresta Shetl'd 64 B8
Tresta Shetl'd 64 D7
Treswell Notts 32 B5
Trethosa Cornw'l 2 D6
Trethurgy Cornw'l 3 D7
Tretio Dyfed 12 D1
Tretire Heref/Worcs 15 B8
Tretower Powys 14 B5
Treuddyn Clwyd 29 D11
Trevadlock Cornw'l 3 B9
Trevalga Cornw'l 3 A8
Trevalyn Clwyd 30 E2
Trevanson Cornw'l 3 B7
Trevarren Cornw'l 2 D6
Trevarrian Cornw'l 2 C5
Trevarrick Cornw'l 3 E7
Trevaughan Dyfed 12 E5
Trevaughan Dyfed 13 E7
Trevellas Cornw'l 2 D4
Trevelmond Cornw'l 3 C9
Treverva Cornw'l 2 F5
Trevethin Gwent 14 D6
Trevigro Cornw'l 3 C10
Trevine Dyfed 12 D2
Treviscoe Cornw'l 2 D6
Trevivian Cornw'l 3 A9
Trevoll Cornw'l 2 D5
Trevone Cornw'l 2 B6
Trevor Gwyn 28 F3
Trewarmett Cornw'l 3 A8
Trewassa Cornw'l 3 A8
Trewellard Cornw'l 2 F1
Trewen Cornw'l 3 A9
Trewennack Cornw'l 2 G4
Trewern Powys 21 A8
Trewetha Cornw'l 3 B7
Trewethern Cornw'l 3 B7
Trewidland Cornw'l 3 D9
Trewilym Dyfed 12 C5
Trewint Cornw'l 2 B2
Trewint Cornw'l 3 B9
Trewithian Cornw'l 2 F6
Trewoon Cornw'l 3 D7
Treyarnon Cornw'l 2 B6
Treyford W Sussex 9 D9
Triangle W Yorks 35 E9
Trickett's Cross Dorset 8 F3

Triermain *Cumb* **44** F4
Trimdon *Durham* **40** B4
Trimdon Colliery *Durham* **40** B4
Trimdon Grange *Durham* **40** B4
Trimingham *Norfolk* **26** B6
Trimley St. Martin *Suffolk* **27** L6
Trimley St. Mary *Suffolk* **27** L6
Trimpley *Heref/Worcs* **22** D1
Trimsaran *Dyfed* **13** F8
Trinafour *Tayside* **52** A2
Trinant *Gwent* **14** D5
Tring *Herts* **17** C10
Tring Wharf *Herts* **17** C10
Trinity *Devon* **6** F3
Trinity *Gramp* **59** L4
Triscombe *Som'set* **6** C5
Trislaig *H'land* **55** M5
Trispen *Cornw'l* **2** E5
Tritlington *Northum* **45** D10
Trochry *Tayside* **52** C5
Troedrhiw *Gwent* **14** D5
Troedyraur *Dyfed* **13** B7
Troed-y-rhiw *Dyfed* **13** B8
Troedyrhiw *Mid Glam* **14** D4
Troon *Cornw'l* **2** F4
Troon *S'clyde* **47** F8
Troqueer *Dumf/Gal* **43** D10
Troquhain *Dumf/Gal* **43** D7
Trossachs Hotel *Central* **51** G12
Trostan *Suffolk* **27** H2
Trottiscliffe *Kent* **10** B5
Trotton *W Sussex* **9** D9
Troughend *Northum* **45** D7
Troutbeck *Cumb* **38** C6
Troutbeck *Cumb* **38** E6
Troutbeck Bridge *Cumb* **38** E6
Trow Green *Glos* **15** D9
Troway *Derby* **32** B1
Trowbridge *Wilts* **15** H11
Trowell *Notts* **32** F2
Trowle Common *Wilts* **15** H11
Trowley Bottom *Herts* **17** C11
Trows *Borders* **49** F9
Trowse Newton *Norfolk* **26** E5
Trudoxhill *Som'set* **7** B10
Trull *Som'set* **6** D6
Trumpan *H'land* **62** B2
Trumpet *Heref/Worcs* **21** H12
Trumpington *Cambs* **25** K6
Trumps *Devon* **6** E4
Trunch *Norfolk* **26** B6
Truro *Cornw'l* **2** E5
Truscott *Cornw'l* **3** A10
Trusham *Devon* **6** H2
Trusley *Derby* **31** G11
Trusthorpe *Lincs* **33** B12
Trysull *Staffs* **22** C2
Tubney *Oxon* **16** D5
Tuckenhay *Devon* **5** K7
Tuckingmill *Cornw'l* **2** F4
Tuddenham *Suffolk* **25** H8
Tuddenham *Suffolk* **27** K5
Tudeley *Kent* **10** D5
Tudhoe *Durham* **40** B3
Tudorville *Heref/Worcs* **15** B9
Tudweiliog *Gwyn* **28** G2
Tuesley *Surrey* **9** B11
Tuffley *Glos* **15** C11
Tufton *Dyfed* **12** D4
Tugby *Leics* **23** B11
Tugford *Shrops* **21** D11
Tughall *Northum* **45** E12
Tulchan *Tayside* **57** M7
Tullibardine *Tayside* **52** F4
Tullibody *Central* **52** H3
Tullich *Central* **51** D12
Tullich *H'land* **54** E3
Tullich *H'land* **57** G2
Tullich *S'clyde* **51** F8
Tullich Muir *H'land* **56** B3
Tulliemet *Tayside* **52** B5
Tullo of Benholm *Gramp* **59** K5
Tulloch *Central* **52** D1
Tulloch *H'land* **55** L7
Tulloch House *Gramp* **58** D5
Tullochgorm *S'clyde* **51** H7
Tullochmacarrick *Gramp* **57** J8
Tullochs *Gramp* **58** C2
Tullochvenus *Gramp* **59** G3
Tullybannocher *Tayside* **52** E2
Tullyfergus *Tayside* **53** B7
Tullymurdoch *Tayside* **53** B7
Tullynessle *Gramp* **58** F3
Tumble *Dyfed* **13** F9
Tumby *Lincs* **33** D9
Tumby Woodside *Lincs* **33** D9
Tumford *Herts* **18** C4
Tummel Bridge *Tayside* **52** A3
Tunbridge Wells *Kent* **10** D5
Tung *W Isles* **63** C5
Tunley *Avon* **15** H10
Tunstall *Humber* **37** D10
Tunstall *Kent* **11** B7
Tunstall *Lancs* **39** H8
Tunstall *N Yorks* **40** F2
Tunstall *Staffs* **31** E7
Tunstall *Suffolk* **27** K6
Tunstall *Tyne/Wear* **45** H12
Tunstall St. Mary *Norfolk* **26** E7
Tunworth *Hants* **9** A8
Tupsley *Heref/Worcs* **21** H10
Tupton *Derby* **32** D1
Tur Langton *Leics* **23** C10
Turgis Green *Hants* **17** H8
Turin *Tayside* **53** B10
Turkdean *Glos* **16** B2
Turnastone *Heref/Worcs* **15** A7
Turnberry *S'clyde* **42** A3
Turnditch *Derby* **31** F11
Turner's Hill *W Sussex* **10** E2
Turners Puddle *Dorset* **7** G11
Turnhouse *Lothian* **48** B4
Turnworth *Dorset* **7** E11
Turriff *Gramp* **58** C5
Turton Bottoms *Lancs* **34** F6
Turvelaws *Northum* **49** F12
Turvey *Beds* **23** G12
Turville *Bucks* **17** E8
Turville Heath *Bucks* **17** E8
Turweston *Bucks* **23** H9
Tushielaw *Borders* **48** G6
Tutbury *Staffs* **31** G10
Tutnall *Heref/Worcs* **22** E3
Tutshill *Gwent* **15** E8
Tuttington *Norfolk* **26** C5
Tutts Clump *Berks* **17** G7
Tutwell *Cornw'l* **3** B11
Tuxford *Notts* **32** C4
Twatt *Shetl'd* **64** D7
Twatt *Orkney* **64** C1
Twechar *S'clyde* **47** B11
Tweeddaleburn *Borders* **48** D5
Tweedmouth *Northum* **49** D12
Tweedshaws *Borders* **48** H3
Tweedsmuir *Borders* **48** G4
Twelveheads *Cornw'l* **2** E5
Twemlow Green *Ches* **30** C6
Twenty *Lincs* **24** C3
Twerton *Avon* **15** H10
Twickenham *London* **18** G2
Twigworth *Glos* **15** B11
Twineham *W Sussex* **10** F1
Twinhoe *Avon* **15** H10
Twinstead *Essex* **27** L2
Twinstead Green *Essex* **27** L2
Twitchen *Devon* **4** B4
Twitchen *Devon* **4** C7
Twitchen *Shrops* **21** D9
Two Bridges *Devon* **5** H5
Two Dales *Derby* **31** D11
Two Gates *Staffs* **22** B5
Two Pots *Devon* **4** B4
Twycross *Leics* **23** B7
Twyford *Berks* **17** G9
Twyford *Bucks* **17** B7
Twyford *Derby* **31** G11
Twyford *Hants* **8** D6
Twyford *Leics* **23** A10
Twyford *Norfolk* **26** C3
Twyford Common *Heref/Worcs* **15** A8
Twyn Llanan *Dyfed* **13** E11
Twynholm *Dumf/Gal* **43** F7
Twyning *Glos* **15** A12
Twyn-mynydd *Dyfed* **13** F10
Twyn-y-Sheriff *Gwent* **15** D7
Twywell *Northants* **23** D12
Tyberton *Heref/Worcs* **21** H9
Tycroes *Dyfed* **13** F9
Ty-croes *Gwyn* **28** C3
Tycrwyn *Powys* **29** H10
Tydd Gote *Lincs* **24** D5
Tydd St. Giles *Cambs* **24** D5
Tydd St. Mary *Lincs* **24** D5
Tyddyninco *Gwyn* **29** G9
Tye Green *Essex* **19** B7
Tye Green *Essex* **25** L7
Ty-hen *Dyfed* **12** E6
Ty-Hen *Gwyn* **28** G1
Tyldesley *Gtr Man* **34** G6
Tyler Hill *Kent* **11** B10
Tyler's Green *Bucks* **17** E10
Tyler's Green *Surrey* **10** C2
Tylorstown *Mid Glam* **14** E3
Tylwch *Dyfed* **20** D5
Ty-nant *Gwyn* **29** H8
Tyndrum *Central* **51** E10
Tynecwm *Powys* **20** D4
Tyneham *Dorset* **7** H12
Tynehead *Lothian* **48** C6
Tynemouth *Tyne/Wear* **45** F11
Tynewydd *Mid Glam* **14** D3
Tyninghame *Lothian* **49** B8
Tynribbie *S'clyde* **50** C6
Tynron *Dumf/Gal* **43** B9
Tynswydd *Dyfed* **20** F2
Ty'n-y-ffridd *Clwyd* **29** G10
Ty'n-y-gongl *Gwyn* **28** B4
Ty'n-y-groes *Gwyn* **29** C7
Tyn-y-wern *Clwyd* **29** G10
Tyrie *Gramp* **58** B7
Tyringham *Bucks* **23** G12
Tythecott *Devon* **4** D3
Tythegston *Mid Glam* **14** F2
Tytherington *Avon* **15** E10
Tytherington *Ches* **31** C7
Tytherington *Wilts* **8** B1
Tytherleigh *Devon* **7** F7
Tywardreath *Cornw'l* **3** D8
Tywardreath Highway *Cornw'l* **3** D8
Tywyn *Gwyn* **20** B2
Tywyn *Gwyn* **29** B7
Uags *H'land* **54** F1
Ubbeston Green *Suffolk* **27** H6
Ubley *Avon* **15** H8
Uckerby *N Yorks* **40** E3
Uckfield *E Sussex* **10** F4
Uckington *Glos* **15** B12
Uddingston *S'clyde* **47** C11
Uddington *S'clyde* **48** F1
Udimore *E Sussex* **11** F7
Udny Green *Gramp* **58** E6
Udston *S'clyde* **47** E12
Udstonhead *S'clyde* **47** E12
Uffcott *Wilts* **16** F2
Uffculme *Devon* **6** E4
Uffington *Lincs* **24** E2
Uffington *Oxon* **16** E4
Uffington *Shrops* **21** A10
Ufford *Cambs* **24** E2
Ufford *Suffolk* **27** K6
Ufton *Warwick* **23** F7
Ufton Green *Berks* **17** G7
Ufton Nervet *Berks* **17** G7
Ugadale *S'clyde* **46** F3
Ugborough *Devon* **5** K5
Uggeshall *Suffolk* **27** G7
Ugglebarnby *N Yorks* **41** D9
Ugley *Essex* **18** A5
Ugthorpe *N Yorks* **41** D8
Uig *H'land* **62** B3
Uig *H'land* **62** C1
Uigshader *H'land* **62** D4
Uisken *H'land* **50** F1
Ulbster *H'land* **61** C12
Ulceby *Humber* **37** F9
Ulceby *Lincs* **33** C11
Ulceby Cross *Lincs* **33** C11
Ulceby Skitter *Humber* **37** F9
Ulcombe *Kent* **11** C7
Uldale *Cumb* **38** B5
Uley *Glos* **15** D11
Ulgham *Northum* **45** D10
Ullapool *H'land* **60** G3
Ullenhall *Warwick* **22** E5
Ullenwood *Glos* **15** C12
Ulleskelf *N Yorks* **36** C3
Ullesthorpe *Leics* **23** C8
Ulley *S Yorks* **32** B2
Ullingswick *Heref/Worcs* **21** G11
Ullinish *H'land* **62** D2
Ullock *Cumb* **38** C3
Ulpha *Cumb* **38** F4
Ulrome *Humber* **37** B9
Ulsta *Shetl'd* **64** C7
Ulston *Borders* **49** G9
Ulva House *H'land* **50** D2
Ulverston *Cumb* **38** G5
Ulwell *Dorset* **8** H2
Ulzieside *Dumf/Gal* **43** A8
Umachan *H'land* **62** C5
Umberleigh *Devon* **4** D5
Unapool *H'land* **60** D4
Under Burnmouth *Borders* **44** E3
Under River *Kent* **10** C4
Underbarrow *Cumb* **39** F7
Undercliffe *W Yorks* **35** D10
Underhills *S'clyde* **47** F9
Underhoull *Shetl'd* **64** A8
Underwood *Notts* **32** E2
Undy *Gwent* **15** F7
Unifirth *Shetl'd* **64** D6
Union Cottage *Gramp* **59** H6
Union Mills *I of Man* **38** H2
Unstone *Derby* **32** C1
Unstone Green *Derby* **32** C1
Unsworth *Gtr Man* **35** F7
Unthank *Cumb* **39** A8
Unthank *Cumb* **39** B7
Unthank *Cumb* **44** H2
Unthank *Northum* **45** A11
Unthank *Northum* **49** E12
Unthank End *Cumb* **39** B7
Up Cerne *Dorset* **7** F10
Up Exe *Devon* **6** F3
Up Hatherley *Glos* **15** B12
Up Holland *Lancs* **34** G4
Up Marden *W Sussex* **9** E9
Up Nately *Hants* **9** A8
Up Somborne *Hants* **8** C5
Up Sydling *Dorset* **7** F9
Upavon *Wilts* **8** A3
Upchurch *Kent* **11** A7
Upcott *Devon* **4** E4
Upcott *Heref/Worcs* **21** G8
Upcott *Som'set* **6** D3
Uphall *Lothian* **48** B3
Uphall Station *Lothian* **48** B3
Upham *Devon* **4** E7
Upham *Hants* **9** D7
Uphampton *Heref/Worcs* **21** F9
Uphampton *Heref/Worcs* **22** F2
Uphill *Avon* **14** H6
Uplawmoor *S'clyde* **47** D9
Upleadon *Glos* **15** B10
Upleatham *Clevl'd* **40** C6
Uplees *Kent* **11** B8
Uploders *Dorset* **7** G8
Uplowman *Devon* **6** E4
Uplyme *Devon* **6** G6
Upminster *London* **18** E6
Upottery *Devon* **6** E5
Uppat *H'land* **61** F8
Upper Affcot *Shrops* **21** D10
Upper Arley *Heref/Worcs* **22** D1
Upper Arncott *Oxon* **17** B7
Upper Astrop *Northants* **23** H8
Upper Badcall *H'land* **60** C3
Upper Barvas *W Isles* **63** B5
Upper Basildon *Berks* **17** F7
Upper Beeding *W Sussex* **10** G1
Upper Benefield *Northants* **24** F1
Upper Bentley *Heref/Worcs* **22** E3
Upper Boddam *Gramp* **58** E4
Upper Boddington *Northants* **23** G8
Upper Borth *Dyfed* **20** D2
Upper Bourne *Surrey* **9** B9
Upper Brailes *Warwick* **22** H6
Upper Breakish *H'land* **62** F6
Upper Breinton *Heref/Worcs* **21** H10
Upper Broughton *Notts* **32** H4
Upper Bucklebury *Berks* **16** G6
Upper Burgate *Hants* **8** D3
Upper Burnhaugh *Gramp* **59** H6
Upper Caldecote *Beds* **25** L3
Upper Canterton *Hants* **8** E4
Upper Catesby *Northants* **23** F8
Upper Chapel *Powys* **20** H6
Upper Cheddon *Som'set* **6** C6
Upper Chicksgrove *Wilts* **8** C1
Upper Church Village *Mid Glam* **14** F4
Upper Chute *Wilts* **8** A4
Upper Clatford *Hants* **8** B5
Upper Clifton *Dumf/Gal* **43** F10
Upper Clynnog *Gwyn* **28** F4
Upper Coll *W Isles* **63** C5
Upper Craigenbay *Dumf/Gal* **42** D6
Upper Cumberworth *W Yorks* **35** F10
Upper Cwmbran *Gwent* **14** E6
Upper Dallachy *Gramp* **58** A1
Upper Dalveen *Dumf/Gal* **43** A9
Upper Dean *Beds* **25** H1
Upper Denby *W Yorks* **35** F11
Upper Denton *Cumb* **44** G4
Upper Derraid *H'land* **56** F6
Upper Diabaig *H'land* **54** D2
Upper Dicker *E Sussex* **10** G4
Upper Dournreay *H'land* **61** A9
Upper Druimfin *H'land* **50** B2
Upper Elkstone *Staffs* **31** D9
Upper End *Derby* **31** C9
Upper Ethie *H'land* **56** C3
Upper Farringdon *Hants* **9** C8
Upper Framilode *Glos* **15** C10
Upper Gornal *W Midlands* **22** C3
Upper Gravenhurst *Beds* **25** L2
Upper Green *Berks* **16** H5
Upper Grove Common *Heref/Worcs* **15** B9
Upper Hale *Surrey* **9** A10
Upper Halistra *H'land* **62** B2
Upper Halliford *Surrey* **17** G11
Upper Halling *Kent* **10** B6
Upper Hambleton *Leics* **23** A12
Upper Hardress Court *Kent* **11** C10
Upper Hartfield *E Sussex* **10** E3
Upper Haugh *S Yorks* **36** G2
Upper Heath *Shrops* **21** D11
Upper Hellesdon *Norfolk* **26** D5
Upper Hemsley *Humber* **36** B5
Upper Hergest *Heref/Worcs* **21** G8
Upper Heyford *Northants* **23** F10
Upper Heyford *Oxon* **16** B6
Upper Hill *Heref/Worcs* **21** G10
Upper Hindhope *Borders* **44** B6
Upper Hopton *W Yorks* **35** E10
Upper Horsebridge *E Sussex* **10** G5
Upper Hulme *Staffs* **31** D8
Upper Inglesham *Wilts* **16** D3
Upper Inverbrough *H'land* **57** G4
Upper Kenley *Fife* **53** F10
Upper Killay *W Glam* **13** H9
Upper Kinkell *Gramp* **58** E5
Upper Knockando *Gramp* **56** E7
Upper Lambourn *Berks* **16** F4
Upper Langford *Avon* **15** H8
Upper Leigh *Staffs* **31** F8
Upper Lochton *Gramp* **59** H4
Upper Longdon *Staffs* **22** A4
Upper Lybster *H'land* **61** D11
Upper Lydbrook *Glos* **15** C9
Upper Lye *Heref/Worcs* **21** F9
Upper Membie *Dumf/Gal* **44** E2
Upper Milovaig *H'land* **62** C1
Upper Minety *Wilts* **16** E1
Upper Moorside *W Yorks* **35** D11
Upper Morton *Avon* **15** E9
Upper Mulben *Gramp* **58** B1
Upper Nisbet *Borders* **49** G9
Upper North Dean *Bucks* **17** D9
Upper Obney *Tayside* **52** C5
Upper Ollach *H'land* **62** E4
Upper Penn *W Midlands* **22** C3
Upper Poppleton *N Yorks* **36** B3
Upper Quinton *Warwick* **22** G5
Upper Ratley *Hants* **8** D5
Upper Rochford *Heref/Worcs* **21** F11
Upper Rusko *Dumf/Gal* **42** E6
Upper Sandaig *H'land* **55** H2
Upper Sapey *Heref/Worcs* **21** F12
Upper Scoulag *S'clyde* **46** C6
Upper Seagry *Wilts* **16** F1
Upper Shader *W Isles* **63** B5
Upper Shelton *Beds* **25** L1
Upper Sheringham *Norfolk* **26** A4
Upper Side *Lothian* **48** D6
Upper Skelmorlie *S'clyde* **47** C7
Upper Slaughter *Glos* **16** B3
Upper Sonachan *S'clyde* **51** E8
Upper Soudley *Glos* **15** C10
Upper Stanton Drew *Avon* **15** H9
Upper Stonall *Staffs* **22** B4
Upper Stondon *Beds* **25** M3
Upper Stowe *Northants* **23** F10
Upper Street *Hants* **8** D3
Upper Street *Norfolk* **26** D7
Upper Strensham *Heref/Worcs* **22** H3
Upper Sundon *Beds* **17** A11
Upper Swell *Glos* **16** B3
Upper Tean *Staffs* **31** F8
Upper Thong *W Yorks* **35** F10
Upper Tillyrie *Tayside* **52** F6
Upper Tote *H'land* **62** B4
Upper Town *Avon* **15** H8
Upper Town *Heref/Worcs* **21** G11
Upper Tysoe *Warwick* **23** H7
Upper Upham *Wilts* **16** F3
Upper Upnor *Kent* **10** A6
Upper Wardington *Oxon* **23** G8
Upper Weald *Bucks* **23** H11
Upper Weedon *Northants* **23** F9
Upper Wield *Hants* **9** B7
Upper Winchendon *Bucks* **17** C8
Upper Woodend *Gramp* **58** F4
Upper Woodford *Wilts* **8** B3
Upper Wootton *Hants* **9** A7
Upper Wyche *Heref/Worcs* **22** H1
Upperby *Cumb* **44** H2
Uppermill *Gtr Man* **35** G8
Uppertack *Gramp* **58** B6
Upperton *Gramp* **59** K5
Upperton *W Sussex* **9** D11
Uppingham *Leics* **23** B12
Uppington *Shrops* **21** A11
Upsall *N Yorks* **40** F5
Upshire *Essex* **18** D4
Upstreet *Kent* **11** B11
Upton *Berks* **17** F10
Upton *Cambs* **24** E2
Upton *Cambs* **25** G3
Upton *Ches* **30** C3
Upton *Cornw'l* **4** E1
Upton *Devon* **6** F4
Upton *Dorset* **7** H10
Upton *Dorset* **8** G1
Upton *Hants* **8** A5
Upton *Hants* **8** D5
Upton *Leics* **23** B7
Upton *Lincs* **32** B6
Upton *Mersey* **30** A1
Upton *Norfolk* **26** D7
Upton *Northants* **23** F10
Upton *Notts* **32** C5
Upton *Notts* **32** E4
Upton *Oxon* **16** E6
Upton *Som'set* **6** C3
Upton *Som'set* **7** D8
Upton *W Yorks* **36** F3
Upton *Warwick* **22** F5
Upton Bishop *Heref/Worcs* **15** B9
Upton Cheyney *Avon* **15** G10
Upton Cressett *Shrops* **21** C12
Upton Grey *Hants* **9** A8
Upton Hellions *Devon* **4** F7
Upton Lovel *Wilts* **8** B1
Upton Magna *Shrops* **21** A11
Upton Noble *Som'set* **7** B10
Upton Pyne *Devon* **6** F3
Upton St. Leonards *Glos* **15** C11
Upton Scudamore *Wilts* **7** A12
Upton Snodsbury *Heref/Worcs* **22** G3
Upton upon Severn *Heref/Worcs* **22** H2
Upton Warren *Heref/Worcs* **22** E3
Upwaltham *W Sussex* **9** E10
Upware *Cambs* **25** H6
Upwell *Norfolk* **24** E6
Upwey *Dorset* **7** H10
Upwood *Cambs* **25** G4
Urafirth *Shetl'd* **64** C6
Urchfont *Wilts* **16** H2
Urgha Beag *W Isles* **63** G3
Urlay Nook *Clevl'd* **40** D4
Urmston *Gtr Man* **34** H6
Urquhart *Gramp* **56** C8
Urquhart *H'land* **56** D1
Urra *N Yorks* **40** E6
Urray *H'land* **56** D1
Ushaw Moor *Durham* **40** A3
Usk *Gwent* **15** D7
Usselby *Lincs* **37** H8
Ussie *H'land* **56** D1
Usworth *Tyne/Wear* **45** G11
Utley *W Yorks* **35** C9
Uton *Devon* **4** F7
Utterby *Lincs* **37** H10
Uttoxeter *Staffs* **31** G9
Uwchmynydd *Gwyn* **28** H1
Uxbridge *London* **18** F1
Uyeasound *Shetl'd* **64** B8
Uzmaston *Dyfed* **12** F3
Vachelich *Dyfed* **12** D1
Valley *Gwyn* **28** B2
Valley Truckle *Cornw'l* **3** A8
Valtos *H'land* **62** B4
Valtos *W Isles* **63** C2
Van *Dyfed* **20** D5
Vange *Essex* **19** E7
Varteg Hill *Gwent* **14** D6
Vatten *H'land* **62** D2
Vaynor *Mid Glam* **14** C4
Velindre *Dyfed* **12** C4
Velindre *Dyfed* **13** C7
Velindre *Powys* **14** A5
Vellow *Som'set* **6** B4
Vementry *Shetl'd* **64** D6
Veness *Orkney* **64** B3
Venn Ottery *Devon* **6** G4
Vennington *Shrops* **21** A9
Venny Tedburn *Devon* **4** F7
Ventnor *I of Wight* **9** H7
Vernham Dean *Hants* **16** H4
Vernham Street *Hants* **16** H4
Verwig *Dyfed* **12** B5
Verwood *Dorset* **8** E2
Veryan *Cornw'l* **2** F6
Vicarage *Devon* **6** G5
Vickerstown *Cumb* **38** H4
Victoria *Cornw'l* **3** D7
Victoria *Gwent* **14** D5
Vidlin *Shetl'd* **64** C7

Vinehall Street E Sussex 10 F6
Vine's Cross E Sussex 10 F5
Viney Hill Glos 15 D9
Virginia Water Surrey 17 G10
Virginstow Devon 5 G3
Vobster Som'set 7 A10
Voe Shetl'd 64 C7
Vowchurch Heref/Worcs 15 A7
Voy Orkney 64 C1
Wackerfield Durham 40 C2
Wacton Norfolk 26 F5
Wadborough Heref/Worcs 22 G3
Waddesdon Bucks 17 B8
Waddingham Lincs 37 G7
Waddington Lancs 34 C6
Waddington Lincs 33 D7
Wadebridge Cornw'l 3 B7
Wadeford Som'set 6 E6
Wadenhoe Northants 25 G1
Wadesmill Herts 18 B4
Wadhurst E Sussex 10 E5
Wadshelf Derby 31 C11
Wadsley S Yorks 31 A11
Wadsley Bridge S Yorks 32 A1
Wadswick Wilts 15 G11
Wadworth S Yorks 36 G3
Waen Clwyd 29 D10
Waen Fach Powys 29 H11
Wainfleet All Saints Lincs 33 D12
Wainfleet Bank Lincs 33 D11
Wainfordrigg Northum 45 C7
Waingroves Derby 32 E1
Wainhouse Corner Cornw'l 2 B2
Wainscott Kent 10 A6
Wainstalls W Yorks 35 D9
Waitby Cumb 39 D10
Wakefield W Yorks 35 E12
Wakerley Northants 24 F1
Wakes Colne Essex 19 A9
Walberswick Suffolk 27 H8
Walberton W Sussex 9 E11
Walbottle Tyne/Wear 45 F10
Walbutt Dumf/Gal 43 E8
Walcot Lincs 24 B2
Walcot Lincs 33 E8
Walcot Shrops 21 A11
Walcot Shrops 21 D9
Walcot Warwick 22 F5
Walcot Wilts 16 F3
Walcote Leics 23 D9
Walcott Norfolk 26 B7
Walden Head N Yorks 39 G12
Walden Stubbs N Yorks 36 E3
Walderslade Kent 10 B6
Walderton W Sussex 9 E9
Walditch Dorset 7 G8
Waldley Derby 31 F9
Waldridge Durham 45 H10
Waldringfield Suffolk 27 L6
Waldron E Sussex 10 F4
Wales S Yorks 32 B2
Walesby Lincs 33 A8
Walesby Notts 32 C4
Walford Heref/Worcs 15 B9
Walford Heref/Worcs 21 E9
Walford Shrops 30 H3
Walford Heath Shrops 30 H3
Walgherton Ches 30 E5
Walgrave Northants 23 E11
Walhampton Hants 8 F5
Walk Mill Lancs 35 D7
Walkden Gtr Man 34 G6
Walker Tyne/Wear 45 G11
Walker Fold Lancs 34 C5
Walkerburn Borders 48 F6
Walkeringham Notts 32 A5
Walkerith Lincs 32 A5
Walkern Herts 18 A3
Walker's Green Heref/Worcs 21 H10
Walkford Dorset 8 G4
Walkhampton Devon 5 J4
Walkington Humber 37 C8
Walkley S Yorks 32 A1
Wall Northum 45 F7
Wall Staffs 22 B4
Wall Bowers Cumb 44 G4
Wall under Heywood Shrops 21 C10
Wallaceton Dumf/Gal 43 C9
Wallacetown S'clyde 42 A4
Wallasey Mersey 30 A2
Wallend Cumb 38 G5
Wallingford Oxon 17 E7
Wallington Hants 9 E7
Wallington Herts 25 M4
Wallington London 18 H3
Walliswood Surrey 9 B12
Walls Shetl'd 64 D6
Wallsall Wood W Midlands 22 B4
Wallsend Tyne/Wear 45 F11
Wallthwaite Cumb 38 C6
Wallyford Lothian 48 B6
Walmer Kent 11 C12
Walmer Bridge Lancs 34 E4
Walmersley Gtr Man 35 F7
Walmley W Midlands 22 C5
Walpole Suffolk 27 H7
Walpole Crosskeys Norfolk 24 D6
Walpole Highway Norfolk 24 D6
Walpole Island Lincs 24 D6
Walpole St. Andrew Norfolk 24 D6
Walpole St. Peter Norfolk 24 D6
Walsall W Midlands 22 B4
Walsden W Yorks 35 E8
Walsgrave on Sowe W Midlands 23 D7
Walsham le Willows Suffolk 27 H3
Walshaw Gtr Man 34 F6
Walshford N Yorks 35 B12
Walsoken Norfolk 24 D6
Walston S'clyde 48 E3
Walsworth Herts 18 A2
Walter's Ash Bucks 17 D9
Walterston S Glam 14 G4
Walterstone Heref/Worcs 15 B7
Waltham Humber 37 G10
Waltham Kent 11 C9
Waltham Abbey Essex 18 D4
Waltham Chase Hants 9 E7
Waltham Cross Herts 18 D4
Waltham Forest London 18 E4
Waltham on the Wolds Leics 32 H5
Waltham St. Lawrence Berks 17 F9
Walthamstow London 18 E3
Walton Bucks 23 H12
Walton Cambs 24 E3
Walton Cumb 44 G3
Walton Derby 32 C1
Walton Leics 23 C9
Walton Powys 21 F8
Walton Shrops 30 H4
Walton Som'set 7 C8
Walton Suffolk 27 L6
Walton W Yorks 35 E12
Walton W Yorks 36 B2
Walton Warwick 22 G6
Walton Cardiff Glos 15 A12
Walton East Dyfed 12 E4
Walton Elm Dorset 7 D11
Walton on the Hill Staffs 31 H8
Walton on the Hill Surrey 10 C1
Walton on the Naze Essex 19 B12
Walton on the Wolds Leics 32 H3
Walton Park Avon 15 G7
Walton upon Trent Derby 31 H10
Walton West Dyfed 12 F2
Walton-in-Gordano Avon 15 G7
Walton-Le-Dale Lancs 34 D4
Walton-on-Thames Surrey 17 G12
Walton-on-the-Hill Mersey 34 H3
Walwen Clwyd 29 C11
Walwick Northum 45 F7
Walwick Grange Northum 45 F7
Walworth Durham 40 C3
Walwyn's Castle Dyfed 12 F2
Wambrook Som'set 6 E6
Wamphraygate Dumf/Gal 43 B12
Wampool Cumb 44 H1
Wanborough Surrey 9 A10
Wanborough Wilts 16 F3
Wandel S'clyde 48 G2
Wandon Northum 45 C11
Wandsworth London 18 F3
Wandylaw Northum 45 A9
Wangford Suffolk 27 G8
Wanlip Leics 23 A9
Wanlockhead S'clyde 48 H2
Wannock E Sussex 10 H4
Wansford Cambs 24 F2
Wansford Humber 37 B8
Wanstead London 18 E4
Wanstrow Som'set 7 B10
Wanswell Glos 15 D10
Wantage Oxon 16 E5
Wapley Avon 15 F10
Wappenbury Warwick 23 E7
Wappenham Northants 23 H9
Warbleton E Sussex 10 F5
Warblington Hants 9 E8
Warborough Oxon 17 E7
Warboys Cambs 25 G4
Warbreck Lancs 34 C2
Warbstow Cornw'l 2 B2
Warburton Gtr Man 30 A5
Warcop Durham 39 D10
Ward Green Suffolk 27 J3
Warden Kent 11 A9
Wardington Oxon 23 G8
Wardlaw Borders 48 H5
Wardlaw S'clyde 47 E8
Wardle Ches 30 E5
Wardle Gtr Man 35 E8
Wardley Leics 23 B11
Wardlow Derby 31 C10
Wardon Northum 45 F7
Wardy Hill Cambs 25 G6
Ware Herts 18 C4
Ware Kent 11 B11
Wareham Dorset 8 G1
Warehorne Kent 11 E8
Waren Mill Northum 45 C12
Warenford Northum 45 C12
Warenton Northum 45 C12
Wareside Herts 18 B4
Waresley Cambs 25 K3
Waresley Heref/Worcs 22 E2
Warfield Berks 17 G9
Warfleet Devon 5 L7
Wargate Lincs 24 C3
Wargrave Berks 17 F9
Warham All Saints Norfolk 26 A2
Warham St. Mary Norfolk 26 A2
Wark Northum 45 E7
Wark Northum 49 E11
Warkleigh Devon 4 D5
Warkton Northants 23 D12
Warkworth Northants 23 H8
Warkworth Northum 45 B10
Warlaby N Yorks 40 F4
Warland W Yorks 35 E8
Warleggan Cornw'l 3 C8
Warley Essex 18 E6
Warley W Midlands 22 C3
Warlingham Surrey 10 B2
Warmfield W Yorks 35 E12
Warmingham Ches 30 D5
Warminghurst W Sussex 9 D12
Warmington Northants 24 F2
Warmington Warwick 23 G7
Warminster Wilts 7 B12
Warmlake Kent 11 C7
Warmley Avon 15 G10
Warmley Tower Avon 15 G10
Warmsworth S Yorks 36 G3
Warmwell Dorset 7 H11
Warndon Heref/Worcs 22 F2
Warnford Hants 9 D8
Warnham W Sussex 10 E1
Warningcamp W Sussex 9 E11
Warninglid W Sussex 10 E1
Warren Ches 31 C7
Warren Dyfed 12 G3
Warren House Inn Devon 5 H5
Warren Row Berks 17 F9
Warren Street Kent 11 C8
Warrington Bucks 23 G12
Warrington Ches 30 A5
Warsash Hants 8 E6
Warslow Staffs 31 D9
Warsop Notts 32 C3
Warsop Vale Notts 32 C3
Warter Humber 36 B6
Warthermarske N Yorks 40 G2
Warthill N Yorks 36 B4
Wartling E Sussex 10 G5
Wartnaby Leics 32 H4
Warton Lancs 34 D3
Warton Lancs 39 H7
Warton Northum 45 C8
Warton Warwick 22 B6
Warwick Cumb 44 G3
Warwick Warwick 22 F6
Warwick Bridge Cumb 44 G3
Warwicksland Cumb 44 E3
Wasbister Orkney 64 B2
Wasdale Head Cumb 38 D4
Wash Common Berks 16 H5
Washaway Cornw'l 3 C7
Washbourne Devon 5 K7
Washerwall Staffs 31 E8
Washfield Devon 6 E3
Washfold N Yorks 40 E1
Washford Som'set 6 B4
Washford Pyne Devon 4 E7
Washingborough Lincs 33 C7
Washington Tyne/Wear 45 G11
Washington W Sussex 9 E12
Wasing Berks 17 H7
Waskerley Durham 40 A1
Wasperton Warwick 22 F6
Wass N Yorks 40 G6
Watchet Som'set 6 B4
Watchfield Oxon 16 E3
Watchfield Som'set 7 B7
Watchgate Cumb 39 E8
Watchhill Cumb 43 G12
Watendlath Cumb 38 D5
Water Devon 5 H6
Water Lancs 35 E7
Water End Herts 18 C2
Water End Humber 36 C6
Water Newton Cambs 24 F2
Water Orton Warwick 22 C5
Water Stratford Bucks 17 A7
Water Yeat Cumb 38 F5
Waterbeach Cambs 25 J6
Waterbeck Dumf/Gal 44 E1
Waterden Norfolk 26 B2
Waterend Bucks 17 C11
Waterfall Staffs 31 E9
Waterfoot Lancs 35 E7
Waterfoot S'clyde 47 D10
Waterford Hants 8 G5
Waterford Herts 18 B3
Waterford S'clyde 47 H10
Waterhead Cumb 38 E6
Waterhead Dumf/Gal 43 B12
Waterhead Dumf/Gal 43 C8
Waterhead Tayside 59 K2
Waterheads Borders 48 D5
Waterhouses Durham 40 A2
Waterhouses Staffs 31 E9
Watering Dyke Houses Lincs 33 B7
Wateringbury Kent 10 C6
Wateringhouse Orkney 64 E2
Waterlane Glos 15 D12
Waterloo Derby 32 D1
Waterloo Dorset 8 G2
Waterloo Dyfed 12 G3
Waterloo H'land 62 F6
Waterloo Mersey 34 G2
Waterloo Norfolk 26 D5
Waterloo S'clyde 48 D1
Waterloo Tayside 52 C5
Waterloo Cross Devon 6 E4
Waterlooville Hants 9 E8
Watermeetings S'clyde 48 H2
Waterperry Oxon 17 C7
Waterrow Som'set 6 D4
Waters Upton Shrops 30 H5
Watersfield W Sussex 9 E11
Waterside Cumb 44 H1
Waterside Gramp 58 E7
Waterside S'clyde 42 A5
Waterside S'clyde 47 B11
Waterside S'clyde 47 E9
Waterstock Oxon 17 D7
Waterston Dyfed 12 F3
Watford Herts 18 D1
Watford Northants 23 E9
Wath N Yorks 40 G3
Wath N Yorks 40 H2
Wath Brow Cumb 38 D3
Wath upon Dearne S Yorks 36 G2
Watley's End Avon 15 F9
Watlington Norfolk 24 D7
Watlington Oxon 17 E8
Watnall Chaworth Notts 32 F2
Watten H'land 61 B11
Wattisfield Suffolk 27 H3
Wattisham Suffolk 27 K3
Wattlesborough Heath Shrops 21 A9
Watton Humber 37 B8
Watton Norfolk 26 E2
Watton-at-Stone Herts 18 B3
Wattston S'clyde 47 B12
Wattstown Mid Glam 14 E3
Wauchan H'land 55 L3
Waun Fawr Dyfed 20 D2
Waunarlwydd W Glam 13 G9
Waun-deg Dyfed 13 D7
Waunfawr Gwyn 28 D5
Waunlwyd Gwent 14 D5
Wavendon Bucks 23 H12
Waverbridge Cumb 44 H1
Waverton Ches 30 D3
Waverton Cumb 44 H1
Wawne Humber 37 C8
Waxham Norfolk 26 C7
Waxholme Humber 37 D11
Way Village Devon 6 E2
Wayfield Kent 10 B6
Wayford Som'set 7 F7
Waytown Dorset 7 F8
Weachyburn Gramp 58 B4
Weacombe Som'set 6 B5
Weald Oxon 16 D4
Wealdstone London 18 E2
Weardley W Yorks 35 C11
Weare Som'set 7 A7
Weare Giffard Devon 4 D3
Wearhead Durham 39 A11
Weasdale Cumb 39 E9
Weasenham All Saints Norfolk 26 C1
Weasenham St. Peter Norfolk 26 C1
Weaverham Ches 30 C5
Weaverthorpe N Yorks 41 H9
Webheath Heref/Worcs 22 E4
Webton Heref/Worcs 15 A7
Wedderlairs Gramp 58 D6
Wedderlie Borders 49 D9
Weddington Warwick 23 C7
Wedhampton Wilts 16 H2
Wedmore Som'set 7 A8
Wednesbury W Midlands 22 C3
Wednesfield W Midlands 22 B3
Weedon Bucks 17 B9
Weedon Bec Northants 23 F9
Weedon Lois Northants 23 G9
Weeford Staffs 22 B5
Week Devon 4 C4
Week Devon 4 D6
Week St. Mary Cornw'l 4 F1
Weeke Hants 8 C6
Weekley Northants 23 D12
Weel Humber 37 C8
Weeley Essex 19 B11
Weeley Heath Essex 19 B11
Weem Tayside 52 B3
Weeping Cross Shrops 21 A10
Weeping Cross Staffs 31 H8
Weeting Norfolk 27 G1
Weeton Lancs 34 D3
Weeton N Yorks 35 B11
Weir Lancs 35 E7
Weirend Heref/Worcs 15 B9
Welbeck Abbey Notts 32 C3
Welborne Norfolk 26 E4
Welbourn Lincs 33 E7
Welburn N Yorks 41 G7
Welburn N Yorks 41 H7
Welbury N Yorks 40 E4
Welby Lincs 33 F7
Welches Dam Cambs 25 G6
Welcombe Devon 4 D1
Weldon Northants 23 C12
Welford Northants 23 D9
Welford on Avon Warwick 22 G5
Welham Leics 23 C11
Welham Green Herts 18 C2
Well Hants 9 A9
Well Lincs 33 C11
Well N Yorks 40 G3
Well End Bucks 17 E9
Well Hill Kent 10 B4
Well Town Devon 6 E3
Welland Heref/Worcs 22 H2
Wellbank Tayside 53 C9
Welldale Dumf/Gal 43 E12
Wellesbourne Warwick 22 G6
Wellfields Durham 40 A4
Wellford Tayside 59 L2
Welling London 18 F5
Wellingborough Northants 23 E12
Wellingham Norfolk 26 C2
Wellingore Lincs 33 E7
Wellington Cumb 38 E3
Wellington Heref/Worcs 21 H10
Wellington Shrops 21 A12
Wellington Som'set 6 D5
Wellington Heath Heref/Worcs 21 H12
Wellington Marsh Heref/Worcs 21 H10
Wellow Avon 15 H10
Wellow I of Wight 8 G5
Wellow Notts 32 D4
Wells Som'set 7 B9
Wellsborough Leics 23 B7
Wells-next-the-Sea Norfolk 26 A2
Wellswood Devon 5 J8
Wellwood Fife 52 H6
Welney Norfolk 24 F6
Welsford Devon 4 D1
Welsh Bicknor Heref/Worcs 15 C9
Welsh Frankton Shrops 30 G2
Welsh Hook Dyfed 12 D3
Welsh Newton Heref/Worcs 15 B8
Welsh St. Donats S Glam 14 G4
Welshampton Shrops 30 G3
Welshpool Powys 21 B8
Welton Avon 7 A10
Welton Cumb 38 A6
Welton Humber 37 D7
Welton Lincs 33 B7
Welton Northants 23 E9
Welton le Marsh Lincs 33 C11
Welton le Wold Lincs 33 B10
Welwick Humber 37 E11
Welwyn Herts 18 B2
Welwyn Garden City Herts 18 C2
Wem Shrops 30 G4
Wembdon Som'set 6 C6
Wembley London 18 E2
Wembury Devon 5 L4
Wembworthy Devon 4 E5
Wemyss Bay S'clyde 47 B7
Wenallt Gwyn 29 F9
Wendens Ambo Essex 25 L6
Wendlebury Oxon 16 B6
Wendling Norfolk 26 D2
Wendover Bucks 17 C9
Wendron Cornw'l 2 G4
Wendy Cambs 25 K4
Wenhaston Suffolk 27 H7
Wennington Cambs 25 G3
Wennington Lancs 39 H8
Wennington London 18 F5
Wensley Derby 31 D11
Wensley N Yorks 40 F1
Wentbridge W Yorks 36 E3
Wentnor Shrops 21 C9
Wentworth Cambs 25 G6
Wentworth S Yorks 35 G12
Wenvoe S Glam 14 G4
Weobley Heref/Worcs 21 G9
Weobley Marsh Heref/Worcs 21 G9
Wereham Norfolk 24 E8
Wergs W Midlands 22 B2
Wern Gwyn 28 F5
Wern Powys 14 C4
Wernffrwd W Glam 13 H8
Wernyrheolydd Gwent 15 C7
Werrington Cambs 24 E3
Werrington Cornw'l 3 A10
Werrington Staffs 31 E8
Wervin Ches 30 C3
Wesham Lancs 34 D3
Wessington Derby 32 D1
West Heref/Worcs 21 G9
West Aberchalder H'land 57 G1
West Aberthaw S Glam 14 H4
West Acre Norfolk 26 D1
West Adderbury Oxon 16 A5
West Adsborough Som'set 6 C6
West Allerdean Northum 49 E12
West Allotment Tyne/Wear 45 F11
West Alvington Devon 5 L6
West Amesbury Wilts 8 B3
West Anstey Devon 4 C7
West Ash Devon 4 D2
West Ashby Lincs 33 C9
West Ashling W Sussex 9 E9
West Ashton Wilts 7 A12
West Auckland Durham 40 C2
West Ayton N Yorks 41 G10
West Badfont Surrey 17 G11
West Bagborough Som'set 6 C5
West Balhagarty Gramp 59 K5
West Barkwith Lincs 33 B8
West Barnby N Yorks 41 D8
West Barns Lothian 49 B9
West Barr Dumf/Gal 42 G4
West Barsham Norfolk 26 B2
West Bay Dorset 7 G8
West Bay Som'set 7 D8
West Beckham Norfolk 26 B4
West Benridge Northum 45 D10
West Bergholt Essex 19 A9
West Bexington Dorset 7 H9
West Bilney Norfolk 24 D8
West Blackadder Borders 49 D11
West Blatchington E Sussex 10 G2
West Bold Borders 48 F6
West Bowhill Dumf/Gal 43 D12
West Bowling W Yorks 35 D10
West Bradenham Norfolk 26 E2
West Bradford Lancs 34 C6
West Bradley Som'set 7 C9
West Bretton W Yorks 35 F11
West Bridgford Notts 32 G3
West Bromwich W Midlands 22 C4
West Browncastle S'clyde 47 E11
West Buckland Devon 4 C5
West Buckland Som'set 6 D5
West Burrafrith Shetl'd 64 D6
West Burton N Yorks 39 F12
West Burton W Sussex 9 E11
West Butsfield Durham 40 A1
West Butterwick Humber 36 G6
West Byfleet Surrey 17 H11
West Byres Lothian 49 C7
West Caister Norfolk 26 D8
West Calder Lothian 48 C3
West Camel Som'set 7 D9
West Cannahars Gramp 58 E7
West Carr Humber 36 F5

West Cauldcoates *S'clyde* **47** E11
West Chaldon *Dorset* **7** H11
West Challow *Oxon* **16** E4
West Chelborough *Dorset* **7** F9
West Chevington *Northum* **45** C10
West Chiltington *W Sussex* **9** D12
West Chiltington Common *W Sussex* **9** D12
West Chinnock *Som'set* **7** E8
West Chisenbury *Wilts* **8** A3
West Clandon *Surrey* **9** A11
West Cliffe *Kent* **11** D12
West Clyne *H'land* **61** F8
West Clyth *H'land* **61** D11
West Coker *Som'set* **7** E8
West Compton *Dorset* **7** G9
West Compton *Som'set* **7** B9
West Cowick *Humber* **36** E4
West Cranmore *Som'set* **7** B10
West Creeting Green *Suffolk* **27** J4
West Cross *W Glam* **13** H9
West Cullerley *Gramp* **59** G5
West Curthwaite *Cumb* **44** H2
West Darlochan *S'clyde* **46** G2
West Dean *W Sussex* **9** E10
West Dean *Wilts* **8** C4
West Deeping *Lincs* **24** E2
West Derby *Mersey* **30** A3
West Dereham *Norfolk* **24** E7
West Ditchburn *Northum* **45** A9
West Down *Devon* **4** B4
West Drayton *London* **18** F1
West Drayton *Notts* **32** C4
West Edington *Northum* **45** E9
West Ella *Humber* **37** D8
West End *Avon* **15** G8
West End *Berks* **17** G9
West End *Gwyn* **28** G3
West End *Hants* **8** E6
West End *Humber* **37** D7
West End *Lincs* **37** G11
West End *Norfolk* **26** D8
West End *S'clyde* **48** E2
West End *Surrey* **17** H10
West End *Wilts* **8** D1
West Fallodon *Northum* **45** A10
West Farleigh *Kent* **10** C6
West Felton *Shrops* **30** H2
West Firle *E Sussex* **10** G3
West Garforth *W Yorks* **36** D2
West Ginge *Oxon* **16** E5
West Grafton *Wilts* **16** H3
West Green *Hants* **17** H8
West Grimstead *Wilts* **8** C4
West Grinstead *W Sussex* **10** F1
West Haddlesey *N Yorks* **36** D3
West Haddon *Northants* **23** E9
West Hagbourne *Oxon* **16** E6
West Hagley *Heref/Worcs* **22** D3
West Hall *Cumb* **44** F4
West Hallam *Derby* **32** F2
West Halton *Humber* **37** E7
West Ham *London* **18** F4
West Hanney *Oxon* **16** E5
West Hanningfield *Essex* **19** D7
West Hardwick *W Yorks* **36** E2
West Harnham *Wilts* **8** C3
West Harptree *Avon* **7** A9
West Harrington *Tyne/Wear* **45** H11
West Hatch *Som'set* **6** D6
West Hay *Wilts* **15** H8
West Head *Norfolk* **24** E7
West Helmsdale *H'land* **61** E9
West Hendred *Oxon* **16** E5
West Heslerton *N Yorks* **41** H9
West Hill *Avon* **15** G8
West Hill *Devon* **6** G4
West Hoathly *W Sussex* **10** E2
West Holme *Dorset* **7** H12
West Hopes *Lothian* **49** C8
West Horrington *Som'set* **7** A9
West Horsley *Surrey* **9** A12
West Horton *Northum* **45** C11
West Hougham *Kent* **11** D11
West Huntspill *Som'set* **6** B6
West Hyde *Herts* **17** E11
West Hythe *Kent* **11** E10
West Ilsley *Berks* **16** F6
West Itchenor *W Sussex* **9** F9
West Keal *Lincs* **33** D10
West Kennett *Wilts* **16** G2
West Kilbride *S'clyde* **47** E7
West Kingsdown *Kent* **10** B5
West Kington *Wilts* **15** F11
West Kinharrachie *Gramp* **58** D7
West Kinnernie *Gramp* **58** F5
West Kirby *Mersey* **30** B1
West Knapton *N Yorks* **41** H9
West Knighton *Dorset* **7** G10
West Knoyle *Wilts* **7** C12
West Kyloe *Northum* **45** B11
West Lambrook *Som'set* **7** D7
West Langdon *Kent* **11** C11
West Langwell *H'land* **61** F7
West Lavington *W Sussex* **9** D10
West Lavington *Wilts* **8** A2
West Layton *N Yorks* **40** D2
West Leake *Notts* **32** G3
West Learmouth *Northum* **49** F11
West Lexham *Norfolk* **26** D1
West Lilling *N Yorks* **36** A4
West Linkhall *Northum* **45** A10
West Linton *Borders* **48** D4
West Liss *Hants* **9** C9
West Littleton *Avon* **15** G11
West Looe *Cornw'l* **3** D9
West Luccombe *Som'set* **6** B2
West Lulworth *Dorset* **7** H11
West Lutton *N Yorks* **41** H9
West Lydford *Som'set* **7** C9
West Lyham *Northum* **45** C12
West Lyng *Som'set* **7** C7
West Lynn *Norfolk* **24** D7
West Mains *Northum* **45** B12
West Mains *S'clyde* **47** D8
West Mains *S'clyde* **48** D2
West Malling *Kent* **10** B5
West Malvern *Heref/Worcs* **22** G1
West Marden *W Sussex* **9** E9
West Markham *Notts* **32** C4
West Marsh *Humber* **37** F10
West Marton *N Yorks* **35** B8
West Meon *Hants* **9** D8
West Mersea *Essex* **19** C10
West Milton *Dorset* **7** G8
West Minster *Kent* **11** A8
West Molesey *Surrey* **17** G12
West Monkton *Som'set* **6** C6
West Moors *Dorset* **8** F2
West Morden *Dorset* **7** G12
West Morriston *Borders* **49** E8
West Ness *N Yorks* **41** G7
West Newton *Humber* **37** C9
West Newton *Norfolk* **24** C8
West Ogwell *Devon* **5** J7
West Orchard *Dorset* **7** E11
West Overton *Wilts* **16** G2
West Panson *Devon* **5** G2
West Parley *Dorset* **8** F2
West Peckham *Kent* **10** C5
West Pelton *Durham* **45** H10
West Pennard *Som'set* **7** B9
West Pentire *Cornw'l* **2** D5
West Porlock *Som'set* **6** B2
West Putford *Devon* **4** D2
West Quantoxhead *Som'set* **6** B5
West Rainton *Durham* **45** H11
West Rasen *Lincs* **33** A8
West Raynham *Norfolk* **26** C2
West Rounton *N Yorks* **40** E4
West Row *Suffolk* **25** H8
West Rudham *Norfolk* **26** C1
West Runton *Norfolk* **26** A5
West Saltoun *Lothian* **49** C7
West Sandford *Devon* **4** F7
West Sandwick *Shetl'd* **64** B7
West Scrafton *N Yorks* **40** G1
West Sessex Co *W Sussex* **10** E1
West Sidewood *S'clyde* **48** D3
West Skelston *Dumf/Gal* **43** C9
West Sleekburn *Northum* **45** E11
West Somerton *Norfolk* **26** D7
West Stafford *Dorset* **7** G10
West Stockwith *Notts* **36** H6
West Stoke *W Sussex* **9** E9
West Stonesdale *N Yorks* **39** E11
West Stoughton *Som'set* **7** A7
West Stour *Dorset* **7** D11
West Stourmouth *Kent* **11** B11
West Stow *Suffolk* **27** H1
West Stowell *Wilts* **16** H2
West Strathan *H'land* **60** B6
West Stratton *Hants* **8** B6
West Street *Kent* **11** C8
West Summer Side *N Yorks* **40** G2
West Tanfield *N Yorks* **40** G3
West Taphouse *Cornw'l* **3** C8
West Tarbert *S'clyde* **46** C3
West Third *Borders* **49** F9
West Thirston *Northum* **45** C10
West Thorney *W Sussex* **9** F9
West Thurrock *Essex* **18** F6
West Tisted *Hants* **9** C8
West Tofts *Tayside* **52** D6
West Torrington *Lincs* **33** B8
West Town *Avon* **15** H8
West Town *Hants* **9** F8
West Town *Heref/Worcs* **21** F10
West Tytherley *Hants* **8** C4
West Tytherton *Wilts* **16** G1
West Walton *Norfolk* **24** D6
West Walton Highway *Norfolk* **24** D6
West Warlington *Devon* **4** E6
West Wellow *Hants* **8** D4
West Wemyss *Fife* **53** H8
West Wick *Avon* **15** H7
West Wickham *Cambs* **25** K7
West Wickham *London* **18** G4
West Williamston *Dyfed* **12** F4
West Willow *Hants* **8** E4
West Winch *Norfolk* **24** D7
West Wittering *W Sussex* **9** F9
West Witton *N Yorks* **40** F1
West Woodburn *Northum* **45** D7
West Woodhay *Berks* **16** H5
West Woodlands *Som'set* **7** B11
West Worldham *Hants* **9** B9
West Wratting *Cambs* **25** K7
West Wycombe *Bucks* **17** E9
West Yell *Shetl'd* **64** C7
Westacott *Devon* **4** C5
Westbere *Kent* **11** B10
Westborough *Lincs* **32** F6
Westbourne *Dorset* **8** G2
Westbourne *W Sussex* **9** E9
Westbury *Bucks* **17** A7
Westbury *Shrops* **21** A9
Westbury *Wilts* **7** A12
Westbury Leigh *Wilts* **7** A12
Westbury on Trym *Avon* **15** G9
Westbury-on-Severn *Glos* **15** C10
Westbury-sub-Mendip *Som'set* **7** A8
Westby *Lancs* **34** D3
Westcliff on Sea *Essex* **19** E8
Westcombe *Som'set* **7** B10
Westcote *Glos* **16** B3
Westcott *Bucks* **17** B8
Westcott *Devon* **6** F4
Westcott *Surrey* **9** A12
Westcott Barton *Oxon* **16** B5
Westdean *E Sussex* **10** H4
Wester Aberchalder *H'land* **57** G1
Wester Balgedie *Tayside* **52** G6
Wester Causewayend *Lothian* **48** C3
Wester Clunie *Tayside* **52** A4
Wester Essenside *Borders* **49** G7
Wester Fintray *Gramp* **58** F6
Wester Fodderletter *Gramp* **57** G7
Wester Greenyards *H'land* **60** G6
Wester Happrew *Borders* **48** E4
Wester Housebryes *Borders* **49** F8
Wester Milton *H'land* **56** D5
Wester Newburn *Fife* **53** G9
Wester Ochiltree *Lothian* **48** B3
Wester Pencaitland *Lothian* **49** C7
Wester Quarff *Shetl'd* **64** E7
Wester Rarichie *H'land* **56** B4
Wester Slumbay *H'land* **54** F3
Westerdale *H'land* **61** C10
Westerdale *N Yorks* **41** E7
Westerfield *Suffolk* **27** K5
Westergate *W Sussex* **9** F10
WesterGreenskairs *Gramp* **58** A5
Westerham *Kent* **10** C3
Westerhope *Tyne/Wear* **45** F10
Westerleigh *Avon* **15** F10
Westerton *Durham* **40** B3
Westerton *Gramp* **58** C3
Westerton *Tayside* **53** B11
Westerton *W Sussex* **9** E10
Westertown *Gramp* **58** C3
Westfield *Cumb* **38** B2
Westfield *E Sussex* **11** F7
Westfield *Gramp* **58** E3
Westfield *H'land* **61** B10
Westfield *Heref/Worcs* **22** G1
Westfield *Lothian* **48** B2
Westfield *Norfolk* **26** D3
Westfields *Dorset* **7** F10
Westfields of Rattray *Tayside* **52** C6
Westgate *Durham* **39** A11
Westgate *Humber* **36** F5
Westgate *Norfolk* **26** B3
Westgate on Sea *Kent* **11** A11
Westgillsyke *Dumf/Gal* **44** F2
Westhall *Suffolk* **27** G7
Westham *Dorset* **7** H10
Westham *E Sussex* **10** H5
Westham *Som'set* **7** B7
Westhampnett *W Sussex* **9** E10
Westhaugh *Gramp* **58** E4
Westhay *Som'set* **7** B8
Westhead *Lancs* **34** F3
Westheath *Hants* **17** H9
Westhide *Heref/Worcs* **21** H11
Westhill *Gramp* **59** G6
Westhill *H'land* **56** E3
Westhope *Heref/Worcs* **21** G10
Westhope *Shrops* **21** D10
Westhorpe *Lincs* **24** B3
Westhorpe *Suffolk* **27** H3
Westhoughton *Gtr Man* **34** G5
Westhouse *N Yorks* **39** H9
Westhouses *Derby* **32** D2
Westhumble *Surrey* **10** C1
Westleigh *Devon* **4** C3
Westleigh *Devon* **6** D4
Westleigh *Gtr Man* **34** G5
Westleton *Suffolk* **27** H7
Westley *Shrops* **21** B9
Westley *Suffolk* **27** J1
Westley Waterless *Cambs* **25** K7
Westlington *Bucks* **17** C8
Westlinton *Cumb* **44** G2
Westmarsh *Kent* **11** B11
Westmeston *E Sussex* **10** G2
Westmill *Herts* **18** A4
Westminister *London* **18** F3
Westmuir *Tayside* **53** B8
Westness *Orkney* **64** B2
Westnewton *Cumb* **43** G12
Westnewton *Northum* **49** F11
Weston *Avon* **15** H10
Weston *Berks* **16** G5
Weston *Ches* **30** B4
Weston *Ches* **30** E6
Weston *Devon* **6** F5
Weston *Devon* **6** G5
Weston *Dorset* **7** H7
Weston *Hants* **9** D8
Weston *Herts* **18** A3
Weston *Lincs* **24** C4
Weston *N Yorks* **35** B10
Weston *Northants* **23** G9
Weston *Notts* **32** C5
Weston *S'clyde* **48** E3
Weston *Shrops* **21** C11
Weston *Shrops* **21** E9
Weston *Shrops* **30** G4
Weston *Staffs* **31** G8
Weston Bampfylde *Som'set* **7** D9
Weston Beggard *Heref/Worcs* **21** H11
Weston by Welland *Northants* **23** C11
Weston Colville *Cambs* **25** K7
Weston Coyney *Staffs* **31** F8
Weston Favell *Northants* **23** F11
Weston Green *Cambs* **25** K7
Weston Heath *Shrops* **22** A1
Weston Hills *Lincs* **24** C4
Weston Jones *Staffs* **30** H6
Weston Longville *Norfolk* **26** D4
Weston Lullingfields *Shrops* **30** H3
Weston Patrick *Hants* **9** B8
Weston Rhyn *Shrops* **30** G1
Weston Sudedge *Glos* **22** H5
Weston Turville *Bucks* **17** C9
Weston under Penyard *Heref/Worcs* **15** B9
Weston under Wetherley *Warwick* **23** E7
Weston Underwood *Bucks* **23** G12
Weston Underwood *Derby* **31** F11
Weston Upon Trent *Derby* **32** G1
Westonbirt *Glos* **15** E11
Westoning *Beds* **25** M1
Weston-in-Gardano *Avon* **15** G8
Weston-on-Avon *Warwick* **22** G5
Weston-on-the-Green *Oxon* **16** B6
Weston-super-Mare *Avon* **14** H6
Weston-under-Lizard *Staffs* **22** A2
Westonzoyland *Som'set* **7** C7
Westow *N Yorks* **36** A5
Westport *S'clyde* **46** G2
Westport *Som'set* **7** D7
Westridge Green *Berks* **16** F6
Westrigg *Lothian* **48** C2
Westruther *Borders* **49** D9
Westry *Cambs* **24** F5
Westville *Notts* **32** E2
Westward *Cumb* **38** A5
Westward *Durham* **45** G9
Westward Ho! *Devon* **4** C3
Westwater *Dumf/Gal* **44** E1
Westwell *Kent* **11** C8
Westwell *Oxon* **16** C3
Westwell Leacon *Kent* **11** C8
Westwick *Cambs* **25** J5
Westwick *Durham* **40** D1
Westwood *Devon* **6** F4
Westwood *S'clyde* **47** D11
Westwood *Wilts* **15** H11
Westwoodside *Humber* **36** G5
Wether Cote *N Yorks* **40** F6
Wetheral *Cumb* **44** H3
Wetherby *W Yorks* **35** B12
Wetherden *Suffolk* **27** J3
Wetheringsett *Suffolk* **27** J4
Wethersfield *Essex* **25** M8
Wethersta *Shetl'd* **64** C7
Wetherup Street *Suffolk* **27** J4
Wetley Rocks *Staffs* **31** E8
Wettenhall *Ches* **30** D5
Wetton *Staffs* **31** E9
Wetwang *Humber* **37** A7
Wetwood *Staffs* **30** G6
Wexcombe *Wilts* **16** H4
Wexham Street *Bucks* **17** F10
Weybourne *Norfolk* **26** A4
Weybread *Suffolk* **27** G5
Weybridge *Surrey* **17** H11
Weycroft *Devon* **6** F6
Weydale *H'land* **61** A10
Weyhill *Hants* **8** A5
Weymouth *Dorset* **7** H10
Whaddon *Bucks* **17** A9
Whaddon *Cambs* **25** K4
Whaddon *Glos* **15** C11
Whaddon *Wilts* **8** C3
Whale *Cumb* **39** C7
Whaley *Derby* **32** C2
Whaley Bridge *Derby* **31** B8
Whaley Thorns *Derby* **32** C3
Whalley *Lancs* **34** D6
Whalton *Northum* **45** E9
Whaplode *Lincs* **24** C4
Whaplode Drove *Lincs* **24** D4
Whaplode St. Catherine *Lincs* **24** D4
Wharfe *N Yorks* **39** H10
Wharles *Lancs* **34** D3
Wharmley *Northum* **45** F7
Wharncliffe Side *S Yorks* **35** H11
Wharram le Street *N Yorks* **36** A6
Wharton *Ches* **30** D5
Wharton *Heref/Worcs* **21** G10
Whashton *N Yorks* **40** E2
Whasset *Cumb* **39** G7
Whatcote *Warwick* **22** H6
Whateley *Warwick* **22** B6
Whatfield *Suffolk* **27** K3
Whatley *Som'set* **7** B10
Whatlington *E Sussex* **10** F6
Whatstandwell *Derby* **31** E11
Whatton *Notts* **32** F5
Whauphill *Dumf/Gal* **42** G5
Wheatacre *Norfolk* **26** F8
Wheathampstead *Herts* **18** C2
Wheathill *Shrops* **21** D11
Wheatley *Hants* **9** B9
Wheatley *Oxon* **17** D7
Wheatley Hill *Durham* **40** A4
Wheatley Lane *Lancs* **35** C7
Wheaton Aston *Staffs* **22** A2
Wheddon Cross *Som'set* **6** B3
Wheedlemont *Gramp* **58** E2
Wheelerstreet *Surrey* **9** B11
Wheelock *Ches* **30** D6
Wheelock Heath *Ches* **30** D6
Wheelton *Lancs* **34** E5
Wheen *Tayside* **59** K1
Wheldrake *N Yorks* **36** C4
Whelford *Glos* **16** D3
Whelpo *Cumb* **38** A5
Whempstead *Herts* **18** B3
Whenby *N Yorks* **40** H6
Whepstead *Suffolk* **27** J1
Wherstead *Suffolk* **27** L5
Wherwell *Hants* **8** B5
Wheston *Derby* **31** C10
Whetsted *Kent* **10** C5
Whetstone *Leics* **23** B9
Whicham *Cumb* **38** G4
Whichford *Warwick* **16** A4
Whickham *Tyne/Wear* **45** G10
Whiddon Down *Devon* **5** G6
Whigstreet *Tayside* **53** C9
Whilton *Northants* **23** F9
Whimble *Devon* **4** F2
Whimple *Devon* **6** F4
Whimpwell Green *Norfolk* **26** C7
Whinburgh *Norfolk* **26** E3
Whinkerstones *Borders* **49** E10
Whinnie Liggate *Dumf/Gal* **43** F8
Whinnyfold *Gramp* **58** D8
Whippingham *I of Wight* **8** G6
Whipsnade *Beds* **17** B11
Whipton *Devon* **6** G3
Whissendine *Leics* **23** A11
Whissonsett *Norfolk* **26** C2
Whistley Green *Berks* **17** G9
Whiston *Mersey* **30** A3
Whiston *Northants* **23** F11
Whiston *S Yorks* **32** A2
Whiston *Staffs* **22** A2
Whiston *Staffs* **31** F9
Whitbeck *Cumb* **38** G4
Whitbourne *Heref/Worcs* **21** G12
Whitbourne Ford *Heref/Worcs* **22** F1
Whitburn *Tyne/Wear* **45** G12
Whitburn *Lothian* **48** C2
Whitburn Colliery *Tyne/Wear* **45** G12
Whitby *Ches* **30** C3
Whitby *N Yorks* **41** D9
Whitcastles *Dumf/Gal* **44** D1
Whitchurch *Avon* **15** G9
Whitchurch *Bucks* **17** B9
Whitchurch *Devon* **5** H4
Whitchurch *Dyfed* **12** D2
Whitchurch *Hants* **8** A6
Whitchurch *Heref/Worcs* **15** C8
Whitchurch *Oxon* **17** F7
Whitchurch *S Glam* **14** F5
Whitchurch *Shrops* **30** F4
Whitchurch Canonicorum *Dorset* **7** G7
Whitchurch Hill *Oxon* **17** F7
Whitcombe *Dorset* **7** G10
Whitcott Keysett *Shrops* **21** D8
White Chapel *Lancs* **34** C4
White Coppice *Lancs* **34** E5
White Cross *Avon* **7** A9
White Cross *Devon* **6** G4
White Lackington *Dorset* **7** F10
White Ladies Aston *Heref/Worcs* **22** G3
White Mill *Dyfed* **13** E8
White Notley *Essex* **19** B8
White Pit *Lincs* **33** B11
White Rock *Heref/Worcs* **15** B7
White Roding *Essex* **18** C5
White Stone *Heref/Worcs* **21** H11
White Waltham *Berks* **17** F9
Whiteacen *Gramp* **56** E8
Whiteacre Heath *Warwick* **22** C5
Whitebridge *H'land* **55** H8
Whitebridge *H'land* **57** H1
Whitebrook *Gwent* **15** D8
Whiteburn *Borders* **49** E8
Whitecairn *Dumf/Gal* **42** F3
Whitecairns *Gramp* **58** F7
Whitecastle *S'clyde* **48** E3
Whitecraig *Lothian* **48** B6
Whitecrashes *Gramp* **58** E6
Whitecroft *Glos* **15** D9
Whitecrook *Dumf/Gal* **42** F3
Whitecross *Cornw'l* **3** B7
Whitecross *Lothian* **48** B2
Whiteface *H'land* **61** G7
Whitefarland *S'clyde* **46** E4
Whitefaulds *S'clyde* **42** A4
Whitefield *Northum* **44** G6

Whitefield Tayside 52 D6
Whitefield under Lyne Gtr Man 35 G7
Whitefirld Som'set 6 C4
Whiteford Gramp 58 E5
Whitegate Ches 30 C5
Whitehall Devon 6 E5
Whitehall Orkney 64 B4
Whitehaugh Borders 44 B3
Whitehaven Cumb 38 C2
Whitehill Dumf/Gal 43 D12
Whitehill Gramp 58 B3
Whitehill Hants 9 C9
Whitehills Gramp 58 A4
Whitehouse Gramp 58 F4
Whitehouse S'clyde 46 C3
Whitekirk Borders 49 E8
Whitekirk Lothian 49 A8
Whiteknowes Gramp 59 G3
Whitelackington Som'set 7 E7
Whitelaw Borders 49 D11
Whitelee Borders 49 F8
Whiteley N Yorks 36 E3
Whiteley Bank I of Wight 9 H7
Whiteley Green Ches 31 B8
Whiteley Village Surrey 17 H11
Whitemans Green W Sussex 10 E2
Whitemire Gramp 56 D5
Whitemoor Cornw'l 3 D7
Whitenap Hants 8 D5
Whiteparish Wilts 8 D4
Whiteshill Glos 15 D11
Whiteside Northum 44 F5
Whiteside Lothian 48 C2
Whitesmith E Sussex 10 G4
Whitestaunton Som'set 6 E6
Whitestone Devon 4 A4
Whitestone Devon 4 F7
Whitestone Gramp 59 H4
Whitestones Gramp 58 B6
Whiteway Glos 15 C12
Whiteway House Devon 6 H2
Whitewell Lancs 34 B5
Whiteworks Devon 5 J5
Whitewreath Gramp 56 D8
Whitfield Avon 15 E10
Whitfield Borders 48 D4
Whitfield Kent 11 D11
Whitfield Northants 23 H9
Whitford Clwyd 29 B10
Whitford Devon 6 G6
Whitgift Humber 36 E6
Whitgreave Staffs 31 G7
Whithorn Dumf/Gal 42 G5
Whiting Bay S'clyde 46 G5
Whitington Norfolk 24 E8
Whitland Dyfed 12 E5
Whitletts S'clyde 47 G8
Whitley Berks 17 G8
Whitley Wilts 15 H12
Whitley Bay Tyne/Wear 45 F11
Whitley Chapel Northum 45 G7
Whitley Lower W Yorks 35 E11
Whitlock's End W Midlands 22 D4
Whitminster Glos 15 D11
Whitmore Staffs 31 F7
Whitnage Devon 6 E4
Whitney Heref/Worcs 21 H8
Whitrigg Cumb 38 A4
Whitrigg Cumb 44 G1
Whitriggs Borders 44 B4
Whitsbury Hants 8 D3
Whitsleigh Barton Devon 4 D4
Whitsome Borders 49 D11
Whitsomehill Borders 49 D11
Whitson Gwent 15 F7
Whitstable Kent 11 A9
Whitstone Cornw'l 4 F1
Whittingham Northum 45 B9
Whittingslow Shrops 21 D9
Whittington Derby 32 C1
Whittington Glos 16 B1
Whittington Heref/Worcs 22 G2
Whittington Lancs 39 H8
Whittington Shrops 30 G2
Whittington Staffs 22 A5
Whittington Staffs 22 D2
Whittlebury Northants 23 H10
Whittle-le-Woods Lancs 34 E5
Whittlesey Cambs 24 F4
Whittlesford Cambs 25 K6
Whittlestone Head Lancs 34 E6
Whitton Borders 49 G10
Whitton Clevl'd 40 C4
Whitton Humber 37 E7
Whitton Northum 45 C9
Whitton Powys 21 F8
Whitton Shrops 21 E11
Whitton Suffolk 27 K4
Whittonditch Wilts 16 G4
Whittonstall Northum 45 G9
Whitway Hants 16 H6
Whitwell Derby 32 C3
Whitwell Herts 18 B2
Whitwell I of Wight 9 H7
Whitwell Leics 23 A12
Whitwell N Yorks 40 E3
Whitwell-on-the-Hill N Yorks 41 H7
Whitwick Leics 23 A8
Whitwood W Yorks 36 E2
Whitworth Lancs 35 E7
Whixall Shrops 30 G4
Whixley N Yorks 36 A2
Whoberley W Midlands 22 D6
Whorlton Durham 40 D1
Whorlton N Yorks 40 E5
Whygate Northum 44 E6
Whyle Heref/Worcs 21 F11
Whyteleafe Surrey 10 B2
Wibdon Glos 15 E9
Wibtoft Warwick 23 C8
Wichenford Heref/Worcs 22 F1
Wichling Kent 11 B8
Wick Avon 15 G10
Wick Dorset 8 G3
Wick H'land 61 C12
Wick Heref/Worcs 22 H3
Wick Mid Glam 14 G3
Wick Som'set 6 B5
Wick Som'set 7 D7
Wick W Sussex 9 F11
Wick Wilts 8 D3
Wick Hill Berks 17 H9
Wick St. Lawrence Avon 15 H7
Wicken Cambs 25 H7
Wicken Northants 23 H10
Wicken Bonhunt Essex 25 M6
Wickenby Lincs 33 B8
Wickersley S Yorks 32 A2
Wickford Essex 19 E7
Wickham Berks 16 G5
Wickham Hants 9 E7
Wickham Bishops Essex 19 C8
Wickham Heath Berks 16 G5
Wickham Market Suffolk 27 K6
Wickham St. Paul Essex 27 L1
Wickham Skeith Suffolk 27 H4
Wickham Street Suffolk 27 H4
Wickham Street Suffolk 27 K1
Wickhambreaux Kent 11 B10
Wickhambrook Suffolk 25 K8
Wickhamford Heref/Worcs 22 H4
Wickhampton Norfolk 26 E7
Wicklewood Norfolk 26 E4
Wickmere Norfolk 26 B5
Wickstreet E Sussex 10 G4
Wickwar Avon 15 E10
Widdington Essex 25 M6
Widdrington Northum 45 C10
Widdrington Station Northum 45 D10
Wide Open Tyne/Wear 45 F10
Widecombe in the Moor Devon 5 H6
Widegates Cornw'l 3 D10
Widemouth Bay Cornw'l 2 A2
Widford Essex 19 C7
Widford Herts 18 B4
Widmer End Bucks 17 D9
Widmerpool Notts 32 G4
Widnes Ches 30 B4
Widworthy Devon 6 F5
Wigan Gtr Man 34 F5
Wigbeth Dorset 8 E2
Wiggaton Devon 6 G4
Wiggenhall St. Germans Norfolk 24 D7
Wiggenhall St. Mary Magdalen Norfolk 24 D7
Wiggenhall St. Mary the Virgin Norfolk 24 D7
Wiggenhall St. Peter Norfolk 24 D7
Wigginton Herts 17 C10
Wigginton N Yorks 36 A4
Wigginton Oxon 16 A5
Wigginton Staffs 22 A6
Wigginton Heath Oxon 16 A5
Wigglesworth Lancs 35 B7
Wiggonby Cumb 44 H1
Wiggonholt W Sussex 9 D12
Wighill N Yorks 36 B3
Wighton Norfolk 26 B2
Wigley Hants 8 D5
Wigmore Heref/Worcs 21 E9
Wigmore Kent 11 B7
Wigsley Notts 32 C9
Wigsthorpe Northants 25 G1
Wigston Leics 23 B9
Wigtoft Lincs 24 B4
Wigton Cumb 44 H1
Wigtown Dumf/Gal 42 F5
Wigtwizzle S Yorks 35 H11
Wike W Yorks 35 C12
Wilbarston Northants 23 C11
Wilberfoss Humber 36 B5
Wilburton Cambs 25 H6
Wilby Norfolk 26 F3
Wilby Northants 23 E12
Wilby Suffolk 27 H5
Wilcot Wilts 16 H2
Wilcott Shrops 30 H2
Wilcrick Gwent 15 E7
Wildboarclough Ches 31 C8
Wilden Beds 25 K2
Wilden Heref/Worcs 22 E2
Wildhern Hants 8 A5
Wildsworth Lincs 36 G6
Wilford Notts 32 F3
Wilkesley Ches 30 F5
Wilkhaven H'land 61 H9
Wilkieston Lothian 48 C4
Willand Devon 6 E4
Willaston Ches 30 B2
Willaston Ches 30 E5
Willen Bucks 23 H12
Willenhall W Midlands 22 B3
Willenhall W Midlands 23 E7
Willerby Humber 37 D8
Willerby N Yorks 41 G10
Willersey Glos 22 H4
Willersley Heref/Worcs 21 H8
Willesborough Kent 11 D9
Willesden London 18 E2
Willett Som'set 6 C4
Willey Shrops 21 C12
Willey Warwick 23 D8
Willey Green Surrey 9 A11
Williamscot Oxon 23 H8
Willian Herts 18 A2
Willingale Essex 18 C6
Willingcott Devon 4 B4
Willingdon E Sussex 10 H5
Willingham Cambs 25 H5
Willingham Lincs 32 B6
Willington Beds 25 K2
Willington Derby 31 G11
Willington Durham 40 B2
Willington Warwick 22 H6
Willington Corner Ches 30 D4
Willitoft Humber 36 D5
Williton Som'set 6 B4
Willmontswick Northum 44 G6
Willoughby Lincs 33 C11
Willoughby Warwick 23 E8
Willoughby on the Wolds Notts 32 H4
Willoughby Waterleys Leics 23 C9
Willoughton Lincs 32 A6
Willows Green Essex 19 B7
Willsbridge Avon 15 G10
Willsworthy Devon 5 H4
Wilmcote Warwick 22 F5
Wilmington Devon 6 F5
Wilmington E Sussex 10 H4
Wilmington Kent 10 A4
Wilmslow Ches 31 B7
Wilnecote Staffs 22 B6
Wilpshire Lancs 34 D6
Wilsden W Yorks 35 D9
Wilsford Lincs 33 F7
Wilsford Wilts 16 H2
Wilsford Wilts 8 B3
Wilshamstead Beds 25 L2
Wilsill N Yorks 35 A10
Wilsley Pound Kent 10 D6
Wilson Heref/Worcs 15 B9
Wilson Leics 32 H1
Wilsontown S'clyde 48 D2
Wilsthorpe Lincs 24 D2
Wilstone Herts 17 C10
Wilton Borders 44 B3
Wilton Clevl'd 40 C6
Wilton Cumb 38 D3
Wilton Heref/Worcs 15 B9
Wilton N Yorks 41 G8
Wilton Wilts 16 H4
Wilton Wilts 8 C3
Wimbish Essex 25 L7
Wimbish Green Essex 25 M7
Wimbledon London 18 G2
Wimblington Cambs 24 F5
Wimborne Minster Dorset 8 F1
Wimborne St. Giles Dorset 8 E2
Wimbotsham Norfolk 24 E7
Wimpole Lodge Cambs 25 K4
Wimpstone Warwick 22 G5
Wincanton Som'set 7 C10
Wincham Ches 30 C5
Winchburgh Lothian 48 B4
Winchcombe Glos 16 A1
Winchelsea E Sussex 11 F8
Winchelsea Beach E Sussex 11 F8
Winchester Hants 8 C6
Winchet Hill Kent 10 D6
Winchfield Hants 9 A9
Winchmore Hill Bucks 17 E10
Wincle Ches 31 D8
Windermere Cumb 38 E6
Winderton Warwick 23 H7
Windlesham Surrey 17 H10
Windley Derby 31 F11
Windmill Derby 31 B10
Windmill Hill E Sussex 10 G5
Windmill Hill Som'set 6 E6
Windrush Glos 16 C3
Windshielknowe Borders 44 C4
Windsor Berks 17 G10
Windsoredge Glos 15 D11
Windy Yet S'clyde 47 D9
Windyedge Gramp 59 H6
Windygates Fife 53 G8
Windywalls Borders 49 F10
Wineham W Sussex 10 F1
Winestead Humber 37 E10
Winewall Lancs 35 C8
Winfarthing Norfolk 27 G4
Winford Avon 15 H8
Winford I of Wight 9 H7
Winforton Heref/Worcs 21 H8
Winfrith Newburgh Dorset 7 H11
Wing Bucks 17 B9
Wing Leics 23 B12
Wingate Durham 40 A4
Wingates Gtr Man 34 F5
Wingates Northum 45 D9
Wingerworth Derby 32 C1
Wingfield Beds 17 B11
Wingfield Suffolk 27 H5
Wingfield Wilts 7 A11
Wingham Kent 11 B11
Wingmore Kent 11 C10
Wingrave Bucks 17 B9
Winkburn Notts 32 D4
Winkfield Berks 17 G9
Winkfield Row Berks 17 G10
Winkhill Staffs 31 E9
Winkleigh Devon 4 E5
Winksley N Yorks 40 H3
Winkton Dorset 8 F3
Winlaton Tyne/Wear 45 G10
Winlaton Mill Tyne/Wear 45 G10
Winless H'land 61 B12
Winmarleigh Lancs 34 B3
Winnall Hants 8 C6
Winnall Heref/Worcs 15 A8
Winnard's Perch Cornw'l 2 C6
Winnersh Berks 17 G8
Winscales Cumb 38 C3
Winscombe Avon 15 H7
Winsford Ches 30 D5
Winsford Som'set 6 C3
Winsham Som'set 7 F7
Winshill Staffs 31 H11
Winsh-wen W Glam 13 G10
Winskill Cumb 39 B8
Winslade Hants 9 A8
Winsley Wilts 15 H11
Winslow Bucks 17 A8
Winson Glos 16 C2
Winsor Hants 8 E5
Winster Cumb 38 F6
Winster Derby 31 D11
Winston Durham 40 D2
Winston Suffolk 27 J5
Winstone Glos 15 C12
Winswell Devon 4 E4
Winterborne Clenston Dorset 7 F11
Winterborne Herringston Dorset 7 G10
Winterborne Houghton Dorset 7 F11
Winterborne Kingston Dorset 7 F12
Winterborne Monkton Dorset 7 G10
Winterborne Stickland Dorset 7 F11
Winterborne Whitechurch Dorset 7 F11
Winterborne Zelston Dorset 7 F12
Winterbourne Avon 15 F9
Winterbourne Berks 16 G5
Winterbourne Abbas Dorset 7 G9
Winterbourne Bassett Wilts 16 G2
Winterbourne Dauntsey Wilts 8 C3
Winterbourne Down Avon 15 F10
Winterbourne Earls Wilts 8 C3
Winterbourne Gunner Wilts 8 C3
Winterbourne Monkton Wilts 16 G2
Winterbourne Steepleton Dorset 7 G9
Winterbourne Stoke Wilts 8 B2
Winterburn N Yorks 35 A8
Wintercleugh S'clyde 48 H2
Winteringham Humber 37 E7
Winterley Ches 30 E6
Wintersett W Yorks 35 F12
Wintershields Cumb 44 F4
Wintershill Hants 9 D7
Winterslow Wilts 8 C4
Winterton Humber 37 E7
Winterton-on-Sea Norfolk 26 D8
Winthorpe Lincs 33 D12
Winthorpe Notts 32 E5
Winton Cumb 39 D10
Winton Dorset 8 G2
Winton N Yorks 40 F4
Wintringham N Yorks 41 H9
Winwick Cambs 25 G2
Winwick Ches 34 H5
Winwick Northants 23 E9
Wirksworth Derby 31 E11
Wirswall Ches 30 F4
Wisbech Cambs 24 E6
Wisbech St. Mary Cambs 24 E5
Wisborough Green W Sussex 9 C11
Wiseton Notts 32 A4
Wishaw S'clyde 47 D12
Wishaw Warwick 22 C5
Wisley Surrey 17 H11
Wispington Lincs 33 C9
Wissett Suffolk 27 G6
Wistanstow Shrops 21 D10
Wistanswick Shrops 30 G5
Wistaston Ches 30 E5
Wistaston Green Ches 30 E5
Wiston Dyfed 12 E4
Wiston S'clyde 48 F2
Wistow Cambs 25 G4
Wistow N Yorks 36 D4
Wiswell Lancs 34 C6
Witcham Cambs 25 G6
Witchampton Dorset 8 E1
Witchford Cambs 25 G6
Witham Essex 19 B8
Witham Friary Som'set 7 B10
Witham on the Hill Lincs 24 D2
Withcall Lincs 33 B10
Witherenden Hill E Sussex 10 E5
Witheridge Devon 4 E7
Witherley Leics 23 B7
Withern Lincs 33 B11
Withernsea Humber 37 D11
Withernwick Humber 37 C9
Withersdale Street Suffolk 27 G6
Withersfield Suffolk 25 K7
Witherslack Cumb 39 G7
Withiel Cornw'l 3 C7
Withiel Florey Som'set 6 C3
Withington Ches 31 C7
Withington Glos 16 C1
Withington Gtr Man 35 H7
Withington Heref/Worcs 21 H11
Withington Shrops 21 A11
Withington Staffs 31 G9
Withington Green Ches 30 C6
Withington Marsh Heref/Worcs 21 H11
Withleigh Devon 6 E3
Withnell Lancs 34 E5
Withybrook Warwick 23 D8
Withycombe Som'set 6 B4
Withycombe Raleigh Devon 6 H4
Withyham E Sussex 10 E4
Withypool Som'set 6 C2
Witley Surrey 9 B11
Witnesham Suffolk 27 K5
Witney Oxon 16 C5
Wittering Cambs 24 E2
Wittersham Kent 11 E7
Witton Heref/Worcs 22 F2
Witton Tayside 59 K3
Witton Bridge Norfolk 26 B7
Witton Gilbert Durham 45 H10
Witton le Wear Durham 40 B2
Witton Park Durham 40 B2
Wiveliscombe Som'set 6 C4
Wivelrod Hants 9 B8
Wivelsfield E Sussex 10 F2
Wivelsfield Green E Sussex 10 F2
Wivenhoe Essex 19 B10
Wivenhoe Cross Essex 19 B10
Wiveton Norfolk 26 A3
Wix Essex 19 A11
Wixford Warwick 22 G4
Wixhoe Suffolk 25 L8
Woburn Beds 17 A10
Woburn Sands Bucks 23 H12
Woking Surrey 17 H11
Wokingham Berks 17 G9
Wolborough Devon 5 J7
Wold Newton Humber 37 G10
Wold Newton Humber 41 H10
Woldingham Surrey 10 C3
Wolfclyde S'clyde 48 F3
Wolferton Norfolk 24 C7
Wolfhill Tayside 52 D6
Wolf's Castle Dyfed 12 D3
Wolfsdale Dyfed 12 E3
Woll Borders 49 G7
Wollaston Northants 23 F11
Wollaston Shrops 21 A9
Wollerton Shrops 30 G5
Wolseley Staffs 31 H9
Wolsingham Durham 40 A1
Wolstanton Staffs 31 E7
Wolston Warwick 23 E7
Wolvercote Oxon 16 C6
Wolverhampton W Midlands 22 B2
Wolverley Heref/Worcs 22 D2
Wolverley Shrops 30 G3
Wolverton Bucks 23 H11
Wolverton Hants 16 H6
Wolverton Warwick 22 F5
Wolverton Common Hants 16 H6
Wolvesnewton Gwent 15 D8
Wolvey Warwick 23 C8
Wolviston Clevl'd 40 C5
Wombleton N Yorks 41 G7
Wombourne Staffs 22 C2
Wombwell S Yorks 36 G2
Womenswold Kent 11 C11
Womersley N Yorks 36 E3
Wonersh Surrey 9 B11
Wonsan Devon 5 G5
Wonston Hants 8 B6
Wooburn Bucks 17 E10
Wooburn Green Bucks 17 E10
Wood Dalling Norfolk 26 C4
Wood End Beds 25 K1
Wood End Beds 25 K2
Wood End Herts 18 A3
Wood End Warwick 22 B6
Wood End Warwick 22 E4
Wood Enderby Lincs 33 D10
Wood Green London 18 E3
Wood Hayes W Midlands 22 B3
Wood Norton Norfolk 26 C3
Wood Street Surrey 9 A11
Wood Walton Cambs 25 G3
Woodacott Devon 4 E3
Woodale N Yorks 39 G12
Woodbastwick Norfolk 26 D6
Woodbeck Notts 32 B5
Woodborough Notts 32 E3
Woodborough Wilts 16 H2
Woodbridge Dorset 7 E10
Woodbridge Suffolk 27 K6
Woodbury Devon 6 G4
Woodbury Salterton Devon 6 G4
Woodchester Glos 15 D11
Woodchurch Kent 11 E8
Woodcombe Som'set 6 B3
Woodcote Oxon 17 F7
Woodcote Shrops 22 A1
Woodcott Hants 8 A6
Woodcroft Glos 15 E8
Woodcutts Dorset 8 D1
Woodditton Cambs 25 J8
Woodeaton Oxon 16 C6
Woodend Cumb 38 F4
Woodend Gramp 59 H3
Woodend Northants 23 G9
Woodend S'clyde 48 F2
Woodfalls Wilts 8 D3
Woodfield Dumf/Gal 44 F1
Woodfield S'clyde 47 G8
Woodfield Surrey 10 B1
Woodford Cornw'l 4 E1
Woodford Glos 15 E10
Woodford Gtr Man 31 B7
Woodford London 18 E4
Woodford Northants 25 H1
Woodford Som'set 7 B9
Woodford Halse Northants 23 G9
Woodgate Heref/Worcs 22 E3
Woodgate Norfolk 26 D3
Woodgate W Sussex 9 F10
Woodgreen Hants 8 D3
Woodhall Lothian 49 B9
Woodhall N Yorks 39 F12
Woodhall Northum 45 B9
Woodhall S Yorks 32 B2
Woodhall Spa Lincs 33 D9
Woodham Surrey 17 H11
Woodham Ferrers Essex 19 D8
Woodham Mortimer Essex 19 C8
Woodham Walter Essex 19 C8
Woodhaven Fife 53 D9
Woodhead Derby 35 G9
Woodhead Gramp 58 D5
Woodhead House Gramp 58 C5

Woodheads *Borders* **49** E8
Woodhill *Avon* **15** G8
Woodhill *Shrops* **22** D1
Woodholme *H'land* **56** D2
Woodhorn *Northum* **45** D11
Woodhouse *Leics* **23** A9
Woodhouse *S Yorks* **32** B1
Woodhouse *W Yorks* **35** D11
Woodhouse Eaves *Leics* **23** A8
Woodhurst *Cambs* **25** H4
Woodingdean *E Sussex* **10** G2
Woodland *Devon* **5** J7
Woodland *Durham* **40** C1
Woodland *Gramp* **58** E6
Woodland *Gramp* **58** F6
Woodlands *Dorset* **8** E2
Woodlands *Dumf/Gal* **43** D11
Woodlands *Gramp* **59** H5
Woodlands *H'land* **56** D1
Woodlands *Hants* **8** E5
Woodlands Park *Berks* **17** F9
Woodlands St. Mary *Berks* **16** G4
Woodlane *Staffs* **31** H10
Woodleigh *Devon* **5** L6
Woodlesford *W Yorks* **35** D12
Woodley *Berks* **17** G8
Woodley *Gtr Man* **35** H8
Woodmancote *Avon* **15** E10
Woodmancote *Glos* **16** A1
Woodmancote *Glos* **16** C1
Woodmancote *W Sussex* **10** G1
Woodmancote *W Sussex* **9** E9
Woodmancott *Hants* **9** B7
Woodmansey *Humber* **37** C8
Woodmansgreen *W Sussex* **9** C10
Woodmansterne *Surrey* **10** B2
Woodminton *Wilts* **8** D2
Woodnesborough *Kent* **11** B11
Woodnewton *Northants* **24** F1
Woodplumpton *Lancs* **34** D4
Woodrising *Norfolk* **26** E3
Wood's Green *E Sussex* **10** E5
Woodseaves *Shrops* **30** G5
Woodseaves *Staffs* **30** H6
Woodsend *Wilts* **16** F3
Woodsetts *S Yorks* **32** B3
Woodsford *Dorset* **7** G11
Woodside *Berks* **17** G10
Woodside *Dumf/Gal* **43** D11
Woodside *Fife* **53** F9
Woodside *Gramp* **58** C8
Woodside *Gramp* **59** G7
Woodside *Northum* **49** E12
Woodside *Tayside* **53** C7
Woodside of Arbeadie *Gramp* **59** H5
Woodslee *Dumf/Gal* **44** F2
Woodstock *Oxon* **16** B5
Woodstock Cross *Dyfed* **12** D4
Woodstock Slop *Dyfed* **12** D4
Woodthorpe *Derby* **32** C2
Woodthorpe *Leics* **32** H3
Woodton *Norfolk* **26** F6
Woodtown *Devon* **4** C4
Woodtown *Devon* **4** D3
Woodtown *Gramp* **59** K3
Woodvale *Mersey* **34** F2
Woodville *Derby* **31** H11
Woodyates *Dorset* **8** D2
Woofferton *Shrops* **21** F10
Wookey *Som'set* **7** B8
Wookey Hole *Som'set* **7** A9
Wool *Dorset* **7** H11
Woolacombe *Devon* **4** B3
Woolage Green *Kent* **11** C11
Woolaston *Glos* **15** D9
Woolavington *Som'set* **7** B7
Woolbeding *W Sussex* **9** D10
Woolbrook *Devon* **6** G5
Woolcotts *Som'set* **6** C3
Wooldale *W Yorks* **35** F10
Wooler *Northum* **49** G12
Woolfardisworthy *Devon* **4** E7
Woolfords Cotts *S'clyde* **48** D3
Woolgarston *Dorset* **8** H2
Woolhampton *Berks* **17** G7
Woolhope *Heref/Worcs* **15** A9
Woolland *Dorset* **7** F11
Woollard *Avon* **15** H9
Woollaston *Northants* **23** F12
Woollaton *Devon* **4** E3
Woolley *Avon* **15** G10
Woolley *Cambs* **25** H3
Woolley *Cornw'l* **4** D1
Woolley *W Yorks* **35** F11
Woolmer Green *Herts* **18** B3
Woolmere Green *Heref/Worcs* **22** F3
Woolpit *Suffolk* **27** J3
Woolpit Green *Suffolk* **27** J3
Woolscott *Warwick* **23** E8
Woolsery *Devon* **4** D2
Woolsington *Tyne/Wear* **45** F10
Woolstaston *Shrops* **21** C10
Woolsthorpe *Lincs* **32** G5
Woolsthorpe *Lincs* **32** H6
Woolston *Ches* **30** A5
Woolston *Devon* **5** L6
Woolston *Hants* **8** E6
Woolston *Shrops* **21** D9
Woolston *Shrops* **30** H2
Woolston Green *Devon* **5** J6
Woolstone *Bucks* **23** H12
Woolstone *Oxon* **16** E4
Woolton *Mersey* **30** B3
Woolton Hill *Hants* **16** H5
Woolverstone *Suffolk* **27** L5
Woolverton *Som'set* **7** A11
Woolwich *London* **18** F4
Woonton *Heref/Worcs* **21** G9
Wooperton *Northum* **45** A8
Wooplaw *Borders* **49** E7
Woore *Shrops* **30** F6
Wootton *Beds* **25** L1
Wootton *Hants* **8** F4
Wootton *Humber* **37** E8
Wootton *Kent* **11** C11
Wootton *Northants* **23** F11
Wootton *Oxon* **16** B5
Wootton *Oxon* **16** D6
Wootton *Shrops* **21** E10
Wootton *Staffs* **31** F9
Wootton *Staffs* **31** G7
Wootton Bassett *Wilts* **16** F2
Wootton Bridge *I of Wight* **9** G7
Wootton Common *I of Wight* **9** G7
Wootton Courtenay *Som'set* **6** B3
Wootton Fitzpaine *Dorset* **7** G7
Wootton Rivers *Wilts* **16** H3
Wootton St. Lawrence *Hants* **9** A7
Wootton Wawen *Warwick* **22** F5
Worcester *Heref/Worcs* **22** G2
Wordsley *W Midlands* **22** C2
Worfield *Shrops* **22** C1
Work *Orkney* **64** C3
Workington *Cumb* **38** B2
Worksop *Notts* **32** B3
Worlaby *Humber* **37** F8
World's End *Berks* **16** F6
World's End *Hants* **9** E8
Worle *Avon* **15** H7
Worleston *Ches* **30** E5
Worlingham *Suffolk* **26** F7
Worlington *Suffolk* **25** H8
Worlingworth *Suffolk* **27** H5
Wormald Green *N Yorks* **35** A11
Wormbridge *Heref/Worcs* **15** A7
Wormegay *Norfolk* **24** D8
Wormelow Tump *Heref/Worcs* **15** A8
Wormhill *Derby* **31** C9
Wormingford *Essex* **27** M2
Worminghall *Bucks* **17** C7
Wormington *Glos* **16** A1
Worminster *Som'set* **7** B9
Wormiston *Borders* **48** E5
Wormit *Fife* **53** E9
Wormleighton *Warwick* **23** G8
Wormley *Herts* **18** C4
Wormley *Surrey* **9** B10
Wormley West End *Herts* **18** C3
Wormshill *Kent* **11** B7
Wormsley *Heref/Worcs* **21** H9
Worplesdon *Surrey* **9** A11
Worrall *S Yorks* **35** H11
Worsbrough *S Yorks* **35** G12
Worsley *Gtr Man* **34** G6
Worstead *Norfolk* **26** C6
Worstead Lodge *Cambs* **25** K6
Worsthorne *Lancs* **35** D7
Worston *Lancs* **34** C6
Worswell *Devon* **5** L4
Worth *Kent* **11** C12
Worth *W Sussex* **10** D2
Worth Matravers *Dorset* **8** H1
Wortham *Suffolk* **27** H4
Worthen *Shrops* **21** B9
Worthenbury *Clwyd* **30** F3
Worthing *Norfolk* **26** D3
Worthing *W Sussex* **9** F12
Worthington *Leics* **32** H1
Worthy *Som'set* **6** A2
Wortley *S Yorks* **35** G11
Wortley *W Yorks* **35** D11
Worton *Wilts* **16** H1
Wortwell *Norfolk* **27** G6
Wotter *Devon* **5** J4
Wotton *Surrey* **9** A12
Wotton Underwood *Bucks* **17** C8
Wotton-under-Edge *Glos* **15** E11
Woughton on the Green *Bucks* **23** H12
Wouldham *Kent* **10** B6
Wrabness *Essex* **27** M5
Wraes *Gramp* **58** D3
Wrafton *Devon* **4** C4
Wragby *Lincs* **33** B8
Wragby *W Yorks* **36** E2
Wragholme *Lincs* **37** G11
Wramplingham *Norfolk* **26** E4
Wrangbrook *W Yorks* **36** F3
Wrangham *Gramp* **58** D4
Wrangham *Northum* **49** F12
Wrangle *Lincs* **33** E11
Wrangle Common *Lincs* **33** E11
Wrangle Lowgate *Lincs* **33** E11
Wrangway *Som'set* **6** D5
Wrantage *Som'set* **6** D6
Wrawby *Humber* **37** F8
Wraxall *Avon* **15** G8
Wraxall *Dorset* **7** F9
Wraxhall *Som'set* **7** C9
Wray *Lancs* **39** H8
Wrayland *Devon* **5** H7
Wraysbury *Berks* **17** G11
Wrea Green *Lancs* **34** D3
Wreay *Cumb* **39** C7
Wreay *Cumb* **44** H3
Wrecclesham *Surrey* **9** B9
Wrekenton *Tyne/Wear* **45** G11
Wrelton *N Yorks* **41** F8
Wrenbury *Ches* **30** E4
Wreningham *Norfolk* **26** F4
Wrentham *Suffolk* **27** G8
Wrenthorpe *W Yorks* **35** E11
Wrentnall *Shrops* **21** B9
Wressle *Humber* **36** D5
Wrestlingworth *Beds* **25** K4
Wretton *Norfolk* **24** E8
Wrexham *Clwyd* **30** E2
Wribbenhall *Heref/Worcs* **22** E2
Wrightington Bar *Lancs* **34** F4
Wrinehill *Staffs* **30** E6
Wrington *Avon* **15** H8
Writhlington *Avon* **7** A10
Writtle *Essex* **19** C7
Wrockwardine *Shrops* **21** A11
Wroot *Humber* **36** G5
Wrotham *Kent* **10** B5
Wrotham Heath *Kent* **10** B5
Wroughton *Wilts* **16** F3
Wroxall *Warwick* **22** E6
Wroxeter *Shrops* **21** B11
Wroxhall *I of Wight* **9** H7
Wroxham *Norfolk* **26** D6
Wroxton *Oxon* **23** H7
Wyaston *Derby* **31** F10
Wyberton *Lincs* **24** B4
Wyboston *Beds* **25** K3
Wybunbury *Ches* **30** E5
Wych Cross *E Sussex* **10** E3
Wychbold *Heref/Worcs* **22** F3
Wychnor *Staffs* **22** A5
Wychnor Bridges *Staffs* **22** A5
Wyck *Hants* **9** B9
Wyck Rissington *Glos* **16** B3
Wycliffe *Durham* **40** D1
Wycombe Marsh *Bucks* **17** E10
Wyddial *Herts* **25** M5
Wye *Kent* **11** C9
Wyesham *Gwent* **15** C8
Wyke *Dorset* **7** D11
Wyke *Shrops* **21** B12
Wyke *Surrey* **9** A10
Wyke *W Yorks* **35** D10
Wyke Champflower *Som'set* **7** C10
Wyke Regis *Dorset* **7** H7
Wykeham *N Yorks* **41** G9
Wykeham *N Yorks* **41** H8
Wykeham Moor *Lincs* **32** C6
Wykey *Shrops* **30** H3
Wylam *Northum* **45** G9
Wylde Green *W Midlands* **22** C5
Wyllie *Gwent* **14** E5
Wylye *Wilts* **8** B2
Wymering *Hants* **9** E8
Wymeswold *Leics* **32** H3
Wymington *Beds* **25** J1
Wymondham *Leics* **32** H6
Wymondham *Norfolk* **26** E4
Wyndham *Mid Glam* **14** E3
Wynford Eagle *Dorset* **7** G9
Wyre Piddle *Heref/Worcs* **22** G3
Wysall *Notts* **32** G3
Wythall *Heref/Worcs* **22** E4
Wytham *Oxon* **16** C6
Wythburn *Cumb* **38** D6
Wythenshawe *Gtr Man* **31** A7
Wyton *Cambs* **25** H4
Wyverstone Street *Suffolk* **27** H3
Wyville *Lincs* **32** G6
Wyvis Lodge *H'land* **54** B8
Yaddlethorpe *Humber* **36** F6
Yafford *I of Wight* **8** H6
Yafforth *N Yorks* **40** F4
Yalberton *Devon* **5** K7
Yalding *Kent* **10** C6
Yanworth *Glos* **16** C2
Yapham *Humber* **36** B6
Yapton *W Sussex* **9** F11
Yarburgh *Lincs* **33** A10
Yarcombe *Devon* **6** E6
Yardley *W Midlands* **22** D5
Yardley Gobion *Northants* **23** H11
Yardley Hastings *Northants* **23** F12
Yardro *Powys* **21** F8
Yardwell's Cross *Devon* **4** C6
Yarkhill *Heref/Worcs* **21** H11
Yarlet *Staffs* **31** G7
Yarlington *Som'set* **7** C10
Yarm *Clevl'd* **40** D4
Yarmouth *I of Wight* **8** G5
Yarnacott *Devon* **4** C5
Yarnbrook *Wilts* **7** A12
Yarnfield *Staffs* **31** G7
Yarnscombe *Devon* **4** D4
Yarnton *Oxon* **16** C6
Yarpole *Heref/Worcs* **21** F10
Yarrow *Borders* **48** G6
Yarrow Feus *Borders* **48** G6
Yarsop *Heref/Worcs* **21** H9
Yarwell *Northants* **24** F2
Yate *Avon* **15** F10
Yateley *Hants* **17** H9
Yatesbury *Wilts* **16** G2
Yattendon *Berks* **16** G6
Yatton *Avon* **15** H7
Yatton *Heref/Worcs* **15** A9
Yatton *Heref/Worcs* **21** F9
Yatton Keynell *Wilts* **15** G12
Yaverland *I of Wight* **9** H7
Yawthorpe *Lincs* **32** A6
Yawthorpe *Lincs* **37** H7
Yaxham *Norfolk* **26** D3
Yaxley *Cambs* **24** F3
Yaxley *Suffolk* **27** H4
Yazor *Heref/Worcs* **21** H9
Yeadon *W Yorks* **35** C10
Yealand Conyers *Lancs* **39** H7
Yealand Redmayne *Lancs* **39** H7
Yealmpton *Devon* **5** K4
Yearby *Clevl'd* **40** C6
Yearsley *N Yorks* **40** H6
Yeaton *Shrops* **30** H3
Yeaveley *Derby* **31** F10
Yeavering *Northum* **49** F12
Yelford *Oxon* **16** D4
Yelland *Devon* **4** C4
Yelling *Cambs* **25** J4
Yelsted *Kent* **11** B7
Yelvertoft *Northants* **23** E9
Yelverton *Devon* **5** J4
Yelverton *Norfolk* **26** E6
Yenston *Som'set* **7** D10
Yeo Mill *Devon* **4** C7
Yeoford *Devon* **4** F6
Yeolmbridge *Cornw'l* **3** A10
Yeovil *Som'set* **7** D9
Yeovil Marsh *Som'set* **7** D9
Yeovilton *Som'set* **7** D9
Yerbeston *Dyfed* **12** F4
Yerbeston Mountain *Dyfed* **12** F4
Yesnaby *Orkney* **64** C1
Yetholm Mains *Borders* **49** F11
Yetlington *Northum* **45** B8
Yetminster *Dorset* **7** E9
Yett *S'clyde* **47** C12
Yett *S'clyde* **47** G9
Yettington *Devon* **6** H4
Yetts of Muckhart *Central* **52** G5
Yffor *Gwyn* **28** F3
Yielden *Beds* **25** J1
Yieldshields *S'clyde* **48** D2
Yiewsley *London* **18** F1
Ynys *Dyfed* **20** F2
Ynys-boeth *Mid Glam* **14** E4
Ynysbwl *Mid Glam* **14** E4
Ynysddu *Gwent* **14** E5
Ynyshir *Mid Glam* **14** E4
Ynyslas *Dyfed* **20** C2
Ynystawe *W Glam* **13** G10
Yockenthwaite *N Yorks* **39** G11
Yockleton *Shrops* **21** A9
Yokefleet *Humber* **36** E6
Yoker *S'clyde* **47** C10
Yonder Bognie *Gramp* **58** C3
York *N Yorks* **36** B3
York Town *Surrey* **17** H9
Yorkeston *Lothian* **48** D6
Yorkletts *Kent* **11** B9
Yorkley *Glos* **15** D9
Youldonmoor Cross *Devon* **4** E2
Youlethorpe *Humber* **36** B5
Youlgreave *Derby* **31** D10
Youlton *N Yorks* **36** A3
Young's End *Essex* **19** B7
Yoxall *Staffs* **31** H10
Yoxford *Suffolk* **27** H7
Ysbyty Cynfyn *Dyfed* **20** D3
Ysbyty Ifan *Gwyn* **29** E8
Ysbyty Ystwyth *Dyfed* **20** E3
Ysceifog *Clwyd* **29** C10
Yspitty *Dyfed* **13** G9
Ystalyfera *W Glam* **13** F11
Ystrad *Mid Glam* **14** E3
Ystrad Aeron *Dyfed* **13** A8
Ystrad Meurig *Dyfed* **20** F3
Ystradfellte *Powys* **14** C3
Ystradffin *Dyfed* **13** B11
Ystradgynlais *Powys* **14** C1
Ystrad-mynach *Mid Glam* **14** E5
Ystradowen *Dyfed* **13** F10
Ystradowen *S Glam* **14** G3
Ystumtuen *Dyfed* **20** D3
Ythanbank *Gramp* **58** D6
Ythanwells *Gramp* **58** D4
Ythsie *Gramp* **58** D6
Zeal Monachorum *Devon* **4** F6
Zeals *Wilts* **7** C11
Zelah *Cornw'l* **2** D5
Zennor *Cornw'l* **2** F2

INDEX TO LONDON MAPS

ABBREVIATIONS

All.	*Alley*
App.	*Approach*
Av.	*Avenue*
Blds.	*Buildings*
Bri.	*Bridge*
Cir.	*Circus*
Cl.	*Close*
Cnr.	*Corner*
Coll.	*College*
Com.	*Common*
Cres.	*Crescent*
Ct.	*Court*
Dri.	*Drive*
E.	*East*
Emb.	*Embankment*
Est.	*Estate*
F.C.	*Football Club*
Flds.	*Fields*
Gdns.	*Gardens*
Grn.	*Green*
Gro.	*Grove*
Gt.	*Great*
Ho.	*House*
Hosp.	*Hospital*
La.	*Lane*
Man.	*Mansions*
Miss.	*Mission*
Mkt.	*Market*
Ms.	*Mews*
Mus.	*Museum*
Nth.	*North*
Par.	*Parade*
Pass.	*Passage*
Pk.	*Park*
Pl.	*Place*
R.C.	*Roman Catholic*
Rd.	*Road*
Res.	*Reservoir*
Sq.	*Square*
St.	*Street*
Sta.	*Station*
Sth.	*South*
Ter.	*Terrace*
Th.	*Theatre*
Vs.	*Villas*
W.	*West*
Wk.	*Walk*
Yd.	*Yard*

Abbey Gdns. *NW8* **73** C3
Abbey Gdns. Ms *NW8* **73** C4
Abbey Orchard St. *SW1* **79** D7
Abbey Rd. *NW8* **73** B3
Abbey St. *SE1* **80** D4
Abbey Wood **67** G12
Abbots La. *SE1* **80** B4
Abchurch La. *EC4* **76** H3
Abercorn Cl. *NW8* **73** C4
Abercorn Pl. *NW8* **73** C3
Aberdeen Pl. *NW8* **73** E5
Aberdour St. *SE1* **80** E3
Abingdon Rd. *W8* **77** D1
Abingdon St. *SW1* **79** D8
Abingdon Vs. *W8* **77** E1
Abridge **68** A1
Abridge Rd. **67** A12
Acacia Gdns. *NW8* **73** B5
Acacia Pl. *NW8* **73** B5
Acacia Rd. *NW8* **73** B5
Academy Rd. **67** H11
Acre La. **70** B6
Acre La. *Carshalton* **70** F5
Acton **66** F3
Acton Central Sta. **66** G3
Acton La. **66** F3
Acton (Main Line) Sta. **66** F3
Acton Pk. **66** G3
Acton St. *WC1* **75** D9
Acton Town Sta. **66** G2
Adam Eve Ms. *W8* **77** D2
Adam St. *WC2* **75** J9
Adams Row *W1* **74** J4
Addington **71** F8
Addington Rd. *Selsdon* **71** G7
Addington Rd. W. Wickham **71** E9
Addington Square *SE5* **80** J2
Addington St. *SE1* **79** C10
Addington Village Rd. **71** F8
Addiscombe **71** E7
Addiscombe Rd. **71** E7
Addiscombe Sta. **71** E7
Addlestone **69** F2
Adelaide Rd. **66** E5
Adelaide St. *WC2* **75** J8
Adeline Pl. *WC1* **75** G7
Adelphi Ter. *WC2* **75** J9
Adelphi Theatre *WC2* **75** J9
Adler St. *E1* **76** G6
Admiralty *SW1* **79** B8
Admiralty Arch *SW1* **79** B8
Adpar St. *W2* **73** F5
Æolian Hall *W1* **74** H5
Agar St. *WC2* **75** J8
Agdon St. *EC1* **75** E12
Air St. *W1* **74** J6
Albany Pk. Sta. **71** C12
Albany Rd. *SE5* **80** H3
Albany St. *NW1* **74** C5
Albemarle St. *W1* **74** J5
Albert Bri. *SW3/SW11* **78** J1
Albert Bri. Rd. *SW11* **78** J1
Albert Court *SW7* **77** D5
Albert Embankment *SE1* **79** F9
Albert Gate *SW1* **78** C3
Albert Memorial *SW7* **77** C4
Albert Pl. *W8* **77** D3
Albert Rd **67** G11
Albert St. *NW1* **74** B5
Albert Ter. *NW1* **74** A3
Albert Ter. Ms. *NW1* **74** A3
Alberta St. *SE17* **79** G12
Albery Theatre *WC2* **75** J8
Albion Cl. *W2* **73** H6
Albion Gate *W2* **73** H6
Albion Ms. *W2* **73** H6
Albion St. *W2* **73** H6
Aldborough Hatch **67** C12
Aldborough Rd. **67** C12
Aldbridge St. *SE17* **80** G4
Aldenham Pk. **66** A2
Aldenham Res. **66** A2
Aldenham Rd. *Bushey* **65** A5
Aldenham Rd. *Elstree* **66** A2
Aldenham St. *NW1* **74** C7
Aldermanbury *EC2* **76** G2
Alderminster Rd. *SE1* **80** F6
Alderney St. *SW1* **78** F5
Aldersbrook **67** D10
Aldersbrook Rd. **67** D10
Aldersgate St. *EC1* **75** F13
Alford St. *W1* **78** A3
Aldgate *EC3* **76** H4
Aldgate High St. *EC3* **76** G5
Aldwych *WC2* **75** H9
Aldwych Theatre *WC2* **75** H9
Alexander Av. **65** D6
Alexander Pl. *SW7* **77** E6
Alexander Sq. *SW3* **77** E6
Alexander St. *W2* **73** G2
Alexandra Gate *SW7* **77** C5
Alexandra Palace **66** C6
Alexandra Pk. **66** C6
Alexandra Pk. Rd. **66** C6
Alfred Ms. *WC1* **74** F7
Alfred Pl. *WC1* **74** F7
Alfred Rd. *W2* **73** F1
Alice St. *SE1* **80** E3
Alie St. *E1* **76** H6
All England Lawn Tennis Club **70** C4
All Saints Rd. **70** E4
All Saints St. *N1* **75** B9
All Souls Av. **66** E4
Allen St. *W8* **77** D1
Allhallows La. *EC4* **76** J2
Allingham St. *N1* **75** B13
Allington St. *SW1* **78** D5
Allitsen Rd. *NW8* **73** B6
Allsop Pl. *NW1* **74** E3
Allum La. **66** A2
Alma Grove *SE1* **80** F6
Alma Sq. *NW8* **73** C4
Alperton **66** E2
Alpha Pl. *NW6* **77** H6
Alsace Rd. *SE17* **80** G3
Alscot Rd. *SE1* **80** E5
Alvey St. *SE17* **80** G4
Ambassadors Th. *WC2* **75** H8
Ambergate St. *SE17* **79** G12
Amberley Rd. *W9* **73** E2
Amberwood Rise **70** E3
Ambrosden Av. *SW1* **78** E6
Amelia St. *SE17* **79** F13
Amhurst Pk. **67** D7
Ampton St. *WC1* **75** D9
Amwell St. *EC1* **75** D11
Anderson St. *SW3* **78** F2
Andover Pl. *NW6* **73** C2
Anerley Rd. **71** D7
Anerley Sta. **71** D7
Angel Hill **70** E4
Angel Rd. **67** B8
Angel Rd. Sta. **67** B8
Angel St. *EC1* **75** G13
Anglesea St. *E1* **76** E7
Ann La. *SW10* **77** J4
Ansdell St. *W8* **77** D3
Ansdell Ter. *W8* **77** D2
Anselm Rd. *SW6* **77** H1
Apex Cnr. **66** B3
Apple Tree Yd. *SW1* **78** A7
Appleby St. *E2* **76** B5
Appold St. *EC2* **76** F4
Apsley House *W1* **78** C4
Apsley Way *SW1* **78** C4
Aquinas St. *SE1* **79** B11
Arch St. *SE1* **80** E1
Archbishop's Pk. *SE1* **79** D10
Archer St. *W1* **74** H7
Archery Cl. *W2* **74** H2
Archway Rd. **66** D6
Ardleigh Green **68** C3
Ardleigh Green Rd. **68** C3
Argyle Rd. *W13* **66** F1
Argyle Sq. *WC1* **75** D9
Argyle St. *WC1* **75** D9
Argyll Rd. *W8* **77** D1
Argyll St. *W1* **74** H6
Arkley **66** A4
Arkley La. **66** A4
Arlington Av. *N1* **76** B2
Arlington Rd. *NW1* **74** B5
Arlington Sq. *N1* **76** B2
Arlington St. *SW1* **78** B6
Arlington Way *EC1* **75** C11
Armadale Rd. *SW6* **77** J1
Arne St. *WC2* **75** H9
Arnold Cir. *E2* **76** D5
Arnolds La. **72** C3
Arnos Grove Sta. **66** B6
Arnside St. *SE17* **80** H2
Arsenal F.C. **67** E7
Artesian Rd. *W2* **73** H1
Arthur St. *EC4* **76** J3
Artillery Ground *EC1* **76** E2
Artillery La. *E1* **76** F4
Artillery Row *SW1* **78** D7
Arundel St. *WC2* **75** H10
Ash **72** F5
Ashbridge St. *NW8* **73** E6
Ashburn Gdns. *SW7* **77** E3
Ashburn Ms. *SW7* **77** E3
Ashburn Pl. *SW7* **77** F3
Ashby St. *EC1* **75** D12
Ashford Hospital **69** B3
Ashford Rd. *Feltham* **69** C4
Ashford Rd. *Laleham* **69** D3
Ashland Pl. *W1* **74** F3
Ashley Pk. **69** E4
Ashley Pl. *SW1* **78** E6
Ashley Rd. *Epsom* **70** G3
Ashley Rd. *Walton* **69** E4
Ashmill St. *NW1* **73** F6
Ashmole St. *SW8* **79** H10
Ashtead **70** H2
Ashtead Common **70** G1
Ashtead Pk. **70** H2
Ashtead Sta. **70** H1
Ashworth Rd. *W9* **73** D3
Astell St. *SW3* **77** G6
Aston Rd. **65** B4
Astwood Ms. *SW7* **77** F3
Atherstone Ms. *SW7* **77** E4
Atterbury St. *SW1* **79** F8
Attneave St. *WC1* **75** D10
Auckland St. *SE11* **79** G9
Audley St. *W1* **78** B4
Audrey St. *E2* **76** B6
Augustus St. *NW1* **74** C5
Aulton Pl. *SE11* **79** G11
Austin Friars *EC2* **76** G3
Austin St. *E2* **76** D5
Austral St. *SE11* **79** E12
Australia House *WC2* **75** H10
Ave Maria La. *EC4* **75** H12
Avebury St. *N1* **76** A3
Aveley **68** G4
Aveley Rd. **68** E4
Aveline St. *SE11* **79** G10
Avenue Cl. *NW8* **73** A6
Avenue Rd. *Bexleyheath* **68** H1
Avenue Rd. *N14* **66** A6
Avenue Rd. *NW8* **73** B6
Avenue, The *EC3* **76** H4
Avenue, The *Sunbury* **69** D5
Avenue, The *SW4* **70** B5
Avery Row *W1* **74** H5
Averyhill Rd. **71** B11
Avon Pl. *SE1* **80** C2
Avondale Square *SE1* **80** G6
Avonmouth St. *SE1* **79** D13
Aybrook St. *W1* **74** F3
Aylesbury Rd. *SE17* **80** G3
Aylesbury St. *EC1* **75** E12
Aylesford St. *SW1* **78** G7
Aylmer Rd. **66** D5
Ayres St. *SE1* **80** C1
Back Church La. *E1* **76** H6
Back Hill *EC1* **75** E11
Back La. **68** G5
Bacon Gro. *SE1* **80** E5
Bacon St. *E1/E2* **76** E6
Badger's Mount **72** G1
Bagshot St. *SE17* **80** G4
Bainbridge St. *WC1* **75** G8
Baker St. *NW1/W1M* **74** F3
Baker's Ms. *W1* **74** G3
Baker's Row *EC1* **75** E11
Balaclava Rd. *SE1* **80** F6
Balcombe St. *NW1* **74** E2
Balderton St. *W1* **74** H4
Baldwin St. *EC1* **76** D2
Baldwin Ter. *N1* **75** B13
Baldwin's Gdns. *EC1* **75** F11
Baldwin's La. **65** A4
Balfe *N1* **75** C9
Balfour St. *SE17* **80** E2
Balgores La. **68** C3
Balham **70** B5
Balham High Rd. **70** C5
Balham Hill **70** B5
Balham Sta. **70** B5
Ballards La. **66** C5
Balls Pond Rd. **67** E7
Baltic Shipping Exchange *EC3* **76** G4
Baltic St. *EC1* **76** E1
Banbury Res. **67** C8
Bank End *SE1* **80** A2
Bank of England *EC2* **76** G3
Bankruptcy Court *WC2* **75** H10
Bankside *SE1* **79** A13
Banner St. *EC1* **76** E2
Banstead **70** G4
Banstead Downs **70** G4
Banstead Hospital **70** G4
Banstead Rd. **70** G3
Banstead Rd. Sth. **70** F5
Barbican Sta. *EC1* **75** F13
Barbican, The *EC2* **76** F1
Barford St. *N1* **75** B11
Barge House St. *SE1* **79** A11
Baring Rd. **71** C9
Baring St. *N1* **76** A2
Bark Pl. *W2* **73** J2
Barking **67** E11
Barking Pk. **67** E11
Barking Rd. **67** F10
Barking Sta. **67** E11
Barkingside **67** C11
Barkston Gdns. *SW5* **77** F2
Barlett Court *EC4* **75** G11
Barley La. **67** D12
Barlow St. *SE17* **80** F3
Barn End *Dartford* **72** C2
Barn Hill Pk. **66** D2
Barnby St. *NW1* **74** C6
Barnehurst **72** A1
Barnes **70** A3
Barnes Bri. **70** A3
Barnes Bri. Sta. **70** A3
Barnes Common **70** A3
Barnes Sta. **70** A3
Barnet **66** B4
Barnet Bypass **66** A3
Barnet Gate **66** A3
Barnet Gro. *E2* **76** D6
Barnet La. *Elstree* **66** A2
Barnet La. *Totteridge* **66** A4
Barnet Rd. **66** A3
Barnet Way **66** A3
Barnetwood La. **70** H1
Barnham St. *SE1* **80** C4
Barnsbury Rd. *N1* **75** B10
Barnwood Cl. *W9* **73** E2
Baroness Rd. *E2* **76** C5
Baron's Pl. *SE1* **79** C11
Barrett St. *W1* **74** H4
Barrow Hill Rd. *NW8* **73** C6
Barrowell Green **67** B7
Barter St. *WC1* **75** G9
Bartholomew Cl. *EC1* **75** F13
Bartholomew La. *EC2* **76** G3
Bartholomew Sq *EC1* **76** D2
Bartholomew St. *SE1* **80** E3
Basil St. *SW3* **78** D2
Basinghall Av. *EC2* **76** G2
Basinghall St. *EC2* **76** G2
Bastwick St. *EC1* **75** E13
Bat & Ball Sta. **72** H2
Batchelor St. *N1* **75** B11
Batchworth **65** B3
Batchworth Heath **65** B4
Batchworth Heath Hill **65** B4
Bateman St. *W1* **74** H7
Bateman's Row *EC2* **76** D4
Bath Ct. *EC1* **75** E11
Bath Rd. *Colnbrook* **65** H2
Bath Rd. *Cranford* **65** H5
Bath St. *EC1* **76** D2
Bath Ter. *SE1* **80** D1
Bathurst Gdns. *NW10* **66** F4
Bathurst Ms. *W2* **73** H5
Bathurst St. *W2* **73** H5
Battersea **70** A5
Battersea Bri. *SW3/SW11* **77** J5
Battersea Bri. Rd. *SW11* **70** A5
Battersea Pk. **70** A5
Battersea Pk. Rd. *SW8/SW11* **70** A5
Battersea Rise **70** B5
Battle Bri. La. *SE1* **80** B3
Battle Bri. Rd. *NW1* **75** C8
Battlebridge Basin *N1* **75** B9
Batty St. *E1* **76** G7
Baxendale St. *E2* **76** C6
Bayham St. *NW1* **74** B6
Bayhurst Wood **65** C3
Bayley St. *WC1* **74** F7
Baylis Rd. *SE1* **79** C11
Bayswater **66** F5
Bayswater Rd. *W2* **73** J4
Beaconsfield Rd. *SE17* **80** G3
Beacontree Heath **68** D1
Beak St. *W1* **74** H6
Bean **72** C4
Bean Rd. *Greenhithe* **72** B4
Bear Gdns. *SE1* **80** A1
Bear La. *SE1* **79** B12
Bear St. *WC2* **75** J8
Beatty St. *NW1* **74** B6
Beauchamp Pl. *SW3* **78** D2
Beauchamp St. *EC1* **75** F11
Beaufort Gdns. *SW3* **78** D2
Beaufort St. *SW3* **77** H5
Beaumont Ms. *W1* **74** F4
Beaumont St. *W1* **74** F4
Beckenham **71** D8
Beckenham Hill Rd. **71** C9
Beckenham Hill Sta. **71** C9
Beckenham Junc. Sta. **71** D8
Beckenham Pl. Pk. **71** C9
Beckenham Rd. **71** D8
Beckton **67** F11
Beckway St. *SE17* **80** F3
Becontree **68** D1
Becontree Av. **68** D1
Becontree Sta. **68** E1
Bedale St. *SE1* **80** B2
Beddington **70** F6
Beddington Cnr. **70** E5
Beddington La. **70** E6
Beddington La. Sta. **70** E5
Beddington Pk. **70** E5
Beddlestead La. **71** H9
Bedfont Rd. **69** B3
Bedfont Rd. *Feltham* **69** C4
Bedford Av. *WC1* **75** G7
Bedford College *NW1* **74** D3
Bedford Gdns. *W8* **77** B1
Bedford Hill **70** C5
Bedford Pl. *WC1* **75** F8
Bedford Row *WC1* **75** F10
Bedford Sq. *WC1* **75** F7
Bedford St. *WC2* **75** J8
Bedford Way *WC1* **75** E8
Bedfordbury *WC2* **75** J8
Bedford's Pk. **68** B3
Bedonwell Rd. **72** A1
Beech Farm Rd. **71** H9
Beech St. *EC2* **76** F1
Beechen Wood **72** F1
Beechenlea La. **72** D2
Beeston Pl. *SW1* **78** D5
Belgrave Ms. Nth. *SW1* **78** D3
Belgrave Ms. Sth. *SW1* **78** D4
Belgrave Ms. W. *SW1* **78** D3
Belgrave Pl. *SW1* **78** D4
Belgrave Rd. *SW1* **78** F6
Belgrave Sq. *SW1* **78** D3
Belgravia **66** G5
Belgrove St. *WC1* **75** C8
Belhus Pk. **68** F4
Bell La. *E1* **76** G5
Bell St. *NW1* **73** F6
Bell Wharf La. *EC4* **76** J2
Bell Yd. *WC2* **75** H11
Belle Grove Rd. **71** A11
Bellingham **71** C8
Bellingham Rd. **71** C9
Belmont **66** C1
Belmont Rise **70** F4
Belmont Sta. **70** F4
Belvedere **68** G2
Belvedere Rd. *SE1* **79** B10
Bemerton St. *N1* **75** A9
Benhill Av. **70** F4
Benhill Rd. **70** E5
Benjamin St. *EC1* **75** F12
Bennet Castle La. **68** E1
Bentinck St. *W1* **74** G4
Berkeley Ms. *W1* **74** G3
Berkeley Sq. *W1* **74** J5

Berkeley St. *W1* 78 A5
Bermondsey 67 G8
Bermondsey Leather Mkt. *SE1* 80 C3
Bermondsey St. *SE1* 80 C4
Bermondsey Wall E. *SE17* 80 C7
Bermondsey Wall W. *SE16* 80 C6
Bernard St. *WC1* 75 E8
Berners Ms. *W1* 74 G6
Berners Pl. *W1* 74 G6
Berners Rd. *N1* 75 B12
Berners St. *W1* 74 G6
Berry St. *EC1* 75 E12
Berryfield Rd. *SE17* 79 G13
Berrylands Sta. 70 D2
Berry's Green Rd. 71 H11
Berry's Hill 71 G11
Berwick Pond Rd. 68 E3
Berwick St. *W1* 74 H6
Bessborough Gdns. *SW1* 79 G8
Bessborough Pl. *SW1* 79 G7
Bessborough Res. 69 D5
Bessborough St. *SW1* 78 G7
Bethlehem Royal Hospital 71 E8
Bethnal Green 67 E8
Bethnal Green Rd. *E1/E2* 76 E5
Bethnal Green Sta. 67 F8
Bethwin Rd. *SE5* 80 J1
Betsham 72 C5
Betterton St. *WC2* 75 G9
Beulah Hill 71 C7
Bevan St. *N1* 76 B2
Bevenden St. *N1* 76 C3
Bevington St. *SE16* 80 D7
Bevis Marks *EC3* 76 G4
Bexley 72 B1
Bexley Hospital 72 C1
Bexley La. 71 C12
Bexley Rd. *Erith* 72 A1
Bexley Rd. *SE9* 71 B11
Bexley Sta. 72 B1
Bexleyheath 72 B1
Bianca Rd. *SE15* 80 H6
Bibury Cl. *SE15* 80 H4
Bickenhall St. *W1* 74 F3
Bickley 71 D10
Bidborough St. *WC1* 75 D8
Biddulph Rd. *W9* 73 D2
Biggin Hill 71 H10
Biggin Hill Airport 71 G10
Billet Rd. *Chadwell Heath* 68 C1
Billet Rd. *E17* 67 C8
Billing Pl. *SW10* 77 J3
Billing Rd. *SW10* 77 J3
Billing St. *SW10* 77 J3
Billiter St. *EC3* 76 H4
Bina Gdns. *SW5* 77 F3
Bind La. 68 C4
Bingham Pl. *W1* 74 F3
Bingham Rd. Sta. 71 E7
Binney St. *W1* 74 H4
Birches, The 72 F2
Birchin La. *EC3* 76 H3
Birchwood Rd. 72 C1
Bird St. *W1* 74 H4
Birdcage Wk. *SW1* 78 C7
Bird-in-Bush Rd. *SE15* 80 J6
Birdlip Cl. *SE15* 80 J4
Birkbeck Coll. *WC1* 74 E7
Birkbeck Sta. 71 D8
Birkenhead St. *WC1* 75 C9
Bishops Av., The 66 D5
Bishop's Bri. Rd. *W2* 73 G3
Bishop's Ter. *SE11* 79 E11
Bishopsford Rd. 70 E4
Bishopsgate *EC2* 76 G4
Bittams La. 69 E2
Black Horse La. 67 C8
Black Horse Rd. Sta. 67 C8
Black Lion Gate *W8* 73 J3
Black Pk. 65 E1
Black Prince Rd. *SE11* 79 F10
Blackall St. *EC2* 76 E3
Blackbird Hill 66 D3
Blackburnes Ms. *W1* 74 J3
Blackfen 71 B11
Blackfen Rd. 71 B11
Blackfriars Bri. *EC4/SE1* 75 H12
Blackfriars La. *EC4* 75 H12
Blackfriars Rd. *SE1* 79 C12
Blackfriars Sta. *EC4* 75 H12
Blackheath 71 A9
Blackheath Hill 67 H9
Blackheath Rd. 67 H9
Blacklands Ter. *SW3* 78 F2
Blackwall 67 F9
Blackwall Reach 67 G9
Blackwall Tunnel 67 G9
Blackwood St. *SE17* 80 G2
Blake Hall 67 D10
Blake's Rd. *SE15* 80 J4
Blandford Estate *NW1* 74 E1
Blandford Sq. *NW1* 74 E1
Blandford St. *W1* 74 G3
Blantyre St. *SW10* 77 J4
Blendon Rd. 71 B12
Blendon Row *SE17* 80 F2
Blenheim Rd. *NW8* 73 B4
Blenheim Ter. *NW8* 73 B3
Bletchley St. *N1* 76 C2
Blithfield St. *W8* 77 E2
Blomfield Rd. *W9* 73 F3
Blomfield St. *EC2* 76 G3
Blomfield Vs. *W2* 73 F3
Bloomfield Ter. *SW1* 78 F4
Bloomsbury 66 F6
Bloomsbury Sq. *WC1* 75 F9
Bloomsbury St. *WC1* 75 G8
Bloomsbury Way *WC1* 75 G8
Blossom St. *E1* 76 E4
Blundell La. 69 G6
Boadicea St. *N1* 75 B9
Board La. 69 C6
Bolingbroke Grove 70 B5
Bolsover St. *W1* 74 F5
Bolters La. 70 G4
Bolton Cres. *SE5* 79 H12
Bolton Gdns. *NW10* 77 F3
Bolton St. *W1* 78 B5
Boltons, The *SW10* 77 G3
Bondway *SW8* 79 H9
Bonhill St. *EC2* 76 E3
Bonnington Sq. *SW8* 79 H9
Boot St. *N1* 76 D3
Borders La. 67 A11
Borehamwood 66 A3
Borough Green 72 H5
Borough High St. *SE1* 80 C2
Borough Mkt. *SE1* 80 B2
Borough Rd. *SE1* 79 D12
Boscobel St. *NW8* 73 E5
Boss St. *SE1* 80 C5
Bostall Hill Rd. 67 G12
Bostall Woods 67 H12
Boston Manor Rd 66 G1
Boston Manor Sta. 66 G1
Boston Pl. *NW1* 74 E2
Boston Rd. 66 G1
Boswell Ct. *WC1* 75 F9
Boswell St. *WC1* 75 F9
Botleys 69 E1
Botley's Hosp. 69 E2
Botolph La. *EC3* 76 J3
Bounces Rd. 67 B8
Boundary La. *SE17* 80 H2
Boundary Rd. 71 G9
Boundary Row *SE1* 79 C12
Boundary St. *E2* 76 D5
Bounds Green Rd. 66 C6
Bourdon St. *W1* 74 J5
Bourne Hill 66 B6
Bourne St. *SW1* 78 F3
Bourne Ter. *W2* 73 F2
Bourne, The 66 B6
Bournebridge 68 A2
Bournebridge La. 68 A2
Bouverie St. *EC4* 75 H11
Bow 67 F9
Bow Bri. 67 F9
Bow Common 67 F9
Bow La. *EC4* 76 H2
Bow Rd. 67 F9
Bow St. *WC2* 75 H9
Bowden St. *SE11* 79 G11
Bowes Pk. Sta. 66 C6
Bowles Rd. *SE1* 80 H6
Bowling Green La. *EC1* 75 E11
Bowling Green St. *SE11* 79 H11
Bowling Green Wk. *N1* 76 D3
Boyd St. *E1* 76 H6
Boyfield St. *SE1* 79 C12
Brackley St. *EC1* 76 F1
Brad St. *SE1* 79 B11
Braden St. *W9* 73 E2
Braganza St. *SE17* 79 G12
Braham St. *E1* 76 G5
Braidwood St. *SE1* 80 B4
Bramble La. 68 E4
Bramerton St. *SW3* 77 H6
Bramham Gdns. *SW5* 77 F2
Bramley Rd. 66 A6
Brampton Rd. 71 A12
Branch Pl. *N1* 76 A3
Brand Drive 70 D3
Brandon Estate *SE17* 79 H12
Brandon St. *SE17* 80 F2
Brands Hatch 72 F4
Brands Hatch Motor Racing Circuit 72 F4
Brasted Hill 71 H12
Brasted La. 71 H12
Bray Pl. *SW3* 78 F2
Bread St. *EC4* 76 H1
Breakspear Rd. Nth. 65 C3
Breakspear Rd. Sth. 65 D3
Bream's Blds. *EC4* 75 G11
Brechin Pl. *SW7* 77 F4
Brecknock Rd. 66 E6
Bremner Rd. *SW7* 77 D4
Brendon St. *W1* 74 G1
Brent 66 D2
Brent Cross Sta. 66 D4
Brent Reservoir 66 D3
Brent St. 66 C4
Brentford 66 G2
Brentford Central Sta. 70 A1
Brentford F.C. 66 H2
Brentwood 68 B6
Brentwood Bypass 68 B5
Brentwood Rd. 68 D3
Brentwood Sta. 68 B5
Bressenden Pl. *SW1* 78 D5
Bretlands 69 E2
Brewer St. *W1* 74 H7
Brick La. *E1/E2* 76 E5
Brick St. *W1* 78 B4
Bride La. *EC4* 75 H12
Bride St. *SW1* 78 E5
Bridewell Pl. *EC4* 75 H12
Bridford Ms. *W1* 74 F5
Bridge Rd. *Chertsey* 69 E2
Bridge Rd. *Chessington* 70 F2
Bridge Rd. *East Molesey* 69 D6
Bridge St. *SW1* 79 C8
Bridgefoot *SE11* 79 G8
Bridgeman St. *NW8* 73 C6
Bridgewater Rd. 66 E2
Bridgewater Sq. *EC2* 75 F13
Bridgeway St. *NW1* 74 C7
Bridle La. *W1* 74 H6
Bridle Rd. 65 D5
Bridport Pl. *N1* 76 B3
Bridstow Pl. *W2* 73 G1
Brighton Rd. *Coulsdon* 70 H5
Brighton Rd. *Purley* 70 G6
Brighton Rd. *Sutton* 70 F4
Brigstock Rd. 70 D6
•Brimsdown Sta. 67 A8
Briset St. *EC1* 75 F12
Bristol Gdns. *W9* 73 F3
Bristol Ms. *W9* 73 E3
Britannia St. *WC1* 75 C9
Britannia Wk. *N1* 76 D2
British Medical Association *WC1* 75 D8
British Museum *WC1* 75 F8
Britten St. *SW3* 77 G6
Britton St. *EC1* 75 F12
Brixton 70 A6
Brixton Hill 70 B6
Brixton Prison 70 B6
Brixton Rd. *SW9* 79 H11
Brixton Sta. 70 B6
Broad La. *Dartford* 72 C2
Broad La. *N15* 67 C8
Broad Mead Rd. 67 C10
Broad Sanctuary *SW1* 79 D8
Broad Wk. The *W8* 77 C3
Broadcasting House *W1* 74 G5
Broadley St. *NW8* 73 F5
Broadley Ter. *NW1* 73 E6
Broadstone Pl. *W1* 74 F3
Broadwall *SE1* 79 B11
Broadway *Bexleyheath* 72 B1
Broadway *SW1* 78 D7
Broadway, The *Southall* 65 G5
Broadway, The *SW19* 70 C4
Broadwick St. *W1* 74 H6
Brockham St. *SE1* 80 D2
Brockley Hill 66 B2
Brockley Rise 71 B8
Brockley Rd. 71 B8
Brockley Sta. 71 A8
Brockwell Pk. 70 B6
Brockworth Cl. *SE15* 80 J4
Bromfield St. *N1* 75 B11
Bromley 71 D9
Bromley *E3* 67 F9
Bromley Common 71 E10
Bromley Hill 71 C9
Bromley Nth. Sta. 71 D9
Bromley Rd. *Beckenham* 71 D9
Bromley Rd. *Chislehurst* 71 D11
Bromley Rd. *SE6* 71 C9
Bromley Sth. Sta. 71 D9
Bromley-by-Bow 67 F9
Brompton 66 G5
Brompton Cemetery *SW10* 77 H2
Brompton Hospital *SW3* 77 F5
Brompton Pl. *SW3* 78 D2
Brompton Rd. *SW3* 77 E6
Brompton Sq. *SW3* 77 D6
Brondesbury 66 E4
Brondesbury Pk. 66 E4
Brondesbury Pk. Sta. 66 E4
Brondesbury Sta. 66 E4
Bronti Cl. *SE17* 80 G2
Brook Dri. *SE11* 79 E11
Brook Fever Hospital 71 A10
Brook Green *W6* 66 G4
Brook Ms. Nth. *W2* 73 H4
Brook St. *W1* 74 H4
Brook St. *W2* 73 H5
Brooke St. *EC1* 75 F11
Brooklands Rd. 69 F3
Brook's Ms. *W1* 74 H5
Brookshill 66 B1
Broom Rd. 70 C1
Broomfield Pk. 66 B6
Broomfield Wood 72 F4
Broomsleigh 72 H4
Brown Hart Gdns. *W1* 74 H4
Brown St. *W1* 74 G2
Brownhill Rd. 71 B9
Browning St. *SE17* 80 F2
Brownlow Ms. *WC1* 75 E10
Brownlow St. *WC1* 75 F10
Broxhill Rd. 68 B3
Broxwood Way *NW8* 74 B1
Bruce Castle Pk. 67 C7
Bruce Grove Sta. 67 C7
Brune St. *E1* 76 F5
Brunel Estate *W2* 73 F1
Brunel University 65 F3
Brunswick Centre *WC1* 75 E8
Brunswick Cl. Estate *EC1* 75 D12
Brunswick Ct. *SE1* 80 C4
Brunswick Gdns. *W8* 77 B2
Brunswick Pk. 66 B6
Brunswick Pl. *N1* 76 D3
Brunswick Sq. *WC1* 75 E9
Brushfield St. *E1* 76 F4
Bruton La. *W1* 74 J5
Bruton Pl. *W1* 74 J5
Bruton St. *W1* 74 J5
Bryanston Ms. E. *W1* 74 G2
Bryanston Ms. W. *W1* 74 G2
Bryanston Pl. *W1* 74 G2
Bryanston Sq. *W1* 74 G2
Bryanston St. *W1* 74 H2
Bryant Av. 68 C3
Buckfast St. *E2* 76 D6
Buckhurst Hill 67 B10
Buckhurst Rd. 71 H11
Buckingham Gate *SW1* 78 D6
Buckingham Palace *SW1* 78 C5
Buckingham Palace Gdns. *SW1* 78 C5
Buckingham Palace Rd. *SW1* 78 E5
Buckingham Pl. *SW1* 78 D6
Buckingham St. *WC2* 79 A9
Buckland St. *N1* 76 C3
Buckle St. *E1* 76 G6
Bucklersbury *EC4* 76 H2
Bucknall St. *WC2* 75 G8
Bug Hill 71 H8
Bugsby's Reach 67 G10
Bulinga St. *SW1* 79 F8
Bull La. 68 D2
Bulstrode St. *W1* 74 G4
Bunhill Fields *EC1* 76 E2
Bunhill Row *EC1* 76 E2
Bunker's Hill La. 72 F5
Burbage Cl. *SE1* 80 D2
Burdett St. *SE1* 79 D11
Burgh Heath 70 H4
Burgh Heath Rd. 70 G3
Burgh St. *N1* 75 B13
Burleigh St. *WC2* 75 H9
Burling La. 71 H11
Burlington Arcade *W1* 74 J6
Burlington Gdns. *W1* 74 J6
Burne St. *NW1* 73 F6
Burnsall St. *SW3* 77 G6
Burnt Ash La. 71 C9
Burnt Oak 66 C3
Burnt Oak Sta. 66 C3
Burntash Hill 71 B9
Burntash Rd. 71 B9
Burntwood La. *Caterham* 71 H7
Burntwood La. *SW17* 70 C5
Burrell St. *SE1* 79 B12
Burton Grove *SE17* 80 G3
Burton St. *WC1* 75 D8
Burtons Court *SW3* 78 G2
Burtons Rd. 69 C6
Burwood Pl. *W2* 73 G6
Burwood Rd. 69 F4
Bury Ct. *EC3* 76 G4
Bury Pl. *WC1* 75 G8
Bury St. *EC3* 76 G4
Bury St. *N9* 67 A7
Bury St. *Ruislip* 65 D4
Bury St. *SW1* 78 B6
Bury Wk. *SW3* 77 F6
Bury Wood 67 A10
Busby St. *E2* 76 E6
Bush Hill 67 A7
Bush La. *EC4* 76 H2
Bushey 65 A6
Bushey & Oxhey Sta. 65 A5
Bushey Heath 66 A1
Bushey Rd. 70 D3
Bushill Pk. 67 A7
Bushill Pk. Sta. 67 A7
Bushy Pk. 69 D6
Bute St. *SW7* 77 F5
Buttesland St. *N1* 76 D3
Button St. 72 D2
Butts La. 68 D3
Buxton La. 71 H7
Buxton St. *E1* 76 E6
Byfleet 69 G3
Byfleet & New Haw Sta. 69 F3
Byfleet Rd. *Byfleet* 69 F3
Byfleet Rd. *Cobham* 69 G4
Byng Pl. *WC1* 74 E7
Byward St. *EC3* 76 J4
Bywater St. *SW3* 78 F2
Cabbel St. *NW1* 73 G6
Cable St. *E1* 76 H6
Cackets La. 71 G11
Cadiz St. *SE17* 80 G2
Cadogan Gdns. *SW3* 78 E2
Cadogan Gate *SW1* 78 E3
Cadogan La. *SW1* 78 E3
Cadogan Pier *SW3* 78 H1
Cadogan Pl. *SW1* 78 E3
Cadogan Sq. *SW1* 78 E2
Cadogan St. *SW3* 78 F2
Cadogan Ter. 67 E9
Caesar St. *E2* 76 C4
Caesar's Camp 70 C3
Caldew St. *SE5* 80 J2
Caledonia St. *N1* 75 C9
Caledonian Rd. & Barnsbury Sta. 66 E6
Caledonian Rd. *N1* 75 B9
Callow St. *SW3* 77 H4
Calmington Rd. *SE5* 80 H4
Calshot St. *N1* 75 B9
Calthorpe St. *WC1* 75 E10
Calvert Av. *E2* 76 D4
Calvin St. *E1* 76 E5
Camberwell 71 A7
Camberwell New Rd. *SE5* 79 H11
Camberwell Rd. *SE5* 80 J2
Cambridge Circus *WC2* 75 H8
Cambridge Gate *NW1* 74 D5
Cambridge Heath Sta. 67 F8
Cambridge Pk. *E11* 67 D10
Cambridge Pk. *Twickenham* 70 B1
Cambridge Pl. *W8* 77 D3
Cambridge Rd. *Kingston* 70 D2
Cambridge Rd. *NW6* 73 C1
Cambridge Sq. *W2* 73 G6
Cambridge St. *SW1* 78 F5
Cambridge Ter. *NW1* 74 D5
Camden 66 E6
Camden High St. *NW1* 74 B5
Camden Rd. 66 E6
Camden St. *NW1* 74 A6
Camden Town 66 E6
Camera Pl. *SW10* 77 H4
Camlet St. *E2* 76 D5
Camley St. *NW1* 75 B7
Camomile St. *EC3* 76 G4
Campden Gro. *W8* 77 C1
Campden Hill *W8* 77 C1
Campden Hill Rd. *W8* 77 C1
Campden St. *W8* 77 B1
Camrose Av. 66 C2
Canada House *SW1* 79 A8
Canal St. *SE5* 80 H3
Cane Hill Hospital 70 H5
Cann Hall 67 D10
Canning Pl. *W8* 77 D3
Canning Town 67 F10
Canning Town Sta. 67 F9
Cannon Row *SW1* 79 C8
Cannon St. *SW1* 76 H2
Cannon St. Sta. *EC4* 76 J2
Canon St. *N1* 76 A1
Canonbury 67 E7
Canonbury Sta. 67 E7
Canons Pk. 66 B2
Canon's Pk. Sta. 66 C2
Canterbury Way *SE17* 79 F12
Capel Rd. 67 E10
Capland St. *NW8* 73 E5
Capper St. *WC1* 74 E6
Carburton St. *W1* 74 F5
Cardigan St. *SE11* 79 G11
Cardington St. *NW1* 74 D6
Carey La. *EC2* 76 G1
Carey St. *WC2* 75 G10
Carlisle Av. *EC3* 76 H4
Carlisle La. *SE1* 79 D10
Carlisle Pl. *SW1* 78 E6
Carlisle St. *W1* 74 G7
Carlos Pl. *W1* 74 J4
Carlton Av. E. 66 D2
Carlton Gdns. *SW1* 78 B7
Carlton Hill *NW8* 73 B3
Carlton House Ter. *SW1* 78 B7
Carlton House Ter. *SW1* 79 B7
Carlton Vale *NW6* 73 C1
Carlyle Sq. *SW3* 77 G5
Carlyle's House *SW3* 77 H6
Carmelite St. *EC4* 75 H11
Carnaby St. *W1* 74 H6
Carnegie St. *N1* 75 B10
Caroline Pl. *W2* 73 J2
Caroline Ter. *SW1* 78 F3
Carpenders Pk. 65 B5
Carpenders Pk. Sta. 65 B5
Carpenters Rd. 67 E9
Carriage Drive E. *SW11* 78 J4
Carriage Drive Nth. *SW1* 78 H4
Carroun Rd. *SW8* 79 H10
Carshalton 70 E5
Carshalton Beeches Sta. 70 F5
Carshalton Ho. 70 F5

*Brill Pl. *NW1* 75 C7

Carshalton on the Hill 70 F5
Carshalton Rd. *Sutton* 70 F5
Carshalton Rd. *Woodmansterne* 70 G5
Carter La. *EC4* 75 H13
Carter Pl. *SE17* 80 G1
Carter St. *SE17* 79 G13
Carteret St. *SW1* 78 D7
Carthusian St. *EC1* 75 F13
Carting La. *WC2* 75 J9
Cartwright Gdns. *WC1* 75 D8
Cartwright St. *E1* 76 J6
Cassiobury Pk. 65 A4
Casson St. *E1* 76 F6
Castellain Rd. *W9* 73 E3
Castelnau *SW13* 70 A3
Castle Bar Pk. Sta. 66 F1
Castle Baynard St. *EC4* 75 H13
Cat Hill 66 A5
Catesby St. *SE17* 80 F3
Catford 71 B9
Catford Bri. 71 B8
Catford Hill 71 B8
Catford Sta. 71 B8
Cathcart Rd. *SW10* 77 H3
Catherine Pl. *SW1* 78 D6
Catherine St. *WC2* 75 H9
Cato St. *W1* 74 G1
Cator St. *SE15* 80 J5
Catos Hill 69 E6
Catton St. *WC1* 75 G9
Causton St. *SW1* 79 F7
Cavaye Pl. *SW10* 77 G4
Cavendish Av. *NW8* 73 C5
Cavendish Cl. *NW8* 73 C5
Cavendish Hotel *SW1* 78 B6
Cavendish Pl. *W1* 74 G5
Cavendish Rd. *NW6* 66 E4
Cavendish Rd. *SW12* 70 B5
Cavendish Sq. *W1* 74 G5
Cavendish St. *N1* 76 C2
Caversham St. *SW3* 78 H2
Caxton Hall *SW1* 78 D7
Caxton St. *SW1* 78 D7
Cayton St. *EC1* 76 D2
Cenotaph *SW1* 79 C8
Centaur St. *SE1* 79 D10
Central Criminal Court *EC4* 75 G12
Central Hill 71 C7
Central Pk. 68 D2
Central Rd. 70 D4
Central St. *EC1* 75 D13
Chadwell Heath 68 D1
Chadwell Heath La. 68 D1
Chadwell St. *EC1* 75 C11
Chadwick St. *SW1* 78 E7
Chagford St. *NW1* 74 E2
Chalfont Common 65 B1
Chalfont Pk. 65 C1
Chalfont St. Peter 65 C1
Chalk Farm Rd. 66 E6
Chalk La. 70 G3
Chalky Hill 71 G11
Chalton St. *NW1* 74 C7
Chamber St. *E1* 76 H6
Chambers St. *SE16* 80 C6
Chambord St. *E2* 76 D5
Chancel St. *SE1* 79 B12
Chancery La. *WC2* 75 G10
Chandos Pl. *WC2* 75 J8
Chandos St. *W1* 74 G5
Chantry St. *N1* 75 B13
Chapel Ct. *SE1* 80 C2
Chapel End 67 C9
Chapel Mkt. *N1* 75 B11
Chapel Side *W2* 73 J2
Chapel St. *NW1* 73 F6
Chapel St. *SW1* 78 D4
Chapter Rd. *SE17* 79 G13
Chapter St. *SW1* 78 F7
Charing Cross Hospital *SW6* 66 H4
Charing Cross Pier *WC2* 79 B9
Charing Cross Rd. *WC2* 75 H8
Charing Cross Sta. *WC2* 79 A9
Charlbert St. *NW8* 73 B6
Charles II St. *SW1* 78 A7
Charles La. *NW8* 73 B6
Charles Sq. *N1* 76 D3
Charles St. *W1* 78 B4
Charleston St. *SE17* 80 F2
Charlotte Ms. *W1* 74 F6
Charlotte Rd. *EC2* 76 D4
Charlotte St. *W1* 74 F6
Charlotte Ter. *N1* 75 B10
Charlton 67 G10
Charlton F.C. 67 G10
Charlton La. 69 D4
Charlton Pk. 67 H10
Charlton Pl. *N1* 75 B12
Charlton Rd. *SE7* 67 H10
Charlton Rd. *Shepperton* 69 D4
Charlton Way 67 H9
Charlwood Pl. *SW1* 78 F6
Charlwood St. *SW1* 78 G6
Charmwood La. 71 F12
Charrington St. *NW1* 74 B7
Chart St. *N1* 76 D3
Charterhouse Sq. *EC1* 75 F13
Charterhouse St. *EC1* 75 F12
Chase Rd. 66 A6
Chase Side 66 A6
Chatham St. *SE17* 80 E3
Cheam 70 F4
Cheam Rd. 70 F3
Cheam Sta. 70 F4
Cheapside *EC2* 76 H2
Chelsea Barracks *SW1* 78 G4
Chelsea Bri. *SW3/SW8* 78 H4
Chelsea Bri. Rd. *SW1* 78 G4
Chelsea College of Science & Technology *SW3* 77 G5
Chelsea Emb. *SW3* 78 H2
Chelsea Manor Gdns. *SW3* 77 G6
Chelsea Manor St. *SW3* 77 G6
Chelsea Pk. Gdns. *SW3* 77 H5
Chelsea Physic Gdns. *SW3* 78 H2
Chelsea Reach 78 H3
Chelsea Sq. *SW3* 77 G5
Chelsfield Hill 71 F12
Chelsfield La. *Badger's Mount* 72 F1
Chelsfield La. *Orpington* 71 E12
Chelsfield Rd. 71 E12
Chelsfield Sta. 71 F12
Chelsfield Village 71 F12
Chelsham 71 H8
Chelsham Ct. Rd. 71 H9
Chelsham Rd. 71 H8
Cheltenham Ter. *SW3* 78 F2
Cheney Rd. *NW1* 75 C8
Chenies Ms. *WC1* 74 E7
Chenies St. *WC1* 74 F7
Cheniston Gdns. *W8* 77 D2
Chepstow Cres. *W11* 73 H1
Chepstow Pl. *W2* 73 H1
Chepstow Rd. *W2* 73 G1
Chepstow Vs. *W11* 73 H1
Chequer St. *EC1* 76 E2
Chequers Rd. 68 B3
Cherbury St. *N1* 76 C3
Chertsey 69 E2
Chertsey Bri. 69 E3
Chertsey La. 69 D2
Chertsey Rd. *Byfleet* 69 G3
Chertsey Rd. *Feltham* 69 C4
Chertsey Rd. *Shepperton* 69 E3
Chesham Ms. *SW1* 78 D3
Chesham Pl. *SW1* 78 D3
Chesham St. *SW1* 78 E3
Cheshire St. *E2* 76 E6
Chessington 70 F2
Chessington Nth. Sta. 70 F2
Chessington Rd. 70 F2
Chessington Sth. Sta. 70 F2
Chessington World of Adventures 70 F1
Chester Cl. *NW1* 74 D5
Chester Cl. *SW1* 78 D4
Chester Gate *NW1* 74 D5
Chester Ms. *SW1* 78 D4
Chester Pl. *NW1* 74 C5
Chester Rd. *NW1* 74 D4
Chester Row *SW1* 78 F3
Chester Sq. *SW1* 78 E4
Chester St. *SW1* 78 D4
Chester Ter. *NW1* 74 D5
Chester Way *SE11* 79 F11
Chesterfield Gdns. *W1* 78 B4
Chesterfield Hill *W1* 78 A4
Chesterfield St. *W1* 78 B4
Cheval Pl. *SW7* 77 D6
Chevening Pk. 71 H12
Cheyne Gdns. *SW3* 77 H6
Cheyne Hospital *SW3* 77 H6
Cheyne Row *SW3* 77 H6
Cheyne Wk. *SW10/SW3* 77 H6
Chicheley St. *SE1* 79 C10
Chichester Rd. *NW6* 73 F3
Chichester St. *SW1* 78 G6
Chicksand St. *E1* 76 F6
Chigwell 67 B11
Chigwell La. 67 A11
Chigwell Rise 67 B11
Chigwell Rd. 67 C10
Chigwell Row 67 B12
Childerditch La. 68 D6
Child's Pl. *SW5* 77 F2
Child's St. *SW5* 77 F2
Chiltern Rd. 70 F4
Chiltern St. *W1* 74 F3
Chilton St. *E2* 76 E6
Chilworth Ms. *W2* 73 H4
Chilworth St. *W2* 73 H4
Chingford 67 B9
Chingford Hatch 67 B9
Chingford La. 67 B10
Chingford Mount Rd. 67 B9
Chingford Rd. 67 C9
Chippenham Ms. *W9* 73 E1
Chippenham Rd. *W9* 73 E1
Chipstead 70 H5
Chipstead Valley Rd. 70 H5
Chislehurst 71 D11
Chislehurst Common 71 C11
Chislehurst Rd. *Bromley* 71 D10
Chislehurst Rd. *Orpington* 71 E11
Chislehurst Sta. 71 D10
Chislehurst W. 71 C10
Chiswell St. *EC1* 76 F2
Chiswick 66 G3
Chiswick Bri. 70 A2
Chiswick High Rd. 66 G3
Chiswick House 70 A3
Chiswick Pk. Sta. 66 G3
Chiswick Sta. 70 A2
Chiswick Steps 66 H3
Chitty St. *W1* 74 F6
Chorleywood Rd. 65 A3
Christchurch Av. 66 C1
Christchurch Rd. 70 B6
Christchurch St. *SW3* 78 G2
Christian St. *E1* 76 H7
Christina St. *EC2* 76 E4
Christopher St. *EC2* 76 F3
Chumleigh St. *SE5* 80 H4
Church Elm La. 68 E2
Church End 66 C4
Church Hill *Dartford* 72 C2
Church Hill *Loughton* 67 A11
Church Hill *Pyrford* 69 H2
Church Hill Rd. 66 A5
Church House *SW1* 79 D8
Church La. 71 H9
Church Rd. *Addlestone* 69 F2
Church Rd. *Ashford* 69 C3
Church Rd. *Byfleet* 69 G3
Church Rd. *Chelsfield* 71 F12
Church Rd. *Noak Hill* 68 A3
Church Rd. *Northolt* 65 E5
Church Rd. *SE19* 71 D7
Church Rd. *SE5* 80 J3
Church Rd. *Sutton-at-Hone* 72 C3
Church Rd. *SW19* 70 C4
Church Rd. *Teddington* 70 C1
Church St. *Edmonton* 67 B7
Church St. *Enfield* 67 A7
Church St. *Epsom* 70 G3
Church St. *NW8* 73 F5
Church St. *Walton* 69 E4
Churchill Gdns. Est. *SW1* 78 G6
Churchill Gdns. Rd. *SW1* 78 G5
Churchill Hotel *W1* 74 G3
Churchway *NW1* 75 D7
Churchyard Row *SE11* 79 E12
Churton St. *SW1* 78 F6
Circus Rd. *NW8* 73 C5
Cirencester St. *W2* 73 F2
City Garden Row *N1* 75 C13
City Rd. *EC1* 75 C12
City Rd. *EC1* 76 D2
City Rd. Basin *N1* 76 C1
City University *EC1* 75 D12
Clabon Ms. *SW1* 78 E2
Clanricarde Gdns. *W2* 73 J2
Clapham 70 A6
Clapham Common 70 B5
Clapham Common Nth. Side 70 B5
Clapham Common Sth. Side 70 B5
Clapham Junc. Sta. 66 H5
Clapham Pk. Rd. 70 B6
Clapham Rd. *SW9* 70 A6
Clapham Sta. 70 A6
Clapton Common 67 D8
Clapton Sta. 67 D8
Claremont Cl. *N1* 75 C11
Claremont Sq. *N1* 75 C11
Clarence Gdns. *NW1* 74 D5
Clarence Gate *NW1* 74 E3
Clarence House *SW1* 78 C6
Clarendon Gdns. *W9* 73 E4
Clarendon Gate *W2* 73 H6
Clarendon Grove *NW1* 74 C7
Clarendon Pl. *W2* 73 H6
Clarendon St. *SW1* 78 G5
Clareville Gro. *SW7* 77 F4
Clareville Ms. *SW7* 77 F4
Clareville St. *SW7* 77 F4
Clarges Ms. *W1* 78 B5
Clarges St. *W1* 78 B5
Claridge's Hotel *W1* 74 H4
Claverton St. *SW1* 78 G6
Clay St. *W1* 74 F3
Claybury Hosp. 67 C11
Claygate 70 F1
Clayhall 67 C11
Clayhall Av. 67 C11
Clayhall Pk. 67 C11
Claylands Pl. *SW8* 79 H10
Claylands Rd. *SW8* 79 H10
Clayton Rd. 70 F1
Clayton St. *SE11* 79 H11
Clearwell Dr *W9* 73 E2
Cleaver Sq. *SE11* 79 G11
Cleaver St. *SE11* 79 G11
Clement St. 72 C2
Clement's La. *EC4* 76 H3
Cleopatra's Needle *WC2* 79 A9
Clere Pl. *EC2* 76 E3
Clere St. *EC2* 76 E3
Clerkenwell Cl. *EC1* 75 E11
Clerkenwell Green *EC1* 75 E12
Clerkenwell Rd. *EC1* 75 E11
Cleveland Gdns. *W2* 73 H3
Cleveland Row *SW1* 78 B6
Cleveland Sq. *W2* 73 H3
Cleveland St. *W1* 74 F6
Cleveland Ter. *W2* 73 G4
Clifford Inn *EC4* 75 G11
Clifford St. *W1* 74 J5
Clifton Gdns. *W9* 73 E3
Clifton Hill *NW8* 73 B3
Clifton Pl. *W2* 73 H5
Clifton Rd. *W9* 73 E4
Clifton St. *EC2* 76 F3
Clifton Vs. *W9* 73 F3
Clink St. *SE1* 80 A2
Clipstone Ms. *W1* 74 F6
Clipstone St. *W1* 74 F5
Clissold Pk. 67 D7
Cliveden Pl. *SW1* 78 E3
Cloak La. *EC4* 76 H2
Clock House Sta. 71 D8
Clockhouse La. 69 C3
Cloth Fair *EC1* 75 F13
Cloudesley Pl. *N1* 75 B11
Cloudesley Rd. *N1* 75 B11
Cloudesley Sq. *N1* 75 A11
Cloudesley St. *N1* 75 B11
Club Row *E2* 76 D5
Cluny Pl. *SE1* 80 D4
Coalbrookdale Gt. *SW7* 77 C5
Coate St. *E2* 76 C7
Cobb St. *E1* 76 G5
Cobham 69 G5
Cobham & Stoke D'Abernon Sta. 69 H5
Cobham Pk. 69 H5
Cobham Rd. 69 H6
Cobourg Rd. *SE5* 80 H5
Cobourg St. *NW1* 74 D6
Cochrane St. *NW8* 73 C5
Cock Hill *E1* 76 G4
Cock La. *EC1* 75 G12
Cockfosters 66 A5
Cockfosters Sta. 66 A6
Cockspur St. *SW1* 79 B8
Code St. *E1* 76 E6
Coin St. *SE1* 79 B11
Coke St. *E1* 76 G6
Colbeck Ms. *SW7* 77 F3
Colchester Rd. 68 C3
Coldblow Maypole 72 B1
Coldharbour La. *Hayes* 65 G5
Coldharbour La. *SW9/SE5* 70 B6
Cole Pk. 70 B1
Cole St. *SE1* 80 D2
Colebrooke Row *N1* 75 B12
Colegrove Rd. *SE15* 80 J6
Coleherne Ms. *SW10* 77 G2
Coleherne Rd. *SW10* 77 G2
Coleman Rd. *SE5* 80 J4
Coleman St. *EC2* 76 G2
Coley St. *WC1* 75 E10
Colham Green 65 F4
Colin Deep La. 66 C3
Colindale 66 C3
Colindale Av. 66 C3
Colindale Sta. 66 C3
Coliseum Theatre *WC2* 75 J8
College Hill *EC4* 76 H2
College of Arms *EC4* 75 H13
College Pl. *NW1* 74 A6
College Rd. *Bromley* 71 D9
College Rd. *Epsom* 70 G3
College Rd. *Hextable* 72 D1
College Rd. *SE21* 71 B7
College St. *EC4* 76 H2
Collier Row 68 C2
Collier Row La. 68 C2
Collier Row Rd. 68 C2
Collier St. *N1* 75 C9
Collier's Wood 70 C5
Collingham Gdns. *SW5* 77 F3
Collingham Pl. *SW5* 77 F2
Collingham Rd. *SW5* 77 F3
Collinson St. *SE1* 79 C13
Colnbrook 65 H2
Colnbrook Bypass 65 H2
Colnbrook St. *SE1* 79 D12
Colney Butts 65 A5
Colney Hatch 66 B5
Colney Hatch La. 66 C6
Colombo St. *SE1* 79 B12
Colonnade *WC1* 75 E8
Columbia Rd. *E2* 76 D5
Colville Pl. *W1* 74 F7
Colwyn Gro. *SE17* 80 F2
Colyers La. 72 A1
Commercial Rd. *E1* 76 G6
Commercial St. *E1* 76 F5
Commercial Way 67 H8
Common La. *Dartford* 72 C2
Common Rd. 66 B1
Commonside E. 70 D5
Commonside W. 70 D5
Compton St. *EC1* 75 E12
Concert Hall Approach *SE1* 79 B10
Conduit Ms. *W2* 73 H4
Conduit Pl. *W2* 73 H5
Conduit St. *W1* 74 H5
Congreve St. *SE17* 80 F4
Connaught Pl. *W2* 74 H2
Connaught Sq. *W2* 74 H2
Connaught St. *W2* 73 H6
Cons St. *SE1* 79 C11
Constitution Hill *SW1* 78 C5
Content St. *SE17* 80 F2
*Coleherne Ct. *SW5* 77 G3
Convent Rd. 69 C4
Conway St. *W1* 74 E6
Cooks Rd. *SE17* 79 H12
Coombe La. 70 D3
Coombe Rd. *Kingston* 70 D2
Coombe Rd. *New Malden* 70 D3
Coomb's St. *N1* 75 C13
Coopers La. *NW1* 75 C8
Cooper's Rd. *SE1* 80 G5
Cooper's Wood 72 G4
Cope Pl. *W8* 77 D1
Copenhagen St. *N1* 75 A9
Copperfield St. *SE1* 79 C13
Copse Hill 70 D3
Copse Wood 65 C4
Copsem La. 69 F6
Copthall Av. *EC2* 76 G3
Copthall Ct. *EC2* 76 G3
Coptic St. *WC1* 75 G8
Coral St. *SE1* 79 C11
Coram St. *WC1* 75 E8
Coram's Field Playground *WC1* 75 E9
Corbet Pl. *E1* 76 F5
Corbets Tey 68 E4
Corbets Tey Rd. 68 E4
Cork St. *W1* 74 J6
Corn Exchange *EC3* 76 H4
Cornhill *EC3* 76 H3
Cornwall Gdns. *SW7* 77 E3
Cornwall Rd. *SE1* 79 B11
Coronet St. *N1* 76 D3
Corporation Row *EC1* 75 E11
Corsham St. *N1* 76 D3
Cosser St. *SE1* 79 D10
Cosway St. *NW1* 73 F6
Cotham St. *SE17* 80 F2
Cottage Pl. *SW3* 77 D6
Cottage Wk. *SW1* 78 D3
Cottenham Pk. 70 D3
Cottenham Pk. Rd. 70 D3
Cottesmore Gdns. *W8* 77 D3
Cottington St. *SE11* 79 F12
Coulsdon 70 H6
Coulsdon La. 70 H5
Coulsdon Rd. 70 H6
Coulsdon South Sta. 70 H6
Coulson St. *SW3* 78 F2
County Hall *SE1* 79 C9
County St. *SE1* 80 E2
Court La. 71 B7
Courtenay St. *SE11* 79 G10
Courtfield Gdns. *SW5* 77 F2
Courtfield Rd. *SW7* 77 F3
Covent Garden *WC2* 75 H9
Covent Garden Mkt. *SW8* 79 H8
Coventry St. *W1* 74 J7
Cowan St. *SE5* 80 H4
Cowcross St. *EC1* 75 F12
Cowley 65 F3
Cowley St. *SW1* 79 D8
Cowper St. *EC2* 76 D3
Craddocks Av. 70 H2
Crail Row *SE17* 80 F3
Cramer St. *W1* 74 F4
Crampton St. *SE17* 79 F13
Cranbourn St. *WC2* 75 H8
Cranbrook Rd. 67 C11
Cranbrook Rd. 67 D10
Cranford 65 H4
Cranford La. 65 H5
Cranham 68 D5
Cranleigh St. *NW1* 74 C6
Cranley Gdns. *SW7* 77 G4
Cranley Ms. *SW7* 77 F4
Cranley Pl. *SW7* 77 F5
Cranwood St. *EC1* 76 D3
Craven Gdns. *W2* 73 H4
Craven Hill *W2* 73 H4
Craven Hill Gdns. *W2* 73 H3
Craven St. *WC2* 79 B8
Craven Ter. *W2* 73 H4
Crawford Pl. *W1* 74 G1
Crawford St. *W1* 74 F2
Crayford 72 A2
Crayford Rd. 72 B2
Creechurch La. *EC3* 76 H4
Creed La. *EC4* 75 H12
Creekmouth 67 F12
Cremer St. *E2* 76 C5
Crescent Pl. *SW3* 77 E6
Crescent Row *EC1* 75 E13
Cresswell Gdns. *SW5* 77 F3

Cresswell Pl. SW10 77 G4
Crestfield St. WC1 75 C9
Cricklewood 66 E4
Cricklewood La. 66 D4
Cricklewood Sta. 66 E4
Crimscott St. SE1 80 E4
Crinan St. N1 75 B9
Cringle St. SW8 78 J6
Cripplegate Institute EC1 76 F1
Criterion Theatre W1 74 J7
Crockenhill 72 E1
Crofton Heath 71 E10
Crofton Pk. Sta. 71 B8
Crofton Rd. 71 E11
Croham Rd. 71 F7
Cromer St. WC1 75 D9
Crompton St. W2 73 E4
Cromwell Cres. SW5 77 F1
Cromwell Gdns. SW7 77 E5
Cromwell Ms. SW7 77 E5
Cromwell Pl. SW7 77 E5
Cromwell Rd. Hounslow 69 B6
Cromwell Rd. SW5/SW7 77 E3
Crondall St. N1 76 C3
Cropley St. N1 76 B2
Crosby Row SE1 80 C3
Crosby Sq. EC3 76 G4
Cross Keys Cl. W1 74 G4
Cross La. 68 D3
Crossdeep 70 C1
Crosswall EC3 76 H5
Crouch End 66 D6
Crouch Hill 66 D6
Crouch Hill Sta. 66 D6
Crow La. 68 D2
Crown Dale 70 C6
Crown La. 70 C6
Crown Office Row EC4 75 H11
Crowndale Rd. NW1 74 B6
Croxley Green 65 A4
Croxley Green Sta. 65 A4
Croxley Sta. 65 A4
Croxted Rd. 71 B7
Croydon 71 E7
Croydon La. 70 G5
Croydon Rd. Beckenham 71 D8
Croydon Rd. Beddington 70 E6
Croydon Rd. Chelsham 71 H9
Croydon Rd. Keston 71 E10
Croydon Rd. Mitcham 70 D5
Croydon Rd. SE20 71 D7
Crucifix La. SE1 80 C4
Cruden St. N1 75 B12
Cruikshank St. WC1 75 C10
Crutched Friars EC3 76 H4
Crystal Palace F.C. 71 D7
Crystal Palace Pk. 71 C7
Crystal Palace Sta. 71 C7
Cubitt St. WC1 75 D10
Cudham 71 G11
Cudham La. Cudham 71 G11
Cudham La. Green Street Green 71 F11
Cudham La. Horns Green 71 H11
Cudham Rd. 71 G11
Culford Gdns. SW3 78 F2
Culham St. EC3 76 H4
Culross St. W1 74 J3
Culverstone Green 72 F6
Culworth St. NW8 73 C6
Cumberland Gate W1 74 H2
Cumberland Hotel W1 74 H3
Cumberland Mkt. NW1 74 D5
Cumberland St. SW1 78 G5
Cumberland Ter. NW1 74 C5
Cumming Mus. SE17 80 F1
Cumming St. N1 75 C10
Cundy St. SW1 78 F4
Cunningham Pl. NW8 73 E5
Cureton St. SW1 79 F8
Curlew St. SE1 80 C5
Cursitor St. EC4 75 G11
Curtain Rd. EC2 76 E4
Curtis St. SE1 80 E5
Curtis Way SE1 80 E5
Curzon Gate W1 78 B4
Curzon St. W1 78 B4
Custom House EC3 76 J4
Custom House Sta. 67 F10
Cut, The SE1 79 C11
Cuthbert St. W2 73 F5
Cutler St. E1 76 G4
Cynthia St. N1 75 C10
Cypress Pl. W1 74 F6
Cyrus St. EC1 75 D12
Dacre St. SW1 78 D7
Dagenham 68 E2
Dagenham Av. 68 E1
Dagenham Dock Sta. 68 F1
Dagenham Heathway Sta. 68 E1
Dagenham Rd. 68 D2
Dagnam Pk. 68 B4
Dallington St. EC1 75 E12
Dalston 67 E7
Dalston La. 67 E8
Daltons Rd. 72 E1
Dame St. N1 75 B13
Danbury St. N1 75 B12
Dane St. WC1 75 F9
Daniel Gdns. SE15 80 J4
Danson Pk. 71 B12
Danson Rd. Bexley Heath 71 B12
Dante Rd. SE11 79 F12
Danvers St. SW3 77 H5
D'Arblay St. W1 74 H6
Darenth 72 C3
Darenth Rd. 72 B3
Dartford 72 B2
Dartford Heath 72 B2
Dartford Rd. Dartford 72 B2
Dartford Rd. Hextable 72 C2
Dartford-Purfleet Tunnel 72 A3
Dartmouth Pk. Hill 66 D6
Dartmouth Rd. 71 C8
Dartmouth St. SW1 78 D7
Darwin St. SE17 80 F3
Datchet 65 H1
Date St. SE17 80 G2
Davenant St. E1 76 F6
Daventry St. NW1 73 F6
Davey St. SE15 80 H5
Davidson Rd. 71 E7
Davies Ms. W1 74 H4
Davies St. W1 74 H4
Dawes Rd. SW6 66 H4
Dawes St. SE17 80 F3
Dawley Rd. 65 G4
Daws Hill 67 A9
Dawson Pl. W2 73 H1
Days La. 71 B11
De Laune St. SE17 79 G12
De Vere Gdns. W8 77 D3
De Walden St. W1 74 F4
Deacon Way SE17 80 E1
Deal St. E1 76 F6
Dean Bradley St. SW1 79 E8
Dean Farrar St. SW1 78 D7
Dean Ryle St. SW1 79 E8
Dean Stanley St. SW1 79 E8
Dean St. W1 74 H7
Deanery St.W1 78 B4
Dean's Buildings SE17 80 F3
Dean's Court EC4 75 H13
Dean's La. 66 B3
Dean's Yd. SW1 79 D8
Deansbrook Rd. 66 B3
Debden Sta. 67 A11
Decima St. SE1 80 D4
Deer Pk. 70 D4
Defence, Ministry of SW1 79 B8
Delaford Pk. 65 F2
Delamere Ter. W2 73 F3
Delancey St. NW1 74 B5
Delaware Rd. W9 73 E2
Delhi St. N1 75 A9
Denbigh Pl. SW11 78 F6
Denbigh St. SW1 78 F6
Denham 65 D2
Denham Areodrome 65 C2
Denman St. W1 74 J7
Denmark Gro. N1 75 B11
Denmark Hill 71 B7
Denmark Hill Sta. 71 A7
Denmark St. WC2 75 G8
Denning Av. 70 F6
Dennises La. 68 E4
Denny Cres. SE11 79 F11
Denny St. SE11 79 F11
Denyer St. SW3 78 F2
Deptford 67 H8
Deptford Sta. 67 H9
Derbyshire St. E2 76 D7
Dereham Pl. EC2 76 D4
Dering St. W1 74 H5
Derry Downs 71 E12
Derry St. W8 77 D2
Deverell St. SE1 80 E2
Devonia Rd. N1 75 B12
Devons Rd. 67 F9
Devonshire Cl. W1 74 F5
Devonshire Ms. Sth. W1 74 F4
Devonshire Ms. W. W1 74 F4
Devonshire Pl. W1 74 F4
Devonshire Pl. Ms. W1 74 F4
Devonshire Row EC2 76 G4
Devonshire Sq. EC2 76 G4
Devonshire St. W1 74 F4
Devonshire Ter. W2 73 H4
Dewey Rd. N1 75 B11
Dial Wk., The W8 77 C3
Diana Pl. NW1 74 E5
Dickens Sq. SE1 80 D2
Dignum St. N1 75 B11
Dilke St. SW3 78 H2
Dingley Pl. EC1 76 D2
Dingley Rd. EC1 76 D1
Diss St. E2 76 C5
Distaff La. EC4 76 H1
Ditton Hill 70 E1
Ditton Pk. 65 G1
Ditton Rd. 70 E2
Dock St. E1 76 J6
Dockhead SE1 80 C6
Dockley Rd. SE16 80 D6
Doddington Gro. SE17 79 G12
Dolben St. SE1 79 B12
Dolland St. SE11 79 G10
Dollis Hill La. 66 D4
Dollis Hill Sta. 66 E3
Dolphin Sq. SW1 78 G7
Dombey St. WC1 75 F9
Dominion St. EC2 76 F3
Domville Grove SE15 80 G5
Donegal St. N1 75 C10
Donne Pl. SW3 78 E1
Doon St. SE1 79 B10
Dorchester Hotel W1 78 B4
Doric Way NW1 74 D7
Dorking Rd. 70 G2
Dorrington St. EC1 75 F11
Dorset Cl. NW1 74 F2
Dorset Est. E2 76 C5
Dorset Ms. SW1 78 D4
Dorset Rise EC4 75 H12
Dorset Rd. SW19 70 D4
Dorset Rd. SW8 79 J9
Dorset Sq. NW1 74 E2
Dorset St. W1 74 F3
Doughty Ms. WC1 75 E10
Doughty St. WC1 75 E10
Douglas St. SW1 78 F7
Douro Pl. W8 77 D3
Dove Ms. SW5 77 F4
Dove Row E2 76 B6
Dovehouse St. SW3 77 G5
Dover House Rd. 70 B3
Dover St. W1 78 A5
Dowgate Hill EC4 76 H2
Down St. W1 78 B4
Downe 71 G10
Downham Estate 71 C9
Downham Way 71 C9
Downing St. SW1 79 C8
Downs Rd. Epsom 70 G3
Downs Rd. Gravesend 72 C6
Downs Rd. Sutton 70 G4
Downs Wood 72 G6
Downside 69 H5
Downside Rd. 69 H5
Doyley St. SW1 78 E3
Draco St. SE17 79 H13
Drake St. WC1 75 F9
Drant St. E1 76 F5
Draper St. SE17 79 E13
Drapers Hall EC2 76 G3
Draycott Av. SW3 78 F1
Draycott Pl. SW3 78 F2
Draycott Ter. SW3 78 F2
Drayson Ms. W8 77 C2
Drayton Gdns. SW10 77 G4
Drayton Green 66 F1
Drive, The 67 D11
Druid St. SE1 80 C5
Drummond Cres. NW1 74 C7
Drummond St. NW1 74 D6
Drury La. WC2 75 H9
Dryden St. WC2 75 H9
Drysdale St. N1 76 D4
Ducal St. E2 76 D5
Duchess of Bedford's Wk. W8 77 C1
Duchess St. W1 74 F5
Duchess Theatre WC2 75 H9
Duchy St. SE1 79 B11
Ducks Hill 65 C4
Ducks Hill Rd. 65 C4
Dudden Hill La. 66 E3
Dufferin St. EC1 76 E2
Duke of York St. SW1 78 A6
Duke of York's H.Q. SW3 78 F3
Duke of York's Th. WC2 75 J8
Duke St. SW1 78 A6
Duke St. W1 74 H4
Duke St. Hill SE1 80 B3
Duke's La. W8 77 C2
Duke's Pl. EC3 76 G4
Duke's Rd. WC1 75 D7
Dulwich 71 B7
Dulwich College 71 C7
Dulwich Common 71 B7
Dulwich Park 71 B7
Dulwich Village 71 B7
Dulwich Wood Pk. 71 C7
Dunbridge St. E2 76 E7
Duncan St. N1 75 B12
Duncan Ter. N1 75 B12
Duncannon St. WC2 79 A8
Dunloe St. E2 76 C5
Dunlop Pl. SE16 80 E6
Dunning's La. 68 D6
Dunraven St. W1 74 H3
Dunstans Hill 70 F4
Dunsterville Rd. SE1 80 C3
Dunston Rd. E8 76 A5
Dunton Green 72 H1
Dunton Rd. SE1 80 F5
Duplex Ride SW1 78 C3
Durant St. E2 76 C6
Durants Pk. 67 A8
Durham Rd. 70 D3
Durham St. SE11 79 G10
Durham Ter. W2 73 G2
Durnsford Rd. N11 66 C6
Durnsford Rd. SW19 70 C4
Dyott St. WC1 75 G8
Dysart St. EC2 76 E3
Eagle St. WC1 75 F9
Eagle Wharf Rd. N1 76 B2
Ealing 66 F2
Ealing Broadway Sta. 66 F2
Ealing Common 66 G2
Ealing Common Sta. 66 G2
Ealing Rd. Brentford 66 G2
Ealing Rd. Greenford 65 E6
Ealing Rd. Wembley 66 E2
Eamont St. NW8 73 B6
Eardley Cres. SW5 77 G1
Earl Rd. SE1 80 F5
Earl St. EC2 76 F3
Earlham St. WC2 75 H8
Earl's Court SW5 77 G1
Earl's Court Gdns. SW5 77 F2
Earl's Court Rd. W8/SW5 77 E1
Earl's Court Sq. SW5 77 G2
Earl's Court Sta. SW5 77 F2
Earl's Path 67 A10
Earl's Wk. W8 77 E1
Earlsfield Rd. 70 B4
Earlsfield Sta. 70 B4
Earnshaw St. WC2 75 G8
East Acton 66 G3
East Acton Sta 66 F3
East Barnet 66 A6
East Bedfont 69 B4
East Croydon Sta. 71 E7
East Dulwich 71 B7
East Dulwich Rd. 71 B7
East Dulwich Sta. 71 B7
East End Rd. 66 C5
East Ewell 70 F4
East Finchley 66 C5
East Finchley Sta. 66 C5
East Hall Rd. 71 E12
East Ham 67 F11
East Harding St. EC4 75 G11
East Hill Dartford 72 B3
East Hill SW18 70 B4
East India Dock Rd. 67 F9
East La. SE16 80 D6
East La. Wembley 66 D2
East Molesey 69 D6
East Putney Sta. 70 B4
East Rd. N1 76 D3
East Rochester Way 71 B12
East Sheen 70 B2
East Sheen Gate 70 B2
East Smithfield E1 76 J6
East St. Epsom 70 G3
East St. SE17 80 F4
East Tenter St. E1 76 H6
East Wickham 67 H12
Eastbourne Ms. W2 73 G4
Eastbourne Ter. W2 73 G4
Eastbury 65 B4
Eastcastle St. W1 74 G6
Eastcheap EC3 76 H3
Eastcote 65 D5
Eastcote La. 65 E5
Eastcote Rd. 65 D4
Eastern Av. 67 D10
Eastern Av. 68 D5
Eastern Av. E. 68 C3
Eastern Av. W. 68 C1
Eastern Way Thamesmead 68 G1
Easthall La. 68 F3
Eastham Manor Way 67 F11
Eastman Dental Hospital WC1 75 D10
Easton St. WC1 75 D11
Eastworth 69 E2
Eastworth Rd. 69 E2
Eaton Gate SW1 78 E3
Eaton La. SW1 78 D5
Eaton Ms. Nth. SW1 78 E3
Eaton Ms. Sth. SW1 78 E4
Eaton Ms. W. SW1 78 E4
Eaton Pl. SW1 78 E3
Eaton Row SW1 78 D4
Eaton Sq. SW1 78 E4
Eaton Ter. SW1 78 E3
Ebenezer St. N1 76 D2
Ebor St. E1 76 E5
Ebury Bri. SW1 78 F4
Ebury Bri. Est. SW1 78 G4
Ebury Bri. Rd. SW1 78 G4
Ebury Ms. SW1 78 E4
Ebury Ms. E. SW1 78 E4
Ebury Sq. SW1 78 F4
Ebury St. SW1 78 E4
Eccleston Bri. SW1 78 E5
Eccleston Ms. SW1 78 D4
Eccleston Pl. SW1 78 E5
Eccleston Sq. SW1 78 F5
Edbrooke Rd. W9 73 E1
Eden Pk. 71 D8
Edge Hill Rd. 70 F6
Edge St. W8 77 B1
Edgware 66 B3
Edgware Rd. NW2 66 D3
Edgware Rd. NW9 66 C3
Edgware Rd. W2 73 F5
Edinburgh Gate SW1 78 C2
Edith Gro. SW10 77 J4
Edith Ter. SW10 77 J3
Edmund St. SE5 80 J3
Eel Pie Is. 70 B1
Effra Rd. 70 B6
Egerton Cres. SW3 77 E6
Egerton Gdns. SW3 77 E6
Egerton Pl. SW3 77 E6
Egerton Ter. SW3 77 E6
Egham 69 C1
Elba Pl. SE17 80 E2
Elder Rd. 71 C7
Elder St. E1 76 E4
Eldon Rd. W8 77 D3
Eldon St. EC2 76 F3
Elephant & Castle Sta. SE17 80 E1
Elephant Rd. SE17 80 E1
Elgin Av. W9 73 D2
Elia Ms. N1 75 C12
Elia St. N1 75 C12
Elizabeth Bri. SW1 78 F5
Elizabeth St. SW1 78 E4
Ellen St. E1 76 H6
Elliotts Row SE11 79 E12
Ellis St. SW1 78 E3
Elm Av. 65 D5
Elm Pk. 68 D3
Elm Pk. Gdns. SW10 77 G5
Elm Pk. La. SW3 77 G4
Elm Pk. Rd. SW3 77 H4
Elm Pl. SW7 77 G5
Elm St. WC1 75 E10
Elm Tree Cl. NW8 73 C5
Elm Tree Rd. NW8 73 C5
Elmers End 71 D8
Elms Ms. W2 73 J4
Elmstead 71 C10
Elmstead La. 71 C10
Elmstead Wood 71 C10
Elmwood Av. 69 C5
Elnathan Ms. W9 73 E3
Elsted St. SE17 80 F3
Elstree 66 A2
Elstree & Borehamwood Sta. 66 A2
Elstree Aerodrome 66 A1
Elstree Hill Sth. 66 A2
Elstree Rd. Bushey 66 A1
Elstree Rd. Stanmore 66 B2
Eltham 71 B10
Eltham Bypass 71 C10
Eltham Common 71 A10
Eltham Hill 71 B10
Eltham Pk. 71 B11
Eltham Rd. 71 B9
Eltham Sta. 71 B10
Eltham St. SE17 80 F2
Elthorne Heights 66 F1
Elvaston Ms. SW7 77 D4
Elvaston Pl. SW7 77 D4
Elvers Way 70 H3
Elverton St. SW1 78 E7
Elwin St. E2 76 C6
Ely Pl. EC1 75 F11
Elystan Pl. SW3 78 F2
Elystan St. SW3 77 F6
Embankment Gdns. SW3 78 H3
Ember La. 69 E6
Emerald St. WC1 75 F10
Emerson Pk. 68 D3
Emerson St. SE1 80 A1
Emery Hill St. SW1 78 E6
Emperor's Gate SW7 77 E3
Empire Pool 66 E2
Endell St. WC2 75 G8
Endlebury Rd. 67 B9
Endsleigh Gdns. WC1 74 D7
Endsleigh Pl. WC1 74 E7
Endsleigh St. WC1 74 D7
Endwell Rd. 71 A8
Enfield 67 A7
Enfield Chase Sta. 67 A7
Enfield Rd. 66 A6
Enfield Town Sta. 67 A7
Enford St. W1 74 F2
Enid St. SE16 80 D6
Ennismore Gdns. SW7 77 D6
Ennismore Gdns. Ms. SW7 77 D5
Ennismore Ms. SW7 77 D6
Ennismore St. SW7 77 D6
Ensign St. E1 76 J6
Environment, Dept of SW1 79 E8
Epping Forest 67 C9
Epping New Rd. 67 A10
Epsom 70 G2
Epsom Common 70 G2
Epsom District Hospital 70 G2
Epsom Downs Race Course 70 H3
Epsom Downs Sta. 70 G3
Epsom La. 70 H3
Epsom Rd. Croydon 70 E6
Epsom Rd. Ewell 70 G3
Epsom Rd. Leatherhead 70 H1
Epsom Rd. Morden 70 E4
Epworth St. EC2 76 E3
Erasmus St. SW1 79 F8
Erbisham Dri. SW8 79 H9
Erith 72 A2
Erith Marshes 68 G1
Erith Reach 68 G2

Erith Rd. *Barnehurst* **68** H2
Erith Rd. *Belvedere* **68** G2
Eros *W1* **74** J7
Errol St. *EC1* **76** E2
Esher **69** F6
Esher Common **69** F6
Esher La. **69** E6
Esher Rd. **69** F5
Esher Sta. **69** E6
Esmeralda Rd. *SE1* **80** F6
Essendine Rd. *W9* **73** D1
Essendine Rd. *W9* **73** D4
Essex Rd. *N1* **75** A12
Essex Vs. *W8* **77** D1
Eustace Rd. **77** J1
Euston Centre *NW1* **74** E5
Euston Rd. *NW1* **74** E6
Euston Sq. *NW1* **74** D7
Euston Sta. *NW1* **74** D6
Euston Station Colonade *NW1* **74** D7
Euston St. *NW1* **74** D6
Euston Tower *NW1* **74** E6
Evelyn Gdns. *SW7* **77** G4
Evelyn St. **67** G8
Evelyn Wk. *N1* **76** C2
Everilda St. *N1* **75** A10
Eversholt St. *NW1* **74** C6
Ewell **70** F3
Ewell Bypass **70** F3
Ewell E. Sta. **70** F3
Ewell W. Sta. **70** F3
Ewer St. *SE1* **79** B13
Exeter St. *WC2* **75** H9
Exhibition Rd. *SW7* **77** D5
Exmouth Mkt. *EC1* **75** D11
Exon St. *SE17* **80** F4
Exton St. *SE1* **79** B11
Eynsford **72** E3
Eyre St. Hill *EC1* **75** E11
Ezra St. *E2* **76** C6
Faggs Rd. **69** B4
Fair St. *SE1* **80** C4
Fairchildes Rd. **71** G9
Fairclough St. *E1* **76** H7
Fairlop Pl. *NW8* **73** D5
Fairlop Sta. **67** C11
Fairmead Rd. **67** A10
Fairmile **69** G5
Fairmile La. **69** G5
Fairoak La. **70** G1
Fairseat **72** G5
Falconwood Sta. **71** B11
Falkirk St. *N1* **76** C4
Falling La. **65** F3
Falmouth Rd. *SE1* **80** E2
Fann St. *EC1* **76** E1
Fanshaw St. *N1* **76** C4
Farleigh **71** G8
Farleigh Court Rd. **71** G8
Farleigh Rd. **71** G8
Farley Rd. **71** F7
Farm La. *Ashtead* **70** H2
Farm La. *SW6* **77** J1
Farm St. *W1* **74** J4
Farmer St. *W8* **77** B1
Farnborough **71** F11
Farnborough Bypass **71** F11
Farnborough Common **71** E10
Farncombe St. *SE16* **80** C7
Farnham Pl. *SE1* **79** B13
Farnham Royal *SE11* **79** G10
Farningham **72** E3
Farningham Rd. **72** D3
Farningham Rd. & Sutton-at-Hone Sta. **72** D3
Farningham Wood **72** D2
Farringdon La. *EC1* **75** E11
Farringdon Rd. *EC1* **75** E11
Farringdon Sta. *EC1* **75** F12
Farringdon St. *EC4* **75** G12
Fashion St. *E1* **76** F5
Faunce St. *SE17* **79** G12
Fawcett St. *SW10* **77** H3
Fawkham Green **72** E4
Featherbed La. **71** F8
Featherstone St. *EC1* **76** E2
Feltham **69** C4
Feltham Rd. **69** C4
Felthamhill **69** C5
Felthamhill Rd. **69** C4
Felton Rd. *SE16* **80** C6
Fen La. **68** E6
Fencepiece Rd. **67** B11
Fenchurch Av. *EC3* **76** H4
Fenchurch Blds. *EC3* **76** H4
Fenchurch St. *EC3* **76** H4
Fenchurch St. Sta. *EC3* **76** H5
Fendall St. *SE1* **80** D4
Fentiman Rd. *SW8* **79** J9
Fernsbury St. *WC1* **75** D11
Fernshaw Rd. *SW10* **77** J3
Ferry La. *N17* **67** C8
Ferry La. *Rainham* **68** F2
Fetter La. *EC4* **75** G11
Fickleshole **71** G9
Field Ct. *WC1* **75** F10
Field End Rd. **65** D5
Field St. *WC1* **75** C9
Fieldgate St. *E1* **76** G7
Fife Ter. *N1* **75** B10
Filston La. **72** G2
Finborough Rd. *SW10* **77** H3
Finch La. *EC3* **76** H3
Finchley **66** C5
Finchley Central Sta. **66** C5
Finchley Pl. *NW8* **73** B4
Finchley Rd. **66** E5
Finchley Rd. & Frognall Sta. **66** E5
Finchley Rd. *NW11* **66** D4
Finchley Rd. *NW8* **73** B4
Finck St. *SE1* **79** D10
Finsbury **67** F7
Finsbury Cir. *EC2* **76** F3
Finsbury Estate *EC1* **75** D12
Finsbury Pk. **67** D7
Finsbury Pk. Sta. **67** D7
Finsbury Pavement *EC2* **76** F3
Finsbury Sq. *EC2* **76** F3
Finsbury St. *EC2* **76** F2
Fire Brigade H.Q. *SE11* **79** F9
Firs La. **67** B7
First St. *SW3* **78** E1
Firtree Rd. **70** G4
Fish St. Hill *EC4* **76** J3
Fisher St. *WC1* **75** F9
Fisherton St. *NW8* **73** E5
Fishmongers' Hall *EC4* **76** J3
Fitzalan St. *SE11* **79** E10
Fitzhardinge St. *W1* **74** G3
Fitzjohn's Av. **66** E5
Fitzmaurice Pl. *W1* **78** A5
Fitzroy Sq. *W1* **74** E6
Fitzroy St. *W1* **74** E6
Flaxman Ter. *WC1* **75** D8
Fleet St. *EC4* **75** H11
Fleming Rd. *SE17* **79** H12
Fletcher St. *E1* **76** H6
Fleur de Lis St. *E1* **76** E4
Flint St. *SE17* **80** F3
Flinton St. *SE17* **80** F4
Flood St. *SW3* **78** G1
Flood Wk. *SW3* **77** G6
Floral St. *WC2* **75** H8
Florida St. *E2* **76** D7
Flower Wk., The *W2* **77** C4
Fochelle St. *E2* **76** D5
Foley St. *W1* **74** F6
Folgate St. *E1* **76** F4
Foots Cray **71** C12
Foots Cray La. **71** C12
Foots Cray Rd. **71** B10
Forbes St. *E1* **76** H6
Ford Bri. Rd. **69** C3
Fordbridge Rd. **69** D4
Fore St. *EC2* **76** F2
Fore St. *N9/N18* **67** B8
Fore St. *Ruislip* **65** C5
Foreign Office *SW1* **79** C8
Forest Gate **67** E10
Forest Hill **71** C7
Forest Hill Sta. **71** C8
Forest Hospital **67** B10
Forest La. **67** E10
Forest Rd. *E17* **67** C9
Forest Rd. *Redbridge* **67** C12
Forest Rd. *Sutton* **70** E4
Forest Side **67** A10
Forest St. *W1* **74** G2
Formosa St. *W9* **73** E3
Forston St. *N1* **76** B2
Fort Rd. *SE1* **80** F6
Fortis Green Rd. **66** C5
Fortress Rd. **66** E6
Fortune Green Rd. **66** E4
Fortune St. *EC1* **76** E2
Forty Av. **66** D2
Forty La. **66** D3
Foster La. *EC2* **76** G1
Foubert's Pl. *W1* **74** H6
Foulis Ter. *SW7* **77** F5
Fournier St. *E1* **76** F5
Fox Ct. *EC1* **75** F11
Fox Hill **69** F4
Fox Hill Rd. **69** F1
Fox La. **66** B6
Foxburrow Wood **68** A1
Foxley Rd. *SW9* **79** H11
Frampton St. *NW8* **73** E5
Francis St. *SW1* **78** E6
Franklin's Row *SW3* **78** G3
Frazier St. *SE1* **79** C11
Frean St. *SE16* **80** D6
Frederick St. *WC1* **75** D9
Fremantle St. *SE17* **80** F4
French St. **69** D5
Frenshaw St. *SE1* **80** H6
Friary Rd. *SE15* **80** J7
Friend St. *EC1* **75** C12
Friends House *NW1* **74** D7
Friern Barnet **66** B5
Frith St. *W1* **74** H7
Frith Wood **71** G8
Frome St. *N1* **75** B13
Front La. **68** D4
Fryent Way **66** D2
Fulham F.C. **70** A3
Fulham Palace **70** A4
Fulham Palace Rd. *W6/SW6* **66** H4
Fulham Rd. *SW10/SW3* **77** G5
Fulham Rd. *SW6* **70** A4
Fuller St. *E2* **76** E6
Fulmer **65** E1
Furnival St. *EC4* **75** G11
Furze Hill **70** H4
Furzehill Rd. **66** A3
Fynes St. *SW1* **78** E7
Gainsford St. *SE1* **80** C5
Gale St. **68** E1
Gallery Rd. **71** B7
Galley Hill **72** B5
Galliard Rd. **67** A8
Gallions Reach **67** G11
Gallows Cnr. **68** C3
Galway St. *EC1* **76** D2
Gambia St. *SE1* **79** B12
Gander Green La. **70** E4
Ganton St. *W1* **74** H6
Gants Hill Sta. **67** D11
Garbutt Pl. *W1* **74** F4
Garden Rd. *NW8* **73** C4
Garden Row *SE1* **79** D12
Garden Wk. *EC2* **76** D4
Garlick Hill *EC4* **76** H2
Garnault Pl. *EC1* **75** D11
Garratt La. **70** C4
Garrett St. *EC1* **76** E1
Garrick St. *WC2* **75** H8
Garrick Theatre *WC2* **75** J8
Garth Rd. **70** E3
Garway Rd. *W2* **73** H2
Gascoigne Pl. *E2* **76** D5
Gasholder Pl. *SE11* **79** G10
Gaston Bri. Rd. **69** D4
Gate St. *WC2* **75** G9
Gateforth St. *NW8* **73** E6
Gates Cnr. **67** C10
Gatliff Rd. *SW1* **78** G4
Gaunt St. *SE1* **79** D13
Gayfere St. *SW1* **79** E8
Gaywood St. *SE1* **79** E12
Gaza St. *SE17* **79** G12
Gee St. *EC1* **75** E13
Geffrye St. *E2* **76** B5
Geological Mus. *SW7* **77** E5
George Row *SE16* **80** C6
George St. *W1* **74** G2
George V Av. **65** C6
George Yd. *W1* **74** H4
Gerald Rd. *SW1* **78** F4
Geraldine Mary Harmsworth Pk. *SE1* **79** E11
Geraldine St. *SE11* **79** E12
Gerpins La. **68** E4
Gerrard Rd. *N1* **75** B12
Gerrard St. *W1* **74** H7
Gerrards Cross **65** D1
Gerridge St. *SE1* **79** D11
Gertrude St. *SW10* **77** H4
Gibson Rd. *SE11* **79** F10
Gidea Pk. **68** C3
Gidea Pk. Sta. **68** C3
Gilbert Pl. *WC1* **75** G8
Gilbert Rd. *SE11* **79** F11
Gilbert St. *W1* **74** H4
Gillingham St. *SW1* **78** E5
Gilston Rd. *SW10* **77** G4
Giltspur St. *EC1* **75** G12
Gladstone Pk. **66** E3
Gladstone St. *SE1* **79** D12
Glasgow Ter. *SW1* **78** G6
Glass Hill St. *SE1* **79** C13
Glasshouse St. *W1* **74** J6
Glasshouse Wk. *SE11* **79** G9
Glasshouse Yd. *EC1* **75** E13
Glebe Pl. *SW3* **77** H6
Gledhow Gdns. *SW5* **77** F3
Glenfinlas Way *SE5* **79** H13
Glengall Rd. *SE15* **80** H6
Glengall Ter. *SE15* **80** H5
Glentworth St. *NW1* **74** E2
Globe Rd. **67** F8
Globe St. *SE1* **80** D2
Globe Theatre *SE1* **80** E3
Globe Theatre *W1* **74** H7
Globe Yard *W1* **74** H5
Gloucester Av. *NW1* **74** A4
Gloucester Gate *NW1* **74** B4
Gloucester Ms. *W2* **73** H4
Gloucester Ms. W. *W2* **73** H4
Gloucester Pl. *NW1/W1* **74** F2
Gloucester Pl. Ms. *W1* **74** G3
Gloucester Rd. *SW7* **77** E3
Gloucester Sq. *W2* **73** H5
Gloucester St. *SW1* **78** G6
Gloucester Ter. *W2* **73** H4
Gloucester Wk. *W8* **77** C1
Gloucester Way *EC1* **75** D11
Godfrey St. *SW3* **77** G6
Goding St. *SE11* **79** G9
Godson St. *N1* **75** B11
Godstone Rd. **71** H7
Godstone Rd. *Purley* **70** G6
Golden La. *EC1* **76** E1
Golden La. Est. *EC1* **75** E13
Golden Sq. *W1* **74** H6
Golders Green **66** D4
Golders Green Rd. **66** D4
Golders Green Sta. **66** D5
Goldhawk Rd. *W12* **66** G4
Goldington Cres. *NW1* **74** B7
Goldington St. *NW1* **74** B7
Goldman St. *EC4* **75** H13
Goldney Rd. *W9* **73** E1
Goldsmiths Hall *EC2* **76** G1
Goldsmiths Row *E2* **76** B6
Goodge Pl. *W1* **74** F6
Goodge St. *W1* **74** F6
Goodmans Yard *E1* **76** H5
Goodmayes **67** D12
Goodmayes Hospital **67** D12
Goodmayes La. **67** D12
Goods Way *NW1* **75** B8
Gopsall St. *N1* **76** B3
Gordon Pl. *W8* **77** C2
Gordon Sq. *WC1* **75** E7
Gordon St. *WC1* **74** E7
Gore Hill **72** C3
Gore St. *SW7* **77** D4
Goresbrook Rd. **68** E1
Gorse Rd. **71** E12
Gorsuch St. *E2* **76** C5
Gosfield St. *W1* **74** F5
Gospel Oak Sta. **66** E6
Gosset St. *E2* **76** D6
Goswell Rd. *EC1* **75** D12
Gough Sq. *EC4* **75** G11
Gough St. *WC1* **75** E10
Goulston St. *E1* **76** G5
Gower Ms. *WC1* **74** F7
Gower Pl. *WC1* **74** E7
Gower St. *WC1* **74** E7
Gowers Wk. *E1* **76** H6
Gracechurch St. *EC3* **76** H3
Grafton Ms. *W1* **74** E6
Grafton Pl. *NW1* **74** D7
Grafton St. *W1* **74** J5
Grafton Way *W1* **74** E6
Grafton Way *W1* **74** F6
Graham Rd. **67** E8
Graham St. *N1* **75** C13
Graham Ter. *SW1* **78** F3
Granby St. *E2* **76** D6
Granby Ter. *NW1* **74** C6
Grandstand Rd. **70** H3
Grange Hill **67** B11
Grange Pk. Sta. **67** A7
Grange Rd. *SE1* **80** D4
Grange Rd. *SE25* **71** D7
Grange, The *SE1* **80** D5
Grange Wk. *SE1* **80** D4
Grange Wk. *SE1* **80** D5
Grange Yd. *SE1* **80** D5
Grangewood **71** D7
Grantbridge St. *N1* **75** B12
Grantully Rd. *W9* **73** D2
Granville Pl. *W1* **74** H3
Granville Rd. *NW6* **73** C1
Granville Sq. *WC1* **75** D10
Grape St. *WC1* **75** G8
Gravel Hill *Bexley* **72** B1
Gravel La. **67** B12
Gravel La. *Abridge* **67** A12
Gravel La. *E1* **76** G5
Gray St. *SE1* **79** C11
Grays **68** H6
Gray's Inn Gdns. *WC1* **75** F10
Gray's Inn Rd. *WC1* **75** D9
Grays Rd. **71** H11
Great Bookham Common **69** H6
Great Cambridge Rd. **67** A8
Great Castle St. *W1* **74** G5
Great Central St. *NW1* **74** F2
Great Chapel St. *W1* **74** G7
Great Chertsey Rd. **70** A2
Great College St. *SW1* **79** D8
Great Cumberland Pl. *W1* **74** H2
Great Dover St. *SE1* **80** D2
Great Eastern St. *EC2* **76** E4
Great George St. *SW1* **79** C8
Great Guildford St. *SE1* **79** B13
Great James St. *WC1* **75** F10
Great Marlborough St. *W1* **74** H6
Great North Rd. **66** A5
Great North Way **66** C4
Great Ormond St. *WC1* **75** F9
Great Percy St. *WC1* **75** C10
Great Peter St. *SW1* **79** D8
Great Portland St. *W1* **74** F5
Great Pulteney St. *W1* **74** H6
Great Queen St. *WC2* **75** G9
Great Russell St. *WC1* **75** G8
Great Scotland Yd. *SW1* **79** B8
Great Smith St. *SW1* **79** D8
Great South West Rd. **69** B4
Great St. Helens *EC3* **76** G4
Great Suffolk St. *SE1* **79** C13
Great Sutton St. *EC1* **75** E12
Great Swan All. *EC2* **76** G3
Great Tattenhams **70** H3
Great Titchfield St. *W1* **74** F6
Great Tower St. **76** J4
Great Warley **68** C5
Great West Rd. **69** A5
Great Winchester St. *EC2* **76** G3
Great Windmill St. *W1* **74** H7
Great Wood **68** A1
Great Wood **72** G6
Greatness **72** H2
Greatorex St. *E1* **76** F6
Greek St. *W1* **75** H7
Green Dragon La. **67** A7
Green Hundred Rd. *SE15* **80** H7
Green La. *Addlestone* **69** E2
Green La. *Goodmayes* **68** D1
Green La. *Hatton* **69** B5
Green La. *Morden* **70** E4
Green La. *Northwood* **65** B4
Green La. *SE9* **71** C11
Green La. *Seven Kings* **67** D12
Green La. *Shepperton* **69** D4
Green La. *SW16* **70** D6
Green Lanes *N21* **67** B7
Green Lanes *N4/N16* **67** D7
Green Pk. *SW1* **78** C5
Green Rd. **72** C3
Green St. *Dartford* **72** C3
Green St. *E7/E13* **67** E10
Green St. *Sunbury* **69** D4
Green St. *W1* **74** H3
Green Street Green *Dartford* **72** C4
Green Street Green *Farnborough* **71** F11
Green Ter. *EC1* **75** D11
Green, The **65** G5
Green Wrythe La. **70** E5
Greenberry St. *NW8* **73** C6
Greencoat Pl. *SW1* **78** E6
Greencoat Row *SW1* **78** E6
Greenfield Rd. *E1* **76** G7
Greenford **65** F6
Greenford Av. **66** F1
Greenford Green **65** E6
Greenford Rd. **65** F6
Greenford Sta. **65** E6
Greenhill **66** D1
Greenhithe **72** B4
Greenwell St. *W1* **74** E5
Greenwich **67** H9
Greenwich High Rd. **67** H9
Greenwich Pk. **67** H9
Greenwich Reach **67** G9
Greenwich Sta. **67** H9
Greenwood Th. *SE1* **80** C3
Greet St. *SE1* **79** B11
Grendon St. *NW8* **73** E6
Grenville Pl. *SW7* **77** E3
Grenville St. *WC1* **75** E9
Gresham St. *EC2* **76** G2
Gresse St. *W1* **74** G7
Greville St. *EC1* **75** F11
Greycoat Pl. *SW1* **78** E7
Greycoat St. *SW1* **78** E7
Greyeagle St. *E1* **76** E5
Grimsby St. *E2* **76** E6
Grittleton Rd. *W9* **73** E1
Groom Pl. *SW1* **78** D4
Grosvenor Bri. *SW1/SW8* **78** H5
Grosvenor Cres. *SW1* **78** C4
Grosvenor Crescent Ms. *SW1* **78** C3
Grosvenor Gdns. *SW1* **78** D5
Grosvenor Hill *W1* **74** J5
Grosvenor House Hotel *W1* **74** J3
Grosvenor Pk. *SE5* **80** J1
Grosvenor Pl. *SW1* **78** D4
Grosvenor Rd. *SW1* **78** H6
Grosvenor Sq. *W1* **74** H4
Grosvenor St. *W1* **74** H5
Grosvenor Ter. *SE5* **80** H1
Grove End Rd. *NW8* **73** C4
Grove Pk. **71** C10
Grove Pk. Hospital **71** C10
Grove Rd. *E3* **67** F8
Grove Rd. *Mitcham* **70** D5
Grove Rd. *Romford* **67** D12
Grovegreen Rd. **67** D9
Gubbins La. **68** C4
Guildford Rd. **69** F2
Guildhall *EC2* **76** G2
Guildhouse St. *SW1* **78** F6
Guilford St. *WC1* **75** E9
Gunnersbury **66** G3
Gunnersbury Av. **66** G2
Gunnersbury Pk. **66** G2
Gunter Gro. *SW10* **77** J3
Gutter La. *EC2* **75** G13
Guy St. *SE1* **80** C3
Guy's Hospital *SE1* **80** C2
Gypsey Hill Sta. **71** C7
Haberdasher St. *N1* **76** C3
Hackbridge **70** E5
Hackney **67** E8
Hackney Downs **67** E8
Hackney Downs Sta. **67** E8
Hackney Marsh **67** E8
Hackney Rd. *E2* **76** C5
Hackney Wick **67** E9
Hacton La. **68** E4
Hadrian Estate *E2* **76** C7
Haggerston Pk. *E2* **76** B6
Haggerston Rd. *E8* **76** A5
Hainault **67** C12

Hainault Estate 67 B12
Hainault Forest 68 B1
Hainault Rd. Chigwell 67 B11
Hainault Rd. Hainault 67 C12
Halcomb St. N1 76 B4
Hale End 67 B9
Half Moon St. W1 78 B5
Halford Rd. SW6 77 H1
Halfway Reach 68 F2
Halfway St. 71 B11
Haling Pk. Rd. 70 F6
Halkin Pl. SW1 78 D3
Halkin St. SW1 78 D4
Hall Gate NW8 73 D4
Hall La. 68 D6
Hall La. E4 67 B9
Hall La. Upminster 68 D4
Hall Pl. Bexley 72 B1
Hall Pl. W2 73 F5
Hall Rd. NW8 73 D4
Hall St. EC1 75 C12
Hall Wood Brentwood 68 B6
Hall Wood Fairseat 72 G6
Hallam St. W1 74 F5
Hallfield Estate W2 73 G3
Halliford Rd. 69 D4
Halsey St. SW3 78 E2
Halstead 72 G1
Ham 70 C1
Ham Common 70 C2
Ham Cross 70 C2
Ham Gate 70 C2
Ham House 70 B1
Hamilton Cl. NW8 73 D4
Hamilton Gdns. NW8 73 C4
Hamilton Pl. W1 78 B4
Hamilton Ter. NW8 73 C3
Hammersmith 66 G4
Hammersmith Bri. Rd. W6 66 G4
Hammersmith Rd. 66 G4
Hampden Way 66 B6
Hampermill La. 65 A5
Hampstead 66 E5
Hampstead Heath 66 D5
Hampstead Heath Sta. 66 E5
Hampstead La. 66 D5
Hampstead Ponds 66 E5
Hampstead Rd. NW1 74 C6
Hampton 69 D6
Hampton Cl. NW6 73 D1
Hampton Court Bri. 69 D6
Hampton Court Palace 70 D1
Hampton Court Pk. 70 D1
Hampton Court Rd. 69 D6
Hampton Court Way 69 E6
Hampton Rd. Hanworth 69 C5
Hampton Rd. Twickenham 69 C6
Hampton St. SE17 79 F13
Hampton Wick 70 D1
Hamsey Green 71 G8
Hanbury St. E1 76 F5
Handel St. WC1 75 E8
Hangar Hill 69 F4
Hanger Hill 66 F2
Hanger La. 66 F2
Hanger La. Sta. 66 F2
Hankey Pl. SE1 80 D3
Hanover Gdns. SE11 79 H10
Hanover Gate NW1 74 D1
Hanover Sq. W1 74 H5
Hanover St. W1 74 H5
Hanover Ter. NW1 74 D2
Hanover Ter. Ms. NW1 74 D2
Hans Cres. SW1 78 D2
Hans Pl. SW1 78 D2
Hans Rd. SW3 78 D2
Hans St. SW1 78 D2
Hanson St. W1 74 F6
Hanway Pl. W1 74 G7
Hanway St. W1 74 G7
Hanwell 66 G1
Hanworth 69 C5
Hanworth Pk. 69 C5
Hanworth Rd. Hanworth 69 C5
Hanworth Rd. Hounslow 69 B6
Harbet Rd. W2 73 F5
Harcourt St. W1 74 F1
Harcourt Ter. SW10 77 G3
Hardwick La. 69 E2
Hardwick St. EC1 75 D11
Hardwide St. SE1 80 C4
Hare Hill 69 F2
Hare La. 70 F1
Hare St. 68 C3
Harefield 65 C3
Harefield Hospital 65 C3
Harefield Rd. 65 B3
Harewood Av. NW1 74 E1
Harewood Hall La. 68 E4
Harewood Pl. W1 74 H5
Harewood Row NW1 73 F6
Harlesden 66 E3
Harlesden Sta. 66 F3
Harley Gdns. SW10 77 G4
Harley Pl. W1 74 G4
Harley St. W1 74 F4
Harleyford Rd. SE11 79 H9
Harleyford St. SE11 79 H11
Harlington 65 H4
Harlington Rd. 65 F4
Harlington Rd. E. 69 B5
Harmondsworth 65 H3
Harmondsworth La. 65 H3
Harmsworth St. SE17 79 G12
Harold Hill 68 B3
Harold Wood 68 C4
Harp La. EC3 76 J4
Harper Rd. SE1 80 D2
Harpur St. WC1 75 F9
Harringay Sta. 67 D7
Harringay Stadium 67 D7
Harringay Stadium Sta. 67 D7
Harrington Gdns. SW7 77 F3
Harrington Rd. SW7 77 E5
Harrington Sq. NW1 74 B6
Harrington St. NW1 74 C6
Harrison St. WC1 75 D9
Harrow 66 C1
Harrow & Wealdstone Sta. 66 C1
Harrow on the Hill 66 D1
Harrow on the Hill Sta. 66 D1
Harrow Pl. E1 76 G4
Harrow Rd. Chelsham 71 G8
Harrow Rd. W2 73 F4
Harrow Rd. W9 73 F1
Harrow Rd. Wembley 66 E2
Harrow School 66 D1
Harrow Weald 66 C1
Harrowby St. W1 74 G2
Hart St. EC3 76 H4
Hartley 72 E5
Hartley Wood 72 D5
Harvey St. N1 76 A3
Harvil Rd. 65 D3
Hasker St. SW3 78 E2
Haslebury Rd. 67 B7
Hastings St. WC1 75 D8
Hatch End 65 C6
Hatch End Sta. 65 C6
Hatch La. 67 B9
Hatch La. Harmondsworth 65 H3
Hatchord Pk. 69 H4
Hatfield St. EC1 76 E1
Hatfields SE1 79 B12
Hatherley Gro. W2 73 G2
Hatton 69 B4
Hatton Cross Sta. 69 B4
Hatton Gdn. EC1 75 F11
Hatton Rd. 69 B4
Hatton St. NW8 73 E5
Hatton Wall EC1 75 F11
Havelock St. N1 75 A9
Havering 68 D3
Havering Pk. 68 B2
Havering Rd. 68 B2
Havering-atte-Bowe 68 B2
Haverstock Hill 66 E5
Haverstock St. N1 75 C13
Hawley 72 C3
Hawley Rd. 72 C3
Hawsted La. 71 F12
Hay Hill W1 74 J5
Haydon's Rd. Sta. 70 C4
Hayes 65 G4
Hayes Bromley 71 E9
Hayes & Harlington Sta. 65 G4
Hayes Common 71 E9
Hayes End 65 F4
Hayes La. Beckenham 71 D9
Hayes La. Bromley 71 E9
Hayes La. Coulsdon 70 H6
Hayes Pl. NW1 73 F6
Hayes Rd. 65 G5
Hayles St. SE11 79 E12
Hayling Rd. 65 B5
Haymarket SW1 74 J7
Haymarket Theatre SW1 75 J7
Haymerle Rd. SE15 80 H6
Hayne St. EC1 75 F13
Hays La. SE1 80 B3
Hay's Ms. W1 78 A4
Hayward's Pl. EC1 75 E12
Hazel Way SE1 80 E5
Hazel Wood 71 G11
Headfort Pl. SW1 78 D4
Headley Rd. 70 H2
Headstone 65 C6
Headstone Drive 66 C1
Headstone La. 65 C6
Headstone La. Sta. 65 C6
Hearn St. EC2 76 E4
Heath La. 72 C2
Heath Pk. 68 D3
Heath Pk. Rd. 68 D3
Heath Rd. Hounslow 69 B6
Heath Row 69 F3
Heath Way 68 E1
Heathbourn Rd. 66 B1
Heathcote St. WC1 75 D9
Heathrow Airport 69 A3
Heaverham 72 H4
Heddon St. W1 74 J6
Hedge La. 67 B7
Hedgemans Rd. 68 E1
Heiron St. SE17 79 H13
Helmet Row EC1 76 E1
Hemingford Rd. N1 75 A10
Hemming St. E1 76 E7
Hemsworth St. N1 76 B3
Hemus Pl. SW3 77 G6
Hendon 66 C4
Hendon Central Sta. 66 D4
Hendon Sta. 66 D3
Hendon Way 66 D4
Hendon Wood La. 66 A3
Hendre Rd. SE1 80 F4
Heneage La. EC3 76 G4
Heneage St. E1 76 F6
Henniker Ms. SW3 77 H4
Henrietta Pl. W1 74 G4
Henrietta St. WC2 75 J9
Henriques St. E1 76 H7
Henshaw St. SE17 80 E2
Herbal Hill EC1 75 E11
Herbrand St. WC1 75 E8
Hercules Rd. SE1 79 D10
Hereford Rd. W2 73 G1
Hereford Sq. SW7 77 F4
Hereford St. E2 76 E6
Hermes St. N1 75 C10
Hermit St. EC1 75 C12
Hermitage Wall E1 80 B7
Herne Hill 71 B7
Herne Hill Sta. 70 B6
Herrick St. SW1 79 F8
Hersham 69 F5
Hersham Rd. 69 E5
Hersham Sta. 69 E5
Hertford Rd. Enfield 67 A8
Hertford Rd. N9 67 B8
Hertford St. W1 78 B4
Heseirs Hill 71 H9
Heseirs Rd. 71 H9
Hesper Ms. SW5 77 F2
Heston 65 H6
Heston Rd. 65 H6
Hewitts Rd. 71 F12
Hextable 72 D2
Heyford Av. SW8 79 J9
Heygate St. SE17 80 F1
Hide Pl. SW1 78 F7
High Barnet Sta. 66 A4
High Elms Rd. Farnborough 71 F11
High Holborn WC1 75 G10
High Rd. Byfleet 69 G3
High Rd. Chigwell 67 B11
High Rd. Eastcote 65 D5
High Rd. Goodmayes 67 D12
High Rd. Leytonstone 67 D9
High Rd. Loughton 67 A10
High Rd. N17 67 C7
High Rd. N2 66 C5
High Rd. N20 66 A5
High Rd. NW10 66 E3
High Rd. Orpington 71 E11
High Rd. Wilmington 72 C2
High Rd. Woodford Bridge 67 C10
High Rd. Woodford Green 67 B10
High St. Aveley 68 G4
High St. Banstead 70 G4
High St. Beckenham 71 D8
High St. Bushey 65 A6
High St. Carshalton 70 F5
High St. Colliers Wood 70 C5
High St. Croydon 71 E7
High St. E11 67 D10
High St. E15 67 F9
High St. Epsom 70 G2
High St. Feltham 69 C4
High St. Fulham 70 A4
High St. Harlington 65 G4
High St. Harrow Weald 66 C1
High St. Hornchurch 68 D3
High St. Hounslow 69 A6
High St. Merton SW19 70 D4
High St. N8 66 C6
High St. New Malden 70 D3
High St. Ponders End 67 A8
High St. Rickmansworth 65 A3
High St. SE15 67 H8
High St. SE27 70 C6
High St. Shepperton 69 E4
High St. Sidcup 71 C12
High St. Stanwell 69 B3
High St. SW18 70 B4
High St. SW19 70 C4
High St. Teddington 70 C1
High St. Walton 69 E4
High St. Watford 65 A5
High St. Welling 71 A12
High St. West Wickham 71 E8
High St. Nth. 67 E10
High St. Sth. 67 F11
Higham Hill 67 C8
Highams Pk. 67 B9
Highams Pk. Sta. 67 B9
Highbury 67 E7
Highbury & Islington Sta. 67 E7
Highgate 66 D6
Highgate Ponds 66 D5
Highgate Rd. 66 E6
Highgate Sta. 66 D6
Highgate Wood 66 D6
Highway, The E1 76 J7
Highwood Hill 66 B3
Hildyard Rd. SW6 77 H1
Hilfield La. 66 A1
Hilfield Reservoir 66 A1
Hill End 65 B3
Hill End Rd. 65 C3
Hill Rd. NW8 73 C4
Hill St. W1 78 A4
Hillgate Pl. W8 77 B1
Hillgate St. 77 B1
Hillingdon 65 F3
Hillingdon Heath 65 F4
Hillingdon Hill 65 F3
Hillingdon Rd. 65 E3
Hillingdon Sta. 65 E4
Hillingdon St. SE17 79 H13
Hillreach 67 G10
Hilly Fields 71 B8
Hilton Hotel W1 78 B4
Hinchley Wood 70 E1
Hinde St. W1 74 G4
Hither Green 71 B9
H.M.S. Belfast SE1 80 B4
H.M.S. Chrysanthemum EC4 75 H11
H.M.S. President EC4 75 H11
Hobart Pl. SW1 78 D4
Hobury St. SW10 77 H4
Hocker St. E2 76 D5
Hoe La. 68 A1
Hoe St. 67 D9
Hogarth House 66 H3
Hogarth Rd. SW5 77 F2
Hogg La. 68 G6
Hogtrough Hill 71 H11
Holbein Ms. SW1 78 F3
Holbein Pl. SW1 78 F3
Holborn EC1 75 G11
Holborn Cir. EC1 75 G11
Holborn Viaduct EC1/EC4 75 G12
Holden's Wood 68 C5
Holders Hill 66 C4
Holders Hill Rd. 66 C4
Holford Pl. WC1 75 C10
Holford St. WC1 75 C10
Holland Park Av. 66 G4
Holland Rd. 66 G4
Holland St. SE1 79 B13
Holland St. W8 77 C1
Hollen St. W1 74 G7
Holles St. W1 74 G5
Hollow Pond 67 D9
Holloway Rd. 66 D6
Hollows Wood 72 F1
Holly La. 70 H4
Hollywood Rd. SW10 77 H3
Holmwood Pk. 71 F10
Holyoake Rd. SE11 79 F12
Holyrood St. SE1 80 B4
Holywell La. EC2 76 E4
Holywell Row EC2 76 E3
Home Rd 72 C2
Homer Row W1 74 F1
Homer St. W1 74 F1
Homerton 67 E8
Homerton High St. 67 E8
Homerton Rd. 67 E8
Honeypot La. 66 C2
Honor Oak Pk. 71 B8
Honor Oak Pk. Sta. 71 B8
Hook 70 E2
Hook Green 72 C5
Hook Green 72 E6
Hook Green Meopham 72 E6
Hook Green Rd. 72 C2
Hook La. Stapleford Abbotts 68 A2
Hook La. Welling 71 B11
Hook Rise 70 E2
Hook Rd. Epsom 70 G2
Hook Rd. Hook 70 E2
Hook Rd. Horton 70 F2
Hookwood Rd. 71 G12
Hooper St. E1 76 H6
Hopkins St. W1 74 H7
Hopton St. SE1 79 A12
Hopwood Rd. SE17 80 H3
Horatio St. E2 76 C6
Horn La. 66 G3
Hornchurch 68 D3
Hornchurch Marshes 68 F2
Hornchurch Rd. 68 D3
Hornchurch Stadium 68 E4
Horns Green 71 H11
Horns Rd. 67 D11
Hornsey 66 D6
Hornsey La. 66 D6
Hornsey Rise 66 D6
Hornsey Rd. 66 D6
Hornton Pl. W8 77 C2
Hornton St. W8 77 C1
Horse Guards Parade SW1 79 B8
Horseferry Rd. SW1 79 E7
Horseguards Av. SW1 79 B8
Horselydown La. SE1 80 B5
Horsenden Hill 66 E1
Horsley St. SE17 80 H2
Hortensia Rd. SW10 77 J3
Horton Epsom 70 F2
Horton Staines 69 A1
Horton Hospital 70 G2
Horton Kirby 72 D3
Horton La. 70 G2
Horton Rd. Horton 69 A1
Horton Rd. Stanwell 69 B2
Hosier La. EC1 75 G12
Hospital Bri. Rd. 69 B6
Hospital for Sick Children WC1 75 E9
Hospital of St. John NW8 73 C5
Hotspur St. SE1 79 F11
Houghton St. WC2 75 H10
Hounsditch EC3 76 G4
Hounslow 69 A6
Hounslow Central Sta. 69 A6
Hounslow East Sta. 69 A6
Hounslow Heath 69 B5
Hounslow Rd. 69 C5
Hounslow Sta. 69 B6
Hounslow W. Sta. 69 A5
Houses of Parliament SW1 79 D9
Howell Hill 70 G3
Howick Pl. SW1 78 E6
Howland St. W1 74 F6
Howley Pl. W2 73 F4
Hows St. E2 76 B5
Hoxton 67 E7
Hoxton Sq. N1 76 D4
Hoxton St. N1 76 B4
H.Q.S. Wellington WC2 75 H10
Hudson's Pl. SW1 78 E5
Hugh Ms. SW1 78 F5
Hugh St. SW1 78 F5
Hull St. EC1 76 D1
Humphrey St. SE1 80 G5
Hungerford Railway Bri. WC2 79 B9
Huntley St. WC1 74 E7
Hunton St. E1 76 E6
Huntsmoor Pk. 65 F3
Huntsworth Ms. NW1 74 E2
Hurlingham House 70 A4
Hurst Rd. Molesey 69 D5
Hurst Rd. Sidcup 71 B12
Hyde Park W2 78 A1
Hyde Pk. Barracks SW7 78 C2
Hyde Pk. Cnr. W1 78 C4
Hyde Pk. Cres. W2 73 H6
Hyde Pk. Gdns. W2 73 H5
Hyde Pk. Gdns. Ms. W2 73 H5
Hyde Pk. Gate SW7 77 D4
Hyde Pk. Hotel SW1 78 C2
Hyde Pk. Sq. W2 73 H6
Hyde Pk. St. W2 73 H6
Hyde Rd. N1 76 B3
Hyde, The 66 C3
Hythe 69 C2
Hythe End 69 C1
Ickenham 65 D4
Idol La. EC3 76 J4
Ifield Rd. SW10 77 H3
Ightham 72 H5
Ilchester Gdns. W2 73 H2
Ilford 67 E11
Ilford La. 67 E11
Iliffe St. SE17 79 F13
Imber St. N1 76 B2
Imperial College SW7 77 D5
Imperial College of Science SW7 77 E5
Imperial College Rd. SW7 77 D4
Imperial Drive 65 D6
Imperial Hotel WC1 75 F8
Imperial War Museum SE1 79 E11
India St. EC3 76 H5
Ingestre Pl. W1 74 H6
Inglebert St. EC1 75 C11
Ingrave 68 B6
Ingrave Green 68 B6
Inner Circle NW1 74 D3
International Hotel SW5 77 E2
Inverness Pl. W2 73 H3
Inverness Ter. W2 73 H3
Inverness Ter. Gate W2 73 J3
Inville Rd. SE17 80 G3
Ironmonger La. EC2 76 G2
Ironmonger Row EC1 76 D1
Ironmonger's Hall EC2 76 F1
Irving St. WC2 75 J8
Isabella St. SE1 79 B12
Island Barn Res. 69 E6
Isle of Dogs 67 G9
Isleworth 70 B1
Isleworth Sta. 70 A1
Islington 67 E7
Islington Grn. N1 75 B12
Islington High St. N1 75 B12
Istead Rise 72 D6
Iver 65 F2
Iver Heath 65 E2
Iver La. 65 F2
Iver Sta. 65 G2
Iverna Ct. W8 77 D2
Iverna Gdns. W8 77 D2
Iverson Rd. 66 E4
Ives St. SW3 78 E1
Ivor Pl. NW1 74 E2
Ivy St. N1 76 B4
Ivyhouse La. 72 H1

Ixworth Pl. SW3 **77** F6
Jackass La. **71** F10
Jacob St. SE1 **80** C6
Jail La. **71** G10
Jamaica Rd. SE16 **80** D6
James St. W1 **74** G4
James St. WC2 **75** H9
Jameson St. W8 **77** B1
Jardin St. SE5 **80** H4
Jay Ms. SW7 **77** D4
Jeannette Cochrane Th. WC1 **75** F9
Jermyn St. SW1 **78** A6
Jerome Cresent NW8 **73** E6
Jerome St. E1 **76** F5
Jersey Rd. **69** A6
Jewry St. EC3 **76** H5
Joan St. SE1 **79** B12
Jockey's Fields WC1 **75** F10
Joel St. **65** C5
John Adam St. WC2 **75** J9
John Carpenter St. EC4 **75** H12
John Fisher St. E1 **76** J6
John Islip St. SW1 **79** F8
John Princess St. W1 **74** G5
John Ruskin St. SE5 **79** H13
John St. WC1 **75** E10
John's Ms. WC1 **75** E10
Jonathan St. SE11 **79** F9
Joyce Green Hosp. **72** A3
Joyce Green La. **72** A3
Joyden's Wood **72** C1
Jubilee Pk. **67** A8
Jubilee Pl. SW3 **78** G1
Judd St. WC1 **75** D8
Junction Ms. W2 **73** G6
Junction Rd. **66** D6
Justice Wk. SW3 **77** H6
Juxon St. SE11 **79** E10
Katherine Rd. **67** E10
Kay St. E2 **76** B6
Kean St. WC2 **75** H9
Keeley St. WC2 **75** G9
Kelso Pl. W8 **77** D2
Kemble St. WC2 **75** H9
Kempsford Gdns. SW5 **77** G2
Kempsford Rd. SE11 **79** F12
Kempton Pk. Race Course **69** C5
Kemsing **72** H3
Kendal St. W2 **73** H6
Kenley **71** H7
Kennings Way SE11 **79** G12
Kennington Gro. SE11 **79** H10
Kennington La. SE11 **79** G10
Kennington Oval SE11 **79** H10
Kennington Pk. SE11 **79** H11
Kennington Pk. Gdns. SE11 **79** H12
Kennington Pk. Pl. SE11 **79** H12
Kennington Pk. Rd. SE11 **79** G12
Kennington Rd. SE11/SE1 **79** E11
Kenrick Pl. W1 **74** F3
Kensal Green **66** F4
Kensal Green Sta. **66** F4
Kensal Rise **66** F4
Kensington & Chelsea **66** G4
Kensington Church St. W8 **77** B1
Kensington Ct. W8 **77** C3
Kensington Court Pl. W8 **77** D3
Kensington Gdns. W2/W8 **77** B3
Kensington Gdns. Sq. W2 **73** H2
Kensington Gate W8 **77** D3
Kensington Gore SW7 **77** C4
Kensington High St. W8 **77** D1
Kensington Mall W8 **77** B1
Kensington Palace **77** B2
Kensington Palace Barracks W8 **77** C2
Kensington Palace Gdns. W8 **77** B1
Kensington Palace Green W8 **77** C2
Kensington Pk. Rd. W11 **73** J1
Kensington Pl. W8 **77** B2
Kensington Rd. W8/SW7 **77** C3
Kensington Sq. W8 **77** D2
Kent House Sta. **71** D8
Kent St. E2 **76** B5
Kent Ter. NW1 **74** D2
Kentish Town **66** E6
Kentish Town Sta. **66** E6
Kenton **66** D2
Kenton La. **66** C2
Kenton Rd. **66** C2
Kenton St. WC1 **75** E8
Kenway Rd. SW5 **77** F2
Kenwood **66** D5
Keston **71** F10
Keston Mark **71** E10
Kew **70** A2
Kew Bri. **66** H2
Kew Bri. Rd. **70** A2
Kew Bri. Sta. **66** G2
Kew Gardens Sta. **70** A2
Kew Palace **70** A2
Kew Rd. **70** A2
Keyse Rd. NW6 **80** E5
Keystone Cresent N1 **75** C9
Keyworth St. SE1 **79** D12
Kidbrooke **71** A9
Kidbrooke Sta. **71** A10
Kilburn **66** E4
Kilburn High Rd. Sta. **66** E5
Kilburn Pk Rd. NW6 **73** D1
Kilburn Sta. **66** E4
Kildare Ter. W2 **73** G2
Killick St. N1 **75** C9
King & Queen St. SE17 **80** F2
King Charles St. SW1 **79** C8
King Edward St. EC1 **75** G13
King Edward Wk. SE1 **79** D11
King George V Dock **67** G11
King George VI Res. **69** B2
King George's Res. **67** A9
King Harolds Way West Heath **68** H1
King James St. SE1 **79** D12
King John's Ct. EC2 **76** E4
King St. EC2 **76** G2
King St. SW1 **78** B6
King St. W6 **66** G3
King St. WC2 **75** H8
King William St. EC4 **76** J3
Kingfieldgreen **69** H1
Kinglake St. SE17 **80** G4
Kingly St. W1 **74** H6
King's Arms Yd. EC2 **76** G2
King's Bench St. SE1 **79** C12
King's Bench Wk. EC4 **75** H11
King's College WC2 **75** H10
King's Cross Rd. WC1 **75** D10
King's Cross Sta. N1 **75** C8
King's Head Hill **67** A9
Kings Head Yd. SE1 **80** B3
Kings Ms. WC1 **75** F10
Kings Pl. SE1 **80** D1
King's Rd. Chingford **67** B9
King's Rd. SW1 **78** E4
King's Rd. SW3 **77** G6
King's Scholar's Pass. SW1 **78** E6
King's Sq. Estate EC1 **75** D13
King's Ter. NW1 **74** B6
Kingsbury **66** C3
Kingsbury Green **66** D3
Kingsbury Rd. **66** D3
Kingsbury Sta. **66** D2
Kingshill Av. **65** F5
Kingsland **67** E7
Kingsland Rd. E2 **76** C4
Kingsley Rd. **69** A6
Kingsmill Ter. NW8 **73** B5
Kingston Bri. **70** D1
Kingston Bypass **70** D3
Kingston Bypass Hinchley Wood **70** E1
Kingston Gate **70** C2
Kingston Hill **70** C2
Kingston La. **65** F3
Kingston Rd. Leatherhead **70** H1
Kingston Rd. New Malden **70** D2
Kingston Rd. Staines **69** C3
Kingston Rd. SW15 **70** B3
Kingston Rd. SW19 **70** D4
Kingston Rd. Teddington **70** C1
Kingston Rd. Tolworth **70** F3
Kingston upon Thames **70** D2
Kingston Vale **70** C2
Kingsway WC2 **75** G9
Kingswood Sta. **70** H4
Kinnerton St. SW1 **78** C3
Kintore Way SE1 **80** E5
Kipling Estate SE1 **80** C3
Kipling St. SE1 **80** C3
Kirby Grove SE1 **80** C3
Kirby St. EC1 **75** F11
Kirkdale **71** C7
Kirtling St. SW8 **78** J6
Kirwyn Way SE5 **79** H13
Kitson Rd. SE5 **80** J2
Kitto Rd. **71** A8
Knaresborough Pl. SW5 **77** F2
Knight's Hill **70** C6
Knights Res. **69** D5
Knightsbridge SW7/SW1 **78** C2
Knipp Hill **69** G5
Knivet Rd. SW6 **77** J1
Knockholt **71** H12
Knockholt Main Rd. **71** H11
Knockholt Pound **71** G12
Knockholt Rd. **71** G12
Knockholt Sta. **71** F12
Knowle Green **69** C2
Knox St. W1 **74** F2
Kynance Ms. SW7 **77** E3
Kynance Pl. SW7 **77** D3
Laburnum St. E2 **76** B5
Lackington St. EC2 **76** F3
Ladbroke Gro. W10/W11 **66** F4
Lafone St. SE1 **80** C5
Laleham **69** D3
Laleham Rd. Shepperton **69** D3
Laleham Rd. Staines **69** C2
Lamb St. E1 **76** F5
Lamb Wk. SE11 **80** C4
Lambeth **70** B6
Lambeth Bri. SW1/SE1 **79** E9
Lambeth High St. SE11 **79** E9
Lambeth Hospital SE11 **79** F12
Lambeth Palace SE1 **79** E9
Lambeth Palace Rd. SE1 **79** E9
Lambeth Pier SE1 **79** E9
Lambeth Rd. SE1 **79** E10
Lambeth Wk. SE11 **79** E10
Lambourne End **68** A1
Lamb's Conduit WC1 **75** E9
Lamb's Passage EC1 **76** E2
Lammas La. **69** F6
Lamont Rd. SW10 **77** H4
Lampton **69** A6
Lampton Rd. **69** A6
Lanark Pl. W9 **73** E4
Lanark Rd. W9 **73** D3
Lanark Ter. W9 **73** E4
Lancaster Gate W2 **73** J4
Lancaster House SW1 **78** C6
Lancaster Ms. W2 **73** H4
Lancaster Pl. WC2 **75** J9
Lancaster St. SE1 **79** C12
Lancaster Ter. W2 **73** H5
Lancelot Pl. SW7 **78** D2
Lancing St. NW1 **74** D7
Land Registry Office WC2 **75** G10
Landor Rd. SW9 **70** A6
Lane, The NW8 **73** C3
Langford Pl. NW8 **73** B4
Langham Pl. W1 **74** G5
Langham St. W1 **74** F5
Langley **65** G1
Langley La. SW8 **79** H9
Langley Pk. Eden Park **71** E9
Langley Pk. Slough **65** F1
Langley St. WC2 **75** H8
Langley Vale **70** H3
Langton Cl. WC1 **75** D10
Langton St. SW10 **77** J4
Lanhill Rd. W9 **73** E1
Lansdowne Rd. **67** C8
Lant St. SE1 **79** C13
Larcom St. SE17 **80** F2
Latchmere Rd. SW11 **70** A5
Lathams Rd. **71** F9
Latona Rd. SE15 **80** H6
Laud St. SE11 **79** G9
Lauderdale Rd. W9 **73** D2
Launceston Pl. W8 **77** D3
Launders La. **68** F3
Laurence Pountney La. EC4 **76** J3
Lausanne Rd. **67** H8
Lavender Hill SW11 **70** A5
Laverton Pl. SW5 **77** F2
Lavington St. SE1 **79** B13
Law St. SE1 **80** D3
Lawn La. SW8 **79** H9
Lawn Rd. **70** H1
Lawrence St. NW7 **66** B3
Lawrence St. SW3 **77** H6
Layhams Rd. **71** G9
Laystall St. EC1 **75** E10
Lea Bri. **67** D8
Lea Bri. Rd. **67** D8
Lea Bri. Sta. **67** D8
Lea Valley Rd. **67** A9
Leadenhall Mkt. EC3 **76** H3
Leadenhall St. EC3 **76** H4
Leake St. SE1 **79** C10
Leas Rd. **71** H8
Leather La. EC1 **75** F11
Leatherhead Common **70** H1
Leatherhead Rd. Chessington **70** F1
Leatherhead Rd. Leatherhead **70** H1
Leathermarket St. SE1 **80** C3
Leaves Green **71** G10
Leaves Green Rd. **71** F10
Ledgers Rd. **71** H8
Lee **71** B9
Lee High Rd. **71** B9
Lee Rd. **71** A9
Leeke St. WC1 **75** C9
Lees Pl. W1 **74** H3
Leesons Rd. **71** D11
Leicester Sq. WC2 **75** J7
Leigh Hunt St. SE1 **80** C1
Leigh St. WC1 **75** D8
Leigham Court Rd. **70** C6
Leinster Gdns. W2 **73** H3
Leinster Ms. W2 **73** J4
Leinster Pl. W2 **73** H3
Leinster Rd. NW6 **73** C1
Leinster Sq. W2 **73** H2
Leinster Ter. W2 **73** J3
Leman St. E1 **76** H6
Lennox Gdns. SW1 **78** E2
Lennox Gdns. Ms. SW1 **78** E2
Leonard St. EC2 **76** E3
Leroy St. SE1 **80** E4
Lessness Heath **68** G2
Lever St. EC1 **76** D1
Lewisham **71** B8
Lewisham High St. **71** B9
Lewisham Rd. **71** A9
Lewisham St. SW1 **79** C7
Lewisham Way SE4/SE14 **71** A9
Lexham Gdns. W8 **77** E2
Lexham Ms. W8 **77** E1
Lexington St. W1 **74** H6
Ley St. **67** D11
Leyden St. E1 **76** G5
Leyton **67** D9
Leyton High Rd. **67** D9
Leyton Marshes **67** D8
Leyton Midland Rd. Sta. **67** D9
Leytonstone High Rd. Sta. **67** D9
Leytonstone Rd. **67** E9
Liberty La. **69** F2
Library St. SE1 **79** D12
Lidlington Pl. NW1 **74** C6
Ligonier St. E2 **76** D5
Lilestone St. NW8 **73** E6
Lillie Rd. SW6 **66** H4
Lillie Rd. SW6 **77** H1
Lillington Gdns. Estate SW1 **78** F7
Lime St. EC3 **76** H4
Limehouse **67** F9
Limehouse Reach **67** G9
Limerston St. SW10 **77** H4
Limpsfield Rd. **71** G7
Lincoln Rd. **67** A7
Lincoln Rd. Ponders End **67** A8
Lincoln St. SW3 **78** F2
Lincoln's Inn WC2 **75** G10
Lincoln's Inn Flds. W2 **75** G10
Linden Gdns. W2 **73** J1
Lindsey St. EC1 **75** F13
Linhope St. NW1 **74** E2
Linsey St. SE16 **80** E6
Linton St. N1 **76** B2
Lisle St. W1 **74** H7
Lisson Green Estate NW8 **73** E6
Lisson Gro. NW8/NW1 **73** E6
Lisson St. NW1 **73** F6
Little Albany St. NW1 **74** D5
Little Boltons, The **77** G3
Little Britain EC1 **75** G13
Little Bushey La. **65** A6
Little Chester St. SW1 **78** D4
Little Ealing **66** G2
Little Edward St. NW1 **74** C5
Little Gaynes La. **68** E4
Little George St. SW1 **79** C8
Little Green La. **65** A4
Little Marlborough St. W1 **74** H6
Little New St. EC4 **75** G11
Little Oxhey La. **65** B5
Little Portland St. W1 **74** G6
Little Russell St. WC1 **75** G8
Little St. James's St. SW1 **78** B6
Little Thurrock **72** A6
Little Trinity La. EC4 **76** H2
Little Woodcote **70** G5
Little Woodmansterne La. **70** G5
Littleton **69** D3
Littleton La. **69** D3
Liverpool Grove SE17 **80** G2
Liverpool Rd. N1 **75** B11
Liverpool St. EC2 **76** G3
Liverpool St. Sta. EC2 **76** F4
Livonia St. W1 **74** H6
Lizard St. EC1 **76** D2
Llewellyn St. SE16 **80** C6
Lloyd Baker St. WC1 **75** D10
Lloyd Baker St. WC1 **75** D11
Lloyd Sq. WC1 **75** D10
Lloyd St. WC1 **75** C11
Lloyd's Av. EC3 **76** H4
Lloyd's Buildings EC3 **76** H3
Lloyds's Row EC1 **75** D12
Loampit Hill **71** A8
Lock La. **69** H3
Locket Rd. **66** C1
Locksbottom **71** E10
Lockwood Res. **67** C8
Lodge Av. **67** E12
Lodge La. **71** F9
Lodge La. Grays **68** G6
Lodge Rd. NW8 **73** D5
Loftie St. SE16 **80** C7
Logan Ms. W8 **77** E1
Logan Pl. W8 **77** E1
Lolesworth Cl. E1 **76** F5
Lollard St. SE11 **79** F10
Loman St. SE11 **79** C13
Lombard La. EC4 **75** H11
Lombard St. EC3 **76** H3
London Bri. EC4/SE1 **80** A3
London Bri. Sta. SE1 **80** B3
London Bri. St. SE1 **80** B3
London Clinic W1 **74** E4
London College of Printing SE11 **79** E12
London Fields Sta. **67** E8
London Planetarium NW1 **74** E3
London Rd. Badger's Mount **72** G1
London Rd. Batchworth **65** B3
London Rd. Cheam **70** E4
London Rd. Croydon **70** E6
London Rd. Dunton Green **72** H1
London Rd. Enfield **67** A7
London Rd. Hackbridge **70** E5
London Rd. Kingston **70** D2
London Rd. Mitcham **70** D5
London Rd. Morden **70** D4
London Rd. Norbury **70** D6
London Rd. Purfleet **68** G4
London Rd. Romford **68** D2
London Rd. SE1 **79** D12
London Rd. SE23 **71** B7
London Rd. Shenfield **68** A6
London Rd. Staines **69** C3
London Rd. Stanmore **66** B2
London Rd. Swanscombe **72** B4
London Rd. West Thurrock **68** H5
London School of Economics WC2 **75** H10
London St. Chertsey **69** E2
London St. EC3 **76** H4
London St. W2 **73** G5
London Tilbury Rd. **68** G4
London Transport Museum WC2 **75** H9
London Wall EC2 **76** G3
Londoner Hotel W1 **74** G4
Long Acre WC2 **75** H8
Long Ditton **70** E1
Long Elmes **65** C6
Long Grove Hospital **70** F2
Long Grove Rd. **70** F2
Long La. Bexley Heath **71** A12
Long La. Croydon **71** D8
Long La. EC1 **75** F13
Long La. Hillingdon **65** E4
Long La. SE1 **80** C3
Long La. Stanwell **69** B3
Long Ridge Rd. SW5 **77** F1
Long St. E2 **76** C5
Long Wk. SE1 **80** D4
Long Water, The W2 **77** B5
Long Yd. WC1 **75** E9
Longbridge Rd. **67** E11
Longcroft Rd. SE5 **80** H4
Longdown Rd. Nth. **70** G3
Longfield **72** D5
Longfield Hill **72** D6
Longfield Rd. **72** D5
Longford **65** H3
Longford St. NW1 **74** E5
Longlands **71** C11
Longleigh La. **67** H12
Longley St. SE1 **80** F6
Longmore Av. **66** A5
Longmore St. SW1 **78** F6
Longwood Gdns. **67** C11
Lord Hills Bri W2 **73** G2
Lord Hills Rd. W2 **73** F2
Lord North St. SW1 **79** E8
Lord's Cricket Ground NW8 **73** D5
Lordship La. N17 **67** C7
Lordship La. SE22 **71** B7
Lordship Rd. **67** D7
Lorenzo St. WC1 **75** C10
Lorrimore Rd. SE17 **79** H13
Lorrimore Sq. SE17 **79** H13
Lothbury EC2 **76** G3
Loudon Rd. NW8 **73** B4
Loudwater La. **65** A3
Loughborough Junc. Sta. **70** A6
Loughborough St. SE11 **79** G10
Loughton **67** A11
Loughton Way **67** A10
Lovat La. EC3 **76** J3
Love La. EC2 **76** G2

Love La. Morden 70 E4
Lovegrove St. SE1 80 G7
Lowdnes Cl. SW1 78 D4
Lower Addiscombe Rd. 71 E7
Lower Ashtead 70 H1
Lower Bedford Rd. 68 C2
Lower Belgrave St. SW1 78 E4
Lower Clapton Rd. 67 E8
Lower Edmonton 67 B8
Lower Feltham 69 C4
Lower Green 69 E6
Lower Green Rd. 69 E6
Lower Grosvenor Pl. SW1 78 D5
Lower Marsh SE1 79 C11
Lower Morden La. 70 E4
Lower Mortlake Rd. 70 B2
Lower Richmond Rd. SW13/SW15 70 A3
Lower Rd. 67 G8
Lower Sloane St. SW1 78 F3
Lower Sunbury Rd. 69 D5
Lower Sydenham 71 C8
Lower Sydenham Sta. 71 C8
Lower Thames St. EC3 76 J3
Lowfield St. 72 B3
Lowlands Rd. 66 D1
Lowndes Pl. SW1 78 D3
Lowndes Sq. SW1 78 D3
Lowndes St. SW1 78 D3
Lucan Pl. SW3 77 F6
Lucey Way SE16 80 E6
Ludgate Cir. EC4 75 H12
Ludgate Hill EC4 75 H12
Luke St. EC2 76 E3
Lullingstone Castle 72 F2
Lullingstone Pk. 72 F1
Lumley St. W1 74 H4
Lunghurst Rd. 71 H8
Lupus St. SW1 78 G6
Luscombe Way SW8 79 J8
Lusted La. 71 H10
Luton St. NW8 73 E5
Luxborough St. W1 74 F3
Luxted Rd. 71 G10
Lyall Gdns. SW1 78 E3
Lyall St. SW1 78 E3
Lynton Rd. SE1 80 F6
Lyons Pl. NW8 73 E5
Lytham St. SE17 80 G2
Lyttelton Rd. 66 C5
Mabledon Pl. WC1 75 D8
Macclesfield Rd. EC1 75 D13
Mackennal St. NW8 73 B6
Macklin St. WC2 75 G9
Macks Rd. SE16 80 E6
Mackworth St. NW1 74 C6
Macleod St. SE17 80 G2
Mad Bess Wood 65 C4
Madame Tussaud's NW1 74 E3
Maddox St. W1 74 H5
Madron St. SE17 80 F4
Magdalen St. SE1 80 B4
Magee St. SE11 79 H11
Maguire St. SE1 80 C5
Maida Av. W2 73 F4
Maida Vale W9 73 D3
Maiden La. WC2 75 J9
Maidstone Rd. 71 C12
Main Rd. Biggin Hill 71 H10
Main Rd. Sidcup 71 C11
Main Rd. Sutton-at-Hone 72 D3
Makins St. SW3 77 F6
Malden 70 E3
Malden Manor Sta. 70 E3
Malden Rd. Cheam 70 F4
Malden Rd. Malden 70 D3
Malden Rushett 70 G1
Malden Way 70 E3
Malet Pl. WC1 74 E7
Malet St. WC1 74 E7
Mall, The SW1 78 B7
Mallord St. SW3 77 H5
Mallory St. NW8 73 E6
Mallow St. EC1 76 E2
Malt St. SE1 80 H6
Malta St. EC1 75 D12
Maltby St. SE1 80 D5
Malvern Ms NW6 73 D1
Malvern Rd. NW6 73 D1
Manchester Rd. 67 G9
Manchester Sq. W1 74 G4
Manchester St. W1 74 G3
Manciple St. SE1 80 D3
Mandela Way SE1 80 F4
Mandeville Pl. W1 74 G4
Manette St. W1 75 H7
Manor Av. 71 A8
Manor Hospital 70 G2
Manor Pk. 67 E11
Manor Pl. SE17 79 G13
Manor Rd. Buckhurst Hill 67 A10
Manor Rd. Lambourne End 68 B1
Manor Rd. Mitcham 70 D5
Manor Rd. N16 67 D7
Manor Rd. Wallington 70 F5
Manor Rd. Woodford Bridge 67 B11
Manor Rd. Nth. 70 E1
Manresa Rd. SW3 77 G6
Mansell St. E1 76 H5
Mansfield Hill 67 B9
Mansfield St. W1 74 F5
Mansford St. E2 76 C7
Mansion House EC4 76 H2
Mansion House Pl. EC4 76 H2
Mansion, The 71 B12
Manson Pl. SW7 77 F4
Maplescombe 72 F3
Marble Hill Pk. 70 B1
Marchmont Ter. WC1 75 E8
Marcia Rd. SE1 80 F4
Margaret St. W1 74 G6
Margaretta Ter. SW3 77 H6
Margery St. WC1 75 D11
Mark La. EC3 76 H4
Mark St. EC2 76 E3
Market Ms. W1 78 B4
Market Pl. W1 74 G6
Markham Sq. SW3 78 G2
Markham St. SW3 78 G2
Markhouse Rd. 67 D9
Marks Gate 68 C1
Marks Gate Rd. 68 C1
Marlborough Av. E8 76 A6
Marlborough Gate W2 73 J5
Marlborough Grove SE1 80 G6
Marlborough Hill NW8 73 B4
Marlborough Ho. SW1 78 B7
Marlborough Pl. NW8 73 B4
Marlborough Rd. SW1 78 B6
Marlborough St. SW3 77 F6
Marle St. W1 74 F6
Marloes Rd. W8 77 E2
Marlpit La. 70 H6
Marriet Wk. SW1 78 D2
Marsh La. NW7 66 B3
Marsh La. Stanmore 66 B2
Marsh Rd. 65 C5
Marsh Side 67 B8
Marshall St. W1 74 H6
Marshalsea Rd. SE1 80 C2
Marsham St. SW1 79 E8
Mart St. WC2 75 H9
Martin La. EC4 76 H3
Martin Way 70 D4
Martindale Rd. 69 B5
Mary St. N1 76 A2
Mary Ter. NW1 74 B5
Maryland Sta. 67 E9
Marylands Rd. W9 73 E1
Marylebone 66 F6
Marylebone Flyover W2/NW1 73 F5
Marylebone High St. W1 74 F4
Marylebone La. W1 74 G4
Marylebone Ms. W1 74 G4
Marylebone Rd. NW1 74 F2
Marylebone Sta. NW1 74 E2
Marylebone St. W1 74 F4
Marylee Way SE11 79 F10
Mascalls La. 68 B5
Mason St. SE17 80 E3
Masons Hill 71 D9
Massinger St. SE17 80 F4
Matilda St. N1 75 A10
Matthew Parker St. SW1 79 D8
Maunsel St. SW1 78 E7
Mawbey Pl. SE1 80 G6
Maybury 69 H1
Mayesbrook Pk. 67 E12
Mayfair 66 G6
Mayfair Hotel W1 78 A5
Mayfair Pl. W1 78 B5
Maygood St. N1 75 B10
Mayney Rd. 68 C2
Maypole Rd. 71 F12
Mays La. 66 A4
Maze Hill Sta. 67 H9
Mead Row SE1 79 D11
Meadcroft Rd. SE5 79 H12
Meadow Ms. SW8 79 H10
Meadow Rd. SW8 79 J9
Meadow Row SE1 80 E1
Meard St. W1 74 H7
Mecklenburg Pl. WC1 75 E9
Mecklenburg Sq. WC1 75 E9
Medburn St. NW1 74 B7
Medical College of St. Bartholomew's EC1 75 E13
Medway St. SW1 78 E7
Melbourne Pl. WC2 75 H10
Melbury Ter. NW1 74 E2
Melcombe Pl. NW1 74 F2
Melcombe St. NW1 74 E2
Melfort Rd. 70 D6
Melina Pl. NW8 73 D4
Melior St. SE1 80 C3
Melton St. NW1 74 D7
Meopham 72 E6
Meopham Green 72 E6
Meopham Sta. 72 D6
Mepham St. SE1 79 B10
Mercer St. WC2 75 H8
Mercers Hall EC2 76 H2
Merchant Taylor's Hall EC3 76 H3
Meredith St. EC1 75 D12
Merlin St. WC1 75 D11
Mermaid Ct. SE1 80 C2
Mermaid Theatre EC4 75 H12
Merrick Sq. SE1 80 D2
Merrington Rd. SW6 77 H1
Merrow St. SE17 80 G3
Merry Hill 65 B6
Merryhill Rd. 65 A6
Merton Pk. Sta. 70 D4
Merton Rd. SW18 70 B4
Merton Rd. SW19 70 C4
Methley St. SE11 79 G11
Metropolitan Police Training School 69 E6
Metropolitan Tabernacle SE11 79 E12
Meymott St. SE1 79 B12
Micawber St. N1 76 C1
Micklethwaite Rd. SW6 77 H1
Middle St. EC1 75 F13
Middle Temple La. EC4 75 H11
Middlesex Hosp. W1 74 F6
Middlesex St. E1 76 G5
Midfield Way 71 D12
Midland Rd. NW1 75 C8
Milborne Gro. SW10 77 G4
Milbourne La. 69 F6
Milcote St. SE1 79 D12
Mildmay Forest 72 G1
Mildmay Miss. Hosp. E2 76 D5
Mile End Rd. 67 F8
Miles La. 69 G5
Miles St. SW8 79 H8
Milford La. WC2 75 H10
Milk St. EC2 76 G2
Mill Hill 66 B3
Mill Hill (Broadway) Sta. 66 B3
Mill Hill E. Sta. 66 C4
Mill La. Aveley 68 G4
Mill La. Thorpe 69 D2
Mill Row N1 76 B4
Mill St. SE1 80 C6
Mill St. W1 74 H5
Millbank SW1 79 E8
Miller St. NW1 74 B5
Millers La. 67 B12
Millman St. WC1 75 E10
Millwall 67 G9
Millwall Dock 67 G9
Millwall F.C. 67 H8
Milmans St. SW10 77 J5
Milner St. SW3 78 E2
Milton Pk. 69 C1
Milton St. EC2 76 F2
Milverton St. SE11 79 G11
Mina Rd. SE17 80 G4
Mincing La. EC3 76 H4
Minerva Ms. SW1 78 E4
Minnow St. SE17 80 F4
Minories EC3 76 H5
Mint St. SE1 80 C1
Mintern St. N1 76 B3
Mitcham 70 D5
Mitcham Common 70 D5
Mitcham Junc. Sta. 70 D5
Mitcham La. 70 C5
Mitcham Rd. Croydon 70 E6
Mitcham Sta. 70 D5
Mitchell St. EC1 76 D1
Mitchley Av. 71 G7
Mitchley Hill 71 G7
Mitre Rd. SE1 79 C11
Mitre St. EC3 76 H4
Moat Mount 66 A3
Molesey Rd. 69 E5
Molyneux St. W1 74 G2
Monck St. SW1 79 E7
Monckton St. SE11 79 E11
Moncorio Gdns. SW7 77 D5
Monmouth Rd. W2 73 H2
Monmouth St. WC2 75 H8
Monnow Rd. SE1 80 F6
Montagu Cl. SE1 80 B2
Montagu Man. W1 74 F3
Montagu Ms. Nth. W1 74 F2
Montagu Ms. Sth. W1 74 G2
Montagu Ms. W. W1 74 G2
Montagu Pl. W1 74 G2
Montagu Pl. WC1 75 F8
Montagu Rd. 67 B8
Montagu Row W1 74 F3
Montagu Sq. W1 74 G2
Montagu St. W1 74 G3
Montagu St. WC1 75 F8
Montclare St. E2 76 D5
Montford Pl. SE11 79 G11
Montpelier Pl. SW7 77 D6
Montpelier Sq. SW7 77 D6
Montpelier St. SW7 77 D6
Montpelier Wk. SW7 77 D6
Montrose Av. 66 C3
Montrose Pl. SW1 78 D4
Monument St. EC3 76 J3
Moor La. Chessington 70 F2
Moor La. EC2 76 F2
Moor La. Rickmansworth 65 B3
Moor Pk. Sta. 65 B4
Moore St. SW3 78 E2
Moorfields EC2 76 F2
Moorfields Eye Hosp. EC1 76 D2
Moorfields Rd. 65 D3
Moorgate EC2 76 G2
Moorhouse Rd. W2 73 G1
Mora St. EC1 76 D2
Morants Ct. Rd. 72 H1
Morden 70 E4
Morden Hall Rd. 70 D4
Morden Pk. 70 E4
Morden Rd. 70 D4
Morden Rd. Sta 70 D4
Morden Sth. Sta. 70 D4
Morden Sta. 70 D4
Morecambe St. SE17 80 F2
Moreland St. EC1 75 D13
Moreton Pl. SW1 78 G6
Moreton St. SW1 78 G6
Moreton Ter. SW1 78 G6
Morgan's La. SE1 80 B4
Morland Rd. 71 E7
Morley St. SE1 79 D11
Mornington Cres. NW1 74 C6
Mornington Pl. NW1 74 B5
Mornington St. NW1 74 B5
Mornington Ter. NW1 74 B5
Morocco St. SE1 80 C4
Morpeth Ter. SW1 78 E6
Morshead Rd. W9 73 D2
Mortimer St. W1 74 G6
Mortlake 70 B2
Mortlake Rd. 70 A2
Mortlake Sta. 70 A2
Morwell St. WC1 74 G7
Moscow Rd. W2 73 J2
Mossop St. SW3 78 E1
Mostyn Rd. SW19 70 D4
Motcomb St. SW1 78 D3
Motspur Pk. 70 D3
Mottingham 71 C10
Mottingham La. 71 B10
Mottingham Rd. 71 C10
Mount Pleasant Southall 65 F6
Mount Pleasant WC1 75 E10
Mount Row W1 74 J4
Mount Royal Hotel W1 74 H3
Mount St. W1 74 J4
Mount Vernon Hospital 65 B4
Moxon St. W1 74 F3
Mulberry St. E1 76 G6
Mulberry Wk. SW3 77 H5
Mulgrave Rd. 70 F4
Munster Sq. NW1 74 D5
Munton Rd. SE17 80 E2
Muriel St. N1 75 B10
Murphy St. SE1 79 D11
Murray Gro. N1 76 C2
Museum of London EC2 75 F13
Museum St. WC1 75 G8
Muswell Hill 66 C6
Muswell Hill Pk. Rd. 66 C6
Myddelton Pass. EC1 75 C11
Myddelton Sq. EC1 75 C11
Myddelton St. EC1 75 D11
Nags Head La. 68 C4
Nags Head Rd. 67 A8
Napier Gro. N1 76 B2
Nash 71 F9
Nassau St. W1 74 F6
National Film Theatre SE1 79 B10
National Gallery WC2 79 A8
National Heart Hospital W1 74 F4
National History Museum SW7 77 E5
National Hospital WC1 75 E9
National Maritime Museum 67 H9
National Portrait Gallery WC2 75 J8
National Postal Museum EC1 75 G13
Navarre St. E2 76 D5
Navestock Common 68 A3
Neal St. WC2 75 H8
Neasden 66 E3
Neasden Sta. 66 E3
Neate St. SE5 80 H4
Neckinger SE16 80 D5
Nelson Gdns. E2 76 C7
Nelson Pl. N1 75 C12
Nelson Rd. 69 B6
Nelson Sq. SE1 79 C12
Nelson Ter. N1 75 C12
Nelson's Column WC2 79 A8
Nether St. 66 C4
Netherland Rd. 66 A5
Netherton Gro. SW10 77 H4
Netley St. NW1 74 D6
Nevern Pl. SW5 77 F1
Nevern Sq. SW5 77 F1
Neville Cl. NW1 75 C8
Neville St. SW7 77 G5
Neville Ter. SW7 77 G5
New Addington 71 F9
New Ash Green 72 E5
New Barn 72 D5
New Barn La. Cudham 71 H11
New Barn La. Swanley 72 D2
New Barnet 66 A5
New Beckenham 71 C8
New Beckenham Sta. 71 C8
New Bond St. W1 74 H5
New Bowyer Pl. SE5 80 J2
New Bri. St. EC4 75 H12
New Broad St. EC2 76 G3
New Burlington St. W1 74 H6
New Cavendish St. W1 74 F5
New Change EC4 76 H1
New Charlton 67 G10
New Compton St. WC2 75 H8
New Cross Gate Sta. 67 H8
New Cross Rd. 67 H8
New Cross Stadium 67 H8
New Cross Sta. 67 H9
New Denham 65 E3
New Eltham 71 C10
New Fetter La. EC4 75 G11
New Haw 69 F3
New Haw Rd. 69 F3
New Horticultural Hall SW1 78 E7
New Inn St. EC2 76 E4
New Inn Yd. EC2 76 E4
New Kent Rd. SE1 80 E2
New King's Rd. SW6 70 A4
New Malden 70 D3
New North Pl. EC2 76 E4
New North Rd. Hainault 67 B12
New North Rd. N1 76 B2
New North St. WC1 75 F9
New Oxford St. WC1 75 G8
New Palace Yard SW1 79 C8
New Quebec St. W1 74 H3
New Ride SW1/SW7 78 C2
New Rd. Croxley Green 65 A4
New Rd. Dagenham 68 F2
New Rd. E4 67 B9
New Rd. Littleton 69 D4
New Rd. West Molesey 69 D6
New Row WC2 75 J8
New Scotland Yard SW1 78 D7
New Southgate 66 B6
New Southgate & Friern Barnet Sta. 66 B6
New Sq. WC2 75 G10
New St. EC2 76 G4
New Wharf Rd. N1 75 B9
New Years La. 71 G11
Newark La. 69 H2
Newburgh St. W1 74 H6
Newburn St. SE11 79 G10
Newbury Pk. 67 D11
Newbury St. EC1 75 F13
Newcastle Pl. W2 73 F5
Newcombe St. W8 77 B1
Newcomen St. SE1 80 C2
Newcourt St. NW8 73 C6
Newent Cl. SE15 80 J4
Newgate St. EC1 75 G13
Newham 67 F10
Newham Way 67 F10
Newington Butts SE11 79 F12
Newington Causeway SE1 79 D13
Newman Passage W1 74 G7
Newman St.W1 74 G6
Newport Pl. WC2 75 H8
Newport St. SE11 79 F10
Newton Rd. W2 73 G2
Newton St. WC2 75 G9
Newyears Green La. 65 D3
Nicholas La. EC4 76 H3
Nicholson St. SE1 79 B12
Nicoll St. E2 76 B6
Nightingale La. 70 B5
Nightingale Rd. Carshalton 70 E5
Nightingale Rd. N9 67 A8
Nile St. N1 76 C2
Nile Ter. SE1 80 G5
Nine Elms La. SW8 78 J7
Noak Hill 68 B3
Noak Hill Rd. 68 B3
Noble St. EC2 76 G1
Nockhill Wood 65 C2
Noel Pk. 67 C7
Noel Rd. N1 75 B12
Noel St. W1 74 G6
Nonsuch Pk. 70 F3
Norbiton 70 D2
Norbiton Sta. 70 D2
Norbury 70 D6
Norbury Cres. 70 D6
Norbury Hill 70 D6
Norfolk Cres. W2 73 G6
Norfolk Pl. W2 73 G5
Norfolk Rd. NW8 73 A5
Norfolk Row SE11 79 E10
Norfolk Sq. W2 73 G5

Norman St. *EC1* **76** D1
North Acton Sta. **66** F3
North Audley St. *W1* **74** H3
North Bank *NW8* **73** D6
North Cheam **70** E4
North Circular Rd. **66** C5
North Circular Rd. *NW10* **66** E2
North Circular Rd. *NW2* **66** D3
North Circular Rd. *Wood Green* **67** B7
North Cray **71** C12
North Cray Rd. **72** C1
North Cres. *WC1* **74** F7
North Down St. *N1* **75** C9
North Ealing Sta. **66** F2
North End *Croydon* **71** E7
North End *Erith* **72** A2
North End La. **71** F10
North End Rd. *NW11* **66** D5
North End Rd. *W14* **66** G4
North End Way **66** D5
North Finchley **66** B5
North Gower St. *NW1* **74** D6
North Harrow Sta. **65** D6
North Hill **66** D6
North Hyde **65** G5
North Hyde La. **65** H5
North Ms. *WC1* **75** E10
North Middlesex Hospital **67** B7
North Ockendon **68** E5
North Orbital Rd. **65** C2
North Ride *W2* **73** J6
North Rd. *Chigwell Row* **68** B2
North Rd. *N6* **66** D6
North Rd. *Purfleet* **68** G4
North Row *W1* **74** H3
North Sheen Sta. **70** B2
North St. *Romford* **68** C2
North Sugden Rd. **70** E1
North Tenter St. *E1* **76** H5
North Ter. *SW3* **77** E6
North View **65** D5
North Wembley Sta. **66** E2
North West Poly. *NW1* **74** A5
North Western Av. **66** A1
North Wharf Rd. **73** G5
North Woolwich **67** G11
North Woolwich Rd. **67** G10
Northampton Rd. *EC1* **75** E11
Northampton Sq. *EC1* **75** D12
Northborough Rd. **70** D6
Northburgh St. *EC1* **75** E12
Northfields Av. **66** G2
Northfields Sta. **66** G2
Northfleet **72** B6
Northington St. *WC1* **75** F10
Northolt **65** E5
Northolt Aerodrome **65** E4
Northolt Pk. **65** E6
Northolt Pk. Sta. **65** E6
Northolt Rd. **65** E6
Northover Rd. **71** C9
Northumberland All. *EC3* **76** H4
Northumberland Av. *WC2* **79** B8
Northumberland Heath **72** A1
Northumberland Pk. Sta. **67** C8
Northumberland Pl. *W2* **73** G1
Northumberland St. *WC2* **79** A8
Northwick Cl. *NW8* **73** E5
Northwick Pk. Hospital **66** D1
Northwick Pk. Sta. **66** D1
Northwick Ter. *NW8* **73** E4
Northwood **65** B4
Northwood Hills Sta. **65** C5
Northwood Rd. **65** C3
Norton Folgate *E1* **76** F4
Norwich Rd. *E8* **76** A7
Norwich St. *EC4* **75** G11
Norwood **71** C7
Norwood Green **65** G6
Norwood Junc. Sta. **71** D7
Norwood Rd. *SE27* **70** C6
Norwood Rd. *Southall* **65** G5
Notting Hill **66** F4
Notting Hill Gate *W11* **77** A1
Nottingham Pl. *W1* **74** F3
Nottingham St. *W1* **74** F3
Nugent Ter. *NW8* **73** C4
Nunhead **71** A8
Nunhead La. **71** A7
Nursery Row *SE17* **80** F2
Nutford Pl. *W1* **74** G2
Nuttall St. *N1* **76** B4
Oak Av. **69** C5
Oak Tree Rd. *NW8* **73** D5
Oakden St. *SE11* **79** E11
Oaken La. **70** F1
Oakend Wood **65** C1
Oakfield La. **72** C2
Oakington Rd. *W9* **73** E1
Oakleigh Pk. **66** A5
Oakleigh Pk. Sth. **66** B5
Oakleigh Pk. Sta. **66** A5
Oakley Crescent *EC1* **75** C12
Oakley Gdns. *SW3* **77** H6
Oakley Pl. *SE1* **80** G5
Oakley Sq. *NW1* **74** B6
Oakley St. *SW3* **77** H6
Oakwood Hill **67** A11
Oakwood Pk. **66** A6
Oakwood Sta. **66** A6
Oat La. *EC2* **76** G1
Oatlands Av. **69** F4
Oatlands Chase **69** E4
Oatlands Drive **69** E4
Oatlands Pk. **69** E4
Occupation Rd. *SE17* **79** G13
Ockendon Rd. **68** E5
Ockham Common **69** H4
Ockham La. **69** H3
Ockham Pk. **69** H3
Offley Rd. *SW9* **79** H11
Ogle St. *W1* **74** F6
Okehampton Cres. **67** H12
Old Bailey *EC4* **75** G12
Old Bond St. *W1* **74** J6
Old Broad St. *EC2* **76** G3
Old Brompton Rd. *SW5/SW7* **77** F3
Old Burlington St. *W1* **74** J6
Old Castle St. *E1* **76** G5
Old Cavendish St. *W1* **74** G5
Old Church Rd. *E4* **67** B9
Old Church Rd. *Romford* **68** D2
Old Church St. *SW3* **77** G5
Old Compton St. *W1* **74** H7
Old Coulsdon **70** H6
Old Court Pl. *W8* **77** C2
Old Deer Pk. **70** A1
Old Farleigh Rd. **71** G8
Old Ford Rd. **67** E8
Old Gloucester St. *WC1* **75** F9
Old Jamaica Rd. *SE16* **80** D6
Old Jewry *EC2* **76** G2
Old Kent Rd. *SE1* **80** F4
Old La. **69** H4
Old Marylebone Rd. *NW1* **73** G6
Old Montague St. *E1* **76** F6
Old Nichol St. *E2* **76** E5
Old Paradise St. *SE11* **79** E10
Old Pk. La. *W1* **78** B4
Old Pye St. *SW1* **78** D7
Old Quebec St. *W1* **74** H3
Old Queen St. *SW1* **79** C7
Old Redding **65** B6
Old Rd. **72** B1
Old Royal Observatory **67** H9
Old St. *EC1* **76** D3
Old Vic Theatre *SE1* **79** C11
Old Woking Rd. **69** G2
Oldbury **72** H4
Oldbury Pl. *W1* **74** F4
Oldfield La. **65** F6
Oldfield Rd. **70** E4
Olmar St. *SE1* **80** H6
Olney Rd. *SE17* **79** H13
Olympia **66** G4
Omeara St. *SE1* **80** B2
Omega Pl. *N1* **75** C9
Ongar Rd. *SW6* **77** H1
Onslow Gdns. *SW7* **77** F4
Onslow Sq. *SW7* **77** F5
Ontario St. *SE1* **79** D13
Opal St. *SE11* **79** F12
Open Air Theatre *NW1* **74** D3
Orange St. *WC2* **75** J7
Oratory, The *SW7* **77** E6
Orb St. *SE17* **80** F2
Orchard St. *W1* **74** H3
Orchardson St. *NW8* **73** E5
Orde Hall St. *WC1* **75** F9
Ordnance Hill *NW8* **73** B5
Orient Football Club **67** D9
Orient St. *SE11* **79** E12
Orme Ct. *W2* **73** J2
Orme La. *W2* **73** J2
Orme Sq. *W2* **73** J2
Orme Square Gate *W8* **73** J2
Ormond Yd. *SW1* **78** A6
Ormonde Gate *SW3* **78** G2
Ormsby St. *E2* **76** B5
Orpington **71** E12
Orpington Bypass *Badger's Mount* **72** F1
Orpington Bypass *Orpington* **71** E12
Orpington Bypass *St. Paul's Cray* **71** D12
Orpington Rd. **71** D11
Orsett Rd. *Grays* **68** G6
Orsett St. *SE11* **79** F10
Orsett Ter. *W2* **73** G3
Orsman Rd. *N1* **76** A4
Osborn St. *E1* **76** G6
Osidge La. **66** A6
Osnaburgh St. *NW1* **74** E5
Ossington St. *W2* **73** J2
Ossory Rd. *SE1* **80** H6
Ossulston St. *NW1* **74** C7
Osterley **70** A1
Osterley La. **66** G1
Osterley Pk. **65** G6
Osterley Pk. Ho. **69** A6
Oswin St. *SE11* **79** E12
Otford **72** H2
Otford La. **72** G1
Othello Cl. *SE11* **79** F12
Ottershaw **69** F2
Otto St. *SE17* **79** H12
Ottways La. **70** H1
Outer Circle *NW1* **74** C4
Outram St. *N1* **75** A9
Outwood La. **70** H4
Oval Cricket Ground, The *SE11* **79** H10
Oval Rd. *NW1* **74** A4
Oval Way *SE11* **79** G10
Ovenden Rd. **71** H12
Ovington Gdns. *SW3* **77** D6
Ovington Gdns. *SW3* **78** D1
Ovington Sq. *SW3* **78** E2
Ovington St. *SW3* **78** E2
Oxendon St. *SW1* **74** J7
Oxford Circus *W1* **74** G5
Oxford Rd. **65** D1
Oxford Sq. *W2* **73** H6
Oxford St. *W1* **74** G6
Oxhey **65** A5
Oxhey Drive **65** B5
Oxhey La. **65** B6
Oxlea Wood **71** A11
Oxshott **69** G6
Oyster La. **69** G3
Packington Sq. *N1* **75** B13
Packington St. *N1* **75** A13
Paddington **66** F5
Paddington General Hospital *W9* **73** F1
Paddington Grn. *W2* **73** F5
Paddington Recreation Ground *W9* **73** C2
Paddington Sta. *W2* **73** G4
Paddington St. *W1* **74** F3
Padnall Cnr. **68** C1
Page St. *SW1* **79** E7
Page's Wk. *SE1* **80** E4
Paget St. *EC1* **75** C12
Painters Rd. **67** C12
Pakenham St. *WC1* **75** D10
Palace Ct. *W2* **73** J2
Palace Gdns. Ms. *W8* **77** B2
Palace Gdns. Ter. *W8* **77** B2
Palace Gate *W8* **77** D3
Palace Green *W8* **77** B2
Palace Parade **71** C7
Palace Rd. **70** B6
Palace St. *SW1* **78** D6
Palace Theatre *W1* **75** H8
Palfrey Pl. *SW8* **79** H10
Palissy St. *E2* **76** D5
Pall Mall *SW1* **78** B7
Pall Mall E. *SW1* **79** A7
Palladium Theatre *W1* **74** H6
Palmer St. *SW1* **78** D7
Palmer's Green **66** B6
Palmers Green & Southgate Sta. **67** B7
Palmerston Rd. **67** B10
Pampisford Rd. **70** F6
Pancras La. *EC4* **76** H2
Pancras Rd. *NW1* **75** B7
Panton St. *SW1* **74** J7
Parade, The *SW11* **78** J3
Paradise Wk. *SW3* **78** H2
Parchmore Rd. **70** D6
Pardoner St. *SE1* **80** D3
Parfett St. *E1* **76** G7
Paris Gdn. *SE1* **79** B12
Park Av. **67** A7
Park Cres. *W1N* **74** E5
Park Crescent Ms. E. *W1* **74** E5
Park Crescent Ms. W. *W1* **74** E4
Park Farm Rd. **68** E4
Park Hill Rd. **71** B12
Park Hospital **71** B9
Park La. *Ashtead* **70** H2
Park La. *N17* **67** C8
Park La. *Romford* **68** D3
Park La. *W1* **78** B4
Park La. Hotel *W1* **78** B5
Park Pl. *SW1* **78** B6
Park Pl. Vs. *W2* **73** F4
Park Rd. *Banstead* **70** G4
Park Rd. *Fickleshole* **71** G9
Park Rd. *NW1* **74** D1
Park Rd. *Stanwell* **69** B3
Park Rd. *Teddington* **70** C1
Park Rd. *Twickenham* **69** C6
Park Royal **66** F2
Park Royal Sta. **66** F2
Park Side **70** C3
Park Sq. E. *NW1* **74** E5
Park Sq. W. *NW1* **74** E4
Park St. *SE1* **80** B2
Park St. *W1* **74** J3
Park Village E. *NW1* **74** B5
Park Village W. *NW1* **74** B5
Park Wk. *SW10* **77** H4
Park West Pl. *W2* **73** G6
Park Wood **65** C4
Parker St. *WC2* **75** G9
Parker's Row *SE1* **80** C6
Parkfield St. *N1* **75** B11
Parkfield Wood **72** E4
Parkhouse St. *SE5* **80** J3
Parklangley **71** D9
Parkway *NW1* **74** A5
Parkway, The **65** G5
Parliament Hill **66** E5
Parliament Sq. *SW1* **79** C8
Parliament St. *SW1* **79** C8
Parr St. *N1* **76** B2
Parry St. *SW8* **79** H9
Parsloes Av. **68** E1
Parsloes Park **68** E1
Parson St. **66** C4
Parvis Rd. **69** G3
Pascal St. *SW8* **79** J8
Passmore Ter. *SW1* **78** F3
Patent Office *EC4* **75** G11
Pater St. *W8* **77** D1
Paternoster Sq. *EC4* **75** G13
Paton St. *EC1* **76** D1
Paul St. *EC2* **76** E3
Paulton's Sq. *SW3* **77** H5
Paultons St. *SW3* **77** H5
Paveley St. *NW8* **73** D6
Pavilion Rd. *SW1* **78** D2
Pea La. **68** E5
Peabody Av. *SW1* **78** G5
Peace St. *E1* **76** E7
Peacock St. *SE17* **79** F13
Pear Tree Ct. *EC1* **75** E11
Pear Tree St. *EC1* **75** D13
Pearman St. *SE1* **79** D11
Pears Rd. **69** A6
Pearson St. *E2* **76** B5
Peckham **71** A7
Peckham Hill St. *SE15* **80** J6
Peckham Pk. Rd. *SE15* **80** J6
Peckham Rd. **71** A7
Peckham Rye **71** B7
Peckham Rye Com. **71** B7
Peckham Rye St. **71** A7
Pedley St. *E1* **76** E6
Peel St. *W8* **77** B1
Peerless St. *EC1* **76** D2
Pelham Cres. *SW7* **77** F6
Pelham Pl. *SW7* **77** F5
Pelham St. *SW7* **77** E5
Pelier St. *SE17* **79** H13
Pembridge Gdns. *W2* **73** J1
Pembridge Pl. *W2* **73** H1
Pembridge Rd. *W11* **73** J1
Pembridge Sq. *W2* **73** J1
Pembridge Vs. *W11* **73** H1
Pembroke Cl. *SW1* **78** C4
Pembroke Pl. *W8* **77** D1
Pembroke Rd. *Ruislip* **65** D4
Pembroke Rd. *W8* **77** E1
Pembroke Sq. *W8* **77** E1
Pembroke Vs. *W8* **77** E1
Pen Ponds **70** B2
Penfold Pl. *NW1* **73** F5
Penfold St. *NW8* **73** E5
Penge **71** C7
Penge E. Sta. **71** C8
Penge W. Sta. **71** C7
Penhill Rd. **71** B12
Penn St. *N1* **76** A3
Pennack Rd. *SE15* **80** H5
Pennant Ms. *W8* **77** E2
Pennington St. *E1* **76** J7
Penrose Grove *SE17* **79** G13
Penrose St. *SE17* **79** G13
Penryn St. *NW1* **74** B7
Penton Pl. *SE17* **79** G13
Penton Rise *WC1* **75** C10
Penton St. *N1* **75** B10
Pentonville Rd. *N1* **75** C10
Penywern Rd. *SW5* **77** F2
Pepys Rd. **70** D3
Pepys St. *EC3* **76** H4
Percival St. *EC1* **75** D12
Percy Cir. *WC1* **75** C10
Percy Rd. *Hampton* **69** C6
Percy Rd. *Twickenham* **69** B6
Percy St. *W1* **74** G7
Perivale **66** E2
Perkins Rents *SW1* **78** D7
Perry Hill **71** C8
Perry St. **71** C11
Peter Pan Statue *W2* **77** A5
Peter St. *W1* **74** H7
Peters La. *EC1* **75** F12
Petersham **70** B2
Petersham La. *SW7* **77** D3
Petersham Ms. *SW7* **77** E4
Petersham Pl. *SW7* **77** D4
Peto Pl. *NW1* **74** E5
Petts Wood **71** D11
Petts Wood Rd. **71** D11
Petty France *SW1* **78** D6
Petyward *SW3* **78** F1
Phelp St. *SE17* **80** H2
Phene St. *SW3* **77** H6
Philbeach Gdns. *SW5* **77** F1
Philip La. **67** C7
Phillimore Gdns. *W8* **77** D1
Phillimore Pl. *W8* **77** D1
Phillimore Wk. *W8* **77** D1
Phillipp St. *N1* **76** B4
Philpot La. *EC3* **76** H3
Phipp St. *EC2* **76** E4
Phoenix Pl. *WC1* **75** E10
Phoenix Rd. *NW1* **74** C7
Phoenix St. *WC2* **75** H8
Piccadilly *W1* **78** B5
Piccadilly Circus *W1* **74** J7
Piccadilly Hotel *W1* **74** J6
Piccadilly Theatre *W1* **74** J7
Pickard St. *EC1* **75** C13
Pickford La. **71** A12
Pickhurst La. **71** E9
Pickle Herring St. *SE1* **80** B4
Pickwick St. *SE1* **80** C1
Picton Pl. *W1* **74** G4
Pike La. **68** E5
Pilgrim St. *EC4* **75** H12
Pilgrimage St. **80** D2
Pilgrims Hatch **68** A5
Pilgrims Way *Knockholt* **71** H12
Pilgrims Way *Otford* **72** H2
Pimlico Garden *SW1* **78** H7
Pimlico Rd. *SW1* **78** F4
Pinchin St. *E1* **76** H6
Pindar St. *EC2* **76** F4
Pindock Ms. *W9* **73** E3
Pine St. *EC1* **75** E11
Pinkham Way **66** C6
Pinner **65** C5
Pinner Green **65** C5
Pinner Hill Rd. **65** C5
Pinner Rd. **65** D6
Pitfield St. *N1* **76** C3
Pitt St. *W8* **77** C1
Pitts Head Ms. *W1* **78** B4
Plaistow **67** F10
Plaistow La. **71** D10
Plaistow Sta. **67** F10
Platt **72** H5
Platt St. *NW1* **74** B7
Plender St. *NW1* **74** B6
Plough La. **69** H5
Plough Yd. *EC2* **76** E4
Plum Tree Court *EC4* **75** G12
Plumbers Row *E1* **76** G6
Plumstead **67** G11
Plumstead Common **67** H11
Plumstead Common Rd. **67** H11
Plumstead High St. **67** G12
Plumstead Marshes **67** G12
Plumstead Rd. **67** G11
Plumstead Sta. **67** G11
Plympton St. *NW8* **73** E6
Pointers Rd. **69** H4
Poiter St. *SE1* **80** D3
Pol Hill **72** G1
Poland St. *W1* **74** H6
Police College **66** C3
Pollard Row *E2* **76** D7
Pollen St. *W1* **74** H5
Polygon Rd. *NW1* **74** C7
Polytechnic of London *W1* **74** F3
Pomeroy St. **67** H8
Pond Pl. *SW3* **77** F6
Ponders End **67** A8
Ponsonby Ter. *SW1* **79** F8
Pont St. *SW1* **78** E2
Poole St. *N1* **76** B2
Pope St. *SE1* **80** D4
Poplar **67** F9
Poplar High St. **67** F9
Poplar Pl. *W2* **73** J2
Porchester Gdns. *W2* **73** H3
Porchester Pl. *W2* **73** H6
Porchester Rd. *W2* **73** G2
Porchester Sq. *W2* **73** G3
Porchester Sq. Ms. *W2* **73** G3
Porchester Ter. *W2* **73** H3
Porchester Ter. Gate *W2* **73** J3
Porchester Ter. Nth *W2* **73** G3
Porlock St. *SE1* **80** C3
Porters Av. **68** E1
Porteus Rd. *W2* **73** F4
Portland Rd. *SE25* **71** D7
Portland St. *SE17* **80** G3
Portman Cl. *W1* **74** G3
Portman Hotel *W1* **74** G3
Portman Ms. Sth. *W1* **74** H3
Portman Sq. *W1* **74** G3
Portman St. *W1* **74** H3
Portmore Pk. Rd. **69** E3
Portnalls Rd. **70** H5
Portpool La. *EC1* **75** F11
Portsea Pl. *W2* **74** H2
Portsmouth Rd. *Esher* **69** F6
Portsmouth Rd. *Thames Ditton* **70** E1
Portsmouth Rd. *Wisley* **69** H3
Portsmouth St. *WC2* **75** G10
Portsoken St. *E1* **76** H5
Portugal St. *WC2* **75** H10
Potter St. **65** C5
Potter's Flds. *SE1* **80** B4
Potterstreet Hill **65** B5
Poultrey *EC2* **76** H2
Pound La. **71** G12
Poverest Rd. **71** D11
Powdermill La. **69** B5
Pownall Rd. *E8* **76** A6
Poyle **69** A2
Poynders Rd. **70** B6
Praed St. *W2* **73** G5
Pratt Ms. *NW1* **74** A6

Pratt St. *NW1* **74** A6
Pratt Wk. *SE11* **79** E10
Pratt's Bottom **71** F12
Prebend St. *N1* **76** A1
Prescot St. *E1* **76** H6
Preston **66** D2
Preston Rd. **66** D2
Preston Rd. Sta. **66** D2
Prestwick Rd. **65** B5
Price's St. *SE1* **79** B12
Prideaux Pl. *WC1* **75** D10
Prima Rd. *SW9* **79** H11
Primrose Hill **66** E5
Primrose Hill *EC4* **75** H11
Primrose Hill Sta. **66** E5
Primrose St. *EC2* **76** F4
Prince Albert Rd. *NW8/NW1* **74** B2
Prince Charles Theatre *WC2* **75** H7
Prince Consort Rd. *SW7* **77** D4
Prince of Wales Gate *SW7* **77** C6
Prince of Wales Theatre *SW1* **74** J7
Prince Regents La. **67** F10
Princelet St. *E1* **76** F5
Princes Coverts **70** G1
Prince's Gdns. *SW7* **77** D5
Prince's Gate *SW7* **77** C5
Prince's Gate Ms. *SW7* **77** D5
Princes Ms. *W2* **73** H2
Princes Rd. **72** B2
Princes Square *W2* **73** H2
Princes St. *EC2* **76** G2
Princes St. *W1* **74** H5
Princess Beatrice Hospital *SW10* **77** G2
Princess Rd. *NW1* **73** C1
Princess St. *SE1* **79** E12
Princeton St. *WC1* **75** F10
Prioress St. *SE1* **80** E3
Priory La. **70** B3
Priory Rd. *N8* **66** C6
Priory Wk. *SW10* **77** G4
Pritchards Rd. *E2* **76** B7
Priter Rd. *SE16* **80** D6
Procter St. *WC1* **75** F9
Provence St. *N1* **75** B13
Provost St. *N1* **76** C2
Public Record Office *EC4* **75** G11
Public Trustee Office *WC2* **75** G9
Pudding La. *Chigwell* **67** A12
Pudding La. *EC3* **76** J3
Puddle Dock *EC4* **75** H12
Puddledock La. **72** C1
Purbrook St. *SE1* **80** D4
Purcell St. *N1* **76** B4
Purchese Rd. *NW1* **74** C7
Purfleet **68** G4
Purfleet Bypass **68** G4
Purfleet Rd. **68** G4
Purley **70** G6
Purley Downs **71** G7
Purley Downs Rd. **71** G7
Purley Oaks Sta. **71** F7
Purley Rd. *SE15* **80** J7
Purley Way **70** E6
Putney **70** B3
Putney Bri. **70** A4
Putney Bri. Rd. **70** B4
Putney Heath **70** B3
Putney High St. **70** B4
Putney Hill **70** B4
Putney Sta. **70** B4
Pyrcroft **69** E2
Pyrford **69** H2
Pyrford Common Rd. **69** H2
Pyrford Rd. **69** G2
Pyrgo Pk. **68** B3
Quaker St. *E1* **76** E5
Queen Anne Ms. *W1* **74** G5
Queen Anne St. *W1* **74** G4
Queen Anne's Gate *SW1* **78** D7
Queen Elizabeth College *W8* **77** C1
Queen Elizabeth II Res. **69** E5
Queen Elizabeth St. *SE1* **80** C5
Queen Mary Gdns *NW1* **74** D3
Queen Mary's Hospital *Sidcup* **71** C12
Queen Mary's Hospital *Wallington* **70** F5
Queen Mother Res., The **65** H1
Queen Sq *WC1* **75** F9
Queen St. *EC4* **76** H2
Queen St. *W1* **78** B5
Queen Victoria St. *EC4* **75** H13
Queens Gdns. *W2* **73** H4
Queen's Gate *SW7* **77** D4
Queen's Gate Gdns. *SW7* **77** E4
Queen's Gate Ms. *SW7* **77** D4
Queen's Gate Pl. *SW7* **77** E4
Queen's Gate Pl. Ms. *SW7* **77** E4
Queen's Gro. *NW8* **75** A5
Queens Head St. *N1* **75** A12
Queen's Ms. *W2* **73** H2
Queen's Pk. Rangers F.C. **66** G4
Queen's Pk. Sta. **66** F4
Queen's Rd. *Richmond* **70** B2
Queens Rd. *SE15* **67** H8
Queens Rd. *Teddington* **69** C6
Queens Rd. *Weybridge* **69** F4
Queen's Ter. *NW8* **73** B5
Queensberry Pl. *SW7* **77** E4
Queensberry Way *SW7* **77** E5
Queensborough Ter. *W2* **73** H3
Queensbridge Rd. *E2* **76** B6
Queensbury **66** C2
Queensbury Sta. **66** C2
Queenstown Rd. *SW8* **78** J4
Queensway *W2* **73** H3
Quilp St. *SE1* **80** C2
Quilter St. *E2* **76** C6
Racton Rd. *SW6* **77** H1
Radley Ms. *W8* **77** E2
Radnor Ms. *W2* **73** H5
Radnor Pl. *W2* **73** H5
Radnor Rd. *SE15* **80** J6
Radnor St. *EC1* **76** D2
Radnor Wk. *SW3* **78** G3
R.A.F. Museum **66** C3
Rag Hill **71** H10
Railway App. *SE1* **80** B3
Railway St. *EC3* **76** H4
Railway St. *N1* **75** C9
Rainbow St. *SE5* **80** J4
Rainham **68** F3
Rainham Marshes **68** F3
Rainham Rd. **68** E2
Rainsford St. *W2* **73** G6
Raleigh St. *N1* **75** B13
Ralph St. *SE1* **80** D2
Ramillies Pl. *W1* **74** H6
Ramillies St. *W1* **74** H6
Rampayne St. *SW1* **78** G7
Ramsey St. *E2* **76** D6
Randall Rd. *SE11* **79** F9
Randall Row *SE11* **79** F9
Randalls Rd. **70** H1
Randolph Av. *W9* **73** D3
Randolph Cres. *W9* **73** E3
Randolph Gdns. *NW6* **73** C2
Randolph Ms. *W9* **73** E4
Randolph Rd. *W9* **73** E4
Ranelagh Bri. *W2* **73** G3
Ranelagh Gdns. *SW3* **78** G4
Ranelagh Gro. *SW1* **78** F4
Rangers Rd. **67** A10
Ranston St. *NW1* **73** F6
Raphael St. *SW7* **78** C2
Rathbone Pl. *W1* **74** G7
Rathbone St. *W1* **74** G7
Ravensbourne Sta. **71** D9
Ravenscourt Pk. **66** G3
Ravenscourt Pk. Sta. **66** G4
Ravenscroft St. *E2* **76** C5
Ravensdon St. *SE11* **79** G11
Ravent Rd. *SE11* **79** F10
Ravey St. *EC2* **76** E4
Rawlings St. *SW3* **78** F2
Rawstorne St. *EC1* **75** D12
Ray St. *EC1* **75** E11
Rayners La. **65** D6
Raynes Pk. **70** D3
Raynes Pk. Sta. **70** D3
Rector St. *N1* **76** A1
Rectory La. *Byfleet* **69** G3
Rectory La. *Loughton* **67** A11
Rectory La. *SW17* **70** C5
Rectory La. *Woodmansterne* **70** G5
Rectory Rd. Sta. **67** E8
Red La. **70** F1
Red Lion Row *SE17* **80** H2
Red Lion Sq. *WC1* **75** F9
Red Lion St. *WC1* **75** F10
Red Lodge Rd. **71** E9
Red Pl. *W1* **74** H3
Redan Pl. *W2* **73** H2
Redbridge **67** C12
Redbridge La. **67** D10
Redbridge Sta. **67** D10
Redburn St. *SW3* **78** G2
Redchurch St. *E2* **76** E5
Redcliffe Gdns. *SW10* **77** G3
Redcliffe Ms. *SW10* **77** G3
Redcliffe Pl. *SW10* **77** H3
Redcliffe Rd. *SW10* **77** G4
Redcliffe Sq. *SW10* **77** G2
Redcliffe St. *SW10* **77** H3
Redcross Way *SE1* **80** C2
Rede Pl. *W2* **73** H1
Redesdale St. *SW3* **78** G2
Redfield La. *SW5* **77** E2
Redhill Rd. **69** G4
Redhill St. *NW1* **74** C5
Redmead La. *E1* **80** B6
Reece Ms. *SW7* **77** F4
Reede Rd. **68** E2
Reedworth St. *SE11* **79** F11
Rees St. *N1* **76** A2
Reeves Ms. *W1* **74** J4
Regal La. *NW1* **74** A4
Regan Way *N1* **76** C4
Regency St. *SW1* **78** E7
Regent Palace Hotel *W1* **74** J6
Regent Sq. *WC1* **75** D9
Regent St. *W1* **74** H6
Regent's Pk. *NW1* **74** C3
Regent's Pk. Barracks *NW1* **74** C5
Regent's Pk. Rd. *N3* **66** C4
Regent's Pk. Rd. *NW1* **74** A4
Regents Row *E8* **76** A6
Reigate Av. **70** E4
Reigate Rd. **70** G3
Remington St. *N1* **75** C12
Remnant St. *WC2* **75** G9
Rendall Ms *NW1* **73** F6
Renfrew Rd. *SE11* **79** F12
Rennie St. *SE1* **79** A12
Reston Pl. *SW7* **77** D3
Reverdy Rd. **80** F6
Rex Pl. *W1* **78** A4
Rheidol Ter. *N1* **75** B13
Rhoda St. *E2* **76** D5
Richard's Pl. *SW3* **78** E1
Richings Pk. **65** G2
Richmond **70** B2
Richmond Bri. **70** B1
Richmond Gate **70** B2
Richmond Ms. *W1* **74** H7
Richmond Pk. **70** B2
Richmond Rd. **70** C2
Richmond Ter. *SW1* **79** C8
Rickett St. *SW6* **77** H1
Ricketts Hill Rd. **71** H10
Rickmansworth **65** A3
Rickmansworth Rd. *Croxley Green* **65** A4
Rickmansworth Rd. *Harefield* **65** C3
Riddlesdown Rd. **70** G6
Riddlesdown Sta. **71** G7
Ridge Av. **67** A7
Ridge Rd. **70** E4
Ridge Wood **72** F6
Ridgeway, The **67** B9
Ridgmount Gdns. *WC1* **74** F7
Ridgmount St. *WC1* **74** F7
Ridgway **70** C3
Riding House St. *W1* **74** G6
Riley Rd. *SE1* **80** D4
Riley St. *SW10* **77** J5
Ring, The *W2* **73** H6
Ripley **69** H3
Ripple Rd. **68** E1
Risinghill St. *N1* **75** B10
Rita Rd. *SW8* **79** J9
Ritchie St. *N1* **75** B11
Ritz Hotel *SW1* **78** B6
River St. *EC1* **75** C11
Riverwalk Gdns. *SW1* **79** G8
Rivington St. *EC2* **76** D4
Robert Adam St. *W1* **74** G3
Robert Ms. *NW1* **74** D6
Robert St. *NW1* **74** D5
Roberta St. *E2* **76** D6
Robin Hood Gate **70** C3
Robin Hood Way **70** C3
Rochester Row *SW1* **78** E6
Rochester St. *SW1* **78** E7
Rochester Way *Bexley* **72** B1
Rochester Way *SE9* **71** A10
Rockingham St. *SE1* **80** E1
Rocliffe St. *N1* **75** C12
Roding La. *Buckhurst Hill* **67** B11
Roding La. North **67** C10
Roding La. Sth. **67** C10
Roding Valley Sta **67** B10
Rodmarton St. *W1* **74** G3
Rodney Pl. *SE17* **80** E2
Rodney Rd. *SE17* **80** F2
Rodney St. *N1* **75** B10
Roehampton **70** B3
Roehampton Gate **70** B3
Roehampton La. **70** B3
Roehampton Vale **70** C3
Roger St. *WC1* **75** E10
Roland Gdns. *SW7* **77** G4
Roland Way *SW7* **77** G4
Rolls Rd. *SE1* **80** F5
Roman Villa Rd. **72** C3
Romford **68** D2
Romford Rd. *Aveley* **68** F4
Romford Rd. *Chadwell Heath* **68** D1
Romford Rd. *Chigwell Row* **68** B1
Romford Rd. *E12* **67** D11
Romford Rd. *E7/E15* **67** E10
Romilly St. *W1* **75** H7
Romney Street **72** G3
Romney St. *SW1* **79** E8
Rood La. *EC3* **76** H4
Roosevelt Memorial *W1* **74** H4
Ropemaker St. *EC2* **76** F2
Roper La. *SE1* **80** C4
Ropley St. *E2* **76** C6
Rosary Gdns. *SW7* **77** F4
Roscoe St. *EC1* **76** E2
Rose All. *SE1* **80** A1
Rose Hill **70** E4
Rose La. **68** C1
Roseberry Av. *EC1* **75** E11
Rosemoor St. *SW3* **78** F2
Rosoman St. *EC1* **75** D11
Rossmore Rd. *NW1* **74** E1
Rotary St. *SE1* **79** D12
Rotherhithe **67** G8
Rotherhithe New Rd. **67** G8
Rotherhithe St. **67** G8
Rothsay St. *SE1* **80** D3
Rotten Row *SW1/SW7* **78** C2
Rouel Rd. *SE16* **80** E6
Round Pond *W2* **77** B3
Roundshaw **70** F6
Roundway, The **67** C7
Roupell St. *SE1* **79** B11
Rousebarn La. **65** A4
Row Hill **69** F2
Row Town **69** F2
Rowan Rd. **70** D6
Rowcross St. *SE1* **80** G5
Rowington Cl. *W2* **73** F2
Rowley Bank **66** A3
Rowley La. **66** A3
Roxeth **66** D1
Roxeth Green Av. **65** D6
Roxley Pl. *SW6* **77** H1
Royal Academy of Arts *W1* **74** J6
Royal Academy of Music *NW1* **74** E4
Royal Albert Dock **67** G11
Royal Albert Hall *SW7* **77** C4
Royal Army Medical College *SW1* **79** F8
Royal Automobile Club *SW1* **78** B7
Royal Av. *SW3* **78** G2
Royal Botanical Gardens **70** A2
Royal Cancer Hospital *SW3* **77** F5
Royal College of Art *SW7* **77** D4
Royal College of Medicine *W1* **74** G4
Royal College of Surgeons *WC2* **75** G10
Royal College St. *NW1* **74** B7
Royal Courts of Justice *WC2* **75** H10
Royal Ear Hospital *WC1* **74** E7
Royal Exchange *EC3* **76** H3
Royal Festival Hall *SE1* **79** B10
Royal Geographical Society *SW7* **77** C5
Royal Hospital *SW3* **78** G3
Royal Hospital Rd. *SW3* **78** G3
Royal Institute of British Architects *W1* **74** F5
Royal Lancaster Hotel *W2* **73** H5
Royal Ms., The *SW1* **78** D5
Royal Military Academy **67** H11
Royal Military School of Music **69** B6
Royal Mint St. *E1* **76** J5
Royal National Theatre *SE1* **79** B10
Royal Naval College **67** G9
Royal Opera House *WC2* **75** H9
Royal Rd. *SE17* **79** H12
Royal St. *SE1* **79** D10
Royal Veterinary College *NW1* **74** A7
Royal Victoria Dock **67** G10
Royal Waterloo Hospital *SE1* **79** B10
Royle St. *W1* **74** H6
Royston Pk. **65** B6
Ruckholt Rd. **67** E9
Rudolf Rd. *NW6* **73** C2
Rufus St. *N1* **76** D4
Rugby St. *WC1* **75** F9
Rugby Union Football Ground (Twickenham) **70** B1
Ruislip **65** D4
Ruislip Common **65** C4
Ruislip Gdns. Sta. **65** E5
Ruislip Lido **65** C4
Ruislip Manor Sta. **65** D5
Ruislip Rd. **65** F6
Runnymede **69** C1
Rupert St. *W1* **74** H7
Rush Green **68** D2
Rush Green Rd. **68** D2
Rushett La. **70** G1
Rushey Green **71** B8
Rushmore Hill Rd. **71** G12
Rushton St. *N1* **76** B3
Rushworth St. *SE1* **79** C12
Ruskin **71** B7
Russell Hotel *WC1* **75** E8
Russell La. **66** B5
Russell Sq. *WC1* **75** F8
Russell St. *WC2* **75** H9
Rust Square *SE5* **80** J2
Rutherford St. *SW1* **78** E7
Rutland Gdns. *SW7* **77** C6
Rutland Gate *SW7* **77** C6
Rutland Ms. *SW7* **77** D6
Rutland St. *SW7* **77** D6
Ruxbury Rd. **69** E2
Ruxley La. **70** F2
Rydens Rd. **69** E5
Ryder St. *SW1* **78** B6
Ryders Ter. *NW8* **73** B3
Rye La. **71** A7
Sackville St. *W1* **74** J6
Saffron Hill *EC1* **75** F11
Sail St. *SE11* **79** E10
St. Agnes Pl. *SE11* **79** H12
St. Alban's Gro. *W8* **77** D3
St. Albans Pl. *N1* **75** A12
St. Alban's St. *SW1* **74** J7
St. Alphage Gdn. *EC2* **76** F2
St. Andrew St. *EC4* **75** G11
St. Andrew's Gdns. *WC1* **75** D10
St. Andrew's Hill *EC4* **75** H12
St. Ann's Rd. *Chertsey* **69** E2
St. Ann's Rd. *N15* **67** D7
St. Ann's St. *SW1* **79** D7
St. Ann's Ter. *NW8* **73** B5
St. Barnabas St. *SW1* **78** F4
St. Bartholomew's Hospital *EC1* **75** G12
St. Bernard's Hanwell Hospital **66** G1
St. Botolph St. *E1* **76** G5
St. Bride St. *EC4* **75** G12
St. Chad's Pl. *WC1* **75** C9
St. Chad's St. *WC1* **75** C9
St. Clare St. *EC3* **76** H5
St. Clement Dane's Church *WC2* **75** H10
St. Clement's Church *EC4* **76** H3
St. Clement's La. *WC2* **75** H10
St. Cross St. *EC1* **75** F11
St. Dunstan's Hill *EC3* **76** J4
St. Edmund's Ter. *NW8* **74** B2
St. George St. *W1* **74** H5
St. George's Av. **69** F4
St. George's Cathedral *SE1* **79** D11
St. George's Cir. *SE1* **79** D12
St. George's Dri. *SW1* **78** F5
St. George's Gdns. *WC1* **75** D9
St. George's Rd. *SE1* **79** D12
St. George's Sq. *SW1* **78** G7
St. George's Way *SE15* **80** H4
St. Giles' High St. *WC2* **75** G8
St. Helena St. *WC1* **75** D11
St. Helen's Pl. *EC3* **76** G4
St. Helier **70** E4
St. Helier Av. **70** E4
St. Helier Hospital **70** E4
St. Helier Sta. **70** E4
St. James Pl. *EC1* **75** E12
St. James's *SW1* **78** B6
St. James's Drive **70** B5
St. James's Palace *SW1* **78** B6
St. James's Pk. *SW1* **78** C7
St. James's Pl. *SW1* **78** B6
St. James's Rd. *Croydon* **71** E7
St. James's Rd. *SE16* **80** E7
St. James's Row *EC1* **75** E12
St. James's Sq. *SW1* **78** B7
St. James's St. *SW1* **78** B6
St. James's St. Sta. **67** D8
St. James's Ter. Ms. *NW8* **74** B2
St. John St. *EC1* **75** D12
St. John's Hill **70** B5
St. John's La. *EC1* **75** F12
St. John's Sq. *EC1* **75** E12
St. John's Sta. **67** H9
St. John's Wood **66** F5
St. John's Wood Barracks *NW8* **73** B5
St. John's Wood High St. *NW8* **73** C5
St. John's Wood Pk. *NW8* **73** A5
St. John's Wood Rd. *NW8* **73** D5
St. John's Wood Ter. *NW8* **73** B6
St. Katherine's Way *E1* **80** B6
St. Leonard St. **67** F9
St. Leonard's Hospital *N1* **76** B4
St. Leonard's Ter. *SW3* **78** G2
St. Loo Av. *SW3* **78** H2
St. Margaret St. *SW1* **79** D8

St. Margarets 70 B1
St. Margaret's Church *SW1* 79 D8
St. Mark St. *E1* 76 H6
St. Mark's Hospital *EC1* 75 C13
St. Martins in the Fields Church *WC2* 75 J8
St. Martin's La. *WC2* 75 J8
St. Martin's le Grand *EC1* 75 G13
St. Martin's Pl. *WC2* 75 J8
St. Martin's Pl. *WC2* 79 A8
St. Martin's St. *WC2* 75 J8
St. Martin's Theatre *WC2* 75 H8
St. Mary Abbots Hospital *W8* 77 E2
St. Mary at Hill *EC3* 76 J3
St. Mary Axe *EC3* 76 G4
St. Mary Cray 71 D12
St. Mary-le-Bow Church *EC4* 76 H2
St. Mary's Gdns. *SE11* 79 E11
St. Mary's Hospital *W2* 73 G5
St. Mary's La. 68 D5
St. Mary's Rd. 70 E1
St. Mary's Ter. *W2* 73 F4
St. Mary's Wk. *SE11* 79 E11
St. Matthew St. *SW1* 78 D7
St. Matthew's Row *E2* 76 D6
St. Michael's St. *W2* 73 G5
St. Mildred's Rd. 71 B9
St. Oswald Pl. *SE11* 79 G10
St. Pancras Gdns. *NW1* 74 B7
St. Pancras Hospital *NW1* 74 B7
St. Pancras Sta. *NW1* 75 C8
St. Pancras Way *NW1* 74 A7
St. Paul St. *N1* 76 B1
St. Paul's Cathedral *EC4* 75 H13
St. Paul's Churchyard *EC4* 75 H13
St. Paul's Cray 71 D12
St. Paul's Cray Rd. 71 D11
St. Paul's Rd. 67 E7
St. Paul's Ter. *SE17* 79 H12
St. Paul's Thameslink Sta. *EC4* 75 H12
St. Paul's Wood Hill 71 D11
St. Peter's Cl. *E2* 76 C7
St. Peter's Hosp. 69 E2
St. Peter's St. *N1* 75 B12
St. Petersburgh Ms. *W2* 73 J2
St. Petersburgh Pl. *W2* 73 J2
St. Philip Way *N1* 76 A2
St. Quinton Av. *W10* 66 F4
St. Stephen's Gdns. *W2* 73 G1
St. Stephen's Hospital *SW10* 77 H4
St. Stephens Ms. *W2* 73 G1
St. Thomas Drive 65 C5
St. Thomas St. *SE1* 80 B3
St. Thomas's Hospital *SE1* 79 D9
St. Vincent St. *W1* 74 G4
Salamanca St. *SE11* 79 F9
Sale Pl. *W2* 73 G6
Salem Rd. *W2* 73 H2
Salisbury Ct. *EC4* 75 H12
Salisbury Pl. *W1* 74 F2
Salisbury St. *NW8* 73 E6
Salmon St. 66 D3
Salmons La. 71 H7
Samford St. *NW8* 73 E5
Sancroft St. *SE11* 79 F10
Sanctuary St. *SE1* 80 C2
Sandell St. *SE1* 79 C11
Sanderstead 71 G7
Sanderstead Hill 71 G7
Sanderstead Rd. 71 F7
Sanderstead Sta. 71 F7
Sandhurst Rd. 71 B9
Sandland St. *WC1* 75 F10
Sandown Pk. Race Course 69 E6
Sandwich St. *WC1* 75 D8
Sandy La. *Aveley* 68 G4
Sandy La. *Fairmile* 69 G5
Sandy La. *Twickenham* 70 D1
Sandy La. Sth. 70 F6
Sandy Lodge La. 65 B4
Sandy Lodge Rd. 65 B4
Sandy Row *E1* 76 F4
Sandycombe Rd. 70 A2
Sangley Rd. 71 B9
Sans Wk. *EC1* 75 E12
Sardinia St. *WC2* 75 G9
Saunders St. *SE11* 79 E10
Savage Gdns. *EC3* 76 H4
Saville Row *W1* 74 J6
Savoy Hill *WC2* 75 J9
Savoy Pl. *WC2* 75 J9
Savoy St. *WC2* 75 J9
Savoy Theatre *WC2* 75 J9
Sawyer St. *SE1* 79 C13
Scadbury Pk. 71 C11
Scala St. *W1* 74 F6
Scarborough St. *E1* 76 H5
Scarsdale Rd. *SE5* 80 H4
Scarsdale Vs. *W8* 77 E1
Scawfell St. *E2* 76 B5
School La. 69 F2
School of Arts & Crafts *WC1* 75 F9
School of Oriental Studies *WC1* 75 E8
Science Museum *SW7* 77 D5
Sclater St. *E1* 76 E5
Scoresby St. *SE1* 79 B12
Scotshall La. 71 G9
Scott Ellis Gdns. *NW8* 73 D5
Scott Lidgett Cres. *SE16* 80 D6
Scotts La. 71 D9
Scotts Lodge 71 H11
Scovell Rd. *SE1* 80 C1
Scratchwood 66 A3
Scratchwood Service Area *NW7* 66 B3
Scrubs La. *NW10* 66 F4
Scrutton St. *EC2* 76 E3
Scudders Hill 72 D4
Seacoal La. *EC4* 75 G12
Seaford St. *WC1* 75 D9
Seagrave Rd. *SW6* 77 H1
Seal 72 H3
Searles Rd. *SE1* 80 E3
Sears St. *SE5* 80 J2
Sebastian St. *EC1* 75 D12
Secker St. *SE1* 79 B11
Sedan Way *SE17* 80 F3
Sedding St. *SW1* 78 F3
Sedlescombe Rd. *SW6* 77 H1
Seething La. *EC3* 76 J4
Sekforde St. *EC1* 75 E12
Selby St. *E1* 76 E7
Selhurst 71 D7
Selhurst Rd. 71 D7
Sellow Ms. *SE11* 79 F10
Selous St. *NW1* 74 A6
Selsdon 71 F8
Selsdon Pk. Rd. 71 F8
Selsdon Rd. 71 F7
Selsdon Sta. 71 F7
Selsdon Wood 71 G8
Selwood Pl. *SW7* 77 G5
Semley Pl. *SW1* 78 F4
Senate House *WC1* 75 F8
Senior St. *W2* 73 F2
Serle St. *WC2* 75 G10
Serpentine Bri. *W2* 77 B5
Serpentine Rd. *W2* 77 B5
Serpentine Rd. *W2* 78 B2
Serpentine, The *W2* 77 B6
Setchell Rd. *SE1* 80 E5
Setchell Way *SE1* 80 E5
Settles Rd. *E1* 76 G7
Seven Dials *WC2* 75 H8
Seven Kings 67 D12
Seven Sisters Rd. 67 D7
Sevenoaks Rd. 71 F12
Severnhills Rd. 69 F4
Seville St. *SW1* 78 C3
Sevington St. *W9* 73 E2
Seward St. *EC1* 75 D13
Sewardstone Rd. 67 A9
Sewardstonebury 67 A9
Seymour Hall *W1* 74 G2
Seymour Ms. *W1* 74 G3
Seymour Pl. *W1* 74 G2
Seymour St. *W2/W1* 74 H2
Seymour Wk. *SW10* 77 H4
Shad Thames *SE1* 80 C5
Shaftesbury Av. *W1/WC2* 74 H7
Shaftesbury St. *N1* 76 C2
Shalcomb St. *SW10* 77 H4
Shand St. *SE1* 80 C4
Shap St. *E2* 76 B5
Sharsted St. *SE17* 79 G12
Shaw La. 71 H7
Shawfield St. *SW3* 78 G2
Sheen Common 70 B2
Sheen Rd. 70 B2
Sheerwater Rd. 69 G2
Sheffield Ter. *W8* 77 B1
Sheldrake Pl. *W8* 77 C1
Shelleys Hill 71 H11
Shelton St. *WC2* 75 H8
Shenfield 68 A6
Shenfield St. *N1* 76 C4
Shenley Rd. 66 A2
Shepherd Mkt. *W1* 78 B5
Shepherd St. *W1* 78 B4
Shepherdess Pl. *N1* 76 D2
Shepherdess Wk. *N1* 76 C2
Shepherd's Bush 66 G4
Shepherd's Bush Rd. *W6* 66 G4
Shepherds Hill 66 D6
Shepperton 69 E4
Shepperton Rd. *Laleham* 69 D3
Sheraton St. *W1* 74 H7
Sherborne La. *EC3* 76 H3
Sherwood Pk. Av. 71 B12
Sherwood St. *W1* 74 J6
Ship Hill 71 H10
Ship La. *Aveley* 68 G4
Ship La. *Sutton-at-Hone* 72 D3
Shipton St. *E2* 76 C6
Shire La. 71 F11
Shirehall Rd. 72 C3
Shirland Rd. *W9* 73 E2
Shirley 71 E8
Shirley Rd. 71 E8
Shoe La. *EC4* 75 G11
Shooter's Hill 67 H11
Shooter's Hill Rd. 67 H10
Shoreditch 67 E7
Shoreditch High St. *E1* 76 E4
Shoreditch Pk. *N1* 76 B2
Shoreham 72 G2
Shorncliffe Rd. *SE15* 80 G5
Short St. *SE1* 79 C11
Shortlands 71 D9
Shortlands Rd. 71 D9
Shortlands Sta. 71 D9
Short's Gdns. *WC2* 75 H8
Shouldham St. *W1* 74 G2
Shrewsbury Rd. *W2* 73 G1
Shroton St. *NW1* 73 F6
Sidcup 71 C11
Sidcup Bypass 71 C11
Sidcup Hill 71 C12
Sidcup Rd. *SE9/SE12* 71 C11
Siddons La. *NW1* 74 E2
Sidford Pl. *SE1* 79 E10
Sidmouth St. *WC1* 75 D9
Sidmouth Wood 70 B2
Silex St. *SE1* 79 C12
Silk St. *EC2* 76 F2
Silver St. 67 B7
Silver St. Sta. 67 B7
Silver Thorne Rd. 70 A5
Silvertown 67 G10
Silvertown Way 67 F10
Silvester St. *SE1* 80 C2
Simms Rd. *SE1* 80 F6
Singer St. *EC2* 76 D3
Single St. 71 G11
Sipson 65 H4
Sipson La 65 G4
Sipson Rd. 65 G4
Sixth Cross Rd. 69 C6
Skeet Hill La. 71 E12
Skibbs La. 71 E12
Skin Mkt. Pl. *SE1* 79 A13
Skinner La. *EC4* 76 H2
Skinner St. *EC1* 75 D11
Skinners Hall *EC4* 76 H2
Slade Green 72 A2
Slaidburn St. *SW10* 77 J4
Slines New Rd. 71 H8
Slines Oak Rd. 71 H8
Slingsby Pl. *WC2* 75 H8
Sloane Av. *SW3* 78 F1
Sloane Court E. *SW3* 78 G3
Sloane Court W. *SW3* 78 G3
Sloane Gdns. *SW1* 78 F3
Sloane Sq. *SW1* 78 F3
Sloane St. *SW1* 78 D2
Sloane Ter. *SW1* 78 E3
Slough 65 G1
Smith Sq. *SW1* 79 E8
Smith St. *SW3* 78 G2
Smith Ter. *SW3* 78 G2
Smitham Sta. 70 G6
Smithfield Central Mkt. *EC1* 75 F12
Smithfield St. *EC1* 75 G12
Smyrk's Rd. *SE17* 80 G4
Snaresbrook 67 C10
Snaresbrook Rd. 67 C9
Snow Hill *EC1* 75 G12
Snowden St. *EC2* 76 F4
Snowfields *SE1* 80 C3
Soho 66 F6
Soho Sq. *W1* 74 G7
Soho St. *W1* 74 G7
Somers Cres. *W2* 73 H6
Somers Ms *W2* 73 G6
Somerset House *WC2* 75 H10
Sondes St. *SE17* 80 H3
South Acton Sta. 66 G3
South Africa House *WC2* 79 A8
South Audley St. *W1* 74 J4
South Bank Poly. *SE1* 79 D12
South Bermondsey Sta. 67 G8
South Bolton Gdns. *SW10* 77 G3
South Carriage Rd. *SW1/SW7* 78 C2
South Carriage Rd. *SW7* 77 C5
South Crescent *WC1* 74 F7
South Croxted Rd. 71 C7
South Croydon 70 F6
South Croydon Sta. 71 F7
South Darenth 72 D3
South Ealing Rd. 66 G2
South Ealing Sta. 66 G2
South Eaton Pl. *SW1* 78 E4
South Eden Pk. 71 D8
South End *Croydon* 71 F7
South End *SE9* 71 B11
South End *W8* 77 D2
South End Rd. 68 E3
South End Row *W8* 77 D2
South Greenford Halt 66 F1
South Hampstead Sta. 66 E5
South Harrow 65 D6
South Hornchurch 68 E3
South Kenton Sta. 66 D2
South Lambeth Pl. *SW8* 79 H9
South Lambeth Rd. *SW8* 79 H9
South La. 70 E3
South Merton Sta. 70 D4
South Molton La. *W1* 74 H4
South Molton St. *W1* 74 H4
South Norwood 71 D7
South Norwood Hill 71 D7
South Ockendon 68 F5
South Oxhey 65 B5
South Par. *SW3* 77 G5
South Pk. Drive 67 E12
South Pl. *EC2* 76 F3
South Ruislip Sta. 65 E5
South Stifford 68 H5
South St. *Culverstone Green* 72 F6
South St. *Ponders End* 67 A8
South St. *Romford* 68 D2
South St. *W1* 78 A4
South Tenter St. *E1* 76 H5
South Ter. *SW7* 77 E6
South Tottenham Sta. 67 D7
South Weald 68 B4
South Weald Common 68 A4
South Wharf Rd. *W2* 73 G5
South Woodford Sta. 67 C10
Southall 65 G5
Southall Green 65 G6
Southall La. 65 H5
Southampton Blds. *WC2* 75 G10
Southampton Pl. *WC1* 75 G9
Southampton Row *WC1* 75 F9
Southampton St. *WC2* 75 J9
Southampton Way 67 H7
Southampton Way *SE5* 80 J3
Southborough *Bromley* 71 D10
Southborough *Kingston* 70 E2
Southborough La. 71 D10
Southborough Rd. 71 D10
Southbury Rd. 67 A7
Southcroft Rd. 70 C5
Southend 71 C9
Southend Rd. *E18* 67 C10
Southend Rd. *Romford* 68 C4
Southern St. *N1* 75 B9
Southfields Sta. 70 B4
Southfleet 72 C5
Southgate 66 A6
Southwark 67 G7
Southwark Bri. *SE1* 76 J2
Southwark Bri. Rd. *SE1* 79 C13
Southwark Cathedral *SE1* 80 B2
Southwark Pk. 67 G8
Southwark Pk. Rd. *SE16* 80 E6
Southwark St. *SE1* 79 B13
Southwell Gdns. *SW7* 77 E3
Southwick Ms. *W2* 73 G5
Southwick Pl. *W2* 73 H6
Southwick St. *W2* 73 G6
Spa Hill 71 D7
Spaniards Rd. 66 D5
Spanish Pl. *W1* 74 G4
Sparrowsherne 65 A6
Spear Ms. *SW5* 77 F1
Spelman St. *E1* 76 F6
Spencer St. *EC1* 75 D12
Spenser St. *SW1* 78 D6
Spinney Hill 69 F2
Spital La. 68 B5
Spital Sq. *E1* 76 F4
Spital St. *E1* 76 E6
Spitalfields 67 F8
Spitalfields Mkt. *E1* 76 F5
Sprimont Pl. *SW3* 78 F2
Spring Gdns. *SW1* 79 B8
Spring Grove 70 A1
Spring St. *W2* 73 H5
Springfield Pk. 67 D8
Springfield Rd. *NW8* 73 A3
Spur Rd. *Orpington* 71 E12
Spurgeon St. *SE1* 80 D2
Squires Bri. Rd. 69 D3
Squirrels Heath 68 C3
Squirrels Heath Rd. 68 C4
Squirries St. *E2* 76 D6
Stables Way *SE11* 79 G11
Stacey St. *WC2* 75 H8
Stafford Cl. *NW6* 73 D1
Stafford Pl. *SW1* 78 D6
Stafford Rd. *Beddington* 70 F6
Stafford Rd. *NW6* 73 C1
Stafford St. *W1* 78 A5
Stafford Ter. *W8* 77 D1
Stag La. 66 C3
Stag Pl. *SW1* 78 D6
Staines 69 C2
Staines Bri. 69 C2
Staines Central Sta. 69 C2
Staines La. 69 D2
Staines Reservoirs 69 B3
Staines Rd. *Hounslow* 69 B5
Staines Rd. *Laleham* 69 D2
Staines Rd. E. 69 D5
Staines Rd. W. 69 C4
Stamford Bri. Stadium *SW6* 77 J2
Stamford Brook Sta. 66 G3
Stamford Hill 67 D7
Stamford Hill Sta. 67 D7
Stamford St. *SE1* 79 B11
Stanford Rd. *W8* 77 D3
Stanhope Gdns. *SW7* 77 E4
Stanhope Gate *W1* 78 B4
Stanhope Ms. E. *SW7* 77 E4
Stanhope Ms. W. *SW7* 77 E4
Stanhope Pl. *W2* 74 H2
Stanhope Pl. Gate *W2* 74 H2
Stanhope Row *W1* 78 B4
Stanhope St. *NW1* 74 D6
Stanhope Ter. *W2* 73 H5
Stanley Pk. Rd. 70 F5
Stanley Pass. *NW1* 75 C8
Stanley Rd 70 C1
Stanmore 66 B2
Stanmore Hill 66 B1
Stanmore Sta. 66 B2
Stannary St. *SE11* 79 G11
Stanstead Rd. 71 B8
Stansted 72 F5
Stanway St. *N1* 76 C4
Stanwell 69 B3
Stanwell New Rd. 69 C2
Stanwell Rd. *Ashford* 69 C3
Stanwell Rd. *West Bedfont* 69 B4
Stanwellmoor 69 B2
Stanworth St. *SE1* 80 D5
Staple St. *SE1* 80 D3
Stapleford Abbotts 68 A2
Staples Cnr. 66 D4
Star & Garter Home 70 B2
Star Hill Rd. 72 H1
Star St. *W2* 73 G5
Starcross St. *NW1* 74 D6
Station Av. 69 E4
Station La. 68 D3
Station Rd. 67 A9
Station Rd. *Addlestone* 69 E3
Station Rd. *Harrow* 66 C1
Station Rd. *New Barnet* 66 A5
Station Rd. *Orpington* 71 E11
Station Rd. *Sidcup* 71 C11
Stationers Hall *EC4* 75 G12
Stead St. *SE17* 80 F2
Steedman St. *SE17* 79 F13
Steels La. 69 G6
Stephen St. *W1* 74 G7
Stephenson Way *NW1* 74 D6
Stepney 67 F8
Stepney E. Sta. 67 F8
Sterling St. *SW7* 77 D6
Sterry St. *SE1* 80 C2
Steward St. *E1* 76 F4
Stewart's Gro. *SW3* 77 F5
Stifford 68 G6
Stifford Rd. 68 G4
Stillington St. *SW1* 78 E6
Stock Exchange *EC2* 76 G3
Stockley Rd. 65 G4
Stockwell Rd. *SW9* 70 A6
Stoke D'Abernon 69 H5
Stoke Newington 67 D7
Stoke Newington Rd. 67 E7
Stoke Newington Sta. 67 D7
Stoke Rd. 69 G5
Stone 72 B4
Stone Blds. *WC2* 75 G10
Stone Crossing Halt 72 B4
Stone Grove 66 B2
Stone Marshes 72 A3
Stonebridge Pk. Sta. 66 E2
Stonecot Hill 70 E4
Stonecutter St. *EC4* 75 G12
Stonehill Rd. 69 F1
Stonehouse La. *Pratt's Bottom* 71 F12
Stonehouse La. *West Thurrock* 68 G4
Stoneleigh Sta. 70 F3
Stones End St. *SE1* 80 D1
Stoney La. *E1* 76 G4
Stoney St. *SE1* 80 B2
Stony Cnr. 72 D6
Store St. *WC1* 74 F7
Storey's Gate *SW1* 79 D8
Stourcliffe St. *W1* 74 G2
Straight Rd. 68 C3
Strand *WC2* 75 J9
Strand Theatre *WC2* 75 H9
Stratford 67 E9
Stratford New Town 67 E9
Stratford Pl. *W1* 74 H4
Stratford Rd. *W8* 77 E1

Stratford Sta. 67 E9
Strathearn Pl. *W2* 73 H5
Strathnairn St. *SE1* 80 F7
Stratton St. *W1* 78 B5
Strawberry Hill Sta. 70 C1
Strawberry Vale 70 C1
Streatfield Rd. 66 C2
Streatham 70 C6
Streatham Common 70 C6
Streatham Common Nth. 70 C6
Streatham Common Sta. 70 C6
Streatham High Rd. 70 C6
Streatham Hill 70 B6
Streatham Hill Sta. 70 C6
Streatham Rd. 70 D5
Streatham Sta. 70 C6
Streatham St. *WC1* 75 G8
Streatham Vale 70 C6
Street, The 70 H2
Stroud Green Rd. 67 D7
Stroude 69 D1
Strutton Ground *SW1* 78 D7
Strype St. *E1* 76 G5
Stuart Rd. *NW6* 73 D1
Stubbers La. 68 E4
Stukeley St. *WC2* 75 G9
Sturt St. *N1* 76 C2
Stutfield St. *E1* 76 H7
Sudbrook Pk. 70 C2
Sudbury & Harrow Rd. Sta. 66 E2
Sudbury Hill & Harrow Sta. 66 E1
Sudbury Hill Sta. 66 E1
Sudbury Town Sta. 66 E2
Sudeley St. *N1* 75 C12
Sudrey St. *SE1* 79 C13
Suffolk La. *EC4* 76 J2
Suffolk St. *SE1* 80 C1
Suffolk St. *SW1* 79 A7
Sultan St. *SE5* 80 J1
Summer Rd. 70 D1
Summers La. 66 B5
Sumner Pl. *SW7* 77 F5
Sumner Rd. *SE15* 80 J5
Sumner St. *SE1* 79 B13
Sun St. *EC2* 76 F3
Sunbury 69 D4
Sunbury Sta. 69 D4
Sunderland Ter. *W2* 73 G2
Sundridge Hill Rd. 71 H12
Sundridge Pk. Sta. 71 D9
Sundridge Rd. 72 H1
Sunnings La. 68 E4
Surbiton 70 E2
Surrendale Pl. *W9* 73 E2
Surrey Gro. *SE17* 80 G4
Surrey Row *SE1* 79 C12
Surrey Sq. *SE17* 80 F4
Surrey St. *WC2* 75 H10
Surrey Ter. *SE17* 80 F4
Sussex Gdns. *W2* 73 H5
Sussex Pl. *NW1* 74 D2
Sussex Pl. *W2* 73 H5
Sussex Sq. *W2* 73 H5
Sussex St. *SW1* 78 G5
Sutherland Av. *W9* 73 E2
Sutherland Pl. *W2* 73 G1
Sutherland St. *SW1* 78 G5
Sutherland Wk. *SE17* 80 G2
Sutton 70 F4
Sutton at Hone Rd. 72 C2
Sutton Av. 68 D3
Sutton Common Rd. 70 E4
Sutton Common Sta. 70 E4
Sutton La. *Hounslow* 69 A5
Sutton La. *Sutton* 70 G4
Sutton Row *W1* 74 G7
Sutton Sta. 70 F4
Sutton-at-Hone 72 D3
Swakeleys 65 E4
Swallow St. *W1* 74 J6
Swan La. *EC4* 76 J2
Swan Mead *SE1* 80 E4
Swan St. *SE1* 80 D2
Swan Wk. *SW3* 78 H2
Swancombe Marshes 72 A5
Swanfield St. *E2* 76 D5
Swanley 72 D2
Swanley La. 72 D2
Swanley Village 72 D2
Swanley Village Rd. 72 D2
Swanscombe 72 B5
Swanscombe Pk. 72 C5
Swanscombe Sta 72 B5
Sweeney Cres. *SE1* 80 D5
Swinton St. *WC1* 75 D9
Swiss Cottage Sta. 66 E5
Sydenham 71 C7
Sydenham Hill 71 C7
Sydenham Hill Sta. 71 C7
Sydenham Rd. 71 C8
Sydenham Sta. 71 C8
Sydney Pl. *SW7* 77 F5
Sydney St. *SW3* 77 G6
Symon St. *SW3* 78 F3
Syon House 70 A1
Syon La. 70 A1
Syon La. Sta. 70 A1
Tabard St. *SE1* 80 D2
Tabernacle St. *EC2* 76 E3
Tachbrook St. *SW1* 78 F6
Talbot Rd. *W11/W2* 73 G1
Talbot Sq. *W2* 73 H5
Talbot Yd. *SE1* 80 B2
Tallis St. *EC4* 75 H11
Tamworth St. *SW6* 77 H1
Tank La. 68 G4
Tanner St. *SE1* 80 C4
Taplow St. *N1* 76 C2
Tarver Rd. *SE17* 79 G13
Tate Gallery *SW1* 79 F8
Tatling End 65 D1
Tatsfield 71 H10
Tatsfield La. 71 H10
Tattenham Cnr. Rd. 70 H3
Tattenham Cnr. Sta. 70 H3
Tattenham Way 70 H4
Tatum St. *SE17* 80 F3
Taunton Pl. *NW1* 74 E2
Tavistock Pl. *WC1* 75 E8
Tavistock Sq. *WC1* 75 E8
Tavistock St. *WC2* 75 H9
Taviton St. *WC1* 74 E7
Teale St. *E2* 76 B7
Teddington 70 C1
Tedworth Sq. *SW3* 78 G2
Telecom Tower *W1* 74 F6
Temple Av. *EC4* 75 H11
Temple Bar *WC2* 75 H11
Temple Gdns. *EC4* 75 H11
Temple La. *EC4* 75 H11
Temple Pl. *WC2* 75 H10
Temple Rd. 70 G2
Temple, The *EC4* 75 H11
Templeton Pl. *SW5* 77 F1
Tenison Way *SE1* 79 B10
Tennis St. *SE1* 80 C2
Tentelow La. 65 G6
Terminus Pl. *SW1* 78 E5
Terrace Rd. 69 E5
Tetbury Pl. *N1* 75 B12
Thackeray St. *W8* 77 D2
Thames Ditton 70 E1
Thames Ditton Sta. 70 E1
Thames St. *Weybridge* 69 E4
Thames Water Authority *EC1* 75 D11
Thamesmead 68 G1
Thanet St. *WC1* 75 D8
Thavies Inn *EC4* 75 G11
Thayer St. *W1* 74 G4
Theatre Royal *WC2* 75 H9
Theed St. *SE1* 79 B11
Theobald St. *Borehamwood* 66 A2
Theobald's Rd. *WC1* 75 F9
Thirleby Rd. *SW1* 78 E6
Thistle Gro. *SW10* 77 G4
Thistlecroft 69 F5
Thomas Doyle St. *SE1* 79 D12
Thomas More St. *E1* 76 J6
Thomas More St. *E1* 80 A6
Thompson Av. *SE5* 80 J1
Thoresby St. *N1* 76 C1
Thorndon Pk. 68 C6
Thorney La. 65 F2
Thorney St. *SW1* 79 E8
Thorngate Rd. *W9* 73 E2
Thornton Heath 70 D6
Thornton Pl. *W1* 74 F2
Thornton Rd. 70 E6
Thorpe 69 D2
Thorpe Pk. 69 D2
Thorpe Rd. *Chertsey* 69 D2
Thorpe Rd. *Staines* 69 C2
Thrale St. *SE1* 80 B2
Thrawl St. *E1* 76 G5
Threadneedle St. *EC2* 76 H3
Three Kings Yd. *W1* 74 H4
Three Oak La. *SE1* 80 C5
Throgmorton Av. *EC2* 76 G3
Throgmorton St. *EC2* 76 G3
Thrush St. *SE17* 79 G13
Thurland Rd. *SE16* 80 D6
Thurloe Pl. *SW7* 77 E5
Thurloe Sq. *SW7* 77 E5
Thurloe St. *SW7* 77 E5
Thurlow St. *SE17* 80 G3
Thurrock Way *Grays* 68 G5
Thurtle Rd. *E2* 76 B5
Tibbetts Cnr. 70 B4
Tilbury 72 A6
Tilney St. *W1* 78 B4
Tinworth St. *SE11* 79 F9
Titchborne Row *W2* 73 H6
Titchfield Rd. *NW8* 74 B2
Tite St. *SW3* 78 H2
Tiverton St. *SE1* 79 D13
Token House Yd. *EC2* 76 G3
Tollington Pk. Rd. 66 D6
Tolmers Square *NW1* 74 D6
Tolpits La. 65 A4
Tolworth 70 E2
Tolworth Rise 70 E2
Tolworth Rd. 70 E2
Tomswood Hill 67 C11
Tonbridge St. *WC1* 75 D8
Tooley St. *SE1* 80 B4
Tooting Bec Rd. 70 C5
Tooting Bec Sta. 70 C5
Tooting Common 70 C5
Tooting Graveney 70 C5
Tooting Graveney Common 70 C5
Tooting High St. 70 C5
Tooting Sta. 70 C5
Topham St. *EC1* 75 E11
Tor Gdns. *W8* 77 C1
Torquay St. *W2* 73 F2
Torrens St. *N1* 75 C12
Torrington Pl. *WC1* 74 F7
Tottenham 67 C7
Tottenham Court Rd. *W1* 74 F6
Tottenham Hale 67 C8
Tottenham Hale Sta. 67 C8
Tottenham Hotspur F.C. 67 C8
Tottenham La. 66 D6
Tottenham St. *W1* 74 F6
Totteridge 66 A4
Totteridge & Whetstone Sta. 66 B5
Totteridge La. 66 B4
Toulmin St. *SE1* 79 C13
Tower Bri. *E1/SE1* 80 B5
Tower Bri. App. *E1* 76 J5
Tower Bri. Rd. *SE1* 80 D4
Tower Hamlets 67 F8
Tower Hill *EC3* 76 J5
Tower St. *WC2* 75 H8
Tower, The *EC3* 76 J5
Town La. 69 B3
Townley Rd. 71 B12
Townsend St. *SE17* 80 F3
Townshend Rd. *NW8* 73 B6
Toynbee St. *E1* 76 G5
Trafalgar Av. *SE15* 80 H5
Trafalgar Rd. 67 G9
Trafalgar Sq. *WC2* 79 A8
Trafalgar St. *SE17* 80 G3
Transept St. *NW1* 73 F6
Traps Hill 67 A11
Traps La. 70 D3
Treasury *SW1* 79 C8
Treaty St. *N1* 75 B9
Trebovir Rd. *SW5* 77 F1
Tregunter Rd. *SW10* 77 G3
Tresham Crescent *NW8* 73 D6
Trevor Pl. *SW7* 78 D1
Trevor Sq. *SW7* 78 D2
Trevor St. *SW7* 78 C2
Trinity Church Sq. *SE1* 80 D2
Trinity House *EC3* 76 H5
Trinity Rd. 70 B5
Trinity Sq. *EC3* 76 J4
Trinity St. *SE1* 80 D2
Trio Pl. *SE1* 80 D2
Triton Sq. *NW1* 74 E5
Trothy Rd. *SE1* 80 F7
Trottiscliffe 72 G6
Tryon St. *SW3* 78 F2
Tubbenden La. 71 E11
Tudor Drive 70 E4
Tudor Rd. 69 C6
Tudor St. *EC4* 75 H11
Tufnell Pk. Rd. 66 E6
Tufton St. *SW1* 79 E8
Tulse Hill 70 B6
Tulse Hill Sta. 70 C6
Turin St. *E2* 76 D6
Turk's Row *SW3* 78 G3
Turnham Green Sta. 66 G3
Turnmill St. *EC1* 75 F12
Turnpike La. 67 C7
Twickenham 69 B6
Twickenham Bri. 70 B1
Twickenham Pk. 70 B1
Twickenham Rd. *Hanworth* 69 C5
Twickenham Rd. *Teddington* 70 C1
Tyburn Way *W2* 74 H2
Tyers Gate *SE1* 80 C4
Tyers St. *SE11* 79 G9
Tyers Ter. *SE11* 79 G10
Tysoe St. *EC1* 75 D11
Udall St. *SW1* 78 F6
Ufford St. *SE1* 79 C12
Underwood Rd. *E1* 76 E6
Underwood St. *N1* 76 C2
Union Sq. *N1* 76 B1
Union St. *SE1* 79 B12
Union Wk. *E2* 76 C4
University College *WC1* 74 E7
University College Hospital *WC1* 74 E6
University of London *WC1* 75 F8
University St. *WC1* 74 E6
Unwin Cl. *SE1* 80 H6
Upbrook Ms. *W2* 73 H4
Upminster 68 D4
Upminster Bri. Sta. 68 D4
Upminster Rd. *Rainham* 68 F3
Upminster Rd. *Upminster* 68 D4
Upney 67 E12
Upney La. 67 E12
Upney Sta. 67 E12
Upper Belgrave St. *SW1* 78 D4
Upper Berkeley St. *W1* 74 G2
Upper Brook St. *W1* 74 J3
Upper Cheyne Row *SW3* 77 H6
Upper Clapton 67 D8
Upper Clapton Rd. 67 D8
Upper Edmonton 67 B8
Upper Elmers End 71 E8
Upper Grosvenor St. *W1* 74 J3
Upper Ground *SE1* 79 A11
Upper Halliford Rd. 69 D4
Upper Halliford Sta 69 D4
Upper Harley St. *NW1* 74 E4
Upper Holloway Sta. 66 D6
Upper Marsh *SE1* 79 D10
Upper Montagu St. *W1* 74 F2
Upper Norwood 70 D6
Upper Phillimore Gdns. *W8* 77 C1
Upper Rainham Rd. 68 D3
Upper Richmond Rd. *East Sheen* 70 B2
Upper Richmond Rd. *Putney* 70 B3
Upper St. *N1* 75 B12
Upper St. Martin's La. *WC2* 75 H8
Upper Sunbury Rd. 69 D5
Upper Sydenham 71 C7
Upper Thames St. *EC4* 76 H2
Upper Tooting Rd. 70 C5
Upper Walthamstow 67 C9
Upper Warlington Sta. 71 H7
Upper Wickham La. 71 A12
Upper Wimpole St. *W1* 74 F4
Upper Woburn Pl. *WC1* 75 D7
Upton 67 E10
Upton La. 67 E10
Upton Pk. Sta. 67 E10
Upton Rd. 71 B12
Urlwin St. *SE5* 80 H1
Uxbridge 65 E3
Uxbridge Rd. *Feltham* 69 C5
Uxbridge Rd. *Hampton* 69 C6
Uxbridge Rd. *Hanwell* 66 G1
Uxbridge Rd. *Harefield* 65 D3
Uxbridge Rd. *Hatch End* 65 C6
Uxbridge Rd. *Hayes End* 65 F4
Uxbridge Rd. *Maple Cross* 65 B2
Uxbridge Rd. *Southall* 65 F5
Uxbridge Rd. *Stanmore* 66 B1
Uxbridge Rd. *W12* 66 G3
Uxbridge St. *W8* 77 B1
Vale Cl. *W9* 73 D3
Vale, The *SW3* 77 H5
Vale, The *W3* 66 G3
Valence Av. 68 D1
Valentine Pl. *SE1* 79 C12
Valentines Pk. 67 D11
Vallance Rd. *E1/E2* 76 E7
Vandon St. *SW1* 78 D6
Vandy St. *EC2* 76 E3
Vanston Pl. *SW6* 77 J1
Varndell St. *NW1* 74 D6
Vauban St. *SE16* 80 E5
Vaudeville Theatre *WC2* 75 J9
Vauxhall Bri. *SW1/SW8* 79 G7
Vauxhall Bri. Rd. *SW1* 78 E6
Vauxhall Gro. *SW8* 79 H9
Vauxhall Pk. *SW8* 79 H9
Vauxhall Sta. *SE11* 79 G9
Vauxhall St. *SE11* 79 G10
Vauxhall Wk. *SE11* 79 F9
Venables St. *NW8* 73 F5
Verdant La. 71 B9
Vere St. *W1* 74 H4
Vernon Rise *WC1* 75 C10
Verulam St. *EC1* 75 F11
Vesta Rd. 71 A8
Vestry St. *N1* 76 C3
Vicarage Farm Rd. 69 A5
Vicarage Gate *W8* 77 B2
Vicarage La. *Chigwell* 67 B11
Vicarage La. *South Weald* 68 B4
Vicarage Rd. 69 C4
Victoria & Albert Museum *SW7* 77 E5
Victoria Coach Station *SW1* 78 F4
Victoria Dock Rd. 67 F10
Victoria Drive 70 B4
Victoria Emb. *SW1/WC2/EC4* 79 B9
Victoria Embankment Gdns. *WC2* 79 A9
Victoria Gate *W2* 73 J5
Victoria Gro. *W8* 77 D3
Victoria Palace Theatre *SW1* 78 D5
Victoria Pk. 67 E8
Victoria Pk. Rd. 67 E8
Victoria Rd. *NW10* 66 F3
Victoria Rd. *Romford* 68 D2
Victoria Rd. *Ruislip* 65 D5
Victoria Rd. *W8* 77 D3
Victoria Sq. *SW1* 78 D5
Victoria Sta. *SW1* 78 E5
Victoria St. *SW1* 78 D6
Victoria Tower Gdns. *SW1* 79 D9
Victory Pl. *SE17* 80 E2
Victory Square *SE5* 80 J3
Vigo St. *W1* 74 J6
Vigo Village 72 G6
Villa St. *SE17* 80 G3
Village Way *Enfield* 67 A7
Village Way *Harrow* 65 D5
Villiers St. *WC2* 79 A9
Vince St. *EC1* 76 D3
Vincent Sq. *SW1* 78 E7
Vincent St. *SW1* 79 F7
Vincent Ter. *N1* 75 B12
Vine Hill *EC1* 75 E11
Vine La. *SE1* 80 B4
Vine St. *EC3* 76 H5
Vine St. *W1* 74 J6
Violet Hill *NW8* 73 C4
Virgil St. *SE1* 79 D10
Virginia Rd. *E2* 76 D5
Virginia Water Sta. 69 D1
Viscount St. *EC1* 75 F13
Wadding St. *SE17* 80 F2
Waddington 70 H6
Waddon 70 E6
Waddon Marsh Halt 70 E6
Wadham Rd. 67 C9
Waite St. *SE15* 80 H5
Wakefield St. *WC1* 75 D9
Wakley St. *EC1* 75 C12
Walbrook *EC4* 76 H2
Walcot Sq. *SE11* 79 E11
Waldgrave Rd. 70 C1
Waldram Pk. Rd. 71 B8
Walham Gro. *SW6* 77 J1
Wallace Collection *W1* 74 G3
Wallend 67 E11
Wallgrave Rd. *SW5* 77 F2
Wallington 70 F5
Walnut Tree Wk. *SE11* 79 E11
Walpole St. *SW3* 78 F2
Walterton Rd. *W9* 73 D1
Waltham Forest 67 C9
Walthamstow 67 D8
Walthamstow Av. 67 C9
Walthamstow Central Sta. 67 C9
Walthamstow Marshes 67 D8
Walthamstow Queen's Rd. Sta. 67 C9
Walton Bri. 69 E4
Walton Downs 70 H3
Walton Pl. *SW3* 78 D2
Walton Rd. 69 D5
Walton St. *SW3* 78 E1
Walton-upon-Thames 69 E5
Walworth 67 G7
Walworth Pl. *SE17* 80 G2
Walworth Rd. *SE17* 80 F1
Wandsworth 70 B4
Wandsworth Bri. 70 A4
Wandsworth Bri. Rd. *SW6* 70 A4
Wandsworth Common 70 B5
Wandsworth Common Sta. 70 B5
Wandsworth Prison 70 B5
Wandsworth Rd. *SW8* 79 H8
Wandsworth Rd. Sta. 70 A6
Wandsworth Town Sta. 70 B4
Wansey St. *SE17* 80 F1
Wanstead 67 D10
Wanstead Flats 67 D10
Wanstead Pk. 67 D10
Wanstead Pk. Sta. 67 E10
Wanstead Sta. 67 D10
Wapping 67 G8
Wapping High St. *E1* 80 B6
Wardour St. *W1* 74 H7
Warham Rd. 70 F6
Warham St. *SE5* 79 H12
Warley Barracks 68 B5
Warley Rd. 68 C5
Warlingham 71 H8
Warner Pl. *E2* 76 C6
Warner St. *EC1* 75 E11
Warren La. *Grays* 68 G5
Warren La. *Pyrford* 69 H2
Warren Rd. 71 F12
Warren St. *W1* 74 E6
Warrington Cres. *W9* 73 E3
Warwick Av. *W9/W2* 73 E3
Warwick Cres *W2* 73 F3
Warwick Est. *W2* 73 F2
Warwick House St. *SW1* 79 B7
Warwick La. *EC4* 75 G12
Warwick La. *Rainham* 68 F4
Warwick Pl. *W2* 73 F3
Warwick Res. 67 D8
Warwick Rd. *SW5* 77 F1
Warwick Row *SW1* 78 D5
Warwick Sq. *SW1* 78 F6
Warwick St. *W1* 74 J6
Warwick Way *SW1* 78 F5
Wash Pond Rd. 71 H9
Water La. 67 D12
Waterden Rd. 67 E9
Watergate *EC4* 75 H12
Waterhouse La. 70 H4

Waterloo Bri. *WC2/SE1* **75** H10
Waterloo Pier *WC2* **75** H10
Waterloo Pl. *SW1* **78** B7
Waterloo Rd. *SE1* **79** C11
Waterloo Sta. *SE1* **79** C10
Waterlow Pk. **66** D6
Waterson St. *E2* **76** D4
Watersplash Rd. **69** D3
Watford **65** A5
Watford Bypass **66** A2
Watford F.C. **65** A5
Watford Heath **65** A5
Watford High St. Sta. **65** A5
Watford Rd. *Harrow* **66** E1
Watford Rd. *Rickmansworth* **65** A3
Watford Way *Edgware* **66** B2
Watford Way *NW4* **66** C4
Watford West Sta. **65** A4
Watling Av. **66** C3
Watling St. **72** B1
Watling St. *Dartford* **72** B4
Watling St. *EC4* **76** H1
Watling St. *Swanscombe* **72** C4
Watts La. **71** D11
Waverley Pl. *NW8* **73** B4
Waverton St. *W1* **78** B4
Weald Pk. **68** A4
Wealdstone **66** C1
Weaver St. *E1* **76** E6
Weaver's La. *SE1* **80** B4
Webb St. *SE1* **80** E4
Webber Row *SE1* **79** D11
Webber St. *SE1* **79** C12
Weigh House St. *W1* **74** H4
Weirs Pass. *NW1* **75** D8
Welbeck St. *W1* **74** G4
Welbeck Way *W1* **74** G4
Well Hall Rd. **71** B10
Well Hill **72** F1
Wellclose Sq. *E1* **76** H6
Weller St. *SE1* **80** C1
Welling **71** A12
Welling Way **71** A11
Wellington Arch *SW1* **78** C4
Wellington Barracks *SW1* **78** D6
Wellington Pl. *NW8* **73** C5
Wellington Rd. *NW8* **73** C5
Wellington Rd. Sth. **69** B5
Wellington Row *E2* **76** D6
Wellington Sq. *SW3* **78** G2
Wellington St. *WC2* **75** H9
Wells Ms. *W1* **74** G6
Wells Rise *NW8* **74** B2
Wells St. *W1* **74** G6
Wells Way *SE5* **80** H3
Welsford St. *SE1* **80** F6
Wembley **66** E2
Wembley Central Sta. **66** E2
Wembley Hill Sta. **66** E2
Wembley Park Sta. **66** D2
Wembley Stadium **66** E2
Wenlock Basin *N1* **76** C1
Wenlock Rd. *N1* **76** C1
Wenlock St. *N1* **76** C2
Wennington **68** F3
Wennington Marshes **68** G3
Wennington Rd. **68** F3
Wentworth St. *E1* **76** G5
Werrington St. *NW1* **74** C7
Wesley's Chapel *EC2* **76** E3
West Acton Sta. **66** F2
West Bedfont **69** B3
West Byfleet **69** G2
West Byfleet Sta. **69** G2
West Common Rd. **71** E9
West Cromwell Rd. *SW5* **77** F1
West Croydon Sta. **71** E7
West Drayton **65** G3
West Drayton Rd. **65** F4
West Drayton Sta. **65** G3
West Dulwich Sta. **71** C7
West Ealing Sta. **66** F1
West Eaton Pl. *SW1* **78** E3
West End *Esher* **69** F6
West End *Southall* **65** F5
West End La. *NW6* **66** E5
West End Rd. **65** E5
West Ewell **70** F3
West Ferry Rd. **67** G9
West Finchley Sta. **66** B5
West Green **67** C7
West Green Rd. **67** C7
West Grove **69** F5
West Halkin St. *SW1* **78** D3
West Ham **67** F10
West Ham F.C. **67** E10
West Ham Pk. **67** E10
West Ham Stadium **67** F10
West Hampstead Sta. **66** E5
West Harrow **65** D6
West Heath *NW3* **66** D5
West Heath *SE2* **68** H1
West Hill *Dartford* **72** B2
West Hill *SW15* **70** B4
West Horndon Sta. **68** D6
West India Docks **67** G9
West Kingsdown **72** F4
West Mall *W8* **77** A1
West Molesey **69** D6
West Norwood **71** C7
West Norwood Sta. **70** C6
West Pk. Hospital **70** G2
West Rd. *SW3* **78** G3
West Ruislip Sta. **65** D4
West Smithfield *EC1* **75** F12
West Sq. *SE11* **79** E12
West St. *WC2* **75** H8
West Sutton Sta. **70** F4
West Tenter St. *E1* **76** H5
West Thurrock **68** H5
West Thurrock Marshes **68** H5
West Wickham **71** E9
West Wood La. **71** B11
Westbourne Bri. *W2* **73** G3
Westbourne Cres. *W2* **73** H4
Westbourne Gdns. *W2* **73** G2
Westbourne Gate *W2* **73** J5
Westbourne Gro. *W11/W2* **73** H2
Westbourne Pk. Rd. *W11/W2* **73** G1
Westbourne Pk. Sta. **66** F4
Westbourne Pk. Vs. *W2* **73** G2
Westbourne St. *W2* **73** H5
Westbourne Ter. *W2* **73** G4
Westbourne Ter. Rd. *W2* **73** F3
Westbury Av. **67** C7
Westcombe Pk. Sta. **67** H10
Westcott Rd. *SE17* **79** H12
Westend La. **69** F5
Westerham Rd. **71** F10
Western Av. **66** F3
Western Av. *Greenford* **66** F1
Western Av. *Uxbridge* **65** E4
Western Rd. *Mitcham* **70** D5
Western Rd. *Southall* **65** G5
Westgate Ter. *SW10* **77** H3
Westhall Rd. **71** H7
Westhorne Av. **71** B10
Westland Pl. *N1* **76** D2
Westmead Rd. **70** F5
Westminster **66** G6
Westminster Abbey *SW1* **79** D8
Westminster Bri. *SE1/SW1* **79** C9
Westminster Bri. Rd. *SE1* **79** D11
Westminster Chapel *SW1* **78** D6
Westminster Hall *SW1* **79** D8
Westminster Hospital *SW1* **79** E8
Westminster Pier *SW1* **79** C9
Westminster R.C. Cathedral *SW1* **78** E6
Westminster School *SW1* **79** D8
Westminster Theatre *SW1* **78** D5
Westmoreland Pl. *SW1* **78** G5
Westmoreland Rd. *Bromley* **71** D9
Westmoreland Rd. *SE17* **80** H2
Westmoreland St. *W1* **74** F4
Westmoreland Ter. *SW1* **78** G5
Westmorland Rd. *SE17* **80** G4
Weston Green **70** E1
Weston Green Rd. **70** E1
Weston Rise *WC1* **75** C10
Weston St. *SE1* **80** C3
Westway *W2* **73** F3
Westwood **72** C5
Westwood Hill **71** C7
Wetherby Gdns. *SW5* **77** F3
Wetherby Pl. *SW7* **77** F4
Weybridge **69** E4
Weybridge Rd. **69** E3
Weybridge Sta. **69** F3
Weymouth Ms. *W1* **74** F5
Weymouth St. *W1* **74** F4
Weymouth Ter. *E2* **76** B5
Whalebone La. **68** C1
Whalebone La. Sth. **68** D1
Wharf Rd. *N1* **75** C13
Wharfdale Rd. *N1* **75** B9
Wharton St. *WC1* **75** D10
Wheatsheaf La. *SW8* **79** J8
Wheler St. *E1* **76** E5
Whetstone **66** B5
Whetstone Pk. *WC2* **75** G10
Whidborne St. *WC1* **75** D9
Whipps Cross **67** D9
Whiskin St. *EC1* **75** D12
Whiston Rd. *E2* **76** B5
Whitby St. *E1* **76** E5
Whitchurch La. **66** C2
Whitcomb St. *WC2* **75** J7
White Church La. *E1* **76** G6
White Conduit St. *N1* **75** B11
White Hart La. *Collier Row* **68** C2
White Hart La. *N17* **67** C7
White Hart La. Sta. **67** C7
White Hart Yard *SE1* **80** B2
White Hill **65** B4
White Hill La. **72** F6
White Horse Hill **71** C10
White Horse St. *W1* **78** B5
White Kennett St. *E1* **76** G4
White Lion St. *N1* **75** C11
White Lodge **70** B2
Whitechapel **67** F8
Whitechapel High St. *E1* **76** G5
Whitechapel Rd. *E1* **76** G6
Whitecross St. *EC1* **76** E2
Whitefoot La. **71** C9
Whitefriars St. *EC4* **75** H11
Whitehall *SW1* **79** B8
Whitehall Court *SW1* **79** B8
Whitehall Gdns. *SW1* **79** B8
Whitehall Pl. *SW1* **79** B8
Whitehall Rd. **67** B9
Whitehart St. *SE11* **79** G11
Whiteheads Gro. *SW3* **78** F1
Whitehorse Rd. **71** D7
Whiteley Village **69** F4
White's Grounds *SE1* **80** C4
White's Row *E1* **76** F5
Whitfield Pl. *W1* **74** E6
Whitfield St. *W1* **74** F6
Whitgift St. *SE11* **79** F9
Whitmore Rd. *N1* **76** A3
Whittaker St. *SW1* **78** F3
Whittlesey St. *SE1* **79** B11
Whitton **69** B6
Whitton Av. **65** E6
Whitton Rd. **69** B6
Whyteleafe **71** H7
Whyteleafe Rd. **71** H7
Whyteleafe Sth. Sta. **71** H7
Wick Rd. **67** E8
Wickham La. **67** H12
Wickham Rd. *Beckenham* **71** D8
Wickham Rd. *Croydon* **71** E8
Wickham Rd. *SE4* **71** A8
Wickham St. *SE11* **79** G10
Wickham Way **71** D9
Wicklow St. *WC1* **75** C9
Widegate St. *E1* **76** F4
Widley Rd. *W9* **73** D1
Widmore Rd. **71** D10
Wightman Rd. **67** D7
Wigmore Hall *W1* **74** G4
Wigmore Pl. *W1* **74** G5
Wigmore St. *W1* **74** G4
Wilbraham Pl. *SW1* **78** E3
Wilbury Way **67** B7
Wild Ct. *WC2* **75** G9
Willersley Av. **71** B11
Willesden **66** E3
Willesden Green **66** E4
Willesden Green Sta. **66** E4
Willesden Junc. Sta. **66** F3
Willesden La. **66** E4
William Girling Res. **67** B8
William IV St. *WC2* **75** J8
William Ms. *SW1* **78** C3
William Rd. *NW1* **74** D5
William St. *SW1* **78** C3
Willoughby La. **67** C8
Willow Gro. *SE1* **71** C10
Willow Pl. *SW1* **78** E6
Willow St. *EC2* **76** D3
Willow Wk. *SE1* **80** E4
Willowbank **65** E3
Willowbrook Rd. *SE15* **80** J5
Wilmer Gdns. *N1* **76** B4
Wilmerhatch La. **70** H2
Wilmington **72** C2
Wilmington Sq. *WC1* **75** D11
Wilson St. *EC2* **76** F3
Wilton Cres. *SW1* **78** D3
Wilton Ms. *SW1* **78** D4
Wilton Pl. *SW1* **78** C3
Wilton Rd. *SW1* **78** E5
Wilton Row *SW1* **78** C3
Wilton Sq. *N1* **76** A2
Wilton St. *SW1* **78** D4
Wilton Ter. *SW1* **78** D3
Wiltshire Row *N1* **76** A3
Wimbledon **70** C4
Wimbledon Chase Sta **70** D4
Wimbledon Common **70** C3
Wimbledon Hill Rd. **70** C4
Wimbledon Pk. **70** C4
Wimbledon Pk. Rd. **70** B4
Wimbledon Pk. Sta. **70** C4
Wimbledon Stadium **70** C4
Wimbledon Sta. **70** C4
Wimbolt St. *E2* **76** C6
Wimbourne St. *N1* **76** B2
Wimpole Ms. *W1* **74** F4
Wimpole St. *W1* **74** G4
Winchester Cl. *SE17* **79** F13
Winchester St. *SW1* **78** G5
Winchester Wk. *SE1* **80** B2
Winchmore Hill **67** A7
Wincott St. *SE11* **79** F11
Windmill La. **66** G1
Windmill St. *W1* **74** F7
Windmill Wk. *SE1* **79** C11
Windsor Ter. *N1* **76** C2
Winfield House *NW1* **74** C1
Wingletye La. **68** D4
Winkworth Rd. **70** G4
Winsland Ms. *W2* **73** G5
Winsland St. *W2* **73** G5
Winsley St. *W1* **74** G6
Wisley **69** G3
Wisley Common **69** H3
Wisley La. **69** G3
Woburn Hill **69** E3
Woburn Pl. *WC1* **75** E8
Woburn Sq. *WC1* **75** E8
Woking **69** H1
Woldingham Rd. **71** H8
Wolseley St. *SE1* **80** C6
Wolsey Way **65** B4
Wood End *Hayes* **65** F4
Wood End *South Harrow* **65** E6
Wood Grange Pk. Sta. **67** E10
Wood Green **66** C6
Wood La. *Becontree* **68** E1
Wood La. *Dagenham* **68** E3
Wood La. *Stanmore* **66** B2
Wood La. *W12* **66** F4
Wood St. *Barnet* **66** A4
Wood St. *E17* **67** C9
Wood St. *EC2* **76** G2
Wood St. Sta. **67** C9
Woodbridge St. *EC1* **75** E12
Woodchester Sq. *W2* **73** F2
Woodcote Grove Rd. **70** G6
Woodcote La. **70** G5
Woodcote Rd. **70** F5
Woodfall St. *SW3* **78** G2
Woodfield La. **70** H2
Woodford **67** C10
Woodford Av. **67** C11
Woodford Bri. **67** B10
Woodford Green **67** B10
Woodford New Rd. **67** C9
Woodford Wells **67** B10
Woodham **69** G2
Woodham La. **69** G2
Woodland Pk. **69** H6
Woodlands **72** G3
Woodlands La. **69** H6
Woodmansterne **70** G5
Woodmansterne La. **70** G5
Woodmansterne Rd. **70** F5
Woodmansterne Sta. **70** G5
Woodridings **65** C6
Woods Ms. *W1* **74** J3
Woodseer St. *E1* **76** F6
Woodside **71** E7
Woodside Av. **66** C5
Woodside Pk. Sta. **66** B5
Woodstock La. **70** E1
Woodstock St. *W1* **74** H4
Woodthorpe Rd. **69** C3
Wooler St. *SE17* **80** G3
Woolwich **67** G11
Woolwich Arsenal Sta. **67** G11
Woolwich Church St. **67** G11
Woolwich Common **67** H10
Woolwich Dockyard Sta. **67** G11
Woolwich Reach **67** G11
Woolwich Rd. *SE2* **68** G1
Woolwich Rd. *SE7* **67** G10
Wootton St. *SE1* **79** B11
Worcester Pk. **70** E3
Worcester Pk. Sta. **70** E3
Worgan St. *SE11* **79** G9
World's End Pass. *SW10* **77** J4
Wormwood Scrubs **66** F3
Wormwood St. *EC2* **76** G4
Woronzow Rd. *NW8* **73** A5
Worple Rd. *Staines* **69** D2
Worple Rd. *SW19/SW20* **70** D3
Worship St. *EC2* **76** E3
Wraysbury **69** B1
Wraysbury Res. **69** B2
Wren St. *WC1* **75** E10
Wright's La. *W8* **77** D2
Wrotham **72** H5
Wrotham Heath **72** H6
Wrotham Hill Pk. **72** G5
Wrotham Rd. **72** D6
Wrythe La. **70** E5
Wrythe, The **70** E5
Wybert St. *NW1* **74** D5
Wyclif St. *EC1* **75** D12
Wymering Rd. *W9* **73** D2
Wynatt St. *EC1* **75** D12
Wyndham Pl. *W1* **74** F2
Wyndham St. *W1* **74** F2
Wyndham's Theatre *WC2* **75** J8
Wynford Rd. *N1* **75** B10
Wynnstay Gdns. *W8* **77** D1
Wythburn Pl. *W1* **74** G2
Wyvil Rd. *SW8* **79** J8
Yalding Rd. *SE16* **80** E6
Yardley St. *WC1* **75** D11
Yeading **65** F5
Yeading La. **65** F5
Yeoman's Row *SW3* **77** E6
Yiewsley **65** F4
York Bri. *NW1* **74** E3
York Buildings *WC2* **75** J9
York Gate *NW1* **74** E3
York House Pl. *W8* **77** C2
York Rd. *SE1* **79** C10
York St. *W1* **74** F2
York Ter. E. *NW1* **74** E4
York Ter. W. *NW1* **74** E3
York Way *N1* **75** B9
Yorkton St. *E2* **76** C6
Young St. *W8* **77** C2
Zoar St. *SE1* **79** B13
Zoological Gardens *NW1* **74** B3